AIRCRAFT Structural Maintenance
THIRD EDITION

Production Staff

Lead Illustrator Amy Siever
Designer/Production Coordinator Roberta Byerly
Designer/Photographer Dustin Blyer

© Copyright 2004, 2006, 2011, 2013 by
Avotek Information Resources, LLC.
All Rights Reserved

International Standard Book Number 1-933189-32-0
ISBN 13: 978-1-933189-32-1
Order # T-AFSTR-0301

For Sale by: Avotek
A Select Aerospace Industries Inc. company

Mail to:
P.O. Box 219
Weyers Cave, Virginia 24486
USA

Ship to:
200 Packaging Drive
Weyers Cave, Virginia 24486
USA

Toll Free: 1-800-828-6835
Telephone: 1-540-234-9090
Fax: 1-540-234-9399

Third Edition
First Printing
Printed in the USA

www.avotek.com

Preface

This textbook, the second in a series of four, was written for the Aviation Maintenance Technician student of today. It is based on the real-world requirements of today's aviation industry. At the same time, it does not eliminate the traditional subject areas taught since the first A&E schools were certificated.

This series of textbooks has evolved through careful study and gathering of information offered by the Federal Aviation Administration, the Blue Ribbon Panel, the Joint Task Analysis report, industry involvement and AMT schools nationwide.

The series is designed to fulfill both current and future requirements for a course of study in Aviation Maintenance Technology.

The 2013 revised edition of this textbook represents a positive step in Avotek's commitment to deliver the most up-to-date material possible. Structural repair has been split into two chapters. The new metallic and nonmetallic structures chapters have both been expanded to provide more thorough coverage of the material. Significant additional material has also been added throughout the text. A number of photographs and illustrations have been added, updated or clarified.

Textbooks, by their very nature, must be general in their overall coverage of a subject area. As always, the aircraft manufacturer is the sole source of operation, maintenance, repair and overhaul information. Their manuals are approved by the FAA and must always be followed. You may not use any material presented in this or any other textbook as a manual for actual operation, maintenance or repairs.

The writers, individuals and companies which have contributed to the production of this textbook have done so in the spirit of cooperation for the good of the industry. To the best of their abilities, they have tried to provide accuracy, honesty and pertinence in the presentation of the material. However, as with all human endeavors, errors and omissions can show up in the most unexpected places. If any exist, they are unintentional. Please bring them to our attention.

Email us at comments@avotek.com for comments or suggestions.

Avotek® Aircraft Maintenance Series
Introduction to Aircraft Maintenance
Aircraft Structural Maintenance
Aircraft System Maintenance
Aircraft Powerplant Maintenance

Avotek® Aircraft Avionics Series
Avionics: Fundamentals of Aircraft Electronics
Avionics: Beyond the AET
Avionics: Systems and Troubleshooting

Other Books by Avotek®
Aircraft Corrosion Control Guide
Aircraft Structural Technician
Aircraft Turbine Engines
Aircraft Wiring & Electrical Installation
AMT Reference Handbook
Avotek Aeronautical Dictionary
Fundamentals of Modern Aviation
Light Sport Aircraft Inspection Procedures

Acknowledgements

Academy of Infrared Training, Inc.

Air Methods (Rocky Mountain Helicopters)

Al Dibble — Snap-On Tools

Alan Bandes — UE Systems, Inc.

Andy Wilson — B/E Aerospace

Bob Blouin — National Business Aircraft Association

Boeing Commercial Airplane Co.

Brian Stoltzfus — Priority Air Charter

Cal Crowder

Champlin Fighter Aircraft Museum

Charlie Witman — Avotek

Chris McGee — USAF Museum

David Jones — AIM

David Posavec — Barry Controls

Debbie Jones — MD Helicopters, Inc.

De-Ice Systems International

Dynamic Solution Systems, Inc.

Eaton Aerospace Fluid Systems (Aeroquip)

Fred Workley — Workley Aviation Mx

Greg Campbell, Sherman Showalter, Stacey Smith — Shenandoah Valley Regional Airport

Harry Moyer, Virgil Gottfried — Samaritan's Purse

Jack Knox — Evergreen Air Center

Jean Watson — FAA

Jim Akovenko — JAARS

Karl Stoltzfus, Sr., Michael Stoltzfus, Aaron Lorson & staff — Dynamic Aviation Group, Inc.

Ken Hyde, Weldon Britton — The Wright Experience

Ken Smoll — Cessna Aircraft Company

Ken Stoltzfus, Jr. — Preferred Airparts

Lee Helm — RAM Aircraft Corporation

Lilbern Design

Lori Johnson, Larry Bartlett — Duncan Aviation

Mary Ellen Gubanic — Alcoa

Michelle Moyer

Micro-Mesh

Pat Colgan, Dennis Burnett — Colgan Air

Paul Geist, J.R. Dodson — Dodson International Parts

PHI Air Medical

Phoenix Composites

Pilgrim's Pride Aviation Department

Precision Airmotive Corp.

Precision Instruments

Raymond Goldsby — AIA

Rich Welsch — Dynamic Solutions Systems, Inc.

Richard Kiser, Steve Bradley — Classic Aviation Services

Richard Milburn — Northrop Grumman Corporation

Robert Kafales — Frontier Airlines

Scott Aviation Enterprises

Select Aerospace Industries, Inc.

Select Airparts

Stern Technologies

Steve Hanson, Jeff Ellis, Tim Travis — Raytheon Aircraft

Susan Timmons — JRA Executive Air

Tom Brotz — U.S. Industrial Tools

Vern Raburn, Andrew Broom — Eclipse Aviation

Virginia State Police Med Flight III

Vought Aircraft Industries, Inc.

Contents

Preface iii

Acknowledgements iv

1 Helicopter Fundamentals

1-1	Rotary Wing Aerodynamics	1-24	Rotor Blades
1-6	Fundamentals of Rotors	1-31	Helicopter Transmissions
1-15	Rotor System Operation		

2 Fabric Covering

2-1	History of Fabric Covering	2-3	Today's Fabric Coverings

3 Materials and Processes

3-1	Aerospace Materials	3-51	Riveting
3-29	Fasteners	3-63	Layout and Forming
3-42	Drilling		

4 Airframe Metallic Structures

4-1	Introduction to Airframe Metallic Structures	4-49	Stress Calculations
		4-56	Back-up Structure
4-10	Airframe Sheet Metal Repair		

5 Airframe Nonmetallic Structures

5-1	Types of Nonmetallic Materials	5-38	Maintaining Transparent Plastic Materials
5-2	Composites		
5-17	Advanced Composites	5-58	Wood Structures

6 Welding Techniques

6-1	Welded Structures	6-27	Gas-shielded Arc Welding
6-7	Oxyacetylene, Welding, Brazing, Soldering and Cutting	6-42	Friction Stir Welding
		6-44	Weld Inspection

7 Painting and Refinishing

7-1	Cleaning and Stripping	7-6	Refinishing Practices

8 Assembly and Rigging

8-1	Rigging and Assembly Data	8-24	Rigging Checks
8-3	Control Surface Balance	8-29	Hardware Installation and Safetying
8-7	Control Surface Installation		
8-11	Control Cables		

Index I-1

1

Helicopter Fundamentals

Section 1

Rotary Wing Aerodynamics

Basic aerodynamics applies to rotary-wing aircraft just as it does to fixed-wing aircraft. The flow of air over an airfoil behaves the same way — the same airfoil, drag, stall and downwash principles apply to all aircraft types. The four principles of lift, weight, thrust and drag also apply. However, rotary-winged aircraft have some unique differences.

Autogyros. The first successful rotary-winged aircraft were *autogyros*. An autogyro is defined as an aircraft that uses a conventional engine/propeller combination for forward thrust, while using an overhead rotary wing for lift. The rotary wing on an autogyro is not powered. Rotation is provided by the windmill effect of airflow from the forward motion flowing upward through the rotor. Once rotation has started, lift will continue as long as there is airflow through the rotor.

The first successful, controlled flight of a rotary wing aircraft was in 1928. While developing a flyable autogyro, a Spanish engineer named Juan de la Cierva (1895-1936) figured out the problem of advancing and retreating rotor blades (Figure 1-1-1). He developed and built more than 100 prototypes and was able to consistently achieve vertical take-offs and landings by 1934. His invention of the flapping hinge paved the way for powered rotary-wing aircraft to fly successfully. Commercial autogyro development continued well into the 1940s, with several models being developed for military use. The main attributes of autogyros were, and still are, their low cost, their relatively simple construction and their excellence at short-field landing and takeoff.

Learning Objectives

REVIEW
- Lift, thrust and drag
- Aircraft stability
- Stress

DESCRIBE
- Gyroscopic precession
- Symmetry and dissymmetry of lift
- Rotor vibration and smoothing
- Flapping

EXPLAIN
- Rotors vs. fixed wings
- The parts of rotors and tail assemblies
- Helicopter flight controls and their effects

APPLY
- Rig and balance a helicopter
- Check a helicopter transmission

Left. The same principles of aerodynamics apply to both rotary-wing and fixed-wing aircraft.

Figure 1-1-1. The development of Juan de la Ciervas' autogyro opened the way for true vertical flight.

Although commercial development all but ceased when helicopters became practical, the autogyro is, to a limited extent, alive and well in the homebuilt market.

Helicopters. A helicopter is a rotary-winged aircraft that uses a powered rotor and can perform both vertical takeoff and landing, as well as hovering. Powered vertical flight was not possible until the basic concept of lead-lag was conceived, and solved, by Cierva. Once controlled flight was possible, rather rapid development produced practical machines capable of true vertical flight.

Professor Heinrick Focke (1890-1979) set records for helicopter flight in 1937 and later teamed up with fellow German Gerd Achgelis to produce the Focke-Achgelis, better known as the Focke-Wulf 61. Russian aeronautical engineer Igor Sikorsky (1889-1972) made more historical flights in his VS-300 helicopter in 1941, establishing a world record for endurance, with a flight of just over an hour. One of his many designs the R-4, became the first mass-produced helicopter, with hundreds built during World War II. Refer to Figure 1-1-2.

It remained for the Bell Aircraft Company to produce the first licensed commercial helicopter, the Bell 47B on March 8, 1946. See Figure 1-1-3. For those interested in helicopter history, a quick search of the internet will provide a wide variety of sites.

From these beginnings, helicopter manufacturers have continued to solve difficulties involved with vertical flight. Worldwide, helicopters have evolved into a vast array of different types and sizes, for many applications. Their military applications and their use in emergency medical evacuation are legendary.

However, all rotary-winged aircraft have one thing in common: They all must obey the same

Figure 1-1-2. One of Sikorsky's YR-4B/HNS-1 helicopters is seen in the full scale tunnel. The technician is setting up camera equipment for stopped-action rotor-blade photos. *Photo courtesy of NASA*

Figure 1-1-3. The Bell 47B was the first U.S. certified commercial helicopter.

basic principles of aerodynamics as those that govern conventional aircraft.

Principles of Helicopter Flight

The principals of helicopter flight are different enough from conventional aircraft to be worthy of their own section on aerodynamics. While the basics of airfoil design and fluid flow are the same, the environment in which they operate is vastly more complicated. For this reason, we will not repeat basic airfoil theory in this section. Instead, we will concentrate on the basic applications to vertical flight.

The keys to the helicopter's success are its vertical takeoff, hover and vertical landing capabilities. Along with these abilities come the added benefits of flying not only forward, but also backward, sideways and in a circular rotation around its vertical axis while in a hover.

Aerodynamics. Aerodynamics deals with the motion of air and with the forces acting on objects moving through air or remaining stationary in a current of air. The same principles of aerodynamics apply to both rotary-wing and fixed-wing aircraft. The four forces that affect an aircraft at all times are weight, lift, thrust and drag.

The definition of *weight* is the same for conventional aircraft as for helicopters; that is, the force of gravity acting downward upon the aircraft and everything in it: the crew, the fuel and the cargo.

Lift is produced by air passing over the wing of an airplane or over the rotor blades of a helicopter. Lift is the force that overcomes the weight of an aircraft so that it can rise in the air.

In a conventional fixed-wing aircraft, *thrust* is provided by a propeller or jet exhaust that moves the plane forward, while the wings supply the lift. In a helicopter, both thrust and lift are supplied by the main rotor blades.

Drag is the force of resistance of an object passing through the air. A thrust force sets an aircraft in motion and keeps it in motion against drag force.

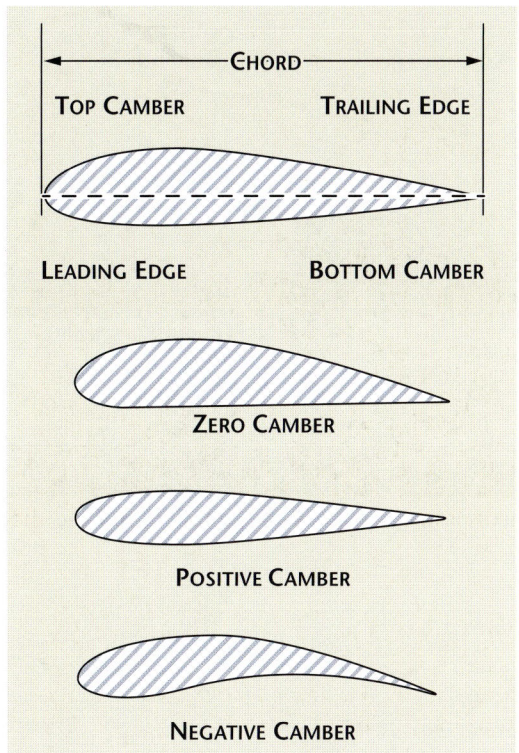

Figure 1-1-4. Different airfoils are used for different purposes. Cambered airfoils, ones with a curved lower surface, do not normally work well for helicopter rotors because of a shift in the aerodynamic center of pressure.

Any device designed to produce lift or thrust when passed through air is an airfoil. Airplane wings, propeller blades and helicopter main and tail rotor blades are all airfoils.

The *empennage* of a conventional airplane is primarily a place to attach the aft controls. While some helicopter designs do have small horizontal and vertical stabilizers, the primary aft control is the tail rotor. Its major function is to overcome rotor torque and provide a means of controlling the direction of the nose of the aircraft.

Chord is the length of the imaginary line between the leading and the trailing edges of an airfoil. The amount of curve, or departure of the airfoil surface from the chord line, is known as the *camber*. Upper camber refers to the upper surface; lower camber refers to the lower surface. If the surface is flat, the camber is zero. The camber is positive if the surface is convex (curves outward from the chord line), and the camber is negative if the surface is concave (curves inward toward the chord line). The upper surface of an airfoil always has positive camber, but the lower surface may have positive, negative or zero camber (Figure 1-1-4).

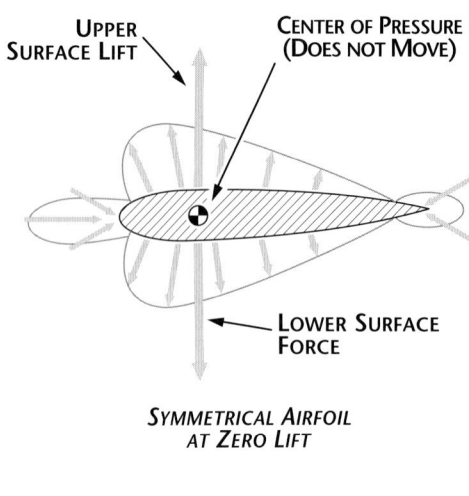

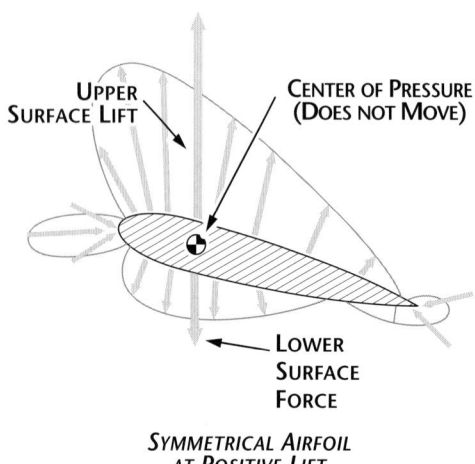

Figure 1-1-5. Bernoulli's principle, as it applies to symmetrical airfoils

Bernoulli's principle. In the physics section, we discussed Bernoulli's principle at length. In this section, we will only do a short review of a symmetrical airfoil, as the basic principles are the same for a helicopter rotor as they are for a wing.

As an airfoil starts moving through the air, it divides the mass of air molecules at its leading edge. In a symmetrical airfoil, there is no lift produced when the rotor has no angle of attack. The distance across the curved top surface is the same as the bottom surface, so no difference exists in the top and bottom airflows. See top illustration, Figure 1-1-5.

When lift is needed, the pilot raises the collective control, increasing the angle of attack of the airfoil. This causes the airflow moving across the top surface to travel a greater distance at a higher velocity. Air pressure below the airfoil is now greater than the pressure above it, and tends to push the airfoil up into the area of lower pressure. As long as air passes over the airfoil, this condition will exist. It is this difference in pressure that causes lift. As the airflow across the top meets the airflow across the bottom, both are deflected downward due to the high velocity air impacting the high pressure air creating a downwash. With the downwash thus created, the helicopter will rise vertically in proportion to the amount of collective control movement. See bottom illustration, Figure 1-1-5.

Most helicopter rotors do not use a conventional airfoil. Instead, they use a symmetrical airfoil. A symmetrical airfoil is one that has the same curve on both the upper and lower surface. A conventional airfoil will produce lift when it has a relative wind striking directly on the leading edge. A relative wind striking the leading edge of a symmetrical airfoil head-on will produce zero lift. The airfoils will streamline. A symmetrical airfoil must have an angle of attack to produce an airflow that will create lift. With an angle of attack, the air will travel a lovnger distance over the top of the airfoil than it will along the under surface, producing a lifting force as it does so.

Not all of the air met by an airfoil is used in lift. Some of it creates resistance, or drag, that hinders forward motion. Lift and drag increase and decrease together. They are affected by the airfoil's angle of attack into the air, the speed of airflow, the air density, and the shape of the airfoil.

Lift and thrust. The amount of lift that an airfoil can develop depends on five major factors:

1. Area (size or surface area of the airfoil)
2. Shape (form or design of the airfoil sections)
3. Speed (velocity of the air passing over the airfoil)
4. Angle of attack (angle at which the air strikes the airfoil)
5. Air density (amount of air in a given space)

Area and shape. The specific shape and surface area of an airfoil are determined by the aircraft manufacturer, though most airfoils are symmetrical. A symmetrical airfoil is designed with an equal amount of camber above and below the airfoil chord line. An asymmetrical airfoil has a greater amount of camber above the chord line. An airfoil with a smooth surface produces more lift than one with a rough surface. A rough surface creates turbulence, which reduces lift and increases drag.

Speed. In helicopters, there are two different speeds to be concerned with. One is the actual speed over the ground or through the air, while the other is the speed of rotation (r.p.m.) of the main rotor blades. Speed over the ground or through the air is controlled by the pilot. Rotor speed is controlled by the engine r.p.m. and is normally governed to a constant r.p.m., no matter what the rest of the helicopter is doing. The speed of advancing and retreating blades is explained later.

Angle of Attack. The difference between the angle of attack and the angle of incidence is critical to the rest of this section, so it is important that these differences stay firmly in your mind.

The *angle of attack* is the angle between the airfoil chord and the direction of relative wind. Direction of airflow in relation to the airfoil is called relative wind. Lift increases as the angle of attack increases, up to a certain point. If the angle of attack becomes too great, airflow over the top of the airfoil tends to lose its streamlined path and break away from the contoured surface to form eddies (burbles) near the trailing edge. When this happens, the airfoil loses its lift, and it stalls. The angle of attack at which burbling takes place is called the *critical angle of attack*.

The *angle of incidence* is the angle at which a wing, or rotor blade, is attached to its structure.

Air density. The density (thickness) of the air plays an important part in the amount of lift an airfoil is able to create. The air nearest the Earth's surface is much more dense than air at higher altitudes. Therefore, an aircraft or helicopter can achieve more lift near the ground than at a high altitude. While keeping at the same speed and angle of attack, an airfoil will slowly make less lift as it climbs higher and higher. This is why high-altitude rescue operations with helicopters are extremely difficult.

Airfoil Stability

Center of pressure. The resultant lift produced by an airfoil is the difference between the drag and lift pressures of its upper and lower surfaces. The point on the airfoil chord line where the resultant lift is effectively concentrated is called the *center of pressure*.

Figure 1-1-7. Stabilizer bar

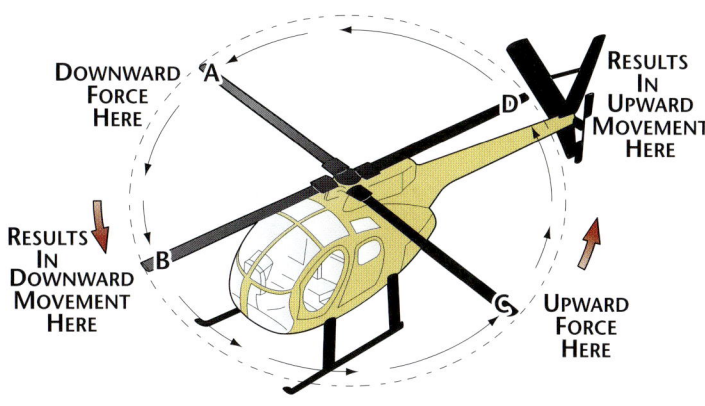

Figure 1-1-6. Because of gyroscopic precession, an input to the rotor disc will not take effect until 90° later, in the direction of rotation.

The center of pressure of a symmetrical airfoil remains in one position at all angles of attack. When the angle of attack of an unsymmetrical airfoil changes, the center of pressure changes accordingly: it moves forward with an increase in angle of attack, and moves backward with a decrease in angle of attack.

Airfoil aerodynamic center. The *aerodynamic center of an airfoil* is the point along the chord line about which the airfoil tends to rotate when the center of pressure moves forward or backward between the leading and trailing edges.

Torque. According to Newton's Third Law of Motion, *for every action there is an equal and opposite reaction*. As a helicopter main rotor, or an airplane propeller, turns in one direction, the aircraft fuselage tends to rotate in the opposite direction. This effect is called *torque*. Solutions must be found to counteract and control torque during flight. In helicopters, torque is applied in a horizontal rather than a vertical plane. The reaction is greater because the rotor is long and heavy in relation to the fuselage, and forward speed is not always present to correct the twisting effect.

Gyroscopic precession. If a force is applied against a rotating body, the reaction will be about 90° from the point of application, in the direction of rotation. This unusual fact is known as *gyroscopic precession*. It pertains to all rotating bodies. In Figure 1-1-6, if a downward force is applied to point "A" the result is a downward motion at "B". 90° later, in the same direction of rotation, the same will be true with inputs "C" and "D". The rotors on helicopters act as gyroscopes and are therefore subject to the action of gyroscopic precession.

Stabilizer bars. Some older Bell helicopters had a stabilizer bar assembly that rotated with the hub. See Figure 1-1-7. Connected to the

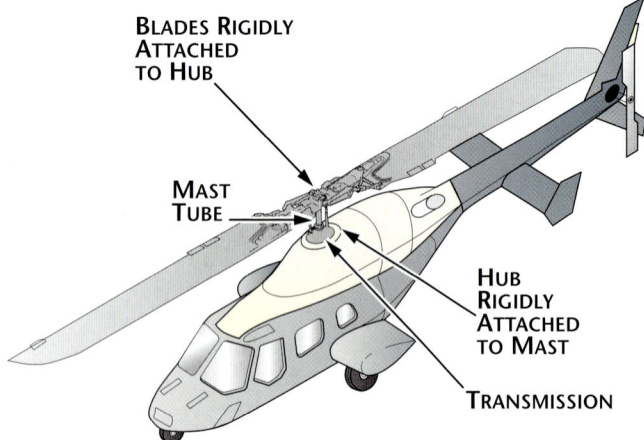

Figure 1-2-1. Hub drive

rotor blade pitch arms, its purpose was to act as a gyroscopic stabilizer. When a movement upset the rotor disc, the stabilizer bar would try to maintain the original path of rotation. This would apply pressure to the pitch-change arms, effectively returning them to the original undisturbed position. In many cases, the stabilizer bars were removed, and they are not used on modern helicopters.

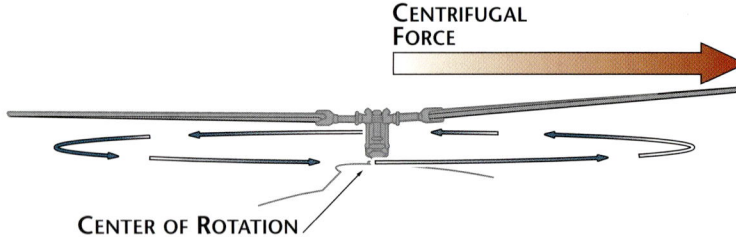

Figure 1-2-2. Centrifugal force

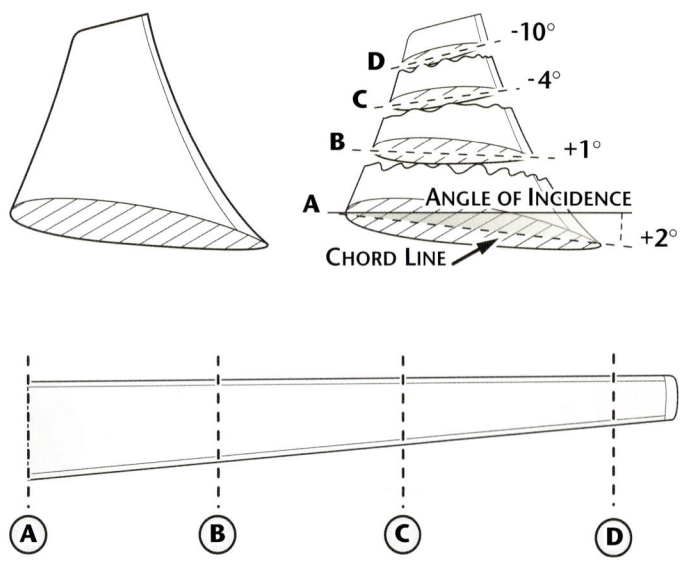

Figure 1-2-3. Angle of incidence

Section 2
Fundamentals of Rotors

Of all airfoils, the rotor blade on a helicopter is unique. Like most airfoils, it provides lift, but it also provides the thrust and directional control needed for helicopter flight.

When talking about rotor systems, there is one important fact to remember: Not all helicopter rotors turn the same direction. In the United States, rotors turn left, or counterclockwise as viewed from above. Most European helicopters turn right, or clockwise as viewed from above. This also makes a difference when we discuss tail rotors later in the chapter.

All of the examples given are for a counterclockwise rotation. If you want to apply any of the discussions to non-U.S. helicopters, simply make the directional switch in your head.

Rotor system. The rotor system includes a rotor head, rotor blades and control systems that drive and control the pitch angles of the blade. The rotor head is the main assembly of the rotor system; it contains the rotor hub, blade attachment fittings and blade controlling mechanisms (Figure 1-2-1). The rotor hub is splined to the mast, which, in turn, rotates the rotor hub and blades.

Forces acting on rotors. Since the rotor system of a helicopter provides both lift and thrust, it is exposed to all of the forces, or stresses, that act on aircraft wings and propellers. When applied to rotor blades, the thrust-bending force that acts on propellers is called coning. The amount of coning is controlled by built-in limit stops. Because of the large mass and weight of the rotating blades, a considerable amount of centrifugal force (Figure 1-2-2) is generated.

Angle of incidence. The angular connection between a reference line on a rotor blade cuff, socket or attachment point and the blade chord line at a specific station is called the angle of incidence (Figure 1-2-3). On most blades, it is determined by design and is not adjustable.

Plane of rotation. The plane formed by the average tip path of the blades is known as the *plane of rotation*. The plane of rotation is at a right angle to the axis of rotation.

Axis of rotation. An imaginary line that passes through a point on which a body rotates is called the *axis of rotation* (Figure 1-2-4), which is at a right angle to the plane of rotation.

Disc area and loading. The *disc area* (Figure 1-2-5) is the total space in the area of the circle formed

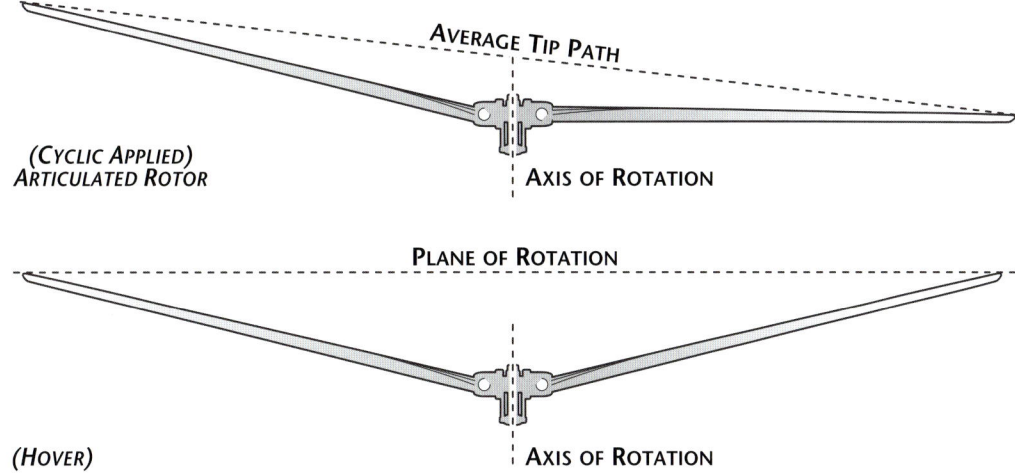

Figure 1-2-4. Axis of rotation

by the rotating rotor blades. The area of the circle equals 3.1416 *(pi)* multiplied by the radius, then squared (multiplied by itself). The span length of one blade is used as the radius. The area of the hub in the disc area is not included, since it doesn't make any lift. Disc loading is the ratio of aircraft gross weight to the disc area.

Symmetry/Dissymmetry of Lift

Symmetry and *dissymmetry of lift* are phenomenona peculiar to rotary-winged aircraft. It is also the problem that de la Cierva solved in 1928. To understand the phenomenon, it is necessary to first divide the disc area into two sections: advancing and retreating. The advancing section starts at the tail of the aircraft and proceeds, in the direction of rotation, to the front of the aircraft. The retreating section starts at the front of the aircraft and proceeds, in the direction of rotation, to the rear. This effectively divides the disc area in half.

Lift varies according to the square of the velocity (speed of blade and forward airspeed of aircraft). Symmetry and dissymmetry of lift are shown in Figure 1-2-6. The example uses a blade-tip speed of 300 m.p.h. The blade speed varies from 300 m.p.h. at the tip station to 0 m.p.h. at the center of blade rotation on the hub. When a helicopter is hovering in a no-wind condition, there is symmetry of lift. The lift is equal on advancing and retreating halves of

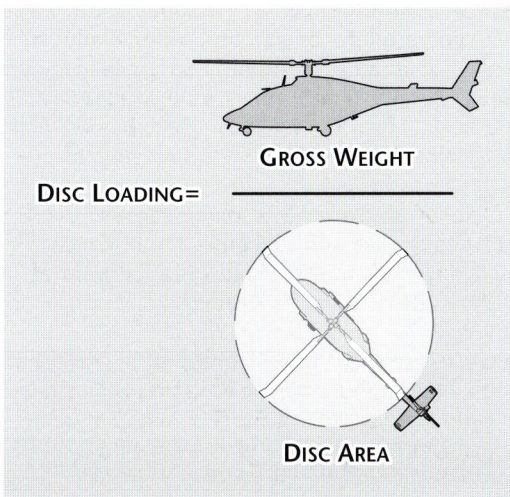

Figure 1-2-5. Disc area and loading

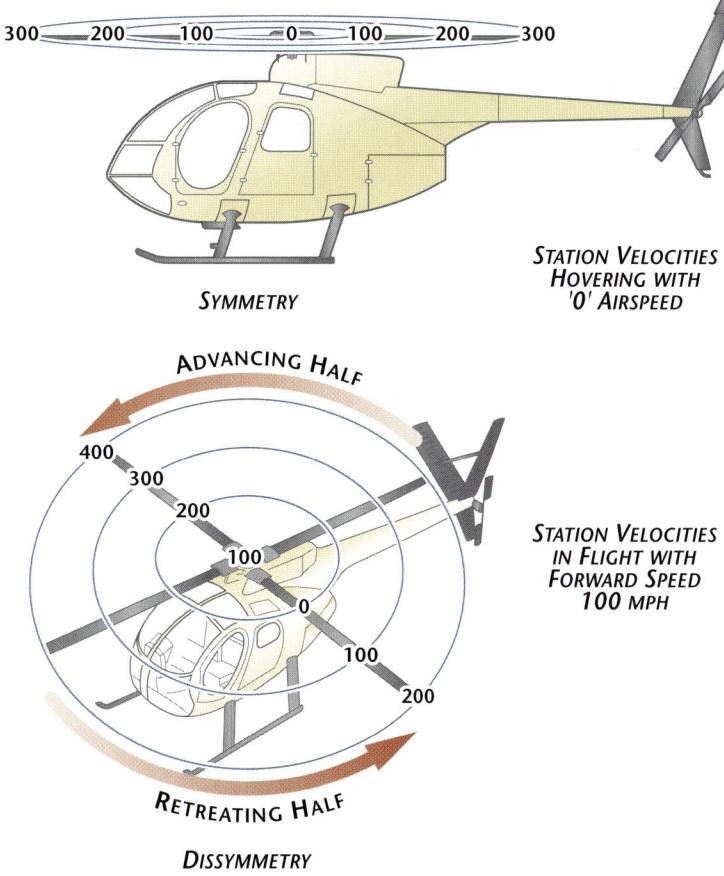

Figure 1-2-6. Symmetry and dissymmetry of lift

the rotor disc area because speed of the blade is the same on both halves.

Dissymmetry of lift is the difference in lift that exists between the advancing half of a rotor disc and the retreating half. Dissymmetry is created by forward movement of the helicopter.

When the helicopter is moving forward, the speed of the advancing blade is the sum of the indicated airspeed of the helicopter plus the rotational speed of the blade. The speed of the retreating blade is the rotational speed of the blade minus the forward speed of the helicopter. In Figure 1-2-6, the advancing half of the disc area has a blade tip speed of 300 m.p.h. plus the indicated helicopter speed of 100 m.p.h. — a total blade-tip speed of 400 m.p.h. The total speed squared is 160,000 m.p.h. The retreating half of the disc has a blade-tip speed of 300 m.p.h. minus the 100 m.p.h.-indicated forward speed of 200 m.p.h., and velocity squared is 40,000 m.p.h. In this example, the advancing blade creates four times as much lift as the retreating blade.

With no allowances for this dissymmetry of lift, the helicopter could only rise into a hover. It could not fly forward, or in any other direction. If directional flight was attempted, the helicopter would roll into the retreating disc side of the disc area and crash.

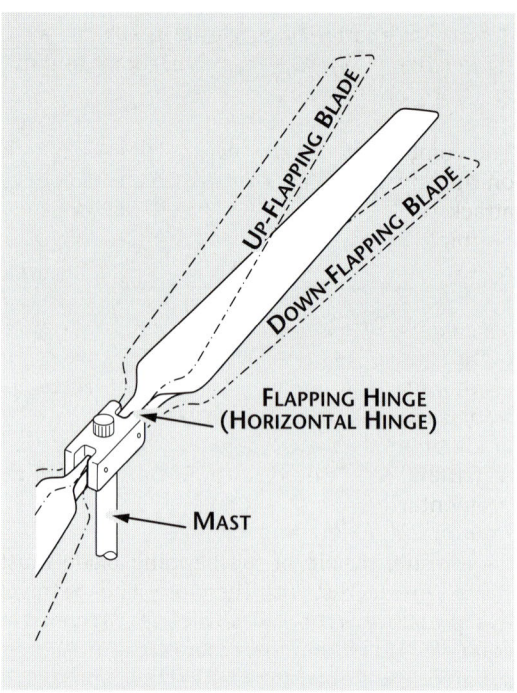

Figure 1-2-7. Flapping (articulated hub)

Flapping. The up-and-down movement of rotor blades positioned at a right angle to the plane of rotation is referred to as *flapping* (Figures 1-2-7 and 1-2-8). This permits the rotor disc to tilt, providing directional control in flight. It also controls the required lift on each blade when in forward flight, thus experiencing dissymmetry of lift. Up-and-down flapping is limited by the large centrifugal force acting against the smaller lifting force.

In a two-bladed system, the blades flap as a unit. As the advancing blade flaps up due to the increased lift, the retreating blade flaps down due to the decreased lift. The change in angle of attack on each blade brought about by this flapping action tends to equalize the lift over the two halves of the rotor disk.

The position of the cyclic pitch-control in forward flight also causes a decrease in angle of attack on the advancing blade and an increase in angle of attack on the retreating blade. This, together with blade flapping, equalizes lift over the two halves of the rotor disk.

In any rotor system with three or more blades, the rotor blades are attached to the rotor hub by a horizontal hinge (flapping hinge) that permits the blades to move in a vertical plane, or flap up or down, as they rotate (Figure 1-2-9). In forward flight, assuming that the blade-pitch angle remains constant, the increased lift on the advancing blade will cause the blade to flap up, decreasing the angle of attack, because the relative wind will change from horizontal to a more downward direction. The decreased lift on the retreating blade will cause the blade to flap

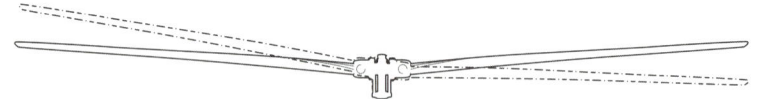

Figure 1-2-8. Flapping (semi-rigid hub)

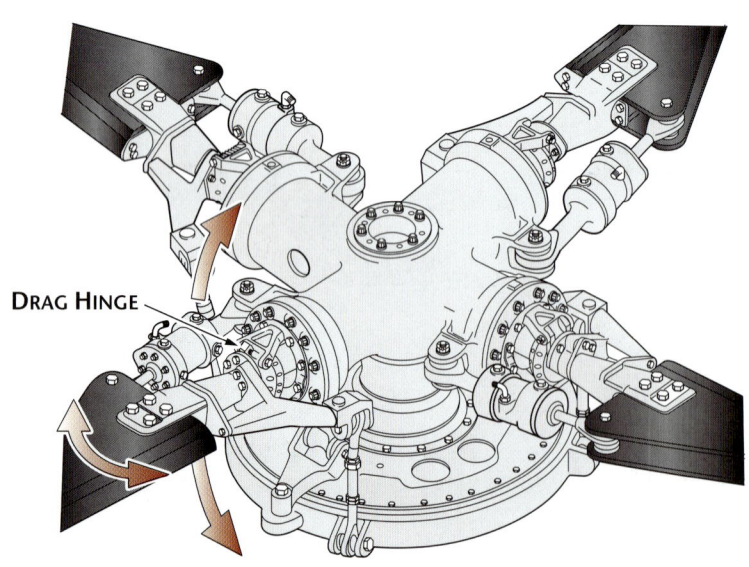

Figure 1-2-9. A four-bladed, articulated rotor head

down, increasing the angle of attack, because the relative wind goes from horizontal to more of an upward direction.

The combination of decreased angle of attack on the advancing blade and increased angle of attack on the retreating blade, through blade flapping action, tends to equalize the lift over the two halves of the rotor disk.

The amount that a blade flaps up is a compromise between centrifugal force, which tends to hold the blade straight out from the hub, and lift forces, which tend to raise the blade on its flapping hinge. As the blades flap up, they leave their normal tip-path plane momentarily.

As a result, the tip of the flapping blade must travel a greater distance. Therefore, it has to travel at a greater speed for a fraction of a second, in order to keep up with the other blades.

The blade flapping action creates a condition of unbalance with resulting vibration. To prevent this vibration, a drag hinge (Figure 1-2-9) is incorporated, which permits the blade to move back and forth in a horizontal plane.

With the blades free to move back and forth on the drag hinges, an unbalanced condition is created, since the center of gravity will not remain fixed but will move around the mast. This center of gravity movement causes excessive vibration. To lessen the vibrations, hydraulic or elastomeric dampers limit the movement of the blades on the drag hinge. These dampers also maintain the geometric relationship of the blades. Blade flapping is not limitless. Their total travel is limited to a fixed total by a flap-stop built into the damper. When a rotor is at rest, it will droop because of the flapping hinge. The total amount of droop is limited by a built-in droop stop.

A main rotor that permits individual movement of the blades from the hub in both a vertical and horizontal plane is called an *articulated rotor*. The hinge points and direction of motion around each hinge are illustrated in Figure 1-2-9.

Coning and preconing. The upward flexing of a rotor blade due to lift forces acting on it is called *coning* (Figure 1-2-10). Coning is the result of lift and centrifugal force acting on a blade in flight. The lift force is almost 7 percent of centrifugal force, which causes the blade to deflect upward from 3° to 4°. Coning is often expressed as an angle. Helicopter manufacturers determine the coning angle mathematically and build a precone angle into the rotor hub that is similar to the coning effect in normal flight. The preconed hub lets the blades operate at normal coning angles without bending, which

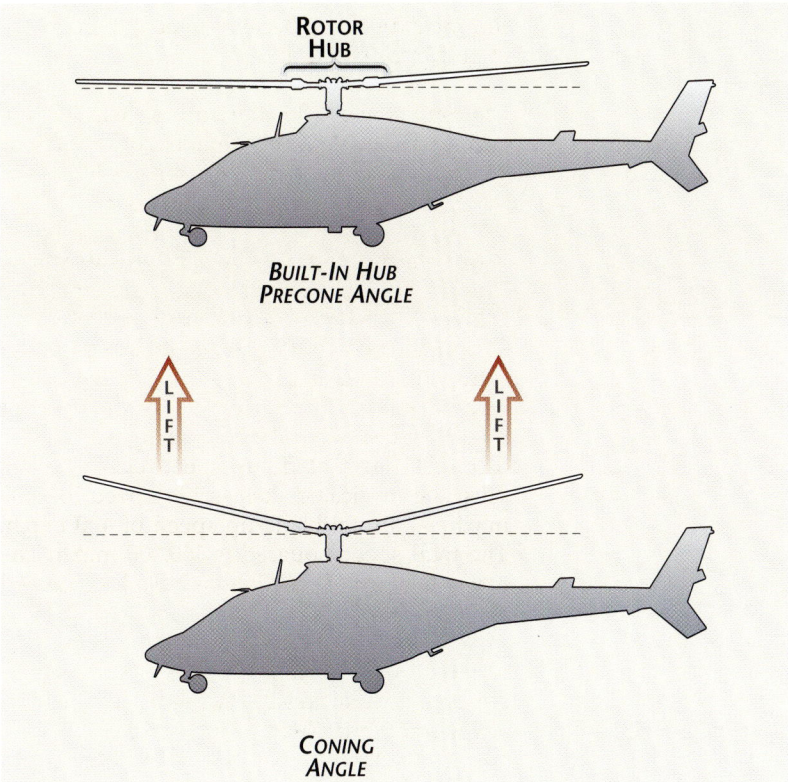

Figure 1-2-10. Coning and preconing angles

reduces stress. It is not necessary to precone the articulated rotor hub, because the blade can flap up on hinges to the correct coning angle.

Lead and lag of blades. The horizontal movement of the blades around a vertical pin is called leading and lagging, or *hunting* (Figure 1-2-11). This is found only on fully articulated rotor heads. During starting, the blades will resist rotational movement and will lag behind their true radial position. As centrifugal force reacts on the blade, the blade will gain momentum and find its own position of rotation. The blade

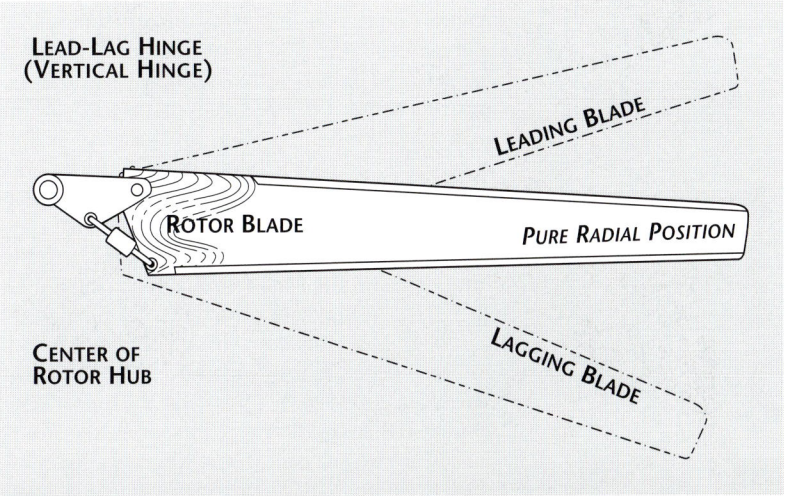

Figure 1-2-11. Blade movement called lead and lag are necessary for an articulated rotor system to be aerodynamically balanced.

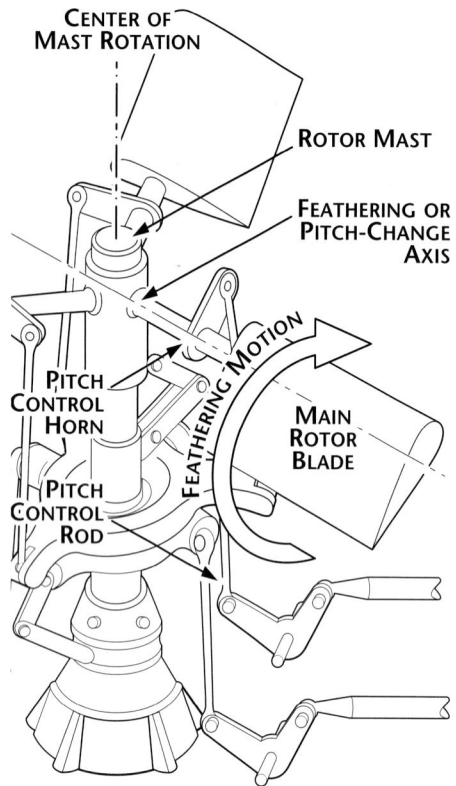

Figure 1-2-12. Feathering axis

will hunt about the vertical hinge in close to a 5° range during normal operation. A hydraulic or elastomeric damper restricts the movement of the blades about the vertical hinge.

Feathering axis. The spanwise axis about which a rotor blade rotates to change pitch is the *feathering axis* (Figure 1-2-12). Feathering varies with the position of the cyclic control in forward flight in proportion to the dissymmetry of lift, and with the collective pitch-control position when the helicopter hovers.

Hover. The versatility of a helicopter is due to its ability to *hover* at a point above the ground. This lets the helicopter use small, unimproved landing areas or prepared helipads. When main rotor angle of attack and engine power are adjusted so that lift equals weight, the helicopter will hover. Hover is considered an element of vertical flight. Assuming a no-wind condition exists during hover, the tip-path plane of the rotor will remain horizontal with the Earth. When the angle of attack of both blades is increased equally while blade speed remains constant, more lift will result, and the helicopter will rise. By upsetting the lift-gravity balance, the helicopter will rise or come down, depending on which force is greater. Hovering takes a great deal of power, because a large mass of air must be drawn through the rotor blades at high speeds.

Ground effect. When hovering near ground or water surfaces at a height no more than one-half of the rotor diameter, the helicopter encounters a condition referred to as *ground effect*. This condition is more pronounced nearer the ground. Helicopter operations within ground effect are more efficient due to reduction of the rotor-tip vortex and the flattening out of the rotor downwash. The benefit of ground effect is lower blade angle of attack, resulting in a reduction of power requirements.

Ground resonance. *Ground resonance* happens in helicopters with *lead-lag hinges*. It occurs only on the ground, and starts when the blades bunch up on one side of the rotor disc. They generate an unbalanced centrifugal force that gets in phase with the natural frequency of the aircraft rocking on skids and landing gear. Modern helicopters avoid this by using dampers on the blades and on the gear (shock-absorbed struts). It is less prominent on wheeled helicopters, although it can still occur. The emergency action is to lift the aircraft to a hover.

Ground resonance has not been solved and is still a big concern for anyone who flies a helicopter with a fully articulated rotor system. It is an out-of-balance condition in the rotor system of a helicopter on the ground that rapidly increases in frequency until the helicopter shakes itself apart. It is usually caused by a hard ground contact and is much more likely in aircraft with improperly maintained landing gear (deflated oleo struts, for example).

It cannot occur in a two-bladed, semi-rigid, seesaw-type rotor system, because the blades do not lead and lag.

Stress

Stress is a force placed on a body measured in terms of force (pounds) per unit area (square inches). Aircraft design engineers design aircraft to meet the stress requirements as specified in the FARs. Maintenance personnel must check constantly for failures and for signs of approaching failure in aircraft structural units. Stress may take the form of compression, torsion, tension, bending, or shear, or it may be a combination of two or more of these forces.

There are two basic types of stress: tension and compression. The three other forms are applications of tension and compression: torsion, bending and shear.

Tension. *Tension* occurs when a force tends to pull a body apart. Tension occurs in many parts of an aircraft and may often occur along with other forces on the same component. In one of its purest forms, tension is applied to a control cable every time the control is moved. Another example of tension is found in the helicopter transmission mount/mast tube, each time the helicopter lifts off the ground.

Compression. *Compression* is the resistance to any external force that tends to push a body together. This also occurs on aircraft structures or components. In fact, many times a part which has tension applied at one point in flight may have compression applied at another point. For example, the same transmission mount and mast tube that experienced tension at take-off will experience compression at landing, when lift and centrifugal force release the rotor blades and gravity acts downward on the apparatus.

Torsion. *Torsion* is a combination force that has both tension and compression acting on

Figure 1-2-14. Lift and centrifugal force cause a helicopter's blades to flex upward during rotation, an example of bending. Here, gravity acts upon the non-rotating blades, bending them downward.

the component at the same time. This torsional force is often referred to as a twisting force. It is usually placed upon driveshafts, crankshafts or propshafts that are common to aircraft, as well as to mast tubes and transmission mounts atop helicopters.

Multiple stresses. It should be noted that most parts of the helicopter are placed under more than one stress at a time and must be designed to withstand these stresses. While one stress may be evident, others may occur at the same time or at different modes of operation. This is quite evident in the example in Figure 1-2-13. This is a helicopter mast used to drive the main rotor. When the mast is first rotated, it is subject to torsion. As the helicopter lifts, a tension load is added, and when it lands a compression load is placed on the mast.

Bending. *Bending* is another combination force that is applied to many components of the aircraft. This force may be applied with one force being greater than the other, or they may be equal. An example of this force is shown on a helicopter's rotor blades at rest (Figure 1-2-14). The skin on the top of the wing is subject to tension, while the bottom of the wing is subject to compression.

Shear. *Shear* is a force that tends to pull a component apart. This is a common force applied to rivets used to join sheet metal used in the helicopter. When the sheet metal is stressed with either a tension or compression load, the rivet is placed in a shear load, as shown in Figure 1-2-15. The combination is not uncommon, since the sheet metal may be stressed differently and at different times during flights and landings. Generally, rivets are subjected to shear only, but bolts may be

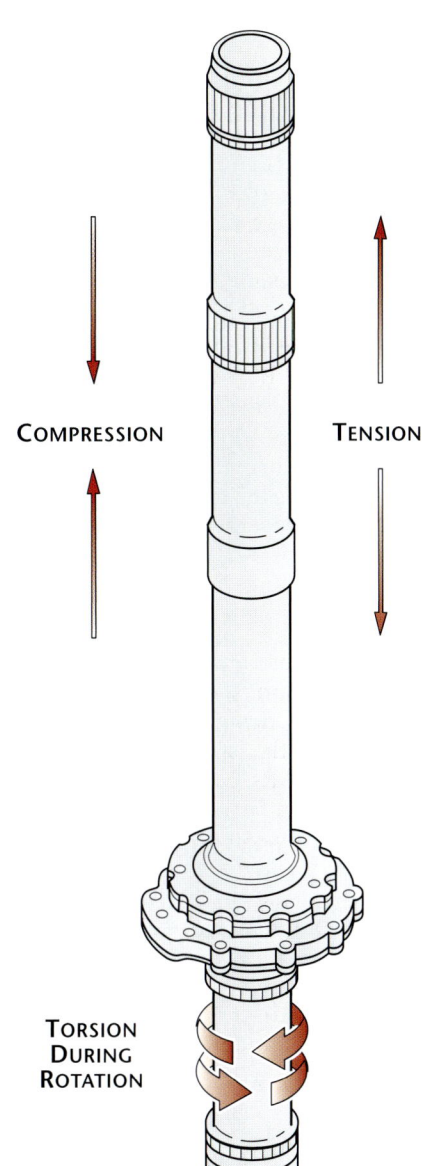

Figure 1-2-13. Examples of torsion, tension and compression on a helicopter's mast

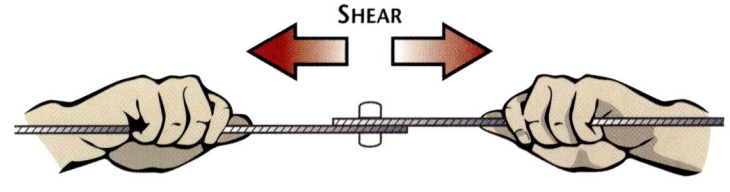

Figure 1-2-15. An illustration of shear

stressed by shear and tension. There is internal shear in all parts being bent, such as the skin of sheet metal structures.

Strain. *Strain* is the consequence of stress. When stress is applied to any body, strain is the result. If strain does not exceed the elastic limit of the body, there will be no visible change. Over a period of time, though, a change will take place. For example, if we bend a piece of wire back and forth, it will eventually yield or break. This will take place with any solid body. In helicopter structures, this may take place as a result of many take-offs and landings. Often, highly stressed parts are assigned a time life, or a finite life, to eliminate the possibility of failure of the component.

Moment of force. The *moment of force* is the product of a force or weight times a distance. To find a lever's moment of force, multiply the applied effort by the distance between the point of effort application and the pivot point (fulcrum). If the moment of force of the applied effort equals the moment of force of the resistance, the lever will balance. If an object to be balanced on a first class lever weighs 4 lbs. and is located 2 inches from the fulcrum, it could be balanced by a 2 lb. effort applied 4 inches from the fulcrum on the opposite side or by a 1 lb. effort applied 8 inches from the fulcrum.

Vibration

Any type of machinery vibrates, though greater than normal vibration usually means that there is a malfunction. Malfunctions can be caused by worn bearings, out-of-balance conditions or loose hardware. If allowed to continue unchecked, vibrations can cause material failure or machine destruction. Aircraft — particularly helicopters — have a high vibration level due to their many moving parts. Designers have been forced to use many different dampening and counteracting methods to keep vibrations at acceptable levels. Some examples are:

- Driving secondary parts at different speeds to reduce harmonic vibrations; this method removes much of the vibration buildup
- Mounting high-level vibration parts, such as drive shafting, on shock-absorbent mounts
- Installing vibration absorbers in high-level vibration areas of the airframe

Lateral vibrations. Lateral vibrations are evident in side-to-side swinging rhythms. An out-of-balance rotor blade causes this type of vibration. Lateral vibrations in helicopter rotor systems are quite common.

Vertical vibrations. Vertical vibrations are evident in up-and-down movement that produces a thumping effect. An out-of-track rotor blade causes this type of vibration.

High-frequency vibrations. These vibrations are made evident by a buzzing sound and a numbing effect on the feet and fingers of crewmembers. High-frequency vibrations are caused by an out-of-balance condition or a high-speed, moving part that has been torqued incorrectly. The balancing of high-speed parts is very important. Any buildup of dirt, grease or fluid on or inside such a part (drive shafting, for example) causes a high-frequency vibration. This type of vibration is more dangerous than a lateral or vertical one because it causes crystallization of metal, which can lead to mechanical failure. This vibration must normally be corrected before the equipment can be operated. It is often said that low frequency vibrations cause discomfort while high frequency vibrations cause accidents.

Helicopter Rotor Smoothing

Over the last 30 years, a variety of methods and techniques have been used to reduce vibrations produced by the main and tail rotors of helicopters.

Main Rotor Tracking Methods

Theoretically, main rotor blades should all fly in the same plane and maintain equidistant angular spacing during flight. Pitch links and tip tabs can be adjusted to compensate for blade differences, to keep the blades in line at all forward speeds. Rotor tracking systems have focused on providing information that can be used to adjust the pitch links and tabs to coax the blades to fly perfectly.

Flag tracking. The earliest technique for rotor tracking was flag tracking. See Figure 1-2-16. The tip of each blade is marked with colored chalk or crayon and a white strip of cloth mounted to a pole is pushed into the edge of the rotor blade path. The marks on the cloth gave a measure of the blade track.

Electro-optical tracking. In the 1960s, an electro-optical method of measuring rotor track height and lead-lag was developed and patented by Chicago Aerial. They built small, single-lens systems that could be mounted to the aircraft and measure track in flight. The system they sold the most of was a large ground-based, dual-lens/dual-sensor system that was very accurate but could only measure track on the ground.

Strobe-light tracking. In the late 1960s and early 1970s, Chadwick-Helmuth adapted a

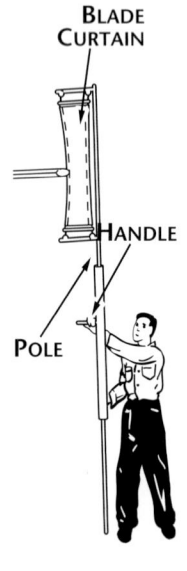

Figure 1-2-16. One of the earliest methods of tracking rotor blades was flag tracking. Fortunately, it has been all but relegated to history.

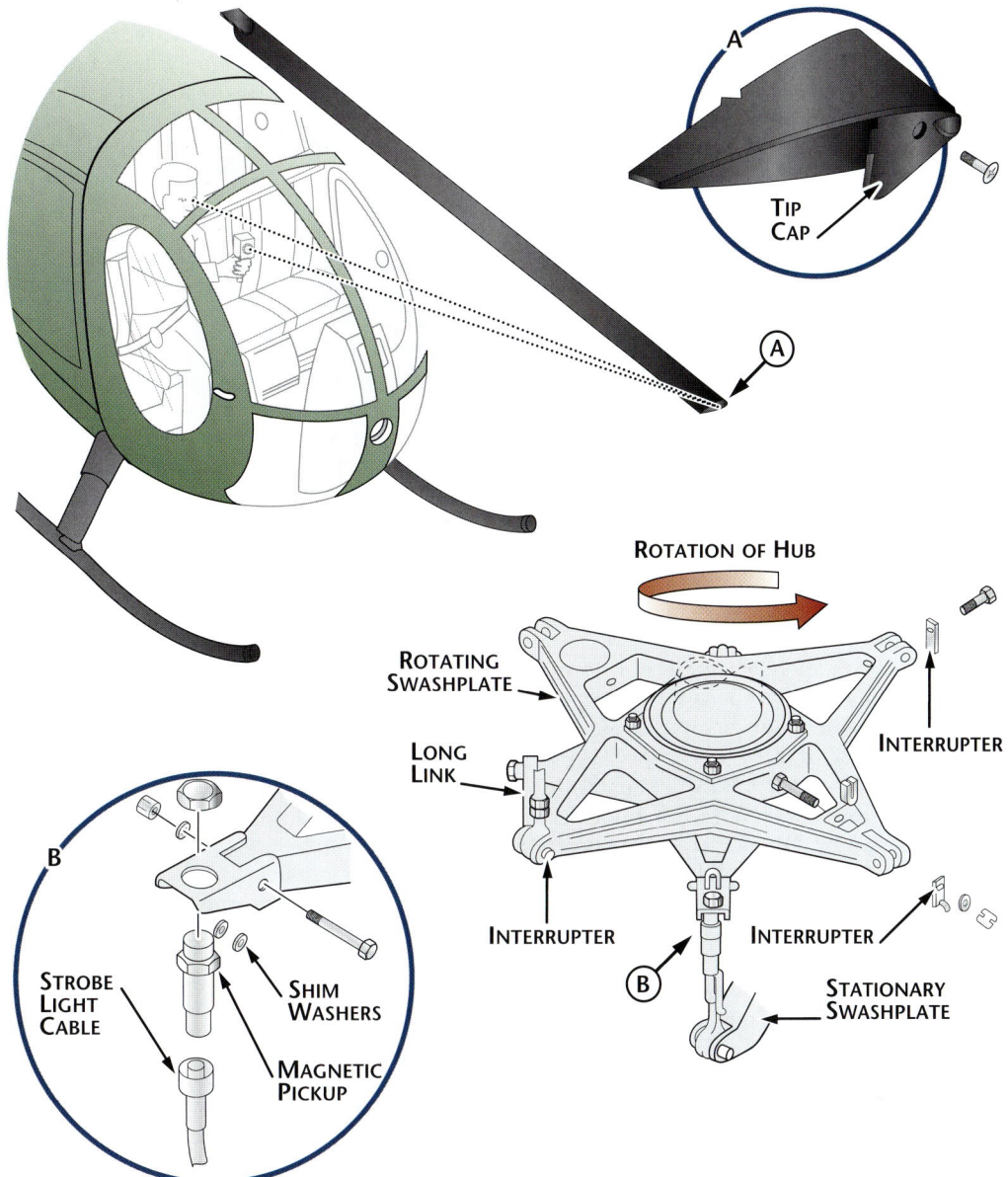

Figure 1-2-17. The development of strobe-light tracking was a major advancement over flag tracking. Track and balance results were much more precise.

strobe light and retro-reflective tip targets to allow blade track and lead-lag to be measured in flight. This technique required the operator to manipulate a dial, visually locate a group of targets in space and remember their relative locations (Figure 1-2-17). This method required significant operator skill and training, often making results unreliable. In the early 1980s, the U.S. Army, along with helicopter manufacturers, was looking for a system that could measure blade track consistently and accurately without highly skilled human operators.

Electro-optical tracking, revisited. Chadwick-Helmuth introduced a system in the early 1990s that utilized the method patented nearly three decades before by Chicago Aerial to measure track optically without using a strobe.

In 1995, Dynamic Solutions Systems, Inc., introduced an optical tracker using a method patented in the 1970s but never produced commercially. This technique uses a hand-held electronic camera. Several advantages over the other methods are:

- No tip targets, tape, or painting blades are required.
- Very little power is required, meaning aircraft power is not used.
- The data are machine-readable, making the results reliable and repeatable, even with unskilled users
- Because it uses daylight, the system is totally passive

Figure 1-2-18. Optical Tracker
Photo Courtesy of Dynamic Solutions Systems, Inc.

- The camera is hand-held, eliminating mounting problems. See Figure 1-2-18.

Tracking using vibration sensors. Users found the track conditions of the rotor directly related to vibrations in the airframe. Experimentally, it was found that the vibration information could be used to adjust pitch links and tabs to produce minimum vibrations at all forward speeds. After this process was complete, the blade track could be measured optically and, surprisingly, the blades were not in perfect track. This leads to a quandary: Which is more desirable — perfect track or minimum vibrations?

The value of tracking. In the process of using these tracking methods and measuring the vibrations that resulted, users found that *perfect track* rarely produced minimum vibrations. Various theories have been proposed to explain this effect. One theory is that each blade has a slightly different shape, twist, flexibility, etc., and only by putting them slightly out of track can these variations in lift be compensated. Another theory is that each blade produces a turbulent wake that the trailing blade must fly through. If alternating blades are set to fly high and then low, each blade will have calmer air to fly through, resulting in smoother flight. This effect is more pronounced on aircraft with four or more blades on the main rotor.

Finding rotor faults. Some manufacturers have concluded that blade tracking is of little value, and the only purpose of rotor smoothing should be to minimize vibrations without regard to blade track. This approach has a few drawbacks. First, a bad blade that must be put way out of track to minimize vibrations can only be detected if a tracking system is used. Second, blade track and lag information may make finding some problems with the rotor much easier. For example, a bad damper may produce a subtle transient vibration effect during turns, but a lead-lag measurement will show the damper problem as a blade obviously unstable in angular position.

Rotor Balancing Methods

Early methods of balancing helicopter rotors were limited to static *bubble balancing* of rotor heads, and weighing the blades to be sure the rotor was symmetrically loaded. In the 1970s, maintenance personnel began attaching vibration sensors and using spin-balancing techniques that were commonly used on large industrial blowers. Using a strobe flash to establish the phase of the vibration, along with a meter reading of the amplitude of the vibration, charts, or *nomograms*, could be used to determine where to add weight and how much.

Early complex algorithms. With helicopter rotors, there is interaction between mass imbalance and blade track at hover. If one blade is flying high and producing more lift, it will also lag its normal position due to higher drag force. This induces an effective mass imbalance, due to the out-of-position blade. Because of this and other interactions, users developed procedures, or *algorithms*, that allowed the rotor to be smoothed by performing certain steps in a particular order. For example:

- Track the blades with pitch links on the ground
- Track the blades with pitch links based on hover and forward-flight track.
- Adjust tabs based on track data or vertical vibration data in forward flight
- Spin-balance the main rotor at hover

These procedures required a good deal of skill and accuracy from the maintenance personnel. Once again, the military did not get consistently good results from trying to execute these complex algorithms. The military and helicopter manufacturers asked for automated, computerized methods that eliminated the need for highly skilled users.

Computer-based algorithms. In the 1980s, hand-held computers were programmed to perform the rotor-smoothing algorithms. In some cases, the engineers programming the new computer systems wanted to leapfrog the algorithms that were currently in use. A new concept became popular, theorizing that all interactions between pitch link, mass balance and tab were linear. If this linearity were valid, a single flight to gather data at several flight regimes would be all that was necessary to make any required adjustments.

Another popular concept was that all helicopters of the same type were sufficiently similar to allow a single computer math model to be used, without adjustments for each individual aircraft. Equipment based on these two concepts was developed and introduced into the market.

Unreliable algorithm. Single-flight computer-based rotor-smoothing algorithms work fine as long as the aircraft is close enough to normal conditions for linearity to hold fairly well, and as long as the aircraft is a fairly good match for the math model contained in the program. The problem is: How often are these two conditions met? Experience has shown these conditions are only met 50-75 percent of the time. When these conditions are not met, the algorithm fails and cannot provide any further assistance in rotor smoothing.

Compounding this problem is that a single-flight method does not lead to any method of verifying that the changes recommended were executed properly. This is because the single-flight method requires the user to make several adjustments at once. Due to the interaction of these adjustments, it is difficult to determine if the adjustments were done correctly, or if the combined adjustments resulted in the correct outcome.

Improved fault-tolerant algorithm. Using the single-move method each flight will only result in instructions to make a single adjustment. The next flight will be used to verify that the change matches the math model. If it does not match but is within a tolerance, the math model will be corrected to match the current aircraft. If it does not match and is radically different from the expected result, the user can double-check that the move was as specified and, if so, the move can be taken back out to see if the original data repeats. This algorithm will allow the math model to learn the particular characteristics of the current aircraft. Any errors in user execution of the change will be caught.

Another advantage of this method is that the first flight may only be pulling the aircraft up into hover for 30 seconds. Forward flight will not be attempted until hover-vertical and lateral vibration are low. This will avoid the safety hazard of trying to fly an aircraft in forward-flight conditions when it is badly out of track or balance.

Development of a single-flight program requires hundreds of flights on many different aircraft of the same type. This is required to arrive at a reasonable average math model of this type of aircraft. Since this method cannot learn from normal use, all this data must be gathered and averaged before the program can be written.

This process is time-consuming and costly. During this process, which may take up to a year or more, the program for this aircraft is unavailable. Even when the process is complete, if the math model does not match the user's particular aircraft, the program will not work. The single-move algorithm will only need to know basic mechanical facts like the number of blades, number of tab stations, type of rotor, whether tabs are adjustable, etc., and can then be used immediately to smooth any helicopter rotor.

Section 3
Rotor System Operation

An understanding of the rotor system is necessary to be able to troubleshoot in a logical manner. It is important to know and understand the operation of rotor heads and how rotor blades are driven. Remember that if the components of the rotor system are not properly maintained, a malfunction may occur while in flight, causing possible loss of life and equipment.

Single and Tandem Rotors

Helicopter configurations are classified as single, tandem, coaxial and side-by-side. The single- and tandem-rotor configurations are the most popular.

Single rotor. Helicopters designed to use a main and tail rotor system are referred to as single-rotor helicopters. See Figure 1-3-1. The

Figure 1-3-1. On a single-rotor helicopter, rotor tilt is fairly simple to understand. It tilts in the direction the helicopter is supposed to go.

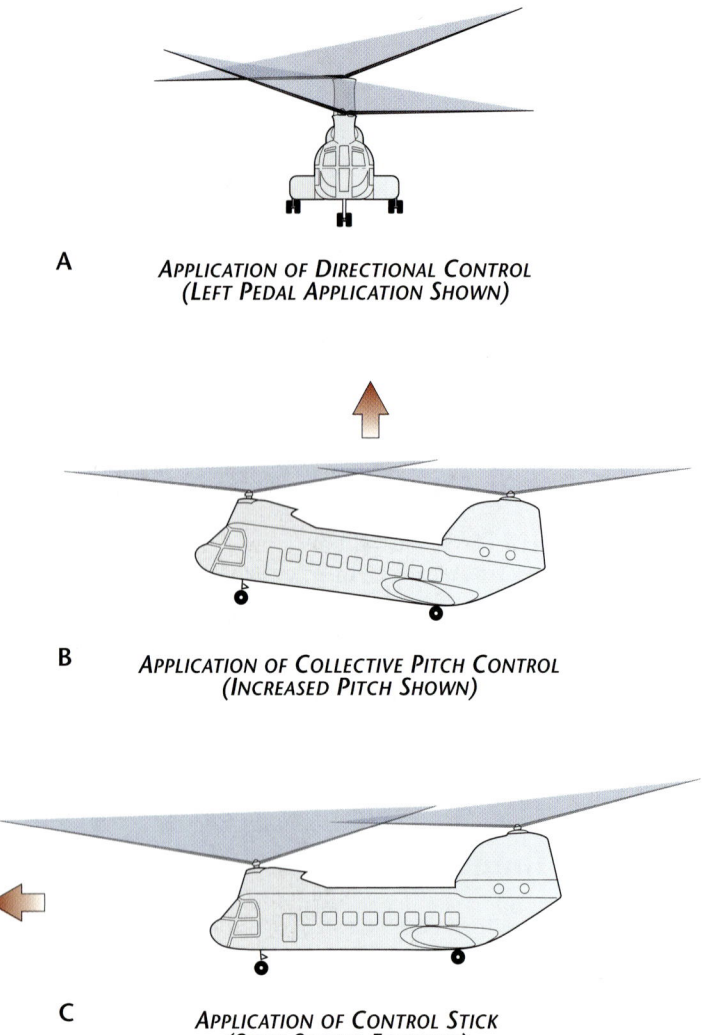

Figure 1-3-2. With no tail rotor, directional control is gained from movements of the rotor disks. With only slight variation between designs, all multiple-rotor helicopters use the same basic directions of rotor tilt for control.

Figure 1-3-3. Tandem-rotor helicopters are typically large, heavy-lift machines.

main rotor provides lift and thrust, while the tail rotor counteracts the torque made by the main rotor. This operation keeps the aircraft from rotating in the opposite direction of the main rotor. The tail rotor also provides the directional control for the helicopter during hovering and engine power changes. Power to operate the main and tail rotors is supplied by the power train system. The single-rotor configuration has the advantage of being simpler and lighter than the tandem-rotor system, and it also requires less maintenance. Since the tail rotor uses a portion of the available power, the single-rotor system has a smaller center-of-gravity range.

Tandem rotor. Most tandem-rotor helicopters are military models. A few civilian examples are operated on oil platforms in the North Sea near Scotland. Some are used in the northwest United States for logging and heavy-lift operations. The tandem-rotor configuration has two main rotor systems, one mounted on each end of the fuselage. Each rotor operates the same as the main rotor on the single-rotor helicopter, except for the direction of rotation of the aft rotor and the method of keeping directional control. The forward rotor turns in a counter-clockwise direction, viewed from below, and the aft rotor rotates in a clockwise direction. See Figure 1-3-2.

A separate anti-torque system is not needed, because the rotor systems rotate in opposite directions, counteracting each other's torque. Advantages of the tandem-rotor system are a larger center-of-gravity range and good longitudinal stability. Because there is no anti-torque rotor, full engine power can be applied to load lifting (Figure 1-3-3). Disadvantages of the tandem-rotor system are a complex transmission and more drag, due to its shape and additional weight.

Tiltrotor. Currently, experimental aircraft/helicopter hybrids are undergoing testing. These aircraft are designed to takeoff vertically like a helicopter, with the ability to transition to horizontal flight like a conventional aircraft. The aircraft would then become a high-speed, conventional, propeller-driven airplane (Figure 1-3-4).

This design concept is an attempt to get around the speed limitations of the conventional helicopter. This limitation is an aerodynamic one caused by the retreating blade. At some point, the retreating blade runs out of lift. When the rotor speed is insufficient to produce an apparent wind on the retreating blade and cannot generate normal lift, the angle of attack will reach a critical point. When the critical point is reached, the retreating blade will stall. With the retreating half of the rotor disc stalled and the

Figure 1-3-4. Tiltrotor transition.

advancing half of the rotor disc creating lift, the helicopter will not fly.

With the tiltrotor, the blades are rotated to the horizontal (down thrust) to produce lift and control, as in a helicopter. Once in flight, the blades can be rotated to vertical (aft thrust) as in a conventional airplane. With a conventional propeller arrangement, the high-speed limitation does not apply.

Coaxial rotor blades. Coaxial rotor blades have both rotors on the same mast, turning in different directions. They do not require torque reaction that needs correcting. Instead of using engine power to drive a tail rotor, all power can be used by the rotors.

While this design solves several problems, it also produces a few. Directional control becomes more difficult, and requires a more complicated control system. While rudder pedals are still used for directional control, they now control torque differential between the two rotors. The pedals, through interconnected linkage, increase collective pitch on one rotor and decrease it on the other. This allows the coaxial system to use torque to rotate the fuselage to the desired heading. Turning the other way is just the opposite, allowing one blade to advance into the torque direction by lessening the correcting factor on the other blade. Figure 1-3-5 illustrates a coaxial-bladed helicopter.

Synchropters. A helicopter with twin masts, each with a rotor turning in an opposite direction, is called a *synchropter*. A classic Kellet synchropter is shown in Figure 1-3-6. To make this arrangement possible, the masts are tilted outwards, while the rotors are timed to intermesh. Like a coaxial-rotor system, a synchropter eliminates the need for a tail rotor. It does, however, require some conventional airplane surfaces to provide better control and stability.

Flight Controls

As a helicopter maneuvers through the air, its attitude in relation to the ground changes. These changes are described with reference to

Figure 1-3-5. Coaxial-rotor systems have some very undesirable control problems in autorotation. As a result, they nearly all have vertical tail surfaces (rudders and vertical fins) to allow autorotation control. This Kamov KA-52 is one of a very few examples of a coaxial-rotor helicopter in flight today.

Figure 1-3-6. Most synchropters have both horizontal stabilizers and vertical fins and rudders. Some can be quite large. Directional control is maintained with differential collective pitch.

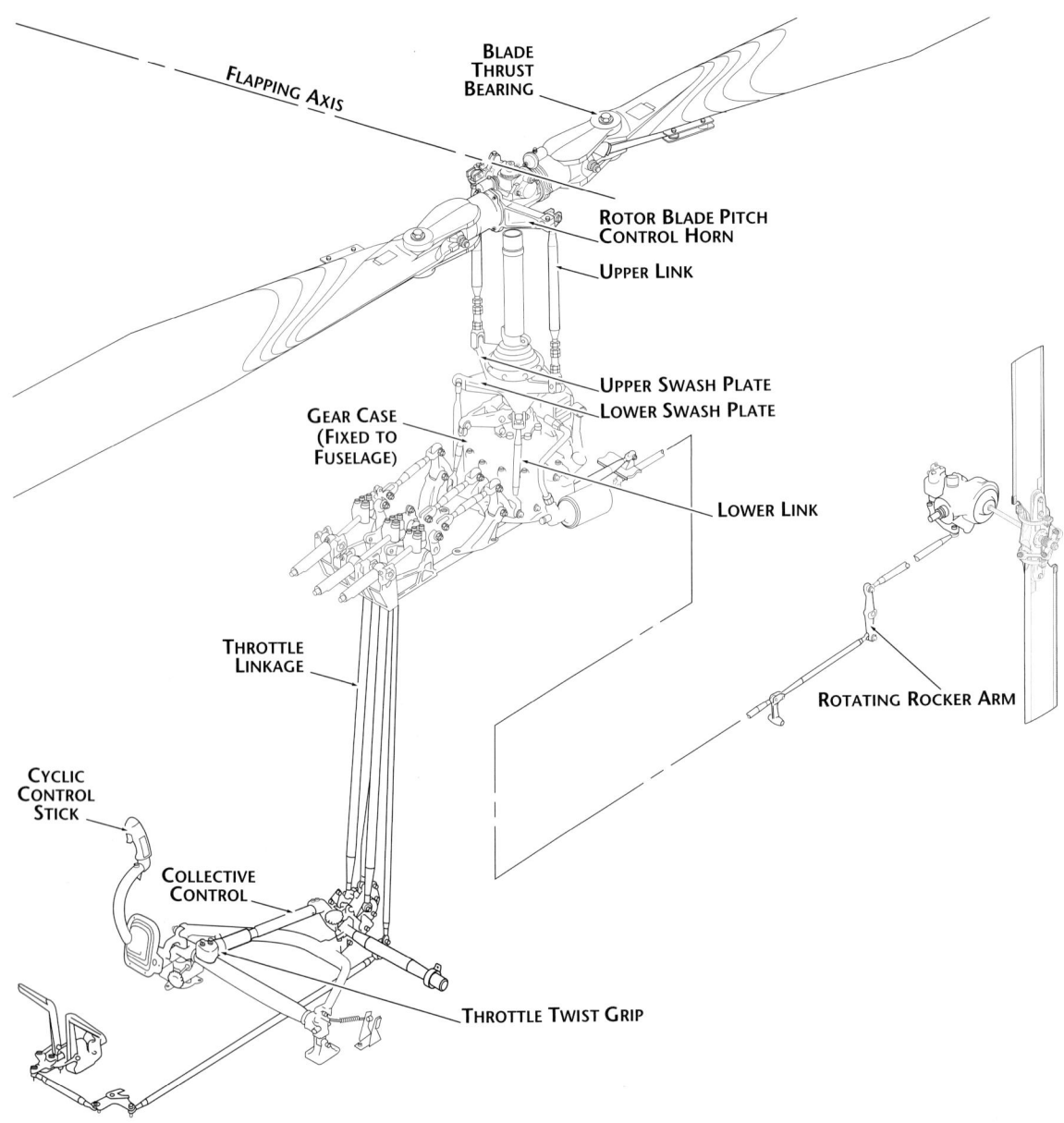

Figure 1-3-7. Two of the three main controls on a conventional helicopter are the collective and its attached throttle control, operated by the left hand, and the cyclic control, operated by the right hand. The torque control pedals, used to control the tail rotor and operated by both feet, are the third.

three axes of flight: lateral, vertical and longitudinal. Movement around the lateral axis produces a nose-up or nose-down attitude, or *pitch*, which is accomplished by moving the cyclic pitch control fore and aft. Movement around the vertical axis produces a nose swing (or change in direction) to the right or left. This movement is called *yaw* and is controlled by the directional control pedals (frequently called rudder pedals, even though there is no rudder on a helicopter). These pedals are used to increase or decrease thrust in the tail rotor of a single-rotor helicopter and to tilt the rotor discs in opposite directions on a tandem-rotor helicopter. Movement around the longitudinal axis is called *roll*. This produces a tilt to the right or left. The movement is accomplished by moving the cyclic pitch control to the right or left.

Cyclic pitch control. The rapidly rotating rotor blades create a disc area that can be tilted in any direction relative to the supporting rotor mast. Horizontal movement is controlled by changing the direction of tilt of the main rotor to produce a force in the desired direction.

The *cyclic pitch control*, shown in Figure 1-3-7, looks like the control stick of a common aircraft. Moving the cyclic control stick changes the angle of attack of the blades. It acts through a mechanical linkage to cause the pitch of each main rotor blade to change during a cycle of rotation. This change tilts the rotor disc.

To move a helicopter forward from a hover, the rotor disc must be tilted forward so that the main rotor provides forward thrust. This change from hovering to flying is called *transition* and is done by moving the cyclic control stick forward.

Collective pitch control. *Collective pitch control* varies the lift of the main rotor by increasing or decreasing the pitch of all blades at the same time. Raising the collective pitch control increases the pitch of the main rotor blades. This increases the lift and causes the helicopter to rise. Lowering the control decreases the pitch of the blades, causing a loss of lift. This produces a corresponding rate of descent. Collective pitch control is also used in coordination with cyclic pitch control to regulate the airspeed. For example, to increase airspeed in level flight, the cyclic is moved forward and the collective is raised at the same time. These controls are illustrated in Figure 1-3-7.

Control plate. If there is a key component that makes controlled helicopter flight possible, it is the *control plate*. Forces from the cyclic and collective pitch controls are carried to the rotor by a control plate, commonly called a *swashplate*, usually located near the bottom of the rotor hub. Essentially, a swashplate is a large, spherical collar that can ride up and down the main mast, while rotating with it. See Figure 1-3-8.

The control plate portion of the swashplate fits around the outside and is moveable in all directions; in essence, the outer portion of a large bearing. The control plate is comprised of an upper and a lower section. Both sections can travel up and down the shaft and swivel, though only the upper section rotates with the hub. The upper plate is attached to the rotor blades by push-pull rods and bell cranks, while the lower non-rotating plate is attached to the cyclic and collective controls, as shown in Figure 1-3-9. All control input to the blades is to the lower plate, through the upper plate and to the push rods.

The collective pitch stick changes the pitch of the blades at the same time by a vertical movement of the entire swashplate. Pressure against the lower plate raises the upper plate, while the push rods twist the blades to a new pitch angle.

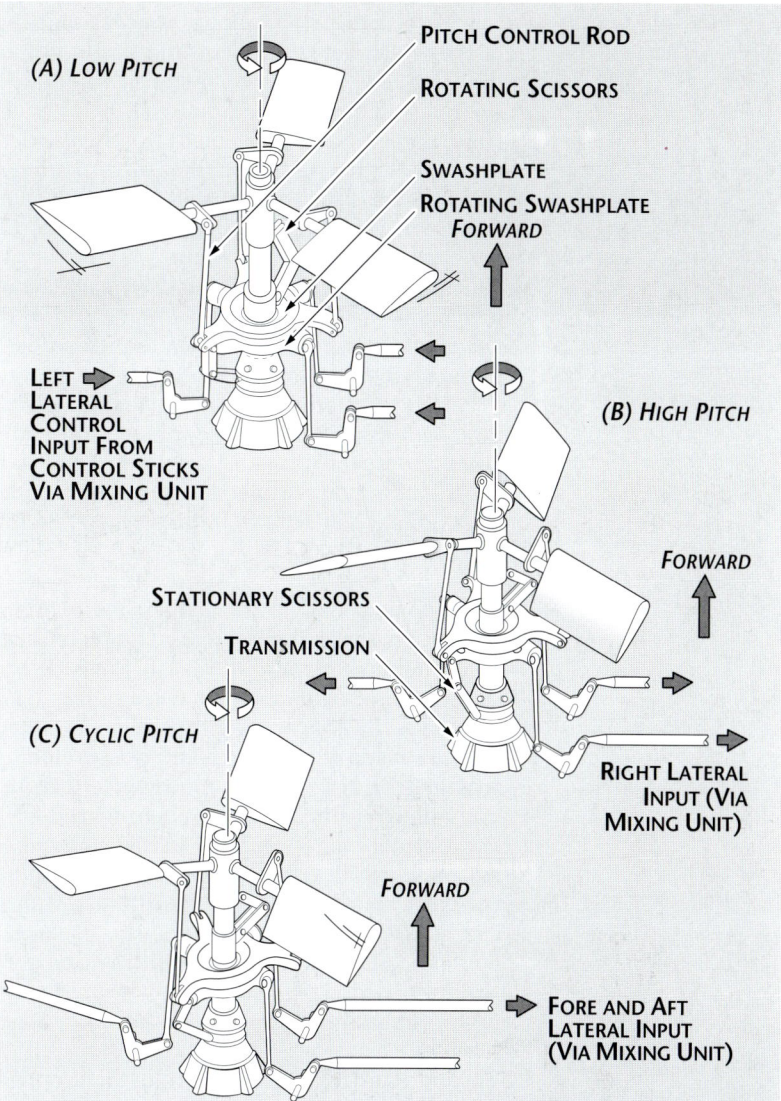

Figure 1-3-8. A swashplate assembly with attached control links. In view (A), the cyclic control is in neutral and the rotor is not lifting. View (B) shows the collective raised, increasing pitch equally in all blades and lifting the helicopter. View (C) shows the cyclic moved to the left, with the collective still UP. This will tilt the rotor disc to the left, and the helicopter will follow.

Figure 1-3-9. Swashplate assembly with collective control

The cyclic pitch stick allows angular shifting of the swashplate to be sent to a single side of the disc. The fixed lower plate is tilted, and the rotating upper plate follows suit. The push rods transmit the movement to the blades, establishing the rotor disc tilt. The direction of tilt of the rotor disc determines the direction of flight: forward, backward, left or right.

Throttle control. By working the throttle control, pilots can keep the same engine and rotor speed, even if a change in blade pitch causes them to increase or decrease engine power. When the main rotor pitch angle is increased, it makes more lift, but it also makes more drag. To overcome the drag and keep the same rotor speed, more power is needed from the engine. This added power is obtained by advancing the throttle.

The opposite is true for a decrease in main rotor pitch-angle. The decreased angle reduces drag, and a reduction in throttle is needed to prevent rotor overspeed. On helicopters with reciprocating engines, the throttle is mounted on the collective pitch grip and is operated by rotating the grip, as on a motorcycle throttle. The collective pitch stick is synchronized with the control of the carburetor so that changes of collective pitch will automatically make small increases or decreases in throttle settings. On turbine engine helicopters, the collective pitch stick is synchronized with the fuel control unit, which controls the power and rotor r.p.m. automatically.

Torque control. In single-rotor helicopters, torque is counteracted by the tail (anti-torque) rotor. It is driven by a power takeoff from the main transmission. The anti-torque rotor runs at a speed in direct ratio to the speed of the main rotor. For this reason, the amount of thrust developed by the anti-torque rotor must be changed as the power is increased or decreased. This is done by the two directional control pedals (anti-torque pedals), which are connected to a pitch-changing device on the anti-torque rotor. Pushing the left pedal increases the thrust of the tail rotor blades, swinging the nose of the helicopter to the left. Pressing the right pedal reduces the angle of the tail rotor blades, decreasing their thrust output and allowing the nose of the helicopter to rotate to the right around the vertical axis.

When a helicopter is in a hover, it is affected by a process known as the *translating tendency*. Simply put, at a motionless hover, the tail rotor wants to cause the helicopter to drift in the direction in which it is producing anti-torque thrust. Manufacturers compensate for this by offsetting the mast a few degrees in the opposite direction. It doesn't always work, and a pilot may sometimes have to compensate by adding a little left cyclic. You can tell if he is doing this because the helicopter will hover with the left landing skid low.

In tandem-rotor, coaxial and synchropter designs, the main rotors turn in opposite directions, thereby neutralizing or eliminating the torque effect.

Emergency Operation

Helicopters are subject to the same failure modes as every other aircraft. In most cases, the results will be the same as a conventional air-

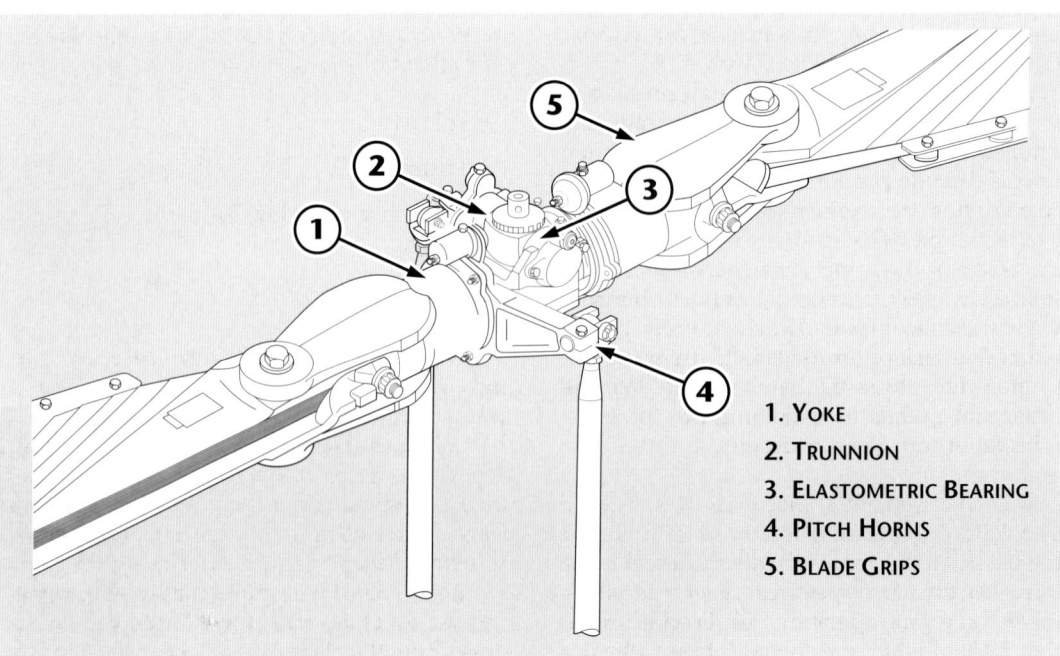

1. Yoke
2. Trunnion
3. Elastometric Bearing
4. Pitch Horns
5. Blade Grips

Figure 1-3-10. Semi-rigid rotor system

plane. The one major area of difference is what happens when an engine fails. The answer is *autorotation*.

Autorotation. All helicopters are fitted with a free-wheeling unit between the engine and the main rotor, usually in the transmission. This free-wheeling unit comes in different forms, but the most popular is the *sprag clutch*. The free-wheeling unit will allow the engine to drive the rotors, but it will not allow the rotors to turn the engine. When the engine(s) fail, the main rotor will still have a considerable amount of inertia and will still turn under its own force and through the aerodynamic force of the air. The free-wheeling unit is designed in such a way as to allow the main rotor to now rotate of its own free will, regardless of engine speed. This is the *autogyro principle*.

Controlled descent. The pilot will still have complete control of the descent and flight controls. The majority of helicopters are designed with a hydraulic pump mounted on the main transmission. As the rotor will still be turning the transmission, the pilot will still have hydraulically assisted flight controls. Descent speed and main rotor r.p.m. can be controlled with the collective control stick, and main rotor r.p.m. can be controlled by increasing the collective pitch, which will increase drag on the rotor blades and thereby slow the main rotor. If the pilot needs to increase rotor r.p.m., collective pitch can be decreased, thereby decreasing drag.

The pilot can usually find a suitable area for a safe landing by normal manipulation of the cyclic control stick and directional, or tail-rotor pedals.

Torque effect is the aircraft's tendency to rotate in the opposite direction to the main rotor due to Newton's Third Law of Motion: *Every action has an equal and opposite reaction.* This is the reason we need a tail rotor or some other form of anti-torque control. The question is, what happens to torque effect during autorotation? Torque effect is directly proportional to the amount of force driving the main rotor. Because of this, when the engine fails, the amount of force driving the main rotor instantaneously decreases, therefore decreasing the torque effect. The fuselage of the helicopter will begin to rotate due to the sudden lack of torque effect. The pilot will therefore have to immediately manipulate the directional pedals to overcome this problem and retain control of the aircraft.

If a helicopter's engine(s) should fail, it is not only possible, but quite easy, for the pilot to retain control and land safely. A fixed-wing aircraft will always need forward speed to safely land, with or without an engine operating. A helicopter can be made to land with zero forward speed whether the engine is operating or not, though it is like a dead-stick landing in a conventional light airplane — the pilot has to be right the first time, because there is only one chance.

Main Rotor Head Assemblies

The main rotor head assembly is attached to and supported by the main gearbox shaft. This assembly supports the main rotor blades and is rotated by torque from the main gearbox. It also provides the means of transmitting the movements of the flight controls to the blades.

Rigid rotor. There have been many attempts, some successful, to produce a helicopter with a rigid rotor assembly. To allow for the necessary blade movement, the hubs are designed using all *elastomeric bearings*. Elastomeric bearings are simply molded, rubber-like material bonded to the appropriate parts. Instead of rotating like conventional bearings, elastomeric bearings flex, or twist, to allow the proper movement. The material composition of elastomeric bearings varies with the specific application. Many conventional helicopters use elastomeric bearings, in conjunction with conventional ball, roller and bronze bearings.

At this point, rigid rotors are still used only on experimental military helicopters.

Semi-rigid. The semi-rigid rotor head gets its name from the fact that the two blades are rigidly interconnected and pivot about a point slightly above their center (Figure 1-3-10). There are no flapping or drag hinges like those on the articulating head. Since the blades are interconnected, when one blade moves upward the other moves downward a corresponding distance. The main rotor hub is of a semi-rigid, underslung design consisting basically of these components:

- Yoke (1)
- Trunnion (2)
- Elastomeric bearing (3)
- Pitch horns (4)
- Blade grips (5)

The yoke is mounted to the trunnion by bearings that permit rotor flapping. Cyclic and collective pitch-change inputs are received through pitch horns mounted on the trailing edge of the grips. The grips, in turn, are permitted to rotate about the yoke extensions on bearings, resulting in the desired blade pitch. Adjustable drag braces are attached to the grips and main rotor blades to maintain alignment. Frequently, blade-centrifugal loads are transferred from the blade grips to the extensions by tension-torsion straps.

Fully articulated. A fully articulated rotor head gets its name from the fact that it is jointed. See Figures 1-2-9 and 1-3-9. Jointing is made with vertical and horizontal pins. The fully articulated rotor head assembly has three or more blades, each acting as a single unit and capable of flapping, feathering, leading and lagging. The assembly is made up primarily of:

- An internally splined hub
- Horizontal and vertical hinge pins
- Extension links
- Pitch shafts
- Pitch housing
- Dampers
- Pitch arms
- Bearing surfaces
- Connecting parts

The extension links are attached to the hub by the horizontal pins, and to the forked end of the extension link. The pitch shafts are attached by the vertical pins. The pitch housing is fitted over and fastened to the pitch shaft by the tension-torsion straps, which are pinned at the inboard end of the pitch shaft and the outboard end of the pitch-varying housing. One end of the dampers is attached to a bracket on the horizontal pins; the other end is fastened to the pitch housing.

Tail Rotor Hubs

The tail rotor hub (anti-torque rotor) is used as a centering fixture to attach the tail rotor blades so that they rotate about a common axis. It accepts the necessary pitch-change mechanism to provide automatic equalization of thrust on the advancing and retreating blade, or equal and simultaneous pitch change to counteract torque made by the main rotor system. Hub design varies with the manufacturer. Typical configurations are the hinge-mounted, flex-beamed and fully articulated types.

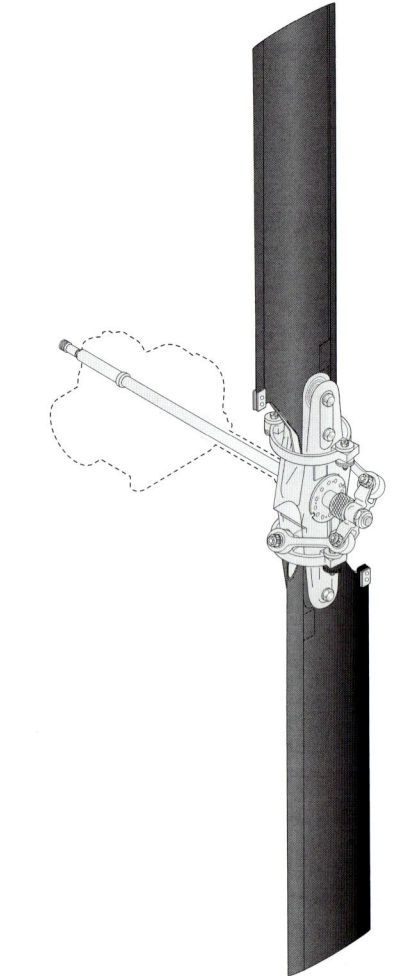

Figure 1-3-11. Hinge-mounted tail rotor system

Hinge-mounted type. A single two-blade, controllable-pitch tail rotor is located on the left side of the tail rotor gearbox (Figure 1-3-11). It is composed of the blades and the hub, and is driven through the tail rotor gearbox.

Blades are of all-metal construction and attached by bolts in blade grips, which are mounted through bearings to spindles of the hub yoke. The tail rotor hub is hinge-mounted to provide automatic equalization of thrust on advancing and retreating blades. Control links provide equal and simultaneous pitch change to both

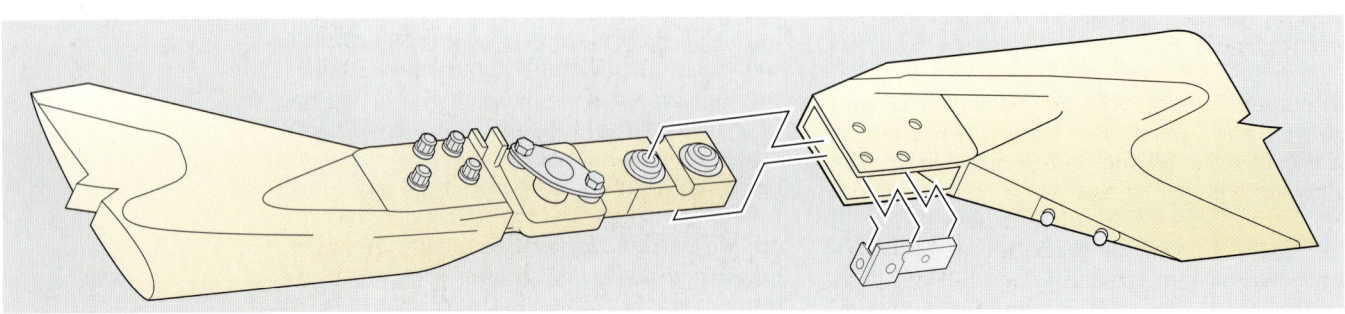

Figure 1-3-12. Flex-beamed-type tail rotor system

blades. The tail rotor counteracts the torque of the main rotor and provides directional control.

Flex-beamed type. The tail rotor hub and blade assembly counteracts torque of the main rotor and provides directional control. It consists of the hub and two blades (Figure 1-3-12). The hub assembly has a preconed, flex-beamed-type yoke and a two-piece trunnion connected to the yoke by self-lubricating, spherical flapping bearings. The *trunnion*, which is splined to the tail rotor gearbox shaft, drives the blades and serves as a flapping stop for the tail rotor. The yoke has two self-lubricating, spherical bearings as attaching the points for each rotor blade. Rotor pitch change is accomplished at these bearings.

Fenestron tail rotor. First used in 1967 by Aerospatiale in its Gazelle and Dauphine helicopters, the fensetron system is a slightly different approach to the tail rotor. At first glance, it looks like a multi-bladed fan surrounded by a duct system that is built into the tail section of the helicopter (Figure 1-3-13). The fan is typically 30-50 percent smaller than a conventional tail rotor. Naturally, it turns somewhat faster. With the higher r.p.m. comes an increase in noise, which is offset somewhat by better airflow around the rotor tips because of the duct. Airflow through the duct also increases overall thrust. The amount of torque control is varied by pitch changes in the fan blades, just as in a conventional tail rotor.

The fan shroud also makes the working environment safer for the ground crew, because it is more difficult to be struck by the tail rotor. Flight safety is also enhanced, because there is less likelihood of tail rotor strikes.

Fully articulated type. The articulated tail rotor system (Figure 1-3-14) counterbalances disturbing forces in the same way that the hinge-type rotor does. The major difference is that the blades can lead and lag individually during rotation.

NOTAR® (NO-TAil Rotor). The McDonnell Douglas Helicopter's NOTAR design is, as its name implies, a rotorless torque-control system. While its operation is simple, there are several things going on at the same time. See Figure 1-3-15.

The system starts with a fan driven by the main rotor transmission. Fan-blade pitch changes are controlled by the anti-torque pedals. The fan supplies low-pressure air to the hollow tail boom. Some of this air is directed through a series of slots in the tail boom, with the balance exiting through a 90° duct, called a *direct jet thruster*, located at the rear of the tail boom.

Figure 1-3-13. Fenestron tail rotor system. The fan shroud protects against damage to the rotors, the most common type of accident for helicopters.

Anti-torque pedals also control the amount of air exiting the jet thruster.

One might think that the air blast from the jet thruster simply blows the tail in the desired direction. As with most things in aviation, it isn't that simple. Fully 70 percent of the torque control comes from the airflow created by the series of slots in the tail boom.

As the downwash from the main rotor blades flows over the tail boom, the air pressure exhausted by the slots in the tail boom redirect it. This redirection results in a classic application of the *Coanda Effect* by producing a downwash (in this case, maybe a sidewash would be a more accurate description). Just as in a normal airfoil, a negative pressure is created, only the resulting lift is applied opposite to the torque.

Figure 1-3-14. Fully articulated tail rotor system

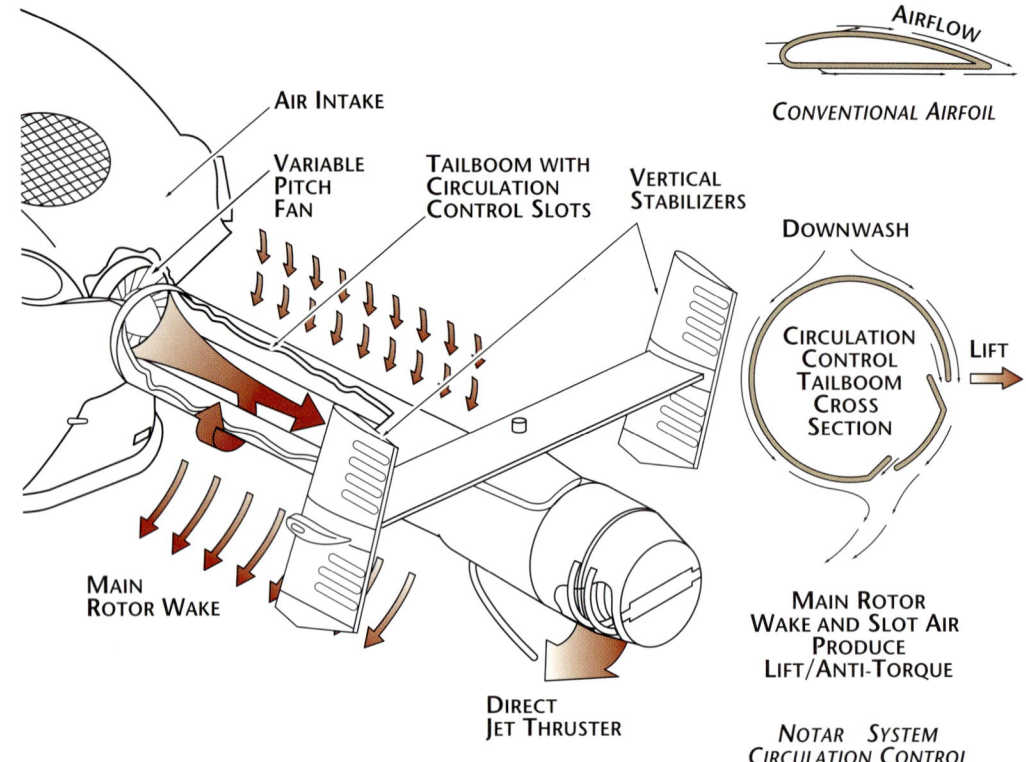

Figure 1-3-15. The NOTAR® system stops accidents from tail rotor strikes by eliminating the tail rotor altogether.

The NOTAR system is almost self-compensating. Higher torque from the main rotor produces more downwash, resulting in more anti-torque pressure, with lower main-rotor torque producing less downwash. The vertical stabilizers are also connected to the anti-torque pedals and provide some additional directional control in flight. They also provide directional control during autorotation.

Section 4
Rotor Blades

Main Rotor Blades

The rotor blade is an airfoil designed to rotate about a common axis to produce lift and provide directional control for a helicopter, thus the name rotary wing. The design and construction of rotor blades vary with the manufacturer, although they all strive to manufacture the most efficient and economical lifting device. The particular helicopter design places certain requirements on the main rotor blades, which influence their design and construction. Most rotor blades are designed as symmetrical airfoils to produce a stable aerodynamic pitching characteristic.

Aerodynamic stability is achieved when the center of gravity, center of pressure and blade-feathering axis all act at the same point. The blade is more stable in flight because these forces continue to act at almost the same point as the blade changes pitch.

There are some helicopters equipped with an unsymmetrical airfoil. This unsymmetrical airfoil blade is capable of producing greater lift than a symmetrical airfoil blade of similar dimensions. Aerodynamic stability is achieved by building a 3° upward angle into the trailing edge section of the blade. This prevents excessive center-of-pressure travel when the rotor blade angle of attack is changed.

Types of Rotor Blades

A variety of material is used in the construction of rotor blades: wood, aluminum, steel, brass, fiberglass and advanced composites are all used at one time or another.

Wooden blades. Various kinds of wood have been used in rotor construction, with spruce and balsa being the most common. Steel fittings

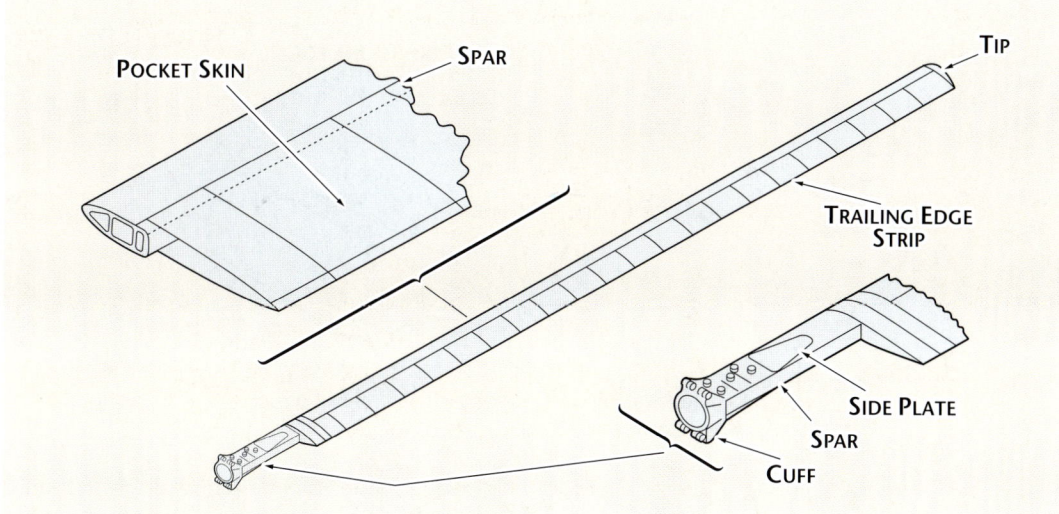

Figure 1-4-1 Metal rotor blades

are screwed to the blade butts for attachment of the blade grips and drag braces. Wooden blades are normally covered with fiberglass, with a stainless steel leading edge attached. The steel is necessary to reduce erosion. Most blades have a steel bar laminated inside the forward portion of the blade. Its purpose is to provide chordwise balance, similar to leading-edge weights in ailerons. Wooden blades are manufactured in pairs and must normally be replaced as a set. Blade repair is limited and should only be performed according to the manufacturer's instructions.

Metal blades. A typical metal blade has a hollow, extruded aluminum spar that forms its leading edge (Figure 1-4-1). Aluminum pockets bonded to the trailing edge of the spar assembly provide streamlining. An aluminum tip cap is fastened with screws to the spar and tip pocket. A steel cuff bolted to the root end of the spar provides a means of attaching the blade to the rotor head. A stainless steel abrasion strip is adhesive-bonded to the leading edge.

Fiberglass blades. The main load-carrying member of a fiberglass blade is a hollow, extruded steel spar (Figure 1-4-2). The *fairing*, or pockets, are fiberglass covers bonded over either aluminum ribs or aluminum foil honeycomb. The fairing assembly is then bonded to the trailing edge of the spar. The trailing edge of the fairing is bonded to a stainless steel strip forming the blade trailing edge. Rubber chafing strips are bonded between the fairings to prevent fairing chafing and provide a weather seal for the blade fairings. A steel socket threaded to the blade spar shank provides an attaching point to the rotor head. A stainless steel tip cap is fastened by screws to the blade spar and blade tip pocket.

Blade Nomenclature

Planform. The blade *planform* is the shape of the rotor blade when viewed from above (Figure 1-4-3). It can be uniform (parallel) or tapered. Uniform planforms are most often selected by the manufacturer because, with all the ribs and other internal blade parts the same size, they are easier to manufacture. The uniform blade requires only one stamping die for all ribs, which reduces cost. This design has a

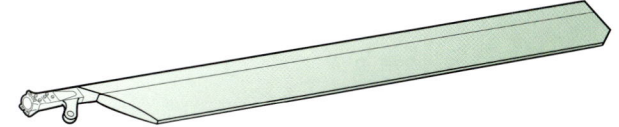

Figure 1-4-2. Fiberglass rotor blade

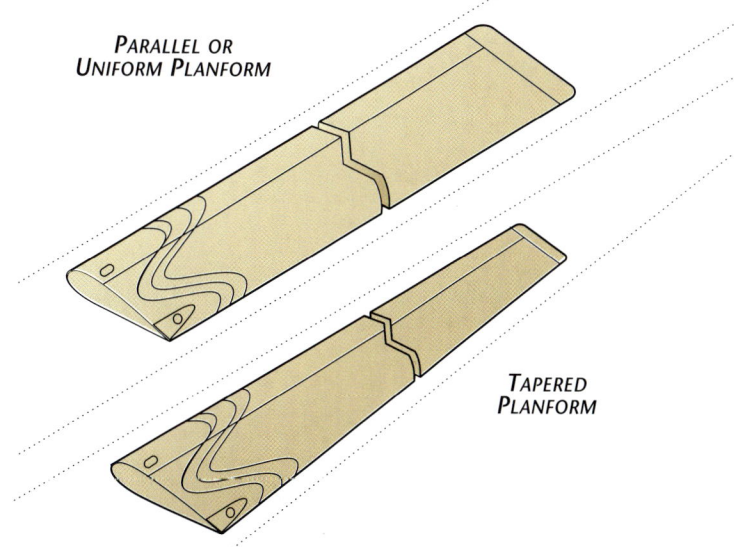

Figure 1-4-3. Blade planform

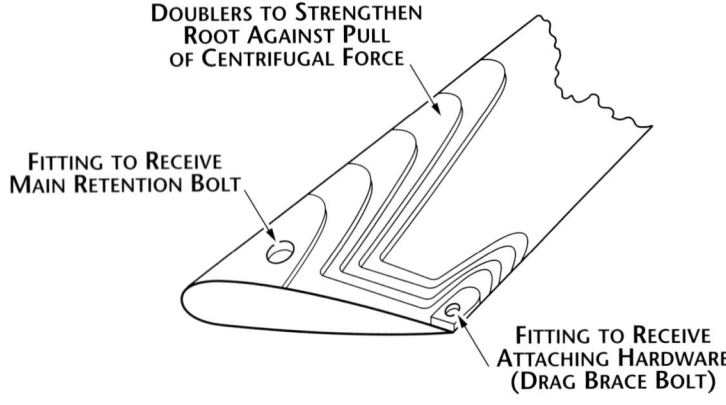

Figure 1-4-4. Blade root

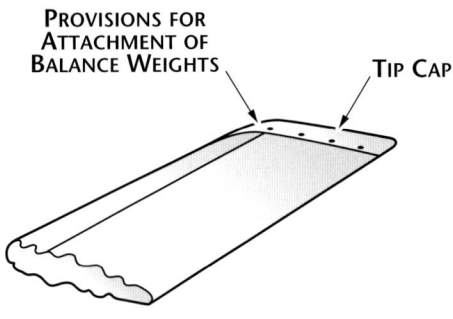

Figure 1-4-5. Blade tip

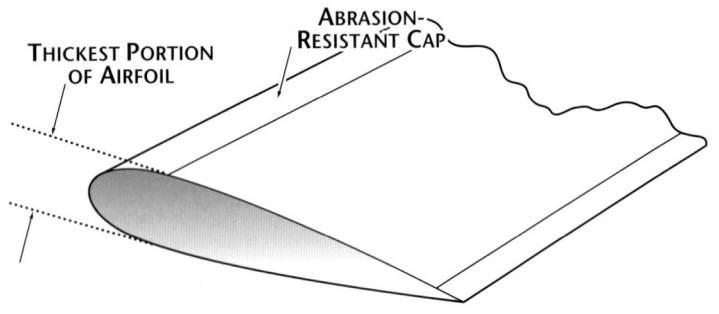

Figure 1-4-6. Blade leading edge

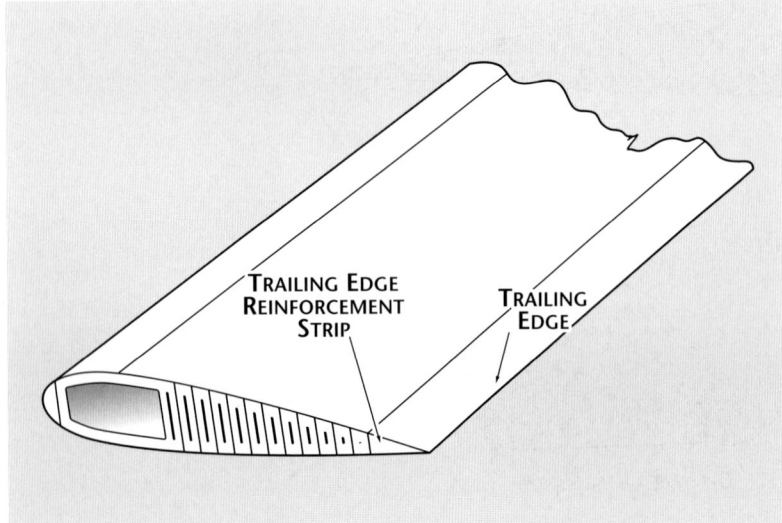

Figure 1-4-7. Blade trailing edge

large blade surface area at the tip. It must therefore incorporate negative tip twists to make a more uniform lift along the blade span.

If the blade angle is the same for the length of the blade, the blade will produce more lift toward the tip because it moves at a higher speed than the blade root. This unequal lift will cause the blade to cone (bend up on the end) too much. The tapered planform blade makes a more uniform lift throughout its length. Few blade manufacturers use it, however, because the manufacturing cost is too high due to the many different-shaped parts required to fit the tapered airfoil interior.

Twist. The blade-element theory applies to a rotor blade as well as to propellers. Therefore, most rotor blades are twisted negatively from root to tip to get more even distribution of lift.

Skin. The skin may be fiberglass or aluminum and may consist of single or multiple layers. The thin skin can easily be damaged by careless ground handling. Three types of blade coverings are used: one-piece wrap-around aluminum alloy, single-pocket and multiple-pocket. Most main rotor blades are of single-pocket or multiple-pocket , or fairing, construction.

Root. The blade root is the section nearest the center of rotation that provides a means of attachment to the rotor head (Figure 1-4-4). It is heavier and thicker than the rest of the blade in order to resist centrifugal forces.

Tip. The tip is located furthest from the center of rotation and travels at the highest speed during operation (Figure 1-4-5). The blade tip cap also has a means for attaching balance weights.

Leading edge. The part of the blade that meets the air first is the *leading edge* (Figure 1-4-6). For the edge to work efficiently, airfoils must have a leading edge that is thicker than the trailing edge. The leading edge of all blades is covered with a hard, abrasion-resistant cap or coating to protect against erosion.

Trailing edge. The *trailing edge* is that part of the blade that follows, or trails, the leading edge and is the thinnest section of the airfoil (Figure 1-4-7). The trailing edge is strengthened to resist damage, which happens most often during ground handling.

Span and span line. The *span* of a rotor blade is its length from root to tip (Figure 1-4-8). The *span line* is an imaginary line running parallel to the leading edge from the root of the blade to the tip. Span line is important in the blade repair, because damages are often located and classified according to their relation to it. Defects paralleling the span line are usually less serious, because stress lines move parallel to the span line and would therefore pass the damage without interruption. Chordwise damage interrupts lines of stress.

Chord and chord line. The *chord* of a rotor blade is its width measured at the widest point (Figure 1-4-9). The *chord line* of a rotor blade is an imaginary line from the leading edge to the trailing edge, perpendicular to the span line. Blade chord line is used as a reference line to make angular measurements.

Spar. The main supporting part of a rotor blade is the *spar* (Figure 1-4-10). Spars are usually made of aluminum, steel or fiberglass, and they always extend along the span line of the blade. Often, the spar is D-shaped and forms the leading edge of the airfoil. Spars are of different shapes, depending on the blade material and on how they fit into the blade airfoil.

Doublers. *Doublers* are flat plates that are bonded to both sides of the root end of some rotor blades

Figure 1-4-8. Span and span line

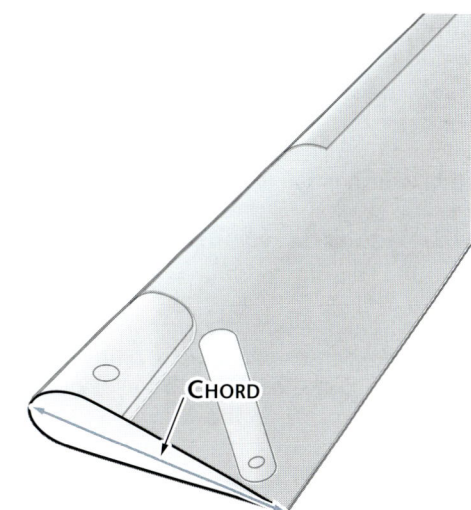

Figure 1-4-9. Rotor-blade chord

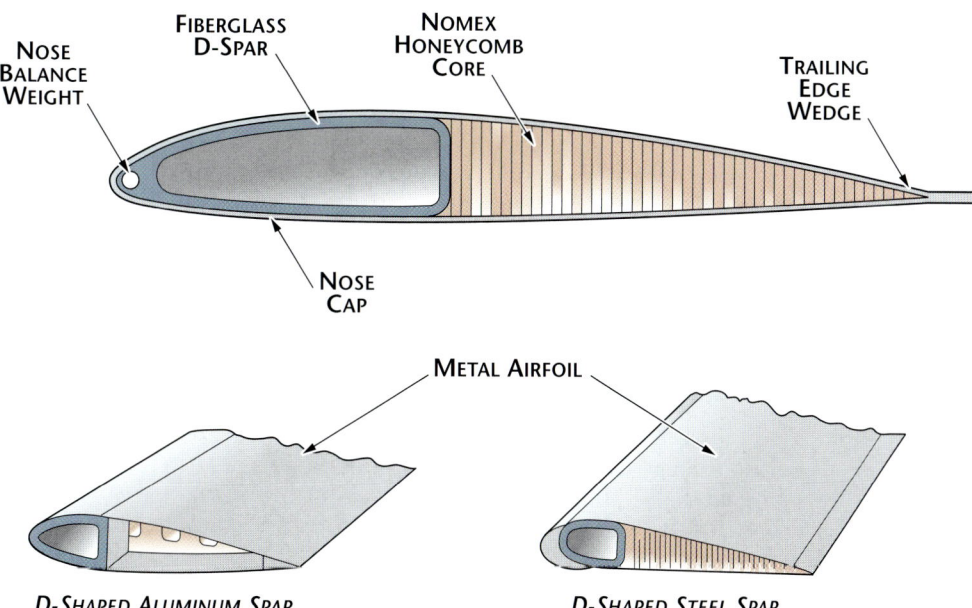

Figure 1-4-10. Blade spars

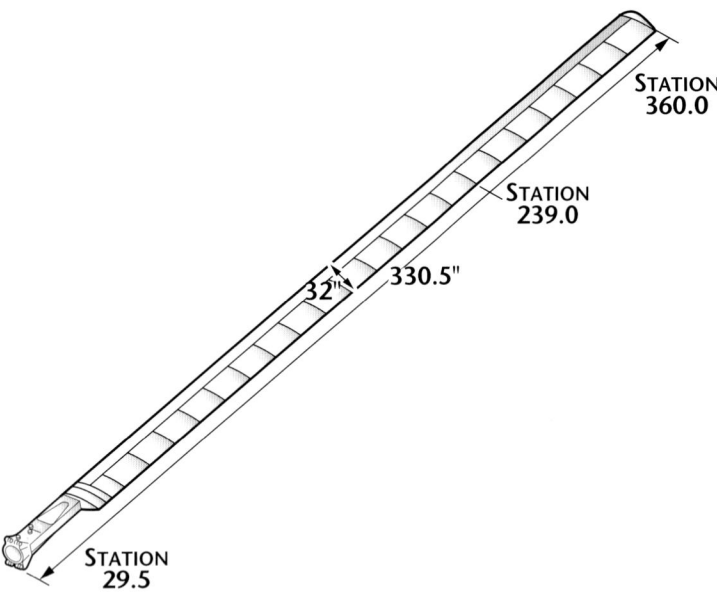

Figure 1-4-11. Rotor blade stations numbered from root end

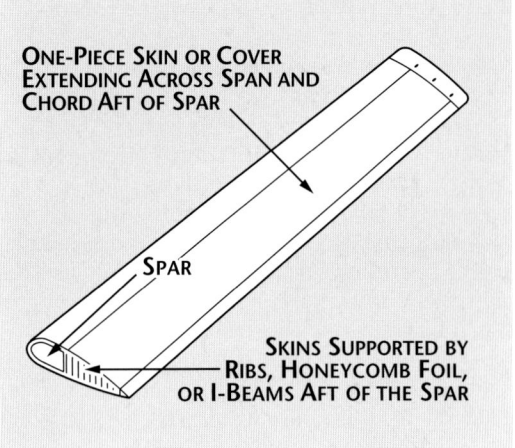

Figure 1-4-12. Single-pocket rotor blade cover

to provide more strength. Not all blades use doublers, since some spars are made thick enough to provide the needed strength at the root end.

Top. The low-pressure side of the blade is the *top*. The top is the surface that is viewed from above the helicopter. It is usually painted white or black when the blade skin is plastic or metal and white for composite blades.

Bottom. The high-pressure side of the blade is the *bottom*. The bottom is viewed from the ground. It is always painted a lusterless black to prevent glare from reflecting off the blade and into crew compartments during flight.

Blade stations. Rotor *blade stations* are numbered in inches or centimeters and are measured from one of two starting points. Some rotor blades are numbered from the center of rotation (center of the mast), which is designated station zero, and outward to the blade tip. Others are numbered from the root end of the blade, station zero, and outward to the blade tip (Figure 1-4-11).

Blade Construction

Single-pocket (fairing). The single-pocket, or *fairing*, blade is made with a one-piece skin on top and bottom. See Figure 1-4-12.

Each skin extends across the entire span and chord, behind the spar. This style is simple and easy to make because of the minimum number of pockets, or fairings, that need positioning and clamping during the bonding process. Minor damage to the skin often results in the blade being thrown away, since replacing the skin costs more than replacing the blade.

Multiple pockets (fairings). Most large rotor blades built with the multiple-pocket or fairing shape behind the spar are costly (Figure 1-4-13). When this type of blade is selected, it is because damage to the skin cover requires that only the pocket (fairing) be replaced. The high-cost blade can then be used repeatedly. This type of blade is more flexible across the span, which cuts down on blade vibrations.

Internal structural components. Rotor blades have internal structural parts that help to support the blade skin: ribs, I-beams, spanwise channels and aluminum honeycomb foil.

Bonds and bonding. *Bonding* is a method of putting two or more parts together with an adhesive compound. Bonding helps reduce the use of hardware like bolts, rivets and screws, which all need holes and therefore weaken the strength of the bond. To ensure full strength, manufacturers never drill holes in load-carrying parts of the blade except at the inboard and outboard ends. However, bonds react to the chemical action of paint thinners and many cleaning solvents. Careless use of these solvents will dis-

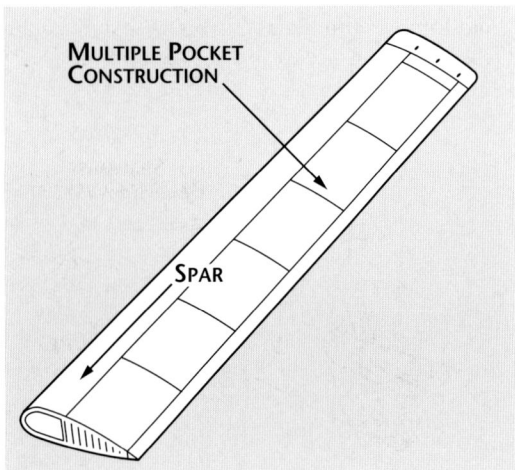

Figure 1-4-13. Multiple-pocket rotor blade cover

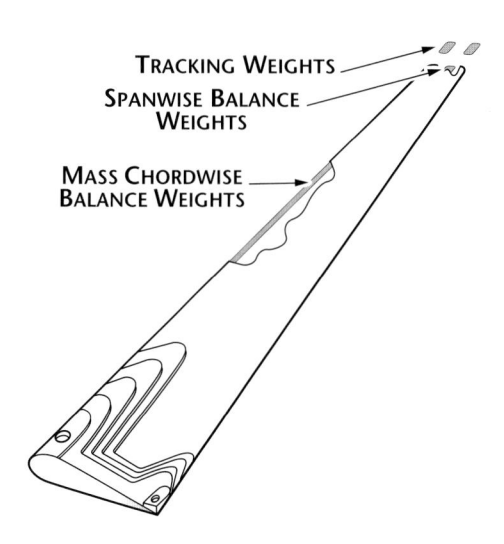

Figure 1-4-15. Blade balance weights

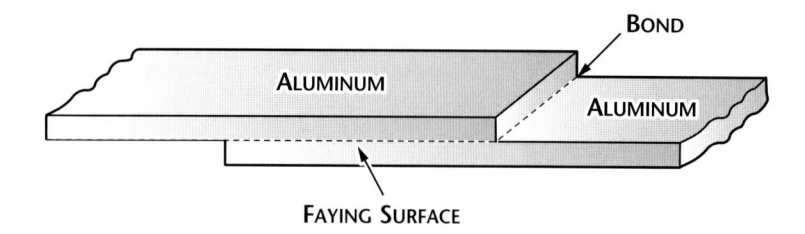

Figure 1-4-14. Faying surface

solve bonded joints. The surface area where two objects are bonded together is known as the *faying surface* (Figure 1-4-14).

Blade Balance

The three types of weights to balance the blade are: mass balance, spanwise and tracking (Figure 1-4-15).

Mass balance weights. Bars are placed into the leading edge of a blade while the blade is being manufactured (Figure 1-4-16). This is to ensure that correct chordwise balance is about 25 percent of chord. The type of metal and its shape and location vary with the manufacturer. The technician is not allowed to move the weights in most helicopter blades. When moving of weights is allowed, however, remember that changing weights will move the center of gravity forward or backward.

Spanwise balance weights. These are mounted at the tip of the blade, usually where they can be attached securely to the spar (Figure 1-4-17). They are normally installed in the blade during manufacture. The technician is not always permitted to move these weights. When movement is necessary, always remember that adding spanwise weight moves the center of gravity outward. Subtracting weight moves the center of gravity inward. When moving the spanwise weight is permitted, the weight change is computed mathematically by the technician after the blade has been weighed.

Tracking weights. To be efficient and vibration-free, all rotating blades should track on approximately the same level or plane of rotation. Failure of blades to track correctly causes vibrations, which can result in the following:

- Damage to parts of the helicopter
- Reduction of riding comfort
- A loss in blade performance due to air turbulence made by the rotating blades

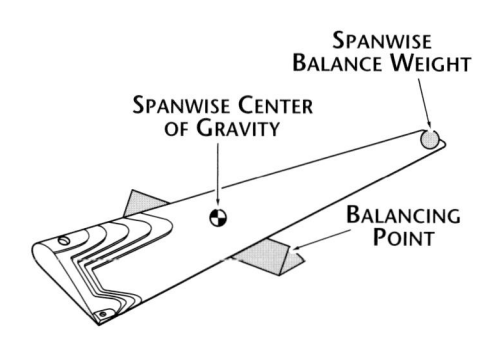

Figure 1-4-17. Spanwise balance weights

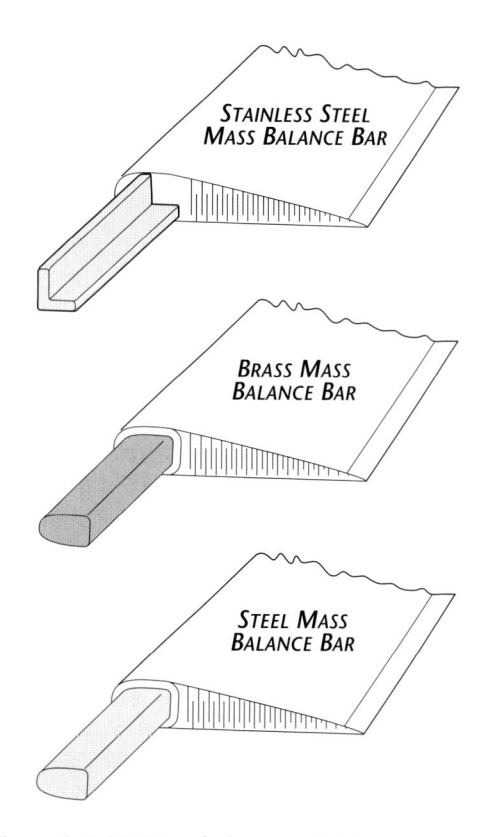

Figure 1-4-16. Mass balance weights

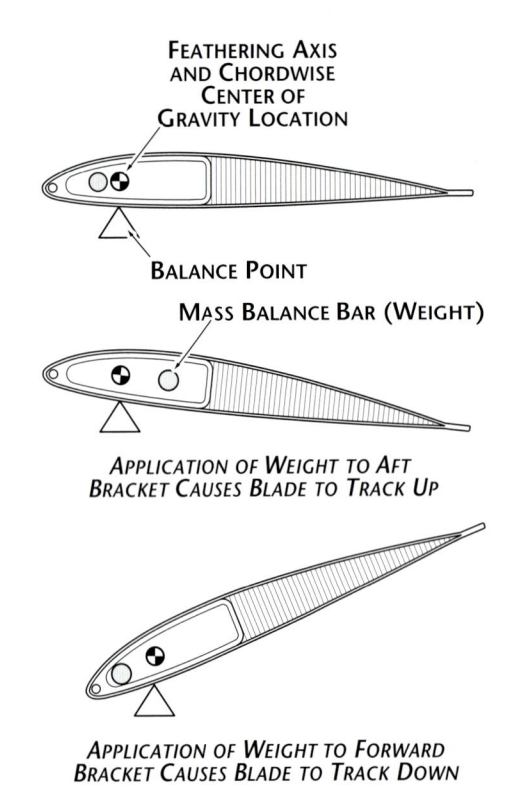

Figure 1-4-18. Tracking weights

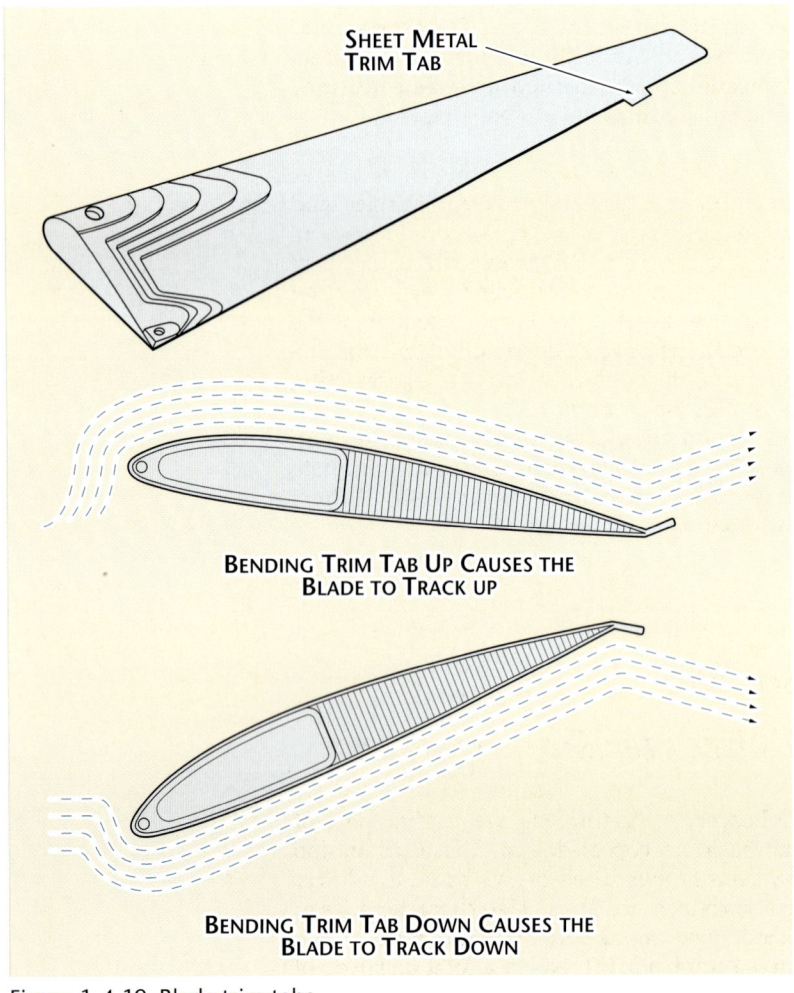

Figure 1-4-19. Blade trim tabs

One way of retaining track is to attach *tracking weights* in front of and behind the feathering axis at the blade tips (Figure 1-4-18). By adding, removing or shifting tracking weights, the technician can move a blade track up or down to match the track of the other blade or blades. This causes all blades to move in the same tip path plane.

Trim tabs. Another method used to align the rotor blade on the same plane of rotation is the use of *trim tabs* (Figure 1-4-19). Using tracking weights adds to building costs, but the same results may be achieved by cheaper methods, such as, putting a sheet metal trim tab on the trailing edge of the blade. The trim tab is usually located near the tip of the blade, where the speed is great enough to get the needed aerodynamic reaction. In tracking operations, the trim tab is bent up to make the leading edge of the rotor blade fly higher in the plane of rotation or bent down to make it fly lower. The trim tabs are adjusted until the rotor blades are all flying in the same plane of rotation.

Tail Rotor Blades

Tail rotor blades are used to provide directional control only. Made of metal or fiberglass, they are built similarly to main rotor blades. Metal tail rotor blades are made of aluminum; the spars can be made of solid aluminum extrusions, hollow aluminum extrusions or aluminum sheet channels. Figure 1-4-20 shows typical tail-rotor blade construction.

Metal blades. The blade skins are formed around and bonded to the spars, which in most cases form the leading edge of the blades. Metal blade skins are supported from the inside with aluminum honeycomb, ribs and some smaller blades that have no bracing or support inside themselves.

Fiberglass blades. The blade skins are formed around and bonded to H-shaped titanium spars. They are supported inside with aluminum honeycomb. The space around the spar is filled with foam plastic.

Blade Balance

Spanwise. On some models, spanwise balance is accomplished by adding or subtracting washers on the blade tip. On others, the washers are added to the blade-cuff attaching bolts.

Some models are balanced chordwise by adding weights to the tips behind the spanwise balance screw. Others are balanced by adding weights to the trailing edge of the blades near the cuff end.

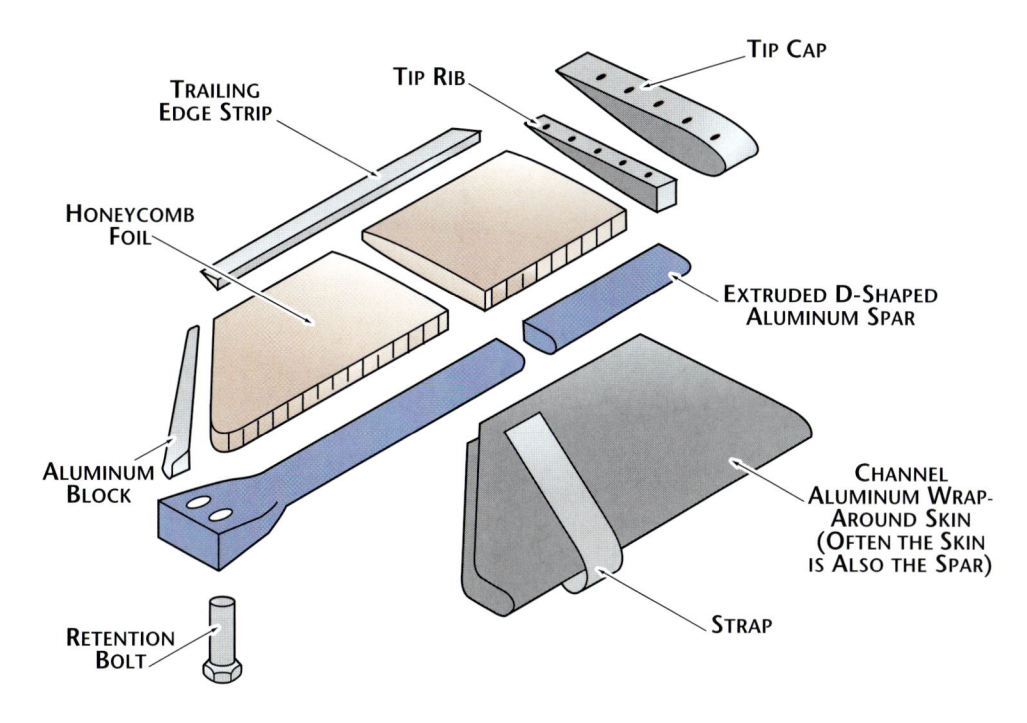

Figure 1-4-20. Tail-rotor blade construction

Trammeling. Fully articulated tail-rotor systems must be trammeled before they are balanced. *Trammeling* consists of aligning the tail-rotor blades an equal distance to one another with a 2° angle of lead to the blades.

Nondestructive Inspection

Nondestructive inspection (NDI) methods determine integrity, composition, physical/electrical/thermal properties and dimensions without causing a change in any of these characteristics in the item being inspected. The different types of NDI used in helicopter maintenance are:

- Liquid penetrant methods
- Magnetic particle methods
- Electromagnetic methods
- Ultrasonic methods
- Penetrating radiation
- Harmonic bond testing

NDI in the hands of a trained and experienced technician is capable of detecting flaws or defects with a high degree of accuracy and reliability. Maintenance technicians should know the capabilities of each method. Equally important, they should recognize the limitations of each method. NDI is not a panacea for inspection ills. It is merely a means of extending the human senses. No NDI method should ever be considered conclusive. A defect indicated by one method must be confirmed by some other method to be reliable.

Further, NDI equipment is highly sensitive and capable of detecting discontinuities and anomalies that may be of no consequence to the particular service for which a component is used. Limits for acceptance and rejection are thus as much a part of an inspection as the method itself. For example, ultrasonic inspection equipment is fully capable of detecting normal grain boundaries in some cast alloys. Inspection criteria must be designed to overlook these normal returns, and to discriminate in favor of those discontinuities that will affect the component in service.

Section 5

Helicopter Transmissions

Helicopter transmissions are a vital part of the basic helicopter design. The transmission converts higher speed engine r.p.m. to a lower speed rotor r.p.m. The design characteristics of blade span, chord and twist needed to maximize rotor blade lift require a rotation speed of between 300 and 400 r.p.m. The blades on the

Helicopter Fundamentals

Figure 1-5-1. Helicopter transmissions are the link between a rotorcraft's engine(s) and its main and tail rotors. The transmission on this Bell 412 is visible during a post-maintenance test run.

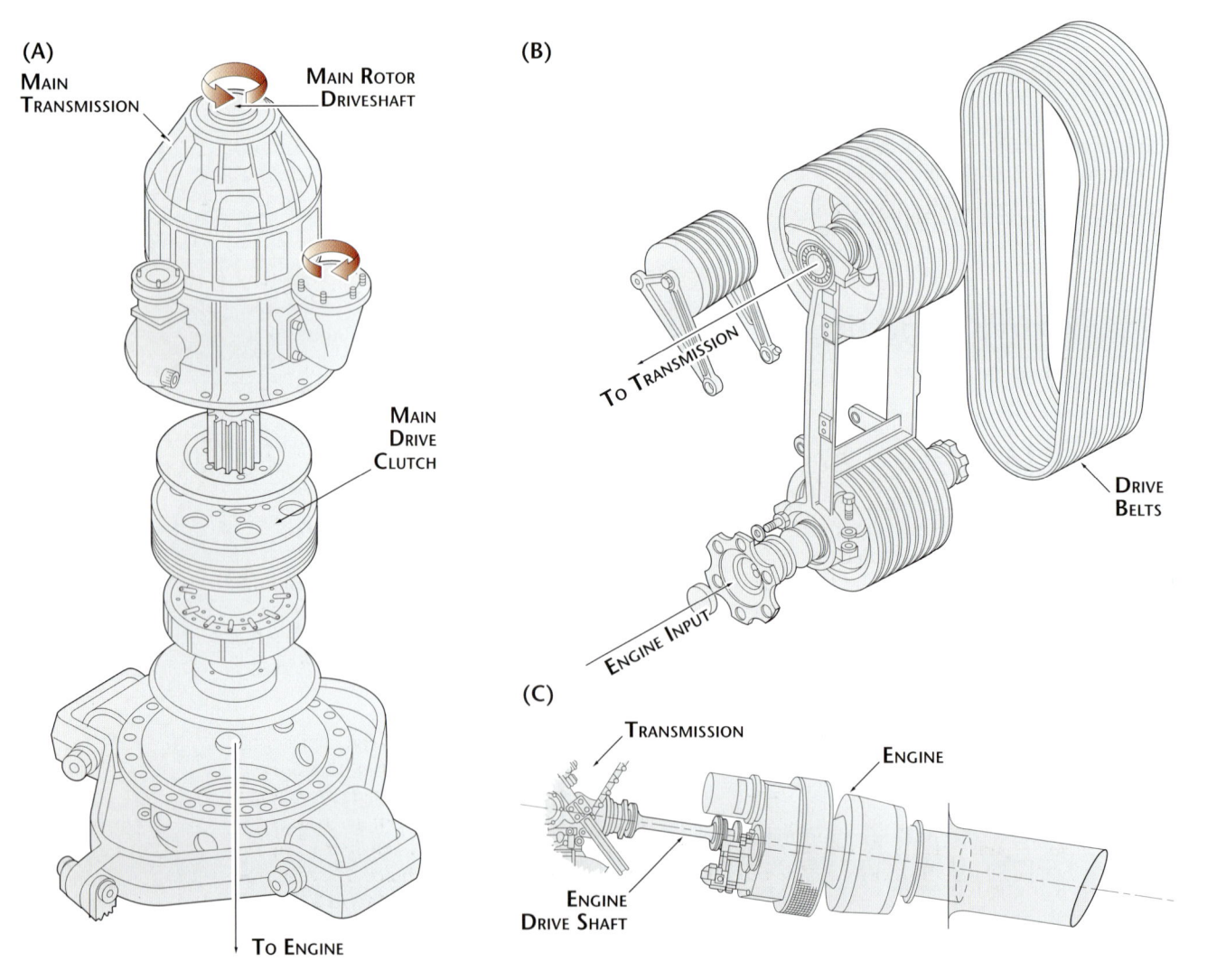

Figure 1-5-2. Transmission configurations: (A) Direct engine to transmission coupling; (B) Arrangement of belts; (C) Short drive shaft

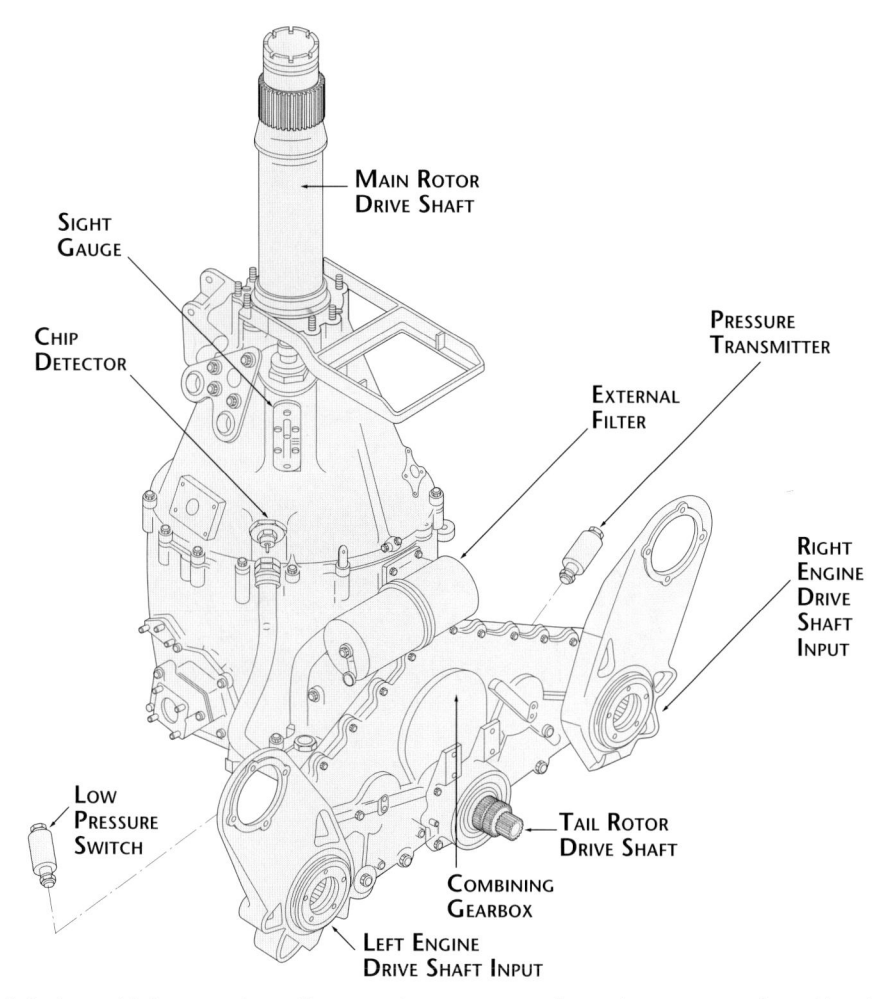

Figure 1-5-3. A combining gear box allows engines to power the main rotor as a shared load.

anti-torque (tail) rotor have a shorter span and chord than the main rotor and must operate at a higher r.p.m. to generate enough lift to counteract the torque of the main rotor.

Reciprocating engines typically operate at around 3,000 r.p.m., while turboshaft engines operate at speeds sometimes approaching as much as 7,000 r.p.m. A transmission, because it has output shafts for both the main and tail rotors, is used to change these speeds to accommodate the different r.p.m. needs of both the main and tail rotors. The same transmission also powers the accessories that are used for helicopter systems.

For both the speed and directional changes, the transmission can be as simple as an arrangement of bevel and helical gears or as complex as a planetary gear system. The power from the engine(s) often needs to be turned 90°, from the horizontal to the vertical or turned as much as 180° to meet up with the anti torque rotor drive shaft so that it can be powered by the engine(s).

Engine power can be directed to the transmission through several configurations. These include an arrangement of belts, a short drive shaft or even a direct engine to transmission coupling. See Figure 1-5-2.

Many small, entry level helicopters use a belt drive arrangement, as shown in Figure 1-5-2 (B). One set of pulleys is connected to the engine drive shaft. The second set of pulleys is connected to the helicopter's transmission. A series of belts connect the two pulleys, transferring power from the engine to the transmission.

Another common method is to directly mount the engine to the transmission housing. Figure 1-5-2 (A) shows this type of transmission. Many early helicopters used this arrangement. It offers a compact installation.

Most modern helicopters use a drive shaft connection as shown in Figure 1-5-2 (C). This allows the designer more flexibility in engine choice and in powerplant location. Some manufacturers offer versions of the same basic helicopter with more than one engine choice. Driveshafts also permit the engine to be located in the ideal location for center-of-gravity issues.

In helicopters that use multiple engines a combining gearbox (Figure 1-5-3) is incorpo-

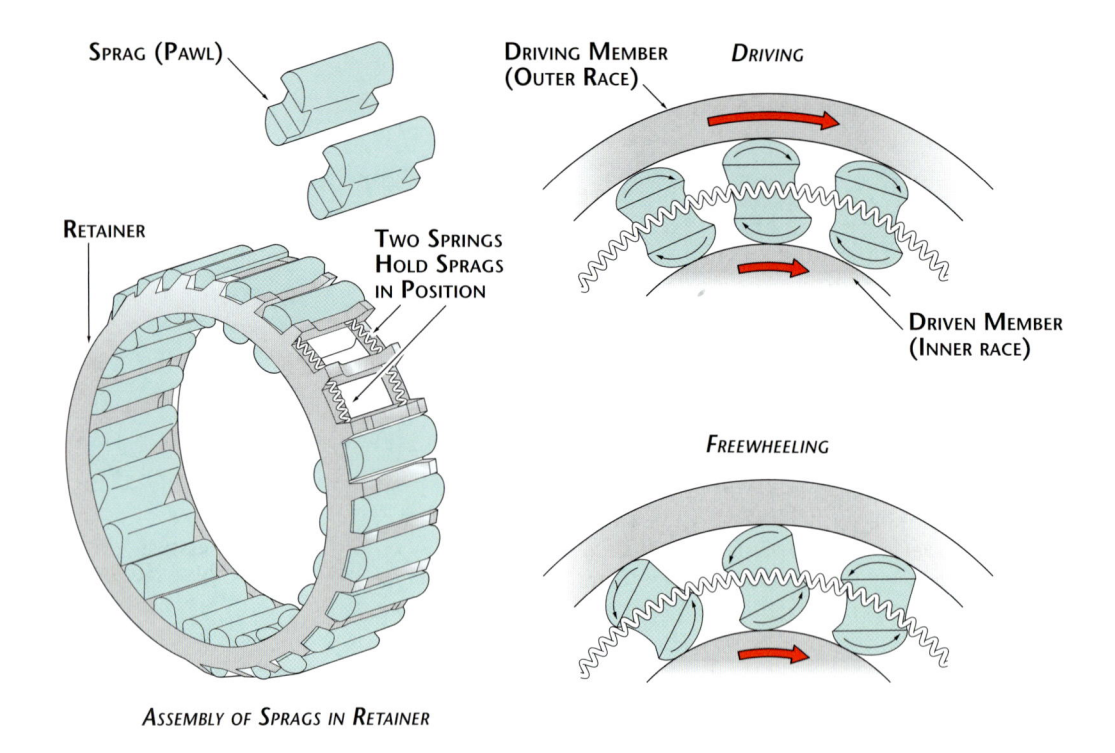

Figure 1-5-4. Sprag clutch assembly and operation

rated that will allow all engines to power the main rotor as a shared load. This gearbox will also permit one engine to provide power to the rotors in the event that the other engine becomes inoperative.

Since the engine drives the main rotor, a device is incorporated that allows the rotor system to spin freely if an engine should fail or when rotor r.p.m. exceeds engine r.p.m. This freewheeling unit, or sprag clutch, allows the rotor system to spin and uses the inertia in the main rotor for autorotation and landing in an emergency. See Figure 1-5-4. The transmission-mounted accessories will continue to power the helicopter systems because the gear train in the transmission is now rotated by the main rotor instead of the engine(s). In some cases, the clutch allows the transmission to be disengaged to relieve the load on the engine while it is being started.

System accessories that are mounted to the transmission include hydraulic pump(s) used to boost the cyclic and collective controls, tachometer generators that monitor engine and main rotor r.p.m., alternators that power electrical systems, and fans that circulate air over the heat exchangers for engine and transmission oil system cooling.

Transmission Oil System

The gear system in the transmission has a lubrication system that reduces friction and dissipates heat. Synthetic oils are well suited for use in the gear system, where operating conditions include high rotational speeds, heavy loads and elevated temperatures. With more turbine-powered helicopters being used, the use of one type of oil for the entire aircraft reduces the possibility of the wrong oil being used.

Most transmissions are lubricated using a wet sump system where the oil tank is part of the transmission. A few helicopters use a dry sump system where the oil tank is separate from the

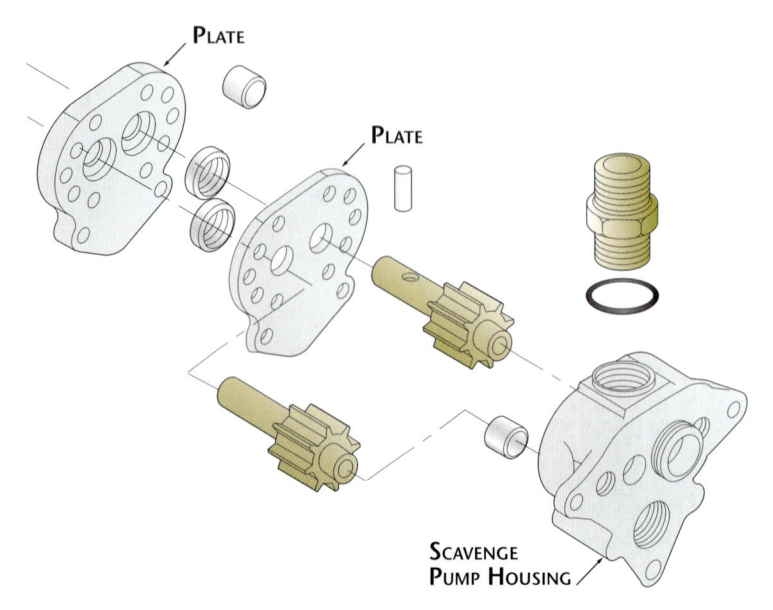

Figure 1-5-5. Gear-type oil pump

transmission. In both cases, the transmission oil system is separate from the engine oil system. This eliminates any chance of cross contamination of oils and systems by dirt or metal particles.

All of the systems have gear type pumps (Figure 1-5-5) that are driven by one of the internal gears or intermediate shafts. From these pumps, oil is directed through the filter and then distributed to the gears through a system of lines, nozzles or jets. Once this oil has been sprayed over the gears, it falls to the bottom of the gearbox or sump where it is collected and run through the cooler to dissipate heat it is then returned to the reservoir for re-use. These oil systems have a pressure regulator and an oil filter with a by-pass indicator. There are temperature and pressure monitors, as well as fluid level indicators, chip detectors and oil coolers for the systems.

Pressure regulator. Any time a positive displacement pump is used in an oil system, it is necessary to have some means of regulating and relieving the pressure. See Figure 1-5-6. These regulators are a piston and spring mechanism that is located in the pump outlet, or pressure line. This valves is set at the factory and seldom needs adjustment in the field. When any adjustment is needed, changing the tension on the spring will change the pressure, the tighter the spring the higher the pressure. The oil must be at its operating temperature and quantity before any adjustment is made, and the maintenance manual must always be consulted.

Filter. Filters require more service than any other part of a helicopter transmission. The maintenance manual will stipulate the intervals and conditions for filter service. Often, the filter is a type of metallic screen that can be removed, inspected, cleaned and re-used,

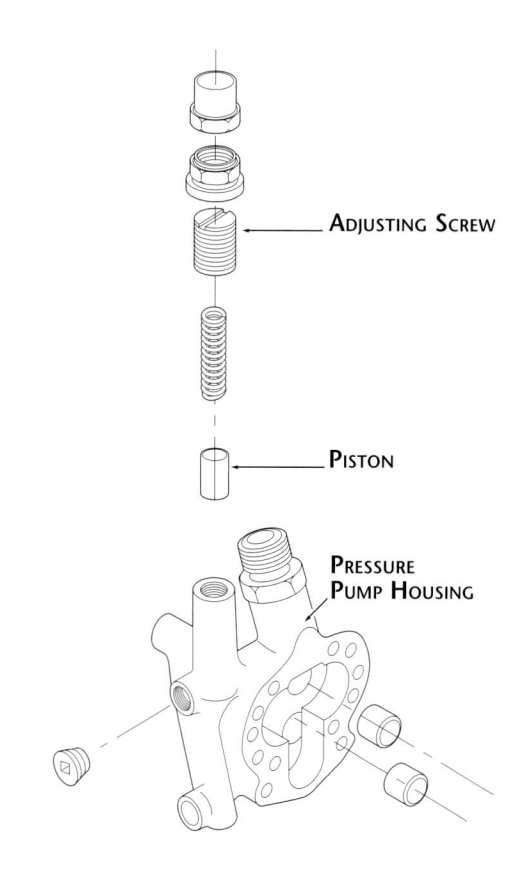

Figure 1-5-6. Pressure regulator

although some are paper elements that are not reusable. The filters are located in between the pump and the transmission on the pressure side of the system. It is here that the oil is cleaned before entering the distribution system of nozzles and jets and being sprayed onto the gears. See Figure 1-5-7.

As is true of most sophisticated filter systems a bypass indicator is incorporated in the filter housing. These indicators will alert the maintenance and flight crews that a filter has become

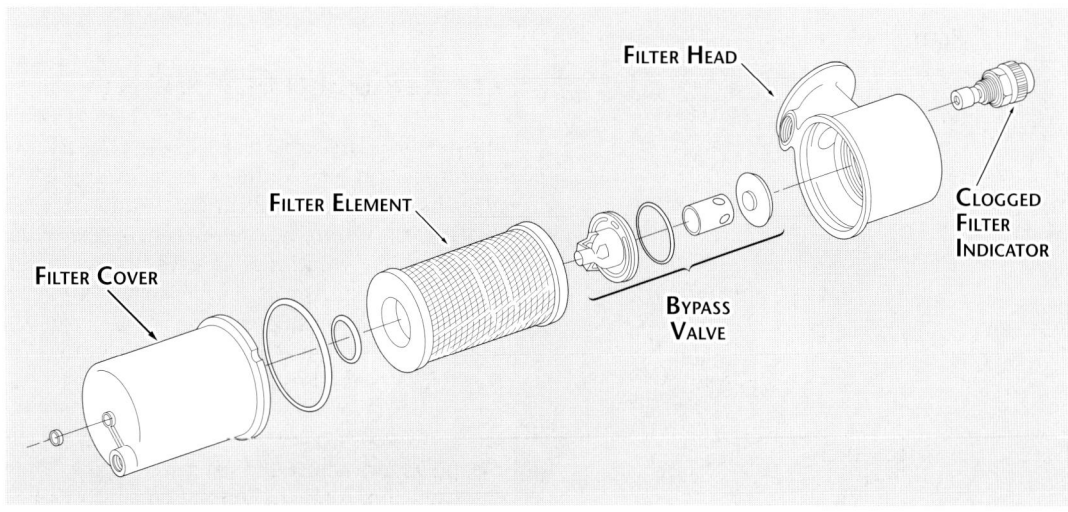

Figure 1-5-7. Oil filter

Figure 1-5-8. Quantity indicator

clogged and is in the bypass mode allowing un-filtered oil into the gearbox. In this case, the need for lubrication is considered superior to the need for filtration. Some bypass systems indicate mechanically with a pop-out button that is checked at every pre-flight, while others indicate electronically in the cockpit and require no pre-flight check. In either case, a positive indication requires follow on maintenance as directed by the maintenance manual: usually a drain and flush of the system should there be dirt in the filter. If the bypass is caused by an excess of metal then a transmission replacement may be in order.

Temperature and pressure indicators. The oil temperature and pressure must be within specifications to function properly for cooling and lubrication. A temperature sensor is installed in the system to monitor the oil and alert the crew of any extremes. A gauge or digital indicator will display the operating temperature range and have a warning for "Hot Oil" so that the flight crew can take appropriate action.

The oil pressure will also be measured by a sensor in the oil pressure line. An operating range will be displayed on a gauge or digital readout that will be marked for the cautionary (yellow) and the low pressure (red line) limits.

Should the temperature or pressure warnings be exceeded then maintenance personnel will be required to perform certain checks of the indicating and pressure systems. The sensors may be faulty leading to an erroneous reading or in extreme cases; the transmission may need to be replaced.

Quantity indicators. The oil quantity in a transmission requires a pre-flight visual check that can be performed very quickly. Most transmissions have a sight glass that can be checked by opening an access panel during the pre-flight or daily inspection. See Figure 1-5-8. Those that do not have a sight glass will have a

Figure 1-5-9. Chip detector

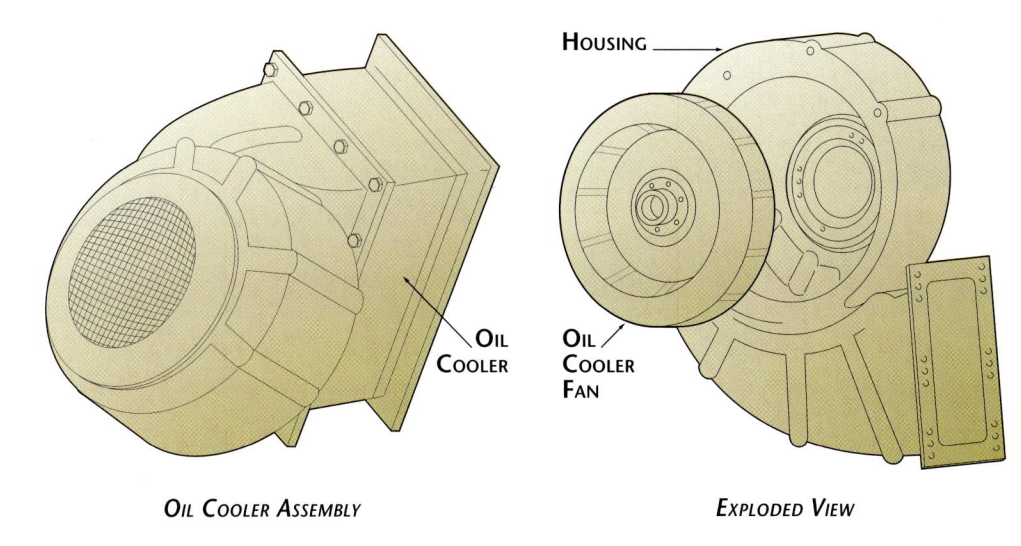

Figure 1-5-10. Oil cooler

dipstick that can be checked. If the level is low oil can be added through a filler neck located on the transmission or oil tank.

Chip detector. Chip detectors are simple devices that consist of a magnetic plug with an electrical contact. Figure 1-5-9 shows a typical chip detector installation. When particles of ferrous metal are attracted to the magnet in such quantity as to bridge the gap between the magnet and the contact, a warning circuit is completed and the "Chip" light illuminates on the instrument panel of the helicopter.

Since all gearboxes will shed small amounts of metal, most chip detectors have an added feature that is known as a chip burner. This allows the flight crew to briefly induce a high voltage current through the detector, which will melt any tiny particles, or fuzz, that have made contact across the detector. However, a larger particle will not be affected and the warning will continue, at which time emergency procedures may be in order for the flight crew.

These detectors are placed in the gearboxes in locations that are washed by oil so that any metal can be attracted to the magnet. They are housed in quick disconnect fittings that allow the detector to be removed and inspected without draining the oil from the gearbox.

Oil cooler. The oil cooler is an air to oil radiator that is mounted close to the transmission or it may be an integral part of the transmission. On many helicopters, the cooler is located in an area that does not have any ram air through it. In this case, a fan is mounted nearby to blow cooling air over the cooler, or the air used for the engine oil coolers is then ducted over the transmission cooler. See Figure 1-5-10. The cooler has a thermostatic valve that controls the supply of oil in order to maintain the temperature. During start up when the oil is cold, very little oil flows through the cooler. As the temperature increases, more oil is allowed into the cooler.

The blower, or fan, that circulates air through the cooler is important because without it the effectiveness of the cooler is dramatically reduced. Often the only clue of a blower going bad is an increase in the vibration of the area. Of equal importance is the ducting for the air from the blower to the cooler. This ductwork needs to be checked for breaks or loose connections that can leak air.

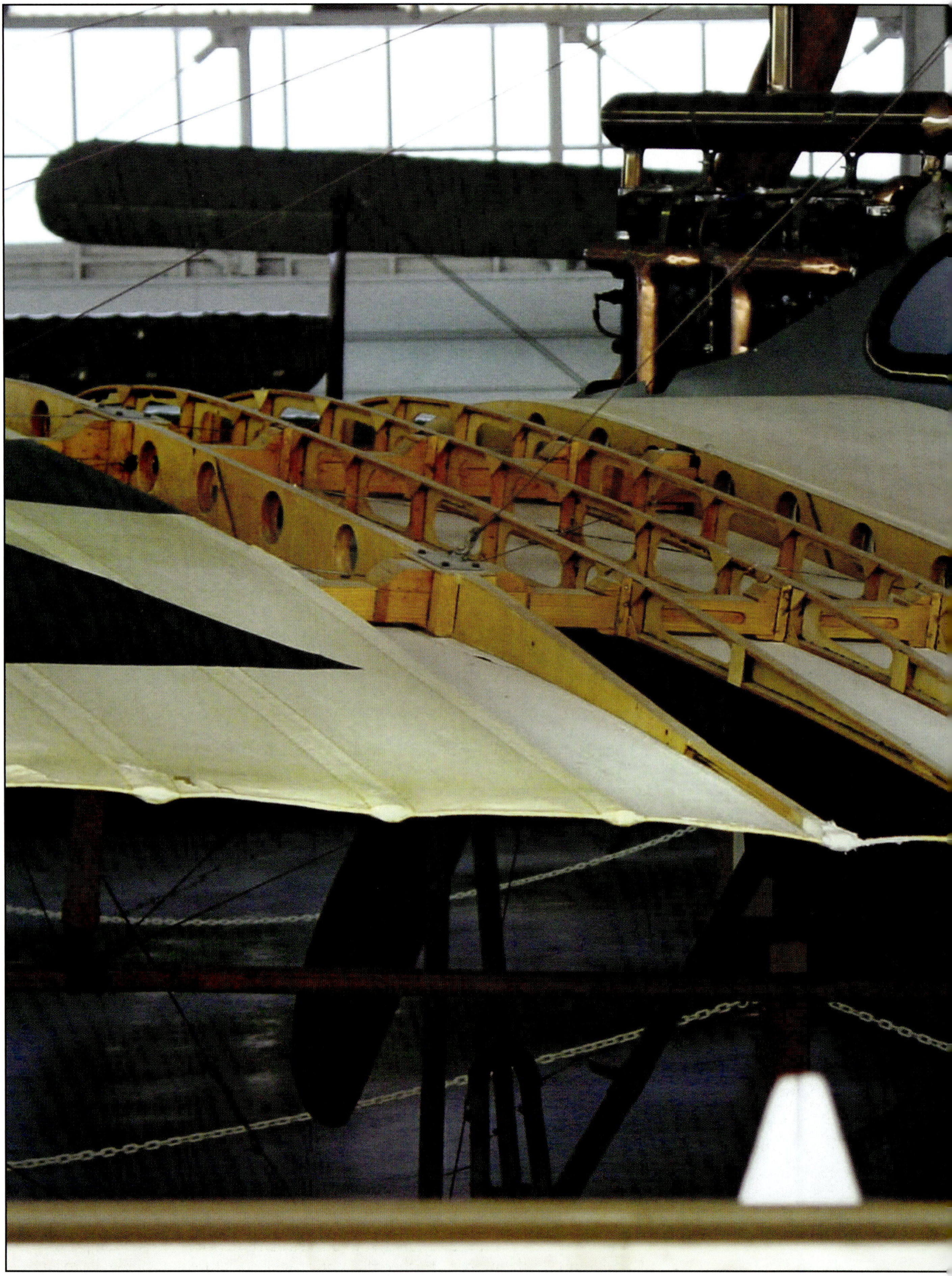

2

Fabric Covering

Section 1

History of Fabric Covering

Since man has been able to look into the sky and marvel at the freedom of the birds, he has dreamed of flying. From the earliest time, there have been myths and legends of men flying. Most of those legends come from the Greeks: among the earliest and best-known are Pegasus, the flying horse, and Daedalus and Icarus, a father and son who made wings of feathers and wax. Leonardo da Vinci made working models of gliders, parachutes and helicopters. In the sixteenth century, men were constructing balloons and going aloft.

All of these early experiments had one thing in common: They all depended upon some sort of fabric covering over a wooden frame to give the aircraft shape. Fabric was stretched over a frame of wood and painted with some sort of protective coating. This was the only method available to early aviation experimenters until the 1930s.

In 1902, American Wilbur Wright (1867-1912) and his brother, Orville (1871-1948), test-launched a series of cloth-covered gliders (Figure 2-1-1) based on wind tunnel tests they made. The next year, the brothers made the first successful, engine-powered, heavier-than-air flight. Because the aircraft needed to be as light as possible, they constructed it of thin pieces of wood or bamboo and covered it with fabric. The fabric was a special tight weave not available today. The Wrights did not use a fabric finish, and changes in humidity caused the fabric to sag and wrinkle.

With the onset of World War I, the demand for aircraft increased dramatically. Aircraft manufacturers set up plants where workers built the structures of planes, sewed fabric coverings for them, then attached the fabric to the structure.

Learning Objectives

DESCRIBE
- FAA-approved fabrics
- Fabric terminology
- Structural protection
- Thread and cord
- Dopes, thinners and finishes

EXPLAIN
- The purpose of a pre-covering inspection
- Types of stitching and seams

APPLY
- Perform a fabric inspection
- Install fabric covering
- Methods for repairing fabric covering

Left. A 1916 German Rumpler Taube, with some of the fabric covering removed to expose underlying wooden ribs. After undergoing wooden rib repairs, this craft will again be a flying example of a museum airplane.

Figure 2-1-1. The Wright brothers' third test glider was launched at Kill Devil Hills, North Carolina, on October 10, 1902. Wilbur is at the controls, Orville is shown on the left and local resident Dan Tate is on the right. *Photo courtesy of NASA*

See Figure 2-1-2. The aircraft were required to operate in all kinds of weather conditions. This spurred research into more acceptable coatings to help the linen fabric retain its aerodynamic shape. In 1916, manufacturers began to use a compound of cellulose dissolved in nitric acid, referred to as *nitrate dope*. This coating proved to be a significant improvement over oils and varnishes. However, the transparent quality of the nitrate dope did nothing to protect the linen fabric from damage done by the ultraviolet rays of the sun.

In 1918, color pigments were added to the nitrate dope. This pigmentation was an advancement and worked well enough. True protection was not achieved until the introduction of aluminum powder into the nitrate dope, providing a good barrier between the fabric and the sun.

Linen was the standard fabric used on aircraft until the introduction of *mercerized cotton*, cotton thread treated with sodium hydroxide to shrink the fiber and increase its color absorption and luster. The process was invented by an English textile maker, John Mercer (1791-1866). This fabric made it easier to fill the weave, resulting in a smoother, cleaner-looking surface. Cotton quickly became the standard for aircraft fabric coverings.

At the same time, a replacement for the nitrate dope was being researched. The nitrate dope proved flammable, in both the liquid and the solid form. Butyrate dope, cellulose fiber dissolved in butyric acid, was found to give the same fabric protection as the nitrate dope. However, it did not have the ability to tighten the fabric. Consequently, it became acceptable to coat the raw fabric with nitrate dope and then finish off with butyrate dope. This combination offered the best protection with the technology of the time.

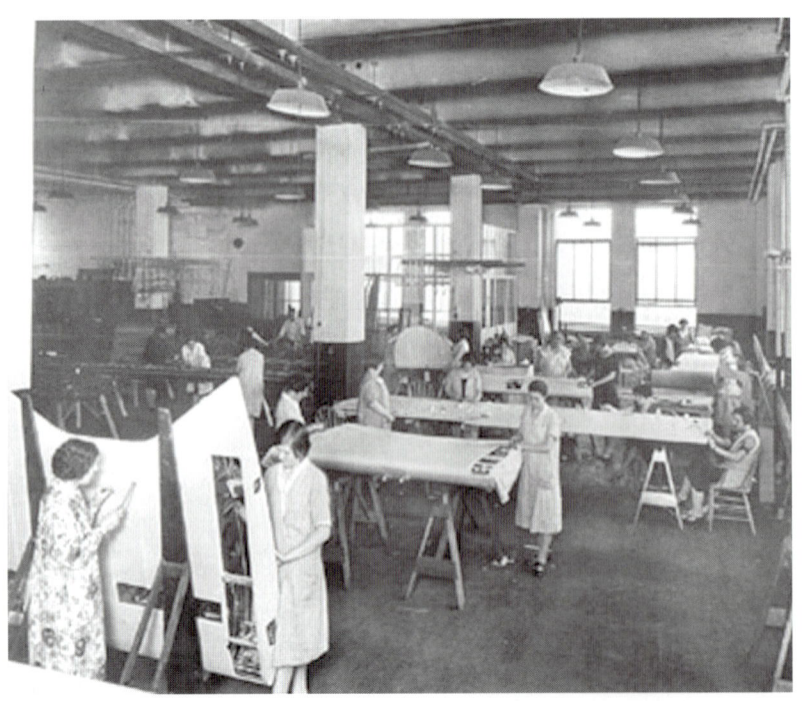

Figure 2-1-2. In 1926, workers at the Chance Vought Corporation's Long Island facility sew, cut and attach fabric on the wings and control surfaces of the newly designed O2U Corsair. During the Golden Age of aviation, the Corsair was the U.S. Navy's most widely flown biplane, used primarily for observation. *Photo courtesy of Vought Aircraft Industries, Inc.*

World War II introduced larger, faster aircraft. The demand for these aircraft was great, and conditions under which they were required to operate were much harsher than in the previ-

Figure 2-2-1. A Maule is an excellent example of a modern fabric-covered utility aircraft. This example is mounted on amphibious floats.

ous war. Thin, lightweight aluminum became the covering material of choice for the higher performance aircraft. This method of covering aircraft proved to be faster and cheaper, and eventually textile fabric was displaced as the covering standard.

Section 2
Today's Fabric Coverings

Today, very few aircraft are manufactured with fabric covers. However, many aircraft that were manufactured 50 years ago are still flying. Many of the so-called classic airplanes are fabric-covered. The Maule shown in Figure 2-2-1 is a major contender in today's utility airplane market. Many are used by state highway patrol departments to patrol major highways: the so-called "Bear in the Air." Stronger and more durable synthetic polyester fabrics have replaced much of the cotton fabrics. These new fabrics have a lifespan that is several times that of cotton.

In the following discussions, Grade A cotton will be the standard, as it is with the FAA. Newer polyester fabrics are not actually approved for airplanes. Instead, polyester coverings are part of an approved system of re-covering that is covered in an *STC* (Supplemental Type Certificate). The holders of the various STCs have all conducted the required experiments and submitted the necessary data to win approval of their processes. The materials used in the STC are covered by a *Technical Standard Order* (TSO-C14b or TSO-C15d). Many of the various finishes and glues are covered by a PMA (Parts Manufacturing Authority) held by the STC holder. Some PMA materials are available from standard aviation supply houses; some are available from the STC holder only.

If fabric removed from an airplane is determined to be polyester, there is some detective work that needs to be done. A search of the aircraft logbook should tell you what STC system was supposedly used in the prior re-cover. A review of the STC holder's manuals will tell you what material should have been used in the re-cover. If the records don't match the actual materials — even if the re-cover was approved by the FAA — it may not have been in compliance with regulations. In that case, you must re-acquire a copy of the STC from the supplier and follow its directions carefully. If you freelance, you will be nullifying the STC and be in violation of the FARs.

Fabric Terms

The following terms and definitions are presented to simplify the discussion of fabrics.

Bias. A bias cut, fold or seam is made diagonally to the warp of fill threads.

Calendering. The calendering process of ironing fabric by threading it, wet, between a series of hot and cold rollers produces a smooth finish.

Count. A count is the number of threads making up a inch.

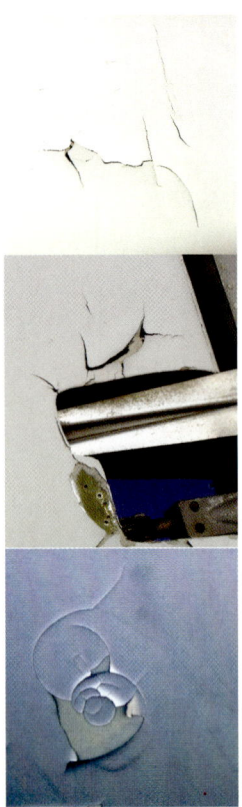

Figure 2-2-2. These three examples of deteriorated fabric are typical of an older airplane that has been left outside year-round. The bottom photo shows a classic case of ringworm. Ringworm is caused from a push, blow or some other kind of pressure strong enough to crack the dope finish without penetrating the fabric.

Denier. A yarn and filament numbering system in which the yarn number is equal to the weight in grams of 9,000 meters of yarn. (100 *denier* is finer than 150 *denier* yarn).

Fill, woof or weft. The fill, woof or weft is the directions across the width of the fabric.

Mercerization. This is the process of dipping cotton yarn or fabric in a hot solution of diluted caustic soda, this treatment causes the material to shrink and acquire greater strength and luster.

Pinked edge. Pinked edge is an edge that has been cut by machine or shears in a continuous series of V's to prevent raveling.

Ply. The ply is the number of yarns making up a thread.

Selvage edge. A selvage edge is an edge of cloth, tape, or webbing woven to prevent raveling.

Sizing. Sizing is a material, such as starch, used to stiffen the yarns for ease in weaving the cloth.

Warp ends. Warp ends are the woven threads that run the length of the fabric.

Warp. The warp is the direction along the length of fabric.

Determining the Strength of Doped Fabric

The condition of doped fabric should be checked at intervals sufficient to determine that the strength of the fabric has not deteriorated to the point where airworthiness of the aircraft is affected. Figure 2-2-2 shows three examples of extreme fabric deterioration. Unfortunately, they are not isolated examples.

The areas selected for test should be those known to deteriorate most rapidly. The top surfaces generally deteriorate more rapidly than the side or bottom surfaces. When contrasting colors are used on an aircraft, the fabric will deteriorate more rapidly under the darker colors. The warmer inner surface of the fabric under the dark color absorbs more moisture from the air inside the wing or fuselage. When the surface cools, this moisture condenses and the fabric under the dark area becomes moist and promotes mildew growth in a localized area. When checking cloth fabric that has been reinforced by applying fiberglass, peel back the glass cloth in the areas to be tested. Test the underlying cloth in the conventional manner.

Checking fabric surfaces is made easier by using a fabric punch tester. There are several acceptable fabric punch testers on the market; one such tester incorporates a penetrating cone. Fabric punch testers are designed for use on the dope-finished-fabric surface of the aircraft and provide only a general indication of the degree of deterioration on the strength of the fabric covering. Their advantage is that they may be used easily and quickly to test the fabric surfaces without cutting samples from the airplane's fabric. If a fabric punch tester indicates that the aircraft fabric strength is marginal, a laboratory test must be performed to determine the actual fabric strength.

When using a punch tester, place the tip on the doped fabric. With the tester held perpendicular to the surface, apply pressure with a slight rotary action until the flange of the tester contacts the fabric. The last exposed band on the color-banded plunger that projects from the top of the tester indicates the condition of the fabric.

The test should be repeated at various positions on the fabric. The lowest reading obtained, other than on an isolated repairable area, should be considered representative of the fabric condition as a whole. Fabrics that test just within the acceptable range should be rechecked frequently to ensure continued serviceability.

The punch tester makes only a small hole (approximately 1/2 inch diameter) or a depression in the fabric that can be repaired quickly by doping on a 2 inch or 3 inch patch.

AC 43.13-1B is most specific about punch testers: they are NOT approved as a testing device. The FAA suggests that they may be used as a first line test to determine if a more serious test needs to be conducted. The FAA goes on to define how to cut out a strip of fabric, and how to make a dead weight test to determine fabric strength. If the strength is still in doubt the FAA gives the standard which an outside testing laboratory must use to make the certified test.

Pre-covering Inspection

A thorough inspection of the aircraft structure is the first step before the covering or recovering can begin. In fact, most FSDOs will insist on a *pre-cover inspection*. Once recovered, many areas cannot be seen easily until the cover is removed again, it is the only way for an inspector to determine the condition of the underlying structure. There, the first thing to do before starting a recover is to contact a mechanic with an FAA Inspection Authorization (IA) and solicit his inspection services. Most do not charge for a pre-cover inspection if they will be doing your final inspection.

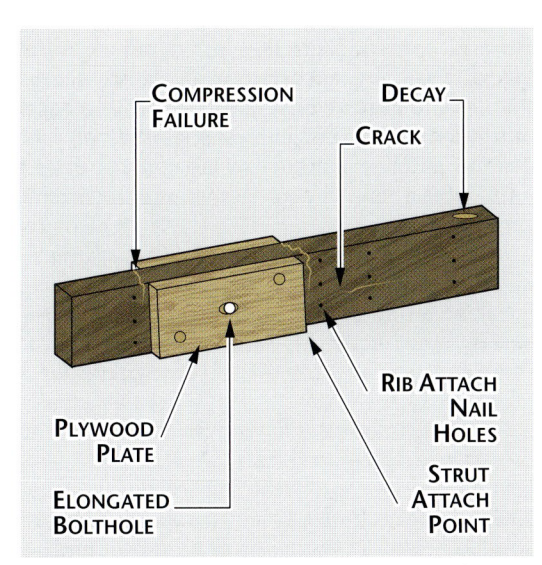

Figure 2-2-3. Likely areas to incur structural damage in wooden components

It is not unusual for the structure to have damage that has not been detected during normal inspection procedures. Structural defects, if not detected during this time, may again be covered up and at some future date cause catastrophic failure of the structure.

Wing inspection. Wings should be inspected for airworthiness conformity in the following areas: alignment, controls, fittings, installation of accessories, bonding, protection and safeties.

The structure to be covered—wings, fuselage or both—should be carefully inspected for material defects. Wood used in the construction of airplanes is susceptible to deterioration over time and should be inspected very carefully for certain types of defects. Rib capstrips should be inspected for excessive cracking around the nails that fasten the capstrip to the spar. Rib diagonals should be inspected for cracks. The spars should be inspected for various forms of damage. The spars have various components attached to them and the attachment points are especially vulnerable to damage. Also, all parts of the wooden structure should be inspected for any form of wood rot.

On metal-constructed wings, check for cracks, loose rivets and corrosion. Repair any damaged components in accordance with the manufacturer's manual and the FAA AC 43.13-1B.

Wing alignment is critical to the proper flight characteristics of the airplane. When checking the alignment, consult the manufacturer's manual for correct dimensions. Most aircraft wings are constructed with a front and rear spar. The distance between these two spars is fixed by the placement of the wing ribs. The alignment of the two spars along the lateral axis of the wing is controlled by the length of the *drag wires* and *anti-drag wires* located in each wing bay. Loosening and tightening these wires will bring the wing spars into correct alignment. Care should be taken to insure that the wires do not vibrate against each other during flight. They should be secured to prevent relative motion.

Fuselage inspection. The fuselage may be constructed of wood, metal or a combination of both. All metal parts should be inspected for damage and corrosion. While the fuselage is uncovered, it is the perfect time to give some protection to the insides of the metal tubing of the fuselage. Coat the tube interior by flushing with hot linseed oil, paralketone or other approved corrosion inhibitor. The flushing liquid is usually introduced through small holes drilled in the tubing. Allow the flushing liquid to drain and plug the holes with a screw or by other means to prevent entry of moisture. Air and watertight sealing of the tubing will also give adequate protection against corrosion if the tubing is internally dry before being sealed. Consult FAA AC 43.13-1B for further instruction in the protection of metal tube interiors.

Wooden stringers, longerons, frames or bulkheads should be inspected for rot cracks and splitting. See Figure 2-2-3. Any defective wooden components should be repaired or replaced in accordance with the Manufacturer's Manual and the FAA AC 43.13-1B.

Any oil or grease that gets on the structures or fabric of an aircraft may be removed with acetone.

While the fuselage is uncovered, it is the perfect opportunity to inspect that area. During the life of the aircraft it is difficult to inspect. These areas include the space beneath the floorboards, behind the instrument panel, the vertical tail post and any other place difficult to get to during normal and routine inspections.

Empennage group. Just as with the wings and the fuselage, the horizontal and vertical stabilizers, the rudder and the elevators should be inspected for damage. Any damage or defect detected during the inspection should be repaired or the part replaced prior to covering the structure. Figure 2-2-4 shows the empennage of a Stearman resplendent in its new cover and finish. In this case pre-cover repairs would include sandblasting and refinishing the basic steel structure.

Controls. Aileron controls are located inside of the wing and should be inspected at this time. These controls should be thoroughly inspected for any defect that may later cause a problem. Once the wing is covered, the aileron controls are difficult to inspect thoroughly and even more difficult to repair and replace should they malfunction. Therefore, every effort should be made to be sure the controls are in perfect condition before covering the wings. The cables, turnbuckles, terminal ends, bellcranks, mounting bolts, nuts and safeties should all be inspected. The attachment of the various fittings to the spars should be inspected for airworthiness.

Bonding jumpers. If the wing is constructed of metal, bonding jumpers should be checked. The bonding jumpers are small and generally do not require maintenance. If the bonding jumper becomes loose, the electrical conductivity of the aircraft structure will be impaired. Inspect all bonding jumpers for integrity and replace any that appear to be frayed or are missing.

Protection

Before the structure can be covered with fabric, the underlying frame must be considered. First, the fabric must be protected from the structure. Inspect for chaffing and sticking. Second, the construction material must be protected from the dope used to coat the fabric.

Fabric protection. The fabric should be protected from the structural material. Check every surface that comes into contact with the material. The technician's hand is run over all surfaces. Defects like sharp edges are filed down. Nails that protrude above the surface are driven in. Any tube ends or ends of other structural members that will come into contact with the fabric are to be padded.

Structural protection. Protection of the structure from the effects of the dope used to coat the fabric is referred to as dope proofing. Dope proofing also serves to prevent the fabric from sticking to the structure in certain places. There are some points on the structure, such as the leading edge and the trailing edge of the wing, where sticking the fabric down is desired. However there are other parts of the wing where this is not desirable, such as the capstrips of the ribs.

There are two common methods of accomplishing dope proofing. One method is to cover those surfaces that come into contact with the fabric, such as, longerons, spars and ribs, with a dope proof paint. A dope proof paint is a neutral base paint that is unaffected by the chemicals used in the manufacture of nitrate or butyrate dope. Use a small brush to apply the dope proof paint. A single application is all that is required, as this paint is not considered a protection coat for the material, just a barrier for the dope.

The second method is the application of a layer of cellulose tape over all parts of the structure that contact fabric. Care should be exercised to use the correct width of tape for the different structural members. This tape is manufactured in various widths, from fractions of an inch to several inches wide. Use the smaller widths on the capstrips and the more appropriate widths on the spars and other members.

A third method that is some times used is to cover the structure with thin sheets of aluminum foil. Some aluminum foils are manufactured with adhesive to allow them to be held in place, or a coat of sticky varnish can be applied to the structure to hold the foil in place.

Once the structure has been thoroughly inspected, repaired or replaced as necessary, and fully and completely protected, it is time to begin the covering process.

Figure 2-2-4. The empennage of this Stearman is constructed of welded steel tubing. It must go through an IRAN (Inspect and Repair As Necessary) before being refinished prior to re-cover. The entire airplane will have a pre-cover inspection before starting on that phase.

Figure 2-2-5. A light plane fuselage in a work-holding fixture being re-covered with Dacron. It has already received its first coat of fill.

Materials

One item that is a standard procedure is a holding fixture for a fuselage (Figure 2-2-5). Without a fixture of some kind the job would be extremely difficult.

Materials preparation. Before the covering process can begin, it is essential to gather all needed materials to allow for a smooth flow of the work. To facilitate a high-quality, professional job, the fabric should have dope applied to it as soon as it is properly attached to the structure and shrunk. If there is any delay, the fabric may begin to sag. Sagging may be so excessive that the dope cannot restore it to the correct fabric tension.

Once the first coat of dope has been applied, all other steps in the covering process should be taken immediately. Surface tape, rib stitching, inspection rings, grommets, patches and reinforcements should be applied with the successive coats.

Covering Materials

Grade A cotton. This is the standard from which all other fabrics are measured. Grade A cotton fabric is the covering method employed on all antique aircraft. As time goes by, it is becoming more difficult to get Grade A cotton fabric. Due to the strength, durability and ease of covering, most aircraft owners are opting for the high tech polyester fabrics rather than recovering with Grade A. Therefore, it is essential that the technician determine the correct widths of fabric available before finalizing the estimation of the amount of fabric needed for a particular project. Specifications for Grade A fabric are detailed in AC 43.13-1B (Table 2-2-1) a useful study tool for any AMT student.

Very often, Grade A cotton is not manufactured in widths that will cover a wing from leading edge to trailing edge in the blanket. For this reason, spanwise seams may have to be sewn in order to create a covering that will extend from butt rib to the wingbow. To estimate the amount of Grade A fabric needed for a particular wing covering, stretch a length of string around the wing, over the top of a major rib, starting at the trailing edge, around the leading edge and back to the trailing edge. If the lower surface of the wing is concaved, tape the string up to the rib to get an accurate measurement. Finally add approximately four inches to allow for seams.

Next, measure the overall length of the wing. Add twelve inches to this measurement to allow for butt rib and seams. If the fabric being used is 60 inches wide, only 59 inches can be calculated for covering, since one inch must be used for the

MATERIALS	SPECIFICATION	MINIMUM TENSILE STRENGTH, NEW (UN-DOPED)	MINIMUM TEARING STRENGTH, NEW (UN-DOPED) ASTM D 1424	MINIMUM TENSILE STRENGTH, DETERIORATED (UN-DOPED)	THREAD COUNT (PER INCH)	USE AND REMARKS
Airplane cloth, mercerized cotton (Grade A)	TSO-C15d, as amended. References Society of Automotive Engineers AMS 3806d, as amended, or MIL-C-5646	80 lbs. per inch warp and fill	5 lbs. warp and fill	56 lbs. per inch	80 minimum, 84 maximum warp and fill	For use on all aircraft. Required on aircraft with wing loading of 9 lbs./sq. ft. or greater, or never-exceed speed of 160 m.p.h. or greater.
Airplane cloth, mercerized cotton	TSO-C14d, as amended. References Society of Automotive Engineers AMS 3804c, as amended.	65 lbs. per inch warp and fill	4 lbs. warp and fill	46 lbs. per inch	80 minimum, 94 maximum warp and fill	For use on aircraft with wing loading of less than 9 lbs./sq. ft., and never-exceed speed of less than 160 mp.h.
Airplane cloth, mercerized cotton	Society of Automotive Engineers AMS 3802, as amended.	50 lbs. per inch warp and fill	3 lbs. warp and fill	35 lbs. per inch	110 maximum, warp and fill	For use on gliders with wing loading of 8 lbs./sq. ft. or less, if the never-exceed speed is 135 m.p.h. or less.
Aircraft linen	British 7F1.	—	—	—	—	This material meets the minimum strength requirements of TSO-C15.

Table 2-2-1. To pass an inspection, a fabric-covered airplane must maintain 70 percent of the minimum tensile strength.

seams. Therefore, divide the 59 into the overall length of the wing and this will give the number of widths of fabric needed. Increase by one width for any remainder from the division. For example: if the wing is 150 inches long, 59 will divide into 150 two and one-half times, with 32 inches left over. That would require three widths to cover one wing.

To get the final number of yards, multiply the length around the wing, expressed in yards, by the number of widths calculated (three in the example) to get the final number of yards. Experience has shown that it is prudent to increase the order amount by 5-10 percent to allow for mistakes, spoilage or waste. This is an especially good practice, because there are so few suppliers. This will eliminate delays in the covering process.

Should the 60 inch width be sufficient to cover the wing from leading edge to trailing edge, with enough for seams, measure the length of the wing, multiply by four, to cover the top and bottom of both wings, allowing enough to cover the wing tip bow and the butt rib.

Of all methods possible for recovering of aircraft, the Grade A cotton is the most time consuming and unforgiving to the carelessness and unskilled. But to restore antique aircraft to their original condition, it is the best method that can be used. Machine-sewn and hand-sewn seams are illustrated in Figure 2-2-6 and Figure 2-2-7, from AC 43.13-1B. Of the machine sewn seams shown, the French fell is the strongest.

Polyester fabric. Polyester fabrics have replaced Grade A cotton on most fabric-covered aircraft flying today. Polyester has several advantages such as strength, durability, weather resistance, ease of application and repair, and the predictability of the shrinking process. Figure 2-2-8 shows a wing tip where the fabric has been notched before being curved around the tip. Some people prefer notching to bias tape because of the rough pinked edges of bias tape.

The method of accurately estimating the length of fabric needed is essentially the same as for Grade A cotton. The primary exception is in the width of the fabric. There are three grades of polyester, 3.4 ounces per square yard, 2.7 ounces per square yard and 1.7 ounces per square yard. Only the 3.4 and 2.7-weight fabrics are approved for re-covering of certified aircraft.

The 3.4-weight fabric is the strongest and most resistant to punctures and tears, and is therefore used most often on aircraft that are operated in rugged environments. Due to the increase in weight, this fabric would not be a

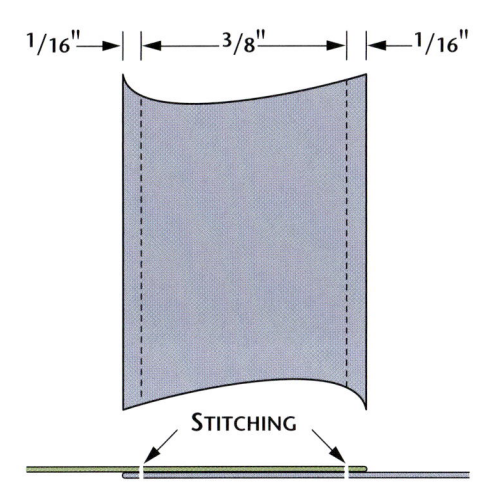

A. PLAIN OVERLAP SEAM, STRAIGHT EDGE

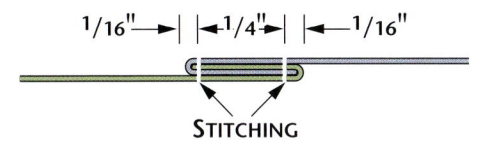

B. FRENCH FELL SEAM

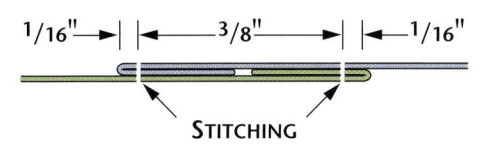

C. FOLDED FELL SEAM

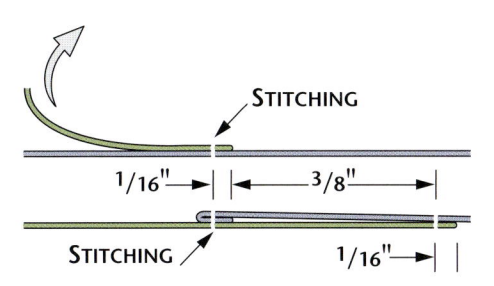

D. MODIFIED FOLDED FELL SEAM SEWN IN TWO STEPS

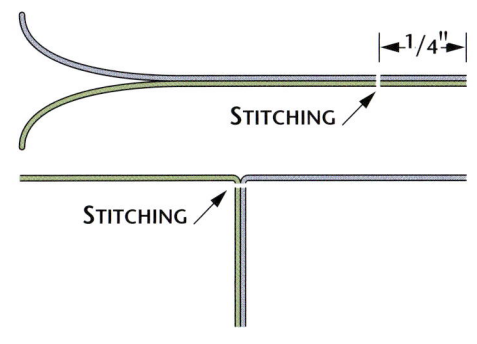

E. SINGLE STITCH SEAM TO CLOSE AN ENVELOPE WHEN THE STITCH WILL BE LOCATED OVER A STRUCTURE

Figure 2-2-6. Machine-sewn seams

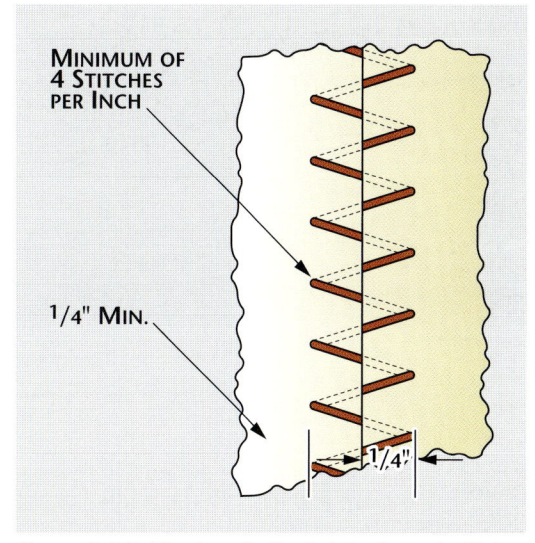

Figure 2-2-7. The baseball stitch is the only FAA-approved hand-sewn seam.

good choice to use for most re-coverings. This fabric is manufactured in 70 inch widths.

The 2.7-weight fabric is the fabric most often chosen to cover certified aircraft still flying today. This fabric exhibits all the qualities of the 3.4-weight fabric, but does not have the same tensile strength. Under less than extreme conditions, this not a matter of any consequence. The 2.7-weight fabric is manufactured in 70 inch widths.

In most cases, the 70 inch width is wide enough to extend from leading to trailing edge with enough material to allow for overlap for proper gluing of the seams.

Fiberglass cloth. Fiberglass cloth may be used to cover aircraft structures with a material that is considered a lifetime material resistant to mold, mildew and most acids.

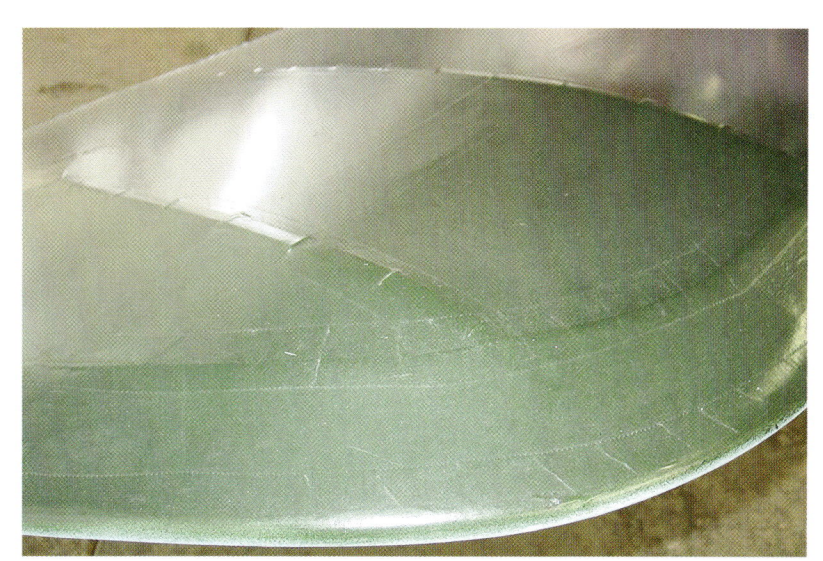

Figure 2-2-8. Notched surface tape curved around a wing tip

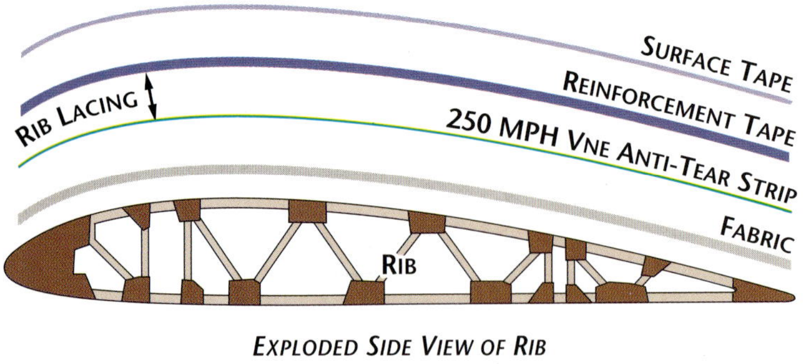

Figure 2-2-9. Tape types and their uses

Due to its slippery nature, several processes have been used to make the cloth less difficult to work with; pre-treatment with a butyrate dope and special weave designs are some of the methods.

The initial shrinking is not done with water or heat, but with several coats of dope. The application and finishing of fiberglass cloth requires different skills and techniques from those used on cotton or polyester fabrics. The steps in the manufacturer's installation manual should be followed carefully for a satisfactory covering and finish.

In order to change from the original type of fabric used on the aircraft to fiberglass cloth, a Supplemental Type Certificate (STC) will have to accompany the covering system for the aircraft.

Tapes. Surface tape, reinforcing tape, inter-rib lacing tape and anti-tear tape (Figure 2-2-9) are a matter of straight measurement, but should be supplemented by a generous amount. It seems that there are always some extra uses found for these materials. Tapes are manufactured for both Grade A cotton and synthetic fabrics. Some natural-fabric tape specifications, also found in AC 43.13-1B, are shown in Table 2-2-2.

MATERIALS	SPECIFICATION	YARN SIZE	MINIMUM TENSILE STRENGTH	YARDS PER POUND	USE AND REMARKS
Reinforcing Tape, Cotton	MIL-T-5661e, Type 1 MIL-Y-1140h	—	150 lbs. per 1/2 inch width	—	Used as reinforcing tape on fabric and under rib-lacing cord. Strength of other widths approx. in proportion.
Lacing Cord, Pre-waxed Braided Cotton	Federal T-C-57 1F	—	40 lbs.	310 minimum	Lacing fabric to structures. Unless already waxed, must be lightly waxed before using.
Lacing Cord, Braided Cotton	MIL-C-5648a	—	80 lbs.	170 minimum	Lacing fabric to structures. Unless already waxed, must be lightly waxed before using.
Lacing Cord Thread, High-tenacity Cotton	MIL-T-5660b	Ticket No. 10	62 lbs.	480 minimum	Lacing fabric to structures. Unless already waxed, must be lightly waxed before using.
Machine Thread Cotton	Federal V-T-276 H	20/4-ply	5 lbs.	5,000 nominal	Use for all machine sewing.
Hand-sewing Thread Cotton	Federal V-T-276 H Type IIIB	8/4-ply	14 lbs.	1,650 nominal	Use for all hand-sewing. Use fully waxed thread.
Finishing (surface) Tape Cotton	Same as fabric used	—	Same as fabric used	—	Use over seams, leading edges, trailing edges, outer edges and ribs, pinked, raveled or straight edges.

Table 2-2-2. Cotton/linen tapes and threads

Inter-rib bracing tape is used to stabilize the ribs before they are covered. If this is not done, the ribs are subject to taking a lateral bow or deflecting into an "S" shape due to compression pressure exerted by spars. This causes the rib stitching to be at angle with the slip steam, inducing excess drag.

Anti-chafe tape is applied under the fabric surface, over sharp and protruding edges that abrade the fabric and eventually cause a puncture. However, pads, patches and strips can be cut from excess fabric to be used for this purpose. It is more costly to purchase the tape; on the other hand, it is less labor intensive than repair and provides a savings in that respect.

Reinforcing tape is a strong, heavy tape available in rolls from 1/4 to 1-1/4 inches in width. It is made in either a straight or a herringbone weave, and is applied over the fabric on top of each rib, to resist the tearing and abrasion of the rib stitching cord or other fastening devices that are used to hold the fabric down onto the ribs of the wing structure. This tape is usually much thicker than other tapes used on the aircraft. Reinforcing tape comes in various widths to accommodate the needs of the aircraft.

Surface tape is made of the same fabric as is used for covering airplane structures. It is manufactured in rolls of standard widths from 1-1/4 to 3-3/4 inches, and is applied over the reinforcing tape and the rib-lacing cord to protect the rib-lacing cord and give the surface a finished appearance. Surface tape is also used to cover all seams, the leading edge and the trailing. Surface tape is manufactured in a variety of widths to meet the needs of the covering project. The wing tip bow is also covered with surface tape, but to avoid puckering, as the tape is curved around the tip bow, a bias-cut surface tape is manufactured. This bias-cut tape gives the finish a much smoother and more professional appearance.

Surface tape may be obtained with either pinked or straight edges impregnated with a sealing compound. The pinked or sealed edges prevent raveling and provide for better adherence of the tape to the fabric cover. Tape is made either uncoated or pre-doped.

Surface tape should be applied over *all* lacing, seams, and all places where it is necessary or desirable to provide reinforcement or to improve the finished appearance, but it should not applied until the first coat of dope has dried. A coat of dope then is brushed locally over that portion of the fabric that is to be covered by the finishing tape. The tape is laid in position on the wet dope. Spanwise tapes should be applied first, whenever possible. A covering coat is applied immediately on the top of the tape and over the entire surface. This latter coat

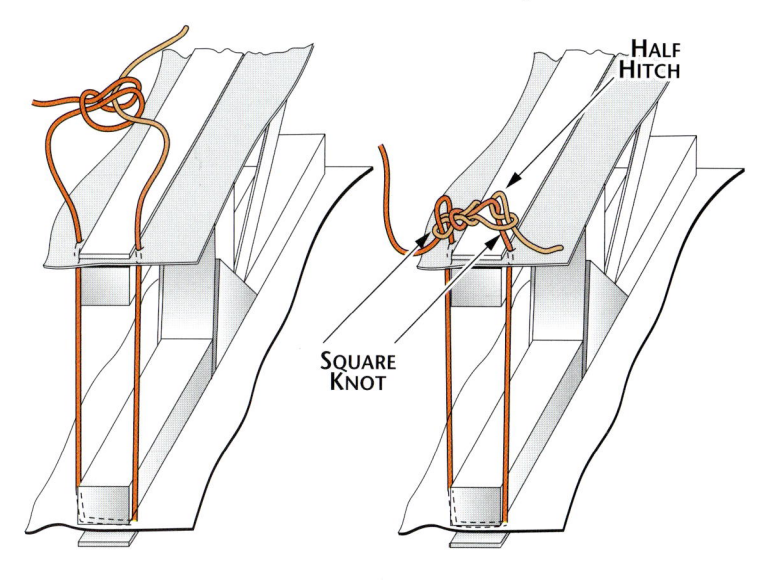

Tie a square knot by passing the short end of the cord through the fold back loop, as illustrated.

Secure the tight square knot with a half hitch at each side.

Figure 2-2-10. One sequence for rib lacing, using a modified seine knot

is the second coat of the specified finish. Care should be taken to assure good adhesion of the pinked edges to the covering by additional brushing and pressing, as necessary.

Anti-tear tape is designed particularly for certain high-speed airplanes that need additional reinforcement to prevent the fabric covering from tearing under the reinforcement tape and rib lacing. The anti-tear tape is applied over the covering and underneath the reinforcement. It may be cut either straight or at a 45° bias, from standard Grade A airplane fabric, which affords greater tear resistance. It should have 8-10 pinks per inch.

Threads and Cords

The three main classifications of thread used in fabric covering are: rib-stitching or rib-lacing cord, machine-sewing thread and hand-sewing thread. Some specifications, also found in AC 43.13-1B, are shown in Table 2-2-2.

Rib-stitching cord. This is a heavy cotton or linen cord ranging in tensile strength from 35-300 lbs. Rib-stitching cord is used to hold the fabric down onto the wing ribs. The rib-lacing cord extends over the top rib cap strip, down the side of the rib, over the bottom cap strip, and back up the other side, where it is tied off with a special knot. See Figure 2-2-10. This maintains the smooth, aerodynamic surface of the wing. Were rib-lacing cord, or some other fastening device, not used to hold the fabric down, it would balloon up, alter the shape of the wing and diminish the airfoil's efficiency. Where approved, other fastening methods, such as PK

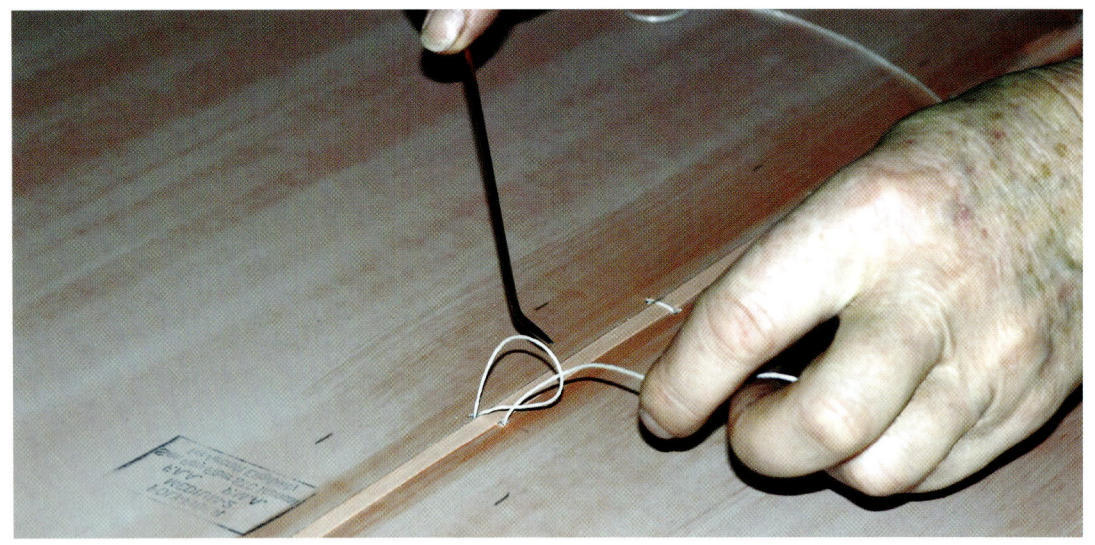

Figure 2-2-11. Rib stitching being applied over reinforcing tape

(sheet metal) screws, pop rivets and wire clips, may be used instead of rib-lacing cord.

Machine-sewing thread. Machine-sewing thread is necessary when the covering method requires (or the technician desires to use) the envelope method for covering the wing. This material is wound onto 500-yard spools and one spool is generally more than will be needed for the covering of the aircraft.

For machine sewing Grade A fabric, a left-hand twist, unbleached cotton thread, four-ply is used. It has a tensile strength of approximately 4-5 lbs., and the sizes range from Nos. 16 to 24. The left twist is necessary, because many sewing machines have the tendency to unravel a right-hand twist.

Hand-sewing thread. The correct grade of cotton or linen thread should be used when it is necessary to sew fabric covering by hand. If cotton is used, it must be an unbleached, left-hand twist, No. 10, three-strand thread. Linen thread must be unbleached, left twist, No. 30, three-strand thread. Each strand has a tensile strength of approximately 9 lbs.

Beeswax. All thread for hand sewing and cord for rib lacing must be coated thoroughly with beeswax before use. The wax repels moisture during service and protects the thread or cord against abrasion during sewing and knotting.

Inter-rib bracing. Before wings are covered, the alignment should be checked. All ribs which do not have permanent inter-rib bracing need to be securely braced in position to resist drifting during the application of covers. This is done with cotton reinforcing tape. Whenever covering fabric is laced to any part of a structure, reinforcing tape is placed over the fabric along the underlying member, under all lacing. This tape prevents rib-lacing cord from tearing through the fabric. The width of the tape should not be less than the width of the structural member to which the cover is being laced. In the case of an extra wide member, two or more tapes may be used to provide the necessary reinforcement width.

Reinforcing tape is used under and over special fabric-fastening methods, such as PK screws and Rivnuts. Reinforcing tape can be seen in Figure 2-2-11, as rib stitching is applied over it.

Tape bracing should be applied alternately to both the top and bottom capstrips. When completed, the tape should form an X between each rib. Tape shall be continuous, with one turn around successive capstrips, arranged so that the tape between the ribs is separated from the cover by a distance equal to the depth of the capstrip. The loop around each capstrip should be tied off in permanent position by means of a short length of lacing cord. See Figure 2-2-12.

Figure 2-2-13 shows surface tape applied over a stitched wing rib.

Grommets and Eyelets

Grommets are installed in fabric surfaces to provide reinforcements around drainage and ventilation holes. They may be made of metal or plastic. Plastic grommets have replaced the metal types in practical use. They can be readily applied because they adhere well to wet dope. Using a small, round, pre-doped *dollar patch* over a drain grommet is sometimes a good idea.

Grommets must be installed in all bottom surfaces in such a position as to provide free drainage when the airplane is in any one of the following positions:

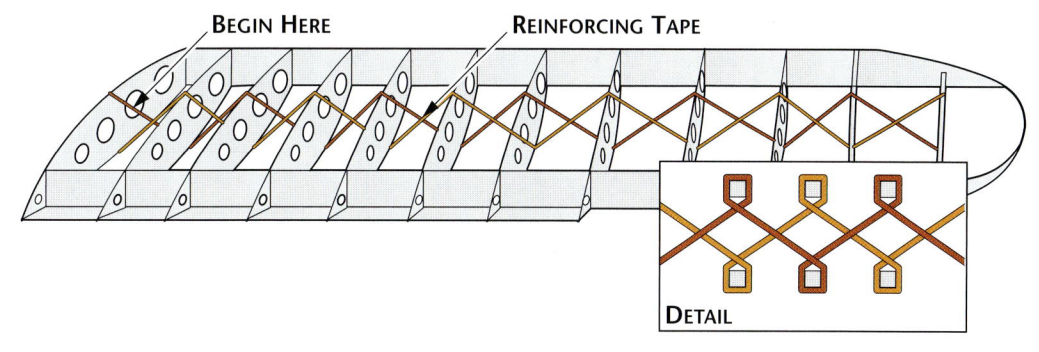

Figure 2-2-12. Inter-rib bracing is done using reinforcing tape; the same tape used over the fabric and under the rib stitching.

- Horizontal flying attitude
- At rest with tail on the ground
- Normal position on beaching gear or on water (flying boats)

For wire trailing edges, one grommet is placed on each side of each rib, as close to the rib as possible. On a wood or metal rigid trailing edge, one grommet is placed at the low point between successive ribs.

Grommets are available in both *flat washer* and *suction* (seaplane) types. The *seaplane grommet* is shielded with a hood opening aft to deflect the salt water or spray from the openings and to dry out the structure quickly. Eyelets may be used for the drainage and ventilation of small surfaces, instead of grommets.

> **NOTE:** *Those materials manufactured for Grade A cotton, such as rib lacing cord, inter-rib bracing tape and so on, will have the necessary strength to be used on synthetic fabrics, but their use is strongly discouraged. While these materials do have the initial strength, their durability is substantially less than that of the same materials specifically manufactured for the synthetic fabrics used to cover the aircraft. This implies that they will drop below required strength long before the Dacron covering will. If used, they will dictate the time to the next re-covering, not the fabric itself. It is strongly recommended that materials not be mixed. Besides, if they are not part of the STC, they should not be used in the first place.*

Dopes, Thinners and Finishes

Dopes, both nitrate and butyrate, are the acceptable mediums for encapsulating the fibers of aircraft covering. The exception is in the use of nitrate dope. When using Grade A cotton, a tautening nitrate dope is used, because the tightness of the fabric is dependant upon the abilities of the dope. When using synthetic fabrics, heat is used to tighten the fabric, not the dope. Therefore, a non-tautening nitrate dope is used.

Nitrate dope is used to encapsulate the fibers of the material and, in the case of cotton, to tighten up the fabric. Nitrate is flammable and care should be exercised in its use. All dopes should be used in a well-ventilated area.

Butyrate dope does not have the tautening ability of nitrate, but once the nitrate dope has done its job, the other coats can be butyrate to fill in and build up the film over the fabric. The main advantage of using butyrate to build up the film is in the fire resistance of butyrate dope.

Fungicide is an additive that is incorporated into the first coat of nitrate dope. This additive is for the purpose of offsetting the effects of mildew or other fungus on cotton fabric. The preferred fungicide is zinc dimethyldithiocarbamate. It comes in a powder form and is added to the dope before it is brushed onto the fabric. It should be mixed in accordance with the manufacturer's recommendations. Pre-mixed fungicidal dope can also be purchased.

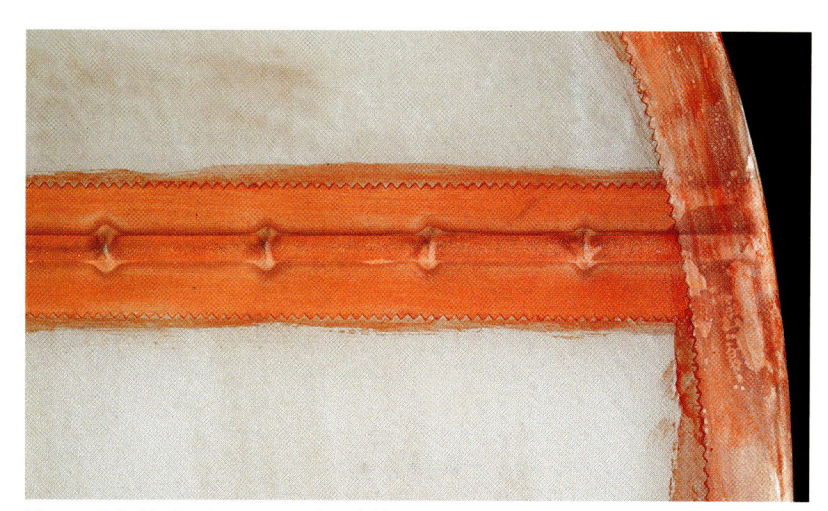

Figure 2-2-13. Surface tape should be applied as soon after rib stitching as practical. Give surface taping some thought in advance. Each end should be covered by another tape. When completed, only a few tape ends should terminate at the butt rib.

2-14 | Fabric Covering

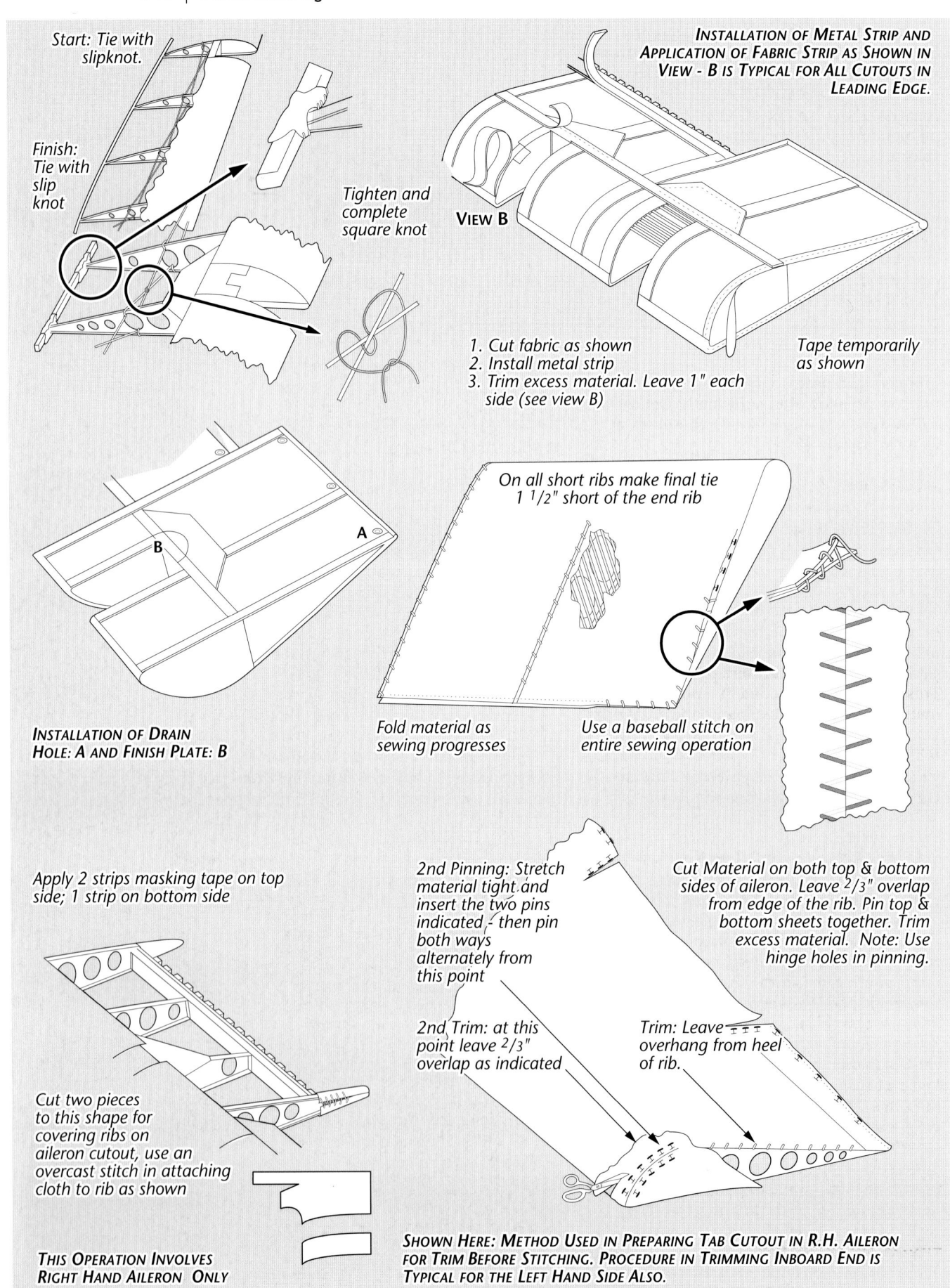

Start: Tie with slipknot.

Finish: Tie with slip knot

Tighten and complete square knot

View B

INSTALLATION OF METAL STRIP AND APPLICATION OF FABRIC STRIP AS SHOWN IN VIEW - B IS TYPICAL FOR ALL CUTOUTS IN LEADING EDGE.

1. Cut fabric as shown
2. Install metal strip
3. Trim excess material. Leave 1" each side (see view B)

Tape temporarily as shown

INSTALLATION OF DRAIN HOLE: A AND FINISH PLATE: B

On all short ribs make final tie 1 1/2" short of the end rib

Fold material as sewing progresses

Use a baseball stitch on entire sewing operation

Apply 2 strips masking tape on top side; 1 strip on bottom side

Cut two pieces to this shape for covering ribs on aileron cutout, use an overcast stitch in attaching cloth to rib as shown

THIS OPERATION INVOLVES RIGHT HAND AILERON ONLY

2nd Pinning: Stretch material tight and insert the two pins indicated - then pin both ways alternately from this point

2nd Trim: at this point leave 2/3" overlap as indicated

Cut Material on both top & bottom sides of aileron. Leave 2/3" overlap from edge of the rib. Pin top & bottom sheets together. Trim excess material. Note: Use hinge holes in pinning.

Trim: Leave overhang from heel of rib.

SHOWN HERE: METHOD USED IN PREPARING TAB CUTOUT IN R.H. AILERON FOR TRIM BEFORE STITCHING. PROCEDURE IN TRIMMING INBOARD END IS TYPICAL FOR THE LEFT HAND SIDE ALSO.

Figure 2-2-14. There is much handwork involved in finishing fabric attachment. It is an important part of the process and must be treated as such.

Pigmented dope is used in the final three or four coats. There must be two coats of aluminum-pigmented dope to shield the fabric against the effects of ultraviolet rays. After the aluminum coats have been applied, the number of colored, pigmented coats is a matter of preference. The color of choice is added to the butyrate dope either as a powder or paste.

Polyurethane finishes are sometimes applied to the fabric. When these finishes are applied, extreme care should be used. These materials can be deadly when the proper gear is not used. Special ventilated masks should be worn to prevent the plasticizers from entering the lungs and suffocating the technician.

Thinners are used to reduce the viscosity of the dope to allow it to sufficiently wet the surface, uniformly encapsulating the fibers of the fabric. Care should be taken to insure that only the appropriate thinner is used for each dope. Nitrate dope should be thinned with nitrate thinner, which is also true for butyrate dope. Urethane finishes will have their own thinners.

Dope proofing of structure. Prior to any fabric being attached to an aircraft structure, all surfaces that will be contacted by dope must be protected. A older method of dope proofing involved the use of cellophane tape over all portions of the structure as a protective barrier. This has been superceded by epoxy zinc chromate primer or other two part dope proof primers. Any wooden sections must be protected with at least two coats of dope proof varnish and allowed to cure completely before being covered with any fabric that will be doped.

Covering Procedures

Storage and cleaning of fabrics. Proper storage of unused fabric is necessary to prevent deterioration or damage. The material should be kept away from sunlight, ultraviolet light or chemicals that could damage the cloth. Unprotected exposure to sunlight and UV will accelerate the deterioration of organic fibers, shortening their useful life. Many chemicals and oils in the work area will create adhesion problems for dopes and finishes leading to fisheyes or blooming and other related problems. Fabric rolls are best kept in the shipping boxes until ready for use and returned to the same box after any fabric is removed. Any dirt or oils on the fabric can be cleaned off with acetone prior to installation and doping.

Fabric Installation

There are two methods that can be used to cover the aircraft structure: the *blanket* and the *envelope* methods. The blanket method consists

1. Allow an overlap of 1/2" beyong the edges of hinge cutout.

2. Fold the material under so that the double edged material will come just to the edge of the cut-out.

3. Cut two pieces of fabric to fit the sides of the cut-out, large enough to allow the edges to be turned 1/2" all around.

4. Fit the two pieces of material (step 3) in the cut out and sew all around as indicated, using a baseball stitch, six stitches per inch, double lock stitch at the start, lock stitch every 5 inches and a double lock stitch at the finish.

5. Cover the retaining strips with 2 in. tape flush with the edge of the opening. Cover all seams with 2 in. doped surface tape, pinked or frayed.

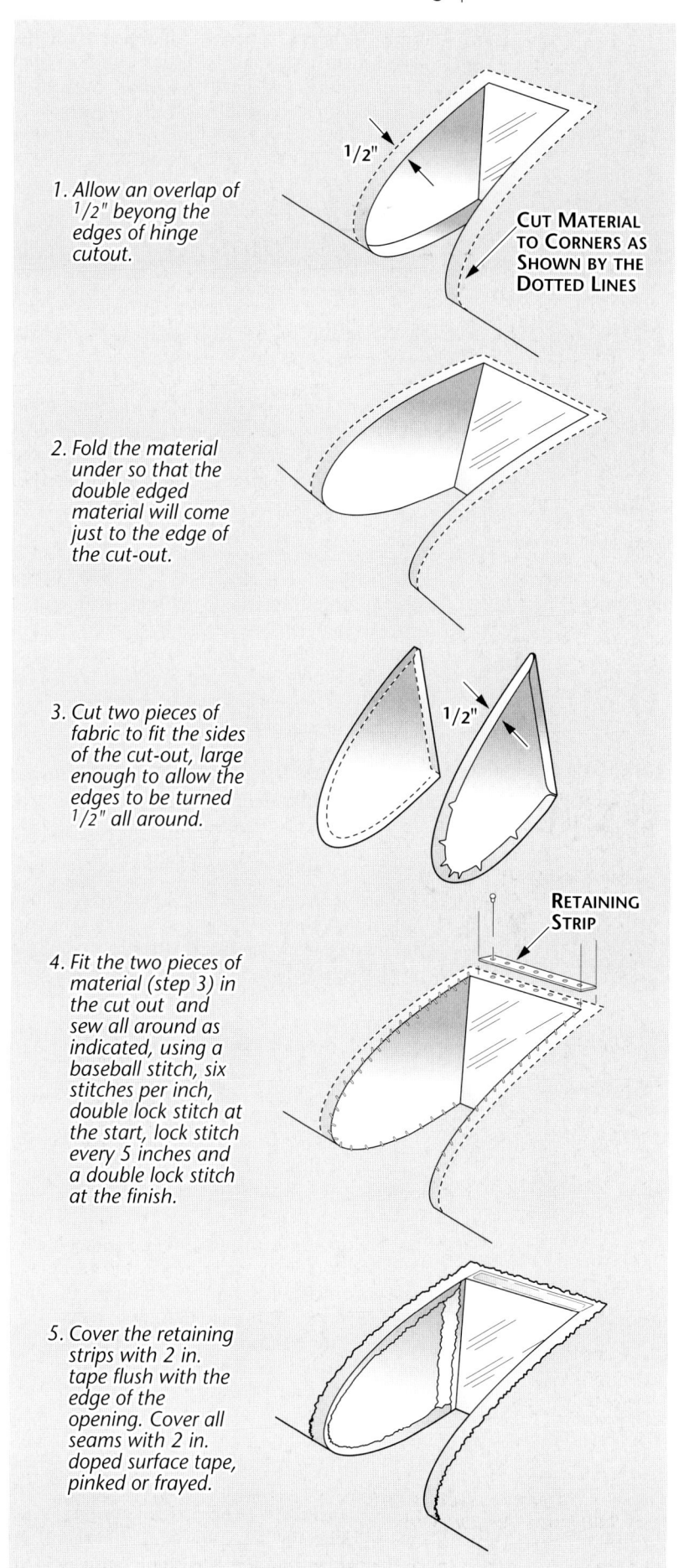

Figure 2-2-15. A typical landing light cutout

simply of laying a length of fabric over the wing structure and attaching it in place. When using Grade A cotton, that would imply that the leading and the trailing edge would have to be hand-stitched to close them up. If the fabric is polyester, the fabric is simply laid over the structure, and the leading and the trailing edge are simply glued in place.

The envelope method consists of carefully measuring and cutting the fabric in the shape of the wing, machine sewing the leading and the trailing edges, and pulling the closed-up tube over the wing like one would pull on a sock.

There are several things to consider before either of these methods is selected. If the goal of the re-covering is authentic restoration, the material and the method of attachment will be selected based upon the original covering. If the original material was made of Grade A cotton using machine-sewn, chordwise seams, then the re-covering method will probably be the same in all details. If the goal is to simply re-cover the structure, there is greater flexibility in the methods chosen for re-covering.

Figure 2-2-14 shows several different ways that ends and cutouts have fabric attached.

Cotton fabric. Cotton fabric is manufactured under Technical Standard Order (TSO) C14 or C15. It can have a thread count from 80-94 for TSO-C14b and 80-84 for TSO-C15d.

Grade A cotton fabric is woven in 60 inch widths, and this is enough to cover many aircraft wings from leading to trailing edge. To cover a wing using the envelope method, a length of fabric is laid over the wing, extending from butt to bow. The top and the bottom pieces are pinned together at the leading and the trailing edge. Then a pencil line is drawn, following the shape of the wing. This line will indicate where the seam will be sewn.

The marked fabric is removed from the wing and machine-sewn using either the folded-fell or the French-fell style of seam. Once the seams have been sewn, the envelope is turned inside out and slipped back over the wing structure. Care should be taken to insure that the seams run straight along the leading and the trailing edge of the wing. The opening at the butt rib will then have to be hand-stitched, using the baseball or roll stitch.

If the blanket method is going to be used, the fabric is pinned in place, and the excess material is trimmed off. Leave 1 inch of fabric to be turned under to make the edge of the seam. The seam will have to be closed using a curved or straight needle. The type of stitch will be the baseball or roll stitch. Hand-sewn seams should have a minimum of four stitches per inch, and the stitch should be locked at a maximum of ten stitches. Once the fabric is fully closed, it is ready for shrinking. Some areas, such as landing light cutouts (Figure 2-2-15) require special fabric attachment.

Aircraft linen. Commonly called *Irish linen*, it is manufactured under British Specification 7F1. It has two different sizes of thread that alternate throughout the fabric. It has a lower nap than cotton, and is somewhat harder to encapsulate with dope. In addition to the fact that it looks like traditional linen fabric, aircraft linen can be recognized by its slightly darker color, the fact that it is smoother than cotton and that the reverse side has small yarn ends protruding. However, it is strong and will last a long time when installed with reasonable care. Irish linen is difficult to obtain and is not used very often.

Polyester fabric. The envelope method is not used with these modern fabrics, due to the advanced methods and materials. These Dacron polyester materials come in 70 inch widths and are installed using the blanket method. The fabric is laid over the wing structure and then glued down using the proper glue material for the particular method. There are two particular methods currently in use, and each one has materials and approved techniques. When using polyester, be sure to follow the instructions carefully.

Both currently popular methods have several things in common. The blanket is laid down over the surface of the wing and the fabric is glued down, using the prescribed cement to stick the fabric to the leading edge. The fabric is then pulled over the trailing edge and likewise cemented down. Finally, the fabric at the butt rib and the wing tip bow are cemented down. The wing structure is then turned over and the process is repeated. Depending on which product is used, the overlap at the leading and the trailing edge must be carefully observed. Once the correct overlap is determined, the fabric is cemented down. Once the cement has had sufficient time to dry, the fabric is ready for shrinking. Care should be taken to not cause the material to tighten up excessively, as this could cause damage to the underlying structure.

Fabric sizing or shrinking. Grade A cotton fabric is sized by the application of water to the fabric. A damp sponge is used to bathe the fabric with water. As the water dries, the cotton fibers shrink up, causing the fabric cover to tighten over the structure.

Polyester fabrics are sized using the heat from an electric iron ~~or an approved heat gun~~. Polyester fabric tends to sag over the structure more than the Grade A cotton does. When heat is applied to the surface of the fabric, the fibers begin to shrink and the material becomes taut.

1. Tie square knot on center of capstrip.

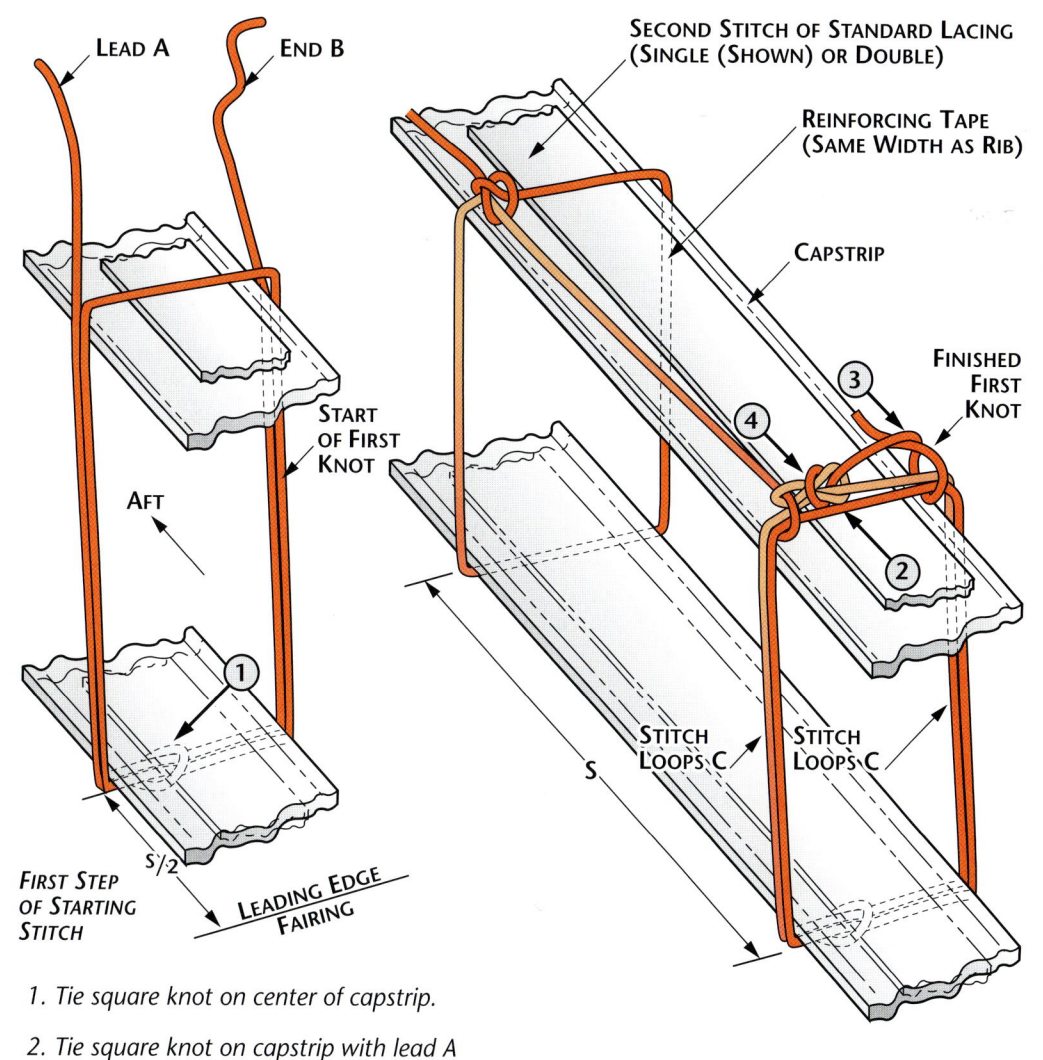

2. Tie square knot on capstrip with lead A and end B.

3. Lock square knot with half hitch around stitch loops C with end B. Cut off surplus of end B.

4. Half hitch around stitch loops C.

S = Normal Stitch Spacing
Schematic Represents Lacing Around Entire Rib.

Figure 2-2-16. Starting stitch for rib lacing

The manufacturer's manual will give instructions as to the calibration of the iron. Be sure to follow these instructions closely and shrink the fabric in the prescribed stages, otherwise the fabric could be over-tightened in isolated spots.

Fabric doping. The main purpose of dope is to shrink the fabric and produce a tight fabric with a closed weave. A tight cover is essential for the fabric cover to hold its smooth airfoil shape. Maintaining the airfoil shape enables the wing to produce the lift in the way that the structure was designed to do.

The *encapsulation* of the individual fibers of the weave produces an increase in strength, especially in cotton fabric, that allows the fabric to withstand the heavy air loads. In essence, the fabric holds the shape, and the doped finish provides the majority of the strength. Further, the encapsulation of the fibers produces an almost waterproof surface that protects the wing and fuselage structure from the damage of moisture.

Dope can be either clear or pigmented. Clear dope is used for the initial tautening process. Aluminum powder, added to clear dope at a ratio of 3 ounces of 325-mesh aluminum powder to 1 gallon of clear un-thinned dope, is used for ultraviolet protection. Pigmented dope, in almost any color desired, is available pre-mixed from aviation suppliers and is used for the final fill and for the decorative color.

Nitrate dope. There are few uses for nitrate dope because of its low fire resistance. However,

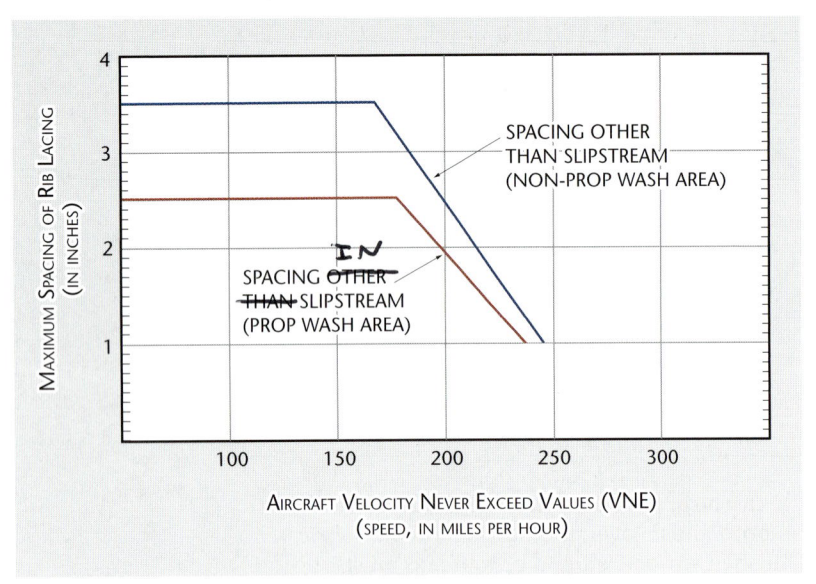

Figure 2-2-17. Fabric attachment spacing

one use is for the first coat on fabric and some Dacron processes. While the FAA states that this is not necessary, many experienced technicians believe that an initial coat of nitrate provides a better encapsulation of the fibers than does an initial coat of butyrate.

CAB dope (Cellulose Acetate Butyrate). Cellulose acetate butyrate is the material of choice because of its superior fire resistance. Cellulose acetate butyrate dope is the product of the action of acetic and butyric acids on the cellulose, plus the addition of the solvent and plasticizer.

Cellulose is the basic structural material of plants, forming the film base.

Acetic acid is an organic acid found naturally in vinegar. The commercial source of this vinegar is the oxidation of acetone, one of the products of the fermentation of corn sugar.

Butyric acid is an organic acid found naturally in rancid butter.

Solvents are the liquid parts of the dope in which the solid cellulose products are dissolved. They have low boiling points and therefore evaporate very quickly. Both solvents and their vapors are flammable and explosive.

Plasticizers are added to slow down the rate of evaporation, allowing the dope to be brushed on the surface. They are castor oil, gum shellac or other similar materials.

Dilutents are composed of butyl-acetate (50 percent by weight) and diacetone alcohol (50 percent by weight). They are used to thin the solution to the correct consistency. A much thinner solution must be used in a spray gun than would be used with a brush.

Anti-blush compounds are added to prevent or control whitening, or blushing, of the dope when drying. They also retard drying of dope in a damp atmosphere, which prevents its turning white and becoming brittle.

Rib Stitching

Rib stitching is a major part of any re-cover. See Figure 2-2-16. Fortunately, it is not really difficult; only tedious. The dope and fabric section of AC 43.13-1B has a wealth of material on rib stitching, so this textbook will cover just the basics found in that manual.

The spacing of rib stitching is important to airworthiness. The FAA mentions that you can duplicate the spacing of the original cover. If that spacing is not known, there is a chart based on the airplane's never-exceed speed (Figure 2-2-17). The problem is that very few airplanes around today still have their original covers. If you cannot verify the original spacing, it might be a good idea to use the chart.

NOTE: *Build a set of wing stands first. It keeps you off of your hands and knees.*

Beeswax-coated linen rib-stitching cord is best for Grade A fabric. For an STC Dacron material, use what they say to use.

Learn to tie the starting knot correctly. If you have to do the job by yourself, use several needles at the same time — it saves a lot of walking around.

That slight bend in the end of the needle seen in Figure 2-2-11 is really handy — just don't bend it too much.

Always put the knot on the bottom surface, never on top. See Figure 2-2-16. Push the knot down along side the reinforcing tape to lower its protrusion. It is possible to make the knots and the running thread inside the wing instead of alongside the reinforcing tape, producing a much better surface. If an airplane did not have that as an original process, get FAA approval before doing it on your re-cover. It is actually a modification and can be hard to explain.

Think hard about what is inside a wing. Don't sew cables, cable sectors, pushrods, etc., so tightly that you will have to cut the new fabric to fix the problem. Allow plenty of room per instructions in AC 43.13-1B.

Figure 2-2-18 shows a rib stitch in process. Notice the completed stitches behind the sewer and the pre-punched holes ahead.

Pigmented dope. Sunlight is the greatest factor in the deterioration of dope and fabric. For this reason, dope transparency must be eliminated. This is done by adding pigment, or coloring material, to the last few coats of dope applied. Pigmented dope should be mixed only in sufficient quantities for immediate use. Aluminum-pigmented dope must be stirred frequently to prevent the aluminum powder from settling to the bottom of the solution.

Application of Dope to Fabric

Working conditions. The room in which doping is performed must be enclosed completely and not used for any purpose other than painting, doping or patching prior to doping. Maintain the room in a clean, neat condition, consistent with the best practices for obtaining dust-free finishes.

The temperature should be 70°-90°F (75°-85°F preferred) with a humidity of 30-55 percent (45-55 percent preferred).

Ventilation of the room is accomplished by forced draft with at least 15 changes of air per hour.

As a means of fire prevention, all electrical equipment, including lights, motors, switches, starters, etc., should be explosion-proof. Under no circumstances are electrical appliances of any kind, including flashlights, permitted in the doping room. Floors, benches and other equipment should be made of spark-proof material, if possible, to prevent explosions.

Static electricity. Provisions should be made for discharging static electricity from the body of any person entering the room by grounding all door pulls. All work in the dope room should be grounded by a flexible cable attached by means of battery clips to the work at one end and to approved ground rod connection at the other.

Overspray particles and sanding dust that have fallen to the floor, can be ignited by static electricity while sweeping a cement floor. Sprinkling water on the floor before sweeping, or using a wet floor-sweeping compound, can greatly reduce the danger of ignition by static.

Painting equipment. Brushes used for applying dope should be of the flat type, 5-6 inches wide, with bristles set in rubber and bound in metal. They should be cleaned after each day's use with the proper thinner.

Spray guns should be adjusted to provide the proper spray distribution for satisfactory coverage.

Application. Successive coats of clear dope must be applied on fabric-covered parts until a film is obtained that produces a uniformly taut, smooth and rigid surface. Whenever possible, pigmented dope should be applied with a spray gun over clear dope. AC 43.13-1B gives the minimum number of coats of dope. The minimum legal requirement for a light aircraft of up to 9 lbs. per square foot of wing load is three to four coats (showing a uniform gloss), in combination with the aluminum-pigmented and finish coats. For higher wing-load aircraft, five to eight clear coats, on average, are recommended. That said, few re-cover jobs will pass an owner's inspection with the minimum FAA requirements.

Colors are to be used for dope fabric surfaces in accordance with customer requirements. Under no circumstances will any airplane surface be finished with clear dope only. The dope should be applied so as to produce a uniformly smooth finish over the surface of the fabric. Finished surfaces should be taut and must ring drum-like when struck.

Panels should be in a horizontal position while doping. If a vertical position is necessary, the dope must be carefully applied in a continuous film to prevent it from running along the bottom edge.

The tautening property of dope is a function of both volatiles and plasticizers. Insufficient thinning causes a loss in tautness. The speed of tautening may be increased greatly by blowing air inside the wing panels or other confined spaces to remove the heavy solvent vapors that accumulate during the drying period.

Drying time between successive coats varies with temperature and humidity. Under good atmospheric conditions, not less than 30 minutes shall be allowed between successive coats. Under unfavorable conditions, this time must be extended. Under all conditions, sufficient time must elapse between coats to allow the surface to become dry to the touch. Unless dope is properly thinned, drying time will be unduly retarded.

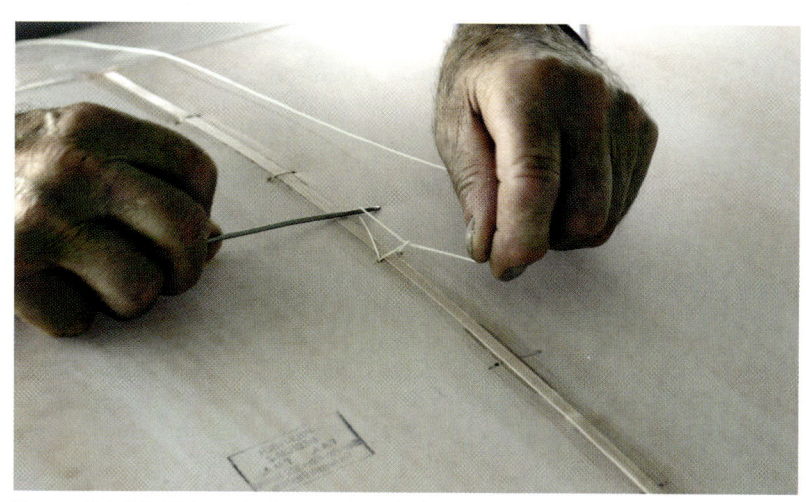

Figure 2-2-18. This technician is rib stitching a Dacron-covered wing, with the FAA PMA stamp on the fabric to the right of the stitch. An STC PMA part is always marked as such.

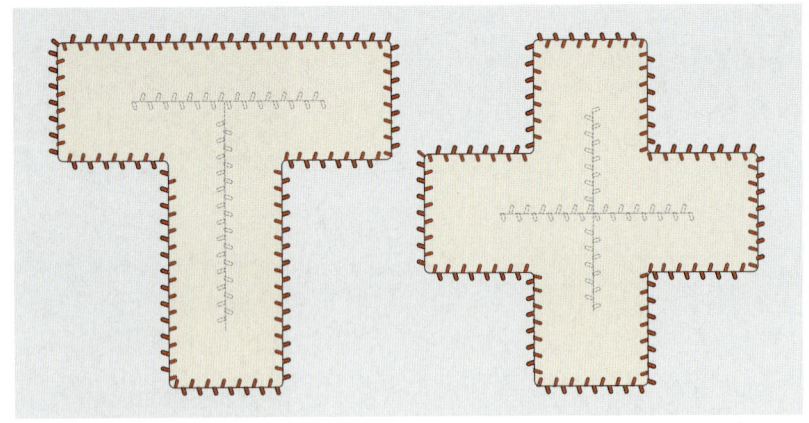

Figure 2-2-19. Typical sewn fabric patches. These types of patches are seldom used because they are difficult to match invisibly to the original surface texture.

Blushing. Blushing has the effect of seriously reducing tensile strength of dope film and is caused by a precipitation of the cellulose ester. Blush must be avoided. It is caused by too-rapid evaporation or by relative humidity conditions being too high. Blushing tendencies are increased if strong currents of air flow over the surfaces during or immediately after spraying.

If roughness appears after the last coat of clear dope or succeeding coats of pigmented dope, the surface may be smoothed by rubbing it lightly with No. 280 sandpaper. No other rubbing materials are to be used for this purpose. All wing panels, while being sanded, rubbed or wiped incident to doping, must be grounded to prevent accumulation of static electricity.

Doping Procedure

==The first coat is applied with a brush.== It should be spread on the surface as uniformly as possible and thoroughly worked into the fabric. Care should be taken not to work the dope through the fabric to the extent that an excessive film is formed on the reverse side. The first coat should be nothing more than a thorough, uniform wetting of the fabric, applied quickly and carefully. The dope should be worked with the warp and with the fill alternately for three or four strokes, and excess material stroked away to avoid piling up or dripping.

> **NOTE:** *These directions are generally acceptable FAA processes. Many experienced technicians will thin dope differently; at least half with thinner/fungicide in the first coat, continuing with that mixture for three more coats before taping. While this consistency requires skill and fast brushwork, it makes encapsulation of the fibers more complete.*

A fungicidal compound may be incorporated only in the first clear coat of dope to prevent loss in strength of fabric through mold growth. This deterioration of fabric is encountered particularly under tropical conditions of high temperature and high relative humidity. Three ounces of salicyanilide added to one gallon of thinned dope ready for application will prevent growth of mold. The fabric will develop a blue, purple or green cast from the fungicide.

The second coat is applied with a brush, laid on smoothly, and worked only enough to secure an even spread. Although the FAA says it can be *dressed out* after the first coat, reinforcing tape, grommets and chafe patches can be applied at this time. Surface tape can be applied with the next coat.

> **NOTE:** *While applying the surface tape, be careful not to allow the dope to drip through the rib stitching holes and hit the other side. The resulting round drip mark will stay forever. It cannot be covered up.*

The third or fourth coats may be applied by brush. The required weight of clear dope coating ordinarily will normally be produced by four coats, though AC 43.13-1B identifies that as the minimum for a 9-lb.-per-square-foot wing loading. As the wing loading goes higher, up to eight coats of dope may be required. Should additional coats be necessary, depending upon the amount of thinning and method of spray gun operation, they should be applied as needed. Clear dope will provide a taut and rigid surface to fabric-covered parts.

The minimum satisfactory weight of clear cellulose butyrate dope coat is normally regarded as being 2.25 ounces per square yard or surface, with 2.50 ounces somewhat more desirable after drying at least 72 hours. The weight of pigmented dope should be 2.00 ounces per square yard, with a slightly higher figure preferable.

Pigmented dope of the proper color is applied to the various surfaces with a spray gun whenever possible. The weight of the film is specified when applied in not less than two coats.

Rejuvenator. A special solvent, called *rejuvenator*, can be sprayed on a fabric surface to soften all coats of dope at the same time. It can help restore the condition of the coating. *but not the fabric*

Precautions

- ==Dope must not be poured on fabric.==
- Dope must not stand in open containers exposed to air for more than one hour.
- When not in use, dope dispensing cans or other containers must be covered carefully to prevent unnecessary evaporation.
- Do not use electrical equipment in the same area as dope.

Repair of Fabric Covers

Repair fabric-covered surfaces so that the original strength and tautness are returned to the fabric. Repair all tears or punctures immediately to prevent the entry of moisture or foreign objects into the interior of the structure. Sewn and un-sewn repairs are permitted. The type of repair technique to be used depends on the size and location of the damage, as well as the never-exceed speed of the aircraft. AC 43.13-1B has specific instructions for each type patch.

When re-covering or repairing control surface fabric, especially on high-performance airplanes, the repairs must not involve the addition of weight aft of the hinge line. The addition of weight disturbs the dynamic and static balance of the surface to a degree that will induce flutter.

Tears in the fabric. Small cuts or tears are repaired by sewing the edges together and doping a pinked- or frayed-edge patch over the area. The baseball stitch is used in repairing tears. The first stitch is started by inserting the needle from the underneath side. All remaining stitches are made by inserting the needle from the top instead of from the bottom so that the points for making the stitch can be more accurately located. The edges are sewn together using the proper thread. The last stitch is anchored with a modified seine knot [dbl half hitch]. Stitches should not be more than 1/4 inch apart and should extend 1/4 inch into the un-torn cover.

Doped-on patch. Un-sewn (doped-on) repairs may be made on all aircraft fabric-covered surfaces, provided the aircraft never-exceed speed is not greater than 150 m.p.h. A doped-on patch repair may be used if the damage does not exceed 16 inches in any direction. Cut out the damaged section, making a round- or oval-shaped opening trimmed to a smooth contour. Use a grease solvent to clean the edges of the opening to be covered by the patch. Sand off the dope from the area around the patch or wash it off with a dope thinner. Support the fabric from underneath while sanding.

Sewn-in patch. Damage to covers where the edges of the tear are tattered beyond joining or where a piece has been completely torn away is repaired by sewing a fabric patch onto the damaged area and doping a surface patch over the sewn insert. A sewn-in repair patch may be used if the damage is not longer than 16 inches in any one direction.

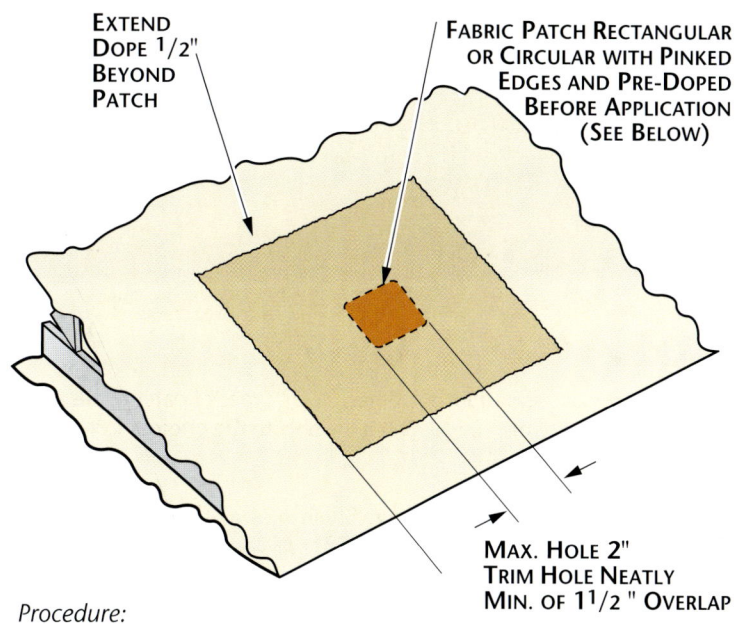

Procedure:
1. *Clean fabric down to clear dope.*
2. *Apply one coat of dope and set patch while dope is fresh*
3. *Apply 3 additional coats, permitting each coat to dry thoroughly.*
4. *Apply 3 additional coats of non specular pigmented dope of desired color.*

Figure 2-2-20. A doped-in panel is preferred by many because a well-finished patch will all but disappear.

Before sewing, fasten the patch at several points with a few temporary stitches to aid in sewing the seams. The edges of the insert are sewn with a baseball stitch (Figure 2-2-19).

Doped-in panel. When the damage exceeds 16 inches in any direction, make the repair by doping in a new panel. This type of repair may be extended to cover both the upper and lower surfaces and to cover several rib bays if necessary. The panel should be laced to all ribs covered, and it should be doped or sewn in the blanket method (Figure 2-2-20).

Sewn-in panel. When the damaged area exceeds 16 inches in any direction, a new panel should be installed. Remove the surface tape from the ribs adjacent to the damaged area and from the trailing and leading edges of the section being repaired. Leave the old reinforcing tape in place.

This type of repair may be extended to cover both the upper and lower surfaces and to cover several rib bays if necessary. The panel must be laced to all ribs covered.

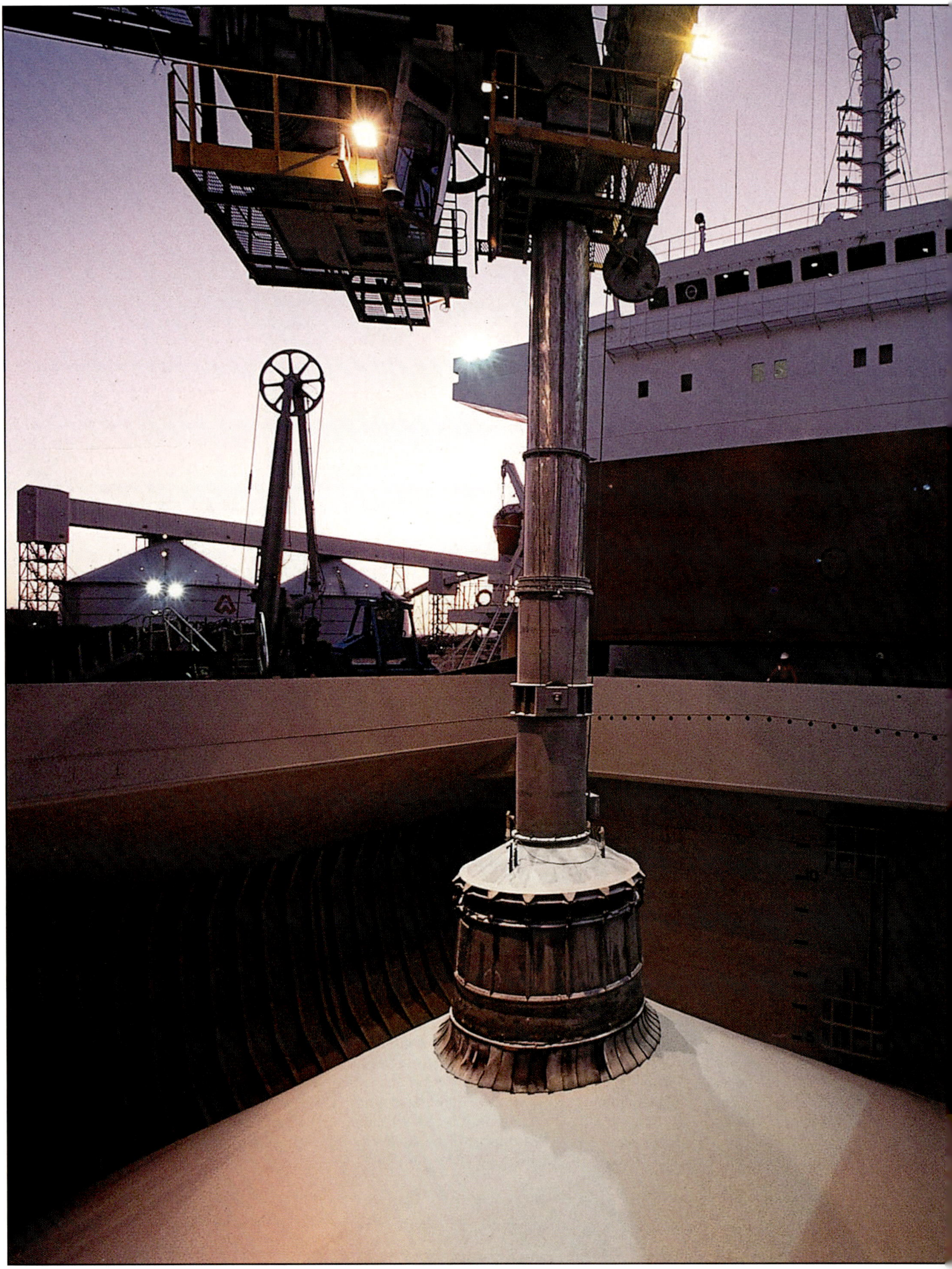

3

Materials and Processes

Section 1

Aerospace Materials

Knowledge and understanding of the uses, strengths, limitations and other characteristics of structural metals are vital to properly construct and maintain any equipment, especially airframes. In aircraft maintenance and repair, even a slight deviation from design specification or the substitution of inferior materials may result in the loss of both lives and equipment. The use of unsuitable materials can readily erase the finest craftsmanship. The selection of the correct material for a specific repair job demands familiarity with the most common physical properties of various metals.

Properties of metals are of primary concern in aircraft maintenance. Of specific importance are such general properties of metals and their alloys as strength, hardness, malleability, ductility, brittleness, conductivity, thermal expansion, elasticity, toughness, fusibility and density. These terms are explained within this section to establish a basis for further discussion of structural metals.

Terms

Strength. The ability of a material to withstand forces which tend to deform it in any direction and the ability of that material to resist stress without breaking is known as *strength*. There are four primary types of strength, which are of importance when working with metals: tensile, yield, shear and bearing strengths.

Tensile strength of a material is its resistance to a force which tries to pull it apart. Tensile strength is measured in pounds per square inch (p.s.i), and is calculated by dividing the

---

Learning Objectives

REVIEW
- Physical and chemical properties of metals

DESCRIBE
- Production of metals used in aircraft structures
- Rivet types
- Rivet installation

EXPLAIN
- How to identify metals, rivets and fasteners
- Heat treatment and hardening
- Rivet patterns
- How to lay out sheet metal

APPLY
- Use drilling tools
- Install rivets and other fasteners
- Form sheet metal

Left. Ships like this one transport aluminum ore from the refinery to the smelter. From there, the ore is turned into ingots, which will be processed into familiar aluminum products.

Photo courtesy of Alcoa

load, in pounds, required to pull the material apart by its cross-sectional area.

Yield strength is that point at which a load would cause an initial indication of a permanent distortion. It is measured in p.s.i.

Shear strength is that point at which a material would fail under a shear force. The shear strength, measured in p.s.i., is found by dividing the shear force or load by the shear area.

Bearing strength is the ability of a material to resist the forces that tend to damage it at the point of an applied load.

The relationship between the strength of a material and its weight per cubic inch, expressed as a ratio, is known as the *strength-to-weight ratio*. This ratio forms the basis for comparing the desirability of various materials for use in airframe construction and repair. Neither strength nor weight alone can be used as a means of true comparison.

Hardness. The ability of a metal to resist abrasion, penetration, cutting action or permanent distortion is referred to as *hardness*. Hardness may be increased by cold-working the metal, and in the case of steel and certain aluminum alloys, by heat-treatment.

Structural parts are often formed from metals in their soft state, and are then heat-treated to harden them so that the finished shape will be retained. Hardness and strength are closely associated properties of metals.

Malleability. A metal which can be hammered, rolled or pressed into various shapes without cracking, breaking or having some other detrimental effect, is said to be *malleable*. This property is necessary in sheet metal that is worked into curved shapes such as cowlings, fairings or wingtips. Copper is an example of a malleable metal.

Ductility. Similar to malleability, *ductility* is the property of a metal which permits it to be permanently drawn, bent or twisted into various shapes without breaking. This property is essential for metals used in making wire and tubing. Ductile metals are greatly preferred for aircraft use, because of their forming ease and resistance to failure under shock loads. For this reason, aluminum alloys are used for cowl rings, fuselage and wing skin, and for formed or extruded parts, such as ribs, spars or bulkheads. Chromium molybdenum steel is also easily formed into desired shapes.

Brittleness. The property of a metal which allows little bending or deformation without shattering is *brittleness*. A brittle metal is apt to break or crack without change of shape. Because structural metals are often subjected to shock loads, brittleness is not a very desirable property. Cast iron, cast aluminum and very hard steel are examples of brittle metals.

Conductivity. The ability of a metal to transmit heat or electricity is known as *conductivity*.

Thermal conductivity is the ability of a metal to transmit heat. The thermal conductivity of a metal must be carefully considered if the metal is to be used in applications where the metal will be welded or where expansion and contraction are critical.

Electrical conductivity is the ability of a metal to freely accept and release electrons when an electrical current is applied. To eliminate radio interference in aircraft, electrical conductivity and bonding of metals parts must be considered.

Elasticity. The property which enables a metal to return to its original shape when the force which causes the change of shape is removed is *elasticity*. This property is extremely valuable, because it would be highly undesirable to have a part permanently distorted after an applied load was removed. Each metal has a point, known as the elastic limit, beyond which it cannot be loaded without causing permanent distortion. In aircraft construction, parts and components are designed so that the maximum loads to which they are subjected will not stress them beyond their elastic limits. This desirable property is present in spring steel.

Toughness. A material which possesses *toughness* will withstand tearing or shearing and may be stretched or otherwise deformed without breaking. This is desirable in aircraft metals.

Density. The mass of a unit volume of a material is its *density*. In aircraft work, the specified mass of a material per cubic inch is preferred. This figure can be used in determining the weight of a part before it is actually manufactured. Density is critical when choosing a material to be used in the design of a part, so that the proper weight and balance of the aircraft can be maintained.

Aluminum Production

Aluminum ore, most commonly bauxite, is plentiful and occurs mainly in tropical and sub-tropical areas: Africa, the West Indies, South America and Australia. There are also some deposits in Europe. Bauxite is refined into aluminum oxide trihydrate (alumina) and then electrolytically reduced into metallic aluminum. Primary aluminum production facilities are located all over the world, often in areas where there are abundant supplies of inexpensive energy, such as hydroelectric power.

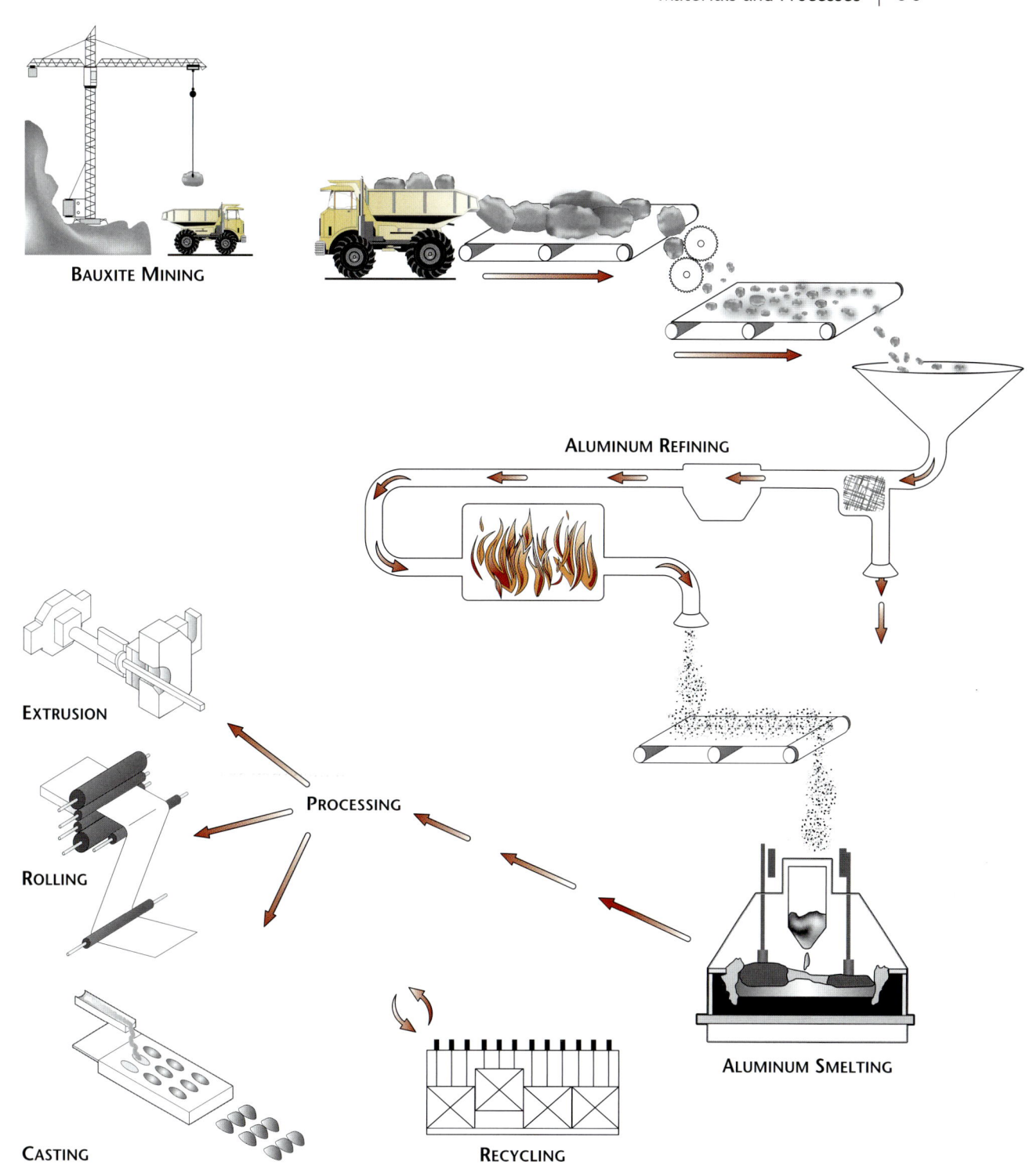

Figure 3-1-1. The process of refining aluminum, from mining to the finished process

Two to three tons of bauxite are required to produce one ton of alumina, and two tons of alumina are required to produce one ton of aluminum metal. Figure 3-1-1 illustrates the complete process.

Bauxite Mining. Bauxite is normally extracted by open cast-mining from strata, typically some four to six meters thick under a shallow covering of topsoil and vegetation. In most cases, the topsoil is removed and stored.

Alumina Refining

The Bayer process. The aluminum industry relies on the Bayer process to produce alumina from bauxite. It remains the most economic means of obtaining alumina, which in turn is vital for the production of aluminum metal.

The aluminum industry is dependent on a regular supply of alumina for four functions:

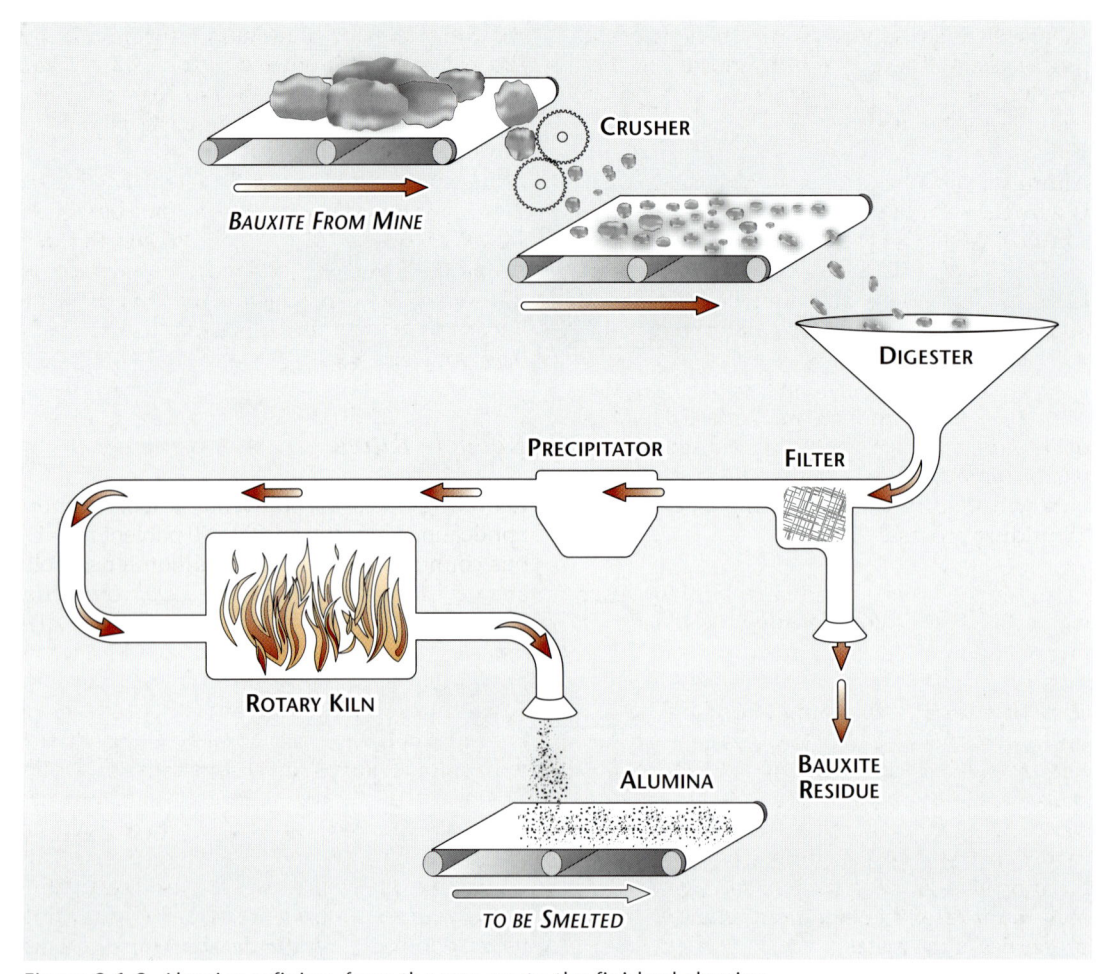

Figure 3-1-2. Alumina refining, from the raw ore to the finished alumina

- Basic raw material for aluminum production
- Thermal insulator for tops of electrolytic cells
- Coating for pre-baked anodes
- Absorbent filter for cell emissions

Bauxite is washed, ground and dissolved in caustic soda (sodium hydroxide) at high pressure and temperature. The resulting liquor contains a solution of sodium aluminate and undissolved bauxite residues containing iron, silicon and titanium. These residues sink gradually to the bottom of the tank and are removed. They are known colloquially as "red mud." The clear sodium aluminate solution is pumped into a huge tank called a precipitator. Fine particles of alumina are added to seed the precipitation of pure alumina particles as the liquor cools.

The particles sink to the bottom of the tank, are removed and are then passed through a rotary, or fluidised calciner, at 1,100°C, to drive off the chemically combined water. The result is a white powder, pure alumina. The caustic soda is returned to the start of the process and used again. Figure 3-1-2 illustrates the aluminum refining process.

Alumina smelting. The basis for all modern primary aluminum-smelting plants is the *Hall-Héroult Process*, invented in 1886. Alumina is dissolved in an electrolytic bath of molten cryolite (sodium aluminum fluoride) within a large carbon- or graphite-lined steel container known as a "pot." An electric current is passed through the electrolyte at low voltage, but very high current, typically 150,000 amperes. The electric current flows between a carbon anode (positive) — made of petroleum coke and pitch — and a cathode (negative), formed by the thick carbon or graphite lining of the pot. Molten aluminum is deposited at the bottom of the pot and is siphoned off periodically, taken to a holding furnace, often but not always blended to an alloy specification, cleaned and then generally cast.

A typical aluminum smelter consists of around 300 pots. These will produce some 125,000 tons of aluminum annually. However, some of the latest generation of smelters are in the 350,000-400,000 ton range.

Aluminum is formed at about 1,652°F, but once formed, it has a melting point of only 1,220°F. In some smelters, this spare heat is used to melt recycled metal. Producing recycled aluminum requires only 5 percent of the energy required to make new aluminum. Blending recycled metal with new metal allows considerable energy savings, as well as the efficient use of process heat. There is no difference between primary and recycled aluminum in terms of quality or properties.

Aluminum smelting is energy intensive, which is why the world's smelters are located in areas which have access to abundant power resources (hydro-electric, natural gas, coal or nuclear). Many locations are remote and the electricity is generated specifically for the aluminum plant.

The smelting process is continuous. A smelter cannot easily be stopped and restarted. If production is interrupted by a power supply failure of more than four hours, the metal in the pots will solidify, often requiring an expensive rebuilding process.

From time to time, individual pot linings reach the end of their useful life and the pots are then taken out of service and relined.

Most smelters produce aluminum of 99.7 percent purity, which is acceptable for most applications. However, super-purity aluminum (99.99 percent) is used for some special applications, typically those where high ductility or conductivity is required. The marginal difference in the purities of smelter-grade aluminum and super-purity aluminum results in significant changes in the properties of the metal.

Value of Scrap: Recycling

Anything made of aluminum can be recycled repeatedly: not only cans, but aluminum foil, plates and pie molds, window frames, garden furniture and automotive components are melted down and used to make similar products again. The recycling of aluminum requires only 5 percent of the energy to produce secondary metal, as compared to primary metal, and generates only 5 percent of the greenhouse gas emissions. Scrap aluminum has significant value and commands good market prices. Aluminum companies have invested in dedicated state of the art secondary metal processing plants to recycle aluminum. In the case of beverage cans, the process uses gas collected from burning off the coating to preheat the material prior to processing. The recycling of aluminum beverage cans eliminates waste. It saves energy, conserves natural resources, reduces the use of city landfills and provides added revenue for recyclers, charities and local town government. The aluminum can is therefore good news for the environment and good for the economy.

Used beverage cans are normally back on supermarket shelves as new beverage cans in six to eight weeks in those countries which have dedicated can collecting and recycling schemes. The recycling rate for aluminum cans is already above 70 percent in some countries. Cans made from aluminum are worth 6 to 20 times more than any other used packaging material.

In Europe, the aluminum beverage can meets the minimum targets set in the European Directive on Packaging and Waste. Sweden (92 percent) and Switzerland (88 percent) are the European can-recycling champions. The European average is 40 percent, a 10-percent increase since 1994.

Recycle Rates

Recycling rates for building and transport applications range from 60 to 90 percent in various countries. Just over 11.6 million tons of old and new scrap were recycled in 1998 worldwide, which fulfilled close to 40 percent of the global demand for aluminum. Of this total, 17 percent came from packaging, 38 percent from transport, 32 percent from building and 13 percent from other products. The aluminum industry is working with automobile manufacturers to enable easier dismantling of aluminum components from cars in order to improve the sorting and recovery of aluminum. In 1997, more than 4.4 million tons of scrap were used in the transport sector and the use of aluminum in automobiles is increasing year upon year. Worldwide, the future of scrap recycling certainly looks promising, especially with growth of packaging expected in South America, Europe and Asia.

Production of Sheets and Plates

Cold-rolling mills. Aluminum is first passed through a hot-rolling mill and then transferred to a cold-rolling mill.

Hot-rolling mills. Prior to rolling, the aluminum is in the form of an ingot, which can be up to 23.62 inches thick. This ingot is then heated to around 932°F and passed several times through the hot-rolling mill. This gradually reduces the thickness of the metal to around 0.24 inch.

This thinner aluminum is then coiled and transported to the cold-rolling mill for further processing.

There are various types of cold-rolling mills, and they produce various types of rolled product, with thicknesses as low as .0020 inches. See Figure 3-1-3. In general the type of product depends on the alloy used, the rolling deformation and thermal treatment used in the process as well as careful adjustments to the mechanics and chemistry of the process. Rolling mills are controlled by very precise mechanisms and measuring systems.

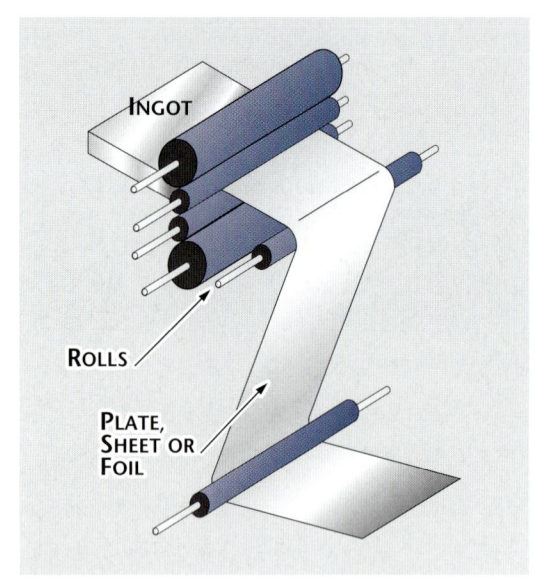

Figure 3-1-3. An illustration of the cold-rolling process required to finish aluminum sheet

Products

Rolled products can be divided into foil, sheet and plate.

Foil is less than 0.0079 inch thick and is used mainly in the packaging industry for foil containers and wrapping. Foil is also used for electrical applications, building insulation and in the printing industry.

Sheet is between 0.0079 inch and 0.24 inch in thickness and has a wide variety of uses in the construction industry, including aluminum siding and roofing. Sheet is also used extensively in transport applications such as automobile body panels, airframes and the hulls of boats.

Figure 3-1-4. Extruded aluminum is a familiar product. Extruding can form lengths of very complicated designs.

Plate is any rolled product over 0.24 inch in thickness. It also is found in a number of applications including airframes, military vehicles and structural components in bridges and buildings.

Aluminum extrusions are made from solid aluminum cylinders called *billets*, which are continuously cast from molten aluminum. Billets are available in a wide variety of alloys, pre-treatments and dimensions, depending upon the requirements of the manufacturer.

Extrusions

The extrusion process involves aluminum metal being forced through a die with a shaped opening. This is made possible by preheating the billet to 842-932°F and then applying a pressure of 72,500-101,500 p.s.i. — equivalent to the pressure found at the bottom of a water tank 37 miles tall. The heated and softened metal is forced against the container walls and the die by a hydraulic ram. The only exit is the geometric cross-section of the die opening, and the metal is squeezed out.

The extrusion leaves the die at a temperature of around 932°F, and the exit temperature is carefully controlled in order to achieve specified mechanical properties, a high-quality surface finish and good productivity. Examples of extruded forms are shown in Figure 3-1-4.

The press. The press supplies the force necessary to squeeze the billet through the extrusion die. It consists of:

- The container where the billet is put under pressure
- The ram for pushing the billet into the container and through the die
- The counter support to the die package
- The main columns fixing the ram and the cylinder
- A series of backers and bolsters, which support the die, for transferring the main press load to the front plate

The principle of an extrusion press can be seen in the schematic diagram. See Figure 3-1-5.

Applications. Aluminum extrusions are used throughout the construction industry, particularly in window and doorframe systems, prefabricated houses/building structures, roofing and exterior cladding and curtain walling. Extrusions are also used in road and rail vehicles, airframes and marine applications.

Aluminum Casting

Applications. Cast parts are used in a variety of applications, including:

- Lightweight components for vehicles, aircraft, ships and spacecraft
- General engineering components where light weight and corrosion resistance are required
- Architectural fittings where light weight and good appearance are important
- High-tech products for office and home
- Tools and motor housings

Casting falls into three main categories: *sand casting, permanent mold casting,* and *die casting*. Of all aluminum castings made, 95 percent are one of these three types.

Sand casting. *Sand casting*, as a process, is a centuries old technique. It was used in both the New and the Old World, making it universal. Sand molds must be bonded together using either synthetic compounds or clay and water. Molds must be rebuilt after each casting.

Pattern making for sand casting, or all casting for that matter, is an exacting process. Not only must the mold contain the shape of the part being cast, it must also contain the sprues and risers to accommodate flow of the molten metal. Sand castings have the greatest potential for *inclusions* (impurities encased in the metal) than other types of casting. Sand castings are also susceptible to *gas holes* and *excess porosity*, both of which are defects.

The design of molds is a very complicated process; but they are filled simply by gravity without the need for any pressure differentials or mechanical action.

Patterns, and the molds made from them, allow for shrinkage of the molten metal as it cools. The way to accomodate this size change is to do all measuring with the *shrink rules* that have a built in allowance. As an example, if the metal will shrink 5/32 inch per foot when it cools, the ruler used to fabricate a foot-long pattern is 12-5/32 inches long. Therefore, when the metal shrinks, it is the correct size.

Permanent mold casting. *Permanent molds* are made from cast iron or steel and may be used any number of times. A higher quality product can be produced because permanent molds have the following benefits:

- Finer grain structure
- Better strength than sand castings

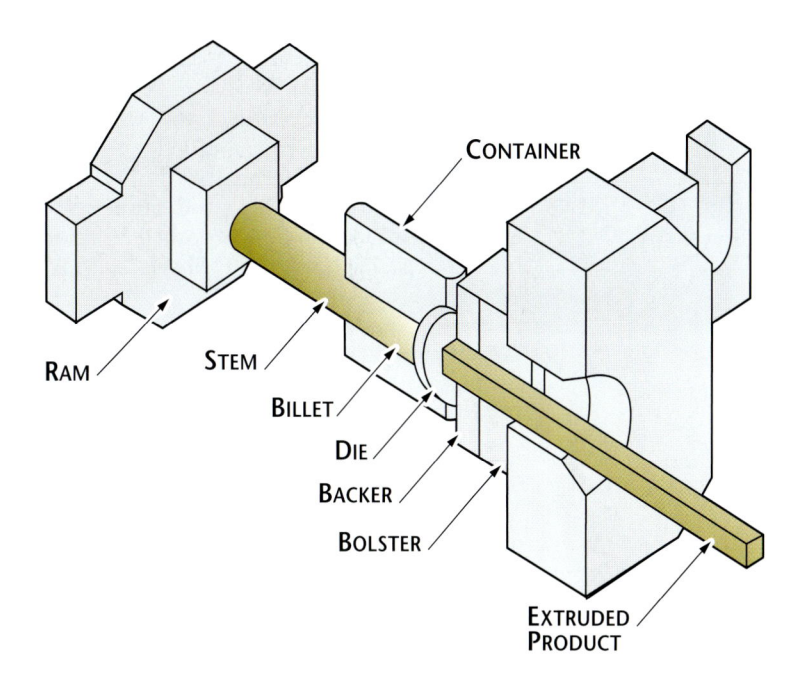

Figure 3-1-5. This illustration shows the basic extrusion process. Very complex parts can be extruded.

- Cast surfaces are smoother and can hold closer dimensional tolerances
- Virtually no inclusions or gas bubbles
- Less shrinkage and lower porosity

An excellent example of the benefits of permanent mold casting over sand casting is aircraft engine crankcases. As reciprocating engines became more sophisticated and produced more horsepower, their sand cast crankcases started to crack in service. The need was for stronger crankcases, and the answer was permanent mold casting. In your career you will come across several of the Per-Mold® crankcases manufactured by Continental Engines.

Die casting. *Die casting* molds are similar to permanent molds and made of either cast iron or steel. There are three main modes of die-casting: high pressure, low pressure and gravity die-casting.

Die-casting can produce very fine-grained structures with amazing accuracy. Of all the cast products you will encounter in the course of a day, most will be die cast. The process is used for most automotive parts, from engine blocks the clock housings. Most consumer cast parts are also die-castings.

High-pressure die-casting. High-pressure die-casting is the most commonly used process, in which molten aluminum is injected at high pressure into a metal mold by a hydraulically powered piston. The machinery needed for the process can be very costly, thus high-pressure die-casting is only used for high volume production.

Low-pressure die-casting. Low-pressure die-casting uses a die, which is filled from a pressurized crucible underneath. The process is particularly suited to the production of rotationally symmetrical products such as automobile wheels. High strength wheels are forged instead of cast.

Gravity die-casting. This process is suitable for mass production and for fully mechanized casting.

Advantages of die-casting. The process has these advantages:

- Almost finished as cast
- Very long die life
- Less shrinkage and porosity
- Virtually no inclusions
- More dimensionally stable
- Higher strength

Heat-treatment. All castings are heat treatable by all the normal processes. They do take more time and care, as the cross sections are naturally thicker than sheet products. Castings take longer to heat up and to cool down. If heated too fast, they can warp; if too hot, porosity can develop; if cooled too quickly, they can crack or warp.

Inspecting Castings

Because of the possibility of inclusions and gas holes, the best method to inspect castings is by x-ray. This is usually done during the manufacturing quality control process. Though infrequent, a casting may have to be x-rayed as the result of an airworthiness directive or special inspection. In service normally they are inspected through the dye penetrant process.

A casting found defective in service can almost never be repaired in the field. However, there are exceptions. Many certified repair stations do weld repairs on aluminum castings, particularly crankcases and cylinder heads. A technician may not weld them.

Forging

Forging is a manufacturing process where metal is pressed, pounded or squeezed under great pressure into high-strength parts known as forgings. The process is normally (but not always) performed hot by preheating the metal to a desired temperature before it is worked. It is important to note that the forging process is entirely different from the casting (or foundry) process. The metal used to make forged parts is never melted and poured, as in the casting process.

The forging process can create parts that are stronger than those manufactured by any other metalworking process. This is why forgings are almost always used where reliability and safety are critical.

Compared to castings, the advantages of forgings are:

- **Strength.** Casting cannot obtain the strengthening effects of hot and cold working. Forging surpasses casting in predictable strength properties.

- **Defect-refining.** A casting has neither grain flow nor directional strength. The process cannot prevent formation of certain metallurgical defects. Preworking forge stock produces a grain flow oriented in directions requiring maximum strength. See Figure 3-1-6.

- **Reliable, less costly.** Because hot working refines grain pattern and imparts high strength, ductility and resistance properties, forged products are more reliable.

- **Better response to heat-treatment.** Castings require close control of melting and cooling processes because alloy segregation may occur. This results in non-uniform heat-treatment response that can affect straightness of finished parts. Forgings respond more predictably to heat-treatment and offer better dimensional stability.

Hand tools and hardware. Forging has traditionally been the mark of quality in hand tools and hardware. Pliers, hammers, sledges, wrenches and garden tools, as well as wire-rope clips, sockets, hooks, turnbuckles and eye bolts, are common examples. Surgical and dental instruments are also often forged.

Aviation and aerospace. High strength-to-weight ratio and structural reliability can favorably influence performance, range and payload capabilities of aircraft. Made of various ferrous, non-ferrous and special alloy materials, forgings are widely used in commercial jets, helicopters, piston-engine planes, military aircraft and spacecraft. Some examples of where a forging's versatility of size, shape and properties make it an ideal component include bulkheads, wing roots and spars, hinges, engine mounts, brackets, beams, shafts, landing gear cylinders and struts, wheels, brake carriers and discs. In jet turbine engines, iron-base, nickel-base and

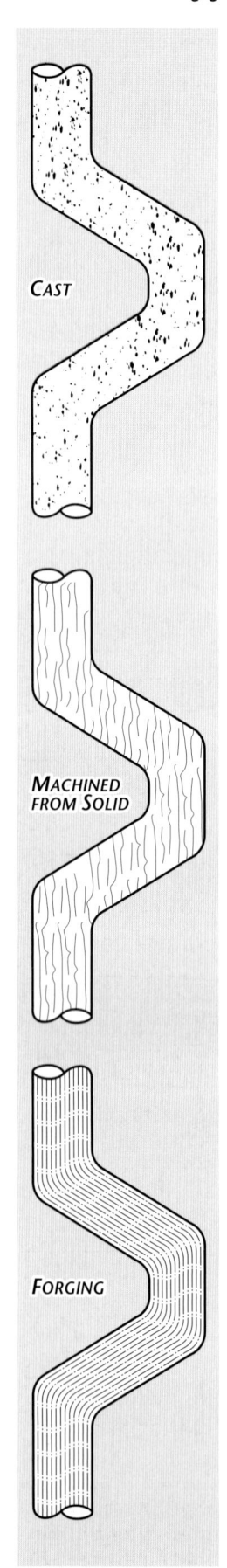

Figure 3-1-6. Comparison of grain structures in different metal processes

cobalt-base superalloys are forged into components such as discs, blades, buckets, couplings, manifolds, rings, chambers and shafts.

Forged parts vary in size, shape and sophistication — from the hammer and wrench in your toolbox to close tolerance precision components in airplanes and NASA's space shuttle. In fact, over 18,000 forgings are contained in a Boeing 747. Some of the largest customer markets include: aerospace, national defense, automotive and agriculture, construction, mining, material handling and general industrial equipment. Even the dies themselves that make forgings (and other metal and plastic parts) are forged. Figure 3-1-7A and Figure 3-1-7B show the visual difference between a forged and a welded nose gear assembly.

Figure 3-1-7A. This welded nose gear assembly, used on many Beechcraft King Air executive turboprops, is prone to cracking and is subject to a repetitive AD inspection.

Figure 3-1-7B. The welded assembly has been replaced by this forged nose gear leg. The greater strength and predictable load bearing characteristics eliminate the need for a repetitive inspection.

Forging Processes

There are basically four methods (or processes) to make a forged part.

- Impression die forging
- Cold forging
- Open die forging
- Seamless rolled ring forging

Impression die forging. *Impression die forging* pounds or presses metal between two dies (called tooling) that contains a precut profile of the desired part. Parts from a few ounces to 60,000 lbs. can be made using this process. Some of the smaller parts are actually forged cold.

Commonly referred to as closed-die forging, impression-die forging of steel, aluminum, titanium and other alloys can produce an almost limitless variety of 3-D shapes that range in weight from mere ounces up to more than 25 tons. Impression-die forgings are routinely produced on hydraulic presses, mechanical presses and hammers, with capacities up to 50,000 tons, 20,000 tons and 50,000 lbs., respectively. Figure 3-1-8 shows a forging sequence. In practice, the complete operation happens extremely fast: one quick blow.

As the name implies, two or more dies containing impressions of the part shape are brought together as forging stock undergoes plastic deformation. Because metal flow is restricted by the die contours, this process can yield more complex shapes and closer tolerances than open-die forging processes. Additional flexibility in forming both symmetrical and non-symmetrical shapes comes from various preforming operations (sometimes bending) prior to forging in finisher dies.

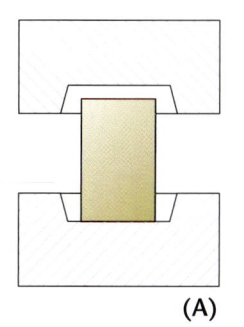

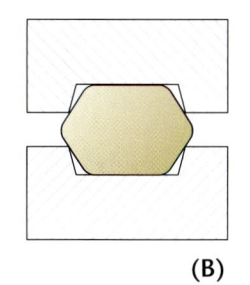

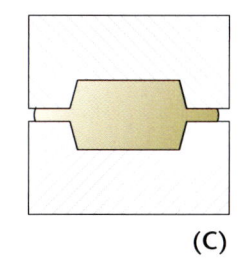

Figure 3-1-8. (A) shows a forging die starting to close. (B) shows the part in process, while (C) shows the completed operation.

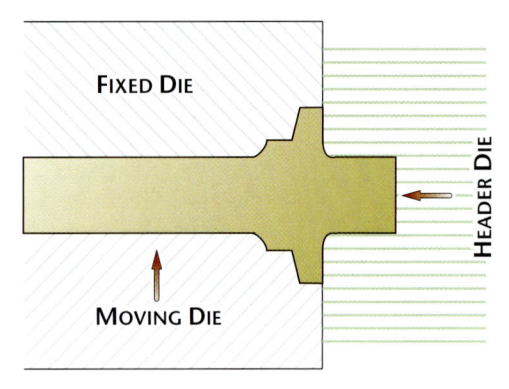

Figure 3-1-9. Cold forging can be both a swaging and a heading operation at the same time.

Cold forging. Most forging is done as hot work, at temperatures up to 2,300°F, however, a variation of impression die forging is *cold forging*. Cold forging encompasses many processes: bending, cold drawing, cold heading, coining, extrusions and more, to yield a diverse range of part shapes. The temperature of metals being cold forged may range from room temperature to several hundred degrees. See Figure 3-1-9.

Open die forging. *Open die forging* is performed between flat dies with no precut profiles in the dies. Movement of the work piece is the key to this method. Larger parts over 200,000 lbs. and 80 feet in length can be hammered or pressed into shape this way.

Open-die forging can produce forgings from a few pounds up to more than 150 tons. Called open-die because impression dies do not confine the metal laterally during forging, this process progressively works the starting stock into the desired shape, most commonly between flat-faced dies.

Practically all forgeable ferrous and non-ferrous alloys can be open-die forged, including some exotic materials like age-hardening superalloys and corrosion-resistant refractory alloys.

Seamless rolled ring forging. *Seamless rolled ring* forging is typically performed by punching a hole in a thick, round piece of metal (creating a donut shape), and then rolling and squeezing (or in some cases, pounding) the donut into a thin ring. Ring diameters can be anywhere from a few inches to 30 ft.

High tangential strength and ductility make forged rings well-suited for torque- and pressure-resistant components, such as gears, engine bearings for aircraft, wheel bearings, couplings, rotor spacers, sealed discs and cases, flanges, pressure vessels and valve bodies. Materials include not only carbon and alloy steels, but also non-ferrous alloys of aluminum, copper and titanium, and nickel-base alloys.

Forging Equipment

Although the styles and drive systems vary widely, a forging can be produced on any of the following pieces of equipment:

- *Hammers* with a driving force of up to 50,000 pounds, pound the metal into shape with controlled high pressure impact blows.

- *Presses* with a driving force of up to 50,000 tons, squeeze the metal into shape vertically with controlled high pressure.

- *Upsetters* are basically forging presses used horizontally for a forging process known as upsetting.

- *Ring rollers* turn a hollow round piece of metal under extreme pressure against a rotating roll, thereby squeezing out a one-piece ring (with no welding required).

Aluminum: Practical Applications in Aviation

The modern commercial aviation industry would never have succeeded without aluminum. The Wright brothers' first airplane, which flew in 1903, had a four-cylinder, 12-horsepower auto engine modified with a 30-lb. aluminum block to reduce weight. Aluminum gradually replaced the wood, steel and other airplane parts in the early 1900s, and the first all-aluminum plane was built in the early 1920s. Since then, airplanes of all kinds and sizes have been made largely of aluminum.

Its combination of lightness, strength and workability makes it the ideal material for mass-produced commercial aircraft. Strong aluminum alloys take the extraordinary pressures and stresses involved in high-altitude flying; wafer thin aluminum panels keep the cold out and the warm air in.

Many internal fittings, like the seating on planes, are made from aluminum or aluminum composite in order to save weight and fuel, reduce emissions and increase the aircraft's payload.

Today, there are around 5,300 commercial passenger aircraft flying in the world, and many thousands of light aircraft and helicopters. The industry continues to grow. Demand for commercial aircraft is forecast to rise by around 60 percent over the next decade.

Aluminum is the primary aircraft material, comprising about 80 percent of an aircraft's unladen weight. The standard Boeing 747 jumbo jet contains approximately 165,000 lbs. (75,000 kg) of aluminum. Because the metal resists corrosion, some airlines don't paint their planes, saving several hundred kilograms of weight.

PHYSICAL PROPERTIES	
Density / Specific Gravity (68°F)	168.5
Melting Point (°F)	1,220°F
Specific Heat at 212 °F, cal/g (J/kg)	32.403 (938)
Latent Heat of Fusion cal/g (kJ/kg)	400.0 (1.67)
Electrical Conductivity at 68°F (percent of international annealed copper standard)	64.94
Thermal Conductivity (cal/sec/cm2/cm/°C)	0.5
Thermal Emmisivity at 100°F (%)	3.0
Reflectivity for Light, Tungsten Filament (%)	90.0

Table 3-1-1. Physical properties of aluminum

The process of producing pure alumina from bauxite has changed very little since the first plant was opened in 1893. The Bayer process can be considered in three chemical stages: *extraction, decomposition* and *calcination*.

Extraction. The hydrated alumina is selectively removed from the other (insoluble) oxides by transferring it into a solution of sodium hydroxide (caustic soda):

$$Al_2O_3 \cdot XH_2O + 2NaOH \Rightarrow 2NaAlO_2 + (X+1)H_2O$$

The process is far more efficient when the ore is reduced to a very fine particle size prior to reaction. This reduction is achieved by crushing and milling the pre-washed ore. This is then sent to a heated pressure digester.

Conditions within the digester (concentration, temperature and pressure) vary according to the properties of the bauxite ore being used. Although higher temperatures are theoretically favored, these produce several disadvantages, including corrosion problems and the possibility of other oxides (other than alumina) dissolving into the caustic liquor.

Modern plants typically operate at 392-464°F and can involve pressures of around 30 atmospheres.

After the extraction stage, the liquor (containing the dissolved Al_2O_3) must be separated from the insoluble bauxite residue, purified as much as possible and filtered before it is delivered to the decomposer. The mud is thickened and washed so that the caustic soda can be removed and recycled.

Decomposition. Crystalline alumina trihydrate is extracted from the digestion liquor by hydrolysis:

$$2NaAlO_2 + 4H_2O \Rightarrow Al_2O_3 \cdot X \cdot 3H_2O + 2NaOH$$

This is the reverse of the extraction process, except that the product's nature can be carefully controlled by plant conditions (including seeding or selective nucleation, precipitation temperature and cooling rate). The alumina trihydrate crystals are then sorted into size fractions and fed into a rotary bed calcination kiln.

Calcination. Alumina trihydrate crystals are calcined to remove their water of crystallization and prepare the alumina for the aluminum smelting process. The mechanism for this step is complex, but the process, when carefully controlled, dictates the properties of the final product.

Aluminum Properties

Pure aluminum is a silvery-white metal with many desirable characteristics. It is light, non-toxic (in metal form), non-magnetic and non-sparking. Although not found free in nature, aluminum is an abundant element in the Earth's crust.

It is decorative, easily formed, machined and cast. Alloys with small amounts of copper, magnesium, silicon, manganese and other elements have very useful properties.

Strength depends on purity. Aluminum of 99.996 percent purity has a tensile strength of about 7,000 p.s.i., rising to 100,000 p.s.i. following alloying and suitable heat-treatment. A key property is low density. Aluminum is only one-third the weight of steel.

Aluminum and most of its alloys are highly resistant to most forms of corrosion. Its natural coating of aluminum oxide provides a very effective barrier to the ravages of air, temperature, moisture and chemical attack.

Aluminum is a superb conductor of electricity. This property, allied with other intrinsic qualities, has ensured the replacement of copper by aluminum in many situations.

Being non-magnetic and non-combustible are properties invaluable in advanced industries such as electronics or in offshore structures.

Aluminum's non-toxic and impervious qualities have established its use in the food and packaging industries.

Other valuable properties include high reflectivity, good heat-barrier properties and excellent heat conduction. The metal is malleable and easily worked by the common manufacturing and shaping processes.

Altering Physical Properties

The properties outlined in Table 3-1-1 can be very significantly altered with the addition of small amounts of alloying materials. Aluminum reacts with oxygen to form a microscopic protective film of oxide, which prevents corrosion.

Aluminum in massive form is non-flammable, though finely divided particles will burn. Carbon monoxide or dioxide, aluminum oxide and water will be emitted. This is a useful property for making rocket fuel.

Non-ferrous Metals

The term non-ferrous refers to all metals that have elements other than iron as their base or principal constituent. This group includes such metals as aluminum, titanium, copper and magnesium, as well as alloyed metals like Monel.

Aluminum Alloys

Commercially pure aluminum is very light, but has no great amount of strength. It is, however, very valuable in the construction of many nonstructural units. In order to increase the strength of aluminum, it is alloyed with various other metals to form the so-called "strong-alloys" for structural use. These alloys are available in both wrought and cast forms.

Alloy Designation System

Wrought Alloys (Sheet and Plate)

- First digit: Principal alloying constituent(s)
- Second digit: Variations of initial alloy (modifications)
- Third and fourth digits: Individual alloy variations (number has no significance but is unique)

First digit alloy identification:

1xxx	Aluminum (99 percent or greater) non-heat-treatable
2xxx	Copper heat-treatable
3xxx	Manganese non-heat-treatable
4xxx	Silicon non-heat-treatable
5xxx	Magnesium non-heat-treatable
6xxx	Magnesium & silicon heat-treatable
7xxx	Zinc heat-treatable

Heat-treatment

Heat-treatment of aluminum is generally used to increase the strength of precipitation-hardenable wrought and cast alloys. These are usually referred to as the *heat-treatable alloys*, to distinguish them from those alloys in which no significant strengthening can be achieved by heating and cooling. The heat-treatable cast alloys are the 2xx0, 3xx0 and 7xx0 series. The basic definitions of the numerous temper codes designating aluminum alloy heat-treatments are listed in Table 3-1-2.

Alloys which are not strengthened by heating and cooling are generally referred to as the *non-heat-treatable* types. When in wrought form, these alloys are hardened by cold work.

NOTE: *A special forging alloy, 4032, is hardened by heat-treatment.*

Heating to reduce strength and increase ductility (*annealing*) and heating to relieve internal stresses (*stress relief*) are commonly used for both heat-treatable and non-heat-treatable alloys.

We will discuss the 2xxx and the 7xxx in more detail, because they are the primary alloys used in aircraft construction.

2xxx aluminum-copper alloys. The 2xxx series are heat-treatable and possess, in individual alloys, good combinations of high strength (especially at elevated temperatures) and toughness; they are not resistant to atmospheric corrosion and are usually painted or clad in such exposures. The higher strength 2xxx alloys are primarily used for aircraft (2024) and truck body (2014) applications; these are usually used in bolted or riveted construction. Specific members of the series (e.g. 2219 and 2048) are readily welded, and so, are used for aerospace applications where that is the preferred joining method.

Alloy 2195 is a new Li-bearing alloy for space applications providing very high modules of elasticity, along with high strength and weld-

NON HEAT-TREATABLE ALLOYS		HEAT-TREATABLE ALLOYS	
Temper Designation	Definition	Temper Designation	Definition
-O	Annealed recrystallized (wrought products only) applies to softest temper of wrought products	-O	Annealed recrystallized (wrought products only) applies to softest temper of wrought products
-H1	Strain-hardened only. Applies to products which are strain-hardened to obtain the desired strength without supplementary thermal treatment	-T1	Cooled from an elevated temperature shaping process (such as extrusion or casting) and naturally aged to a substantially stable condition
-H12	Strain-hardened one-quarter-hard temper	-T2	Annealed (castings only)
-H14	Strain-hardened half-hard temper	-T3	Solution heat-treated and cold-worked by the flattening or straightening operation
-H16	Strain-hardened three-quarters-hard temper	-T36	Solution heat-treated and cold-worked by reduction of 6 percent
-H18	Strain-hardened full-hard temper	-T4	Solution heat-treated
-H2	Strain-hardened and then partially annealed. Applies to products which are strain-hardened more than the desired final amount and then reduced in strength to the desired level by partial annealing	-T42	Solution heat-treated by the user regardless of prior temper (applicable only to 2014 and 2024 alloys)
-H22	Strain-hardened and partially annealed to one-quarter-hard temper	-T5	Artificially aged only (castings only)
-H24	Strain-hardened and partially annealed to half-hard temper	-T6	Solution heat-treated and artificially aged
-H26	Strain-hardened and partially annealed to three-quarters-hard temper	-T62	Solution heat-treated and aged by user regardless of prior temper (applicable only to 2014 and 2024 alloys)
-H28	Strain-hardened and partially annealed to full-hard temper	-T351, -T451, -T3510, -T3511, -T4510, -T4511	Solution heat-treated and stress relieved by stretching to produce a permanent set of 1 to 3 percent, depending on the product
-H30	Strain-hardened and then stabilized. Applies to products which are strain-hardened and then stabilized by a low temperature heating to slightly lower their strength and increase ductility	-T651, -T851, -T6510, -T8510, -T6511, -T8511	Solution heat-treated, stress relieved by stretching to produce a permanent set of 1 to 3 percent, and artificially aged
-H32	Strain-hardened and then stabilized; Final temper is one-quarter hard	-T652	Solution heat-treated, compressed to produce a permanent set and then artificially aged
-H34	Strain-hardened and then stabilized; Final temper is one-half hard	-T8	Solution heat-treated, cold-worked and then artificially aged
-H36	Strain-hardened and then stabilized; Final temper is three-quarters hard	-T4	Solution heat-treated, cold-worked by the flattening or straightening operation, and then artificially aged
-H38	Strain-hardened and then stabilized; Final temper is full-hard	-T86	Solution heat-treated, cold-worked by reduction of 6 percent, and then artificially aged
-H112	As fabricated; with specified mechanical property limits	-T9	Solution heat-treated, artificially aged and then cold-worked
-F	For wrought alloys; as fabricated. No mechanical properties limits; For cast alloys; as cast	-T10	Cooled from an elevated temperature shaping process artificially aged and then cold-worked
		-F	For wrought alloys as fabricated; No mechanical properties limits; For cast alloys; as cast

Table 3-1-2. Temper designations and definitions for non-heat-treatable and heat-treatable alloys

TYPICAL SOAKING TIMES FOR SOLUTION HEAT-TREATMENT	
Thickness (Inch)	Time (Minutes)
Up to 0.125	30
1/8 to 1/4	40
Over 1/4	60

Table 3-1-3. Reheat-treatment

ability. There are also high-toughness versions of several of the alloys (2124, 2324, 2419). Developed specifically for the aircraft industry, these alloys have fewer impurities that may diminish resistance to unstable fractures. Alloys 2011, 2017 and 2117 are widely used for fasteners and screw-machine stock.

Properties of 2xxx aluminum copper alloys are:

- Heat-treatable
- High strength at room and elevated temperatures
- Aircraft, transportation applications
- Representative alloys: 2014, 2017, 2024, 2195, 2219
- Typical ultimate tensile strength range: 27,000-62,000 p.s.i.

7xxx aluminum-zinc alloys. The 7xxx alloys are heat treatable and, among the Al-Zn-Mg-Cu versions, provide the highest strengths of all aluminum alloys. There are several alloys in the series that are produced especially for their high toughness, notably 7150 and 7475, both with controlled impurity level to maximize the combination of strength and fracture-resistance.

The widest application of the 7xxx alloys has historically been in the aircraft industry, where fracture-critical design concepts have provided the impetus for the high-toughness alloy development. These alloys are not considered weldable by routine commercial processes and are regularly used in riveted construction.

The atmospheric corrosion resistance of the 7xxx alloys is not as high as that of the 5xxx and 6xxx alloys, so in such service they are usually coated or, for sheet and plate, used in an Alclad version. The use of special tempers such as the T73-type is required in place of T6-type tempers whenever stress corrosion cracking may be a problem.

Properties of 7xxx aluminum-zinc alloys are:

- Heat-treatable
- Very high strength; special high-toughness versions
- Aerospace; automotive applications
- Representative alloys: 7005, 7075, 7150, 7475
- Typical ultimate tensile strength range: 32,000-88,000 p.s.i.

Specific Heat-treatments for Aluminum

Specific instructions for the heat-treatment of various aluminum alloys used in aircraft construction are beyond the capabilities of this textbook, but can be found in MIL Handbook 5.

Although general procedures for heat-treating aluminum remains the same, differences in composition demand that factors, such as time, temperature and quenching media, be defined for each material.

Solution heat-treating. To take advantage of the *precipitation-hardening* reaction, it is necessary to first produce a solid solution. This process is referred to as *solution heat-treating*. The objective is to take into solid solution the maximum practical amounts of the soluble hardening elements in the alloy. The process consists of soaking the alloy at a temperature sufficiently high and for a time long enough to achieve a nearly homogeneous solid solution.

Solutionizing temperatures vary with alloy composition, but the specific temperature must be carefully controlled within ±10°F. If the solution temperature is lower than required, insufficient solute will be dissolved and the final aging treatment will not reach the desired hardness. If overheated, low melting-point phases called eutectics at the grain boundaries will liquefy and ruin the material.

The time at the nominal solution heating temperature is called soak time, and is a function of microstructure before heat-treatment, the thickness of the material being heated and the loading of the furnace being used. The time at temperature must be sufficient to completely dissolve the solute phases and homogenize the solid solution.

Reheat-treatment. The treatment of material that has been previously heat-treated is considered a *reheat-treatment*. The unclad heat-treatable alloys can be solution heat-treated repeatedly without harmful effects.

The number of solution heat-treatments allowed for clad sheet is limited, due to increased diffusion of core and cladding with each reheating. Existing specifications allow one to three reheat-treatments of clad sheet, depending on thickness. Cladding will be discussed later in more detail.

Soak time for Alclad sheet and for parts made from Alclad sheet must be held to a minimum, because excessive diffusion of alloying elements from the core into the cladding reduces corrosion protection (Table 3-1-3). For the same reason, reheat-treatment of Alclad sheet less than 0.030 inches thick is generally prohibited, and the number or reheat-treatments permitted for thicker Alclad sheet is limited.

NOTE: *Heat-treatment of a previously heat-treated material is classified as a reheat-treatment. Therefore, the first heat-treatment of material purchased in the heat-treated condition is a reheat-treatment. As far as Table 3-1-3 is concerned, annealing and precipitation treatments are not considered heat-treatments.*

Quenching. In most instances, to avoid the types of precipitation which are detrimental to strength or corrosion resistance, the solid solution formed during solutionizing must be *quenched* rapidly and without interruption to produce a supersaturated solution at room temperature. Most frequently, parts are quenched by immersion in cold water. Large aluminum production facilities use water spray quenching. For parts with complex shapes and abrupt changes in thickness, somewhat slower cooling may be required to prevent cracking. In these instances, boiling water or an aqueous solution of polyalkaline glycol is used. Some forgings and castings, which require maximum dimensional stability, are air-cooled. The hardening response of these parts is limited, but satisfactory for the applications.

Lag between soaking and quenching. The time interval between the removal of the material from the furnace to the quenching media, quench delay, is critical for some alloys and should not exceed 15 seconds. This is to prevent precooling into a critical temperature range with un-wanted results. For instance, when solution heat-treating 2017 or 2024 sheet material, the elapsed time must not exceed 10 seconds. The extent of the temperature range varies with the alloy, but the temperatures between 750°F and 500°F should be avoided for virtually all aluminum alloy quenches.

Allowing the metal to cool slightly before quenching promotes re-precipitation from the solid solution. The precipitation occurs along grain boundaries and in certain slip planes, causing poor formability. In the case of 2017, 2024 and 7075 alloys, their resistance to intergranular corrosion is decreased.

Straightening after solution heat-treatment. Some warping occurs during solution heat-treatment, producing kinks, buckles, waves or twists. These imperfections are generally removed by straightening and flattening operations.

When the straightening operations produce an appreciable increase in the tensile and yield strengths and a slight decrease in the percent of elongation, the material is designated T3 temper. When the above values are not materially affected, the material is designated T4 temper.

The solution heat-treatment process that results in the metal becoming age-hardened goes through three events: heating, quenching and aging. The heating range is usually about 940°F. The quenching medium is cold water. During this step, the operator wants to get the metal cooled down as soon as possible to prevent early corrosion from starting. The aging period varies for each thickness of metal, but it usually levels out to about 12-16 hours. After the metal has age-hardened, it is suitable for aircraft structural work.

Precipitation hardening. After quenching, the material is a supersaturated, solid solution of alloying elements dissolved in aluminum. This is an unstable condition. The chemical balance of the material is out of equilibrium, and the elements suspended in solid solution will have a tendency to precipitate in order to restore the equilibrium. When this precipitation occurs at room temperature, it is referred to as *natural aging*. Depending upon the alloy, this process can take from one hour to many years to reach completion. Of course, alloys which would require years to naturally age couldn't be used in this condition and would require further heat-treatment. The heat energy required to drive the chemical reactions in these more sluggish alloys is supplied by *artificial aging* heat-treatments.

In both natural and artificial aging, the precipitates harden the material by setting up sub-microscopic strains throughout the aluminum matrix. The secondary phases that fall out of the solution actually crowd and stretch the surrounding material. This serves to reduce the elasticity or ductility of the metal, which, in turn, increases hardness and structural strength. There is an optimum particle size, neither too small nor too large, which imparts the best compromise between strength and corrosion properties.

Strain hardening. Mechanically working metals at temperatures below their critical range (the temperature at which crystals begin to form) results in *strain hardening* of the metal. The mechanical working may consist of *rolling*, *drawing*, *stamping* or *pressing*. During strain hardening, the metal becomes so hard that it becomes difficult to continue the forming process without softening the metal by annealing.

Strength, hardness and elasticity are increased by strain hardening. Ductility decreases. Since this makes the metal more brittle, it must be heated sometimes during certain operations to remove the undesirable effects of the working.

Natural aging. The more highly alloyed members of the 6xxx wrought series, the copper-containing alloys of the 7xxx group, and all of the 2xxx series are almost always solution heat-treated and quenched. For some of these alloys, particularly the 2xxx alloys, the precipitation hardening that results from natural aging alone produces useful tempers (T3 and T4 types of temper). The tensile property specifications for the T3 and T4 types of tempers of most alloys are based on a nominal natural aging time of four days. Aluminum aircraft rivets, however, age within hours.

Heat-treatment of Rivets

Rivets requiring heat-treatment are usually heated in small screen wire baskets, which allow free and rapid circulation of water during the quenching process. The load should be held at the specified temperature for at least one hour in a still air furnace, and then quenched in the coldest water available. Rivets removed from the cold water and held at room temperature should be driven within 15 minutes after quenching, or it may be held for much longer periods without hardening if stored under refrigeration. Rivets will harden completely at room temperature in about 24 hours due to the effects of natural aging. Rivets driven in the full hardened or partially hardened condition show a much greater tendency to crack than those driven within 15 minutes after quenching. Rivets made from 2017 (D) and 2024 (DD) alloy must be heat-treated before use; 1xxx, 4xxx and 5xxx alloy rivets may be driven in the condition in which they are received.

Artificial aging. Precipitation heat-treatment is also called *artificial aging*. The process consists of heating the aluminum alloy into a narrow temperature range (±10°F) and holding for several hours, sometimes days. This treatment produces the T6 and T7 types of tempers. The heat causes a fine dispersion of strengthening particles to precipitate out of solution. The times and temperatures for specific alloys were developed to produce an optimum particle size. If the alloys are heated to above the proper temperature, or held for too long a period of time, the suspended particles will become too large and the metal will lose both strength and corrosion properties. This excessive heat-treatment is called *overaging*.

Annealing

Annealing treatments employed for aluminum alloys are of several types that differ in objective. Annealing times and temperatures depend on alloy type, as well as initial structure and temper. The types of annealing are full, partial and stress-relief annealing.

Full annealing. The softest, most ductile and workable condition of both non-heat-treatable and heat treatable wrought alloys is produced by *full annealing* to the temper designated "O." For work-hardened material like 1xxx-, 3xxx-, 4xxx- and 5xxx-series aluminums, the heating removes the hardening strains induced by deformation. A temperature in the range of 650°F for a time just long enough to insure that the entire load comes to temperature will be sufficient to accomplish full annealing of these types. The rate of cooling in this case is not important.

The heat-treatable alloys are annealed by thoroughly precipitating the solutes into coarse, widely spaced particles. This removes the effects of heat-treatment and prevents natural age hardening. The temperatures required for the treatment are in the 750°-850°F range for a time of not less than one hour. Slow enough cooling at about 50°F per hour maximum is required. Although material annealed from the precipitation-hardening condition usually has sufficient ductility for most forming operations, this ductility is often slightly lower than the ductility of metal which has received a prior heat-treatment. Therefore, when maximum ductility is required, annealing of a previously heat-treated product is sometimes unsuccessful.

Partial annealing. Partial annealing is also referred to as *recovery annealing*. Partial annealing is performed on the non-heat-treatable alloys, which have been severely *work-hardened* (H18 temper). Heating to between 350°F to 550°F restores some of the ductility, and gives the material an intermediate hardness value (H2-type temper). Bendability and formability of an alloy annealed to an H2-type temper generally are significantly higher than those of the same alloy in which an equal strength level is developed by a final cold working operation (H1-type temper). Times and temperatures for partial annealing must be carefully controlled in order to achieve the desired strength.

Stress-relief annealing. For cold-worked wrought alloys, annealing merely to remove the effects of strain hardening is referred to as stress-relief annealing. Such treatments employ heating to 650°F and cooling to room temperature. No appreciable holding time is required.

Annealing of castings. The suggested annealing treatment for most aluminum alloy castings is 600°F to 650°F for two to four hours. This provides the most complete release of residual stresses. Such annealing treatments produce maximum dimensional stability at high temperatures and are designated as the "O" temper.

Cladding

Pure aluminum has such a very high resistance to corrosion that under normal conditions it rarely ever corrodes. Due to this excellent corrosion-resistant characteristic, sheet metal manufacturers apply, or clad, pure aluminum to the surface of most aluminum alloy flat stock in a process known as cladding.

In the cladding process, this pure aluminum alloy sheet is clad to a thickness approximately 5 percent on each side.

Alclad versus clad. Aluminum products sometimes are coated on one or both surfaces with a metallurgically bonded, thin layer of pure aluminum or aluminum alloy. If the combination of core and cladding alloys is selected so that the cladding is anodic to the core, it is called *Alclad*. Alclad products are designed for corrosion protection.

Clad products resemble Alclad products in many respects, but they are distinguished by a cladding alloy that is not intentionally anodic to the core. Clad products are designed to provide improved surface appearance.

Aluminum Sheet Identification Marks

Aircraft aluminum alloy is marked the full length of the sheet with an ink roller after all manufacturing operations are completed. If it weren't marked, it would not be possible to know what you really had.

The markings consist of the alloy, its temper condition, clad or Alclad and the federal specification number under which it was manufactured (QQA number). The aluminum manufacturer is also identified by name, and the batch number is included. Figure 3-1-10 shows the markings on the reverse side of the sheet.

Tests to distinguish heat-treatable and non-heat-treatable aluminum alloys. Clad aluminum alloys have surface layers of pure aluminum or corrosion-resistant aluminum alloy bonded to the core material to inhibit corrosion. Presence of such a coating may be determined under a magnifying glass by examination of the edge surface that will show three distinct layers. In aluminum alloys, the properties of any specific alloy can be altered by work-hardening (often called strain-hardening), heat-treatment or by a combination of these processes.

If, for any reason, the identification mark of the alloy is not on the material, it is possible to distinguish between some heat-treatable alloys and some nonheat-treatable alloys by immersing a sample of the material in a 10-percent solution of caustic soda (sodium hydroxide).

Those heat-treated alloys containing several percent of copper (2014, 2017 and 2024) will turn black due to the copper content. High-copper alloys are not based primarily on the use of copper as an alloying agent. These include, among others, 6053, 6061 and 7075 alloys. The composition and heat-treating ability of alloys that do not turn black in a caustic soda solution can be established by a testing laboratory.

Specifications and Inspection

All material ordered on the basis of Alcoa specifications will comply with corresponding government specifications.

Quantitative inspection items include chemical composition, mechanical properties, dimensional requirements (which sometimes include straightness), and packing and shipping requirements. The limits to which these factors must conform are set forth in detail in government specifications.

Qualitative inspection items include general surface appearance, specific surface abra-

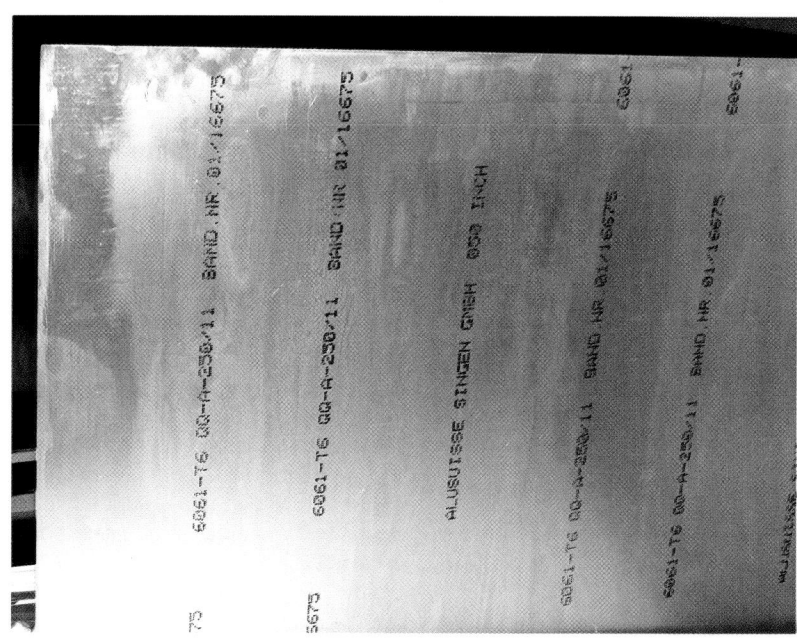

Figure 3-1-10. Manufacturer's markings on an aluminum sheet

sions and blemishes, flatness and straightness. Government specifications discuss these items under workmanship. The following, among others, are not normally considered grounds for rejection:

- Surface discoloration of heat-treated materials. Alclad sheet is less susceptible than other heat-treated sheet.
- A few small surface blisters on heat-treated Alclad sheet
- Shallow scratches on Alclad sheet. The surface of Alclad sheet is relatively soft and is therefore somewhat susceptible to handling scratches. Extensive investigations have shown that these scratches do not detract from the resistance to corrosion and do not have a measurable effect on the tensile strength, yield strength or elongation.
- Light die scratches and minor surface abrasion on extrusions, tubing, rods, bars and rolled shapes
- Small residual heat-treating buckles and lack of perfect flatness, particularly on thin-gauge (less that 0.040 inch think) heat-treated alloy sheet
- Lack of perfect flatness on annealed sheets of any gauge

Those not familiar with accepted standards for these qualitative items of inspection are urged to consult with the local company representative. Special inspection requirements are sometimes included in contracts for material to be used for special purposes for which commercial grades are not applicable.

Substitution of Aircraft Metals

In selecting substitute metals for the repair and maintenance of aircraft, it is very important to check the appropriate structural repair manual. Most manufacturers will have a skin plating chart or diagram listed. As a general rule, 2024-T3 can be substituted for 7075-T6 if the next heavier gauge is used. There are exceptions, so consult the manual first.

Aircraft manufacturers design structural members to meet a specific load requirement for a particular aircraft. The methods of repairing these members, apparently similar in construction, will thus vary with different aircraft.

Four requirements must be kept in mind when selecting substitute metals:

1. The most important is maintaining the original strength of the structure.
2. Maintaining contour or aerodynamic smoothness
3. Maintaining original weight, if possible, or keeping added weight to a minimum
4. Maintaining the original corrosion-resistant properties of the metal

Magnesium Alloys

Magnesium, the world's lightest structural metal, is a silvery-white material weighing only two-thirds as much as aluminum. Magnesium does not possess sufficient strength in its pure state for structural uses, but when alloyed with zinc, aluminum and manganese, it produces an alloy having the highest strength-to-weight ratio of any of the commonly used metals. Magnesium is not used as much today due to its poor corrosion characteristics.

Magnesium alloys produced in the United States consist of magnesium alloyed with varying proportions of aluminum, manganese, and zinc. These alloys are designated by a letter of the alphabet and with the number 1, indicating high purity and maximum corrosion resistance.

Magnesium alloys are subject to such treatments as annealing, quenching, solution heat-treatment, aging, and stabilizing. Sheet and plate magnesium are annealed at the rolling mill. The solution heat-treatment is used to put as much of the alloying ingredients as possible into solid solution, which results in high tensile strength and maximum ductility. Aging is applied to castings following heat-treatment where maximum hardness and yield strength are desired.

Magnesium embodies fire hazards of an unpredictable nature. When in large sections, its high thermal conductivity makes it difficult to ignite and prevents it from burning. Magnesium will not burn until the melting point is reached, which is 1,204°F. However, magnesium dust and fine chips are ignited easily. Extreme caution must be taken to prevent this from occurring. Should a fire occur, it can be extinguished with an extinguishing powder, such as powdered soapstone or graphite powder. Water or any standard liquid or foam fire extinguisher will cause magnesium to burn much more rapidly, and can even cause the magnesium to explode.

Titanium Alloys

Weighing 0.63 lbs. per cubic inch, titanium has a very high strength, particularly in an alloyed form. In addition, it has excellent corrosion-resistant characteristics. Certain forms of titanium alloys are used extensively in many aerospace applications. Sensitive to both nitrogen and oxygen, titanium has to be converted to titanium dioxide with chlorine gas and a reducing agent, usually carbon, to be used effectively as a strong metal. Not as lustrous as chromium or stainless steel, pure titanium is soft and ductile, and its weight is between that of aluminum and iron.

Titanium alloys are classified as alpha, alpha-beta, and beta alloys. These classifications are based on the specific chemical bonding within the alloy itself.

Alpha titanium alloy. *Alpha alloys* have medium strength, and good elevated-temperature strength. They can be welded, and are used mostly for forgings.

Alpha-beta titanium alloy. *Alpha-beta alloys* are the most versatile of the titanium alloys. In the annealed condition they have medium strength, but when heat-treated their strength greatly increases. This form of titanium is generally not weldable, but it has good forming characteristics.

Beta titanium alloy. *Beta alloys* have medium strength, and excellent forming characteristics. Beta titanium can be heat treated to a very high strength.

Nickel Alloys

Monel®. Combining the properties of high strength and excellent corrosion resistance, Monel is the leading high-nickel alloy. This metal consists of 68 percent nickel, 29 percent copper, 0.2 percent iron, 1 percent manganese, and 1.8 percent of other elements. It cannot be hardened by heat-treatment.

Monel is adaptable to castings and either hot or cold working, and it can be successfully welded. It has working properties similar to those of steel, and when forged and annealed, has a tensile strength of 80,000 p.s.i. This can be increased by cold-working to 125,000 p.s.i, which is sufficient for it to be classified among the tough alloys.

Monel has been successfully used for gears and chains to operate retractable landing gears, and for structural parts subject to corrosion. Monel is often used for rivets to rivet stainless steel parts.

Inconel®. Closely resembling stainless steel in appearance, Inconel is a nickel-chromium-iron alloy. Its tensile strength is 100,000 p.s.i. annealed, 125,000 p.s.i. when hard-rolled. It is highly resistant to salt water and is able to withstand temperatures as high as 1,600°F. Inconel welds readily and has working qualities quite similar to those of corrosion-resistant steel.

Because Inconel and stainless steel look very much alike, a distinguishing test is often necessary. One method of identification is to use a solution of 10 grams of cupric chloride in 100 cubic centimeters of hydrochloric acid. The procedure is as follows:

1. Using a medicine dropper, place one drop of the solution on a sample of each metal to be tested and allow it to remain for 2 minutes.

2. At the end of the 2-minute period, slowly add three or four drops of water to the solution on the metal samples, one drop at a time.

3. Wash the samples in clear water and dry them.

4. If the metal is stainless steel, the copper in the cupric chloride solution will be deposited on the metal, leaving a copper-colored spot. If the sample is Inconel, a shiny spot will be seen.

Ferrous Aircraft Metals

Many different metals are required in the repair of aircraft. This is a result of the varying needs with respect to strength, weight, durability and resistance to deterioration of specific structures and parts. In addition, the particular shape or form of the material plays an important role. In selecting materials for aircraft repair, these and many other factors are considered in relation to the mechanical and physical properties. Among the common materials used are ferrous metals. The term *ferrous* applies to the group of metals having iron as their principal constituent.

Iron. One of the basic chemical elements, iron is extracted from iron ore. When combined with limestone and melted down, iron ore can be converted into what is commercially known as *pig iron*. Depending on how the iron ore is melted and what its intended use is, the pig iron is then used for castings, wrought iron or in the manufacture of steel.

Steel. If carbon is added to iron in percentages ranging up to approximately 1 percent, the product is vastly superior to iron alone and is classified as *carbon steel*. Just as with the previously discussed non-ferrous metals, a base metal (such as iron) to which small quantities of other metals have been added is called an alloy. The addition of other metals changes, or improves, the chemical or physical properties of the base metal for a particular use. Steel alloys are produced by combining carbon steel

SERIES DESIGNATION	TYPES OF STEEL
10xx	Non-sulphurized carbon steels
11xx	Re-sulphurized carbon steels (free machining)
12xx	Re-phosphorized and re-sulphurized carbon steels (free machining)
13xx	Manganese (1.75%)
*23xx	Nickel (3.50%)
*25xx	Nickel (5.00%)
31xx	Nickel (1.25%); Chromium (0.65%)
33xx	Nickel (3.50%); Chromium (1.55%)
40xx	Molybdenum (0.20 or 0.25%)
41xx	Chromium (0.50 or 0.95%); Molybdenum (0.12 or 0.20%)
43xx	Nickel (1.80%); Chromium (0.50 or 0.80%); Molybdenum (0.25%)
44xx	Molybdenum (0.40%)
45xx	Molybdenum (0.52%)
46xx	Nickel (1.80%); Molybdenum (0.25%)
47xx	Nickel (1.05%); Chromium (0.45%); Molybdenum (0.20 or 0.35%)
48xx	Nickel (3.50%); Molybdenum (0.25%)
50xx	Chromium (0.25, 0.45 or 0.50%)
50xxx	Carbon (1.00%); Chromium (0.50%)
51xx	Chromium (0.80, 0.90, 0.95 or 1.00%)
51xxx	Carbon (1.00%); Chromium (1.05%)
52xxx	Carbon (1.00%); Chromium (1.45%)
61xx	Chromium (0.60, 0.80 or 0.95%); Vanadium (0.12%, 0.10% min. or 0.15% min.)
81xx	Nickel (0.30%); Chromium (0.40%); Molybdenum (0.12%)
86xx	Nickel (0.55%); Chromium (0.50%); Molybdenum (0.20%)
87xx	Nickel (0.55%); Chromium (0.05%); Molybdenum (0.25%)
88xx	Nickel (0.55%); Chromium (0.05%); Molybdenum (0.35%)
92xx	Manganese (0.85%); Silicon (2.00%); Chromium (0 or 0.35%)
93xx	Nickel (3.25%); Chromium (1.20%); Molybdenum (0.12%)
94xx	Nickel (0.45%); Chromium (0.40%); Molybdenum (0.12%)
98xx	Nickel (1.00%); Chromium (0.80%); Molybdenum (0.25%)

*Not included in the current list of standard steels

Table 3-1-4. SAE numerical index of steel alloy designations

with elements which are known to improve the properties of steel. Carbon steel forms the base of those steel alloys.

Alloying Agents in Steel

Carbon. Steel containing carbon in percentages ranging from 0.10-0.30 percent is classified as *low-carbon steel*. The equivalent SAE numbers range from 1010 to 1030. (SAE numbers will be discussed in a later paragraph.) Steels of this grade are used for making such items as safety wire, certain nuts, cable bushings or threaded rod ends. This steel, in sheet form, is used for secondary structural parts, clamps and in tubular form for moderately stressed structural parts.

Steel containing carbon in percentages ranging from 0.30-0.50 percent is classified as *medium-carbon steel*. This steel is especially adaptable for machining or forging and where surface hardness is desirable. Certain rod ends and light forgings are made from SAE 1035 steel.

Steel containing carbon in percentages ranging from 0.50-1.05 percent is classified as *high-carbon steel*. The addition of other elements in varying quantities adds to the hardness of this steel. In the fully heat-treated condition, it is very hard, will withstand high shear and wear, and will have little deformation. It has limited use in aircraft. SAE 1095 in sheet form is used for making flat springs and in wire form for making coil springs.

Sulfur. During the refining process, as much sulfur as possible is removed from the steel, because it causes steel to be brittle during some forming processes. The effect of any sulfur that cannot be removed is counteracted by adding manganese. The manganese will draw the sulfur to it, creating *manganese sulfides*, which have no appreciable detrimental effects in the later forming processes.

Manganese. As carbon steel is processed, if manganese is added, the steel becomes very brittle. As the quantity of manganese is increased, the brittleness increases (up to a point). At a manganese content of about 5.5 percent, the brittleness begins to decrease, with the steel becoming more ductile and very hard. Manganese steel reaches its maximum hardness and ductility at a manganese content of about 12 percent.

Silicon. When this non-metallic chemical is added to steel (often manganese steel), it aids in the hardening and ductility qualities of the steel. Silicon is usually added to steel in amounts as small as fractions of 1 percent.

Phosphorus. Used to increase the resistance of low-carbon steel to corrosion, phosphorus is added in minute quantities of 0.05 percent or less. Quantities of phosphorus greater than 0.05 percent will cause the steel to become brittle.

Nickel. The various nickel steels are produced by combining nickel with carbon steel. Steels containing from 3 to 3.75 percent nickel are commonly used. Nickel increases the hardness, tensile strength and elastic limit of steel without appreciably decreasing the ductility. It also intensifies the hardening effect of heat-treatment. SAE 2330 steel is used extensively for aircraft parts, such as bolts, terminals, keys, clevises and pins.

Chromium. High in hardness, strength and corrosion-resistant properties, chromium steel is particularly adaptable for heat-treated forgings that require greater toughness and strength than may be obtained in plain carbon steel. It can be used for such articles as the balls and rollers of anti-friction bearings. The amount of chromium used in chromium steels varies greatly, dependent upon the desired usage of the final product.

Molybdenum. In combination with chromium, small percentages of molybdenum are used to form *chromium-molybdenum steel*, which has various uses in aircraft. Molybdenum is a

Figure 3-1-11. This pallet of steel tubing is marked with its four-digit number and with the heat-treat condition.

strong alloying element that raises the ultimate strength of steel without affecting ductility or workability. Molybdenum steels are tough and wear resistant, and they harden throughout when heat treated. Because they are especially adaptable for welding, molybdenum steels are used principally for welded structural parts and assemblies. This type steel has practically replaced carbon steel in the fabrication of fuselage tubing, engine mounts, landing gears and other structural parts. For example, a heat-treated SAE 4130 chromium-molybdenum steel tube is approximately four times as strong as a carbon steel tube of the same weight and size. (4130 is commonly called chrome-moly steel.)

Vanadium. When used to alloy steel, vanadium will increase the strength, toughness and resistance to wear and fatigue. Vanadium steel normally consists of 0.16-0.25 percent vanadium and is often alloyed with chromium. A special grade of this steel in sheet form can be cold-formed into intricate shapes. It can be folded and flattened without signs of breaking or failure. Vanadium steel is used for making springs, gears subjected to severe service conditions and for all parts which must withstand constant vibrations, variance, loads and repeated stresses.

Titanium. When alloyed with stainless steel, a small amount of titanium will keep the steel from becoming brittle under high-temperature conditions. This is used extensively in tail pipe and exhaust stack applications.

Tungsten. Able to withstand high temperatures without losing strength, tungsten is used extensively in high-speed metal-cutting tools and metals to be used for magnets. Tungsten steels normally contain 5 to 15 percent tungsten, although as much as 24 percent is not unusual.

SAE Classification of Steels

In order to facilitate the discussion of steels, some familiarity with their nomenclature is desirable. A numerical index, sponsored by the Society of Automotive Engineers (SAE) and the American Iron and Steel Institute (AISI), is used to identify the chemical compositions of the structural steels. See Table 3-1-4.

In the SAE numerical index system, a four-numeral series is used to designate the plain carbon and alloy steels; five numerals are used to designate certain types of alloy steels. The first two digits indicate the type of steel, the second digit also generally (but not always) gives the approximate amount of the major alloying element and the last two (or three) digits are intended to indicate the approximate middle of the carbon range. However, a deviation from the rule of indicating the carbon range is sometimes necessary. See Figure 3-1-11.

Small quantities of certain elements are present in alloy steels that are not specified as required. These elements are considered as incidental and may be present to the maximum amounts as follows: copper, 0.35 percent; nickel, 0.25 percent; chromium, 0.20 percent; molybdenum, 0.06 percent.

The list of standard steels is altered from time to time to accommodate steels of proven merit and to provide for changes in the metallurgical and engineering requirements of industry.

Carbon Steel

The element which provides the greatest influence on steel is carbon. The greater the amount of carbon in the steel, the harder the steel will be. However, the harder the steel, the more difficult it is to weld. Carbon steels vary from soft (low carbon) steels, with between 0.06 and 0.60 percent carbon content, to high-grade razor steel at about 1.25 percent carbon content.

Alloy Steels

Chromium-molybdenum steel. The series of chromium molybdenum steels (chrome-moly) most widely used in aircraft construction contains 0.25-0.55 percent carbon, 0.15-0.25 percent molybdenum and 0.50-1.10 percent chromium. These steels, when suitably heat-treated, are deep-hardening, easily machined, readily welded by either gas or electric methods and are especially adapted to high-temperature service.

Nickel steel. Sensitive to heat-treatment, nickel steels are primarily used in aviation for hardware, such as rod ends, nuts, bolts and screws. Chromium-nickel steels are corrosion-resistant metals. The anti-corrosive degree of this steel is determined by the surface condition of the metal, as well as by the composition, temperature and concentration of the corrosive agent.

Stainless steel. The principal alloy of stainless steel is chromium. The corrosion-resistant steel most often used in aircraft construction is known as 18-8 steel because of its content of 18 percent chromium and 8 percent nickel. One of the distinctive features of 18-8 steel is that its strength may be increased by cold-working.

Stainless steel may be rolled, drawn, bent or formed to any shape. Because these steels expand about 50 percent more than carbon steel and conduct heat only about 40 percent as rapidly, they are more difficult to weld. Stainless steel can be used for almost any part of an aircraft. Some of its common applications are in the fabrication of exhaust collectors, stacks, manifolds, structural and machined parts, springs, castings, tie rods and control cables.

Heat-treatment of Steel

Heat-treatment is a series of operations involving the heating and cooling of metals in the solid state. Its purpose is to change a mechanical property or combination of mechanical properties so that the metal will be more useful, serviceable and safe for a definite purpose. By heat-treating, a metal can be made harder, stronger and more resistant to impact. Heat-treating can also make a metal softer and more ductile. However, no single heat-treating operation can produce all of these characteristics. In fact, one property is often improved at the expense of another. For example, in the process of being hardened, a metal may be made brittle.

The various heat-treating processes are similar in that they all involve the heating and cooling of metals. They differ, however, in the temperatures to which the metal is heated, the rate at which it is cooled, and, of course, in the final result.

The most common forms of heat-treatment for ferrous metals are annealing, normalizing, hardening, tempering and casehardening. An advantage of ferrous metals over non-ferrous metals is that most ferrous metals can be annealed, and many of them can be hardened by heat-treatment; however, there is only one non-ferrous metal, titanium, that can be case-hardened, and none can be tempered or normalized.

Knowing the chemical composition is the first important consideration in the heat-treatment

Materials and Processes | 3-23

STEEL DESIGNATION NUMBER	TEMPERATURES			QUENCHING MEDIUM (N)	TEMPERING (DRAWING) TEMPERATURE FOR TENSILE STRENGTH (p.s.i.)				
	Normalizing Air Cool °F	Annealing °F	Hardening °F		100,000 (p.s.i.)	125,000 (p.s.i.)	150,000 (p.s.i.)	180,000 (p.s.i.)	200,000 (p.s.i.)
1020	1,650-1,750	1,600-1,700	1,575-1,675	H₂O	-	-	-	-	-
1022(X1022)	1,650-1,750	1,600-1,700	1,575-1,675	H₂O	-	-	-	-	-
1025	1,600-1,700	1,575-1,650	1,575-1,675	H₂O	(a)	-	-	-	-
1035	1,575-1,650	1,575-1,625	1,525-1,625	H₂O	875	-	-	-	-
1045	1,550-1,600	1,550-1,600	1,475-1,550	Oil/H₂O	1,150	-	-	(n)	-
1095	1,475-1,550	1,450-1,500	1,425-1,500	Oil	(b)	-	1,100	850	750
2330	1,475-1,525	1,425-1,475	1,450-1,500	Oil/H₂O	1,100	950	800	-	-
3135	1,600-1,650	1,500-1,550	1,475-1,525	Oil	1,250	1,050	900	750	650
3140	1,600-1,650	1,500-1,550	1,475-1,525	Oil	1,325	1,075	925	775	700
4037	1,600	1,525-1,575	1,525-1,575	Oil/H₂O	1,225	1,100	975	-	-
4130 (X4130)	1,600-1,700	1,525-1,575	1,575-1,625	Oil (c)	(d)	1,050	900	700	575
4140	1,600-1,650	1,525-1,575	1,525-1,575	Oil	1,350	1,100	1,025	825	675
4150	1,550-1,600	1,475-1,525	1,500-1,550	Oil	-	1,275	1,175	1,050	950
4340 (X4340)	1,550-1,625	1,525-1,575	1,475-1,550	Oil	-	1,200	1,050	950	850
4640	1,675-1,700	1,525-1,575	1,500-1,550	Oil	-	1,200	1,050	750	625
6135	1,600-1,700	1,550-1,600	1,575-1,625	Oil	1,300	1,075	950	800	750
6150	1,600-1,650	1,525-1,575	1,550-1,625	Oil	(d) (e)	1,200	1,000	900	800
6195	1,600-1,650	1,525-1,575	1,500-1,550	Oil	(f)	-	-	-	-
8620	-	-	1,525-1,575	Oil	-	1,000	-	-	-
8630	1,650	1,525-1,575	1,525-1,575	Oil	-	1,125	975	775	675
8735	1,650	1,525-1,575	1,525-1,575	Oil	-	1,175	1,025	875	775
8735	1,625	1,500-1,550	1,500-1,550	Oil	-	1,200	1,075	925	850
30905	-	(g) (h)	(i)	-	-	-	-	-	-
51210	1,525-1,575	1,525-1,575	1,775-1,825 (j)	Oil	1,200	1,100	(k)	750	-
51335	-	1,525-1,575	1,775-1,850	Oil	-	-	-	-	-
52100	1,625-1,700	1,400-1,450	1,525-1,550	Oil	(f)	-	-	-	-
Corrosion Resisting (16-2) (l)	-	-	-	-	(m)	-	-	-	-
Silicon Chromium (for Springs)	-	-	1700-1725	Oil	-	-	-	-	-

(a) Draw at 1,150°F for tensile strength of 70,000 p.s.i.
(b) For spring temper draw at 800-900°F. Rockwell hardness C-40-45
(c) Bars and forgings may be quenched in water from 1,500-1,600°F.
(d) Air-cooling from the normalizing temperature will produce a tensile strength of approx. 90,000 p.s.i.
(e) For spring temper draw at 858-950°F. Rockwell hardness C-40-45.
(f) Draw at 350-450°F to remove quenching strains. Rockwell hardness C-60-65.
(g) Anneal at 1,600-1,700°F to remove residual stresses due to welding or cold-work. May be applied to steel containing titanium or columbium.
(h) Anneal at 1,900-2,100°F to produce maximum softness and corrosion resistance. Cool in air or quench in water.
(i) Harden by cold-work only.
(j) Lower side of range for sheet 0.06 inch and under. Middle of range for sheet and wire 0.125 inch. Upper side of range for forgings.
(k) Not recommended for intermediate strengths because of low impact.
(l) An-QQ-S-770. It is recommended that, prior to tempering, corrosion-resisting (16 Cr2Ni) steel be quenched in oil from a temperature of 1,875-1,900°F, after a soaking period of 1/2 hour at this temperature. To obtain a tensile strength of 115,000 p.s.i., the tempering temperature should be approximately 525°F. A holding time at these temperatures of 2 hours is recommended. Tempering temperatures from 700-1,100°F will not be approved.
(m) Draw at approximately 800°F and cool in air for rockwell hardness of C-50.
(n) Water used for quenching shall not exceed 65°F. Oil used for quenching shall be within a range of 80-150°F.

Table 3-1-5. Heat-treatment procedures for steels

of a steel part. This, in turn, determines its *upper critical point*. When the upper critical point is known, the next consideration is the rate of heating and cooling to be used. Carrying out these operations involves the use of uniform heating furnaces, proper temperature controls and suitable quenching mediums.

Annealing

Metals are annealed to relieve internal stresses, soften the metal, make it more ductile and refine the grain structure. In the annealed state, steel has its lowest strength. In general, annealing is the opposite of hardening.

Annealing of steel is accomplished by heating the metal to just above the upper critical point, soaking at that temperature and cooling very slowly in the furnace. See Table 3-1-5 for recommended temperatures. Soaking time is approximately 1 hour per inch of thickness of the material.

To produce maximum softness in steel, the metal must be cooled very slowly. Slow cooling is obtained by shutting off the heat and allowing the furnace and metal to cool together to 900°F or lower, then removing the metal from the furnace and cooling in still air. Another method is to bury the heated steel in ashes, sand or other substance that does not conduct heat readily.

Normalizing

The process of *normalizing* steel removes the internal stresses caused by welding, machining, forming or any type of handling. These stresses, if not reduced or eliminated, will eventually cause extreme brittleness, which in turn will lead to cracking. The application of the normalizing process does exactly what the name implies. It brings the metal back to a normal, shock-resistant state.

Applying to ferrous metals only, normalizing is accomplished by heating the steel above the upper critical point and cooling it in still air. The more rapid quenching obtained by air-cooling, as compared to furnace-cooling, results in a harder and stronger material than that obtained by annealing. Recommended normalizing temperatures for the various types of aircraft steels are listed in Table 3-1-5.

One of the most important uses of normalizing in aircraft work is in welded parts. Welding causes strains to be set up in the adjacent material. Additionally, the weld itself is a cast structure, as opposed to the wrought structure of the rest of the material. These two types of structures have different grain sizes, and to refine the grain as well as to relieve the internal stresses, all welded parts should be normalized after fabrication.

Hardening. Pure iron, wrought iron and extremely low-carbon steels cannot be appreciably hardened by heat-treatment, since they contain little or no hardening element. Since the maximum hardness depends almost entirely on the carbon content of the steel, as the carbon content increases, the ability of the steel to be hardened increases, to a point. When the carbon content is increased beyond that point (which is about 0.85 percent) there is no appreciable increase in hardness.

For most steels, the hardening treatment consists of heating the steel to a temperature just above the upper critical point, soaking or holding at that temperature for the required length of time and then cooling it rapidly by plunging the hot steel into oil, water or brine. Hardening increases the strength of the steel but makes it less ductile.

When hardening carbon steel, it must be cooled to below 1,000°F in less than 1 second. Should the time required for the temperature to drop to 1,000°F exceed 1 second, the hardness will vary and will not reach the maximum hardness possible. After the 1,000°F temperature is reached, the rapid cooling must continue if the final structure is to reach the maximum hardness.

When alloys are added to steel, the time limit for the temperature drop to 1,000°F increases above the 1-second limit for carbon steels. Therefore, a slower quenching medium will produce hardness in alloy steels.

Because of the high internal stresses in the as-quenched condition, steel must be tempered just before it becomes cold. The part should be removed from the quenching bath at a temperature of approximately 200°F, since the range from 200°F down to room temperature is where most cracks occur. Hardening temperatures and quenching mediums for the various types of steel are listed in Table 3-1-5.

Tempering

Tempering reduces the brittleness imparted by hardening and produces definite physical properties within the steel. Tempering always follows, never precedes, the hardening operation. In addition to reducing brittleness, tempering softens the steel. Another name for tempering is *drawing* (i.e. *drawing* the temper).

Tempering is always conducted at temperatures below the low critical point of the steel.

When hardened steel is re-heated, tempering begins at 212°F and continues as the temperature increases toward the low critical point. By selecting a definite tempering temperature, the resulting hardness and strength can be predetermined. Approximate temperatures for various tensile strengths are listed in Table 3-1-5.

The minimum time at the tempering temperature should be 1 hour. If the part is over an inch in thickness, the time should be increased by 1 hour for each additional inch of thickness. Tempered steels used in aircraft work have 125,000-200,000 p.s.i. ultimate tensile strength.

The rate of cooling from the tempering temperature generally has no effect on the resulting structure; therefore, the steel is usually cooled in still air after being removed from the furnace.

Determining the Temperature of Steel

If temperature-measuring equipment is not available, it becomes necessary to estimate temperatures by some other means. An inexpensive, yet fairly accurate, method involves the use of commercial crayons, pellets or paints that melt at various temperatures within the range of 125°-1,600°F. The least accurate method of temperature estimation is by observing the color of the hot hearth of the furnace, or color of the work. The heat colors observed are affected by many factors, such as the conditions of artificial or natural light, the character of the scale on the work, etc.

Steel begins to appear dull red at about 1,000°F and, as the temperature increases, the color changes gradually through various shades of red, to orange, to yellow and finally, to white. A rough approximation of the correspondence between color and temperature is indicated in Figure 3-1-12.

It is also possible to find the temperature of a piece of carbon or low-alloy steel from the color of the thin oxide film that forms on the cleaned surface of the steel when heated to the low temperature range used for tempering. The approximate temperature/color relationship for a given time at temperature is indicated in Figure 3-1-12.

Judging temperature from color is a holdover from the days of blacksmithing and ironworking. It is an outdated process that simply will not go away. Modern steels and alloys require more precise process controls than temperature-by-color guessing will allow. The best

Figure 3-1-12. Approximate temperature/color relationship for steel

method to indicate temperature in the field is to obtain a set of temperature indicating crayons. To use them, you mark the steel and then heat it. When the color changes, the steel is at the correct temperature for that particular crayon.

Casehardening

Producing a hard wear-resistant surface, or case, over a strong, tough core, casehardening is ideal for parts which require a wear-resistant surface and, at the same time, must be tough enough internally to withstand the applied loads. The steels best suited to case-hardening are the low-carbon and low-alloy steels. If high-carbon steel is casehardened, the hardness penetrates the core and causes brittleness.

Carburizing. Carburizing is a casehardening process in which carbon is added to the surface of low-carbon steel. Thus, a carburized steel has a high-carbon surface and a low-carbon interior. When the carburized steel is heat-treated, the case is hardened while the core remains soft and tough.

A common method of carburizing is called *pack carburizing*. When carburizing is performed using this method, the steel parts are packed in a container with charcoal or some other material rich in carbon. The container is then sealed with fire clay, placed in a furnace, heated to approximately 1,700°F and soaked at that temperature for several hours. As the temperature increases, carbon monoxide gas forms inside the container and, being unable to escape, combines with the gamma iron on the surface of the steel. The depth to which the carbon penetrates depends on the length of the soaking period. For example, when carbon steel is soaked for 8 hours, the carbon penetrates to a depth of about 0.062 inch.

Another method of carburizing is called *gas carburizing*, in which a carbon-rich atmosphere is introduced into the furnace. The carburizing atmosphere is produced by the use of various gases, or by the burning of oil, wood or other materials. When the steel parts are heated in this atmosphere, carbon monoxide combines with the gamma iron to produce practically the same results as those described under the pack carburizing process.

A third method of carburizing is called *liquid carburizing*. In this method, the steel is placed in a molten salt bath that contains the carbon-based chemicals required to produce a case comparable with one resulting from pack or gas carburizing.

Alloy steels with low-carbon content, as well as low-carbon steels, may be carburized by any one of these three processes. However, some alloys, such as nickel, tend to retard the absorption of carbon. As a result, the time required to produce a given thickness of case varies with the composition of the metal.

Nitriding. Nitriding is unlike other casehardening processes in that, before nitriding, the part is heat-treated to produce definite physical properties. Thus, parts are hardened and tempered before being nitrided. Most steels can be nitrided, but special alloys are required for best results. These special alloys contain aluminum

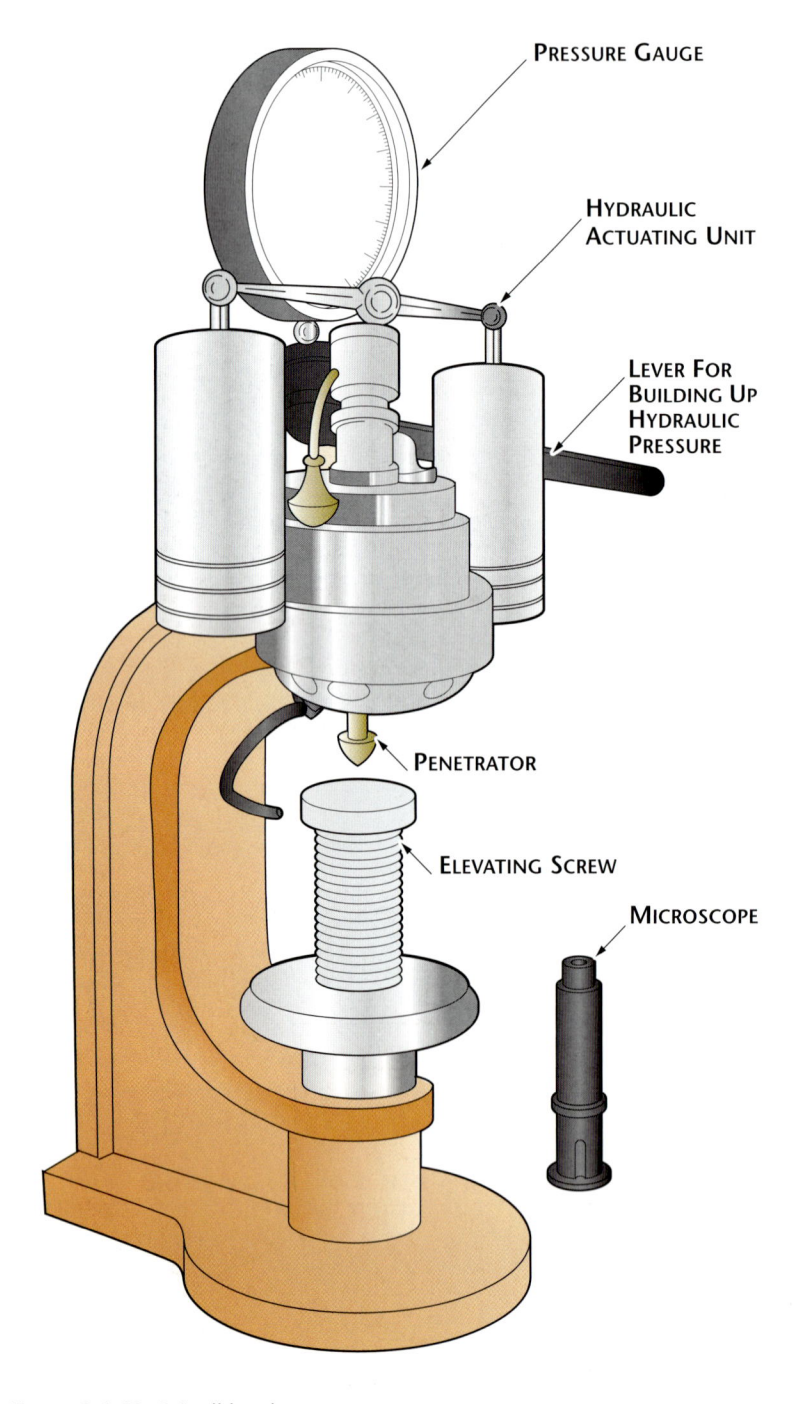

Figure 3-1-13. Brinell hardness tester

as one of the alloying elements and are called nitralloys.

In the nitriding process, the part is placed in a special nitriding furnace and heated to a temperature of approximately 1,000°F. With the part at this temperature, ammonia gas is circulated within the specially constructed furnace chamber. The high temperature cracks the ammonia gas into nitrogen and hydrogen. The nitrogen reacts with the iron to form iron nitride. The iron nitride is dispersed as minute particles at the surface and works inward. The ammonia that does not break down is caught in a water trap below the regions of the other two gases. The depth of penetration depends on the length of the treatment. In nitriding, soaking periods as long as 72 hours are frequently required to produce the desired thickness of case.

Nitriding can be accomplished with a minimum of distortion because of the low temperature at which parts are casehardened, and because no quenching is required after exposure to the ammonia gas.

Hardness Testing

The results of heat-treatment, as well as the state of a metal prior to heat treatment can be determined by hardness testing. Since hardness values can be tied in with tensile strength values and, in part, with wear resistance, hardness tests are a valuable check of heat-treat control and of material properties.

Methods of Hardness Testing

Most hardness-testing equipment uses the resistance to penetration as a measure of hardness. Included among the better-known hardness testers are the Brinell and Rockwell testers, both of which are described and illustrated in this section.

The Brinell hardness testing system. The Brinell tester (Figure 3-1-13) uses a hardened spherical ball, which is forced into the surface of the metal. This ball is 10 millimeters (0.3937 inch) in diameter. A pressure of 3,000 kilograms is used for ferrous metals and 500 kilograms for non-ferrous metals. The pressure must be maintained at least 10 seconds for ferrous metals and at least 30 seconds for non-ferrous metals.

Pressure for the test is supplied by hydraulic pressure from either a hand pump or an electric motor, depending on the model of tester, and is monitored through a pressure gauge. A release mechanism is included in the hydraulic system for relieving the pressure after the test has been made, and a calibrated microscope is provided for measuring the diameter of the impression in millimeters.

The machine uses various shaped anvils for supporting the specimen and an elevating screw for bringing the specimen in contact

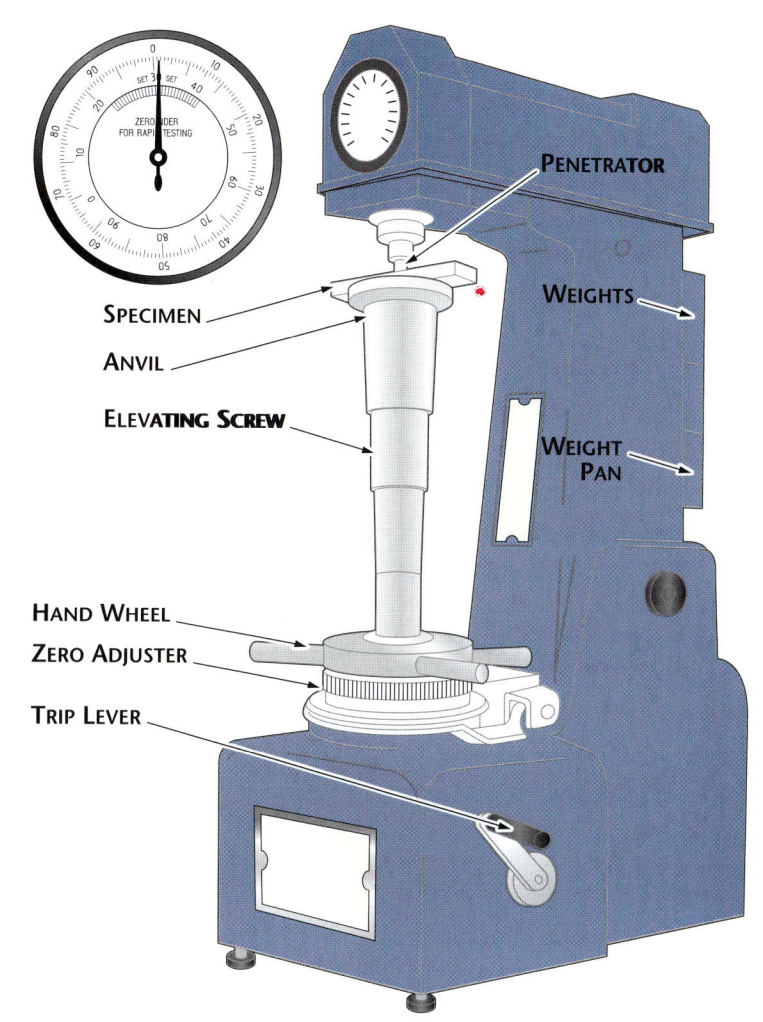

Figure 3-1-14. Rockwell hardness tester

ROCKWELL HARDNESS SCALES				
Scale Symbol	Penetrator	Major Lead (kg)	Dial Number
A	Diamond	60	Black
B	1/16 inch ball	100	Red
C	Diamond	150	Black
D	Diamond	100	Black
E	1/8 inch ball	100	Red
F	1/16 inch ball	60	Red
G	1/16 inch ball	150	Red
H	1/8 inch ball	60	Red
K	1/8 inch ball	150	Red

Table 3-1-6. Standard Rockwell hardness scales

HARDNESS VALUES FOR ALUMINUM ALLOYS		
Material (Commercial Designation)	Hardness (Temper)	Brinell Number (500 kg Load, 10 mm Ball)
1100	O	23
	H18	44
3003	O	28
	H16	47
2014	O	45
	T6	135
2017	O	45
	T6	105
2024	O	47
	T4	120
2025	T6	110
6151	T6	100
5052	O	47
	H36	73
6061	O	30
	T4	65
	T6	95
7075	T6	135
7079	T6	135
195	T6	75
220	T4	75
C355	T6	80
A356	T6	70

Table 3-1-7. Hardness values for aluminum alloys (ref. Mil-H-6088G)

with the ball penetrator. The various anvils and other attachments are used for each of the variety of tests that the tester can perform.

The Brinell hardness number for a metal is determined by measuring the diameter of the impression left by the ball, using the calibrated microscope furnished with the tester. The measurement is converted into a Brinell hardness number using the conversion table furnished with the tester.

The Rockwell hardness testing system. The Rockwell hardness tester (Figure 3-1-14,) measures the resistance to penetration, as does the Brinell tester. But instead of measuring the diameter of the impression, the Rockwell tester measures the depth. The hardness is indicated directly on a dial attached to the machine. The dial numbers in the outer circle are black, and the inner numbers are red. Rockwell hardness numbers are based on the difference between the depth of penetration at major and minor loads. The greater this difference, the less the hardness number, and the softer the material.

Two types of penetrators are used with the Rockwell tester, a diamond cone (used on materials known to be hard and on materials of unknown hardness) and a hardened steel ball (used to test soft materials). The load which forces the penetrator into the metal is called the *major load* and is measured in kilograms. The results of each penetrator and load combination are reported on the separate red and black scales and are designated by letters. The penetrator, the major load and the scale vary with the kind of metal being tested. The scales, penetrators, major loads and dial numbers to be read are listed in Table 3-1-6.

The metal to be tested in the Rockwell tester must be ground smooth on two opposite sides and be free of scratches and foreign matter. The surface should be perpendicular to the axis of penetration, and the two opposite ground surfaces should be parallel. If the specimen is tapered, the amount of error will depend on the taper.

A curved surface will also cause a slight error in the hardness test. The amount of error depends on the curvature; i.e., the smaller the radius of curvature, the greater the error. To eliminate such error, a small flat should be ground on the curved surface, if possible.

Clad aluminum-alloy sheets cannot be tested directly with any accuracy by a Rockwell hardness tester. See Table 3-1-7 for the Brinell numbers for aluminum alloys. If the hardness value of the base metal is desired, the pure aluminum coating must be removed from the area to be checked prior to testing.

Vickers hardness test. In this test, a small pyramidal diamond is pressed into the metal being tested. The *Vickers hardness number* (HV) is the ratio of the load applied to the surface area of the indention. This is done with the following formula:

$$HV = \text{Constant} \times \text{Test Force}/\text{Indent Diagonal}^2$$

The indenter is made of diamond, and is in the form of a square-based pyramid, having an angle of 136° between faces. The facets are highly-polished, free from surface imperfections and the point is sharp. The loads applied vary from 1 to 120 kg; the standard loads are 5, 10, 20, 30, 50, 100 and 120 kg. For most hardness testing, 50 kg is maximum.

A Vickers hardness tester should be calibrated to meet ASTM standard E10 specifications, acceptable for use over a loading range.

Webster hardness gauge. If a part is too large to use in a standard bench tester, the portable Webster style of tester can be used. In appearance, a Webster hardness gauge looks like a pair of pliers with a dial attached.

Before use, the gauge must be calibrated using a strip of the same material being tested, but with a known Rockwell hardness. The pliers are squeezed until they bottom out, and the hardness is read on the gauge.

The Webster gauge is especially useful in testing heat-treated aluminum.

Microhardness testing. This is an indentation hardness test made with loads not exceeding 1 kg (1,000 grams). Such hardness tests have been made with a load as light as 1 gram, although the majority of microhardness tests are made with loads of 100-500 grams. In general, the term is related to the size of the indentation rather than to the load applied.

Fields of application. Microhardness testing is capable of providing information regarding the hardness characteristics of materials which cannot be obtained by hardness tests, such as the Brinell or Rockwell, and are as follows:

- Measuring the hardness of precision work pieces that are too small to be measured by the more common hardness-testing methods
- Measuring the hardness of product forms, such as foil or wire, that are too thin or too small in diameter to be measured by more conventional methods
- Monitoring of carburizing or nitriding operations, which is sometimes accomplished by hardness surveys taken on cross sections of test pieces that accompanied the work pieces through production operations
- Measuring the hardness of individual microconstituents
- Measuring the hardness close to edges, thus detecting undesirable surface conditions such as grinding burn and decarburization
- Measuring the hardness of surface layers, such as plating or bonded layers

Indenters

Microhardness testing can be performed with either the Knoop or Vickers indenter. The *Knoop indenter* is used mostly in the U.S.; the Vickers indenter is the more widely used in Europe.

Knoop indentation testing is performed with a diamond, ground to pyramid form, that produces a diamond-shape indentation with an approximate ratio between long and short diagonals of 7:1. The indentation depth is about 1/30 of its length. Due to the shape of the indenter, indentations of accurately measurable length are obtained with light loads.

The Knoop hardness number (HK) is the ratio of the load applied to the indenter to the unrecovered projected area of indentation.

The Vickers indenter penetrates about twice as far into the work piece as does the Knoop indenter. The diagonal of the Vickers indentation is about one-third of the total length of the Knoop indentation. The Vickers indenter is less sensitive to minute differences in surface conditions than is the Knoop indenter. However, the Vickers indentation, because of the shorter diagonal, is more prone to errors in measuring than is the Knoop indentation

Section 2
Fasteners

Riveted joints have been the preferred construction method for many years. Testing of joints has shown that accurately prepared and riveted joints will withstand more loading/unloading cycles before failure than any other joining system. Following riveted joints in durability are interference pins in *stressed holes* and interference pins in *non-stressed holes*. The list continues down to screws in nut plates and sheet metal screws.

Joints are subject to many variables. Type of load, temperature, vibration, etc., must be factored in. If we add availability, cost, special tooling and component access, it becomes even more complicated.

Riveted joints have their limitations. While they are optimal in shear they are less than ideal in tension (clamp up). When other attachments are involved, bending loads anticipated, etc., other fasteners will often he used. Hi-Loks® are often the choice.

Hi-Lok® Fasteners

Hi-Lok fasteners are intended to provide the strength of a bolt, with less weight and a quicker assembly time. They are a permanent structural fastener that allows for a degree of disassembly. They are designed as a pin/collar assembly (Figure 3-2-1). The threaded collar has a fracture section that will shear at a predetermined torque (Figure 3-2-2). These fasteners are easily installed with basic hand tools. They

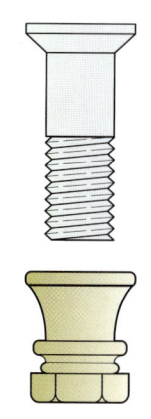

Figure 3-2-1. The two parts of a Hi-Lok fastener, before being screwed together

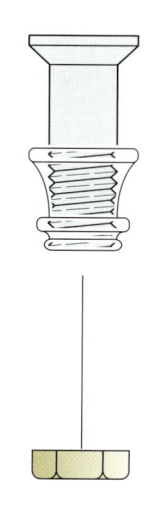

Figure 3-2-2. A Hi-Lok fastener, after being torqued down and the hex collar breaking off

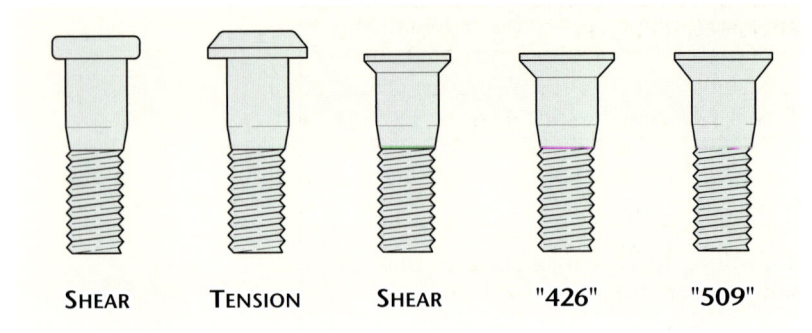

Figure 3-2-3. Different types of Hi-Lok fasteners

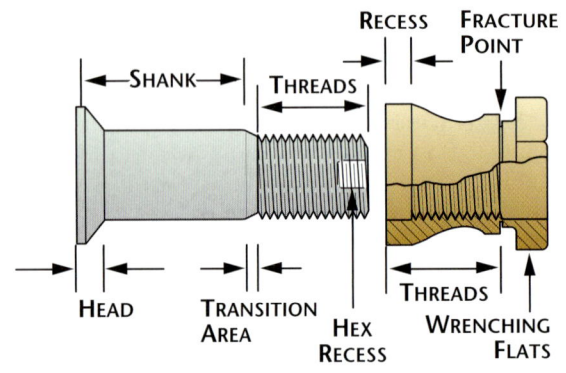

Figure 3-2-4. The nomenclature of the various parts of a Hi-Lok fastener

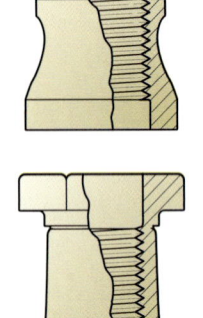

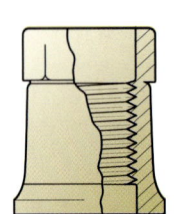

Figure 3-2-5. Hi-Lok collars

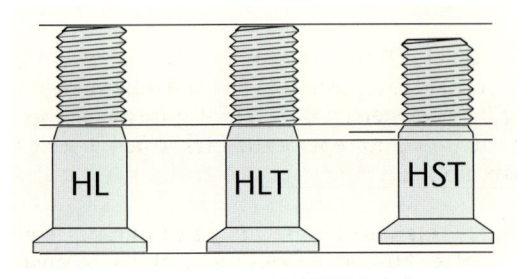

Figure 3-2-6. HL, HLT and HST Hi-Lok fasteners

Pins. The pins come with various types of protruding- and flush-head styles and many standard and oversized shank diameters. See Figure 3-2-3.

The pins are made of high-quality, rolled alloy steel, corrosion-resistant steel (CRES) or titanium alloy. Table 3-2-1 shows different finishes and their codes.

The pin is divided into sections, the head, shank, transition area, threads and the hexagonal recess.

The head counteracts the pull of the collar and allows the fastener to be properly tightened. The type of head is directly related to the designed load. These loads, shear or tension, are reflected in the pin/collar choice (sheer pins/shear collars, tension pin/tension collars). Flush heads match the size of most rivets and bolts.

The shank of the fastener should fill the entire length and diameter of the hole. This is where the load is transferred from one element (part) to another. An installed fastener with any portion of thread in the hole will not allow full load transfer.

The transition area is the portion between the straight portion of the shank and the first load bearing thread and provides a smooth transition from the shank to the threads. It will be either beveled or filleted into the minor thread diameter. The area is the first point of contact when starting the pin into an interference fit hole.

The end opposite the head is threaded to accept a collar or nut. The thread length can vary depending on the intended usage. The threaded end contains a hexagonal recess. This recess allows the installer to use a hex wrench to prevent pin rotation while the collar is being installed. See Figure 3-2-4.

Collars. The collars are made of an aluminum alloy, CRES or alloy steel. The collars have wrenching flats, fracture point, threads and a recess. Wrenching flats are used to install the collar (Figure 3-2-5).

The fracture point has been designed to allow the wrenching flats to shear when the proper torque has been reached.

The threads match the threads of the pin and have been formed into an ellipse that will be distorted to provide a "safety" when installed.

The recess serves the function of a built-in washer. This area is designed to contain a portion of the shank and/or the transition area of the fastener. This eliminates the need for a washer, although a washer may occasionally be used. The diameter of the recess must be larger

can, with proper authorization, replace a variety of other fasteners.

The original Hi-Lok has evolved into a class of fasteners. This classification consists of:

- Hi-Lok
- Hi-Tigue Hi-Lok (normally referred to as just Hi-Tigue®)
- The Light-Weight® series

When installed in aluminum, they go into interference fit holes approximately .003 inch smaller than the fastener. The primary reason for the interference fit is to maximize "instant-load-moment," The second is a slight "cold working" of the hole. A benefit to us as technicians is that it minimizes fastener spinning while the collar or nut is being installed.

CODES AND DIFFERENT FINISHES FOR PINS

Types of Pins	Code	Description
Alloy Steel	PB	Cadmium plated, Type II, plus cetyl alcohol lubed
A-268 CRES	V	Solid film lubed
A-268 CRES	BC	Passivated, plus cetyl alcohol lubed
H-11 Steel	M	Nickel-zinc plated, plus cetyl alcohol lubed
H-11 Steel	—	Diffused nickel - cadmium plated, plus cetyl alcohol lubed
Titanium	V or VAZ	Aluminum coated, plus cetyl alcohol lubed
Titanium	VRA	Phosphate-fluoride treated, plus cetyl alcohol lubed
Titanium	—	Cadmium plate (now inactive)

Table 3-2-1. Codes for different finishes

than the shank diameter to prevent interference. The depth of the recess, in conjunction with the overall thread length, determine *grip variation.*

Hi-Lok® (HL)

The Hi-Lok has been around for many years. The variety of pins and collars exceeds one-thousand. It is the standard by which all others are compared.

The Hi-Lok fastener assembly consists of a pin (bolt) and collar (nut). The distinctive difference is the transition area which would best be described as a bevel. See Figure 3-2-6.

Hi-Tigue® (HLT)

The Hi-Tigue fastener assembly also consists of a pin (bolt) and collar (nut). Hi-Tigue pins have a radius (are rounded) at the transition area. This radius was designed to "cold-work" the hole during installation. This process was found to be less effective than anticipated with these fasteners. The visual difference is difficult to detect and should not be used for identification. Use part numbers.

Most of the Hi-Tigue pins are made of titanium.

> **NOTE:** *Early vendor literature, and some A&P books, show and describe a "slight bead" at the threaded end of the pin. These are incorrect and have not been used in aircraft.*

Light-Weight® Series (HST)

The Light-Weight series fasteners also consist of a pin (bolt) and collar (nut). The series consists of the Hi-Lite (HST), and the Very-Lite (VL) fasteners. All Light-Weight series pins are made of titanium.

The differences between Hi-Lok/Hi-Tigue pins and the Light-Weight series are:

- A shorter (by half) transition area between the shank and the first load bearing thread
- Approximately one less thread

These differences reduce the pin weight without lessening the shear strength. The clamping forces are less, but sufficient for certain jobs. Companion collars have also been redesigned to reduce weight while maintaining the necessary strength. The pins and collars from different vendors within the series are interchangeable. They come in a variety of colors. They are not to be interchanged with the collars of Hi-Lok/Hi-Tigue pins. Be sure to match the proper collar with its respective pin.

The Hi-Lites are identified by an orange band around the threaded end of the fastener. The Very-Lites are identified by a black band around the threaded end of the fastener.

Substitution

Hi-Lok and Hi-Tigue pins are considered interchangeable under most circumstances. The most important considerations are the compatibility of the pin material and the material in which it will be installed. The General Notes in the Maintenance Manual (GN/MM) is the primary authority for substitutions. Information can also be found in the manufacturer's SRMs.

Hi-Lok/Hi-Tigue assemblies have normally been used to replace Lockbolt and other swaged collar fasteners. Hi-Lok/Hi-Tigue assemblies can be used to replace the Light-Weight series assemblies.

Light-Weight series assemblies cannot be used to replace Hi-Lok/Hi-Tigue assemblies because of their reduced clamp-up strength.

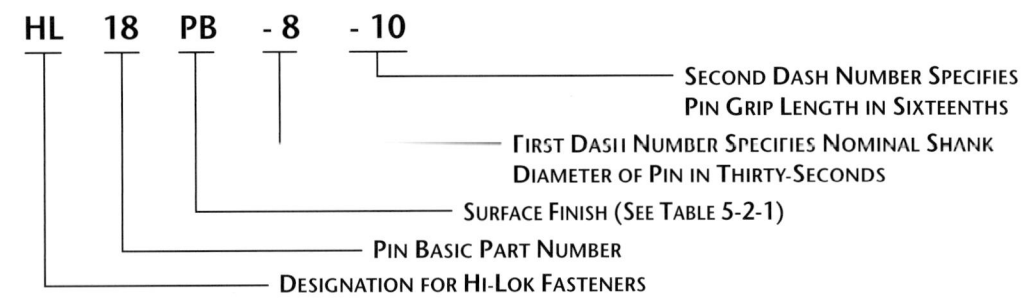

```
        HL   18   PB   -8   -10
         │    │    │    │    └─── SECOND DASH NUMBER SPECIFIES
         │    │    │    │          PIN GRIP LENGTH IN SIXTEENTHS
         │    │    │    └──────── FIRST DASH NUMBER SPECIFIES NOMINAL SHANK
         │    │    │               DIAMETER OF PIN IN THIRTY-SECONDS
         │    │    └───────────── SURFACE FINISH (SEE TABLE 5-2-1)
         │    └────────────────── PIN BASIC PART NUMBER
         └─────────────────────── DESIGNATION FOR HI-LOK FASTENERS
```

Figure 3-2-7. The pin part number

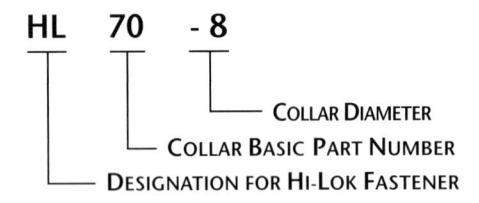

```
        HL   70   -8
         │    │    └── COLLAR DIAMETER
         │    └─────── COLLAR BASIC PART NUMBER
         └──────────── DESIGNATION FOR HI-LOK FASTENER
```

Figure 3-2-8. Collar part number

Identification

Pin part number. Pin part numbers break down like the example in Figure 3-2-7.

Collar part number. A collar part number breakdown is shown in Figure 3-2-8. Boeing's SRMs and prints will use a Boeing assigned number. Example: BACB30FM*-*. A comprehensive list of part numbers can be found in GN/MM 1-0-8-23, 1-0-8-51 & 1-0-8-69.

Installation

Hole preparation. Use Table 3-2-2, Table 3-2-3 and Table 3-2-4 for proper hole sizes.

NOTE: *Interference fit fasteners can cause significant reduction in the static strength of carbon/graphite composites. Typically, a .003 inch interference can result in a 25 percent loss in static strength with no improvement in fatigue life. Refer to Table 3-2-3 for hole sizes in carbon fiber substrates.*

Table 3-2-3 provides hole size limits when all members of the joint (part through which the pin goes) are aluminum (except 7079 aluminum). Typical standard holes are approximately .001 inch to .003 inch smaller than the basic pin (shank) diameter.

STANDARD INTERFERENCE FIT HOLE SIZES FOR ALUMINUM						
Normal Diameter	Standard Size		1/64" Oversize		1/32" Oversize	
	Min.	Max.	Min.	Max.	Min.	Max.
5/32" (-5)	0.1600	0.1620	—	—	—	—
3/16" (-6)	0.1860	0.1880	0.1990	0.2010	0.2145	0.2165
1/4" (-8)	0.2460	0.2480	0.2615	0.2635	0.2770	0.2790
5/16" (-10)	0.3085	0.3105	0.3240	0.3260	0.3395	0.3415
3/8" (-12)	0.3710	0.3710	0.3865	0.3885	0.4020	0.4040

Table 3-2-2. Standard hole sizes for aluminum (except for 7079 alloy)

MODIFIED FIT HOLE SIZES FOR STEEL, TITANIUM AND COMPOSITES						
Normal Diameter	Standard Size		1/64" Oversize		1/32" Oversize	
	Min.	Max.	Min.	Max.	Min.	Max.
5/32" (-5)	0.1635	0.1645	—	—	—	—
3/16" (-6)	0.1890	0.1905	0.2020	0.2035	0.2180	0.2195
1/4" (-8)	0.2490	0.2505	0.2650	0.2665	0.2800	0.2815
5/16" (-10)	0.3115	0.3130	0.3270	0.3285	0.3430	0.3445
3/8" (-12)	0.3740	0.3755	0.3900	0.3915	0.4050	0.4065

Table 3-2-3. Non-interference fit hole sizes – for steel, titanium, 7079 aluminum and carbon/graphite composite laminates

GRIP RANGE		
Grip Number	Minimum	Maximum
2	0.063	0.125
3	0.126	0.188
4	0.189	0.250
5	0.251	0.312
6	0.313	0.375
7	0.376	0.438
8	0.439	0.500
9	0.501	0.562
10	0.563	0.625
11	0.626	0.688
12	0.689	0.750
13	0.751	0.812
14	0.813	0.875
15	0.876	0.938
16	0.939	1.000
17	1.001	1.062

Table 3-2-4. Grip range

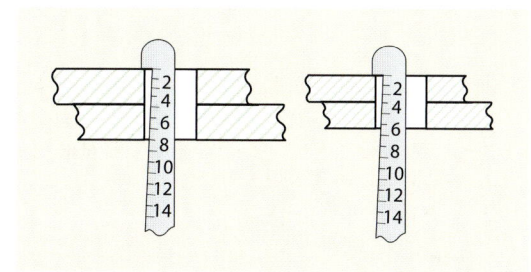

Figure 3-2-10. This illustration shows a –7 grip on the left and a grip between –5 and –6 on the right. When this happens use a longer Hi-Lok and adjust for pin protrusion with a washer.

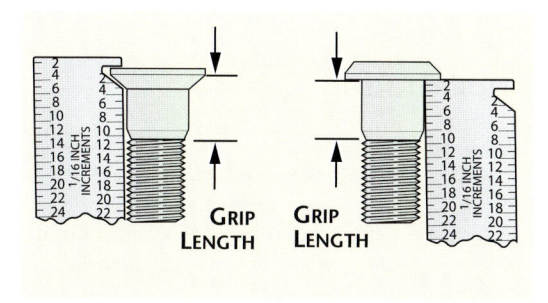

Figure 3-2-11. How both standard and flush-head pins are measured

NOTE: *7079 aluminum alloy was used on early Boeing aircraft. It was highly susceptible to stress corrosion and is no longer used.*

Table 3-2-3 shows hole size limits when one or more members of the joint are steel, stainless steel, titanium, 7079 aluminum or carbon/graphite composite structure.

Pins are available in 1/16 inch length increments. The maximum grip length is indicated by the last dash number of the part number. The grip range is from 1/16 less than maximum to maximum.

To accurately choose a correct length pin, a special *grip gauge* is used (Figure 3-2-9, Figure 3-2-10 and Figure 3-2-11) and how it is used. Pin length and dash number are listed in Table 3-2-4.

To correct grip length variations, the use of washers is permissible provided the washer is galvanically compatible with the material surface against which it will be installed. Washer thickness of .032 inch (thin) or .064 inch (thick) is permissible with .064 being the maximum. Washers are not to be used in an integral fuel tank unless specifically called for in an approved engineering document. See Figure 3-2-12.

NOTE: *Two GO/NO-GO gauge sets are available. They are labeled for the appropriate type fastener and are color coded. The black set is used for Hi-Loks. The red set is used for Hi-Lites®.*

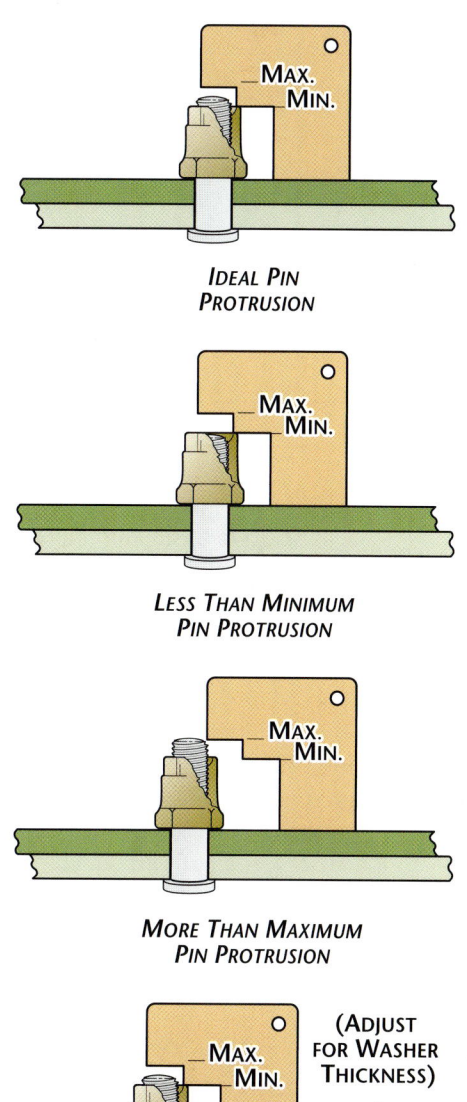

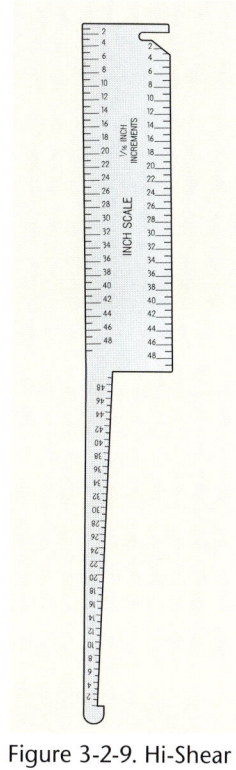

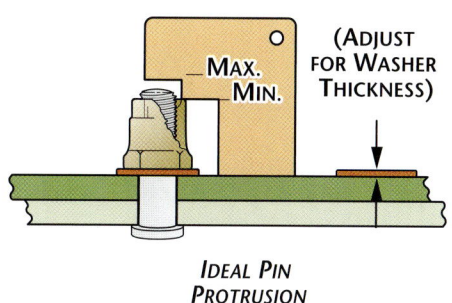

Figure 3-2-12. Correcting for grip variations

Figure 3-2-9. Hi-Shear 2-612 grip gauge

Properly installed fasteners will fall within the protrusion limits of Table 3-2-5. One to four exposed threads was the pin height standard for many years, however many of the newer collars have a lower installed profile. Thread count cannot be used with these collars. Flushness standards for Hi-Loks and Lockbolts is normally ± .003 inch.

Installation

Installation is a five-step process:

1. Insert the pin into the prepared hole. It is permissible to use a hammer and brass drift or flush set and a rivet gun to tap it

Size	PIN PROTRUSION LIMITS			
	Hi-lok/hi-tigue Pins		Lightweight Pins	
	Min	Max	Min	Max
5/32"-5	0.302	0.384	0.270	0.352
3/16"-6	0.315	0.397	0.280	0.362
1/4"-8	0.385	0.467	0.310	0.392
5/16"-10	0.490	0.572	0.370	0.452
3/8"-12	0.535	0.617	0.410	0.492
7/16"-14	0.625	0.707	0.475	0.557
1/2"-16	0.675	0.757	0.515	0.597

Table 3-2-5. Pin protrusion limits

TORQUE-OFF VALUES FOR HI-LOK COLLARS (IN-LBS)		
Size	Shear Collars	Tension Collars
5/32"-5	15-20	30-40
3/16"-6	25-30	40-50
1/4"-8	60-80	115-130
5/16"-10	130-160	200-250
3/8"-12	200-240	360-420

Table 3-2-7. Twist-off torque values for collars (collar twist-off torque is less than that shown in Table 3-2-6 for the equivalent size self-locking nut)

SELF-LOCKING NUT TORQUE (IN-LBS)	
Diameter	Interference Fit
5/32"	30-40
3/16"	40-50
1/4"	80-100
5/16"	145-200
3/8"	240-280

Table 3-2-6. Torque values for self-locking nuts

into the hole. Use care to protect the head and the surrounding structure.

2. Screw the collar onto the pin a minimum of two threads.
3. Tighten the collar using the appropriate tooling. If the pin turns while tightening the collar it can be held in place with a hex wrench.
4. Torque off the collar's wrenching device using a Hi-Lok ratchet and socket, ratcheting box end wrench (dogbone), power driver or hand-wrench.
5. Check for proper protrusion and head seating.

Alternate Installation

When access is not adequate to install a collar or the appropriate collar is not available, it is permissible to use self-locking nuts. Make sure to replace tension collars with tension nuts and shear collars with shear nuts. Torque nuts per aircraft manufacturer's specification. See Table 3-2-6 and Table 3-2-7.

Thread count cannot be used to check protrusion limits when using nuts because they have a lower profile.

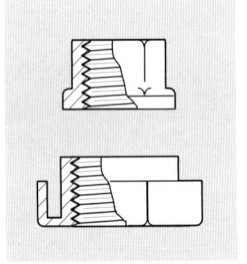

Figure 3-2-13. Nuts for alternate installation

When using a nut there is a requirement to use a minimum of one washer under the nut. The reason is to avoid interference with the nut and the shank/shank transition area. The washer(s) used must be compatible with the base metal. See Figure 3-2-13.

EXAMPLE: *Aluminum or cadmium-plated steel against aluminum. Stainless steel against stainless steel. No cadmium-plated washers against titanium.*

It may be necessary to ream the washer to size. Especially when using oversized Hi-Loks. Table 3-2-8 and Table 3-2-9 show how to measure the clearance under the installed pin head after installation using a feeler gauge.

Removal

Removing the collar. The preferred way to remove the collar is to unscrew it. This can be accomplished by the use of several different tools: Vise Grips®, Shop-made Hi-Lok pliers, grip pliers (Snap-on), 8-point 1/4 or 5/6 inch sockets. Another way is to use a collar shaver for the appropriate size pin. The least desirable way is to use a collar splitter or a chisel.

Using a collar splitter is not recommended because of the damage it can cause to the surrounding structure. It can also elongate the hole if not backed-up. That would require the use of oversized pins for replacement.

Removing the pin. Once the collar has been removed, the pin can be removed by tapping the threaded end with a (brass) drift and a hammer.

Alternate removal. If the collar cannot be removed, drill the head using a drill smaller than the shank diameter to avoid damaging the hole. Remove the head with a punch, then drive the pin out.

HEAD GAP TOLERANCES FOR PROTRUDING HEAD FASTENERS	
3/16"	0.004
1/4"	0.005
5/16"	0.006
3/8"	0.007
7/16"	0.008
1/2"	0.009

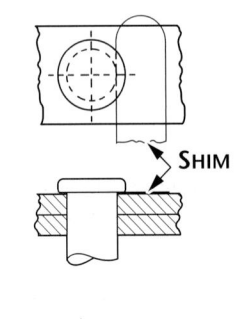

Table 3-2-8. Head gap tolerances for protruding-head fasteners

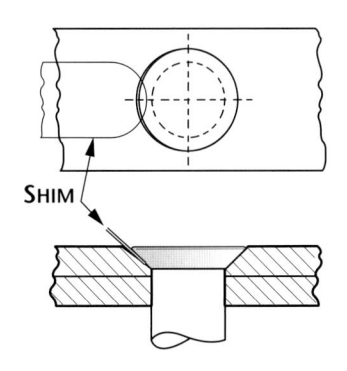

Materials and Processes | 3-35

HEAD GAP TOLERANCES FOR FLUSH HEAD FASTENERS	
3/16"	0.010
1/4"	0.011
5/16"	0.011
3/8"	0.011
7/16"	0.012
1/2"	0.012
9/16"	0.013

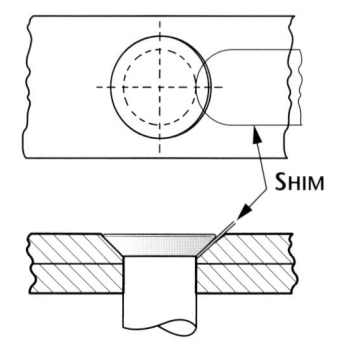

ACCEPTABLE, THE SHIM DOES NOT CONTACT THE SHANK OF THE FASTENER

UNACCEPTABLE, THE SHIM CONTACTS THE SHANK OF THE FASTENER

Table 3-2-9. Head gap tolerances for flush-head fasteners

Inspection

Properly installed fasteners will fall within the pin protrusion limits for hex drive bolts listed in Table 3-2-5. Pin protrusion is measured from sheet (or washer, if used) to the end of pin.

Protruding-head Hi-Loks must seat in at least one location on the periphery of the head with the remaining gap in accordance with the illustration and Table 3-2-8.

Flush-heads must be seated so that a .002 inch shim cannot be inserted between the fastener head and the countersink for more than 40 percent of the head circumference and contact the fastener shank. See Table 3-2-9. Consult the appropriate GN/MM, and/or the SRM for specific information about the aircraft on which the work is being performed.

Head dishing is allowed, provided there is no distinct ring (as shown on right side of Figure 3-2-14) and that it does not exceed the limits stated in the appropriate Structural Repair Manual.

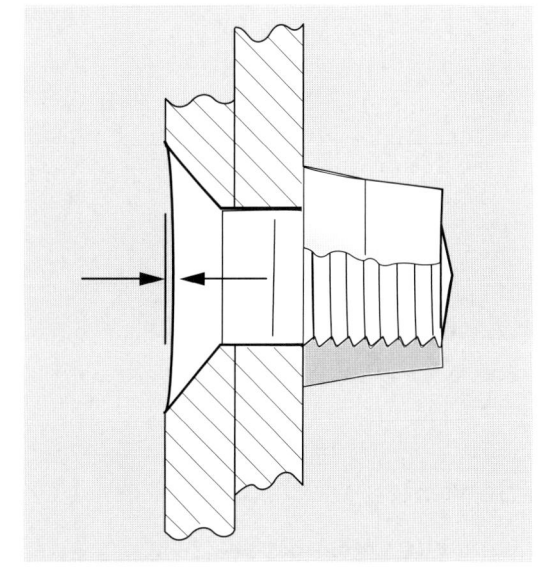

Hi-Lok Pin and Collar Identification

Hi-Shear identification charts (Figure 3-2-15) can run several pages and still be difficult to figure out. The best way to identify a fastener or nut that has become disassociated from its packaging is to compare it with a Mil Spec sheet. The Hi-Shear Corporation (*www.hi-shear.com*) maintains a complete set of Mil Spec sheets on its web site.

Hi-Lok Tools

There are standard installation tools available commercially. Most were developed for manufacturers, but will work equally well for maintenance personnel. Figure 3-2-16 shows a few shop-built tools that also come in handy if proper fabrication is within the abilities of shop personnel.

Figure 3-2-14. An example of head dishing

Hi-Lok ratchets are standard tools and can be purchased from any aviation tool distributor.

Helpful Hints

No matter if you have one or one-hundred holes to countersink, how do you get the proper countersink without having to drive the Hi-Lok into the hole to check it? Here are three different ways:

1. The first and most simple is to take a used Hi-Lok, chuck the threads in your drill motor, then, using a file or abrasive paper,

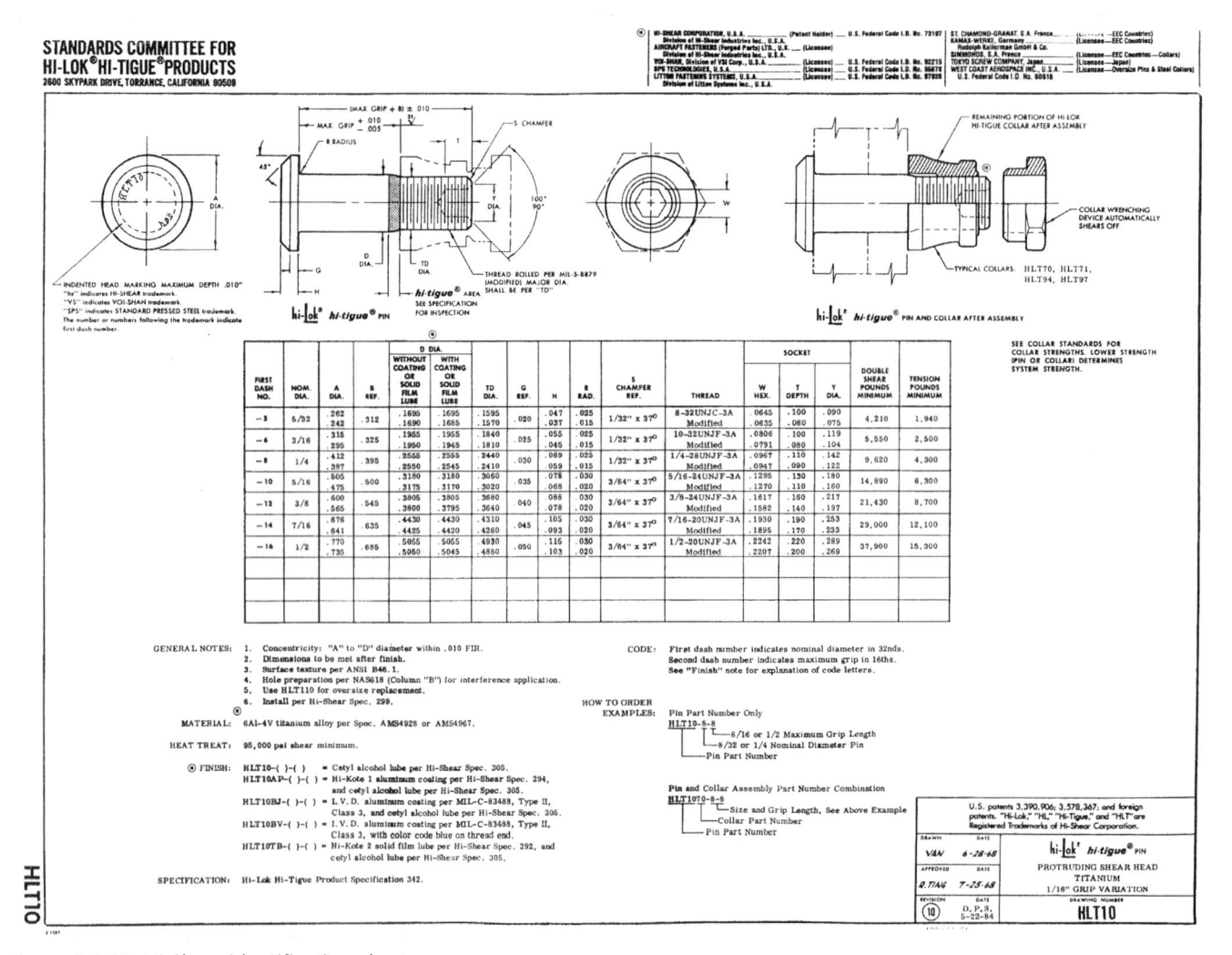

Figure 3-2-15. Hi-Shear identification chart

grind or file the down the shank leaving the head of the fastener intact and undisturbed. Now you have a Hi-Lok to put into the hole and check the countersink. You may want to bond a handle to the top of the head to help remove it from the hole. Don't throw the head away. Keep it so you can use it again.

2. The second way is to use a microstop countersink. You may be wondering how you can use a piloted countersink if the hole is larger or smaller than the pilot. If you are installing an oversized 3/16 Hi-Lok (remember the head size is the same, only the shank diameters are different) for a nominal size 3/16, prepare the hole with a number 13 drill then put a number 13 piloted countersink in your microstop. Set it for proper depth, using your ground down Hi-Lok pin as a gauge. Countersink the holes, then drill or ream them to the final size.

3. The third way is to get a piloted countersink the next size larger than the hole size and file/grind down the pilot the same way you did with the Hi-Lok. Make the pilot approximately .003 inch smaller than the hole to prevent friction heat from binding or galling. Don't throw it away either. Keep it in your toolbox for the next time you need it.

Lockbolts

Lockbolts are permanent-type fastener assemblies. The assembly consists of a headed pin with a collar swaged into annular locking grooves on the pin shank as shown in Figure 3-2-17. They are often incorrectly called *Huck bolts*.

Their primary use is in heavy structures requiring higher shear and clamp-up values than can be obtained from rivets. The lack of threads on the pin and collar make them less expensive to produce.

Pins. Lockbolts are made in various head styles, alloys and finishes. Figure 3-2-18 shows various head styles. They are available in *pull-type* and *stump-type* for shear and tension applications (Figure 3-2-19). Visually, the easiest way to differentiate between tension and shear pins is the number of locking groves. Tension pins normally have four locking grooves and shear pins have two locking grooves.

Pull-type pins are the preferred types. The installation tooling preloads the pin while swaging the collar. The surplus end of the pin, called the *pintail*, is then fractured. Dispose of the pintail properly so it doesn't turn into FOD.

The newest variations of lockbolts are called G.P. lockbolts. G.P. stands for *groove-proportioned*. The annular locking grooves vary in spacing and depth toward the pin end, which distributes clamping forces more evenly over the length of the grooved shank.

Collars. There are two types of collars made in different materials and styles. One type is for tension pins and one for shear applications. The styles are beaded collars and double-end collars, as shown in Figure 3-2-20. The figure also shows the correct installation direction of a beaded collar.

Substitution

In many cases, Hi-Lok and Hi-Tigue fasteners are used to replace lockbolt fasteners. The manufacturer's *Standard Processes Manual* (SPM) is the primary authority for substitutions. Information can also be found in the manufacturer's *Structural Repair Manual* (SRM).

NOTE: *A tension Hi-Lok is needed as a replacement for a tension Lockbolt.*

Installation

Hole preparation is the same as is used for Hi-Loks. Specifications will normally be for an interference fit in aluminum parts and clearance fit in steel, titanium or composite materials. Flushness requirements for flush pins are usually ± 0.003 inch.

The installation sequence, shown in Figure 3-2-21, is as follows:

1. The pin is placed in the hole from the back side of the work and the collar slipped on. The hold-off bead must be toward the gun. This allows the gun to preload the pin before swaging. The gun is then applied and the chuck jaws engage the pull grooves of the projecting pintail. The gun is held loosely and the trigger pulled.

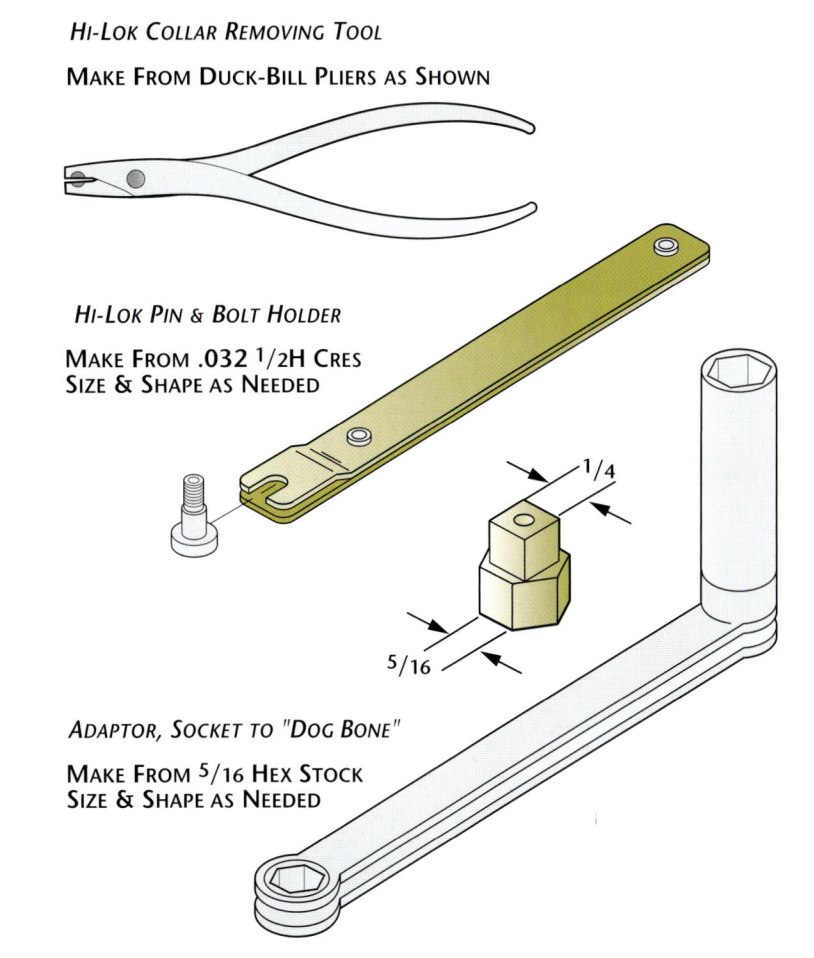

Figure 3-2-16. Hi-Lok tools

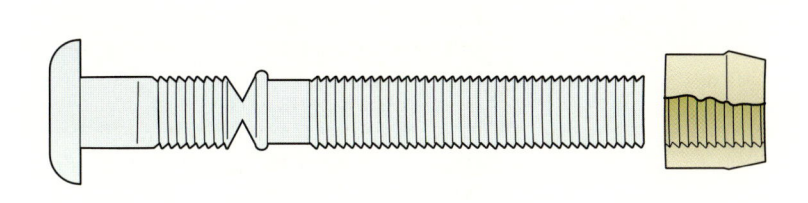

Figure 3-2-17. Lockbolts have serrations instead of threads.

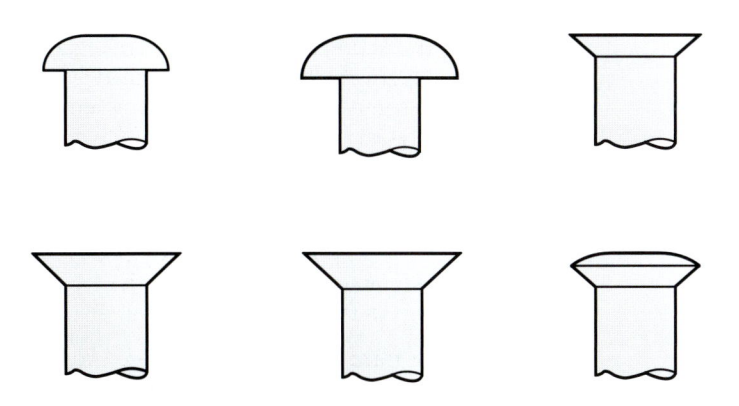

Figure 3-2-18. A variety of head styles

3-38 | Materials and Processes

SHEAR AND TENSION PULL TYPE PINS

SHEAR AND TENSION STUMP TYPE PINS

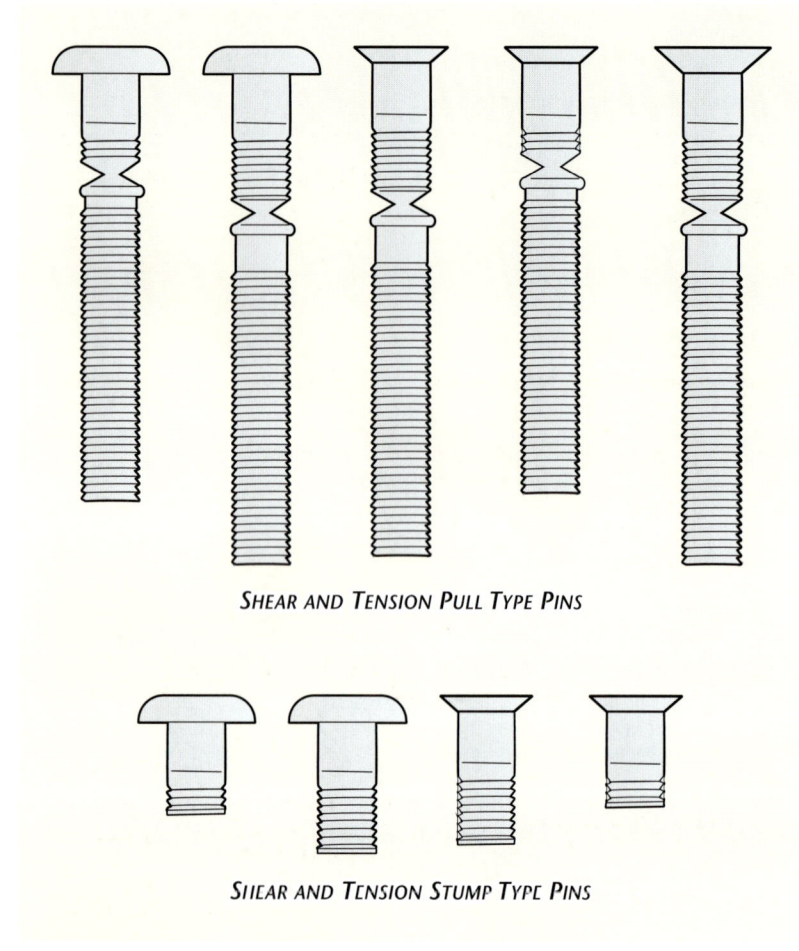

Figure 3-2-19. Shear and tension pull- and stump-type pins

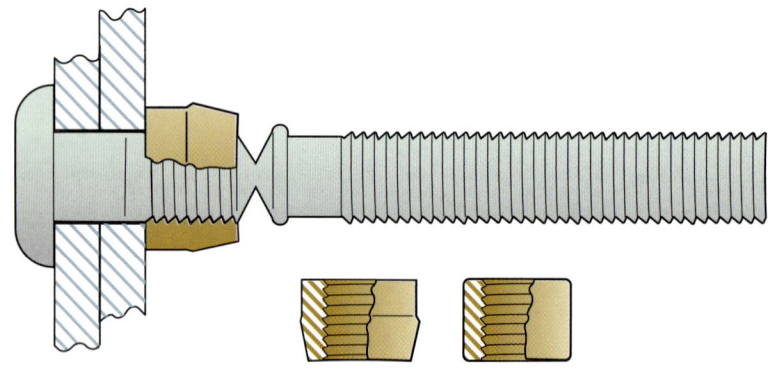

Figure 3-2-20. There are two types of collars: beaded (left) and double-end (right). Beaded collars are to be installed as shown on the lockbolt.

LOCKBOLT/COLLAR ACCEPTANCE CRITERIA				
Nominal Fastener Diameter	Y	Z	R	T
5/32"	0.324/0.161	0.136	0.253	0.037
3/16"	0.280/0.208	0.164	0.303	0.039
1/4"	0.374/0.295	0.224	0.400	0.037
5/16"	0.492/0.404	0.268	0.473	0.110
3/8"	0.604/0.507	0.039	0.576	0.120

Table 3-2-10. The dimensions of an installed collar

2. The initial pull draws the work up tight and pulls that portion of the shank under the head into the hole.
3. Further pull swags the collar into the locking grooves to form a permanent lock.
4. Continued force breaks the pin and ejects the pintail. The anvil returns and disengages from the swaged collar.

When installed, the collar will be swaged as shown in the cutaway illustration in Figure 3-2-22. When needed to correct for grip variations, washers may be used. A .032 inch or .064 inch thick washer is allowed by most SRMs. As always, use only galvanically compatible materials.

Grip lengths for tension pins are not the same as other fasteners. A correct grip gauge must be used (Figure 3-2-23). They have one side labeled for tension lockbolts and the other side for shear lockbolts.

Tooling

Lockbolt pullers are readily available from aviation tools supply companies, but are expensive. They normally have a nose-piece for one particular size fastener. Special rivet gun sets are used to swage collars on stump-type pins.

Inspection After Installation

Post-installation inspection (Figure 3-2-24) is a three-step process:

1. The head must be firmly seated.
2. The collar must be tight against the material and have the proper shape and size (Table 3-2-10).
3. Pin protrusion must be within limits.

Removal

The preferred method is to remove the collars, then drive out the pin. The best way is to mill off the collar with a cutter. If that is not possible, a collar splitter or small chisel can be used. Care should be taken to prevent hole elongation by backing up the pin with a suitable bar. Alternatively, the head may be drilled off.

ASP® Fastener System

ASP stands for Adjustable clamping force, Self-sustaining, Positive lock. Their primary use is in assemblies where common fasteners might crush softcore panels and fastener clamp-up tension must be limited.

The assembly consists of a pin, threaded sleeve, and a locking collar. A sleeve driver is used to install and torque the collar and the specified puller is used to set the locking collar and break the pintail.

They are removed by drilling out the locking collar and unthreading the sleeve. An ASP fastener is illustrated in Figure 3-2-25.

Eddie-Bolt®2

Boeing used a variation of the Hi-Lok in composite floor beams of its early B-777 aircraft. These fasteners look similar to Hi-Loks but have flutes formed on the threaded end of the pin. A companion threaded collar deforms into the flutes at a predetermined torque. This locks the collar into place. They also use a less expensive swaged collar. See Figure 3-2-26.

Either collar can, and should, be removed by un-screwing it if it is installed in composite material.

These fasteners can be identified by their head markings. Replacement fasteners are equivalent Hi-Lok fasteners.

> **CAUTION:** *Never use a collar splitter or chisel to remove a collar when installed in fiberglass or carbon graphic composite materials.*

PT® Fasteners

Boeing uses a variation of a Hi-Tigue Hi-Lok fastener in 747 aircraft wings. The difference is a unique head style (Figure 3-2-27). It is called a 70°-head radius lead-in bolt, BACB30PT, shortened to PT fastener. It is also known as a BRL fastener.

The 70° head is self-explanatory, and the radius lead-in refers to the generous radius (.030 ± .005) at the head/shank junction. These fasteners can be identified by their head markings.

Special countersinks are needed to cut the countersink wells. The Boeing numbers for the countersink cutters are ST1219Y-1CA or ST1219Y-1CB.

Jo-Bolts®

Jo-Bolt fasteners, and their variants, are blind fasteners composed of a nut, sleeve and a draw bolt. See Figure 3-2-28.

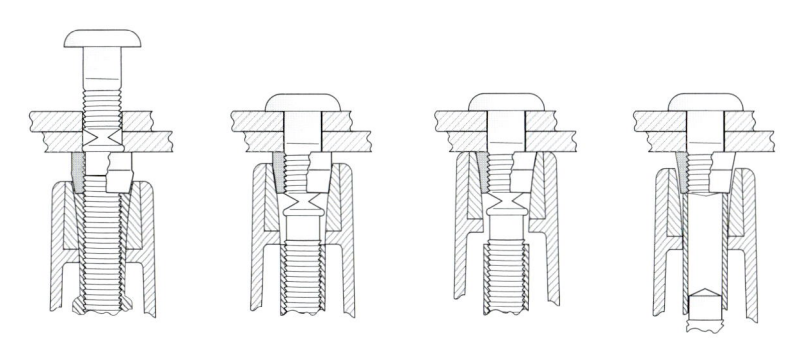

Figure 3-2-21. The installation sequence of a lockbolt

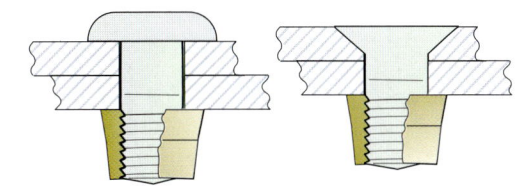

Figure 3-2-22. An installed lockbolt — the collar will swag down and fill the grooves as shown.

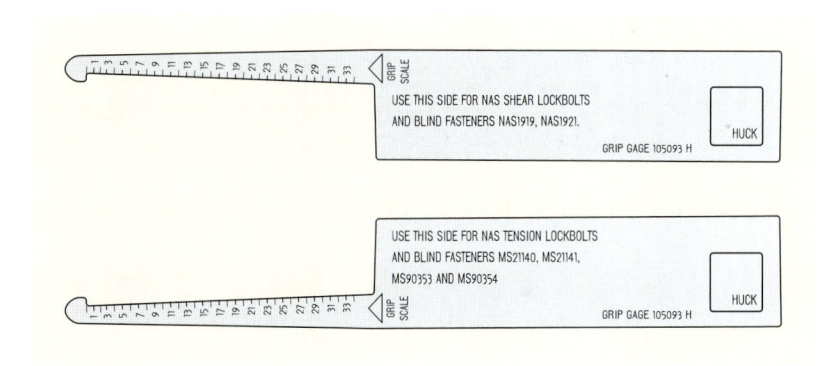

Figure 3-2-23. Lockbolt gauge

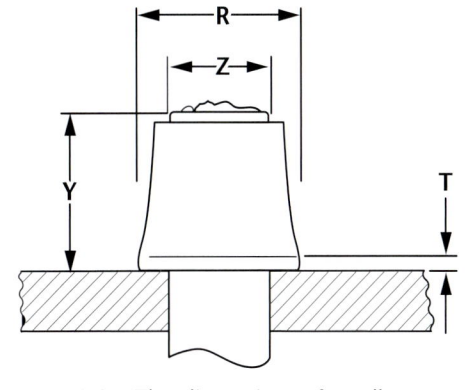

Figure 3-2-24. The dimensions of a collar on an installed lockbolt

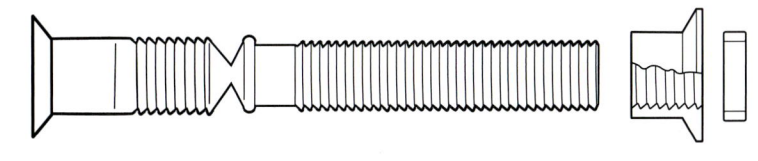

Figure 3-2-25. An ASP fastener

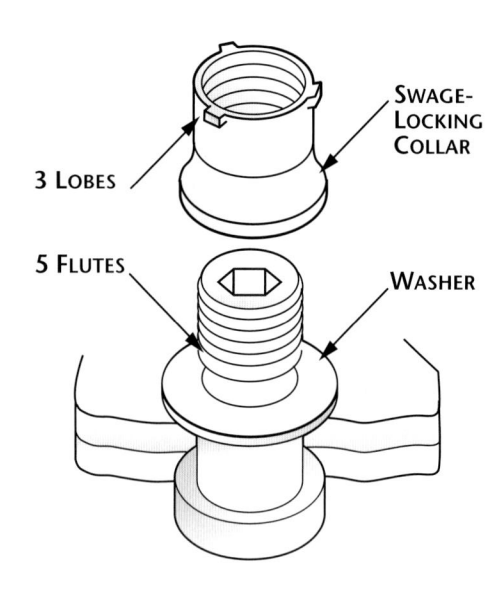

Figure 3-2-26. An Eddie-Bolt is designed to replace HiLok fasteners in composite floors.

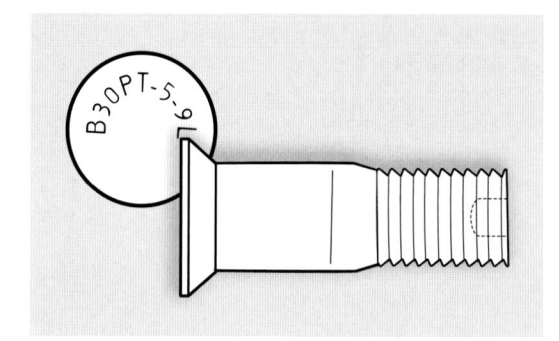

Figure 3-2-27. The PT fastener requires a special countersink because of its 70° head.

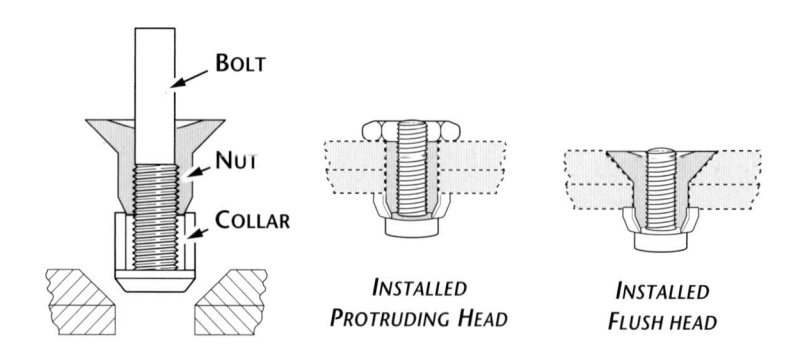

Figure 3-2-28. Jo-Bolts have been in use for some time. They are installed in a reamed hole.

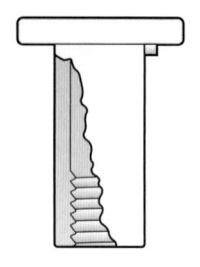

Figure 3-2-29. Rivnuts, originally designed for attaching rubber de-ice boots, have been around since WWII. They are still in use.

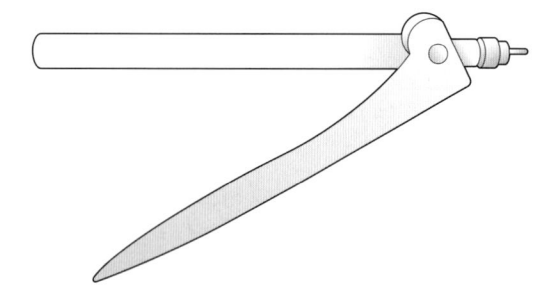

Figure 3-2-30. A notcher is used to cut the keyway that keeps a Rivnut® from rotating.

The nut resembles a conventional screw of a bolt which has been drilled through lengthwise and tapped with a left hand thread. There are no external threads and the shank end has a conical tip to receive the sleeve.

The sleeve is a short collar which is forced over the shank of the bolt on installation.

The bolt, or *center core*, is used to draw the sleeve into the installed position and continues to retain the sleeve for the life of the fastener. The bolt has left hand threads and driving flats on the threaded end. A break-off relief allows the driving portion of the bolt to break off when the sleeve is properly seated. They are installed in precisely sized holes by using either the supplied adaptor or installation tool to hold the nut stationary and rotate the core bolt.

The newest variants are the COMPOSI-LOK®, VISU-LOK®, RADIAL-LOK® and the OSI-BOLT™. These are brand names and the fasteners are made for specific applications.

The lengths of most Jo-Bolts are the same as tension lockbolts and will need the same grip gauge. COMPOSI-LOKs use a different standard (tenths of an inch) and require a completely different grip gauge.

Rivnut® Fasteners

The Goodrich Rivnut is an internally threaded sleeve having a flush or shallow protruding head. They can also have an open or closed end. Rivnuts are installed by crimping from one side. They provide a threaded hole into which machine screws can be used for screw attachments. Rivnuts also serve to hold parts together. Where a flush fit is required, the countersink head style is used. A standard Rivnut is illustrated in Figure 3-2-29.

Rivnuts were originated by the Goodrich Rubber Company for the attachment of rubber de-ice boots. They were soon found to be very handy for other purposes, such as the installation of fairing, trim and lightly loaded fittings which must be put on after an assembly is completed. Rivnuts of steel alloy are made for uses where increased tensile and shear strength are required.

They are valuable for attaching parts which require frequent removal. A good feature of the Rivnut is that installation exerts only a compressive force, thus it does not have a tendency to split the materials being joined

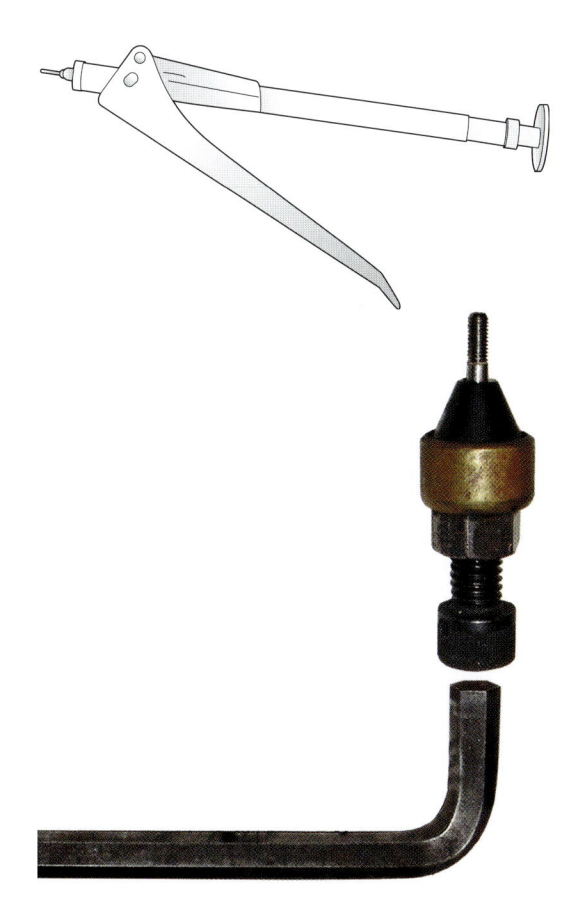

Figure 3-2-31. The two types of Rivnut® installation tools in common use

Keyway preparation. Most Rivnuts have a formed protrusion, or *key*, on the underside of the head. After the hole is drilled the key prevents the Rivnut from rotating. A keyway or notch must be cut in the material to accommodate this key. It is made with a key cutting tool called a notcher (Figure 3-2-30).

Installation. Rivnuts are installed with an upsetting tool, or puller. Blind heading occurs when the mandrel retracts, or spins, pulling the threaded portion of the Rivnut shank toward the work. This forms a bulge around the unthreaded shank area where the wall is thinner. This bulge locks the Rivnut securely in place. There are two types of installation tools in common use, hand and wrench (Figure 3-2-31). Many technicians are familiar with the common hand-operated lever type. This type has a *rotating* threaded mandrel on which the Rivnut is screwed. Heading occurs when the lever is squeezed. The mandrel will rotate to disengage the threads of the Rivnut when the knob is pulled outward. Care must he taken during installation to assure the key and notch are properly aligned, or the Rivnut will loosen and spin. The wrench type is self explanatory.

SLEEVbolt® Fasteners

SLEEVbolt assemblies are the evolutionary development of Taper-Lok bolts. These fasteners can be identified by their head markings. SLEEVbolt assemblies are used, on the newer Boeing aircraft, in the same locations that Taper-Lok fasteners had been used.

The assembly consists of a tapered bolt in an expandable sleeve. The sleeve is internally tapered and externally straight. The assembly is installed in a standard tolerance straight hole. During installation, the bolt is forced into the sleeve. It expands the sleeve, which fills the hole. Straight tooling used to drill and ream the holes cost far less than tapered tooling.

Taper-Loks are high-strength bolts with a taper of 1/4 inch per foot. They are usually used in high stress areas of fuel tanks. When installed they look similar to Hi-Loks. The most obvious difference is the lack of the hex recess at the threaded end. These fasteners can be identified by their head markings (Figure 3-2-32).

They are installed in precision-reamed, tapered holes, with a controlled interference fit. The interference fit compresses the material around the hole, resulting in excellent load transfer, fatigue resistance and sealing. The companion nut has a captive washer, and no additional washer is required.

Hole preparation. Flat-head Rivnuts require only *the proper size hole*. Flush Rivnut installations can be made into either countersunk or dimpled sheet. Metal thinner than the Rivnut head requires a dimple.

Recommended hole sizes are shown in Table 3-2-11.

Rivnuts should be a snug push-fit into their hole. Satisfactory installation requires good hole preparation, removal of burrs and holding the sheets in contact while heading.

Rivnuts are selected according to the thickness of material and the size of screw to be used. The part number identifies the type of rivnut and the maximum gap with which it can be used.

RIVNUT RECOMMENDED HOLE SIZES		
Rivnut Size	Drill Size	Hole Tolerance
No. 4	5/32	0.155 - 0.157
No. 6	No. 12	0.189 - 0.193
No. 8	No. 2	0.221 - 0.226

Table 3-2-11. Rivnut recommended hole sizes

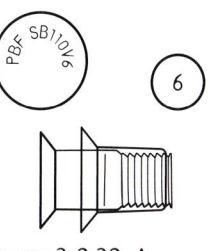

Figure 3-2-32. A Taper-Lok fastener

New Taper-Lok bolt installation or rework of a Taper-Lok hole is not to be attempted on aircraft structure without prior training. Pre-installation proof of tooling must be made on a test plate.

Removal and reinstallation of an existing Taper-Lok bolt for maintenance do not require special training. However, care must be used to make sure that each bolt is reinstalled in its respective hole.

Section 3

Drilling

In any complex skill, there are many tricks of the trade—techniques and desirable practices that can only be learned through experience. A multitude of small details, when performed properly, contributes toward excellent workmanship. Each detail by itself is simple and must be learned. Good habits established early are better than bad habits to unlearn later.

One the first operations when accomplishing structural repairs is to locate and drill good fastener holes. *Drilling* is a simple matter of pushing a rotating twist drill through material at the desired point. However, the successful joining of critical and high-stressed parts requires top-quality holes. Wasted time and material will result from inaccuracy or carelessness when drilling.

Feeds and Speeds

For efficient drilling, the speed and feed combination is important. If the speed is too slow unnecessary time is consumed. Also, there is an increased tendency to break smaller drills even with normal pressure. If the speed is too high the drill will overheat and become dull. As a general rule, the larger the drill the slower the speed and the smaller the drill the higher the speed. Often the equipment available does not adjust to the most desirable speed. Choose a portable drill, which has a speed most suitable for the twist drill size and the material to be drilled.

Technically, the speed of a drill means its speed at the circumference, in *surface feet per minute* (SFM). The recommended speed for drilling aluminum alloy is from 200-300 SFM, for mild steel: 30-50 SFM. In practice, this must be converted into revolutions per minute (r.p.m.) for each size drill. Drill r.p.m. charts are included in machinist's handbooks and many mechanic's handbooks. Drill r.p.m. may also be computed by use of the formula:

r.p.m. = 4CS/D

CS = The recommended cutting speed in SFM

D = The diameter in inches

EXAMPLE: *At what r.p.m. should a 1/8 inch drill turn to drill aluminum at 300 SFM?*

r.p.m. = 4CS/D = 4 X 300/.125 = 9600 r.p.m.

In real life, few will calculate the speed and feed rates during normal hand drilling.

With practice, a feel for drill speed and the pressure needed can be acquired. In general, drilling speed should be suited to the size of the twist drill as nearly as your equipment permits. If the drill speed is too high, the excess peripheral speed will cause burning of the outer corners of the drill. With high speed, it is difficult to maintain sufficient feed pressure to keep the drill cutting. This is especially so in drilling corrosion-resistant steels and titanium. The required drill feed pressure for corrosion-resistant steel and titanium is greater than for aluminum alloy. For example, at least 35 lbs. thrust is recommended for use of a No. 30 drill in corrosion-resistant steel and 56 lbs. for a No. 10 drill. The drill feed pressure should be applied steadily all the way through the metal so that the drill will continue to cut and not spin in the hole. Spinning will work-harden the metal at the bottom of the hole, dull the drill bit and cause the familiar trouble of burned drills. Table 3-3-1 is a drill size chart that gives hole sizes in decimal numbers.

Excessive pressure may result in breaking of the drill or elongation of the hole. Smaller drills will actually bow under too much pressure, causing off-center drilling. Because of the ease of penetrating aluminum alloys, feeds up to three times those for steel may be used.

A well-formed spiral chip will be produced if the feed and speed are correct, the drill is straight and properly sharpened.

Chips may tend to pack in the flutes when drilling in thick material and the drill needs to be withdrawn and cleared.

Drill feed pressure should be relieved as the drill starts to break through the work. If this is not done it may cause a large burr to be formed, the drill to be bent or broken, the drill chuck to mar the surface or the hole to be damaged.

Remember these general rules:
- Big drill, low speed, high pressure
- Small drill, high speed, light pressure
- Hard material, lower speed, higher pressure

STANDARD TWIST DRILL SIZES

Designation	Diameter (In)	Area (sq. in.)	Designation	Diameter (in.)	Area (sq. in.)	Designation	Diameter (in.)	Area (sq. in.)
1/2	0.5000	0.1963	3	0.213	0.03563	3/32	0.0938	0.00690
31/64	0.4844	0.1843	4	0.209	0.03431	42	0.0935	0.00687
15/32	0.4688	0.1726	5	0.2055	0.03317	43	0.0890	0.00622
29/64	0.4531	0.1613	6	0.204	0.03269	44	0.0860	0.00581
7/16	0.4375	0.1503	13/64	0.2031	0.03241	45	0.0820	0.00528
27/64	0.4219	0.1398	7	0.201	0.03173	46	0.0180	0.00515
Z	0.413	0.1340	8	0.199	0.03110	47	0.0785	0.00484
13/32	0.4063	0.1296	9	0.196	0.03017	5/64	0.0781	0.00479
Y	0.404	0.1282	10	0.1935	0.02940	48	0.0760	0.00454
Z	0.397	0.1238	11	0.191	0.02865	49	0.0730	0.00419
25/64	0.3906	0.1198	12	0.189	0.02806	50	0.0700	0.00385
W	0.386	0.1170	3/16	0.1875	0.02861	51	0.0670	0.00353
V	0.377	0.1116	13	0.185	0.02688	52	0.0635	0.00317
3/8	0.375	0.1104	14	0.182	0.02602	1/16	0.0625	0.00307
U	0.368	0.1064	15	0.1800	0.02554	53	0.0595	0.00278
23/64	0.3594	0.1014	16	0.1770	0.02461	54	0.0550	0.00238
T	0.358	0.1006	17	0.1730	0.02351	55	0.0520	0.00212
S	0.348	0.09511	11/64	0.1719	0.02320	3/64	0.0473	0.00173
11/32	0.3438	0.09281	18	0.1695	0.02256	56	0.0465	0.001698
R	0.339	0.09026	19	0.1660	0.02164	57	0.0430	0.001452
Q	0.332	0.08657	20	0.1610	0.02036	58	0.0420	0.001385
21/64	0.3281	0.08456	21	0.1590	0.01986	59	0.0410	0.001320
P	0.323	0.08194	22	0.1570	0.01936	60	0.0400	0.001257
O	0.316	0.07843	5/32	0.1563	0.01917	61	0.0390	0.001195
5/16	0.3125	0.07670	23	0.1540	0.01863	62	0.0380	0.001134
N	0.302	0.07163	24	0.1520	0.01815	63	0.0370	0.001075
19/64	0.2969	0.06922	25	0.1495	0.01755	64	0.0360	0.001018
M	0.295	0.06835	26	0.1470	0.01697	65	0.0350	0.000962
L	0.29	0.06605	27	0.1440	0.01629	66	0.0330	0.000855
9/32	0.2813	0.06213	9/64	0.1406	0.01553	67	0.0320	0.000804
K	0.281	0.06202	28	0.1405	0.01549	1/32	0.0313	0.000765
J	0.277	0.06026	29	0.1360	0.01453	68	0.0310	0.000755
I	0.272	0.05811	30	0.1285	0.01296	69	0.0292	0.000670
H	0.266	0.05557	1/8	0.1250	0.01227	70	0.0280	0.000616
17/64	0.2656	0.05542	31	0.1200	0.01131	71	0.0260	0.000531
G	0.261	0.05350	32	0.1160	0.01057	72	0.0250	0.000491
F	0.257	0.05187	33	0.1130	0.01003	73	0.0240	0.000452
E 1/4	0.2500	0.04909	34	0.1110	0.00968	74	0.0225	0.000398
D	0.246	0.04753	35	0.1100	0.00950	75	0.0210	0.000346
C	0.242	0.04600	7/64	0.1094	0.00940	76	0.0200	0.000314
B	0.238	0.04449	36	0.1065	0.00891	77	0.0180	0.000254
15/64	0.2344	0.04314	37	0.1040	0.00849	78	0.0160	0.000201
A	0.234	0.04301	38	0.1015	0.00809	1/64	0.0156	0.000191
1	0.228	0.04083	39	0.0995	0.00778	79	0.0145	0.000165
2	0.221	0.03836	40	0.0980	0.00754	80	0.0135	0.000143
7/32	0.2188	0.03758	41	0.0960	0.00724			

Note: Designations are in fractions of an inch, in standard twist drill letters, or in standard twist drill numbers, the latter being the same as steel wire gauge numbers.

Table 3-3-1. Drill size chart

Drill Lubrication

Normal drilling of sheet material does not require lubrication. However, lubrication should be provided for all deeper drilling. Lubricants serve to assist in chip removal, which prolongs drill life, insures a good finish and dimensional accuracy of the hole. It will not prevent overheating. The use of a lubricant is always a good practice when drilling castings, forgings or heavy-gauge stock. A good lubricant should be thin enough to help in chip removal and still stick to the drill.

For aluminum, titanium and corrosion-resistant steel, a *cetyl alcohol* based lubricant is the best. Cetyl alcohol is a non-toxic, fatty alcohol chemical and is produced in liquid, paste and solid forms. The solid stick and block forms quickly liquefy at drilling temperatures.

For steel, a sulfurized mineral *cutting oil* is superior. Sulfur has an affinity for steel, which aids in holding the cutting oil in place. In the case of deep drilling, the drill should be withdrawn at intervals to relieve chip packing and to insure that the lubricant reaches the point. As a general rule: if the drill is large or the material hard, use a lubricant.

Drills

There are a wide variety of drill bits available, with specialty bits for many specific jobs. Figure 3-3-1 shows some commonly used drills. Drill (A) is a jobber's-length drill with a reduced diameter shank and a 59° split-point. Drill (B) is a 135° split-point, high-speed, high-helix drill designed especially for aluminum. The high-helix angle makes the cutting edge a sharper angle. The flutes have more relief than normal, which reduces chip clogging. Drill (C) is a standard 135° split-point aircraft extension drill.

Split-point. A split-point is created by a double grinding technique that reduces the heel drag by grinding part of the heel away. Figure 3-3-1 (D) and (E) shows two views of a split point. At the same time, the sharpening stone grinds away a very small part of the cutting edge of the drill. Additionally, a small part of the web is ground back, reducing the web thickness. The end result is a better angle for starting a hole in flat sheet metal. It reduces walking and drill chatter as the drill point exits the back side of the sheet.

High-speed steel drills can withstand temperatures nearing the critical range of approximately 1,400°F (full cherry red) without losing their hardness. These are the industry standard for drilling metal (aluminum, steel, etc).

CoVan® drills are especially designed for hard, tough metals like corrosion-resistant steel and titanium. The shank is longer and the webs thicker than standard drills. These drills are expensive and should be treated with care.

Drill and Hole Sizes

Drill diameters are grouped by three size standards: number, letter and fractional. The decimal equivalents of standard drill sizes are shown in Table 3-3-1.

Drill sizes for rivet holes should be the smallest size that permits easy insertion of the rivet. This is about 0.003 inch greater than the largest tolerance of the shank diameter. The recommended clearance drills for the common rivet diameters are shown in Table 3-3-2. These should be memorized. Hole sizes for other fasteners will normally be found on work documents, prints or in manuals.

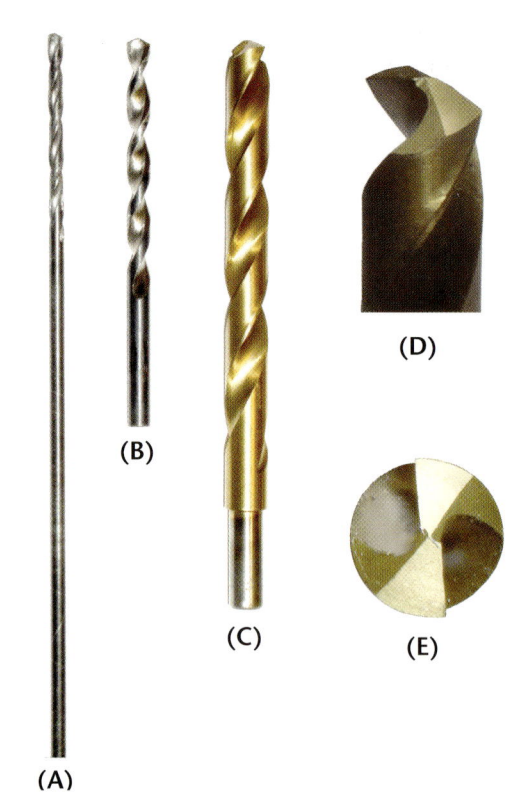

Figure 3-3-1. (A) is a standard jobber's-length drill, (B) is a special high-helix drill for aluminum, while (C) is an aircraft extension drill. (D) and (E) are two views of a 59° split-point.

Extension Drills

Extension drills are widely used for drilling holes in locations where it is necessary to reach through small openings or around projections. These drills, which come in 6- and 12-inch lengths, are high-speed drills with spring-tempered shanks.

Extension drills are ground to a special notched point, which reduces end thrust to a minimum. When using extension drills, always:

- Select the shortest drill that will do the job. It is easier to control.

DRILL SIZE FOR VARIOUS RIVET DIAMETERS			
Drill	Rivet	Drill	Rivet
No. 40	3/32 inch	No. 11	3/16 inch
No. 30	1/8 inch	No. 2	7/32 inch
No. 21	5/32 inch	F	1/4 inch

Table 3-3-2. Drill size for various rivet diameters

- Check the drill for straightness. A bent drill will make an oversized hole and may whip, making it much more difficult to control.
- Be sure to keep the drill under control. Extension drills smaller than 1/4 inch must be supported by a drill guard made from a piece of tubing or spring to prevent whipping.

Drilling the Hole

Holes drilled with hand-held drill motors will generally be larger than the drill or reamer. A steady hand and proper technique will help minimize wobbling and help insure good holes.

Holding the drill. Holding the drill properly is one of the first steps in learning to drill straight, true holes. See Figure 3-3-2.

- The center of pressure must be concentric with the drill rotational center line.
- The drill must be held perpendicular to the surface being drilled.
- The drill must be steadily supported.

Starting the drill, normal drilling. In normal drilling operations *pencil line accuracy* is all that is required and should be practiced. The procedure is as follows:

- Measure and layout the locations carefully and mark with crossed lines.

  NOTE: *The chisel edge is the least efficient operating surface element of the twist drill because it does not actually cut; but, instead squeezes or extrudes the work material.*

- Place the drill point at the center of the crossed lines, perpendicular to the surface, and with light pressure, start drilling slowly. Stop drilling after a few turns and check to see if the drill is starting on the mark. It should be, but if not, it is necessary to walk the hole a little by pointing the drill in the direction it should go and rotating it carefully and intermittently until properly lined up.

- For holes 3/16 inch and larger, pilot-drilling is recommended. Select a drill equal to the width of the chisel edge of the final drill size. Avoid using too large a pilot drill since this would cause the corners and cutting lips of the final drill to be dulled, burnt or chipped. It will also contribute to chattering and may cause the drill motor to stall.

- Enlarge each pilot-drilled hole to final size.

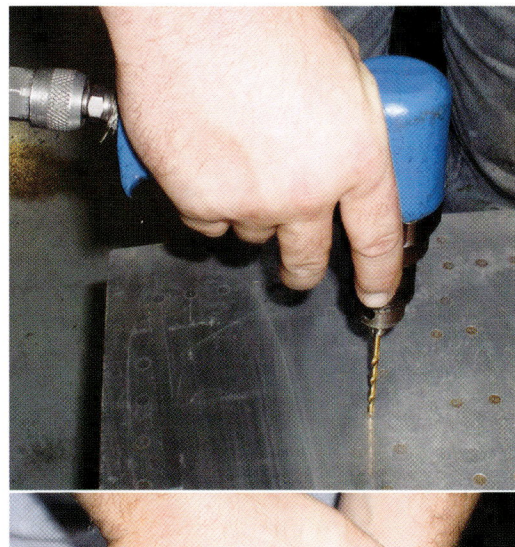

Figure 3-3-2. The proper way to hold and handle a drill

Starting the hole, precise location. Precise location of drilled holes is sometimes required. When locating holes to close tolerances, accurately located punch marks will need to be made. If a punch mark is too small, the chisel edge of the drill may bridge it and *walk off* the exact location before starting. If the punch mark is too heavy, it may deform the metal and/or result in a local strain-hardening at the point where the drill is to start cutting. The best size for a punch mark is about the width of the chisel edge of the drill to be used. This will hold the drill point in place while starting. The procedure which will insure accurate holes is as follows:

- Measure and carefully mark layout locations with crossed lines.
- Use a sharp prick punch or spring-loaded center punch and magnifying glass to further mark the holes.
- Seat a properly ground center punch (120°-135°) in the prick punch mark and, holding the center punch perpendicular to the surface, strike a firm square blow with a hammer.

Materials and Processes

(A) DRILL BIT AND BUSHING

(B) STEP DRILL

(C) STEP REAMER

(D) BULLET REAMER

(E) STRAIGHT REAMER

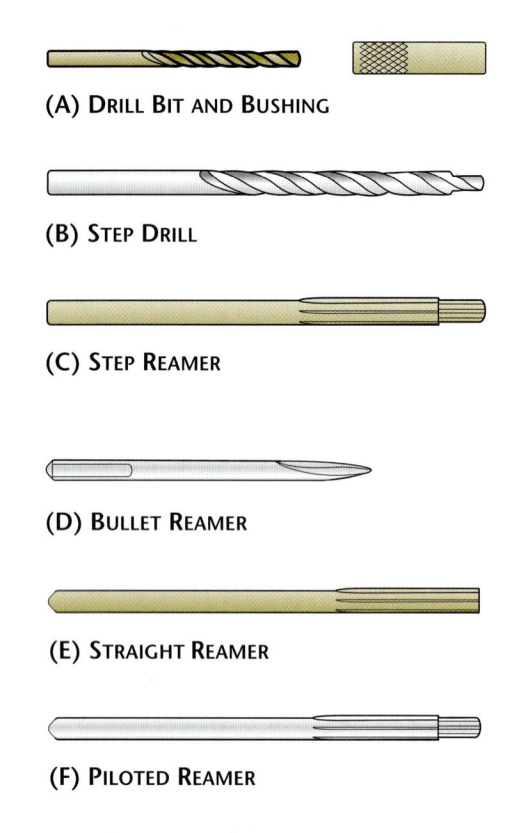

(F) PILOTED REAMER

Figure 3-3-3. Types of reamers

- Mark each hole with a small drill (1/16 inch) to check and adjust the location prior to pilot drilling.
- Pilot drill at each mark.
- Enlarge each pilot drill to final size.

Drilling large holes, precise location. Drilling large holes from existing locations is best done using the following steps and tooling. Tools have been developed to work together to achieve the process.

- A *drill bushing* is used to pilot drill holes. Bushings are sized for 1/8 inch, 3/16 inch or 1/4 inch drills. See Figure 3-3-3, illustration (A).
- *Core drills*, also called *step drills*, are used to "step" the hole to approximately 1/64" less than the final hole size. The aligning step diameter will match the pilot drill size. See Figure 3-3-3, illustration (B).
- Finish ream to size using a *step reamer*. See Figure 3-3-3, illustration (C). The aligning step diameter will match the core drill size. Reamers should be available for both clearance and interference fit hole sizes.
- Three or four fluted production *"bullet" reamers* are customarily used where finer finish and/or size is needed than can be achieved with a standard drill. See Figure 3-3-3, illustration (D).

- A *straight reamer* is used to size a hole to the finish diameter. See Figure 3-3-3, illustration (E). To use a straight reamer, the hole needs to be accessible enough to allow the reamer to be started and driven easily.
- A *piloted reamer* (shown in Figure 3-3-3, illustration (F)) is used where a reamer needs to follow the pilot hole closely, as in a bushing. Piloted reamers can generally remove more material than straight reamers.

NOTE: *Holes can also be enlarged by using a series of step reamers.*

Reamers

Reamers are made in far too many styles to cover here. They can be straight or tapered, solid or expansive, and come with straight or helical flutes. Reamers are used for enlarging holes and finishing them smoothly to a required size.

The cylindrical part of most straight reamers does not have cutting edges, but merely grooves cut for the full length of the reamer body. These provide a way for chips to escape, and a channel for lubricant to reach the cutting edge. Actual cutting is done on the end of the reamer. The cutting edges are normally ground to a 45° ± 5° bevel.

Reamer flutes are not designed to remove chips like a drill. Attempts to withdraw a reamer by turning it in a reverse direction is an unacceptable practice. Chips can be forced into the surface, scarring the hole.

Countersinking

Countersinking is the method of creating a conical well at an end of a hole to accommodate a fastener head or provide an area for a rivet head to be formed. These are produced by a tool appropriately called a countersink.

Countersinking is an important factor in the design of fastener patterns, as the removal of material in the countersinking process will necessitate an increase in the number of fasteners used to assure the required load-transfer strength. If done on metal less than a certain thickness, it may result in a knife edge with less than the minimum bearing surface or enlarging of the hole may result. The edge distance required when using flush fasteners is greater than when protruding-head fasteners are used.

A general rule for countersinking has been that the fastener head must be contained within the outer sheet. See Figure 3-3-4. In recent years

Figure 3-3-5. 82° Countersinks

countersunk holes have been responsible for many fatigue cracks in aircraft pressurized skin. A combination of countersinks too deep (creating a knife edge), number of pressurization cycles, fatigue, deterioration of bonding materials, and working fasteners has caused a high stress concentration leading to skin cracks and fastener failures. This has resulted in the reevaluation of countersinking and flush fastener installation procedures.

In primary structure and pressurized skin repairs, some manufacturers are currently recommending that the countersink depth be no more than 2/3 the outer sheet thickness, or down to .020 inch minimum fastener shank depth, whichever is greater. These will be reflected in fastener call-outs in the Maintenance Manual, applicable Structural Repair Manual or Engineering Documents.

Countersunk holes are usually called out on drawings by degree and maximum diameter. Other repair specifications may only call out a fastener type and size. Countersink sizes can be checked by measuring the diameter at the top with a scale or by inserting the appropriate fastener.

Rivet countersinks in critical areas (exposed to the airstream) should be cut so the finished rivet head is about .004 inch higher than the surface of the skin on smaller holes and .008 inch higher on larger holes. This differs from the .001-.003 inch that many have learned in the past. Rivet countersinks in non-critical areas (not exposed to the airstream) should be cut so the finished rivet head is .008 to .016 inch higher than the surface. Driving a rivet with the head above the surface assures the driving force being directed to the rivet head. Under no circumstances should one attempt to install a rivet that is flush or under flush before driving. This would result in a weak joint and/or unnecessary work-hardening of the surrounding skin. If flushness is critical the head may be shaved with a *rivet shaver*.

NOTE: *Restrictions may prevent some rivets from being shaved.*

There are many types of countersinks, but the type most commonly used has an included angle of 100°. Sometimes types of 82° or 120° are used to form countersunk wells. Figure 3-3-5 illustrates a standard 82° countersink bit. These are extremely difficult to use, as both depth and angle are hard to control.

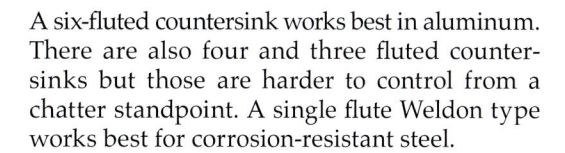

A six-fluted countersink works best in aluminum. There are also four and three fluted countersinks but those are harder to control from a chatter standpoint. A single flute Weldon type works best for corrosion-resistant steel.

The preferred method of countersinking is with a *microstop countersink*, commonly called a *stop-countersink* (Figure 3-3-6). It has an adjustable sleeve cage that functions as a limit stop, and holds the revolving countersink in a vertical position. Countersink cutters are replaceable. Cutters may have either a removable or an integral pilot that keeps the cutter centered in the hole. The pilot should be approximately .002 inch smaller than the hole size. It is recommended that you test adjustments on a piece of scrap material before countersinking repair or replacement parts.

NOTE: *The threaded countersinks can often be used in many offset drilling attachments, and angle drill motors can be used where standard tooling will not reach.*

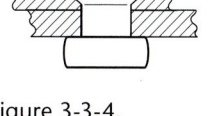

Figure 3-3-4. Countersinking

Figure 3-3-6. Microstop countersink

Figure 3-3.8. An air-powered angle drill
Photo courtesy of U.S. Industrial Tools

Figure 3-3.7. A snake drill can reach places inaccessible to standard drill motors.
Photo courtesy of U.S. Industrial Tools

Figure 3-3-9. Drill stops

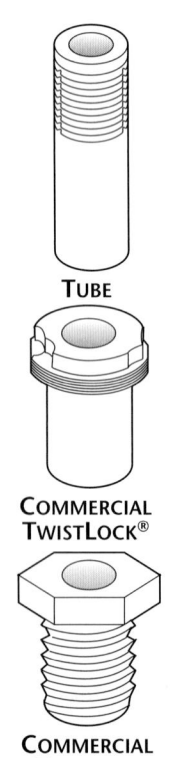

Figure 3-3-10. Drill bushings and guides
TUBE
COMMERCIAL TWISTLOCK®
COMMERCIAL THREADED

A *back-countersink* can be used where there is insufficient room for other tools. The bayonet diameter should match the hole size.

Freehand countersinking is needed where a microstop countersink cannot fit. This method requires practice. Holding the drill motor steady and perpendicular is as critical during this operation as when drilling.

Chattering is the most common problem encountered when countersinking. Here are some of the precautions that can minimize or even eliminate it:

- Use sharp tooling.
- Use a slow speed and steady, firm pressure.
- Use a piloted countersink with a pilot approximately 0.002 inch smaller than the hole.
- Use back-up material to hold the pilot steady when countersinking thin sheet metal.
- Use a cutter with a different number of flutes.
- Pilot drill an undersized hole, then countersink it, and then enlarge the hole to final size.

Drill Attachments and Aids

Because of the design of aircraft structure, some rivets, fasteners, etc. can be very difficult to install or remove. Several drill attachments have been designed to help make it possible to reach difficult locations.

Snake drill. A snake drill is a long flexible attachment that uses threaded drills installed on a straight or 90° angle head. Naturally, the threaded drills are called snake bits. Snake drills are not designed for continuous duty, but work very well in cases where it is impossible to use a standard drill motor. Figure 3-3-7.

Angle drills. Where it is only necessary to reach down into a space, like a wing bay, an angle drill is the answer. Using the same threaded drills as a snake drill, an angle drill can also make it possible to reach a seemingly impossible place. Both electric and air driven versions are available. The air driven versions are the smallest. See Figure 3-3-8.

Drill stops. A spring *drill stop* is shown in Figure 3-3-9. It is a wise investment. Properly adjusted, drill stops can prevent excessive drill penetration that might damage underlying structure or injure personnel. They also prevent the drill chuck from marring the surface of the material. They can be made from tubing, fiber rod or hard rubber if needed.

Drill bushings and guides. Many tools are available to aid in holding the drill perpendicular. They consist of a hardened bushing, which is anchored in a holder. The following drill bushing types are shown in Figure 3-3-10:

- Tube - Handheld in an existing hole
- Commercial TwistLock®
- Commercial threaded

Drill Bushing Holder Types

A drill bushing needs a holder before it can be used. There are many different kinds. A common type drill bushing is shown in Figure 3-3-11.

Standard. Standard bushing holders are fine for drilling flat stock or tubing/rod. They use insert-type bushings.

Egg cup. Improvement on standard tripod base allows drilling on both flat and curved material. Interchangeable bushings allow flexibility, and are normally available in tool rooms. This is the type of bushing shown in Figure 3-3-11.

Plate. Used primarily for interchangeable production components; *plates* use commercial bushings and self-feeding drills.

Arm. Used when drilling critical structure; *arms* can be locked into position. They use interchangeable commercial bushings that are normally available in tool rooms, or can be machined.

Sheet holders (Clecos®). Drilling and joining requires the parts to be held tightly in place and hole alignment to be maintained while the holes are being drilled and fasteners installed. Any separation between the sheets allows rivets to swell between them. Any misalignment of holes complicates or ruins the job. Clamps, threaded fasteners, sheet-metal screws or sheet metal holders can be used.

Sheet holders, traditionally called Clecos, can be quickly installed in or removed from a single side of the material. Figure 3-3-12 shows the standard spring type, along with installation pliers.

Clecos are color-coded and available in the following sizes:

Size	Color
3/32 inch and 7/32 inch	Silver/Zinc
1/8 inch and 1/4 inch	Copper
5/32 inch and 5/16 inch	Black
3/16 inch and 3/8 inch	Brass/Gold

Transfer pins. *Transfer pins* are used for back-marking hole locations when direct-marking or drilling is impractical. They are placed in an existing hole. The new part (doubler plate, etc.) is then placed over them. A light tap with a soft-faced hammer is then used to transfer the hole location onto the new part. They are normally sized the same as rivets (Figure 3-3-13).

Strap duplicators (hole finders). Three types of *strap duplicators,* also called *hole finders*, are shown in Figure 3-3-14. From top to bottom the figure shows a hole finder, a strap duplicator and a hole punch. They permit the marking of hole locations or drilling pilot holes from hidden holes in overlapping sheets or marking the location of the hidden hole.

Cautions for Safety

Protect your eyes. ALWAYS WEAR EYE PROTECTION WHEN DRILLING. Safety glasses are the minimum, with goggles or a face shield being added when drilling overhead or when conditions dictate.

Protect your hands. Secure your work. Never attempt to drill small pieces unless they are securely clamped. Never brush chips away with your hands. Be sure to check to see that your fingers are not in line with the drill when it breaks through the work.

Protect your back. Time spent setting up for drilling is a wise investment. Your work posture should be adjusted so that, as much as possible, you are in a balanced, non-straining position.

Protect your chin. Large, slow-speed drill motors develop enormous torque. Don't lean over them. Use auxiliary handles when available to help keep the motor under control.

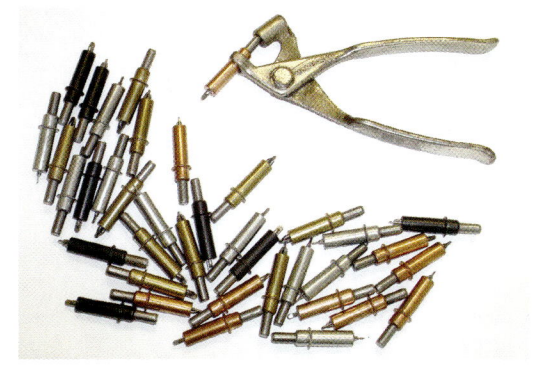

Figure 3-3-12. Clecos

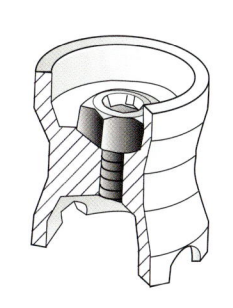

Figure 3-3-11. Bushing holder

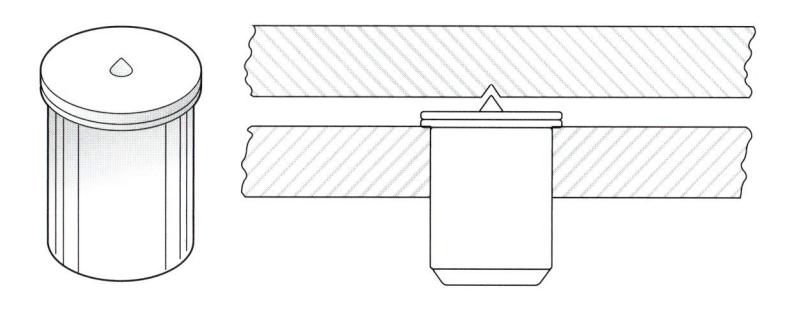

Figure 3-3-13. Transfer pins

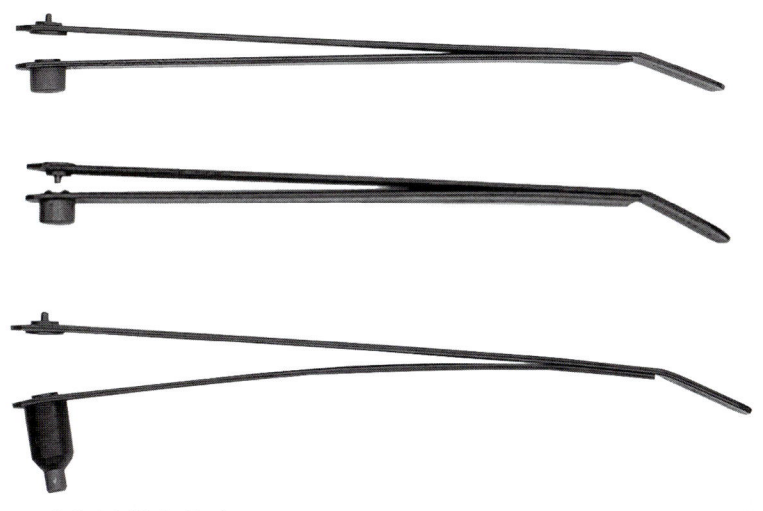

Figure 3-3-14. Hole finders

Photo courtesy of U.S. Industrial Tools

Figure 3-3-15. Hole saws

Protect your coworker and yourself. Avoid letting the drill penetrate the work far enough to damage anything beyond. Always investigate to see what the drill point is apt to hit when it goes through the work. Structural damage at thoughtless moment or by careless operators can occur. It can be expensive to repair as well as being embarrassing. Personnel injures caused by careless operators are even more unwelcome and may result in serious consequences for the operator.

Rules for Drilling

- Layout lines should be clear and sufficiently heavy to clearly indicate the point of drilling. They should be made with a Sharpie® or flow pen. Hard lead pencils and ball point pens will emboss aluminum which may leave stress risers. Scribed lines must never be used.

- Never disregard minimum edge distances or fastener spacing. Recommended edge distances are found in Manufacturer's Structural Repair Manuals and vary with the application. Normal spacing is four to six times the fastener diameter, with three diameters the absolute minimum.

- Parts to be drilled must be held tightly together. Sufficient clamps, Clecos or temporary fasteners should be used to prevent the parts from separating during the drilling operation.

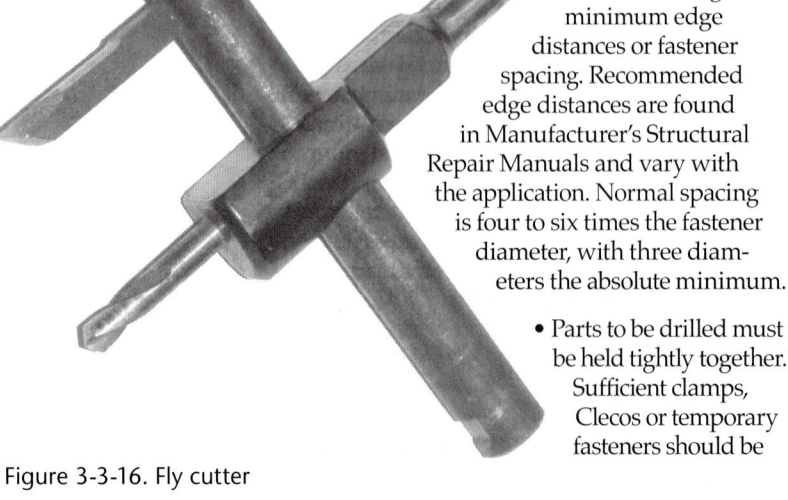

- Parts to be drilled in a vice must be clamped in such a position as to prevent them from bending when pressure is exerted from the drill motor.

- Check the drill size (number, fraction or letter) before drilling.

- Check the first hole drilled before continuing the drilling operation.

- Never drill a hole without first looking behind the material to be drilled.

- Never drill out a fastener without first making sure it can be replaced.

- Be sure that the drill is held perpendicular to the surface being drilled.

- When deburring holes, care must be taken not to deburr too deeply.

Summary

Drill safely. Protect your eyes & fingers.

Use only sharp, straight drill bits. They are necessary to produce true holes.

Use the right size. Shear forces can only be transferred when the fastener shank is contacting the hole sides.

Start on the mark. Turning the chuck several times by hand will make a slight indentation to show you where the drill is cutting.

Start straight. Check to see that the drill is held at 90° to the surface of the material. Drilling aids are available to help when needed.

Drill straight. Apply pressure in line with the center of rotation.

Control the drill. Never allow the drill to break through so far that the chuck marks the surface, the drill damages something on the far side, or the drill breaks. These may be avoided by using a drill stop.

Remove the burrs. Burrs should always be removed, as they will prevent proper sheet face contact. Care must be taken not to remove stock from around the hole, as the resulting countersink effect will reduce the bearing area and weaken the joint.

Hole Cutters

Drilling holes in sheet metal is limited to hole sizes less than 1/2 inch. Anything larger and

Figure 3-3-16. Fly cutter

the drill starts to chatter and will not produce a round hole.

There are two types of hole cutters used to cut holes in sheet metal. These are the circular hole saw and the fly cutter. Each has its advantages and disadvantages.

Hole saw. The circular hole saw, Figure 3-3-15, has a pilot bit used to center the hole cutter and provide stability when the circular saw contacts the sheet metal. Hole saws can be difficult to steady and sometimes cut a rough hole, particularly if they are dull. A drill press, instead of a hand drill, should be used when possible.

Sometimes the pilot bit in a hole saw will rout out the center shaft and make the hole saw wobble slightly. To get a cleaner cut with a hole saw, first drill a pilot hole with a hand drill, then replace the drill in the shaft with a piece of steel rod. Use a lubricant.

Fly cutter. The fly cutter (Figure 3-3-16) is an adjustable hole cutter. The pilot bit functions the same as it does on the circular hole cutter. The radius is adjusted by moving the arm with the cutting bit attached. When using this type of cutter, use a drill press with the sheet metal backed by a piece of wood, and feed the bit very slowly into the metal.

A cleaner hole can result by using a rod, as explained in the preceding section on hole saws. It is also safer.

> **NOTE:** *When using a hole saw or a fly cutter, ALWAYS clamp down the work piece, NEVER hold it with your hand. If the cutters grab, and they will, the sheet metal work becomes a large rotating knife and will cause serious cuts to your hands and arms.*

Hole Punches

Punching is the preferred method of making a large hole. Not only is it safer and cleaner, it is also faster and more accurate than drilling. Most larger shops will have some type of punching equipment. A common tool is a *turret punch*. See Figure 3-3-17. These have been around for years and are a staple in many shops.

Operation of a turret punch is simplicity itself: Just rotate the proper size dies to the front, insert the sheet and pull the handle down. The result is a nice, clean hole.

Whitney punch. A Whitney punch is another item that has been in use for many years. Figure 3-3-18 shows why they are popular. They come with a variety of different punches, and are simple to operate and maintain. A Whitney

Figure 3-3-17. A turret punch

punch is especially useful for making rivet holes in thin sheets. A good example is found on the trailing edges of light airplanes, where both control surface skins are riveted together with a filler strip between. The punch will not bend the thin sheet metal.

Section 4
Riveting

Rivets are the oldest mechanical fastener used to fasten metals together. When installed properly, they are an excellent and effective fastener. A *rivet* may be defined as "a pin of malleable material that becomes a fastener when the ends are upset to form heads."

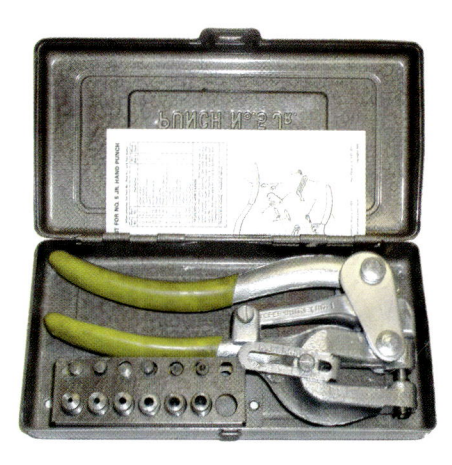

Figure 3-3-18. A Whitney hand punch with interchangeable punches

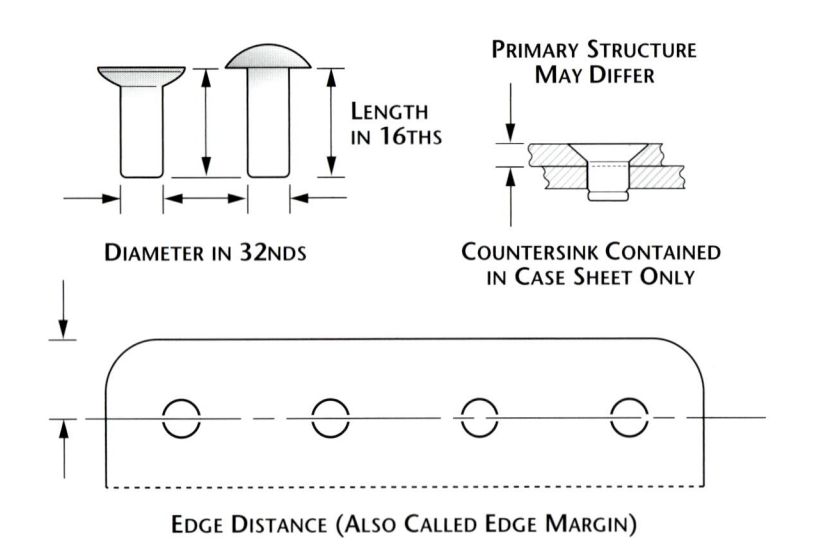

Figure 3-4-1. A quick reference of basic riveting information

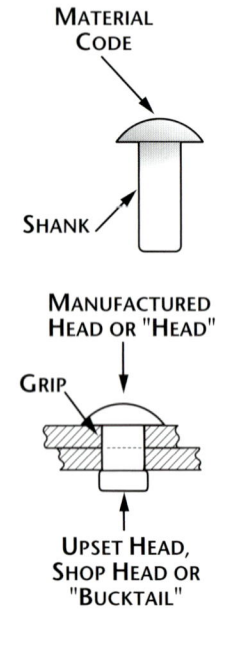

Figure 3-4-2. Rivet terminology

Usually, the first head is formed when the rivet is manufactured, and the second head, the *shop head*, is formed at the time of driving. The evolution of rivets starts with hand-formed heads on pin-shank material, progressing to machine-formed heads.

Aluminum rivets are commonly used for aircraft structure because of their lightweight and resistance to corrosion. Monel rivets are used for joining corrosion resistant steel and titanium parts because they have comparable strength but greater ductility than these metals.

Today's standard rivet may not be the standard of tomorrow. Manufacturers are constantly looking for ways to improve rivets and riveting practices. Each new generation of aircraft introduces rivets of improved head design. This helps enable the manufacturer to produce stronger, lighter aircraft and reduce production time. This evolutionary process will ultimately obsolete some rivets as others take their place.

Under certain flight conditions, the maximum design strength of every rivet is required. Proper hole fill is essential in attaining design strength. When a rivet does not fill the hole, it is the weak link in a chain of several fasteners. Rivets cannot fill the holes properly unless the hole is round, perpendicular and of correct diameter. Good workmanship is essential in drilling and installing rivets.

Good habits will allow one to rivet in a manner which prevents damage to the airplane itself. This requires constant attention and the personal desire of the AMT doing the riveting. The damage that may be done with the rivet gun can be readily understood when you consider that the power of the rivet gun is sufficient to upset the end of a rivet and could exert this same pressure against the surface of the airplane. Driving action must be confined to the rivet alone. Damage of this sort, even though only occasional, can cause uncountable hours of rework or replacement of parts.

Rivets

The information in Figure 3-4-1 is a quick reference of basic riveting information. Details are explained throughout the text.

Rivet terminology. The terms used for the various parts of a rivet are shown in Figure 3-4-2.

Rivet Cutters

A standard tool for a sheet metal technician is a pair of rivet cutters. They have a rivet length gauge that allows several rivets to be cut to the exact same length. They are not ideal for cutting all rivets in an an entire job, but are designed for when occasionally a different length rivet is needed. To operate them, simply insert the rivet, set the gauge and squeeze the handles (Figure 3-4-3).

Rivet part numbers. Rivets differ in style, material and size. In order to identify them, we use an alpha/numeric coding system. This code describes the rivet by basic part number, material and size. These numbers are used on work documents and manufacturers' prints.

The basic part number identifies the head style and may be based on a *Military Specification (MS)*, *National Aerospace Standards (NAS)* or a manufacturer's assigned code. Many previously used *Army-Navy (AN)* standards are not currently being used and have been replaced by MS standards. For example, an AN426 rivet is now a MS20426 rivet.

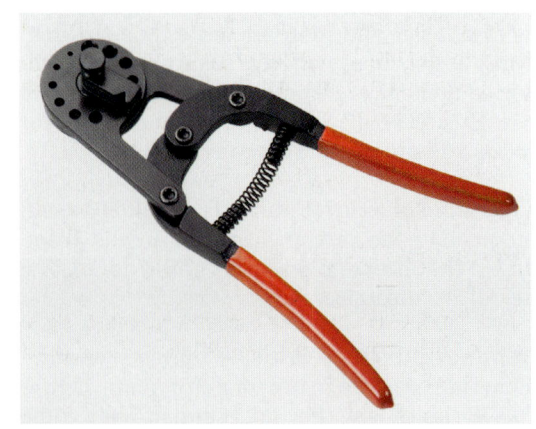

Figure 3-4-3. A pair of rivet cutters can save time and eliminate a lot of walking back and forth.

Alloy Code: A
Alloy: 1100 Or 3003 Aluminum
Head Marking: None
Shear Strength: 10 KSI
Non-structural uses only

Alloy Code: B
Alloy: 5056 Aluminum
Head Marking: Raised Cross
Shear Strength: 28 KSI

Alloy Code: AD
Alloy: 2117 Aluminum
Head Marking: Dimple
Shear Strength: 30 KSI

Alloy Code: D
Alloy: 2017 Aluminum
Head Marking: Raised Dot
Shear Strength: 38 KSI (when driven as received, 34 KSI when re-heat treated)

Alloy Code: DD
Alloy: 2024 Aluminum
Head Marking: Two Bars
Shear Strength: 41 KSI (must be driven in "W" condition (ice-box))

Alloy Code: E
Alloy: 7050 Aluminum
Head Marking: Raised Ring
Shear Strength: 43 KSI (replacement for DD rivet to be driven in "T" condition)

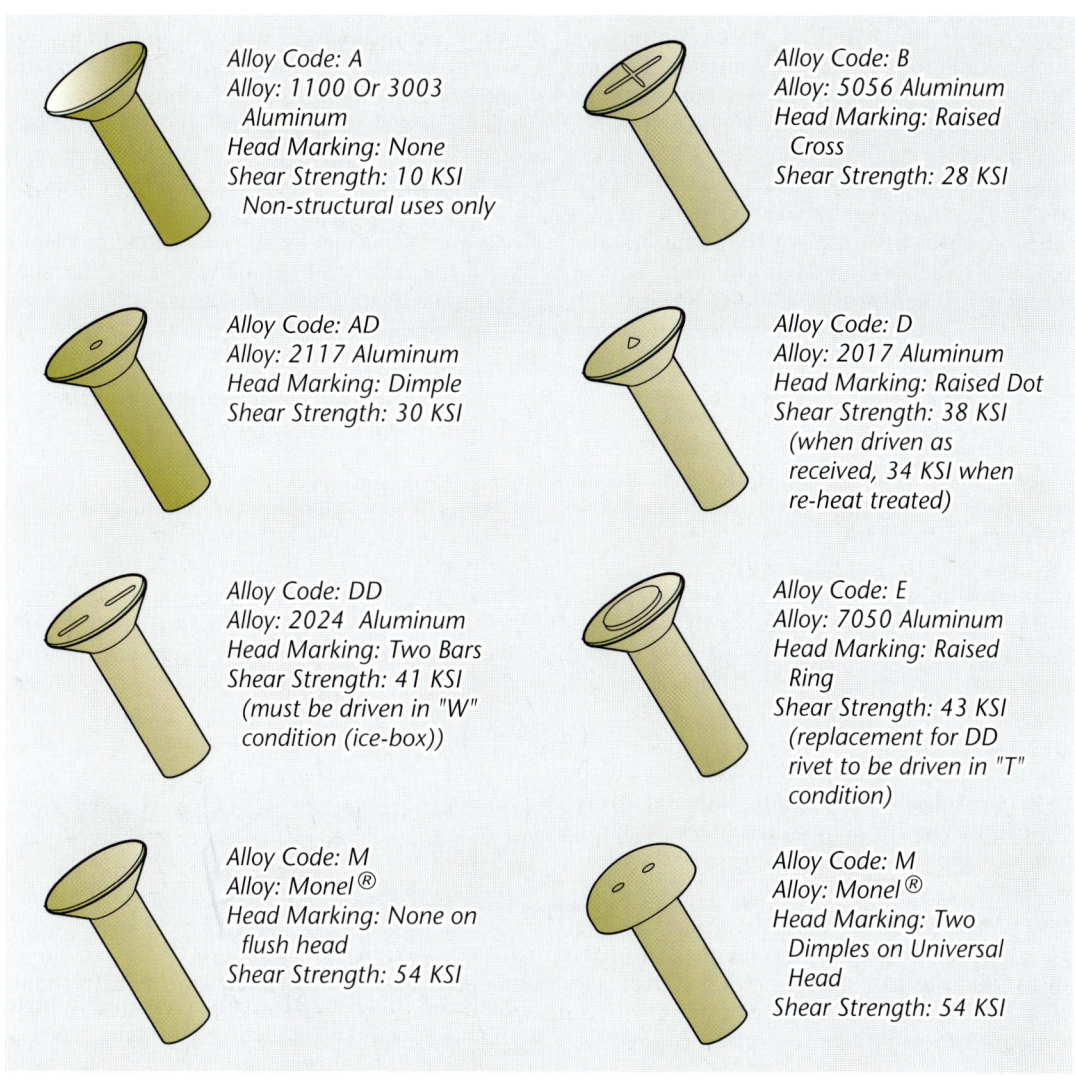

Alloy Code: M
Alloy: Monel®
Head Marking: None on flush head
Shear Strength: 54 KSI

Alloy Code: M
Alloy: Monel®
Head Marking: Two Dimples on Universal Head
Shear Strength: 54 KSI

Figure 3-4-4A. Standard rivet alloy code markings

The material/alloy letter code identifies the material and alloy from which the rivet is made. The most common alloys used in aircraft structures are shown in Figure 3-4-4A. Every mechanic involved with structural repair should be familiar with these codes and know their strength relationships.

The rivet size is indicated by diameter, then length. The diameter is in 1/32 of an inch and the length is in 1/16 of an inch. Thus, a size 6-6 indicates a diameter of 6/32 (3/16) inch and a length of 6/16 (3/8) inch.

EXAMPLE: *MS20426DD6-6*

Aircraft Rivets

Rivets can be divided into two general categories, those with protruding heads and those with flush heads.

Protruding-head. *Protruding-head* rivets were copied from the steel rivets used by the construction industry. For many years we used round or button head rivets that looked like a half-sphere on a shank or brazier and modified brazier head rivets that looked like quarter-sphere on a shank. We now use universal and modified universal head rivets. These are the first choice for all riveting applications.

Flush-head. *Flush-head rivets* were needed as aircraft speeds became greater, placing a greater demand on aerodynamic smoothness. There were two methods to achieve this needed flushness. One was to manufacture a flush head rivet and install it in a countersink well or dimple. The other was to use a conventional protruding head or slug rivet and form the head by driving or squeezing into a tapered well (countersink). Manufactured heads have been made to fill wells from 80°-120°.

Rivet alloys. *Rivet alloys* in common use are shown in Figure 3-4-4a. The alloy marking on the rivet and its letter code should be memorized. The aluminum alloy number has minimal value and is seldom used or needed.

Monel rivets are used to fasten nickel-steel alloys, while steel parts are fastened with mild steel rivets. Magnesium is riveted with 5056 aluminum rivets. While 2017 rivets below 3/16 inch diameter can be driven as received, larger diameters (and all 2024 rivets) must be kept in dry ice or refrigerated until use. Otherwise, they must be reheat-treated just prior to installation. All 2024 rivets will age-harden after driving, reaching full hardness in about four days.

Rivet Types

The following styles of rivet constitute the highest percentage of rivets used in aircraft structures and components. Figure 3-4-4B illustrates these types.

Universal-head rivets. These were designed as a universal replacement for both the round- and brazier-head rivets. They were developed specifically for the aircraft industry. They look similar to modified brazier-head rivets.

Universal-head rivets have a flat area on the head one-half times the shank diameter, a head diameter twice the shank diameter and a head height approximately 42.5 percent of the shank diameter.

UNIVERSAL-HEAD RIVETS	
MS20470	Aluminum rivets
MS20615	Monel rivets
BACR15BB	Aluminum rivets (Boeing code)

Modified universal-head rivets. These rivets were developed for use in areas where aerodynamic smoothness is unimportant. They look like universal head rivets with the head diameter reduced. By reducing the outer diameter, a small weight savings is realized. Small reductions like this add up to many pounds and lighter aircraft.

Modified universal-head rivets share dimensions with the universal head rivets, the difference being the head diameter, which is 1.5 times the shank diameter.

MODIFIED UNIVERSAL-HEAD RIVETS
BACR15FT

Standard flush-head rivets. Standard flush-head rivets are an ideal compromise for use in dimpled structures but have an installed shear value that is much lower than a universal head rivet when installed in a countersink-well. The 100° angle is ideal for dimpling, and the nesting dimples contribute a portion of shear strength. The head size offers optimal shear/clamp-up strength ratio when used in this manner.

STANDARD 100° FLUSH-HEAD RIVETS	
MS20426	Aluminum rivets
MS20427	Monel rivets
BACR15BA	Aluminum rivets (Boeing code)

Reduced flush-head rivets. When the plate thickness could not contain the head of a rivet of the desired shank diameter, standard flush-head rivet head sizes were reduced to produce a *shear rivet*, in order to increase joint shear strength in thin skins. These rivets sacrifice *clamp-up* (tension) strength for increased shear strength.

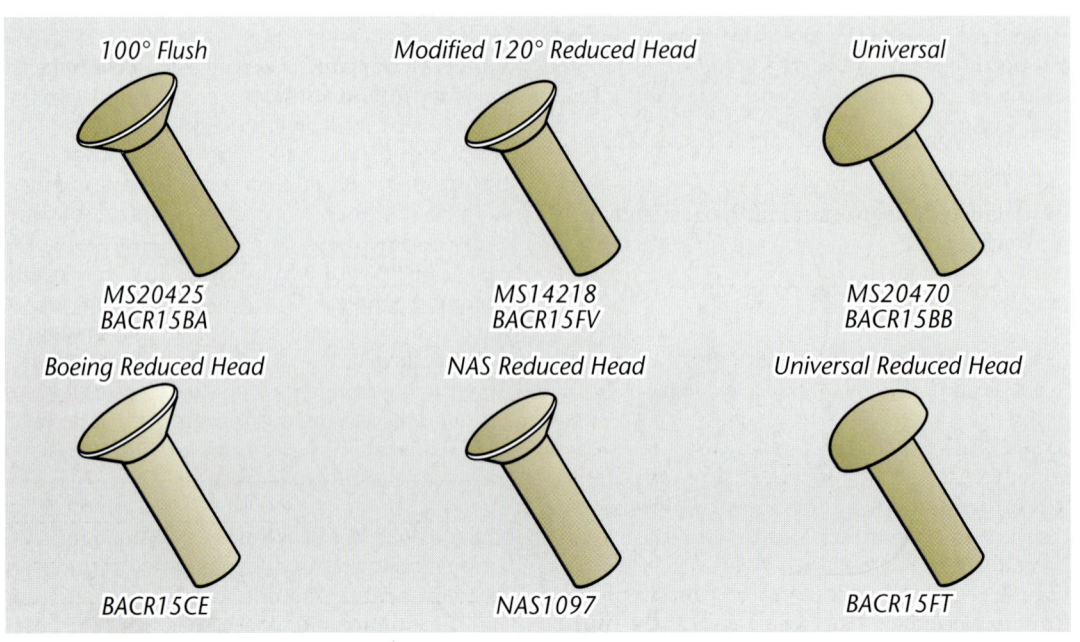

Figure 3-4-4B. Rivet types

REDUCED FLUSH-HEAD RIVETS	
NAS1097	Aluminum & Monel Rivets
BACR15CE	Aluminum & Monel Rivets

Modified 120° countersink rivets. Many styles of flush heads have been used over the years. One of the latest and more successful was developed by Frank Briles. It has a modified 120° head and is being used on several new aircraft. It is called the *Briles Fast Rivet*.

MODIFIED 120° COUNTERSINK RIVETS
MS14218
BACR15FV
Briles BRFZ Series Fast Rivet

Methods of Installing

Two primary processes are used to install solid rivets: squeezing with a pneumatic or hand squeezer, or driving with a rivet gun. Both accomplish the same objective.

Driving is done with a *rivet gun*. A rivet gun with the correct header (rivet set) must be held snugly against the head and perpendicular to the surface. A *bucking bar* of the proper weight is held against the opposite end. When the gun is triggered, the rivet is driven.

The dynamic of the driving process has the gun hitting (vibrating) the rivet and material, which causes the bar to bounce (counter-vibrate). These opposing blows (low frequency vibrations) squeeze the rivet, causing it to swell and then form the upset, or shop, head.

These skill elements must be learned and practiced to proficiently drive rivets:

- Holding and controlling the gun and/or bar in correct relationship to the material surfaces.
- Balancing the pressure of the gun and bucking bar.
- Triggering the gun the proper amount of time.

Countersunk flush riveting method. This is accomplished by cutting a countersink well of the required size (as covered in the section on drilling) and then installing the rivets. Remember to pay attention to minimum thickness to countersink.

Protruding-head riveting method. If two or more sheets are being joined, the standard practice is to place the factory head against the thinner sheet. This is the simplest method of all.

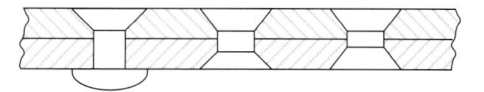

Figure 3-4-5. Several different types of driven rivets, including the NACA-type of rivet heading

NACA riveting method. NACA is an acronym for National Advisory Committee of Aeronautics, the predecessor of today's NASA.

A rivet installation technique known as the *NACA method* has primary applications in tank areas. To make a NACA rivet installation, the shank is upset into a 82° countersink. In driving, the gun may be used on either the head or shank side. The upsetting is started with light blows, then the force is increased and the gun or bar is moved on the shank end so as to form a head inside the countersink well. If desired, the upset head may be shaved flush after driving. See Figure 3-4-5.

The optimal strength is achieved by cutting the countersink well to the dimensions given in Table 3-4-1. Material thickness minimums must be carefully adhered to.

Slug rivets are sometimes driven into two 82° countersink wells when double flushness is required in tank areas. A flush-head rivet may also be driven into an 82° countersink well (100° one side, 82° the other).

Dimpling method. *Dimpling* is the process of making an indentation around a rivet hole so that the top of the rivet head will be flush. Dimpling removes no metal, and due to the *nestling effect*, gives a stronger joint than the non-flush type. A dimpled joint reduces the shear loading on the rivet and places more on the riveted sheets.

NOTE: *Dimpling is also done for flush bolts and other flush fasteners.*

Dimpling is required for sheets that are thinner than the minimum specified thickness

MINIMUM SHEET THICKNESS FOR COUNTERSUNK RIVET SIZE		
Rivet Size	Minimum Thickness	Countersink Diameter ±.005
3/32"	0.032	0.141
1/8"	0.040	0.189
5/32"	0.050	0.236
3/16"	0.063	0.288
1/4"	0.090	0.400

Table 3-4-1. Minimum sheet thickness for countersunk rivet size

DIMPLING AND SUB-COUNTERSINKING DEPTHS		
Rivet Diameter	Maximum Thickness of Outer (Face) Sheet	Minimum thickness of Inner Sheet
1/16"	0.028	0.032
3/32"	0.032	0.040
1/8"	0.040	0.050
5/32"	0.050	0.063
3/16"	0.063	0.071
1/4"	0.071	0.100

Table 3-4-2. Dimpling and sub-counter sinking depths

Figure 3-4-6. Countersink rivet dies for a squeeze riveter

Photo courtesy of U.S. Industrial Tools

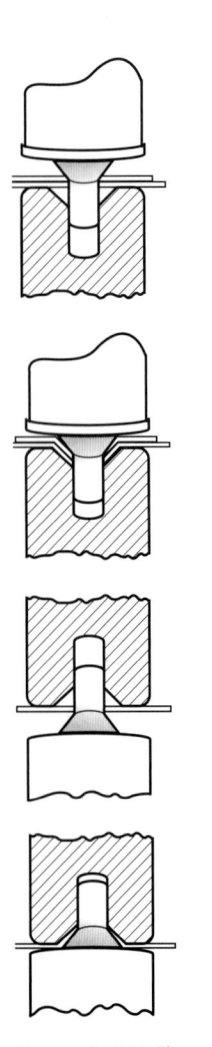

Figure 3-4-7. Shop-made countersink dies

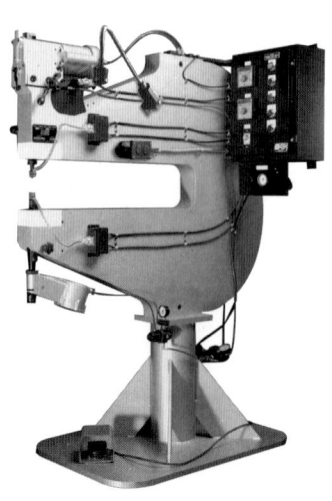

Figure 3-4-8. A large floor-mounted countersink press with heated dies

Photo courtesy of U.S. Industrial Tools

thin gap seals, wear strips and repairs for worn countersinks.

Sheet thicknesses for dimpling and sub-countersinks are specified in Table 3-4-2.

Dimpling Techniques

There are two primary ways of forming dimples— squeezing and drawing.

Squeezing. The preferred squeezing method uses a set of dies (Figure 3-4-6) and a suitable stationary pedestal or portable squeezer.

Drawing. The preferred drawing method involves the use of a flush rivet, or other suitable fastener, in such a way that it becomes a dimpling punch, forming metal into a countersunk with a draw die. This technique is used where accessibility does not permit squeeze dimpling, equipment is unavailable, or the job requires expediency.

The illustrations in Figure 3-4-7 show how dimples can be formed using shop-made tooling. A *countersink well* is cut into a rod (old bolt, etc.) or a piece of bar stock to form the draw die. A rivet (Monel preferred), bolt or Hi-Lok with the needed head size is used to form the dimple.

Whichever way you choose to form your dimple, there are several limitations and cautions that must be followed.

- Aluminum alloys heat-treated to T6, T62, T6511, titanium or magnesium MUST be *hot dimpled* using heated dies (Figure 3-4-8).
- Aluminum alloys that are not heat-treated (O condition), and treated T3 & T4 are dimpled at room temperature.
- The working surfaces of dimpling tools should be highly polished to improve metal flow. Some mechanics will also lubricate the tool faces before using them.

Dimple Inspection

To determine the quality of a dimple, it is necessary to make a close visual inspection. Several features must be checked:

- The rivet head should fit flush and there should be a sharp break from the surface into the dimple. The sharpness of the break is affected by dimpling pressure and metal thickness.
- Selected dimples should be checked by inserting a fastener to make sure that the flushness requirements are met.

for countersinking. However dimpling is not limited to thin materials. Heavier parts may be dimpled without cracking by specialized hot dimpling equipment. The temper of the material, rivet size and available equipment are all factors to be considered in dimpling.

100° combination pre-dimple and countersink method. Metals of different thickness are sometimes joined by a combination of dimpling and countersinking. A countersink well made to receive a dimple is called a *sub-countersink*.

These are most often seen where a thin web is attached to heavy structure. It is also used on

Cracked dimples are caused by poor dies, rough holes or improper heating. Both radial and circumferential cracks may form during dimpling.

Radial cracks. *Radial cracks* start at the edge and spread outward as the metal within the dimple stretches. They are most common in 2024-T3. A rough hole or too-deep dimple will cause such cracks. A small tolerance is usually allowed for radial cracks.

Circumferential cracks. Downward bending into the draw die causes tension stresses in the upper portion of the metal. Under some conditions, a crack, called a *circumferential crack*, may be created that runs around the edge of the dimple. Such cracks do not always show; they may be underneath the cladding. When found, they are cause for rejection. These cracks are most common in hot-dimpled 7075 T6 material. The usual cause is insufficient dimpling heat.

Team Riveting

Some jobs, such as driving rivets through a fuselage or tank, may require two persons for *team riveting*. Communication is essential during these operations. Normal conversation is not always possible. The traditional way of communicating has been by tapping. The bucker (person bucking the rivets) should tap on the structure to let the driver (person driving the rivets) know how the rivets look and what is needed. The driving code should be learned:

- One tap = Drive the rivet
- Two taps = Good rivet
- Three taps = Bad rivet

Today, two-way radios or other communication equipment are being used.

Installation

Rivets are the most widely used fastening devices for assembling aircraft. Large aircraft may contain more than a quarter of a million rivets. A sound riveted joint calls for skill on the part of the riveter. Some rivets are comparatively simple to drive, while others present a challenge. In every case, however, good riveting requires a careful setup before the actual driving begins. The ability to drive rivets with one continuous burst is the objective. It can only be developed by practice.

Tooling

Traditional tooling has not visibly changed from what was used in factories during WWII. However, significant changes have been made in rivet gun ergonomics. Reduced vibration rivet guns and bucking bars are available. They have been developed to reduce Carpal Tunnel Syndrome and enhance operator comfort.

Compression riveters. Commonly called *rivet squeezers*, these tools are one of the best ways to drive, or squeeze, a solid rivet. Available in a wide variety of sizes and styles, both hand and power operated, they are relatively inexpensive. They all use interchangeable tooling and can be used for many different jobs. See Figure 3-4-9.

Rivet hammer (rivet gun). The *rivet guns* used should be high-quality *pneumatic hammers*. Well-made rivet guns should last for many years of continuous usage. A plunger in the bore of the gun strikes the rivet header, then impact is transmitted through the header, through the rivet, and into the bucking bar. The structure being riveted deflects slightly so that the inertia of the bar upsets the rivet shank. Figure 3-4-10 shows the most common sizes of air hammers (rivet guns).

Slow-hitting rivet guns are the most common type. They strike from 900-2500 blows per minute.

Figure 3-4-9. The two most common types of compression riveters
Photo courtesy of U.S. Industrial Tools

Figure 3-4-10. The basic operation of short-stroke, medium-stroke and heavy-duty rivet guns is the same.

Photo courtesy of U.S. Industrial Tools

Materials and Processes

RIVET GUN COMPARISON							
Rivet Capacity		Gun Size Codes					Set Shank Diameter
Aluminum	Steel	Ingersol Rand	Chicago Pneumatic	Cleco	Atlas Copco	DAPT (APT/ Deutsch Jiffy)	
1/8"	3/32"	AVC 10	2X 4444RUS RA	E2AJ E2BWD	RRH-04P Recoilless	100,100B 200, 0200B	0.401
3/16"	5/32"	AVC 12	3X 4444RUS A	E3AJ E3BWD	RRH-06P Recoilless	300	0.401
1/4"	3/13"	AVC 13	4X 4444RUT A	E4BWB G4CF	NONE	400 LSSR-400	0.401
3/8"	5/16"	AVC 26	7X 4444RU RA	—	—	—	0.498

Table 3-4-3. Rivet gun comparison between manufacturers

These blows are slow enough to be easily controlled and heavy enough to do the job. These guns are sized by the largest rivet size they will continuously drive. The gun size reference often used is based on Chicago Pneumatic Company's old "X" series. A 4X gun (-8 or 1/4 inch rivet) is used for normal work. The less powerful 3X gun is used for smaller rivets in thinner structures. 7X guns are used for large rivets in thicker structures. See Table 3-4-3.

A rivet gun should upset a rivet in 1-3 seconds. With practice, you can soon determine how long the trigger should be held down. Driving force is adjusted by a needle valve on the handle. To avoid header damage, adjustments should never be tested against anything harder than a wooden block. If the best driving force cannot be obtained with this adjustment, a different size gun is needed. Too powerful a gun is hard to control and may damage the work. Force of the gun must be absorbed by the bucking bar and NOT the structure being riveted. On the other hand, if the gun is too light, it may work-harden the rivet before the head can be fully formed.

Figure 3-4-11 shows *rivet set-spring retainers*. NEVER pull the trigger on a rivet gun without a rivet set and retainer spring installed. Even then, don't pull the trigger without the rivet set being placed against something that will not damage the rivet set. A piece of 2 x 4 works well.

A quality rivet gun should have a teasing trigger that will hit harder the more it is depressed.

Header (Rivet Set)

An appropriate rivet set must be a correct match for the rivet being driven. The working face of a set should be properly designed and smoothly polished. Rivet sets are made of forged steel, heat-treated to be tough but not brittle.

Flush sets. Flush rivet sets come in various sizes. Many technicians will have several of them. You want to select the best match for your job. Smaller ones concentrate the driving force in a small area for maximum efficiency. Larger ones spread the driving force over a larger area, thus minimizing the potential to dent or mar thin plates and skins.

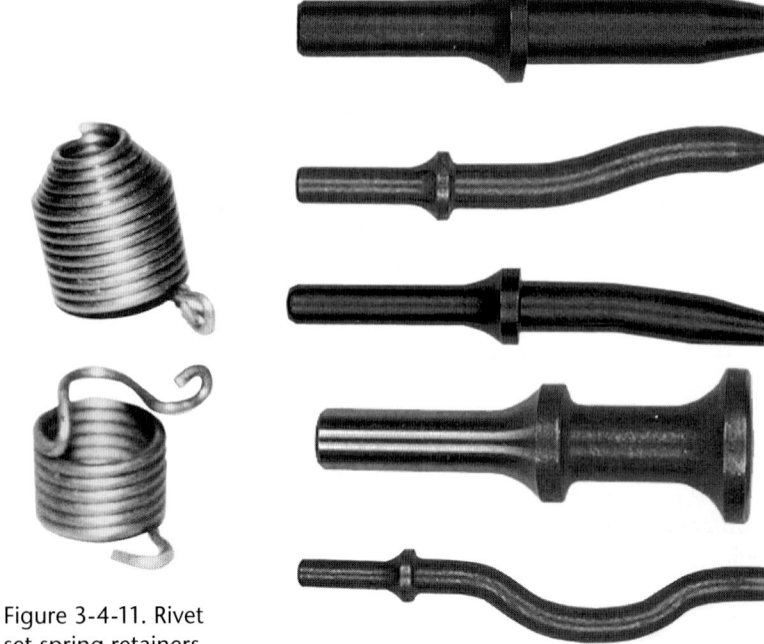

Figure 3-4-11. Rivet set-spring retainers
Photo courtesy of U.S. Industrial Tools

Figure 3-4-12. Rivet sets
Photo courtesy of U.S. Industrial Tools

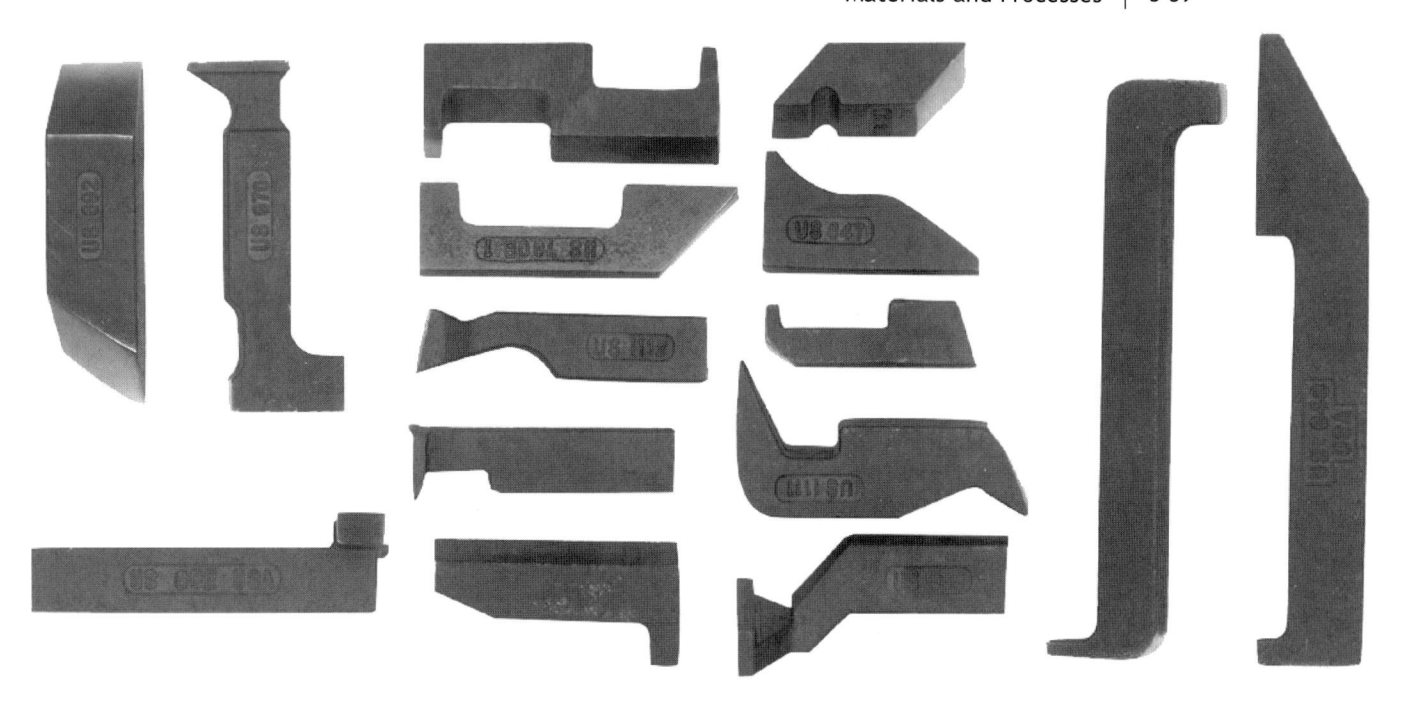

Figure 3-4-13. Bucking bars

Photo courtesy of U.S. Industrial Tools

Non-flush sets. Non-flush rivet sets should fit so as to contact about the center 2/3 of the rivet head. They must be shallow enough to allow for slight upsetting of the head in driving, and for some misalignment without eyebrowing (or smiling) the riveted surface. Care must be taken to match the size of the rivet. Too small a rivet set will mark the rivet, while too large will mark the material.

Rivet sets are made in a variety of styles. See Figure 3-4-12. The short, straight rivet set is best when the gun can be brought close to the work. Offset rivet sets may be used to reach rivets in obstructed places. Long sets are sometimes necessary when the gun cannot be brought close to the work because of structural interference. Rivet sets should be kept clean.

> **WARNING:** *Shop-made punches, chisels, etc. that do not have provisions for retainer springs are absolutely forbidden.*

Bucking Bars (Dollies)

Bucking bars come in a variety of shapes to suit different jobs. They are most often made from low-carbon, case-hardened steel. Bucking faces must be hard enough to resist indentation and remain smooth, but not so hard as to shatter. Sometimes, the more complicated bars must be forged or built up by welding.

A bar must be so shaped that a smooth face can be held at right angles to the rivet shank. Light sander marks are desirable in the bucking face of bars. If they are buffed to a high polish, they will slip off the rivet easily. A buffed surface also interferes with forming the rivet. All corners of a bucking bar should be carefully radiused so that it will not make tool marks on the work. See Figure 3-4-13.

When selecting a bucking bar, the first consideration is whether it is shaped to do the job. It must be heavy enough for the size rivet being driven, but not so heavy as to be hard to handle. Trouble is more often experienced by using a bucking bar that is too light than too heavy. If it is too light it will fail to absorb the force of the gun and may allow parts to be damaged. It also causes rivets to become excessively work-hardened so that they will not form to the proper head shape.

Driven Rivet Standards

The size of the formed head is the visual standard of a proper rivet installation. The minimum and maximum size, as well as the ideal, are shown in Figure 3-4-14. Carefully measure your *bucktails (shop heads)* when starting, and soon the proper proportions will be apparent.

Pre-drive protrusion. The size of the rivet's driven head (bucktail) is directly proportional to the distance the rivet extends, or protrudes, beyond the material and the size of the hole. Recommended distances are reflected in Figure 3-4-14.

Standard practices. Rivets may be replaced as corrective action for repairs, rework or installation without the need for specific approval, as long as the replacement rivets are of the same

3-60 | Materials and Processes

D, E, (KE), M Rivets

Pre-Drive Protrusion: 1.33d, 1.5d

Formed Head Dimension:
- Minimum: 1.25d × .66d
- Preferred: 1.5d × .5d
- Maximum: 1.66d × .33d

A, AD, B, DD Rivets

Pre-Drive Protrusion: 1.25d, 1.33d

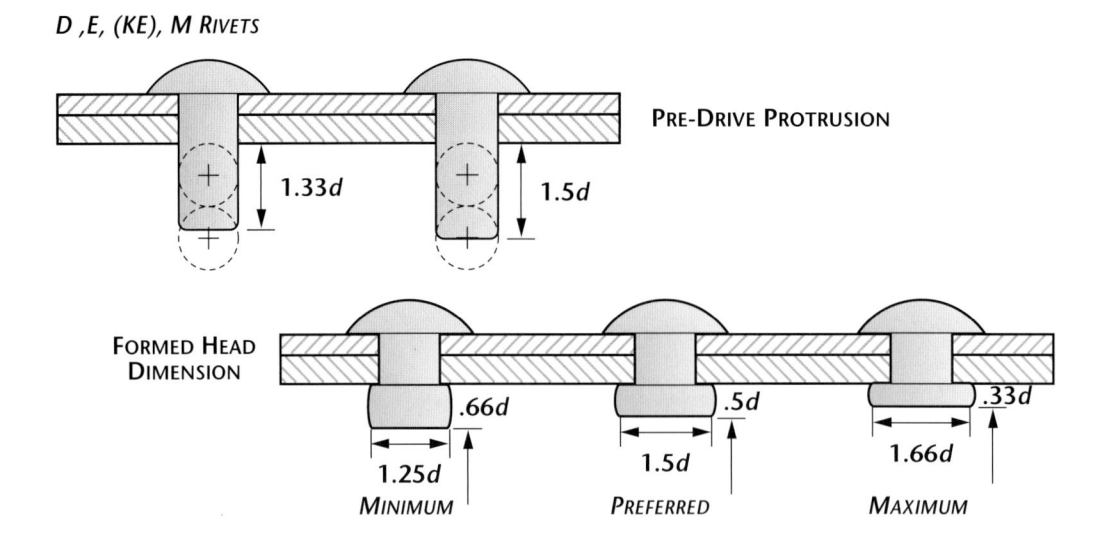

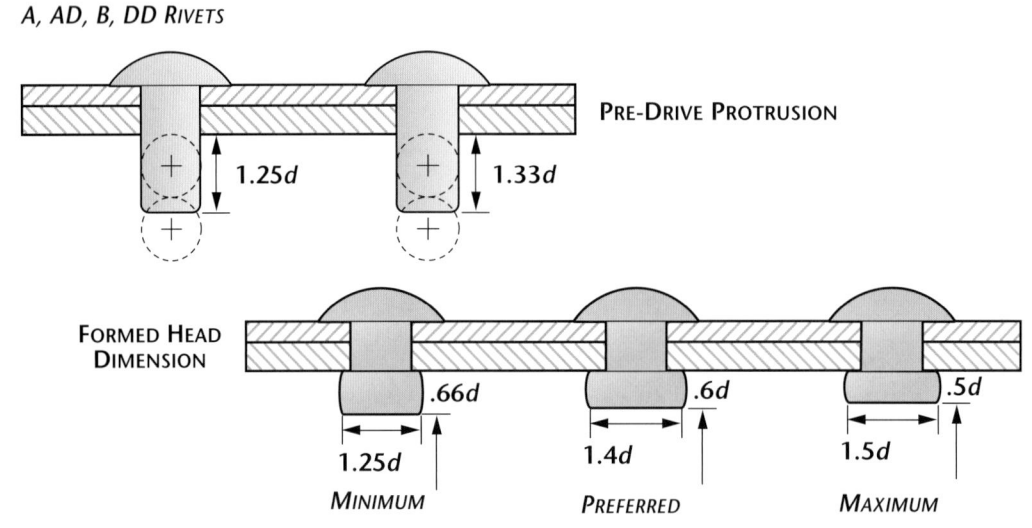

Formed Head Dimension:
- Minimum: 1.25d × .66d
- Preferred: 1.4d × .6d
- Maximum: 1.5d × .5d

Figure 3-4-14. Driven rivet standards

Figure 3-4-15. An adjustable air-powered rivet shaver
Photo courtesy of U.S. Industrial Tools

size, type and material as the existing rivets or a permissible substitute. If more than a small number of rivets in a scattered pattern are to be replaced it is essential that consideration be given to shoring, replacing a few at a time or equivalent provisions to avoid possible trouble from overloads or deflections.

Shaving rivets. It may occasionally be necessary to *shave rivets* after driving to obtain the required flushness. A rivet shaver looks like a combination of tools. See Figure 3-4-15. It is basically an air drill motor with a microstop countersink adjustment attached. When a cutter is installed and the height adjusted, a simple pull of the trigger and a downward feed are all that is necessary. However, practice before trying a real cut. Shaving is normally restricted to MS20426 head rivets. Shear head rivets should never be shaved. When driving rivets NACA style, they will also be shaved.

Always check the cutting depth of a rivet shaver on scrap material before using it. The adjustment is similar to a microstop countersink. Cutter marks are unacceptable.

Driving as received. All rivets, except DD (2024) aluminum rivets, should be driven as received. DD rivets are heat-treated first and then quick-frozen after being quenched. They are stored in this condition, (called AQ) until driven.

Riveting in close patterns. Where rivets are to be installed in a close pattern, care must be taken to avoid over-driving as this causes undesirable *oil canning* or *wrinkling* of the sheet, particularly in thin sheets.

Re-hitting rivets. Under most conditions, AD rivets can be re-hit to obtain a better *upset head*. Hard rivets (D, DD, Monel, etc.) are extremely difficult to upset further once they have been driven. As the chances of causing defective conditions are high, re-hitting is to be avoided. Do not re-hit a rivet when the head is below the skin surface. After re-hitting, the rivet must meet the acceptable standards.

Rivet accessibility. Every effort should be made to avoid covering existing structural rivets with a doubler, wherein later inspection would be impossible.

Rivet Removal

Caution must be used when removing rivets. To avoid damage to holes, countersinks, structure, etc., use the following steps:

1. The drill and punch method should be used on all aircraft. Do not use a chisel.

2. The old standard was to use a drill the same size as the rivet diameter. The latest generation of aircraft with their thin skins will develop small cracks if this is done.

3. Select a drill about 0.003 smaller than the rivet shank diameter.

4. Drill into the exact center of the rivet head to the approximate depth of the head.

5. Remove the head by breaking it off. Use a punch as a lever.

6. Punch out the shank. Use a suitable backup, preferably wood, or a dedicated backup block. If the shank doesn't come out easily, use a small drill and drill through the shank. Be careful not to elongate the hole. Figure 3-4-16 shows the correct way to remove rivets.

Rivet Inspection Standards

The following inspection standards are typical of those used by an airline. Always consult the maintenance manual for actual inspection standards.

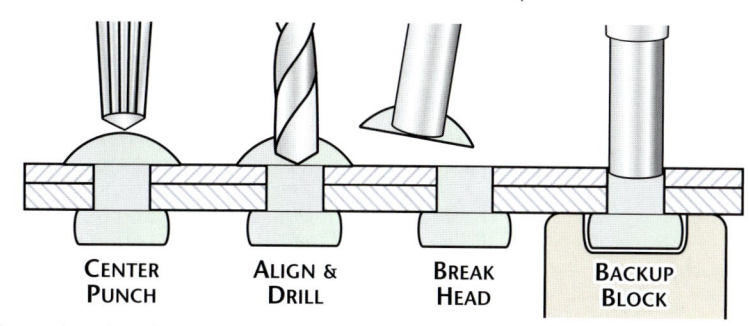

Figure 3-4-16. The preferred procedure for removing rivets

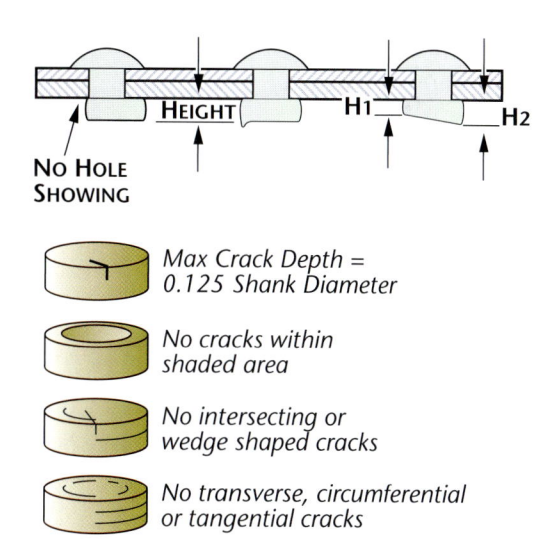

Figure 3-4-17. Upset head variations and reasons for removal

Upset head variations. The following variations in the rivet head, while undesirable, are acceptable, provided they are not widespread in the rivet pattern. See Figure 3-4-17.

Eccentricity. Off-center upset heads are acceptable providing no part of the hole is visible.

Stepped. Stepped upset heads are acceptable providing the flat section is within the tolerance given for the height dimension in Figure 3-4-17.

Sloped. Sloped upset heads are acceptable provided the average height is within tolerance. (H1 not less than minimum, H2 not more than maximum)

Cracks in the upset head. Fine radial cracks in the upset head of driven rivets are acceptable providing:

- Maximum crack depth does not exceed 1/8 (0.125) of the rivet shank diameter.
- Maximum crack width does not exceed 1/16 (0.063) of the rivet shank diameter.

- No cracks exist within a circle concentric within 1.1 times the shank diameter.
- There are no intersecting, wedge-shaped, or similar cracks that would permit chipping out of a piece of the rivet head.
- No circumferential, tangential or transverse cracks exist.

Manufactured head variations. After driving, some variations in the manufactured head are permitted. See Figure 3-4-18. These variations are to be avoided, but are allowable if they are not widespread in the rivet pattern.

Marred. Cut or ringed heads are acceptable providing depth of cut or ring does not exceed 1/4 of the manufactured head height. This variation is not acceptable for flush head rivets.

Flattened. On round or universal head rivets, flattening of the head is acceptable providing the final height is not less than 1/3 of the rivet shank diameter.

Open heads. Open head rivets are acceptable providing a 0.002 feeler gauge cannot be inserted to the rivet shank, the gap at the edge is not over 0.005, and at least 50 percent of the rivet head is tight against the structure. This condition is not acceptable where fluid sealing is required.

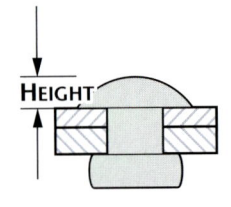

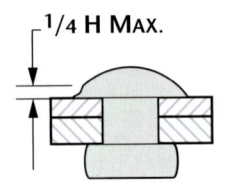

Flushness Variations

Rivet heads should be either flush or slightly high after driving. Heads which are more than 0.001 inch below the sheet surface (curved section) are not acceptable. See Figure 3-4-19.

Limits. Specific limits for maximum head heights will vary from aircraft to aircraft and with location on the airplanes. An ideal practice is to use a microstop countersink set to +0.003 for all flush rivets. A general rule has been to keep small rivets to 0.004 and larger rivets to 0.008 in critical areas. In non-critical areas the respective values of 0.008 to 0.016 should be acceptable. Specific locations of critical/non-critical areas as well as flushness requirements can be found in Manufacturer's Structural Repair Manuals.

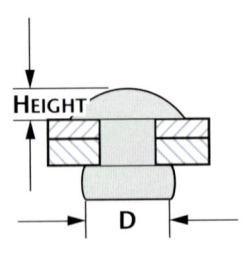

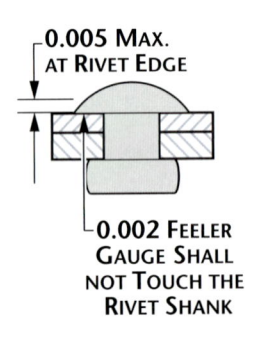

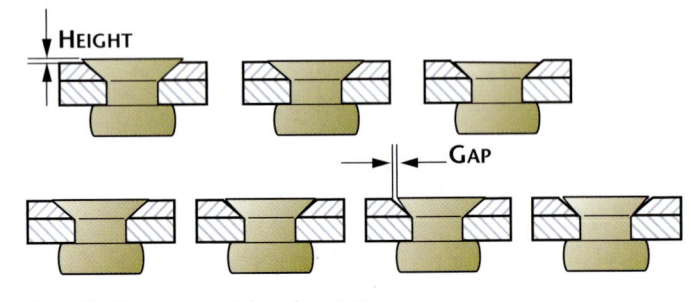

Figure 3-4-18. Manufactured head variations

Figure 3-4-19. Countersunk head variations

Annular rings. The edge of flush rivet heads have their sharp edge broken. Because of this, a small annular ring will exist and is acceptable.

Gaps. Open gaps and eccentric gaps under the heads of flush rivets are not acceptable.

Heads below surface. This condition is not acceptable, nor is a counterbored condition acceptable.

Sheet Discrepancies (After Driving Rivets)

Edge gaps. Skin edge gaps of 0.015 inch maximum at the edge adjacent to the rivet are permitted providing that the following conditions are met:

When a faying surface sealant is used, the fastener installation is not acceptable if a 0.005 inch feeler gauge can be inserted between the sheets far enough to contact the rivet shank.

When a faying surface sealant is not used, the fastener installation is not acceptable if a .002 inch feeler gauge can be inserted between the sheets far enough to contact the rivet shank.

Gaps between sheets. Swelling of rivets between sheets or sheets separated by chips is not acceptable.

Eyebrows or smiles. Marring of the skin, other than superficial, may require special re-work.

Voids around shanks. Do not leave voids around a rivet shank. A riveted joint cannot transfer loads properly if the shanks are not in full contact. For example, do not use an un-dimpled doubler over a countersink or dimpled skin where existing rivet holes are used. Where possible, dimple the doubler to nest into the existing structure. If this cannot be done, use filler washers to occupy the voids. Forming a bevel when deburring also allows voids around shanks.

Safety

Protect your eyes. ALWAYS WEAR EYE PROTECTION WHEN DRILLING AND RIVETING. Safety glasses are the minimum, with goggles or a face shield being added when working overhead or conditions dictate.

Protect your hands and arms. Use protective gloves to avoid overexposure to sealant, some of which contains lead or other harmful ingredients. Too much vibration may be harmful. Use a flexible, rather than, a rigid grip when holding bucking bars. Wear padded gloves, take breaks or trade positions to reduce strain. Use vibration-dampened tools if available.

Protect your back. Time spent setting up is a wise investment. Your work posture should be adjusted so that, as much as possible, you are in a balanced non-straining position. Use ladders, stands, adjustable work platforms, etc., to your best advantage to minimize strain.

Protect your fellow worker and yourself. Disconnect air tools when not in use.

Prevent injury from flying tools. Always use a retainer spring. Inspect the retainer spring for wear or damage regularly.

Do not trigger a rivet gun unless the rivet set is being held against a surface (idle blows). A broken retainer spring can turn a header into a weapon.

Always keep your tools under control. Structural damage at thoughtless moments or by careless operators can occur. It can be expensive to repair as well as being embarrassing. Personnel injures caused by careless operators are even more unwelcome and may result in serious consequences for the operator.

Section 5

Layout and Forming

Aircraft structure and components are composed of numerous small parts. An aircraft has often been referred to as "a multitude of parts flying in tight formation." Many of these parts, or elements, as they are sometimes called, are formed by cutting and bending sheets of metal. Technicians are sometimes called upon to fabricate replacements or repair damaged parts.

Bending Sheet Metal

When making bends, the thickness, alloy composition, and temper conditions of the material must be considered. Thinner pieces of aluminum alloy that are very malleable can be given a radical bend. With thicker sheets, careful consideration must be given to the type of bend required. The following guidelines should be observed when bending sheet metal:

- Maintain a work area free of dirt, chips, grit and other foreign material.
- Use clean, smooth, rust-free forming equipment.
- Sheared or cut edges shall be sanded and filed or polished prior to bending.
- Form material across the direction of grain flow when possible.

It is the accepted practice in aircraft repair to form flanges or bends with a radius that will leave the formed shape of the material as strong as the original shape. Sheet metal that has been formed to a sharp angle is not as strong as it is when shaped using a larger radius. The sharply bent piece will have the stresses concentrated at the bend. Even though most aircraft sheet metals are malleable, they will crack if bent too sharply.

All aircraft metals cannot be bent to the same radius. The minimum radius depends on both the temper and the thickness of the metal. The radius of the bend is usually proportional to the thickness of the material. The type of material is also important. If it is soft, it can be bent very sharply. If it is hard, the radius of bend and the bend allowance will have to be greater. The degree of bend will affect the overall length of the metal, while the metal's thickness affects the radius of bend.

When bending metal to exact dimensions, the length of the *neutral line* must be determined so that enough material can be allowed for the bend. The following paragraphs will discuss these terms and the methods for producing quality bends in sheet metal.

A straight-line bend in sheet metal is called a *brake*. So is the tool that is used to form it. Bends are ordinarily made on the *cornice brake* and *box and pan brake*. However, a considerable amount of bending is also completed by hand-forming methods. Hand forming may be accomplished by using stakes, blocks of wood, angle iron, a vise or the edge of a bench.

Bend radius. When sheet metal is bent, the angle formed will not be sharp but will follow the arc of a circle. The radius of this arc is called the bend radius. The bend radius is measured from the radius center to the inside surface of the metal.

Bending both stretches and shrinks the metal. The material on the inside of the bend shrinks, or is squeezed together, while the material on the outside of the bend is stretched. Figure 3-5-1 shows the changes that take place in a bend.

Most sheet metal used in aircraft is made of strong and correspondingly brittle alloys, which may crack or become so weakened as to fail in service if bent too sharply. Bending has the effect of strain-hardening the material with a resulting increase in brittleness.

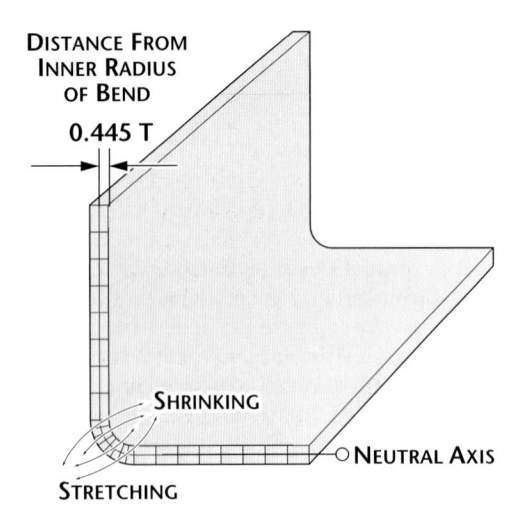

Figure 3-5-1. Neutral axis and stresses resulting from bending

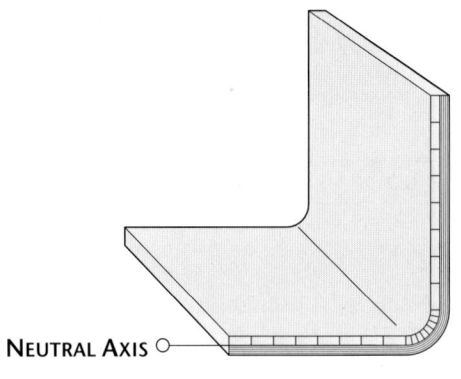

Figure 3-5-2. Neutral axis of the bend

With clad aluminum it is possible for cracks to have occurred in the alloy but not be visible through the soft coating. With aluminum alloy, its thickness and temper determine the minimum safe bending radius. The minimum radius for aluminum alloy 2024-T3 and 7075-T6 are shown in Table 3-5-1. Drawings used for fabrication of aircraft parts will normally call out for the radius to be used for each part. If it is not called for in the drawing, the technician should consult a minimum bend radius chart.

MINIMUM INNER BEND RADII FOR ALUMINUM SHEET					
Gauge	2024-O 5052-H34	2024-T3 2024-T4	5052-O	7178-O 7075-O	7178-T6 7075-T6
0.016	0.030	0.060	0.030	0.030	0.090
0.018	0.030	0.060	0.030	0.030	0.120
0.020	0.030	0.060	0.030	0.030	0.120
0.022	0.060	0.090	0.030	0.060	0.120
0.025	0.060	0.090	0.030	0.060	0.120
0.028	0.060	0.090	0.030	0.060	0.160
0.032	0.060	0.120	0.030	0.060	0.160
0.036	0.060	0.160	0.060	0.060	0.190
0.040	0.060	0.160	0.060	0.060	0.190
0.045	0.090	0.190	0.060	0.090	0.250
0.050	0.090	0.190	0.060	0.090	0.250
0.056	0.120	0.220	0.060	0.120	0.280
0.063	0.120	0.220	0.060	0.120	0.310
0.071	0.120	0.280	0.090	0.120	0.380
0.080	0.160	0.340	0.090	0.190	0.440
0.090	0.190	0.380	0.090	0.190	0.500
0.100	0.220	0.440	0.120	0.220	0.620
0.112	0.250	0.500	0.120	0.280	0.750
0.125	0.250	0.560	0.120	0.280	0.880
0.140	0.340	0.620	0.120	0.380	1.000
0.160	0.380	0.750	0.160	0.440	1.120
0.180	0.440	0.880	0.190	0.500	1.250
0.190	0.500	0.880	0.190	0.560	1.250

Table 3-5-1. Minimum bend radius chart

Sheet Metal Terminology

Before we start the study of flat pattern layout, you must understand the terminology and techniques involved. To successfully use this method there are four mandates:

1. Your math must be absolutely correct.
2. Your layout lines must be absolutely correct.
3. Your brake must be adjusted correctly.
4. Your material must be located precisely in the brake.

Bend radius. When sheet metal is bent, the angle formed will not be sharp but will follow the arc of a circle. The radius of this arc is called the bend radius. The bend radius is measured from a radius center to the inside surface of the metal. See Figure 3-5-1.

Always use a minimum bend radius table to determine the minimum bend radius for the alloy you are going to use. See Table 3-5-2.

Neutral line. Within the curved portion of metal which has been bent, there is an imaginary line called the neutral line. At this line or axis, the compression on the inside of the bend changes to tension on the outside of the bend.

The neutral line represents that part of the metal, in the bend, which is the same length after bending as it was before bending. (See Figure 3-5-2). When metal is bent the bend area is 10 to 15 percent thinner than before bending. This is because the metal moves more easily in tension than in compression. After the metal moves beyond its elastic limit, the strength of the metal on the inside of the bend (compressive strength) becomes greater than the strength of the metal on the outside of the bend (tension strength). Due to this thinning the neutral line of the metal moves in toward the radius center.

Mold-line dimensions. There are several ways of dimensioning formed sheet metal parts on draw-

MINIMUM BEND RADII FOR CORROSION-RESISTANT STEEL		
Thickness	Annealed Cold-Formed	Annealed Hot-Formed
0.016	0.090	0.030
0.020	0.120	0.060
0.025	0.160	0.060
0.032	0.190	0.060
0.036	0.220	0.090
0.040	0.220	0.090
0.050	0.280	0.090
0.056	0.310	0.120
0.063	0.340	0.120
0.071	0.380	0.160
0.080	0.440	0.160
0.090	0.500	0.190
0.100	0.560	0.220
0.112	0.620	0.220
0.125	0.690	0.250
0.140	—	0.310
0.160	—	0.310
0.180	—	0.380
0.190	—	0.380
0.200	—	0.410

Table 3-5-2. Minimum bend radius for corrosion-resistant steel

ings. The most common is the outside, called the *mold-line dimension* (MLD). A mold-line dimension is the distance from the edge of the metal to a point in space called the *mold point*. The mold point is the point of intersection of lines extended from the outside surfaces on either side of the bend. A mold line is an imaginary line in space, parallel to the unbent sides and passing through the mold points. The mold line would be the outside corner of the part if there were no radius.

Inside dimensions. On some parts, the most critical dimension may be to an inside surface, for example, between the flanges of a channel that is to fit over something. Such a part would be dimensioned from inside surface to inside surface. This is called an inside dimension.

Total developed width. The *total developed width* (TDW) is the width of material, measured around the bends from edge to edge. Finding the TDW answers the question of what size to cut the stock. The TDW will be less than the sum of mold line dimensions since the metal is bent on a radius and not to a square corner as mold line dimensions indicate.

Bend tangent lines. Lines can be drawn across flat metal, which will indicate the boundaries of a bend to be made. Such lines must be located where the surface of the unbent section is tangent to the arc of the radius. These lines, where the bent and unbent metal meet, are called *bend tangent lines* (BTL). Dimensions which give the length of the unbent section are known as Bend Tangent Line Dimensions (BTLD). In Figure 3-5-3, sections A and C are BTLD.

Bend allowance. *Bend allowance* (BA) is the term referring to the flat distance or *allowance* of the curved section of metal within the bend (The portion of metal, which will be curved in bending.) The bend allowance may be considered as being the length of the curved portion of the neutral line. As illustrated in Figure 3-5-4, section B is the bend allowance for a 90° bend A bend allowance chart is found in Table 3-5-3.

Bend allowance can be determined by the use of either of two formulas or a chart.

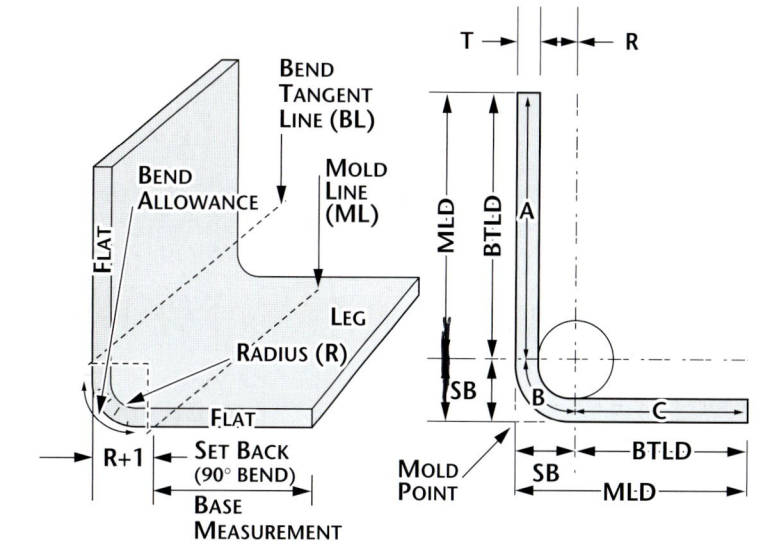

Figure 3-5-3. Bend allowance terms for a 90° bend

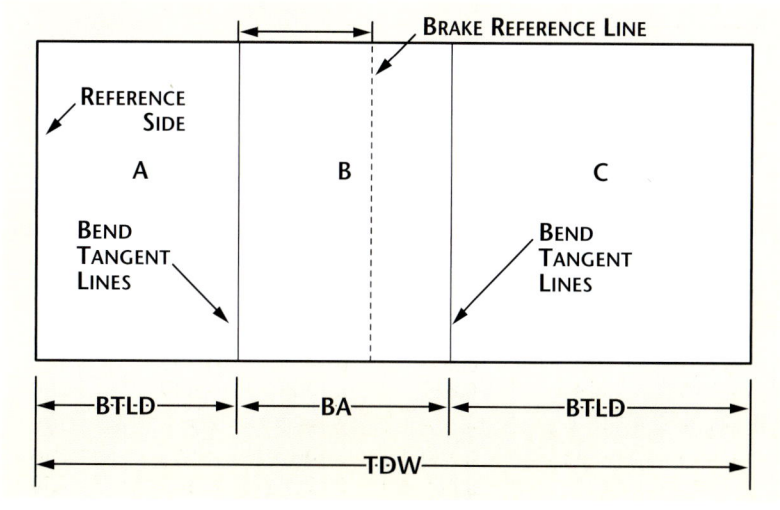

Figure 3-5-4. Bend allowance laid out on flat pattern

Materials and Processes

Formula No 1. To the radius of bend (R), add 1/2 the thickness of the metal (1/2T). This gives R+1/2T, or the radius of the circle, of the neutral axis. See Figure 3-5-5. Compute the circumference of this circle by multiplying the radius of the neutral line by 2π.

(Note: $\pi = 3.1416$)

This gives:

$$2\pi (R + 1/2T)$$

Since a 90° bend is a quarter of the circle, divide the circumference by 4. This gives:

$$\frac{2\pi (R + 1/2T)}{4}$$

This, therefore, is the bend allowance for a 90° bend. To use the formula for a 90° bend having a radius of 1/4 inch for material 0.051 inch thick, substitute in the formula as follows.

BA = 2 × 3.1416 (0.250 + 1/2 × 0.051)/4 =

6.2832 (0.250 + 0.0255)/4 =

6.2832 × (0.2755)/4 = 0.4327 (rounded 0.4328)

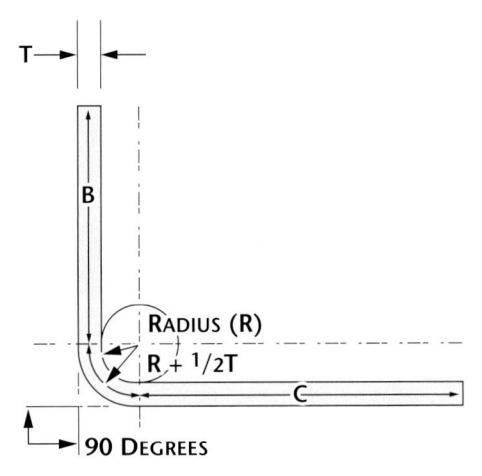

Figure 3-5-5. Bend allowance for 90°

Thus bend allowance, or the length of material required for the bend, is 0.4327 or 7/16 inch.

NOTE: *This formula is slightly in error because the neutral axis is not exactly in the center of the material. However, the amount of error incurred is so slight that, for most work, the formula is satisfactory.*

Metal Thickness	BEND ALLOWANCE CHART								
	Radius Gauge								
	0.031 1/32	0.063 1/16	0.125 1/8	0.156 5/32	0.188 3/16	0.250 1/4	0.313 5/16	0.344 11/32	0.500 1/2
0.020"	0.062 0.000693	0.113 0.001251	0.210 0.002333	0.259 0.002874	0.309 0.003433	0.406 0.004515	0.505 0.005614	0.554 0.006695	0.799 0.008877
0.025"	0.066 0.000736	0.116 0.001294	0.214 0.002376	0.263 0.002917	0.313 0.003476	0.410 0.004558	0.509 0.005657	0.558 0.006198	0.803 0.008920
0.032"	0.071 0.000787	0.121 0.001345	0.218 0.002427	0.267 0.002968	0.317 0.003526	0.415 0.004608	0.514 0.005149	0.562 0.006249	0.807 0.008971
0.040"	0.007 0.000853	0.127 0.001411	0.224 0.002493	0.273 0.003034	0.323 0.003593	0.421 0.004675	0.520 0.006315	0.568 0.006856	0.813 0.009037
0.051"	—	0.134 0.001413	0.232 0.002575	0.280 0.003116	0.331 0.003675	0.428 0.004756	0.527 0.005855	0.576 0.006397	0.821 0.009119
0.064"	—	0.144 0.00595	0.241 0.002680	0.290 0.003218	0.340 0.003776	0.437 0.004858	0.536 0.005957	0.585 0.006498	0.830 0.009220
0.072"	—	—	0.247 0.002743	0.296 0.003284	0.346 0.003842	0.443 0.004924	0.542 0.006023	0.591 0.006564	0.836 0.009287
0.091"	—	—	0.260 0.002891	0.309 0.003432	0.359 0.003990	0.456 0.005072	0.555 0.006172	0.604 0.006713	0.849 0.009435
0.102"	—	—	0.268 0.002977	0.317 0.003518	0.367 0.004076	0.464 0.005158	0.563 0.006257	0.612 0.006798	0.857 0.009521
0.109"	—	—	0.273 0.003031	0.321 0.003572	0.372 0.004131	0.469 0.005213	0.568 0.006312	0.617 0.006853	0.862 0.009575
0.125"	—	—	0.284 0.003156	0.333 0.003697	0.383 0.004256	0.480 0.005338	0.579 0.006437	0.628 0.006978	0.873 0.009700
0.250"	—	—	—	—	—	0.568 0.006313	0.667 0.007412	0.716 0.007953	0.961 0.010675

Note: The top numbers in each box are for a 90° bend. The bottom numbers are the bend allowance for 1 degree of bend.

Table 3-5-3. Bend allowance chart

Formula No 2. By experimentation with actual bends in metals over a period of years, aircraft engineers have found that two constant values exist which are the relationship between the degrees in the bend and the thickness of the metal. This formula can be used for any degree of bend between 1°-180°. The formula is:

Bend allowance = (0.01743R + 0.0078T) N where:

R = The desired bend radius

T = The thickness of the metal

N = Number of degrees of bend

To use this formula for a 90° bend having a radius of 1/4 inch for material 0.051 inch thick, substitute in the formula as follows:

Bend allowance = (0.01743 x 0.250) + (0.0078 x 0. 051) x 90

= (0.0043575 + 0.0003978) x 90

= (0.0047553) x 90

= 0.427977 or 0.428

Thus, the bend allowance is 0.428 or $7/16$ inch.

Bend allowance table. In Table 3-5-3, the radius of bend in a decimal and fraction is shown on the top line and the metal thickness is shown on the left hand column. The upper numbers are the bend allowance for a 90° bend. The lower numbers are the bend allowance per 1° of bend. To determine the bend allowance for a 90° bend simply use the top number in the chart. For any specific angle besides a 90° bend, multiply the bottom number by the number of degrees in the angle required. Thus, if a sheet 0.051 inch thick is to be bent to a 120° angle with a bend radius of 1/4 inch, the bend allowance of 0.004756, as shown, must be multiplied by 120. Therefore, the bend allowance for a 120° bend will be 120 x 0.004756 or 0.570 inch.

Setback. When computing a layout from mold line dimensions, the distance from the mold point to the bend tangent line is called setback (SB). When a part has more than one bend, setback must be subtracted for each bend. See Table 3-5-4. The majority of bends in sheet metal are 90° bends. Setback for all 90° bends is equal to the sum of the metal thickness plus the radius of the bend. See Figure 3-5-6.

Setback formula. Setback for all 90° bends can be calculated from the formula:

Setback = R + T

For example, for a piece of 0.032 inch thick material that is to be bent to a radius of 1/8 (0.125) inch, setback equals 0.125 + 0.032, which is 0.157 inch. When setback is subtracted from the base measurement, the remainder will be the length of the flat.

K-chart. To calculate setback for all bends other than 90°, a K-chart (Table 3-5-5) must be consulted to find a value called K that must be substituted in the formula, or you can directly find the setback with a flat pattern setback chart.

SB = K (R + T)

NOTE: *The "K" Value is the tangent of one-half the bend angle.*

Material growth. This is defined as a comparison of the dimension given on a drawing to the actual material needed to make the part. It results in the amount a piece of metal seems to grow after each bend has taken place.

Flange. A flange is a stiffening member bent at the edge of a part. It can be used for purposes of attachment to another part, or it can be used principally for stiffness, such as the area around a lightening hole.

Web. The major load-carrying portion of a spar, wing rib, beam, etc., usually is the principal depth unit.

Brake Reference Line (Sight Line)

The correct marking of a brake reference line (sight line) is of utmost importance; it is here that most mistakes are made. Metal to be bent with a cornice brake must be positioned in the brake so that the bend will start at one bend tangent line and end at the other. When the metal is clamped in the brake and bent, the bend will start under the nose at a distance exactly equal to the radius of the nose. One bend tangent line should coincide with this point. Since this point is hidden under the nose of the brake, a sight or

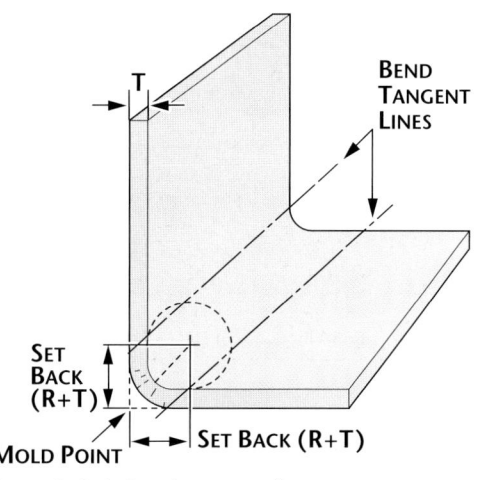

Figure 3-5-6. Bend tangent lines

3-68 | Materials and Processes

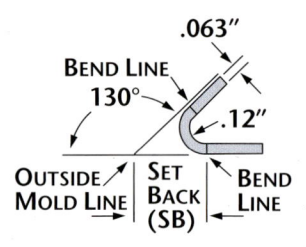

SB = Distance from Mold Line to Bend Line
BA = Bend Angle
R = Bend Radius
T = Thickness

1. Enter Chart at Bottom on Appropriate Scale Using Sum of T + R
2. Read up to Bend Angle
3. Determine Set Back from Corresponding Scale on Left

Example:
T (0.063) + R (0.12) = 0.183
BA = 135°
Set Back = 0.453

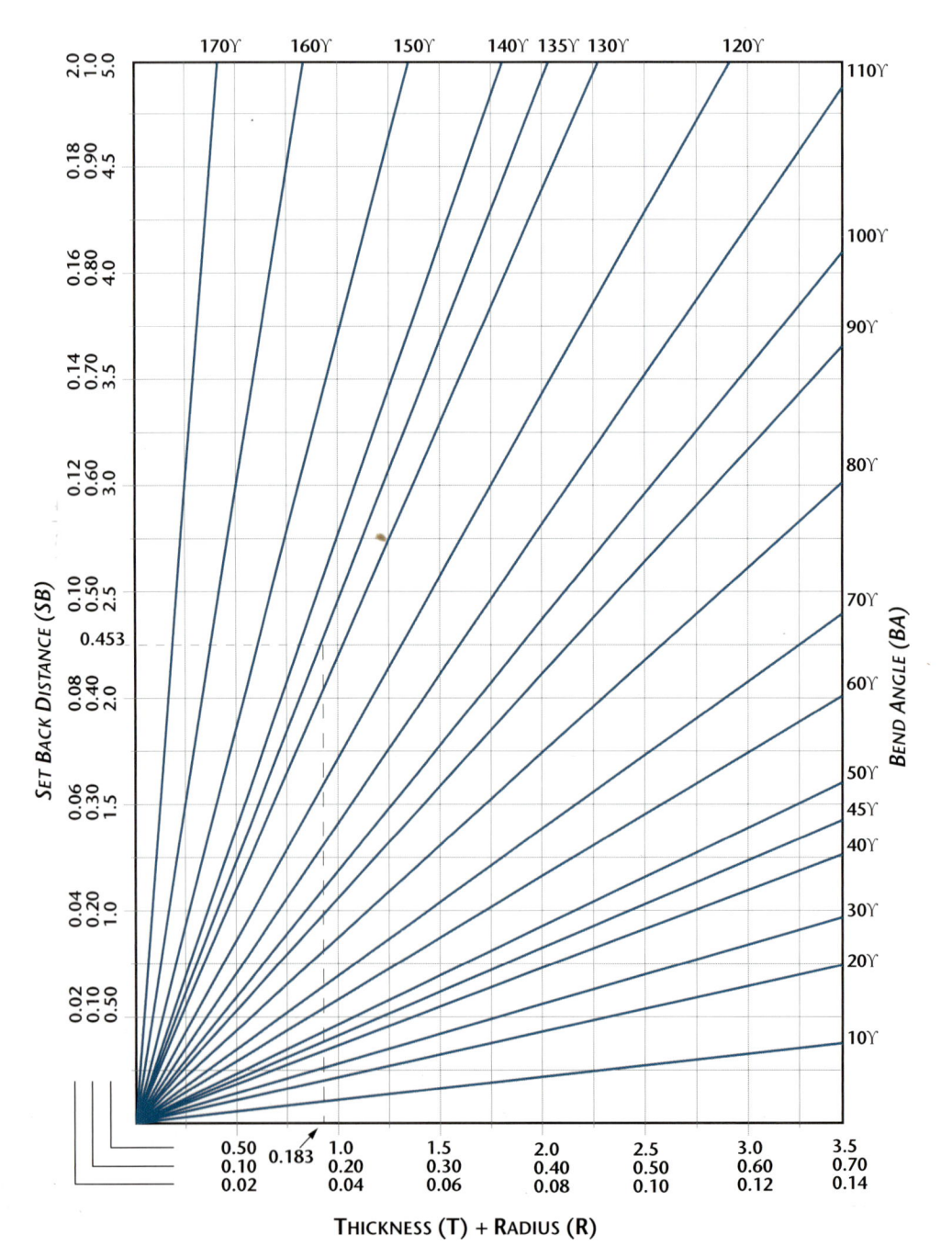

Table 3-5-4. Flat pattern setback graph

reference line is needed to properly position the metal for bending. This line, called the brake reference line (BRL), is located at a distance equal to the radius of the brake measured outward from the bend tangent line beneath the clamping bar. This distance can most conveniently be calculated and measured from the edge of the metal. See Figure 3-5-7.

In order to best understand the technique of sheet-metal layout, consider a channel such as that seen in Figure 3-5-8. This channel is made of 0.040 inch-thick 2024-T4 aluminum alloy. The dimension across the bottom of the channel is 2 inches and each side of the channel is 1 inch high.

To lay out this channel, follow these steps:

1. Choose the correct bend radius
2. Find the setback
3. Find the length of each of the flats
4. Find the bend allowance
5. Lay out the flat pattern
6. Draw the sight lines on the flat pattern

Choose the correct bend radius. Use the minimum radius chart in Table 3-5-1 to choose the correct bend radius for the alloy and temper and the metal thickness. For 0.040, 2024-T4 the minimum allowable radius is 3/32 inch.

Find the setback. Since all of the angles in this channel are 90° angles, the setback is simply the bend radius of 3/32 plus the metal thickness of 0.040 or 0.134 inch back from the brake leaf hinge.

$$SB = K(R + T)$$

$$SB = (0.09375 + 0.040)$$

$$SB = 0.134 \text{ inch}$$

NOTE: *K = 1 for a 90° bend. For other than 90° bends use a K factor chart. See Table 3-5-5.*

Find the length of each of the flats. The flats, or flat portions of the channel, are equal to the

SETBACK CHART (K CHART)							
1°	0.00873	37°	0.33459	73°	0.73996	109°	1.4019	145°	3.1716
2°	0.01745	38°	0.34433	74°	0.75355	110°	1.4281	146°	3.2708
3°	0.02618	39°	0.35412	75°	0.76733	111°	1.4550	147°	3.3759
4°	0.03492	40°	0.36397	76°	0.78128	112°	1.4826	148°	3.4874
5°	0.04366	41°	0.37388	77°	0.79546	113°	1.5108	149°	3.6059
6°	0.05241	42°	0.38386	78°	0.80978	114°	1.5399	150°	3.7320
7°	0.06116	43°	0.39391	79°	0.82434	115°	1.5697	151°	3.8667
8°	0.06993	44°	0.40403	80°	0.83910	116°	1.6003	152°	4.0108
9°	0.07870	45°	0.41421	81°	0.85408	117°	1.6318	153°	4.1653
10°	0.08749	46°	0.42447	82°	0.86929	118°	1.6643	154°	4.3315
11°	0.09629	47°	0.43481	83°	0.88472	119°	1.6977	155°	4.5107
12°	0.10510	48°	0.44523	84°	0.90040	120°	1.7320	156°	4.7046
13°	0.11393	49°	0.45573	85°	0.91633	121°	1.7675	157°	4.9151
14°	0.12278	50°	0.46631	86°	0.93251	122°	1.8040	158°	5.1455
15°	0.13165	51°	0.47697	87°	0.94896	123°	1.8418	159°	5.3995
16°	0.14054	52°	0.48773	88°	0.96569	124°	1.8807	160°	5.6713
17°	0.14945	53°	0.49858	89°	0.98270	125°	1.9210	161°	5.9758
18°	0.15838	54°	0.50952	90°	1.00000	126°	1.9626	162°	6.3137
19°	0.16734	55°	0.52057	91°	1.0176	127°	2.0057	163°	6.6911
20°	0.17633	56°	0.53171	92°	1.0355	128°	2.0503	164°	7.1154
21°	0.18534	57°	0.54295	93°	1.0538	129°	2.0965	165°	7.5957
22°	0.19438	58°	0.55431	94°	1.0724	130°	2.1445	166°	8.1443
23°	0.20345	59°	0.56577	95°	1.0913	131°	2.1943	167°	8.7769
24°	0.21256	60°	0.57735	96°	1.1106	132°	2.2460	168°	9.5144
25°	0.22169	61°	0.58904	97°	1.1303	133°	2.2998	169°	10.385
26°	0.23087	62°	0.60086	98°	1.1504	134°	2.3558	170°	11.430
27°	0.24008	63°	0.61280	99°	1.1708	135°	2.4142	171°	12.706
28°	0.24933	64°	0.62487	100°	1.1917	136°	2.4751	172°	14.301
29°	0.25862	65°	0.63707	101°	1.2131	137°	2.5386	173°	16.350
30°	0.26795	66°	0.64941	102°	1.2349	138°	2.6051	174°	19.081
31°	0.27732	67°	0.66188	103°	1.2572	139°	2.6746	175°	22.904
32°	0.28674	68°	0.67451	104°	1.2799	140°	2.7475	176°	26.636
33°	0.29621	69°	0.68728	105°	1.3032	141°	2.8239	177°	38.188
34°	0.30573	70°	0.70021	106°	1.3270	142°	2.9042	178°	57.290
35°	0.31530	71°	0.71329	107°	1.3514	143°	2.9887	179°	114.590
36°	0.32492	72°	0.72654	108°	1.3764	144°	3.0777	180°	Infinite

Table 3-5-5. K-chart

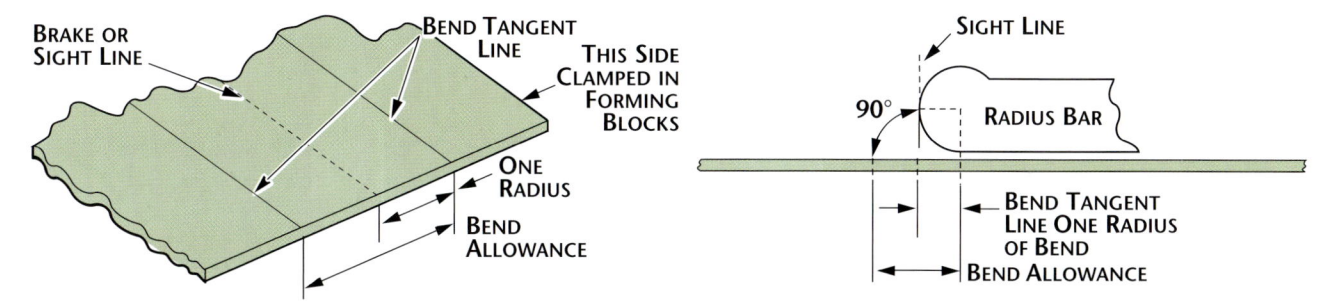

Figure 3-5-7. Brake reference line

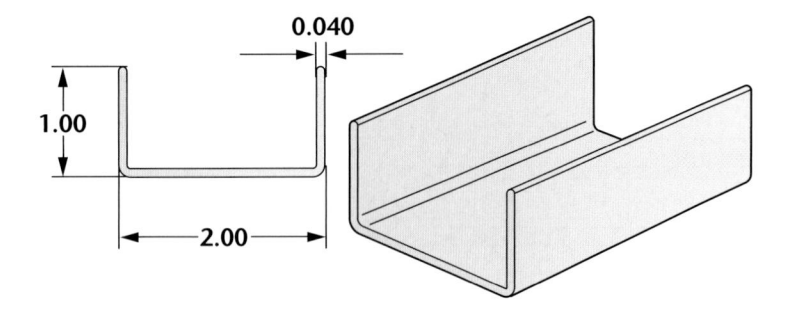

Figure 3-5-8. Traditional layout of a sheet metal U-channel

mold line length minus the setback for each of the sides and the mold line length minus two setbacks for the bottom.

Flat 1 = 1.00 − 0.134 = 0.866 inch

Flat 2 = 2.00 − (2 × 0.134) = 1.732 inch

Flat 3 = 1.00 − 0.134 = 0.866 inch

Find the bend allowance. Use the bend allowance chart in Table 3-5-3. Use the top number for 90° bends. The bend allowance is 0.176 inch, which rounds off to the practical dimension of 0.18 inch.

Lay out the flat pattern. When you know the lengths of the flats and the bend allowance, you can lay out the flat pattern. Note that the metal needed to make the channel is less than the dimensions of the outside of the channel. This is because the metal follows the radius of the bend rather than going from mold line to mold line. The larger the bend radius, the less material used for the channel. See Figure 3-5-9.

Draw the sight lines on the flat pattern. The pattern laid out in Figure 3-5-9 is complete, except for a very handy line you can draw to help position the bend tangent line directly at the point the bend should start. Draw a line inside the bend allowance that is one bend radius away from the bend tangent line for the sides of the channel. Put the metal in the brake with the flat for one side of the channel under the clamp and adjust the position of the metal until the sight line is directly below the edge of the radius bar, as is shown in Figure 3-5-10. Now clamp the brake on the metal and you can raise the leaf to make the bend. The bend will begin exactly on the bend tangent line.

> **NOTE:** *A common mistake made is that people draw the sight line exactly in the middle of the Bend Allowance area, instead of 1 radius away from the bend tangent line that will be placed under the brake nose bar.*

Shortcut Method to Calculate Total Developed Width (TDW)

Material growth (bend deduction). Material growth, or bend deduction, is a comparison of the dimensions given on a drawing (to the mold points) to the actual material needed to make the part. It results in the amount that a piece of metal seems to grow after each bend has taken place. The metal does not actually grow at all.

A common mistake is to find the length of metal necessary to bend up a part by adding up the mold line dimensions. These dimen-

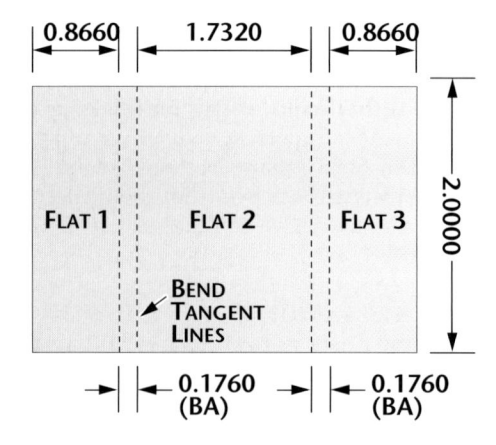

Figure 3-5-9. Flat pattern layout of the channel

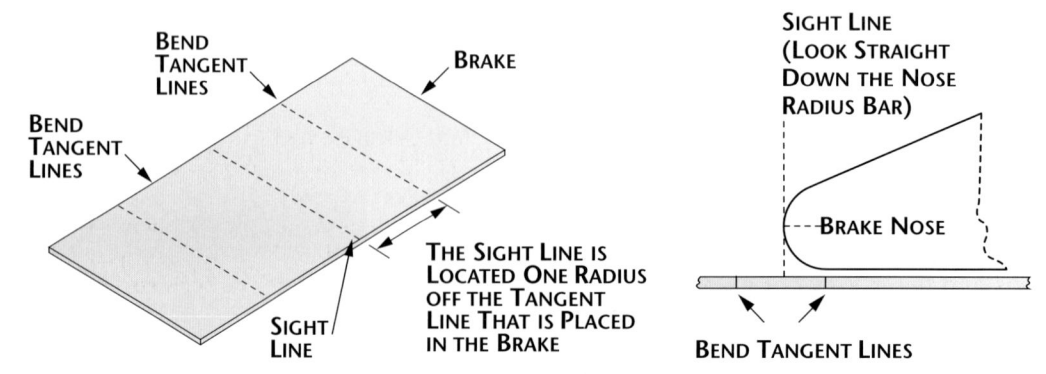

Figure 3-5-10. Sight lines

MATERIAL GROWTH FACTOR (90° ONLY — SAME AS BEND DEDUCTION)									
	Material Thickness								
Radius	0.032	0.040	0.050	0.063	0.071	0.080	0.090	0.100	0.125
1/32"	1/16 0.055	1/16 0.065	—	—	—	—	—	—	—
1/16"	1/16 0.068	5/64 0.079	3/32 0.093	7/64 0.110	1/8 0.120	—	—	—	—
3/32"	5/64 0.082	3/32 0.092	7/64 0.107	1/8 0.124	9/64 0.134	9/64 0.146	5/32 0.159	—	—
1/8"	3/32 0.095	7/64 0.106	1/8 0.124	9/64 0.137	9/64 0.147	5/32 0.159	11/64 0.172	3/16 0.186	7/32 0.216
5/32"	7/64 0.109	1/8 0.119	9/64 0.134	5/32 0.150	5/32 0.161	11/64 0.173	3/16 0.186	13/64 0.200	15/64 0.230
3/16"	1/8 0.122	9/64 0.133	9/64 0.147	5/32 0.164	11/64 0.174	3/16 0.186	13/64 0.199	7/32 0.213	1/4 0.243
7/32"	9/64 0.136	9/64 0.146	5/32 0.161	11/64 0.177	3/16 0.188	13/64 0.199	7/32 0.212	15/64 0.227	1/4 0.257
1/4"	5/32 0.149	5/32 0.160	11/64 0.174	3/16 0.191	13/64 0.201	7/32 0.212	15/64 0.226	15/64 0.240	17/64 0.270
9/32"	5/32 0.163	11/64 0.173	3/16 0.187	13/64 0.204	7/32 0.215	15/32 0.226	15/64 0.239	1/4 0.254	9/32 0.284
5/16"	11/64 0.176	3/16 0.187	13/64 0.201	7/32 0.218	15/64 0.228	15/64 0.240	1/4 0.253	17/64 0.267	19/64 0.297
11/32"	3/16 0.190	13/64 0.200	7/32 0.214	15/64 0.231	1/4 0.242	1/4 0.253	17/64 0.266	9/32 0.281	5/16 0.311
3/8"	13/64 0.203	7/32 0.214	15/64 0.228	1/4 0.245	1/4 0.255	17/64 0.267	9/32 0.280	19/64 0.294	21/64 0.324
1/2"	1/4 0.257	17/64 0.268	9/32 0.282	19/64 0.299	5/16 0.309	21/64 0.321	21/64 0.334	11/32 0.348	3/8 0.378

Table 3-5-6. Material growth chart

sions continue beyond the bend tangent line and end at the mold point. Since it is impossible to bend a square corner, it is this segment (the setback) that is erroneous to us. The metal does not go to the mold point, instead it takes a short cut around a radius (the bend allowance). This is why the metal seems to grow when a bend is made. See Table 3-5-6. The material growth (or bend deduction) tells us how much shorter this dimension is than what seems necessary. Figure 3-5-11, shows four examples.

The material necessary to go from bend tangent line A to bend tangent line B is not 5/16 + 5/16 or 10/16 (2 x SB), but 7/16 (BA). This means that the material growth is 3/16.

The material growth can be calculated for any degree of bend by the use of this formula:

MG = (2 x SB) – BA

For 90° bends, it can simply be looked up on the material growth chart by using the required radius and the material's thickness. To calculate the length of metal necessary to bend a 90° angle, it is as simple adding the two legs (mold line dimensions) and subtracting one material growth.

R = 3/16 inch

Total Developed Width =
  Mold Line Dimensions – Material growth

T = 0.063 inch

MG = 0.164 inch

Total Developed Width = 1 + 1 - 0.164

Total Developed Width = 1.836 inch

For a U-channel, just add the three mold line dimensions and since it has two bends, subtract 2 x MG.

Total Developed Width =
  Mold Line Dimensions – Material growth

Total Developed Width =
  (1 + 2 +1) – 0.328 = TDW = 3.672

It doesn't matter how many 90° bends there are or which way that they are bent, just add up the mold line dimensions then subtract a MG for each bend.

Total Developed Width =
  Mold Line Dimensions – Material growth

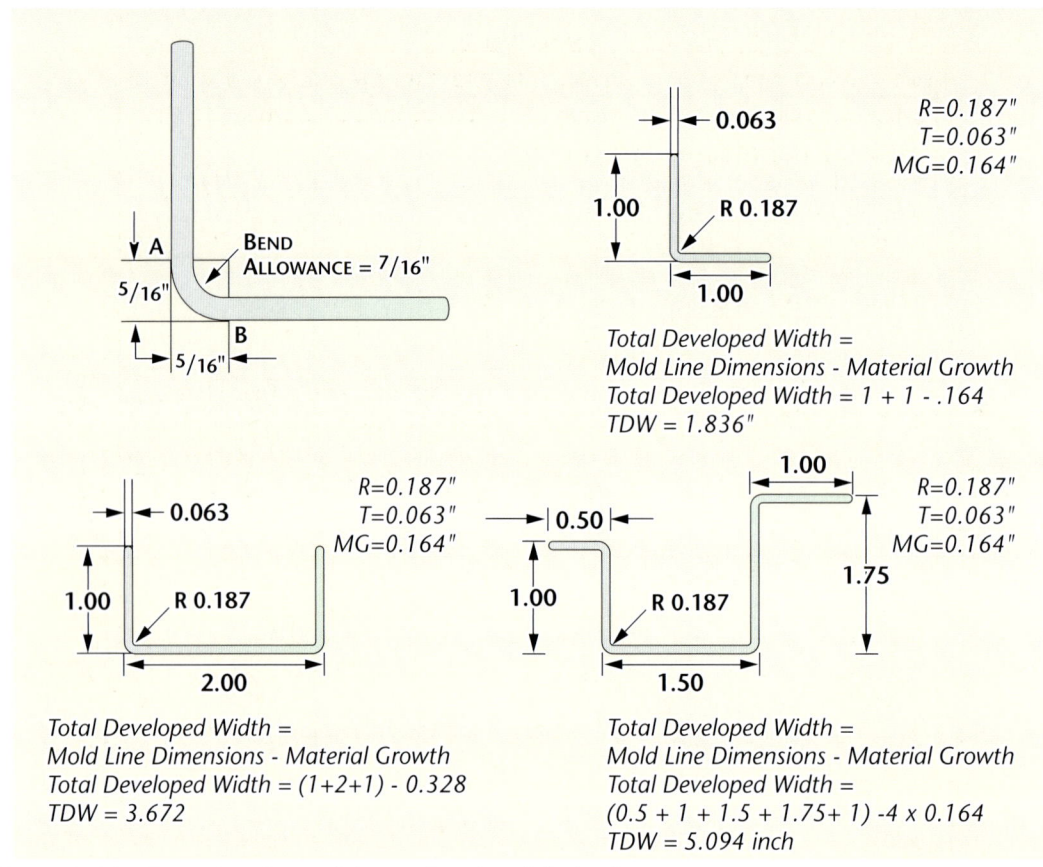

Figure 3-5-11. Examples of material growth or bend deduction

Total Developed Width =
(0.5 + 1 + 1.5 + 1.75 + 1) – (4 x .164)

TDW = 5.094 inch

Using a J-chart to find the TDW. The J-chart is often found in Manufacturers' Structural Repair Manuals and it is a simple and quick way to find the TDW of a flat pattern layout. See Table 3-5-7. It is not as accurate as the traditional layout method, but it will be sufficient for most applications. The main advantage of the J-chart is that you don't have to do any calculations, remember formulas or looking up information in charts and tables. The only things that you need to know are bend radius, bend angle, material thickness and mold line dimensions, which you can find in a drawing or by measuring them with simple measuring tools. Examples are shown in Figure 3-5-12

There are several steps to find the total developed width using a J-chart:

- Place a straight edge across the chart and connect the bend radius on the top scale with the material thickness on the bottom scale

- Locate the angle on the right hand scale and follow this line horizontally until it meets the straight edge

- The factor X (bend deduction) is then read on the diagonally curving line

- Interpolate when the X factor falls between lines

- Add up the mold line dimensions and subtract the X factor to find the TDW

Open and Closed Bends

Open and closed bends present some unique problems that require more calculations than were needed when only 90° bends were encountered. These pages show three typical bends. They are all symmetrical and share the same mold line dimensions, but that is where the similarity ends. Note the mold point location on the end-views. Also notice on the flat layouts that all the dimensions are different. See Figure 3-5-12.

Start by studying the open bend example. The bend allowance is calculated by multiplying the number of degrees in the bend and the bend allowance per 1°. This is always the number of degrees the material is bent from the flat. In our examples the material is 0.050 thick and the bend radius is 3/16 inch.

The bend allowance for 1° from the bend allowance chart is 0.0036581, so multiply this times the number of degrees (45) and we find our

BEND RADIUS

0.50 0.47 0.44 0.40 0.38 0.34 0.31 0.28 0.25 0.22 0.19 0.16 0.12 0.09 0.06 0.03 0.00

X = Amount to be Deducted from Sum of Flange Dimension
A + B − X = Developed Length
Example:
0.063 Material
0.12 Angle
X = 0.035

Instruction: Place a straight edge across chart connecting the radius on upper scale and thickness on lower scale. Then locate the angle on the right hand scale and follow this line horizontally until it meets the straight edge. The factor x is then read on the diagonally curving line. Interpolate when the factor x falls between lines.

0.130 0.120 0.110 0.100 0.090 0.080 0.070 0.060 0.050 0.040 0.030 0.020 0.010 0.000

THICKNESS

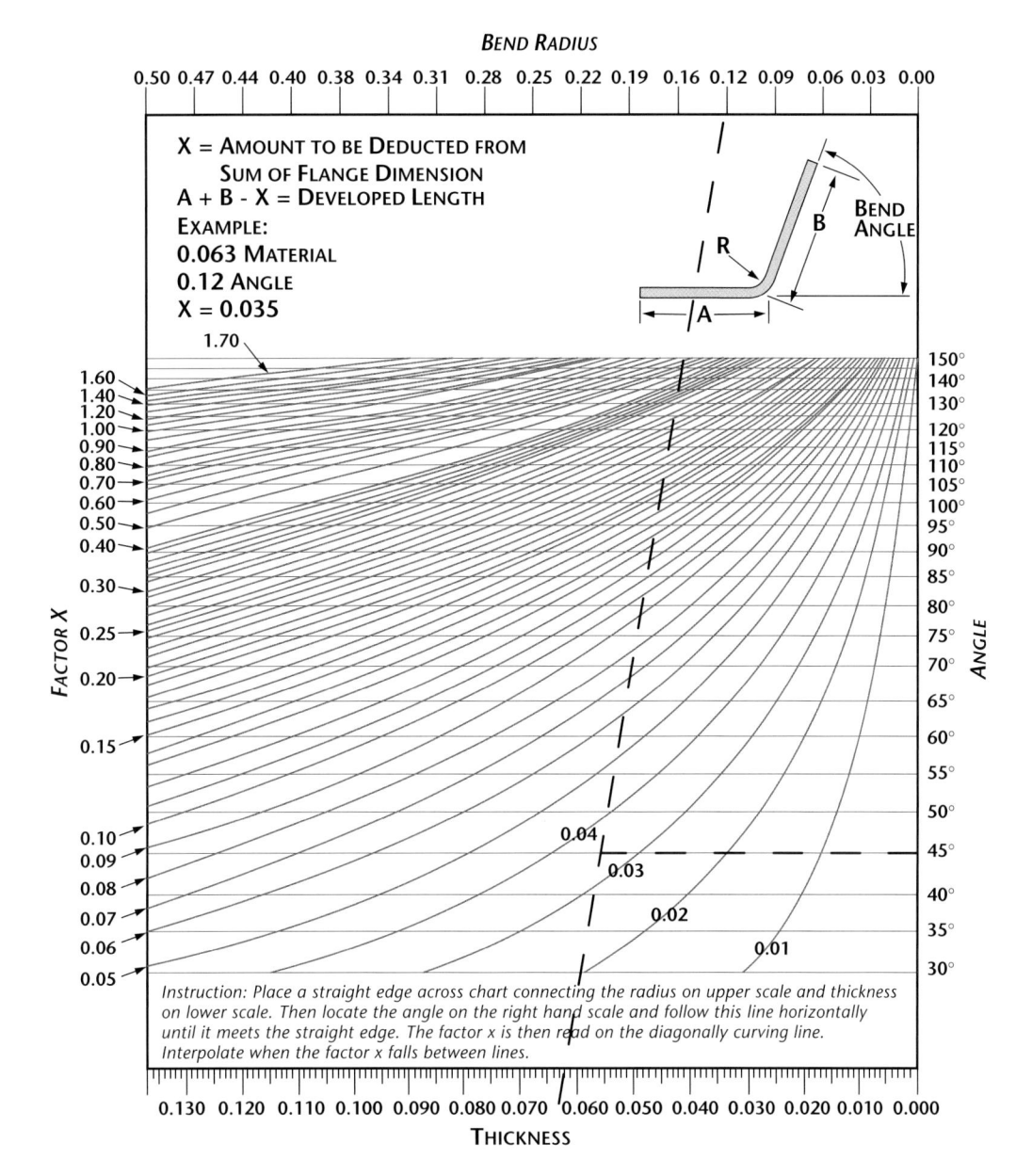

Table 3-5-7. J-chart

bend allowance is 0.1646". The bend tangent line dimensions are found by using trigonometry. The simplest way is by using a setback chart sometimes called a K-chart (Table 3-5-5). The setback formula is K (T + R). The K factor for 45° is 0.41421 inch, the thickness is 0.050 inch and the radius is 3/16 inch or 0.1875 inch. The sum of 0.050 and 0.1875 is 0.2375, which multiplied by 0.41421 equals 0.0983749, which subtracted from 1.5 is our bend tangent line dimension of 1.4016 inch.

Observe that the brake reference line is still located one radius from the bend tangent line.

A flat layout for a closed angle is done the same way, just remember the number of degrees is always the number of degrees the material is bent from the flat.

Layout Example for Open and Closed Bends

In this example, we will make a reinforcing channel six inches long, to the dimensions shown in Figure 3-5-13. We will start by making a flat layout. Complete all the calculations, in order, before rounding them.

NOTE: *This procedure is for a cornice/pan and box brake.*

T + R = 0.063 + 0.1875 = 0.2505
BA per degree (from chart) = 0.0037595

The following are for the closed left side bend:

The bend is 30° more than 90°, which equals 120°.
Setback Factor for 120° = 1.73205 (See Table 3-5-5)

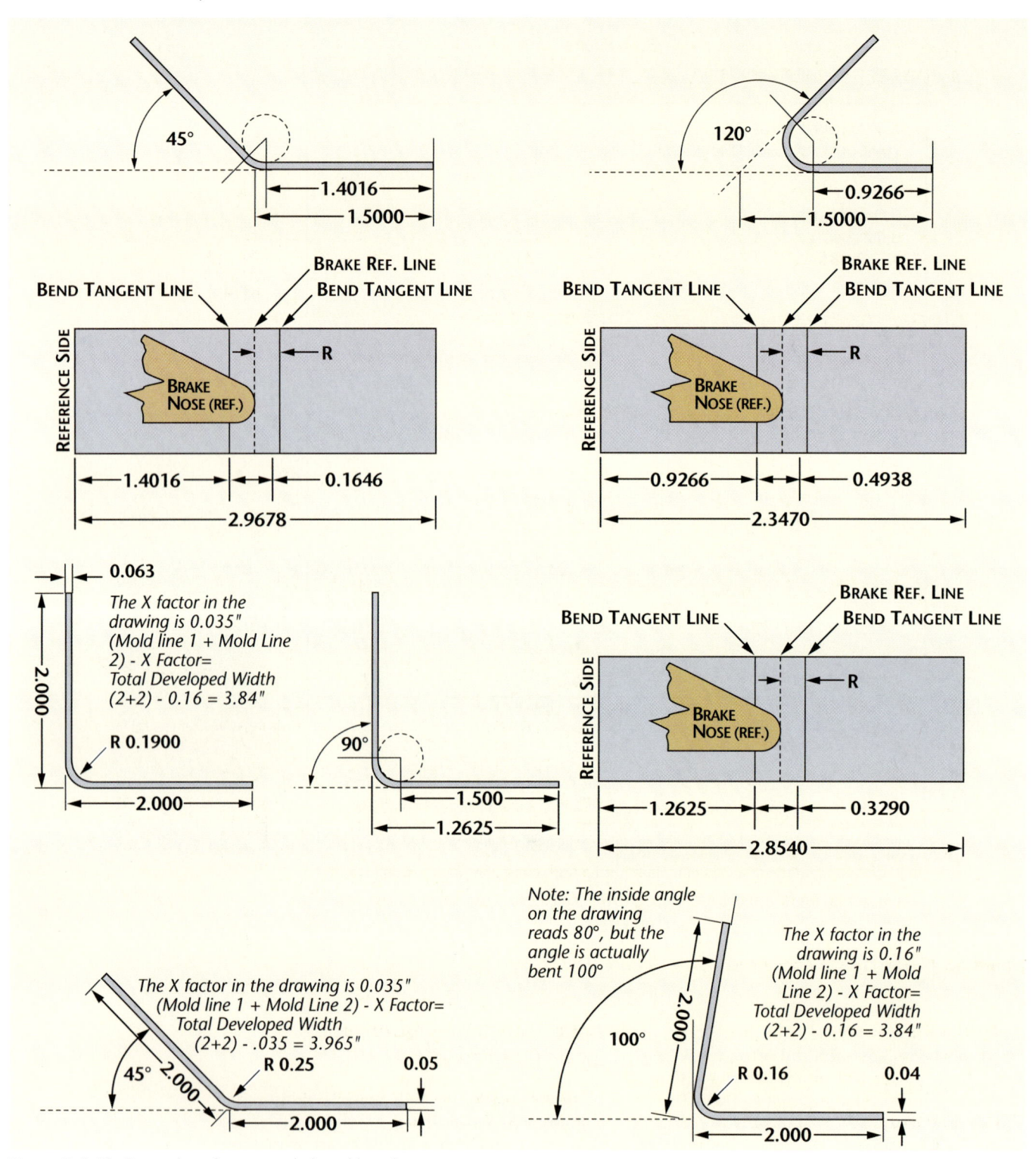

Figure 3-5-12. Examples of open and closed bends

1.73205 x 0.2505 = 0.4338785 is the setback for this side.

0.0037595 x 120 = 0.45114 is the bend allowance for this side.

The following are for the open right side bend:

The bend is 30° less than 90°, which equals 60°.

The setback factor for 60° from the "K" chart is 0.57735.

0.57735 x 60 = 0.22557 is the setback for this side.

0.0037595 x 60 = 0.22557 is the bend allowance for this side.

Now it is necessary to dimension the flat layout segments.

Materials and Processes | 3-75

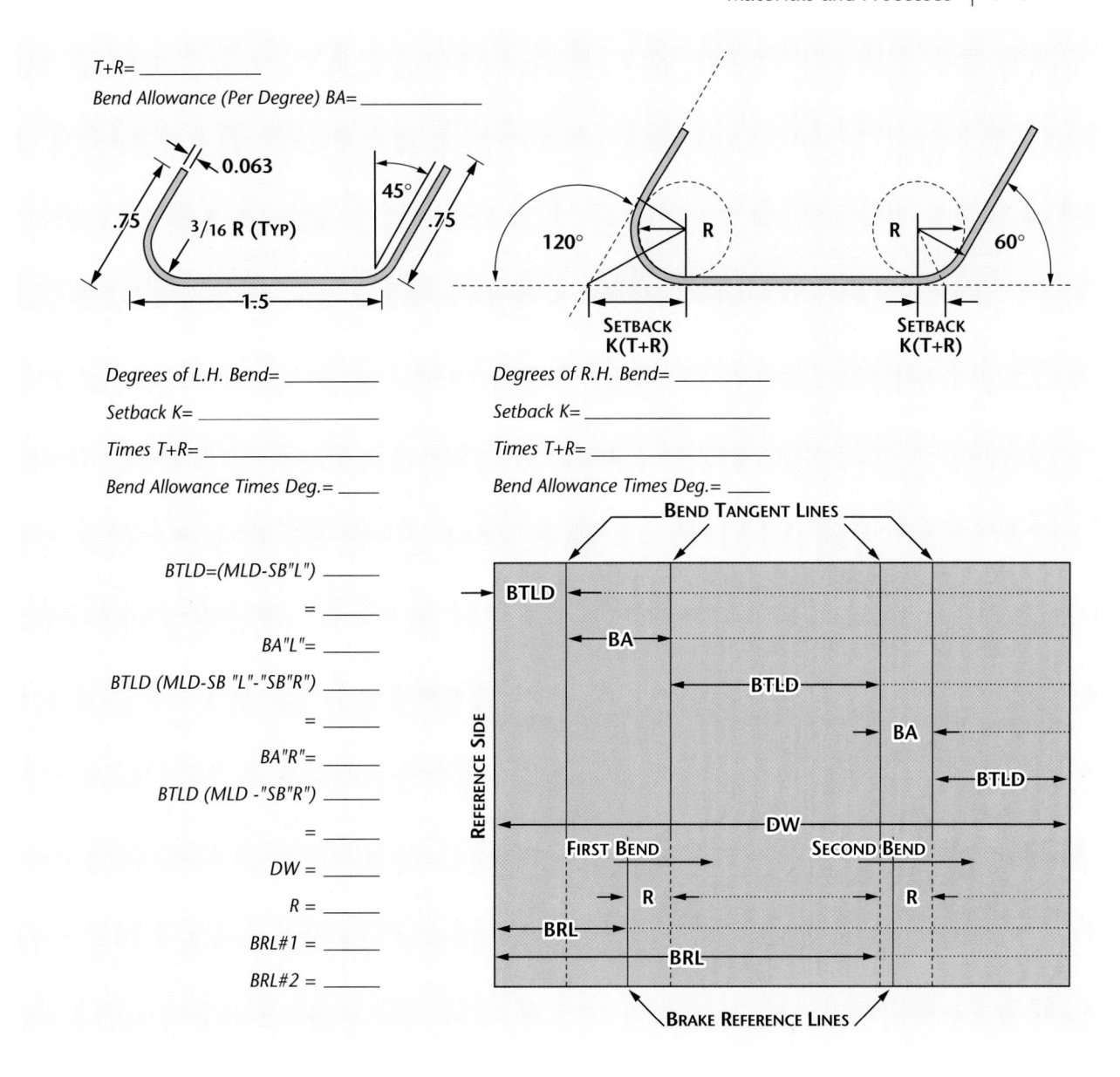

T+R= _____
Bend Allowance (Per Degree) BA= _____

Degrees of L.H. Bend= _____
Setback K= _____
Times T+R= _____
Bend Allowance Times Deg.= _____

Degrees of R.H. Bend= _____
Setback K= _____
Times T+R= _____
Bend Allowance Times Deg.= _____

BTLD=(MLD-SB"L") _____
= _____
BA"L"= _____
BTLD (MLD-SB "L"-"SB"R") _____
= _____
BA"R"= _____
BTLD (MLD -"SB"R") _____
= _____
DW = _____
R = _____
BRL#1 = _____
BRL#2 = _____

Figure 3-5-13. Flat layout of open and closed bends

BTLD = 0.75 − 0.4338785
 = 0.3161215

BA"L" = 0.45114

BTLD = 1.5 − 0.4338785 − 0.1446262
 = 0.9214953

BA"R" = 0.22557

BTLD = 0.75 − 0.1446262
 = 0.6253738

DW = 0.3161215 + 0.45115 + 0.9214953
 + 0.22557 + 0.6253738
 = 2.5397

Now, lay out the brake reference lines:

R = 0.1875

BRL #1 = 0.3161215 + 0.45115 − 0.1875
 = 0.5797715

BRL #2 = 0.3161215 + 0.45115 + 0.9214953
 + 0.22557 − 0.1875
 = 1.7268268

Sheet Metal Bending Equipment

There are many types of bending equipment that are used to form or bend sheet metal.

Vise. Vises are used for holding sheet metal when it is being shaped or riveted. Figure 3-5-14 shows a common bench vise. The machinist's bench vise is the one most generally used for forming sheet metal. The machinist's bench vise is a large steel vise

Figure 3-5-14. Common bench vise

Figure 3-5-15. Cornice brake

with rough jaws that prevent the work form slipping. It has a swivel base, allowing the user to position the vise in a better working position. Machinist's vises are usually bolted to a workbench or table.

Cornice brake. The cornice brake is designed to bend large sheets of metal. See Figure 3-5-15. It can be adjusted to handle a variety of metal thicknesses and to bend to a variety of radii.

The brake is equipped with a stop gauge, which consists of a rod, a yoke and a setscrew. The stop gauge limits the travel of the bending leaf. This feature is used to make a number of pieces with the same angle of bend.

The cornice brake has been accepted as the standard of simplicity and economy for bending aircraft sheet metal. While it may not be the very best method in all circumstances it is still essential for sheet metal technicians to be comfortable with its operation. The standard cornice brake is extremely useful for making single hems, double hems, lock seams and various other shapes, some of which require the use of molds. The molds are fastened to the bending leaf of the brake by friction clamps

Box and pan brake. Box and pan brakes in Figure 3-5-16 are often called finger brakes because they do not have solid upper jaws, as do cornice brakes. Instead, they are equipped with a series of steel fingers of varying widths. Finger brakes can be used to do everything that cornice brakes can do and several things that cornice brakes cannot do.

The box and pan brake is used to form boxes, pans and other similar shaped objects. If these shapes were formed on a cornice brake, you would have to straighten part of the bend on one side of the box in order to make the last bend. With a finger brake, you simply remove the fingers that are in the way and use only the fingers required to make the bend.

The fingers are secured to the upper leaf by thumbscrews. All the fingers that are not removed for an operation must be securely seated and firmly tightened before the brake is used. The radius of the nose on the clamping fingers is normally rather small and will frequently require nose radius shims to be custom-made for the total length of the bend.

Sheet metal brake setup. After selection of the correct type of material and thickness, the proper radius must be chosen. Normally, this information can be found in the drawings, but if it is not mentioned you could consult the structural repair manual for the minimum bend radius chart. This chart lists the smallest radius allowable for each thickness and type of metal that is normally used. To bend tighter than this radius would jeopardize the integrity of the part. Stresses left in the area of the bend may cause it to fail while in service, even if you are lucky enough that it doesn't crack while bending it. An excellent technique to avoid concentrating stresses at the edge of the part, which could lead to cracking, is to *deburr* the edges of the part. This should be done even to the point of polishing in highly stressed areas before bending. See Figure 3-5-17.

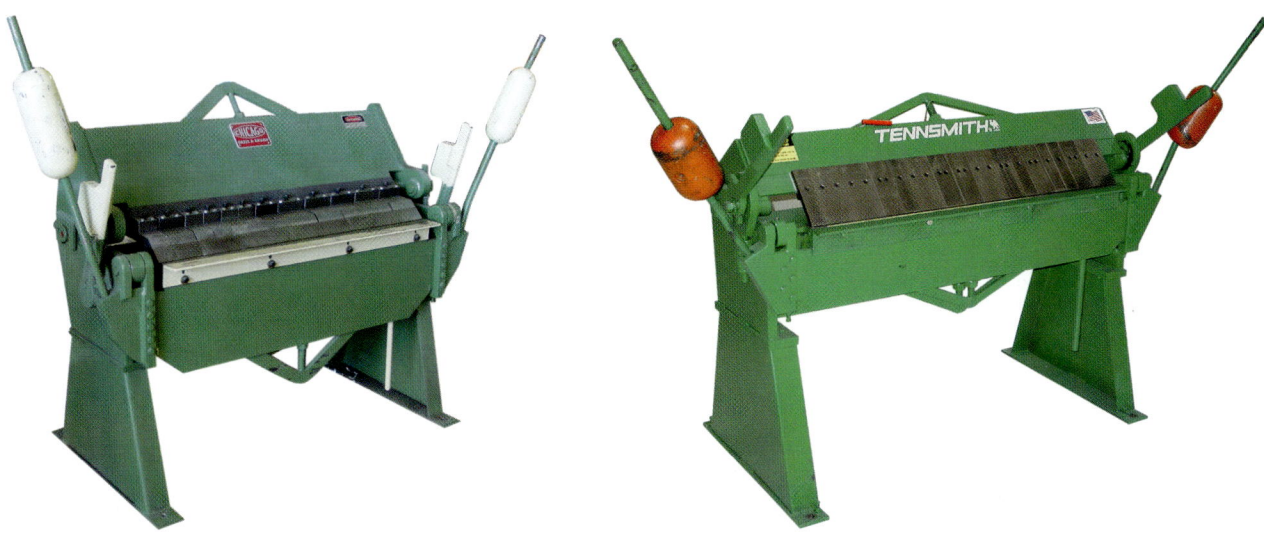

Figure 3-5-16. Box and pan brakes (finger brake)

If different nose radius bars are not available and the existing radius is smaller than required, it will be necessary to bend some *nose radius shims*. If the radius is so small that it would tend to crack even annealed aluminum, mild steel would be a good choice of material. It takes some experimentation with a small piece of scrap material to come up with a thickness that will increase the radius to precisely 1/16 inch or 1/8 inch. Use *radius and fillet gauges* to check this dimension. It is easy to size-up the nose shims from this point on. Each additional shim is added to the radius before it. See Figure 3-5-18.

EXAMPLE: *If the original nose was 1/16 inch and we bent a piece of 0.063 inch (1/16 inch) material around it, our new outside radius would now be 1/8 inch. If we added another 0.063 inch (1/16 inch) layer it would then be a 3/16 inch radius. If we used a piece of 0.032 inch (1/32 inch) instead of 0.063 inch (1/16 inch) bent around the 1/8 inch radius, we would have a 5/32 inch radius.*

Figure 3-5-17. Forming crack from improper radius

A good sheet metal technician will often bend a set of these radius shims up to keep in his/her toolbox as a permanent tool.

The next step is setting clamping pressure. See Figure 3-5-19. With the radius shims nested over the sharp nose, slide a piece of the material to be bent under them. Pull the clamping lever toward you to test the pressure. This is an over-center type clamp, and when properly set, will not feel springy or spongy when pulled to its fully clamped position. You must be able to pull this lever over center with a firm pull and have it bump its limiting stops. This adjustment has to be made on both sides. Place test strips on the table 3 inches from each end and 1 inch in the center between the bed and the clamp. Then adjust clamp pressure until it is tight enough to prevent the work piece from slipping while you are bending. This is

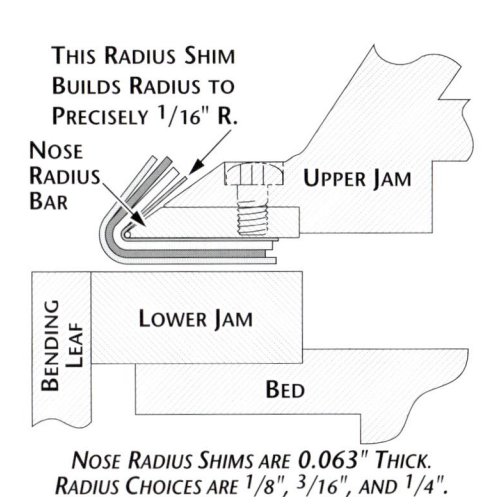

Figure 3-5-18. Adding radius shims

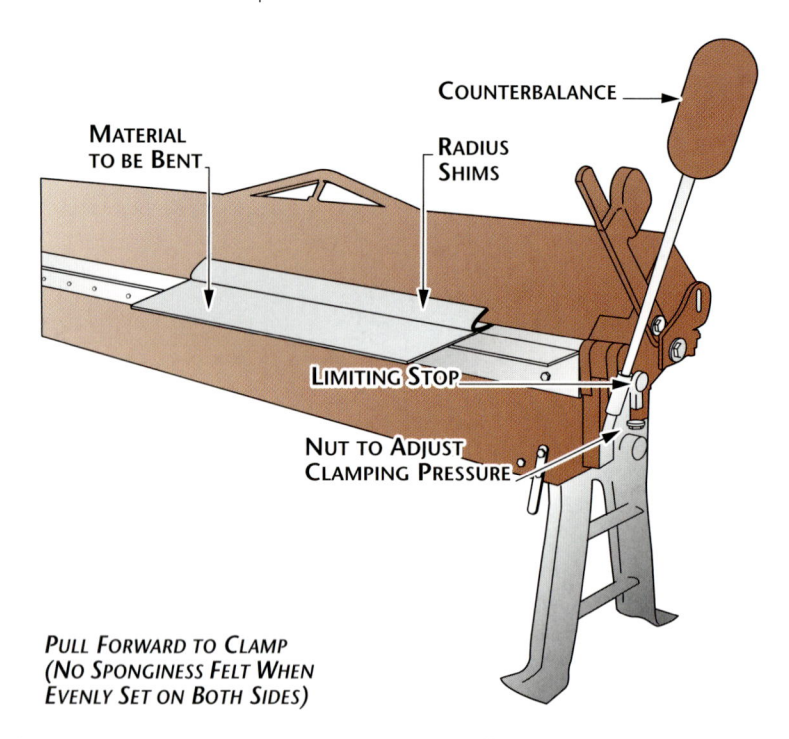

Figure 3-5-19. Operating an over center type clamp

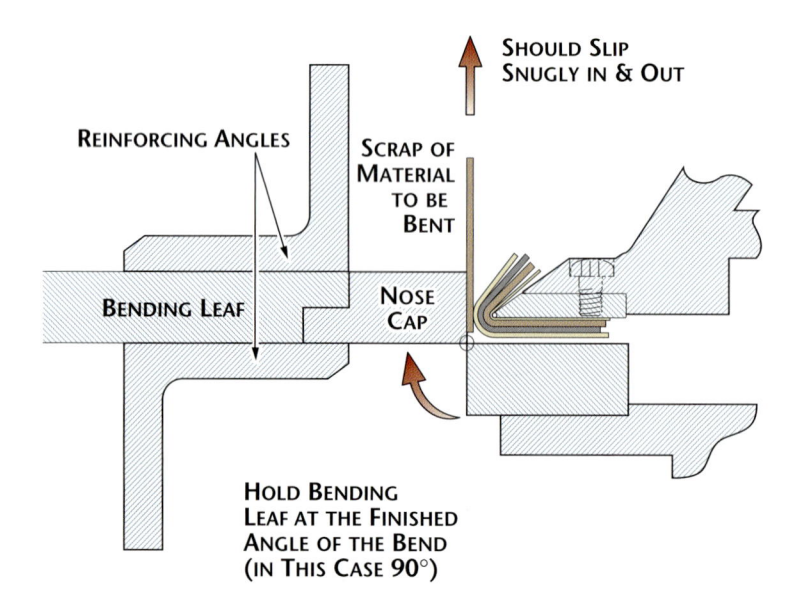

Figure 3-5-20. Checking the adjustment of the nosepiece

Care must be taken not to be misled by any fore and aft *play* (looseness) of the upper jaw. Remember, when setting this nose gap, push the upper jaw back to remove any slop and get the correct setting. The pressure exerted on the nose during the bend will have a tendency to shift it to the aft position if play exists. An easy way to assure this setting is correct is to slightly lift the upper jaw with the clamping pressure lever. Then twist the scrap metal feeler gauge to take out all of the play, then while still applying a light pressure with the scrap, set the upper jaw down on the bed. If the scrap metal gauge can be pulled out and snugly reinserted between the nose and the bending leaf, you have the proper setting. This setting will assure that your material will be forced to conform to the radius of the nose.

It is essential that this nose gap is perfectly even across the length of the part to be bent. Check by clamping two test strips between the bed and the clamp 3 inches from each end of the brake, bend 90°, remove test strips and place one on top of the other—they SHOULD match. If they do not match, adjust the end with the sharper bend back slightly.

With the brake properly set up, it is time to clamp your part into position. See Figure 3-5-21. This can be very easy, if you are bending a 90° angle. Always remember that the bending leaf will establish the outside plane of your finished part. Therefore, if you set up the nose gap properly, the outside of the finished part will be one material thickness outside of the nose after being bent.

Simply mark the metal with a line at exactly the dimension that you want the finished part to measure as shown in Figure 3-5-22. This is the mold line dimension. This side of the part will have to be placed under the nose of the brake. Since the clamping pressure has been set to assure that the metal can't move or change underneath the upper jaw, you can have confidence that you will have an accurate leg if your line was set at one material thickness outside of the nose.

Bending a U-channel is no different than with any other bend. As previously discussed, cut your metal to length by adding up the 3 mold line dimensions, and subtract a material growth for each bend.

Press brake. Most cornice and box and pan brakes are limited to a maximum forming capacity of about .090 inch annealed aluminum, .063 inch 7075-T6 and .063 inch stainless steel. For operations requiring heavier materials, a press brake will be used. See Figure 3-5-23.

adjustable by using the cams located at each end of the brake.

The next step is to set the *nose gap*. Turn the large knobs at the rear of the upper jaw to achieve its proper alignment. The perfect setting is obtained when the bending leaf is held up to the angle of the finished bend and there is one material thickness between it and the final inside nose radius. To achieve a high degree of accuracy, use a feeler gauge made from a material the same thickness as the part to be bent.

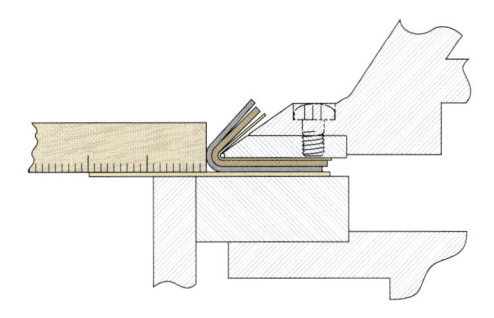

Figure 3-5-21. Checking the nose gap

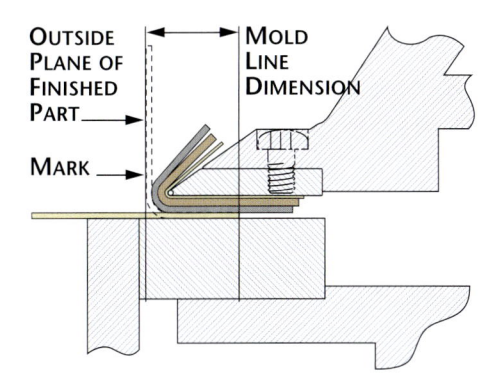

Figure 3-5-22. Setup on a cornice brake

We are also sometimes limited by the shape of a certain part, because of interference with the upper jaw or other parts of the cornice brake. Narrow U-channels (especially with long legs) and hat channel stringers can not be bent on a cornice or box and pan brake. However, by using special gooseneck, or offset dies, they can be formed on the press brake. Power press brakes can be set up with back stops (some are computer controlled) for high volume production.

Bar folder. The *bar folder.* See Figure 3-5-24) is designed for use in making bends or folds along edges of sheets of metal. This machine is best suited for folding small hems, flanges, seams and edges to be wired. Most bar folders have a capacity for metal up to 22 gauge in thickness and 42 inches in length. Before using the bar folder, you must make several adjustments for thickness of material, width of fold, sharpness of fold and angle of fold. See Figure 3-5-25.

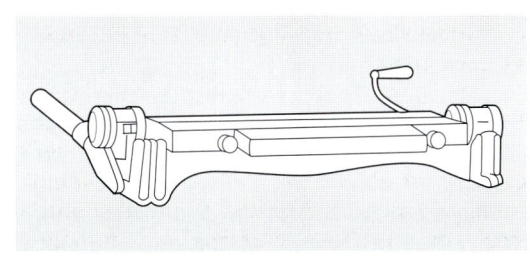

Figure 3-5-24. A bar folder, used primarily for sheet steel and stainless steel

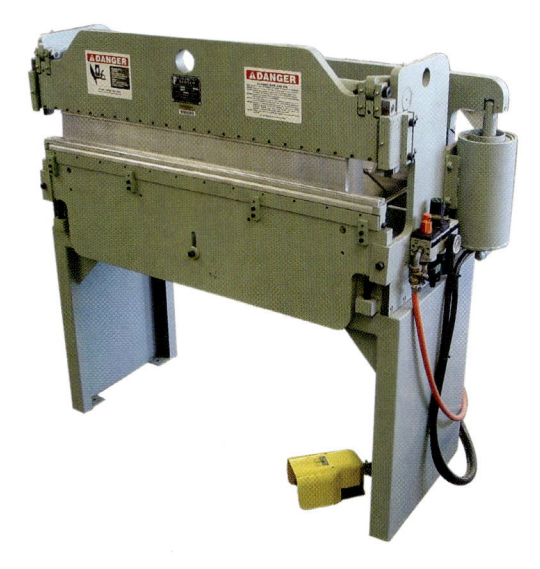

Figure 3-5-23. Press brake

Folding a Box

You can form a box the same way as the channel just described, but you must also drill relief holes at the intersection of the inside bend tangent lines and bend it in a box brake. The relief holes, whose diameter is approximately twice the bend radius, relieve stresses in the metal as it is bent and prevent the metal from tearing. An example is shown in Figure 3-5-26. Two opposite sides of the box are bent first, and then the fingers of the brake will be adjusted so the folded-up sides will ride up in the cracks between the fingers when the leaf is raised to bend the other two sides.

Bend relief radius. Where a sheet metal part has intersecting bend radii, it is necessary to have a bend relief radius. This *bend relief radius* prevents an intense concentration of stresses that would be allowed if it were a square corner (the most abrupt cross sectional change possible).

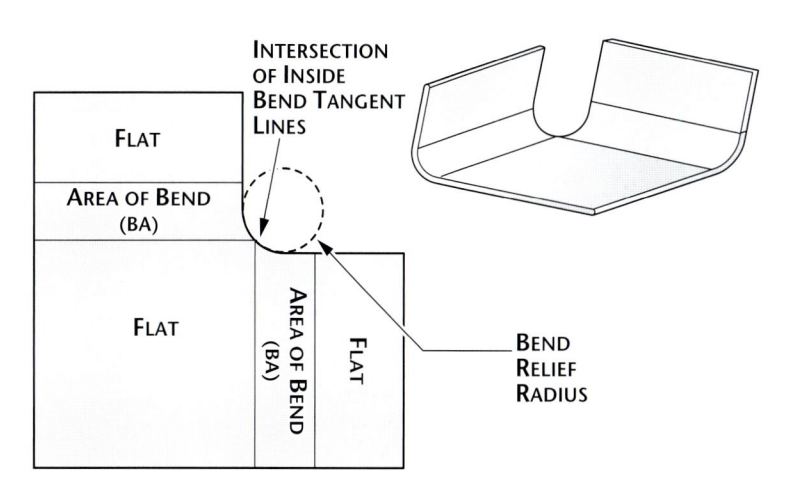

Figure 3-5-25. Creating angular folds

3-80 | Materials and Processes

The larger and smoother this radius the less likely a crack will form in the corner.

This radius is specified on the drawing. Its positioning is important. It should be located so its outer perimeter touches the intersection of the inside bend tangent lines. This will keep any material from one bend from interfering with the bend allowance area of the other bend. If these bend allowance areas intersect with each other, substantial compressive stresses would accumulate in that corner during bending. This could cause the part to crack while bending or at some later date because of its pre-stressed, weakened state.

Layout Method

Layout the basic part using traditional layout procedures. This will give you the width of the flats and the bend allowance. It is the intersection of the inside bend tangent lines that indexes the bend relief radius' position. Bisect these intersected lines and move outward the distance of the radius on this line. This will be the center of the hole. Drill at this point.

Finish by trimming off the remainder of the corner material. This trim out is often tangent to the radius and perpendicular to the edge (as pictured). This will leave an open corner. If the corner must be closed or a slightly longer flange is necessary, then trim out accordingly. If the corner is to be welded, it will be necessary to have touching flanges at the corners. The length of the flange should be one material thickness shorter than the finished length of the part so only the insides of the flanges will touch. See Figure 3-5-27.

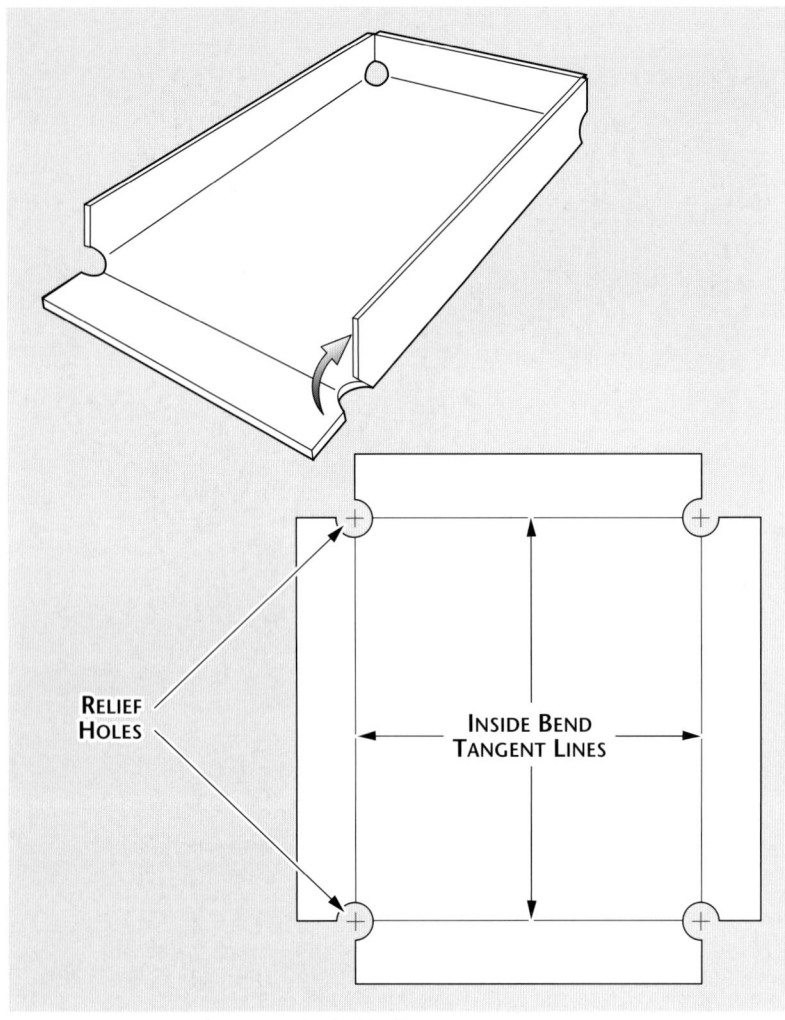

Figure 3-5-26. Application of relief holes

Forming Compound Curves

Large *compound curves* are formed in sheets of metal in the aircraft factories with *drop hammers*. The metal to be formed is placed over a heavy metal female die, and a matching male die is dropped onto the sheet metal. It drives the metal down into the female die and forms the compound curves with a minimum of work hardening of the material.

Smaller parts with more drastic curves are formed on a *hydro press*. The metal to be formed is cut to shape and all of the burrs are removed from its edges. This piece, called a *blank*, is then placed over a hard steel male die and is held in place by locator pins on the die fitting through index holes in the blank. The die with the blank is placed on the bed of the hydropress and a rubber pad in the ram of the press is forced down over the die with several thousand tons of pressure. The sheet metal is forced down into

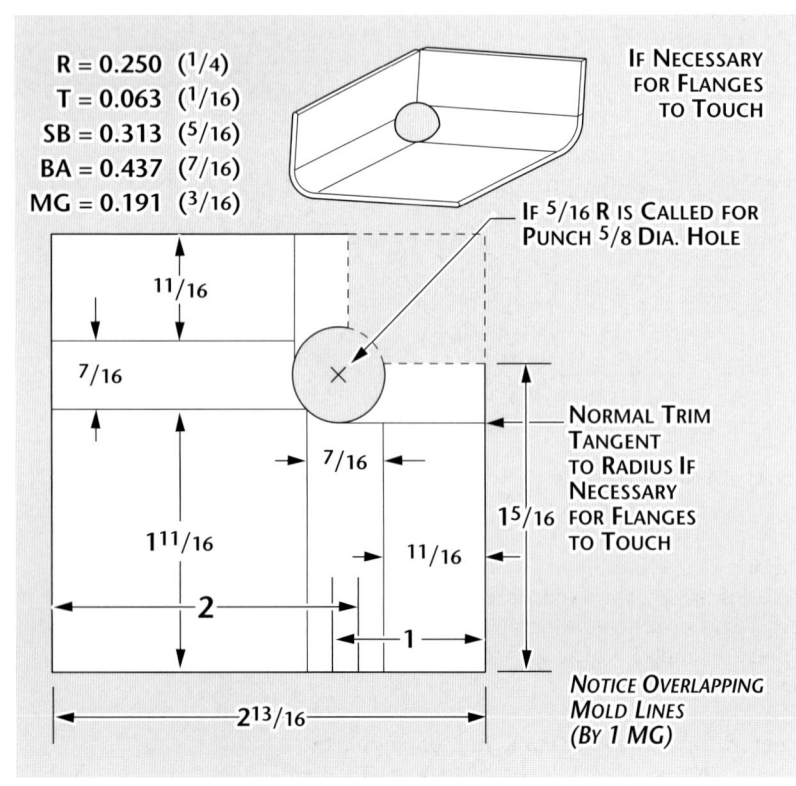

Figure 3-5-27. Application of bend relief holes

all of the recesses of the die and down along its sides.

Flanging lightening holes. Thin sheet metal used for aircraft components usually has plenty of strength, but it often lacks stiffness or rigidity. To increase the stiffness of a part, the metal is often corrugated, and the edges of holes are *flanged*.

The web of a stamped metal wing rib does not carry an excessive amount of load, and the rib can be made much lighter by cutting large *lightening holes* that remove a considerable amount of metal. With these holes cut, the rib is still strong enough, but it lacks rigidity. If the edges of these lightening holes are flanged, the rib will be made stiff.

A set of *flanging dies* are used to flange the lightening holes. The hole is cut in the rib with a hole saw, a punch or a fly cutter and the edges are smoothed to prevent cracking or tearing. The hole is placed over the tapered die, which is placed in the female die. Pressure is applied with an arbor press, which forces the dies together and flanges the edges of the lightening holes. See Figure 3-5-28.

Hand-forming Operations

The methods used in forming operations include bumping, crimping, stretching, shrinking and folding. Any of these methods of cold working a metal will result in the material becoming harder and more brittle than it was. To prevent the metal from cracking, it must be annealed from time to time.

Bumping. Shaping or forming metal by hammering or pounding is called bumping. During this process, the metal is supported by a dolly, a sandbag or a die. Each contains a depression into which the hammered portion of the metal can sink. Bumping can be done by hand or by machine.

Crimping. *Folding, pleating* or *corrugating* a piece of sheet metal in a way that shortens it is called crimping. Crimping is often used to make one end of a pipe smaller so that it may fit inside the end of another identical pipe. As seen in Figure 3-5-29, crimping one side of an angle with *crimping pliers* will cause it to curve.

Stretching. Hammering a flat piece of metal in one location will cause the material in that area to become thinner. See Figure 3-5-30. However, since the amount of material has not changed, it covers a greater area because the metal has been stretched. As Figure 3-5-30 illustrates, the vertical face of the angle has not changed, so the piece will bend as a result of the stretching on the horizontal face.

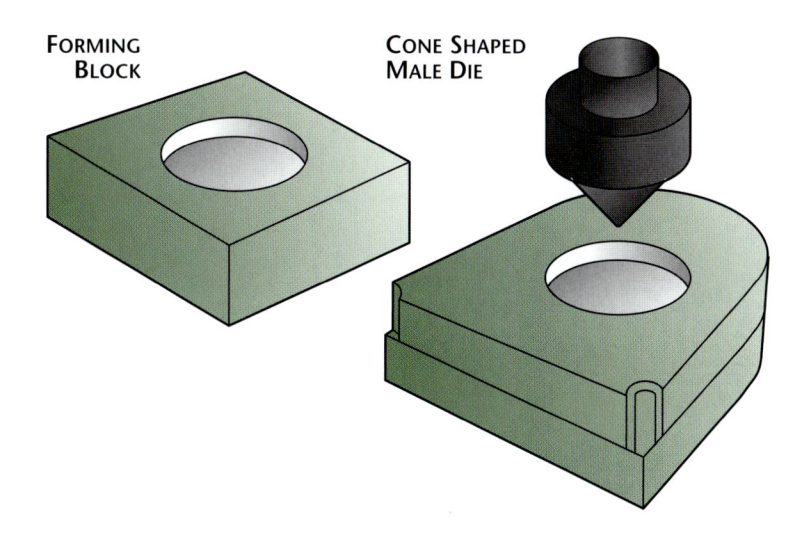

Figure 3-5-28. Chambered flanging block

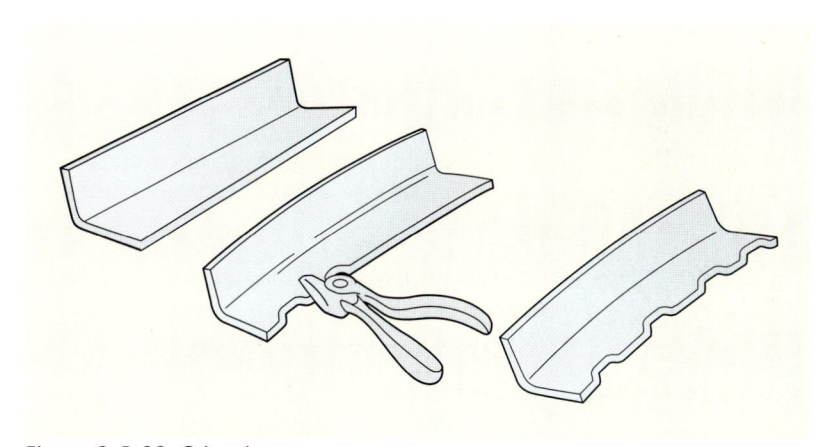

Figure 3-5-29. Crimping

Figure 3-5-30. Stretching

Shrinking. During the *shrinking* process, material is forced or compressed into a smaller area. This process is used when the length of a piece of metal, especially on the inside of a bend, is to be reduced.

Sheet metal can be shrunk in two ways: by hammering on a *V-block*, or by crimping and then using a V-block.

V-block. To curve a formed angle on a V-block, place it on the V-block and gently hammer on the upper edge directly above the V, as shown in Figure 3-5-31. While hammering, move the angle back and forth across the V-block to compress the material along the upper edge. Compression of the material along the upper edge of the vertical flange will cause the formed angle to curve.

Crimping and V-block. To make a sharp curve or a sharply bent flanged angle, crimping and the V-block can be used. Crimps are placed in one flange, and then by hammering the metal on the V-block, the crimps will be driven out one at a time.

Folding. Making bends in sheets or plates is called folding. Folds are usually thought of as sharp, angular bends, and they are generally made on folding machines.

Hand-forming Procedures

All forming revolves around the process of shrinking and stretching. Large metal-working machines are normally used to simplify these processes. However, in their absence, metal can still be worked by hand. The following paragraphs discuss some of these techniques.

Straight-line bends. Hand-formed folds and bends can be made in the following manner using wooden or metal bending blocks.

- Layout: The material should be laid out as required and the blank piece cut out. Clamp the material rigidly along the bend line between two wooden forming blocks by placing and holding it in a vise. The wooden forming block should have one edge rounded as needed for the desired radius of bend. It should also be curved slightly beyond the 90° point to allow for springback.

- Work: With the metal sheet held firmly in the vise by the forming blocks, use a rubber, plastic, or rawhide mallet and lightly tap the sheet. This will cause the metal to begin protruding beyond the forming blocks to the desired angle. Start tapping at one end and work back and forth along the edge, thus gradually and evenly making the bend. Continue doing this until the protruding metal is forced down to the desired angle against the forming block. Allow for springback by driving the material slightly farther than the actual bend. If a large amount of metal extends beyond the forming blocks, maintain hand pressure against the protruding sheet to prevent it from bouncing. Remove any irregularities by holding a straight block of hardwood edgewise against the bend and striking it with heavy blows of a mallet or hammer. If only a small amount of metal protrudes beyond the forming block, use the hardwood block and hammer to make the entire bend.

Curving formed or extruded angles. Both formed and extruded types of angles can be curved (not bent sharply) by stretching or shrinking either of the flanges. Curving by stretching the one flange is usually preferred since the process requires only a V-block and a mallet and is easily accomplished.

- Stretching: In the *stretching* process, place the flange to be stretched in the groove of the V-block. Using a stretching mallet, strike the flange directly over the V portion with light, even blows while gradually forcing it downward into the V. Too heavy a blow will buckle the angle strip. Keep moving the angle strip across the V-block, but always strike the spot directly above the V. Form the curve gradually and evenly by moving the strip slowly back and forth, distributing the hammer blows at equal spaces on the flange.

- Pattern: Lay out a full-sized, accurate *pattern* on a sheet of paper or plywood and periodically check the accuracy of the curve. Comparing the angle with the pattern will determine exactly how the curve is progressing, and just where it needs to be increased or decreased. It is better to get the curve to conform roughly to the desired shape before attempting to finish any one portion, because the finishing or smoothing of the angle may cause some other portion of the angle to change shape. If any part of the angle strip is curved too much, reduce the curve by reversing the angle strip on the V-block, placing the bottom flange up, and striking it with light blows of the mallet.

Figure 3-5-31. Shrinking

- **Work-hardening:** Try to form the curve with a minimum amount of hammering, because excessive hammering will *work-harden* the metal. Work-hardening can be recognized by a lack of bending response or by springiness in the metal. It can be recognized very readily by an experienced worker. In some cases, the part may have to be annealed during the curving operation. If so, be sure to heat-treat the part again before installing it on the aircraft.

- **Shrinking:** Curving an extruded or formed angle strip by shrinking may be accomplished by either of two methods: the V-block method or the shrinking block method. Of the two, the V-block is, in general, more satisfactory because it is faster, easier and affects the metal less. However, very good results can be obtained by the shrinking block method.

V-block method. In the V-block method, place one flange of the angle strip flat on the V-block with the other flange extending upward, as shown in Figure 3-5-31. Hold it firmly so that it does not bounce when hammered, and strike the edge of the upper flange with light blows of a round, soft-faced mallet.

1. Begin at one end of the angle strip and, working back and forth, strike light blows directly over the V-portion of the block.

2. Strike the edge of the flange at a slight angle, as this tends to keep the vertical flange from bending outward.

3. Occasionally, check the curve against the pattern for accuracy. If a sharp curve is made, the angle (cross section of the formed angle) will close slightly.

4. To avoid such closing of the angle, clamp the angle strip to a hardwood board using small C-clamps. The hammered flange should be facing upward.

5. The jaws of the C-clamps should be covered with masking tape.

6. If the angle has already closed, bring the flange back to the correct angle with a few blows of a mallet or with the aid of a small hardwood block.

7. If any portion of the angle strip is curved too much, reduce it by reversing the angle on the V-block and hammering with a suitable mallet, as explained in the previous paragraph on stretching.

8. After obtaining the proper curve, smooth the entire angle by planishing or smoothing with a soft-faced mallet.

Shrinking block method. If the curve in a formed angle is to be quite sharp or if the flanges of the angle are rather broad, the shrinking block method is generally used. In this process, crimp the flange which is to form the inside of the curve.

- **Crimping:** When making a crimp, hold the crimping pliers so that the jaws are about 1/8 inch apart. By rotating the wrist back and forth, bring the upper jaw of the pliers into contact with the flange, first on one side and then on the other side of the lower jaw. Complete the crimp by working a raised portion into the flange, gradually increasing the twisting motion of the pliers. This is shown in Figure 3-5-29. Do not make the crimp too large because it will be difficult to work out. The size of the crimp depends upon the thickness and softness of the material, but usually about 1/4 in. is sufficient. Place several crimps spaced evenly along the desired curve with enough space left between each crimp so that jaws of the shrinking block can easily be attached.

- **Shrinking:** After completing the crimping, place the crimped flange in the shrinking block so that one crimp at a time is located between the jaws. Flatten each crimp with light blows of a soft-faced mallet, starting at the apex (the closed end) of the crimp and gradually working toward the edge of the flange. Check the curve of the angle with the pattern periodically during the forming process, and again after all the crimps have been worked out. If it is necessary to increase the curve, add more crimps and repeat the process. Space the additional crimps between the original ones so that the metal will not become unduly work-hardened at any one point. If the curve needs to be increased or decreased slightly at any point, use the V-block.

Forming flanged angles. The forming process for the following two flanged angles is slightly more complicated than that just discussed, in that the bend is shorter (not gradually curved), and necessitates shrinking or stretching in a small or concentrated area. If the flange is to point toward the inside of the bend, the material must be shrunk. If it is to point toward the outside, it must be stretched.

In forming a flanged angle by shrinking, use wooden forming blocks similar to those shown in Figure 3-5-32 and proceed as follows:

1. Cut the metal to size, allowing for trimming after forming. Determine the bend allowance for a 90° bend and round the edge of the forming block accordingly.

2. Clamp the material in the form blocks as shown in Figure 3-5-32, and bend the exposed flange against the block. After bending, tap the blocks slightly. This induces a setting process in the bend.

3. Using a soft-faced shrinking mallet, start hammering near the center and work the flange down gradually toward both ends. The flange will tend to buckle at the bend because the material is made to occupy less space. Work the material into several small buckles instead of one large one and work each buckle out gradually by hammering lightly and gradually compressing the material in each buckle. The use of a small hardwood wedge block, as shown in Figure 3-5-32, will aid in working out the buckles.

4. Once the wrinkles are worked out and the material is relatively flat, the final flattening can be done. Use a hardwood or lead paddle and a mallet to work the flange into finished form. See Figure 3-5-33.

5. Planish the flange after it is flattened against the form block to remove small irregularities. If the form blocks are made of hardwood, use a metal planishing hammer. If the forms are made of metal, use a soft-faced mallet. Trim the excess material away and file and polish.

Stretching. To form a flanged angle by stretching, use the same forming blocks, wooden wedge block and mallet as in the shrinking process and proceed as follows:

1. Cut the material to size (allowing for trim), determine bend allowance for a 90° bend, and round off the edge of the block to conform to the desired radius of bend.

2. Clamp the material in the form blocks as shown in Figure 3-5-34.

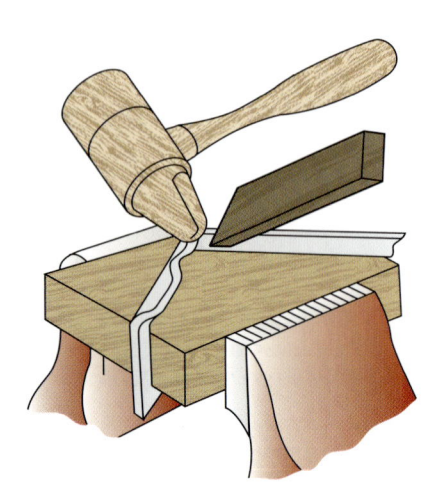

Figure 3-5-32. Forming a flanged angle by shrinking

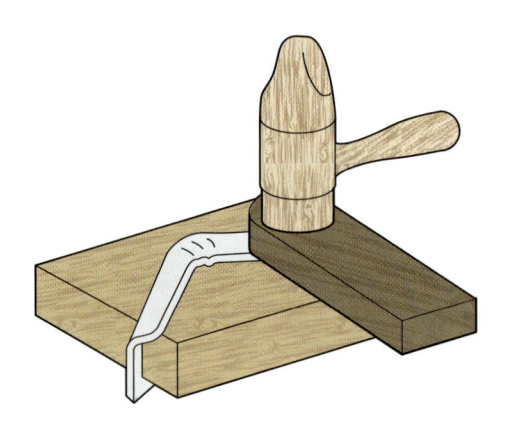

Figure 3-5-33. The last of the wrinkles are worked out with a paddle and a mallet.

3. Using a soft-faced stretching mallet, start hammering near the ends and work the flange down smoothly and gradually to prevent cracking and splitting. Planish the flange and angle as described in the previous procedure, and trim and smooth the edges, if necessary.

Forming curved flanged parts. Curved flanged parts are usually hand-formed. They usually have a *concave flange* (the inside edge), and a *convex flange* (the outside edge). Note the various types of forming represented in the following figures. Figure 3-5-35 shows a plain nose rib.

Only one convex flange is used, but because of the great distance around the part and the potential of buckles in forming, it is rather difficult to form. The flange and the beaded portion of this rib, however, provide sufficient strength to make this a very good type to use.

In Figure 3-5-36 the concave flange gives difficulty in forming, however, the outside flange is broken up into smaller sections by relief holes. The notches that prevent strain in a bend in the type shown in Figure 3-5-36. Note that crimps are inserted at equally spaced intervals. The crimps are placed to absorb material and cause curving while also giving strength to the part. In the nose rib shown in Figure 3-5-37 and Figure 3-5-38, note that a combination of the four common forming methods is applied.

They are crimping, beading, putting in relief holes, and using a formed angle riveted on at each end. The beads and the formed angles supply strength to the part.

Forming blocks. These blocks are made in pairs similar to those used for straight angle bends and are identified in the same manner. They differ in that they are made specifically for the particular part to be formed, they fit each other exactly, and they conform to the actual dimensions and

Figure 3-5-34. Forming a flanged angle by stretching

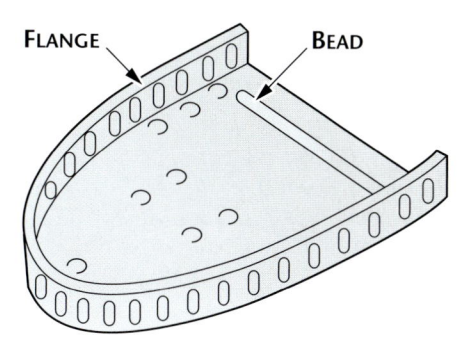

Figure 3-5-35. Plain nose rib

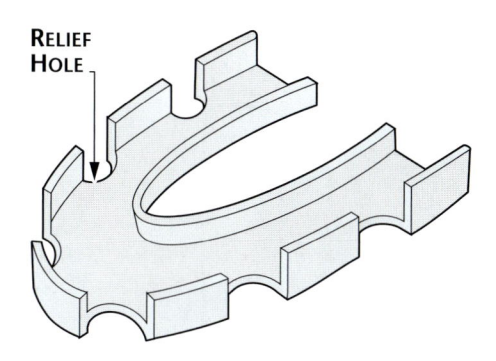

Figure 3-5-36. Nose rib with relief holes

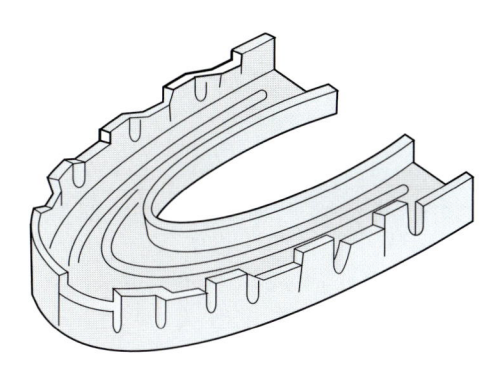

Figure 3-5-37. Nose rib with crimps and beads

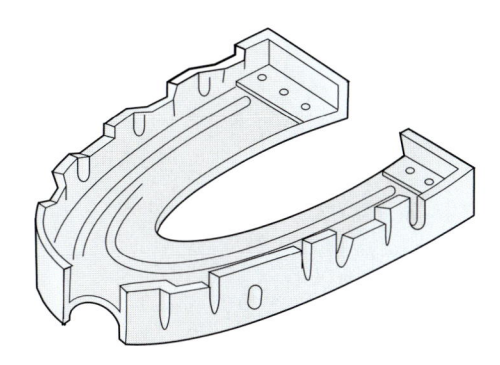

Figure 3-5-38. Nose rib using beads, crimps, relief holes and riveted angles

contour of the finished article. The mating parts may be equipped with aligning pins to aid in lining up the blocks and holding the metal in place. The blocks may be held together by C-clamps or a vise. They also may be held together with bolts by drilling through both forms and the metal, provided the holes do not affect the strength of the finished part. The edges of the forming block are rounded to give correct radius of bend to the part, and are undercut to allow for spring back of the metal. The undercut is especially necessary if the material is hard or if the bend must be highly accurate.

Forming procedures. See Figure 3-5-39. The major steps in forming a curved flanged part are explained as follows:

1. Cut the material to size (allowing for trim), locate and drill holes for alignment pins, and remove all burrs (jagged edges) from the metal and the forming blocks to be put together.

2. Place the material between the wooden blocks. Clamp blocks tightly in a vise so that the material will not move or shift. Clamp the work as closely as possible to the particular area being hammered to prevent strain on the form blocks and to keep the metal from slipping.

3. Bend the flange on the concave curve first. Using a soft mallet or wooden wedge block, start hammering at a point a short distance away from the beginning of the concave bend and continue toward the center of the bend. Continue hammering until the metal is gradually worked down over the entire flange, flush with the form block.

4. Starting at the center of the curve and working toward both ends, hammer the convex flange down over the form. Strike the metal with glancing blows, at an angle of approximately 30° off perpendicular, and with a motion that will tend to pull the part away from the block.

5. Stretch the metal around the radius bend and remove the buckles gradually by hammering on a wedge block.

6. While working the metal down over the form, keeping the edges of the flange as nearly perpendicular to the block as possible, to lessen the possibility of buckles and of splitting or cracking the metal, and aids in removing buckles.

7. Finally, trim the flanges of excess metal, planish, remove burrs, round the corners (if any) and check the part for accuracy.

Forming by bumping. The two commonly used methods of bumping are on a form block or female die and bumping on a sandbag. Either method requires only one form: a wooden block, a lead die or a sandbag. The blister or streamlined cover plate is an example of a part made by the block or die method of bumping. Wing fillets are an example of parts that are usually formed by bumping on a sandbag.

Form block bumping. This is done with a wooden block or lead die. Such a die or block designed for bumping must have the same dimensions and contour as the outside of the blister. To provide enough bucking weight and bearing surface for fastening the metal, the block or die should be at least 1 inch larger in all dimensions than the form requires (Figure 3-5-40).

Preparing the form block. The following procedures should be followed to create a form block:

1. Hollow the block out with tools such as saws, chisels, gouges, files and rasps.

2. Smooth and finish the block with sandpaper. The inside of the form must be as smooth as possible, because the slightest irregularity will show up on the finished part.

3. Prepare several templates (patterns of the cross-section) as shown in Figure 3-5-40 so that the form can be checked for accuracy.

4. Shape the contour of the form at points 1, 2 and 3, shown in Figure 3-5-40.

5. Shape the areas between the template check points to conform the remaining contour to template 4.

Bumping procedure. After the form is prepared and checked, perform the bumping as follows:

1. Cut a metal blank to size, allowing an extra one-half to 1 inch to permit drawing.

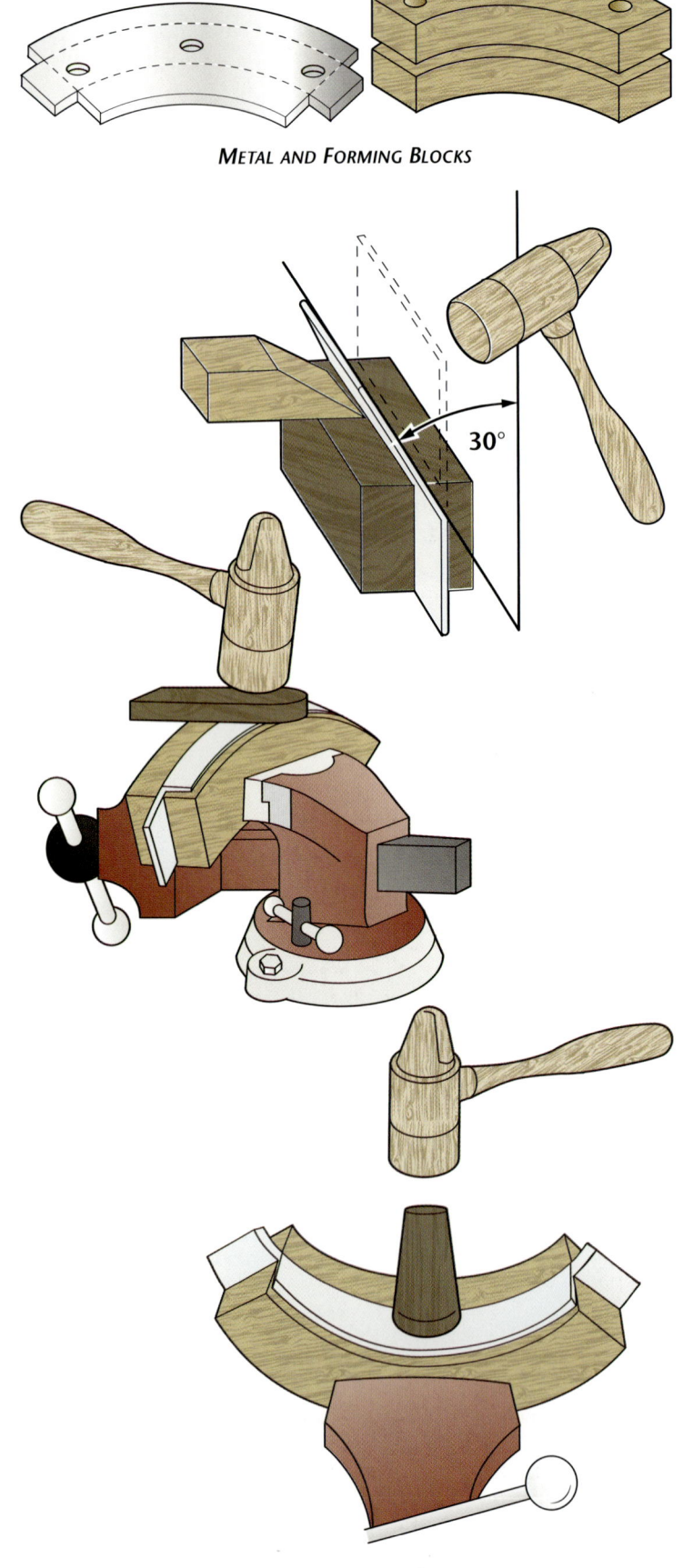

Figure 3-5-39. Forming convex and concave flanges

2. Apply a thin coat of light oil to the block and the aluminum to prevent galling (scraping on rough spots).

3. Clamp the material between the block and steel plate so that it will be firmly supported and yet able to slip a little toward the inside of the form.

4. Clamp the bumping block in a bench vise. Use a soft-faced rubber mallet or a hardwood drive block with a suitable mallet to start bumping near the edges of the form.

5. Work the material down gradually from the edges with light blows of the mallet. Remember that the purpose of bumping is to work the material into shape by stretching rather than forcing it into the form with heavy blows. Always start bumping near the edge of the form. Never start near the center of the blister.

6. Before removing the work from the form, smooth it as much as possible by rubbing it with the rounded end of either a maple block or a stretching mallet.

7. Remove the blister from the bumping block and trim to size.

Sandbag bumping. This is one of the most difficult methods of hand-forming sheet metal because there is no exact forming block to guide the operation. Therefore, a depression must be driven into the sandbag to take the shape of the hammered portion of the metal. The following procedure for bumping sheet metal parts on a sandbag includes certain basic steps that can be applied to any part, regardless of its contour or shape.

1. Layout and cut the contour template (This can be made of sheet metal, medium-heavy cardboard or thin plywood).

2. Determine the amount of metal needed, lay it out and cut it to size, allowing at least 1/2 inch in excess.

3. Place a sandbag on a solid foundation capable of supporting heavy blows, and make a pit in the bag with a smooth-faced mallet. Analyze the part to determine the correct radius the pit should have for the forming operation. The pit will change shape with the hammering it receives and must be readjusted occasionally.

4. Select a soft round-faced or bell-shaped mallet with a contour slightly smaller than the contour desired on the sheet metal part. Hold one edge of the metal in the left hand and place the portion to be bumped near the edge of the pit on the sandbag. Strike the metal with light glancing blows about one-half to 1 inch from the edge. An example of this process is shown in Figure 3-5-41.

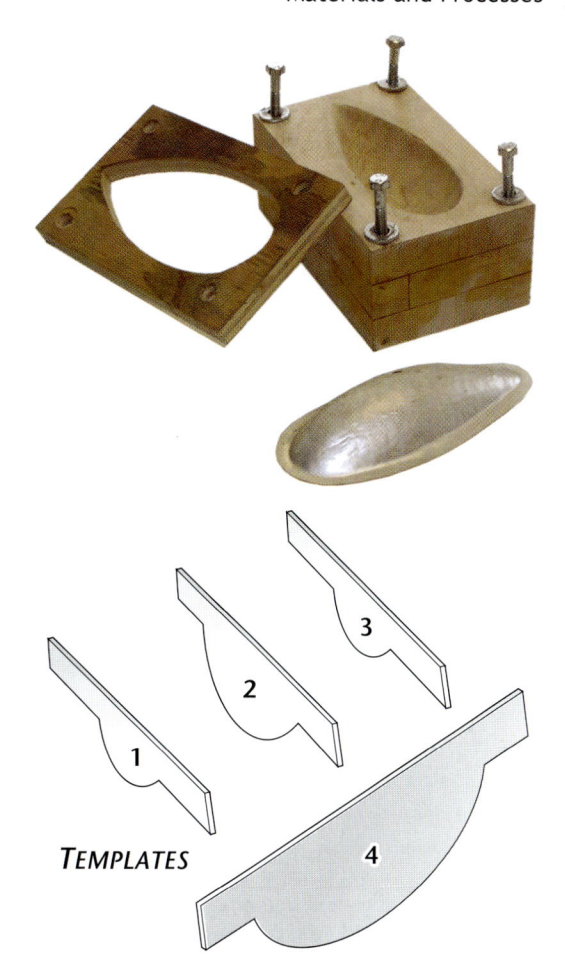

Figure 3-5-40. Form block and finished blister

5. Continue bumping toward the center, revolving the metal and working gradually inward until the desired shape is obtained. Shape the entire part as a unit.

6. Check the part often for accuracy of shape during the bumping process by applying the template. If wrinkles form, work them out before they become too large.

7. Finally, remove small dents and hammer marks with a suitable stake and planishing hammer or with a hand dolly and planishing hammer.

8. After bumping, use a pair of dividers to mark around the outside of the object.

9. Trim the edge and file it smooth. Clean and polish the part.

Joggle

Joggling is the process of offsetting a plane of sheet metal to provide room for another sheet on the same plane. It is a simple, light and effective method of joining because only half the number of fasteners and half of the material overlap is used when compared to a traditional butt joint with doubler.

Figure 3-5-41. Sandbag bumping

Joggles can be utilized on not only flat sheets of metal and skins, but also on angles and channels as well. Special tooling such as matched metal dies may be necessary to form wide joggles, double joggled 90° angles and triple joggled U-channels. Many times, this tooling is made in-house for particular jobs (Figure 3-5-42).

The distance between the two bends of a joggle is called the allowance. This dimension will normally be called out on the drawing. However, a general rule of thumb is 4 times the thickness of the displacement of flat sheets. For 90° angles it must be slightly more because of the stress built up at the radius while joggling. For extrusions, the allowance can be as much as 12 times the material thickness. So it is important to follow the drawing.

Joggling a single leg of a 90° angle can be accomplished as simply as clamping that leg in a vise using a strip of metal taped to each side at the proper location. These strips would have to be thicker than the desired offset to allow for some spring back. A wooden joggling block could also be used. The disadvantage of these methods is that the other leg will be free to warp and distort as the joggle takes place. So it will require some tapping and prying on that leg to attempt to bring it back into alignment. The superior method to form this type of joggle is with a hydraulic joggling machine. With this method, the non-joggled leg is trapped between two dies to limit its distortion.

When joggling a flat sheet in a cornice brake, set the nose gap a little wider than would normally be called for to allow the use of a relatively small nose radius. This will allow the part to be bent 20°-30° without overstressing the metal by forcing too tight of a radius.

Bending over stakes. Stakes are used to back up sheet metal to form many different curves, angles and seams. Stakes are available in a wide variety of shapes. The stakes are held securely in a stake holder or stake plate, which is anchored in a workbench. The stake holder contains a variety of holes to fit a number of different types of shanks. Although stakes are by no means delicate, they must be handled with reasonable care. They should not be used as backing when you are chiseling holes or notches in sheet metal.

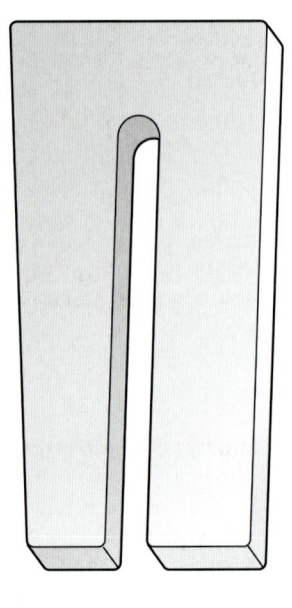

Figure 3-5-42. A simple joggling die

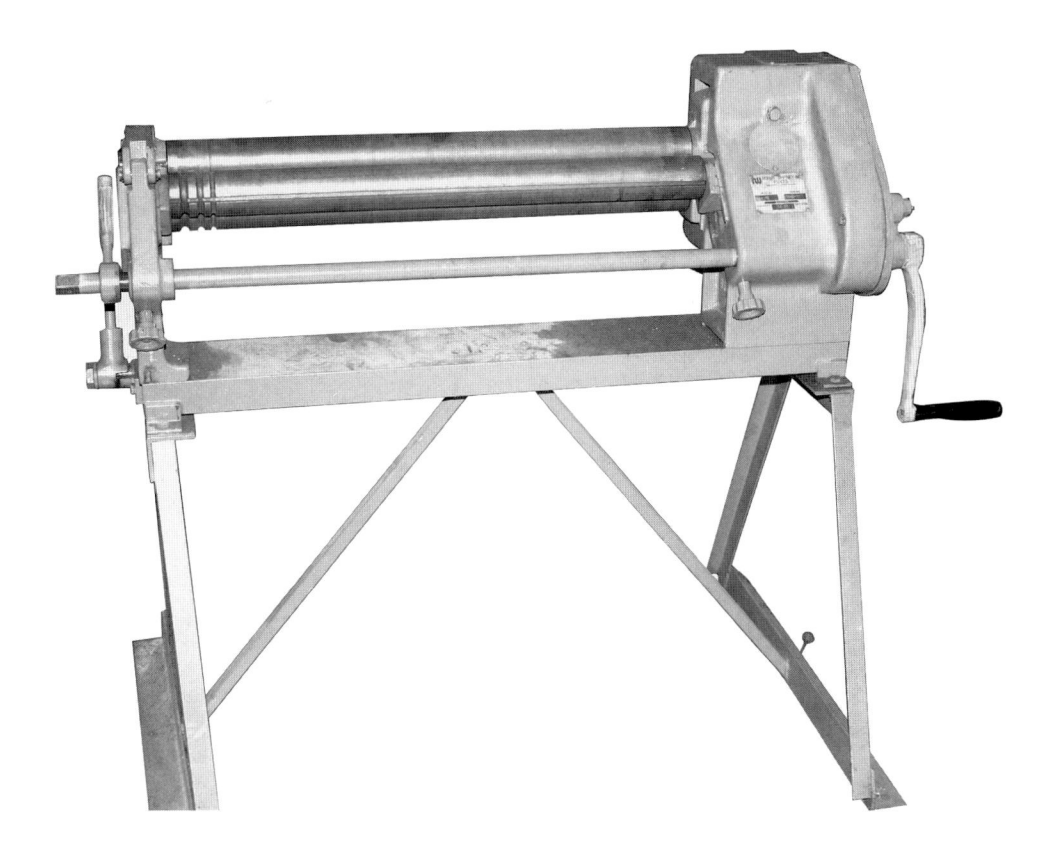

Figure 3-5-43. A slip-roll can form a wide variety of cylindrical or conical shapes.

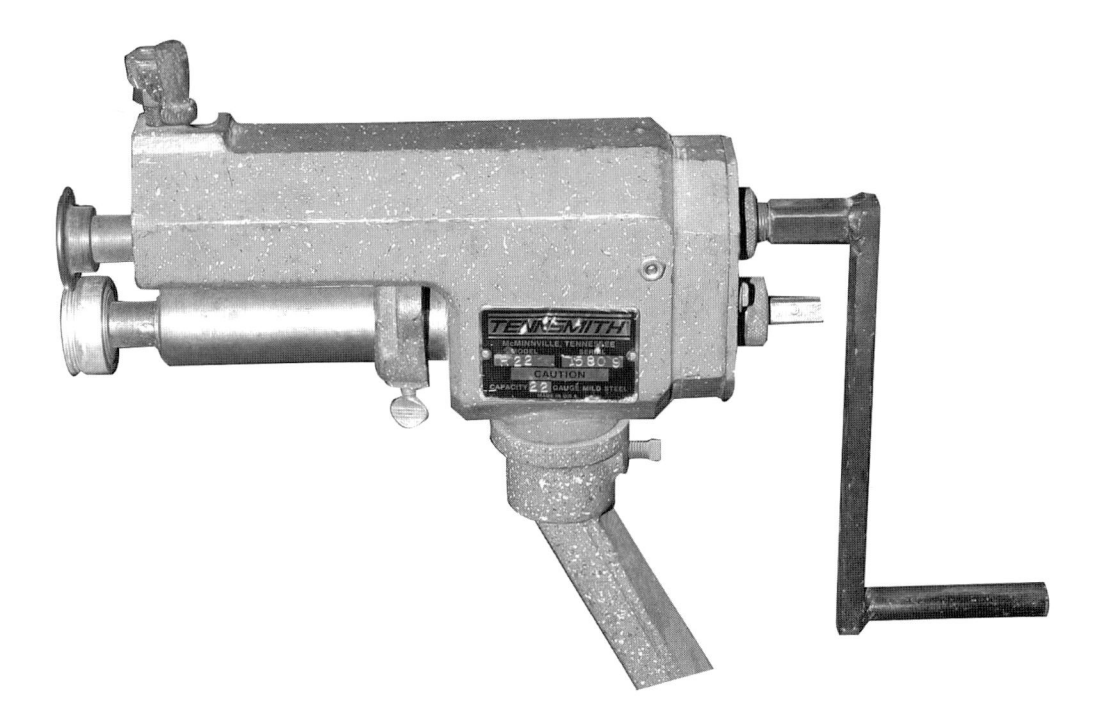

Figure 3-5-44. A rotary machine for rolling edges, forming flanges and making beads around large tubing.

Forming Machines

A sheet metal object made on a brake will have corners (bends) and sides (flanges). On a forming machine, it is possible to make an object without sides, such as a funnel. The two most common forming machines are the slip-roll and the rotary.

Slip-roll forming machine. Sheet metal can be formed into curved shapes over a pipe or a mandrel, but the slip-roll forming machine, Figure 3-5-43, is easier to use and produces more accurate bends. Most slip-rolls are regular commercial machines that have grooves for wired edges. Rolling machines are available in various sizes and capacities. Some are hand operated, and others are power operated.

Rotary machine. The rotary machine shown is used on cylindrical and flat sheet metal to shape the edge or to form a bead along the edge. Various shaped rolls can be installed on the rotary machine to perform different operations. See Figure 3-5-44.

Eckold "piccolo" sheet metal former. The piccolo (Figure 3-5-45) is available for cold forming sheet metal and other profile sections (extrusions). The power is transmitted mechanically by V-belts from the electric motor to the eccentric wheel and pressure lever. The position of the ram is adjustable in height by means of a foot pedal permitting control of the working pressure. Be sure to utilize the adjusting ring situated in the machine head to control the maximum working pressure. The forming tools are located in the moving ram and the lower tool holder. They are the quick-change magnetic type and are available in either fiberglass faced (to prevent marring the surface) or steel faced (for working harder materials).

Shrinking tools. Shrinking dies repeatedly clamp down on the metal, then shift inward. This compresses the material between the dies, which will actually slightly increase the thickness of the metal. Strain-hardening takes place during this process, so it is best to set the working pressure high enough to complete the shape rather quickly (eight passes could be considered excessive).

> **CAUTION:** *Avoid striking dies on the radius itself when forming a curved flange. This will damage the metal in the radius and decrease the angle of bend.*

Stretching tools. Stretching dies repeatedly clamp down on the surface and then shift outward. This stretches the metal between the dies, which decreases the thickness in the stretched area. Caution should be used to avoid striking the same point too many times or the part will weaken and eventually crack. It is advantageous to deburr, or even polish, the edges of a flange undergoing even moderate stretching in order to avoid crack formation. Forming flanges with existing holes will cause the holes to distort and possibly crack or substantially weaken the flange.

Shrinkers and Stretchers

The only dies available are steel-faced, and therefore tend to mar the surface of the metal. When they are used on aluminum, it will be necessary to gently blend out the surface irregularities (primarily in the cladding), then treat and paint the part.

Since this is a manual machine, it relies on your arm power repeatedly pulling on the lever. If the dies are in good condition, it may amaze you how effective this tool is. The harder you pull on the lever, the more stresses will concentrate at that single point. It will yield a better part with a series of smaller stretches (or shrinks) than with a few intense ones. Be careful not to squeeze the dies over the radius or it will damage the metal and flatten out some of the bend. It may be handy to tape a thick piece of plastic or micarta to the opposite leg to shim the radius of the angle away from the clamping area of the dies. See Figure 3-4-46 and Figure 3-5-47.

Figure 3-5-45. An Eckold piccolo forming machine. Smoother results in heavier stock can be obtained than with a hand shrinker/stretcher.

Photo courtesy of U.S. Industrial Tools

Figure 3-5-46. A manually operated bench-mounted stretcher *Photo courtesy of U.S. Industrial Tools*

Figure 3-5-47. A manually operated bench-mounted shrinker *Photo courtesy of U.S. Industrial Tools*

Operation. Watch the part change shape while you slowly apply pressure. A number of small stretches works more effectively than one large one. If you apply too much pressure, the metal has the tendency to buckle. Take your time.

Forming Compound Curves on Sheet Metal

English wheel. A forming tool called an English wheel is one of the best tools for hand forming sheet stock to specific compound curves, such as engine cowling, nacelles or forward fuselage skin. The English wheel is a large machine that basically works by pulling sheet metal back and forth between two rollers. Each roller has a curved surface. See Figure 3-5-48.

By moving the sheet between the rollers and gradually increasing pressure, the sheet metal curves. With skillful observation and manipulation of the process, an experienced operator can produce almost any bend or combination of bends.

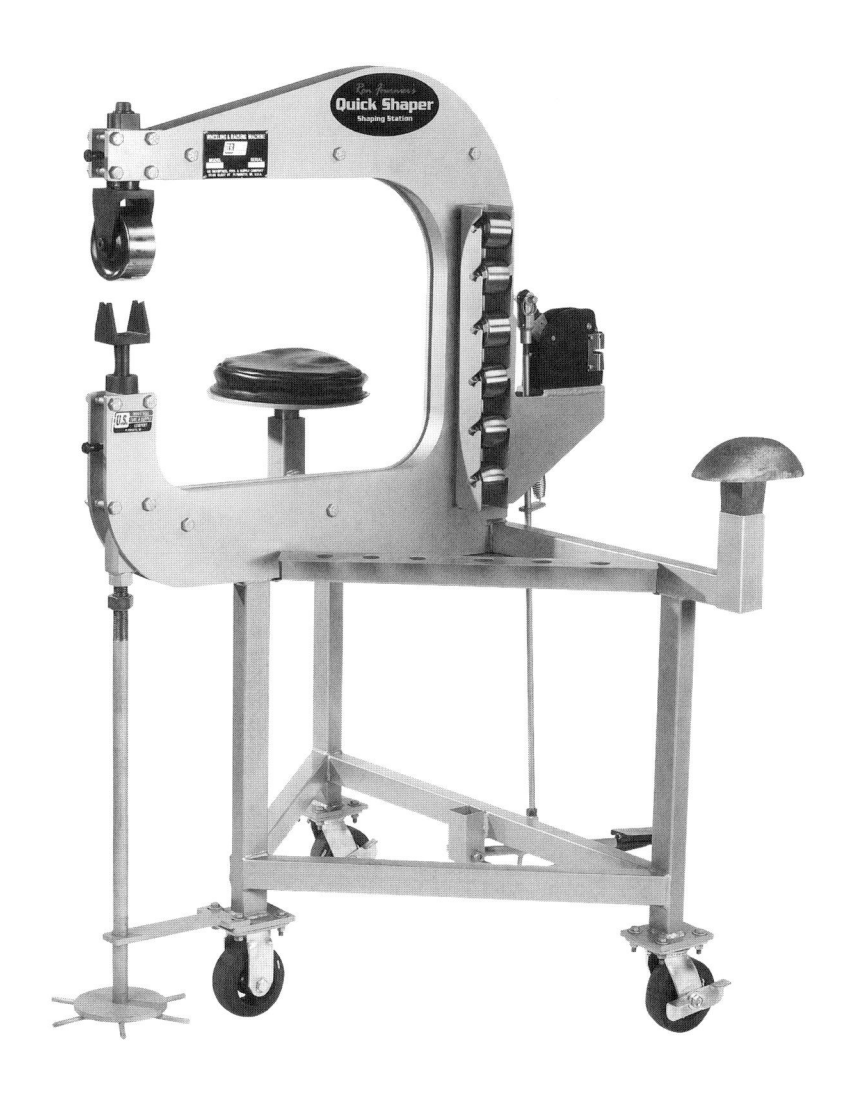

Figure 3-5-48. An English wheel allows the operator to form compound curves. *Photo courtesy of U.S. Industrial Tools*

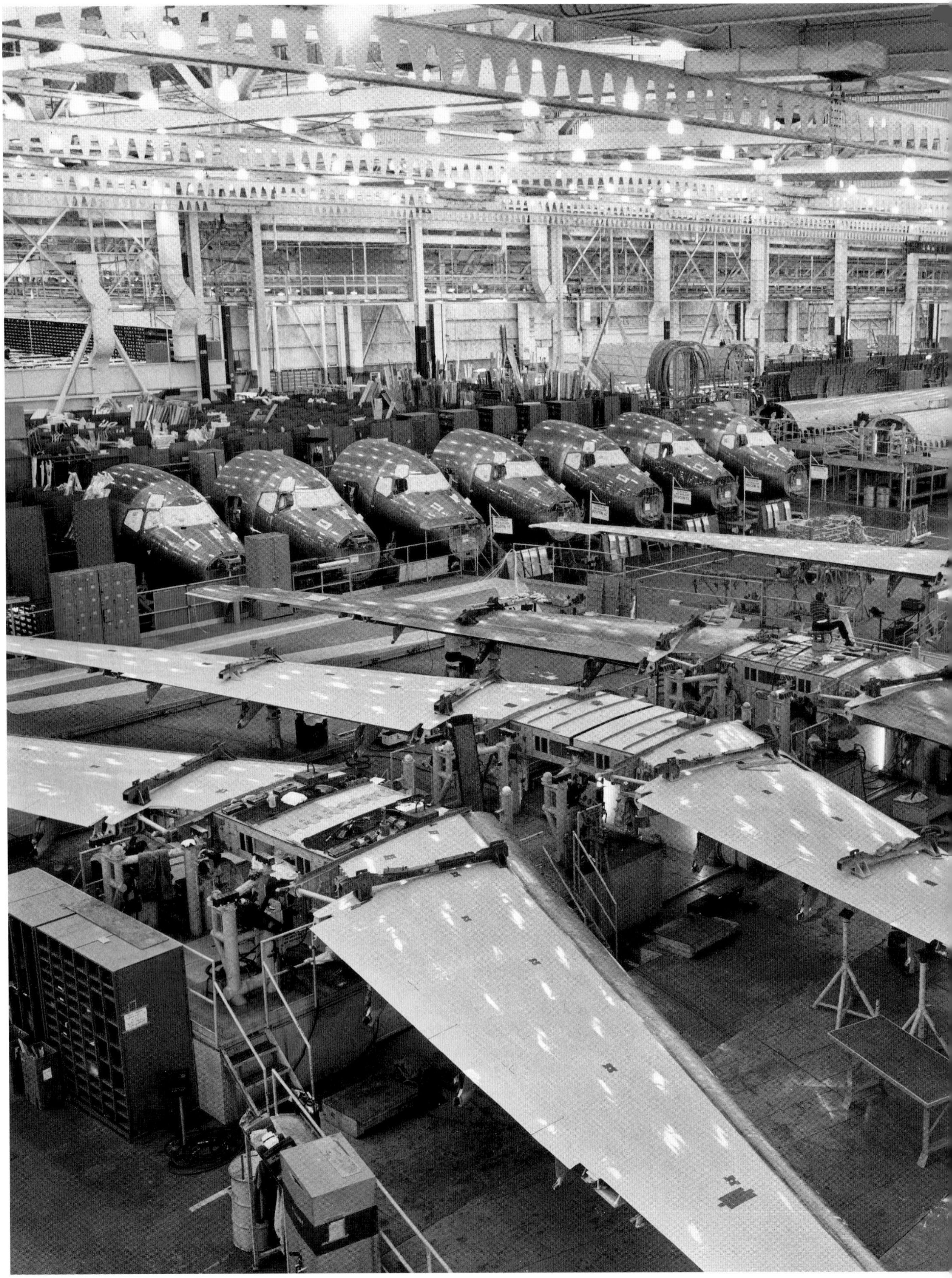

4

Airframe Metallic Structures

Section 1

Introduction to Airframe Metallic Structures

An aircraft is constructed of many parts that are either riveted, bolted, screwed, glued, bonded or welded together with connectors, or fasteners. Because these connected parts make up the structure of the aircraft, they are called structural members. Modifications to these parts are undertaken for several reasons. Some are done as improvements; some extend the life of the airframe; others correct potential problems. Some changes are made to keep us competitive in an ever-changing market place.

Structural repair is performed to restore and maintain structural integrity. The need for repairs is normally determined during a planned inspection period and is the result of normal stress, erosion and corrosion. Sometimes, damage is the result of an incident or mishap. The guideline that airframe technicians follow is based on a principle called *as-designed*.

There are only a few different types of construction, though they vary considerably in complexity. Obviously, the complexity depends on the type of aircraft. A small, two-seat private airplane can be very simply constructed, while large commercial airplanes are quite complex.

Structural materials have evolved and developed as aviation has progressed. The earliest aircraft structures were made of wood and fabric. Within a few decades lightweight metallic materials became prevalent. In recent decades there have been significant developments in composite structures.

Learning Objectives

REVIEW
- Metals used in aircraft structures
- Types of stress
- Rivet installation

DESCRIBE
- Parts of the fuselage
- Structural members
- Back-up structures and typical repairs to them

EXPLAIN
- Types of wing design
- Preparing for structural repairs
- Rivet spacing in metal skin repairs

APPLY
- Inspect an aircraft's structure
- Patch an aircraft's skin
- Repair major structural parts of an aircraft
- Calculate the stress on a joint

Left. New construction methods and alloys are rapidly finding their way into aircraft production. However the mainstay of aircraft structures is still aluminum alloy.

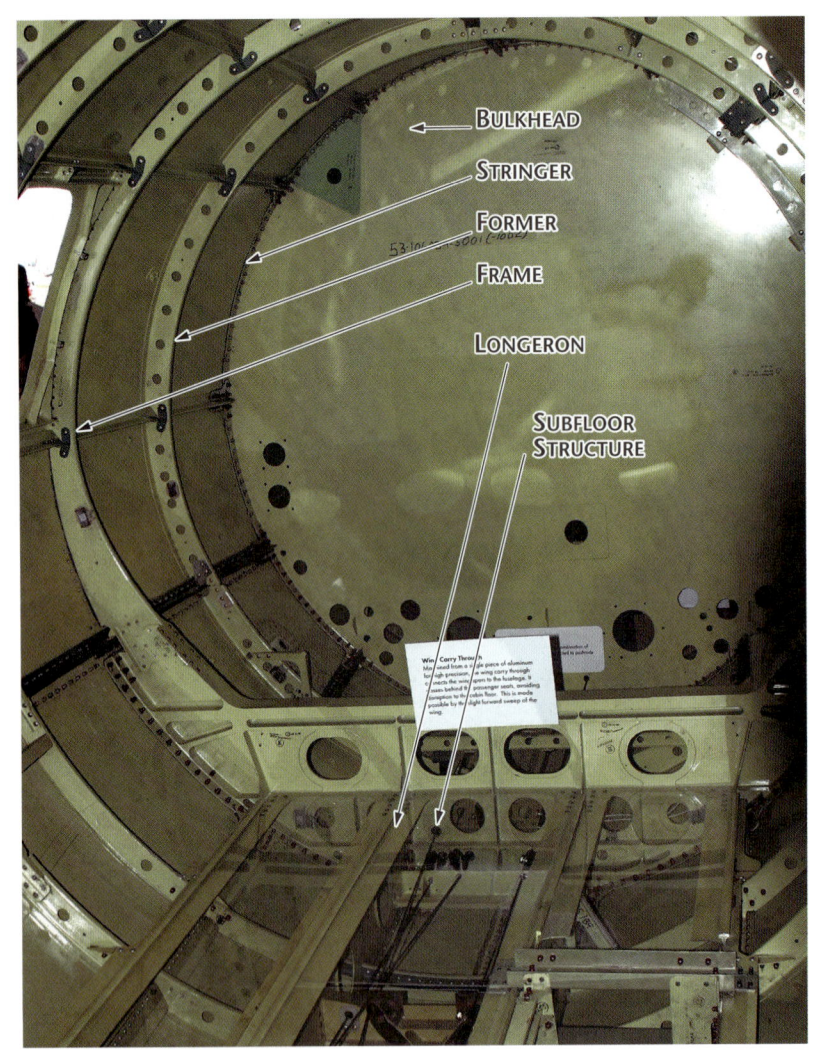

Figure 4-1-1. Monocoque construction

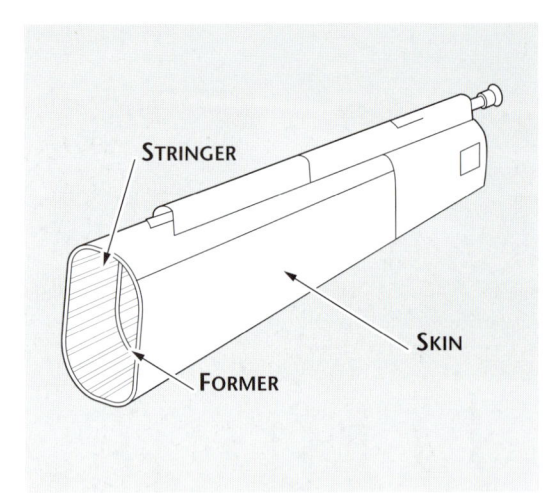

Figure 4-1-2. Semi-monocoque construction

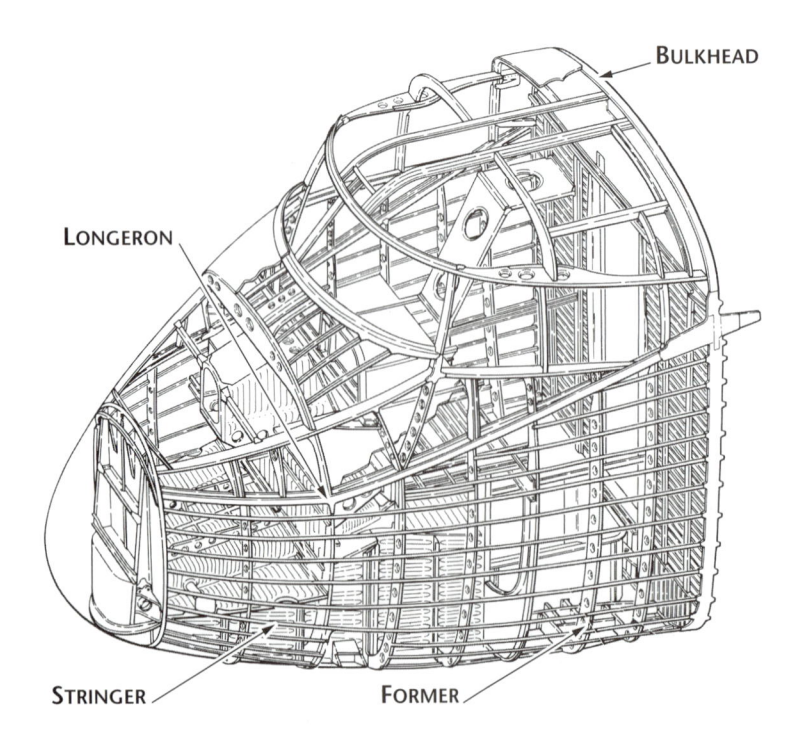

Figure 4-1-3. Reinforced-shell construction

This chapter covers the basic terminology of aircraft structures as well as design and repair of primarily metallic structures. The following chapter covers non-metallic structures such as wood, plastics and composites.

Fuselage

The basic type of fuselage construction now in use in helicopters and airplanes is the monocoque. This type of construction, shown in Figure 4-1-1 is like a shell in which the skin carries the major stresses and functions as part of the airframe. The classic example of a full monocoque construction is the aluminum beverage can. Undented, it is extremely strong in almost all directions. However, even a slight dent will cause it to lose its strength and collapse.

In the full monocoque construction shown in Figure 4-1-1, the formers and bulkhead merely provide the shape; the skin carries the primary stress. This type of construction is rarely used because of its limited load-carrying capability. Therefore, two modifications of this construction were developed: *semi-monocoque* and *reinforced-shell construction*.

The semi-monocoque type is the most widely used type of construction in aviation today and has formers, with the skin reinforced by stringers, as shown in Figure 4-1-2. The semi-monocoque fuselage is constructed primarily of aluminum alloy; however, on newer aircraft graphite epoxy composite material is often used. Steel and titanium are found in areas subject to high temperatures.

Primary bending loads are absorbed by the longerons, which usually extend across several points of support. The longerons are supplemented by other longitudinal members, called

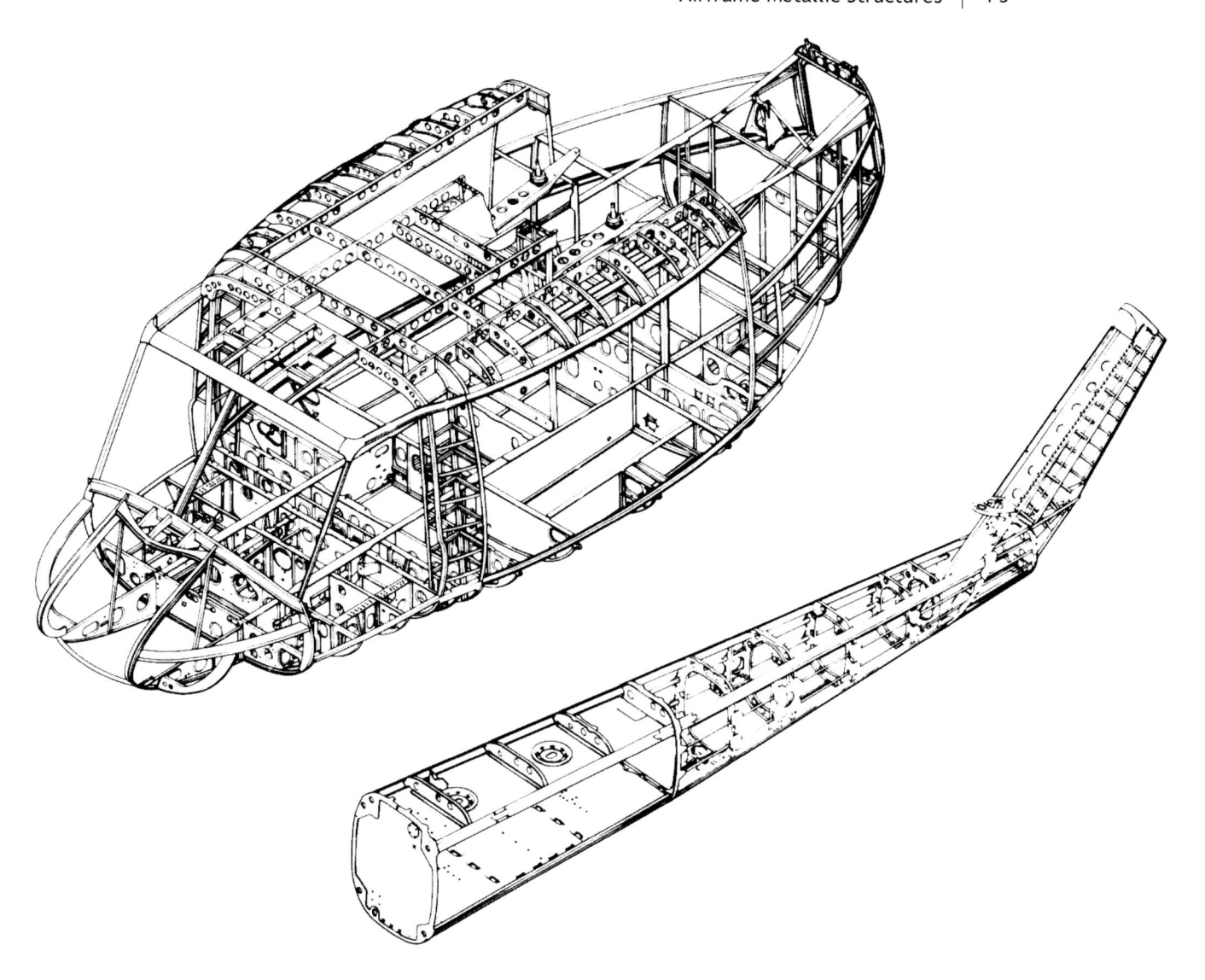

Figure 4-1-4. Helicopter airframe sections

stringers. Stringers are lighter in weight and are used more extensively than longerons. The vertical structural members are referred to as bulkheads, frames, and formers. These vertical members are grouped at intervals to carry concentrated loads and at points where fittings are used to attach other units, such as the wings, engines, and stabilizers.

The skin is attached to the longerons, bulkheads, and other structural members and carries part of the load. Skin thickness varies with the loads carried and the stresses supported. There are many advantages in the use of the semi-monocoque fuselage. The bulkheads, frames, stringers, and longerons aid in the construction of a streamlined fuselage. They also add to the strength and rigidity of the structure. The main advantage of this design is that it does not depend only on a few members for strength and rigidity. All structural members aid in the strength of the fuselage. This means that a semi-monocoque fuselage may withstand considerable damage and still remain strong enough to hold together.

Figure 4-1-3 shows the reinforced-shell construction, where the skin is reinforced by a complete framework. While similar to semi-monocoque construction, this type relies much more on the underlying framework for its strength. The skin helps tie all of the structural members together and provides aerodynamic streamlining.

Helicopters

The fuselage of a helicopter has two or more main sections, as shown in Figure 4-1-4. The cabin section contains the passenger or cargo compartments, with space for the crew, passengers, cargo, fuel, oil tanks, controls and power plant. The cone is attached to the cabin in such a manner that it can be removed, inspected, repaired or replaced as necessary.

Figure 4-1-6. Engine mount

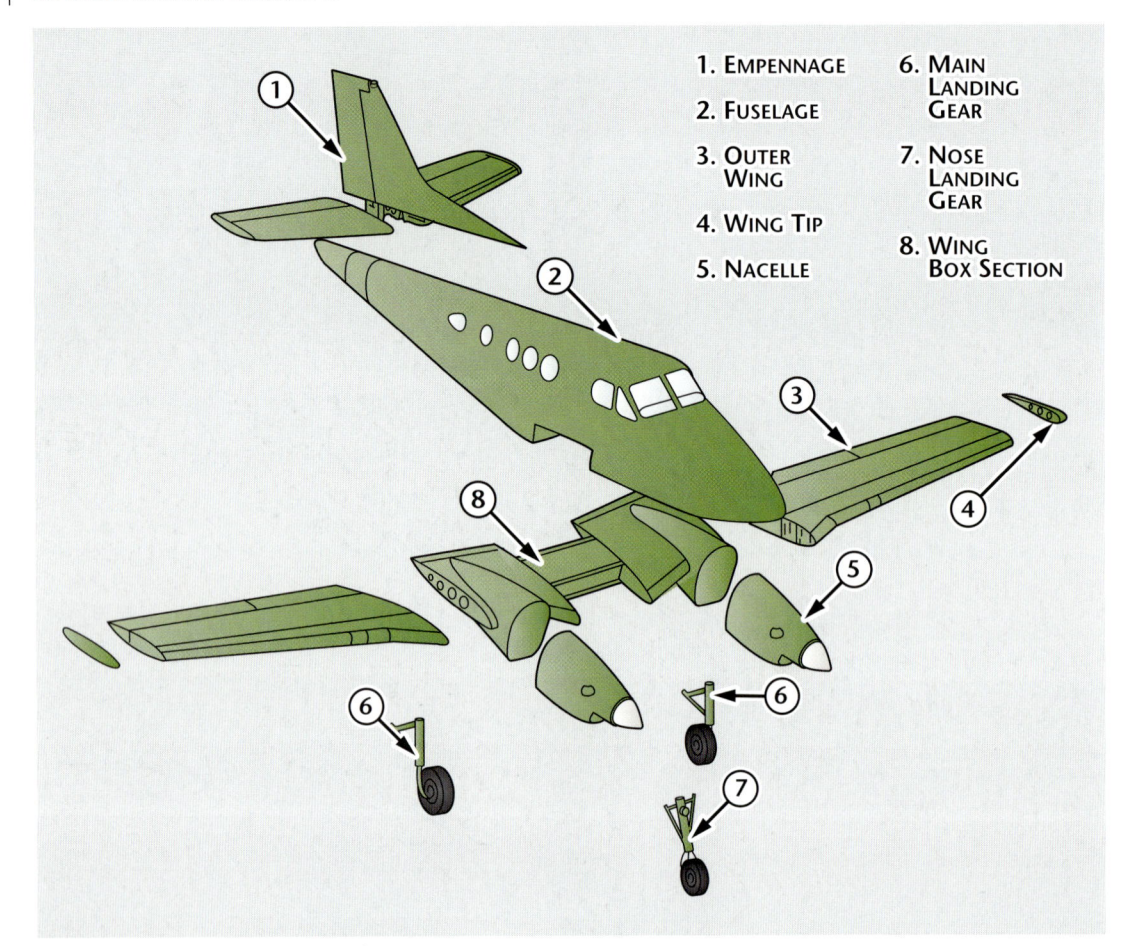

1. EMPENNAGE
2. FUSELAGE
3. OUTER WING
4. WING TIP
5. NACELLE
6. MAIN LANDING GEAR
7. NOSE LANDING GEAR
8. WING BOX SECTION

Figure 4-1-5. Airframe structural parts

The cone supports the tail rotor, tail rotor drive shafts and the stabilizer. The aft fuselage supports the aft pylon.

Airplanes

The fuselage is the main structural unit of any airplane. As Figure 4-1-5 shows, the other structural units are directly or indirectly attached to it. On most multi-engine airplanes, the power plants are housed in nacelles, which are either built into the wings or suspended in pods from the wings or fuselage. The basic internal structure of an airplane fuselage is the same as that of a helicopter.

Construction Materials

The metal in general use for fuselage construction is aluminum alloy, principally one of the two alloys commercially known as 7075-T and 2024-T. These are about three times lighter than steel and, after being heat-treated, have strength approximately equal to that of mild steel. Skin sheet metal is usually Alclad aluminum. Extrusions are generally of 2024-T, however, 2014-T is being used for extrusions with web thickness greater than 1/8 inch.

Engine Mounts

Engine mounts are designed to meet particular conditions of installations, such as location on aircraft, methods of attachment, and size, type and characteristics of the engine they are intended to support. A typical engine mount is shown in Figure 4-1-6. Although they vary widely in their appearance and in arrangement of their members, the basic features of engine mount construction are similar.

Piston-engine mounts. A primary consideration in design of engine mounts is to render the engine and its equipment accessible for maintenance and inspection. A framework construction of welded chrome-molybdenum steel tubing is well adapted to this purpose and is used extensively. Forgings of chrome-nickel molybdenum are used for the more highly stressed fittings, these being accurately machined at points of rigid connection to the engine or other structures.

Turbine-engine mount. Some important features of turbine-engine mounts are as follows:

- They operate in a high-temperature environment.

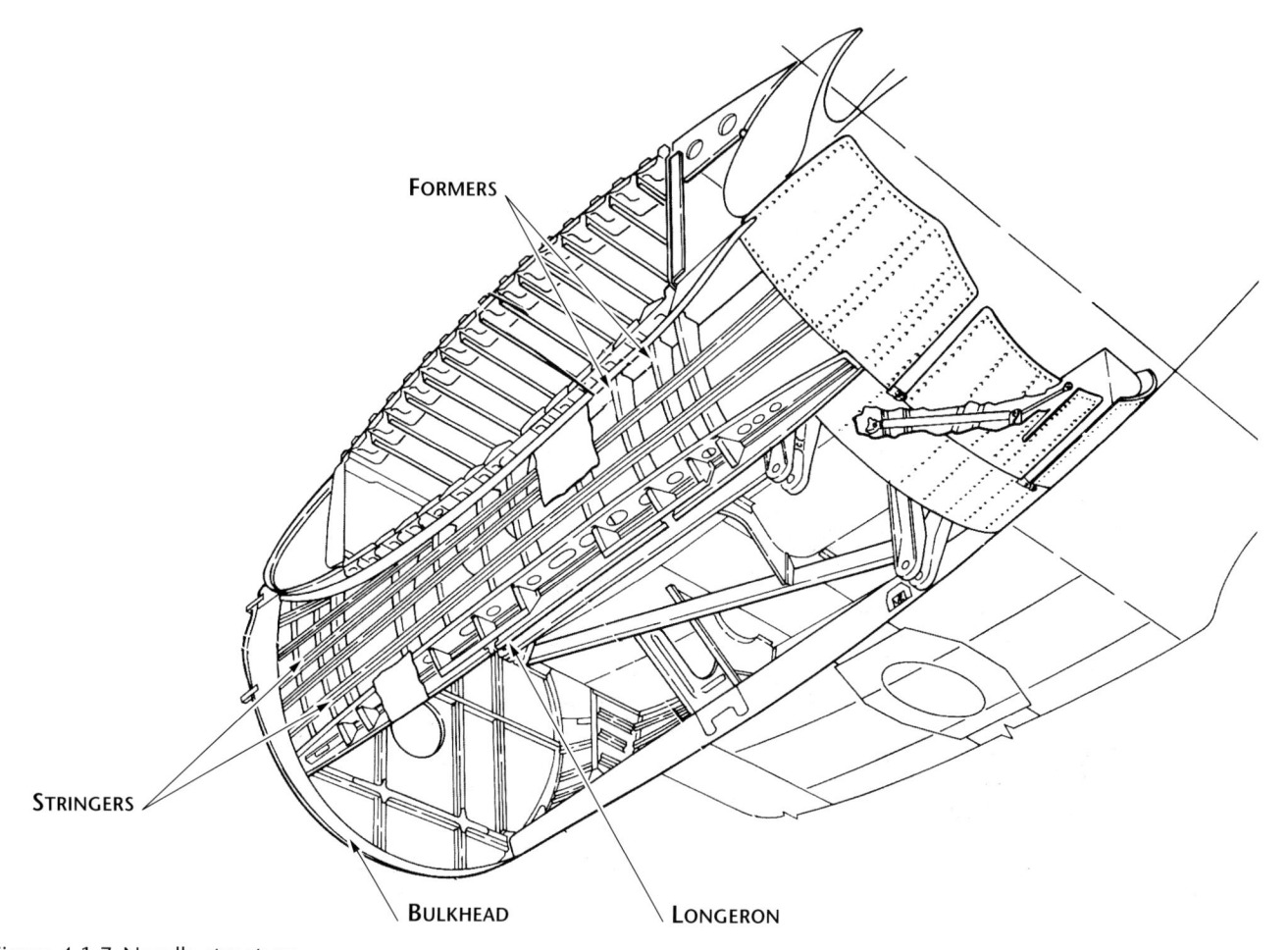

Figure 4-1-7. Nacelle structure

- They are subjected to high-vibration inertial loads.
- They are susceptible to fatigue failure from their loading environment.
- Corrosion properties must be of the highest quality to prevent stress-corrosion failures.
- Improper torque of fittings and fasteners, coupled with flight load, can cause fastener failure. This is critical to safety of flight.

Maintenance

Cracked, bent or broken members of these structures constitute a highly dangerous condition and, without exception, must be replaced or repaired by those authorized to do such work before the aircraft will be permitted to be flown. The point at which the loads of the airframe's individual parts are transferred is called a *joint*. In order to transfer the load properly, connectors (nuts, bolts, screws, rivets, glue bonds or welds) are used.

In general, cracks are most likely to occur at the welded joints. Small cracks, in particular, may be difficult to see through the protective coating. This is especially true if the structure is not kept thoroughly clean, and special care must be exercised in making inspections at these points. Mounting clamps and bolts, if not properly tightened, will allow movement of the mount with consequent rapid wear of the bolts, elongation of bolt holes and a resultant serious vibration. Protective coatings, if damaged, should be retouched promptly to prevent corrosion of exposed steel surfaces.

Nacelles. Nacelles are enclosed, streamlined structures that primarily house the engines on multi-engine aircraft. They are used on helicopters and airplanes as required by the engine configuration. On airplanes, they may even house the landing gear and some cargo. As Figure 4-1-7 shows, the structure is essentially the same as for a fuselage.

Nacelles vary with the size of the aircraft. Larger aircraft require less fairing, and therefore relatively smaller nacelles. The structural design of a nacelle is similar to that of the fuselage. In certain cases the nacelle is designed to transmit engine loads and stresses to the wings through the engine mounts.

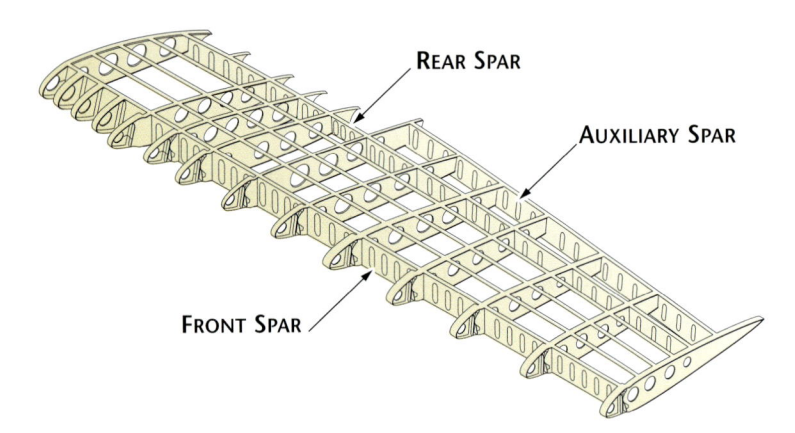

Figure 4-1-8. Multi-spar wing construction

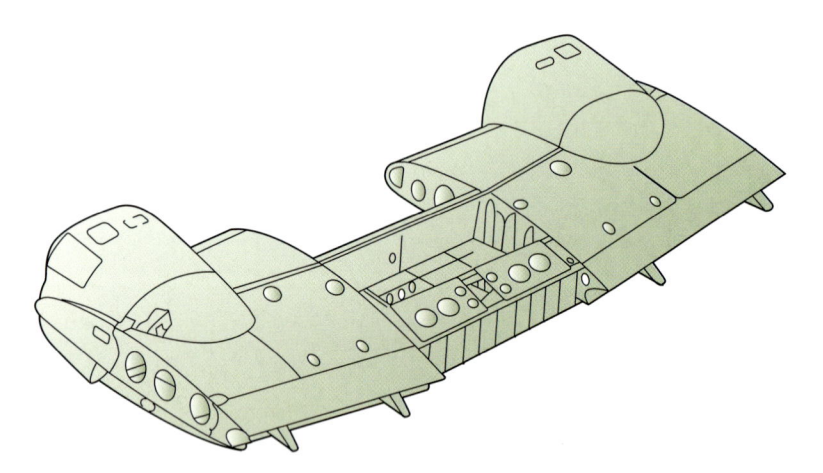

Figure 4-1-9. Box beam construction

support all distributed loads as well concentrated weights, such as a fuselage, landing gear, and nacelle.

Inspection and access panels are usually provided on the lower surface of a wing. Drain holes are also placed in the lower surfaces. Walkways are provided on the areas of the wing where personnel should walk or step. The substructure is stiffened or reinforced in the vicinity of the walkways to take such loads. Walkways are usually covered with a nonskid surface.

Some aircraft have no built-in walkways. In these cases removable mats or covers are used to protect the wing surface. On some aircraft, jacking points are provided on the underside of each wing. The jacking points may also be used as tiedown fittings for securing the aircraft.

Types of Design

In general, wing construction is based on one of three fundamental designs: *mono-spar*, *multi-spar* and *box beam*.

Mono-spar. The mono-spar wing uses only one main longitudinal member in its construction. Ribs or bulkheads provide the necessary contour, or shape, to the airfoil. Wings of the strict mono-spar type of construction are not in common use; however, they are often used, when modified by adding false spars or light shear webs along the trailing edge as support for the control surfaces.

Multi-spar. The multi-spar wing, shown in Figure 4-1-8, uses more than one main longitudinal member in its construction. Ribs or bulkheads are included to give contour to the wing. This type of construction is used in lighter aircraft.

Box beam. The box beam construction, shown in Figure 4-1-9, uses two main longitudinal members with connecting bulkheads to provide additional strength and give contour to the wing. A corrugated sheet may be placed between the bulkheads and the smooth outer skin to enable the wing to carry tension and compression loads better. In some cases, heavy longitudinal stiffeners are substituted for the corrugated sheets, or a combination of corrugated sheets on the upper surface of the wing and stiffeners on the lower surface is used.

Wings. The wings of an airplane are airfoils designed to provide lift at operating speeds of the aircraft. Design and construction of the wings depend on the size, weight, intended use, operating speeds and rate of climb of the airplane. Modern aircraft today have wings of cantilever construction, meaning they have no external bracing. In some aircraft, the larger compartments of the wings are used as fuel tanks. The wings are designated as right and left, corresponding to the right- and left-hand sides of a pilot seated in the aircraft.

Usually wings are of the stress-skin type. This means that the skin is part of the basic wing structure and carries part of the loads and stresses. The internal structure is made of spars and stringers running spanwise, as well as ribs and formers running chordwise. The spars are the main structural members of the wing, and are often referred to as beams.

The skin is attached to all the structural members and carries part of the wing loads and stresses. During flight, the loads imposed on the wing structure act primarily on the skin. From the skin, the loads are transmitted to the ribs and then to the spars. The spars

Spars. Spars are the principal structural members of the wing. They run parallel to the lateral axis, toward the wing tip, and are usually attached to the fuselage by wing fittings, plain beams or by part of a truss system. The I-beam type of spar construction consists of a web and

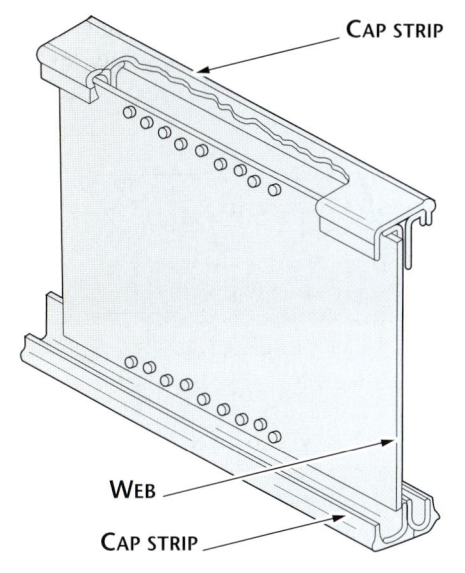

Figure 4-1-10. The I-beam spar, with web and cap strips labeled

Figure 4-1-11. Three types of rib construction

cap strips, as shown in Figure 4-1-10. The web is the portion of the I-beam that is between the cap strips. Cap strips are extrusions, formed angles or milled sections to which the web is attached. They carry the loads caused by the wing bending and provide a foundation for attaching the skin.

Ribs. Ribs are the crosspieces that make up the framework of a wing. They run from the leading edge of the wing toward its trailing edge (front to rear). The ribs give the wing its contour, or shape, and transfer the load from the skin to the spars. Ribs are also used in ailerons, elevators, fins and stabilizers. There are three general types of rib construction: *reinforced*, *truss* and *formed*, as shown in Figure 4-1-11. The reinforced and truss ribs are both relatively heavy compared to the formed rib, and are located only at points where the greatest stresses are imposed.

The construction of *reinforced ribs* is similar to that of spars, consisting of upper and lower cap strips joined together by a web plate. The web is reinforced between the cap strips by vertical and diagonal angles. Reinforced ribs are much more widely used than truss ribs.

Truss ribs consist of cap strips reinforced only by vertical and diagonal cross members. An example of a truss rib is pictured in Figure 4-1-12).

Formed ribs are made of formed sheet metal and are very light in weight. The bent-up portion of a formed rib is known as the *flange*; the vertical portion is called the *web*. The web is generally constructed with *lightening holes*, as shown in Figure 4-1-11, with beads formed between the holes. The lightening holes lessen the weight of the rib without decreasing its strength. The lightening hole areas are made rigid by flanging the edges of the holes. The beads stiffen the web portion of the rib.

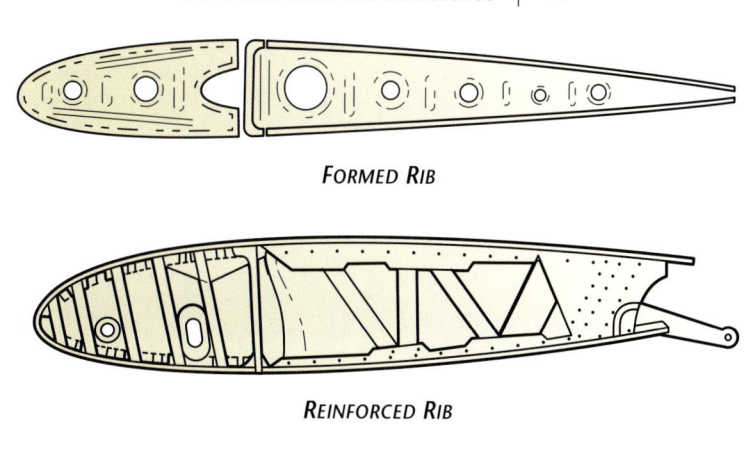

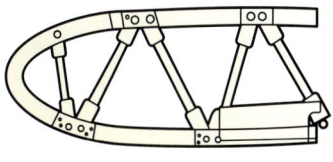

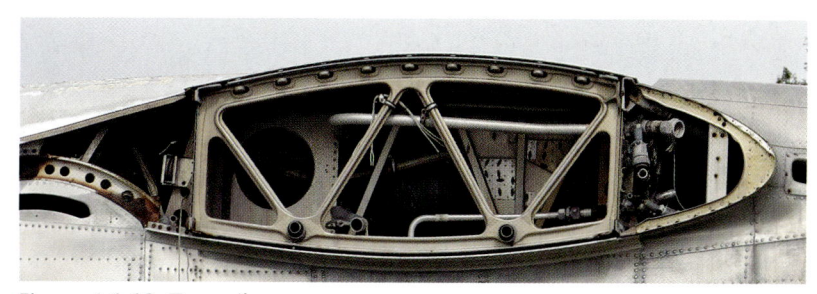

Figure 4-1-12. Truss rib

Empennage. The stabilizing surfaces of an aircraft consist of vertical and horizontal airfoils. These are known as the vertical stabilizer or fin and the horizontal stabilizer. These two airfoils, together with the rudder and elevators, form the tail section. For inspection and maintenance purposes, the entire tail section is considered a single unit of the airframe, and is referred to as the *empennage*.

The primary purpose of the stabilizers is to stabilize the aircraft in flight; that is, to keep the aircraft in straight and level flight. The vertical stabilizer maintains the stability of the aircraft about its vertical axis. This is known as "directional stability." The vertical stabilizer usually serves as the base to which the rudder is attached. The horizontal stabilizer provides stability of the aircraft about the lateral axis. This is "longitudinal stability." It usually serves as the base to which the elevators are attached.

Generally speaking, the empennage structures are the same as those of wings. They are usually of all-metal construction and cantilever design,

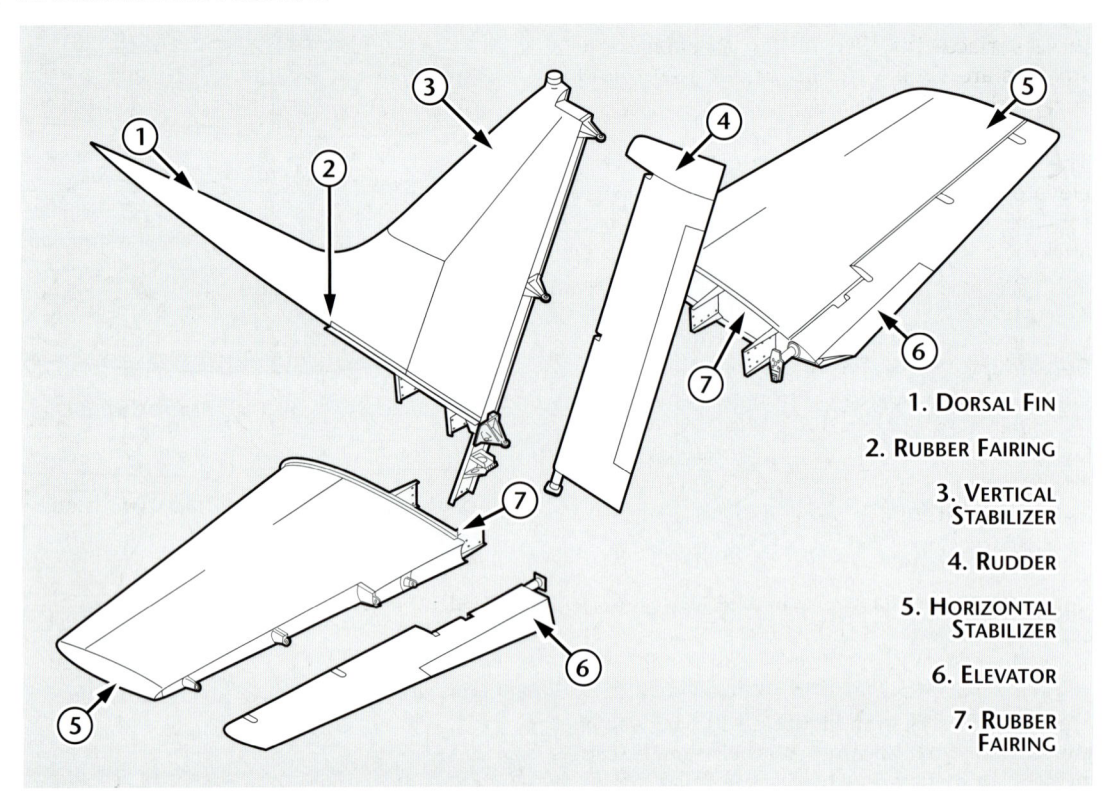

Figure 4-1-13. Empennage assembly

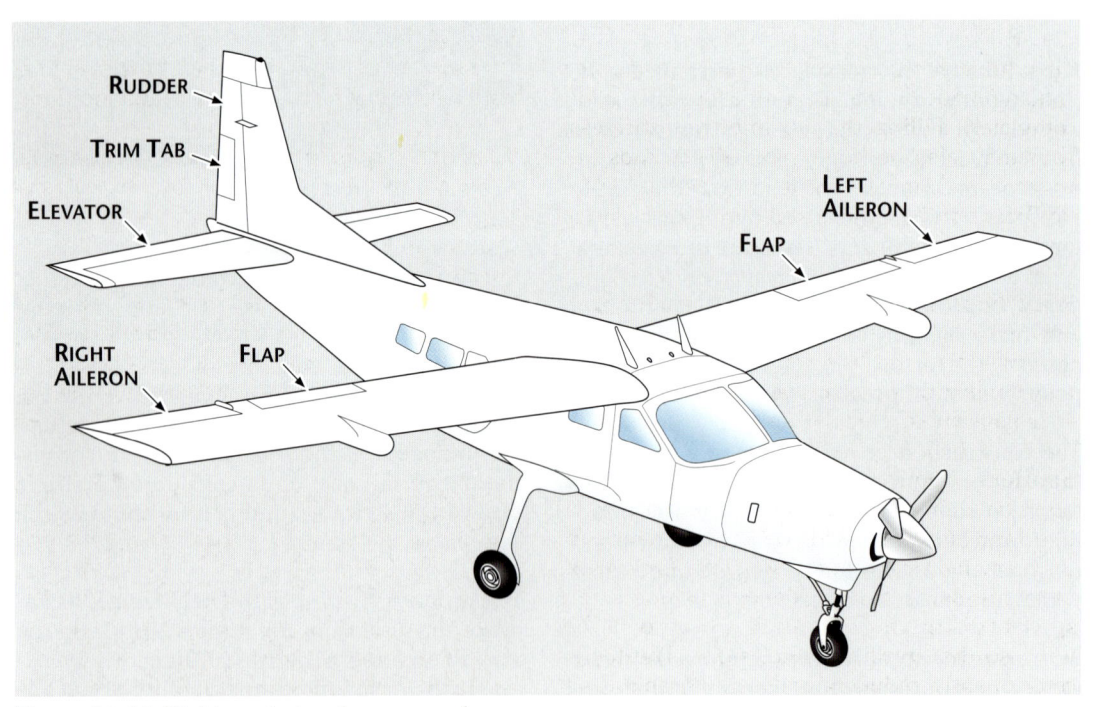

1. DORSAL FIN
2. RUBBER FAIRING
3. VERTICAL STABILIZER
4. RUDDER
5. HORIZONTAL STABILIZER
6. ELEVATOR
7. RUBBER FAIRING

Figure 4-1-14. Flight-control surfaces on a plane

although mono-spar and multi-spar construction are also both commonly used. Ribs give shape to the cross section. Figure 4-1-13 shows a typical empennage assembly and its components.

Flight-control surfaces. Flight-control surfaces are hinged or movable airfoils designed to change the attitude of the aircraft during flight. Flight control surfaces are grouped as systems and are classified as being either primary or secondary. Primary controls are those that provide control over the yaw, pitch, and roll of the aircraft. Secondary controls include the trim tabs, spoilers, slats and flap systems. All systems consist of the control surfaces, cockpit controls, connecting linkage, and other necessary operating mechanisms. They consist of ailerons, elevators, rudders, trim tabs and flaps. Figure 4-1-14 shows these surfaces installed on the aircraft. These surfaces are similar in structure to the control surface shown in Figure 4-1-15.

The primary flight controls are the ailerons, elevators, and rudder. The ailerons and elevators are operated from the cockpit by a control stick or a wheel and yoke assembly. The rudder is operated by rudder pedals on all types of aircraft.

Secondary Flight Controls. Secondary flight controls include those controls not designated as primary controls. The secondary controls supplement the primary controls by aiding the pilot in controlling the aircraft. Various types are used on aircraft, but only the most common are discussed here.

Trim Tabs. Trim tabs are small airfoils recessed in the trailing edge of a primary control surface. Their purpose is to enable the pilot to neutralize any unbalanced condition that might exist during flight, without exerting any pressure on the control stick or rudder pedals. Each trim tab is hinged to its parent control surface, but is operated independently by a separate control.

Construction of trim tabs is similar to that of the other control surfaces, although greater use is being made of plastic materials to fill the tab completely. Filling the tab improves stiffness. Tabs may also be honeycomb filled. Tabs are covered with either metal or reinforced plastic. Trim tabs are actuated either electrically or manually.

Wing flaps. Wing flaps are used to give the aircraft extra lift for take-off or landing. Most flaps are hinged to the lower trailing edges of the wings inboard of the ailerons; however, leading edge flaps are in use on some heavy aircraft.

Spoilers. Spoilers are used for decreasing wing lift; however, their specific design, function, and use vary with different aircraft. In the retracted position, the spoiler is flush with the wing skin, In the extended position, the spoilers disturb the smooth flow of air over the wing so that burbling takes place. The lift is consequently reduced, and considerable drag is added to the wing. They may be independently operated or they may be interconnected with the ailerons.

Slats. Slats are movable control surfaces attached to the leading edge of the wing. When the slat is retracted, it forms the leading edge of the wing. When the slat is opened (extended forward), a slot is created between the slat and the leading edge of the wing. This improves airflow over the wing at low speeds. Slats are normally used during take-off or landing.

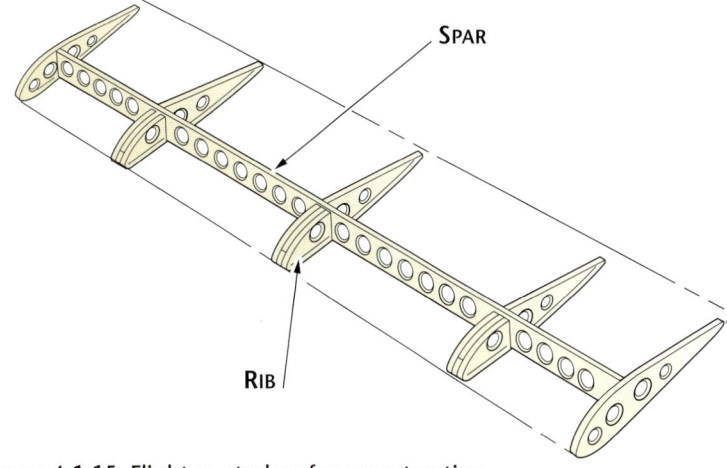

Figure 4-1-15. Flight-control surface construction

Structural Members

Specific structural members consist of bulkheads, frames, formers, stringers and longerons.

Bulkheads, Frames and Formers

Bulkheads, frames and formers serve a dual purpose. They give cross-sectional shape to the fuselage, and they add rigidity and strength to the structure. The shape and size of these structures vary depending on their function and location.

Formers. Formers are the lightest of these units. They are used primarily for support between larger members and for skin attachment and give the surface its form or shape.

Frames. Frame assemblies are the most numerous and important members in the fuselage. They provide the major cross-sectional structure, as shown in Figure 4-1-16, and outline structural features, such as doors and windows.

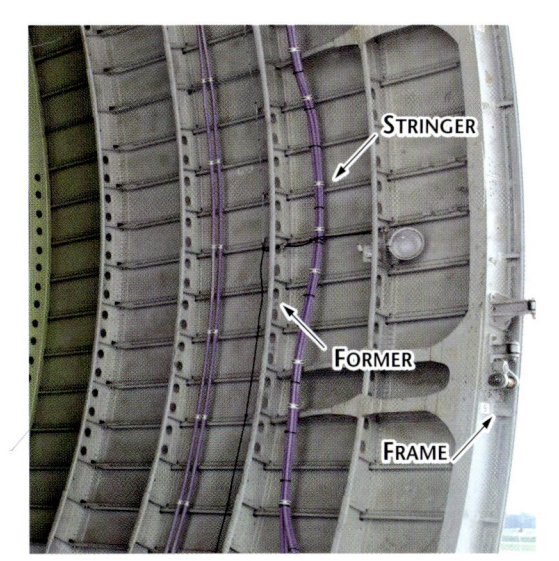

Figure 4-1-16. Typical frame installations

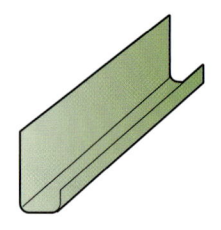

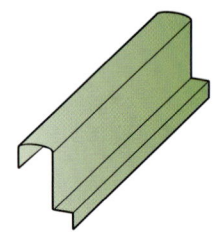

Figure 4-1-18. Stringers

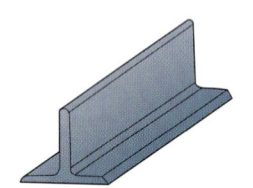

T Extrusion

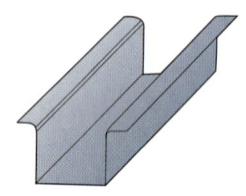

Hat Section

Figure 4-1-19. Longerons

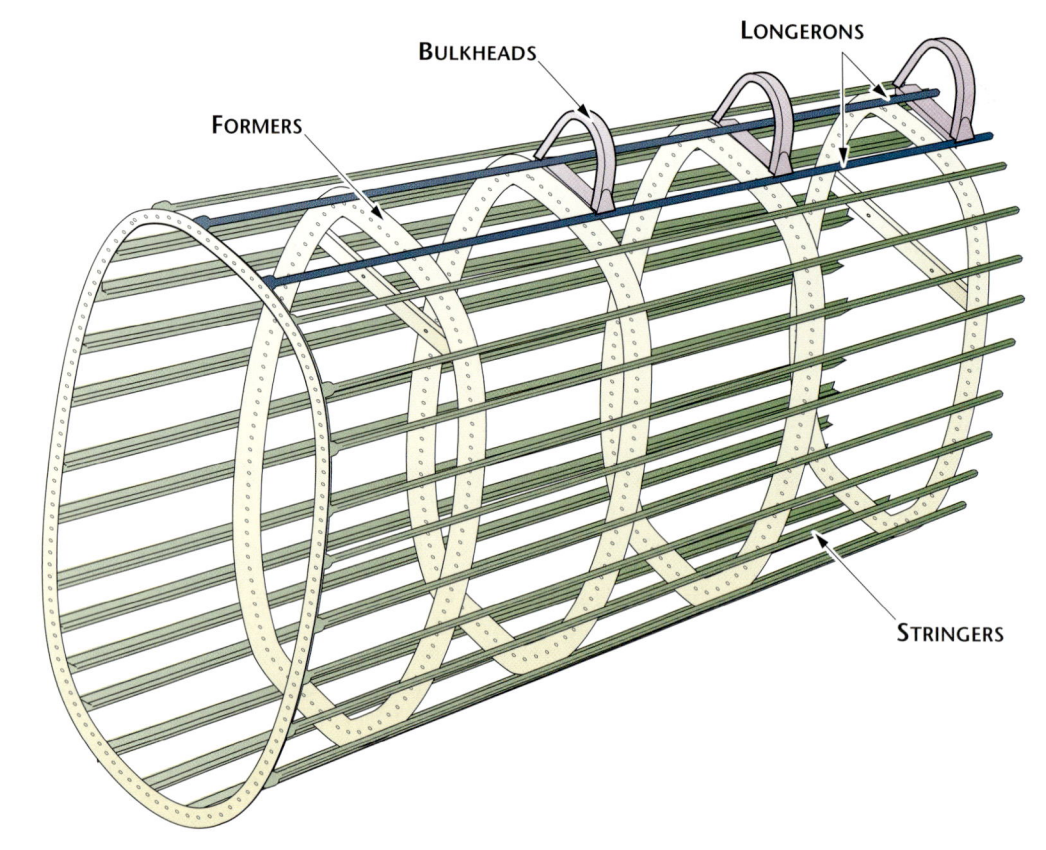

Figure 4-1-17. Longerons and stringer installation

Bulkheads. When frame assemblies are used to separate one section from another section, they are called bulkheads. Their construction is heavier than that of formers, and they provide a location for doors, windows, or other means of access.

Gussets. Gussets are used to strengthen attach points or to allow for the attachment of intersecting structural members (stringers and longerons).

Stringers & Longerons

Stringers and longerons are the main lengthwise members of a structure. Figure 4-1-17 shows these members installed.

Stringers. Stringers are smaller, lighter and weaker than longerons. They have some rigidity, but are mainly used to shape the structure and attach the skin. Stringers usually have a cross-section in the shape of a J or a Z, as shown in Figure 4-1-18, but other shapes may be used.

Longerons. Longerons are fairly heavy. Several longerons usually run the full length of the structure. They hold the bulkheads and formers, which, in turn, hold the stringers. Longerons usually take the form of a T extrusion or a formed-hat section, as shown in Figure 4-1-19.

Section 2
Airframe Sheet Metal Repair

Technicians with sheet metal skills modify and repair our aircraft. Sheet metal is a tactile skill that is quite different from ordinary repair-and-replace mechanics.

The purpose of this chapter is to provide general instructions for typical aircraft structural repairs, the materials required, and the methods to be used. The methods and procedures outlined are presented as general instructions on structural repair, and are not directed to specific aircraft. For specific instructions on structural repairs of a particular aircraft, refer to the applicable Aircraft Structural Repair Manual (SRM).

Basic Principles of Repair

There are three specific qualities of a repair which must be kept in mind during all phases of the repair process, and which apply to virtually all repairs of an aircraft structure: It is critical to maintain the original strength and contour, and to minimize the weight.

Maintaining Original Strength

The following paragraphs contain the rules to be observed in order to maintain the original strength.

Patch design. Ensure that the cross-sectional area of a splice or patch is at least equal to, or greater than, that of the damaged part. Avoid abrupt changes in cross-sectional area to eliminate dangerous stress concentration by tapering splices and making small skin patches round- or elliptical-shaped, instead of rectangular.

Stresses on repaired member. If the member is subjected to compression or bending loads, the patch should be placed on the outside of the member to obtain a higher resistance to such loads. If the patch cannot be placed there, material one gauge thicker than the original shall be used for the repair.

Buckling. Replace or reinforce with a member of equal strength any member that has buckled. A buckled part of the structure shall not be depended upon to carry its load again, no matter how well the part may be strengthened.

Replacement material. The material used in all replacements or reinforcements must be similar to that used in the original structure. If an alloy weaker than the original must be substituted for it, a heavier thickness must be used to give equivalent cross-sectional strength. A material that is stronger, but thinner, must not be substituted for the original, because one material can have greater tensile but less compressive strength than another, or vice versa. Also, the buckling and torsional strength of many sheet metal and tubular parts depends primarily on the thickness of the material rather than its allowable compressive and shear strengths.

Forming. Care must be taken when forming. Heat-treated and cold-worked aluminum alloys will stand very little bending without cracking. On the other hand, soft alloys are easily formed, but they are not strong enough for primary structure. Strong alloys can be formed in their annealed condition and heat-treated before assembling to develop their strength.

Riveting. Use the size and type of rivets used by the manufacturer in the row of rivets immediately adjacent to the damaged area; or, use a size three times the thickness of the sheet.

Excessive strength. Extensive repairs which are made too strong can be as undesirable as repairs weaker than the original structure. All aircraft structure must flex slightly to withstand the violent and excessive forces imposed during takeoff, flight and landing. If a repaired area is too strong, excessive flexing will occur only at the edge of the completed repair, causing acceleration of metal fatigue.

Maintaining Original Contour

All repairs must be formed to fit the original contour perfectly. A smooth contour is essential when making patches on the smooth external skin of an aircraft.

Minimizing Weight

The weight of all repairs should be kept to a minimum. Patches should be as small as possible, and no more rivets should be used than necessary.

In many cases, repairs disturb the original balance of the structure. Adding excessive weight may make the aircraft so unbalanced that the trim and balance tabs will require readjustment. In an area such as the spinner of a propeller, a repair will require application of balancing patches so that a perfect balance of the propeller assembly can be maintained.

Structural Inspection

Whether specific damage is suspected or not, an aircraft structure must occasionally be inspected for structural integrity. The following paragraphs provide general guidelines for this inspection.

Corrosion. When inspecting the structure of an aircraft, it is very important to watch for evidence of corrosion on the inside. This is most likely to occur in pockets and corners where moisture, dirt and salt spray may accumulate; therefore, drain holes must always be kept clean.

Damage to airframe components and the structure caused by corrosion will develop into permanent damage or failure if not properly treated. The corrosion control section of the maintenance manual or structural repair manual describes the maximum damage limits. These limits should be checked carefully, and if they are exceeded, the corroded component or structure must be repaired or replaced.

Surface indications. While an injury to the skin covering caused by impact with an object is plainly evident, a defect such as distortion or failure of the substructure may not be apparent until some evidence develops on the surface, such as canted, buckled or wrinkled covering, and loose rivets or working rivets. A *working* or *smoking rivet* is one which has movement under

Figure 4-2-1. Damage inspection.

structural stress, but has not loosened to the extent that movement can be observed. This situation can sometimes be noted by a dark, greasy residue or deterioration of paint and primers around rivet heads. External indications of internal injury must be watched for and correctly interpreted when found. When found, an investigation of the substructure in the vicinity should be made and corrective action taken.

Skin wrinkles. Warped wings are usually indicated by the presence of parallel wrinkles running diagonally across the wings and extending over a major area.

This condition may develop from unusually violent maneuvers, extremely rough air or extra hard landings, and while there may be no actual rupture of any part of the structure, it may be distorted and weakened. Similar failures may also occur in fuselages.

Fatigue. This type of damage is more noticeable as the operating time of the aircraft accumulates. The damage will begin as small cracks, caused by vibration and other loads imposed on skin fittings and load-bearing members, where the fittings are attached. Small cracks in the skin covering are frequently found leading away from rivets.

Commercial aircraft in high volume service or operating in severe environments are particularly subject to fatigue damage. Aging aircraft inspections, with an emphasis on fatigue and corrosion issues are required for some types of aircraft.

Heat. Certain areas of the aircraft are exposed to high temperatures. These areas usually include the fuselage sections around the engine, especially in areas where the exhaust flows from the engine. Flaps on twin engine aircraft often extend into the exhaust flow area and can have heat damage. Exhaust stains and flows on higher performance turboprop aircraft can be found as far back as the horizontal stabilizer. Turbine exhaust areas are often areas of suspect for heat damage.

Some aircraft structural repair manuals include diagrams that illustrate the heat danger areas. Heat damaged structures should be evaluated per the manufacturer's instructions and repaired as necessary.

Protective coatings. Aluminum alloy surfaces having chipped protective coating, scratches or worn spots which expose the surface of the metal should be recoated at once, as corrosion may develop rapidly. The same principle is applied to Alclad surfaces. Scratches which penetrate the pure aluminum surface layer will permit corrosion to take place in the alloy beneath.

Non-destructive inspection. A simple visual inspection cannot accurately determine whether or not suspected cracks in major structural members actually exist, nor can it measure the full extent of the visible cracks.

Damage Inspection

When investigating damage to an aircraft, it is necessary to make an extensive inspection of the structure. When any component or group of components has been damaged, it is essential that both the damaged members and the attaching structure be investigated, since the damaging force may have been transmitted over a large area, sometimes quite remote from the point of original damage. Wrinkled skin, elongated or damaged bolt or rivet holes, or distortion of members will usually appear in the immediate area of such damage, and any one of these conditions can result in damage being transmitted to adjacent areas. Check all skin, dents and wrinkles for any cracks or abrasions (Figure 4-2-1).

The adjacent structure should be inspected to determine if secondary damage has resulted from the transmission of shock or the load that caused the primary damage. A shock at one end of a structural member may be transmitted to the opposite end of the member and cause rivets to shear or other damage. When estimating the extent of damage, be sure that no secondary damage remains unnoticed.

Additionally, precautions must be taken during the inspection to ensure that all corrosion is detected, especially in places where it will not be visible after repair. Past experience has proven that corrosion occurs more often in parts of the structure that are poorly ventilated and in inaccessible corners of internal joints that prevent proper water drainage.

When investigating damage, proceed as follows:

- Remove all dirt, grease and paint from the damaged and surrounding areas so that the exact condition of each rivet, bolt and weld may be determined.
- Inspect skin for wrinkles throughout a large area.
- Check the operation of all movable parts in the area.
- Determine whether the best procedure would be to repair the damaged area or to remove and replace compromised parts.

Non-destructive inspection will be used as required when inspecting damage. A borescope can be used for the inspection of the internal structure. By using this instrument, some areas may be examined without being disassembled. Some damage may require hardness testing or other NDT methods.

Hardness Testing. When fire has damaged the airframe, the paint will be blistered or scorched and the metal will be discolored. When these conditions exist, the affected area should first be cleaned and the paint removed. Following this, a hardness test should be conducted to determine if the metal has lost any of its strength characteristics. This test can be performed with a portable hardness tester. If the material to be tested is removed from the airframe, then a more reliable test can be made by using a standard bench tester. If the alloy to be tested is either clad or anodized, the surface coating must be removed to the bare metal at the point of penetrator contact. This is necessary because clad surfaces are softer and anodized surfaces are harder than the base alloy.

Damage Classification

After the extent of damage is determined, it should be classified under one of the following categories: negligible damage, damage repairable by patching, damage repairable by insertion, or damage that requires replacement of parts (Figure 4-2-2). In many cases, the availability or lack of repair materials and time are the most important factors in determining whether a part should be repaired or replaced. The following paragraphs contain general descriptions of these types of damage.

Negligible damage. Negligible damage is that which does not affect the structural integrity of the member involved, or that can be corrected by a simple procedure without placing flight restrictions on the aircraft. This class of damage includes small dents, scratches, cracks or holes that can be repaired by burnishing, sanding, stop-drilling, hammering or other means of repair that do not require the use of additional materials. It is important to know the alloy that you are working with when doing small repairs. Most members that are bent may be straightened cold and examined with a magnifying glass for cracks, and tears to the material. If cracks are found after completing a negligible repair, you will need to reinforce as necessary.

Damage repairable by patching. This type of damage is any damage exceeding the limits of negligible damage, which is usually stated as 25 percent or less of the total panel section. Repair is accomplished by bridging the damaged area with a splice material. The splice or patch material used for riveted or bolted repairs is normally of the same type as the original material, but one gauge heavier. In a patch repair, filler plates of the same gauge and type of material as the damaged component can be used for bearing surfaces or to restore the damaged part to its original contour.

Damage repairable by insertion. This type of damage can be repaired by cutting away the damaged section, replacing the removed portion with an identical section of the damaged

4-14 | Airframe Metallic Structures

Negligible Damage

Damage Repairable By Patching

Damage Repairable By Insertion

Damage Requiring Replacement

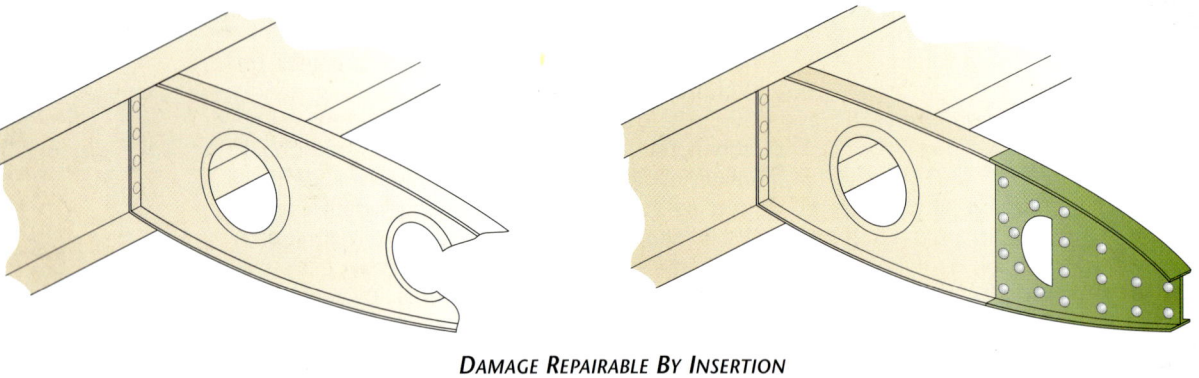

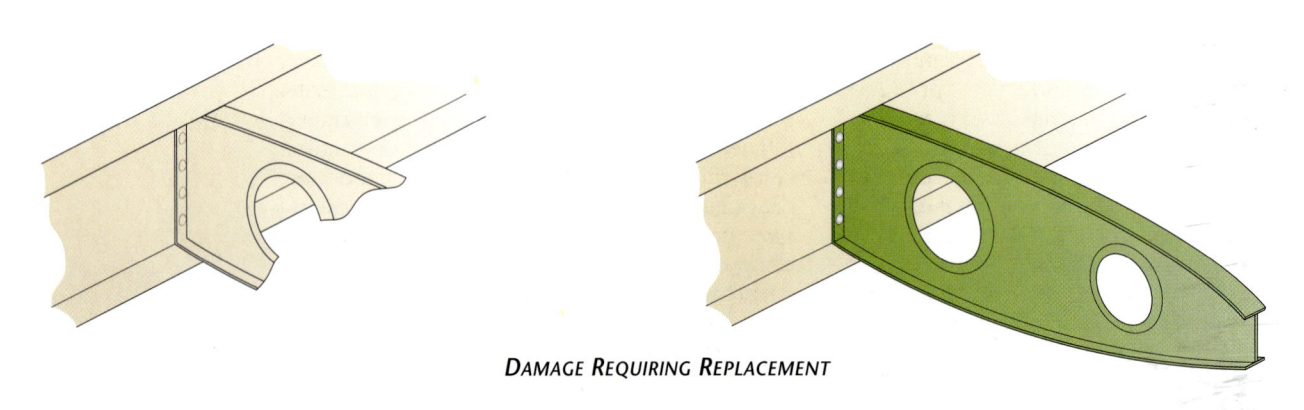

Figure 4-2-2. Damage classification

Figure 4-2-3. Aircraft repair jig

component and securing the insertion with splices at each end.

Damage requiring replacement of parts. This damage involves one or more of the following conditions:

- A complex part has been severely damaged
- The surrounding structure of a part or its inaccessibility makes repair impractical
- It is economically feasible to replace the damaged part, i.e.: local manufacture is available
- Forged or cast fittings are damaged beyond the limits of negligible damage

Structural Support During Repair

During repair, the aircraft must be adequately supported to prevent further distortion or damage. It is also important that the structure adjacent to the repair is supported when it is subject to static loads. The aircraft structure can be supported adequately by the landing gear or by jacks where the work involves a repair such as removing the control surfaces, wing panels or stabilizers. Cradles must be prepared to hold these components while they are removed from the aircraft. When the work involves extensive repair of the fuselage, landing gear or wing center section, the hoisting provisions may be constructed to distribute the loads while repairs are being accomplished (Figure 4-2-3). Docking systems for complete airframe allows full access to elevated areas of the aircraft. Workers can walk the entire perimeter without having to travel up and down the stairs.

Always check the applicable aircraft maintenance manual for specific support requirements.

Damage evaluation. Before starting any repair, the extent of damage must be fully evaluated to determine whether repair is authorized or even practical. This evaluation should identify the original material used and the type of repair required.

Damage removal. To prepare a damaged area for repair, proceed as follows:

- Remove all distorted skin and structure in damaged area.
- Remove damaged material in such a manner that the edges of the completed repair will match existing structure and aircraft lines.
- Round all squared corners.
- Smooth out any abrasions and/or dents.
- Remove and incorporate into the new repair any previous repairs adjoining the area of the new repair.

Repair material selection. The repair material must duplicate the strength of the original structure. If an alloy weaker than the original material has to be used, a heavier gauge must be used to give equivalent cross-sectional strength. A lighter gauge material should not be used, even when using a stronger alloy.

Repair parts layout. All new sections fabricated for repairing or replacing damaged parts in a given aircraft should be carefully laid out to the dimensions listed in the applicable aircraft manual before fitting the parts into the

Figure 4-2-4. Sheet metal marked for drilling, cutting and bending

structure. Information needed to fabricate replacement parts is usually found on blueprints, while information concerning repairs may be found in the aircraft structural repair manual. The manual contains information on extrusions and the necessary data for the fabrication of various sheet metal equivalents. The aircraft structural repair manual will indicate the type of material to be used in each repair.

The fabrication of sheet metal parts for internal structural repair requires careful adherence to the accepted standards of aircraft sheet metal work. This includes accurate calculation of bend allowance and careful layout of all dimensions. Layout is the interpreting and transcribing of information from blueprints, drawings, or written instructions to the metal that will be made into a part for an aircraft. If several parts are to be fabricated, the dimensions may be transferred to a template. Working from a template ensures a higher degree of uniformity and speeds production. The procedure for making a layout either for a template or for the actual part is essentially the same. Layout of a part or a template consists principally of marking the flat sheet so that all drilling, cutting, bending, and forming operations are indicated on the sheet (Figure 4-2-4).

The sheet metal layout may be made from printed instructions, but it is more often made directly from the blueprint. Accuracy in all details is essential. Measurements indicated on the blueprint are made on the layout. Details are often left out and must be developed in the shop. You may, for example, find that you must add several dimensions, and then figure the bend allowance for the material consumed in each bend before you are able to lay out the overall length or width of a part. On very accurate layouts, a magnifying glass is frequently used as an aid to precision work. A magnifying glass enlarges the graduations on a scale and makes them easier to read. It helps locate center punch marks, and it allows a close inspection of the accuracy of the completed layout.

In the layout of a part, you should plan the bending and forming operations so that each step is made in the proper sequence. If the steps are not made in the proper sequence, the part may become so bulky that it will be impossible to insert in the brake to make the final bend. It is important to keep drawings for all parts fabricated as copies of these will need to be submitted to the FAA with your major repair and alteration forms.

Rivet selection. Normally, the rivet size and material should be the same as the original rivets in the part being repaired. If a rivet hole

Figure 4-2-5. This shows how a piece of sheet metal should be prepared for use. No square corners, inside or outside.

has been enlarged or deformed, the next larger size rivet must be used after reworking the hole. When this is done, the proper edge distance for the larger rivet must be maintained. Where access to the inside of the structure is impossible and blind rivets must be used in making the repair, always consult the applicable aircraft maintenance manual. Check for the recommended type, size, spacing, and number of rivets needed to replace either the original installed rivets or those that are required for the type of repair being performed.

Rivet spacing and edge distance. The rivet pattern for a repair must conform to instructions in the applicable aircraft manual. The existing rivet pattern is used whenever possible.

Corrosion treatment. Prior to assembly of repair or replacement parts, make certain that all existing corrosion has been removed in the area and that the parts are properly insulated from each other. Proceed as follows:

- Where corrosion exists, remove the corrosive products and finishes.

- Where magnesium alloys are involved, apply a minimum of two coats of epoxy primer (MIL-P-23377) on each faying surface. In addition, insert tape or pressure-sensitive adhesive (for dissimilar metals) (MIL-T-23142) between faying surfaces. The tape must extend beyond the edge of faying surfaces at least 1/4 inch. Where the use of tape is impractical, assemble parts wet with epoxy primer and provide an adequate primer fillet at joint boundaries.

- Where steel alloys are involved, apply two coats of epoxy primer (MIL-P-23377) to each surface.

- Apply an additional coat of epoxy primer (MIL-P-23377) on the exterior edges of faying surfaces where magnesium and steel alloy parts are assembled.

- Install all rivets, bolts, nuts and washers wet with epoxy primer (MIL-P-23377).

- Apply an additional coat of epoxy primer (MIL-P-23377) to the heads of aluminum alloy rivets driven through corrosion-resistant steel.

Riveting. When riveting all parts together in the final steps of repair, neatness of the repair must be ensured. The edges of sheet metal parts should be free of burrs and tooling marks. Polished edges — those with shear marks removed — are the mark of a quality product. Sharp corners should be rounded. Internal cutouts should have a radius to avoid *stress risers*, which are potential crack-starting points. See Figure 4-2-5.

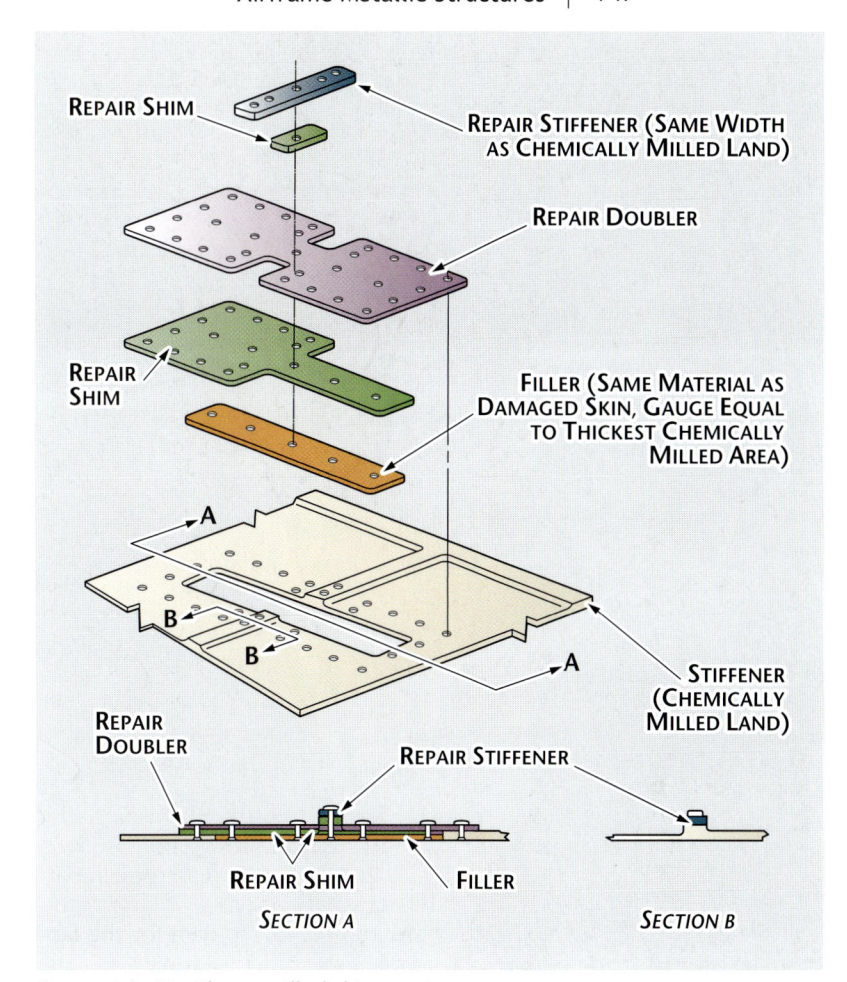

Figure 4-2-6A. Chem-milled skin repair

Any time two or more pieces of metal are clamped together and drilled, the burrs and chips must be removed. The pieces must be taken apart, cleaned, deburred then reassembled for fastening. If chips and burred hole edges are not cleaned, a strong, tight joint is impossible.

Tolerance. Unless otherwise stated by the applicable aircraft manual or engineering specifications, all measurements and repairs should be made with a tolerance ±1/64 inch.

Chem-milled Skin Repair

A chem-milled structural member varies in thickness from end to end or side to side. Therefore, repair requires a procedure slightly different from standard procedures. The repair material must be as thick as the thickest part of the chem-milled structure. The repair material is applied to the thickest part of the damaged member, using normal riveting procedures. Shimming is used to fill the gap between the repair material and the thin part of the member. The shim material is secured with rivets that pass through the damaged part, the shim material and the repair material. Figure 4-2-6A Illustrates a typical chem-milled

Figure 4-2-6B. Aircraft with Chem-milled skin

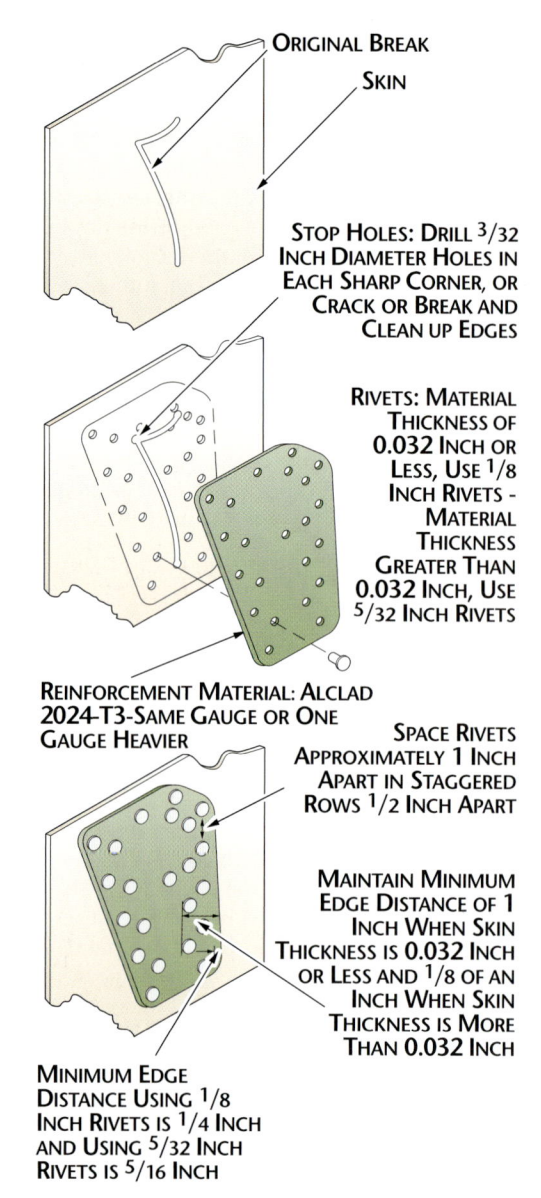

Figure 4-2-7. Lap patch for a surface crack

skin repair. Figure 4-2-6B pictures an aircraft with chem-milled skin.

Stressed Skin Repair

Stressed skin carries a large portion of the load imposed upon an aircraft structure. Various specific skin areas are classified as highly critical, semi-critical or non-critical. To determine specific repair requirements for these areas, refer to the applicable aircraft maintenance manual.

Patches

Skin patches may be classified as two types: the lap (scab) patch, and the flush patch.

Lap (scab) patch. This type of patch is an external patch where the edges of the patch and the skin overlap each other. The overlapping portion of the patch is riveted to the skin. Lap patches may be used in most areas where aerodynamic smoothness is not important. In areas where it is permitted, the lap patch may be used in repairing cracks as well as small holes. Figure 4-2-7 shows a typical patch for a crack, and Figure 4-2-8 shows a typical patch for a hole.

Flush patch. A flush patch is a filler patch that is flush, or smooth, with the surrounding skin. When applied, it is supported by and riveted to a reinforcement plate which is, in turn, riveted to the inside of the skin. This reinforcement plate is often referred to as a doubler or backup plate. Flush patches should be used where aerodynamic smoothness is required. Some high-performance aircraft require flush patch repairs for all skin repairs. Figure 4-2-9 shows a typical flush patch repair.

The type of flush patch used depends on the location of the damaged area. One type is

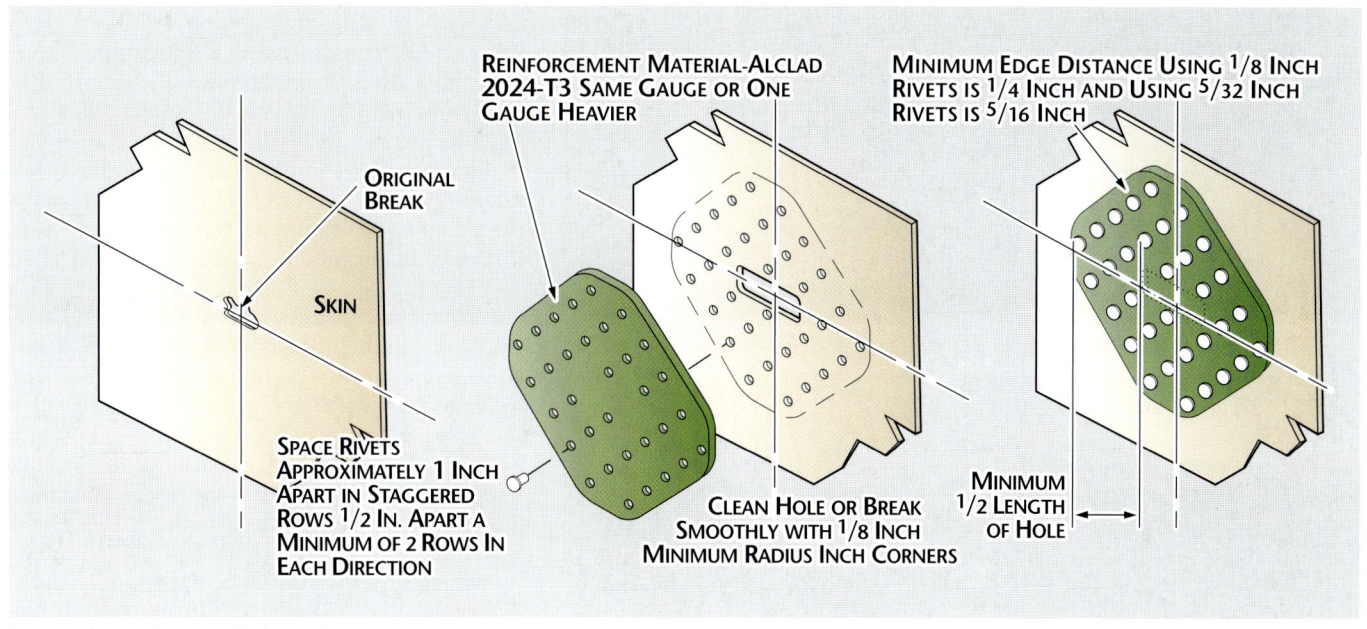

Figure 4-2-8. Lap patch for hole

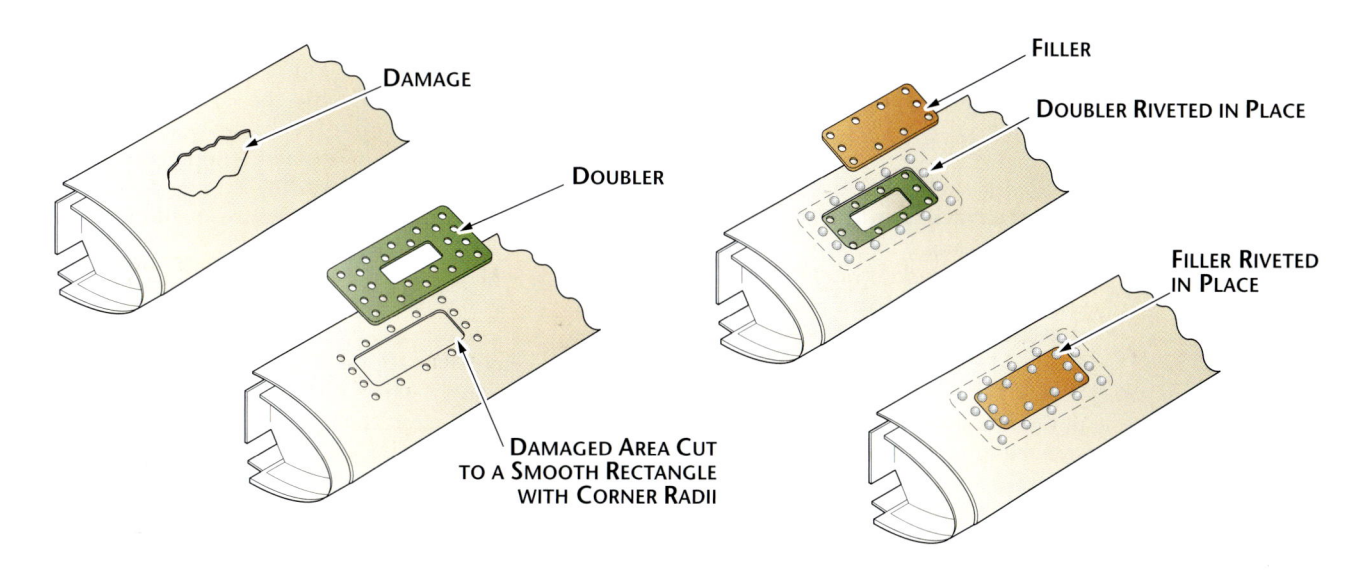

Figure 4-2-9. Flush patch

clear of internal structures, and the other is not. Like all repairs, applicable aircraft structural repair manual must be referenced for the necessary repair information. The repairs discussed in this section are typical of most repairs.

Open- and closed-skin area repair. The factors that determine the methods to be used in skin repair are accessibility to the damaged area and the instructions found in the aircraft maintenance manual. The skin on most areas of an aircraft is inaccessible for making the repair from the inside. This is known as *closed skin*. Skin that is accessible from both sides is called *open skin*. Usually, repairs to open skin can be made in the conventional manner using standard rivets, but in repairing closed skin, some type of special fastener must be used. The exact type to be used will depend on the type of repair being made and the recommendations of the aircraft manufacturer.

Patching Procedures

The following paragraphs provide general procedures for installing lap-type and flush-type patches.

Lap-type patches. When repairing cracks or small holes with a lap or scab patch, the damage must be cleaned and smoothed. In repairing cracks, a small hole must be drilled in each end of the crack before applying the patch. These

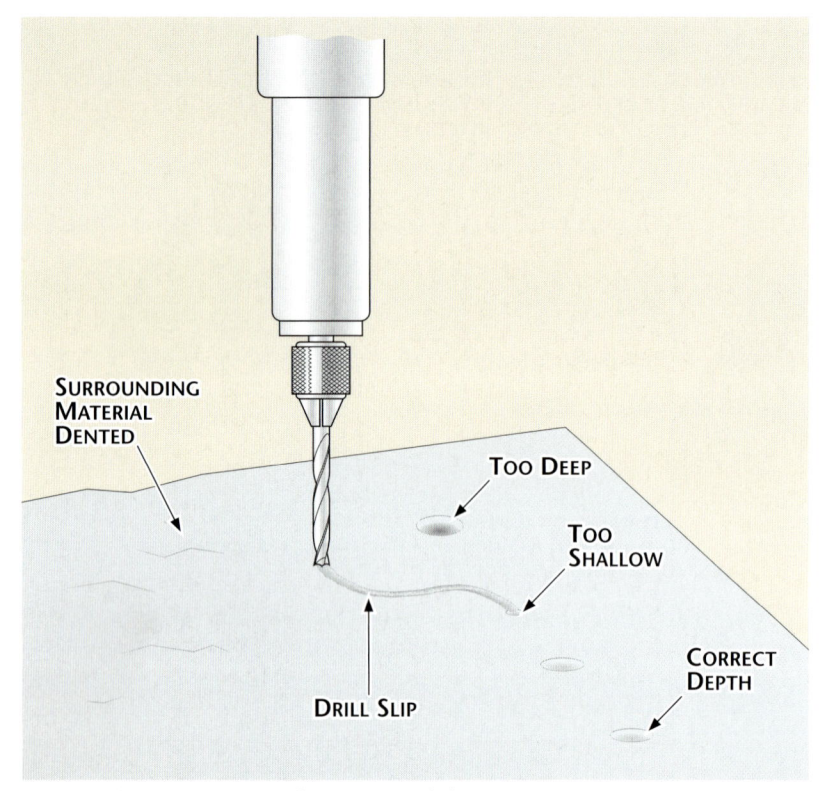

Figure 4-2-11. Center punching to avoid slippage

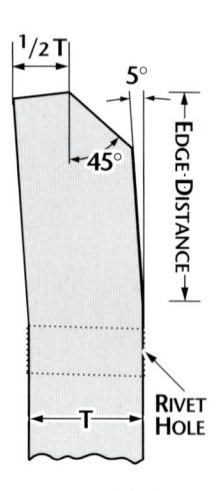

Figure 4-2-10. Lap patch edge preparation

When the patch is temporarily secured, drill the remaining rivet holes through the patch and the surface being repaired. Remove the patch and deburr all rivets holes with a deburring tool or a large drill bit. Prime the repair materials with the proper corrosion-preventive material before the riveting operation. Secure the patch in position with temporary fasteners to maintain alignment during riveting.

Holes may be repaired in either stressed or nonstressed skin that is less than three-sixteenths of an inch in diameter by filling with a rivet. Drill the hole and install the proper size rivet to fill the hole. For holes three-sixteenths of an inch and larger, you should consult the applicable structural repair manual for the necessary repair information. The damaged area is removed by cutting and trimming the hole to a circular, square, rectangular, or diamond shape. The corners of the hole should be rounded to a minimum of one-fourth of an inch in radius. The lap patch is fabricated and installed in the same manner as previously explained for repairing cracks.

Flush patches. Flush patches are designed to be smooth with the original skin when installed. Unlike scab or lap patches, this requires an additional support behind the original surface. Adding this support will vary depending on the structures behind the skin.

Flush patch clear of internal structures. Flush patch repairs are relatively simple in areas that are clear of internal structure. This is especially true where there is an access door or plate through which the rivets can be bucked. In closed areas, the flush patch may be attached by substituting blind rivets or other special fasteners as instructed in the structural repair manual.

The size and shape of the opening dictates the type of doubler. Some openings require a split doubler. One method of using a split doubler is shown in Figure 4-2-12. To insert the doubler, slip the split edge under the skin and twist the doubler until it slides in place under the skin. Temporarily install a screw in the center of the doubler to serve as a handle for inserting the doubler through the hole. This type of patch is normally recommended for holes up to 1-1/2 inches in diameter.

Repair larger opening by trimming the hole to a rectangular or elliptical shape and round the corners to a generous radius. When laying out the size of the opening and the doubler, the length should exceed the width. Slip the doubler by its narrowest dimension through the opening in the skin and position it for installation. This eliminates the splitting and manipulation of the patch required for round or square doublers. A large opening rectangular repair was shown previously in Figure 4-2-9.

holes relieve the stress at these points and prevent the crack from spreading. This is normally done by using a No. 30 or No. 40 drill bit. This prevents the concentration of stresses at the apex of the crack and distributes the stresses around the circumference of the hole. The patch must be large enough to install the required number of rivets. It may be cut circular, square or rectangular. If it is cut square or rectangular, the corners will be rounded to a radius no smaller than 1/4 inch. The edges must be chamfered to an angle of 45° for half the thickness of the material, and bent down 5° over the edge distance to seal the edges. This reduces the chance that the repair will be affected by the airflow over it. These dimensions are shown in Figure 4-2-10.

The rivet pattern is laid out on the patch by using the proper edge distance and spacing. The installation position of each rivet is marked with a center punch. The impression in the material made with the center punch helps to keep the drill from slipping away from the hole being drilled (Figure 4-2-11).

Drill only a minimum number of rivet holes in the patch. Normally four will suffice at an angle of 90 degrees to each other. Position the patch over the surface being repaired, and ensure that the correct edge distances are being maintained. Drill four holes in the surface being repaired, using the predrilled holes in the patch as a pattern for alignment. As each hole is drilled, using the proper temporary fasteners, secure the patch in place.

On the larger repair areas, it is usually possible to buck the doubler rivets by inserting and holding the bucking bar through the center of the doubler. The filler is then riveted in place with blind fasteners. When blind rivets are used as substitutes for solid rivets, the structural repair manual normally specifies the next larger size. The proper edge distances for the substitute fasteners must be maintained.

In all flush patches, the filler in normally the same gauge and material as the original skin. The doubler, generally, should be of the same material and one gauge heavier than the skin. Structural repair manuals will specify the allowable substitution of materials. This can be in the form of a note on the repair diagram.

The filler is fabricated slightly less than the dimensions of the hole being repaired. Generally, the maximum clearance between the skin and the filler is one thirty-second of an inch. This will allow a 1/64-inch clearance on each end of the filler and eliminate any possibility of stress developing from contact between the two parts. The doubler is fabricated larger than the hole being repaired to allow for the specified number of rivets required to attach the doubler to the skin being repaired.

The doubler, filler, and attaching skin rivet pattern may be laid out, drilled, and deburred in the identical manner as described for a lap patch. After the required corrosion-preventive materials have been applied, the doubler is positioned in the structure's interior and secured with temporary fasteners. Inspect the rivet holes for proper alignment, and rivet the doubler in place with solid rivets. The filler can then be riveted in place with blind fasteners.

If the flush repair is in an open area, the filler may be riveted to the doubler prior to installing the doubler.

Flush patch over internal structures. Fabricating a flush patch over internal structures increases the complexity. In some instances, it may be done simply with a split doubler and a filler, as shown in Figure 4-2-13. Frequently a split doubler, filler strips, and filler are used in the repair. The filler strip is used as a spacer if a structural component under the skin has been damaged. In all cases, the existing structure's rivet holes should be used when the rivet pattern is laid out. The flush patch over internal structure is installed with the same methods as described for a flush patch clear of internal structure, except for modification of the doubler.

Flush access door. Installing a flush access door, if it is permitted by the applicable aircraft maintenance manual, can make it easier to repair the aircraft's internal structure and

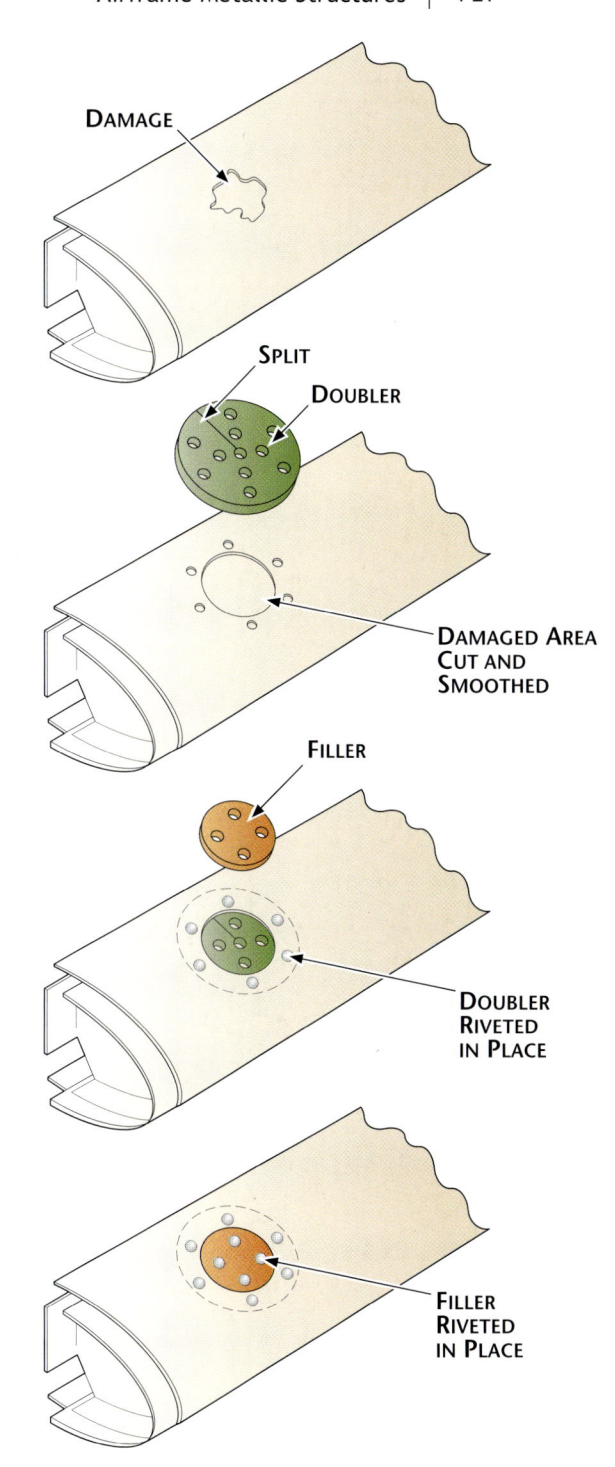

Figure 4-2-12. Flush patch repair using a split doubler

damage to the skin in certain areas. Some manufacturers have issued service bulletins requiring additional inspection panels for in service aircraft. These access panels are usually installed using these techniques.

The installation consists of a doubler and a stressed cover plate. A single row of nut plates is riveted to the doubler, and the doubler is riveted to the skin with two staggered rows of rivets. This installation is shown in Figure 4-2-14. The cover plate is then attached to the doubler

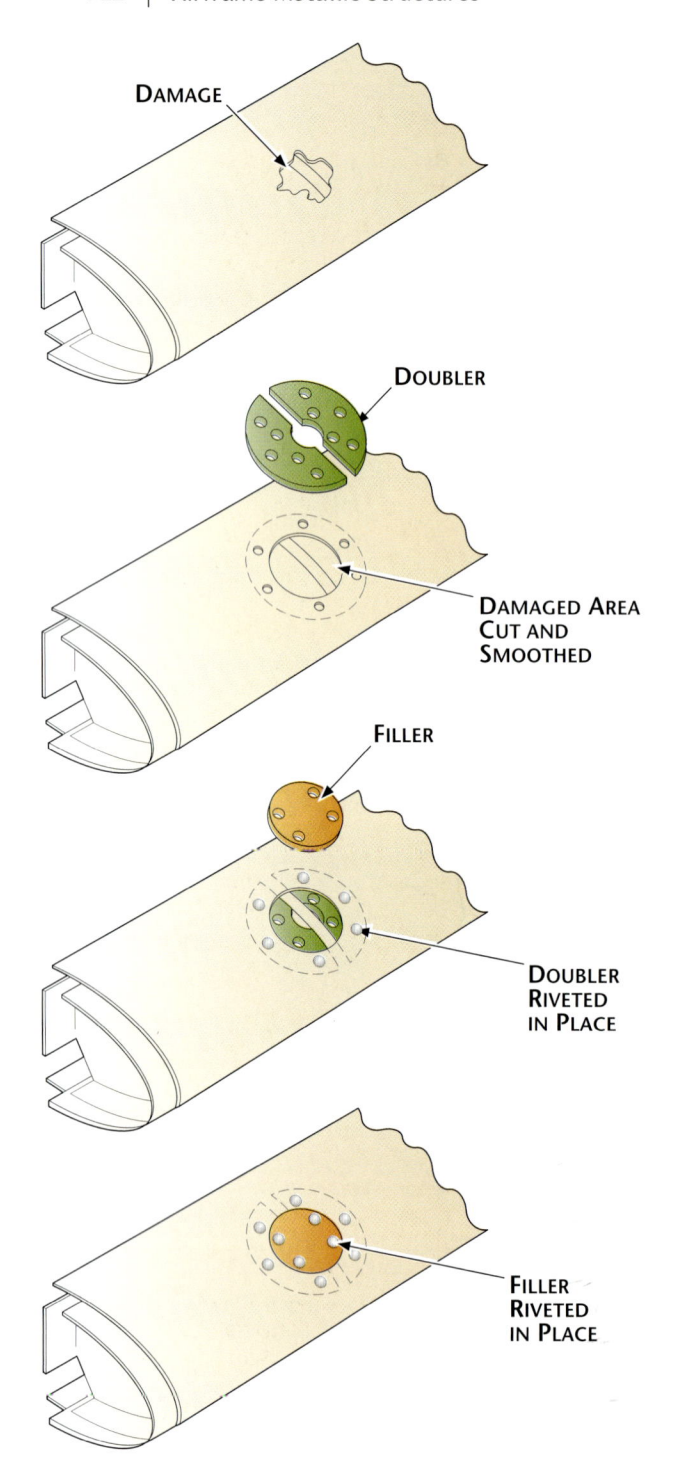

Figure 4-2-13. Flush patch repair over an internal structure

with machine screws. The primary difference between the patch and the access door is the way the door is attached to the doubler. Patches are permanently attached, doors are attached with removable fasteners.

Skin Replacement

Damage to metal aircraft skin that exceeds repairable limits requires replacement of the entire panel. A panel must also be replaced when there are too many previous repairs in a given section or area. The following paragraphs outline skin replacement.

Inspection. As in all other forms of repairs, the first step is to inspect the damaged area thoroughly to determine the extent of the damage. Inspect the internal structure for transmittal damage or signs of induced strain. Structural members must be replaced or repaired when bent, fractured, or wrinkled. All rivets in the damaged area must be inspected for signs of failure. They may be sheared considerably without visible external evidence of that shearing.

Therefore, rivets must be removed at points in the damaged area and examined for signs of shear failure. During the inspection, note carefully all unusual riveting problems or conditions that make riveting difficult or impossible. Any fixtures that will hinder riveting and prevent the use of straight bucking bars will be apparent in a thorough inspection. There will also be places where flanges or reinforcing members, intersection of stringers, longerons, formers, frames, or rings make the bucking of rivets very difficult. This problem can be solved by designing and making bucking bars to suit these particular situations.

Removal of damaged skin. As the skin panel is being removed, the rivet holes in stringers, longerons, bulkheads, formers, frames and other internal members must be kept in the best possible condition. If any of these members are loosened, their locations should be marked so that they can be reinstalled in their original positions. The skin must not be mutilated when being removed; in most cases, it can be used as a template for laying out and drilling holes in the new piece of skin.

Selecting proper skin material. Refer to the applicable skin panel diagram in the specific aircraft maintenance manual for the gauge and alloy of material to be used for the replacement panel. The size and shape of the panel may be determined in either of two ways: the dimension can be measured during inspection, or the old skin can be used as a template for laying out the new sheet. The latter method is preferable and more accurate. In both cases, the new sheet may be cut with an overlap of 1-2 inches of material outside the rivet holes.

Laying out the new panel. If the old sheet is not too badly damaged, it should be flattened out and used as a template. The new sheet, having been cut approximately 1 inch larger than the old, should then be drilled near the

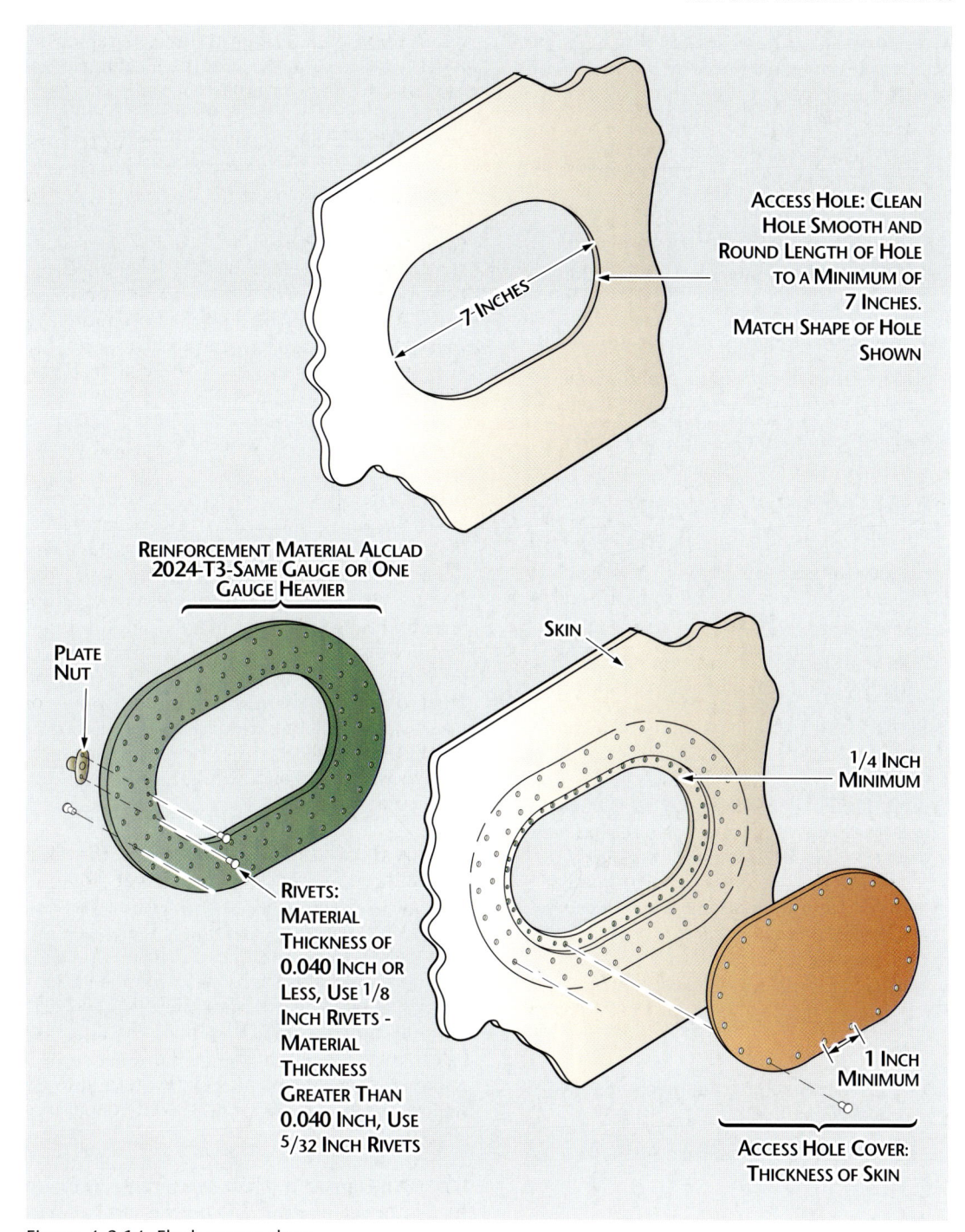

Figure 4-2-14. Flush access door

center of the sheet by using the holes in the old sheet as a guide. The two sheets are then held together with Cleco® fasteners. The drilling should then proceed from the center to the outside of the sheet, with Cleco® fasteners inserted at frequent intervals.

Hole Duplication Methods

If the old sheet cannot be used as a template, there are a number of methods of duplicating the holes from the aircraft structure. These include back-drilling and marking.

Back-drilling. Back-drilling uses the holes in the reinforcing members as guides, with occasional installation of Cleco® fasteners. The reinforcing members must be aligned and flush at the points where they intersect; otherwise, the holes in the new sheet will not be accurately aligned. For the same reasons, the new sheet should have the same contour as the old one before the rivet holes are drilled. The skin should be held firmly against the framework while drilling, which can be done by placing a block of wood against the skin and holding it firmly while drilling.

Transfer pins. When back-drilling isn't feasible, *transfer pins* can be used with good results. It is imperative, however, that you not skip any steps when substituting.

1. Use doubler material larger than needed. It will be trimmed later.
2. Drill one hole in a corner for a Cleco®.
3. Mark and drill one hole in the diagonal corner.
4. Divide the area into three or four fields.
5. Place transfer pins in the holes of one field. Use putty to hold in place if needed.
6. Cleco®-fasten doubler in place, and tap field area with a soft-faced hammer.
7. Remove doubler, and carefully circle each mark.
8. Move transfer pins into the next field, then repeat steps 6 and 7 until the entire doubler is marked.
9. Re-mark each hole location with a spring-loaded center-punch or a prick-punch.
10. Mark each hole location using a common center-punch and hammer.

CAUTION: *If a punchmark is too small, the chisel edge of the drill may bridge it and "walk" off the exact location before starting. If the punchmark is too heavy, it may deform the metal and or result in a local strain-hardening at the point where the drill is to start cutting. The best size for a punchmark is about the width of the chisel edge of the drill to be used.*

11. Drill a partial hole at each mark with a No. 51 drill.
12. Pilot-drill each partial hole with a No. 40 or No. 30 drill.
13. Drill each hole to final size, trim countersink, prime, etc.

Another option to consider when back-drilling isn't feasible is the use of *plastic* (Polyvinyl Chloride Acetate, or Vinylite). It is imperative, however, that no steps be skipped in the process.

1. Clean the area to remove grease, dirt, etc.
2. Tape the plastic tightly to the area.
3. Carefully drill the holes the same size as the existing holes in the aircraft. If they don't come out in the right place, do the following:
   - Elongate the holes in the plastic so that a drill will line up with both holes.
   - Mark the end of the elongated hole slot with a felt pen.
   - Double-check that all the holes are either perfectly round or marked.
   - Remove the plastic from the airplane and place on the doubler material. Clamp or tape it in place.
   - Get drill-guide bushing(s) from the tool crib the same size as the holes you drilled.
   - Pilot-drill all the holes using a drill-guide bushing. Locate the bushing at the marked end of all marked holes.
   - Step the pilot-drilled holes to final size.
4. Now you can lay out and drill additional holes, trim, countersink, prime, etc.

Marking

If all or part of the frame is not accessible from the inside, the new panel can be marked from the old one using a variety of methods. Marking lines and hole locations directly on aluminum with a No. 2 pencil was the standard method for many years. It is not acceptable nowadays. The recommended methods are:

- Marking directly on the protective membrane, if it is still on the material
- Marking directly on the material with a fiber-tipped pen (an ultra-fine point Sharpie works well)
- Covering the material with tape, then marking on the tape (2 inch masking tape works well)

A scribe should be used only when marks will be removed by drilling or cutting, since scribes make objectionable scratches that weaken the material.

Pencil. An aircraft marking pencil (MIL-P-8395) can be used to mark through the holes in the old panel onto the new one.

Transfer punch. Another way to mark the location of the new holes is to use a transfer punch, as shown in Figure 4-2-15. The punch is centered in the old hole and the new sheet lightly tapped with a mallet. The result should be a mark that will serve to locate the hole in the new sheet.

Hole finder. This device allows holes to be drilled in the new section of skin that are perfectly aligned with the holes in the old section. See Figure 4-2-16. The hole finder is made in two sections: an upper part and a lower part, which are bolted together at one end. At the free end of the bottom section of the finder is a guide rivet, which drops into the old holes in the sheet that are still in place. The free end of the top section of the hole finder has a

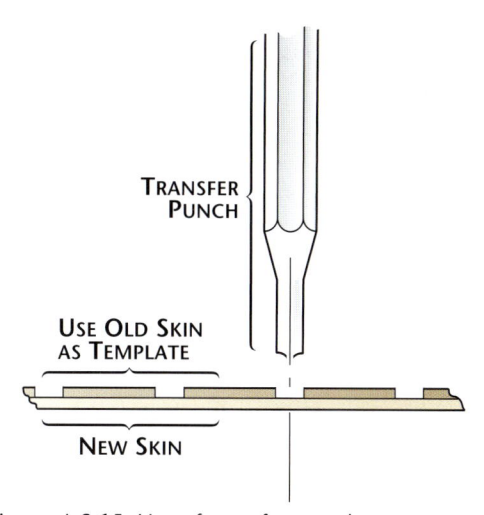

Figure 4-2-15. Use of transfer punch

hole in a position that exactly matches that of the guide rivet. The new hole is drilled through this opening. Thus, as the hole finder travels along, the guide rivet drops into an old hole and automatically determines the position of the new holes.

Deburring. After all the holes have been drilled, the Cleco® fasteners are removed and the sheet is removed from the framework. The holes in the skin, the stringers and the ribs must be deburred on both sides to prevent faulty attachment of the skin to the framework.

Riveting. The new skin is then ready to be riveted onto the structure in accordance with accepted techniques.

Skin Repair

Circular external repair. This repair, also called the *coin patch repair*, is intended for dents, punctures, tears and small cracks that can be cut out within a minimum of 1/2 inch but not exceeding 1-3/4 inch diameter. All patches must clear adjacent structural members by 1/8 inch and be sealed. Refer to the applicable aircraft maintenance manual for information on watertight sealing. The following procedure is shown in Figure 4-2-17.

- Cut out the damage and make a coin patch of the same material and thickness as the skin. The patch should have a diameter 1/16 inch less than the cutout.
- Make a circular backing plate three times the diameter of the coin patch and from the same material, but in the next heavier thickness.
- Smooth the edges of the cutout, coin patch and backing plate with a file.
- Center the coin patch on the backing plate and drill rivet holes through them.

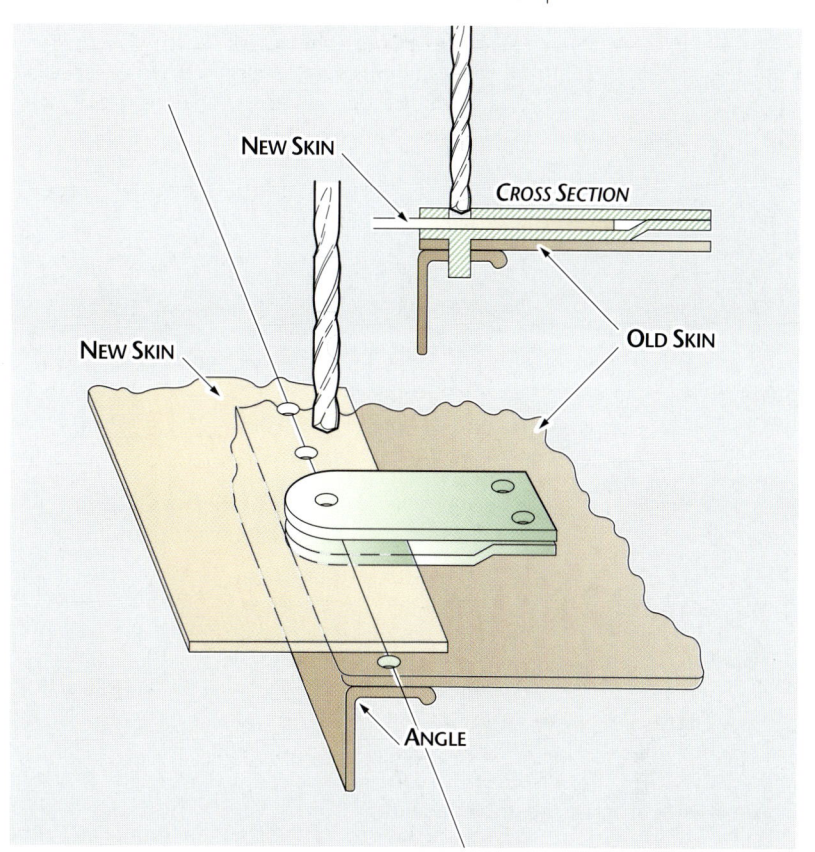

Figure 4-2-16. Use of a hole finder (strap duplicator)

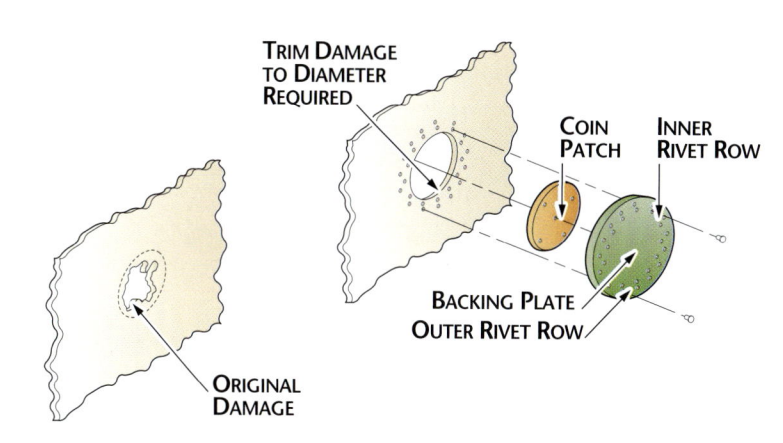

COIN PATCH DIAMETER	RIVET ROW DIAMETER				BACKING PLATE	
	Inner		Outer		Diameter	
0.500	1.000	1.120	1.500	1.620	2.000	2.120
0.625	1.125	1.245	1.625	1.745	2.125	2.245
0.750	1.250	1.370	1.750	1.870	2.250	2.370
0.875	1.375	1.495	1.875	1.995	2.375	2.495
1.000	1.500	1.620	2.000	2.120	2.500	2.620
1.250	1.750	1.870	2.250	2.370	2.750	2.870
1.500	2.000	2.120	2.500	2.620	3.000	3.120
1.750	2.250	2.370	2.750	2.870	3.250	3.370

Note: Dimensions in white are for material thickness less than 0.032 inch; those in grey are for material thickness greater than 0.032 inch.

Figure 4-2-17. Circular external repair

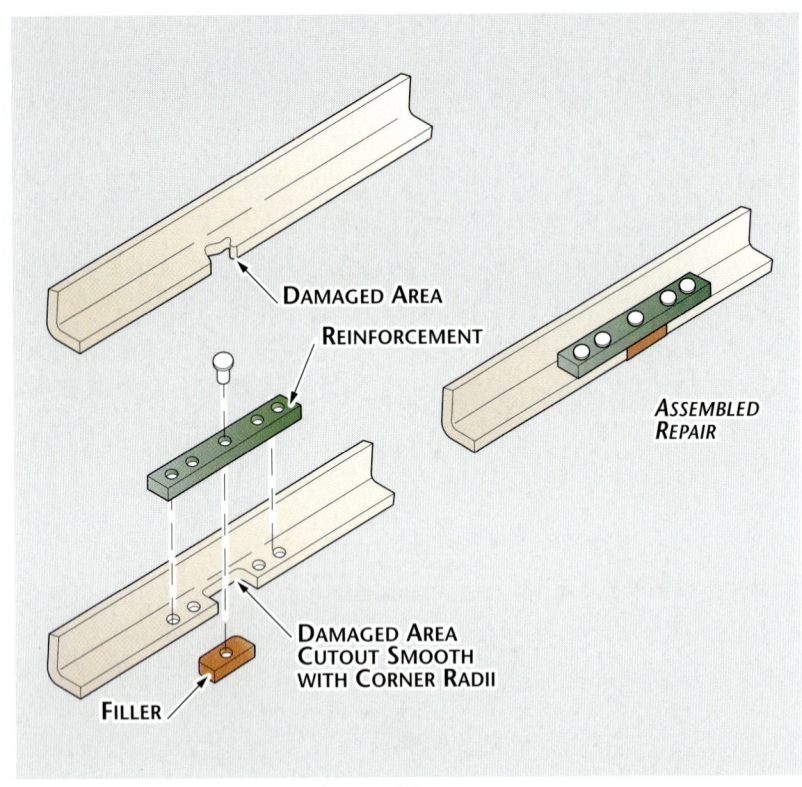

Figure 4-2-18. Stringer repair by patching

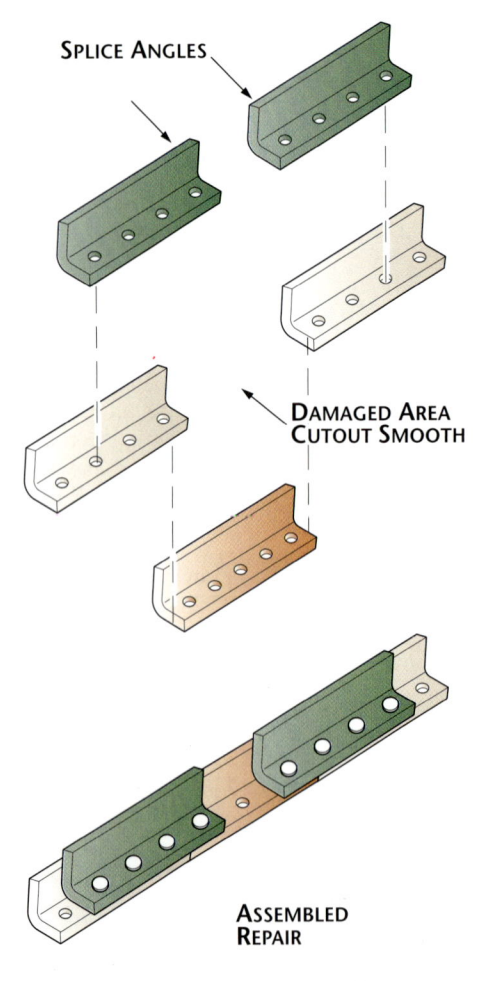

Figure 4-2-19. Repair by insertion, after a portion of the stringer is removed

- Install and set the rivets.
- Spray or brush a thin coat of epoxy primer (MIL-P-23377) on all surfaces of the coin patch. Allow the primer to dry.
- Insert the coin patch in the cutout from inside the skin. Drill rivet holes through the backing plate and skin.
- Remove the coin patch from the cutout after establishing a rivet pattern, and seal the faying surface of the cutout and patch.
- If the damage is less than 1/2 inch and larger than 3/16 inch and located over an undamaged frame or stiffener, repair the damage by omitting the backing plate. Rivet the coin patch to the frame or stiffener.
- Install and set the rivets.

Temporary Patch Repairs

Holes or cracks in the skin panels within the negligible limits applicable to the area can be repaired temporarily using fabric or tape patches. Damage considered allowable for one-time flights can also be repaired by this method. The repaired area should not be painted so it can easily be detected later for permanent repair.

Fabric patches. Repair holes and cracks with fabric patches as follows:

- Stop-drill the cracks or trim the hole. Smooth the edges of the hole with a file.
- Remove the paint from the area surrounding the damage using acetone or thinner.
- Cut a pinked-edge patch from cloth (MIL-C-5646).
- Apply a coat of clear cellulose nitrate dope (MIL-D-5549) to the area surrounding the damage.
- Apply the patch while the dope is wet. Smooth the patch to remove all wrinkles.
- Remove excess dope and allow the patch to dry.
- Apply two additional coats of dope to the patch. Allow sufficient drying time between coats.

Tape patches. Repair holes and cracks with tape patches as follows:

- Cut an oval or round patch from an aluminum-backed, pressure-sensitive adhesive tape.
- Apply the patch to the damaged area, exerting pressure with a rubber roller, particularly around the edges of the patch.
- Repeat steps, as required.

Airframe Metallic Structures | 4-27

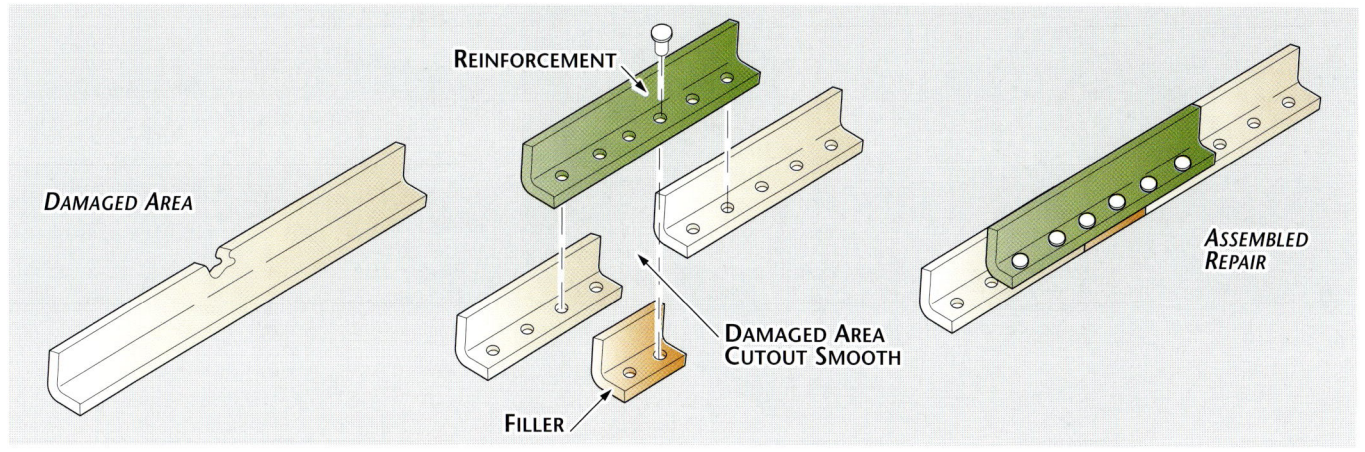

Figure 4-2-20. Stringer repair by insertion when damage affects only one stringer but exceeds 12 inches

Internal and External Repairs

This paragraph describes typical repairs of the major structural parts of an airplane and helicopter. These repairs are typical and general in nature. The applicable aircraft structural repair manual must always be consulted for specific requirements and procedures for a particular repair situation.

Stringer Repair

Stringers may be damaged by vibration, corrosion or collision. Usually the damage involves other parts, such as the skin, a bulkhead or a former. Repair methods differ by the shape of the stringer and the extent of the damage.

Patching. Figure 4-2-18 shows a stringer repair by patching. This requires replacing the damaged section and adding reinforcement to tie the structure together. This repair is permissible when the damage does not exceed 2/3 of the width of one leg and is not more than 12 inches long. Damage exceeding these limits can be repaired by one of the other methods.

Insertion. Repair damaged stringers by insertion where damage exceeds two thirds of one leg in width, or where damage affects only one stringer. This repair requires removal of the damaged section. A replacement section is purchased or fabricated. The replacement piece is tied into the existing structure with splice angles (Figure 4-2-19).

See Figure 4-2-20 for repair of a stringer when the damage exceeds 12 inches in length. This type of repair requires a full-length reinforcement.

See Figure 4-2-21 for assembled repair by insertion where damage affects more than one stringer. The stringers should be cut back in a staggered fashion. This creates a better load distribution throughout the repaired structure.

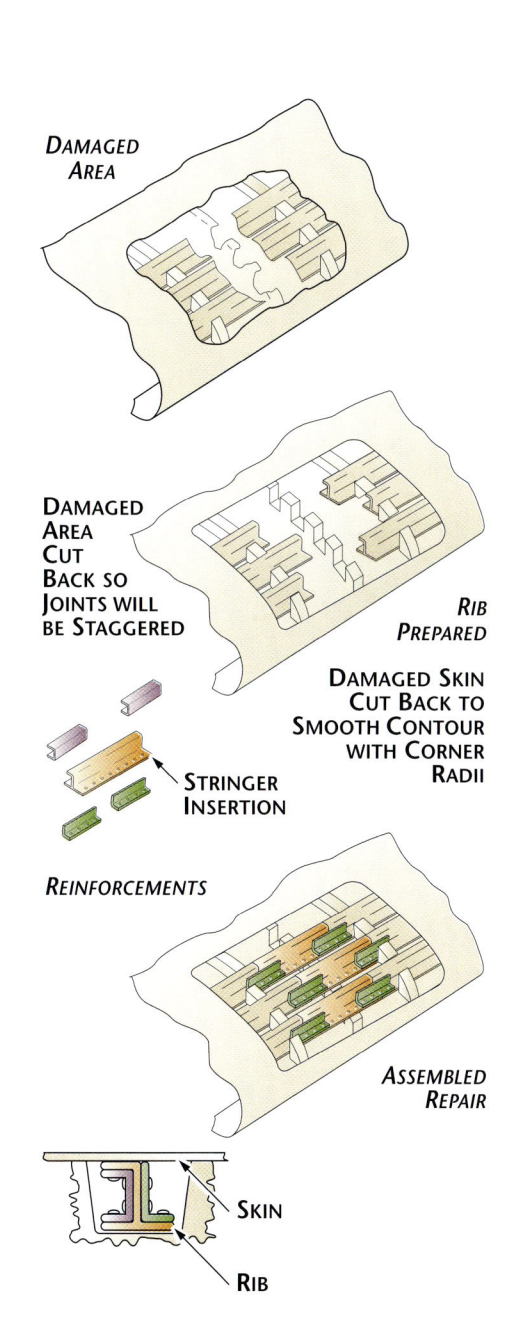

Figure 4-2-21. Stringer repair by insertion when damage affects more than one stringer

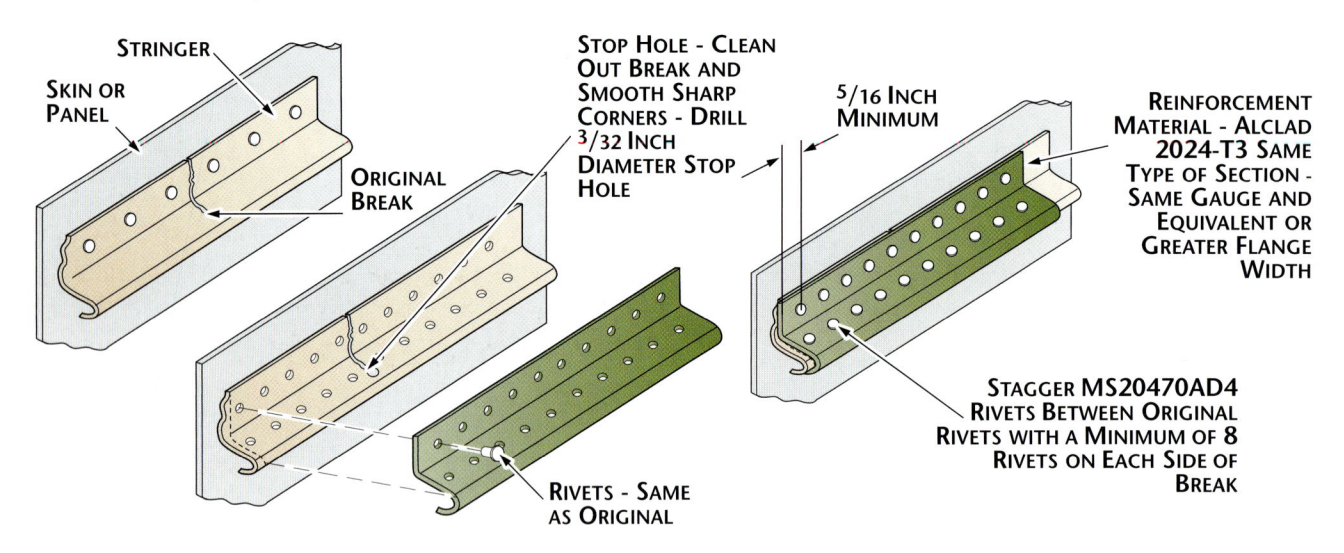

Figure 4-2-22. J-section stringer splice repair

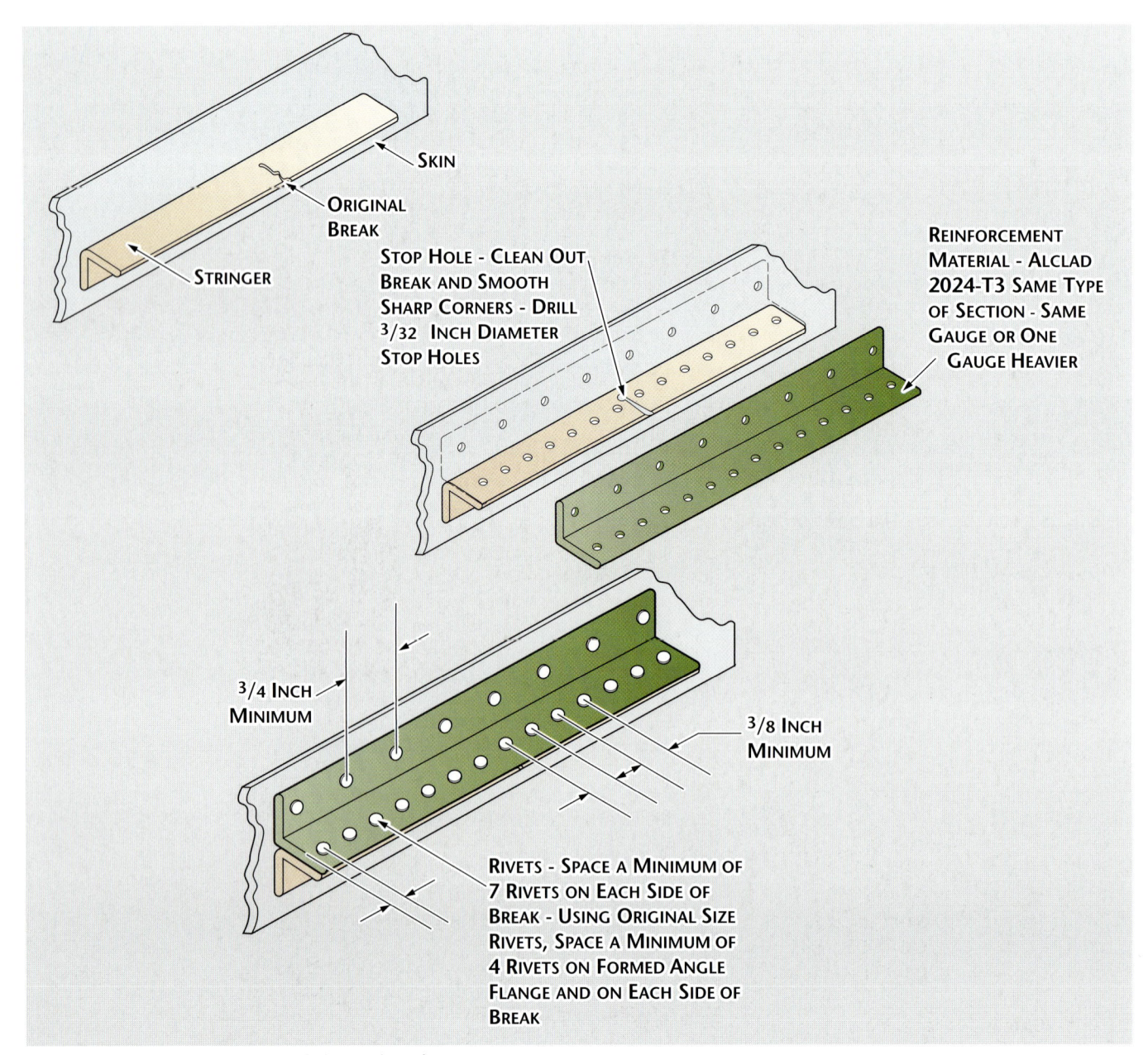

Figure 4-2-23. Stringer repair with formed angle

J-section stringer splice repair. Cracks in J-sections can be repaired by stop drilling and adding a reinforcement section over the original structure. See Figure 4-2-22 for this type of repair.

Stringer repair with formed angle. Cracks or breaks in stringers can be repaired by stop drilling and adding a reinforcement backing to the original structure. This repair is shown in Figure 4-2-23.

Cracks in radius of stringer ends. This type of defect requires installing a reinforcement patch to hold the stringer end in place. It is shown in Figure 4-2-24.

Longeron repair. *Longerons* are usually fairly heavy and serve as the primary lengthwise structural members. They serve approximately the same purpose as stringers, but they can be differentiated from stringers by their heavier size and continuous length through the aircraft or structural section. If the longeron consists of a formed section and an extruded angle section, it is known as a *composite structural member,* in which each sec-

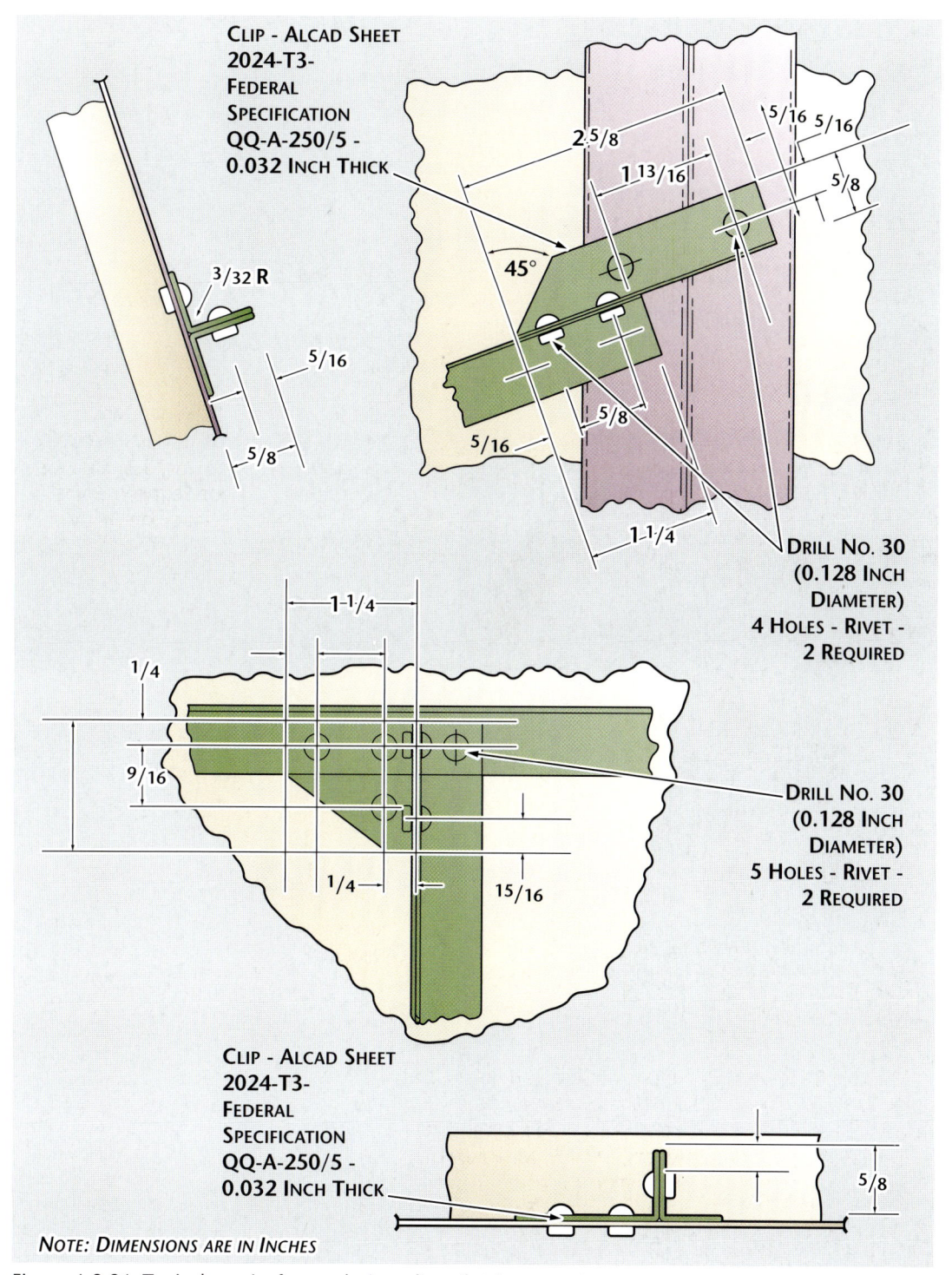

Figure 4-2-24. Typical repairs for cracks in radius of stringer end

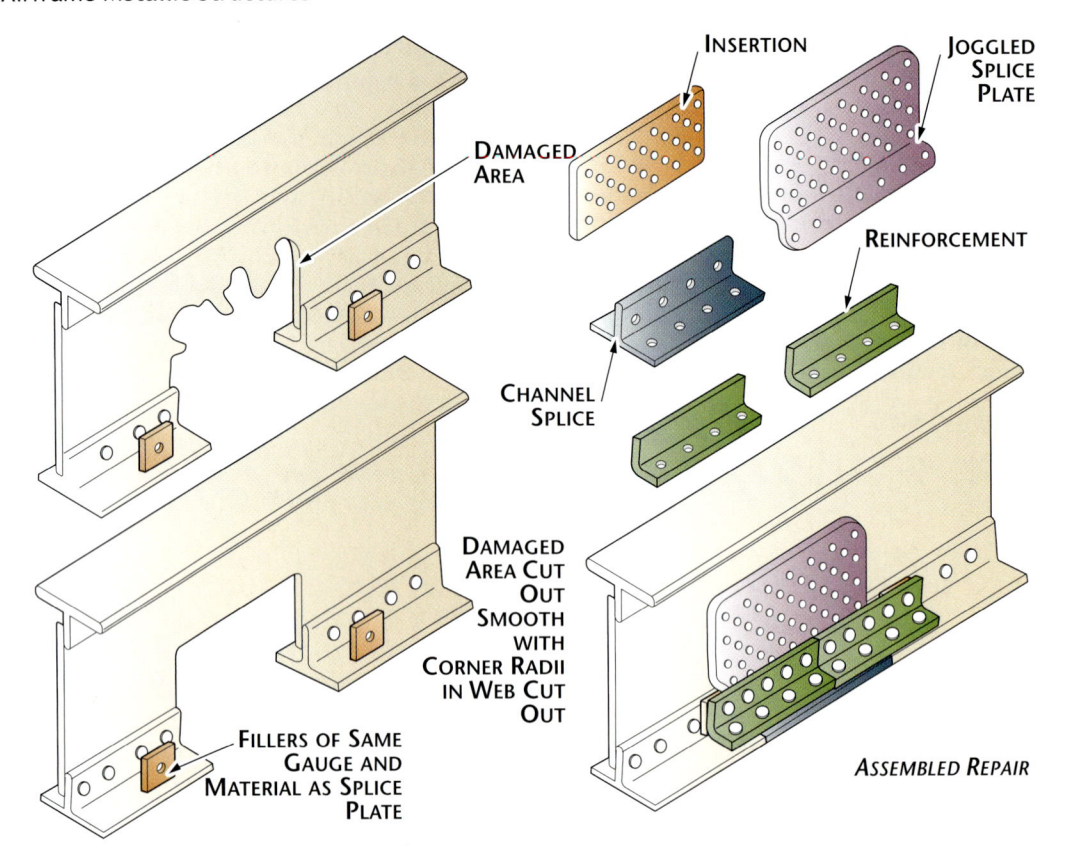

Figure 4-2-25. Spar repair by insertion

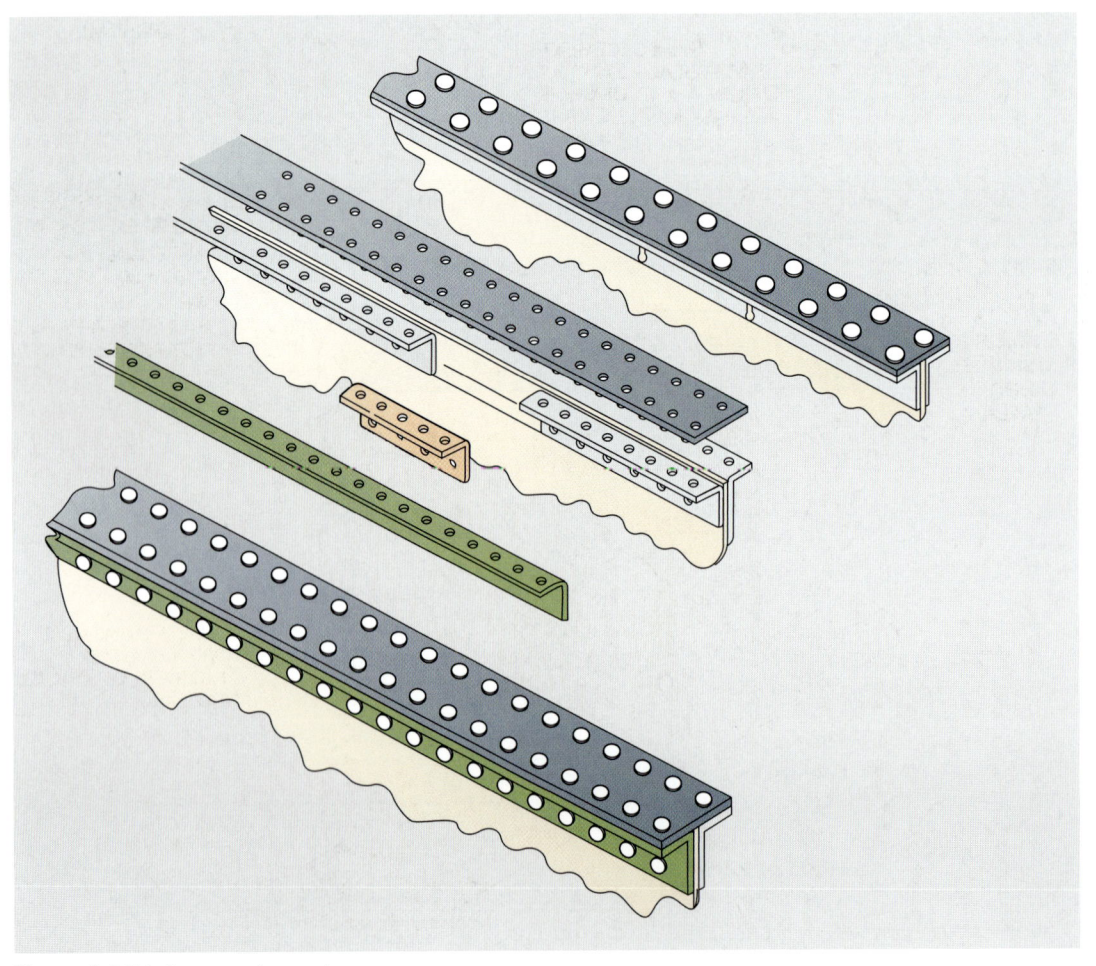

Figure 4-2-26. Spar angle repair

Airframe Metallic Structures | 4-31

tion will normally be evaluated separately. The extruded section in such a composite member will be repaired in the same manner as the stringer.

Spar repair by insertion. Repairs on spars may not be permitted because of the critical stresses imposed on them. However, if repairs are made, they are usually made by insertion, as shown in Figure 4-2-25, and they must be made according to instructions in the applicable aircraft maintenance manual.

Spar angle. Figure 4-2-26 shows this repair.

Spar web repair. Some spar web damage is repairable. When small cracks occur, the most common repair is to stop drill the cracks and add a reinforcing doubler over the damaged area. Repair of the spar web is detailed in Figure 4-2-27. Always consult the aircraft maintenance manual for permissible repairs and proper procedures for that type of aircraft.

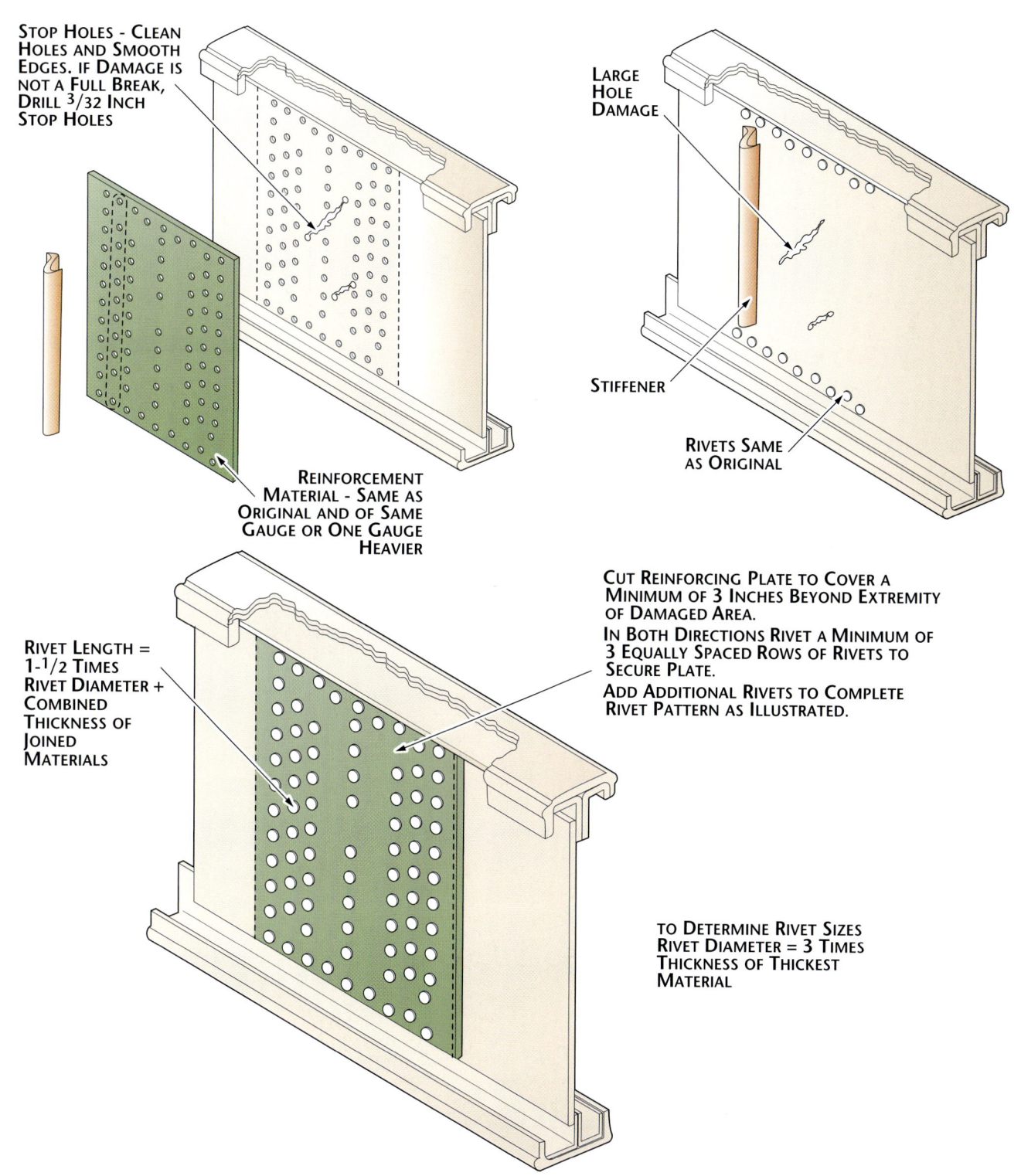

Figure 4-2-27. Spar web repair

Rib repair by patching. Figure 4-2-28 and Figure 4-2-29 show repair of nose and wing ribs by patching.

Rib repair by insertion. This type of repair, shown in Figure 4-2-30, is required when an entire portion of the rib is damaged.

Former repair. Former repair by patching is shown in Figure 4-2-31.

Figure 4-2-28. Example of nose rib repair

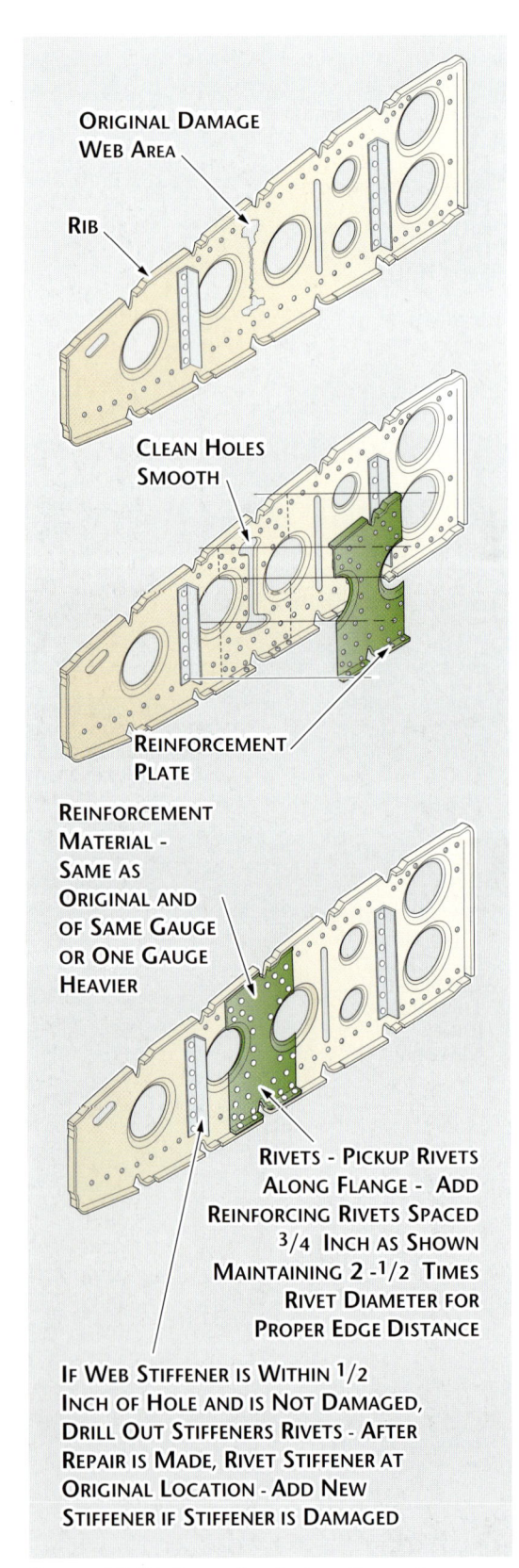

Figure 4-2-29. Example of wing rib repair

Bulkhead repair. A typical repair of a bulkhead flanged member is shown in Figure 4-2-32. Damage involves a bulkhead or frame and the aircraft skin shown in Figure 4-2-33 and Figure 4-2-34.

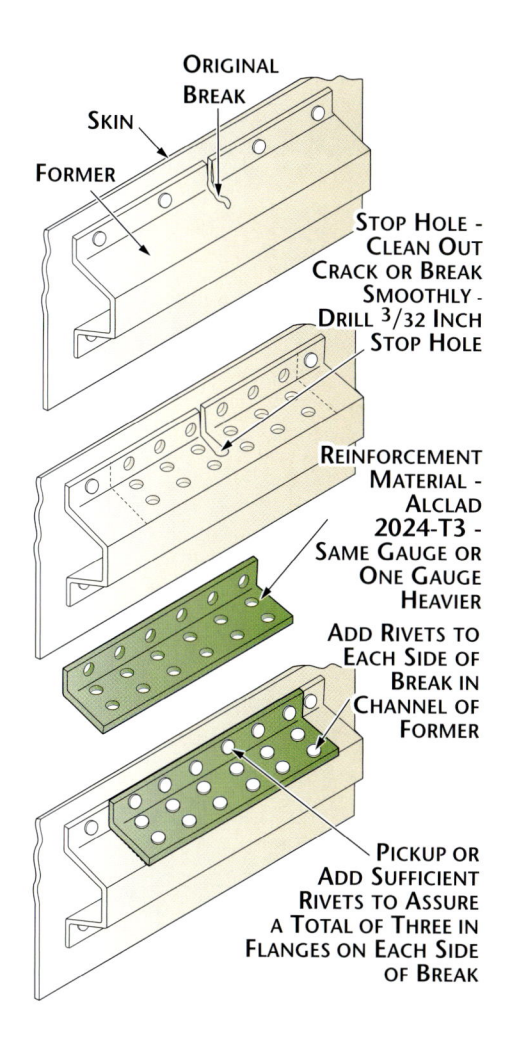

Figure 4-2-31. Illustration of a former repair

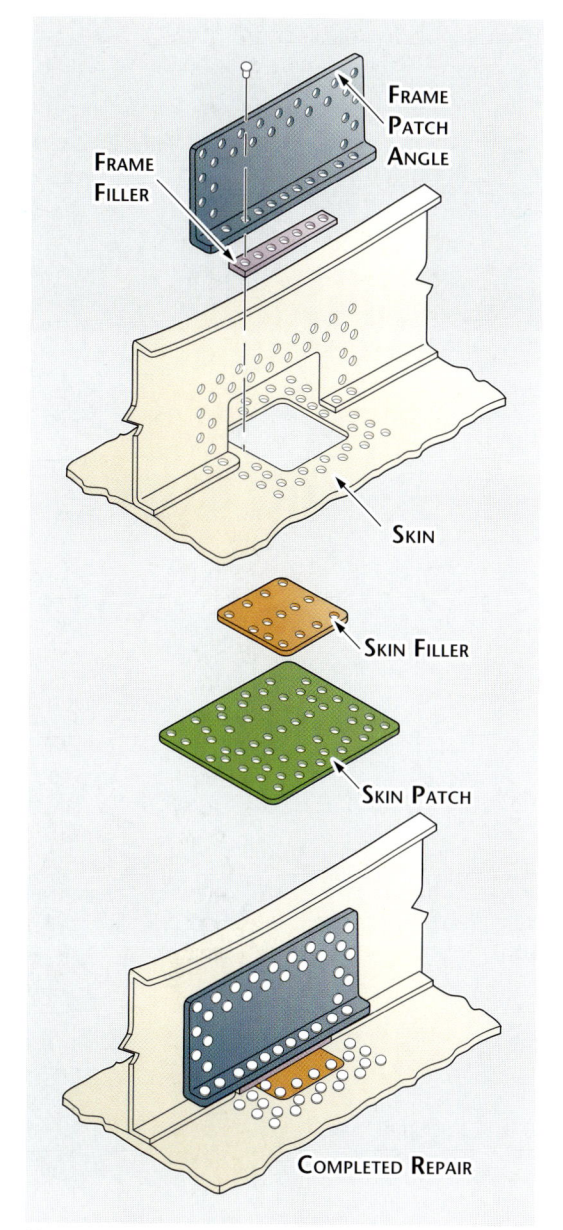

Figure 4-2-33. Frame and skin repair

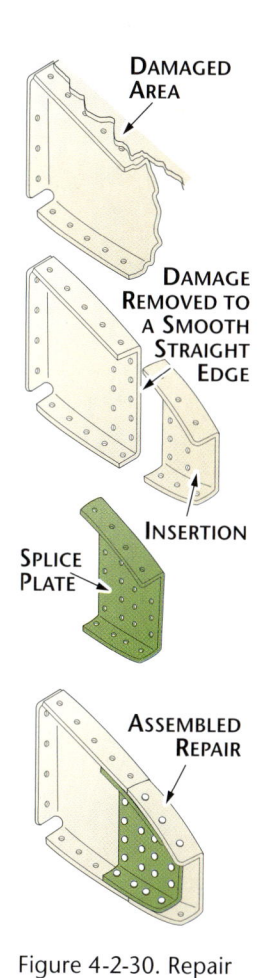

Figure 4-2-30. Repair of a rib with complete damage

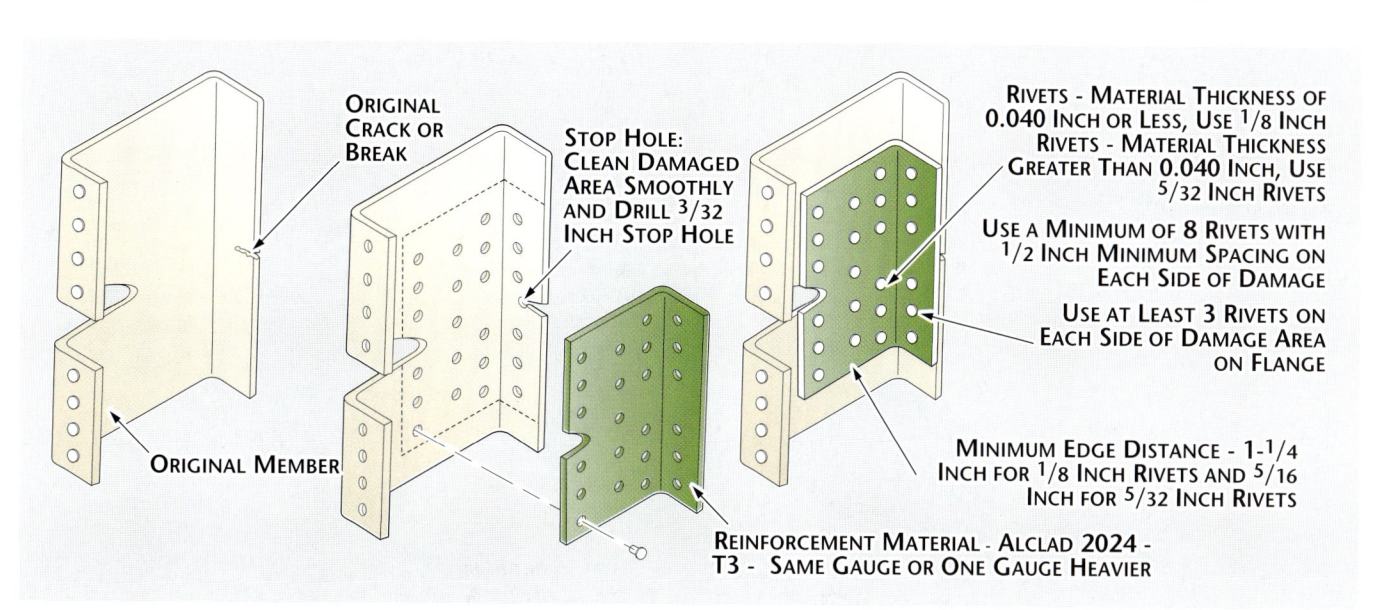

Figure 4-2-32. Bulkhead flanged member repairs

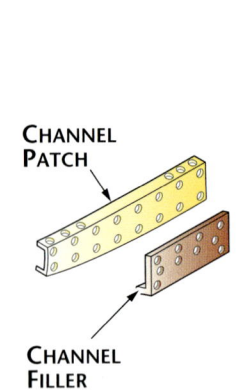

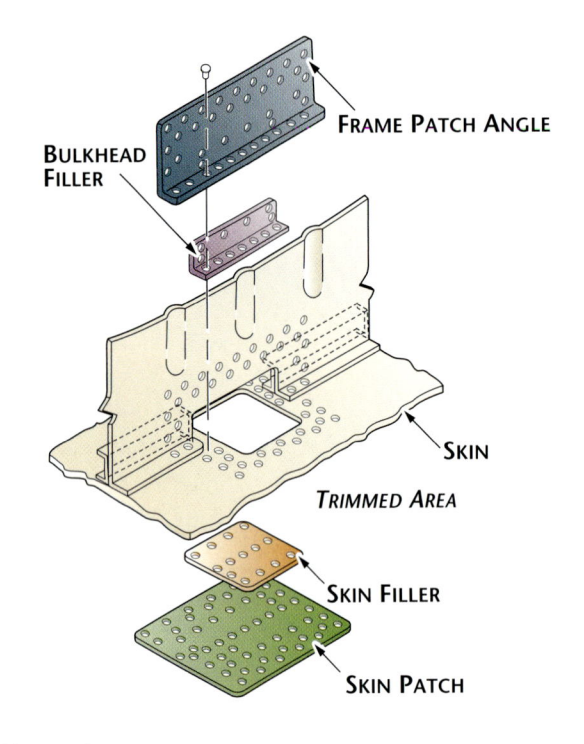

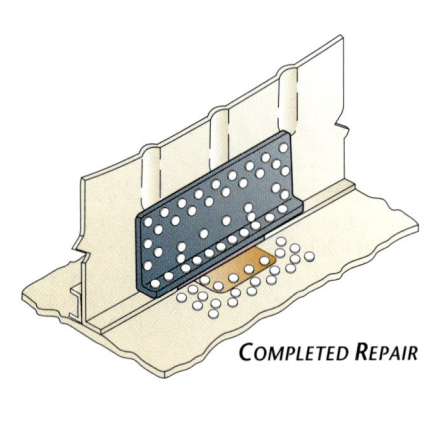

Figure 4-2-34. Bulkhead and skin repair

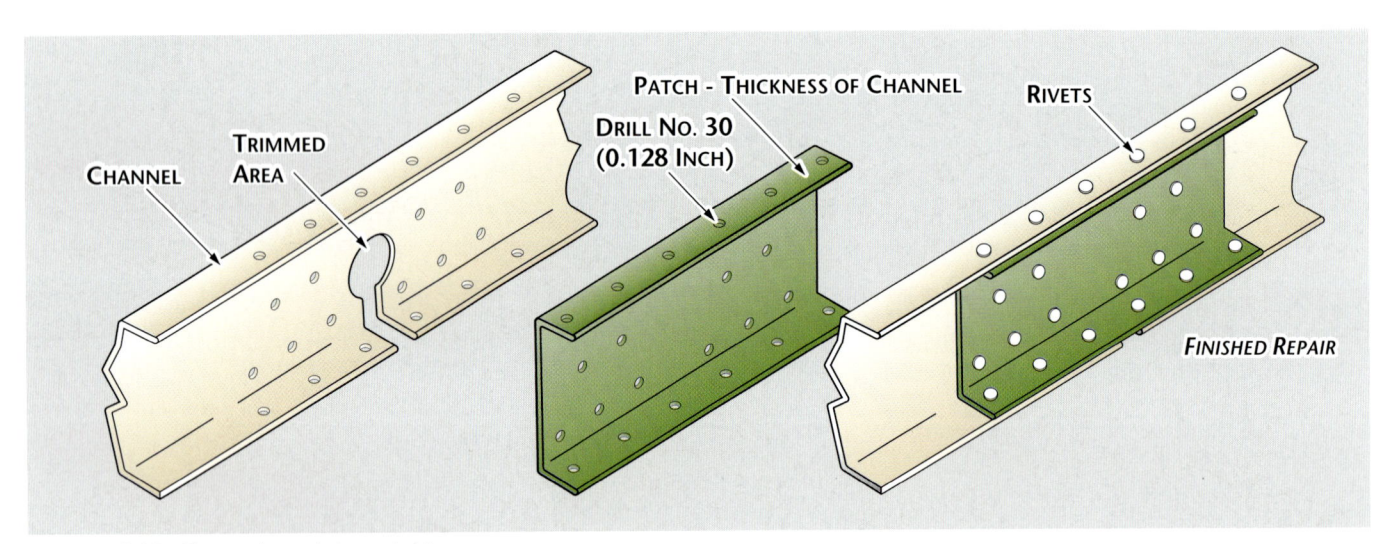

Figure 4-2-35. Channel repair by patching

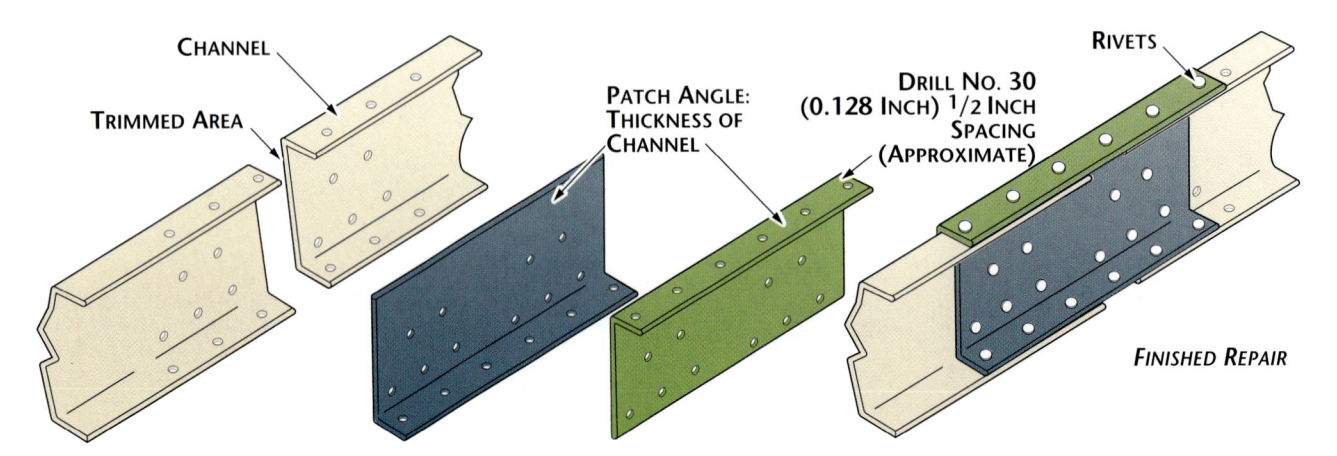

Figure 4-2-36. Channel repair by insertion

Repair of damaged channels. Channels can be repaired by the patching method of repair. See Figure 4-2-35, or the insertion method. See Figure 4-2-36.

Repair of cracks by stop-drilling. A crack develops at the point where stress is concentrated, and it is usually compounded by repetitive stress, such as vibration. This stress must be relieved to prevent the crack from continuing. This procedure is called stop-drilling, and is shown in Figure 4-2-37A and Figure 4-2-37B. In normal circumstances, a 3/32 or 1/8 inch hole drilled at each end and sharp turn of a crack will accomplish this. Stop drilling is a temporary repair. It requires follow-up with another reinforcing repair.

Repair of dents and creases. In most situations involving dents and creases, the repair procedure is basically the same. As shown in Figure 4-2-38, the dent or crease is tapped out with a mallet, using a wood block for support, and a reinforcement is riveted in place. The exact procedure is subject to the applicable aircraft structural repair manual.

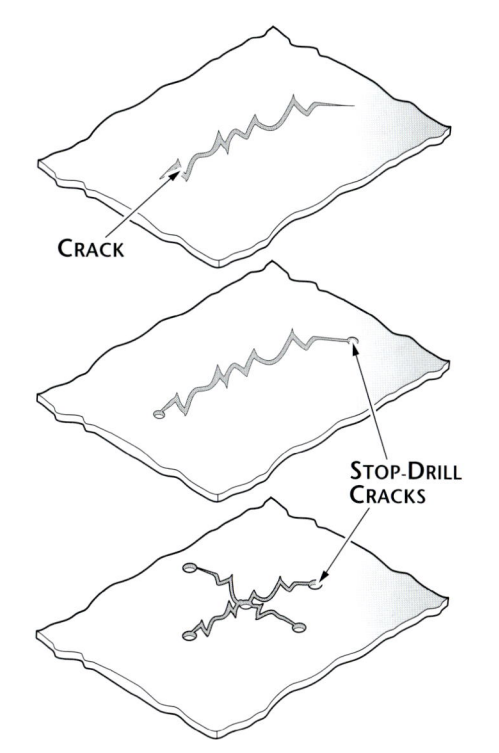

Figure 4-2-37A. Repair of cracks by stop-drilling

Figure 4-2-37B. Example of a stop-drilled crack

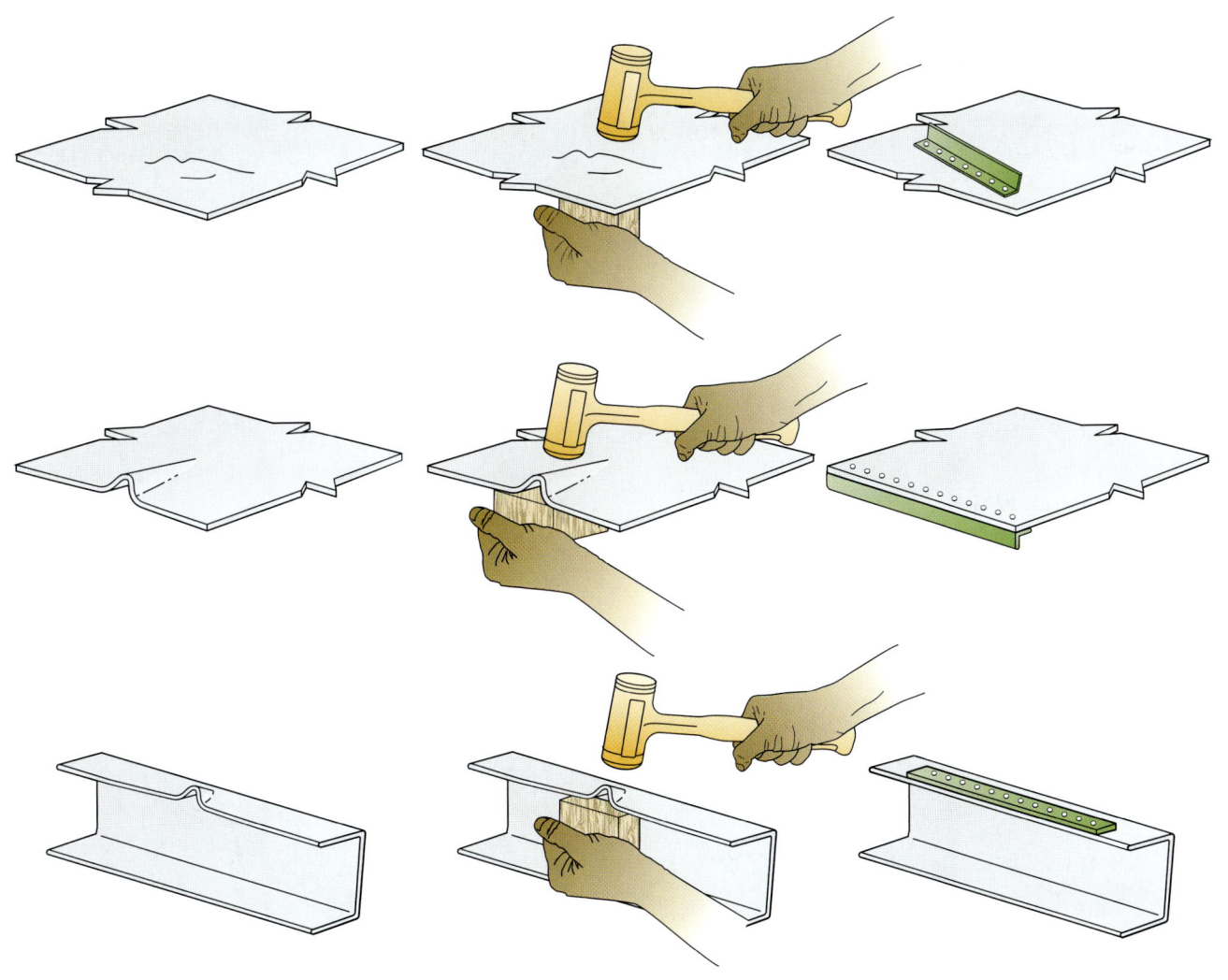

Figure 4-2-38. Repair of dents and creases

Repair of damaged frame or beam. Figure 4-2-39 shows the typical repair for a non-stressed frame. Figure 4-2-40 shows a typical stressed-beam repair.

Repair of frame and stringer joint. When damage involves the skin and the intersection of a stringer with a frame, the repair shown in Figure 4-2-41 can be used.

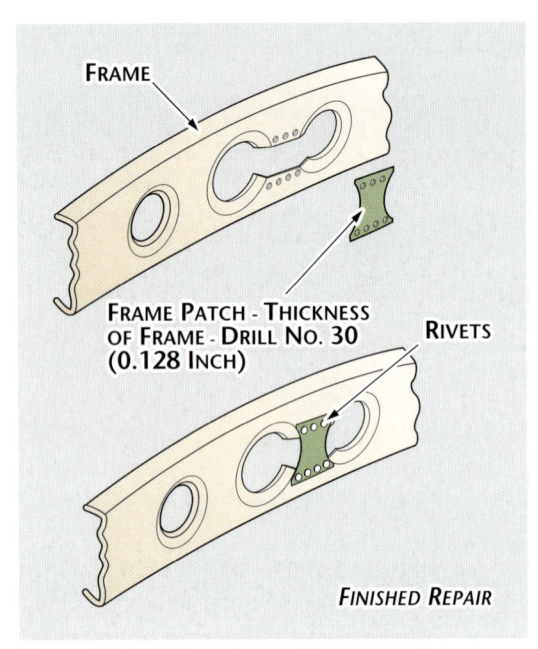

Figure 4-2-39. Non-stressed frame repair

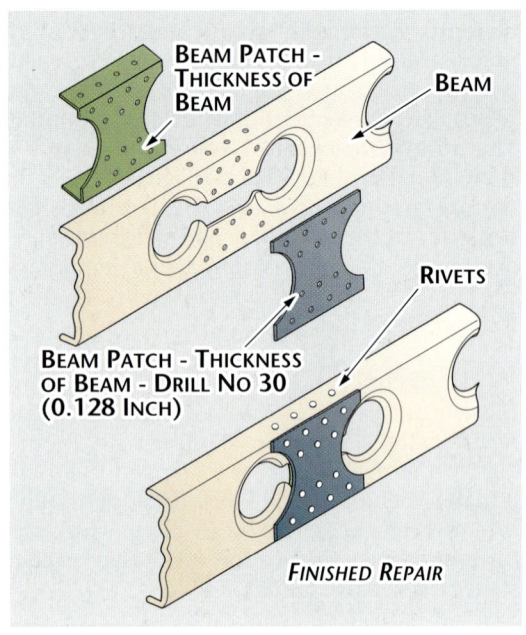

Figure 4-2-40. Stressed-beam repair

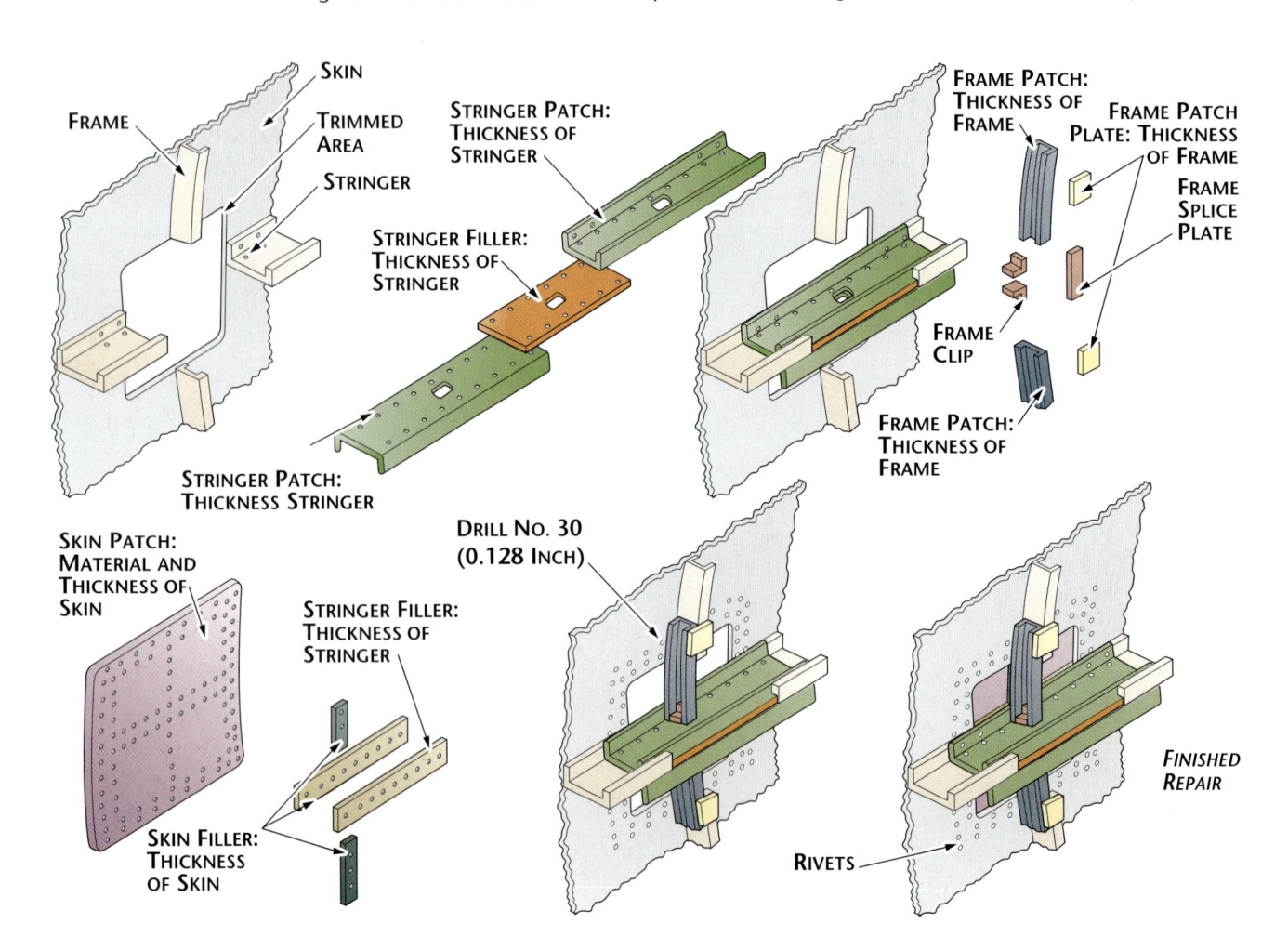

Figure 4-2-41. Repair of frame and stringer joint

Floor channel repair. The floor channel repair shown in Figure 4-2-42 involves typical patching procedures.

Splice repair of hat section. A typical splice repair of a cracked or broken hat section is shown in Figure 4-2-43. If it is partially cracked, the crack must be stop-drilled prior to installation of the splice.

Non-stressed skin and frame repair. Figure 4-2-44 shows the appropriate repair of damage incurred to non-stressed skin and its supporting structure.

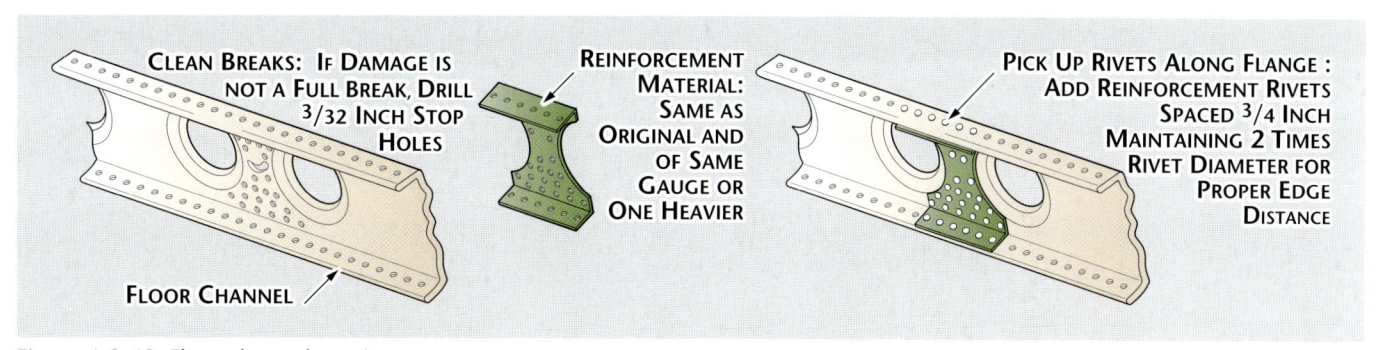

Figure 4-2-42. Floor channel repair

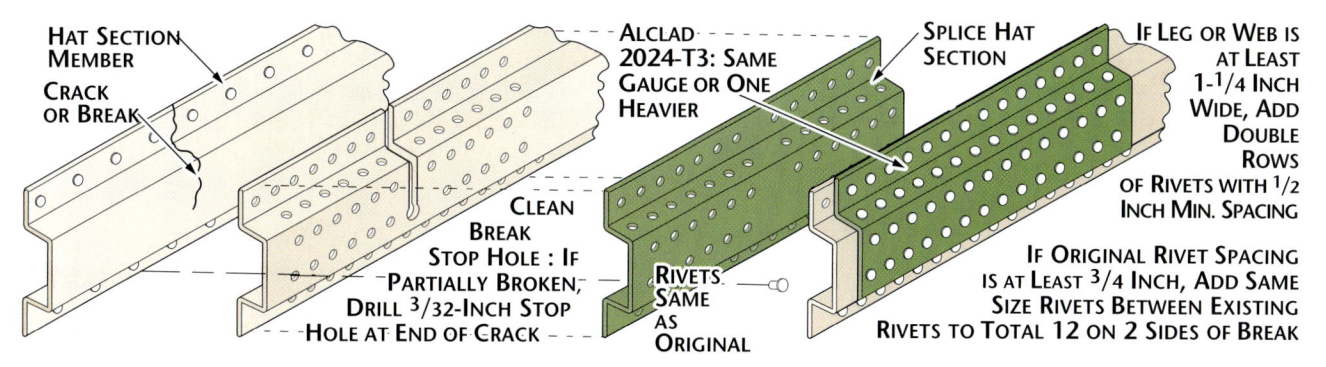

Figure 4-2-43. Splice repair of hat section

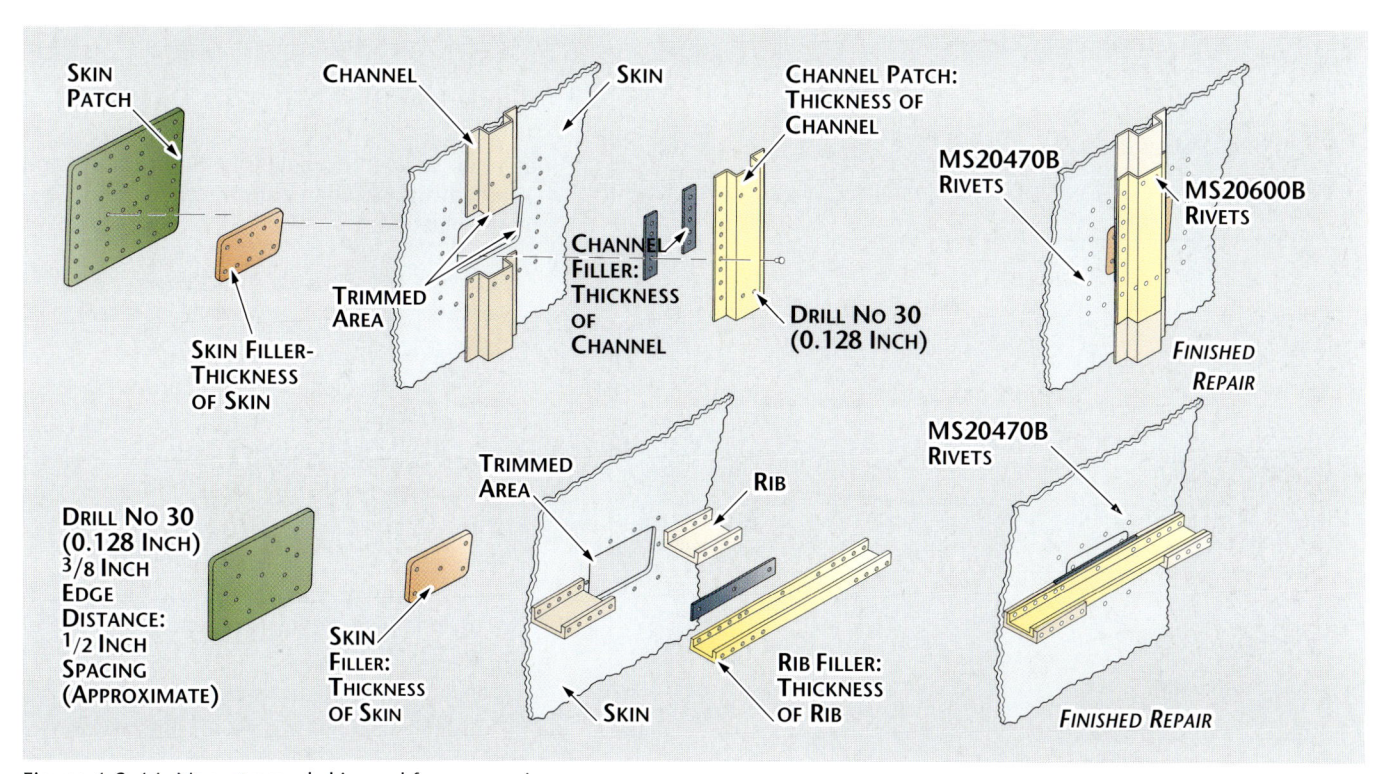

Figure 4-2-44. Non-stressed skin and frame repair

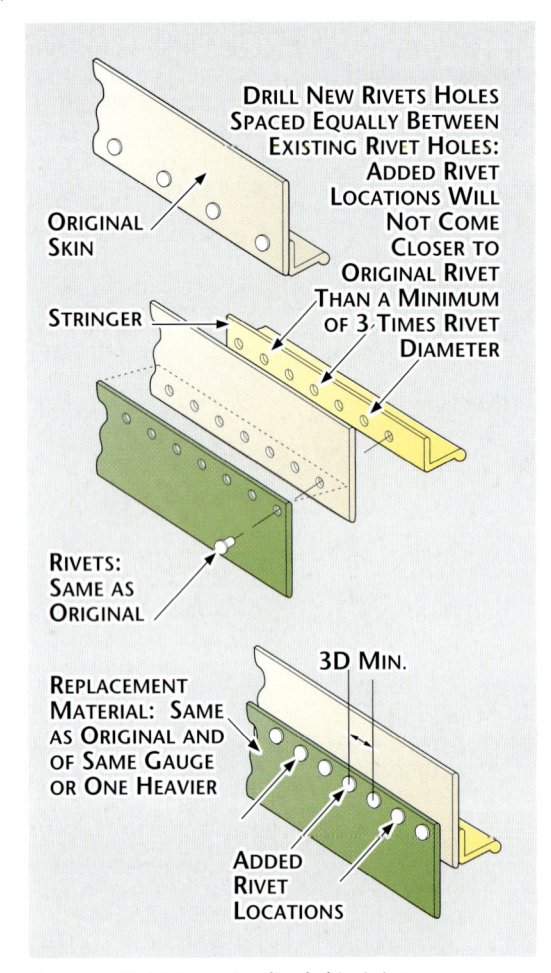

Figure 4-2-45. Longitudinal skin joint

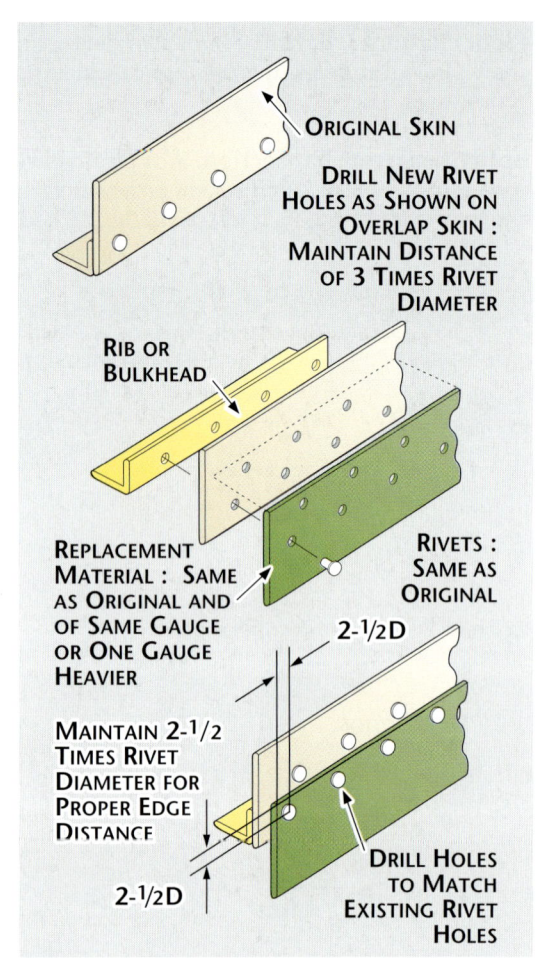

Figure 4-2-46. Transverse skin joint

Longitudinal skin joint. A longitudinal skin joint is created when a sheet is added using the same line of rivets as the original, as shown in Figure 4-2-45.

Transverse skin joint. A transverse skin joint uses two staggered rows of rivets to add a sheet, as shown in Figure 4-2-46.

Fastener Layout and Patterns

Evenly spaced fasteners, straight rows, and aesthetically pleasing patterns are marks of fine craftsmanship.

> **EXAMPLE:** *A repair specification calls for installing eight equal spaces between fasteners.*

- Note that with eight space locations, there will be nine fasteners. See Figure 4-2-47, illustration A.

- Start by measuring and marking the end locations. See Figure 4-2-47, illustration B.

- Divide the distance between the end locations (5.8 inch) by eight. See Figure 4-2-47, illustration C. This will give you the distance between fasteners. 5.8 inch ÷ 8 = 0.725 inch.

- This measurement can be stepped off with dividers. See Figure 4-2-47, illustration D.

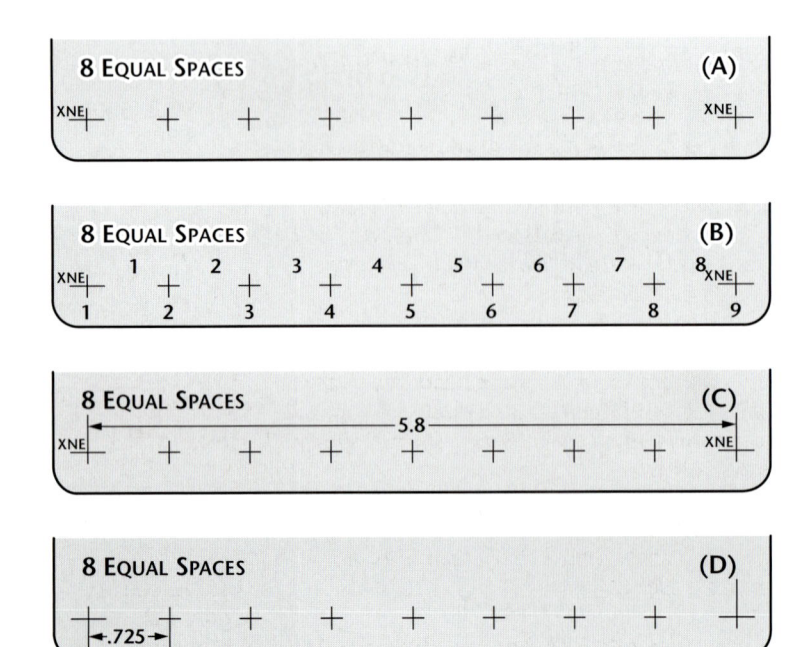

Figure 4-2-47. Evenly spacing a number of holes

| RIVET SPACING 6D | RIVET SPACING 6D | RIVET SPACING 4D |
| DISTANCE BETWEEN ROWS 6D | DISTANCE BETWEEN ROWS 3D | DISTANCE BETWEEN ROWS 4D |

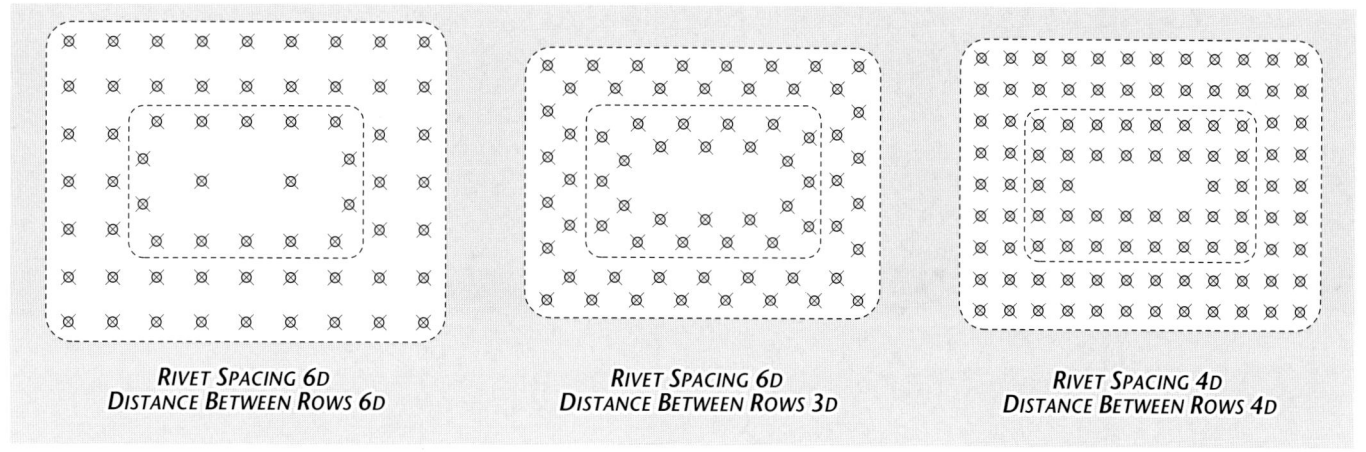

Figure 4-2-48. Examples of rivet spacing

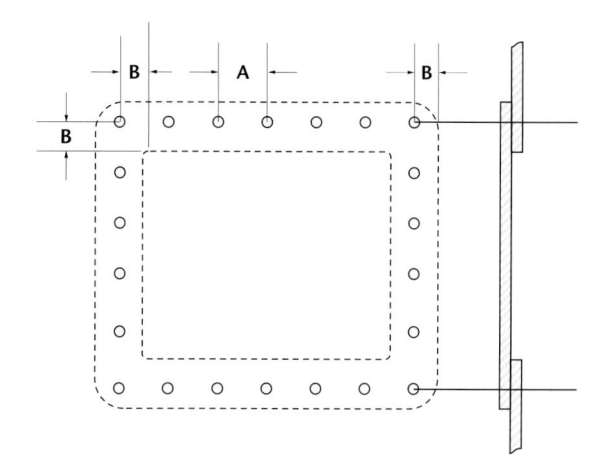

PATCH GAUGE	RIVET DIAMETER (INCHES)	A (INCHES)	B (INCHES)
0.020	3/32	1	3/16
0.025	1/8	1	1/4
0.032	1/8	1	1/4
0.040	1/8	1	1/4
0.051	1/8	1	1/4
0.064	3/16	1	3/8
0.072	3/16	1	3/8
0.081	3/16	1	3/8

Figure 4-2-50. Rivet spacing for repair with single row of rivets

Fasteners are typically placed between four to six fastener diameters (4D-6D) apart (pitch), but can be as far as 18D apart. This measurement is from hole centerline to hole centerline. When optimal strength is required, they may be pitched as close as 3-1/2D apart. They can, in rare instances, be placed 3D apart.

Normally, four to six fastener diameters (4D-6D) are used for repair work. Later in this chapter, illustrations, instructions and tables will be provided to determine the exact number, size and type of fasteners needed in typical repair projects, as well as the material to be used.

The three examples of rivet spacing in Figure 4-2-48 use the 4D-6D spacing guidelines. In these examples, all three repairs are identical in size. When two or more rows are used, they can be straight or staggered. The distance between staggered rivet rows is known as transverse pitch and is usually 75% of the rivet pitch or spacing.

Edge Distance

Placing the fastener too far from the edge or making a repair larger than needed carries a weight penalty (weight is directly related to fuel consumption).

Placing the fastener too close to the edge can cause the joint to fail by spontaneous bending (buckling in thin material), and tear-out (in thicker material). See Figure 4-2-49.

Edge distance (ED) is the distance from the edge of the material to the centerline of the fastener hole. Boeing also calls it the Edge margin. It is related to spacing in that it is often the first measurement determined when making a repair or modification.

Edge distance rules. The recommended minimum distance for protruding head fasteners is normally two diameters (2D), plus 1/16 inch or 2D of the next larger size fastener. The maximum distance is 4D.

> **EXAMPLE:** *The center of a 1/8 inch rivet would never be placed closer than 5/16 inch from the edge.*

The recommended minimum distance for flush head fasteners would normally be no closer than 2-1/2D, plus 1/16 inch or 2-1/2D of

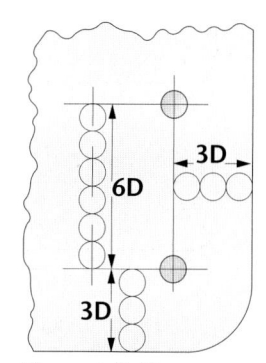

Figure 4-2-49. Measuring edge distance using rivet diameters

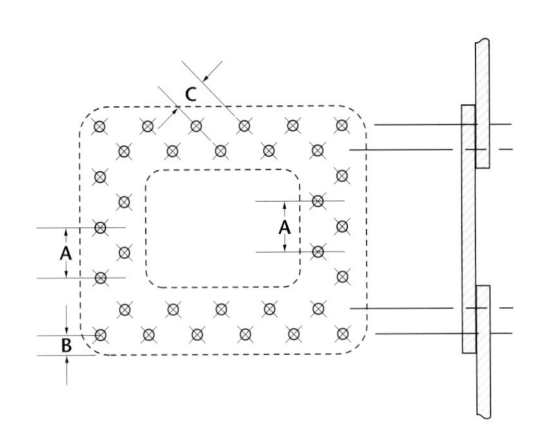

PATCH GAUGE	RIVET DIAMETER (INCHES)	A (INCHES)	B (INCHES)	C (INCHES)
0.020	3/32	1	3/16	3/8
0.025	1/8	1	1/4	1/2
0.032	1/8	1	1/4	1/2
0.040	1/8	1	1/4	1/2
0.051	1/8	1	1/4	1/2
0.064	3/16	1	3/8	3/4
0.072	3/16	1	3/8	3/4
0.081	3/16	1	3/8	3/4

Figure 4-2-51. Rivet spacing for repair with double row of rivets

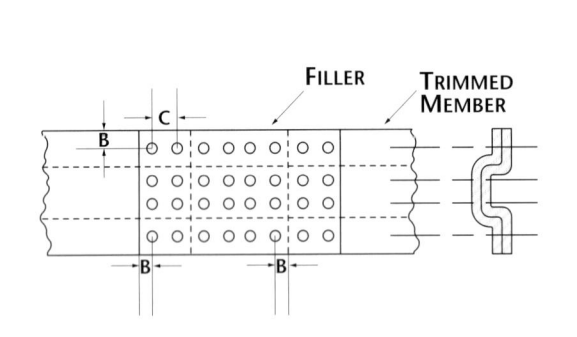

PATCH GAUGE	RIVET DIAMETER (INCHES)	A (INCHES)	B (INCHES)	C (INCHES)
0.020	3/32	3/8	3/16	3/8
0.025	3/32	3/8	3/16	3/8
0.032	1/8	1/2	1/4	1/2
0.040	5/32	3/4	5/16	3/4
0.051	5/32	3/4	5/16	3/4
0.064	3/16	3/4	3/8	3/4
0.072	3/16	3/4	3/8	3/4
0.081	3/16	3/4	3/8	3/4

Figure 4-2-52. Rivet spacing for repair using formed patch

SHEET THICKNESS	NON-FLUSH-TYPE RIVETS				FLUSH-TYPE RIVETS			
	3	4	5	6	3	4	5	6
0.020	0.156	0.218	0.265	—	0.187	0.281	0.328	—
0.025	0.156	0.218	0.265	0.328	0.187	0.281	0.328	0.390
0.032	0.140	0.218	0.265	0.328	0.171	0.281	0.328	0.390
0.040	0.125	0.187	0.234	0.328	0.156	0.250	0.328	0.390
0.051	0.109	0.156	0.203	0.312	0.140	0.218	0.296	0.375
0.064	—	0.140	0.187	0.265	—	0.203	0.265	0.328
0.072	—	0.125	—	0.250	—	0.203	0.250	0.312
0.081	—	0.125	—	0.234	—	—	0.234	0.296
0.102	—	—	—	0.203	—	—	—	0.256

Table 4-2-1. Minimum rivet edge distances for protruding and countersink head rivets

the next larger size fastener. When practical, many AMTs will use a distance of 3D. Though not optimal, it is safe, easy to remember, and if needed, allows a larger diameter to be used.

EXAMPLE: *A 1/8 inch rivet would be centered 3/8 inch from the edge.*

Typical Repair Samples

Rivet spacing, selection and acceptability limits for a non-stressed skin patch. Figure 4-2-50, Figure 4-2-51 and Figure 4-2-52 contain the rivet spacing requirements for various types of patch repairs. Table 4-2-1 shows minimum rivet edge distances for protruding and countersunk head rivets. These edge distances are applicable only to rows of three or more rivets, where a row contains a maximum of 30 percent of the total number of rivets. Table 4-2-2, Table 4-2-3 and Table 4-2-4 show the recommended types of repair rivets and their spacing for the repairs of aluminum alloy, corrosion-resistant steel and magnesium al-loy parts.

GAUGE OF THICKEST PIECE	STANDARD RIVET	BLIND RIVET	MINIMUM PITCH	MAXIMUM PITCH	ROW DISTANCE
0.020	3[1]	4[2]	0.375	0.500	0.437
0.025	4[1]	5[2]	0.500	0.625	0.500
0.032	4[1]	5[2]	0.562	0.687	0.500
0.040	5[1]	6[2]	0.687	0.812	0.625
0.051	5[1]	6[2]	0.687	0.750	0.625
0.064	6[3]	6[2]	0.812	1.062	0.625
0.072	6[3]	6[2]	0.750	1.062	0.687
0.081	6[3]	6[2]	0.625	0.937	0.687
0.091	6[3]	6[2]	0.625	0.750	0.687
0.102	10	6[2]	1.562	1.812	0.875
0.250	10	—	1.187	1.375	0.875

[1]MS20470AD or MS20426AD   [2]MS20600AD or MS20601AD   [3]MS20470ADD or MS20426DD; AN Hex-Head Bolt or Steel Lockbolt

Table 4-2-2. Rivet selection and spacing when repairing aluminum alloy parts

GAUGE OF THICKEST PIECE	STANDARD RIVET	BLIND RIVET	MINIMUM PITCH	MAXIMUM PITCH	ROW DISTANCE
0.024	4[1]	5[2]	0.562	0.687	0.437
0.030	4[1]	5[2]	0.437	0.562	0.500
0.036	5[1]	6[2]	0.750	0.875	0.625
0.042	5[1]	6[2]	0.687	0.812	0.625
0.042	6[1]	6[2]	0.875	1.000	0.687
0.060	6[1]	6[2]	0.812	1.062	0.687

[1]MS20615M or MS20427M   [2]MS20600M

Table 4-2-3. Rivet selection and spacing when repairing corrosion-resistant steel parts

GAUGE OF THICKEST PIECE	STANDARD RIVET	BLIND RIVET	MINIMUM PITCH	MAXIMUM PITCH	ROW DISTANCE
0.020	3[1]	4[2]	0.375	0.500	0.437
0.030	4[1]	5[2]	0.500	0.625	0.500
0.036	4[1]	5[2]	0.625	0.687	0.500

[1]MS20470B or MS20426B   [2]MS206008 or MS20601B

Table 4-2-4. Rivet selection and spacing when repairing magnesium alloy parts

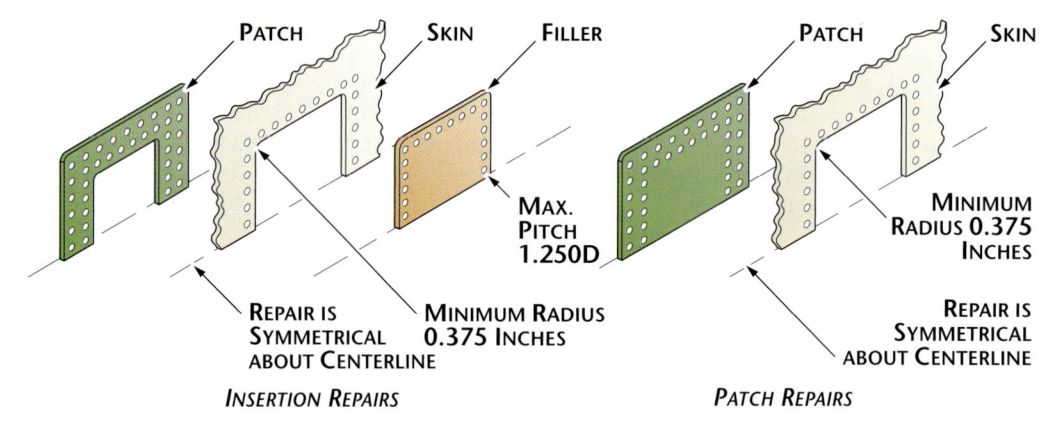

Figure 4-2-53. Rectangular damage cutout repair in lightly stressed area

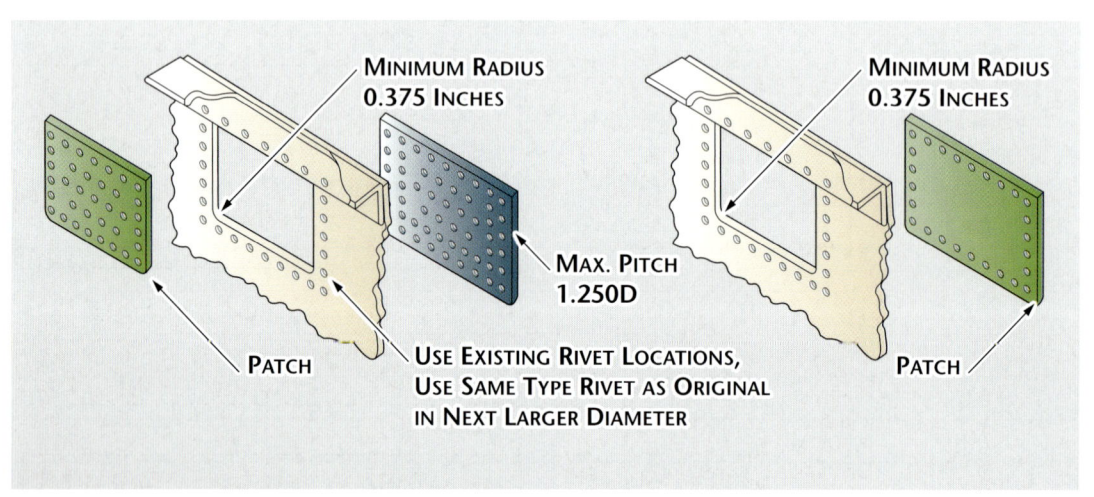

Figure 4-2-54A. Repair of damage near structure in lightly stressed area

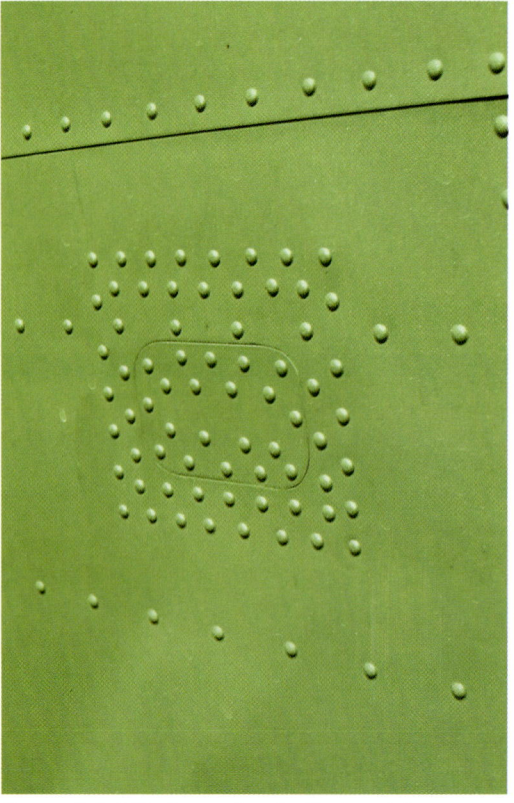

Figure 4-2-54B. Example of a flush patch

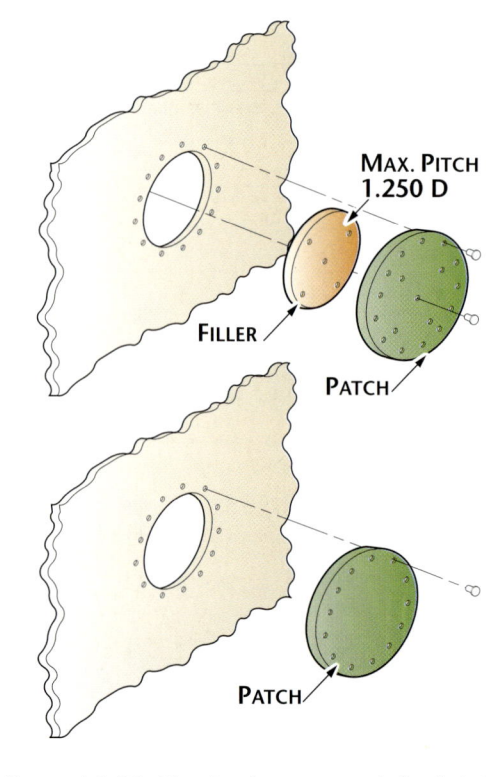

Figure 4-2-55. Circular damage repair for lightly stressed area

Skin and web repairs. Skin and web repairs are generally divided into classifications for lightly stressed and heavily stressed areas. Figure 4-2-53, Figure 4-2-54, Figure 4-2-55 and Figure 4-2-56 show general repair layout for lightly stressed areas. Figures 4-2-57 through 4-2-63 show general repair layout for heavily stressed areas. Table 4-2-5 shows the material selections for the

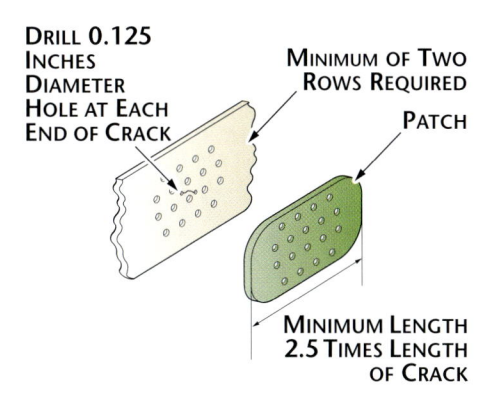

Figure 4-2-56. Crack repair for lightly stressed area

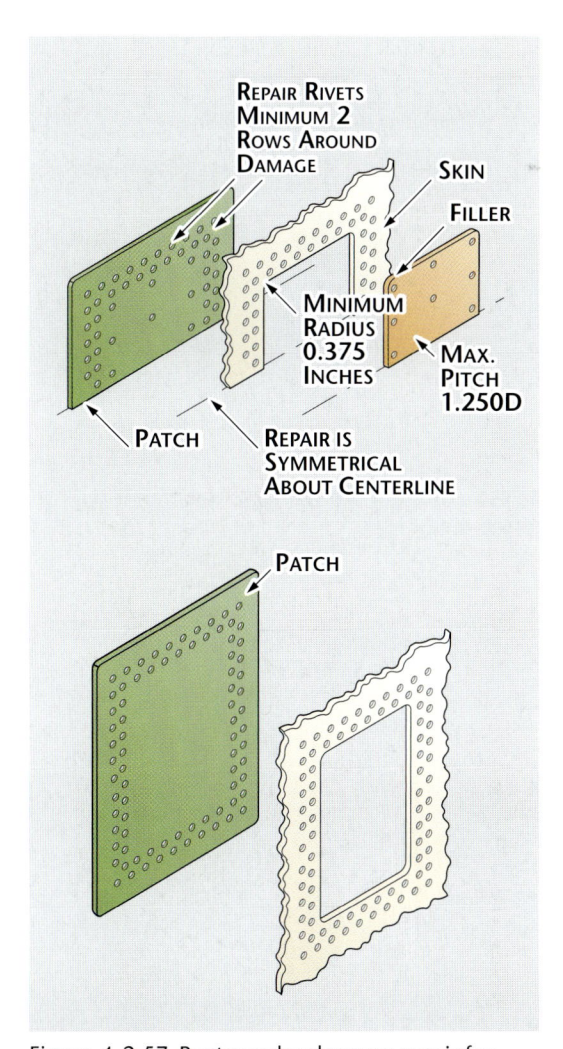

Figure 4-2-57. Rectangular damage repair for heavily stressed area

ORIGINAL THICKNESS	PATCH MATERIAL SELECTION
2024-T3/T4 & 7075-T6, Repair with 2024-T3 Clad or 7075-T6 Clad	
0.012	0.016
0.016	0.020
0.032	0.040
0.040	0.050
0.050	0.063
0.063	0.071
0.071	0.080
0.080	0.090
0.090	0.100
0.100	0.125
0.125	0.160
7075-T6 Repair with 2024-T3 Clad	
0.012	0.020
0.016	0.025
0.032	0.050
0.040	0.063
0.050	0.071
0.063	0.080
0.071	0.090
0.080	0.100
0.090	0.125
0.100	0.160
0.125	0.160
Corrosion-resistant Steel 301 & 302; Replace with Same Material	
0.012	0.016
0.016	0.020
0.020	0.025
0.025	0.032
0.032	0.036
0.036	0.040
0.040	0.050

Table 4-2-5. Material selections for patches

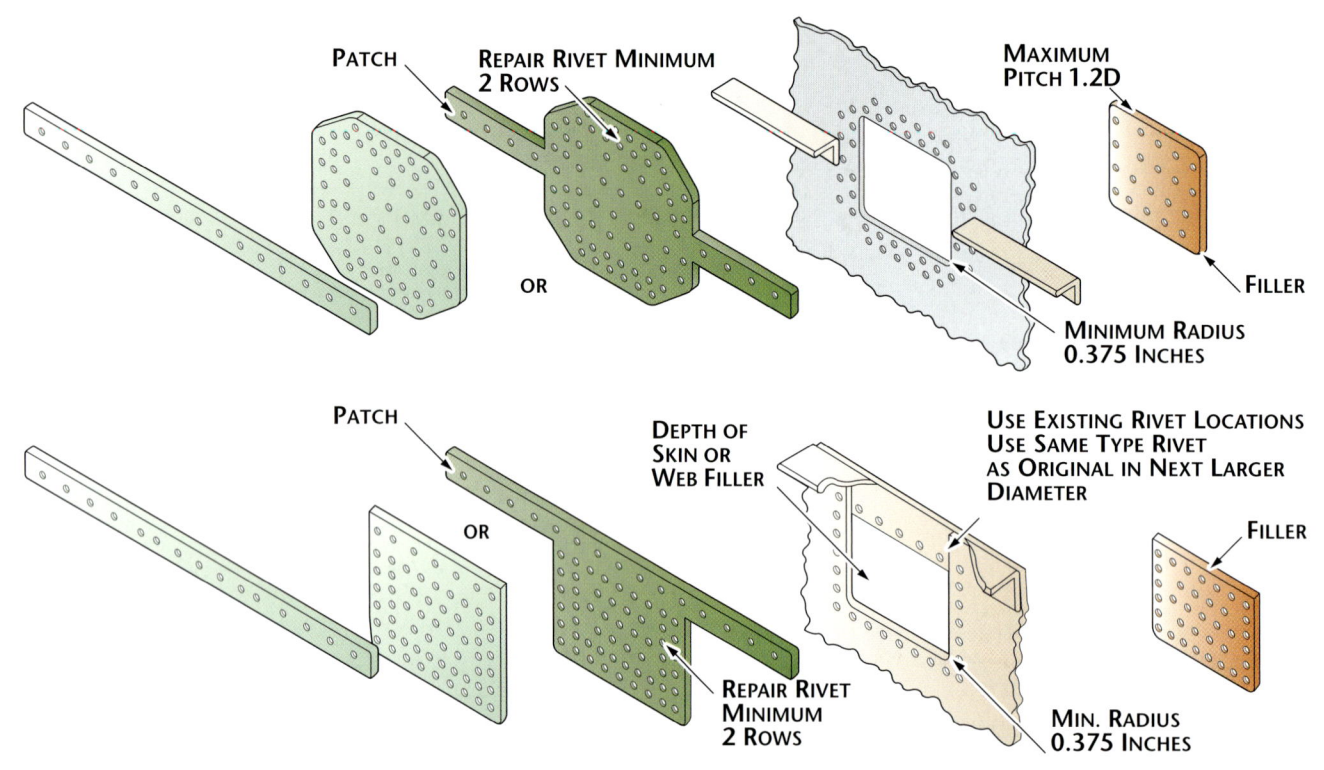

Figure 4-2-58. Damage repair near existing structure in heavily stressed area

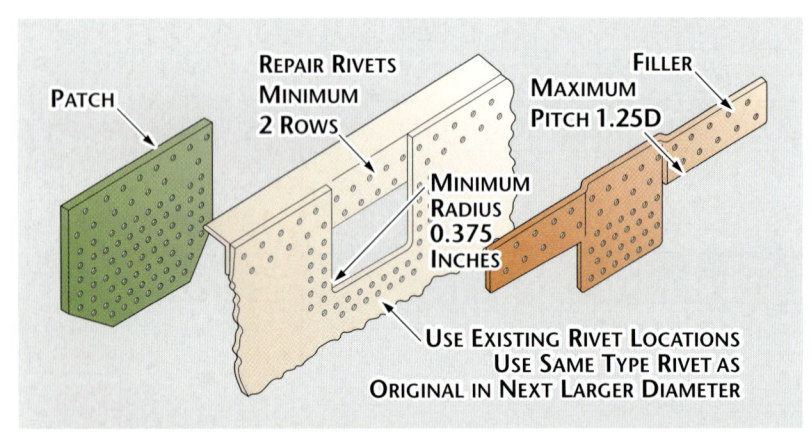

Figure 4-2-59. Damage repair near primary horizontal member in heavily stressed area

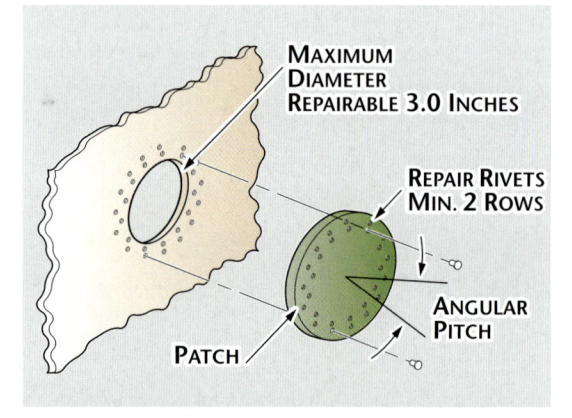

Figure 4-2-60. Circular damage repair in heavily stressed area

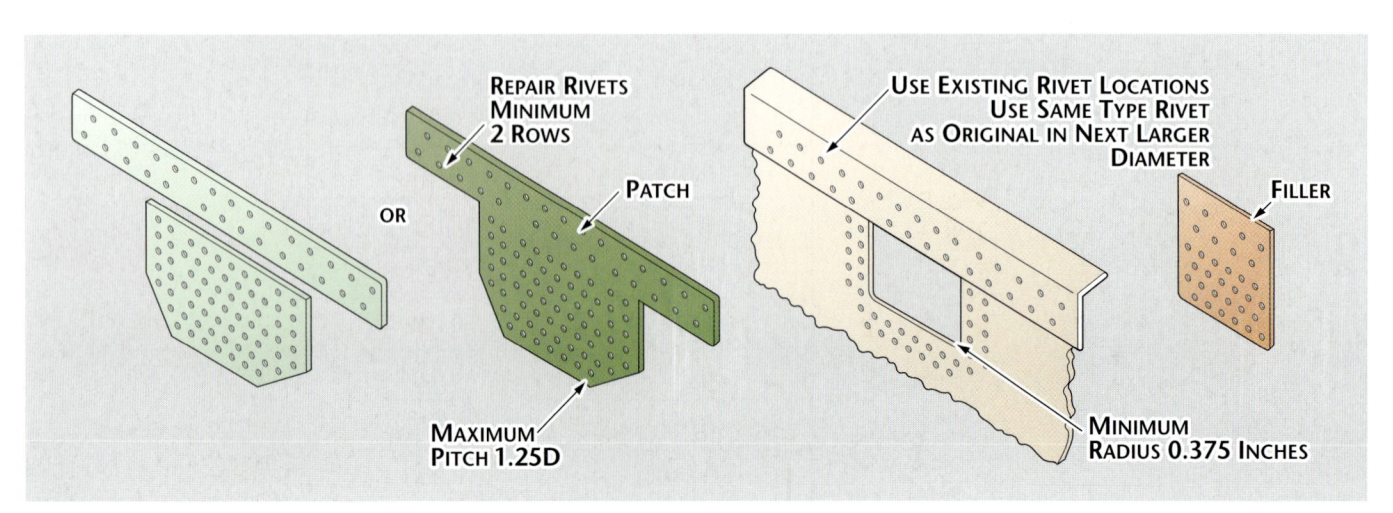

Figure 4-2-61. Damage repair near adjacent member in heavily stressed area

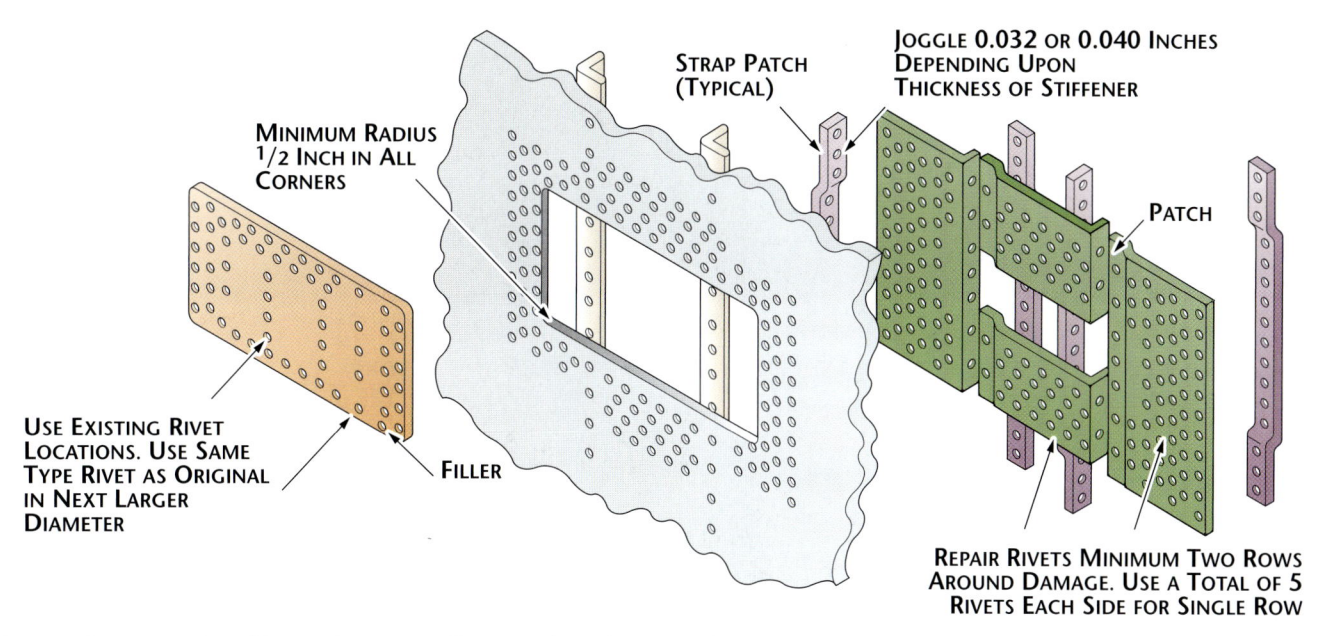

Figure 4-2-62. Insertion skin repair across stiffeners in heavily stressed area

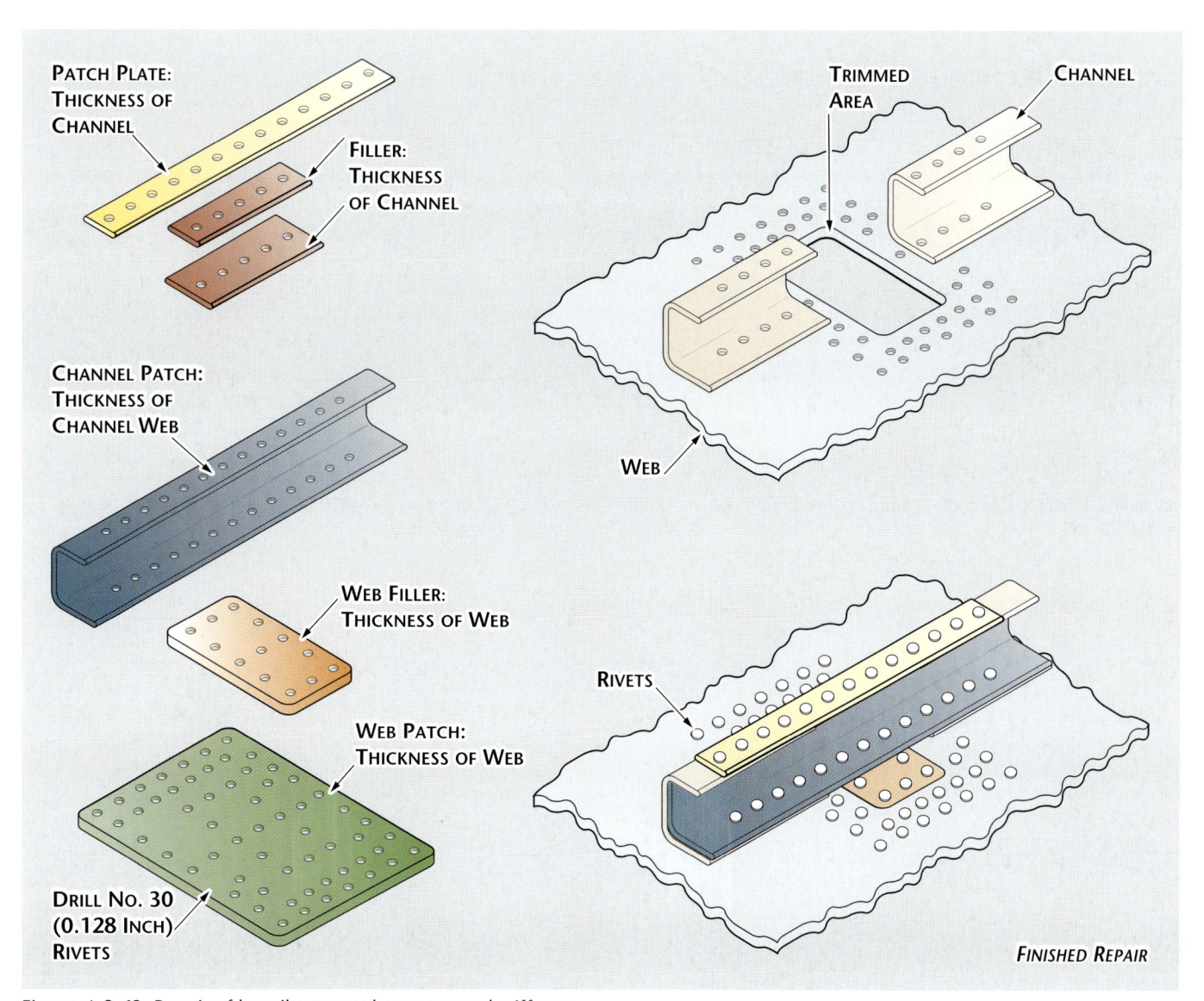

Figure 4-2-63. Repair of heavily stressed support and stiffener

patches shown in these figures. This table is for reference only. Refer to SRM, AC 43.13-1B, or ANC-5 for actual thicknesses.

Figures 4-2-64 through 4-2-67 are illustrations of common repairs to control surfaces. Figure 4-2-68 shows how to solve the problem of a repair not producing a level surface when completed.

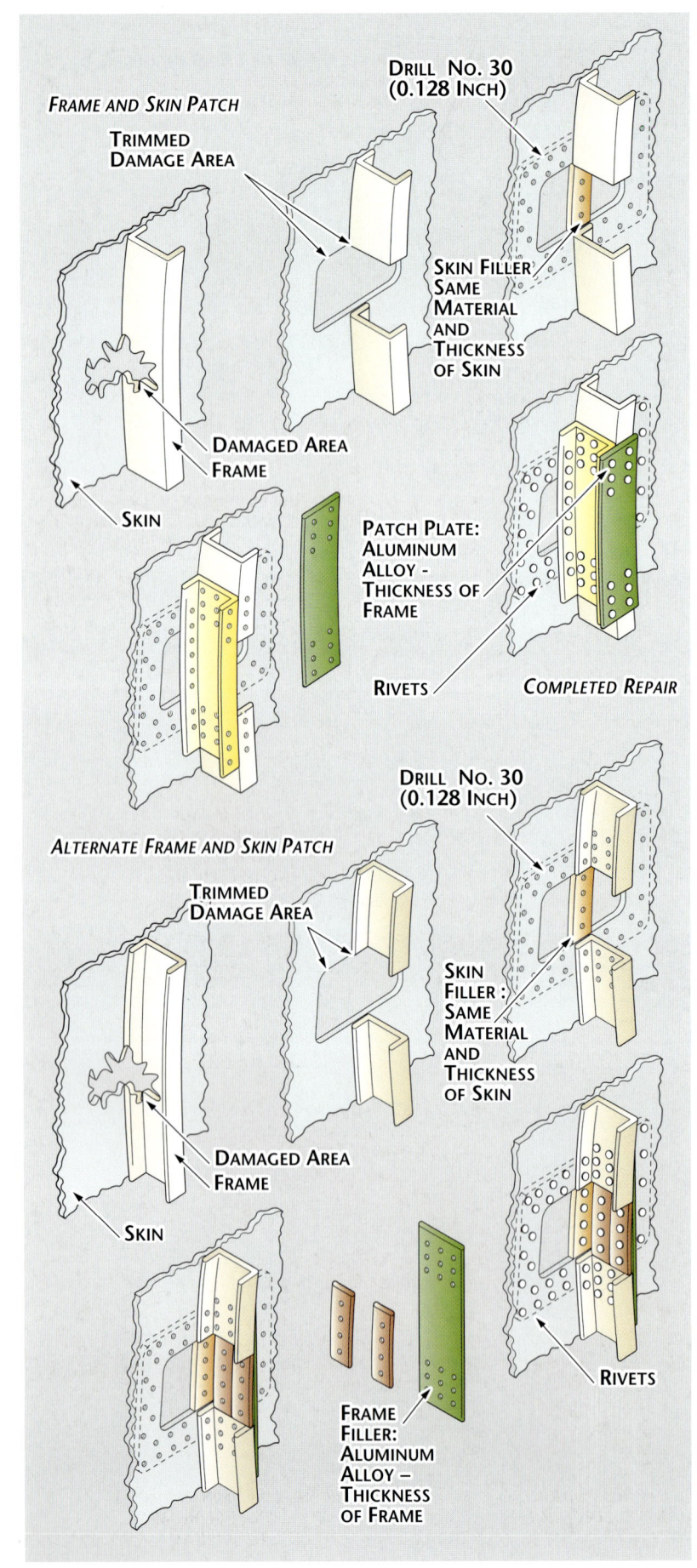

Figure 4-2-64. Two methods for producing a frame and skin patch in a stressed area

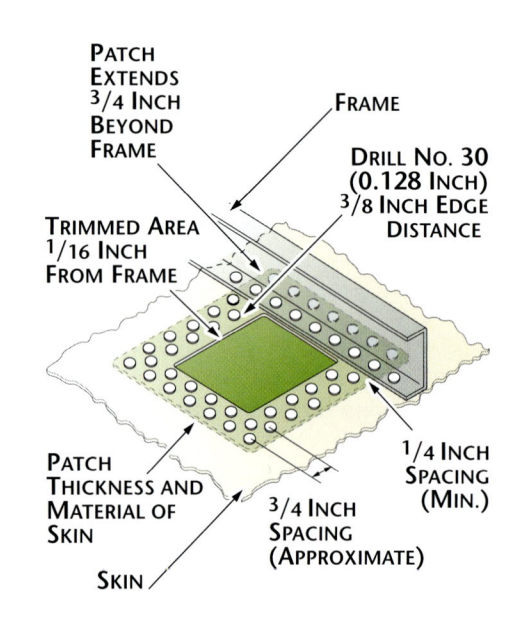

Figure 4-2-65. Repair of skin close to a frame

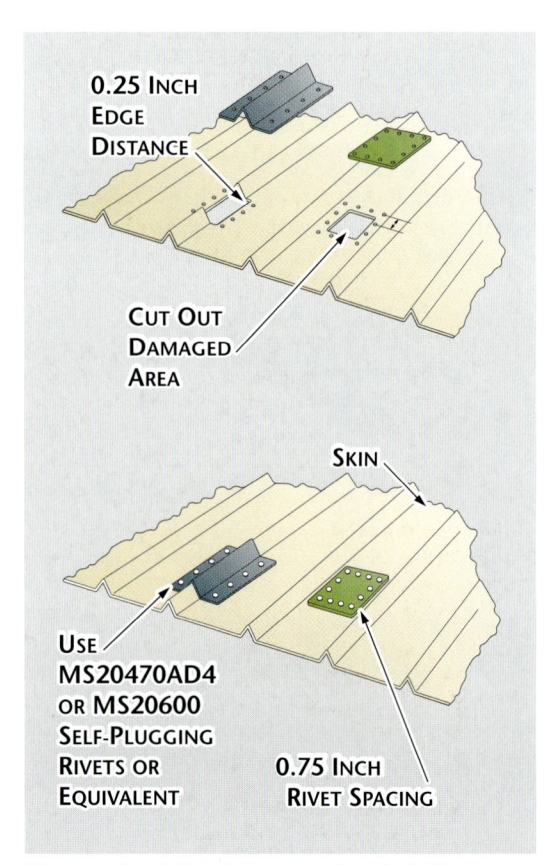

Figure 4-2-66. Patch repair to beaded skin, common on some flight-control surfaces on smaller aircraft

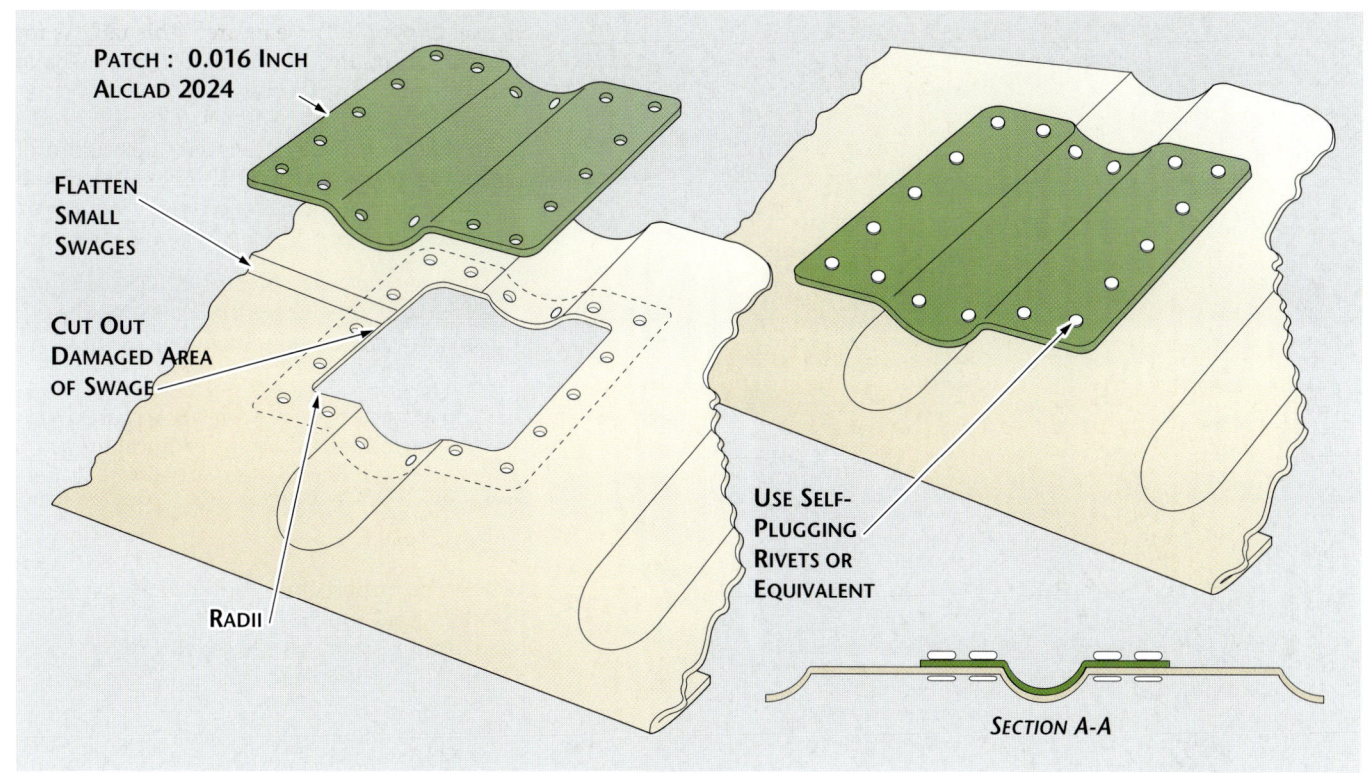

Figure 4-2-67. A patch repair to a damaged swage in aileron and flap skin

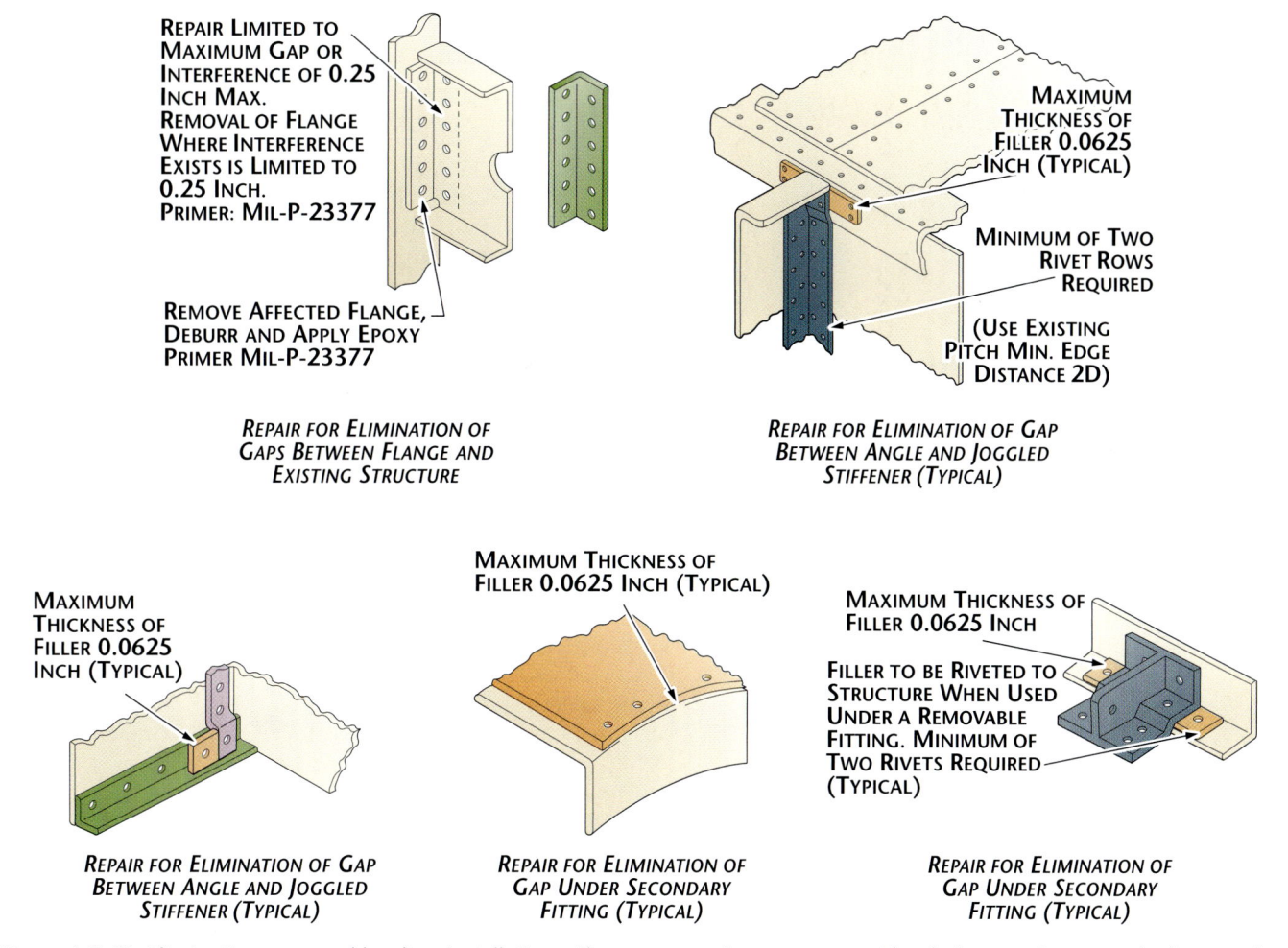

Figure 4-2-68. Eliminating gaps and leveling installations. If gaps appear in a structure, either before or after a repair, they can be repaired by the various methods shown.

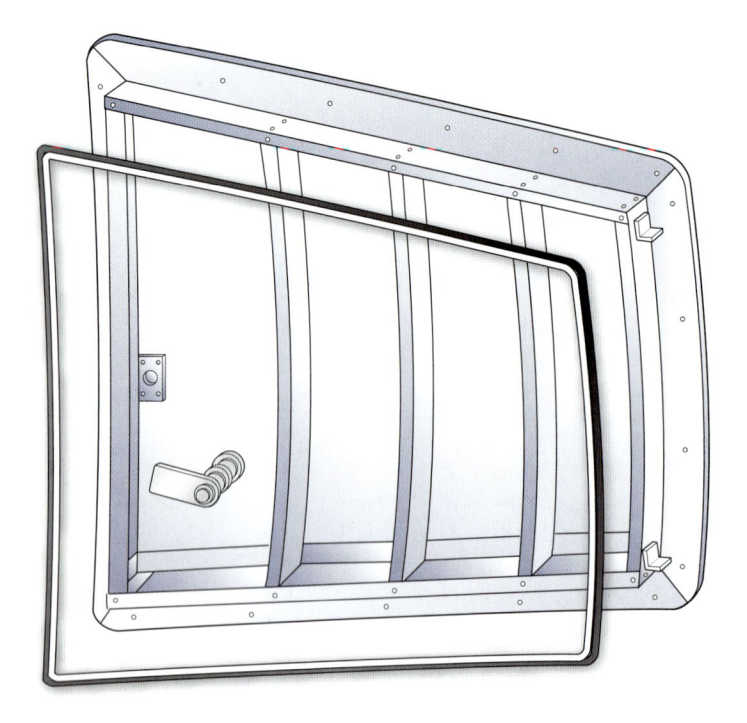

Figure 4-2-69. Typical hatch seal

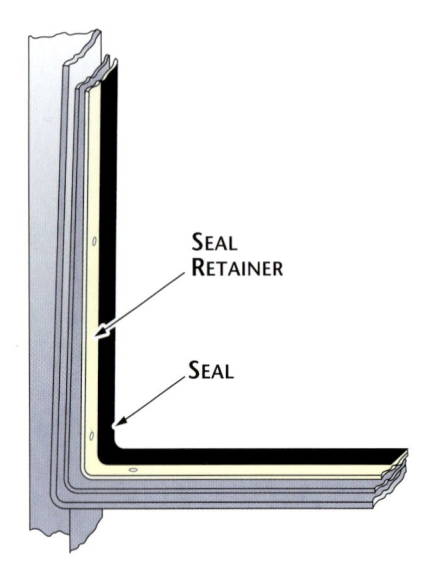

Figure 4-2-70. Seal retainer

Structural Sealing

Various areas of airframe structures are sealed compartments where fuels or air must be confined. Some of these areas contain fuel tanks, while others consist of pressurized compartments, such as the cabin. Because it is impossible to seal these areas completely airtight with a riveted joint alone, a sealing compound or sealant must be used. Sealants are also used to add aerodynamic smoothness to exposed surfaces, such as seams and joints in the wings and fuselage.

Types of seals. The types of seals ordinarily used are rubber seals, sealing compounds and special seals.

- *Rubber seals.* Rubber seals are installed at points where frequent breaking of the seal is necessary, such as emergency exits and entrance doors.

- *Sealing compounds.* Sealing compounds are used at points where the seal is broken only for structural maintenance or part replacement.

- *Special seals.* Special seals are required for passing cables, tubing, mechanical linkages or wiring out of the pressurized or sealed areas.

Wires and tubes. Wires and tubes are passed through pressure bulkheads by using bulkhead fittings, such as Cannon plugs for wiring and couplings for tubing. These fittings are sealed to the bulkhead, and the wires and tubes are fastened to them from each side. All seals of moving components — such as flight controls — are subject to wear, and utmost care must be used when they are installed. They must also be inspected regularly.

Sealant Defects

Pressure tightness of an area or section is checked before and after a repair is made. Ground pressurization is accomplished by filling the section with air from an external source through ground-pressure test fittings.

General pressurization procedures. With the sections pressurized to a given pressure, locate leaks on the outside of the aircraft by applying a soapless bubble solution to all seams and joints in the suspected area. Air bubbles will locate the general area of leakage. A specific leak is then isolated on the inside of the aircraft by passing the free end of a stethoscope or similar listening device along the seams in the leakage area. The leak can be detected by the change in sound when the instrument passes over it. After completing the test, remove the soapless bubble solution from the outside of the aircraft by washing with clear water to prevent corrosion.

Precautions. Observe the following precautions when pressurizing an aircraft:

- Never pressurize higher than the limit established by previous testing.

- No person who has a cold or who has recently had one, or whose sinuses are impaired in any way, should work in the pressurized section of the aircraft.

- A qualified operator should be at the pressurization control panel at all times while the aircraft is being pressurized.

Other sealant defects. Pressurization may not always be necessary to locate defective seals. Seals should be repaired when one or more of the following conditions exist:

- Sealants have been peeled away from the structure
- Seams are exposed through the sealant fillet
- Fillet or hole-filling sealant is exposed through the smooth overcoating
- Sealant becomes damaged by the removal and reinstallation of fasteners, access doors or other sealed parts
- Cracks or abrasions exist in the sealant

Sealant Repair or Replacement

For instructions in the use of sealing compounds, refer to the MM. Only the most common procedures for the use of rubber seals, used mostly in emergency exits and entrance doors, are covered here. Seals of this type should be replaced any time there is any degree of damage. Such a seal is not usually repairable, because it must be continuous around the opening. See Figure 4-2-69.

Seal removal. The seal can be removed as follows:

- Remove the seal retainers from the frame, as seen in Figure 4-2-70.
- Pull off the old seal.
- Use aliphatic naphtha (TT-N-95) and clean rags to clean the frame. This should be done immediately before cement application.
- Allow the rubber cement to dry until tacky, and then join the seal to the metal, pressing it firmly along all contact points.
- Install the seal retainers and allow to cure for approximately 24 hours prior to use.

Sealing of Hardware

Rivets, bolts or screws do not always seal properly when used in these critical areas or sections. When pressure leaks occur around the fasteners, they should be filled with sealing compound and new fasteners installed. Remove excess sealant as soon as possible to avoid the difficulty encountered after it becomes cured.

Section 3
Stress Calculations

Stress calculations are fairly easy to understand. The main objective is to manipulate the cross-sectional area of a joint. Fastener strength must be correct for the material being joined. As a rule, the strength of the fasteners should be such that their *total shear strength* approximates the *total bearing strength* of the material.

Instructions for determining the allowable stresses of various materials and fasteners used in a joint can be found in Manufacturer's Structural Repair Manuals. These should be understood by those engaged in structural engineering and are used when repairs cannot be made within the normally used parameters.

Technicians should look for guidelines in this sequence:

1. Maintenance Manual (MM) for a specific repair
2. Manufacturer's Structural Repair Manual (SRM) for a specific repair
3. Maintenance Manual General Notes (GN) for typical repair information
4. Manufacturer's Structural Repair Manuals for typical repair information
5. FAA Advisory Circular 43.13-1B & -2B

Joint design involves an attempt to straddle the line between being critical in shear and critical in bearing. These are determined by the failure manner affecting the joint involved, most simply, fastener (joint connector) or material (material within the joint) failure.

In a riveted joint (two or more sheets of aluminum joined by rivets), there are four different failure modes. See Figure 4-3-1. If a load is applied, one of the following may occur:

1. Sheets will separate or break. This is called *tensile failure*.
2. Rivets will shear. This is called *rivet shear failure*. This is the most common type.
3. Holes in the sheet will elongate. This is called *bearing failure*.
4. Sheet will tear (*tear-out failure*).

In the design or repair of aircraft structures, it is vital to know how and where a joint will fail. Most joints are designed so that the bearing strength of the sheet is about the same as the combined shear strength of the rivets.

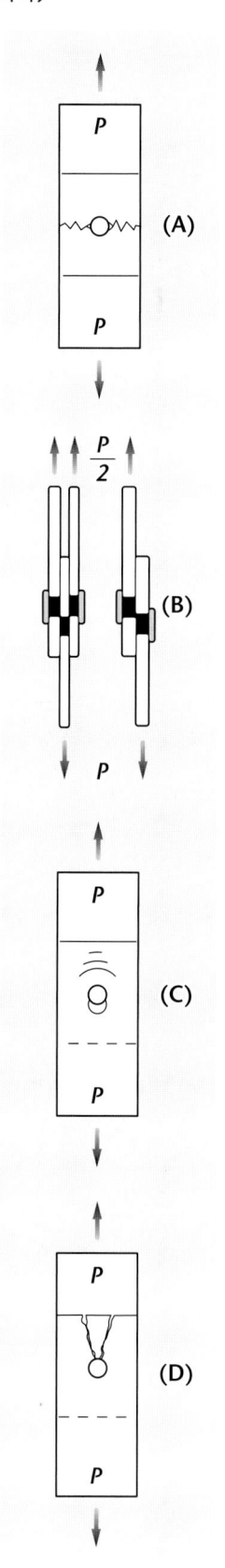

Figure 4-3-1. Methods of failure of bolted or riveted joints: (A) sheet tension, (B) rivet single- or double-shear, (C) sheet bearing failure, (D) sheet tear-out

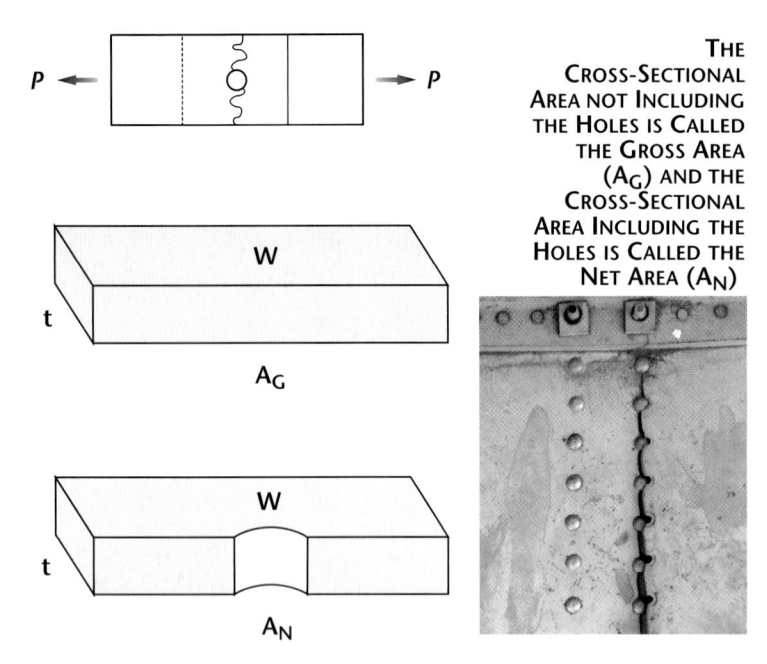

Figure 4-3-2. An example of a tension failure

To calculate the stress experienced by a joint, the general formula is:

$$F = \frac{P}{A} \quad \text{Stress} = \frac{\text{Load (pounds)}}{\text{Area (inches squared)}}$$

The unit of measure used is pounds per square inch (p.s.i.).

NOTE: *Most calculations have to do with the cross-sectional area.*

Cross-sectional area of a rectangle = width x length (W x L)

Cross-sectional area of a circle = $1/4\pi d^2$ or $1/2\pi r^2$

Tensile Stress Calculation

Tension failure of the connecting sheets can occur when the sheets are weakened by holes. See Figure 4-3-2.

The cross-sectional area, not including the holes, is called the *gross area* (A_g). The cross-sectional area, including the holes, is called the *net area* (A_n).

The formulas for area are:

$A_g = W \times T$

$A_n = [W - (d_h \times n)] \times T$

W = width of the sheet

T = thickness of the sheet

d_h = hole diameter (drill size)

n = number of rivets

EXAMPLE 1: *Two sheets of 2024-T3 aluminum alloy are riveted together with two MS20470AD4-4 rivets (Figure 4-3-3). The width of the sheets are 2 inches, and the thickness is 0.032 inches. A load of 500 lbs. is applied to the joint. The edge distance is 2D.*

What is the tension stress (F) in this joint?

$$F = \frac{P}{A}$$

$$F = \frac{P}{[W - (d_h \times n)] \times T}$$

$$F = \frac{500}{[2 - (0.128 \times 2)] \times 0.032}$$

$F = 8,959.289$ p.s.i.

Rivet Shear Stress Calculation

If we install less than the optimal number of fasteners of a given size, then subject our joint to a shear load to the point of failure, we say that the joint has *failed in shear*. The material will remain intact and the fasteners will deform

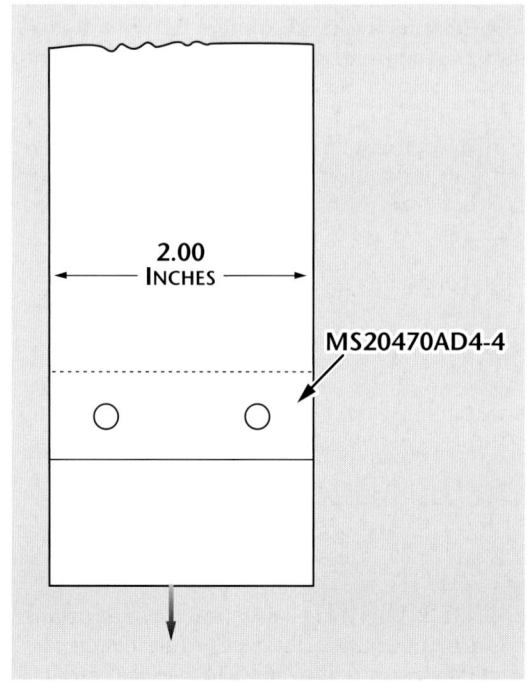

Figure 4-3-3. Two pieces of aluminum, riveted together for the purpose of illustrating a shear load

or shear. This type of joint is considered to be *critical in shear*.

Shear failure of the rivet plane can take place in either single- or double-shear, depending on the number of shear planes included (Figure 4-3-4).

Although in theory all three rivets would shear at the same time, in practice they do not. The hole dimensions, rivet material, riveting technique and load direction can all affect the shear of the rivets.

This is what can happen when holes are misaligned and/or oversized. These sheets are locked into place by friction from the clamping action of rivets holding them together (Figure 4-3-5).

If we attempt to pull these sheets apart in the direction of the arrows, the joint would fail long before it should. Why?

The first (left) rivet seems to be the only one resisting the shearing action. The initial pulling force will cause this rivet to tip in the misaligned hole. This would allow the sheets to move and bring the second rivet into play.

The second rivet, in its oversized hole, will then help resist the shearing action. If the first rivet has been fractured, it will then carry the entire shear load.

The third rivet will only resist the shearing action when the other rivets have been deformed or fractured. If they have failed and this is the only fastener left in the joint, it is sure to fail. In Figure 4-3-6 all rivets will carry their full load.

To calculate the shear stress experienced by the rivet, you must again use the formula F=P/A, but you must change the value of A to reflect the difference in the rivet's cross-sectional area. See Figure 4-3-7.

The cross-sectional area of a rivet formula is:

$$A = \frac{\pi \times (d_{hole})^2}{4} \times n$$

Formula for rivet shear is:

$$F = \frac{P}{\left(\frac{\pi \times d_{hole}^2}{4}\right) \times n}$$

NOTE: *Use the hole diameter, not the rivet diameter, because the rivet will expand as it is driven and will fill the hole. The hole size is always a little larger than the rivet diameter. (Example: MS20426AD4-4 rivet diameter = 0.125, and hole size = 0.1285)*

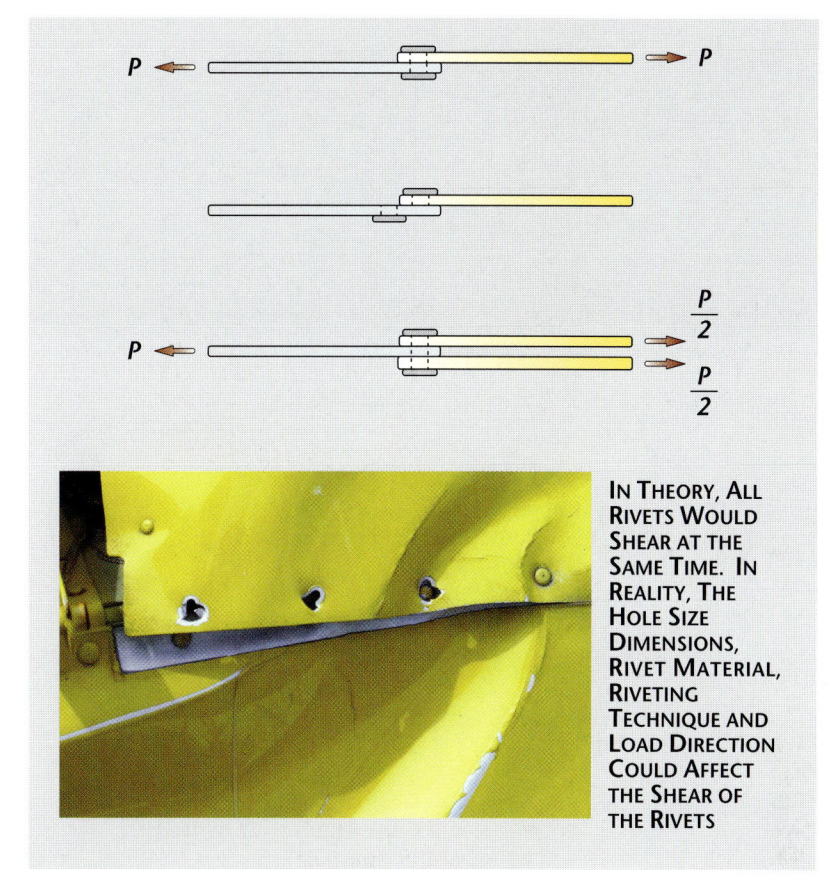

Figure 4-3-4. Rivets that failed in the shear plane

IN THEORY, ALL RIVETS WOULD SHEAR AT THE SAME TIME. IN REALITY, THE HOLE SIZE DIMENSIONS, RIVET MATERIAL, RIVETING TECHNIQUE AND LOAD DIRECTION COULD AFFECT THE SHEAR OF THE RIVETS

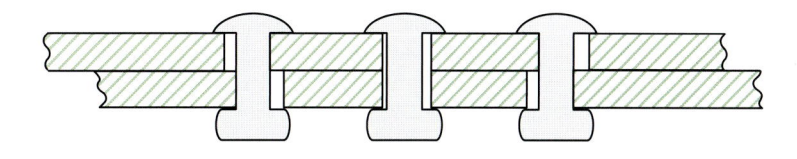

Figure 4-3-5. An example of bad drilling and hole alignment that will result in early shear failure

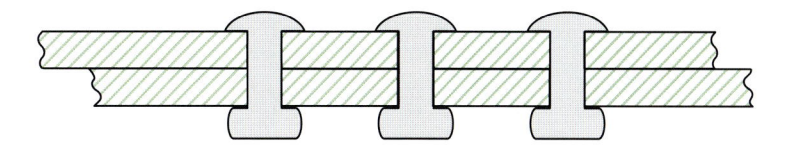

Figure 4-3-6. When all holes are the correct size, straight and filled with properly driven/pulled rivets, all three rivets are *in bearing*, and each can equally resist the shear load.

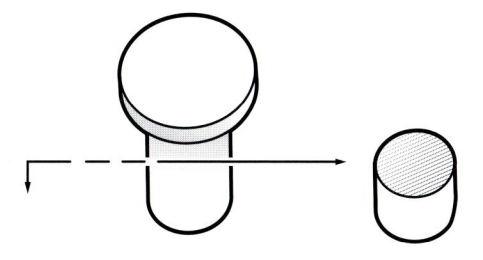

Figure 4-3-7. Cross-sectional area of a rivet

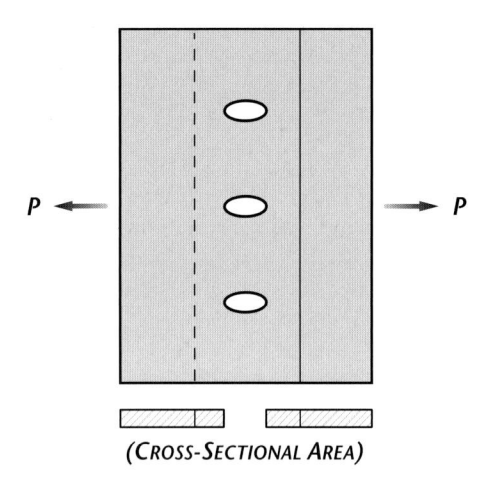

Figure 4-3-8. Sheet elongated from bearing failure

EXAMPLE 2: Calculate the stress the rivets experience using the data in Example 1

$$F = \frac{500}{[(3.1416 \times 0.128^2)/4] \times 2}$$

$$F = 19{,}428 \text{ p.s.i.}$$

Bearing Stress Calculation

Bearing failure of the connected sheets occurs when the sheets elongate due to the bearing force of the rivet on the sheet (Figure 4-3-8). The bearing area is the cross-sectional area of the hole, perpendicular to the direction of the applied force.

If we install more than the optimal number of fasteners of a given size, then subject our joint to a shear load to the point of failure, we say that the joint has *failed in bearing*. The material may crack and tear between holes, or fastener holes distort and stretch while the fasteners remain intact. This type of joint is considered to be *critical in bearing*.

Again, use the following formula:

$$F = \frac{P}{A}$$

This is the formula to use for calculation of the cross-sectional area:

$$A = d_h \times T \times n$$

This is the formula to use for calculation of the bearing stress:

$$F = \frac{P}{d_h \times T \times n}$$

EXAMPLE 3: *Use the information given in Example 1 and calculate the bearing stress.*

$$F = \frac{P}{d_h \times T \times n} = \frac{500}{0.128 \times 0.032 \times 2}$$

$$F = 61{,}035 \text{ p.s.i.}$$

Tear-out or Sheet Shear Calculations

Tear-out, or shear of the connected sheets, can take place when the distance from the rivet to the edge of the sheet, in the direction of stress, is too small. Tear-out can be avoided by providing an adequate *edge distance* (ED). Thin sheets will buckle, and thicker sheets will actually tear-out, as illustrated in Figure 4-3-9.

To calculate the tear-out stress, use the general formula:

$$F = \frac{P}{A}$$

To calculate the cross-sectional area use the following formula:

$$A = 2 \times [ED - (d_h / 2)] \times T \times n$$

NOTE: *ED = edge distance, expressed in rivet diameters. This is the only time in all calculations that you will use the rivet diameter instead of the hole diameter.*

The 2 in front of the formula is there because, if tear-out occurs, two cracks develop. This means that the actual cross-sectional area will be twice as large.

Formula for the calculation of tear-out stress:

$$F = \frac{P}{2 \times [ED - (d_h / 2)] \times T \times n}$$

EXAMPLE 4: *Using the data from Example 1, figure the tear-out stress.*

$$F = \frac{P}{2 \times [ED - (d_h / 2)] \times T \times n}$$

$$F = \frac{500}{2 \times [0.25 - (0.128 / 2)] \times 0.032 \times 2}$$

$$F = 21{,}001 \text{ p.s.i.}$$

Stress Risers

From the these exercises, you should be able to understand how important it is to avoid scratches, gouges and other damage to sheet metal. A scratch will reduce the cross-sectional area of the sheet and also introduce a place for stress to concentrate. That is why a scratch is called a *stress riser*.

If possible, always protect the sheet material with a primer before starting your work. If there are scratches or gouges, blend them out. After blending, check the material thickness and consult the maintenance manual to see if the scratches are within limits after rework.

Additional Exercises

Two sheets of Aluminum 2024-T4, 0.032 inch thick and 2 inches wide, are joined by three MS20470AD4-3 rivets. The edge distance is 2D. Determine the tensile stress, rivet-shear stress, bearing stress and sheet tear-out stresses if the joint is less than 1,000 lbs. tensile load.

Two sheets of 7075-T6 are joined by two MS20426AD6-6 rivets. The thickness of the sheets is 0.064 inches, and they are 1 inch wide. The edge distance is 2D. A tensile load of 1,500 lbs. is applied. Calculate the tensile load stress, the rivet shear stress, the bearing stress and the tear-out stress.

Calculation of Load

Until now, joint stress has been calculated when the applied load is a known factor. It is also important to know how to calculate the bearable load. For most commonly used aircraft materials, the data is available in a publication called *Metallic Materials and Elements for Aerospace Vehicle Structures*, more commonly known as *MIL Handbook 5*. The material in MIL Handbook 5 was collected by actual testing and is the principal repository of design data.

At the end of this section are three tables from MIL Handbook 5 (Table 4-3-1 through Table 4-3-3). Use the information from them to solve the following problems:

FORMULA: *The general formula $F = P/A$ will have to be adjusted. The new formula is:*

$P = F \times A$

With this formula, you can calculate the maximum load that the joint can withstand before failure. You can calculate the tensile, rivet shear, bearing and tear-out loads.

Use the following to calculate the load:

Ultimate tensile strength (F_{tu}), used to calculate the ultimate tensile load:

$P = F \times A \Rightarrow P = F_{tu} \times [W - (d_h) \times n] \times T$

F_{tu} = Ultimate tensile strength

Ultimate sheet strength (F_{su}), used to calculate the ultimate tear-out load:

$P = F \times A \Rightarrow P = 2 \times F_{su} \times [ED - (d_h / 2)] \times T \times n$

F_{su} = Ultimate sheet shear strength

Ultimate bearing strength (F_{bu}), used to calculate the ultimate bearing load:

$P = F \times A \Rightarrow P = F_{bu} \times d_h \times T \times n$

F_{bu} = Ultimate bearing strength

Ultimate rivet strength (F_{su}), used to calculate the ultimate rivet load:

$P = F \times A \Rightarrow P = F_{su} \times [(\pi \times d_h^2) / 4] \times n$

F_{su} = Ultimate rivet shear strength

NOTE: *In the tables, you will find information about bearing strength for ED 2.0 and 1.5. In accordance with AC 43.13-1B, only ED 2.0 can be used for aircraft repairs, but the data concerning ED 1.5 is there to design specific repairs. For ED between 2.0 and 1.5, you can take the average of ED 2.0 and 1.5.*

EXAMPLE: *Two sheets of 2024-T3 clad are joined together with two MS20470AD4-4 rivets. The edge distance is 2D. The width of the sheets is 1 inch, and they are .032 inch thick. Calculate the maximum tensile, rivet shear, bearing and tear-out loads of this joint if tested to failure.*

Tensile load:

$P = F_{tu} \times [W - (d_h) \times n] \times t$

$P = 59,000 \times [1 - (.128 \times 2)] \times .032$

$P = 1,405$ pounds

Rivet shear load:

$P = F_{su} \times [(\pi \times d^2) / 4] \times n$

$P = 30,000 \times [(\pi \times .128^2) / 4] \times 2$

$P = 772$ pounds

Bearing load:

$P = F_{bu} \times d_h \times T \times n$

$P = 121,000 \times .128 \times .032 \times 2$

$P = 991$ pounds

Tear-out load:

$P = 2 \times F_{su} \times [ED - (d_h / 2)] \times T \times n$

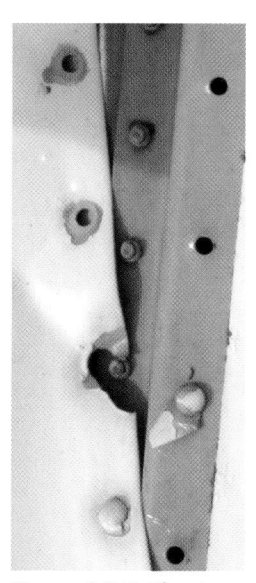

$P = 2 \times 37,000 \times [2 \times .125 - (.128 / 2)] \times .032 \times 2$

$P = 881$ pounds

Figure 4-3-9. Sheet tear-out failure

SPECIFICATION	AMS-QQ-A-250/5															
FORM	Flat Sheet & Plate															
TEMPER	T3								T351							
THICKNESS (INCHES)	0.008-0.009		0.010-0.062		0.063-0.128		0.129-0.249		0.250-0.499		0.500-1.000$_a$		1.001-1.500$_a$		1.501-2.000$_a$		2.001-3.000$_a$		3.001-4.000$_a$
BASIS	A	B	A	B	A	B	A	B	A	B	A	B	A	B	A	B	A	B
Mechanical Properties																		
F_{tu}, KSI:																		
L	59	60	60	61	62	63	63	64	62	64	61	63	60	62	60	62	58	60	55	57
LT	58	59	59	60	61	62	62	63	62	64	61	63	60	62	60	60	58	60	55	57
ST	—	—	—	—	—	—	—	—	—	—	—	—	—	—	—	—	52$_b$	54$_b$	49$_b$	51$_b$
F_{ty}, KSI:																		
L	44	45	44	45	45	47	45	47	46	48	45	48	45	48	45	47	44	46	39	41
LT	39	40	39	40	40	42	40	42	40	42	40	42	40	42	40	42	40	42	39	41
ST	—	—	—	—	—	—	—	—	—	—	—	—	—	—	—	—	38$_b$	40$_b$	38$_b$	39$_b$
F_{cy}, KSI:																		
L	36	37	36	37	37	39	37	39	37	39	37	39	37	39	36	38	35	37	33	35
LT	42	43	42	43	43	45	43	45	43	45	42	45	42	44	42	44	41	43	39	41
ST	—	—	—	—	—	—	—	—	—	—	—	—	—	—	—	—	46	48	44	47
F_{su}, KSI:	37	37	37	38	38	39	39	40	37	38	36	37	35	37	35	37	34	35	32	34
$F_{bru\ c}$, KSI:																		
(e/D = 1.5)	96	97	97	99	101	102	102	104	94	97	92	95	91	94	91	94	88	91	83	86
(e/D = 2.0)	119	121	121	123	125	127	127	129	115	119	113	117	111	115	111	115	107	111	102	106
$F_{bry\ c}$, KSI:																		
(e/D = 1.5)	68	70	68	70	70	73	70	73	69	72	69	72	69	72	69	72	69	72	67	70
(e/D = 2.0)	82	84	82	84	84	88	84	88	82	86	82	86	82	86	82	86	82	86	80	84
e, Percent (S-BASIS):																		
LT	10	—	$_d$	—	15	—	15	—	12	—	8	—	7	—	6	—	4	—	4	—
E, 10^3 KSI:																		
Primary	10.5								10.7									
Secondary	9.5				10.0				10.2									
E_c, 10^3 KSI:																		
Primary	10.7								10.9									
Secondary	9.7				10.2				10.4									
G, 10^3 KSI:	—																	
μ	0.330																	
Physical Properties																		
V, LB./INCH^3	0.100																	
C, K & α	—																	

a = These values, except in the ST direction, have been adjusted to represent the average properties across the whole section, including the 2.5-percent nominal cladding thickness.

b = CAUTION: This specific alloy, temper and product form exhibits poor stress-corrosion cracking-resistance in this grain direction. It corresponds to an SCC resistance rating of D, as indicated in Table 3.1.2.3.1(a) in MIL Handbook 5.

c = Bearing values are "dry pin" values, per Section 1.4.7.1, Table 3.1.2.1.1. in MIL Handbook 5.

d = See Table 3.2.3.0(f) in MIL Handbook 5.

Table 4-3-1. Mechanical, physical, and design properties of clad 2024 sheet and plate

SPECIFICATION	AMS 4296						
FORM	Sheet & Plate						
TEMPER	T3						
THICKNESS (INCHES)	0.032-0.062	0.063-0.128		0.129-0.249		0.250-0.310	
BASIS	S	A	B	A	B	A	B
Mechanical Properties							
F_{tu}, KSI:							
L	59	61	62	62	62	62	63
LT	59	61[c]	62	62	62	62	63
F_{ty}, KSI:							
L		44	45	47	45	46	45	46
LT		39	40[D]	42	40	41	40	41
F_{cy}, KSI:							
L		38	39	41	39	40	39	40
LT		42	43	45	43	44	43	44
F_{su}, KSI:		40	41	42	42	42	42	43
$F_{bru\ A}$, KSI:							
(e/D = 1.5)		93	97	98	98	98	98	100
(e/D = 2.0)		117	121	123	123	123	123	125
$F_{bry\ A}$, KSI:							
(e/D = 1.5)		65	67	70	67	69	67	69
(e/D = 2.0)		76	78	82	78	80	78	80
e, Percent (S-Basis):							
LT		15	15	—	15	—	15	—
E, 10^3 KSI:							
Primary	10.3						
Secondary	9.8						
E_c, 10^3 KSI:							
Primary	10.5						
Secondary	10.0						
G, 10^3 KSI:	—						
μ	0.35						
Physical Properties							
V, LB./INCH^3	0.100						
C, K & α	Not Available						

A = Bearing values are "dry pin" values, per Section 1.4.7.1, Table 3.1.2.1.1. in MIL Handbook 5.
B = Determined in accordance with ASTM B 831-93
C = S-Basis. The rounded T_{99} value is 61.80 ksi.
D = S-Basis. The rounded T_{99} value is 41.20 ksi.

Table 4-3-2. Mechanical, physical, and design properties of clad 2524-73 sheet and plate

SPECIFICATION	AMS 4049							
FORM	Sheet							
TEMPER	T6							
THICKNESS (INCHES)	0.008-0.011	0.012-0.039		0.040-0.062		0.063-0.187		0.188-0.249	
BASIS	S	A	B	A	B	A	B	A	B
Mechanical Properties									
F_{tu}, KSI:									
L	—	71	74	71	75	74	77	75	77
LT	68	71	74	71	75	74[a]	77	75	77
F_{ty}, KSI:									
L	—	62	65	63	66	66	69	66	68
LT	58	60	63	61	64	64	67	64	66
F_{cy}, KSI:									
L	—	61	64	62	65	65	68	65	67
LT	—	64	67	65	68	68	71	68	70
F_{su}, KSI:	—	42	44	42	45	44	46	45	46
$F_{bru\ b}$, KSI:									
(e/D = 1.5)	—	110	115	110	116	115	119	116	119
(e/D = 2.0)	—	142	148	142	150	148	154	150	154
$F_{bry\ b}$, KSI:									
(e/D = 1.5)	—	90	94	91	96	96	100	96	99
(e/D = 2.0)	—	105	110	106	112	112	117	112	115
e, Percent (S-Basis):									
LT	5	8	—	9	—	9	—	9	—
E, 10^3 KSI:									
Primary		10.3				10.3		10.3	
Secondary		9.5				9.8		10.0	
E_c, 10^3 KSI:									
Primary		10.5				10.5		10.5	
Secondary		9.7				10.0		10.2	
G, 10^3 KSI:		—				—		—	
μ		0.33				0.33		0.33	
Physical Properties									
V, LB./INCH^3	0.101								
C, K & α	—								

a = S-Basis. The rounded T_{99} value is 75 ksi.
b = Bearing values are "dry pin" values, per Section 1.4.7.1, Table 3.1.2.1.1. in MIL Handbook 5.

Table 4-3-3. Mechanical, physical, and design properties of clad 7075

Joint Analysis

Now that the maximum loads of tensile, rivet shear, bearing and tear-out are calculable, how a joint will fail can be determined.

A joint can fail in four different ways (modes):

- Tensile
- Rivet shear
- Bearing
- Tear-out

The joint will fail in the failure mode with the lowest maximum load (weakest link in the chain). When you look back at the example, you see that this joint will fail in rivet shear, because 772 lbs. is the lowest value.

Exercises

Two sheets of .040 inch Al 7075-T6 are riveted with three MS20470DD4-4 rivets. The sheets are 1.5 inches wide and the ED = 2D. Will this joint, if tested to failure, fail in tensile, rivet shear, bearing or tear-out mode?

Two sheets of .063 inch AL 23024-T3 clad are riveted with 10 MS20470AD6-6 rivets. The sheets are 4 inches wide and the ED is 2D. The joint is placed in a tension tester and pulled to failure. Determine the rivet shear load, tensile load, bearing load and tear-out load. In what mode will the joint fail?

Section 4

Back-up Structure

The reason for aircraft structural repair is to restore and maintain structural integrity. The goal is to return the component parts to their original strength. A typical repair is designed to be adapted for use on different structural members with the same general cross-sectional shape. These components include general back-up structure, such as brackets, ribs, formers and intercostals. These are used in many applications throughout the aircraft.

This section shows typical repairs that can be applied to structures having configurations, materials and gauges like the ones shown. They are only to be referenced as training examples, and the manufacturer's structural repair manuals must always be the final word.

These repairs are not authorized for Principle Structural Elements (PSE) as listed in

ORIGINAL MATERIAL GAUGE	RIVET DIAMETER			
	3/32	1/8	5/32	3/16
0.032	X	X	—	—
0.036	X	X	—	—
0.040	—	X	X	—
0.045	—	—	X	—
0.050	—	—	X	X
0.056	—	—	—	X
0.064	—	—	—	X

Table 4-4-1. Rivet size selection

Manufacturer's Structural Repair Manuals. Principle elements include: pressurized skin, stringers, frames, spars and any primary load-carrying member. A full list can be found in ATA Chapter 51 of each Structural Repair Manual.

Repair Procedural Considerations

Material identification. This can be determined in the Material Identification section of the Manufacturer's Structural Repair Manual, or by chemical testing. If the material used for the original part is not available, a different material can sometimes be substituted.

Rivets

The size and type rivet to be used must be one of the first determinations made. Table 4-4-2 contains both AD, D and E rivet tables.

Rivet size. Use a rivet diameter of approximately three times the sheet (part being repaired). Example: thickness, 3 X .050 = .150 inch. Use 5/32 inch rivets (3/16 inch rivets would also be satisfactory). See Table 4-4-1 for examples. Preferably, the surrounding structure should be examined and the same size rivets used, whenever possible.

Rivet spacing. Normal spacing will be four-to-six times the diameter of the rivet being used in the repair. Check the surrounding structure and try to use similar spacing.

Rivet selection. Rivet material selection can best be determined by examining the surrounding structure and employing the same type rivet as the manufacturer used during assembly. Fasteners for these repairs are either universal-head rivets (MS20470) or modified universal-head rivets (BACR15FT). If flush fasteners are

	2117AD RIVETS					2017D RIVETS & 7050E RIVETS			
Original Material Gauge	Rivet Diameter				Original Material Gauge	Rivet Diameter			
	3/32	1/8	5/32	3/16		3/32	1/8	5/32	3/16
0.032	8.4	4.7	—	—	0.032	6.8	3.8	—	—
0.036	9.4	5.3	3.4	—	0.036	7.5	4.3	3.0	—
0.040	—	5.8	3.8	—	0.040	—	4.6	3.0	—
0.045	—	—	4.3	3.1	0.045	—	—	3.5	2.5
0.050	—	—	4.8	3.4	0.050	—	—	3.9	2.5
0.056	—	—	5.5	3.8	0.056	—	—	4.4	3.0
0.064	—	—	—	4.2	0.064	—	—	—	3.4

Table 4-4-2. Number of protruding head rivets required on each side of damage, per inch of damage penetration, in 2024-T6, 2024-T3/T4, or 7075-T6 aluminum alloy.

required, the material thickness may be insufficient for countersinking. Existing fasteners' arc must be considered when determining rivet requirements. See Table 4-4-2.

Repair/Replacement Principles

Sometimes it may be more cost-effective to replace a part rather than attempt to repair it. In that case, the part should be carefully removed so as not to damage adjacent structures, and a new part of the same design as the original should be manufactured and installed.

Cross-sectional determinations. The prime objective of aircraft repair is to restore parts to their original condition. When repairing formed sections, care must be taken to maintain equivalent cross-sectional areas.

Gauge requirements in the repair figures in this chapter are based upon maintaining or restoring cross-sectional areas. When repairing extruded sections, the cross-section area must be multiplied by 1.25 on 2024-T3 extrusions, or 1.35 times greater than the original 7075-T6 extrusion.

The following material thicknesses are the most common ones used in aircraft: 0.025 inches, 0.032 inches, 0.036 inches, 0.040 inches, 0.045 inches, 0.050 inches, 0.056 inches, 0.064 inches. These gauges are used for determining repair thickness. Some of these gauges are not commonly available or stocked by a supplier. When not available, use the next higher thickness gauge.

EXAMPLES:

- The original gauge is 0.040 inches. One gauge thicker is 0.045 inches (not stocked). Use a 0.050 inch gauge.

- The original gauge is 0.040 inches. Two gauges thicker is 0.050 inches. Use a 0.050 inch gauge.

- The original gauge is 0.045 inches. One gauge thicker is 0.050 inches. Use a 0.050 inch gauge.

- The original gauge is 0.045 inches. Two gauges thicker is 0.056 inches (not stocked). Use a 0.064 inch gauge.

Other Considerations

Repairs in wet areas should be installed with a faying surface sealant.

When the damage is near the end of a member, it may not be possible to install the complete repair, in such cases terminate the repair at the end of the member.

Sometimes, the substitution of a fastener of a different type than original may be necessary. This may be due to availability or access restrictions. If substitution is necessary, fasteners of equal or greater strength should be substituted on a one-for-one basis.

You must always be alert for work document instructions for clearance, stop-drills, radius, finish, etc.

Repair Figures

The repair figures shown here may have several different choices of repair, depending on the extent of the damage, and are presented as examples only. They may not be used to repair any aircraft. Always consult the proper approved manuals.

NOTE: *All the repair procedural considerations must be read and understood before going to the repair itself. All the notes for each repair must be considered when developing your repair.*

Some of the repair figures contain examples. The sample illustrations will show the same number of fastener locations as in the text. It is imperative to understand the reason and location of the additional row of fasteners. Some of the repair types are defined by damage or cut-outs within the radius. Material within a formed radius is less strong than the unbent areas of the sections.

Reinstalling fasteners in a crack, or closer than the minimum edge distance to a crack, should be avoided. Trim out the damage while maintaining edge distances, when possible.

Circular Repairs

A circular repair is typically used where a hole must be cut for access to an interior structure. It is also used to repair skin punctures and some types of cracks. See Figure 4-4-1.

NOTES:

- Cracks/damage of up to 2 inches should be cleaned up with a circular hole.
- For damage up to 1 inch, use the same material and gauge thickness for cracks.
- For damage of 1-2 inches, use the same material, one gauge thicker.
- Select fastener sizes per Table 4-4-1. Two rows are required.
- A filler may be used where flushness is required, installed with a single row of fasteners.
- Replace any existing attachments with the same type and diameter fasteners as originally used.
- Cracks/damage up to 1 inch at an edge of a web, etc., can be repaired with a semi-circular repair. Use the same material, one gauge thicker, for doubler. (Do not use this repair on pressurized surfaces.)

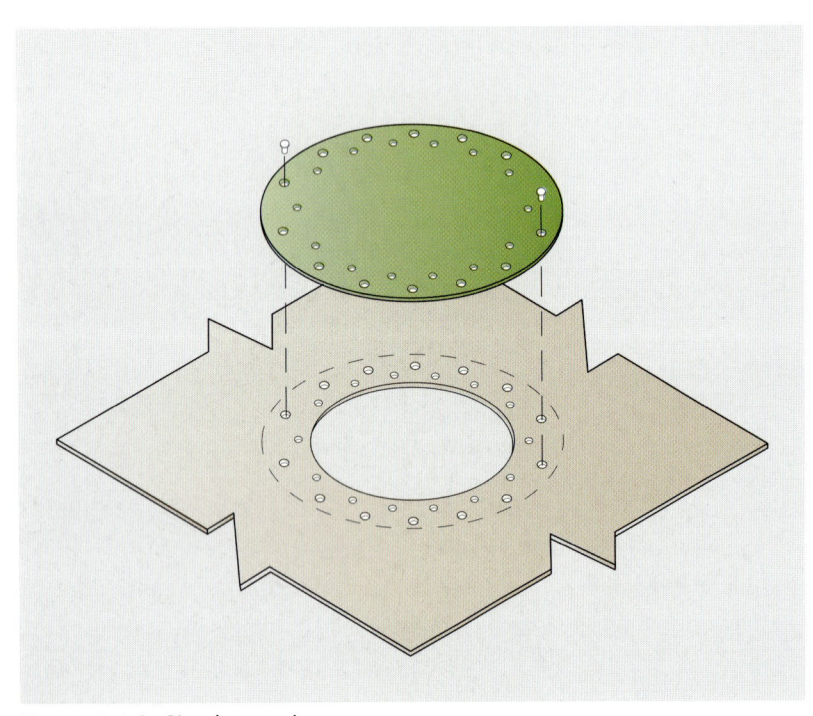

Figure 4-4-1. Circular repair

Rectangular Repairs

A rectangular repair can be used when a crack of any length forms. The crack is generally cleaned out first. Figure 4-4-2 illustrates a rectangular crack repair.

NOTES:

- Single cracks up to 4 inches should be cleaned up, resulting in a slot with a 1/4 inch stop-drill at each end.
- A 1/2 inch radius should be maintained in corners when a rectangular cutout is used to remove damage.

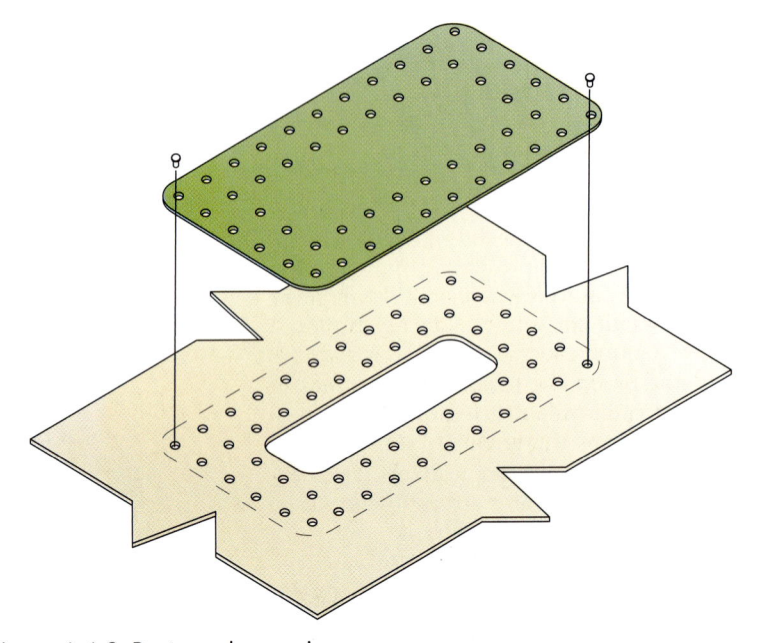

Figure 4-4-2. Rectangular repairs

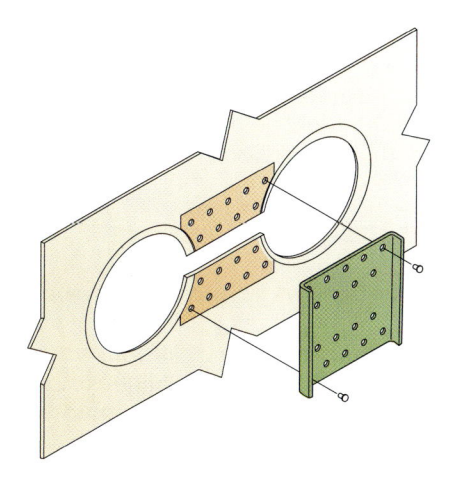

Figure 4-4-3A. Type 1. Repair of damage between holes

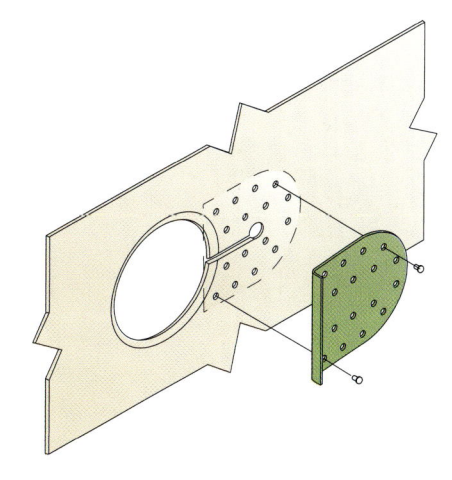

Figure 4-4-3B. Type 2. Repair of radial crack

- Use the same material, one gauge thicker, for doublers.
- Select fastener sizes per Table 4-4-1. Two rows are required.
- Where flushness is required, a filler may be used and installed with a single row of fasteners.
- Replace any existing attachments with the same type and diameter fasteners as originally used.
- This type of repair cannot be used on a pressurized surface.

Lightening Hole Repairs

Cracks between flanged lightening holes are frequently caused by vibrations. Depending on the crack progression, two different types of repairs are common. See Figures 4-4-3A and 4-4-3B.

NOTES:

- Clean up damage (optional: stop-drill or slot).
- Where practical, maintain the original contour of the hole flange. Alternately, a flanged edge 90° by 0.375 inch can be formed to restore lost stiffness. See Figures 4-4-3A and 4-4-3B.
- Use the same material, one gauge thicker, for doublers.
- Select fastener sizes per Table 4-4-1. Two rows are required.
- Fastener spacing should be 4D to 6D.
- Replace any existing attachments with the same type and diameter fasteners as originally used.

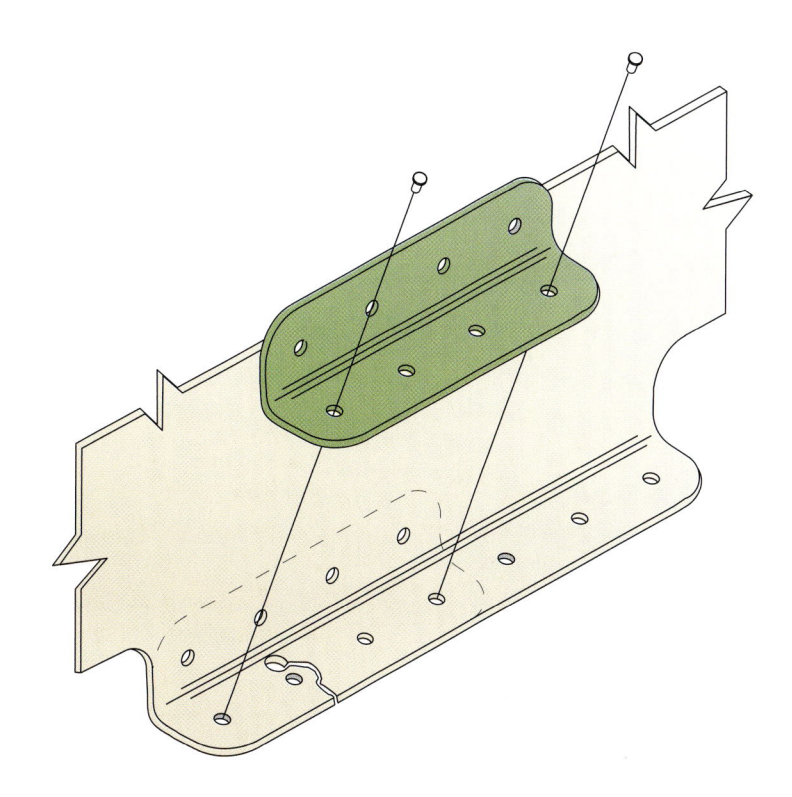

Figure 4-4-4A. Type 1. Stop-drill and doubler. Cracks that intersect fastener holes must use a Type 2 repair.

Flange Repair

Flange repairs are common on ribs, formers, bulkheads and equipment attachment structures. A common cause is either an incorrectly formed radius on the cracked part, or excess pressure from installation. Figures 4-4-4A, 4-4-4B and 4-4-4C are examples.

NOTES:

- Stop-drill. Cut out/off damage.
- Use the same material, one gauge thicker, for doubler on Type 1 and Type 2 repairs.

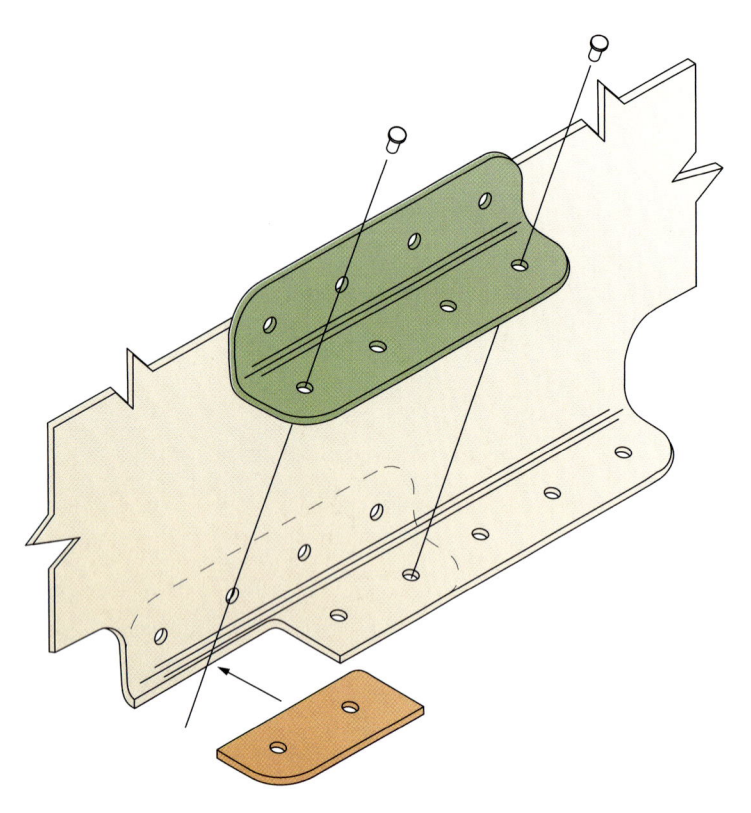

Figure 4-4-4B. Type 2. Cutout, filler and doubler

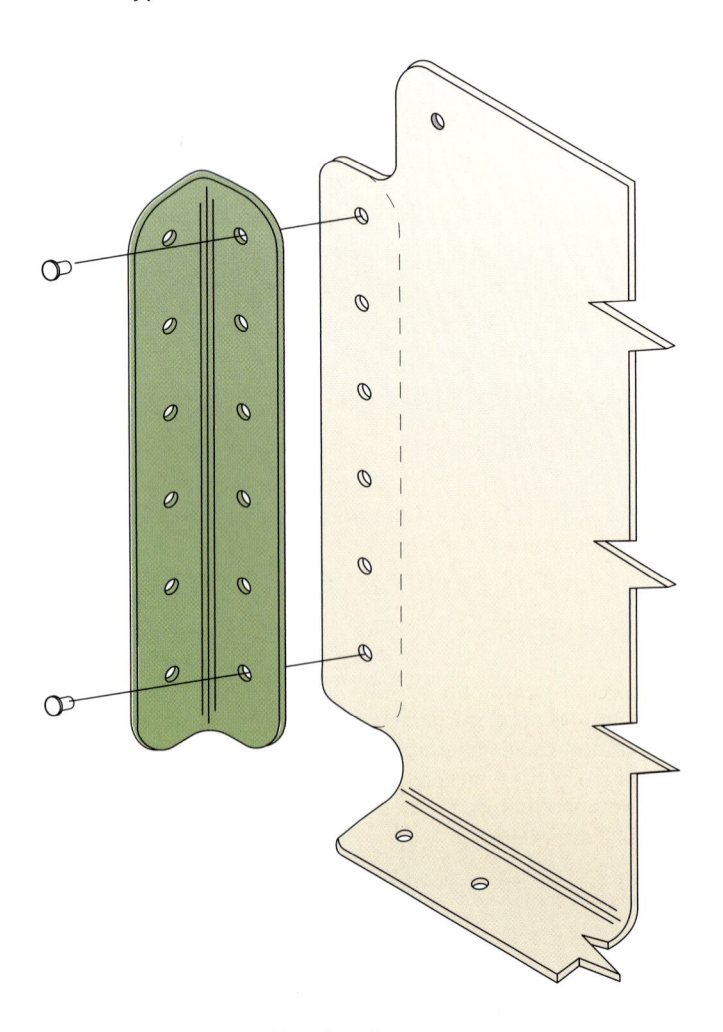

Figure 4-4-4C. Type 3. Cut off and replace

Use the same material and gauge for Type 3 repairs.

- The repair and the original member radii should nest together. Repair rivet heads should not encroach on radii.

Corner Repair

Figure 4-4-5 shows a typical corner repair, such as might be found on a rib. Corner cracks are typically from either unequal pressure against one side, setting up an unequal stress in the relief hole, or from improperly aligned rivet lines, resulting in side pressure.

NOTES:

- For crack lengths of 25T or less, stop-drill or route.
- Use the same material, same gauge for 2024-T3, one gauge thicker for 7075-T6.
- Web area: Use one row of rivets around the crack/clean-out area. Use Table 4-4-1 for rivet size, 4D-6D spacing.
- Flange area: Use the original size and type rivets, with two rivets installed in each flange for each 1 inch of crack length (a minimum of two required).

Bend-Radius Repair

A cracked bend-radius is common on a former, particularly when attached to a removable panel. They usually result from careless

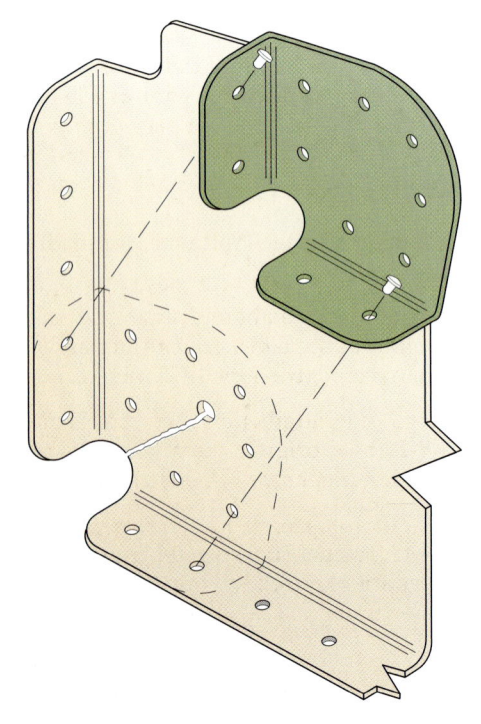

Figure 4-4-5. Corner repair

handling. Figure 4-4-6 shows a typical bend-radius repair.

NOTES:

- For crack lengths of 25T or less, stop-drill.
- Use the same material, same gauge, as damaged member.
- Fasteners should be the same type, size and spacing as those originally installed. A minimum of four is required, with at least two beyond stop-drill.
- A nutplate with a screw or bolt installed is considered a fastener.

Channel Repairs

Channel repairs are common and can be caused by a wide variety of things. Outside pressure causing a kink in a leg is a good example. Repair methods are shown in Figures 4-4-7A, 4-4-7B, 4-4-7C and 4-4-7D.

Figure 4-4-7A is a typical example. Assume damage, when cleaned-up, is 5 inches across and extends 2-3/4 inches (damage width) into a 0.050 inch 7075-T6 channel. Undertake a Type 2 repair. Determine the number of 5/32 D rivets needed from Table 4-4-2. Multiply that tabulated number, 3.9, by 2.75 (inches of damage), for a result of 10.7. The technician should install 11 rivets on each side of the damage (always round up to the next higher number).

NOTES:

- For Type 1 or Type 2 damage, repair members should extend beyond damage to allow the insertion of one continuous longitudinal row of repair fasteners. Do not include this row in repair fastener requirements.
- Repair members and fillers should be the same material as original, but repair members should be the next thicker gauge on formed sections, and two gauges thicker for extrusions.
- Select rivet number and size, per Table 4-4-2. If the original material is extruded, multiply rivet requirements by 1.15.
- Lay out rivet pattern around any original attachments. Replace any original attachments with the same diameter and type fasteners. Use fillers as necessary.
- Repair and original member radii should nest together. Repair rivet heads should not encroach on radii.

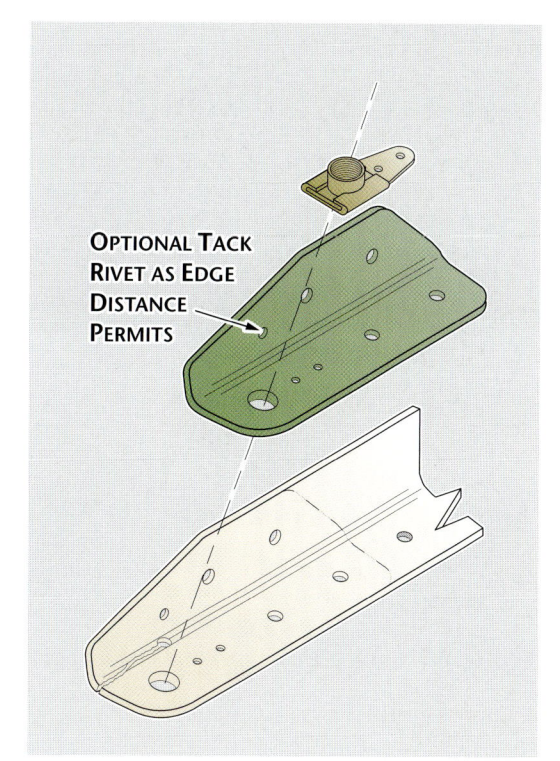

Figure 4-4-6. Bend-radius repair

Figure 4-4-7A. A typical example of a channel repair

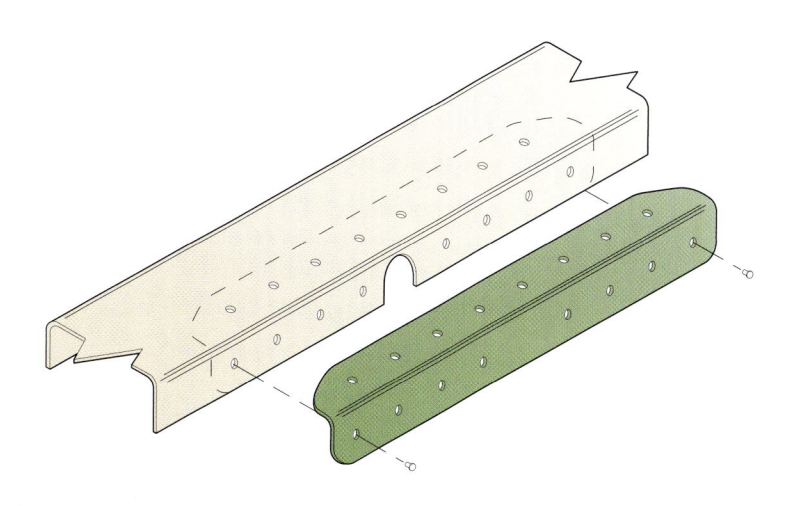

Figure 4-4-7B. Type 1 repair, with damage to one flange, which must not penetrate into radius

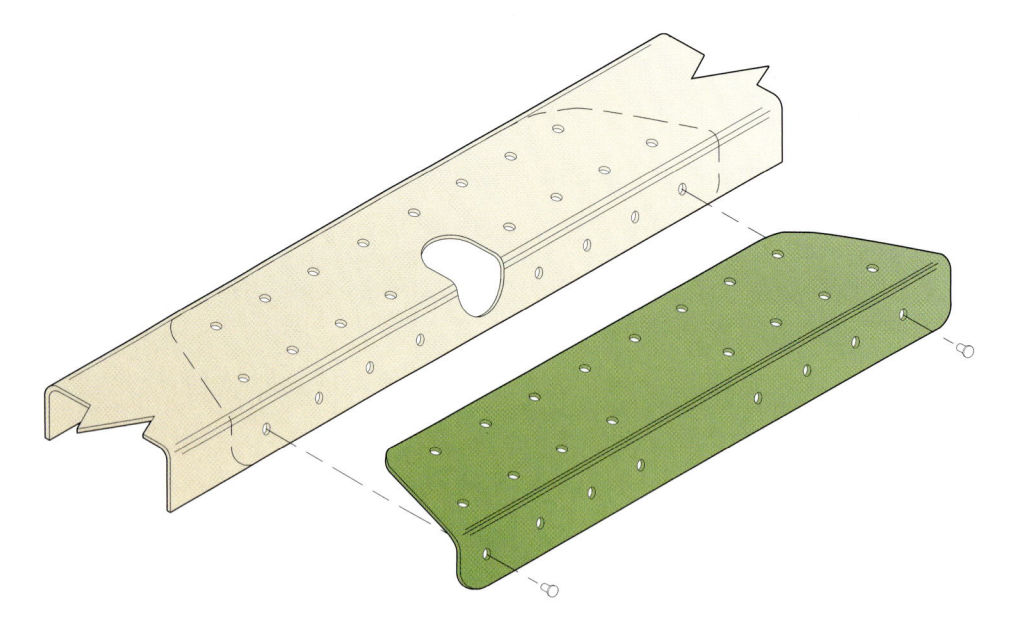

Figure 4-4-7C. Type 2 repair, with damage to flange and web

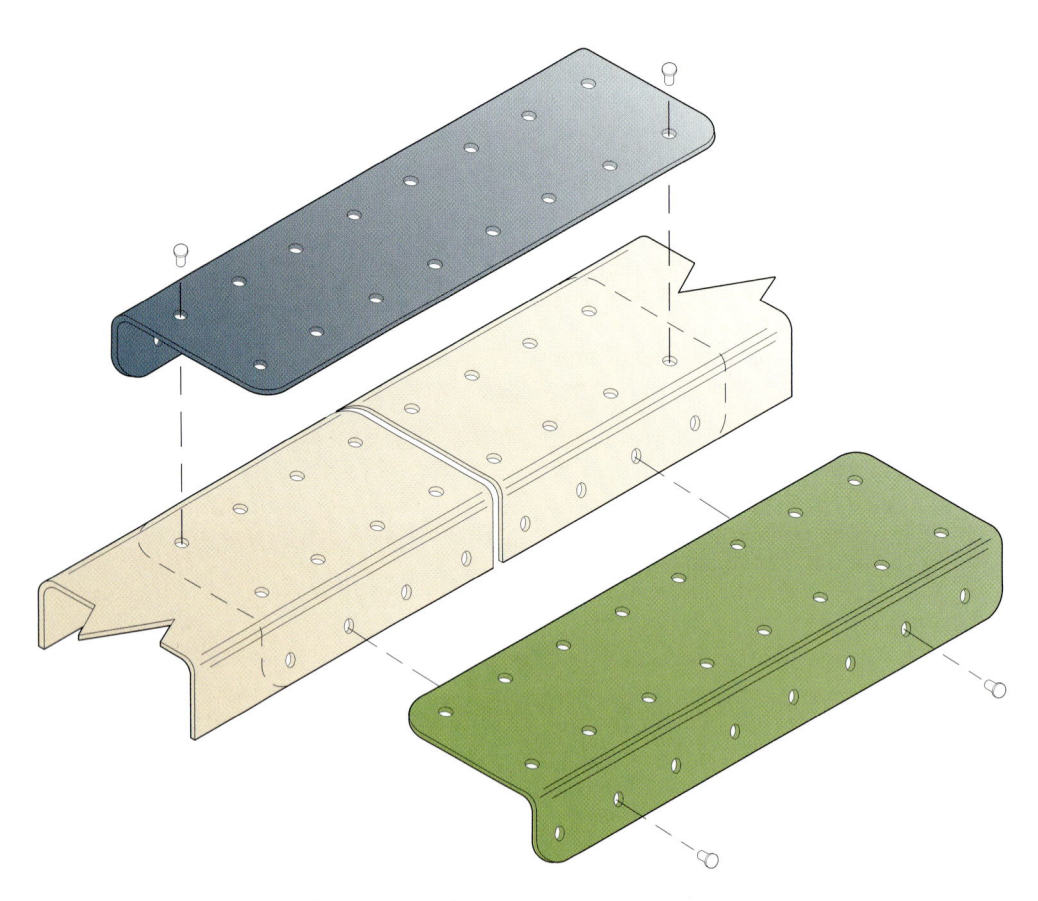

Figure 4-4-7D. Type 3 repair, with complete fracture

Z-Section Repairs

Z-sections are typically formed parts. They are generally used as stiffeners for things like floorboards, equipment and cargo bays, or anything that is a flat area. Figures 4-4-8A, 4-4-8B, 4-4-8C and 4-4-8D are common repairs.

Assume damage, when cleaned-up, is 0.5 inch across and extends 0.875 inches (damage width) into a 0.050 inch extruded 2024-T4 Z-section. This requires a Type 1 repair. Determine the number of 3/16 inch AD rivets needed from Table 4-4-2. Multiply that tabulated number, 3.4, by 0.875, which equals

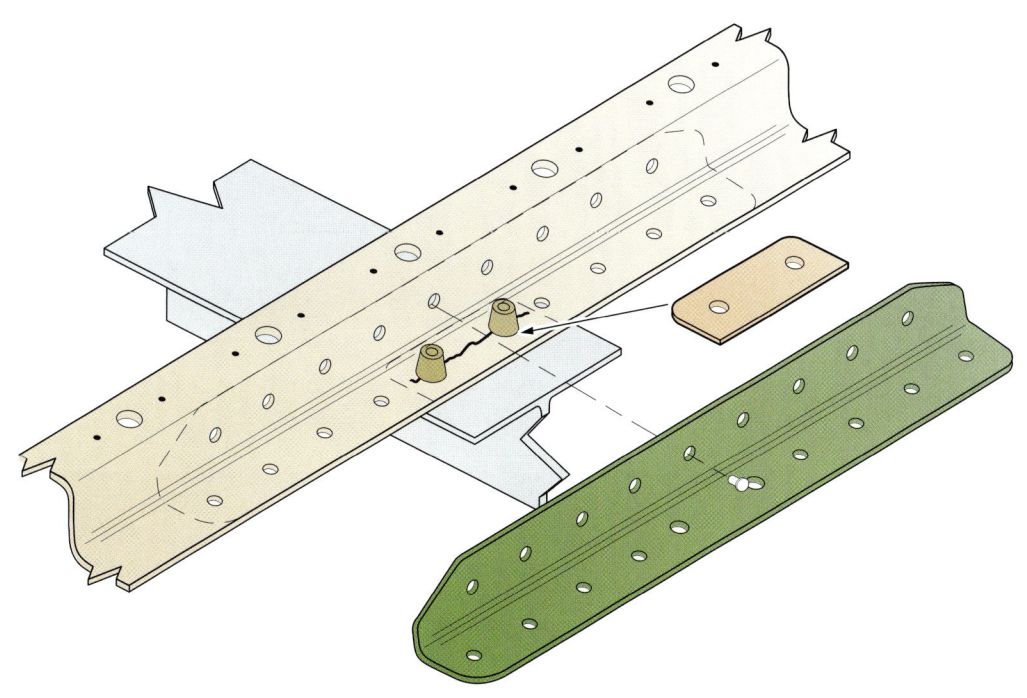

Figure 4-4-8A. Z-section repairs

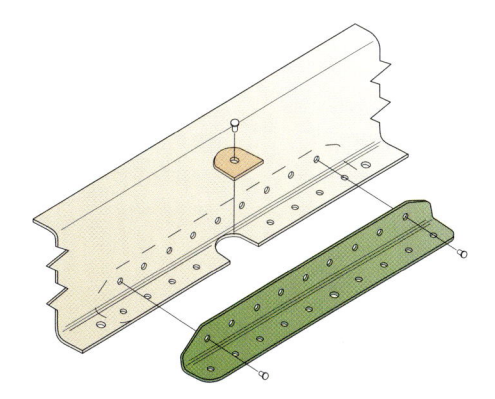

Figure 4-4-8B. Repair example using 3/16 inch AD rivets

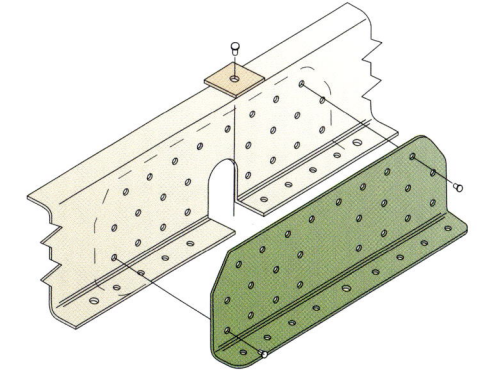

Figure 4-4-8C. Repair where damage extends past bend

2.975. Multiply 2.975 by 1.15, for a total of 3.42. Rounding up, install four rivets on each side of the damage.

NOTES:

- For Type 1 or Type 2 repair, members should extend beyond damage to allow the insertion of one continuous longitudinal row of repair fasteners. Do not include this row in repair fastener requirements.

- For a complete fracture, repair members must be riveted with a minimum of one longitudinal row, carried through the damaged area by use of suitable fillers if a single Z-section repair is not used.

- Repair members and fillers should be of the same material as originally used, but repair members should be the next thicker gauge on formed sections, two gauges thicker for extrusions.

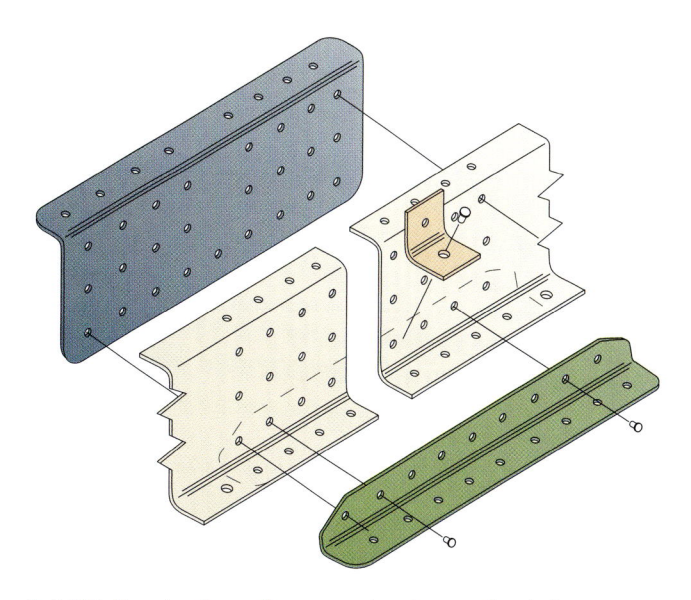

Figure 4-4-8D. Repair where damage extends completely from top to bottom

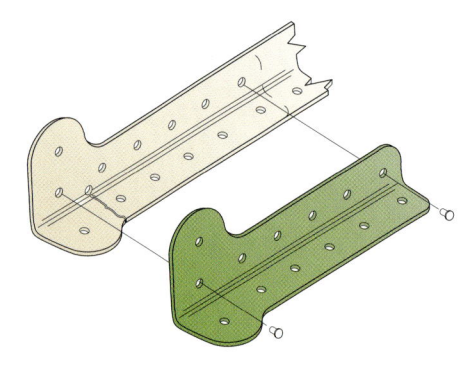

Figure 4-4-9A. Repair example, with 5/32 inch D rivets

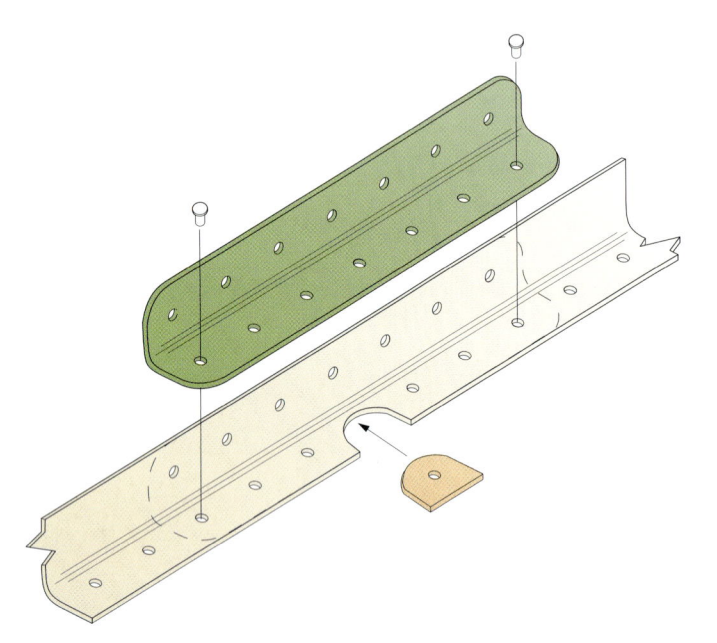

Figure 4-4-9B. Type 1 repair, with damage to one flange, which must not penetrate into radius

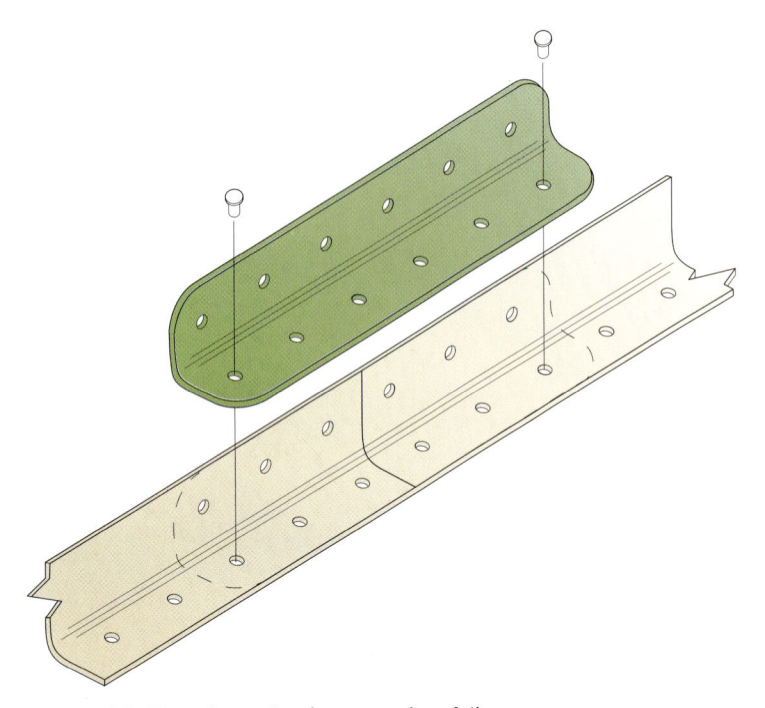

Figure 4-4-9C. Type 2 repair, after complete failure

- Select the rivet number and size, per Table 4-4-1. If the original material is extruded, multiply rivet requirements by 1.15.
- Lay out the rivet pattern around any original attachments. Replace any original attachments with fasteners of the same diameter and type, use fillers as necessary.
- Radii of the repair and that of the original member should nest together. Repair rivet heads should not encroach on radii.

Angle Repairs

Angles in structural assemblies are extremely common. So are angle repairs. Some, like Figure 4-4-9B, use inserts as fillers. Angle repairs are illustrated in Figures 4-4-9A, 4-4-9B and 4-4-9C.

In the repair example shown in Figure 4-4-9A, assume the damage is a stop-drilled crack that extends 1.12 inches (damage width) into a 0.050 inch 7075-T6 angle. A Type 2 complete fracture repair must be used, since the crack has penetrated the radius. The developed width of the angle measures 2.38 inches. Determine the number of 5/32 inch D rivets needed from Table 4-4-2. Multiply the number tabulated, 3.9, by 2.38, which equals 9.28. Rounding up, install 10 rivets on each side of the damage.

NOTES:

- For Type 1 damage, repair members should extend beyond damage to allow the insertion of one continuous longitudinal row of repair fasteners. Do not include this row in repair fastener requirements.
- Repair members and fillers should be the same material as original, but repair members should be the next thicker gauge on formed sections, and two gauges thicker for extrusions.
- Select rivet number and size, per Table 4-4-2. If the original material is extruded, multiply rivet requirements by 1.15.
- Lay out the rivet pattern around any original attachments. Replace any original attachments with same diameter and type fasteners. Use fillers as necessary.
- The radii of the repair and the original member should nest together. Repair rivet heads should not encroach on radii.

Hat-Section Repairs

Hat sections are used where something stronger than angles is needed. A hat section is nothing more than a channel with two flanges. Figure 4-4-10A is an example of a typical repair, while Figures 4-4-10B, 4-4-10C, 4-4-10D, and 4-4-10E are Type 1 and Type 2 examples.

This repair example, with 5/32 inch AD rivets, assumes that the damage, when cleaned up, is 1 inch across and extends 1.70 inch (damage width) into an 0.050 inch 2024-T4 hat section.

Begin a Type 2 repair. Determine the number of 5/32 inch AD rivets needed from Table 4-4-1. Multiply the number tabulated, 4.8, by 1.70 (inches of damage), which equals 8.16. Rounding up to the nearest whole number, install 9 rivets on each side of the damage.

NOTES:

- For Type 1, Type 2 or Type 3 damage, repair members should extend beyond damage to allow the insertion of one continuous, longitudinal row of repair fasteners. Do not include this row in repair fastener requirements.

- Damage to crown of hat section (Type 3) must be such that it is possible to insert one continuous, longitudinal row of repair rivets along each longitudinal edge of the damaged area. Otherwise, repair as a complete fracture (Type 4).

- Repair members and fillers should be the same material as original, but repair members should be the next thicker gauge on formed sections and two gauges thicker for extrusions.

- Select rivet number and size, per Table 4-4-2. If the original material is extruded, multiply rivet requirements by 1.15.

- Lay out rivet pattern around the original attachments. Replace any original attachments with the same diameter and type fasteners. Use fillers as necessary.

- The radii of the repair and original member should nest together. The repair rivet heads should not encroach on radii.

Strap Repair

Straps are used for attaching various equipment and parts, such as oil tanks, brake and hydraulic fluid reservoirs, etc. Figure 4-4-11 is a common repair.

NOTES:

- Repair members and fillers should be the same material as original, but repair members should be the next thicker gauge on formed sections, two gauges thicker for extrusions.

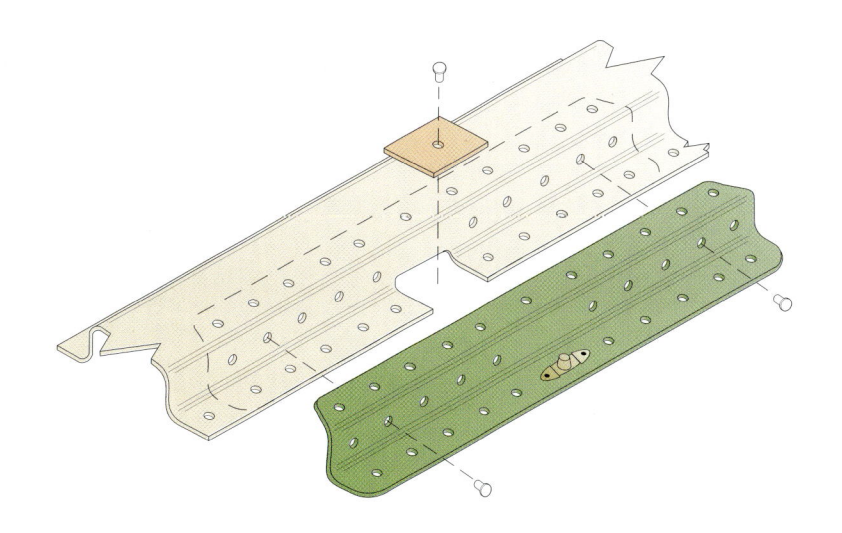

Figure 4-4-10A. Typical repair example

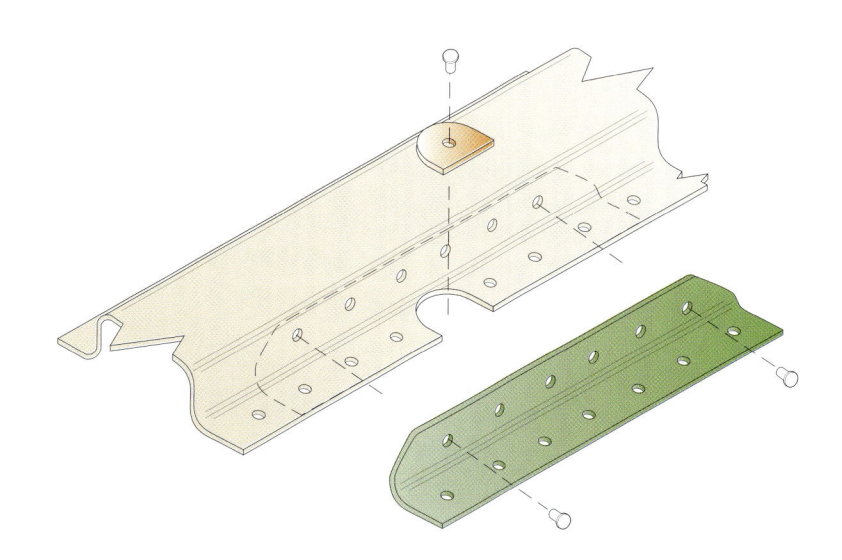

Figure 4-4-10B. Type 1 repair, with damage to flange (which must not penetrate into radius)

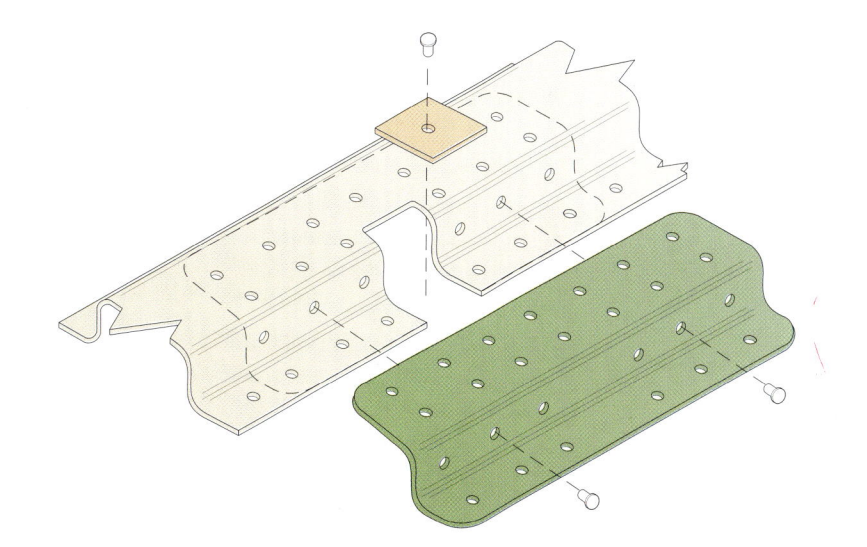

Figure 4-4-10C. Type 1 repair, with damage to one flange, web and crown

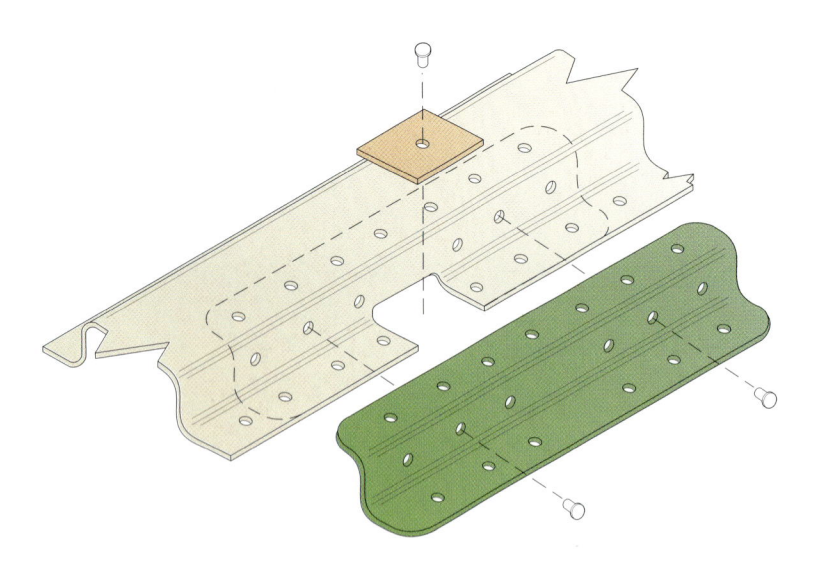

Figure 4-4-10D. Type 2 repair, with damage to one flange and web

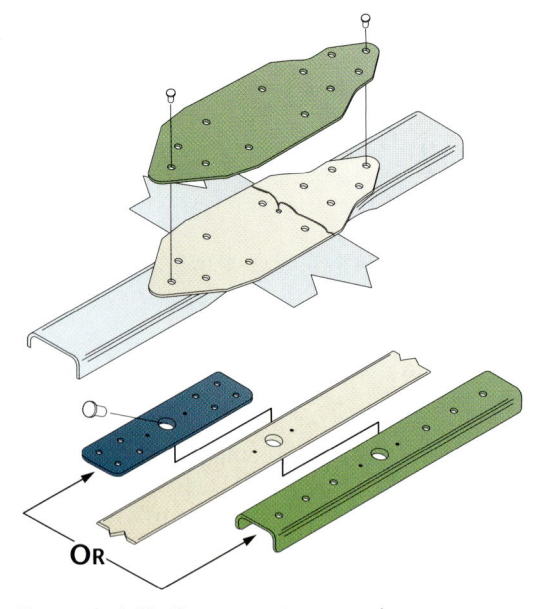

Figure 4-4-11. Common strap repair

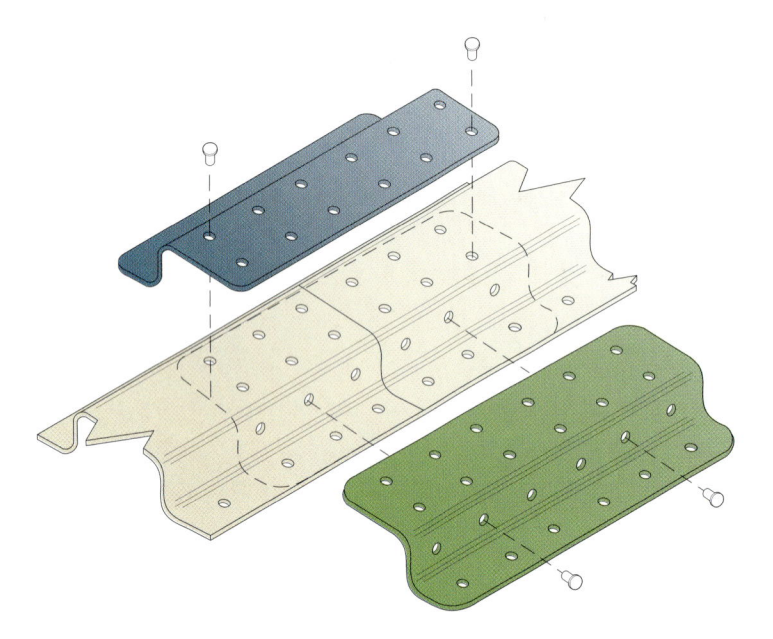

Figure 4-4-10E. Type 2 repair of a complete fracture. Overlapping repairs are shown. Single-hat use is permissible.

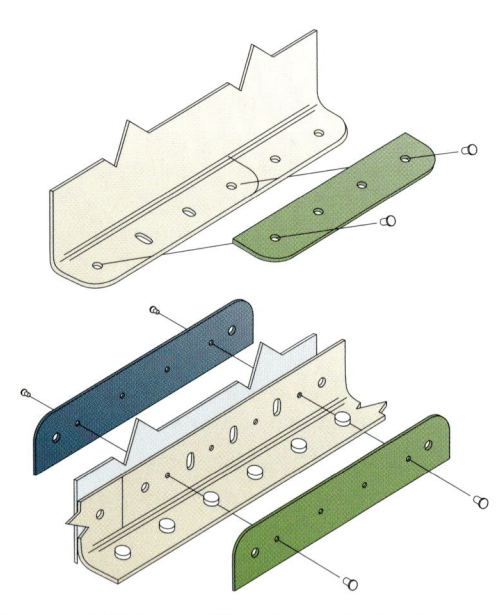

Figure 4-4-12. Two different oversized hole repair methods

- Select rivet number and size, per Table 4-4-2. If the original material is extruded, multiply rivet requirements by 1.15.
- Lay out the rivet pattern around any original attachments. Replace any original attachments with same diameter and type fasteners. Use fillers as necessary.
- The radii of the repair and original member should nest together. The repair rivet heads should not encroach on the radii.

Oversize Hole Repair

Oversized or elongated holes are rather common, particularly after an airplane has been in service for a while. When you find one, the cause is obvious: poorly drilled hole, loose fastener, pulled rivet, etc. Two typical methods of repair are illustrated in Figure 4-4-12.

NOTES:

- The combined thickness of repair member(s) should be one gauge thicker than the next standard gauge of the combined thickness of all damaged members.
- Damaged holes should be smooth and free of ragged edges.
- Voids should be filled with a structural filler containing 10 percent (by weight) fiberglass mill fibers.

- Install fasteners between the original holes if edge distance permits and both sides are covered.

Safety

Working with sheet metal can be very dangerous — a shear-cut piece of sheet metal can cut like a knife. Small, sharp edges are left after using almost any cutting tool.

- Use shears, bandsaws, belt-sanders, routers and drill-presses properly. No one should use such potentially dangerous equipment without first being properly checked out on the equipment. Each tool has its own list of safety rules. Know what they are, and follow them.

- Handle sheet materials with care. Gloves are recommended. Figure 4-4-13 is an example of cut-resistant gloves recommended for sheet metal use.

- Wear eye protection when appropriate.

- Use file handles on your files.

- Rings or other personal jewelry are not a good idea. They can snag on parts and cause considerable personal injury, particularly during machine operations.

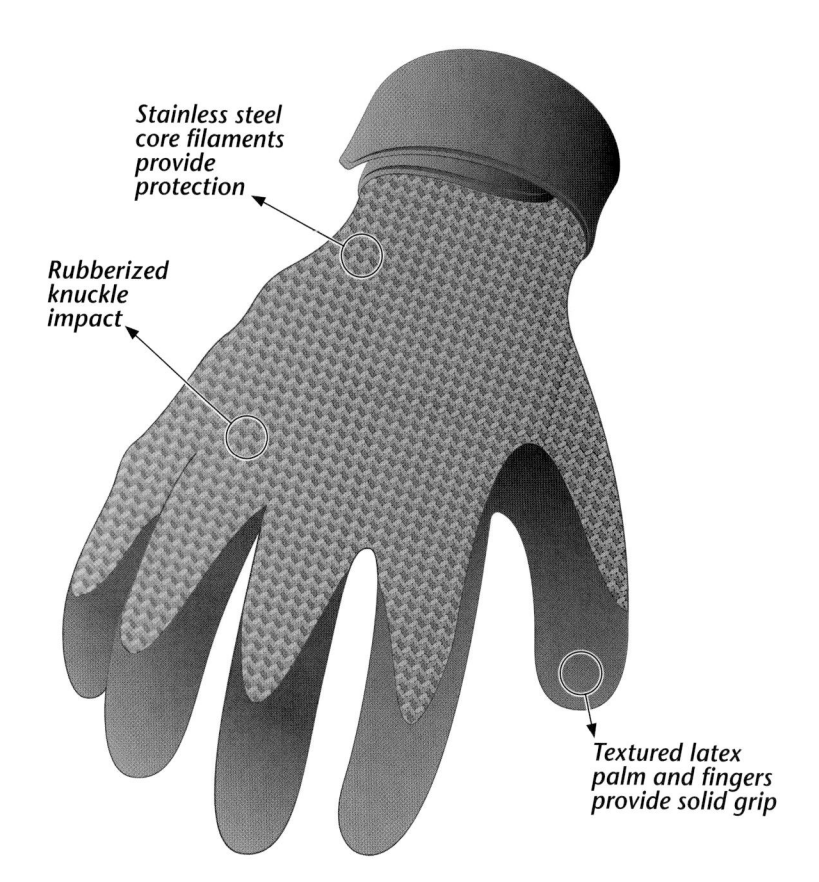

Figure 4-4-13. Cut-resistant gloves

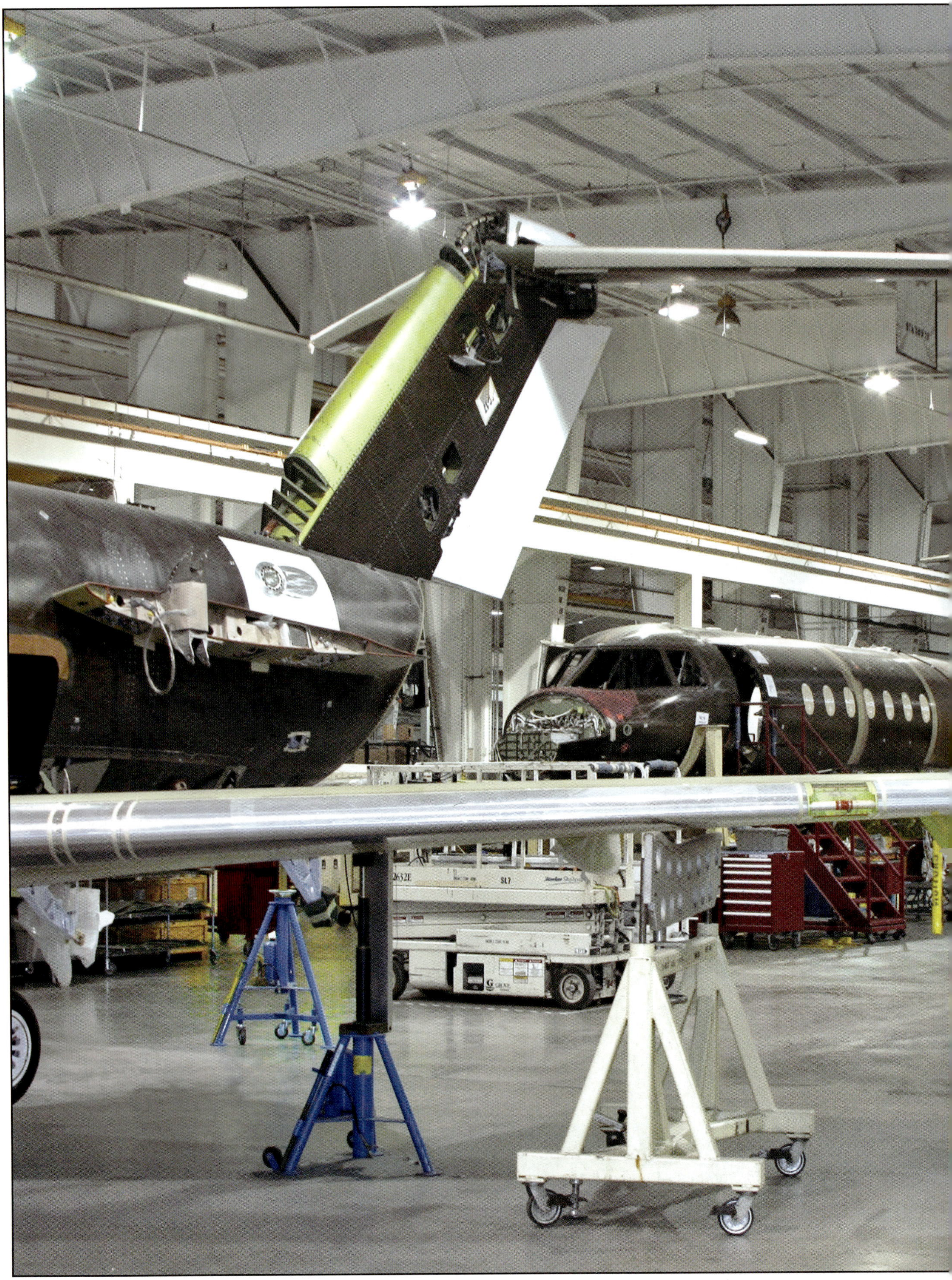
SL7

5

Airframe Nonmetallic Structures

While metallic structures have been the predominant method for most of aviation, early aircraft were built using nonmetallic materials. There has also been a renewed emphasis on nonmetallic materials in recent decades. In addition to the early materials such as wood, plastics and fiberglass, modern nonmetallic materials include advanced composites that exhibit high strength to weight ratios. This allows designers to create stronger, yet lighter, structures improving fuel economy and payload capabilities for comparable sized aircraft.

This chapter deals with the materials and procedures to be used in the repair of nonmetallic and advanced composite materials used in aircraft construction. The procedures discussed are general in nature. When actually repairing nonmetallic or advanced composite materials, you should always refer to the applicable manufactures maintenance manual (MM) and structural repair manual (SRM).

Section 1
Types of Nonmetallic Meterials

Nonmetallic structural materials are present on most aircraft, whether their primary structure is metallic or nonmetallic. Some aircraft use nonmetallic materials for their primary structure. The most common types of nonmetallic structures are:

- Composites
- Plexiglass
- Wood

Photo. Composites are a significant material in new aircraft construction.

Learning Objectives

REVIEW
- Aircraft structural components

DESCRIBE
- Common nonmetallic structural materials
- Types of advanced composite materials
- Safe handling and storage of composite materials
- The types of wood used in aircraft structures

EXPLAIN
- Benefits and limitations of nonmetallic materials
- Hot bonding process
- The classification system for damaged parts
- Tools and chemical products used to work with plexiglass

APPLY
- Use standard terminology to describe composite materials
- Repair reinforced plastic structures
- Inspect composite structures using nondestructive testing

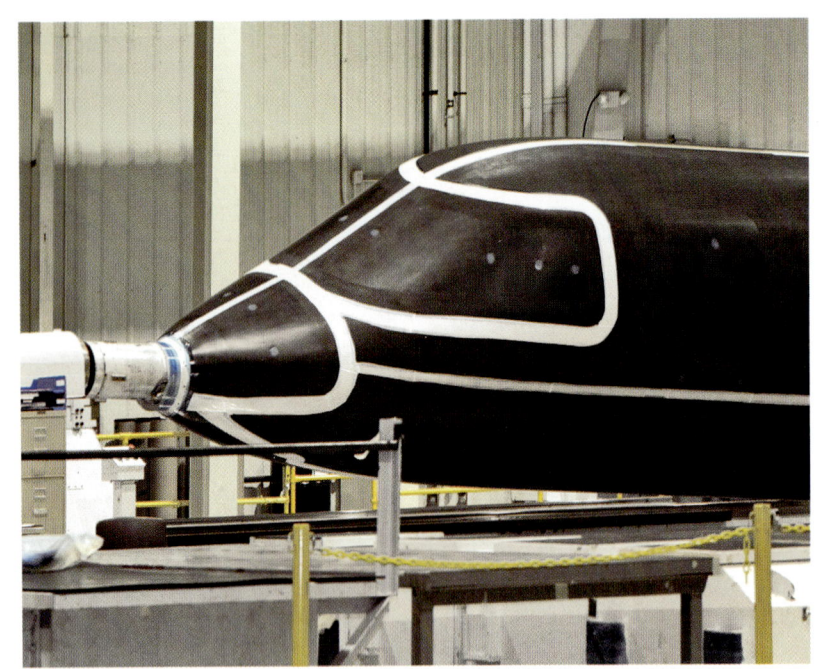

Figure 5-1-1. Composite structures are manufactured in large, monolithic structures

In some cases cost is driven by the cost of the material and in others by the cost of the manufacturing or assembly processes. Advanced composites can be constructed using automated equipment. This can dramatically reduce the labor element in the manufacturing process. Figure 5-1-1 shows the forward fuselage of a Hawker Beechcraft Horizon that was manufactured using computer controlled robotic equipment.

The combination of high strength to weight ratios and automated manufacturing processes make advanced composites a popular structural design for many modern aircraft. A number of newer in-service aircraft have all composite fuselage structures. Composite wing designs are also becoming more common.

Structural Comparisons

The basic types of structures used are similar to those found in metallic designs. Nonmetallic materials can be used to create monocoque, semi-monocoque and reinforced shell construction structures. Monocoque structures are more prevalent using advanced composites than in metallic structures. Fig 5-1-b shows a Hawker Beechcraft Premier forward fuselage that uses a composite monocoque structure.

Many advanced composites can be tailored to provide the necessary structural strength without adding stringers and frames that are needed for metallic structures. In other cases, those additional structural members can be formed as part of a single piece structure that has integral stringers or frames. This greatly simplifies manufacturing, but can add complexity during repairs.

Composites are used as a primary structural material. They include a wide variety of materials ranging from basic fiberglass reinforced plastics to advanced materials such as carbon fiber and Kevlar. Some have been in use for since prior to World War II, others have been developed in the last few decades.

Plexiglass is commonly used for windows and canopies. In some cases it is part of a self-supporting structure. In other cases it is an element of a larger structure. It is not commonly used as a primary structural material. When used in pressurized aircraft it may be subjected to significant pressures and becomes an important part of the basic fuselage structure.

Wood is also used as a primary structural material. It was very prevalent prior to World War II. Today's AMT will primarily see wood structures when called upon to repair antique aircraft. It is not a common structural material in current production aircraft except for limited use in cabin interiors.

Structural Differences with Nonmetallic materials

Nonmetallic materials all offer some attribute that is different than traditional metallic materials. In some cases it is higher strength to weight ratios, others offer transparency and still others can be worked using different types of tools and methods. Aircraft designers choose the material that offers the best combination of weight, strength, workability and cost for their application.

Section 2

Composites

Reinforced Plastics

Structural materials are an evolving process. Reinforced plastics are one of the materials that have evolved significantly. Structural materials are part of an evolving process. Reinforced plastic is part of that process. In a very short period, it has gone from simple fiberglass laminations to the art and science of advanced composites. With this progress has evolved an entire industry, with its own language, processes, design engineering and fabrication techniques. Today's technician needs to be as familiar with composites as they are with sheet metal.

Fabric terms. All advanced composites start as a fabric. Naturally, they all use the same fabric terms. The basic terms are derived from the weavers trade and are the same worldwide.

- **Warp.** The threads that run from one end of a roll of fabric to the other.
- **Woof.** Also known as *fill* or *weft*, the threads that run from side-to-side and actually make the collection of long threads into cloth.
- **Selvage.** When the woof runs to the side of the cloth and turns around and goes back to the other side, it produces a *selvaged edge*. The selvaged edge doesn't lay down well and is generally trimmed.
- **Bias.** Warp and woof threads run parallel to the length, or 90°, and are difficult to form around a curve. By cutting the material at a 45° angle to the warp, it can be made to smoothly fit a curve.

Figure 5-2-1. Fiberglass fabric

Fiberglass

Fiberglass is just what the name implies; it is glass fibers that have been spun into yarn and woven into fabric. The resulting fabric is a smooth, white material that, when encased in a resin matrix, has strength that can exceed aluminum. A fiberglass part is a true composite part, i.e., it is composed of two or more materials that combine into one.

As with most reinforced plastics, a fiberglass part is composed of several layers of material laminated together in a mold. The binding agent in the laminations is a catalyzed resin, and the process is called a lay-up.

Types of fiberglass cloth. For many years, there was only one type of fiberglass that was in general use. It had three forms: one was a coarse cloth, the second was a much finer and lighter cloth, and the third was simply chopped fiber sprayed from a gun and mixed with resin in the process. Figure 5-2-1 shows fiberglass cloth. While all cloth is not the same, much of it looks similar.

Today fiberglass comes in three types, with a wide variety of weaves available in each type. Figure 5-2-2 shows a number of common weaves. The three types of fiberglass cloth are:

E-glass. E-glass has a high electrical resistance. It has good strength and is low cost. Naturally it is used in places where its electrical resistance makes no difference.

WARP SIDE FILL SIDE
5 HARNESS SATIN WEAVE CONSTRUCTION

WARP SIDE FILL SIDE
8 HARNESS SATIN WEAVE CONSTRUCTION

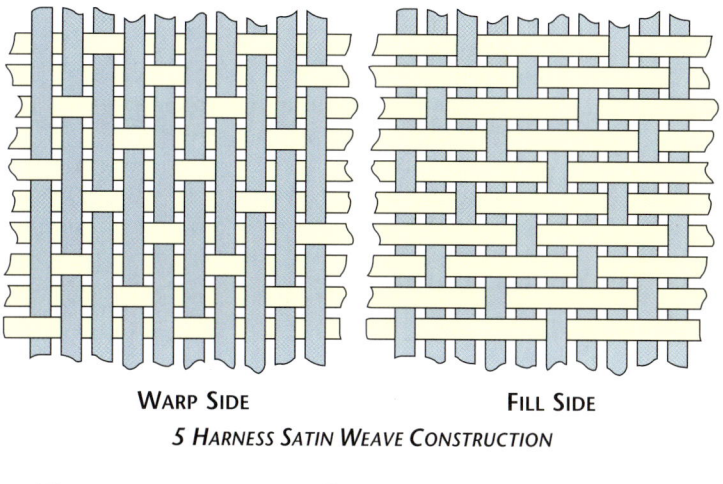

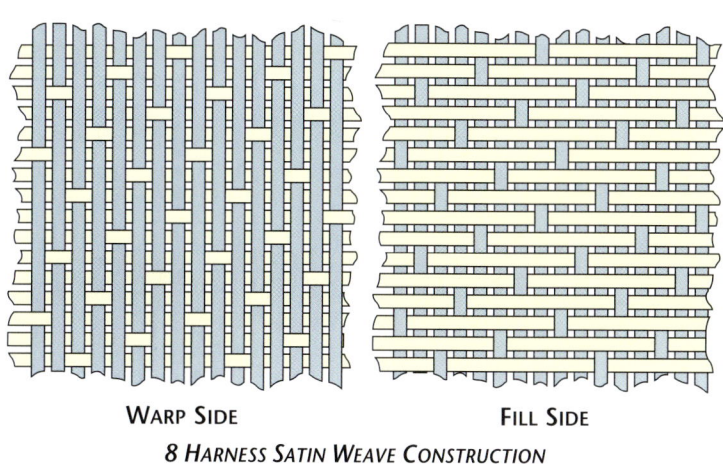

Figure 5-2-2. In five-harness satin weave construction, each yarn goes over four and under one yarn in both directions. In eight-harness satin weave construction, each yarn goes over seven and under one yarn in both directions.

Figure 5-2-3. Typical non-aircraft polyester resin

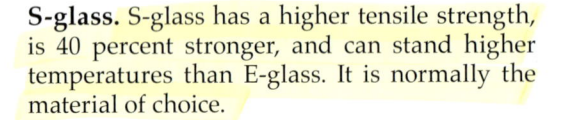

Figure 5-2-4. One type of aircraft epoxy resin

S-glass. S-glass has a higher tensile strength, is 40 percent stronger, and can stand higher temperatures than E-glass. It is normally the material of choice.

C-glass. C-glass has a higher chemical resistance than the other two. It is only used where the higher chemical resistance is needed.

Differences between E-glass, S-glass, and C-glass are not apparent. The material markings should not be removed from the material or the identity may be lost.

Resins

The resin matrix is actually the heart of the entire process. Its purpose is not only to give the flexible glass cloth form, but also to carry loads from one fiber to the next.

All resins require a catalyst, or hardener, to turn them from a liquid to a solid. Resin mixtures are proportional, that is, a specific amount of resin mixes with a specific amount of hardener. Two types of resin are commonly used in fiberglass lay-ups. Each of the two resins in common use has a different mixing ratio.

Polyester resin. This type of resin isn't used in structural components of aircraft. It is material you find in your local hardware store. It is principally used for boats, golf carts, and other commercial fabrications. In aviation it can be used for fabricating forms and other tooling.

Polyester resin uses a peroxide catalyst and cures at room temperature. By varying the amount, and chemistry, of the catalyst, it can be made to harden at different rates. Normal cures are at room temperature and take only a few minutes.

The hardening process generates its own heat from the chemical reaction of the resin and hardener. A promoter that can be mixed with the resin is available. It shortens the setup time. Figure 5-2-3 shows a typical non-aircraft polyester resin.

For this reason, it is critical that you measure the ratio of hardener to resin accurately, and that you follow the temperature tables that should be on the resin container. Not enough catalyst will slow down the hardening process to the point of unsuitability, too much hardener and the mixture will generate so much heat that you will have a thermal runaway. It is even possible to start a fire right in the container.

Epoxy resin. An epoxy matrix has become dominant in the advanced composite industry. Epoxy resin is completely different from polyester resin. To begin with, it hardens not from heat, but by a chemical process known as *cross-linking*. The resin-versus-hardener ratio is critical in epoxy resins. There are special proportional pumps made just for dispensing the two in the correct amount. Unlike polyester resin, epoxy may not cure at all if too much resin is used.

There is a mind-staggering amount of epoxies available. Everything from the tubes found in the grocery store checkout line to the material used to make the stealth airplanes is epoxy. They are not all the same. Five-minute epoxy is not structural epoxy. Depending on time and temperature, structural epoxy may take up to 45 minutes to cure. Figure 5-2-4 shows one type of aircraft epoxy resin.

Once a resin is catalyzed, it has a specific time period in which it must be used. This time period is called a *pot life*. A sample of mixed resin should be kept for quality control purposes after any repair.

Repairing Reinforced Plastic

This section deals with repairing fiberglass-reinforced plastic and sandwich construction components. The procedures discussed are general in nature. When actually repairing reinforced plastic and/or sandwich construction components, refer to the applicable aircraft maintenance manual (MM) or structural repair manual (SRM).

The repair of any damaged component made of reinforced plastic requires the use of identical materials, or of approved substitutes, for rebuilding the damaged portion. Abrupt changes in cross-sectional areas must be avoided by tapering joints, by making small patches round or oval instead of rectangular, and by rounding the corners of all large repairs. Uniform thickness of core and facings is exceedingly important in the repair of radomes. Repairs of punctured facings and fractured cores necessitate removal of all the damaged material, followed by replacement with the same type of material and in the same thickness as the original. When repairing large portions of composite structures with compound curves; it is recommended to use multiple short strips of fiberglass to minimize warping of the component during the curing process. All repairs to components housing radar or radio gear must be made in accordance with the manufacturer's recommendations. This information may be found in the aircraft's SRM. Figure 5-2-5 shows a punctured radome that will require particular care as it involves all of these issues.

Before a thorough inspection of the damage can be made, the area should be cleaned with a cloth saturated with methyl-ethyl-ketone (MEK). After drying, the paint should be removed by sanding lightly with No. 280-grit sandpaper, and the sanded area should be cleaned with MEK. The extent of damage can then be determined by tapping the suspected areas with a blunt instrument. You could use a coin, such as a quarter, as a blunt instrument to perform the tap test. This is referred to as the *coin tap* method. There is a special mallet made just for doing a coin tap. Never use a regular hammer as a blunt instrument.

The damaged areas will have a dull or dead sound, while the undamaged areas will have a clear, metallic sound.

Damages are divided into four general classes:

1. Surface damage
2. Facing and core damage
3. Puncture damage (both facings and core)
4. Damage requiring replacement

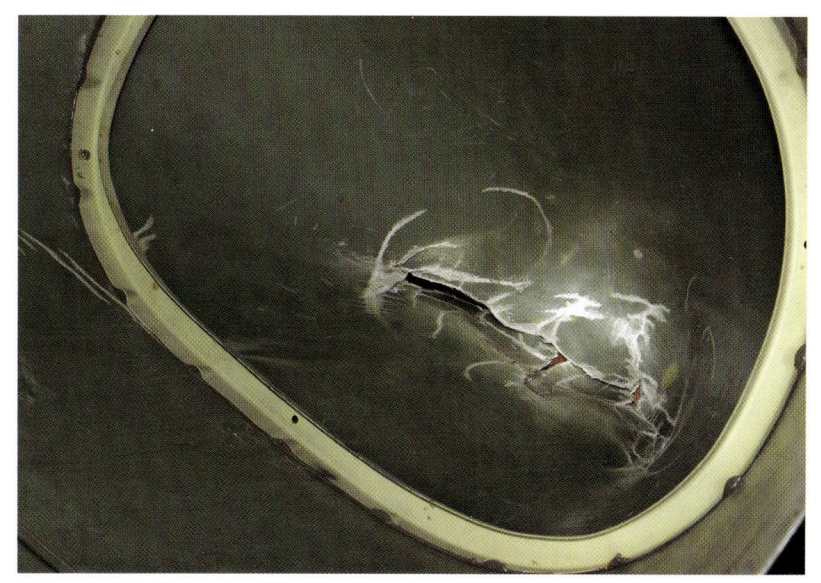

Figure 5-2-5. Radome with puncture damage

Figure 5-2-6. Abraded fiberglass fairing with filler applied

Repairing Surface Damage

The most common types of damage to the surface are abrasions, scratches, scars, dents, cuts and pits. Minor surface damages may be repaired by applying one or more coats of room-temperature catalyzed resin to the damaged area. Figure 5-2-6 shows a fiberglass fairing that has been abraded and is in the process of being repaired.

Fillers. More severe damages may be repaired by filling with a paste made from one part room-temperature resin and two parts short-chopped cotton or milled fiberglass fibers. The mixture is called *FLOX*.

Over this coated surface, apply a sheet of cellophane, extending 2 or 3 inches beyond the

Figure 5-2-7. Filler repair that is being sanded

repaired area. After the cellophane is taped in place, start in the center of the repair and lightly brush all the air bubbles and excessive resin out toward the edge of the repair with your hand or a rubber squeegee. Allow the resin to cure at room temperature or, if necessary, the cure can be hastened by the use of infrared lamps or hot sandbags. After the resin has been cured, remove the cellophane and sand off the excess resin; then, lightly sand the entire repaired area to prepare it for refinishing. Figure 5-2-7 shows a filler repair that is being sanded.

Another filler material common to both reinforced plastics and advanced composites is made from resin and *microspheres*. More commonly called microballoons, they are actually very small spheres of glass. The resulting material has the consistency of powder, is extremely lightweight, and a respirator must be worn at all times when handling it.

Once mixed with resin, the resulting material is referred to as *Micro* and is a mainstay of the homebuilt composite builders. Micro falls into three ranges, depending on how it is mixed:

1. Five parts Micro to one part resin (5:1) is called *dry Micro* and is used for filler.

2. Mixed two or three parts Micro to one part resin (2-3:1), it is called *wet Micro* and is used as a non-structural glue.

3. Mixed one part Micro to one part resin (1:1), it is called *slurry* and is used as a surface filler.

Worn fastener holes may be repaired by filling them with dry micro and then redrilling. Small holes less than 1" in diameter, that do not extend into the core material, may be repaired by using a dry Micro, or potting compound, sanded and painted as needed.

Peel ply. Peel ply is a polyester material like surface tape. Its purpose is to provide a surface that is suitable for bonding another part without all that sanding. In fact, it is better than sanding. Peel ply is installed as the last piece of a lay-up while the resin is still wet. It needs to be completely impregnated. Peel ply should be used on both parts to be joined.

When the parts are ready to be bonded, the peel ply is removed and the resulting surfaces are ready to accept bonding.

Ply Damage (Sandwich Laminates)

When the damage has penetrated more than one ply of the cloth in sandwich-type laminates, the repair may be made by using the scarfed method, shown in Figure 5-2-8. This repair is made in the following manner:

- Clean the area thoroughly.
- Sand out the damaged laminate plies, as shown in Figure 5-2-8B. The area should be sanded to a circular or oval shape, then tapered uniformly down to the deepest penetration of the damage.

Figure 5-2-8. Ply repair (scarfed method)

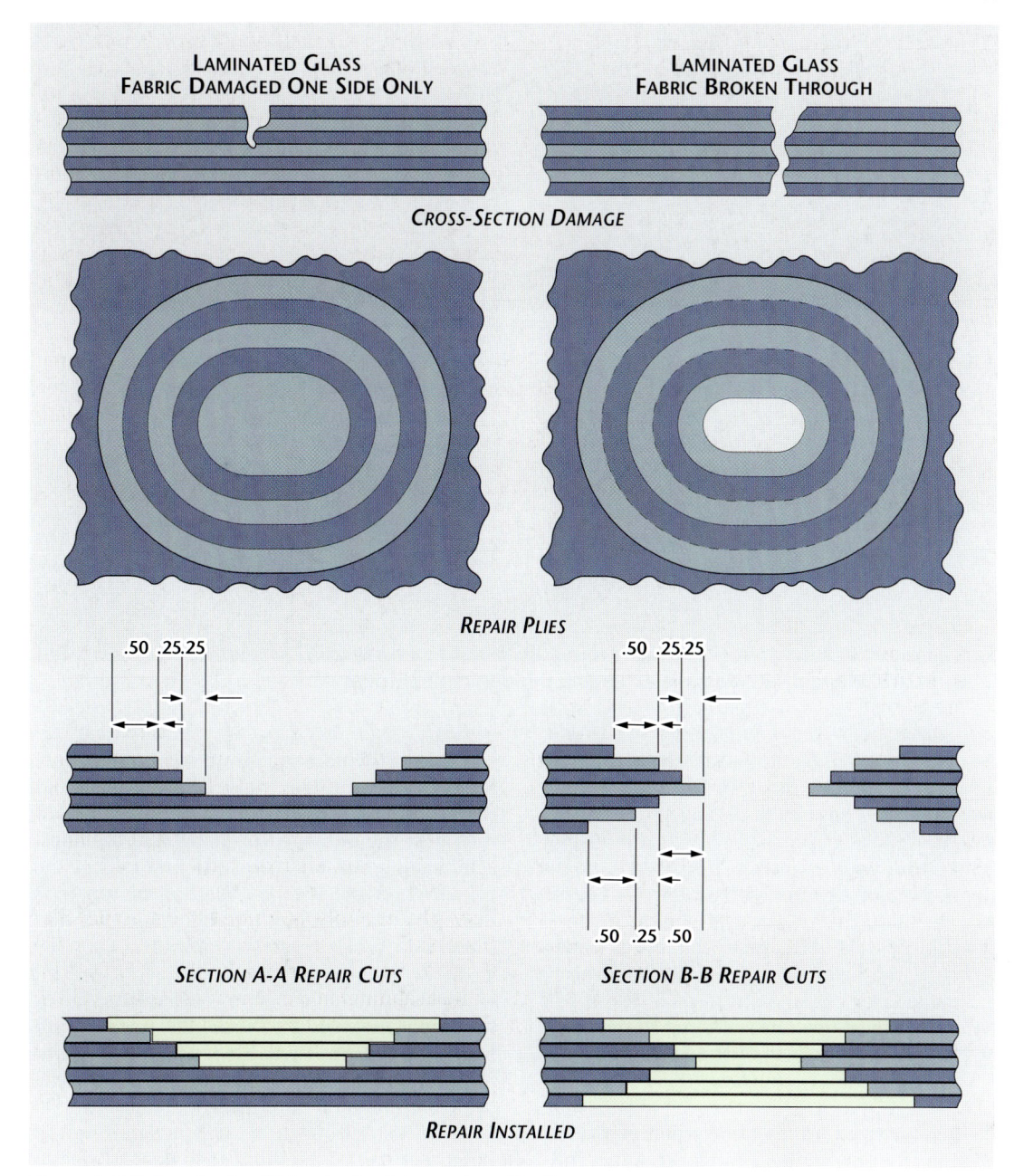

Figure 5-2-9. Repair of solid laminates (stepped method)

NOTE: *The diameter of the scarfed (tapered) area should be at least 100 times the depth of the penetration. Exercise care when using a mechanical sander. Excess pressure on the sander can cause the sandpaper to grab, resulting in the delamination of undamaged plies.*

CAUTION: *The sanding of glass cloth-reinforced laminates produces a fine dust that can cause skin irritation. In addition, if you breathe an excessive amount of this dust, it can be injurious; observe skin, eye and respiratory protection.*

- Clean the area thoroughly.
- Brush coat the sanded area with one coat of room-temperature catalyzed resin, and apply the contoured pieces of resin-impregnated cloth, as shown in Figure 5-2-8C.
- Tape a sheet of cellophane over the built-up repair and work out the excess resin and air bubbles.
- Cure the repair in accordance with the resin manufacturer's instructions, and then sand the surface down (if necessary) to the original surface of the facing.

Ply Damage (Solid Laminates)

Ply damage to solid laminates may be repaired by using the scarfed method described for sandwich-type laminates shown in Figure 5-2-8. The stepped method, shown in Figure 5-2-9

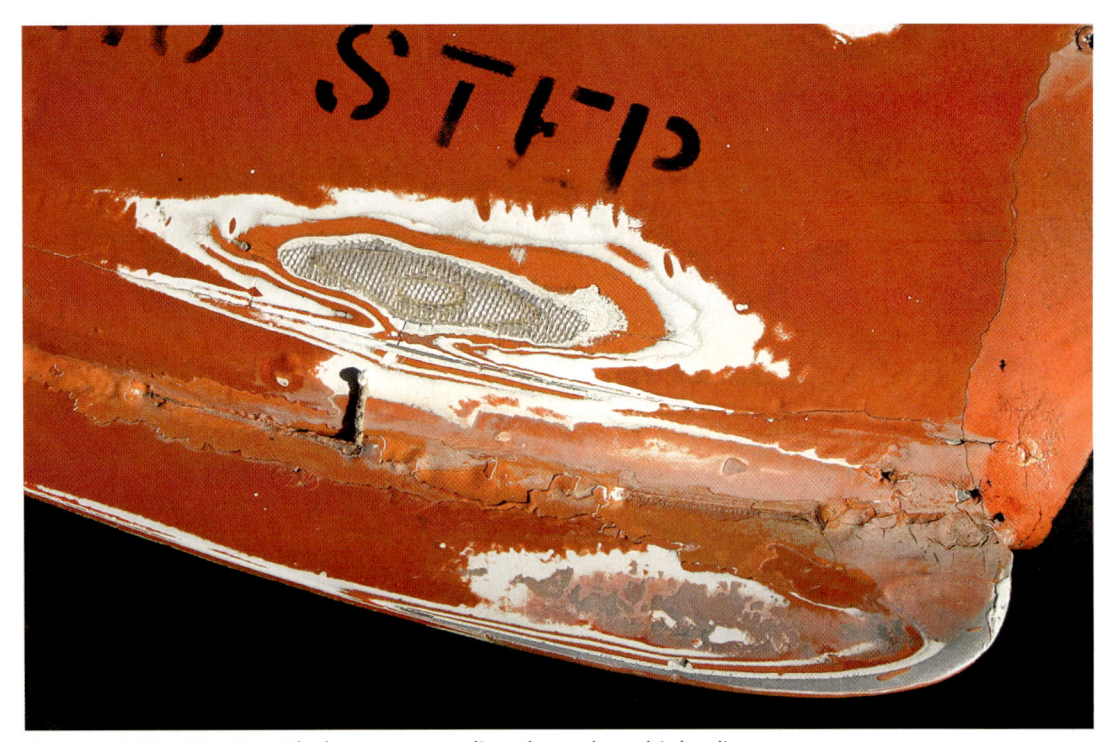

Figure 5-2-10. Wingtip with damage extending through multiple plies

also may be used. Figure 5-2-10 shows a wingtip that may require this type of repair as multiple laminates have been damaged.

When the wall is being prepared for the stepped repair, a router with a controlled depth will facilitate the cutout and should be used to avoid possible damage to the layers underneath. If the layer of glass cloth underneath is scratched or cut, the strength of the repair will be lessened. Exercise care not to peel back or rupture the adhesion of the laminate layers beyond the cutout perimeter.

Removal of the cutouts can be accomplished by peeling from the center and working carefully to the desired perimeter of the cutout. Scrape each step, wipe clean with cloths moistened with MEK, and allow the area to dry thoroughly.

Cut the replacement glass fabric pieces to an exact fit, with the weave directions of the replacement plies running in the same direction as the existing plies. Failure to maintain the existing weave direction will result in a repair that is greatly under strength. Replace each piece of fabric, being careful to butt the existing layers of fabric plies together, but do not overlap them. The laminate layers should be kept to the proper matching thickness.

When the entire wall has been penetrated, as shown in Figure 5-2-9, half of the damaged plies should be removed from one side and the replacement build-up completed. Then, repeat removal and build-up procedure on the opposite side. If the damage occurs over a relatively large or curved area, make up a plaster mold that conforms to the contour and extends 1 inch past the damage, inserting it in the damaged area when repairing the first half of the plies. When the stepped method of repair is used, the dimensions should be maintained as illustrated.

In areas that have become delaminated, or that contain voids or bubbles, clean with MEK and determine the extent of the delamination. Drill holes at each end or on the opposite sides of the void by using a No. 55 drill bit, extending through the delaminated plies. Figure 5-2-11 shows the procedure for repair of delaminated plies.

Additional holes may be needed if air entrapment occurs when you inject the resin. Use a hypodermic needle or syringe and slowly inject the appropriate amount of resin until the void is filled and the resin flows freely from the drilled holes. After the voids are completely filled, bring the area down to proper thickness by working the excess resin out through the holes, then cure and refinish.

Repairing Facing and Core Damage

The repair of facings and cores requires more than one method of repair. Special attention must be given to the type of core used.

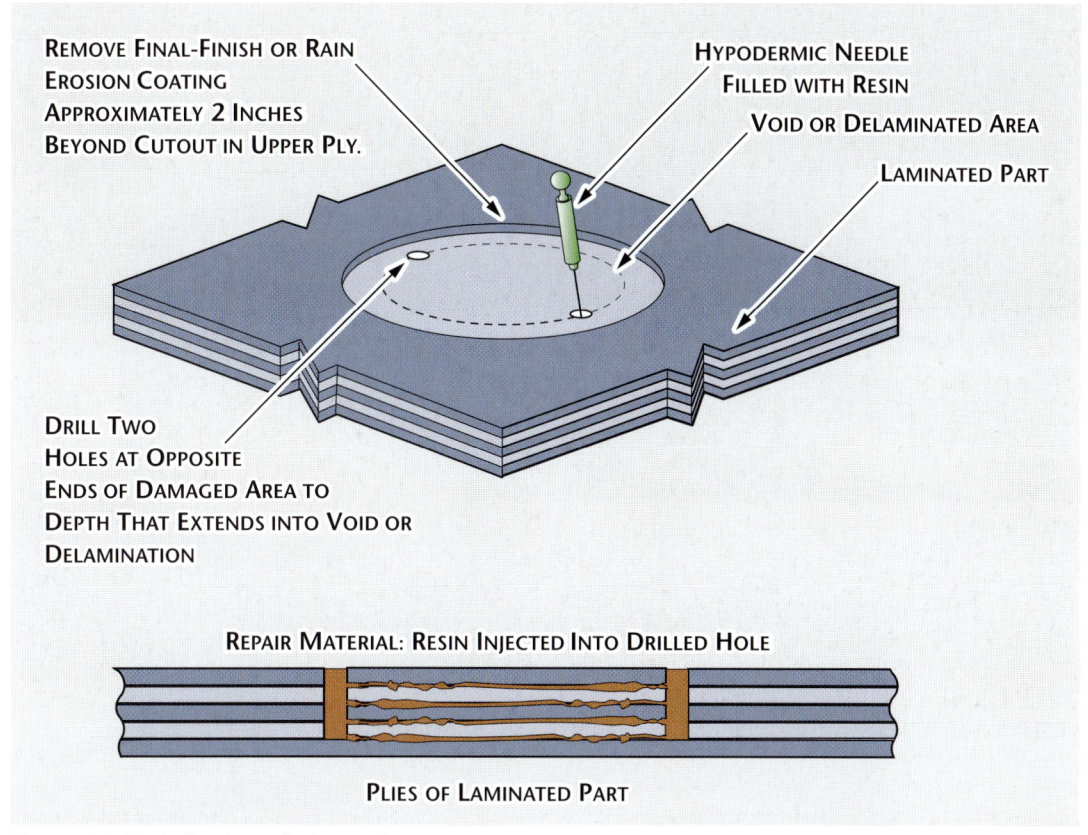

Figure 5-2-11. Delaminated ply repair

Honeycomb core. The repair of facings and cores requires more than one method of repair. Special attention must be given to the type of core used. Damages extending completely through one facing of the material and into the core require removal of the damaged core and replacement of the damaged facings in such a manner that normal stresses can be carried over the area. The scarfed method, illustrated in Figure 5-2-12, is the preferred method for accomplishing small repairs of this type. Repairs of this type may be accomplished as follows:

- Carefully trim out the damaged portion to a circular or oval shape and remove the core completely to the opposite facing. Be careful not to damage the opposite facing. The damaged facing around the trimmed hole is then scarfed back carefully by sanding. The length of the scarf should be at least 100 times the facing thickness, as shown in Figure 5-2-12B This scarfing operation must be done very accurately to a uniform taper.

- Cut a piece of replacement core material to fit snugly in the trimmed hole, and align the ribbon direction.

- Replacement core material should be equal in thickness to the original core material. Brush coat the repair area and the replacement honeycomb, exercising care to prevent an excessive amount of resin from entering the honeycomb cells. To prevent corrosion inside a repaired metal honeycomb structure, the repair must be primed with a corrosion inhibiting primer and finish that will completely seal the atmosphere away from the repaired area.

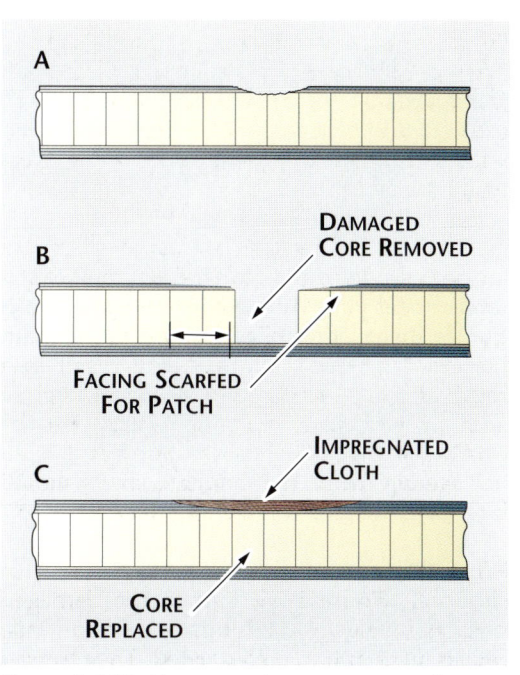

Figure 5-2-12. Honeycomb-type core repair

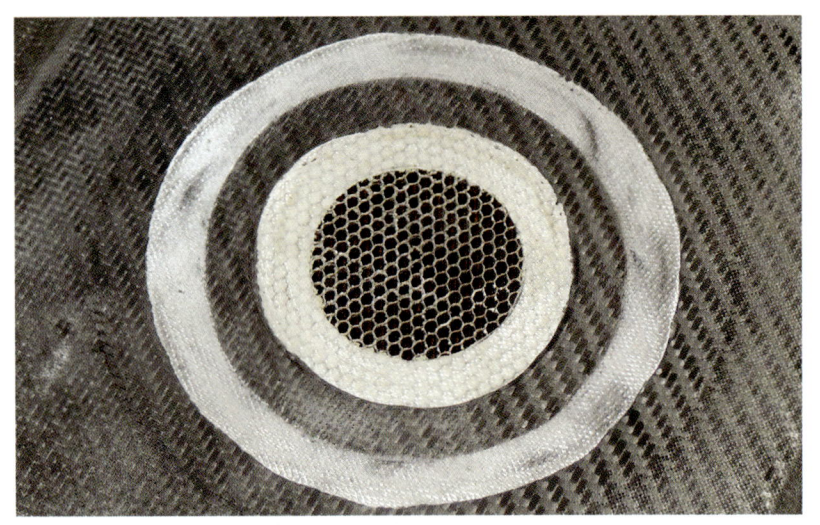

Figure 5-2-13. Honeycomb core repair

- Insert the honeycomb repair section and place the resin-impregnated cloth over the repair area. Cover the area with cellophane sheeting. Cure the repair in accordance with the resin manufacturer's instructions.

Figure 5-2-13 shows a honeycomb core repair where the damaged area has been removed and the surface plies have been stepped back. This piece is ready to have the resin-impregnated cloth placed over the repaired section.

After the repair has been cured, sand the surface to its original contour. The entire area should be lightly sanded before refinishing.

Foam core. Some structures us a foam core faced with fiberglass or other composites. Raw foam core material is shown in Figure 5-2-14.

FORMED IN PLACE FILLER OR HONEYCOMB CORE DAMAGED
LAMINATED GLASS FABRIC SKIN BROKEN

DAMAGE

CUT AWAY DAMAGED CORE AREA AND FILL WITH SPECIFIED FILLER

REMOVE LAYERS OF LAMINATE AS SHOWN

REPAIR MATERIAL

REPAIR INSTALLED

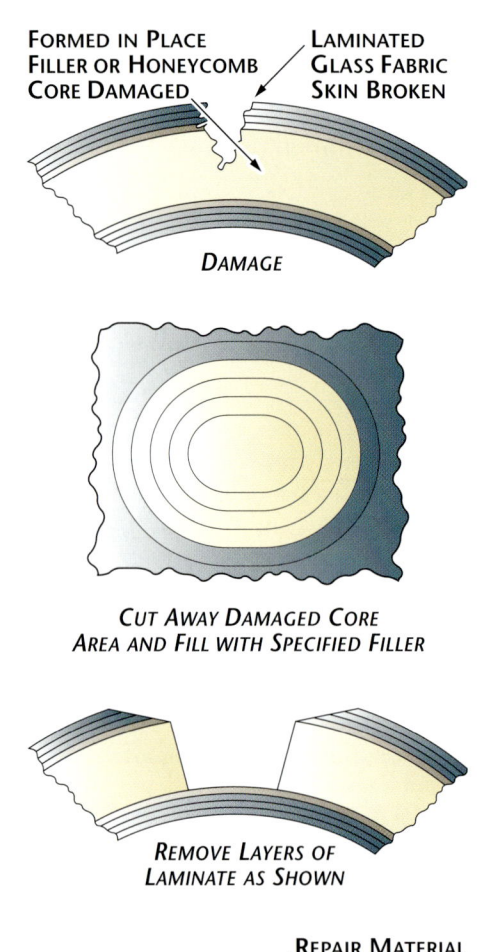

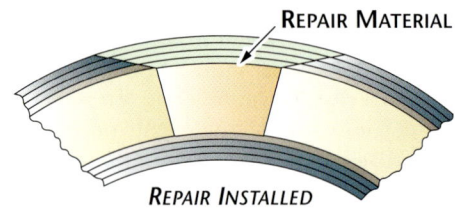

Figure 5-2-15. Foam-type core repair

Figure 5-2-14. Raw foam core material comes in many sizes

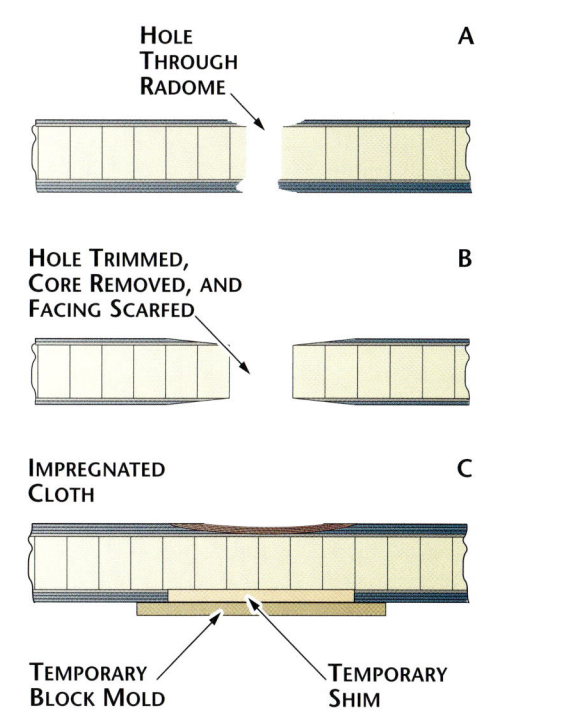

Figure 5-2-16. Scarfed repair method

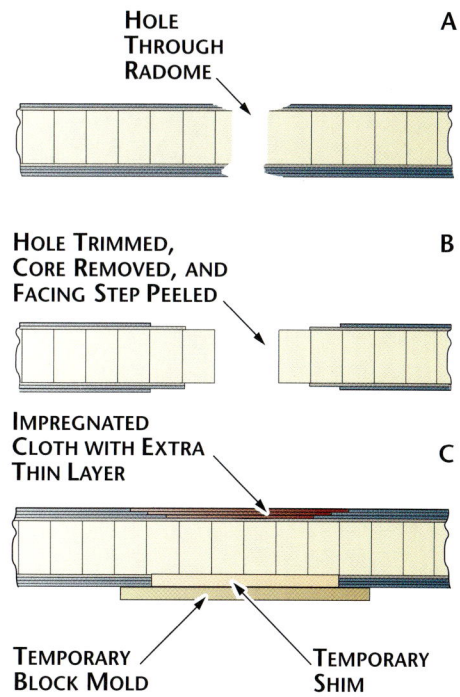

Figure 5-2-17. Stepped repair method

When foam core structures are damaged, the damaged core should be removed by cutting perpendicularly to the surface of the face laminate opposite the damaged face. Scrape the inner facing surface clean, making sure there is no oil or grease film in the area, to ensure good bondage of the foam to the laminate. Fill the area where the core has been removed with the filler material specified in the aircraft SRM. Figure 5-2-15 shows the replacement of a foam core.

NOTE: *Do not use MEK to clean the damage, as it may soften and weaken the foam.*

Repairing Puncture Damage

The repair of punctures differs as to the method used. Repair of honeycomb cores is different than the repair of foam cores.

Honeycomb core. Repairs to damages completely through the sandwich structure may be accomplished either by the scarfed method (similar to the repair described for damage extending into the core) or the stepped method.

The scarfed method is normally used on small punctures up to 3-4 inches in maximum dimension and in facings made of thin cloth (which are difficult to peel). The stepped method is usually employed on larger repairs to facings composed of thick cloth. The scarfed method of repair for punctures is the same as that used for damage extending into the core, with the exception that the opposite side of the sandwich is provided with a temporary mold or block to hold the core in place during the first step. See illustration C in Figure 5-2-16.

After the first facing repair is cured completely, the mold and the shim (temporarily replacing the facing on the opposite side) are removed. The repair is then completed by repeating the procedure used in the first step. When this facing is cured, the surface should be sanded down to the original contour and the repair area lightly sanded in preparation for refinishing.

When using the stepped method of repair, the damaged area is first trimmed out to a round, oval, rectangular, or square shape (preferably having rounded corners).

The individual plies are then cut out, as shown in Figure 5-2-17. Each ply is *stepped* back 1-1/2 inches and trimmed out by using a sharp knife. The sides of the repair should be parallel with the weave of the cloth, if possible.

NOTE: *Do not cut through more than one layer of cloth. If the layer of cloth underneath is scratched, the strength of the repair will suffer.*

The opposite facing is shimmed and backed up with a mold, and the core material is inserted as previously described. The outer repair plies are soaked in the resin and laid over the damaged area. An extra layer of thin cloth is laid over the repair area to extend 1/2 inch over the undam-

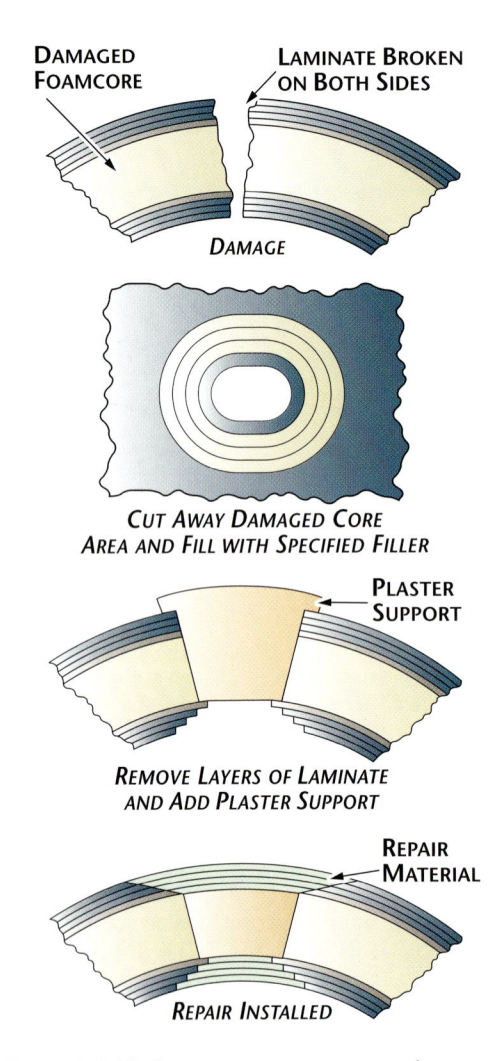

Figure 5-2-18. Foam-type puncture repair

aged facing. The repair area is then covered with a sheet of cellophane to apply pressure, and then it is allowed to cure. The inner facing is then replaced in the same manner as the outer facing. After the inner repair has been cured, the entire repair area should be sanded to the original contour and prepared for refinishing.

Foam core. When the puncture penetrates the entire wall, remove the damaged core and face laminates to 1/4 inch past the perimeter of the hole on the inner face. Make a plaster support to replace the removed core, conforming to the curvature of the inside layer of the inner face. Figure 5-2-18 shows a punctured repair with a plaster support. After repair to the inner face has been completed, remove the plaster support and continue the repair on the opposite side.

Finishing Repaired Areas

In the repair of reinforced plastic parts, the final step is to refinish the part with a finish identical to the original, or an acceptable substitute. In refinishing radomes, consult the equipment manufacturer's repair data. Do not use metallic-pigmented paints or other electronic reflective-type materials because of undesirable shielding and interference effects. Always use the materials recommended in the applicable structural repair manual for refinishing both the interior and exterior surfaces of reinforced plastic components.

Reinforced plastic components whose frontal areas are exposed to high speeds are frequently coated with a rain erosion coating. Rain erosion coatings protect the component against pits that are caused by raindrops hitting the component at high aircraft speeds. These pits or eroded areas can cause delamination of the component glass cloths if allowed to progress unchecked.

The following general safety precautions should be observed when making repairs to reinforced plastic components. Review these safety precautions before attempting any repairs to reinforced plastics:

1. Local safety regulations as to fire and health hazards must be followed.

2. All solvents are flammable; therefore, observe proper handling procedures.

3. Personnel involved in the mixing or handling of catalyzed resin prior to the curing operations should wear rubber gloves. After using rubber gloves, personnel should clean their hands with soap and water and rinse with vinegar to neutralize any catalyst particles.

4. Never mix the catalyst and promoter together, as they are explosively reactive as a mixture. Always mix the promoter with the resin first, and then add the catalyst to the mixture.

5. The toxicity of resin formulations has not been definitely established. Some of the components are known to cause nasal or skin irritation to certain individuals. Adequate ventilation should be provided.

6. The sanding operation on glass cloth-reinforced laminates gives off a fine dust that may cause skin, eye or respiratory irritations. Inhalation of excessive amounts of this dust should be avoided. Protection should be provided for respiration, eyes and skin.

7. Do not store catalyzed resin in an airtight container or an unvented refrigerator.

Repairing Sandwich Construction Materials

Repairs covered in this section are applicable to structural-type sandwich construction consisting of aluminum alloy facings bonded to aluminum honeycomb and balsa wood cores.

Repairing Minor Surface Damage

The most common types of damage to the surface are abrasions, scratches, scars and minor dents. These minor surface damages require no repair other than the replacement of the original protective coating to prevent corrosion if no breaks, holes or cracks exist. The procedures and materials used in replacing the original protective coating are outlined later in this chapter.

Repairing Delaminations

Facing-to-core voids of less than 2.5 inches in diameter can usually be repaired by drilling a series of holes 0.06-0.10 inch in diameter in the upper facing over the void area. An expandable forming resin is then injected through the holes with a pressure-type caulking gun. When the void is on the lower surface of the panel, only sufficient resin must be injected so as to completely fill the void. With voids on the upper surface, the core area should be filled until the resin comes out of the injection holes. These holes should be sealed with a thermosetting epoxy resin adhesive, and the entire assembly cured with lamps, as required for the adhesive system.

When the void areas are large, it is necessary to remove the facing over the damaged area and follow the repair procedures for a puncture. See Figure 5-2-19.

Repairing Punctures

A puncture is defined as a crack, break or hole through one or both skin facings with resulting damage to the honeycomb and/or balsa wood core. The size of the puncture, amount of damage to the core, assembly to be repaired (rudder, elevator, etc.) and previous repairs to the damaged assembly are factors to be considered in determining the type of repair to be made. If damage to a honeycomb and/or balsa wood core assembly exceeds a specified length or diameter in inches, or the total number of repairs exceeds a specified percentage of the total bonded area, the assembly must be replaced.

NOTE: *These figures are found in the applicable structural repair manual.*

Honeycomb core. The repair shown in Figure 5-2-19, at top, is used when a puncture through

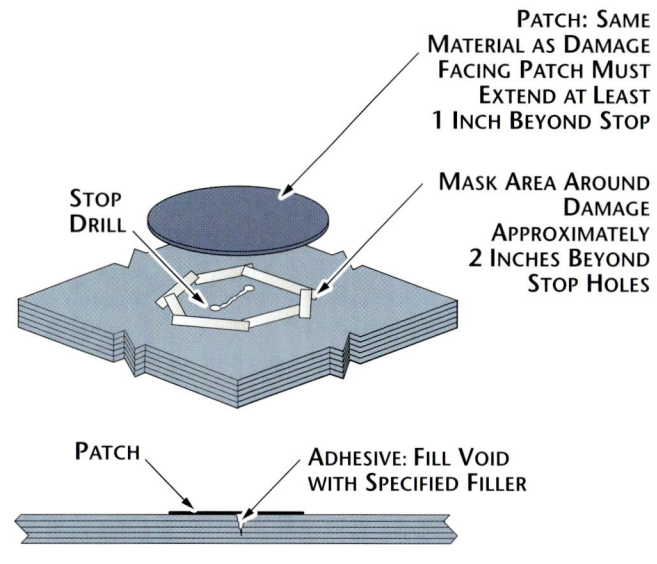

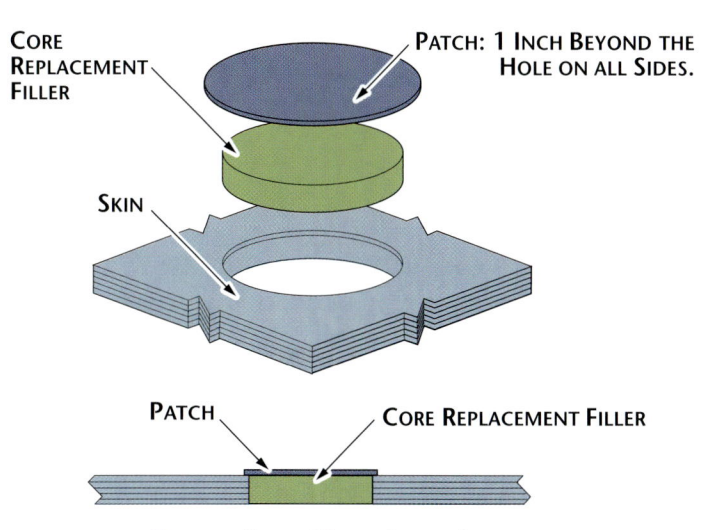

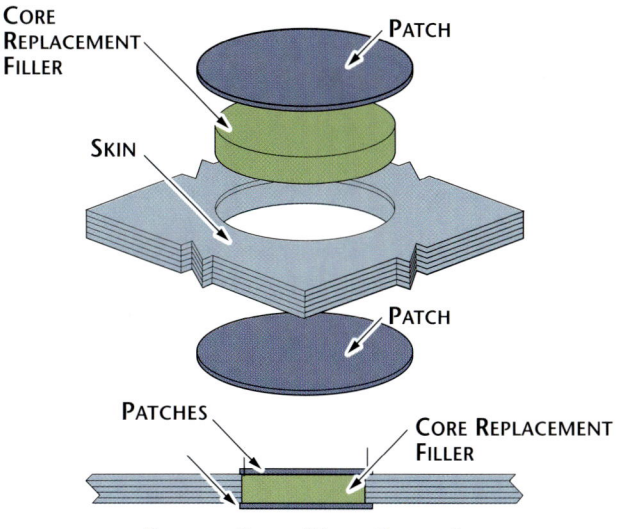

Figure 5-2-19. Sandwich construction puncture repair (honeycomb core)

one skin facing has caused only minor damage to the core material. To repair this type of damage, proceed as follows:

- Cover the component with a suitable protective covering (polyvinyl sheet or kraft paper). Cut out a section of the protective covering that will extend approximately 2 inches beyond the damaged area. Use masking tape to hold the cutout in place. Stop-drill as necessary through the skin facing only.

- Strip the paint and protective coating 1-1/2 inches beyond the stop-drilled holes. Then, clean the stripped area with a special cleaning paste. Fill the void with the specified filler material to within approximately 0.063 inch of the skin facing. Cure as directed.

- Prepare a round or oval patch large enough to overlap the damaged area at least 1 inch. Apply sealant to the undersurface of the patch and to the filler and skin surface. Install the repair patch, maintaining correct overlap, and clamp to the assembly to assure contact with the skin facing. Cure as directed. Remove the excess adhesive, and refinish as necessary.

The repair shown in the middle of Figure 5-2-19 is used when a puncture through one skin facing has caused extensive damage to the honeycomb core. When the core has been damaged extensively, the damaged material must be replaced.

- Prepare the assembly as previously described. Cut out the damaged skin facing with a hole saw or aviation snips. File the edges of the hole smoothly. Using a pocketknife, carefully cut out the damaged core.

CAUTION: *Do not damage the opposite facing. Install a new core filler and complete the repair as previously described for Figure 5-2-19.*

The repair shown at the bottom of Figure 5-2-19, is used when both skin facings and the core have been damaged. Use the same procedures as described above to make this repair.

Balsa wood core. The repair shown in Figure 5-2-20 is used when no gain in structural strength is desired, and it is only to be used for sealing holes of 1 square inch or less in external surfaces. The damaged area (part 1) should be cut out to a smooth, circular or rectangular shape. A 3/8 inch minimum radius (part 2)

1. Damaged Area
2. 3/8 Inch Minimum Radius
3. Inspect for Separation of Skin Facing from Balsa Wood Core.
4. Filler Material
5. Fabric Patch

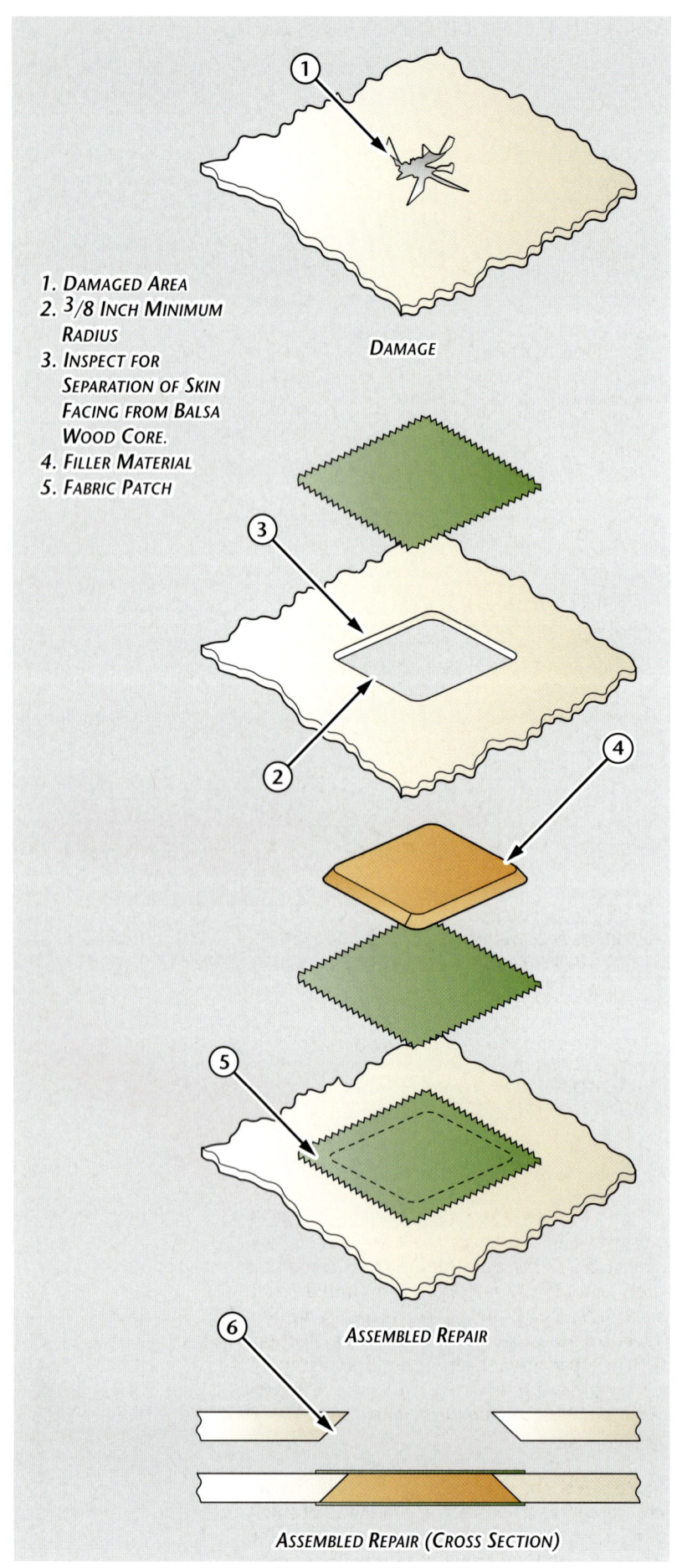

Figure 5-2-20. Balsa wood repair with filler plug and fabric patch

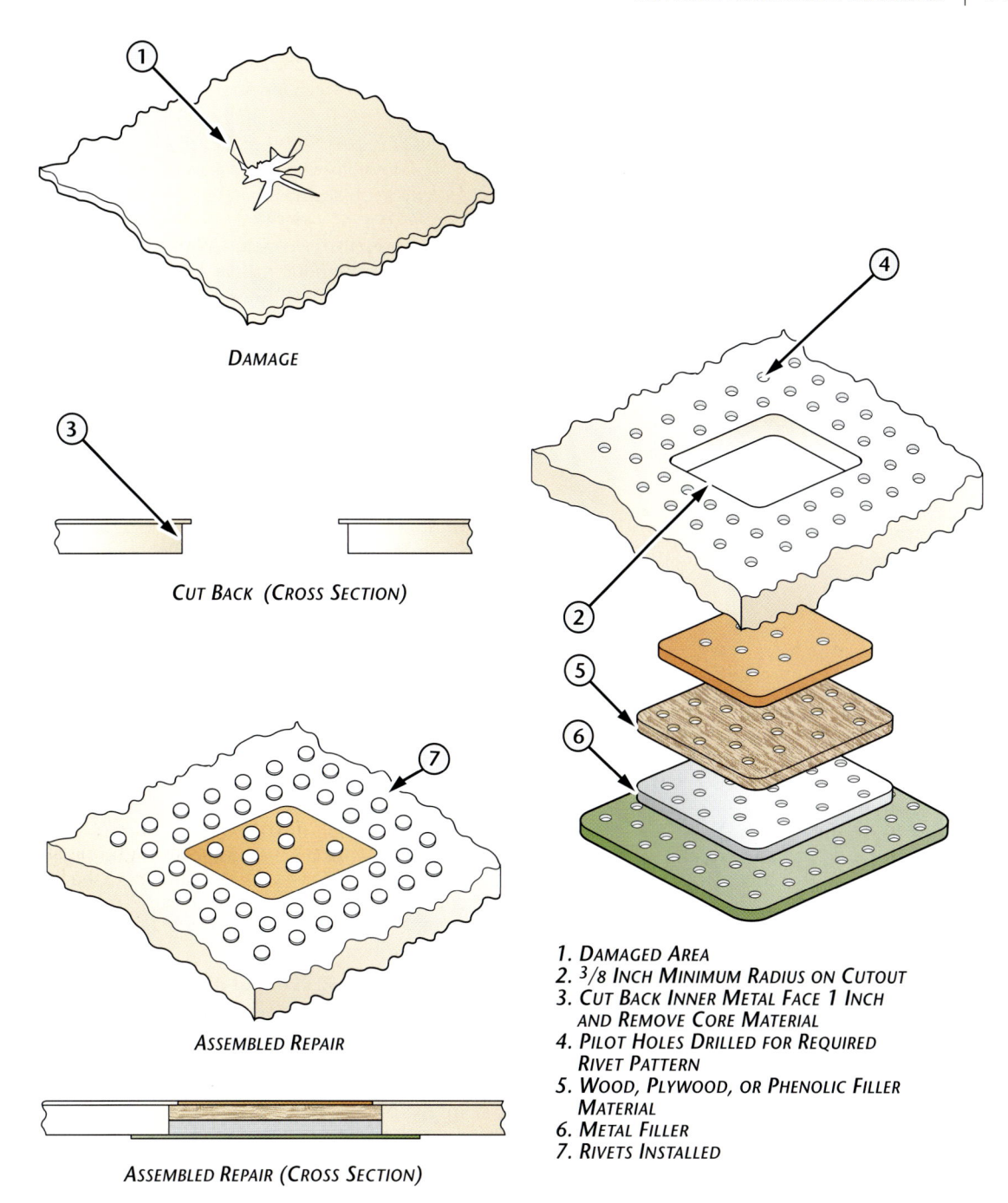

Figure 5-2-21. Balsa wood repair with flush patch

1. Damaged Area
2. 3/8 Inch Minimum Radius on Cutout
3. Cut Back Inner Metal Face 1 Inch and Remove Core Material
4. Pilot Holes Drilled for Required Rivet Pattern
5. Wood, Plywood, or Phenolic Filler Material
6. Metal Filler
7. Rivets Installed

must be provided at the corners of rectangular cutouts.

NOTE: *This information applies to all repairs made to balsa wood core panels. In cutting out the damaged area, you must take care not to separate the metal faces from the core. You can accomplish this by using a very fine-toothed coping or hacksaw blade for straight cuts, and cylindrical saws (hole saws) for cutting holes or rounding corners.*

After the damaged section has been cut out, file the edges smooth by using a fine-cut file only. Then, inspect the area (part 3) for separation of the skin facing from the balsa wood core. If the facing has separated from the core, re-bond the two surfaces, using the procedures outlined in the previous section on skin separation. Then, complete the repair by using the approved filler material and two fabric patches, as shown in parts 4 and 5 of Figure 5-2-20.

Figure 5-2-21 shows one flush-type balsa wood core repair that is used on puncture damages larger than 1 inch. To make this type of repair, cut out the damaged area as previously described. After the damaged area has been

rivet pattern and drill pilot holes in the panel (Figure 5-2-21).

> **NOTE:** *Solid rivets or bolt type fasteners are not normally used on composite repairs. They tend to cause delaminations.*

Next, prepare two patch plates: a wood, plywood or phenolic filler, and a metal filler (Figure 5-2-21). The outer patch plate should fill the hole in the core, and the inner patch plate should overlap the hole in the core approximately 1 inch for each row of rivets.

Locate the patch plates and wood filler. Using the pilot holes in the panel as a guide, drill pilot holes through the patch plates and wood filler. The patch plates and wood filler are then bonded to the panel using the specified adhesive. Next, locate the metal filler and drill pilot holes through both patch plates and the wood filler.

All pilot holes are then size-drilled and machine- or press-countersunk, as applicable. Complete the repair by installing the specified rivets. See Figure 5-2-21.

When aerodynamic smoothness is not desired, a non-flush patch can be used. Notice that this type of repair uses two patch plates, a wood filler and non-flush rivets. Otherwise, the procedures described for the repair shown in Figure 5-2-22 are applicable to this type of repair.

Repairing the Trailing Edge of an Airfoil

A trailing edge is the rearmost edge of an airfoil (wing, flap, rudder, elevator, etc.). It might be a formed or machined metal strip, or possibly a metal-covered honeycomb or balsa wood core material that forms the shape of the edge by tying the ends of a rib section together and joining the upper and lower skins. These trailing edges are very easily damaged. The majority of this type of damage can be avoided if care is taken when moving aircraft in confined spaces and/or when positioning ground support equipment around parked aircraft.

A typical trailing edge repair to a sandwich construction assembly is shown in Figure 5-2-23.

You may use the lap or flush patch, depending on the size of the damage, the type of aircraft and the assembly or control surface to be repaired. Normally, the flush patch is used on control surfaces to ensure aerodynamic smoothness.

DAMAGE

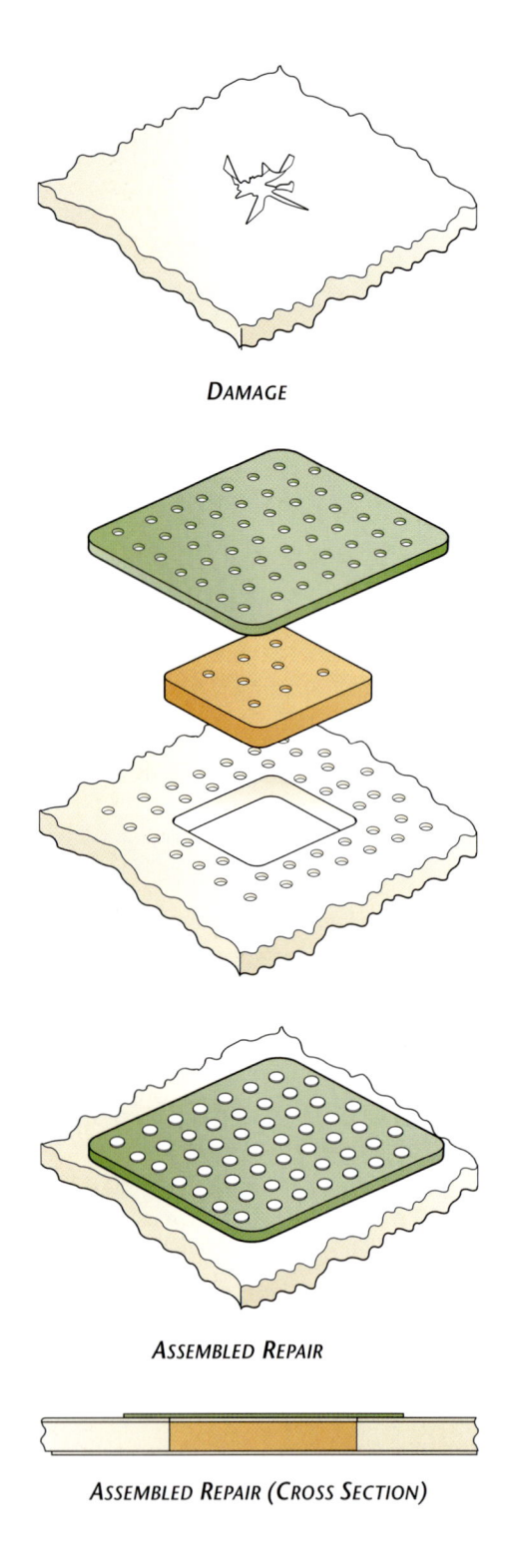

ASSEMBLED REPAIR

ASSEMBLED REPAIR (CROSS SECTION)

Figure 5-2-22. Balsa wood repair with non-flush patch

cut out, cut back the inner metal face 1 inch and remove the core material.

Inspect for adhesion of the face to the core, and seal the exposed filler material to prevent the entry of moisture. Lay out the required

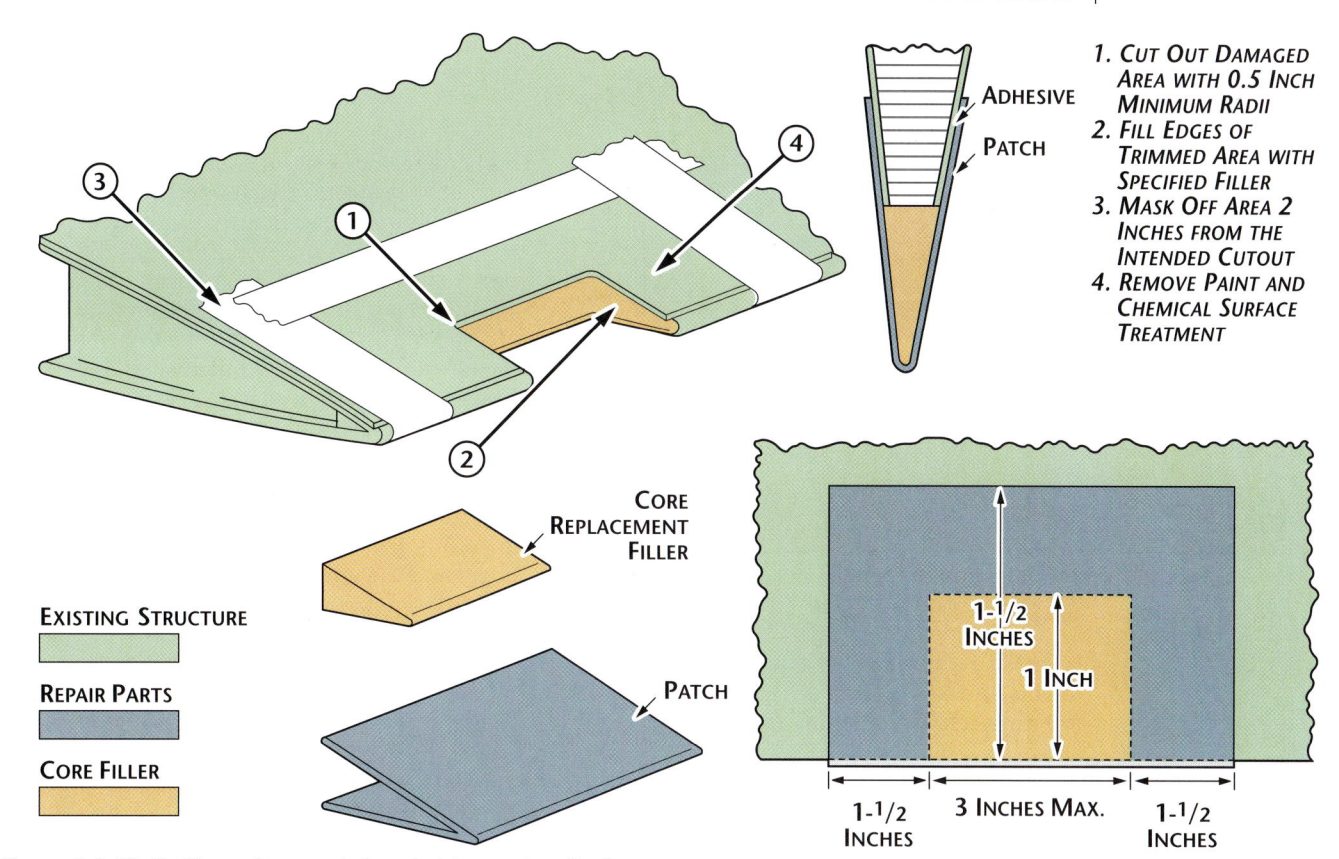

Figure 5-2-23. Trailing edge repair (sandwich construction)

Section 3
Advanced Composites

Advanced Composite Structures

The increasing costs of production, and the cost to fabricate high strength-to-weight metallic components necessitated the development of new materials to meet the demands of aerospace technology. These materials are called *advanced composites* and are replacing some of the metals currently used in aircraft construction.

Advanced composites are materials consisting of a combination of high-strength stiff fibers embedded in a common matrix (binder) material, generally laminated with plies arranged in various directions to give the structure strength and stiffness.

The much stiffer fibers of boron, carbon (graphite) and Kevlar have given composite materials structural properties superior in strength to the metal alloys they have replaced. Specific applications of advanced composite materials and approximate percentages of total aircraft structures for some of our modern-day aircraft are shown in Table 5-3-1.

Composites are attractive structural materials because they provide a high strength-to-weight ratio and offer design flexibility. The function of a composite is to replace heavy/dense metals with stronger, lighter-weight structural components, allowing lightweight aircraft to carry payloads farther distances using less fuel. In contrast to traditional construction materials, these materials can be adjusted to more efficiently match the requirements of specific applications. Figure 5-3-1 shows a closeup of the unpainted nose structure of a Hawker Beechcraft Premier business jet that has a fuselage constructed from advanced composites.

These materials are highly susceptible to impact damage, with the extent of damage being visually difficult to determine. A nondestructive inspection (NDI) is required to analyze the extent of damage and effectiveness of repairs.

Composites are classed by the type of reinforcing elements. These elements may be fiber, particle, flake or laminar materials. They are further classified by the composition of the reinforcing materials and by the type of matrix materials.

The primary factors taken into consideration when designing composites are the costs (research and development, production, fuel economy), type of application (load requirements of the structure, adjoining materials, ser-

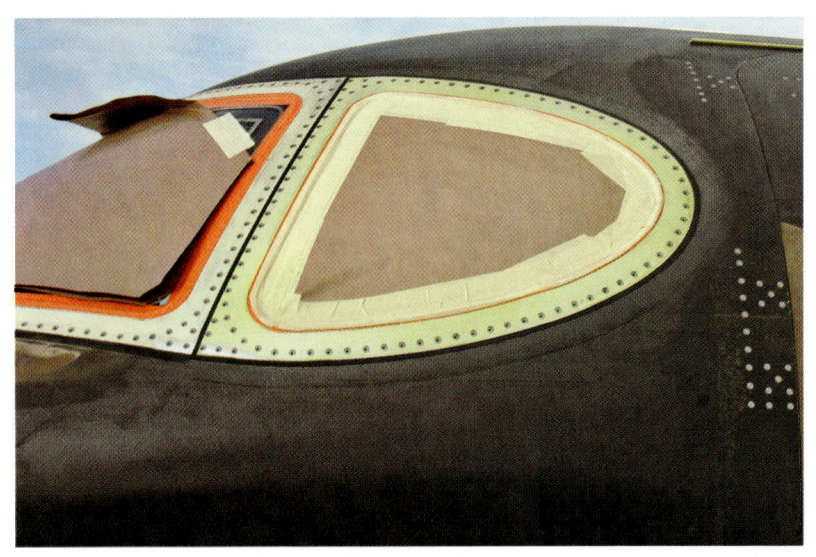

Figure 5-3-1. Unpainted composite nose structure

the fibers, and loads at right angles to the fibers tend to break only the matrix.

The advantages of composites over metals are: higher specific strengths, flexibility in design, ease of manufacturing, lighter-weight materials, easier repair, excellent fatigue and corrosion resistance, fewer use of parts, and production cost reduced. The disadvantages are: higher start-up costs, difficulty of inspection, expense of materials, many of the materials require refrigeration and have limited shelf lives, curing often requires heat and special equipment, poor impact resistance, sensitivity to chemicals and solvents especially paint strippers, susceptibility to environmental attacks, curing often requires heat, and the low conductivity of the materials. *Advanced composites* are made up of fibers and the matrix.

A fiber is a single, homogeneous strand of material, rolled or formed in one direction, and used as the principal constituent in composites. Fibers carry the physical loads and provide most of the strength of composites. Composite materials are made up of many thousands of fibers arranged geometrically, woven or columnated (in columns). The various types of fibrous materials used today are discussed in the following paragraphs.

vice-life requirements), maintenance requirements and operational environment (hot/cold weather, relative humidity and altitude).

Composites and metals used in aircraft structures have almost the same mechanical strengths. These strengths are generally equal in all directions. Stresses and strains are equally transmitted in all directions. Composites can have different physical and mechanical strengths in different directions, and are considered to be *anisotropic* (different strengths when measured in different directions) or *quasi-isotropic* (same strength in different directions). These strengths are determined by the fiber orientation patterns. The patterns are unidirectional, bidirectional or quasi-isotropic. Maximum strength is parallel to

Boron Fibers

Boron was developed in 1959. Boron fibers are made by using a 0.0005 inch tungsten filament, heated to about 2,200°F and drawn through a gaseous mixture of hydrogen and boron tri-

AIRCRAFT	ADVANCED COMPOSITE APPLICATION*	PERCENTAGE USED
Boeing 747	CFRP - winglets, main deck floor panels graphite/phenolic & kevlar/graphite - cabin fittings, engine nacelles	
Boeing 757/767	CFRP -Landing Gear Doors, Rudder, Elevators, Fan Cowls, Spoilers, Floor Panels AFRP -Wing LE Panels, Nacelle Strut Fairings, Stabilizer Tips	
Boeing 777	CFRP - rudder, elevators, ailerons, flaps, nacelles, landing gear doors GFRP -wing LE, tail and fin panels, wing aft panels, engine pylon fairings, radome Carbon/resin-tailplane skins, cabin floor beams	10% of structural weight is composites
Airbus A319/A320	CFRP - spoilers, landing gear doors, cowling panels, elevators, fin box, tailplane, flaps, ailerons, rudder AFRP -belly skins, pylon fairings, radome GFRP - fin LE, fin/fuselage fairing, some upper wing skins, fin & wing tips	
Airbus A330/A340	CFRP -flaps, ailerons, spoilers, LE/TE panels, winglets, fin, tailplane	13% of wing structure is composites
Beechcraft Premier	CFRP -entire fuselage structure, tailplane graphite/epoxy -ailerons, flaps	100% of fuselage structure is composites
*CFRP-Carbon Fiber Reinforced Plastic, AFRP-Aramid Fiber Reinforced Plastic, GFRP-Glass Fiber Reinforced Plastic		

Table 5-3-1. Aircraft advanced composite application usage

chloride. A coating of black boron is deposited over the tungsten filament. The resulting fiber is about 0.004 inch in diameter, has excellent compressive strength and stiffness, and is extremely hard.

Carbon (Graphite) Fibers

High-strength carbon fibers were not developed until the early 1970s. Fibers of carbon are produced by *graphitizing* filaments of rayon or other polymers in a high-temperature furnace. The fibers are stretched to a high tension while slowly being heated through a stabilization process at 475°F in ambient air. The fibers are carbonized at 2,700°F in an inert, oxygen-rich atmosphere, and the graphitization process takes place at 5,400°F in an inert atmosphere. Then the carbon fibers are subjected to a treatment process that involves cooling and cleaning the carbon dust particles to improve the inter-laminar shear properties. These shear properties relate to the shear strength between adjacent plies of laminate. The resulting fibers are black in color and only a few microns in diameter. They are strong, stiff and brittle; through control of the process, graphite of higher tensile strength can be produced at the cost of lower stiffness. Aircraft parts are generally produced with fibers of intermediate strength and stiffness.

Carbon and graphite fabric are the same thing, it just has two different names. Carbon is the preferred one, but many manuals and catalogs will use the names interchangeably. Carbon fiber (Figure 5-3-2) is a stiff, black fabric that is very good for primary structural applications. It has a good compressive strength, is highly rigid when in a matrix and has a high fatigue resistance. Because it is carbon, it is conductive and requires lightening protection.

Because carbon is corrosive to aluminum it is often used with titanium in the build process. In areas where it is used with aluminum, the SRM should outline special corrosion-resistance treatments any time the two are in contact.

Ceramic Fibers

Use of ceramic fibers, though not common, is increasing. Because ceramic fibers have a very high heat resistance, they can be used in areas of up to 2,200°F. Ceramic composite materials (Figure 5-3-3) are popular for firewalls and are very popular with the home-built market.

Kevlar® Fibers

Kevlar® fibers are a registered trademark of DuPont, which maintains exclusive production rights for the fibers. Structural grade

Figure 5-3-2. Carbon Fiber

Figure 5-3-3. Ceramic Fiber

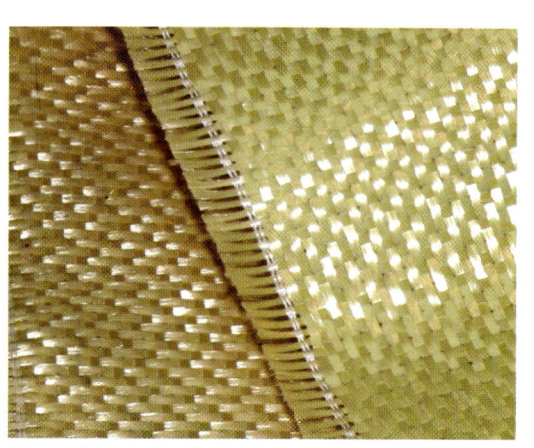

Figure 5-3-4. Kevlar fabric

Kevlar fiber is characterized by excellent tensile strength and toughness, but it has inferior compressive strength when compared to graphite. The stiffness, density and cost of Kevlar® are all lower than graphite; hence, Kevlar® may be found in many secondary structures, replacing fiberglass or as a hybrid with fiberglass. The fibers are golden yellow in color and measure 0.00047 inch in diameter. Figure 5-3-4 is an example of Kevlar® fabric.

Kevlar® has caught the public's fancy because of its use in bulletproof vests. However,

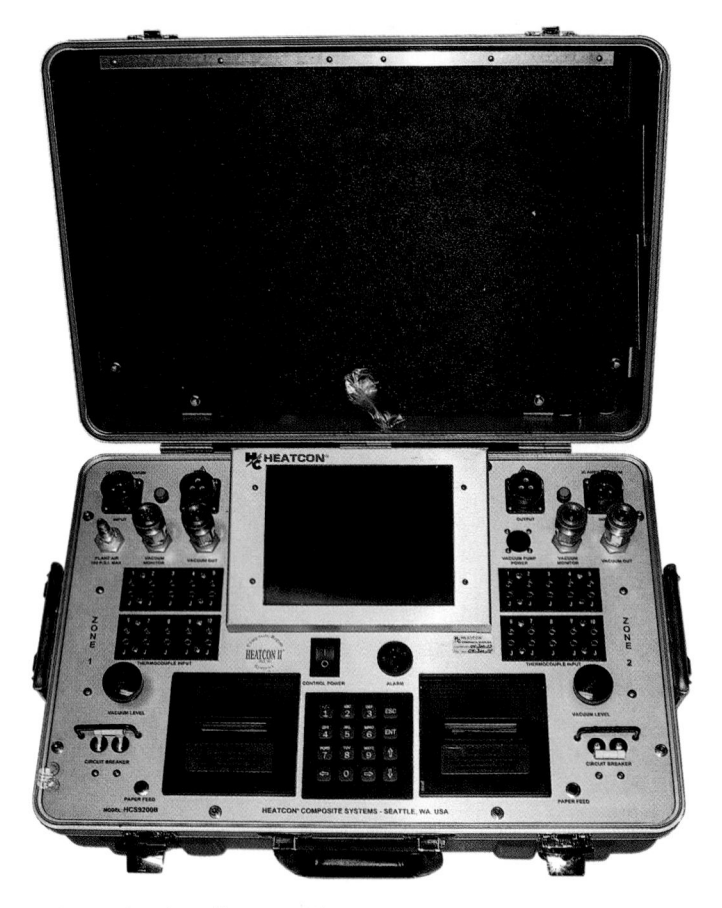

Figure 5-3-5. A hot bonding machine

Kevlar® is made in a wide variety of weaves, and only one is bulletproof.

Kevlar® can be made into a part that is as strong as metal but only a fraction of its weight. It is also extremely strong and flexible. It has a high tensile strength and can stretch a considerable amount before it breaks. The stretching ability can cause problems in fabrication.

Trying to cut Kevlar® is a special problem. It takes special scissors designed for the job. Don't even try to use regular shears. The stretching also causes a drill to catch and pull a fiber instead of cutting it. This results in rough, fuzzy holes that can absorb moisture. The moisture will cause the matrix to de-laminate and require more repairs.

The answer is to use a brad-point drill made for Arimid fabric. It looks similar to a brad-point drill made for wood, but it is not the same. The special drills are available from most aircraft tool suppliers.

Matrix (Resin)

Although the fibers are the principal load-carrying material, no structure could be made without the *matrix*. The matrix is a homogeneous resin that, when cured, forms the *binder* that holds the fibers together and transfers the load to the fibers.

The most common matrix material in current use is *epoxy*. Epoxies provide high mechanical and fatigue strength, excellent dimensional stability, corrosion resistance and *inter-laminar* (between two or more plies) bond, good electrical properties and very low water absorption. The changing of the matrix properties (hardening) by a chemical reaction is called the *cure*. Curing is usually accomplished with heat and vacuum pressure. The finished product may be a single-ply (*lamina*) or a multi-ply product called a *laminate*. The process is called *hot bonding* and is the method of choice.

Hot Bonding Repairs

Hot bonding is a process that allows the technician to actually control the bonding and curing process. By applying a controlled amount of heat under pressure, the cure of an advanced composite repair can be speeded up. Heat lamps, hot sand bags and some other methods of applying heat cannot be controlled. Because you cannot control the heat, you cannot control the cure.

Hot bonding machines (Figure 5-3-5) fix these problems by using a heat blanket that allows full control of the process. Heat blankets are a common method used to apply heat for repairs in the field. Heat is transferred from the blanket via conduction. Consequently, the heat blanket must conform to and be in 100 percent contact with the part. Lack of contact between the heat blanket and the area to be cured will result in inadequate heating of the repair area and an overheating of the heat blanket.

With built-in programs and timers, heat can be applied slowly at first, then increased in a programmed ramp-up. Once the desired amount of heat is obtained, it can be held there while the cure progresses. At the proper time, the program will start a gradual reduction in heat until the process is complete. Figure 5-3-6 shows a heat blanket applied over a small repair sample.

Heat Blanket Inspections:

1. Inspect the blanket's wires, connectors, for loose or frayed wires and pad for silicone cracking.

2. Ensure all areas of the heating pad are working. It is possible for a defective heating pad to heat one side and be cool on another.

Blanket Guidelines:

1. Ensure the heat blanket overlaps the repair areas by a minimum of 2 inches

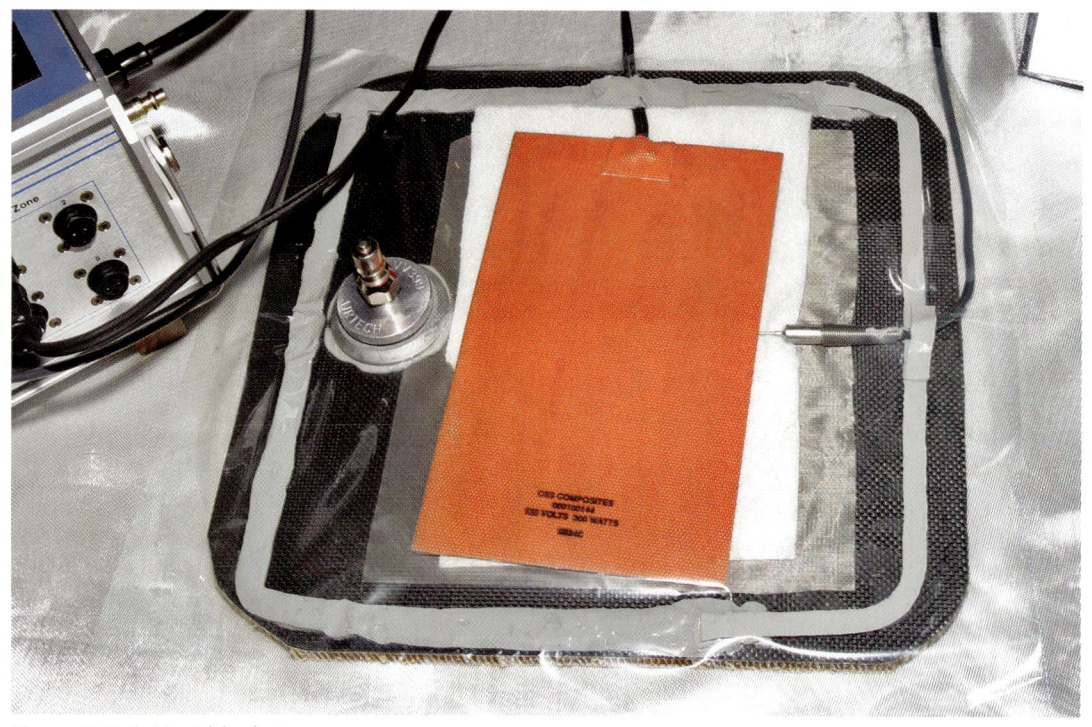

Figure 5-3-6. Heat blanket

on each side of the repair. This is necessary as temperatures on the edges of the heat blanket, can be as much as 50°F cooler than the rest of the heat blanket. For structures thicker than 0.100 inch, an overlap greater than 2 inches may be needed. A thermal survey should be performed to ensure adequate heating in all cases.

2. Hot or cold spots caused by uneven heating within the heat blanket can be corrected by placing a thin copper or aluminum sheet under the heat blanket known as a Caul Plate. The sheet metal will aid in conducting the heat more evenly. The sheet metal must match the contour of the part being repaired. Annealed metal is preferred.

3. When using blankets in a hazardous environment, such as areas where fuel is preset, personnel shall use heat blankets designed for these areas. These blankets often have a secondary safety device that ensures the heat blanket does not reach the auto-ignition temperature of aviation fuel.

4. Do not use heat blankets on components that have a radius smaller than 0.5 inch, as forming the blanket around too tight a radius could damage the heating elements.

5. Do not fold, crush or pinch the blankets. Always store the blankets flat or loosely rolled when not in use to avoid damage to the blankets heating elements.

Figure 5-3-7. Curing oven

Curing Oven

Composite material can be cured in ovens using various pressure application methods. Vacuum bagging can be used to remove volatiles and trapped air, and utilize atmospheric pressure for consolidation. Curing ovens are typically outfitted with vacuum outlets to supply vacuum pressure during the cure. The oven temperature is controlled by an oven controller that can be programmed to run a cure recipe. The oven controller will use an oven air sensor or can use thermocouples placed on the part to control the part temperature. Figure 5-3-7 shows a walk in curing oven with vacuum.

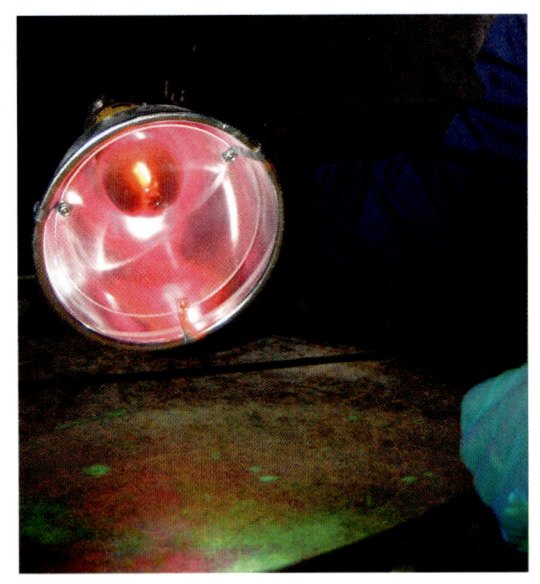

Figure 5-3-8. Heat lamp

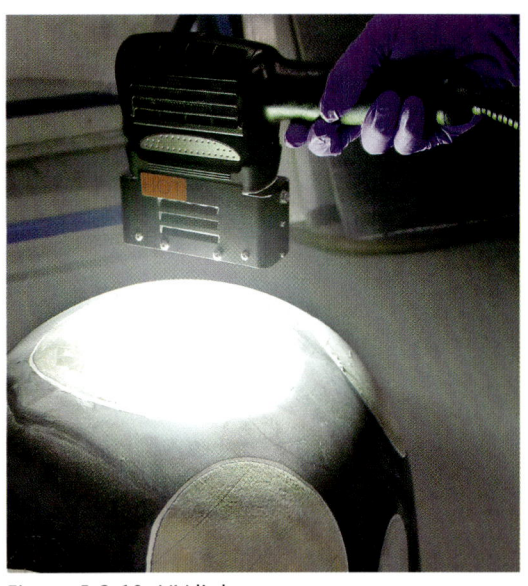

Figure 5-3-10. UV light

Heat Lamps

In field repairs Infrared heat lamps are also used for curing of composites if a vacuum bag is not utilized. The downside is they are generally not effective for producing curing temperatures above 150°F or for areas larger than 2 square feet. It is also difficult to control the heat applied with a lamp, and lamps tend to generate high-surface temperatures quickly. If controlled by thermostats, heat lamps can be useful in applying curing heat to large or irregular surfaces. Figure 5-3-8 pictures a heat lamp being used during a dye-penetrant inspection.

Hot Air Units (HAM)

HAM units (Figure 5-3-9) are generally used to heat large areas of any contour or material. HAMs will supply controlled heat to over 900°F. HAMs lend themselves very well to heating and curing of materials that require noncontact such as paints and coatings. When using hot air for curing of composite laminates, care should be taken to not insulate the repair by using excessive breather materials.

Heat Guns

Heat guns that are thermostatically controlled can be used to cure small areas. Most heat guns will supply air in the temperature range of 130 to 500°F. Heat guns are useful for warming materials but overheating of an area must be avoided, as it will cause the resin to bubble. Keeping the proper distance away from material to heated is necessary.

UV curing

UV curing typically uses UVA light (320-400 nm) or short wave visible light (blue 400-450 nm). UV cured materials contain what is known as photo initiators that starts the curing reaction when exposed to a specific wavelength of light. The intensity of the UV light can also be affected by distance, intensity decreases as the distance increases for both spot lamps and flood lamps. Depth of Cure is typically about 1/2" to 3/4" with special formulas capable of curing up to the depth of 1". Once the material changes from a liquid to a solid, it is considered cured. Advantages of UV cure are that it is very fast and easy to accomplish. The disadvantages are that it

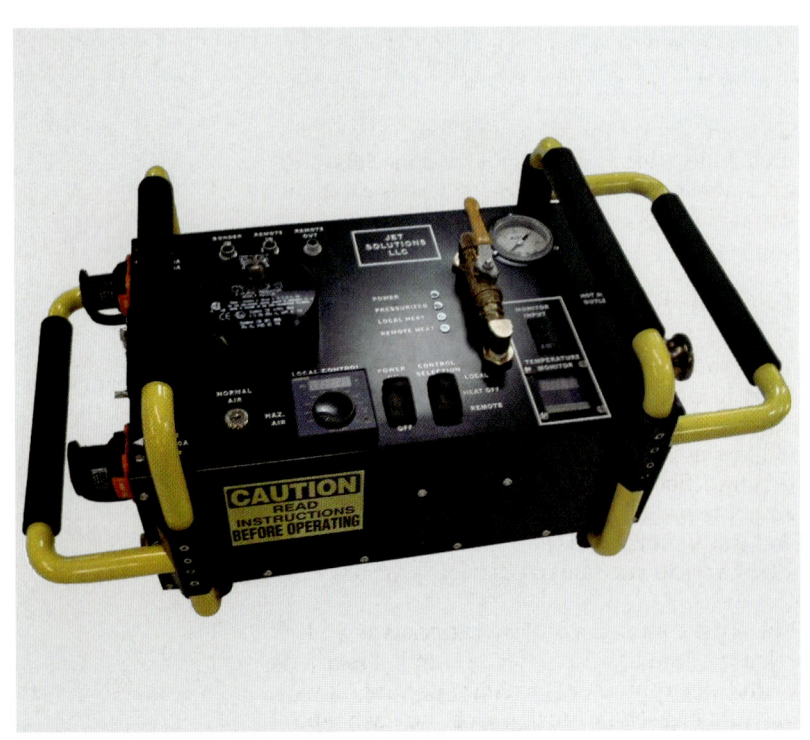

Figure 5-3-9. Hot-air unit (HAM) *Courtesy of Jet Solutions, LLC*

can only be used with fiberglass, as it does not work with carbon fiber materials. Figure 5-3-10 shows a composite repair being cured with a UV light.

Hot bonding machines are so superior to any other curing method, for field work, that they have become the standard for composite repair curing. However, they are only one part of a system of curing composite repairs. The items that are critical to the integrity of the cured repair are:

- Resin quantity
- Fiber contact
- Vacuum pressure
- Excess resin removal
- Applied heat

Resin quantity. A good repair must not be rich in resin; that is, it must not have a large amount of excess resin. When the fibers are correctly orientated, encapsulated in the correct amount of resin and in close contact, a good repair will result. Applied loads will be transferred from fiber to fiber to structure in the correct manner. If there is too much resin there is a possibility that, under load, the resin will crack before the proper amount of pressure is transferred to the next fiber. Remember, the strength is in the fibers, not the resin. The resin is only there to form the matrix.

Fiber contact. Correct fiber contact while the matrix is curing is the most important part of the process. It is almost impossible to obtain without outside pressure. Many types of set-ups were devised over the years in an attempt to apply pressure with clamps. Put simply, mechanical pressure just doesn't work.

What does work is *vacuum pressure*. Called *vacuum bagging* or simply *bagging*, a sheet of flexible film is placed over the repair. When vacuum power is applied, the film will suck down tight over the repair. Because the film conforms to the shape of the repair, even pressure is applied.

Excess resin removal. Obviously, with a repair sealed inside a plastic bag there needs to be a way to remove the excess resin. There are a couple of different ways. One is a coil spring that is laid around the repair, under the bag. A drain tube is connected to a vacuum source and then to the spring. As the pressure squeezes the excess resin out of the repair, it is collected in the area inside the spring and sucked away from the repair by a plastic tube. Figure 5-3-11 shows this method.

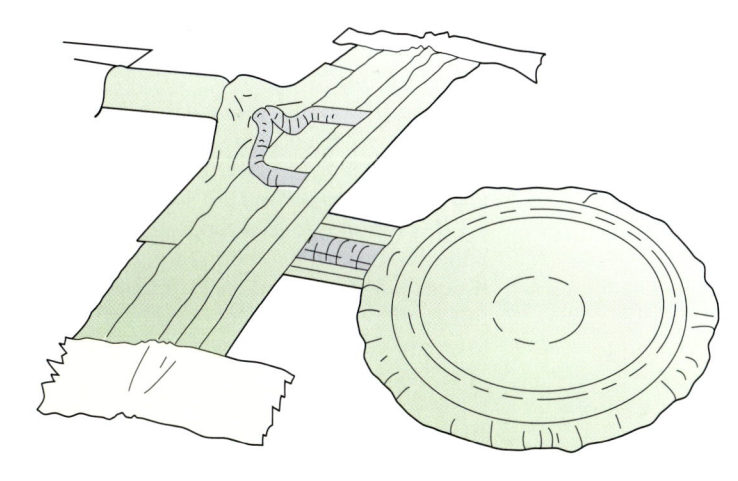

Figure 5-3-11. Resin being collected by a spring laid under the film on a bagged repair

Vacuum Bagging Process

The following is provided to assist in understanding how to design and build a typical vacuum bag used to cure a composite repair. This information is provided for informational purposes only. All repair lay-ups, vacuum bagging materials and procedures should be accomplished in accordance with the original equipment manufacturer's (OEM's) Structural Repair Manual (SRM) or other approved data.

NOTE: *To prevent vacuum bag failure and possible damage to structures, always consult the original equipment manufacturer's structural repair manual or material supplier's technical data sheets for specifications and capabilities of any materials used in the vacuum bagging process.*

To correctly perform a repair, the technician must have a broad knowledge of materials and the knowledge of how these materials can and cannot be used.

Vacuum Bagging Materials

There are many ancillary materials that are used in a vacuum bag cure process. Ancillary materials are those materials that are used to aid and assist the curing process to achieve the required fiber-resin ratio and also provide the ability to produce a patch that bonds to the part and not to other materials. Refer to Figure 5-3-12 for typical vacuum bag lay-up for a cure.

The most common ancillary materials include: release films/fabrics, bleeder and breather cloths, peel-ply fabrics, vacuum bagging films, vacuum bag sealant (tacky) tape and flash tape. Each of these materials is available in various composition, thickness and temperature ranges.

Release films and release fabrics. A release film or fabric is used in direct contact with the resin/adhesive or where control of resin flow is desired. Non-porous (NP) release film/fabric is often referred to as a separator, in that resin/adhesive contact can be made on one side, but it does not pass through. Porous or perforated release films/fabrics allow resin and air to pass through, yet it is easily removed from the part after the cure.

Bleeder and breather materials. Bleeders and breathers may be the same material, but are used in different applications. Both are absorbent, highly porous and are typically made of polyester random mat-type material (often referred to as baby blanket). Breather is used where contact with the resin is not likely, usually between the vacuum bag film and the rest of the bagging materials to provide a chamber for air to be withdrawn from the lay-up. Bleeder is typically placed on top of a porous release film/fabric next to the part so as to allow removal of excess resins, air and volatile gases from the patch. This aids compaction and helps to produce a void-free structure. Some OEMs allow fiberglass fabric to be used for both bleeder and breather applications.

Peel-ply fabrics. Peel-ply materials are fine, open-weave fabrics usually consisting of fiberglass, polyester or nylon construction. Peel-plies are layed-up in direct contact with an uncured part surface ply and cured with the part. Upon completion of the cure, the peel-ply is bonded into the surface resin of the part. The peel-ply is removed from the part immediately prior to secondary bonding, leaving a clean surface that does not require sanding or cleaning prior to bonding.

Vacuum bagging films. Vacuum bagging film comes in many different types, materials, thicknesses and colors. Most common vacuum bagging film is a general-purpose film, which is a green nylon blown film and is suitable for temperatures up to 350°F (176°C). This material will perform satisfactorily in most applications.

Heat blanket. The heat blanket provides the heat source during a vacuum bag cure. The blanket is typically made of silicone rubber with small Nickel-Chromium (NiChrom) wires embedded inside the rubber. These wires will heat due to the resistance of the material when electricity is passed through them. It is a good idea to use a release film/fabric on top and bottom of the heat blanket to protect it from any resins that might get through the lay-up. Cut the material the same size as the heat blanket or wrap the blanket in the material.

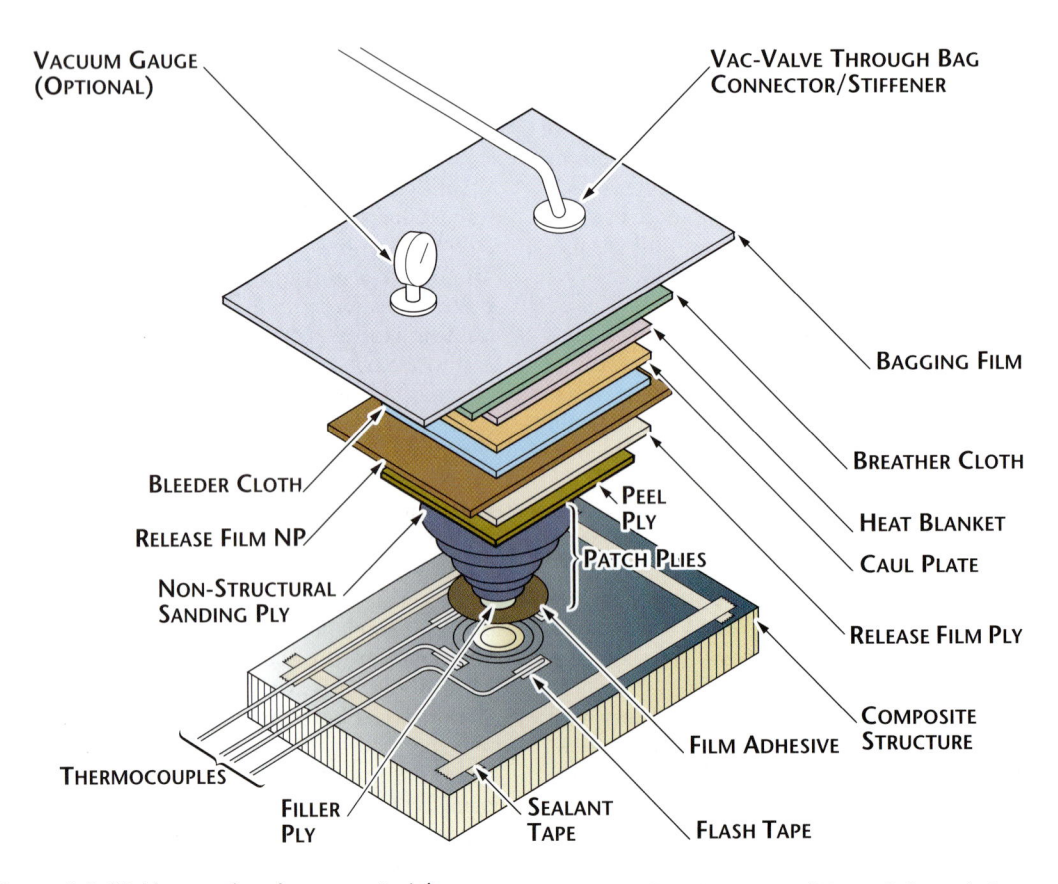

Figure 5-3-12. Vacuum bag lay-up materials. *Illustration courtesy of Heatcon® Composite Systems*

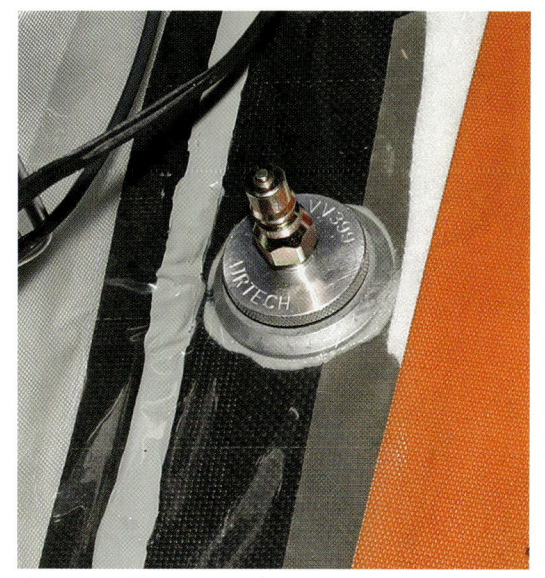

Figure 5-3-13. Vacuum bag connector

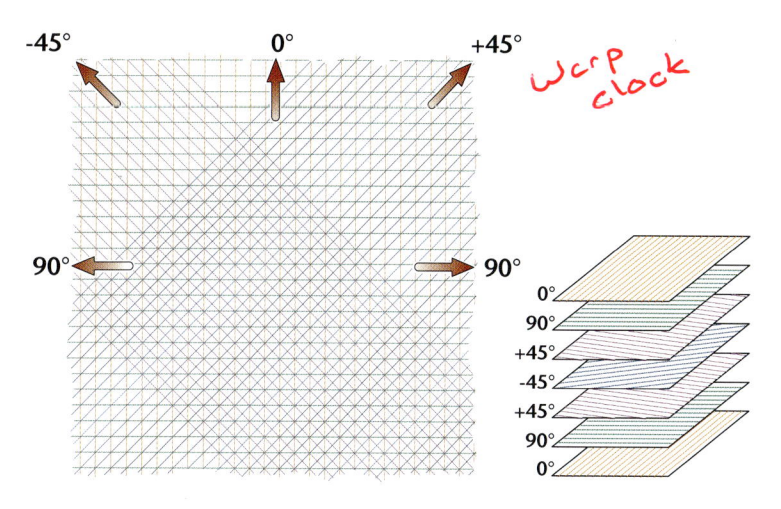

Figure 5-3-14. Standard ply orientation

Vacuum valve through-bag connectors/sniffer. These quick-lock and -unlock connectors provide a method of sealing the vacuum bagging film where the connection between the vacuum bag and the bonder is made. The vacuum valve consists of a base and a top with a check valve that attaches to the vacuum hose from the bonder. A high-temperature rubber gasket provides a vacuum-tight seal with the vacuum valve on the top, the vacuum bag film in the middle, and the base inside the vacuum bag. This seal is necessary to ensure integrity of the bag. Figure 5-3-13 shows a typical vacuum bag connector.

Two vacuum valves should be installed in each vacuum bag. One is connected to the vacuum out port and the other is connected to the vacuum return monitor port on the bonder. If vacuum is provided by a source other than the bonder, only the vacuum monitor port is connected to the bonder. The base should be positioned outside the repair area on top of the breather so that it does not leave an imprint on the repair.

Caul plate. A caul plate is a thin copper, aluminum or composite plate typically between 0.010/0.020 inch (0.254/0.508-mm) thick that is used to evenly distribute temperature and pressure over the repair area. Caul plates may or may not be used in repairs, depending on the contour of the part being repaired and SRM requirements.

Vacuum bag sealant tape. This sealant tape (tacky tape) is used to provide an airtight seal between the part or tool and the vacuum bagging film, thus creating a vacuum chamber, which allows atmospheric pressure (14.7 p.s.i. at sea level) to apply compacting pressure to the repair patch. Vacuum bag sealant tape is a putty-type extruded tape. The tape is typically 25 ft. (3.04 m) long and 1/4 inch (6.35 mm) wide.

Flash tape. Flash tape is a high-temperature Teflon tape that is used inside the vacuum bag to hold thermocouples and bagging materials in place during the vacuum bag lay-up process. It is especially helpful if the repair is not a flat surface, such as on the side of an aircraft or when the repair is overhead.

Laminate

A *lamina* is a single-ply arrangement of unidirectional or woven fibers in a matrix. A lamina is usually referred to as a ply. A laminate is a stack of lamina, or plies, with various in-plane angular orientations bonded together to form a structure. Figure 5-3-14 shows a shop-made compass for determining ply direction, as well as an example of a composite stack with plies in various directions.

Drawings specify ply-stacking angles and the sequence of the lay-up. A standard laminate orientation code is used to ensure standardization in the industry. The orientation code denotes the angle, in degrees, between the fibers and the *X axis* of the part. The X axis is usually spanwise of the part, or in the direction of applied loads. See Figure 5-3-14. The laminate ply orientation, or stacking sequence, is denoted in brackets, with the angle of each ply separated by a slash (/), for example, [+45/-45/+45/-45]. Laminae are listed in sequence from the first lamina to the last. The brackets or parentheses indicate the beginning and the end of a code. The plus (+) and minus (-) angles are relative to the X axis. Plus (+) signs are to

Figure 5-3-15. Delamination

the right of zero, and minus (-) signs are to the left of zero. Adjacent laminae of equal angles but opposite signs are identified as ±, (±45 = +45, -45). The directional strengths and stiffness of the laminate can be altered by changing the ply orientation.

Categories of Composite Material Damage

Advanced composite materials continue to be increasingly popular with designers of new aircraft. It is estimated that new airframes will be 75 to 80 percent composites. As a structural technician, you will be required to maintain these new types of aircraft. To be proficient, you must be able to recognize the types of damage, understand the processes involved in damage assessment, inspection and repair of composite materials. As new materials are introduced, new repair procedures will be required. It will be your responsibility to keep abreast of developments.

Damage to composite materials may be categorized as either *environmental* or *physical*. Environmental damage includes crazing and cracking caused by solar and ultraviolet radiation, water absorbed through humidity and rain, and lightning-strike damage. Lightning strikes can cause holes to be burned in the structure, puncturing and splintering, and it has been known to weld bearings and hinges. Physical damage is caused by an applied force or deficiency in fabrication, such as dents, scratches, cracks, cuts and abrasions, pits, voids, *disbonds, delamination* (Figure 5-3-15), *core crush* on sandwich structures and impact damage.

Assessment of Composite Material Damage

The task of repair begins when you determine that the structure has been damaged and that the damage is sufficient to require repair. The existence of damage may be obvious, such as a skin penetration, a gouge, a crack or a dent. Conversely, the proper identification and classification of the damage may be difficult. Because of the brittle, elastic nature of composite laminate materials, for example, the fibers may break upon impact, but then spring back, leaving little visible indication of damage.

There are four distinct steps involved in damage assessment:

1. Locate the damage. This is usually done by performing an initial visual inspection. Caution must be exercised as non-visible subsurface damage may exist beneath the impact area. Areas suspected of having been impacted should be further evaluated for delamination and cracks beyond the initial visual inspection.

2. Evaluate the defect to determine the defect type, depth and size. This information will be needed in determining the method of repair. Once the damage has been located, the extent of the damage must be determined. The depth of delamination and possible presence of disbonds should be determined in characterizing the damage. Damage to honeycomb core materials should be characterized using radiographic or other techniques. Understanding the extent of damage and

characterizing the damage is an important part of the assessment process. This evaluation will have a direct bearing on the repair procedures to be used.

3. After the damage assessment has been accomplished, the repair zone in which the damage is located needs to be determined by using the part specific Structural Repair Manual (SRM). Overlapping damage from one repair zone to another requires the damage limits for the most severely damaged zone to be used. If the damage limits are exceeded for any zone, engineering support is needed from aircraft manufacturer. Any damage assessed to be in a non-repairable zone, must be removed and replaced with a new part.

4. Following damage removal, a re-inspection of the damage area needs to be accomplished to ensure all the damage was removed. Current NDI methods used to detect subsurface delamination are capable of only finding the first delamination nearest the surface on which the probe was applied. Delamination may be masked that may have occurred deeper in the material therefore it is necessary to re-inspect the area to ensure no delamination remains below the originally defined damage.

Damage Inspection Methods

There are many methods available for locating and evaluating the damage. Some of the inspection methods to be discussed are:

- Visual inspection
- Tap test
- X-ray
- Ultrasonic inspection

Visual inspections. Visual inspections are a methodical search for defects, checking for obvious damages. A visual inspection is the most common type of inspection method for metallic and composite aircraft structures. Be suspicious of any scorch, stain, dent, penetrate, abrade, or chip in the composite surface. If there is a suspicion of underlying damage, the paint or protective coating should be removed from area and shine a strong light through the structure to illuminate possible damage.

Flashlights, magnifying glasses, mirrors, and bore scopes are commonly used in the visual inspection of composites. These tools help magnify defects which otherwise might not be seen easily and allow access of areas that are not readily accessible. Shining a flash light under an angle through the composite is a great aid in finding damage. Many types of defects, such as impact damage, corrosion and de-lamination, cannot be detected by visual inspection alone.

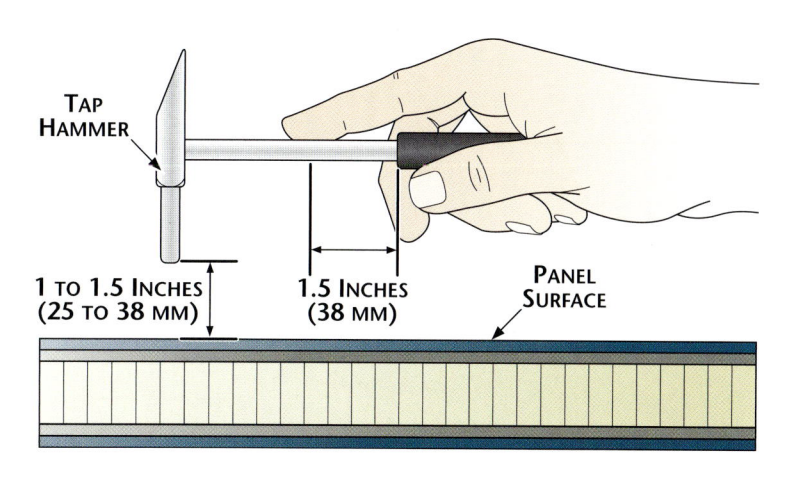

Figure 5-3-16. Tap test

Tap testing. A tap test (Figure 5-3-16) is used in conjunction with a visual inspection, and is an elementary approach to locating de-laminations, dis-bonds, core damage, water or corrosion. Tapping should be done with a small hammer about the weight of a U.S. 50-cent coin. An acoustically flat or dull response is considered unacceptable. A dull sound is a good indication that some delamination or dis-bond exists. A clear sharp tapping sound should be double checked especially in thicker panels. The acoustic response vary dramatically with changes in thickness and geometry of the part, therefore, the thickness and geometry must be known before performing the tap test. Questionable results can be compared to a tap test of other like parts which are known to be good or use another inspection method. The entire area of concern should be tapped in order to map the damage. Tap testing is limited to finding defects close to the surface, and is ineffective in areas of sharp contours and changes in shape.

X-ray inspections. X-ray inspections use the same basic process as a dentist uses to X-ray teeth. The penetrating power of the radiation is used to reveal the interior of objects and to record it on film. Defects in material essentially change the thickness of the material, thus changing the degree of absorption of radiation. More radiation passes through the thinner area of a part, and shows up as a darkened area on the developed film.

Adjusting the radiation intensity, focusing the area to be x-rayed, and exposure times are critical to the outcome of the inspection results. Highly specialized skills are required to set up x-ray tests and to properly interpret test results. As in all NDT inspections, interpretation of the

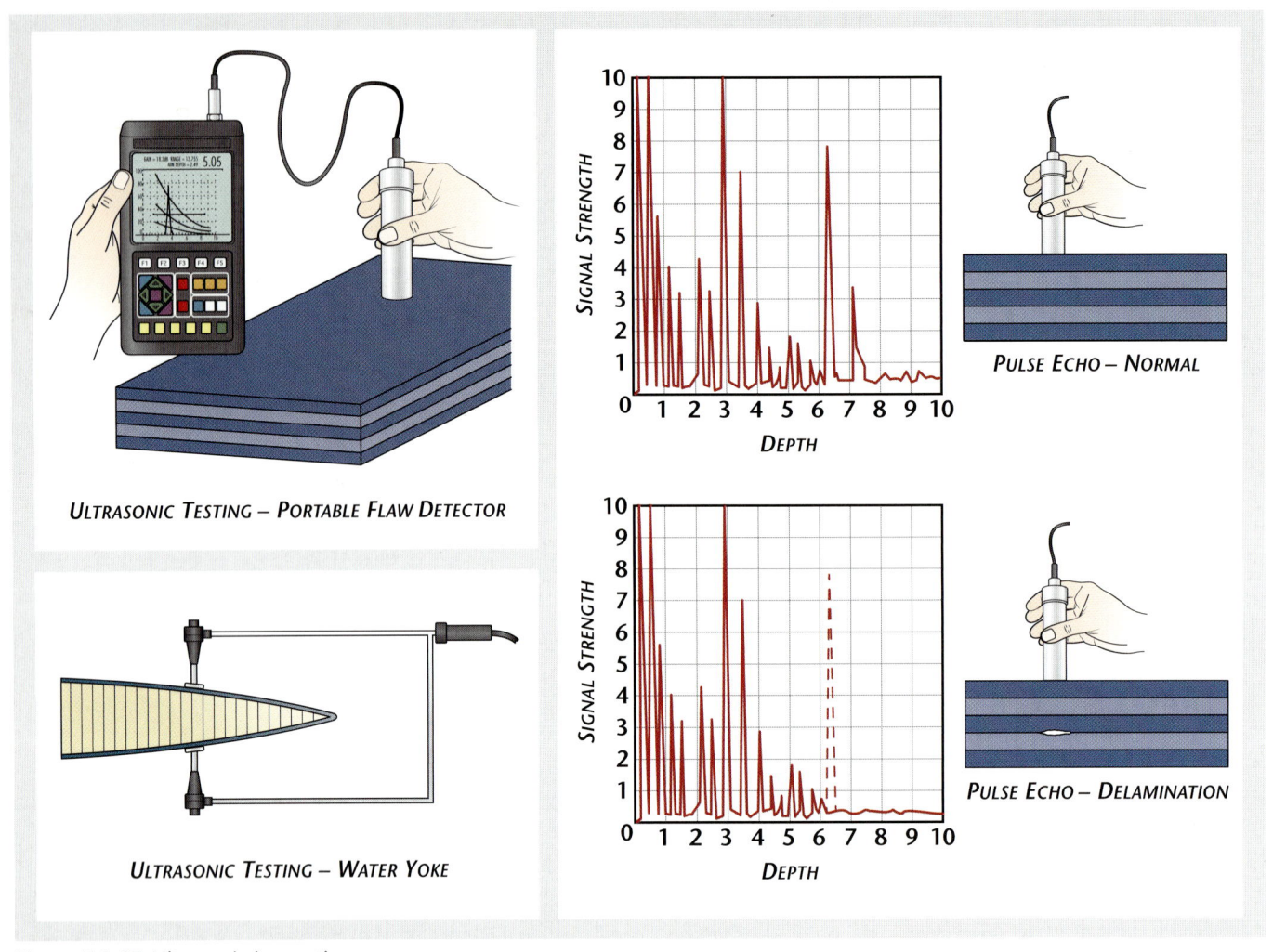

Figure 5-3-17. Ultrasonic inspection

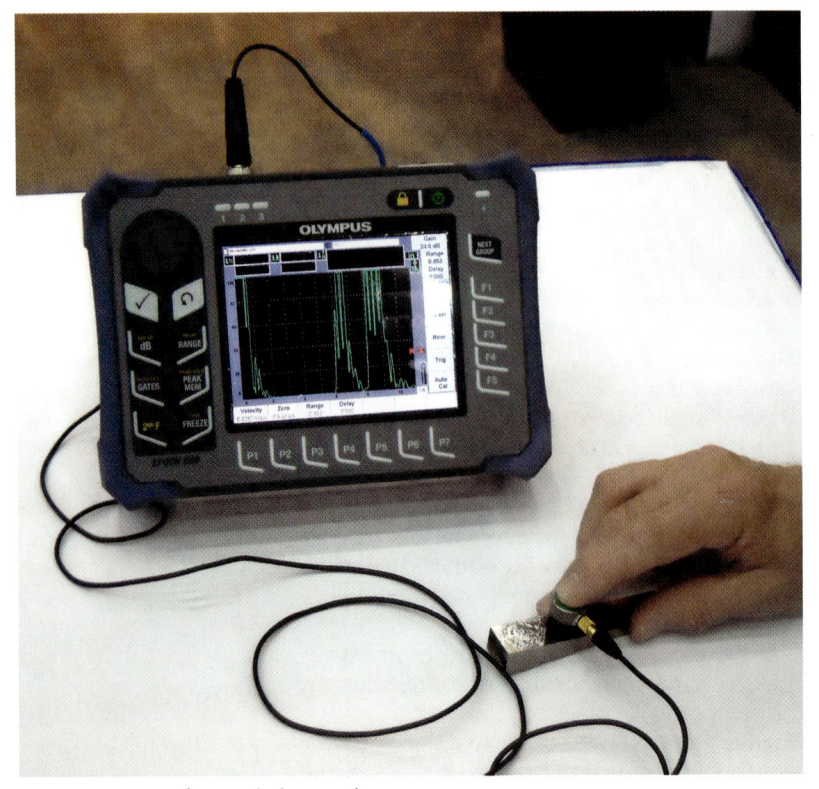

Figure 5-3-18. Ultrasonic inspection

results is the most critical portion. X-ray involves equipment that is high in cost and radiation may pose a safety hazard to personnel. X-ray methods are more practical for small parts that can be brought to a fixed facility. They are least practical for large, complex structures that require on-site inspection because of safety concerns with scattered radiation leakage. X-ray technicians should always be protected by sufficient lead shields. Maintaining a minimum safe distance from the X-ray source is always essential.

Ultrasonic inspections. Ultrasonic inspection (Figure 5-3-17) has proven to be one of the best methods for detecting de-laminations, voids, or inconsistencies in composite components not otherwise discernible using visual or tap inspection methods. Ultrasonic testing uses sound wave energy with a frequency above the audible range. A high frequency sound wave is introduced into the part and directed to travel along the surface of the part, or at some predefined angle to the part surface. Different directions are used as the damage may not be visible only from one direction. The sound is then monitored as it travels through the part for any significant change in sound or frequency.

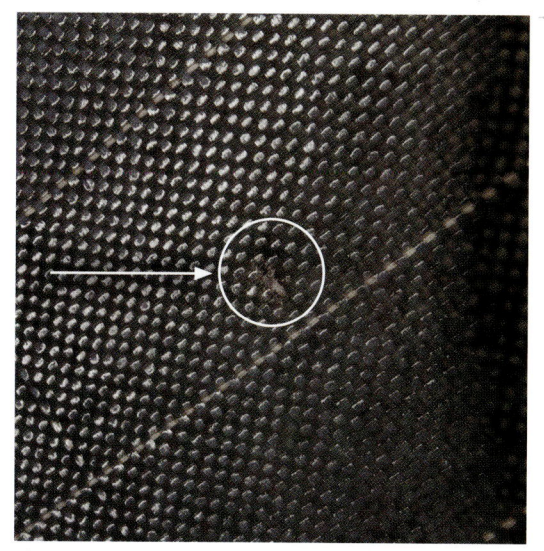

Figure 5-3-19. Negligible damage

Figure 5-3-20. Non-repairable damage

When an ultrasonic wave strikes a flaw within the object, the wave is either absorbed or reflected back to the surface. The disruption in the wave is then picked up by a receiving transducer and converted into a display on an oscilloscope or a chart recorder. The display allows the operator to compare discrepant indications against those from areas that are known to be good. Reference standards are established and utilized to calibrate the ultrasonic equipment.

Handheld miniature ultrasonic devices (Figure 5-3-18) are commonly used in checking repairs made to composite structures in a field environment. These ramp check devices can quickly determine if a repair is airworthy. The normal defects found with these are voids in the bond line of the repair. Some of these devices are used simply as a go no-go indicator.

Repair. All field repairs of composite or bonded assemblies should be accomplished in accordance with instructions outlined in the Structural Repair Manual (SRM). Any damage exceeding the limits of repair specified in the SRM, must be approved by the manufacture or a FAA Designated Engineer Representative (DER) for the repair procedure. It is important that all personnel conducting structural repairs be properly trained and certified in the repair procedure. All engineering instructions and guidelines must be followed to accomplish an approved repair. An incorrectly accomplished repair can often result in a second more extensive and complicated repair.

The first task of any repair is to inspect and evaluate the extent and type of damage to the composite. The objective of the repair is to restore the damaged structure as close as possible original form, strength, stiffness, functionality, performance ability and safety. In other words, the repair will return the structure to original form, fit and function. To start the repair process the components structural design must be known for the appropriate damage classification and repair criteria to be selected.

Damage Classifications

All damage must be classified to determine what repair action should be taken. Ultimately, all discrepancies will be placed into one of three categories:

1. Negligible damage
2. Non-repairable damage
3. Repairable damage

The decision concerning disposition must be made considering the requirements of the aircraft, the particular parts involved, the limitations that can be placed on the repaired aircraft, the degree of urgency and any other circumstances impacting the situation.

Negligible damage. Negligible damage is damage that can be permitted to exist *as is*, or can be corrected by a single cosmetic refinishing procedure with no restrictions on flight operations. This damage may include some de-lamination, disbonds and voids. Figure 5-3-19 shows a minor cosmetic issue in an avionics compartment.

Non-repairable damage. Non-repairable damage exceeds published criteria or established limits. Normally, non-repairable damage requires the changing of components because it has been established that the item is not repairable in the field. This does not, however, mean that the item is not *rebuildable*.

Figure 5-3-20 shows a lower fuselage that was damaged by a landing gear collapse. While not field repairable, a repair may be possible.

Class I Damage
- Cuts, Scratches, Pits, Erosion or Abrasions (Composite Skin)
- Dents (Honeycomb Core)

Class II Damage
- Dents

Class III Damage
- Delamination Between Skin Ply Open to Edge (Composite Skin Plies)

Class IV Damage
- Cuts, Scratches, Cracks, Delaminations, or Skin Erosion

Class V Damage
- Skin Damage, Full Penetration with Honeycomb Core Damage

Class VI Damage
- Skin Damage, Full Penetration of Both Skins with Honeycomb Core Damage

Class VII Damage
- Water in Honeycomb Core

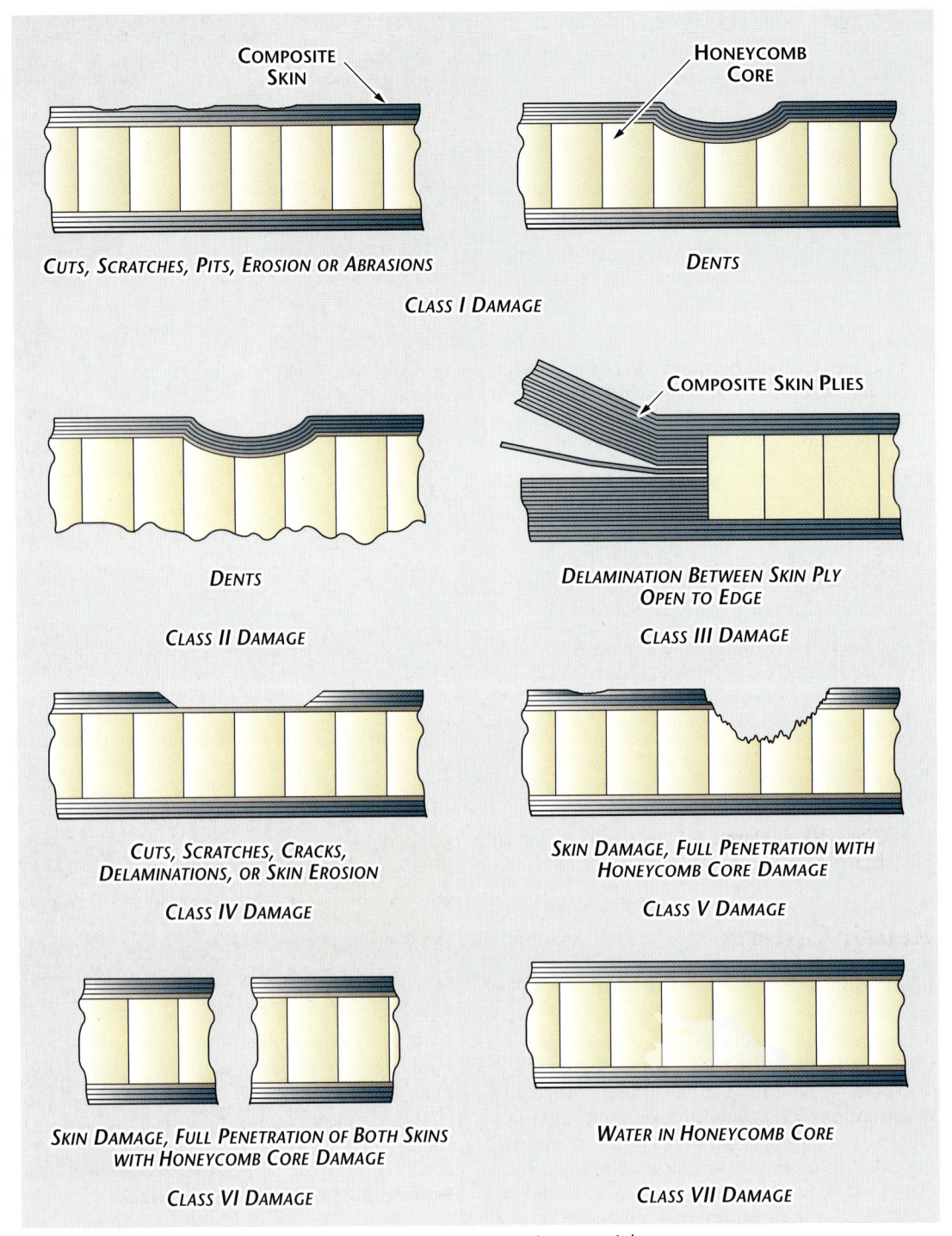

Figure 5-3-21. Examples of repairable damage on composite material

Many times the item can be sent to a certified repair station (CRS). There, major repairs can be undertaken that cannot be accomplished in a shop. Additionally, many Advanced Composite-Rated CRSs are equipped with an autoclave, an item not normal to a repair shop.

Repairable damage. Repairable damage is any damage to the skin, bond or core that cannot be allowed to exist as is without placing performance restrictions on the aircraft. All permanent repairs must be structural, restore load-carrying capabilities, meet aerodynamic smoothness requirements and meet the environmental durability requirements of the aircraft. See Figure 5-3-21.

Repairable damage is divided into several classifications. The SRM provides the approved repair procedures for all levels of maintenance. Information contained in the SRM includes damage classifications, inspection procedures, typical repair procedures and tool and material lists. The examples listed below may vary depending upon the type of aircraft and the specific location of the damage on the aircraft.

- Class I - Cuts, scratches, pits, erosion or abrasions not exceeding 0.005 inch in depth and 5 inches in length
- Class II - Dents in the skin up to 3 inches in diameter and 0.010 inch in depth, with no de-lamination between skin plies, no cracks or graphite fiber breakage, and no skin-to-honeycomb core separation
- Class III - De-lamination between plies, including the skin land area, opened up to external edge and up to 1-1/2 inches in diameter
- Class IV - Skin damage, including delamination, cracks, cuts, scratches or skin erosion exceeding 0.015 inch in depth, but less than full penetration, with no damage to honeycomb core
- Class V - Damage is single skin damage, including full penetration, accompanied by honeycomb core damage. Figure 5-3-22 shows multiple punctures that would be considered class V damage.
- Class VI - Damage to both skins, including full penetration, accompanied by honeycomb core damage. Figure 5-3-23 shows a long crack visible in a skin. This damage included the honeycomb as well the underlying skin making it class VI damage.
- Class VII - Damage is water trapped in honeycomb area

Repair Criteria

Repair criteria differ in the same way that initial design requirements for aircraft differ. Criteria for a repair can be less demanding if the repair is considered to be temporary. Temporary repairs are performed for such requirements as a one-time flight to a repair facility (*ferry permit*). However, most repairs are intended to be permanent and, except for special conditions, criteria are applied so that the repair will remain acceptable for the life of the aircraft. Figure 5-3-24 shows a typical damage flow chart for determining repairability.

One of the major factors that influences the repair quality is the environment where the repairs are to be made. For example, the presence of moisture is critical to bonded repairs. Epoxy resins can absorb 1.5 to 2 times their weight in moisture, thereby reducing the ability of the resins to support the fibers. Dirt and dust can seriously affect bonded repairs. Oils, vapors and solvents prevent good adhesion in bonded surfaces and can lead to voids or delamination. To perform quality repairs, personnel must have a knowledge of the composite system to be repaired, type of damage, damage

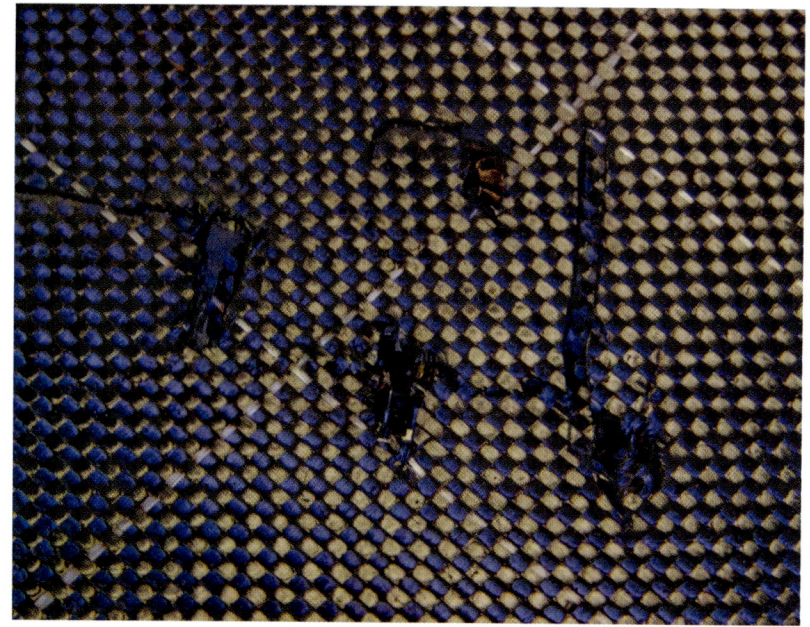

Figure 5-3-22. Class V punctures in carbon fiber

Figure 5-3-23. Carbon fiber skin crack

limitations/ classifications, repair publications, materials, tools and equipment and repair procedures.

The repair facilities where the work is to be performed will be clean and climate-controlled if possible. The relative humidity should be 25 to 60 percent and temperatures stable at 65-75°F.

Strength restoration. Repair manuals for specific aircraft frequently zone the structure to show the amount of strength restoration needed or the kinds of standard repairs that are acceptable. Repair zones help to identify and classify damage by limiting repairs to the

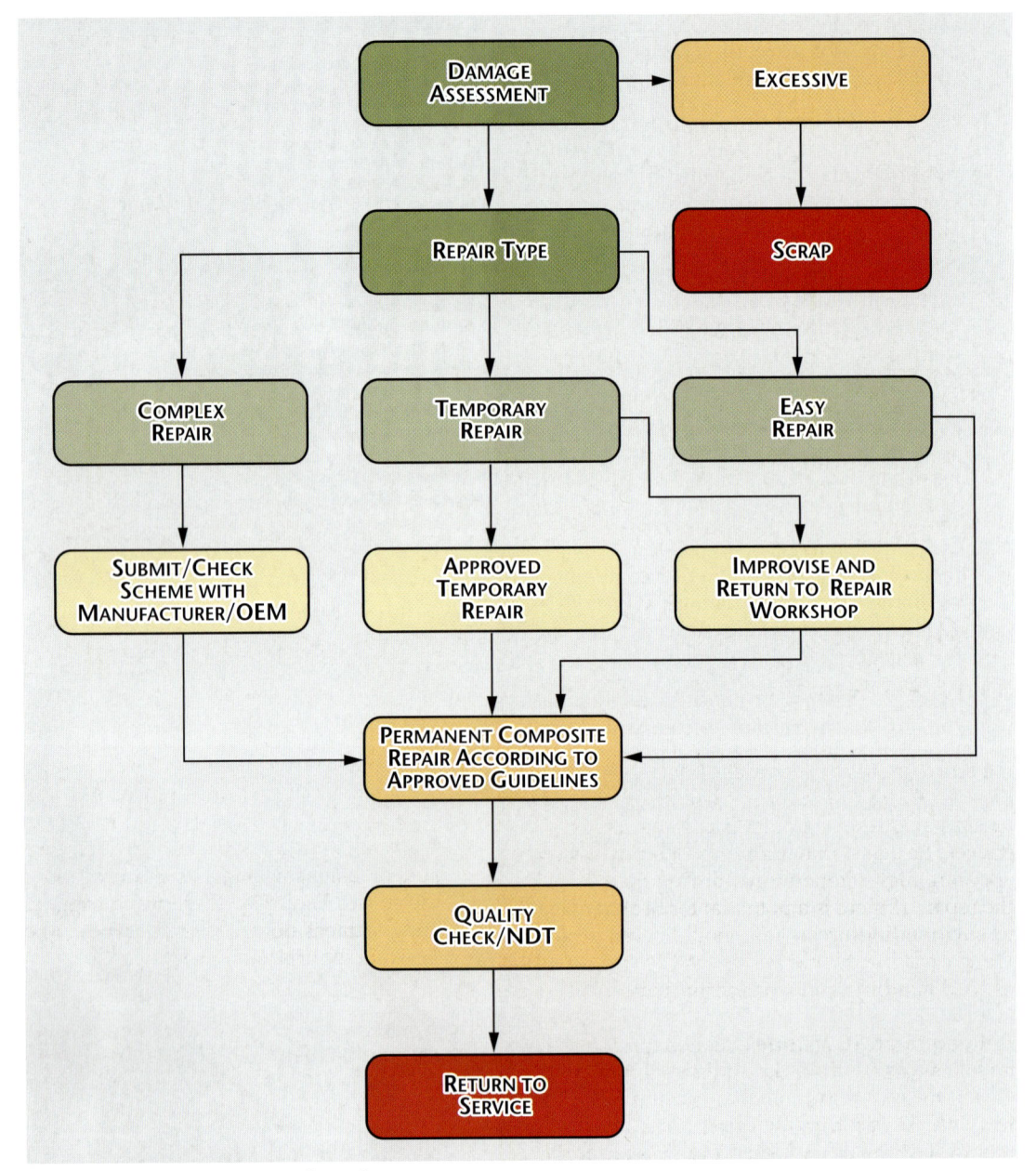

Figure 5-3-24. Aircraft repair flow chart

load-carrying requirements. Repair zone borders indicate changes in load-carrying requirements due to changes in the structure, skin thickness, ply drop-offs, location of supporting members (ribs and spars), ply orientation, core density, size and type of materials. Damage in one zone may be repairable, whereas the same type of damage in an adjacent zone may not be repairable. See Figure 5-3-25. The techniques and practices used on fiberglass structures may result in an un-airworthy repair when used on advanced composites. The instructions in the SRM must be followed carefully in order to restore the original strength and airworthiness to the repair area.

Aerodynamic smoothness. All aircraft depend on smooth external surfaces to minimize drag. During initial fabrication, smoothness requirements are specified, usually by defining zones where different levels of aerodynamic smoothness are required. Most SRM's will specify a smoothness requirement. These most critical zones include leading edges of wings and tails, forward nacelles and inlet areas, forward fuselages and over-wing areas of the fuselage. The least critical zones include trailing edges and aft fuselage areas.

Whatever the SRM requirements, all repairs should restore the aerodynamic contour and structural integrity. Sometimes the repair may cause a slight reduction in performance in order to accept a repair that is more structurally sound and is easier and quicker to accomplish.

Surrounding structure. An important part of the repair criteria is to assure that the surround-

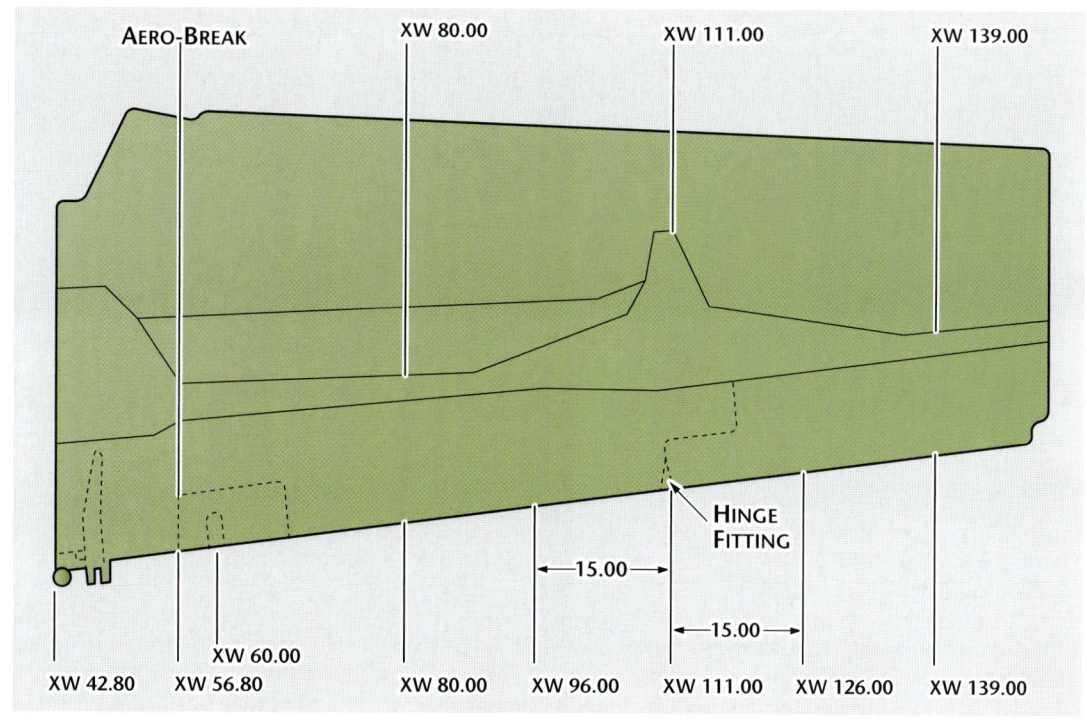

Figure 5-3-25. Repair zones

ing structure to the repair does not sustain any damage. Areas around the repair are often damaged by mishandling of tools causing scratches, gouges, or dents. Attention must be paid when applying high temperatures during the cure of the repair. If there is a potential for heat damage to surrounding areas you should select resins that cure at low temperatures while still capable of good handling and work performance.

Related aircraft systems. Related aircraft systems have to be evaluated in the repair criteria. Complying with structural criteria, compatibility with related aircraft systems may also be required of the repair. Some examples of these systems include:

1. Fuel System. Is the repair material compatible with fuel? Will the repair adequately seal the fuel bay to prevent leakage? Are there structural considerations to the repair in wet wing environments? Will the repair be subjected to fuel pressure loading?

2. Lightning Protection System. Some composite structure has provision for conducting lightning strikes. Does the repair restore the electrical continuity as well as the structural strength? If a bolted repair is used near a fuel tank, it must not provide an electrical path to the fuel.

3. Mechanical Systems. Mechanically actuated components, such as landing gear doors, control surfaces, or entrance and exit doors to the aircraft must function and fit properly after the repair. Clearances and fit to adjacent structures must be checked as they may be critical in operation of the component repaired. Checking the rigging and or balancing may be required after the repair. Figure 5-3-26 shows a baggage compartment door where clearances and fit would be critical.

Figure 5-3-26. Carbon fiber baggage compartment door

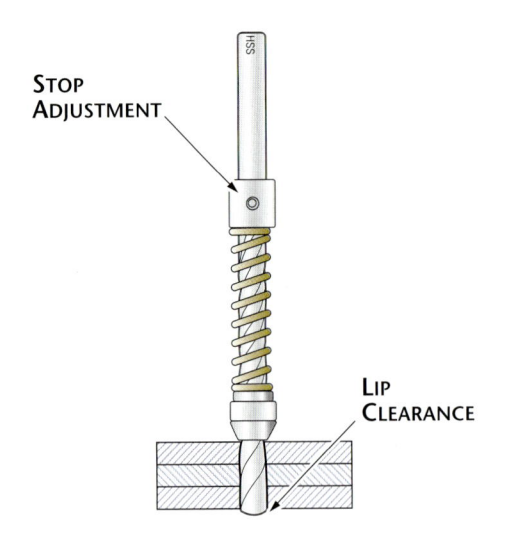

Figure 5-3-27. Drill stop

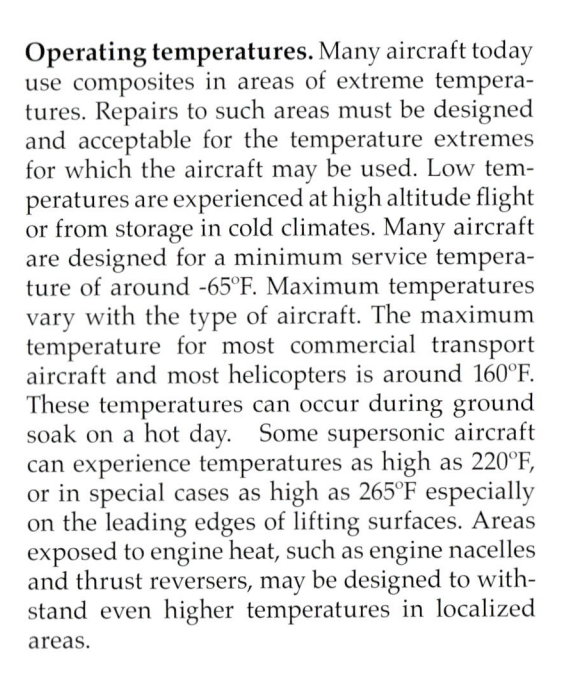

Figure 5-3-28. Router

Operating temperatures. Many aircraft today use composites in areas of extreme temperatures. Repairs to such areas must be designed and acceptable for the temperature extremes for which the aircraft may be used. Low temperatures are experienced at high altitude flight or from storage in cold climates. Many aircraft are designed for a minimum service temperature of around -65°F. Maximum temperatures vary with the type of aircraft. The maximum temperature for most commercial transport aircraft and most helicopters is around 160°F. These temperatures can occur during ground soak on a hot day. Some supersonic aircraft can experience temperatures as high as 220°F, or in special cases as high as 265°F especially on the leading edges of lifting surfaces. Areas exposed to engine heat, such as engine nacelles and thrust reversers, may be designed to withstand even higher temperatures in localized areas.

Operating temperature has a major influence on the repair criteria. Selection of materials that develop adequate strength and durability for the required temperature must be considered during the repair. The combination of temperature extremes with environmental exposure is a critical condition for which the repair must be designed.

Weight and balance. The weight added by most repairs is insignificant. The weight of repair becomes a major concern when the repair is accomplished to components where balance is critical such as moveable control surfaces, rotor blades, and rotating shafts. In such cases, it is of utmost importance to remove as much damaged material as will be added by the repair. This will aid in limiting change in weight and moments of inertia. After repair to any weight critical component the part must be re-balanced after repair.

If large repairs are accomplished to the aircraft structure, the aircraft should have a post maintenance weight and balance performed prior to being returned to service.

Repair tools. Drill motors should be capable of speeds of 2,000-5,000 rpm. These drills should be controlled to prevent backside breakout caused by feeding the drill too fast and excessive heat build-up from feeding the drill too slow. Feed rates should not exceed 30 seconds per inch, with 10-15 seconds per inch producing the best results on graphite-epoxy composites. The drill should be turning full speed prior to surface contact and during withdrawal from completed holes. These holes should be drilled slightly undersize and reamed to the finish size. The various types of drill bits used for drilling composites are either twist, flat fluted/spade/dagger, single flute or piloted countersink, and they are made out of carbide or carbon steel. Cooling of the drill bit is only done after consultation with the SRM. Water is the only type of coolant used and then the area must be dried by applying low temperature heat and vacuum bagging the area to remove all traces of moisture.

A drill stop (Figure 5-3-27) is an adjustable spring damper that is attached to the drill bit shank. This mechanically stops the drill at a predetermined depth prior to exiting the material backside, thus reducing backside breakout caused by the follow through. Firm pressure is required to overcome this spring tension for the drill to penetrate the laminate's backside.

Routers are high-speed, hand-held, portable cutters used for removing damaged skin or core materials. They are designed to operate at speeds of 25,000-40,000 r.p.m. Routers are normally used with a template to define a smooth, regular cut, with the depth of the cut set and locked. An example of a router is pictured in Figure 5-3-28.

Hole saws are good for removing small areas of damage on laminates, although they have a tendency to damage honeycomb rather than cut it. Hole saws also easily clean up damages, providing a good surface for repairs. Backup plates should be taped to the backside of the material being sawed to prevent backside breakout. Fine tooth metal or diamond saws work the best for sawing laminates.

Power Sanders are good for removing paint during repairs. DA or jitterbug sanders with a fine grit sand paper are best for this application. A disk sander is too aggressive and should not be used for paint removal. With any sanding of a composite material, always sand in the direction of the surface fibers to avoid damaging them. Power sanding is used as a rapid means of removing paint and surface preparation for repair. When using powered sanders, caution must be used to prevent gouging or sanding material that is deeper than the needed repair. Figure 5-3-29 is an example of an orbital sander being used on a composite repair.

Abrasive blasting may be accomplished on composites by using wheat starch. Media blasting provides a quick removal rate, with a moderate prep and cleanup time. One of the cost saving benefits of this process is the fact that the blast media may be reused. Media blasting does not harm the composite surface. Any type of blast media should be practiced on a test sample before being used on the aircraft.

Hazards and Safety Precautions

The issue of personal health and safety is paramount when working with composite materials. With the rapid development of the new material systems, the full effect of hazards to personnel has not been determined; however, sensible shop practices and procedures have to be employed to prevent problems now and those that may appear later. Following these safety precautions may prevent future health problems, such as those encountered in the case of asbestos fibers.

Personnel hazards. Airborne dust and fibrous particles are the principal sources of hazards. These particles are generated by drilling, sanding, routing or sawing the composite structures. Fine, lightweight fiber particles are easily circulated into the atmosphere, causing skin irritation and inflammation, eye irritation, respiratory system inflammation, pulmonary diseases (black lung), cancer of the lung and abdominal disorders. Personal protective equipment (PPE) including, eye protection, gloves, aprons, and respirators, need to be worn during handling and repair of all composite materials. The PPE required to safely handle a specific material is provided in the supplier's Material Safety and Data Sheet (MSDS) as seen in Figure 5-3-30.

Your skin needs to be protected from hazardous materials at all times while working with composite materials. Always wear protective gloves and articles of clothing that offer maximum protection against toxic materials. Use

Figure 5-3-29. Orbital sander

Figure 5-3-30. Personal protective equipment (PPE) and Material Safety and Data Sheet (MSDS)

only approved gloves recommended by the MSDS as not to contaminate the composite material. Always wash your hands after handling materials even if wearing gloves and protective clothing, especially prior to eating.

Handle damaged composite components with care. Single fibers can easily break off and penetrate the skin becoming splinters lodged under the skin. These splinters are difficult to remove, perhaps needing to be cut out and the wound disinfected to prevent infections. Sometimes fibers that are not extremely brittle may be removed from the skin by using tape. Simply stick the tape down on the skin, then remove the tape. The fibers, including many that were sticking into your skin, will be removed with the tape.

Use of Gloves. Gloves are one of the most important defenses used for protection during the repair of advanced composite materials. Different stages of the repair may require different style gloves for protection. There is no all-purpose glove in composite repair. Leather palmed gloves on the initial portion of the repair while lose stands and fiber are removed and trimmed may be used. A chemical resistant glove may be needed, for use with cleaning solvents while prepping the area for lay-up or during the lay-up process to keep material and resins off of your skin. As you can see the selection of the proper glove is dependent upon the operation being performed as well as the type of material that is being handled.

Respirators. Respirators just like gloves and protective clothing are a necessity when working with composites. The best protection against dusts and fibers is attained by wearing a respirator equipped with a HEPA filter (Figure 5-3-31). A good respirator will utilize a chemical cartridge, normally organic, to protect against chemical vapors or gases. A half mask is the minimum recommended. Try to use respirators approved by the National Institute of Occupational Safety and Health/Mine Safety and Health Administration (NIOSH/MSHA). It is important to have training on how to properly care for, fit and wear your respirator. It is important to adhere to the time change requirements on all cartridges.

Even when wearing protective equipment it is important to maintain a good flow of air where the work is being performed. Always use forced fresh air equipment to help you breathe when working in a confined spaces. Filtered ventilation systems to remove the dust from the air should be used when repairing composites.

Eye Protection. Full eye protection such as googles or a full faced respirator should be worn when performing damage removal, machining, drilling or sanding of advanced composite materials. Goggles and/or face shields should be worn when working with liquids. Safety glasses with side shields should be worn at all times while in the shop environment.

Clothing. Long-sleeved and long-legged protective clothing or cover-all suits should be worn to minimize skin contact. Openings in suits should be taped closed with masking tape. When dealing with liquid chemicals a chemical protective apron should be worn.

Personal hygiene includes washing your hands before and after working with composites, and your hair should be washed at the end of each day. Wash dust-contaminated clothing separate from other clothing. Do not eat, drink or smoke in the composite repair area.

Equipment hazards. Graphite dust and particles are conductors and can cause shorts in electrical motors and avionics circuitry. Also, these dust particles can affect the aircraft's fluid systems. In the hydraulic system where contamination is critical, actuating cylinder rods can draw the dust particles into the system, causing premature seal failures. The abrasiveness of these dust particles can also cause failures to valves, pumps and other close tolerance parts. In the fuel system, these particles can be introduced during wet wing repairs, causing clogged filters and erroneous readings in capacitance fuel-quantity probes. The abrasiveness of these dust particles can cause failures to fuel controls and other close tolerance fuel valves.

Solvents. Because of the necessity to use solvents while accomplishing bonded repairs, potential health and fire dangers must be given special consideration.

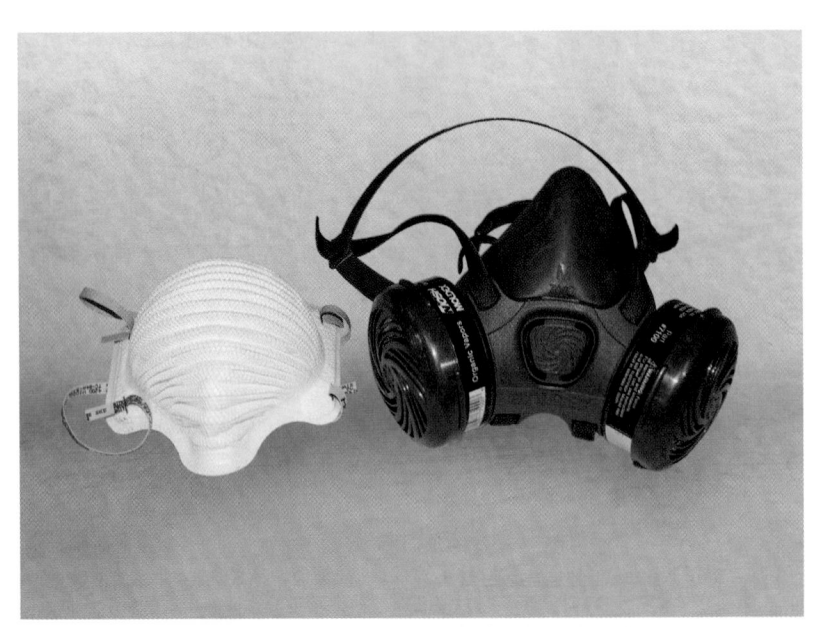

Figure 5-3-31. Respirators (dusk mask and filter type)

Figure 5-3-32. Composite materials create toxic smoke when burning

Solvents dissolve natural skin oils and result in drying and cracking of the skin, rendering it susceptible to infection. Additionally, these solvents may cause irritation and allergic reactions to individuals.

If the vapors are inhaled during prolonged and repeated exposure to moderate concentrations, solvents can cause headache, fatigue, nausea or visual and mental disturbances. Extreme exposure may result in unconsciousness and even death. Solvent vapors may also act as an anesthetic or cause irritation of the eyes or respiratory system. In addition, they can result in blood, liver and kidney damage. Therefore, adequate ventilation should be provided during mixing and use of adhesives, solvents and cleaning solvents.

To minimize or eliminate the danger of fire and subsequent destruction of life and property, flammable solvents should be used only in approved areas and with methods recommended by local fire safety authorities. Composite material fire hazards are usually limited to solvents and resins. Flashpoints of solvents and resins vary, but are usually around 200°F or above. High-temperature resins have higher flashpoints.

Burning composite surface temperatures can exceed 1,000-1,400°F and generate high internal combustion temperatures (830°F and above). Burning composites generate dense smoke-drawing particles into the air, presenting hazards to shop personnel (Figure 5-3-32).

Besides being hazardous to shop personnel, they also affect the quality of repairs. Bonding repairs will not be performed in the same area as machining operations. Vacuuming is used during all machining operations.

Some of the fire prevention and suppression requirements are as follows:

- Eliminate all flames, smoking, sparks and other sources of ignition from areas where solvents are used.
- Use non-spark-producing tools.
- Eliminate static electricity creating clothing.
- Solvents should be used in approved ways and stored in approved containers.
- Ensure adequate ventilation wherever vapors are present.
- Ensure aircraft and equipment are static-grounded.
- Composite materials produce hot fires. Combat fires with chemical foam, dry chemicals, CO_2 or low-velocity water fog.
- Fight fires from the upwind position.
- Wear self-contained breathing apparatus when fighting fires.

Waste disposal. Carbon or graphite fibers cannot be disposed of by incineration. All composite material particles and dust must be packaged, tagged and buried in an approved landfill. Do not allow fibers to contaminate water supplies.

Coolants used in machining composites also contain fibers and particles. When disposing of these particles, allow them to settle to the bottom, drain off the liquid without disturbing the particles, then bag and dispose of them properly.

Epoxy resins cannot be disposed of in their liquid form. Once cured, the problem goes away as the liquid becomes a solid that can be disposed of in a normal manner.

Section 4

Maintaining Transparent Plastic Materials

Because of the many uses of plastic materials in aircraft, optical quality is of great importance. These plastic materials are similar to plate glass in many of their optical characteristics. Ability to locate and identify other aircraft in flight, to land safely at high speeds all depend upon the surface cleanliness, clarity, and freedom from distortion of the plastic material. These factors depend entirely upon the amount of care exercised in the handling, fabrication, maintenance, and repair of the material (Figure 5-4-1).

Transparent plastics have many advantages over glass for aircraft application, particularly the lightness in weight and ease of fabrication and repairs. They lack the surface hardness of glass, though, and are very easily scratched, with resulting impairment of vision. The original transparent plastic is Plexiglas®. It was invented by the Rohm & Haas Company in Germany during the early 1930s. The current favorite is a material called Lexan®, manufactured by the DuPont Company. While Lexan is stronger, more flexible and not as prone to breakage as Plexiglas®, Plexiglas® is still a favorite. For the purposes of this section, it really doesn't matter. They work nearly the same.

The type of plastic can be determined by a couple of simple tests. A sample of the material can be rubbed with zinc chloride, if it turns white but does not soften then its an acrylic plastic. Acetone will soften most acetate plastics without any change in color.

The following are general rules in handling transparent plastics:

- Transparent plastic materials should be handled only with clean cotton gloves.
- The use of harmful liquids, such as cleaning agents, should be avoided.
- Fabrication, repair, installation and maintenance instructions must be closely followed.
- Operations that tend to scratch or distort the plastic surface must be avoided. You must take care to avoid scratching plastic surfaces with finger rings or other sharp objects.

Just as woods split and metals crack in areas of high, localized stress, plastic materials develop, under similar conditions, small surface fissures called *crazing* (Figure 5-4-2). These tiny cracks are approximately perpendicular to the surface, very narrow in width, and usually not over 0.01

Figure 5-4-1. Plexiglass is the material of choice for window and windshields in aircraft"

Figure 5-4-2. Crazing

Figure 5-4-3. Good Plexiglas® cleaners are available from multiple suppliers

inch in depth. These tiny fissures are not only an optical defect, but also a mechanical defect, as there is a separation or parting of material. If the crazing is in a random pattern, it is usually caused by the action of solvent or solvent vapors.

If the crazing is in a random pattern, it is usually caused by the action of solvent or solvent vapors. If the crazing is approximately parallel, it is usually caused by directional stress, set up by cold forming, excessive loading, improper installation, improper machining or a combination of these with the action of solvents or solvent vapors.

Once a part has been crazed, neither the optical nor the mechanical defect can be removed permanently; therefore, prevention of crazing is very important.

Cleaning Plastic Surfaces

New material is always covered with a self-adhesive masking paper. Masking paper should be left on the plastic as long as possible. When it is necessary to remove the masking paper from the plastic during fabrication or installation, the surface should be re-masked as soon as possible. Either replace the original paper or apply masking tape. If the masking paper adhesive deteriorates, making removal of paper difficult, moisten the paper with aliphatic naphtha. Plastic treated with the aliphatic naptha should be washed immediately with clean water.

For exterior surfaces, flush with plenty of water, and use your bare hand to gently feel and dislodge any dirt, sand or mud. Then wash the plastic with a wetting agent and clean water.

A clean, soft cloth, sponge or chamois may be used to apply the soap and water to the plastic. The cloth, sponge or chamois should not be used for scrubbing; use the hand method as described for removing dirt or other foreign particles.

Dry with a clean, damp chamois, a soft, clean cloth or a soft tissue by blotting the surface until dry. Rubbing the surface of the plastic will build up an *electrostatic charge* that attracts dust particles to the surface. If the surface does become charged, patting or gently blotting with a damp, clean cloth will remove this charge as well as the dust.

To clean interior plastic surfaces, dust lightly with a soft cloth. Do not wipe the surface with a dry cloth. Next, wipe carefully with a soft, damp cloth or sponge. Keep the cloth or sponge free from grit by rinsing it frequently in clean water.

Windshield Cleaner and Scratch Removal

Minor surface scratches can be filled with paste wax to improve the appearance of the part. There are several good paste or liquid wax windshield cleaners available in the aftermarket. These materials will actually fill small scratches and make them all but disappear. The wax has the same refractory index as the base material, so a small scratch doesn't show much.

Most cleaners approved for Plexiglas® or Lexan will leave an antistatic coating that will make the dust repel, instead of attract, from the material (Figure 5-4-3).

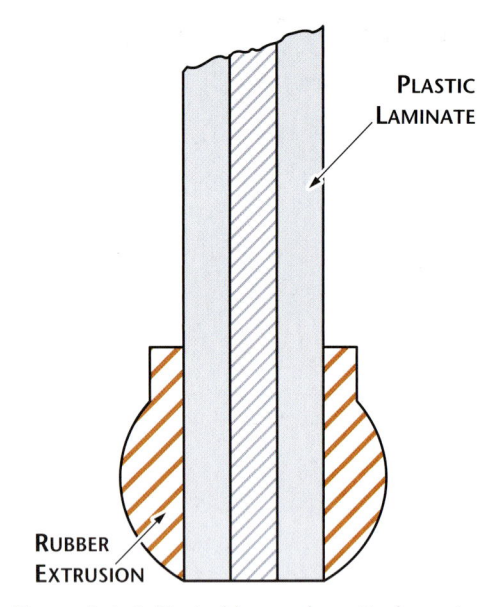

Figure 5-4-4. Typical loop edge attachment

Installing Plastic Panels

There are a number of methods for installing transparent plastic panels in aircraft, one of which is shown in Figure 5-4-4. Which method the aircraft manufacturer uses depends upon the position of the panel in the aircraft, the stresses to which it will be subjected, and a number of other factors. When installing a replacement panel, always follow the same mounting method used by the manufacturer of the aircraft.

The following paragraphs apply to all types of mountings. Fitting and handling should be done with masking paper in place, although the edges of the paper may be peeled back slightly and trimmed off for installation.

Since transparent plastic is brittle at low temperatures, installation of panels should be done at normal temperatures. Plastic panels should be mounted between some type of gasket material to make the installation waterproof, to reduce vibration and to help distribute compressive stresses on the plastic. Minimum packing thickness is 1/16 of an inch. Rubber, fiberglass impregnate and nylon are the most commonly used gasket materials. Figure 5-4-5 shows a window gasket installation.

Since plastic expands and contracts three times as much as metal, suitable allowances for dimensional changes with temperature must be made. Minimum clearances between the frame and plastic are listed in the applicable Maintenance Manual. Clearances should be equally divided on all sides.

Screw torquing procedures should be in accordance with the applicable MM. Plastic panels should never be installed under unnatural stresses. Each screw must be torqued, as specified in the MM, to enable it to carry its portion of the load. If a plastic panel is installed in a binding or twisted position and screws are not torqued correctly, the plastic panel may fail while the aircraft is undergoing normal taxiing and flight operations.

When you remove a plastic panel, there may be several different lengths of screws to be removed. You will save a lot of time by acquiring the habit of keeping screws separated. An easy way to do this is to draw a diagram of the panel on cardboard. Puncture each screw hole, with an awl, through the cardboard. As each screw is removed from the panel, it is installed in its respective position on the cardboard.

During installation of the panel, remove each screw from the cardboard and reinstall it in the same hole from which it was removed until all of the screws are reinstalled. If any screws or other fasteners are damaged during removal or reinstallation, the part replaced must be the same part number as the damaged part. Some fasteners are required to be of non-magnetic material because of their location near compasses and other instruments. The specific part number for each fastener can be found in the IPB for the aircraft.

Repair of Damaged Transparent Surfaces

While it is possible to completely restore the visual clarity of transparent plastic, it must first be checked to see if the part must be rejected. For a low-speed general aviation airplane, the manufacturer may simply want to rely on a visual inspection. However, on part 121 airplanes, there could be an entire NDT course in checking plastic windows.

There are certified repair stations that grind, polish and remove scratches from aircraft windows and windshields. They have developed products and procedures that allow them to restore most windows to their original clarity. Included in the process is an inspection for structural integrity.

Figure 5-4-5. Typical gasket installation

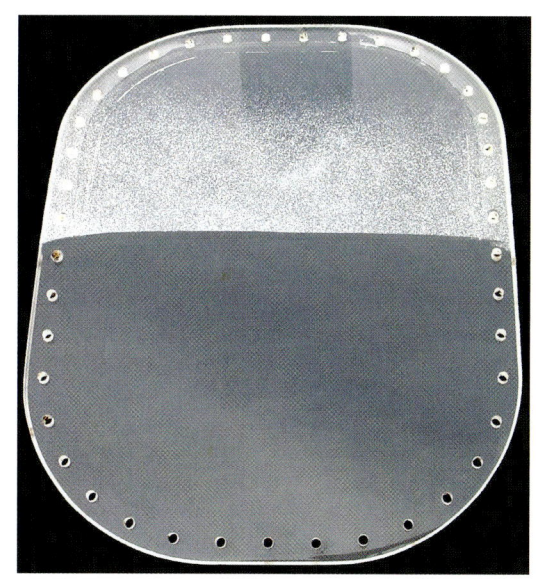

Figure 5-4-6. Paint overspray on an airliner side window, shown before and after restoration.
Photo courtesy of Micro-Surface Finishing Products, Inc.

Repair materials. While materials can be purchased piecemeal and used as needed, it is almost better — certainly less expensive in the long run — to purchase a restoration kit from a supplier. That way everything is available at the same time, materials are not contaminated or dried out and the job is easier.

Each kit will have all the necessary items to repair or restore a windshield or side window.

Types of Damage

Listed below are three of the most common types of damage to transparent plastic.

Paint overspray. Paint overspray, as shown in Figure 5-4-6, is more common than you think. A careless moment, inadequate masking or a loose corner can cause a considerable amount of damage in a hurry. Unfortunately, just wiping it off with paint thinner would likely cause more damage because of the chemical reaction between the thinner and the plastic.

Chemical damage. Chemical damage is one of those things that is almost always preventable. It is caused by simply allowing a non-compatible chemical to come in contact with the plastic. Sometimes it doesn't have to come in contact — just the fumes can damage the plastic surface badly enough to require restoration. Inadequate or poor quality masking materials used prior to paint stripping are a common cause of this type of damage. See Figure 5-4-7.

Scratches and crazing. As mentioned before, stress, old age and some environmental items can cause crazing. More general aviation windows and windshields are ruined by scratches resulting from improper cleaning than most other reasons combined. A lot of airline windows end up scratched from improper airplane washing.

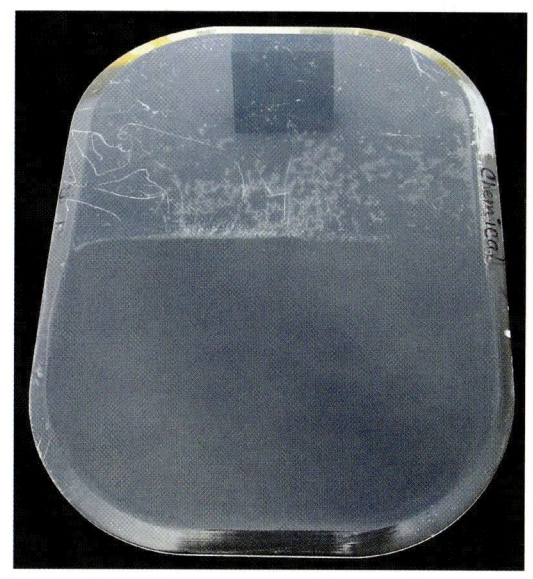

Figure 5-4-7. Damage caused from an incompatible chemical material. The easiest way to not contaminate a plastic window is to treat all chemicals as if they will damage your windows, because most will.
Photo courtesy of Micro-Surface Finishing Products, Inc.

Figure 5-4-8. An example of both scratching and crazing on the same window
Photo courtesy of Micro-Surface Finishing Products, Inc.

Many FBOs, in an effort to provide customer service and mitigate their liability exposure, hold classes in windshield washing. Non-completion of the class often means a technician won't be allowed to wash windows.

Figure 5-4-8 is an example of a restored side window. The window appears to have been wiped off with a dry rag and scratched

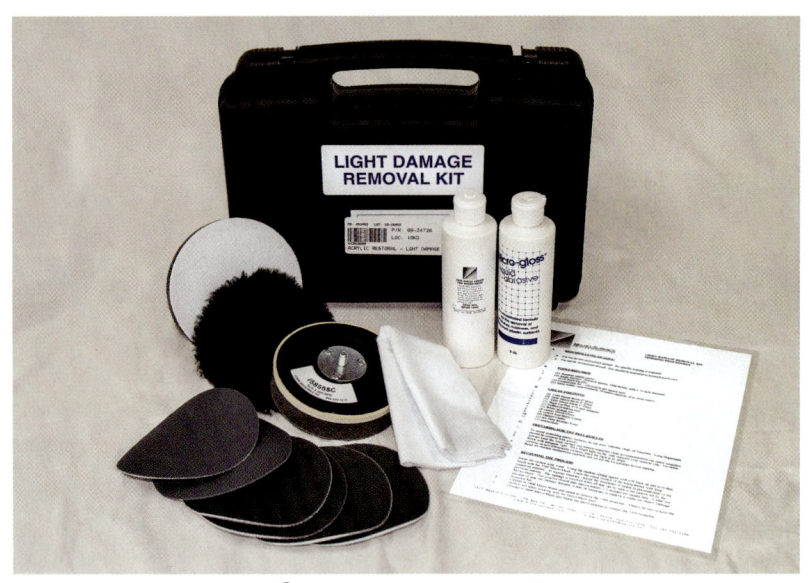

Figure 5-4-9. Micro-Mesh® light damage removal kit

severely. The crazing is also significant. Both were repaired by a CRS.

Figure 5-4-6, Figure 5-4-7 and Figure 5-4-8 are examples of actual acrylic window repairs that can be accomplished by technicians in the field. To be successful in this type of process requires some special materials and directions. While it may be possible to acquire the items separately, it is generally better to buy them in kit form, because you can have everything at one time and it will be correct.

One popular product line goes under the trade name of Micro-Mesh®. They provide a kit for restoration that contains the necessary items. Figure 5-4-9 shows a light damage removal kit.

Restoration kit. The restoration kit includes contents and instructions for use with Micro-Mesh® 5 inch discs: 1500, 2400, 3600, back-up pad, TufBuf polishing pad, spong pad, anti-static cream, Micro-Gloss® and two cotton flannel wipes (sandpaper is not included in this kit).

Extent of Damage and Repair Procedure

Crazing. Crazing is a series of very fine lines, stars or haze when viewed at an angle in bright light. It is below the surface and usually cannot be felt with the fingernail, and it requires aggressive sanding to remove. Begin with 220-grit wet/dry sandpaper.

Deep scratches. They can be easily felt with the fingertip. Begin repair with 220-grit wet/dry sandpaper.

Minor scratches. These can be readily detected with a fingernail. Begin with 1500 Micro-Mesh.

If the scratch is not easily removed, use 400-grit wet/dry sandpaper followed by Micro-Mesh 1500.

Hairline scratches & light scuffs. For light scratches and hazing, begin with 2400 or 3600 Micro-Mesh.

Very fine scratches. Fine scratches are usually caused by improper cleaning methods. Begin with 4000 or 6000 Micro-Mesh.

Crazing is the most common and objectionable problem with regards to aircraft transparencies. It appears as scratches — either large or small — which, when highlighted by the sun, show up as bright lines. In reality, they are shallow fractures just under the surface layer. Crazing can be classified in two categories: minor and severe.

Minor crazing has the appearance of thousands of tiny scratches on the surface. When viewed at an angle to the sun or a bright light, they look like a network of very fine shiny lines, stars or haze. *Severe crazing*, on the other hand, has fewer scratches, but they are much larger and appear to be deep gouges in the surface. In both cases, it is rare that these can be felt with the fingernail; they are *under* the surface. This will be the hardest type of damage to remove.

Severe crazing will require sandpaper, possibly as coarse as 120 grit. Crazing removal will take time. An equal amount of material must be removed from the entire surface to prevent distortion.

> **NOTE:** *This much stock removal can only be done with sandpaper. Don't be afraid to use sandpaper on your transparency.*

After damage removal and completion of the sandpaper sequence, the cloudy appearance will be removed as you continue with the Micro-Mesh procedure.

Step 1: Damage Removal

Most of the restoration time is actually spent removing the degraded acrylic material. Take your time and make sure that this first step removes all of the damaged material — the most essential part of the whole process. This may take as much as 70 percent of the total restoration time.

1. Determine the type and extent of damage, and determine your starting abrasive grade. Open-coat sandpaper must be used dry. Wet/dry sandpaper and Micro-Mesh can be used wet or dry, but best results are obtained if used wet. This will also help keep the surface cool and the abra-

sive flushed free of abraded particles. Clean, fresh water is an excellent lubricant and coolant for Micro-Mesh (Figure 5-4-10). Water may be sprayed or misted on the surface with a spray bottle, or Micro-Mesh may be dipped in fresh water occasionally during use. A drop of mild dish detergent can be added to water for lubrication, if needed.

2. Once the starting abrasive grade has been determined, attach the abrasive and soft back-up pad to a random orbital sander (Figure 5-4-11). Cover the entire surface of the transparency with long, sweeping motions until the damaged layer has been totally removed. This damage removal step is critical. If it is incomplete, the final results will not be satisfactory. After 3-5 minutes, check your progress. If it seems the damage is not being removed at an acceptable rate, you may want to proceed to a coarser grade of abrasive.

In the case of crazing, the time needed to remove the damage will be longer. Since more material will be removed to eliminate damage, you may want to alternate with vertical and horizontal straight-line motion. Once the damage has been removed, end with a vertical sanding pattern.

CAUTION: *Take care not to sand in a circular pattern. If using an orbital sander, use long sweeping motions.*

Spot sanding in a localized area is not recommended. To remove a single scratch or small scratch area, sand in an area large enough (8 inches by 8 inches) to prevent waviness or distortion. Work across the damaged area 4-5 inches each way from the damage. This may mean sanding the entire surface. Work an area slightly larger (at least 2 inches) with each consecutive step. You may find you are sanding the entire surface before you are finished.

1. Clean the surface by flushing with water or blowing with air. This will prevent abraded particles from being picked up with the next abrasive step and causing scratches.

2. Proceed to the next step of abrasive. If sandpaper was used, it will be necessary to continue through all of the grades listed to 400-grit sandpaper before beginning with the Micro-Mesh abrasives. Attach the Micro-mesh disk abrasive and sand at a 90° angle from the previous step. Continue sanding until the previous sanding pattern has been completely removed.

The approximate time for each step is 3-5 minutes per square foot. If water is being used, it

Figure 5-4-10. Damage removal using a Micro-Mesh abrasive disc

Figure 5-4-11. Attaching a Micro-Mesh abrasive disc to an orbital sander

will be necessary to dry the surface completely to determine that the previous pattern has been removed. The use of 100 percent cotton flannel is recommended. Avoid synthetics and paper towels, as these both tend to cause scratches in plastic.

Step 2: Surface Restoration

1. After the surface has been sanded with 400-grit sandpaper, begin with the Micro-Mesh abrasives. Attach the 1500 to the soft back-up pad, and sand at a 90° angle from the previous sanding pattern. Continue until the previous pattern is again removed.

2. Proceed as above through all grades of Micro-Mesh included in the kit. Be sure to change the sanding direction 90° with

Figure 5-4-12. Using a TufBuf polishing pad during surface restoration

each step and check for total removal of each scratch pattern. If coarser scratches remain at any step, they will probably still be visible at the end, leaving an incomplete restoration and a hazy finish.

3. When you have finished with the final step of the Micro-Mesh series and are satisfied with the surface appearance, attach the TufBuf polishing pad to the right angle polisher. Wet the surface with water. Apply approximately 1 tablespoon of Micro-Gloss and buff for 2-4 minutes (Figure 5-4-12).

4. Attach the white foam sponge pad and wet the surface with water. Apply approximately 1 tablespoon of Micro-Gloss and buff for 2-4 minutes. Rinse the surface off with water. Wipe clan with a dry flannel cloth. All fine scratches should be gone. If not, repeat the buffing process.

5. Apply Anti-Static sparingly to the surface, using a clan, dry, flannel cloth. Polish surface by hand to remove the static charge that has built up during the process. Clean sponge, TufBuf, and flannel cloths with mild detergent and rinse for future use.

NOTE: *Keep the flannel clean and you can use it many times. Rinsing is needed to remove dirt and abrasive particles that are trapped in the flannel.*

Characteristics of Plexiglas®

Table 5-4-1 is a quick reference guide to some plexiglas® characteristics discussed in more detail in the following paragraphs.

Resistance to breakage. Plexiglas® has six to 17 times greater impact resistance than ordinary glass in thicknesses of .125 inch to .250 inch. When subjected to blows beyond its resistance, Plexiglas® reduces the hazard of injury because it breaks into large, relatively dull-edged pieces that disperse at low velocity, due to the light weight of the material.

Transparency. In colorless form, Plexiglas® is as transparent as the finest optical glass. Its total white light transmittance is 92 percent.

Weather resistance. Plexiglas® withstands exposure to weather and sun. Fifteen-year outdoor exposure tests of colorless transparent Plexiglas® show negligible loss in light transmission.

Light weight. Plexiglas® is less than half as heavy as glass: it is 43 percent as heavy as aluminum and 70 percent as heavy as magnesium.

Ease of fabrication. Plexiglas is a *thermoplastic* material. When heated to a pliable state, Plexiglas® can be formed to almost any shape. It can be sawed, drilled and machined like wood or soft metals.

Dimensional stability. Plexiglas® is notable for its freedom from shrinking and deterioration through long periods of use. Many drawing instruments requiring exact dimensional stability have been fabricated from Plexiglas®.

Chemical resistance. Plexiglas® has excellent resistance to most chemicals, including solutions of inorganic alkalies and acids such as ammonia and sulphuric acid, and aliphatic hydrocarbons such as hexane, octane and naphtha. It is attacked by these chemicals:

- Chlorinated hydrocarbons such as methylene chloride and carbon tetrachloride
- Aromatic solvents such as turpentine, benzene, toluene ethyl and methyl alcohol
- Organic acids such as acetic acid, phenols and Lysol lacquer thinners, ketones and ethers

Electrical properties. Plexiglas® is affected to only a minor degree by weathering or moisture. Its surface resistivity is higher than that of most other plastic materials.

Heat resistance. The maximum recommended continuous service temperature is 180° to 200°F, depending on the particular use.

Fire resistance. Plexiglas® is a combustible material classified as a slow-burning plastic.

Bowing. Different temperature and/or humidity conditions on the inside and outside surfaces of Plexiglas® may cause the sheet to bow somewhat in the direction of the higher temperature and/or humidity. However, this type of bowing is reversible, and the panel will return to approximately original flatness when the temperatures and humidities on both sides of the panel are equalized. Bowing does not affect visibility through the material but may cause reflections to appear distorted.

Plexiglas® has some properties that must be considered in design and installation. A number of factors involved in the design, assembly and installation of Plexiglas® are:

- Stress limits
- Thermal expansion
- Cold flow
- Mounting or attachment methods
- Edge finishing

Stress limits. Plexiglas® offers good tensile, impact and flexural strength properties, as may be seen from the following table:

- Tensile strength — 10,500 p.s.i.
- Flexural strength — 16,000 p.s.i.
- Compressive strength — 18,000 p.s.i.
- Modulus of elasticity — 450,000 p.s.i.

However, stress considerably below the test values shown will produce light surface checking. To avoid stress-crazing, stress limits for continuously imposed loads should not exceed 1,500 p.s.i. at normal operational temperatures.

Coefficient of thermal expansion. Like all organic plastics, Plexiglas® has a relatively large coefficient of thermal expansion: .00005 in./in./°F. Therefore, installations require adequate provision for expansion and contraction of the plastic, particularly when used outdoors in very large sizes, like bubble windshields. Allowance for this is made by installing Plexiglas® in a channel frame that engages the edges of the sheet so that it can expand and contract without restraint. Bolting or other inflexible fastening of the plastic sheet which does not allow for expansion and contraction may result in failure of the installation.

In framing a sheet, the depth of edge engagement must be sufficient to provide for thermal expansion and contraction. A practical rule to follow in outdoor installations is that the frame depth should be 1/4 inch plus 1/8 inch

CHARACTERISTICS OF PLEXIGLASS®	
CHARACTERISTIC	DESCRIPTION
Resistance to Breakage	Plexiglas® has a six to 17 times greater impact resistance than ordinary glass.
Transparency	Plexiglas® is as transparent as the finest optical glass.
Weather Resistance	Plexiglas® can withstand 15 years of out-door exposure with negligible loss in light transmissionl
Weight	Plexiglas® is less than half as heavy as glass.
Ease of Fabrication	Plexiglas® can be formed to almost any shape.
Dimensional Stability	Plexiglas® resists shrinkeage and deterioration.
Chemical Resistance	Plexiglas® is resitant to most chemicals.
Electrical Properties	Plexiglas® has a surface resistivity that is higher than that of most other plastics.
Heat Resistance	Maximun recommended continuous service temperature is 180° – 200°F.
Bowing	Different temperature and/or humidity between the inside and outside surfaces of Plexiglas®
Mounting	Plexiglas® sheets should be frame-mounted.
Edge finishing	Scraping, sanding or joining the edges of Plexiglas® increase the impact resistance

Table 5-4-1. Plexiglas® Characteristics

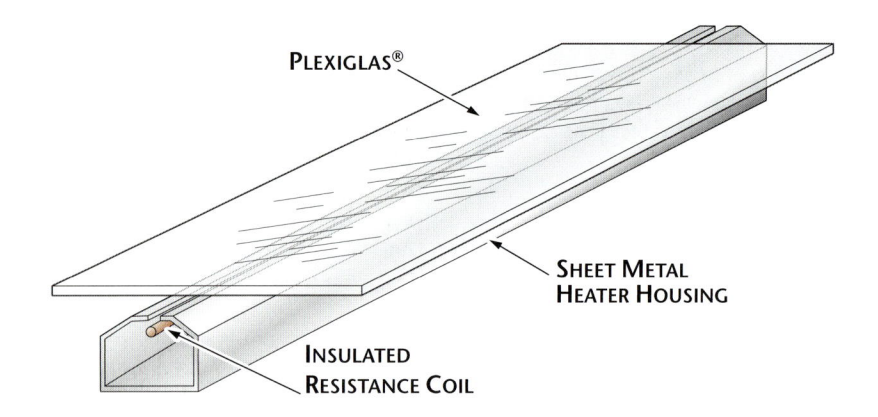

Figure 5-4-13. Use of a strip heater to bend Plexiglas®

per running foot of Plexiglas® in length and width. To provide expansion clearance, the flat Plexiglas® sheet should be cut 1/16 inch per running foot shorter than the frame depth in both dimensions.

Cold flow. Under many conditions, loads far less than 1,500 p.s.i. under the stress limit, may result in undesirably large deflection. Large, flat, horizontally installed sheets of Plexiglas® will take on a permanent deformation under continuously imposed loads such as snow, ice, water or even under their own weight.

These deflection problems can be avoided by shaping the Plexiglas® sheet to increase its rigidity, as in dome-shaped or corrugated sheets.

Forming Transparent Plastics

Many times in the general aviation world, you could well be forced to fabricate, modify or fit a replacement windshield or window. This is especially true in the experimental or restoration market. The process isn't as hard as you might imagine, but it does require adherence to a set of procedures that are a little bit different. The following fabrication procedures are for forming a transparent plastic part from Plexiglas®.

Mounting plexiglas®. Plexiglas® sheet should be frame-mounted, not only because of thermal expansion and contraction, but also because this method gives the material its greatest resistance to impact. Through-fastening of the material causes impact to localize stress at the bolt holes, resulting in breakage. Four-sided channel framing of Plexiglas® sheet distributes shock around the periphery of the sheet, thereby reducing the likelihood of breakage under impact.

Edge finishing. Notches in the edges of Plexiglas® sheet, such as are produced by crude saw cuts, make the material very crack-sensitive under impact. Scraping, sanding or jointing the rough-cut edges will eliminate these notches and increase the impact resistance of panels.

Cold forming. Plexiglas® can be bent while cold to simple cylindrical shapes by springing the material into a curved frame. The radius of the curvature should be at least 180 times the thickness of the sheet for sheets up to .250 inch in thickness.

Heat forming. One of the most useful properties of Plexiglas® is its formability. When it is heated to forming temperature, approximately 340°F, it becomes soft and pliable and can then be formed to almost any desired shape. As the material cools in its formed state, it stiffens and retains the shape to which it has been formed.

Reheating a formed part to forming temperature will cause the material to return to its original flat-sheet condition. This property is called elastic memory, which is useful when it is desirable to correct a forming error by reforming the sheet. Formed parts should be permitted to cool slowly. Forced cooling should not be employed.

Heating Plexiglas® for forming. The following general principles should be observed:

- Blanks should be cut about 2.2 percent larger in length and width than the required blank size to allow for shrinkage on heating.

- The whole sheet should be heated uniformly from 320°-360°F, except for strip-heated parts.

- The sheet should be completely formed before it cools below the minimum forming temperature.

Forced-circulation air oven heating. This is preferred for temperature uniformity and least danger of overheating the sheet. Sheets should be hung vertically from racks with clamps or supported in trays lined with soft cloth to protect the surface of the plastic from scratching.

Sheets may also be heated with radiant heaters. However, radiant heaters may cause overheating of the material; therefore, care should be exercised in their use.

If a suitable oven is not available for heating Plexiglas® sheet, hot oil is a practical and economical means of heating the material. Boiling water will not be sufficiently hot, and high-pressure steam is difficult to handle with Plexiglas®.

Forming Methods

Bending. The simplest method of bending Plexiglas® along a straight line is to use a strip heater which locally heats the Plexiglas® to forming temperature, so that it can be formed along that line. See Figure 5-4-13. The process is usually used for small parts where the length of the bend is relatively short. Long bends (over 24 inches) tend to bow.

The Plexiglas® is placed over the heating element and allowed to remain until it softens or wilts. After heating, the sheet should be bent to the required shape quickly and held, usually in a jig, until cool. Sheets .250 inch thick or more may have to be turned over during the heating period, or they may be heated between two heaters to assure uniform heating through the material. A number of strip heaters and jigs can be arranged so as to make several folds in one operation. Strip heaters are commercially available or can be constructed from resistance-type heating elements or a coil wound from high-resistance wire. Regardless of the heat source, the heating element should never make direct contact with the Plexiglas® sheet.

Only in strip heating is it sufficient to heat the Plexiglas® in one isolated area (strip). For all the following processes, the entire sheet should be uniformly heated.

Drape forming. This is used for all other two-dimensional shapes and for forming straight line bends over 24 inches in length. After heating to the proper temperature, the Plexiglas® sheet should be removed from the oven and carefully draped over the form. See Figure 5-4-14 The edges of the sheet should be held against the form by a clamping ring or rubber bands until the part is cool. Forms for this forming method are usually built by wrapping sheet metal, thin plywood or sheet laminates over contour ribs and fastening the covering to the ribs. Stiffeners inside the mold should not make contact with the covering material, to assure uniform heat transfer and smooth contours. Plaster cast forms are also used in drape forming. Wrapped sheet molds or plaster cast forms are usually covered with cotton flannel, felt or similar soft materials to insulate and form a cushion, which decreases any tendency to mark the hot sheet.

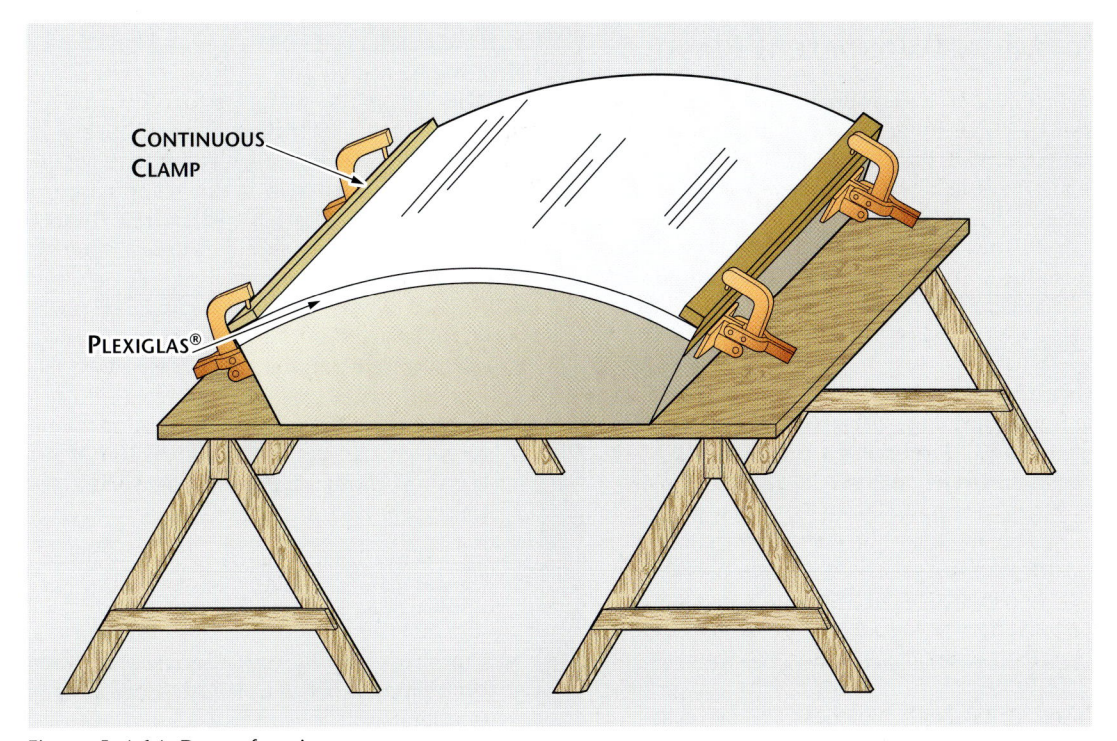

Figure 5-4-14. Drape forming

Manual stretch forming. Manual stretch forming is often used when the compound curvature is not great, when optical distortion is not objectionable and the number of parts to be made does not warrant setting up mechanical equipment. The sheet is heated to forming temperature and placed on the compound curved male drape mold. Refer to Figure 5-4-15. The yoke is placed over the Plexiglas® sheet to stretch and form it to the compound curve and to hold it in position during the cooling period.

Molds for compound curved shapes are usually cast from plaster-of-paris fashioned from wooden patterns. A clamping frame which will fit outside the mold may be required to hold the formed part after stretching until the cooling cycle is finished.

Plug-and-ring forming. A hot sheet of Plexiglas® is clamped over an opening in a flat plate. See Figure 5-4-16. This plate opening is designed to correspond with the outside shape of the formed part. A male plug, smaller than the clamping ring opening to provide a clearance approximately equal to twice the Plexiglas® sheet thickness, is forced downward into the ring, stretching the heated sheet to the desired cross section. Figure 5-4-17 represents a variation of plug-and-ring forming called ridge forming that gives a minimum amount of mark-off.

Materials used for construction of the clamping ring include masonite, hardwood plywood or a combination of the two. The ring is supported on a boxlike structure to give clearance for the formed part. The plug may be made from wood, metal weldment skeleton or cast from plaster, metal or phenolic resin.

Free blowing. Free blowing is used to form three-dimensional shapes by the use of positive air pressure — without the use of male or female forms. The heated sheet is held to a piece of plywood or masonite die stock by a clamping ring, through which the heated sheet is blown to shape. See Figure 5-4-18. Clamping rings are made much like plug-and-ring forming plates.

When the opening in the clamping ring is circular, the finished part takes the shape of a hemispherical section for depths up to approximately one-half the diameter. Figure 5-4-19 shows shapes obtained from blowing through random-shaped openings. Air should be admitted slowly so that the Plexiglas® sheet is brought gradually to its final shape, but fast enough to assure that the sheet does not cool.

Blowing onto a form. This method is based on air pressure differentials. The heated Plexiglas® sheet is clamped directly to the edges of a form, and the sheet is forced down by air pressure onto the form. See Figure 5-4-20.

Blowing onto a form is often used for forming parts that differ quite radically from surface tension shapes. Close approximation of geometric shapes can be produced, but corners will tend to be round. Clamping pressure

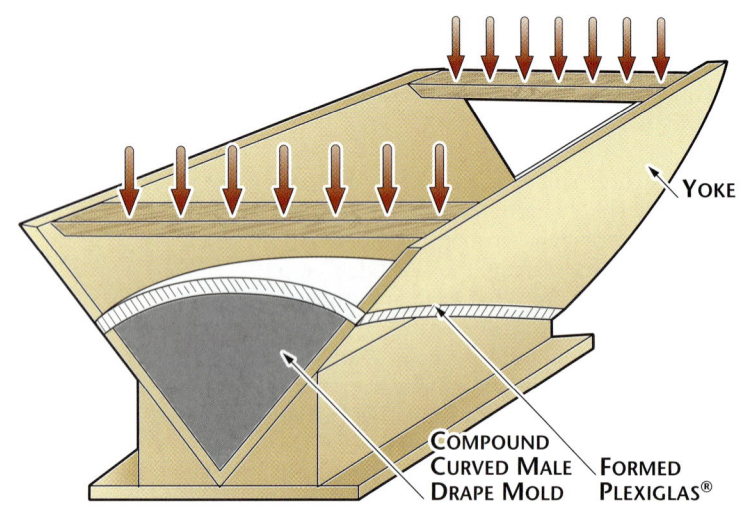

Figure 5-4-15. Manual stretch forming

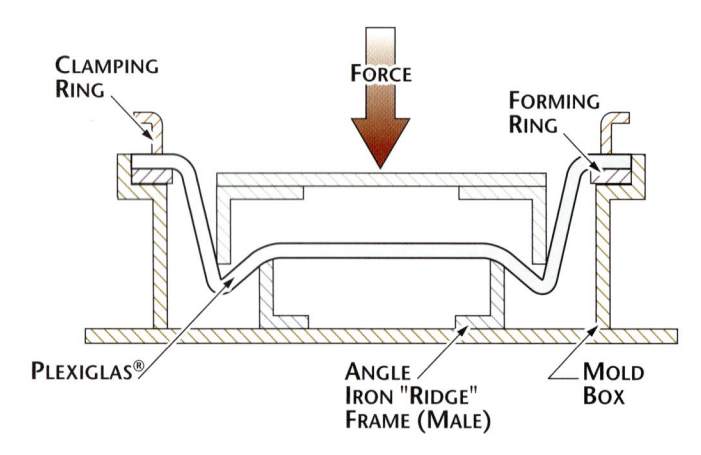

Figure 5-4-16. Plug-and-ring forming

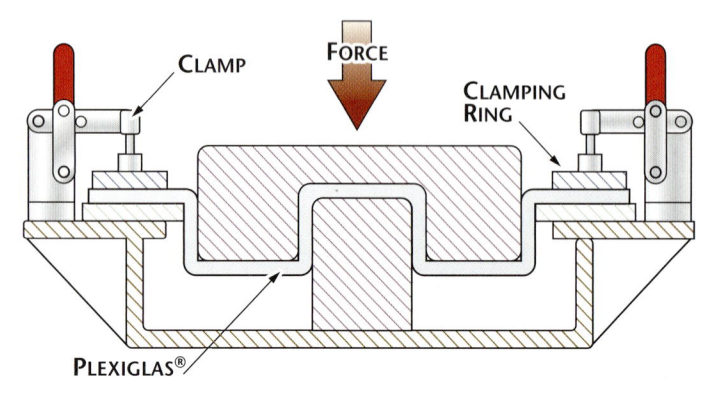

Figure 5-4-17. Ridge forming

should exceed the product resulting from multiplying the air pressure (in p.s.i) and the Plexiglas® sheet size (in square inches). Pressures as high as 150 p.s.i are used for sharp details.

Tools for this process are usually cast from hard compositions such as metal or phenolic resins. Plaster and phenolic molds must be cast into metal boxes for additional strength. Vent passages should be provided at the point or points where the hot Plexiglas® touches the form last.

Mark-Off

When a sheet of Plexiglas® is heated to forming temperature, its surface is soft enough to be indented by any irregularities of the mold surface. These imperfections, when transferred, are called *mark-off*. Even on a smooth mold surface, mark-off can be caused by dust particles. On opaque or translucent sheets, mark-off on the surface away from the normal view offers no problem. It is advisable to determine which surface of the formed part will be visible and then select a tooling method that will bring only the non-visible surface into contact with the mold surface.

Where this is not possible or where transparent Plexiglas® is to be formed, molds should be designed to minimize contact with the hot Plexiglas® sheet. Weldment skeleton plugs used in the plug-and-ring forming process described in Figure 5-4-16 help to keep mark-off to a minimum. Solid molds can be covered with flannel cloth stapled around the periphery. Molds with compound shapes or other complex contours can be covered with a stretchable material such as felt or flocked rubber. Where optical quality is necessary, the surface of the mold can be covered with grease, which insulates the Plexiglas® against mark-off. The mold and grease must be hot (150°F) to insure good flow.

Clamping Rings and Clamps

To hold the edges of the sheet against the form during forming and cooling, a clamping ring that fits the contours of the form is used, and is brought to bear on the edges of the sheet. The ring may be hinged or located by guide pins on the form to facilitate correct positioning in relation to the form, with allowance being made for the thickness of the sheet.

Figure 5-4-21 shows several different types of clamps and clamping rings that can be used to hold the Plexiglas® sheet during forming. If only one or a few parts are to be formed, wood clamps or C-clamps are commonly used. Frequently, forming rings are grooved periph-

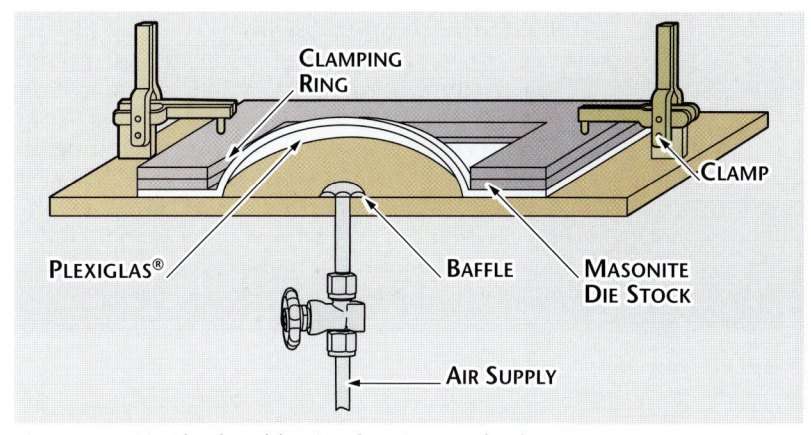

Figure 5-4-18. The free-blowing forming method

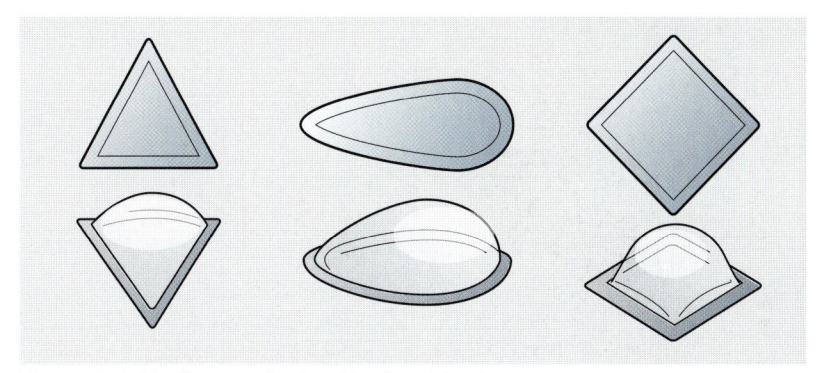

Figure 5-4-19. Shapes obtained by free blowing

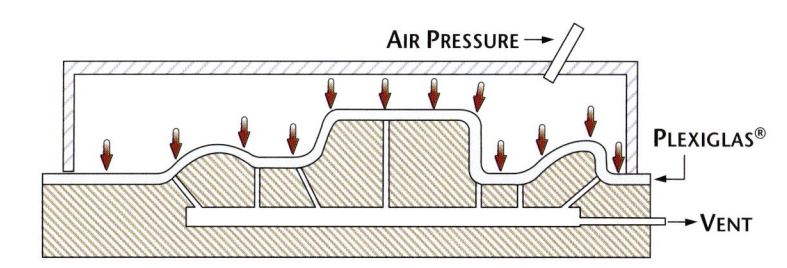

Figure 5-4-20. Blowing onto a form

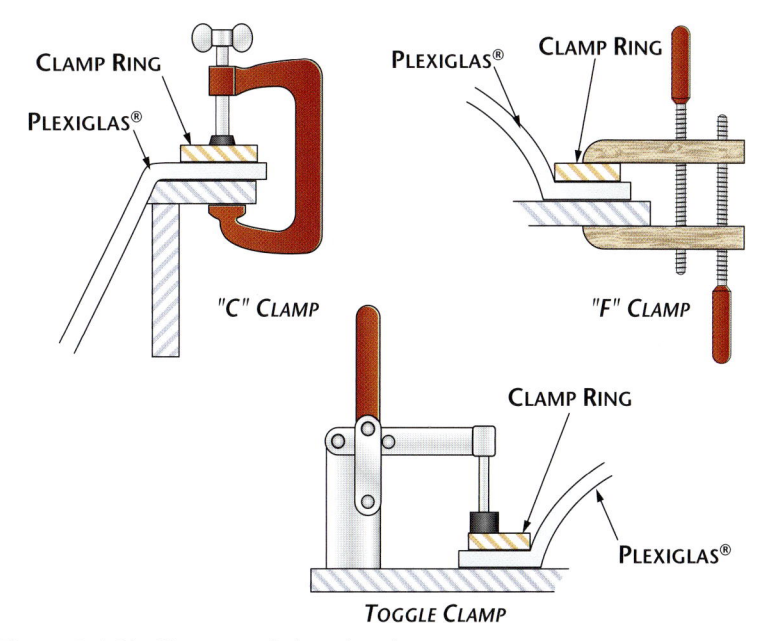

Figure 5-4-21. Clamps and clamping rings

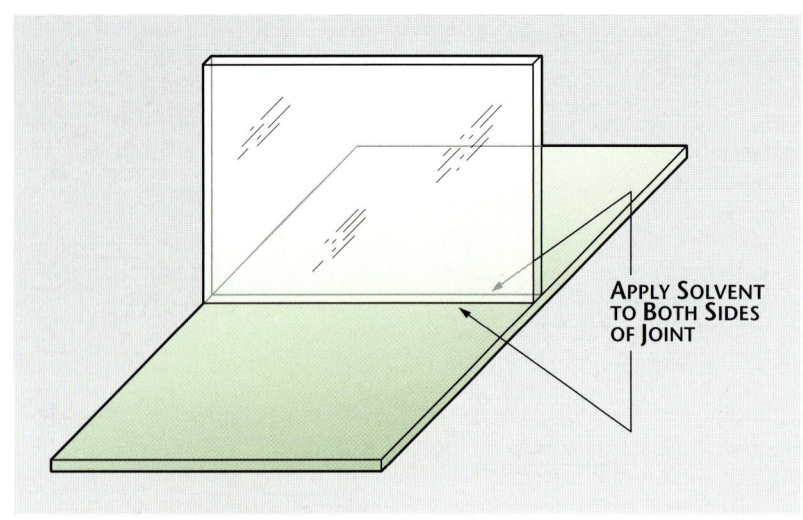

Figure 5-4-22. Capillary cementing

erally under the clamping ring location to cause the hot Plexiglas® sheet to form a bead, thus increasing the resistance to slippage.

Forms for Plexiglas®

Contour tolerances. Contour tolerances of ±1/8 inch can be maintained in many forming operations, but free-blown sections, particularly in large sizes, tolerances of up to ±1/2 inch may have to be allowed.

Shrinkage allowances. When the final dimensions of the formed parts are critical, forms must be built sufficiently oversize to allow for shrinkage when the parts cool from the forming temperature to room temperature. A shrinkage allowance of approximately 3/32 inch per foot should be made in designing forms for Plexiglas®. Also, surfaces of the forms should extend beyond the trim line. It is best to cut the Plexiglas® sheet oversize to assure that it extends beyond the trim line.

Cementing Plexiglas®

There are three basic methods of cementing Plexiglas® to Plexiglas®. These are:

1. Capillary or surface-tension application of a solvent, such as ethylene dichloride, for quick, clean joints of low strength for parts to be used indoors.

2. Soak-cementing, using a monomer-solvent mixture such as Rohm & Haas Company Acrifix 116 for medium- to high-strength joints, to be used either indoors or outdoors. High-strength soaked cement joints are obtained by heat curing (annealing).

3. Reactive cements, such as Cement PS-18 for high-strength structural parts. These may be cured at room temperature and further improved by annealing.

Preparation of joints for cementing. The protective masking paper on Plexiglas® should be removed from any surface that may contact the cement. Solvent-resistant masking tapes may be applied to within 1/16 inch of the areas to be cemented. The surfaces to be cemented must be smooth, free of chips and must fit together without gaps and without application of pressure.

Description of Cementing Methods

Capillary cementing. Solvents for Plexiglas® (ethylene dichloride or 1-1-2 trichloroethylene)

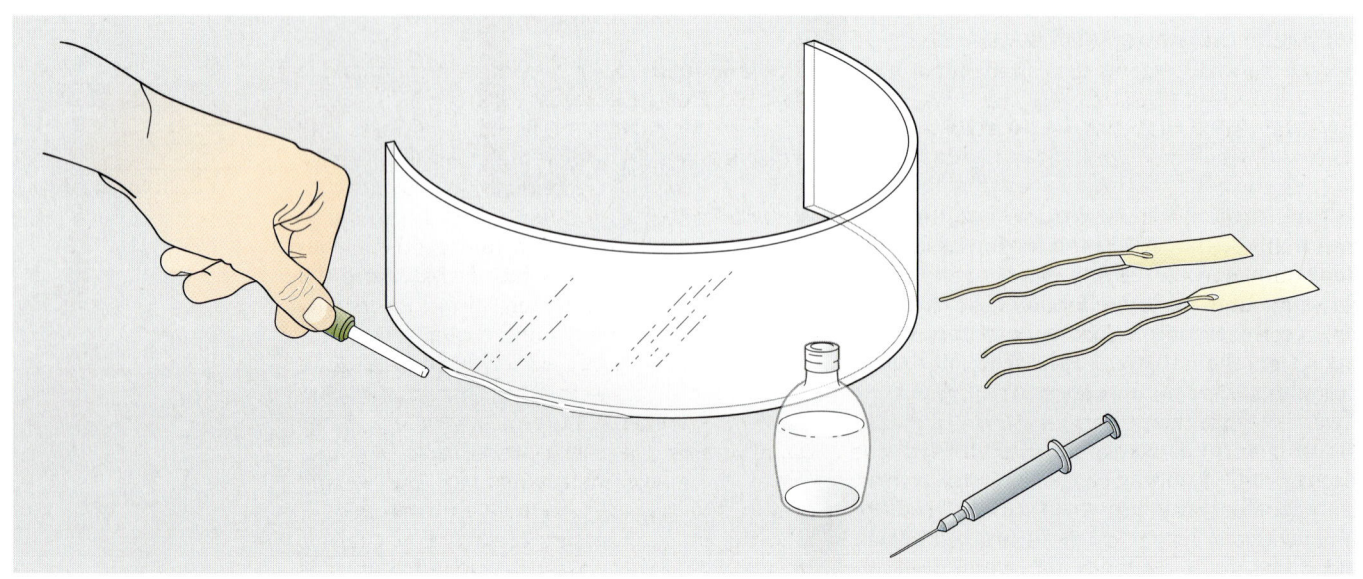

Figure 5-4-23. Multiple applications of cement to a joint

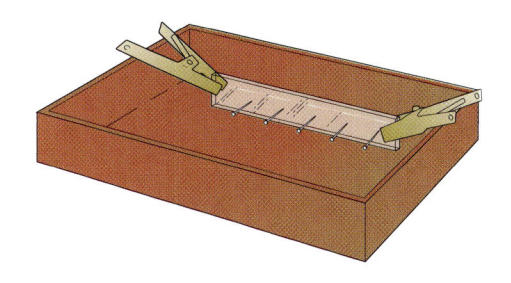

Figure 5-4-24. An example of soak cementing

are applied with a brush, pipe cleaner or eyedropper to the butted edges to be joined. See Figure 5-4-22. Wherever possible, the solvent should be applied to both sides of the joint to be cemented.

Simple jigs or fixtures, exerting only light pressure, should be used to hold the parts together until the cement sets sufficiently to allow handling of the assembly. This setting time varies from a few minutes to an hour or longer, depending on the solvent used, the size of the assembly and the ambient temperature in the room where the cementing operation is performed. Under no circumstances should cementing be attempted when the temperature is below 60°F.

A variation of capillary cementing can be used to improve the strength of the joint (Figure 5-4-23). Fine wires, such as those used to attach shipping tags, are placed between the parts to be cemented, separating them by about .020 inch. Several applications of solvent are made and each is allowed to soak into the Plexiglas® joint areas for several minutes. The wires are then pulled out and light pressure applied to the joint. When cured, the additional solvent at the joint will result in higher joint strength than would be possible with a single application of cement.

Soak cementing. Plexiglas® Cement II should be used for soak cementing to obtain maximum strength and weathering characteristics of the joints. It is important that the instructions supplied with Cement II are followed with care.

To soak straight joints or those in one plane, small nails are placed in the bottom of a shallow aluminum, galvanized or porcelainized steel or glass pan (do not use copper or brass). Then sufficient cement is poured in the level pan until it just covers the nails. The Plexiglas® edge to be soaked is placed on the nails so that the edge is in contact with the cement as shown in Figure 5-4-24. Clamps or blocks are used to hold the piece upright. It should be soaked in the cement for approximately 7 minutes. The part should be removed from the pan carefully to avoid splash, and it should be inclined at a slight angle to allow excess cement to drain off.

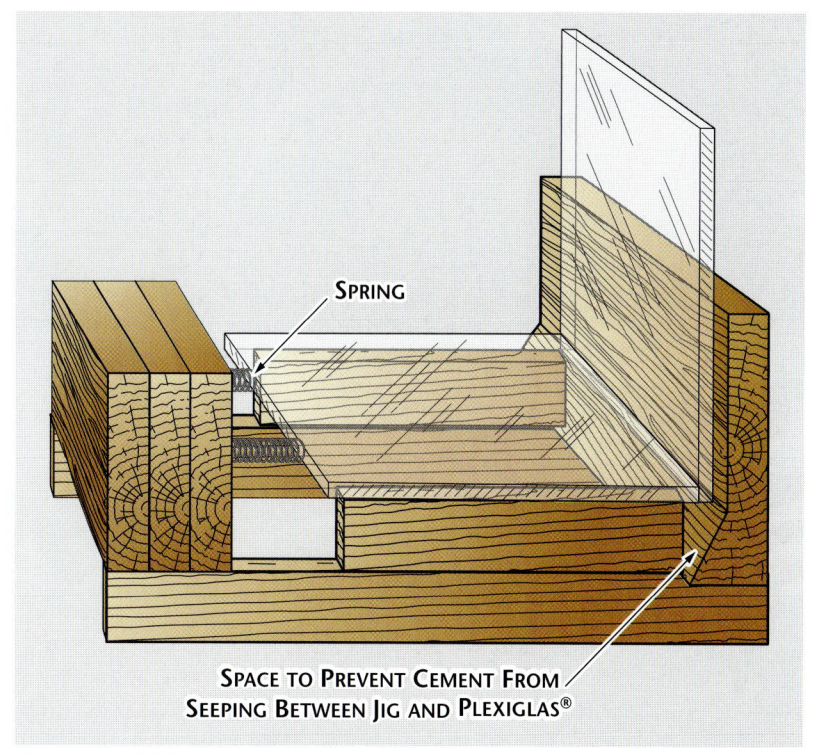

Figure 5-4-25. Joining cemented surfaces

The surfaces to be cemented should then be joined. Only contact pressure should be applied for a minute to allow the soft edge to wet and soften the surface of the other part. Additional pressure of 1-5 lbs. per square inch of cemented area should be maintained for at least one hour. Weights or springs are most useful for applying pressure, because their follow-up compensates for the shrinkage that takes place during the curing period. See Figure 5-4-25.

When exposed to air for short periods, Cement II loses its effectiveness due to evaporation of one of its components. Cement remaining in the soak pan, after cementing operations have been performed, should be discarded.

PS-18 cement. This cement is recommended for all critical load-bearing joints. PS-18 is used in the construction of liquid containers and pressure vessels, for example. As this cement sets by chemical reaction (not evaporation), it shrinks less than other cements and therefore can be used to fill in minor mismatches or crevices. The cement has the advantage of a fast initial set; cemented joints are usually hard enough for machining within four hours of assembly. The cement also provides good weather resistance and high strength. PS-18 cement is prepared by carefully mixing three components: the *base resin*, *catalyst* and *promoter*. Complete instructions for the mixing and proper use of the cement are contained in the shipping containers of several packaging companies. In all cases, the mixed cement is applied to one of the surfaces to be cemented

Figure 5-4-26. Cutting Plexiglas®

by any convenient method, such as polyethylene squeeze bottles, cone funnels made from cellophane or aluminum foil, or by spatula. The parts are then assembled. Moderate pressure may he necessary to remove entrapped air. This cement is also used to fillet joints cemented by the capillary or soak method, to increase joint strength.

PS-18 cement, mixed and ready for use, must be applied within 30 minutes.

Annealing Cemented Joints

The strength of cemented joints is usually improved markedly by annealing. Annealing consists of prolonged heating of the Plexiglas® part at temperatures lower than those used for forming, followed by slow cooling. Annealing improves the strength of cemented joints by evaporating trapped solvent.

Cutting Plexiglas®

Plexiglas® can be cut with any of the saws used for wood or metal. Where a considerable amount of Plexiglas® cutting is being done, it is advisable to select and reserve special saws for Plexiglas®. Circular saws are preferred for straight cutting. Band saws are suited for curves and for straight cuts in thick material. Figure 5-4-26 shows Plexiglas® being cut using a table saw.

Circular Saws

Steel blades. Steel blades are recommended for circular saw cutting of Plexiglas® sheets where large volume cutting operations are not performed. If a considerable amount of cutting is required, carbide-tipped, square- and advance-tooth blades are superior to steel blades.

Most steel blades are made of alloy steel tempered to permit filing, and most have teeth with 0 inch to 10 inch rake. All teeth should have uniform height. Teeth of uneven height will cause excessive chipping and possibly cracked blades because of the cutting strain being concentrated on a few teeth rather than distributed evenly over all the teeth. Similarly, all teeth should be the same shape. The hook, or *rake*, of the teeth should be uniform and preferably in radial line with the center of the blade. Saws should be machine-filed or ground.

To prevent chipping, the height of circular saw blades above the table should be just a little greater than the thickness of the sheet. The work must be held firmly so that the saw moves through the Plexiglas® in a straight line parallel with the saw blade. In some cases, a slitter directly behind the saw blade will prevent the kerf from closing on the retreating edge. Such closing results in a gummed cut, which not only destroys the good surface of the cut but also tends to heat up and dull the saw. See Table 5-4-2 for recommended blade specifications.

More power is required to cut acrylic plastic as fast as wood. A two-horsepower motor is recommended to drive a 10 inch or 12 inch diameter circular saw. As with other materials, several sheets of acrylic plastic can be cut at one time by stacking one on top of another up to approximately 1 inch of thickness. Multiple sawing, especially with suitably designed jigs, can prove economical and will more than pay for the increased power required.

The masking paper is usually left on masked Plexiglas® when sawing. This means that for every sheet of masked Plexiglas®, two sheets of masking paper must be cut. The adhesive tends to stick to the blade, and the paper tends to dull it. Gumming of the blade by the adhesive can be minimized by applying a small amount of oil or grease to the blade. This may be done with wick oilers or, more simply, by touching a stick of tallow or white soap against the revolving blade. If a deposit starts to collect on the saw, it should be cleaned off before it builds up to such an extent that it fills the clearance space between adjacent teeth.

Circular saws should be run at 8,000-12,000 feet-per-minute (that is, a 12 inch diameter circular blade should run approximately 3,000-4,000 r.p.m.). The plastic should be fed slowly enough to prevent overheating.

The feed should be reduced as the blade is leaving the cut to avoid chipping of the corners. An even, steady feed will produce smoother cuts and a longer blade life than a jerky feed. Masked Plexiglas® does not slide evenly on a saw table, so a better cut can usually be obtained if a sliding fixture or fixture is arranged to slide on the table. The fixture should be located and guided by runners sliding in the grooves of the table.

Although carbide-tipped blades cost more than steel blades, experience has shown that the carbide-tipped blade produces a superior cut and has a much longer life between sharpenings than does the steel blade. The extra initial cost of carbide-tipped blades is worth the investment. Carbide-tipped blades are supplied in 8 inch, 10 inch, 12 inch and 14 inch diameters. The square and advance teeth are designed so that alternate teeth start and finish the cut. The teeth are diamond ground to close tolerance and must be returned to the factory for regrinding as soon as they begin to dull.

Circular saw cuts up to 2 or 3 feet in length can be made in single Plexiglas® sheets with the usual type of saw table. Traveling saws are recommended for cuts longer than 2-3 feet and for cutting several sheets in a stack.

Since the sheets remain stationary during cutting and the saw is moved, a hold-down bar can be positioned to clamp the sheets in place on the saw table and prevent chattering, which will cause uneven cutting and chipping.

Cutting Unmasked Sheets

When unmasked sheets are to be trimmed or cut to smaller size, the fabricator should exercise caution to minimize the possibility of damage in handling.

Working surfaces can be covered with a medium-density felt to prevent the sheet from being scratched. These surfaces should be kept free of chips and dirt by frequent brushing or blowing with compressed air.

Saw dust and chips remaining on the surface of the sheets after cutting can he removed by blowing with compressed air. A damp cloth can be used to remove the sawdust if it tends to stick to the sheet because of static charges, which may build up during very dry weather. The moisture in the cloth will dissipate the static as well as clean the sheet. A traveling circular saw should be used for straight cuts in unmasked sheets so that the unprotected surfaces of the sheets need not be moved during sawing.

Band Saws

Where flat sheets are to be cut in curves or where formed parts are to be rough trimmed, band saws can be used. Large saws with a 30-36 inch throat are best for production work. Some of the newer band saws are arranged so that the speed can be changed to suit the work.

In general, the thicker the material, the slower the speed, to insure against overheating. Speed, feed and thickness of stock should be such that each tooth cuts a clean chip. If the speed is too high in proportion to the feed, the teeth will rub and heat up, rather than cut free. The blade should run at speeds of from 2,300-5,000 feet per minute.

Metal-cutting blades have been found best for Plexiglas®. They stay sharp longer than the softer wood-working blades. When dull, they should be thrown away.

Blade thickness, width and number/type of teeth will depend on the size of the saw, the thickness of the material to be cut and the minimum radius. All metal handsaws are set to give side clearance. Always use the widest blade allowed.

CIRCULAR SAWS			
Thickness to be Cut	Blade Thickness	Teeth per Inch	Type Blade
0.040 - 0.080"	1/16 - 3/32"	8-14	hollow ground
0.100 - 0.150"	3/32 - 1/8"	6-8	hollow ground
0.187 - 0.375"	3/32 - 1/8"	5-6	spring set
0.438 - 0.750"	1/8"	3-4	spring set or swaged
1 - 4"	1/8 - 5/32"	3-3.5	spring set, swaged or cemented carbide

Table 5-4-2. Circular saws for cutting Plexiglas®

Figure 5-4-27. Turning Plexiglas®

Internal cuts can be made with a saber saw or plunge router. Use a drilled starting hole, and drill holes at each change of direction or corner.

The usual rules of good machining practice apply to the machining of Plexiglas®, which has working qualities like those of hardwood, brass or copper.

Tools and work should be held firmly to prevent chattering. Standard metal- or woodworking equipment can be used, such as milling machines, lathes, planers and shapers. The general rule of fast tool speed and slow material feed should be followed. Tools should be sharp, clean and free from nicks and burrs.

When proper speed, feed and cutters are used, machined surfaces will have an even, semi-matte surface which can be brought to a high polish by sanding and buffing.

Plexiglas®, like most plastics, is a poor conductor of heat and, being a thermoplastic, tends to soften if frictional heat is generated during machining operations. Excessive heat usually results in gumming and tearing of the plastic, or sticking of the tool.

If the tools are sharp and properly ground, Plexiglas® can be machined at reasonable speed without a coolant. Where excessive heat is encountered, water or soluble oils are recommended. Other coolants may contain chemicals harmful to Plexiglas® or to the masking paper adhesive. When coolants come in contact with masking paper, they reduce the effectiveness of the paper and make its removal difficult.

Specifications for parts to be machined to close tolerances should include temperature and humidity conditions at which the parts are to be inspected.

In order to maintain close tolerances, it is necessary to anneal Plexiglas® before machining, following up with all rough machining operations. After a subsequent re-annealing operation, the Plexiglas® should be finish-machined, removing as little material as practical. The part should then be subjected to a final annealing operation.

Figure 5-4-28. Edge finishing using a router

Turning

Plexiglas® can be turned on a lathe (Figure 5-4-27) to produce an excellent semi-matte surface. Cutting tools should have a zero or slightly negative rake angle.

Surface speeds of 500 feet per minute with feeds of .004 inch to .005 inch per revolution will cut a clean, continuous chip. The feed of the work should be kept constant throughout the cut. If the feed stops, the Plexiglas® may be marked. The maximum permissible depth of cut is controlled by the rigidity of the section being turned.

Routing and Shaping

Woodworking shapers (also called table routers) are used for a variety of edge-finishing operations to predetermined cross-section and cutting-to-size of both flat and formed parts as seen in Figure 5-4-28.

These machines should have a no-load spindle speed of 10,000-22,000 r.p.m. Two- or three-flute cutters less than 1-1/2 inch in diameter running at these speeds will produce the smoothest cut. At slower spindle speeds, the cutter should have more flutes or blades and should be larger in diameter to produce the necessary surface speed.

Cutters should be kept sharp and should have a back-clearance angle of about 10° and a positive rake angle up to 15°.

Portable routers can be used wherever the Plexiglas® part is too large or awkward to bring to a table router. They are useful for obtaining a normal or right angle cut when trimming the edge of a formed piece.

Deflanging operations can be performed on all of the above-mentioned machines by using a veneer saw blade (3 or 4 inch diameter) attached with a suitable arbor to the router spindle.

Where close tolerances are not essential, the use of jigs or fixtures is not required.

For flange trimming operations, a standard woodworking router bit is most commonly used. A trimming fixture should be built, incorporating a template cut to the outlines specified for the trimmed part. If a pilot of the same diameter as the router cutter is inserted in the machine table, the template can be slid along the pilot while the router cutter trims the flange to size.

Where a wood shaper or a table router is to be used for flange-trimming operations, a ball bearing router flush-trimming tool may be used. Some machines have provisions by which a collar may be inserted concentric with the spindle to act as a template pilot.

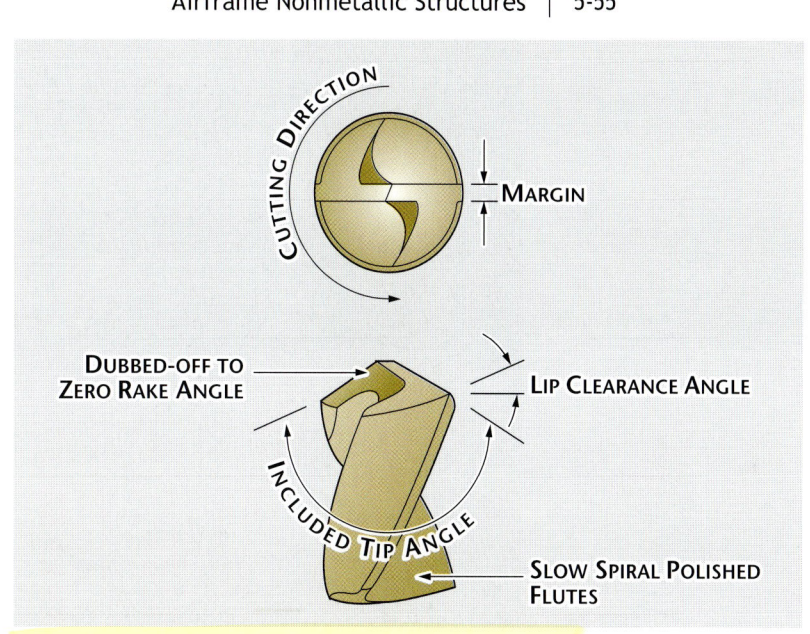

Figure 5-5-29. Special drills are available for Plexiglas®

The part is located by a fixture incorporating a template. Care should be taken that the template is designed to allow for the difference between the radius of the cutter and the radius of the bearing or pilot collar to produce the correct finished size.

When trimming cemented assemblies, where the outlines of the cemented panel should he flush with those of the returns of a formed or fabricated part, a ball bearing router is also used. In this case, however, the tip of the router bit is ground down to provide a pressed fit with the bore of the inner race of a ball bearing whose outside diameter is the same as the diameter of the router bit. The bearing is used as a guide to trim the part.

Drilling

Twist drills commonly used for metals can be used for Plexiglas®, but better surface finish and higher production rates can be obtained if special techniques and modified standard twist drills or special drills are used. See Figure 5-4-29.

For drilling Plexiglas®, the cutting edges of the twist drills should be dubbed off to zero rake angle to prevent catching the material. Bits recommended for different hole depths are as follows:

For shallow holes use slow, spiral-twist drills with wide, polished flutes. An included tip angle of 55°-60° is recommended. Shallow holes have a depth/hole diameter ratio less than 1-1/2:1. The lip clearance angle should be ground to 15°-20°. Chip removal is no problem in drilling shallow holes, and no coolant is needed.

Figure 5-4-30. Drilling Plexiglas® using a hole saw

Figure 5-4-31. Tapping Plexiglas®

For medium-deep holes, use a slow, spiral-twist drill with polished flutes, which should be as wide as possible to aid in removing a continuous ribbon of material. Medium-deep holes have a depth/hole diameter ratio from 1-1/2:1 up to 3:1. The optimum included tip angle, between 60° and 140°, will depend on the size of the flute. Lip clearance angles should be ground to 12°-15°. The feed of the drill should be controlled so that a continuous chip is cut and cleared without overheating the plastic at the tip of the drill. No coolant is needed for drilling holes up to 3:1 depth/diameter ratios, although a jet of compressed air directed into the hole as it is being drilled is helpful. Drills with extra wide spirals and compressed air cooling can clear a continuous chip from holes with depth/diameter ratios up to 5:1.

For deep holes use a slow, spiral-twist drill with wide polished flutes and include a tip angle of 140°. Deep holes have a depth/hole diameter ratio greater than 3:1. The wider tip angle results in a shorter cutting edge and narrow chip. The lip clearance angle should be ground to 12°-15°. The feed should be slow — approximately 2-1/2 inches per minute so that powder, rather than shavings or continuous chips, will be formed. A coolant is necessary for drilling deep holes, to avoid scoring or burning the surface of the hole.

Compressed air car be used as a coolant for holes with depth diameter ratios up to 5:1. Water or a soluble oil-water coolant can also be used. When applied at the entry hole, however, a liquid coolant is actually pumped out of the hole by the drill and seldom reaches the drill point. A standard oil hole drill can be used to insure delivery of the coolant to the drill point. The coolant can also be applied by filling a pilot hole drilled 95 percent of the way through the material or through a pilot hole drilled through from the opposite surface.

Cleaner, more transparent, deep holes can be produced by first drilling a pilot hole a little more than half the diameter of the final hole, filling this pilot hole with a wax stick, then redrilling to the final diameter. If the pilot hole is drilled all the way through, the Plexiglas® must be backed with wood to close the hole and make the wax stick effective. The wax lubricates the cut and supports and expels the chips during drilling. In clear Plexiglas®, the resulting hole is cleaner, smoother and more transparent than holes produced by other methods.

Large diameter holes can be cut with hollow-end mills, hole saws (Figure 5-4-30), fly cutters or trepanning tools. The cutters of the latter should be ground to zero rake angle and adequate back clearance, just as lathe tools are ground. All these tools can be used in the standard vertical spindle drill press or in flexible-shaft or portable hand drills.

In general, the speed at which Plexiglas® sheets can be drilled depends largely on the quality of the equipment used. Plexiglas® can be drilled at the highest speed at which the drill will not wobble enough to affect the finish of the hole. However, large diameter drills require slower rotative speeds for best results. Also, the Plexiglas® should be backed with wood and the feed slowed as the drill point breaks through the underside of the sheet.

For accuracy and safety, Plexiglas® parts should be clamped or held rigidly during drilling.

Tapping and Threading

Standard machine shop tools and procedure may be used for these operations (Figure 5-4-31).

Wherever possible, the National Coarse Thread System should be applied. On diameters of more than 1 inch, Acme threads are preferred to V-formulations.

When tapped threads are to be transparent, a wax stick should be inserted in the drilled holes before tapping. As in drilling, the wax lubricates the cuts and supports and expels the chips during tapping, resulting in cleaner, more transparent threads. The wax stick is particularly useful for blind holes, for it tends to clean out the chips as they are formed.

Sanding

Standard belt or disk sanding machines may be used. For parts too large to be handled by these machines, portable sanders or hand-sanding blocks may be preferred. Small, machined pieces are frequently sanded by rubbing them over sandpaper taped to a flat surface.

Sawed edges and other severe tool marks may be removed by sanding with medium grit (60-80) paper or belt. To further improve the surface (or edge), this operation may be followed by wet-sanding with wet-or-dry sanding paper or belt. It is often advisable to start with medium-fine grits (about 150) and use progressively finer grits. If transparent surfaces are to be produced, grits to 400 should be used when the material is to be machine buffed. Otherwise, as a preliminary operation to hand buffing, 600-grit abrasive should also be used. Round parts are most easily sanded in the lathe. Care must be taken to assure that all scratches left by the coarser grits are removed by the next finer grade of sandpaper. Sanded areas must be spread out to eliminate local hollows that would produce distorted areas. When power sanders are used, light pressure should be applied to reduce frictional heat. Dry sandpaper will tend to clog and drag, particularly in the finer grits.

Buffing

After sanding, the Plexiglas® part should be buffed on a muslin wheel dressed with tallow and abrasive, to bring the surface to a high polish. This should be followed by use of a clean, soft cotton flannel buffing wheel. See next paragraph). The Plexiglas® should be kept constantly in motion relative to the wheel to prevent overheating from friction. Light pressure against the buff will allow the polishing compound to produce the finish. The buffs should be cleaned, using the edge of a piece of Plexiglas® scrap, to remove dry, caked compound. A surface speed of 1,800-2,000 ft. per minute should be used.

Finish wheel. The Plexiglas® is next brought to a high polish on a soft, loose buff on which no abrasive or tallow is used (Figure 5-4-32). These cleaning buffs should be very loose and made of imitation chamois or flannel, 10-12 inches in diameter, running at 2,000-2,400 surface ft. per minute. Smaller buffs may be made to fit portable or flexible shaft equipment.

Hand polishing. If power buffing equipment is not available, a good polish can be obtained on small areas by hand polishing.

Painting

In spray or brush painting, acrylic-based lacquers provide finishes with the best adhesion attainable. Where painted Plexiglas® parts are not exposed to weather, most slow-drying enamels will perform satisfactorily.

Clean Plexiglas® parts are essential to obtain good paint adhesion. Soap, water and naphtha are recommended for cleaning Plexiglas® before painting.

Paint adhesion to Plexiglas® can be tested with masking tape. After the paint is thoroughly dry, apply the tape to the painted surface and then strip it off. If the tape does not pull the paint film off, the adhesion may be considered satisfactory.

Paint should be kept thoroughly stirred, because light transmittance through painted Plexiglas® will reveal non-uniform pigment distribution.

Brush painting. Acrylic-based lacquers are available in brush formulation and should be specified where this method of painting is to

Figure 5-4-32. Buffing Plexiglas®

be used. Mottled or grain effects are readily achieved on Plexiglas® by brush application.

Spray painting. Adequate paint mixing, proper air pressure, correct gun opening and paint viscosity are important factors in good quality spray painting of Plexiglas®. Suction-feed guns are satisfactory for small work and short runs. Longer runs and large work require pressure-feed tanks and automatic stirring. Application of uniform paint layers is more readily achieved when the Plexiglas® is located over a light box.

Annealing

Annealing consists of prolonged heating of the Plexiglas® part at temperatures lower than those used for forming, followed by slow cooling. See Table 5-4-3. Internal stresses set up during forming or machining of the part are reduced or eliminated by this treatment. This results in products of greater dimensional stability and greater resistance to crazing. Annealing also improves the strength of cemented joints by evaporating trapped solvent.

To obtain the benefits of annealing, the Plexiglas® parts must be annealed after all fabrication, including polishing, is completed. In addition to annealing after final finishing, machined parts should be annealed before cementing, to reduce stresses due to machining in the cemented joint area.

Formed parts may show objectionable deformation when annealed at these temperatures. Use caution in annealing formed parts in the higher temperature ranges.

RECOMMENDED HEATING TIMES FOR ANNEALING PLEXIGLAS®					
Thickness (inches)	Heating Time in Hours for a Forced Air Oven Maintained at the Indicated Temperature*				
	230°F	210°F	195°F	175°F	160°F
0.060 to 0.150	2	3	5	10	24
0.187 to 0.375	2.5	3.5	5.5	10.5	24
0.500 to 0.750	3	4	6	11	24
0.875 to 1.125	3.5	4.5	6.5	11.5	24
1.250 to 1.500	4	5	7	12	24
*Includes period of time required to bring part up to annealing temperature.					

Table 5-4-3. Time and temperature chart for annealing Plexiglas®

Section 5
Wood Structures

Not surprisingly, the first airplanes were made of wood and bamboo. After all, wood was familiar, strong and easily worked using the tools and technology of the day. Besides, the material for metal structures had not been developed to the extent necessary to build an airplane. Wood continued to be the principal structural material for the first 35 years of aviation. Even with the introduction of welded steel tubing for fuselages and tail surfaces, wood continued to be the primary material for wing spars and ribs for several more years.

With the advent of WWII and on through the 1940s, wooden airplanes became popular again; this time because wood was a non-strategic material. Several major aircraft designs were produced from all wood, or a combination of wood and steel tubing. Many designs used molded plywood fuselages: a perfect example of semi-monocoque construction.

In this chapter, we are not going to dwell on a bygone era, because the likelihood that an Aircraft Maintenance Technician will ever see an example of these machines is rare. What few that survive are in museums or private collections. Flying examples are hard to come by.

Even if you had the opportunity, there is a regulatory process that makes it difficult. FAR Part 65, section 65.81, says that to do a process or procedure for the first time, you must be under the supervision of someone else who has satisfactorily performed it in the past. Those people are going to be hard to find.

Working on airplanes with some type of wooden construction that are in the system today is not a problem. The ever-popular Boeing Stearman biplane trainer of 1941 (Figure 5-5-1) is still flying in large numbers today. It has all-wooden wings and center section. Many light, general aviation airplanes flying these days have wooden spars and metal wing ribs. In the experimental aircraft movement, there are a large number of wooden designs that are still popular.

As long as these types of airplanes are still in the fleet, AMTs need to know about wooden structures.

The Nature of Wood

There is a little bit more to understanding wood than simply cutting a tree into boards. To start with, we need to know which trees can be

Figure 5-5-1. The Boeing Stearman trainer is still one of the most popular biplanes today. Its wings and center section are all-wood construction.

turned into airplanes. The principal species of wood used in aviation today are:

Hardwoods

White ash. The heartwood of white ash is grayish brown (occasionally with a reddish tinge), and the sapwood, which varies in thickness from less than an inch to several inches, is white. Ash is somewhat similar in appearance to oak and hickory. It ranks high in weight, strength, hardness and shock resistance, retains its shape well, wears well, is flexible and is easy to bend. It does not take glue as readily as spruce. Ash is used for sheet metal dies and forms, for propellers, bearing blocks, wing leading and trailing edges, and reinforcing for structural members.

Basswood. The heartwood of basswood is creamy brown, and the sapwood is creamy white. Basswood has a slight characteristic odor, even when dry. It is light in weight, low in strength, straight-grained, easily workable and can be nailed without splitting. It is a satisfactory low-density species for use in plywood and for filler blocks and corner blocks.

Birch. The woods of the yellow birch and sweet birch are very similar; generally, no distinction is made between the two. The sapwood is almost white and the heartwood is light to moderately deep reddish-brown. The annual rings are indistinct. The wood of both is heavy, hard, stiff and strong, has good shock-resisting ability but is low in natural resistance to decay. The wood does not split easily and glues well. Sweet and yellow birch are used for propellers and in plywood construction.

Mahogany. Mahogany is a lustrous reddish-brown wood that turns darker after exposure to light. It is a heavy wood, varying greatly in weight. The pores are distinctly visible; numerous pores contain dark amber-colored gum. The growth rings are defined by light-colored lines and are widely variable in width. The wood is easy to work and glue. Mahogany is a basic structural material, used mainly in plywood form for rib gussets, webs, skin covering and propellers.

Hard maple. The heartwood of hard maple is light reddish-brown, and its sapwood is white with a slight reddish-brown tinge. The annual rings are defined by a thin, reddish layer usually conspicuous on dressed longitudinal surfaces, and the rays appear as reddish brown flakes on radial faces. The grain is usually straight, but occasionally curly and wavy grains occur. The wood is heavy, hard, strong, and stiff, has good resistance to shock, and wears well under abrasion. It has moderate shrinkage, good gluing properties and, although hard, does not dull tools excessively. It is used in plywood construction, for propellers, jigs, bearing blocks and miscellaneous other uses where an extremely hard wood is desired.

Oak. There are numerous species of oak that commonly are divided into two groups: red oak and white oak. The heartwood of white oak is grayish brown, while that of the red oak usually has a reddish tinge. The sapwood is white. The pores in the heartwood of white oak are less permeable to liquids than that of red oak. The rays are quite pronounced in the sawed lumber. The wood is heavy, hard, stiff and strong. It is used for propellers and test clubs.

Yellow poplar. The heartwood of yellow poplar is a yellowish-brown with a greenish tinge; the sapwood is white. The annual rings are limited by light-colored lines. The wood is slightly heavier than spruce and, while rather low in shock-resisting ability, has good working qualities, retains its shape well, is comparatively free from checks and shakes and glues well. It is easy to nail because it does not split readily, and is easy to glue. It is regarded as a satisfactory substitute for spruce but is slightly less strong in compression and shear. Such substitution involves no necessity for engineering changes. Poplar is used in plywood construction (core and faces) and as a substitute for spruce.

Black walnut. The heartwood of black walnut varies from light, to dark brown; the sapwood is lighter in color. The annual rings are fairly distinct, for the pores in the springwood decrease in size gradually as the springwood merges into the summerwood. The color and distinct pores are usually sufficient to distinguish black walnut from other woods. The wood is heavy, strong, stiff and has the quality to retain its shape under varying conditions of moisture. It is easily worked and glues satisfactorily. It is used for propellers and may be used as a substitute for mahogany plywood.

Softwoods

Spruce. Sitka spruce is the standard by which all other woods are measured. In white spruce and red spruce, the heartwood is as light-colored as the sapwood, whereas in Sitka spruce, the heartwood has a light reddish tinge, rendering it slightly darker than the sapwood. Split or smoothly dressed tangential surfaces of Sitka spruce usually have numerous slight indentations that give it a pocked appearance. Red, white and Sitka spruce possess excellent strength properties, with a high ratio of strength to weight. They may be glued with facility. Spruce is a basic structural wood used for highly stressed parts such as spars, struts and compression ribs; it is also used for capstrips and in plywood. Spruce is considered the most desirable of all softwoods used in aircraft construction.

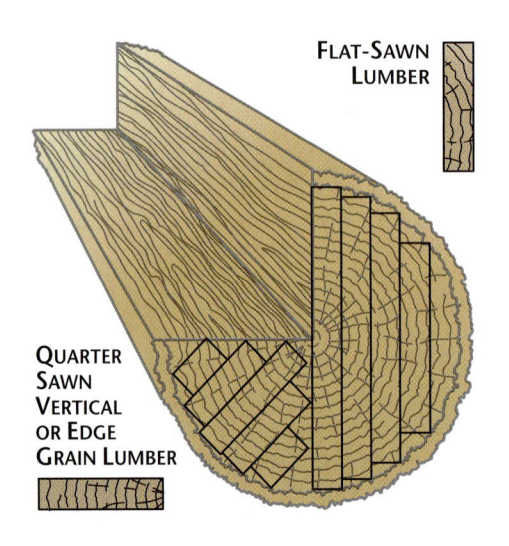

Figure 5-5-2. The difference between flat-sawn and quarter-sawn wood

Balsa. There are no annular rings in balsa. The biggest feature is its extremely light weight: approximately 1/2 that of cork. Balsa is never used where strength is a factor. Its most common use is not in wooden structure, but as a core material for laminated composite panels. It has been supplanted by various kinds of honeycomb core material. Its gluing qualities are excellent.

Port Orford cedar. The sapwood of Port Orford cedar is not clearly defined from the heartwood and is very pale brown in color. Highly resistant to decay, it has a spicy odor. Moderately lightweight (heavier than spruce), it has slightly less strength than spruce, except in compression and shear loads. It is used as a spruce substitute, but gluing can be difficult.

Douglas fir. Wood from the Pacific coast is somewhat heavier than spruce, but its strength is equal or higher to that of spruce. More likely to develop checks, Douglas fir can split and splinter during fabrication. It is excellent for spars, particularly routed or laminated blanks, and is found in many original Boeing Stearman wings. Large, solid sizes should be avoided because they are difficult to inspect internally.

Noble fir. Generally a western tree, it is easier to work than Douglas fir. It can be used as a direct substitute for spruce, providing shear is not critical, because it is rated 8 percent deficient compared to spruce. It does, however, glue well.

Western hemlock. Though becoming difficult to obtain, western hemlock can be used as a direct substitute for spruce. Annular rings are clearly defined, with narrow bands of summerwood. Somewhat heavier than spruce, quarter-sawn lumber is straight-grained, resin-free, and glues well.

White pine. There is little difference between eastern and western white pine. Both are moderately lightweight, straight-grained and actually smell like pine. Lighter weight than spruce, it is rated between 5-15 percent lower in strength; particularly in hardness (compression) and shock (shear). It cannot be used as a direct replacement for spruce, but must be increased in size accordingly. It glues well.

Working with Wood

While many AMTs have knowledge and experience in working with wood from their school shop days, some do not. Because of the limited exposure to wooden airplanes, it is beyond practicality to teach woodworking machines and processes in an aviation textbook. It is even difficult to cover the various repair processes used. For the most part, these examples are thoroughly covered in FAA AC 43.13-1B. Most

Figure 5-5-3. A newly constructed wing with the ribs being fitted over the spar

of the material necessary to cover testing can also be found in the same Advisory Circular. At best, we can only cover that which is different from other facets of woodworking, and maybe offer some advice along the way.

To begin, minor repairs to wooden structures could conceivably be accomplished by anyone who knows how to work with their tools. Carefully studying AC 43.13-1B could get you through the simple things. If a major repair or reconstruction is in your future, first think critically about your woodworking skill levels. If you do not deem them sufficient, you should think about taking a course in woodworking from your local community college. There, you can learn how to work the tools and develop the skills necessary in working with the materials. Classes need not be lengthy.

Many woodworkers' supply stores have free classes in seemingly mundane things that are extremely important. One of the best is a class on how to sharpen your tools. An old saying among woodworkers is "First you buy a tool, then you sharpen it." Once learned, it is a lifelong skill that most people don't have and AMTs would be wise to exercise.

Purchasing Aircraft Wood

There is a difference between how lumber and aircraft wood are cut at the sawmill. Figure 5-5-2 shows it better than it can be explained.

Flat-sawn lumber. Regular lumber is flat, or slab, sawn. This method produces the most lumber in the widest boards possible from a log. This is what you get when you go to the home supply store or regular lumberyard. It also shrinks, warps, splits and crawls all over the place as the internal stresses try to equalize. Almost nothing that comes from a flat-sawn log can be used in aircraft construction or repair.

Quarter-sawn lumber. To get the best lumber that will not shrink excessively or exhibit any of the undesirable tendencies of flat-sawn lumber, it is necessary to *quarter-saw* a log. This is a process that must start at the sawmill. Quarter-sawing produces the best wood available, but the process is somewhat wasteful and time consuming. It is a specialty practiced only by craftsmen that supply the specialty market. The most common use for quarter-sawn wood is for quality furniture and cabinet making.

Commercial aircraft wood. While it is possible to purchase your own spruce at a specialty lumberyard, it is not really a good use of your time. There are specialty stores that supply the home-built market who stock aircraft lumber and plywood. The wood has already been graded and, in the case of spars, cut to size for the particular airplane you are working on. You are, however, responsible for inspecting it when it arrives. Figure 5-5-3 is an example of a wing made from commercial aircraft spruce.

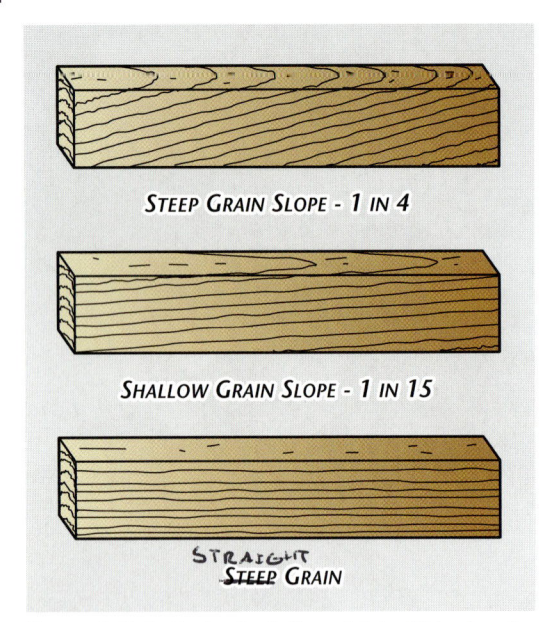

Figure 5-5-4. Grain deviation of 1 in 15 inches is allowable. Any more slope in a shorter length is cause for rejection.

Grain deviation (slope). One of the main standards for aircraft wood is grain deviation. Quarter-sawn wood that has grain structure that runs straight to the end of the board is rare. Most boards have deviation, or grain that runs off the edge. The standard for deviation is set by FAA AC 43.13-1B. Figure 5-5-4 shows how to measure deviation. Grain deviation is the major cause of rejection of otherwise good spruce.

Drilling spars. Good quality drills are available that will drill a quality hole in spar material without tearing out wood splinters. Always use a drill press with a wooden backup to prevent tear-out as the drill exits the back side. If the installation uses aluminum bushings, make sure they fit correctly before assembly.

Between the material covered so far and that provided by the FAA, you should know enough to be able to buy aircraft quality wood.

Gluing

While the amount, and the quality, of available wood have decreased through the years, two things have vastly improved: glue- and varnish-type finishes.

Types of glue. Early wooden structures used Casein glue. Casein glue is not waterproof and can support fungus growth. It has been avoided for several years. In its place came plastic resin glue (urea-formaldehyde) and resorcinol adhesive (resorcinol-formaldehyde). Of these two, only resorcinol has survived. There is another glue mentioned by the FAA, phenol-formaldehyde, but it is used in plywood manufacture and you will never come across it in normal use.

Figure 5-5-5. Gluing ribs to the spar with epoxy glue

FAA AC 43-13.1B lists a method for choosing a newer epoxy wood glue without actually endorsing any specific brand. It even lists the government specifications the material should meet, along with performance guidelines. Figure 5-5-5 shows rib verticals being glued to the spar with an epoxy glue.

Joint preparation. One of the reasons for the prior discussion about learning how to sharpen tools has to do with joint preparation prior to gluing. A joint should never be sanded prior to gluing. Sanding will leave small dust particles on the surfaces. These will actually plug up pores in the wood, making an inferior joint. For a full strength joint, glue on a cut surface, not a sanded one.

Gluing a joint. Again, AC 43-13.1B has an extensive section on gluing and clamping. The advice is good and not much can be added. There are excellent clamps on the market today. Figure 5-5-6 shows a spar splice being clamped using Jorgensen-type cabinetmakers' clamps. When clamping something, adjust the blocks to clamp against the repair and let the blocks apply the pressure. It is more uniform that way.

All splices, from cap-strips and plywood inserts to wing spars, must have a scarfed joint where they are spliced. In aircraft woodwork, a scarf is a joint cut on an angle. This increases the surface area of the joint for gluing, allowing it to develop 100-percent strength. The angle is 10 to 1, meaning that a piece of wood 1 inch thick has a scarf cut 10 inches long. Before you ever do one for real, do a practice one, because it takes a little time getting familiar with the process.

Once splices are ready to glue up, they have to be aligned. Figure 5-5-7 shows how they can be misaligned. By first applying pressure to the scarf, it will tend to slide away from the center. The joint must be clamped on both sides of the scarf before the pressure is actually applied to the joint itself.

Repair and Finishing

Nothing can be added to this subject that isn't covered in the AC. It goes into great length on common repairs and protective finishes. It even includes the federal specifications for the varnish. The AC also goes into detail on how to clean a structure that has been contaminated by oil or grease.

If you wonder why so much emphasis has been placed on AC 43-13.1B, it is because it is acceptable data for common operations on airplanes that do not have a maintenance manual. Diagrams may be referenced as support for repairs that are the same as the AC examples. If anything not addressed in the AC is required, it would be best to discuss it with your local Flight Standards District Office prior to starting the project.

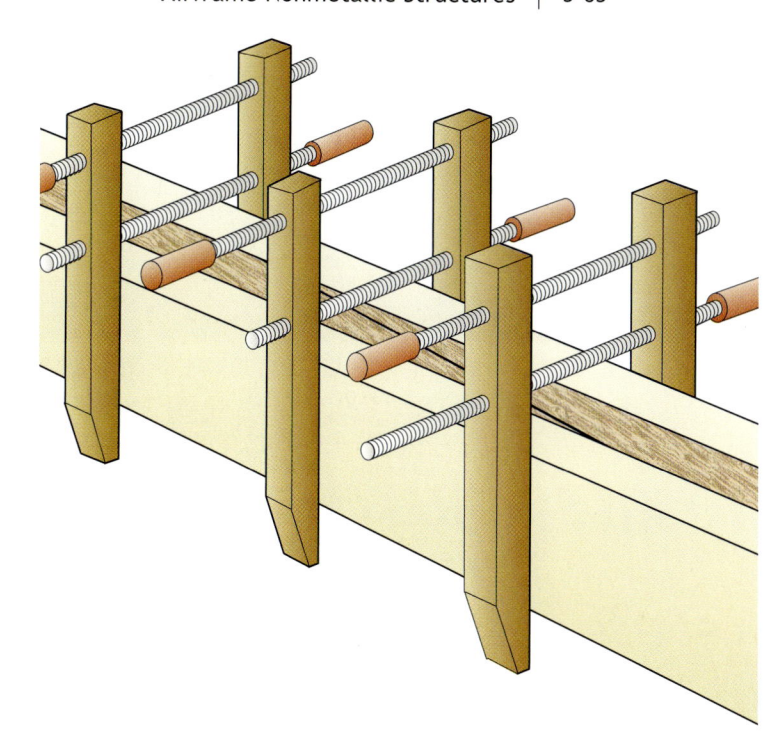

Figure 5-5-6. Cabinetmakers' clamps applied to a spar splice

Inspection

Once again, the AC has about the best information on inspecting wooden structures available. Remember that no decay is acceptable.

Not much has changed over time except the use of a *moisture meter* to inspect a wooden structure for excessive moisture content. A corrected moisture content anywhere close to 20 percent means that there is the likelihood of fungus establishing itself somewhere in the structure. Fungus means wood decay, and decay means replacing the rotted member.

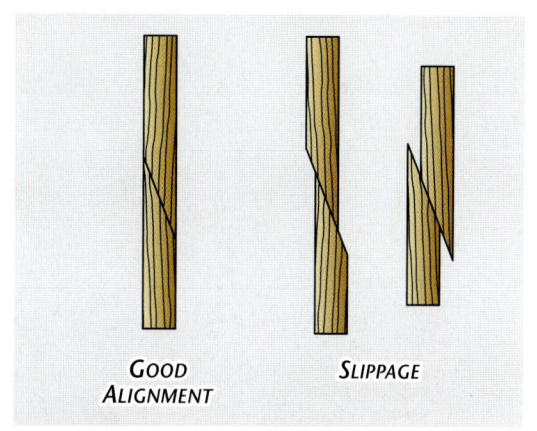

GOOD ALIGNMENT   SLIPPAGE

Figure 5-5-7. Examples of scarf joints showing end slippage

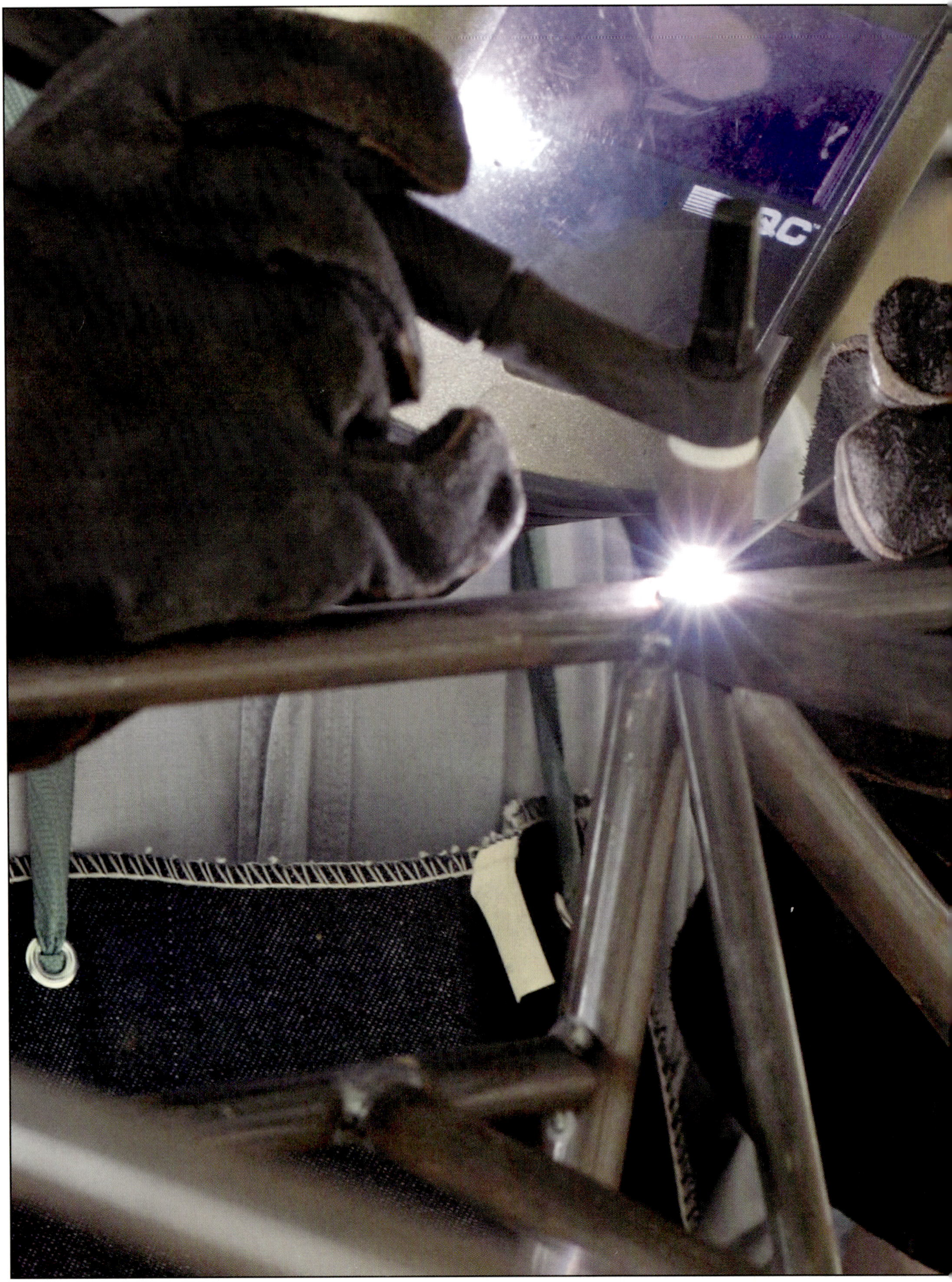

6

Welding Techniques

Section 1

Welded Structures

Welded steel tubing, as an aircraft construction method, first started with Dutch-born airplane designer/manufacturer Anton Herman Gerard Fokker (1890-1939) with the invention of his first monoplane, "The Spider," in 1910. See Figure 6-1-1. He went on to perfect the process, opening his first aircraft factory in 1912. The airplanes his company designed and produced for Germany during World War I were some of the best in the world at the time. In fact, English pilots began to refer to themselves as "Fokker Fodder," fearing airbattle against the fast-climbing, highly maneuverable Fokker Dr. I. and its most famous pilot, Manfred von Richtofen. See Figures 6-1-2 and 6-1-3. The construction methods continued to improve, and most aircraft in the 1920s and '30s were constructed in the same manner, with Fokker's Trimotor (Figure 6-1-4) being used for many record-setting flights and by most commercial airlines.

Figure 6-1-1. Anton "Anthony" Fokker's first aircraft was a monoplane called Die Spinne, or The Spider, manufactured in 1910.

Photo courtesy of Paul von Weezepoel

Learning Objectives

REVIEW
- Metallic aircraft components

DESCRIBE
- How stress is created in metal by welding and how it can be relieved
- Gasses used in welding
- Common welding equipment
- Safe handling and storage of welding gasses

EXPLAIN
- Types of welding flames
- Characteristics of unacceptable welds
- Basic welding techniques
- Gas-shielded arc welding

APPLY
- Inspect a weld
- Weld a joint
- Solder a joint

Far left. Welding steel tube structures is still more of an art than a science. While oxy-acetylene welding has largely been replaced by the TIG process, both are an important facet of the aviation maintenance trade.

Figure 6-1-2. The Fokker Dr. I triplane had an unmatched rate of climb, high-speed diving ability, ease of handling and good pilot visibility.
Photo courtesy of the U.S. Air Force Museum

Figure 6-1-3. The Fokker Dr. I's most famed and feared pilot, Manfred von Richtofen, more commonly remembered as The Red Baron.
Photo courtesy of the U.S. Air Force Museum

Welded tubing fuselages and empennages continued in favor until well into the 1950s. Indeed, some specialty airplanes — and a good number of homebuilts — are still fabricated that way today. The reason welded tubing airframes have retained their popularity for such a long time is simple: They are strong, lightweight, can be fabricated with simple tooling and are fairly easy to maintain and repair.

Fuselage construction evolved around two basic design principles, both borrowed from the bridge builders of the day. They are the *Pratt truss*, which is a design of cross-bracing brought forward from wooden bridge construction, and the *Warren truss*, which is based on the N-brace principal used in steel bridges. In airframe use, the Pratt truss was redesigned to include only one diagonal, because steel tubing can take both a tension and compression load. Figure 6-1-5 shows both types.

During the late '30s and '40s came the peak of what has been called *The Golden Age of Aviation*. This is when the airplanes that have become today's classics were designed and built. Figure 6-1-6 shows the steel fuselage of a Bellanca JE-1 after welding and painting were completed. Notice how all of the clamps and brackets are actually welded to the basic structure, including wing and landing gear fittings and all the interior control attach points. Figure 6-1-7 is the same fuselage with the interior appointments installed and the airplane ready for fabric covering. Notice the *wooden stringers* that attach to the welded formers. They set the outside form of the fuselage, allowing a more rounded structure to evolve from the square frame.

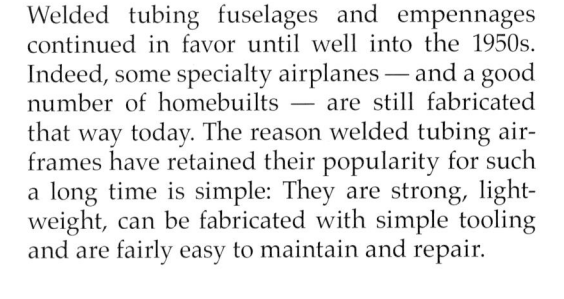

Figure 6-1-4. A flight crew at Langley installs an experimental low-drag cowling on a Fokker Trimotor in 1929. Photo courtesy of NASA

Structural Examples

While the structural detail of an aircraft like the Bellanca JE-1 could be a bit daunting to the beginner, one needs to look at it on a piece-by-piece basis. When an airplane is broken down into individual items, the scope of the process can be more easily understood.

Most airframes were built with four longerons that ran from the firewall to the tailpost. This produced a square or rectangular interior, with the outside shape being decided by the attached formers and stringers. Because the same size tubing for the aft section of the airframe wasn't needed for the forward (cabin) section, diameter was reduced by splicing in smaller tubing for the aft section. Figure 6-1-8 shows a longeron size reduction, as well as various types of welded tubing structural samples. For the record, when one tube connects to another (at any angle) it is called a *joint*. When more than two tubes connect at the same place, it becomes a *cluster*. The cluster is named by the number of tubing projections it has. Thus, a *five-tube cluster* only has four actual tubes in it.

Expansion and Contraction

When metal is heated, it increases in size, both in length and in breadth. If the heating is continued, the expansion will continue until the metal reaches a plastic state. Inversely, as the temperature falls, the metal will contract slightly more that it expanded. Terrific pressure is exerted by metal as it is expanding. Unless the entire piece is being heated uniformly, the section that is being heated will exert enough pressure to distort or crack the piece. If the metal is reasonably ductile, the result of the pressure will be a buckling of the metal in the heated area or a stretching of the metal in the surrounding area. If the metal is brittle, the result will be that a crack is likely to occur.

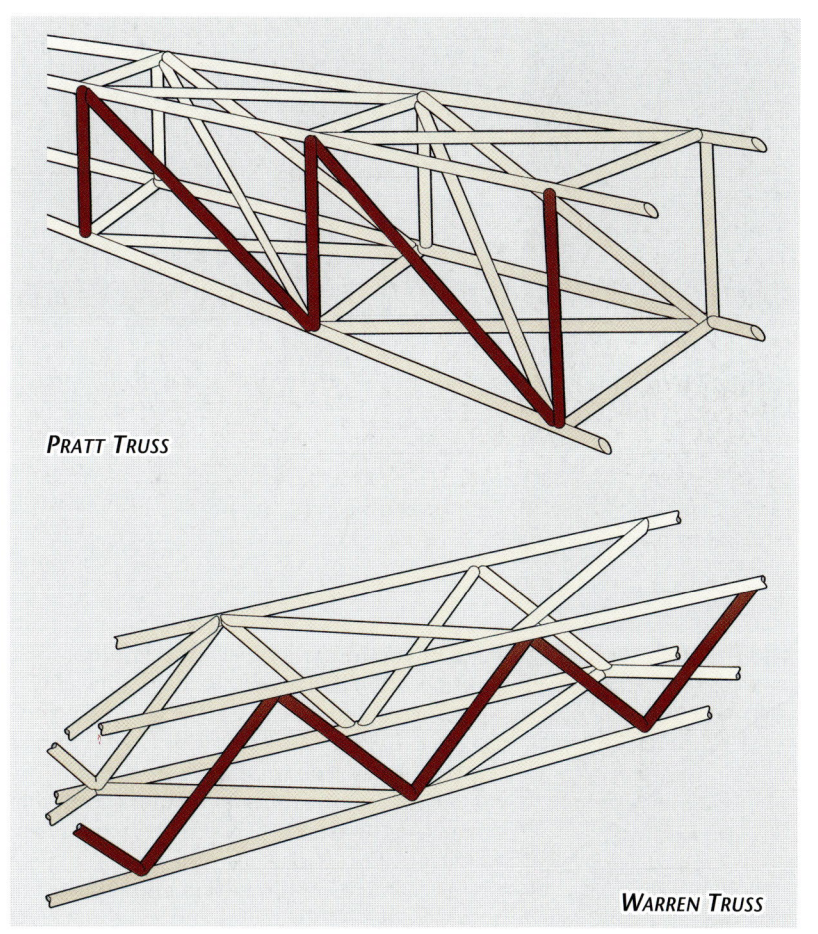

Figure 6-1-5. A Pratt truss and a Warren truss

Figure 6-1-6. This picture of a Bellanca JE-1 shows a welded fuselage back when this construction method produced the jewels of the industry.

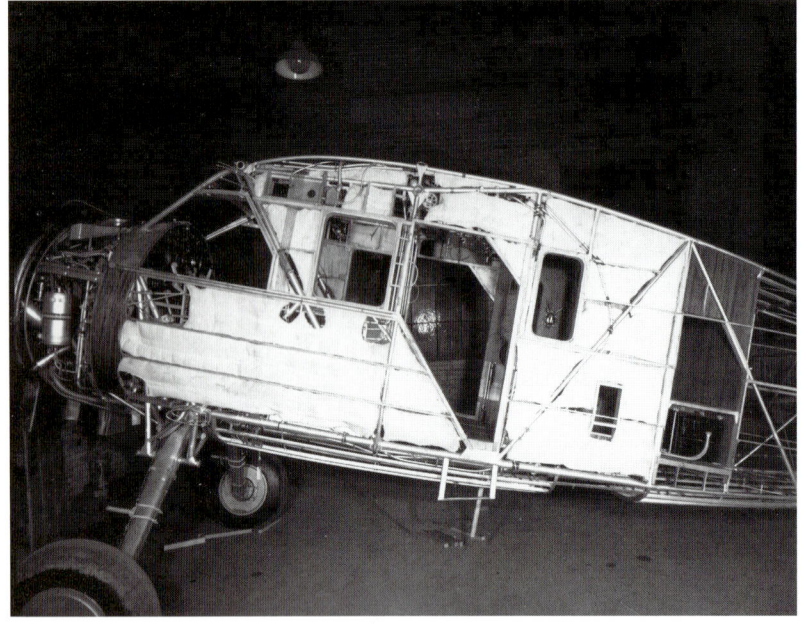

Figure 6-1-7. After welding and painting were completed, the airframe interior appointments were installed. From here, the airframe got its fabric covering.

Now let us assume that the metal is heated to the welding temperature. Obviously, the metal a short distance from the weld will be heated only slightly and will resist the expansion of the weld area. As the metal at the center of the heated area becomes hot enough to be plastic, it will become less resistant to the pressure surrounding it, and it will be squashed, compressed and thickened. This condition continues throughout the progress of the weld.

Of course, not all the pressure or stress will be taken up by this squashing process, and as long as the weld area is hotter than the surrounding area, there will be a slight distortion. Figure 6-1-9 is a good example of this condition. It shows the shape assumed by the base tube during the process of welding the branch tube to it. Arrows show the direction of pressure. The underside of the base tube is not nearly as hot as the top side, and it will expand very little. As the metal cools and contraction begins, the piece attempts to return to its original shape. Owing to the fact that the plastic-state metal was compressed to relieve the pressure and is now cooled to the extent that it is no longer plastic, the tube will necessarily have to contract past its original shape to make up for the shortage of metal caused by that compression. These stresses continue in the cold state. They are called *internal stresses*.

Normalizing. *Normalizing is a process similar to annealing.* The material being normalized is heated to a temperature slightly above critical temperature until it is evenly heated throughout. According to Machinery's Handbook, normalizing temperature is 1,600°F. Do not exceed

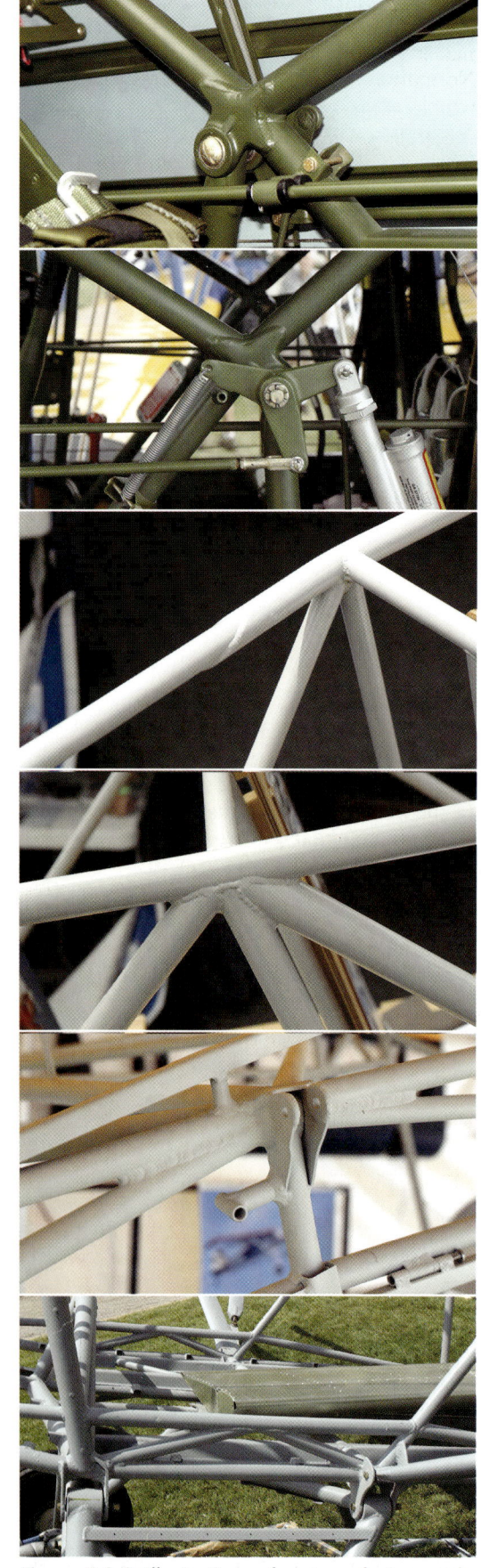

Figure 6-1-8. Illustrations of various clusters and combinations in a welded fuselage. Notice that some sections have cast or forged fittings and weldments included in/on the tubing structure.

the temperature by more than 50-75°F. Do not guess. Use a *temperature indicating crayon*. The material is then allowed to cool in still air. Normalizing will produce a hard, strong metal which is less ductile then when annealed. Normalizing relieves internal stresses and produces a greater uniformity of grain structure in the metal. Almost all SAE 4130 aircraft tubing is normalized when it is produced in the mill. Normalizing reduces the chances of failure from fatigue and built-up internal stresses. Normalizing of the weld and tube beside the weld will relieve the internal stress but will not relieve the distortion.

Straightening bent tubing. Straightening may be accomplished by the method shown in Figure 6-1-10. A steel bar of somewhat greater strength than the tubing, two vee blocks and a clamp large enough to clamp over the entire setup are all that is necessary to straighten this type of distortion.

Remember that the contraction will always exceed the expansion. Therefore, the tube will not only be distorted, but its length will also be shortened. This shrinkage will obviously be dependent on several factors: namely, the temperature to which the piece was heated, the size of the heated area, the location of the heated area in relation to the rest of the piece and the amount of outside stress that is applied to the members during the welding operation. The branch tube (Figure 6-1-9) will also shrink, and the angle at which it sets with the base tube will be slightly changed. The extent of contraction in welded joints in general is dependent on so many factors that it is impossible to have a rule that will determine it, so each joint must be analyzed individually.

Now consider the effect of several joints of this type, all on one base tube, as in the case of a longeron in a fuselage, with the various vertical tubes arising from it. Figure 6-1-11 shows the side view of a fuselage. The horizontal tubes at the top and bottom are the longerons, and the tubes that set at about 90° to them are called *vertical tubes*, whereas the tubes that are set diagonally between the vertical tubes are the *diagonals*. The longerons show the effect of having been welded, with a bow beneath each of the joints.

Shrink allowance. Allowance is made in the fixture for shrinkage that inevitably will follow the welding. This means that the entire fuselage, as it sets in the fixture before being welded, is oversized in every direction. The fixture holds each piece in its proper place and at its proper angle to the rest of the structure. The average weld in a fuselage will shrink the tubes from 1/32 to 1/16 inch each; therefore the vertical tubes, because they are welded at each end, should be cut from 1/16 to 1/8 inch longer than the dimension called for. A *shrink allowance* must be made for each weld on the longeron, since the accumulative shrink will sometimes be as much as 1/2 inch.

Judgment in allowing for shrinkage comes only with experience. The fastest way to familiarize yourself with the variations caused by the different sizes and weights of tubing is to start measuring any and every welding job you do, or that anyone else does. This will add to your practical knowledge and give you a basis for future projects.

Stress

Two-torch method. Many times the stresses set up by the welding are so great and the surrounding metal so rigid that the piece will not distort enough to relieve the pull of contraction, and a crack or series of cracks may develop. Many of these may be eliminated by the use of a flame playing on the underside of the piece that is being welded. An additional welding torch

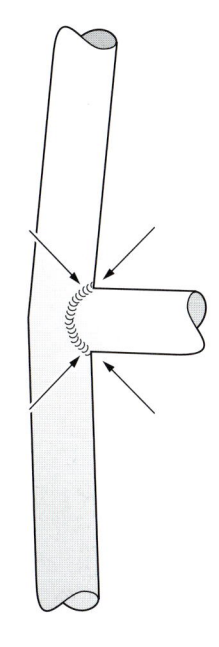

Figure 6-1-9. Tube warp

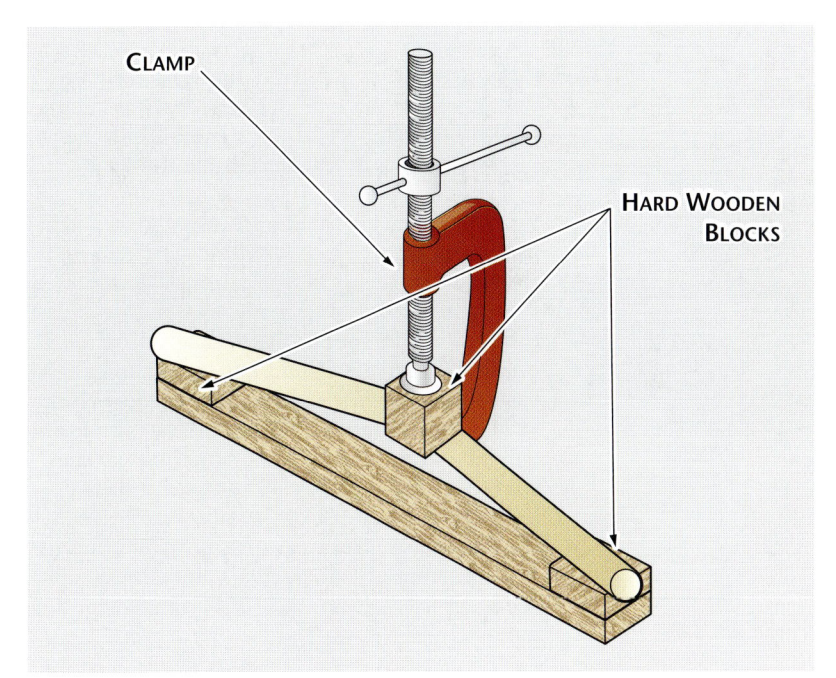

Figure 6-1-10. One method of straightening a bent tube involves placing the tube between two vee blocks and tightening the clamp on past straight to allow for springback of the tube.

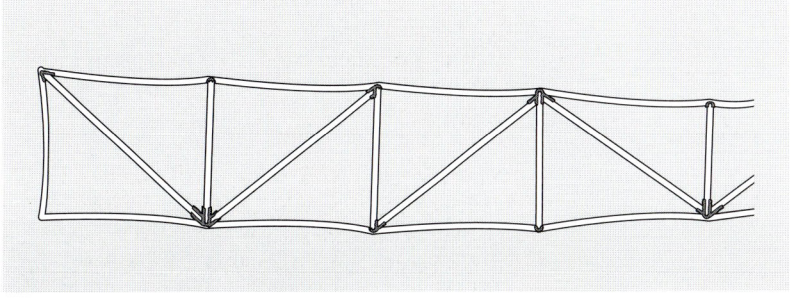

Figure 6-1-11. Warping of a longeron

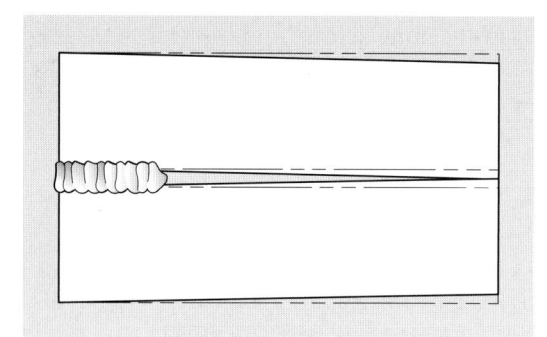

Figure 6-1-12. Warpage in sheet steel

with a large tip and a soft flame will work, as will a propane or a MAPP torch. When using an additional torch, don't overheat the piece. Remember that the second torch is only warming it up, not melting it down. The flame, playing upon the highly heated surface, unites with the oxygen in the air that surrounds it, thus preventing the formation of scale or iron oxide that is so common on the underside of welds. This flame not only helps eliminate cracks but also has the peculiar quality of reducing the amount of distortion to a noticeable degree.

Preheating with a second flame is frequently the only way to weld a large complicated cluster. Without the second torch there would never be enough heat in the piece to do the weld.

Subassemblies. Another method of controlling the contraction of welding, particularly in the case of large, complex assemblies in which it is necessary to hold the work to close finish dimensions for subsequent machining, is to break down these assemblies into smaller subassemblies in which the welding becomes more or less self-contained. These subassemblies are welded, straightened and sometimes normalized to relieve the internal stresses and strains. In the final assembly of the subassemblies into the one whole structure, only simple, not dangerous compounded strains, can be set up, and the likelihood of the structure being warped is averted.

Expansion and contraction, with the resulting shrinkage, cannot be eliminated but only allowed for.

Welds in sheet steel. Butt welds in sheet steel produce a different type of contraction. As the weld progresses, the two edges will be pulled together. If there has been no spacing, they will even overlap. This action causes no difficulties in the case of short welds, but in longer welds it is very noticeable. The reason for this is easily explained. The first inch or so of the weld does not react in so great a degree as it will from there on. As the weld moves along, the metal that has been molten and fully expanded solidifies. As the weld gets farther away, the temperature quite naturally becomes less. We know that as soon as a piece starts to cool, it starts to contract; therefore, as soon as the weld solidifies, the contraction sets in. The part previously welded is now reasonably cool and stiff, and the contracting metal cannot relieve itself in that locality. It therefore relieves itself in any area that is too weak to resist it, and that is obviously the metal ahead of the weld. The area that is contracting is so much greater than the area that is expanding that the force of expansion, being much less than that of contraction, will relieve itself in the area that is plastic. Thus, the farther the weld progresses, the more the edges will pull together. See Figure 6-1-12.

It is possible to tack the edges at frequent intervals and thus eliminate this pulling together, but the forces of expansion and contraction will still be at work and will manifest themselves by exceptionally large and numerous buckles. In the case of metal thick enough to withstand the warping effect, the finished piece will be full of internal stresses that will detract much from its strength. The most successful method of welding is to allow extra space between the edges at the end toward which the weld is progressing (usually 1/8-1/4 inch to the foot, as an average)

This method eliminates both the buckling and the internal stresses, since it allows the metal to assume the shape that the stresses force it to take. Some experimentation will be necessary to determine the proper spacing, since the contraction is dependent on the thickness of the metal, the width of the pieces and the speed with which the weld progresses. A weld that is made with a tip of as large a size as possible and at a rapid forward speed will not pull together so much as a weld made with a smaller size tip with the resulting slower rate of forward speed.

Another method that is widely used to prevent buckling is to remove the excess heat from the base metal adjacent to the weld by the use of heavy pieces of metal placed on either side of the weld, in direct contact with the base metal. Welding jigs often utilize this principle and, in the case of parts in which the surface is uneven, the fixture will be shaped to match the contour of the piece in order that perfect contact may be made along the entire weld. Clamps are used to secure the piece in the jig, thus eliminating undue movement of the parts.

Replacing Tubes

Anytime a tube, or section of tube, is removed, the remaining structure must be braced in order to retain its shape. Depending on the amount removed, bracing can be significant or simple. Sometimes it is best to do one repair piece at

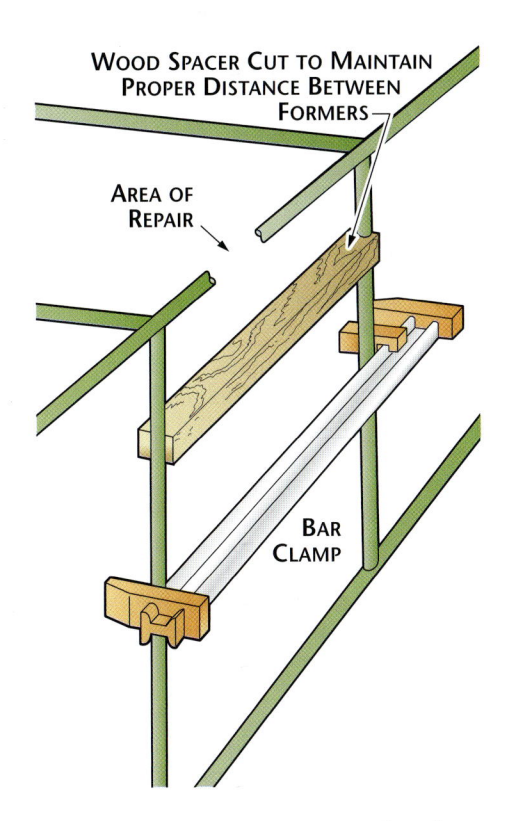

Figure 6-1-13. Bracing a structure to allow for tube replacement

a time and not remove everything needing replacement at one time.

FAA AC 43.13-1B contains many illustrations of acceptable tube repairs and splices.

When bracing for a tube replacement, as shown in Figure 6-1-13, it is possible to allow for shrinkage. The brace can be longer by the amount of estimated shrinkage.

Section 2
Oxyacetylene Welding, Brazing, Soldering and Cutting

Welding is the most practical metal joining process available. A welded joint offers rigidity, simplicity, low weight and high strength. Consequently, welding has been universally adopted in the manufacturing of all types of aircraft. Many structural and non-structural parts are joined by some form of welding.

In addition to the repair of aircraft parts and assemblies, there are almost limitless other welding jobs around an aircraft facility. Fabricating jigs and fixtures and repairing maintenance equipment and machinery are common everyday duties.

Oxyacetylene (Gas) Welding

Gas welding is a fusion process in which heat is supplied by burning a mixture of oxygen and acetylene; hence, the term oxyacetylene. A welding torch is used to mix the gases in the proper proportions and to direct the flame against the parts to be welded. The molten edges of the parts then literally flow together and, after cooling, form one solid piece. Usually, it is necessary to add material to the joint. The correct material in rod form is dipped in and fuses with the puddle of molten metal from the parent metal parts, hence the name *welding rod*.

Acetylene is widely used as the combustible gas because of its high flame temperature when mixed with oxygen. The temperature, which ranges from approximately 5,700-6,300°F, is so far above the melting point of all commercial metals that it provides a means for the rapid localized melting essential in welding.

The oxyacetylene flame is also used in cutting ferrous metals. The oxyacetylene welding and cutting methods are widely used by all types of manufacturing and maintenance activities because the flame is easy to regulate, the gases are inexpensive and the equipment can be transported easily and safely.

Equipment

Oxyacetylene welding equipment may be either stationary or portable. A portable outfit is fastened on a hand truck and pushed around from job to job. It consists of two cylinders: one contains oxygen, the other acetylene. Figure 6-2-1 shows a portable outfit mounted on a hand truck.

Stationary equipment is similar to a portable outfit except that the acetylene and oxygen are piped to several welding stations from a central supply. Master regulators are used to control the flow of gas and maintain a constant pressure at each station. This is known as a manifold system and is used in manufacturing and instruction.

Oxygen

As explained in previous chapters, oxygen will not burn by itself, but it will support combustion by combining with other gases. This means that it aids in burning, and this burning gives off considerable heat and light. Oxygen unites with the acetylene gas in oxyacetylene welding, causing it to burn and raising the temperature of the flame to the point where it will melt metal.

Oxygen is obtained for commercial use by one of two methods:

- It may be obtained by the liquid-air process, in which atmospheric air is compressed and cooled until it is in a liquid state. In this state, the liquid is heated slightly and pure oxygen is distilled out and compressed in cylinders.

- Oxygen may be produced by the electrolytic process, in which the hydrogen and oxygen in water are separated by passing a direct current through the water.

Hydrogen gas is collected by means of an inverted container at the negative terminal, oxygen at the positive terminal, and each is then piped off and compressed in cylinders.

Oxygen can also be separated from the atmosphere by passing air through a special sieve. Because oxygen molecules are smaller than the molecules of other gasses, only oxygen will emerge from the outlet.

Oxygen cylinders. Standard oxygen cylinders used in welding operations are made of seamless steel and come in two sizes. The smaller size holds 220 cubic feet of oxygen at 2,000 lbs. per square inch (p.s.i.) pressure; the larger size holds 250 cubic feet of oxygen at 2,265 p.s.i. All oxygen cylinders are painted green for identification.

Each oxygen cylinder has a high-pressure valve located at the top of the cylinder. This valve is protected by a metal safety cap, which should always be in place when the cylinder is not in use. If an oxygen cylinder should fall and the valve break off, it will take off like a rocket. The jet from the escaping high-pressure gas can turn it into a lethal weapon.

CAUTION: *Oxygen should never be brought in contact with oil or grease. In the presence of pure oxygen, these substances become highly combustible. Oxygen hose and valve fittings should never be oiled or greased or handled with oily or greasy hands. Even grease spots on clothing may flare up or explode if struck by a stream of oxygen.*

Acetylene Gas

Acetylene is a flammable, colorless gas. It has a distinctive, disagreeable odor that is easily detected, even when the gas is greatly diluted with air. Unlike oxygen, *acetylene* does not exist free in the atmosphere; it must be manufactured. The process is neither difficult nor expensive. *Calcium carbide* is made to react chemically with water to produce acetylene.

The gas is either used directly in a manifold system from an acetylene generator or stored in cylinders. If it is ignited in this state, the result is a yellow, smoky flame with a low temperature. When the gas is mixed with oxygen in the proper proportions and ignited, the result is a blue-white flame with a temperature of approximately 6,000°F.

Under low pressure at normal temperatures, acetylene is a stable compound, but when compressed in an empty container to pressures greater than 15 p.s.i., it becomes dangerously unstable. For this reason, manufacturers fill the

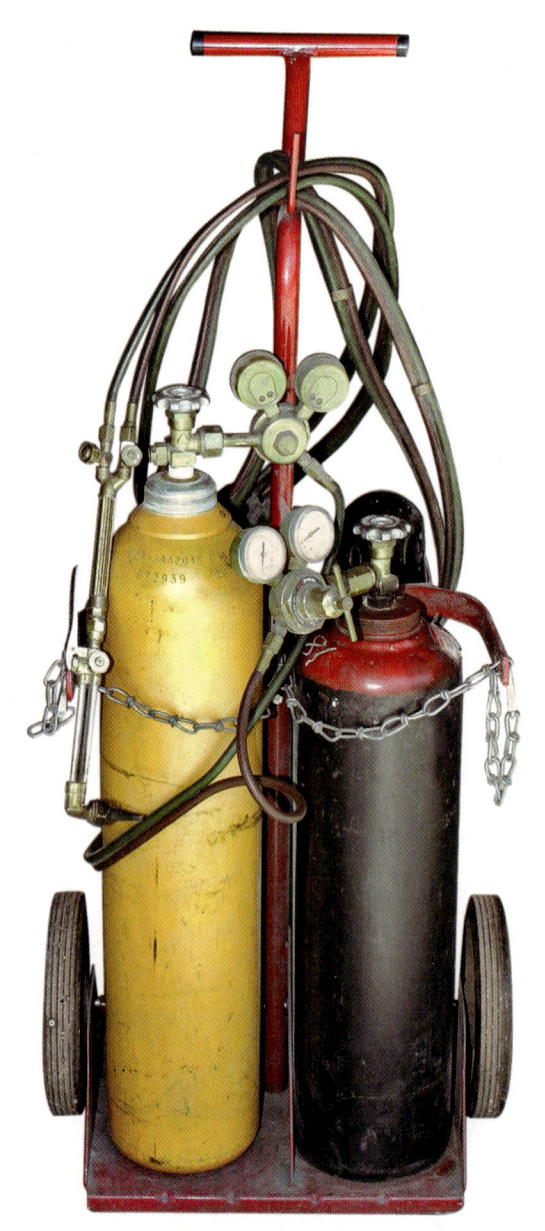

Figure 6-2-1. Portable oxyacetylene welding outfit

acetylene cylinders with a porous substance (generally a mixture of asbestos and charcoal) and saturate this substance with acetone. Since acetone is capable of absorbing approximately 25 times its own volume of acetylene gas, a cylinder containing the correct amount of acetone can be charged to a pressure of 250 p.s.i. without fear of the acetylene becoming unstable.

Acetylene Safety Precautions

Acetylene safety precautions should be rigidly observed and enforced. Some of the more important things to remember follow:

- Store acetylene cylinders in an upright position. They must be securely fastened to prevent shifting or falling under any circumstances. Do not lay them on their sides, drop them or handle them roughly. If horizontal storage is necessary or an acetylene cylinder is inadvertently left lying in a horizontal position, it must be placed in an upright position for a minimum of two hours before using. Otherwise, the acetone in which the acetylene is dissolved will be drawn out with the gas.
- Store acetylene cylinders in a well protected, well-ventilated, dry place, away from heating devices or combustible materials.
- Use acetylene from cylinders only through pressure-reducing regulators. Do not use acetylene at pressures greater than 15 p.s.i.
- Open the acetylene valve slowly, 1/4 to 1/2 turn. This will permit an adequate flow of gas. Never open the valve more than 1-1/2 turns of the spindle. Use the special wrench provided, and leave it in place on the spindle so that the acetylene may be turned off quickly in an emergency.
- Keep sparks, flames and heat away from acetylene cylinders.
- Turn the acetylene cylinder so that the valve outlet points away from the oxygen cylinder.
- Do not interchange hose, regulators or other apparatus intended for oxygen with those intended for acetylene.
- Use only approved hoses and fittings with acetylene equipment. Pure copper or copper alloys containing 67 to 99 percent copper must not be used in piping or fittings for handling acetylene (except blowpipe or torch tips). Acetylene reacts with pure or slightly alloyed copper to form cuprous acetylide, a violent explosive.
- Test for leaks with leak check — not with an open flame.

- Make no attempt to transfer acetylene from one cylinder to another, refill an acetylene cylinder or mix any other gas or gases with acetylene.
- Keep valves closed on empty cylinders.
- Should an acetylene cylinder catch fire, use a wet blanket to extinguish the fire. If this fails, spray a stream of water on the cylinder to keep it cool.
- Crack each cylinder valve for an instant to blow dirt out of nozzles before attaching the pressure regulator. Do not stand in front of the valve when opening it.

Acetylene cylinders. The standard acetylene cylinder is a seamless steel shell with welded ends, approximately 12 inches in diameter and 36 inches long. It is painted red and the name of the gas is indicated black letters painted on the cylinder. A fully changed acetylene cylinder contains 225 cubic feet of gas at pressures up to 250 p.s.i. In the event of fire or any excessive temperature rise, special safety fuse plugs installed in both the top and bottom of the cylinder melt, allowing the excess gas to escape or burn off, thereby minimizing the chances of an explosion. The holes in the safety plugs are made so small that they will not allow the flames to burn back into the cylinder. Acetylene cylinders should not be allowed to become completely empty, or a loss of filler material may result.

Pressure Regulators

Acetylene and oxygen regulators reduce pressures and control the flow of gases from the cylinders to the torch. Acetylene and oxygen regulators are of the same general type, although those designed for acetylene are not made to

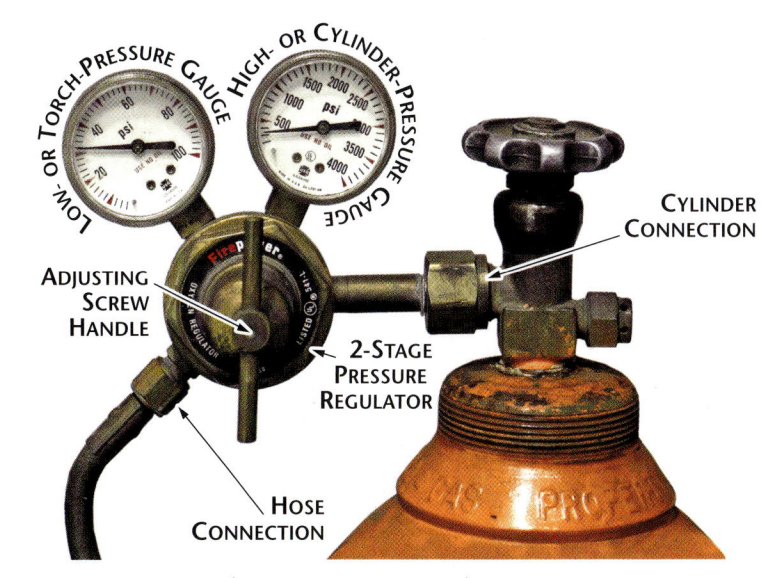

Figure 6-2-2. A typical oxygen pressure regulator

withstand such high pressures as are those designed for use with oxygen. The fittings on acetylene regulators have left-hand threads; oxygen regulators have right-hand threads, so you can't mix them up.

Each regulator is equipped with two pressure gauges, a high-pressure gauge to indicate the cylinder pressure, and a low-pressure gauge to indicate the pressure in the hose leading to the torch, or the *working pressure*.

A typical regulator, complete with pressure gauges and connections, is shown in Figure 6-2-2. The adjusting screw shown on the front of the regulator is for adjusting the working pressure. When this adjusting screw is turned to the left (counterclockwise) until it runs free, the valve mechanism inside the regulator is closed. No gas can then pass to the torch. As the handle is turned to the right (clockwise), the screw presses against the regulating mechanism, the valve opens, and gas passes to the torch at the pressure shown on the working pressure gauge. Changes in this pressure may be made at will, simply by adjusting the handle until the desired pressure is registered.

Before opening the valve on a cylinder, the adjusting screw on the regulator should be fully released by turning to the left. As noted previously, this closes the valve inside the regulator, thus protecting the mechanism against possible damage.

Regulators are either *single-stage* or *two-stage* type. Single-stage regulators reduce the pressure of the gases from cylinder pressure to working pressure in one step (stage).

In two-stage regulators, the pressure reduction is accomplished in two separate steps. Pressure regulators are available in both the single- and two-stage type. Two-stage regulators are the most common and are generally used with portable outfits.

Welding Torches, Hoses and Equipment

The welding torch is the unit used to mix the two gases in the proper proportions and control the volume of the gases and the direction of the flame. The torch has two needle valves, one for adjusting the flow of oxygen (O_2), the other for adjusting the flow of acetylene. Tips are interchangeable and come in various styles and sizes for welding a wide range of metal thicknesses. Figure 6-2-3 shows an aircraft welding torch.

Torch tips. The torch tip delivers and controls the final flow of gases. It is important that the correct tip be selected and used with the proper gas pressures. The nature of the weld, the material, the experience of the welder and the position in which the weld is to be made all determine the correct size of the tip opening. The size of the tip opening, in turn, determines the *amount* of heat (not the temperature) applied to the work. If a too-small tip is used, the heat provided will be insufficient to produce penetration to the proper depth. If the tip is too large, the heat will be too great and holes will be burned in the metal.

There is no standard system for indicating the size of the opening in the torch tip; each manufacturer has its own numbering system. A comparison of the tips supplied by various manufacturers appears in Table 6-2-1. The thickness of the metal for which each tip is adaptable is only approximate, since the nature of the weld, its position and the conductivity of the metal are all factors in the selection of a torch tip. Such approximations may be used until the welder is experienced enough to know which size tip will produce the best weld for each situation.

With use, the torch tip will become clogged with carbon deposits and, if it is brought in contact with the molten pool, particles of slag may lodge in the opening. A split or distorted flame is an indication of a clogged tip. Tips should be cleaned with *wire tip cleaners* of the correct diameter, or with soft copper wire. Tips should not be cleaned with drills or other hard, sharp instruments. These devices may enlarge or scratch the tip opening and greatly reduce the efficiency of the torch tip.

Fine steel wool may be used to remove oxides from the outside of the tip. These oxides hinder the heat dissipation and cause the tip to overheat.

Welding hose. Welding hoses are specially made to connect the cylinders to the torch. Oxygen hose is green and acetylene hose is red. The hoses are attached to their respective regulators at one end and to the torch at the other.

NOTE: *Acetylene hose fittings have left-hand threads and the nut is marked with a groove. Oxygen hose fittings have right-hand threads, and the nut is plain (no groove).*

Lighters. A flint lighter is used for igniting the torch. The lighter consists of a file-shaped piece of steel, usually recessed in a cuplike device, and a piece of flint that can be drawn across the steel, producing the sparks required to light the torch.

CAUTION: *Matches should never be used to ignite a torch; their length requires bringing the*

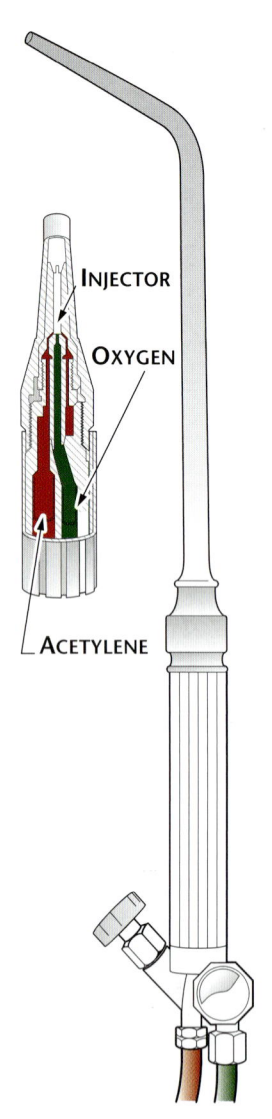

Figure 6-2-3. An aircraft welding torch

hand too close to the tip in order to ignite the gas. Accumulated gas may envelop the hand and, when ignited, cause a severe burn.

Goggles. Welding goggles are fitted with colored lenses to keep out heat and light rays and to protect the operator's eyes from sparks and molten metal. Regardless of the shade of lens used, it should be protected by a clear cover glass.

The welding operator should select the shade or density of color that is best suited for his or her particular work. The desired lens is the one of the darkest shade that will still show a clear definition of the work without eyestrain. Goggles should fit closely around the eyes and should be worn at all times during welding and cutting operations.

Special goggles, utilizing standard lenses, are available for people who wear glasses. *Do not try to use sunglasses.* Sunglasses are made to filter differently and the dark lens shade alone is not enough to protect your eyes.

Welding (filler) rods. The use of the proper type filler rod is very important. It not only adds reinforcement to the weld area but also adds desired properties to the finished weld.

Welding rods may be classified as ferrous and non-ferrous. The ferrous rods include carbon and alloy steel rods, as well as cast iron rods. Non-ferrous rods include brazing and bronze rods, aluminum and aluminum alloy rods, magnesium and magnesium alloy rods, copper rods and silver rods.

Rods are manufactured in standard 24 inch and 36 inch lengths and in diameters from 1/16 inch to 3/8 inch. The diameter of rod used is governed by the thickness of the metals being joined. If the rod is too small, it will not conduct heat away from the puddle rapidly enough, and a burned weld will result. A rod that is too large will chill the puddle. As in selecting the proper size of welding torch tip, experience will enable you to select the proper diameter welding rod.

Welding Flame

The welding flame is classified as *neutral*, *oxidizing* or *carburizing*, each having its own special function. See Figure 6-2-4. Adjustment of the torch enables the operator to produce the type of flame best suited for the job at hand.

The neutral flame, in which a balanced mixture of oxygen and acetylene is burned, is used for most welding operations. The oxidizing flame, in which an excess of oxygen is burned, is used

TORCH TIP SIZES					
Tip Sizes	Drill Size	Smith Tip No.	Victor Tip No.	Airco Tip No.	Thickness of Sheet Steel
0.0210	75	—	000	00	1/64-1/32
0.0225	74	100	—	—	1/64-1/32
0.0250	72	—	—	0	1/32-3/32
0.0260	71	101	—	—	1/64-3-32
0.0280	70	—	00	—	1/64-3/64
0.0292	69	102	—	—	1/16-1/8
0.0310	68	—	—	1	1/16-1/8
0.0320	67	103	—	—	1/32-5/64
0.0350	65	—	0	—	1/32-5/64
0.0370	63	104	—	—	3/32-5/32
0.0370	62	—	—	2	3/32-5/32
0.0400	60	—	1	—	3/64-3/32
0.0430	57	105	—	—	1/16-1/8
0.0465	56	106	2	3	5/32-7/32
0.0550	54	107	—	4	1/8-3/16
0.0595	53	—	3	—	1/8-3/16
0.0635	52	108	—	—	1/8-3/16
0.0670	51	—	—	5	3/16-5/16
0.0730	49	109	4	—	3/16-1/4
0.0760	48	—	—	6	1/4-3/8

Table 6-2-1. Torch tip sizes

for welding bronze or fusing brass and bronze. The carburizing flame, in which an excess of acetylene is burned, is used when welding nickel alloys.

Neutral flame. The *neutral flame* does not alter the composition of the base metal to any great extent and is therefore the best suited for most metals. The neutral flame burns at approximately 5,850°F. A balanced mixture of one volume of oxygen and one volume of acetylene is supplied from the torch when the flame is adjusted to neutral.

The neutral flame is divided into two distinct zones. The inner zone consists of the cone — a white, clearly defined, round, smooth cone, 1/16 to 1/8 inch in length. The outer zone, made up of completely burned oxygen and acetylene, is blue with a purple tinge at the point and edges.

A neutral flame melts metal without changing its properties and leaves the metal clear and clean. If the mixture of oxygen and acetylene is correct, the neutral flame allows the molten metal to flow smoothly, and few sparks are produced when welding most metals.

Carburizing flame. The *carburizing flame*, produced by burning an excess of acetylene, may be recognized by its three distinct colors. There is a bluish-white inner cone, a white intermediate cone, and a light-blue outer flame. It may also be recognized by the feather at the tip of the inner cone. See Figure 6-2-4. The degree of carburization can he judged by the length of the feather.

Oxidizing flame. The *oxidizing flame* is produced by burning an excess of oxygen. It has the general appearance of the neutral flame, but the inner cone is shorter, slightly pointed and has a purplish tinge as shown in Figure 6-2-4. This flame burns with a hissing sound. When welding ferrous metals, an oxidizing flame can be recognized by the numerous sparks that are thrown off as the metal melts, and by the foam, or scum, which forms on the surface.

Flame adjustment. To adjust the flame, light the torch by opening the torch acetylene valve 1/4-1/2 turn. With only the acetylene valve open, the flame will be yellow in color and will give off smoke and soot.

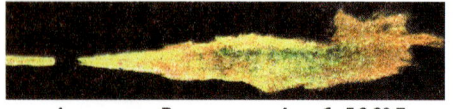

ACETYLENE BURNING IN AIR. 1,500°F

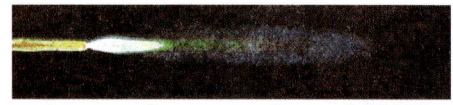

STRONGLY CARBURIZING FLAME. 5,700°F

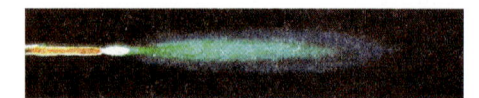

SLIGHT EXCESS ACETYLENE FLAME. 5,800°F

NEUTRAL FLAME. 5,900°F

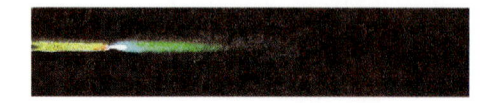

OXIDIZING FLAME. 6,300°F

Figure 6-2-4. Characteristics of oxyacetylene flames

Next, open the torch's oxygen valve slowly. The flame will gradually change in color from yellow to blue and will show the characteristics of the excess acetylene flame described earlier.

> **NOTE:** *With most torches, there will still be a slight excess of acetylene when the oxygen and acetylene valves are wide open and the recommended pressures are being used.*

Then, close the acetylene valve on the torch very slowly. Notice that the secondary cone gets smaller until it finally disappears completely. Just at this point of complete disappearance, the neutral flame is formed.

In order to see the effect of an excess of oxygen, close the acetylene valve still further. A change will be noted, although it is by no means as sharply defined as that between the neutral and excess acetylene flames. The entire flame will decrease in size, and the inner cone will become much less sharply defined.

Because of the difficulty in making a distinction between the excess oxygen and neutral flames, an adjustment of the flame to neutral should always be made from the excess acetylene side. Always adjust the flame first so that it shows the secondary cone characteristic of excess acetylene, then increase the flow of oxygen until just after this secondary cone disappears.

With each size of tip, a neutral, oxidizing or carburizing flame can be obtained. It is also possible to obtain a *harsh* or *soft* flame by increasing or decreasing the pressure of both gases.

For most regulator settings, the gases are expelled from the torch tip at a relatively high velocity, and the flame is called harsh. For some work, it is desirable to have a soft, or low-velocity, flame without a reduction in thermal output. This may be achieved by using a larger tip and closing the gas needle valves until the neutral flame is quiet and steady. It is especially desirable to use a soft flame when welding aluminum, to avoid blowing holes in the metal when the puddle is formed.

Backfire and Flashback

Improper handling of the torch may cause the flame to backfire or, in very rare cases, to flashback. A *backfire* is a momentary backward flow of the gases at the torch tip, causing the flame to go out. Sometimes, the flame may immediately come on again, but a backfire is always accompanied by a snapping or popping noise. A backfire may be caused by touching the tip against the work, by overheating the tip, by operating the torch at other than recommended pressures, by a loose tip or head, or by dirt or slag in the end of the tip. A backfire is rarely dangerous, but the molten metal may be splattered when the flame pops.

A *flashback* is the burning of the gases within the torch, and it is dangerous. It is usually caused by loose connections, improper pressures or overheating of the torch. A shrill hissing or squealing noise accompanies a flashback. Unless the gases are turned off immediately, the flame may burn back through the hose and regulators, causing great damage. The cause of a flashback should always be determined and the trouble remedied before relighting the torch.

Setting up equipment. Setting up welding equipment and preparing for welding must be done systematically and in a definite order to avoid costly mistakes. Follow the instructions in the order given to assure your own safety and the safety of the equipment.

1. Secure the cylinders so they cannot be upset. Remove the protecting caps from the cylinders, then remove the outlet connection caps.

2. Crack the cylinder valves by opening (cracking) the valve for an instant to blow it out. Close the valves and wipe off the connections with a clean oil free cloth.

3. Connect the acetylene pressure regulator to the acetylene cylinder, and the oxygen regulator to the oxygen cylinder. Use a regulator wrench and tighten the connecting nuts tightly enough to prevent leakage.

4. Connect the red hose to the acetylene pressure regulator and the green hose to the oxygen regulator. Tighten the connecting nuts enough to prevent leaks.

CAUTION: *Notice the left-hand threads on the acetylene hose connections. Do not force them, as these threads are made of brass and are easily damaged.*

5. Release both pressure regulator-adjusting screws by turning the adjusting screw handle on each regulator counterclockwise until it runs free. This is to avoid damage to the regulators and pressure gauges when the cylinder valves are opened.

6. Open the cylinder valves slowly and read each of the cylinder pressure gauges to check the contents in each cylinder.

7. Stand to one side of the regulator while opening a cylinder valve to avoid possible injury.

8. Blow out each hose by turning the pressure-adjusting screw handle inward (clockwise) and then turning it out again.

9. Connect both hoses to the torch and check the connections for leaks by turning the pressure-regulator screws in, with the torch needle valves closed. When 20 p.s.i. shows on the oxygen working-pressure gauge and 5 p.s.i. on the acetylene gauge, close the valves by turning the pressure-regulator screws out. A drop in pressure on the working gauge indicates a leak between the regulator and torch tip. A general tightening of all connections should remedy the situation. If it becomes necessary to locate the leak, use an oxygen safe leakcheck solution to check for it.

CAUTION: *Do not hunt for an acetylene leak with a flame, as a serious explosion can occur in the hose or in the cylinder.*

10. Adjust the working pressure on both the oxygen and acetylene regulators by turning the pressure-adjusting screw on the regulator clockwise until the desired settings are obtained.

11. Light the torch, using the friction lighter. The torch is lighted by opening the acetylene needle valve and igniting the acetylene as it leaves the torch tip. Adjust the flame for the welding operation at hand, as described earlier.

CAUTION: *When lighting the torch, always point the tip away from your body, other persons and flammable materials.*

Shutting down. Extinguish the torch flame by closing the *acetylene needle valve first*, then close the *oxygen needle valve last*.

When welding is stopped and will not be resumed within 15 minutes, or when the equipment is to be left unattended for any period of time, the equipment must be secured as follows:

1. Close both acetylene and oxygen cylinder valves. Leave regulators open momentarily.

2. Open acetylene valve on torch and allow gas to escape (5-15 seconds) to outside atmosphere, then close the valve.

3. Open oxygen valve on torch and allow gas in hose to escape (5-10 seconds), then close the valve.

4. Close both regulators.

NOTE: *Regulators are closed when adjusting screws are backed out (turned counterclockwise) until loose.*

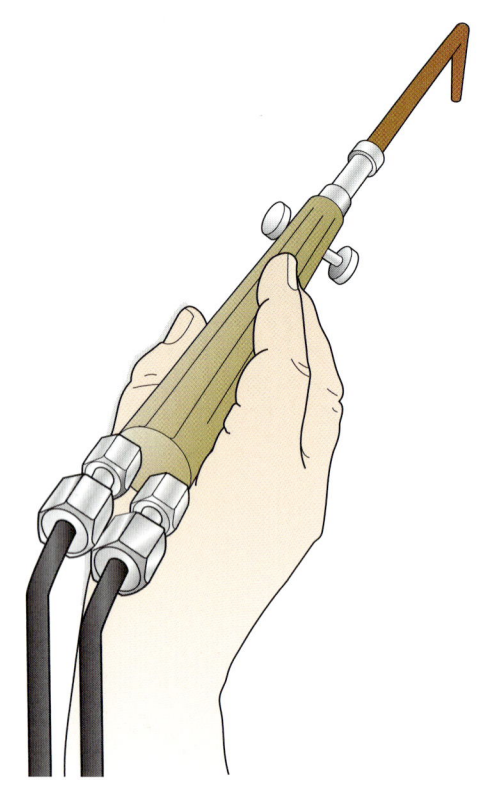

Figure 6-2-5. Correct grip for welding light-gauge metals

Figure 6-2-6. Forehand welding

Basic Welding Technique

The composition, thickness, shape and position of the metal to be welded govern the techniques to be used.

Holding the torch. The proper method to use in holding the torch depends upon the thickness of the metal being welded. For light-gauge metal, hold the torch as shown in Figure 6-2-5, with the hose draped over the wrist.

Hold the torch so that the tip is in line with the joint to be welded, inclined between 30° and 60° degrees from the perpendicular. The exact angle depends upon the type of weld to be made, the amount of preheating necessary and the thickness and type of metal. The thicker the metal, the more nearly vertical the torch must be for proper heat penetration. The white cone of the flame should be held about 1/8 inch from the surface of the base metal.

If the torch is held in the correct position, a small puddle of molten metal will form. The puddle should be composed of equal parts of the two pieces being welded. After the puddle appears, begin the movement of the tip in a semicircular or circular motion. This movement assures an even distribution of heat on both pieces of metal. The speed and motion of the torch are learned only by practice and experience.

Forehand welding. Forehand welding is the technique of pointing the torch flame forward in the direction in which the weld is progressing. The filler rod is added to the puddle as the edges of the joint melt before the flame. See Figure 6-2-6. The forehand method is used in welding most of the lighter tubing and sheet metal, or when the weld is to be made in certain positions.

Backhand welding. Backhand welding is the reverse of forehand welding. The welding rod is added to the puddle between the flame and the finished weld. Backhand welding is seldom used on sheet metal, because the increased heat generated in this method is likely to cause overheating and burning. You might never use or see a backhand weld in your aviation maintenance career.

Welding Positions

The four basic welding positions are shown in Figure 6-2-7. Also shown are four commonly used joints. Notice that the *edge joint*, *corner joint* and *butt joint* are classified as *groove welds*, while the *tee joint* and *lap joint* are classified as *fillet welds*.

Always weld in the flat position whenever possible. The puddle is much easier to control, and you can work longer periods without tiring. Quite often, though, it is necessary to weld in the overhead, vertical or horizontal position.

The *flat weld* position is used when the material is to be laid flat or almost flat and welded on the topside. The welding torch is pointed downward toward the work.

The *overhead weld* position is used when the material is to be welded on the underside with the torch pointed upward toward the work. In welding overhead, the puddle can be kept from sagging if it is not permitted to get too large or assume the form of a large drop. The rod is used to control the molten puddle. Less heat is required in an overhead weld, because the heat naturally rises.

The *horizontal weld* position is used when the line of the weld runs horizontally across a piece of work, and the torch is directed at the material in a horizontal position. The weld is made from right to left across the plate (for the right-hand welder). The flame is inclined upward at an angle of 45-60°, and the weld is made with a normal forehand technique. Adding the rod to the top of the puddle will prevent the molten metal from sagging to the lower edge of the bead. If the puddle is to have the greatest possible cohesion, it should not be allowed to get too hot.

In a *vertical weld*, the pressure exerted by the torch flame must be relied upon to a great extent to support the puddle. It is highly important to keep the puddle from becoming too hot, in order to prevent the hot metal from running out of the puddle onto the finished weld. It may be necessary to remove the flame from the puddle for an instant to prevent overheating, then return it to the puddle. Vertical welds are begun at the bottom, and the puddle is carried upward with a forehand motion. The tip should be inclined from 45-60° degrees, the exact angle depending upon the desired balance between correct penetration and control of the puddle. The rod is added from the top and in front of the flame with a normal forehand technique.

Welded Joints

The five fundamental types of welded joints are the butt joint, tee joint, lap joint, corner joint and edge joint.

Butt joints. A *butt joint* is made by placing two pieces of material edge to edge, so that there is no overlapping, and then welding. Some of the various types of butt joints are shown in Figure 6-2-8. The flanged butt joint is used in welding thin sheets, 1/16 inch or less. The edges are prepared for welding by turning up a flange equal to the thickness of the metal. This type is usually made without the use of filler rod.

A *plain butt joint* is used for metals from 1/16 to 1/8 inch in thickness. A filler rod is used in making this joint, in order to obtain a strong weld.

If the metal is thicker than 1/8 inch, it is necessary to bevel the edges so that the heat from the torch can penetrate completely through the metal. These bevels may be either single- or double-bevel types or single- or double-V types. The V-type joint is generally used on very thick metals. Penetration of the weld bead on a butt joint should be 100%.

Lap joints. The *lap joint* is seldom used in oxyacetylene welding of flat stock, but it is commonly used in spot welding. The *single-fillet lap joint*, shown in Figure 6-2-9, has very little resistance to bending and will not withstand

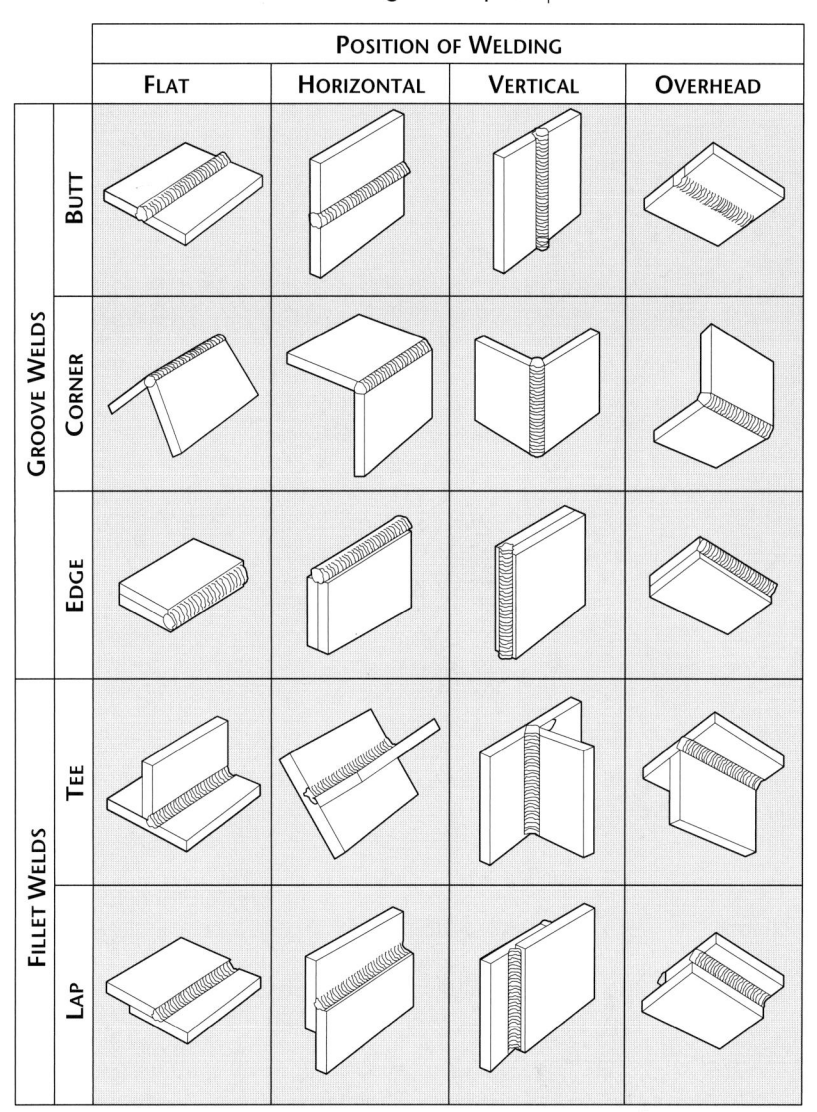

Figure 6-2-7. Four basic welding positions and types of joints

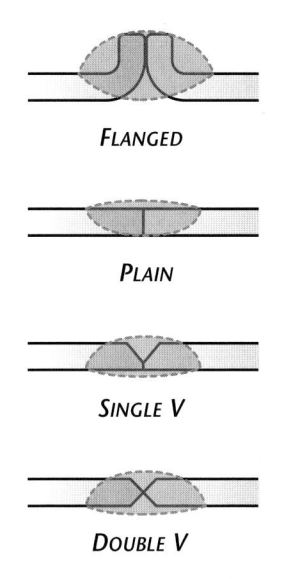

Figure 6-2-8. Types of butt joints

Figure 6-2-9. Single- and double-fillet lap joints

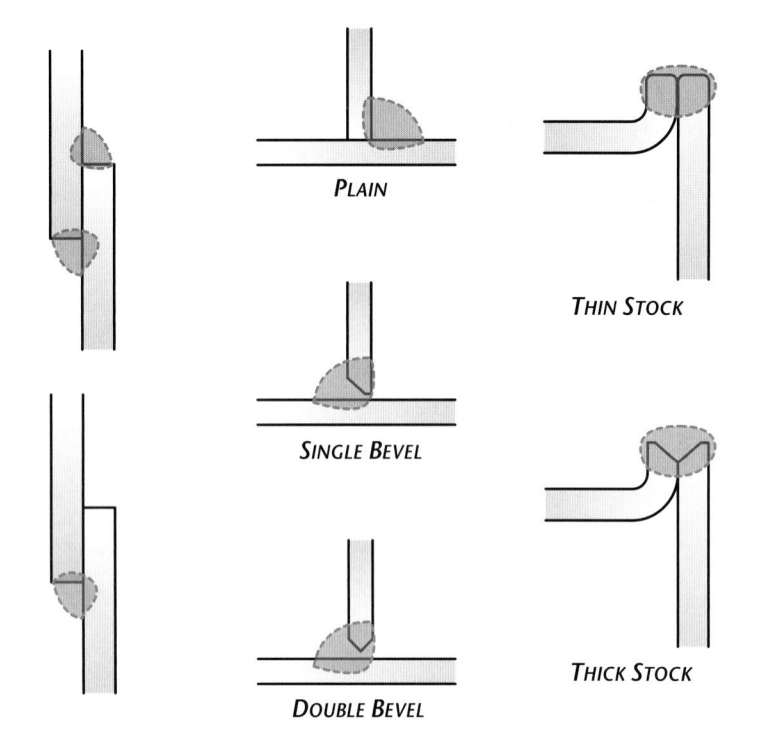

Figure 6-2-10. Types of tee joints

Figure 6-2-11. Types of edge joints

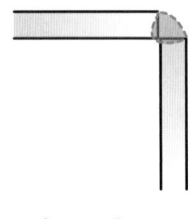

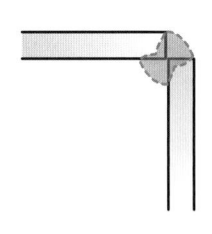

Figure 6-2-12. Types of corner joints

the shearing stress to which the weld is subjected under tension or compression loads.

The double-fillet lap joint (Figure 6-2-9) offers more strength, but it requires twice the amount of welding required on the simpler, more efficient butt weld.

Tee joints. A *tee joint* is formed when the edge or end of one piece is welded to the surface of another, as shown in Figure 6-2-10. These joints are quite common in tubular structures. The plain tee joint is suitable for thin plate metal, but heavier metals require the vertical member to be single- or double-beveled, in order to permit the heat to penetrate deeply enough. The dark areas in the illustrations show the depth of heat penetration and fusion required.

Edge joints. An *edge joint* may be used when two pieces of sheet metal must be fastened together and load stresses are not important. Edge joints are usually made by bending the edges of one or both parts upward, placing the two bent ends parallel to each other (or placing one bent end parallel to the upright unbent end) and welding along the outside of the seam formed by the two joined edges.

Figure 6-2-11 shows two types of edge joints. Thin stock, shown at top, requires no filler rod; the edges can be melted down to fill the seam. Thick stock, shown at the bottom, is made of thicker metal and must be beveled for heat penetration. Filler rod must be added for reinforcement.

Corner joints. A *corner joint* is made when two pieces of metal are brought together so that their edges form a corner of a box or enclosure as shown in Figure 6-2-12.

The corner joint shown on the top of Figure 6-2-12 requires little or no filler rod, since the edges fuse to make the weld. It is used where load stress is unimportant. The joint shown in the middle of Figure 6-2-12 is used on heavier metals, and filler rod is added for roundness and strength. If much stress is to be placed on the corner, the inside is reinforced, as shown in the bottom illustration of Figure 6-2-12.

Melting point. The melting point of any substance is the temperature at which the solid substance becomes liquid. A welder should know the approximate melting points of the various metals, because it is often necessary to weld together metals that differ in this respect. Table 6-2-2 shows the melting points of the most commonly used aircraft metals.

Expansion and Contraction

Heat causes metals to expand; cooling causes them to contract. Uneven heating will, therefore, cause uneven expansion, and uneven cooling will cause uneven contraction. Under such conditions, stresses are set up within the metal. These forces must be relieved, and unless precautions are taken, warping or buckling of the metal takes place. Likewise, when cooling, if nothing is done to take up the stress set up by the contraction forces, further warping may result. If the surrounding cool sections of the metal are too heavy to permit this change in shape, the stresses remain within the metal itself. Such stresses may cause cracking while cooling, or may remain within the metal until further force is applied, as when the piece is put into use.

Sheet metal (1/8 inch and less in thickness) has such a large surface area per unit of weight that heat stresses tend to produce warping or buckling of the sheet. This and the contraction effect encountered on long seams are the main points to be considered in sheet metal welding.

The effect of welding a long seam (more than 10-12 inches) is to draw the seam together as the weld progresses. If the edges of the seam are placed in contact with each other throughout their length before welding starts, the far ends of the seam will actually overlap before the weld is completed.

One way of overcoming this effect is illustrated in Figure 6-2-13. The two pieces to be welded are placed with an increased allowance at the far end. As the welding progresses, the two

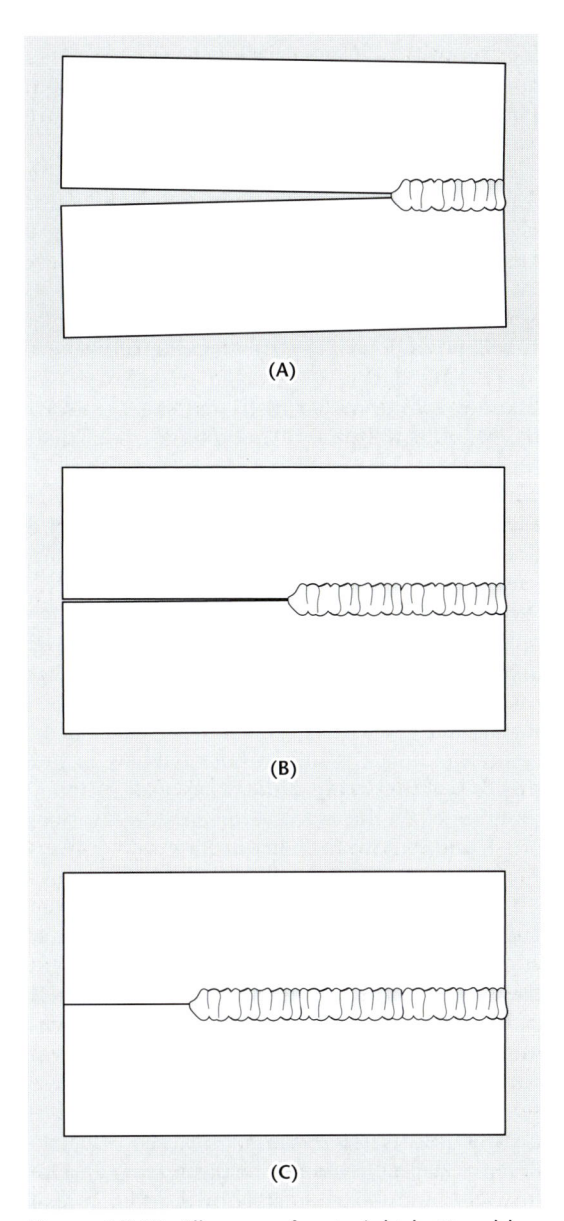

Figure 6-2-13. Allowance for straight butt weld

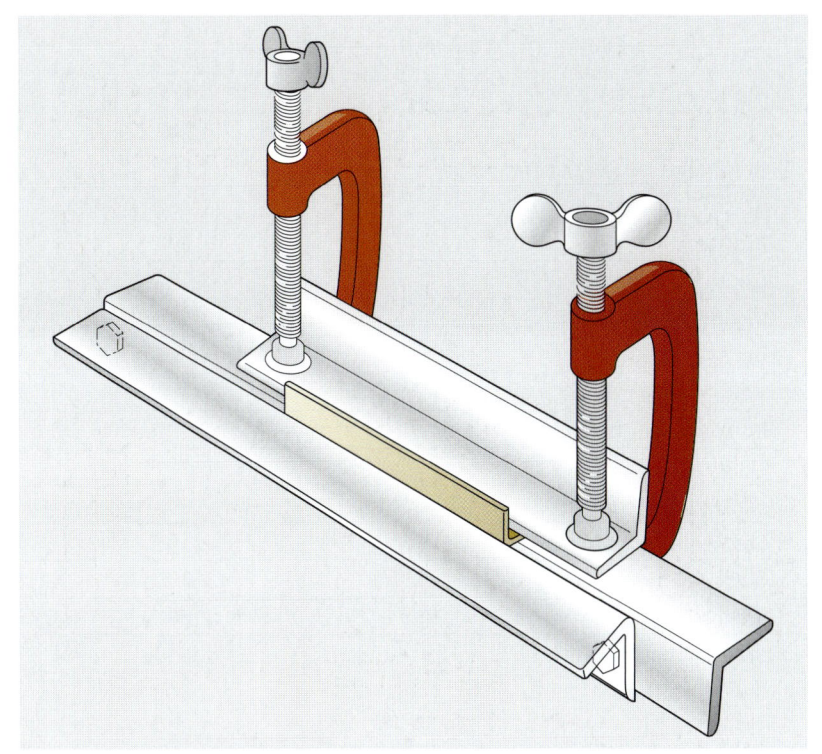

Figure 6-2-14. Example of the use of jigs and chill bars

pieces are drawn together. This allowance is generally one metal thickness per foot of seam.

Another method of controlling expansion and contraction is by the use of *chill bars*. Heavy pieces of metal are placed on either side of the weld; they absorb the heat and keep it from spreading across the whole surface area. Copper is commonly used for chill bars because of its ability to absorb heat readily. Welding jigs sometimes use this same principle to remove heat from the base metal. See Figure 6-2-14.

Preheating is another method of controlling expansion and contraction. Preheating is especially important in welding tubular structures and in welding castings. Contraction still takes place at the weld, but there is also shrinking in the rest of the structure at approximately the same rate.

Weld Characteristics

A completed, well-executed weld should have the following characteristics:

- The seam should be smooth, the bead ripples evenly spaced and of a uniform thickness
- The weld should be built-up, thus providing extra thickness at the joint
- The weld should taper off smoothly into the base metal
- No oxide should be formed on the base metal close to the weld
- The weld should show no signs of blowholes, porousness or projecting globules
- The base metal should show no signs of burns, pits, cracks or distortion

Although a clean, smooth weld is desirable, this characteristic does not necessarily mean that the weld is a good one; it may be dangerously weak inside. However, when a weld is rough, uneven and pitted, it is almost always unsatisfactory inside. Welds should never be filed, nor should they be filled with filler of any sort to give them a better appearance. Filing or filling deprives the weld of its strength.

Rewelding. When it is necessary to reweld a joint, all old weld material must be removed before the operation is begun. Remember, however, that continued reheating of the area

MELTING POINT OF AIRCRAFT METALS °F	
Aluminum — cast 8% copper	1,175
Aluminum — pure	1,218
Aluminum — 5% silicon	1,117
Brass	1,660
Bronze	1,598
Copper	1,981
Inconel	2,540
Iron — cast	2,300
Iron — malleable	2,300
Iron — wrought	2,900
Lead	620
Nickel	2,646
Steel — high-carbon	2,500
Steel — low-carbon	2,700
Steel — medium-carbon	2,600
Steel — manganese	2,450
Steel — nickel	2,600
Steel — cast	2,600
Steel — stainless	2,640
Tin	450
Zinc — cast or rolled	786

Table 6-2-2. Melting points of aircraft metals

Welding Ferrous Metals

Low-carbon steel, low-alloy steel, cast steel and wrought iron are easily welded with the oxyacetylene flame. As the carbon content of steel increases, welding becomes more difficult. For this reason, parts made of steel may be repaired by welding only under certain conditions. Factors involved are carbon content and hardenability. For corrosion and heat resistant nickel-chromium steels, the allowed weldability depends upon their stability, carbon content or reheat treatment.

Preparation For Welding

Proper preparation for welding is an important factor in every welding operation. The edges of the parts must be prepared in accordance with the joint design chosen. The edges must be clean. Arrangements must be made for holding the parts in proper alignment and for preheating, if required.

The first step in preparing a part for welding is to strip it of all dirt, grease or oil, and remove any protective coating, such as cadmium plating, enamel, paint or varnish. Such coatings not only hamper welding, but also mingle with the weld to prevent good fusion.

Cadmium plating can be chemically removed by dipping the edges to be welded in a mixture of 1 pound of ammonium nitrate mixed in 1 gallon of water.

CAUTION: *Both cadmium and zinc plating will produce fumes that are toxic to breathe.*

Enamel, paint or varnish may be removed by sandblasting, by using paint or varnish remover, or by treating the pieces with a 10 percent caustic soda solution followed by a thorough washing with hot water to remove the solvent or residue.

Sandblasting is the most effective method for removing rust or scale from steel parts. Grease or oil may be removed with a suitable grease solvent.

If you sandblast a piece, it must be further cleaned before welding. The silica residue bubbles up and makes welding more difficult, as well as intermingling with the weld puddle. A stainless steel brush will remove the silica residue.

Welding Techniques

Some types of ferrous metals are more difficult to weld than others. For this reason, the techniques used for welding these metals differ in some respects.

Carbon steels. In general, the carbon steels that are weldable require no preheating and no flux. Use a low-carbon steel filler rod containing a small percentage of vanadium. Adjust the torch flame to neutral.

Use the forehand method, holding the torch at an angle of 60° to the surface of the work. Be sure that the tip of the inner cone of the flame does not quite touch the molten metal. If the edges of the metal have been beveled, use a swinging motion of the torch to melt the metal on each side of the groove.

While breaking down the edges, grasp the filler rod in the other hand and hold it in the outer cone of the flame to heat it. The filler rod should almost reach the melting point by the time that the puddle of molten metal has formed in the bottom of the groove.

Move the torch in one direction while moving the rod in the opposite direction. Dip the tip of the filler rod below the surface of the weld puddle just before the rod begins to melt, and move it from side to side in the puddle with a motion exactly opposite to the motion of the

causes the base metal to lose its strength and become brittle.

torch. If the filler rod is held above the surface of the puddle, it will melt and fall into the puddle a drop at a time. This ruins the weld.

Add filler metal until the surface of the joint is built up slightly above the edges of the parts being joined. Gradually advance the puddle of molten metal along the seam until the end is reached.

As the end of the seam is approached, raise the torch slightly, chilling the molten steel to prevent it from spilling over the edge and/or melting through the work.

Chrome-molybdenum steel. The welding technique for *chrome-molybdenum* (*chrome-moly*) is practically the same as that for carbon steels, except that the surrounding area must be preheated to a temperature between 300° and 400°F before beginning to weld. To preheat the metal, direct the flame at such an angle that preheating takes place just ahead of the weld. Use a rod of the same material as the base metal. Use a soft, neutral flame just large enough to melt the base metal and to obtain good fusion. Do not allow the flame to shift to an oxidizing flame.

If jigs or fixtures are used, they should be designed to prevent any strains from contraction while the metal is cooling. The metal should not be clamped too tight.

Chrome-moly thicker than 0.093 inch should be *TIG welded*. In TIG (tungsten inert-gas) welding, the heat zone is narrower, the heat strains are lower and a better weld will be obtained.

Stainless steel. The procedure for welding stainless steel is basically the same as that for carbon steels. There are, however, some special precautions that must be taken in order to obtain the best results.

Only stainless steel used for non-structural members can be welded satisfactorily — the stainless steel used for structural components is cold-worked or cold-rolled and, if heated, loses some of its strength. Non-structural stainless steel is obtained in sheet and tubing form and is often used for exhaust collectors, stacks or manifolds. Oxygen combines very readily with this metal in the molten state, and extreme care must be taken to prevent this combination. By and large, these metals are better for the TIG process.

A slightly carburizing flame is recommended for welding stainless steel, and the welder should adjust the flame so that a feather of excess acetylene, about 1/16 inch long, forms around the inner cone. Too much acetylene, however, will add carbon to the metal and cause it to lose its resistance to corrosion. The torch tip size should be one or two sizes smaller than that prescribed for a similar gauge of plain steel. The smaller tip lessens the chances of overheating and subsequent loss of the stainless qualities of the metal.

Stainless steel must be protected from the atmosphere to prevent the nitrogen and oxygen in the air from combining with the hot metal. This is done by welding in an atmosphere of inert gas (TIG), or by using a suitable flux.

The flux used with stainless steel is compounded especially to dissolve the chromium oxide which forms on the molten metal. It is mixed with water or alcohol until it forms a thin paste. Apply the flux to the underside of the seam and to the filler rod. Allow the flux to dry a few minutes after brushing it on.

Welding Non-ferrous Metals

Aluminum alloys. Gas welding of aluminum alloy is usually confined to materials 0.031-0.125 inch in thickness. Thicker material may be gas-welded if necessary, but thinner material is usually spot, TIG or seam-welded.

Aluminum alloys best suited for gas welding are 1100, 3003, 5052, 6056, 6061 and 6063. Gas welding of 2014, 2017, 2024 and 7075 is not normally permitted, since the strength of the metal in the vicinity of the weld is lowered considerably and cannot be restored. Corrosion resistance is also seriously impaired.

Melting characteristics of aluminum. The biggest problem in welding aluminum is that aluminum melts at around 1,200°F and boils at around 2,880°F, while the surface oxide melts at around 3,200°F. That means that if you wait for a puddle to form, as in welding ferrous metal, the aluminum will melt and boil underneath the oxide before the oxide melts. Before attempting to weld aluminum alloy for the first time, you should become familiar with the action of the metal under the welding flame.

Place a small piece of sheet aluminum on the welding table, light the torch and adjust the flame to neutral. With the flame held perpendicular to the surface of the sheet, bring the tip of the inner cone almost in contact with the metal. Observe that, almost without warning, the metal suddenly melts and runs away, leaving a hole in the sheet. Now repeat the operation with the torch held at an angle of about 30° to the plane of the surface.

With a little practice, you will be able to melt the surface metal without forming a hole. Now try moving the flame slowly along the surface of the sheet, melting a small puddle. Observe how quickly the puddle solidifies when the

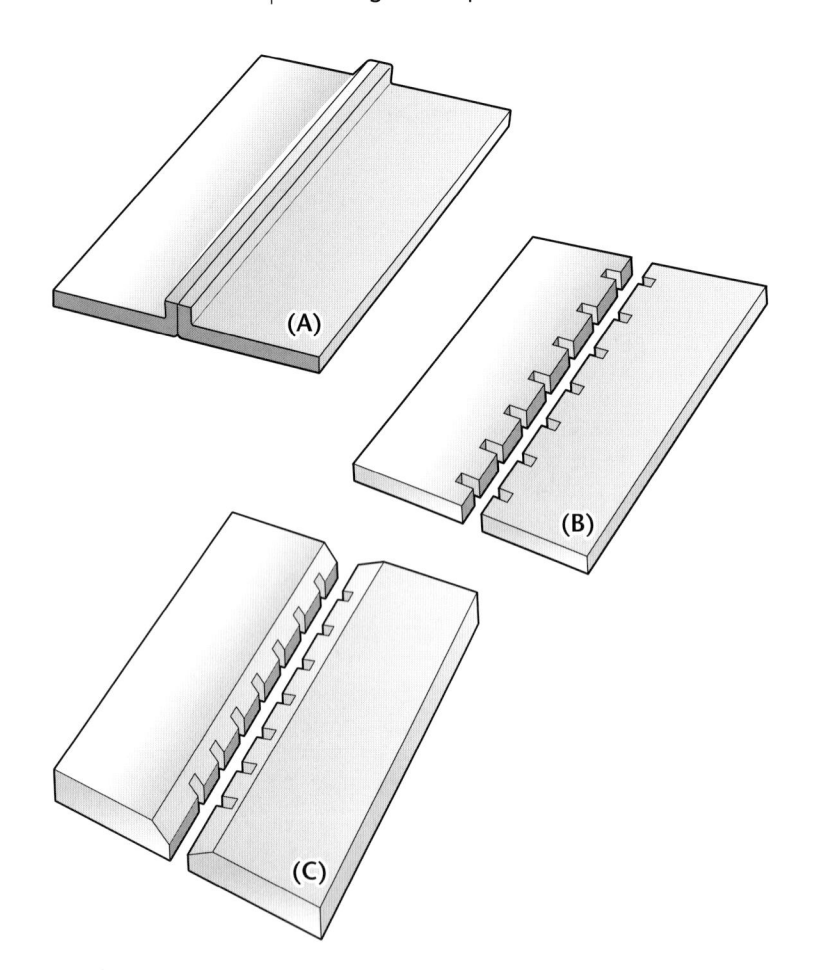

Figure 6-2-15. Edge preparation for gas-welding aluminum

flame is removed. Continue this practice until able to control melting, then proceed with practice in actual welding, starting with simple flanged and notched butt joints that do not require a welding rod. Then proceed with the use of a welding rod, at first with thin sheet metal, subsequently with castings.

Preparation of aluminum for welding. Thickness of the material determines the method of edge preparation. On material up to 0.062 inch, the edges should be formed to a 90° flange about the same height as the thickness of the material or higher. See Figure 6-2-15, illustration (A) The only requirement for the flanges is that the edges be straight and square. If desired, material up to 0.125 inch may be welded with a flange-type joint. No filler rod is necessary when the edges are flanged.

Unbeveled butt welds may be made on thicknesses of 0.062-0.188 inch, but in these applications it is necessary to notch the edges with a saw or cold chisel in a manner similar to that shown in illustration (B) of Figure 6-2-15. Edge notching is recommended in aluminum welding because it aids in getting full penetration and also prevents local distortion. All butt welds in material over 0.125 inch thick are generally notched in some manner. For anything over 0.188 inch thick, bevel the edges and notch them as shown in illustration (C) of Figure 6-2-15.

After the edges of the pieces have been properly prepared, the surfaces to be welded should be cleaned. If heavy oxide is present on the metal surface, it may be necessary to use a stainless steel wire brush. A solvent-soaked rag will remove dirt, grease or oil.

Preheating. Aluminum plate 1/4 inch thick and over should be preheated in order to prevent cracks and to assure more complete penetration. Thin materials should be warmed with the torch prior to welding; even this slight preheat helps to prevent cracks.

Welding rods. Two types of welding rods are available for gas welding aluminum alloys: the 1100 and 4043 rods. The 1100 rod is used when maximum resistance to corrosion and high ductility are of prime importance. The 1100 rod is used for welding 1100 and 3003 only. The 4043 rod is used for greater strength and to minimize the tendency for cracking. It is used for all other wrought aluminum alloys and may be used for castings.

Welding fluxes. The use of the proper flux in welding aluminum is extremely important. Aluminum welding flux is designed to remove the aluminum oxide by chemically combining with it. In gas welding, the oxide forms rapidly in the molten metal. It must be removed, or a defective weld will result. To insure proper distribution of the flux, it should be brushed on the surface to be welded and also applied to the welding rod.

Aluminum flux is generally obtained in powder form. It is best prepared for use by mixing the powder with water to form a paste. The paste should be kept in an aluminum, glass or earthenware container, since steel or copper containers tend to contaminate the mixture.

After welding is finished, it is important that all traces of flux be removed by using a stiff bristle brush and hot water. If aluminum flux is left on the weld, it will corrode the metal.

Welding technique for aluminum. After the pieces to be welded have been properly prepared and fluxed, pass the flame in small circles over the starting point until the flux melts. Then scrape the rod over the surface at about 3 or 4 second intervals, permitting the rod to come clear of the flame each time; otherwise, the rod will melt before the parent metal, and it will be difficult to note when the welding should start. The scraping action will reveal when welding can be started without overheating the aluminum. Maintain the same cycle throughout the

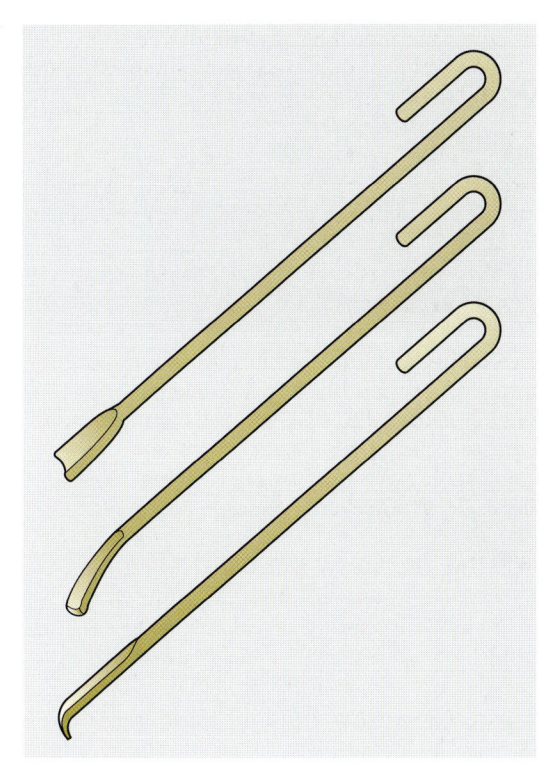

Figure 6-2-16. Puddling rods

course of welding, except for allowing the rod to remain under the flame long enough to melt the amount of metal needed. The movement of the rod can easily be mastered with practice.

Welding lenses for aluminum. While some success can be had using regular green colored welding lenses, they are not the best. Rose or cobalt blue colored lenses work better. With either color, it is possible to actually see aluminum melt. If you follow the directions in the preceding paragraph, just before the metal melts you will see it change surface appearance. At that instant it is ready to weld. Your rod should be hot and ready to drag through the zone, melting the end off. Then continue along the area to be welded.

In welding aluminum alloys up to 0.188 inch thick, there is little need to impart any motion to the torch other than moving it forward. On flanged material, care must be taken to break the oxide film as the flange melts down. This may be accomplished by stirring the melted flange with a *puddling rod*, as illustrated in Figure 6-2-16 (a puddling rod is essentially a paddle flattened and shaped from a 1/4 inch stainless steel welding rod).

The angle of the torch has much to do with welding speed. Instead of lifting the flame from time to time in order to avoid melting holes in the metal, it may be advantageous to hold the torch at a flatter angle to the work. The speed of welding should be increased as the edge of the sheet is approached. The inner cone of the flame should never be permitted to come in contact with the molten metal, but should be held about 1/8 inch away from the metal.

In the vertical position, the torch is given an up-and-down rather than a rotating motion. In the overhead position, a light back-and-forth motion is employed the same as in flat welding.

Whenever possible, heat-treatable alloys should be held in a fixture for welding. This helps to eliminate the possibility of cracking.

Cracking may also be reduced by tack welding the parts while they are in the fixture and then loosening the clamps before completing the seam.

Magnesium Alloys

Gas welding was once a widely used method of joining magnesium alloys, but because of corrosion difficulties caused by flux, it is not currently favored. Magnesium alloy parts used as structural members on aircraft cannot be repaired by gas welding, since these parts are heat-treated and it is impossible to regain the required strength after welding. Any welding of magnesium should be contracted out to a certified repair station that specializes it that type of operation.

Cutting Ferrous Metals

Oxyacetylene flame cutting is a quick, inexpensive way to cut iron or steel where the effect of burning or heating the edge of a piece of metal is not objectionable.

Ferrous metals combine with oxygen so readily that the oxygen in the air can start the reaction, as rusty pieces of iron in scrap piles will attest.

Cutting iron or steel with an oxyacetylene torch is simply a speeding up of this process in a localized area, because iron oxidizes much more readily when it is hot. Pure oxygen, if directed on a hot piece of iron, increases the rate of oxidation so enormously that the metal is actually burned away.

The metal is heated to a bright red (1,400-1,600°F), which is the kindling or ignition temperature, and a jet of high-pressure oxygen is directed against it. This oxygen blast combines with the hot metal and forms an intensely hot oxide. The molten oxide is blown down the sides of the cut, heating the metal in its path to a kindling temperature. The metal thus heated also burns to an oxide, which is then blown away on the underside of the piece. This action

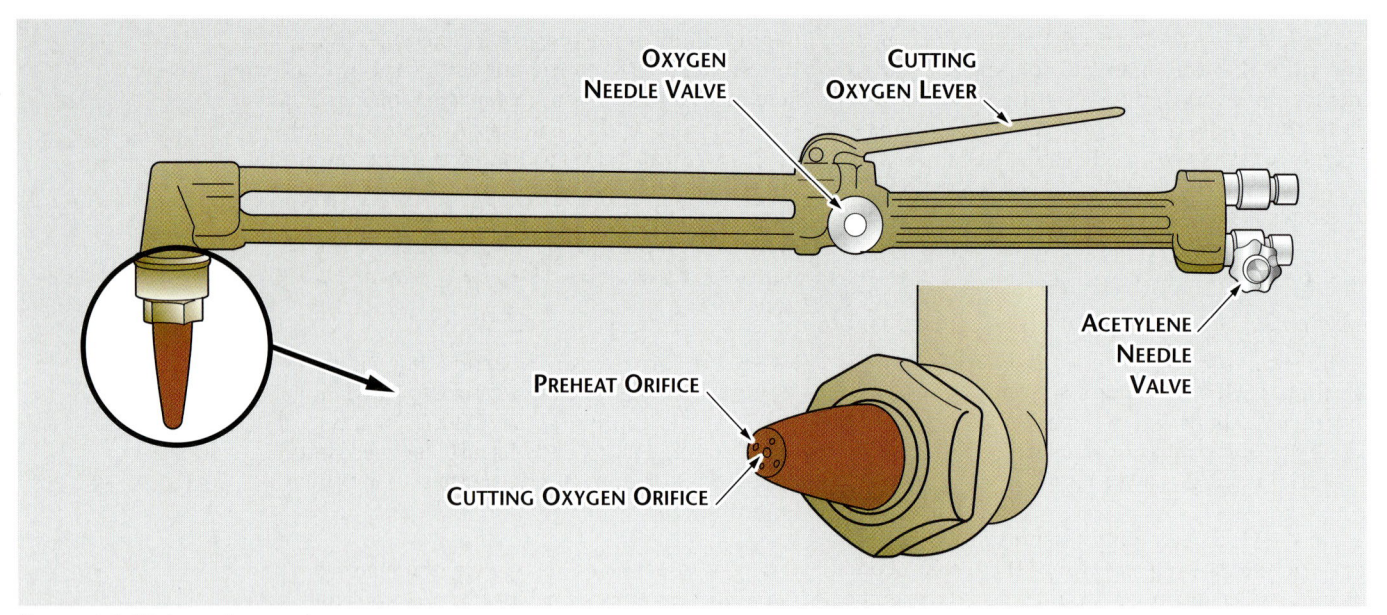

Figure 6-2-17. A cutting torch

is precisely that which the torch accomplishes when the mixing head is replaced with a cutting attachment or when a special cutting torch is used.

Figure 6-2-17 shows an example of a *cutting torch*. It has the conventional oxygen and acetylene needle valves, which control the flow of the two gases. Many cutting torches have two oxygen needle valves so a finer adjustment of the neutral flame can be obtained.

A cutting torch combines a heating flame with a jet of pure oxygen under pressure. The heating flame preheats the metal to a bright red, and the oxygen jet is directed upon the hot metal to burn it away, thus forming a slit, known as a *kerf*, in the metal.

The heating flame in a cutting tip is generally not fed by a single hole as in a welding tip, but instead comes through several holes, arranged in a ring around a larger central hole for oxygen. See Figure 6-2-17. The central oxygen tube tapers as it reaches the tip opening, which increases the velocity.

The high-pressure cutting oxygen jet is regulated by an auxiliary oxygen control valve generally operated by a lever.

Four different size tips are generally supplied for cutting metals of varying thicknesses. There are also special tips for cleaning metal; cutting rusty, scaly or painted surfaces; rivet cutting and other special jobs.

In cutting, as in welding, the pressure of oxygen and acetylene and the size of tip are determined by the thickness and quality of the metal to be cut. Table 6-2-3 shows the approximate pressures for various size tips.

Cutting procedure. Before beginning a cutting operation with an oxyacetylene cutting torch, a thorough inspection of the area should be made. There should be no combustible material which could be ignited by the sparks and slag produced by the cutting operation.

Insert the proper size tip in the cutting torch. Next, adjust the oxygen and acetylene pressures for the thickness of material to be cut (the tip size and pressures should be in accordance with the cutting torch manufacturer's recommendations). Put goggles and gloves on, then light the torch.

APPROXIMATE PRESSURE FOR VARIOUS TIP SIZES			
Tip Number	Thickness of Metal (In Inches)	Acetylene Pressure (In Pounds)	Oxygen Pressure (In Pounds)
1	1/8	4	10
1	1/4	4	15
1	3/8	4	20
1	1/2	4	25
2	3/4	5	30
2	1	5	40
2	1-1/2	5	50
2	2	5	60
3	3	6	70
3	4	6	80
3	5	6	90
4	6	7	100
4	8	7	130
4	10	8	160

Table 6-2-3. Approximate pressure for various tip sizes

To light the torch, turn on the acetylene needle valve, light the gas and adjust the flame to neutral, as in welding. When the neutral flame is burning smoothly, actuation of the cutting oxygen control will disclose the type of cutting flame created. It may be necessary to readjust the neutral preheating flame while the control lever is depressed, to make sure that it remains neutral while cutting.

The line to be cut should be marked on the metal with soapstone or chalk. Place the metal so that this line is beyond the end of the welding bench. If an exceptionally straight cut is desired, clamp a bar of steel across the piece of material to guide the torch.

Hold the torch in the right hand so that there is instant and positive control of the oxygen control lever. The left hand should be used to steady and guide the cutting torch. A fire brick or some other similar object placed on top of the material to be cut will provide a good rest for the left hand and help steady the torch. If the cutting tip wavers from side to side, a wide kerf will be made. This will result in a wide cut, slower speed, and greater oxygen consumption.

Begin cutting at the edge of the piece. Hold the tip perpendicular to the surface of the metal, keeping the inner cone about 1/16 inch from the line. Hold the flame at this point until a spot in the metal turns bright red, and then gradually depress the oxygen control lever. As soon as the cutting starts, there will be a shower of sparks from the lower side of the material, and the oxygen control level should then be fully depressed.

When the cut has been started all the way through the material, move the torch slowly but steadily along the line (Figure 6-2-18). The motion of the cutting torch should be just fast enough so that the cut continues to penetrate completely without excessive oxidation or melting.

If the torch is moved too slowly, the heat from the preheating flame will tend to melt the edges of the cut, producing a ragged appearance or, at times, fusing the metal together again. On the other hand, if the torch is moved too rapidly, the cutting jet will fail to go through the material and cutting will be stopped. Should this happen, immediately release the lever, closing the cutting oxygen valve, and reheat at

Figure 6-2-18. Finishing the cut

Figure 6-2-19. A plasma torch is easier to master than an oxyacetylene cutting rig

the point where the cutting stopped until it is a bright red. When the oxygen valve is reopened, the cutting will start again.

When the cut is finished, the cut section may stick to the main piece. This means that some of the slag produced by the cutting action has bridged across the bottom of the two pieces and on cooling has formed a thin crust which holds them together. The crust is quite brittle, however, and a smart blow from a hammer will break it and separate the pieces.

Safety Precautions

- Use no oil, grease or any other lubricant on welding or cutting apparatus. Never allow oil or grease to come in contact with oxygen under pressure.

- Always use the proper tip or nozzle, and operate it at the proper pressure for the particular work involved. This information should be taken from tables supplied with the equipment.

- Always wear goggles when working with a lighted torch. Use only goggles designed specifically for welding use.

- Do not light torches from hot metal, especially in a confined space. An explosive mixture of acetylene and oxygen in a confined space may cause damage or personal injury when ignited. Do not allow such a mixture to accumulate.

- When extinguishing the torch, close the acetylene valve, then the oxygen valve.

Plasma Cutting

One major advantage of a *plasma cutter* is that it can cut almost any metal that will conduct electricity. This includes both aluminum and stainless steel, neither of which can be cut with an oxyacetylene cutting torch.

Any shop that does any variety of metal cutting can afford a plasma cutting machine. In normal use, a plasma cutter is easier for a novice to master, will make better cuts on thin materials, do it faster and do it without any fuel gas.

Most plasma cutters use compressed air and electricity. They don't have the heat input of an oxyacetylene cutting torch. As a result, the heat damage to the work is considerably less.

Plasma Cutter Technology

The plasma in the cutting process is created by ionizing a stream of compressed air and blowing it through a nozzle. The ionized airstream, having a surplus of positive charged atoms, is then heated by a high-voltage discharge passing through the nozzle. The high voltage heats the ionized air and creates the plasma. The hot *plasma* (ionized air with an arc going through it) melts the metal to be cut, while the ionized air part of the plasma blows the molten metal out the other side. A plasma torch in operation is shown in Figure 6-2-19.

Since a plasma torch is an electrical device similar to a welder, there are some duty cycle considerations, with most smaller units running around 50 percent. The Lincoln Electric website (*www.lincolnelectric.com/knowledge*) has a great deal of general information on plasma cutters.

Operation and Safety

The operation of a plasma torch is fairly straightforward. A few minutes reading the machine's instructions is about all that is needed to get started. A novice can produce good-looking results after a few tries, while an oxyacetylene cutting rig takes considerable practice to operate proficiently.

Operator safety equipment and procedures are about the same as for a TIG/MIG unit: goggles, shoes, gloves and no nylon shirts.

Brazing

Originally, *brazing* meant joining with brass. As the process was improved and new joining alloys were developed, the term assumed its present meaning — a group of thermal joining processes in which the bonding material is a non-ferrous metal or alloy with a melting point higher than 800°F, but less than the metals being joined. Brazing, therefore, includes silver soldering, bronze welding and hard soldering.

Brazing requires less heat than welding, and therefore may be used to join metals that are injured by high heat. The strength of brazed joints is not as great as welded joints, though, so brazing is not used for critical structural repairs on aircraft. Newer brazing alloys and silver solder are used on some tubing connections, particularly primer and instrument lines.

As the definition of brazing implies, the base metal parts are not melted. The brazing metal adheres to the base metal by molecular attraction and intergranular penetration; it does not fuse and amalgamate with them. For this reason, it is not normally possible to weld an item that has been brazed. The weld will be contaminated by the brazing material remaining within the metal pores.

The usefulness of brazing is easily recognized when the many metals that can be joined by this process are considered. Brazing is applicable to the joining of cast iron, malleable iron, carbon steels, alloy steels, wrought iron, galvanized iron and steel, copper, and brass, bronze and nickel alloys. It is also used to join dissimilar metals, such as cast iron to steel, or steel to copper.

Its principal use is in maintenance, making and repairing tools, jigs and machinery. In this field, it has many applications and attendant advantages. Among these are the relatively low temperatures involved, reduced chance of an excessively annealed area near the brazed joint and the ability of a properly prepared brazed joint to stand heavy compression and impact loads. Before welding an area that has been brazed, all the old braze material must be removed to prevent contamination of the weld area.

Brazing Technique

In brazing a joint, first bevel down the edges as in welding steel. Clean the surrounding surfaces of dirt, rust and debris, then select the proper brazing alloy for the job.

A brazing flux is necessary to obtain a good union between the base metal and the filler metal. It is still possible to buy flux that can be used to coat the rod.

The bare rod is heated, then dipped in the powered flux. A commercial brazing rod that is precoated with flux is the most common general-purpose rod. It is available virtually anywhere.

Preheat the base metal slowly with a mild flame, and when it reaches a dull red heat (in the case of steel), heat the rod to a dark or purple color and dip it into the flux. Enough flux adheres to the rod, making it unnecessary to spread it over the surface of the metal.

LAP JOINT

FLANGED BUTT JOINT

EDGE JOINT

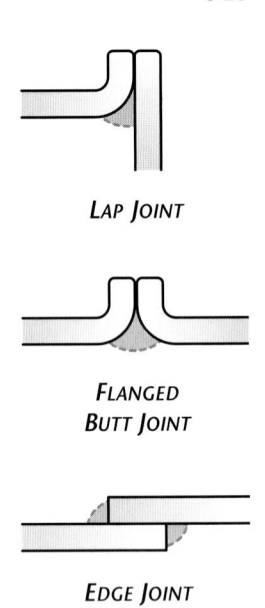

Figure 6-2-20. Silver solder joints

Bring the filler rod near the tip of the torch and let the molten bronze flow over a small area of the seam. The base metal must be at the flowing temperature of the filler metal before it will flow into the joint. The brazing metal melts when applied to the steel and runs into the joint by capillary attraction.

Continue adding the rod, as the braze progresses, with a rhythmic dipping action so that the bead will be built to a uniform width and height. Complete the job rapidly and with as few passes of the rod and torch as possible.

The ideal brazing job is completed in one pass. Avoid multiple layers, and if the job requires more than one pass, always remove and replace the spent flux before applying succeeding layers of filler metal.

It is important that the brazing temperature be carefully controlled. If the base metal is heated excessively above the flow temperature of the brazing alloy, the bronze will boil when added and the low melting point alloys of the bronze will burn out. This will cause the bronze to be porous and brittle. On the other hand, if the base metal is not hot enough, the bronze will not flow smoothly. It will form elusive drops, which roll off as fast as the bronze can be applied.

After finishing the job, allow it to cool slowly.

Silver Soldering

Silver soldering is one of several methods of brazing. The principal use of silver solder is the fabrication of high-pressure oxygen lines, and other parts which must withstand vibration and high temperatures. Silver solder is used extensively to join copper and its alloys, nickel and silver, as well as various combinations of these metals and thin steel parts. Silver solder, or hard solder, is very different from soft solder which is a mixture of lead, tin and antimony or cadmium. Soft solder is used in electrical systems and components and is done with a well tinned soldering iron. In order for the iron to conduct heat properly it must not be sharpened to a fine point. The tip must be clean and have a layer of clean solder, or tinned, on it as well.

Silver solder can be obtained in several different grades with silver content, ranging from 14.5-66 percent, and melting points varying from 1,160-1,430°F. The standard forms of silver solder are strips and wires, but it is also made in rod form.

If the job to be performed is one in which the solder may be placed in the joint before applying heat, use the strip form. For joints requiring the solder to be applied after heating, use the wire form.

It is necessary to use flux in all silver soldering operations because of the necessity for having the base metal chemically clean without the slightest film of oxide to prevent the silver solder from coming into intimate contact with the base metal.

A paste flux is used generally in most silver soldering. Prepared flux begins to melt at 800°F, becomes fluid at 1,100°F and remains stable up to 1,600°F. It melts at a slightly lower temperature than the solder.

The joint must be physically clean, which means free of all dirt, grease, oil and paint, and also chemically clean — minus all traces of oxide film. After removing the dirt, grease and paint, remove any oxide which may be present by grinding or filing the piece until bright metal can be seen. During the soldering operation, the flux continues the process of keeping oxide away from the metal.

Joints to be silver soldered must have smooth edges and must fit tightly together. Only a film of silver solder is usually needed for a sound joint. Strength is not added to the joint and expensive solder is wasted if it is used as filler metal.

In Figure 6-2-20, three recommended types of joints for silver soldering are shown. They are flanged, lap and edge joints. With these, the metal may be formed to furnish a seam wider than the base metal thickness and furnish the type of joint that will hold up under all kinds of loads.

If a lap joint is used, figure the amount of lap according to the strength needed in the joint. Here is a handy rule of thumb: For strength equal to that of the base metal in the heated zone, the amount of lap should be four to six times the metal thickness for sheet metal and small diameter tubing.

The oxyacetylene flame for silver soldering should be neutral, but it may have a slight excess of acetylene. It must be soft, not harsh.

During both preheating and application of the solder, hold the tip of the inner cone of the flame about one-half inch from the work. Keep the flame moving so that the metal will not be overheated.

If the piece is large, preheat a considerable area around the joint before applying the solder, especially if the base metal conducts heat rapidly. When soldering two pieces which have different thicknesses, or which conduct heat with unequal speed, gauge the preheating so that both parts reach the soldering temperature at the same time.

When both parts of the base metal are at the right temperature (indicated by the flow of flux), begin applying solder to the surface of the under or inner part at the edge of the seam. It is necessary to simultaneously direct the flame over the seam and keep moving it so that the base metal remains at an even temperature.

Safety Precautions

Gas welding, brazing and soldering operations can be very dangerous. Strict adherence to all applicable safety precautions must be observed when performing these operations. Practically all of the welding and cutting operations performed by the AMT are conducted in specifically designated locations. If welding or cutting is to be done in any other location, approval of the job and the precautions to be taken must be obtained from higher authority.

Some of the common hazards encountered and the precautions to be followed when operating welding equipment and/or supervising a welding shop are as follows:

- Use only approved apparatus, such as torches, regulators, hose, valves and accessories that have been examined, tested and found to be safeguarded in accordance with accepted standards.
- Only qualified operators should perform welding, brazing and soldering operations.
- While the equipment is in use, it must be frequently inspected for evidence of leaks in the hose, couplings, valve stems or other points of the system. Otherwise, an explosive mixture of gas and air may accumulate with serious results.
- Positive ventilation of the welding shop or area must be provided and maintained during all welding, cutting or heating operations to prevent suffocation, fire and explosion due to gas leaks; heat prostration and/or illnesses such as metal fume fever or metal poisoning caused by breathing toxic vapors which may be formed under certain conditions.
- If all fire hazards cannot be removed from the area of welding operations, fire watches must be properly instructed and posted in the vicinity.
- Never weld anything inside an airplane. The danger of catching fire is high. With the normal fuel load, an airplane can create a tremendous fire that cannot be controlled.
- Suitable fire-extinguishing equipment of approved types must be maintained near all welding and/or cutting operations.
- Protective clothing must be provided and worn at all times when welding and/or cutting operations are being performed.
- Not only welding and cutting operators, but also other personnel such as helpers, inspectors, etc., who remain in the vicinity, must use suitable helmets, hand-held shields or goggles during all welding/cutting operation, in order to protect their eyes from stray flashes, reflected glare and flying particles.
- After welding/cutting operations are completed, the operator should mark the hot metal or provide some other means of warning other workers who may inadvertently come in contact with the hot metal.

Section 3
Gas-shielded Arc Welding

Gas-shielded arc welding is a metal joining development which has become one of the most important welding processes, especially for aluminum and stainless steel alloys and other hard-to-weld materials. In the gas-shielded arc welding process, a shielding gas is used to protect the electrode, arc, molten weld metal and weld area from exposure to the atmosphere. The shielding gas is non-combustible and may or may not be inert (chemically inactive). The electrode used for this process may be non-consumable, or it may be a consumable wire electrode that is fed automatically into the weld.

There are two different types of gas-shielded arc welding processes. One is the *gas tungsten-arc* (GTA) process, which employs the use of a non-consumable tungsten electrode. The electrode does not burn off or supply metal to the joint. Necessary filler metal is added to the joint, as required, by the operator in a fashion similar to that used in oxyacetylene welding.

The other type is the *gas metal-arc* (GMA) process, which employs the use of a consumable wire electrode that is fed automatically into the weld.

The two processes mentioned above were formerly known as *tungsten inert-gas* (TIG) welding and *metal inert-gas* (MIG) welding. These names were changed by the American Welding Society, because carbon dioxide is used as a shielding gas when welding mild steel by the gas metal-arc process, and carbon dioxide is not an inert gas. The acronyms TIG and MIG have become part of the language, and because they are so readily recognized, that is how we will refer to the processes throughout the rest of the text.

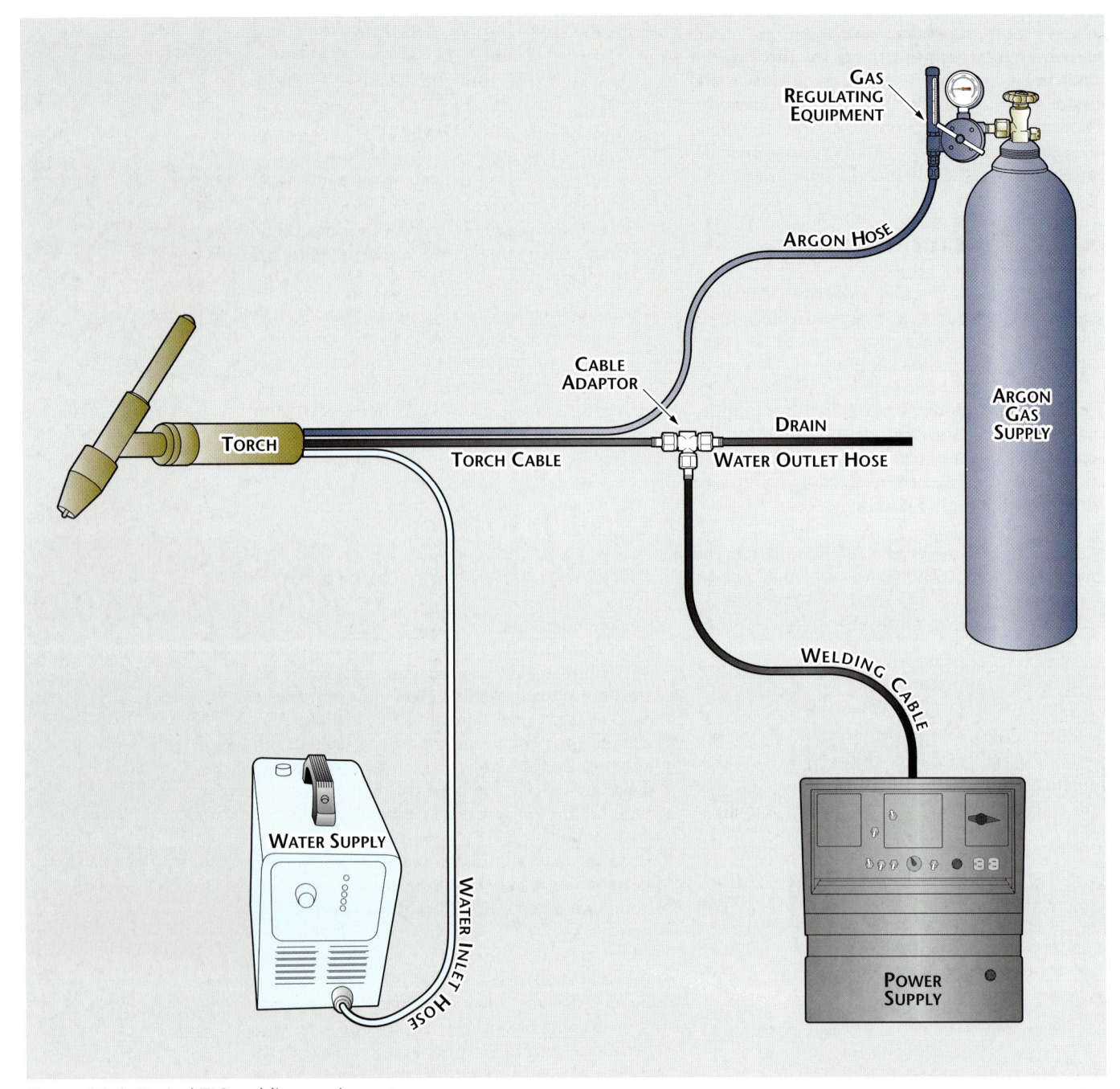

Figure 6-3-1. Typical TIG welding equipment

Gas Tungsten-arc Welding

TIG welding is a gas-arc welding process that uses an inert gas to protect the weld zone from the atmosphere. Heat for welding is provided by a very intense electric arc struck between a virtually non-consumable tungsten electrode and the work. The principle of the inert arc is the same as the conventional electric arc. The arc is actually the passage of electricity through atmospheric resistance between the electrode and the base metal. The current used may be either AC or DC, depending on the material to be welded. TIG welding is also incorrectly called Heli-arc®. Heli-arc® is a trademarked process that uses helium as a shielding gas.

This process differs from MIG welding (discussed later in this chapter) in that the electrode is not melted and used as a filler metal. On joints where filler metal is required, a filler rod is fed into the weld zone and melted with the base metal in much the same manner as used with oxyacetylene welding.

In any type of welding, the best obtainable weld is one that has the same chemical, metallurgical and physical properties as the base metal. To obtain these conditions, the molten weld puddle must be protected from the atmosphere; otherwise, atmospheric oxygen and nitrogen will combine readily with the molten weld metal and a weak, porous weld will result.

In TIG welding, the weld zone is shielded from the atmosphere by an inert gas fed through the torch. Either of two inert gases may be used, argon or helium. An arc in argon or helium gas is smooth and quiet. In argon the arc has an appearance similar to the oxyacetylene welding flame. In helium the arc is more ball-like in shape.

The TIG welding process has several advantages over the conventional arc-welding process; however, it also has some disadvantages, which are discussed in the following paragraphs.

Advantages

TIG welds are stronger, more ductile and more corrosion-resistant than welds made by the conventional arc-welding process. The weld zone has 100-percent protection from the atmosphere; therefore, no flux is required. It is applicable to a wider variety of joints, and no post-weld cleaning is required. Since no flux is required, it eliminates flux or slag inclusions in the weld and there are no sparks, fumes or spatter. Little or no filler metal is needed.

Efficient use is made of welding current; with AC power the machine operates only during actual welding operations. Other advantages are: high speed, 3-12 inches per minute, with a minimum of distortion; efficient use of welding heat; and smooth, even welds with excellent strength and in some cases with only slight reinforcement.

With the improvements in welding machine manufacturing, a general use TIG welder can be purchased from any tool supplier. You can even buy one in a home center.

Disadvantages

Different types of machines and currents are required for different materials to be welded. For example, alternating-current high-frequency (ACHF) is used for welding aluminum, while direct-current straight-polarity (DCSP) is used for heavy gauge stainless steel. The initial cost of equipment is higher, and the gases used can be expensive.

Application

As previously mentioned, the TIG welding process can be used to weld most metals, particularly the hard-to-weld metals such as aluminum, magnesium, corrosion-resistant steels, titanium, nickel and nickel-base alloys. This process is also used for welding various combinations of dissimilar metals, and for applying hard-facing and surfacing materials to steel.

Equipment Requirements

Basic equipment requirements for TIG welding consist of the torch, plus the additional apparatus to supply electric power, inert gas and, in some units, water. See Figure 6-3-1.

The torch feeds both the welding current and the inert gas to the weld zone. The current is fed to the weld zone through the electrode, which is held firmly in place by a collet in the electrode holder. The inert gas is fed to the weld zone through a replaceable gas cup which screws on the end of the torch.

Power unit. The power unit supplies the welding current and has a built-in, or add-on, high-frequency transformer. The high-frequency current is used for welding aluminum. It is also used to start the weld on other materials. The power unit, commonly called the welder, can be anything from a relatively inexpensive *buzz box* to a commercial unit costing several thousand dollars. Best results are obtained with an open circuit voltage of not more than 80 volts.

For alternating-current (AC) welding power, any standard transformer with an adequate amperage capacity for the job may be used. For best results, the open circuit voltage should be 60-100 volts, and the transformer should be a balanced wave type. Regular AC power for TIG welding should have high-frequency current for stabilizing the welding arc.

In direct-current (DC) welding, the welding current circuit can be hooked up as either straight polarity or reverse polarity. The machine connection for DC straight polarity welding is electrode-negative and work-positive. For DC reverse polarity, the connections are reversed and the electrode is positive and the work negative.

In straight polarity welding, the electrons hitting the workpiece at high velocity exert a heating effect on the plate. In reverse-polarity welding, just the opposite occurs. The electrode has to absorb the extra heat, which tends to melt off the end of the electrode. Therefore, reverse polarity requires a larger electrode diameter than straight polarity. For example, a 1/16 inch diameter pure tungsten electrode can handle 125 amperes of welding current with straight polarity. If the polarity is reversed, this amount of current would melt off the electrode and contaminate the weld. A 1/4 inch diameter electrode is required to handle 125 amperes of reverse polarity current safely.

Hand welding torches. There are various types of TIG welding torches available and, although not all torches have the same external appearance, their principle of operation is much the same. Inexpensive torches are

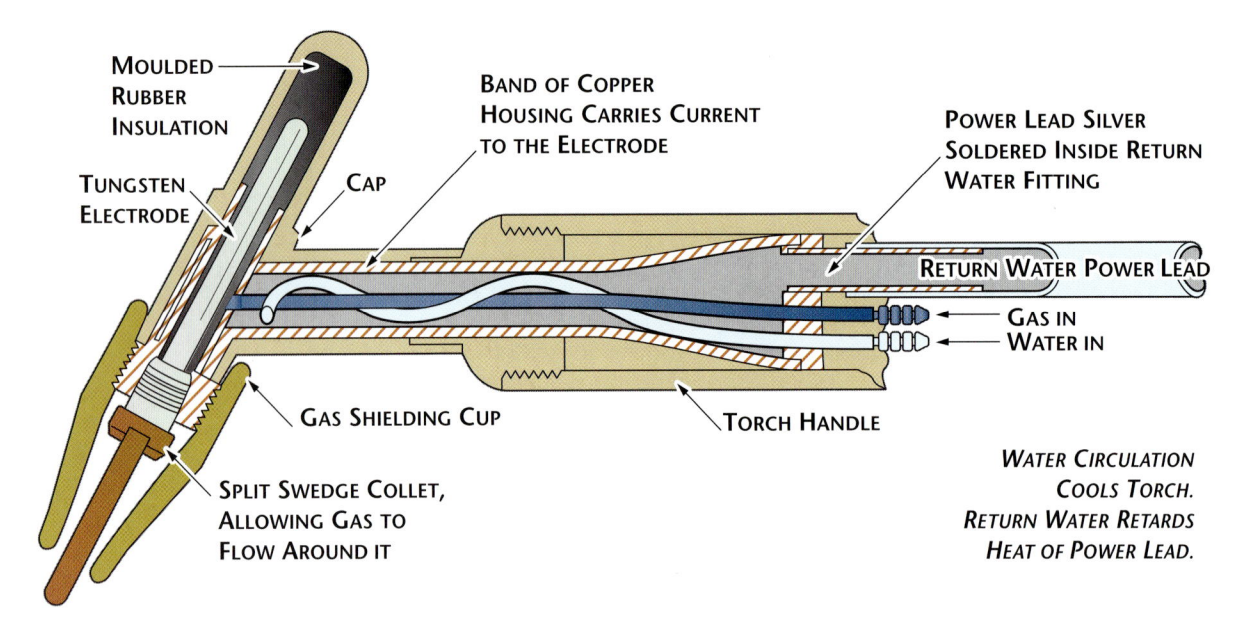

Figure 6-3-2. Typical water-cooled TIG welding torch

gas-cooled, while the better torches use water cooling. Fortunately, you can use an upscale torch on an inexpensive power supply and get good results. Figure 6-3-2 shows a schematic of a typical water-cooled TIG welding torch. The torch illustrated is designed to perform several functions:

- Hold the electrode
- Introduce an envelope of shielding gas around the electrode
- Transmit current to the electrode
- Circulate cooling water throughout the holder

The water-cooled torch is designed for TIG welding using either alternating current or direct current with straight or reverse polarity. Gas enters through a hose fitted to the rear of the handle, passes through the body of the torch and emerges from the gas orifice in the torch head. Gas is then guided down toward the weld puddle by the shielding gas cup which surrounds the electrode.

Cooling water circulates through the torch and out around the power cable. The water cooling protects parts of the torch from excessive heat and permits the use of a minimum of insulation in the body of the torch. The torch is light and easy to manipulate.

The power cable is contained in the water discharge hose and is water-cooled in such a manner that extremely high currents can be used without excessive power loss.

CAUTION: *Be sure water lines are hooked up properly. Do not weld with water flow reversed. The water should cool the torch body before it flows over the power cable.*

The torch is fully insulated to safeguard the operator against shock, and to prevent damage to the work from accidental arcing. Use of the torch at high amperages tends to deteriorate the shielding gas cup.

Electrodes for TIG welding are available in three types: pure tungsten (99.5 percent), tungsten with 1-2 percent thorium and tungsten with 0.3-0.5 percent zirconium. These electrodes have a very high melting point and are practically non-consumable — normal consumption is 0.001-0.005 inch per hour.

Tungsten electrodes of 99.5 percent purity are less expensive and are generally used on less critical operations than tungsten electrodes that are alloyed with thorium or zirconium. A pure tungsten electrode has a relatively low current-carrying capacity and a low resistance to contamination.

Tungsten electrodes with 1-2 percent thorium are superior to pure tungsten electrodes in several respects. They have higher electron emissivity, better current-carrying capacity, longer life and greater resistance to contamination. With these electrodes, arc starting is easier, and the arc is more stable.

The current-carrying capacity of all types of tungsten electrodes is affected by the type of electrode holder, the extension of the electrode from the holder, the position of welding, the shielding gas and the type of welding current. The electrodes are held in place by a collet (Figure 6-3-2). Electrode length is adjusted by extending or retracting the electrode through the collet-clamping device.

The electrode, particularly in manual operations, will pick up contamination from the work caused in most cases by touching the workpiece. The life of the electrode can be extended by making sure that the electrode does not come in contact with the work during welding operations and by choosing an electrode of the proper size for the current range being used. The electrode will deteriorate more rapidly when the welding current is too high or too low for the particular size electrode being used.

If the electrode comes in contact with the workpiece or worktable, a small bead or ball will appear at the contact end. This causes the arc to become unstable. This ball may be removed by grooving the electrode just above the fouled point with a file, then breaking it off with pliers. It is essential that the electrode be grooved to prevent splitting when the burned metal is broken off. This operation can be repeated as often as necessary until the electrode can no longer be clamped or held in the torch.

Ceramic and metal cups. Ceramic and metal cups are available in various diameters, shapes and lengths. The cup should be large enough to provide complete inert-gas coverage of the molten weld metal. Ceramic cups are acceptable when the welding current is less than 250 amperes. When higher currents are used, or when welding conditions are unusually severe, metal cups are used. Metal cups should never be allowed to come in contact with the metal being welded when the current is on.

Regulator. The regulator used on the inert-gas cylinder is identical in design to those used on oxygen cylinders. It is ruggedly built and combines high sensitivity of control with a large flow capacity.

> **CAUTION:** *Always stand to the side when cracking the cylinder valve. Gauge faces sometimes blow out when pressure is suddenly applied.*

The function of the regulator is to reduce pressure in the cylinder to the desired working pressure and hold that pressure, without fluctuation or readjustment, until the cylinder is almost exhausted. Figure 6-3-3 shows a typical regulator, flowmeter and pressure gauge combination.

Flowmeter. Along with pressure reduction, successful TIG welding requires a constant flow of shielding gas. The gas flow rate is indicated by a graduated glass tube flowmeter (Figure 6-3-3). As shown, the flowmeter is usually attached to the regulator, but it may be installed elsewhere in the gas line. The flowmeter should always be

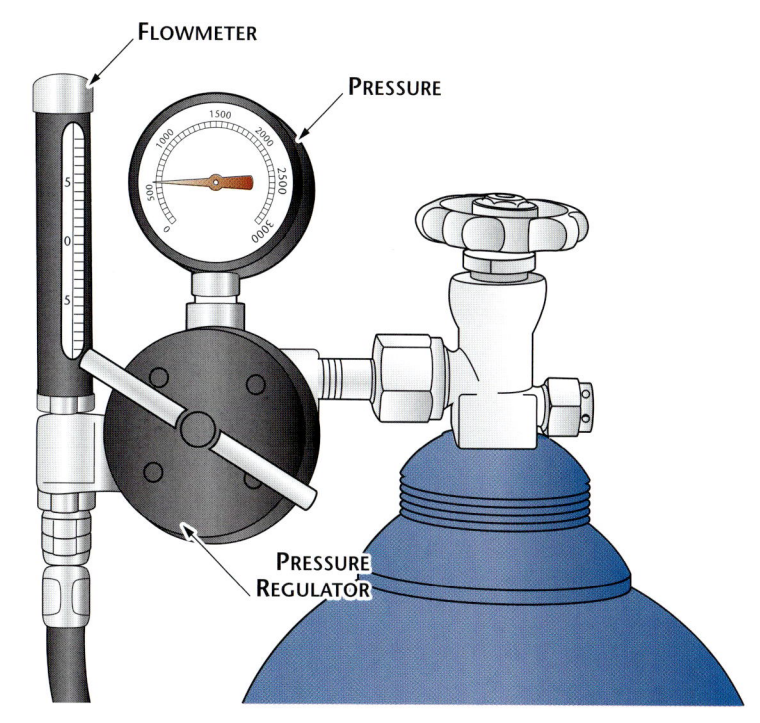

Figure 6-3-3. Regulator, flowmeter and pressure gauge

mounted vertically. Be sure you have the proper flowmeter for the gas being used, or the flow indicated will be incorrect.

Flowmeters are calibrated in liters per minute (l.p.m.) or cubic feet per hour (c.f.h.). The selection of gas flow is a critical factor. A sufficient flow of gas is required during the welding operation to prevent oxidation of the weld metal. The weld zone must have 100 percent protection from the atmosphere. This flow will be found in the range of 4-15 liters per minute for argon and 8-40 liters per minute for helium.

The exact flow setting will depend on the type of joint, fit of the joint and the material to be welded. Small differences in conditions can make considerable difference in the required flow. The distance the torch is held from the work will change the required flow sharply. A drafty shop will increase the required flow. An increase in welding speed, while generally acting to reduce gas consumption, will usually require an increase in gas flow.

Inert gases. The inert gases used in TIG welding are argon or helium. An inert gas is defined as a gas that will not combine chemically with any known substance.

Whether the gas used in TIG welding is helium or argon, the gas must be of high purity and free of moisture, hydrogen and hydrocarbons. Each gas has advantages for certain applications.

Argon's density (weight per volume) is considerably greater than that of helium, but it offers

TIG CURRENT TYPE BY WELDABLE MATERIAL TYPE			
Material	High-frequency Stabilized Alternating Current	Direct Current	
		Straight Polarity	Reverse Polarity
Aluminum	1	N.R.	N.R.
Aluminum casting	1	N.R.	N.R.
Stainless steel 0.015–0.050 Inch	1	2	N.R.
Stainless steel 0.050–1.000+ Inch	2	1	N.R.
High-carbon steel 0.015–0.050 Inch	1	N.R.	N.R.
High-carbon steel 0.050+ Inch	2	1	N.R.
Cast iron	2	1	N.R.
Monel®	2	2	N.R.
Hastelloy alloys	1	2	N.R.
1 — Excellent operation. First preference. 2 — Good Operation. Second preference. N.R. — Not recommended.			

Table 6-3-1. Current requirements for commonly used metals

less resistance to the passage of electricity than does helium. Because of the difference in electrical resistance, the heat produced by the arc in an atmosphere of helium is hotter than that developed in argon. The helium-shielded arc also produces deeper penetration, but at the same time has a greater tendency to spatter. Because of its greater density, argon remains in the weld vicinity longer and provides a better cleaning action when welding aluminum and magnesium with alternating current. For these reasons, about one-third less argon than helium is needed to provide equal shielding.

No inflexible rule governs the choice of gas for any application. Either argon or helium may be used successfully for most applications with the possible exception of the welding of extremely thin material, for which argon is essential.

Water-gas shut-off valves. Shut-off valves for water and gas are of two types: solenoid and manual. The *solenoid valve* is controlled electrically. The *manual valve* is shut off by hanging the torch on the hook provided on the valve. A water drain, or recirculating system, is necessary to carry away the water coming from the cooling system of the torch.

Gas should be permitted to flow after the arc is broken for a minimum of 5 seconds to a maximum of 40 seconds, depending on the diameter of the electrode. The electrode should be brought to a silvery-white appearance, without blue-black discoloration, which indicates oxidation.

Protective equipment. The protective equipment used for gas-shielded arc welding is similar to that used in regular arc welding. The operator should be properly protected from the arc rays. This requires suitable clothing to cover all exposed skin surfaces, and a welder's helmet with the proper shade of glass to protect the eyes and face. The recommended welding lens shade numbers for various welding applications are included the in welding equipment manufacturer's instructions.

High-frequency unit. The high-frequency unit of the TIG welding machine is used to introduce a high-voltage, high-frequency, low-power additional current into the welding current. The high frequency produces a low-intensity arc, which jumps the gap between the electrode and the workpiece and pierces the oxide film, forming a path for the welding current to follow.

Introducing this high-voltage, high-frequency current into the welding current gives the following advantages:

- The arc can be started without touching the electrode to the work
- Better arc stability is obtained
- A longer arc is possible
- The tungsten electrodes will have a longer life
- Use of wider current ranges for a specific diameter electrode is possible

Controlling the high-frequency unit of a TIG welder depends on the sophistication of the machine. On small units, it is simply turned on or off. Expensive units have built-in switches and timers to control water, gas and the high-frequency unit.

Welding current controls. If all a TIG unit is to be used for is welding aluminum, it is possible to just use the shop AC stick welder as a power source. However, an AC/DC unit will make welding a more varied selection of materials possible.

On some machines, the high-frequency option is not automatically selected along with the alternating current. On these machines, the selector should be set to the AC position and a manually operated switch will have to be actuated to provide the high frequency.

Welding Procedures and Techniques

Aluminum and aluminum alloys. The TIG welding process is particularly adapted to the welding of aluminum and aluminum alloys. Sound welds may be made without the use of flux. Dispensing with flux is a definite advantage, since flux removal from aluminum welded joints is extremely important to avoid corrosion. Although all of the aluminum alloys except 2024 and 7075 are considered weldable by the gas-shielded arc process, there are certain restrictions, as described in the following paragraphs.

Effects of welding. The heat of welding decreases the strength of both the non-heat-treatable and heat-treatable aluminum alloys, except when the alloy is in the annealed condition. In some cases, the resistance to corrosion is also lowered.

The effects of strain hardening in the non-heat-treatable alloys are partially or wholly destroyed by heat, depending upon the temperature attained, coupled with the time at temperatures above 400°F. These alloys are not affected as far as corrosion resistance is concerned.

The positive effects of solution heat-treatment and precipitation treatments for heat-treatable aluminum alloys are adversely affected by the heat of welding. The extent increases with temperature and time at temperatures above 400°F.

The alloys containing substantial amounts of copper (alloys 2014 and 2017) suffer not only from loss of strength but also from loss in resistance to corrosion when subjected to the heat of welding.

In view of the above, heat-treatable aluminum alloys that have been welded must be properly reheat-treated before being used on aircraft.

> **NOTE:** *Alloys 2024 and 7075 are not fusion-welded because of hot cracking and impairment of corrosion resistance. However, both of these alloys are spot- and seam-welded extensively.*

Current requirements. Current requirements for the most commonly used metals are shown

GENERAL OPERATING DATA FOR ALUMINUM				
Thickness (in Inches)	Current Range (in Amperes)	Argon Flow (C.F.H.)	Rod Size	Arc Speed (in Inches per Minute)
0.025	10-75	10	1/16	10-40
0.031	20-75	10	1/16	10-40
0.037	35-75	10	1/16	10-40
0.050	50-125	14	3/32	10-40
0.062	70-130	14	3/32	10-40
0.078	80-150	14	1/8	10-40
0.109	150-175	14	1/8	20-30
0.125	160-200	14	3/16	6-25
0.195	175-200	14	3/16	4-20
0.250	150-200	20	3/16	2-10
0.375	150-225	25	3/16	2-8
0.500	300-450	30	1/4	5-10

Table 6-3-2. General operating data for aluminum

in Table 6-3-1. As shown in the table, first preference for aluminum is high-frequency, stabilized alternating current.

The low-intensity arc produced by this high-frequency current provides a path easily followed by the main welding current. The welding arc can be started easily without the electrode actually contacting the work, and a longer arc can be used during welding. With alternating current stabilized in this manner, good welds can be made.

Current range (amperage) depends upon the size electrode, thickness of the metal and the type of joint to be welded. Table 6-3-2 lists the general operating data for aluminum.

Torch adjustment. The correct size electrode and corresponding gas cup are selected according to the thickness of the material to be welded.

The electrode should be polished with steel wool before installing it into the torch. Cleaning the electrode is important, since the appearance of the finished weld is improved by the cleanliness of the electrode.

Install the electrode in the torch so that the extension is 1/8-1/4 inch beyond the end of the gas cup for butt welding and 1/4-3/8 inch beyond for fillet welding.

> **CAUTION:** *Always make certain that the welding current is off before adjusting the electrode.*

STARTING POSITION · STRIKING THE ARC

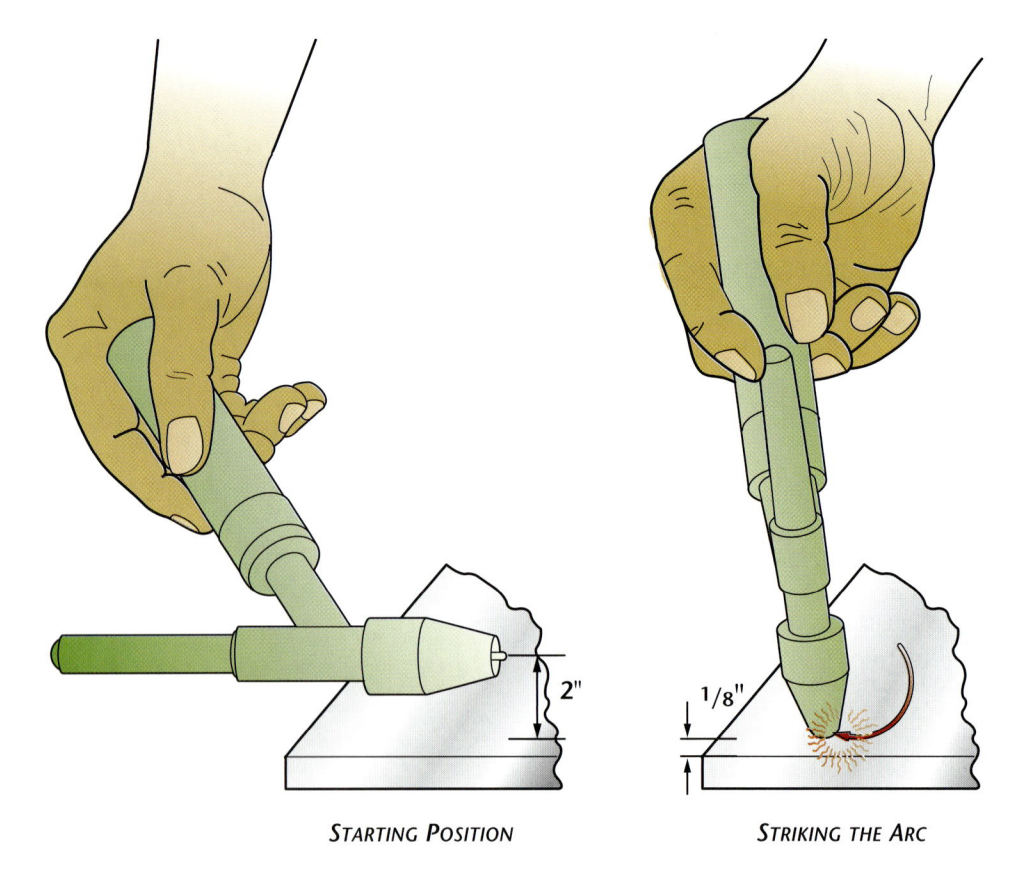

Figure 6-3-4. Starting the arc

Selection of filler rod. The selection of the proper filler rod is necessary in order to obtain a weld of high strength and good corrosion resistance. For alloys 1100 and 3003, 1100 filler rod may be used. For other aluminum alloys, 4043, 5154, 5356 or 5456 rod should be used.

Preparation of metal. Cleanliness is very important. Parts to be welded should be free of oil, grease and dirt. Combustible materials in the path of the arc will burn and contaminate the gas shielding. If filler rod is used, it should also be cleaned.

Oil or grease should be mechanically or chemically removed. An abrasive disc sander is recommended for mechanical cleaning. Chemical cleaning should be performed, using a caustic bath followed by a sulfuric acid brightening bath. Do not use a wire brush or nitric acid, as this will contaminate the weld. If the part has been grit blasted, the residue from the grit must be removed.

Starting the arc. It is possible to start the arc without actually contacting the work. Grasp the torch in a comfortable position. Hold the torch in a horizontal position about 2 inches above the work, or starting block, then quickly swing the torch down toward the work or starting block, so that the end of the electrode is 1/8 inch above the work. This motion will start the arc. Figure 6-3-4 illustrates the procedure for starting the arc.

The downward motion should be made rapidly to provide the maximum amount of gas protection to the weld zone. If the end of the electrode is too far from the work when the arc starts, it will cause oxidation of the weld.

The arc can be started with AC or DC power on the work itself or on a heavy piece of copper or scrap steel, then carried to the starting point of the weld. Do not use a carbon block for starting the arc, as the electrode will become contaminated, causing the arc to wander.

In making the first start with AC power with a cold electrode, the distance the arc will start is much shorter than when the electrode is hot. When starting to weld with a hot electrode, the motions must be rapid, as the arc tends to start before the torch is in the proper welding position. This procedure for starting the arc can be used on all types of materials to be joined by the TIG welding process.

Breaking the arc. To stop the arc, merely snap the electrode rapidly back to the horizontal position, as shown in Figure 6-3-5. This motion is just the reverse of the starting procedure. This motion must be fast, so that the arc will not mar or damage the weld surface or work.

When the electrode is hot, the arc will jump a greater distance. This procedure for breaking the arc can be used on all types of materials.

Arc blow. With the torch held stationary, the points at which the arc leaves the electrode and strikes the work may often shift and waver without apparent reason. This is known as arc blow, and is generally caused by one of the following reasons:

- Low electrode current density — amperage for the electrode diameter is too low
- Carbon contamination of the electrode caused by starting the arc on a carbon block
- Magnetic effects — usually caused by improper location of the ground
- Air drafts — when exposed to excessive air drafts, the arc becomes erratic

The first two causes are distinguished by a very rapid movement of the arc from side to side. The third cause will usually displace the arc along the entire length of the weld. The fourth will cause various amounts of arc wandering, depending on how severe the air drafts are.

Preheating. It is possible to weld aluminum up to 3/4 inch thick by hand without preheating. However, thicknesses over 3/4 inch will require a preheat of 300-400°F.

By preheating, the operator can work more easily and complete the weld much faster. Preheating can be accomplished in special preheat ovens or by gas flames directed on the work in such a manner that they do not disturb the gas shield.

Welding procedure. After the arc has been started, hold the torch at an angle of approximately 75° to the surface of the work. The starting point on the work is first preheated by moving the torch in a small circular motion until a molten puddle three to five times the thickness of the material is developed.

The end of the electrode should be held approximately 1/8 inch above the work. When the puddle becomes bright and fluid, move the torch slowly and steadily along the joint at a speed that will produce a bead of uniform penetration and width. No oscillating or other movement of the torch except for a steady motion forward is required.

When filler rod is required, the rod is held at an angle of approximately 15° to the work, and just clear of the arc stream. Once the puddle has been developed, move the torch to the rear of the puddle, and add filler rod by quickly touching the leading edge of the puddle. Add only a small amount of rod. Remove the rod and bring the torch back up to the leading edge. When the puddle is again bright, repeat the above steps.

BREAKING THE ARC

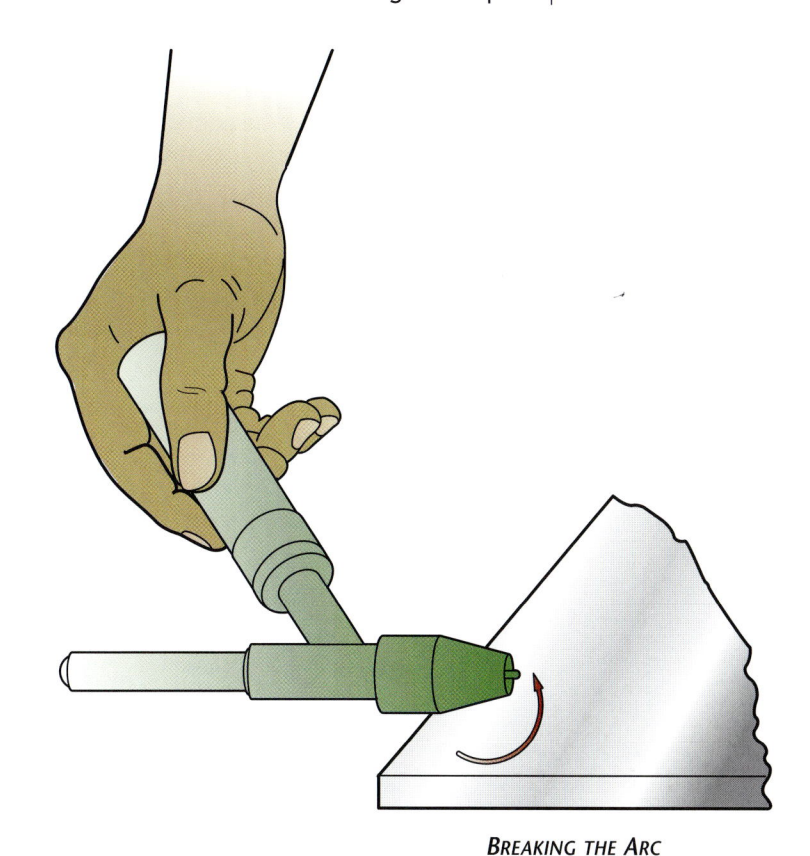

Figure 6-3-5. Breaking the arc

Arc speed is governed by the amount of current and thickness of material. Speed should be adjusted to obtain a bead of uniform height and width. The penetration should be uniform on the underside of the work. Good penetration is indicated by a very small, smooth bead. The controlling factors affecting a good weld are as follows:

- Torch angle
- Arc length
- Arc speed
- Electrode condition
- Joint design

Some of the precautions to observe when running the bead follow. No attempt to add filler rod should be made until the puddle has been developed. Do not insert the filler rod in the arc stream or considerable spatter and excessive melting of the filler rod will result. Do not attempt to hold the filler rod in the molten puddle. The amount of filler rod determines the buildup of the bead, and it is necessary to have little or no buildup.

Inspection of weld. Inspection of the finished weld is very important, not only to make certain that it meets all specifications, but also to determine if the proper welding procedures were used. Some possible defects in the weld and their probable causes are:

- Bead too narrow — usually indicates an excessive rate-of-welding speed
- Bead too wide — usually indicates too slow a rate-of-welding speed
- Weld contamination — indicated by a black deposit on the weld and caused by the electrode coming in contact with the weld metal
- Oxidation of the weld, caused by an insufficient supply of gas

Magnesium Alloys

Weldable types. Magnesium alloys in virtually all forms can be successfully welded by the TIG welding process. All types of joints commonly employed on steel can be used on magnesium.

There are, however, some types of magnesium alloys that have poor weldability. Manufacturers' maintenance, component repair and overhaul manuals should specify whether or not a magnesium part is repairable. In addition, many certified repair stations have approved methods of repair that are not available outside of their establishments. It is generally best to have them do any welding necessary on a magnesium part.

POST-WELD TREATMENTS FOR AUSTENITIC STAINLESS STEEL	
AISI Type	Recommended Heat Treatment
301 302	Cool rapidly from 1,950°F-2,000°F when corrosion conditions are moderate to severe
304	Cool rapidly from 1,850°F-2,000°F only when corrosion conditions are severe
304L	Not required for corrosion resistance
316	Cool rapidly from 1,950°F-2,100°F only when corrosion conditions are severe
316L	Not required for corrosion resistance
321 327	Not required for corrosion resistance

Table 6-3-3. Recommended post-weld heat treatments for austenitic stainless steels

Corrosion-resistant (Stainless) Steel

The wrought stainless steels are of three principal types: austenitic, martensitic and ferritic. In aircraft work, you will not be concerned with the martensitic and ferritic steels.

Austenitic steels are used extensively in aircraft where strength or resistance to corrosion at high temperatures is required. Austenitic steels contain both chromium and nickel and are non-magnetic. The minimum content of chromium is 16 percent; of nickel, 7 percent. The 18 percent chromium and 8 percent nickel composition is the most popular example of this class of steels. Types 302, 303, 304, 316, 321 and 347 are probably the most extensively used 18-8 steels.

All of the above stainless steels can be satisfactorily welded by the TIG process. The one serious difficulty encountered is intergranular corrosion of the metal in or alongside the weld in some specific stainless steels.

When an 18-8 stainless steel with more than 0.08 percent carbon is heated between 1,000-1,500°F, the excess carbon is precipitated, or segregated, out of solution and deposited along the grain boundaries in the form of carbides. These carbides are less resistant to corrosion than the parent metal.

In making a weld, the metal deposited and the joint itself are heated to the melting, or fusing, temperature (approximately 2,690°F) while the body of the work remains cold. Hence, there is a zone parallel to and near the weld that is heated between 1,000-1,500°F. It is in this area that carbides are precipitated. This region may be wide or narrow, near to or some distance from the weld, depending upon the type of joint and method of welding. If welding is rapid, the zone will be narrow and close to the weld; if slow, it will be wide and farther away.

This carbide can be put into solution again by heating to a temperature of approximately 1,900°F or higher and cooling quickly through the critical range. Table 6-3-3 lists the recommended post-weld heat treatments for the most commonly used austenitic steels.

It should be noted that alloys 304, 316, 321 and 347 require no post-weld treatment. Alloys 304 and 316 have a lowered carbon content (0.03 percent maximum), alloy 321 has titanium added and alloy 347 has columbium added. When either of these procedures is employed, the steel is virtually free from intergranular attack.

Current requirements. Either DC straight-polarity or high-frequency, stabilized AC may be used in welding stainless steels by the TIG process. Slightly greater penetration and welding speed can be obtained with direct current, and high frequency alternating current has a tendency to cause hot tearing or stress cracks in or near the weld. DC straight-polarity is therefore considered first preference. Table 6-3-4 lists the general operating data for welding the austenitic stainless steels.

Torch adjustment. The proper size electrode and corresponding gas cup are determined by the thickness of the material to be welded. The electrode should extend about 1/8 inch below the gas cup in most applications. It is important to select the correct size, as it is difficult to start and maintain the arc with an oversized electrode.

Selection of filler rod. Filler rods for general-purpose welding usually have the same composition as the base metal. Strips cut from parent metal may be used in some cases.

Preparation of metal. As with all other materials to be welded with this process, corrosion-resistant steel must be clean. Parts to be welded must be free from oil, grease, or dirt. The surface to be welded may be cleaned either by chemical or mechanical means as previously discussed in this chapter.

Welding procedure. After starting the arc, the torch should be held at an angle of approximately 75° to the work to run the bead. When filler rod is used, it should be held at an angle of approximately 10° to the work. The length of the arc should be approximately 1/8 inch.

The procedure for manipulating the torch is almost the same as that used for other materials. The puddle is developed and the rod is dipped rapidly in and out of the forward edge of the puddle. Care must be taken not to pull the filler rod too far from the puddle. A cold filler rod chills the puddle and makes it difficult to maintain. Dipping in and out of the puddle rapidly will assure the addition of filler metal at a uniform rate to form a weld with good contour.

Weld back-up. For TIG welding applications on corrosion-resisting steels, the joint should be backed up. On light-gauge materials, backing is used to protect the underside of the weld from atmospheric contamination, which results in poor surface appearance. On heavier materials, it prevents the weld puddle from dropping through by drawing away some of the heat.

Some of the materials used for weld back-up are: metal back-up bars; gas shielding; a combination of metal back-up bars and gas shielding; and fluxes.

GENERAL OPERATING DATA FOR STAINLESS STEEL				
Thickness (in Inches)	Current Range (in Amperes)	Argon Flow (C.F.H.)	Rod Size (in Inches)	Arc Speed (Inches per Minute)
0.025	20-40	10	1/32	15-40
0.031	20-40	10	1/32	15-40
0.037	50-130	10	1/16	15-40
0.050	80-165	10	1/16	15-40
0.062	90-170	10	1/16	15-40
0.078	125-200	10	3/32	15-40
0.109	140-250	10	3/32	10-35
0.125	160-200	10	1/8	10-20
0.195	100-225	10	1/8	4-20
0.250	400-500	10	3/16	12-20
0.375	400-500	10	3/16	*7-14
0.500	—	—	—	—

*Two Passes

Table 6-3-4. General operating data for stainless steels

On applications where the final weld composition must conform to rigid specifications, extra care must be taken to exclude all atmospheric oxygen from the underside of the weld. There are a number of gases and methods of applying them that will give 100 percent protection of the weld zone.

Inspection of weld. Good weld penetration is indicated by either the oxide deposit (color bands) or a small, smooth bead on the underside of the work. A finished weld should have a regular bead pattern and may require some cleaning. Cleaning can usually be accomplished by wire brushing.

Gas Metal-arc Welding (MIG)

Gas metal-arc (GMA) welding is another process that is commonly known by its former name: MIG welding. It uses a direct current and a gas shield of argon, helium or carbon

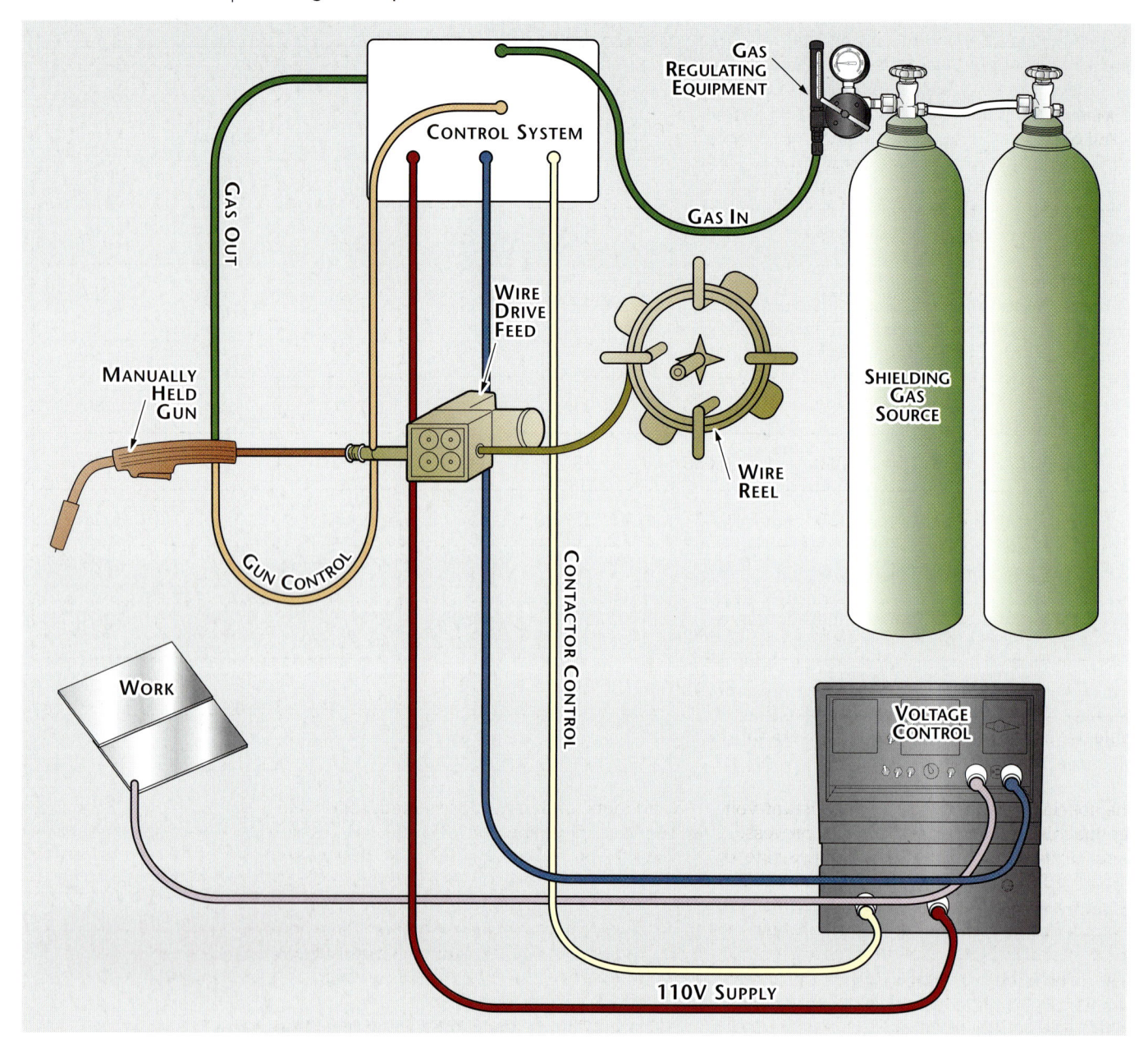

Figure 6-3-6. MIG welding equipment

dioxide (CO_2). A small diameter wire serves both as electrode and filler metal and is fed continuously and automatically from a spool or reel through a flexible cable to the torch or electrode holder. A welding pool is formed immediately when the arc is established. Welding progresses by moving the welding gun along the line of the joint at a rate to build up a bead of the desired dimensions. The electrode and weld pool are protected from oxidation by the shield of gas during welding. No flux is required.

MIG Welding Equipment

There are numerous types and models of MIG welding equipment. Each must have a source of direct current, reverse polarity (DCRP) welding current, a wire feed unit for feeding the wire filler metal, a control unit that controls the automatic feed of the wire filler metal and shielding gas, and a welding gun for directing the wire filler metal and shielding gas to the weld area. Figure 6-3-6 illustrates MIG welding equipment.

The power source, or welding machine, must be the DC, constant-voltage type; however, it can be a DC rectifier or a motor- or engine-driven generator. The output welding power of this type machine has essentially the same voltage regardless of the welding current. Output voltage is regulated by a rheostat on the welding machine. The range is 15-40 volts, depending on the type of shielding gas used. The constant voltage machine has no current control; therefore, it cannot be used for manual shielded metal-arc (stick) welding.

| AMPERE SETTINGS FOR MIG WELDING ||||||||||
| Material Thickness (in Inches) | Electrode || Deposit (Approx. lb./ft.) | CO_2 Gas Flow | Welding Conditions (DCRP) || Reactance | Travel Speed (Inches per Minute) |
	Size (in Inches)	Feed (Inches per Minute)			Amps	Volts		
18 ga. 0.050	0.045	360	0.010	35	300	26	Yes	190
16 ga. 0.062	0.045	360	0.013	35	325	26	Yes	150
14 ga. 0.078	0.045	360	0.017	25	325	27	Yes	100
1/8	1/16	200	0.026	35	380	30	No	80
3/16	1/16	260	0.036	35	425	31	No	75
1/4	3/32	150	0.077	35	500	32	No	45
3/8	3/32	205	0.189	35	550	34	No	25
1/2	1/8	160	0.294	35	625	36	No	23
5/8	1/8	175	0.411	35	675	36	No	18

Table 6-3-5. Ampere settings for MIG welding

The special wire feeder and the constant voltage machine form the heart of this process. A fixed relationship exists between the rate of electrode burn-off and welding current. At a given wire feed speed rate, the machine will produce the current required to maintain the arc; consequently, the electrode wire feed rate determines the welding current. Wire feed speed is set by the control knob on the wire feeder. The welding current is indicated on the machine's ammeter (while welding) and ranges from approximately 100-800 amperes, depending on the diameter size of the electrode. See Table 6-3-5. DC with reverse polarity (DCRP) is used for this process.

The reverse polarity arc supplies heat to melt the consumable filler wire and the workpiece. The arc also breaks up the surface oxide on the workpiece. This cleaning action is due to the electrical characteristics of the DCRP arc; arc action in DCRP is not intermittent, as in AC TIG welding. It is continuous, because there is no change in current direction using DC MIG welding.

Filler metal. The MIG welding process uses a consumable electrode wire ranging in size from 0.030 to 1/8 inch. The sizes 0.030, 0.035 and 0.045 are referred to as microwire. The wire is solid and bare, except for a very thin copper coating on the surface to prevent corrosion. It contains deoxidizers to help clean the weld metal and to produce sound, solid welds. The wire should be carefully selected to assure that the composition of the wire will have similar mechanical properties to the base metal.

The distance from the contact tip to the work is called stickout. This distance is controlled by the welder and should be 1/4 to 3/8 inch.

The contact tip is recessed up to 1/8 inch inside the cup or nozzle.

Special attention must be given to see that the wire used is clean. Unsound welds result from the use of wire that has been contaminated by oil, grease, dust or shop fumes. Wire should be stored in a hot locker or in a warm, dry area, and it should be kept covered. If welding is stopped for any length of time, remove the wire and place it in the original carton to prevent possible contamination.

Shielding gas. The MIG welding gun deposits molten filler metal where directed on the workpiece. The gas shields the arc and weld pool while the filler wire is being melted and transferred in spray or droplet form. Helium, argon or mixtures of the two are suitable for MIG welding of aluminum and stainless steel. At any given current, the helium-shielded arc has a higher voltage than the argon arc. A smoother, more stable arc is obtained with argon.

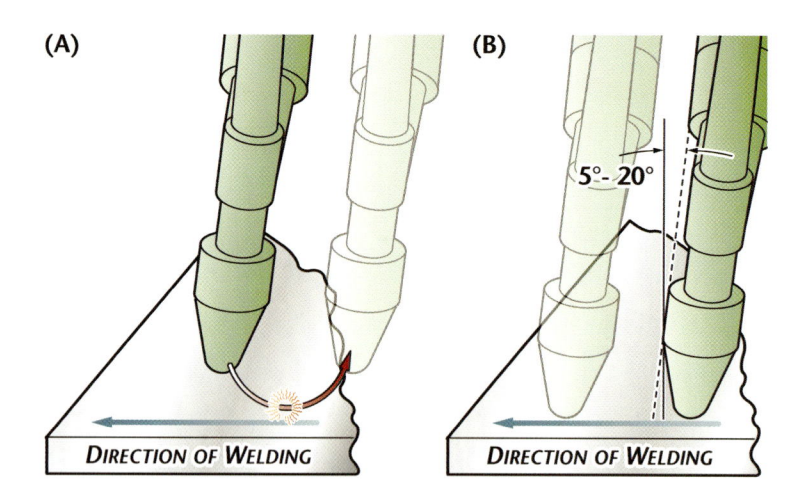

Figure 6-3-7 Gas metal-arc welding, with striking the arc (A) and gun angle (B) illustrated

Pure argon is used most widely on plates less than 3/4 inch thick. Combinations of argon and helium are often employed for welding heavy plate, particularly for out-of-position welding, to obtain the hotter arc characteristics of helium with the stabilizing effects of argon. Mixtures of 75 percent helium and 25 percent argon are commercially available. Other gas mixtures (for example, 60 percent helium and 40 percent argon) are mixed by combining flows from separate tanks of helium and argon. Helium additions of more than 10 percent markedly change the arc characteristics.

Carbon dioxide (CO_2) is suitable for MIG welding of mild steel. Because of carbon dioxide's (welding grade) low moisture content, its flow rate must be between 25-50 cubic feet per hour (C.F.H.).

The outstanding features of the CO_2 process are: (1) higher welding speed, (2) high metal deposition rates, (3) deep penetration and (4) greater production.

The flow of gas necessary for good quality MIG welding depends upon the gas used, welding current, diameter of gun nozzle, joint design, welding position, speed of welding and freedom from draft in the welding area. This last factor can affect gas usage and weld quality considerably, so it is recommended that the welding area be essentially draft-free.

MIG Welding Techniques

Before starting to weld with MIG equipment, be sure that all controls are properly adjusted, that all connections are correctly made and that all safety precautions are being observed. Wear protective clothing, including a helmet with suitable filter lens. Support the weight of the welding cable and gas hose across your shoulder to insure free movement of the welding gun. Hold the gun close to, but not touching, the workpiece. Lower your helmet and squeeze the trigger on the gun. Squeezing the trigger starts the flow of shielding gas and energizes the welding circuit. The wire-feed motor is not energized until the wire electrode comes in contact with the workpiece. Move the gun toward the work, touching the wire electrode to the work with a sidewise scratching motion, as illustrated in Figure 6-3-7, illustration A. To prevent sticking, it is necessary to pull the gun back about 1/2 inch quickly, the instant contact is made between the wire electrode and the workpiece. The arc will strike as soon as contact is made and the wire-feed motor will feed the wire automatically as long as the trigger is held.

To break the arc, just release the trigger. This breaks the welding circuit and de-energizes the wire-feed motor. If the wire electrode sticks to the work when striking the arc, or at any time during welding, release the trigger and clip the wire with a pair of pliers or side cutters.

A properly established arc has a soft, sizzling sound. The arc itself is about 1/4 inch long, or about one-half the distance between the gun nozzle and the work. Adjustment of the wire-feed control dial or the welding machine itself is necessary when the arc does not sound right.

For example, a loud, crackling sound indicates that the arc is too short and that wire-feed speed is too fast. Correct this by moving the wire-feed dial slightly counterclockwise. This decreases wire-feed speed and increases arc length. A clockwise movement of the dial has the opposite effect. With experience, you will soon be able to recognize the sound of the proper length of arc to use.

Welding is accomplished by use of the forehand technique. The gun should be held at an angle of 5 to 20 degrees from the vertical position, as shown in illustration B of Figure 6-3-7. For a right-handed person, the direction of welding is from right to left. The forehand technique provides the best coverage of shielding gas to the weld area, and the operator has a better view of the weld joint. Left-handed persons hold the gun in the same position relative to the surface of the base metal, but the direction of welding is from left to right.

After some skill has been gained in striking and establishing an arc and in adjusting the wire feed and welding current to obtain the proper arc characteristics, new welders should learn to run a bead. To run a practice bead, select the proper current setting, gas flow and correct size filler wire. Then, proceed as follows:

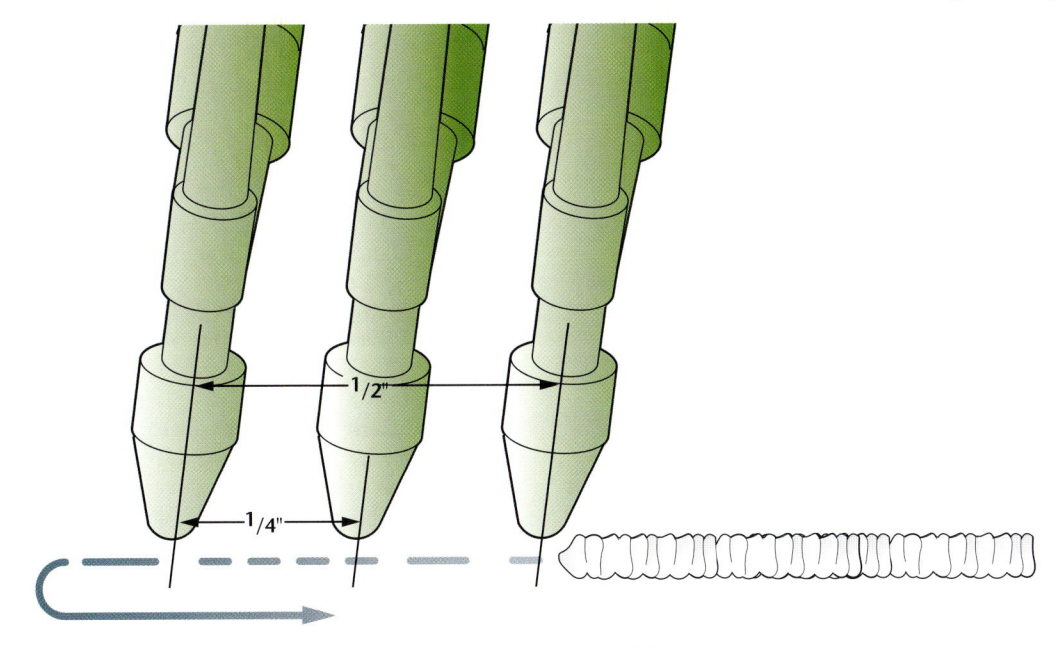

Figure 6-3-8. Reciprocating technique for gas metal-arc welding

- Hold the gun in the proper position, close to (but not touching) the surface of the work, and squeeze the trigger.
- Lower your helmet and strike the arc.
- Hold the gun at the starting point until a puddle forms.
- As soon as a puddle becomes visible, move the gun forward steadily at a rate that permits the work and the electrode to melt at the same time. Keep the arc in the pool of weld metal. Do not direct it into the base metal. A thin, irregular bead will result if you move forward too rapidly. Undercutting may result if you move the gun forward too slowly. A good bead is uniform in width and height, the ripple is uniform, and there is no overlap or undercut at the edges.

Instead of moving the gun along the line of weld with a steady forward motion, some operators prefer to run a bead with a reciprocating technique like that shown in Figure 6-3-8. With this technique, strike the arc and then slowly move the gun forward along the line of weld about 1/2 inch and then back about 1/4 inch. Continue this 1/2 inch forward, 1/4 inch backward motion along the line of weld. If a wide bead is desired, use a side weave. Here, the gun is moved uniformly back and forth across the line of weld while steadily moving along the line of weld. The width of the bead desired determines the amount of sidewise movement.

Although MIG welding does not require the use of a flux, it does require that the base metal be clean. Aluminum and aluminum alloys should be cleaned with an approved compound or with a rotary stainless steel wire brush. If grease is present, it should be removed with a solvent prior to cleaning with a compound. Rotary stainless steel wire brushes that have picked up grease should be cleaned with a solvent before they are used to clean aluminum for welding.

Once you get the feel of welding with MIG equipment, you will probably find that the techniques are less difficult to master than any of the other welding procedures. There are some pitfalls, however. Porous welds may result from the following causes:

- Low arc voltage (less than 26 volts)
- Low welding current
- Inadequate shielding gas flow resulting from a low cylinder pressure, from restrictions in the gas passages of the equipment or from improper adjustment of the flowmeter
- Excessive weaving or whipping of the welding gun
- Poor fit-up of parts
- Improperly cleaned base metal or dirty welding wire
- Non-uniform wire-feed speed

Welder fatigue is often the cause of poor weld quality and low output. You will learn that the quality and quantity of work improves as you learn to weld comfortably. Out-of-position welding is usually more awkward than flat-position welding; therefore, arrange the work for flat-position welding whenever possible for economy and quality.

Safety Precautions

Safety must be observed in TIG and MIG welding, just as in any other welding process. The following are general precautions that should be observed

- The welding area must be properly ventilated without excessive drafts affecting the welding arc and shielding gas. Radiation from the arc causes instantaneous decomposition of chlorinated solvents, such as *perchloroethylene*, *trichloroethylene* and *methyl chloroform*, into highly toxic *phosgene gas* and other irritating products. Welding should not be done in any area where fumes from such solvents are present.

- The voltage required for operating TIG and MIG welding equipment can cause severe or fatal injuries, so do not work on any wiring in an energized circuit. The area being welded must be dry.

- Welding transformers or rectifiers must have a power ground so that welders cannot get a shock should stray current develop.

- Do not lay the torch on the work or work table. Hang it up in a safe place so the electrode will not touch metal and grounded material.

- Do not change a tungsten electrode before it has cooled or while the transformer switch is in the *on* position. Do not change spools of filler wire while the generator or rectifier is on.

- Do not use defective welding cable. If any of the connections are operating hot, a poor electrical connection may exist.

- Use a welding helmet when looking at the arc. Use the correct shade of lens. If your eyes become irritated, see a doctor immediately. If not treated promptly, the irritation caused by burning rays of the arc becomes very painful and feels like hot sand in the eyes. There are eye drops the doctor can give you that will relieve unnecessary suffering.

- Wear suitable clothing as protection from the spatter of molten particles and to shield the body from rays of the arc.

- Do not strike an arc on a compressed gas cylinder.

- Do not weld in the vicinity of flammable or combustible materials. Degreasing with alcohol or other flammable solvents in an improperly ventilated welding area creates a fire hazard.

- Do not weld on containers which have held combustible or flammable materials without first exercising the proper precautions.

- Do not weld in confined spaces without adequate ventilation or individual respiratory equipment.

- Do not weld on workpieces without first wiping the degreasing solvent off.

- Do not chip or grind without safety goggles.

- Do not move individual cylinders unless valve protection cap is in place and tight.

- Do not drop or abuse cylinders in any way.

- Make certain that cylinders are well fastened in their stations so that they will not fall.

- Do not use a hammer or wrench to open cylinder valves.

- Never force connections that do not fit easily.

- Never tamper with cylinder safety devices.

- Always protect hose and welding cable from being trampled or run over. Avoid tangles and kinks. Do not leave the hose and cable so they can trip people.

- Protect the hose, cable and cylinders from flying sparks, hot metal or objects and open flame.

- Do not allow the hose to come in contact with oil or grease; these rot the rubber and are hazards.

- Be sure that the connections between the regulators, adaptors and cylinder valves are gas-tight. Test with oxygen compatible leak-check under gas pressure.

- When welding is to be stopped for an extended length of time, release the pressure-adjusting screws of the regulators.

Section 4

Friction Stir Welding

While most welding processes take a long time to mature, a new process developed by The Welding Institute, an English corporation, is gaining rapid acceptance in automotive, aviation and other aerospace industries. It is called friction stir welding (FSW).

As a process, FSW allows previously unweldable aluminum alloys (like 7075 and 2024) not only to be welded, but to be welded to each other. It all but eliminates extensive riveting in aircraft structural fabrication. Instead, seams are butt or lap welded with a high degree of precision and dependability.

The system consists of a shouldered tool with a profiled pin that is inserted into the seam that is to be welded. The pin is rotated, and as it rotates it creates friction (Figure 6-4-1). The friction does not actually melt the aluminum; instead it plasticizes the aluminum with the heat generated from the friction. As the pin travels down its programmed course, it takes the plasticized metal and moves it around to the rear of the pin, where the plasticized metal consolidates, cools and forms a solid-state weld. The pin, in the meantime, continues traveling down its programmed path, adding more metal to the bead behind it.

Weld is only a slight misnomer, as the material never actually melts, as in conventional fusion welding. It is more akin to the extrusion process without the die. The two metals to be joined actually do join. They become one piece with a fusion area that is as dense, if not more dense, than the parent metal. The result also is not heat-damaged as it would be with a fusion welding process. The grain structure is unmodified, and the strength remains.

Usage

Boeing and Airbus are actively engaged in FSW research and process application. Airbus is currently in the lead, as they have applied the process to stir-welding wing panels. Both companies have advanced the process in welding fairly heavy skins in assemblies. Another company, Eclipse Aviation Corporation, has worked out the process for fabricating thin-skinned structures.

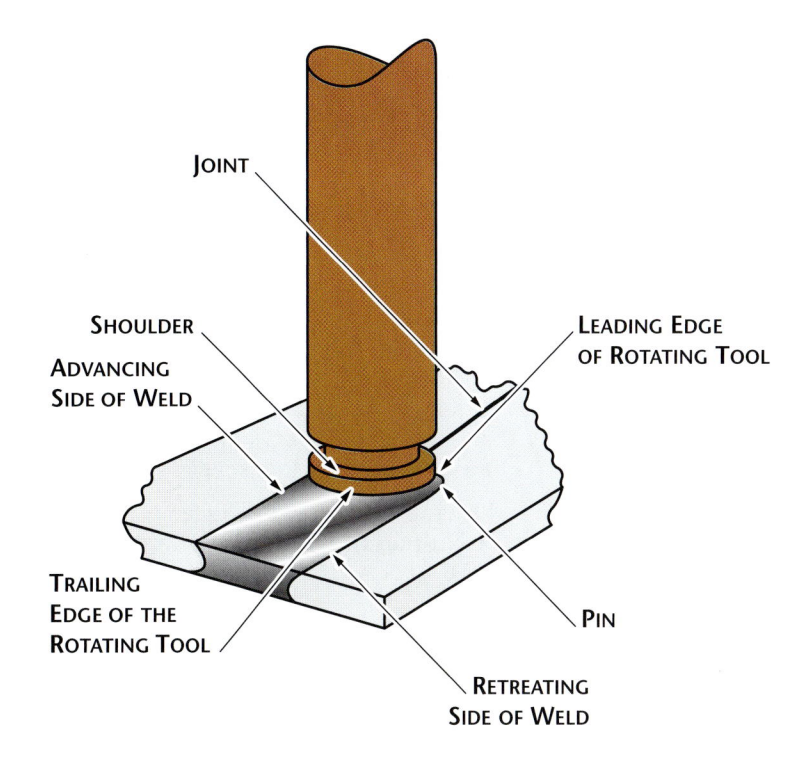

Figure 6-4-1. The heart of friction stir welding is the pin. The pin doesn't actually melt the metal. Instead, it plasticizes it and then mixes the metals together, forming one piece.

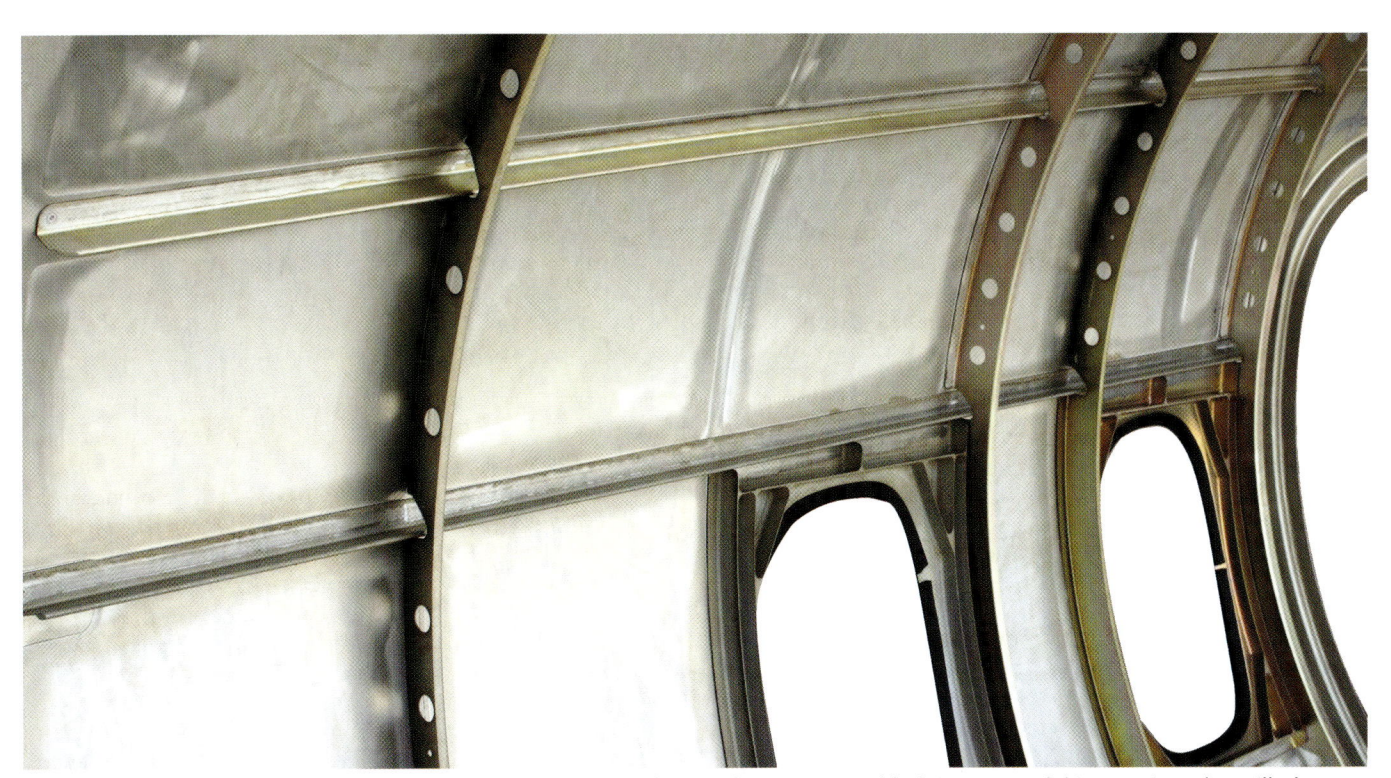

Figure 6-4-2. In this Eclipse interior view, everything in the photo is friction stir welded. Upon careful inspection, the milled sections between the structural attachments can be identified.

Figure 6-4-3. A close-up view of a friction stir welded window opening

Eclipse is using FSW to build skin panels by joining stringers and frames with pocketed skins. The skin pockets are chem-milled or machined into the skins between the stiffeners as a weight reduction technique. The pockets can be seen in Figure 6-4-2.

Reliability

Naturally, there are no long-term studies yet on FSW's reliability as a manufacturing process. That is not to say that it has not been tested extensively. The initial tests included x-ray inspection of the joints produced. The results have been so outstanding that x-ray inspection is now considered unnecessary. The joint quality is very good as compared to conventional welding. Once set up, there are only about three variables that have to be monitored during the process. Conventional welding has more than three variables just in the flame or current adjustment. Figure 6-4-3 shows the welding around a window opening in the fuselage.

Advantages. Smoothness of the finished skin is a major advantage. As you learned from the aerodynamics section, manufacturers go to great lengths to retain that smooth, streamlined look. It makes airplanes go faster and use less fuel. Initial painting or refinishing should be significantly easier, as there are no protruding rivets or countersunk heads to mar the finish.

Disadvantages. On heavy structures, one of the main design problems was corrosion resistance. The lap joints left an open edge that could be susceptible to corrosion. Suitable corrosion-proofing procedures will be worked out and the process will continue. As the technology matures, other equipment designs will evolve that will make the FSW usage widespread.

Equipment

To take advantage of FSW manufacturing, it is necessary to use production robots to control the process. Many of these have to be custom-designed, because the current process requires heavy down-pressure on the pin.

Repair Considerations

While Airbus has developed specific repair procedures for their stir-welded structures, Eclipse proclaims that, through careful design, any of theirs can be repaired using conventional sheet metal repair procedures and tooling.

Section 5
Weld Inspection

Virtually any method of inspection can be used for a weld. It depends on what you are looking for. In the case of complying with an Airworthiness Directive or a specific Operational Directive, it may be chosen for you. If so, it will be spelled out in detail. If not defined, then a visual inspection is assumed. If a visual inspection finds a suspicious area, then it should be followed up with an appropriate NDT inspection.

Visual inspection. Even with a basic visual inspection, you need some kind of an idea of what it is you are looking for, otherwise you won't know what it is when you see it.

OEM parts. In visually inspecting an OEM part, installed or uninstalled, a technician is not normally concerned so much with the quality of the welding as would be the case with a repair. An OEM part has normally undergone a series of inspections that almost precludes a bad weld from getting into the supply chain. Therefore, what you are looking for is environmental or service-induced defects. These can vary from cracks in the weld bead itself to cracks alongside the weld, cracks from poor heat-treatment that show up a short distance from the end of the weld bead, or corrosion on anything related to the entire area. In the case of a part that has an OEM finish, a cracked weld or other defect may appear as a crack or blister in the paint. Obviously, cracked or blistered paint requires further examination.

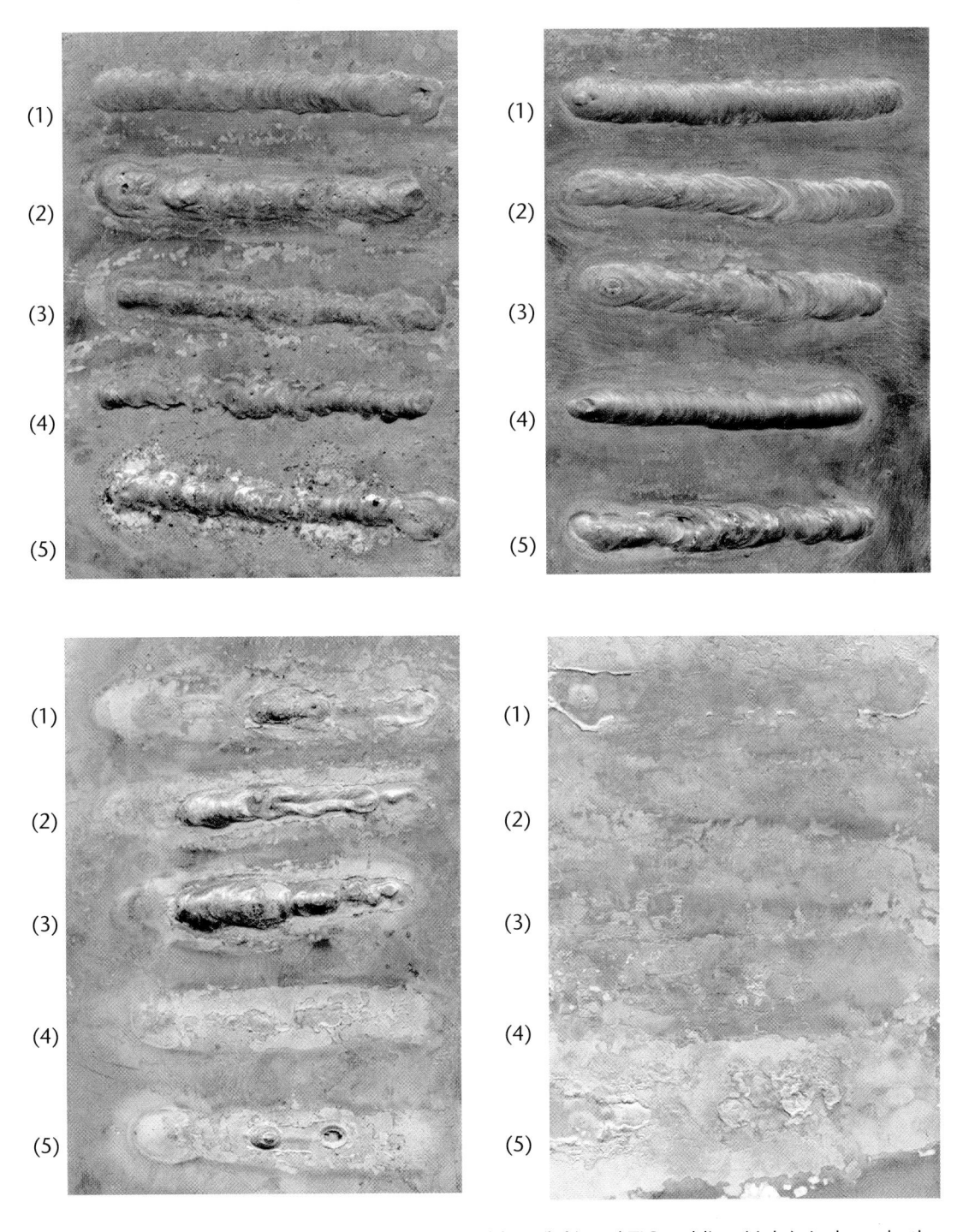

Figure 6-5-1. These samples are from both torch welding (left) and TIG welding (right). It shows both the top (above) and bottom (below) sides of the welds.

An initial visual inspection aid is a 10-power magnifying glass. If it cannot be determined whether or not a crack exists, then an NDT process is in order — either dye check or magnaflux. Frequently, testing methods are outlined in the AMM.

Weld bead examples. Generally, it isn't too difficult to judge a bad weld from a good one if you consider the appearance of either. A weld that looks good will normally be sufficient, while a bad-looking weld will not.

An example of a bad welding repair that isn't obvious is when the welder can actually weld a good bead but can't control their shrinkage and expansion. When a repaired part doesn't fit well, too many times the tendency is to make it fit. The resulting pressures generated by an ill-fitting part may well result in environmental damage to adjoining pieces. Shrinkage and expansion are covered in another section.

Other examples of good and bad welds can be found in FAA AC 43.13-1B paragraph 4-74.

6-46 | Welding Techniques

A

B

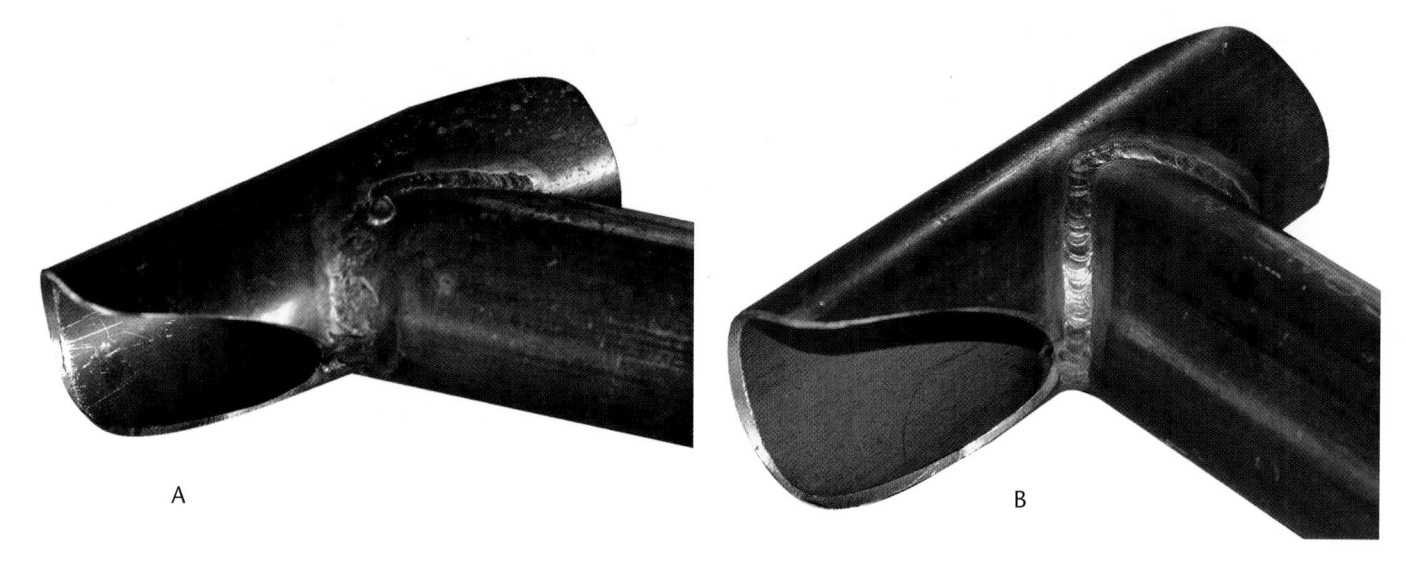

Figure 6-5-2. Two examples of heat control on like welds. Weld A was torch welded with a bit too much heat, while B was TIG welded with good heat control.

Repairs can be a different problem. Many times repairs may be poorly executed — the repairer may not be a good welder. Some of the most common things to look for are shown in Figure 6-5-1.

1. Proper weld bead has good height, width and penetration.
2. The weld was too hot and not enough filler rod was applied. Torch weld shows excess penetration on the back side of the bead (left). The TIG weld (right) has collapsed into itself and appears cracked in the center of the bead.
3. The weld was too hot, too much filler rod was used and the weld traveled too fast. See above for bead condition.
4. Cold weld. Not enough heat and very poor penetration on both welds.
5. Contaminated weld. Torch weld wasn't cleaned after bead blasting, while TIG weld was contaminated by touching the tungsten to the puddle.

Tubing clusters. Welding tubing clusters isn't difficult if you can control the heat. Figure 6-5-2 shows two clusters that are very similar. Illustration A was welded with a torch and had a bit too much heat, while illustration B was TIG welded and heat control was excellent.

In the good cluster in illustration B, the smooth bead with even ripples in the filler metal is consistent with a good weld. Weld A shows excess heat from the reduced mass on that side. The welder should have reduced the heat to allow for it. They also could have carried a bit more heat on the tee tube and used more filler rod to reduce the heat by the necessary amount.

When first learning to weld, there is a tendency not to take practice very seriously. This practice weld (Figure 6-5-3) will allow the welder to

Figure 6-5-3. This lap weld shows a good bead with good heat control.

Figure 6-5-4. Common example of beginning welders' work

gain proficiency and enable him to do the tube joint also. Controlling the heat at the beginning and end of a practice weld will allow beginners to learn how to handle heat in the tube joint.

While Figure 6-5-4 shows extreme examples from beginning welders, it also illustrates the common problems: excess heat, slow travel, burn through and excess filler rod. These same problems frequently follow a person throughout their lifetime.

Unless you become a practiced welder, any aluminum welding should be accomplished with a TIG welder. The skill required to produce a good TIG weld is considerably less than with a torch. Figure 6-5-5 shows an aluminum weld that is progressing correctly. The rod was left attached to the puddle in order to show its size, angle and where it is added into the puddle. When welding an outside corner weld such as the one shown in Figure 6-5-5, there is a natural tendency not to use enough rod. A good bead should be formed instead of just filling up the crack. Notice that expansion has cracked the tack weld on the left corner.

Fuel and Oil Tank Repair

Unless absolutely necessary, never weld any fuel or oil tank that has any flammable liquid or vapor still in it, since the danger of explosion and injury is quite high. If welding such tanks is necessary, the tank must first be cleaned with water based caustic liquid, rinsed and dried. Before actually welding, the tank must be purged with nitrogen or argon. The purging should continue during the entire welding operation.

After welding, tanks must be leak checked as part of the return to service inspection. All inspections must be done in accordance with the manufacturer's recommendations. When using air pressure to leak check a fuel tank be very careful not to over pressurize the tank. As little as 5 psi in a soft aluminum fuel tank can cause a permanent deformation of the tank. Oil tanks that are not pressurized are tested for leaks using 5 psi of pressure while those used in turbine aircraft, with a pressurized tank, must be tested at 5 psi over the maximum pressure of the tank.

All inspection is a matter of looking for an irregularity and correctly identifying it. In the case of welds, get in the habit of looking at each one individually. You will almost never find a bad one, but the one you do find will be worth all the looking.

Figure 6-5-5. This aluminum weld is correctly done with an adequate amount of filler rod.

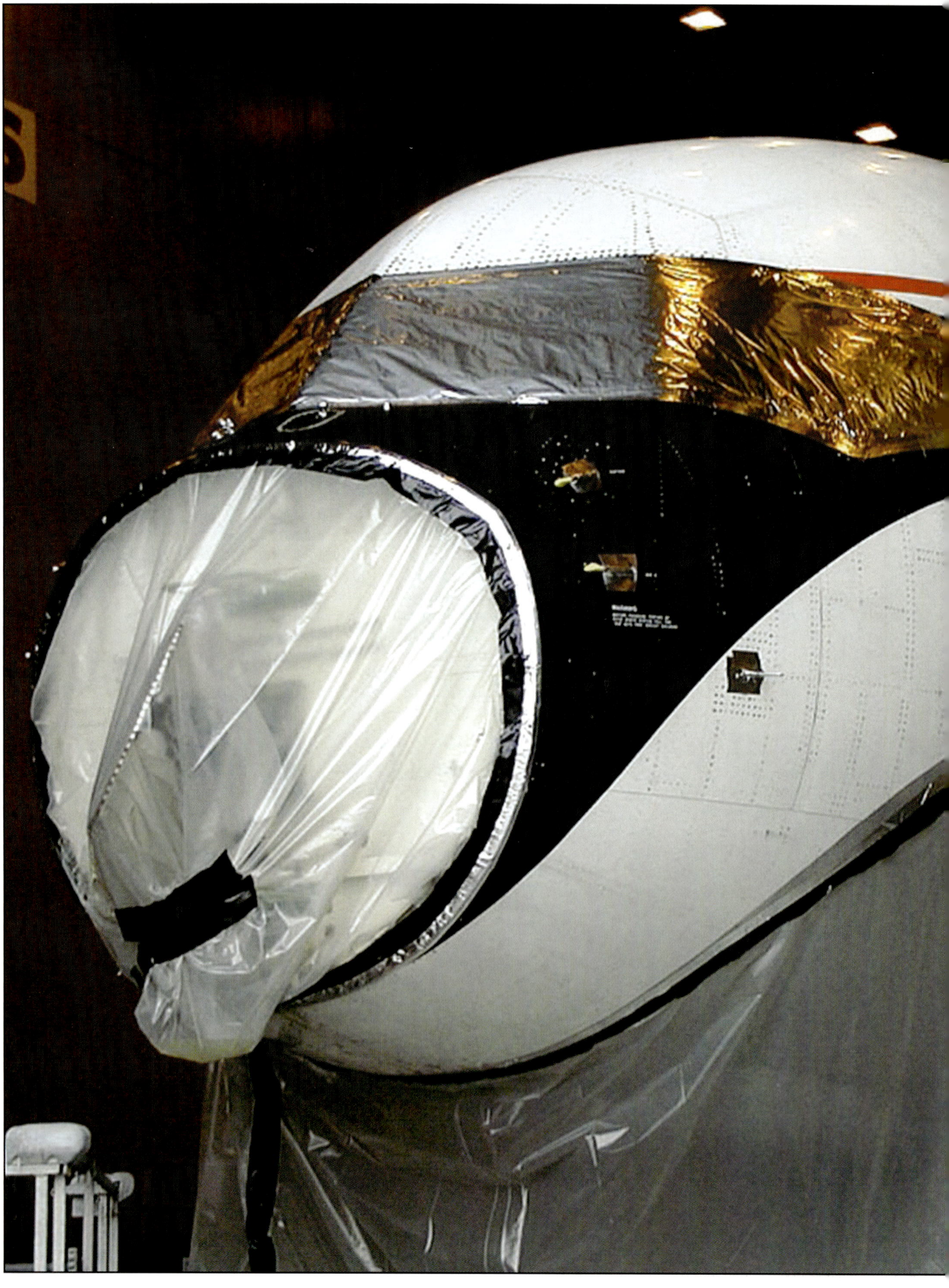

7

Painting and Refinishing

Section 1

Cleaning and Stripping

The primary objective of any paint finish is to protect exposed surfaces against corrosion and other forms of deterioration. It takes less maintenance to keep a properly painted airplane clean and corrosion-free than it does an unpainted one. However, most airplanes are repainted for the sake of cosmetic appearance, and some paint schemes are very elaborate.

Because of age or exposure, some finishes fail to perform their protective function. The maintenance and repair of paint finishes is important, because repainting and/or refinishing an airplane is a time-consuming and expensive proposition.

Out of all the colors available, white is the most popular base color. That is because it is the most visible, hence the safest, color to use. With the popularity of the "wet look" urethane paints, a newly refinished airplane can be a thing of beauty, or it can be just another airplane. It depends on the care used in its refinishing and trim. Figure 7-1-1 shows a corporate jet making its grand exit from the paint shop.

Touch-up Painting

Touch-up painting is the repair of small areas where the paint has been worn or removed because of corrosion, weathering or erosion. The paint system will consist of a primer and a compatible topcoat. Touch-up painting can be difficult, because matching the original color of the finish is sometimes tricky. Besides, nobody wants to have an airplane that looks like it has had its finish touched up.

Learning Objectives

DESCRIBE
- Methods for paint removal
- Types of primers and topcoats
- Common painting equipment

EXPLAIN
- How to prepare a surface for painting
- Types of paint defects
- Masking
- The use of sealants

APPLY
- Inspect the finish on an aircraft
- Remove paint from an aircraft part
- Apply primer and topcoat materials

Left. A Boeing 757 is masked, prepped and ready for painting.

Photo courtesy of Gregg Stansbery

Figure 7-1-1. With a polyurethane finish, this airplane will have a "wet look" for years.
Photo courtesy of JRA Executive Air

Unlike in the auto body profession, it is difficult to do a touch-up on an airplane finish. A touch-up color never quite matches the original finish in color or surface quality. This is mainly because of the paint itself. Newer formulations of urethane finishes make it difficult to spot match. Because of this difficulty, airplanes are generally touched-up by redoing the finish on a complete section or surface. A touch-up finish becomes more a partial repaint operation. With the newer "wet look" finishes, even the auto body shops have started doing more complete refinishes instead of spot, or partial repainting.

Complete Refinishing

A complete refinish is beyond the capability of most shops. That is why most complete refinishes are done by a Certified Repair Station (CRS) that specializes in that type of work. The washing and stripping operations alone, not to mention the experience levels required, are complex beyond most maintenance shops' facilities.

It is important, however, that an aspiring AMT understand the process. The same techniques are required for major touch-up as for a complete job.

Surface Preparation

The effectiveness and adhesion of a paint finish depends upon careful surface preparation. Before you begin to paint, you should remove all soils, lubricants and preservatives from the surface. You should treat corroded areas and replace defective seam sealants. Any maintenance or repair required on exterior items should be completed prior to refininshing. In most cases, the Aircraft Maintenance Manual (AMM) will list acceptable cleaning materials. Many times, they have recommendations for refinish. At the very least, they are likely to contain the requirements for sealing and caulking before a major project is undertaken. Figure 7-1-2 shows the cleaning, inspection and minor repair process prior to a complete refinishing.

Figure 7-1-2. A thorough cleaning and inspection is the first item on the schedule for a complete refinish.
Photo courtesy of JRA Executive Air

Figure 7-1-3. Because of the possibility of creating an imbalanced condition, control surfaces must always be rebalanced after repair and refinishing.
Photo courtesy of JRA Executive Air

Control Surfaces

It is impossible to paint an airplane with everything assembled. With myriad faying surfaces, gaps, cracks and crevices, almost anything that can be removed must be. The process starts with control surfaces and extends to anything that can't be stripped or properly cleaned after stripping.

In the case of control surfaces, they are removed, stripped, cleaned, refinished and then rebalanced as sub-tasks of the total job. It takes an A&P or a certified repairman to do the rebalance, which is mandatory. Figure 7-1-3 shows a full set of control surfaces that have been removed and stripped, awaiting refinish, rebalance and reinstallation.

Paint Removal

Paint removal should be accomplished by the mildest mechanical or chemical means. While we cover chemical stripping and sanding here, there are several other methods of paint removal in use.

Media blasting. One of the most popular is called *media blasting*, which consists of using some type of trajectory medium in a machine that removes everything, right down to the metal. At the same time, most blasting processes have a *media reclamation* process that reclaims, or at least collects, the used media and the material it removes.

The blast media can consist of anything from rice hulls and ground-up walnut shells to much more sophisticated media, such as dry ice crystals.

The main advantage to media blasting is its thoroughness and its environmentally friendly disposability. All of the used and removed materials are more easily handled than a liquid or paste remover washed off with water. There is also a lot less of it to deal with. Any removed paint becomes part of a HAZMAT disposal process. The specific removal process depends on which method and media were used.

In certain parts of the country, media blasting is about the only way paint can be removed because of state and local regulations dealing with hazardous material and effluent discharge. Not everything can simply be flushed down the drain. Learn and observe the local regulations concerning waste disposal.

Paint stripper. All paint removers are toxic and caustic, some more than others. Both personnel and material safety precautions must be observed in their use. You should wear eye protection, gloves and a rubber apron. Depending on the material and your location, you may have some additional HAZMAT regulations to follow.

Figure 7-1-4. Masking prior to stripper

Photo courtesy of JRA Executive Air

Most shops will have already chosen the paint strippers and paint systems that they like to use. Ordinarily, they also will have a paint system that they like to use.

If you have to go it alone, here are some suggestions. A MIL-R-81294-compliant paint remover is an epoxy remover. It will strip acrylic and epoxy finishes satisfactorily. Acrylic windows, plastic surfaces and rubber products are adversely affected by this material and are not generally strippable. They must be masked with a material that is impervious to the stripper's action. Because the wrong stripper on the wrong surface can cause so much damage, masking becomes an important function. Figure 7-1-4 shows an airplane in the process of being masked prior to stripping. At this point, all non-metal and all magnesium materials that can be removed, have been. It is especially important to identify magnesium, because it can become very reactive when it comes in contact with a stripper. The rest are masked for protection from the stripper.

There are other removers available. Each remover has a specific, intended use. For example, MIL-R-81294 is used for removing epoxy finishes, but it may be damaging to synthetic rubber; another nonflammable water-soluble paint remover is usable in contact with synthetic rubber. In all cases, you should use the remover that meets the requirements of the job.

General Stripping Procedures

When stripping an aircraft surface, consult the applicable AMM for the specific procedures to be used. Be careful of faying surfaces, as stripper may be difficult to remove later.

> **CAUTION:** *Prior to cleaning and stripping, you should ensure the aircraft is properly grounded to dissipate any static electricity produced by the cleaning and stripping operations.*

Stripping should be done outside whenever possible. If stripping must be done in a hangar or other enclosure, you must have adequate ventilation.

Paint remover may contact adhesives at seals, joints, skin laps and bonded joints. In these areas, you should mask with approved tapes and papers.

Stripper should be applied liberally with a fiber brush for small sections. Completely cover the surface to a depth of 1/32 to 1/16 inch. The stripper should not be spread in a thin coat. A thin coat will not sufficiently loosen the paint. If the coat is too thin, the remover may dry on the surface of the metal. To keep the stripper from drying before it has finished loosening the paint, it can be covered with a sheet of plastic to block out the air. Obviously, the plastic won't be good for anything else afterwards.

When stripping large areas and undersides of surfaces, a brush just won't do the job. Special stripper spray guns are used to apply the material. Figure 7-1-5 shows a stripper gun being used on the underside of a stabilizer.

Allow the stripper to wrinkle and lift the paint. This may take from 10-40 minutes, depending upon the temperature, the humidity and the condition of the paint.

Remove loosened paint and residual paint remover by washing and scrubbing the surface with fresh water, non-metallic scrapers, fiber brushes or abrasive pads. If water spray is available, use a low- to medium-pressure stream of water directly on the surface while it is being scrubbed.

After thoroughly cleaning the surface, remove the masking materials and any residual paint.

Rinse the surface with a freshwater and alkaline solution (one part MIL-C-25769 to nine parts water) to neutralize the paint remover.

Having gotten this far, you may discover that not all of the paint has been removed. It doesn't necessarily mean that anything is wrong. It does mean that it will have to be re-stripped. Sometimes an old finish just doesn't want to let go.

Water Break Test

A water break test is an important process in checking something (almost anything) for cleanliness. It is really easy. Take clean water and pour, spray or wipe it on a surface. If the water beads up anywhere, the surface isn't clean. If the water flattens out and covers the entire area with a thin, unbroken film, it is clean. Most paint manufacturers want a water break test to ensure cleanliness before painting. Once the job passes the water break test, do not touch the surface with your bare hands.

Treat and Seal

Chemical conversion treatment is an extremely important part of the corrosion-control process. It improves the adhesion of the paint system.

Alodizing. Alodizing is a simple chemical treatment for all aluminum alloys to increase their corrosion resistance and to improve their paint-bonding qualities. Because of its simplicity, it has all but replaced anodizing in aircraft work. Figure 7-1-6 shows a conversion coating being applied to a complete airplane.

The process consists of precleaning with and acidic or alkaline metal cleaner that is applied by either dipping or spraying. The parts are then rinsed with fresh water under pressure for 10 to 15 seconds. After thorough rinsing, alodine is applied by dipping, spraying, or brushing. A thin, hard coating results, ranging in color from light, bluish-green with a slight iridescence on copper-free alloys to an olive green on copper-bearing alloys.

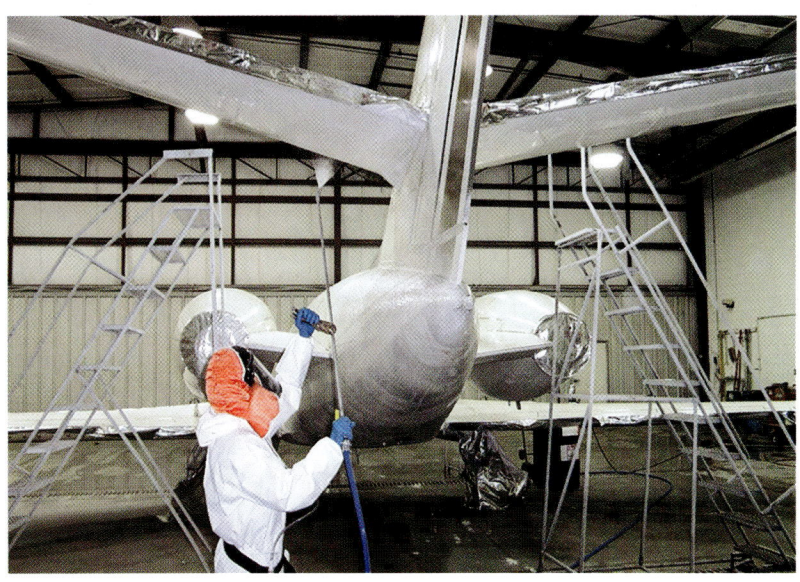

Figure 7-1-5. A stripper gun in operation *Photo courtesy of JRA Executive Air*

The alodine is first rinsed with clear, cold or warm water for a period of 15 to 30 seconds. An additional 10 to 15 second rinse is then given in Deoxylyte bath. This bath is to counteract alkaline material and to make the alodyzed aluminum surface slightly acid on drying.

Overcoating Existing Finishes

Scuff-sanding. Aged paint surfaces should be scuff-sanded to ensure the adhesion of the overcoating paint. Scuff-sanding is the roughening of a paint surface, as evidenced by a

Figure 7-1-6. Once stripped and cleaned, a conversion coating is necessary. Primer doesn't stick well to aluminum without it. Additionally, the surface needs the corrosion protection provided by the conversion coating.

Photo courtesy of JRA Executive Air

Painting and Refinishing

significant reduction of the gloss. To scuff-sand, use aluminum oxide cloth, ScotchBright® pads, or an oscillating sander with aluminum oxide cloth. Scuff-sanding to a depth greater than necessary may result in complete removal of the paint. Since underlying metal is then exposed, corrosion may develop. Unevenly matched faying surface joints or fasteners and sharply protruding objects or corners should be scuff-sanded by hand to avoid sanding through the paint. After sanding, remove the residue with a clean, cotton cheesecloth dampened with thinner.

Paint feathering. Feather the paint along the edge of an area that has been chemically stripped to ensure a smooth, overlapping transition between the old and new paint surfaces. The smooth, overlapping paint film will prevent soil from accumulating in the junction between the old and new paint films. Feathering should be accomplished with 280 or 320-grit aluminum oxide cloth, hand-sanded wet, or with a flap brush.

The major portion of thick paint films may be removed with an oscillating sander, as shown in Figure 7-1-7, with 240 or finer grit aluminum oxide cloth. Do not allow the oscillating sander to touch bare metal. The contact between an operating sander and bare metal will damage the metal, which, in turn, may cause future corrosion. The oscillating sander should not be used after first indications of primer exposure. Use a flap brush or hand-held 240-grit or finer aluminum oxide cloth for final feathering operations. Final operations should always consist of wet sanding to reduce scratches.

Figure 7-1-7. Pneumatic sanders are used to rapidly remove thick paint films.
Photo courtesy of JRA Executive Air

Paint feathering becomes even more important for those items that couldn't be stripped. Plastic and composite parts must have the old finish removed by hand. At the very least, they need to be feathered so the final finish will be smooth, without bumps and dips.

Touch-up Procedures

A paint system for repainting and paint touch-up has been developed by several manufacturers. While each system varies somewhat, they basically consist of the following materials:

Epoxy-polyamide primer. The epoxy-polyamide primer is supplied as a two-part kit. Each part must be stirred or shaken thoroughly before mixing. One component contains the pigment in an epoxy vehicle, while the other component consists of a clear polyamide, used as a hardener for the epoxy resin. These components are packaged separately and have excellent storage stability. However, when the two parts are mixed, the pot life is limited. Only the amount that you can use within that time limit should be mixed. The established mixing ratios must be followed closely, otherwise poor adhesion, poor chemical resistance or inadequate drying may result. The clear polyamide hardener should always be added to the pigmented component — not the other way around.

CAUTION: *Do not mix components from different manufacturers.*

Mixed epoxy-polyamide primer can be thinned to obtain the proper viscosity for spraying. You should check the local air pollution regulations for restrictions and regulations regarding the use of certain solvents and thinners.

Section 2

Refinishing Practices

Thinning Paint Correctly

How to use a Zahn cup. To spray epoxy-polyamide primer, thin it with the correct thinner specified by the paint manufacturer. The thinned primer should be stirred thoroughly, strained and allowed to stand for a minimum of 15 minutes prior to spraying it. The thinning ratio may vary to obtain the proper spraying viscosity, which is when it takes 17-18 seconds to drain out of a No. 2 Zahn cup. A Zahn cup is a cup with a controlled orifice in the bottom (Figure 7-2-1). Dip it full of the thinned paint and, while holding it over the container, time how long it takes for the cup to drain empty. The paint directions will normally give you the time you want to match. If the time is too long, you need to add more thinner. If the time is too short, you have already made a mistake, thinning it too much. It will be difficult to apply the finish and obtain the correct film thickness, shine, drying time and produce a run-free finish.

The 15-minute standing time permits the components to enter into chemical reaction, reduce cratering, preclude the clear resin component from separating, and allows any bubbles formed while stirring to escape. This waiting period is common with many paints and primers and is called the *bloom time*.

> **WARNING:** *Wear goggles when mixing or using thinners and solvents. You should also wear goggles or a face shield, respirator, rubber gloves and coveralls during all paint touch-up and paint spraying. Eating, drinking or smoking should NOT be allowed in areas where paint or solvent is being used or stored.*

Before you apply the primer, ensure that the surface has been cleaned, chemically treated and prepared for spraying. Then, apply a crosscoat of epoxy-polyamide primer and allow the coat to air dry for one hour. The total dry-film thickness of primer should be 0.6-0.9 mil. If the temperature is below 70°F, allow 2-3 hours for drying. Do not spray if the temperature is below 50°F. Figure 7-2-2 shows an airplane after a coat of leveling primer. The primer smoothes all the minute scratches and scrapes left after preparation.

There are a number of other additives for paints that will change the curing or drying process as well as the appearance of the finish.

The addition of a retarder, or leveling agent, will slow the drying time of the paint, which will allow the paint film to flow out longer. The result is a finish that is glossier than normal. However, too much retarder will increases the cure time to the point that it takes a long time to cure, delaying the entire painting process.

Dryers or accelerants can also be added to a paint to speed up the drying time of the color coats. These will have the opposite effect of the retarders, the color coats will dry faster and have a duller appearance. An advantage to these is that the time between painting and masking for the trims can be decreased by many hours. A major drawback, however, is that the paint surface can appear wrinkly, or very orange peeled, if to much is added. This will cause the skin to dry quicker than the material below it. Changing from the manufactures recommendations for additives can create more problems and re-work, than just following the directions in the first place.

Polyurethane Paint Systems

The polyurethane systems used on aircraft consist of two types: the *aromatic type* and the *aliphatic type*. The aromatic type is used in rain erosion-resistant coatings. These materials generally present no special hazard to health when they are cured (dried). They require special precautions during their preparation, application and curing, because isocyanate vapors are produced. The untreated *isocyanates* released can produce significant irritation to the skin, eyes and respiratory tract even in very small concentrations. They may also induce allergic sensitization.

The aliphatic-type polyurethane is the standard general-purpose exterior protective coating for aircraft surfaces. Its unique combination of flexibility, gloss retention and resistance to fuels and lubricating oils make the coating extremely suitable for the exterior surfaces of aircraft. It is supplied as a two-component kit of base and catalyst. Use polyurethane over epoxy-polyamide primer and for touch-up over other polyurethane systems with special directions.

Polyurethane paint is available in kits consisting of pigmented material and *catalyst* (clear resin) component. When mixing polyurethane paint, the catalyst component should always be added to the pigmented component. Only materials from the same kit should be mixed together. Two or more kits of the same color and manufacturer may be mixed in the same vessel.

Do not mix clear resin components and pigmented components from different manufacturers. Follow the prescribed mixing ratios to prevent long drying times, poor chemical resistance or loss of flexibility. Use a mechanical shaker to agitate the pigmented component for at least 20 minutes, then add the clear resin slowly to the

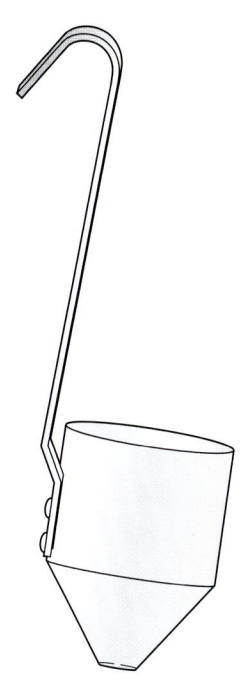

Figure 7-2-1. A Zahn cup allows paint to be thinned consistently from batch to batch.

Figure 7-2-2. After being masked, this airplane has been coated with a leveling primer. Leveling primers help fill the minute discontinuities that are always present.
Photo courtesy of JRA Executive Air

pigmented component while stirring the pigmented component. Ensure the pigmented component and clear resin are thoroughly mixed.

Mix only the amount of paint that can be used in the 4-hour (typical) pot life of the mixed paint. When painting with polyurethane paints, clean the paint gun at the end of each use or every 4 hours, whichever comes first.

To spray polyurethane paint, thin it to the desired spray viscosity. Then stir the mixture, strain it through a paint strainer, and allow it to stand for a minimum of 15 minutes. If the viscosity of the mixed paint is too thick for spraying within 3 hours after mixing, it may be thinned again. Do not attempt to re-thin paint after 3 hours because it tends to produce "orange peel" or dry spots.

Polyurethane paint should be applied over a clean primer within 8 hours of primer application. For the best results, most paint manufacturers recommend applying the topcoat as soon as the primer is dry. Apply the thickness of each coat, and the number and direction of coats, according to the directions on the can. Do not apply a mist coat, because it may cause a low-gloss finish. A primer or topcoat that has aged longer than 24 hours is usually scuff-sanded and cleaned before it is painted. Allow approximately 8 hours for painted surfaces to dry. Additional time, usually 1-2 hours, will be required if the temperature is below 70°F.

Paint Defects

During the application of a polyurethane topcoat, discrepancies may appear on the finish because of faulty application methods. The most common defects, probable causes and preventions are listed next.

Runs. A run is just what its name implies: too much paint in one place, too thinly applied or too quickly top-coated, which allows gravity to make the paint run down the side.

Sags. Almost as bad as a run, a sag is when the paint on an entire panel starts moving down at the same time. The most common causes are too much paint, or paint that is too thin. An uneven spray pattern caused by a partially clogged gun tip will also cause the paint to sag or run. As with a run, the only true fix is to wipe the paint off and start over. The lost time could be days.

Orange peel. True to its name, this imperfection looks like the peel of an orange. Typically caused by too much air pressure, this improper application causes a pass to impinge the first pass with atomized paint, resulting in a bunch of little craters in the new surface that won't flatten out.

Rough surface. This condition is normally caused by paint drying while it is still in the air because of the use of too much air when sprayed or an improper thinner. This results in the paint not flowing on contact. The finish is rough and can even look like coarse sandpaper.

Light and dark streaks. Not using cross-coats and/or not overlapping enough. Adjust your speed and get the overlaps right.

Wrinkling. This defect comes from overcoating either too quickly or not quickly enough. Solvents from the first coat may not have flashed off sufficiently before the surface tacks up. The next pass does the same thing, and the solvents trying to escape the first coat cause the second one to wrinkle. The same undesirable effect can result from completing the process with too much paint and insufficient drying between coats.

Fisheyes. These are small, dark spots where the paint not only didn't stick, it actually pulled away from the center of the spot. They are normally caused by insufficient cleaning, or from oil in the air hose. Old silicon wax not sufficiently removed can also cause fisheyes.

If any of these defects are found, they should be corrected before you continue to paint.

Acrylic Nitrocellulose Lacquer

Acrylic nitrocellulose lacquers are the preferred topcoat materials for aircraft markings and propeller safety stripes, and for paint touch-up of avionic components and instruments. They were also used as original equipment finishes on metal airplanes many years ago.

The exact thinning ratio should be determined by the user and adjusted to the temperature, relative humidity and spraying equipment.

Acrylic nitrocellulose lacquer that has been thinned to spraying viscosity should be applied to a thickness of 1-2 mils. Acrylic nitrocellulose lacquer applied with an aerosol container may require three to four coats to cover the primer. The drying time of lacquer (and airplane dope) can be slowed by using a slow-drying thinner called retarder. It is good for hot weather and high humidity conditions.

Be careful not to apply lacquers over enamels. The solvents in the lacquer will soften and "lift" the enamel paint off the surface.

Zinc Chromate Primer

Zinc chromate primer is intended for use as a general-purpose interior protective coating for metal surfaces. Depending on the location, zinc chromate primer may or may not require a topcoat. This kind of primer is relatively easy to apply and remove, and the surface can be scratched. Zinc chromate primer is a single component.

You should thin primer with zoluol. Do not breath the fumes or overspray produced during painting zinc chromate. It can be very hazardous to your respiratory system. Do not use zinc chromate primer on exterior aircraft surfaces, wheel wells, wing butts or in areas that are exposed to temperatures exceeding 175°F (79.4°C).

Epoxy zinc chromate. Zinc chromate primer is also available in an epoxy finish. The epoxy is a much better material for a corrosion-proof finish. It is also available in a color that closely matches regular zinc chromate. As an epoxy, it comes in a two-part system and applies similarly to other epoxy material. Because it is an epoxy, it doesn't require a topcoat to provide a corrosion-proof finish.

Wash Primers

High volume production of metal aircraft created the need for a surface etch and a primer that could be applied in one step, and also provide corrosion protection and good top coat adhesion.

The solution was the creation of a system, known as a wash primer, that would allow for the application of the color top coats in as little as one half hour after priming. These are a group of acidic primers that etch the skin of the aircraft and in the presence of high humidity, the acid is converted to a phosphoric film that aids in the corrosion protection of the aircraft. When applied over a properly prepared surface the compounds in the wash primer adhere well to the surface and provide an excellent film to which the finish can adhere, providing a high gloss, blush free finish.

The most critical aspect of using these primers is the necessity of having the correct moisture content in the air of the paint booth to properly convert all the acid before being covered with epoxy or polyurethane color coats. Since these paint systems are not as porous as acrylics, any humidity that penetrates the finish gets trapped against the skin and reacts with the un-converted acids. This will result in a form of corrosion that is known as filiform corrosion. Filiform is characterized by fernlike threads under the paint, often coming out of the skin laps or around rivets. The presence of this form of corrosion can result in the entire aircraft being striped and re-painted. Even with the drawbacks, wash primers are an integral part of the aircraft painting industry.

Enamel Finishes

Most enamel finishes used on aircraft surfaces cannot be touched up with good results. Minor damage to conventional enamel finishes ordinarily used on engine housings is repaired with epoxy topcoat material or air-drying enamel. Engine manufacturers provide complete directions for touching-up the paint on their products.

General Safety Precautions

General safety precautions for all painting as well as those for special types of paints must be observed and include the following:

- No eating, drinking or smoking is allowed in areas where paint or solvent is being used.
- Prolonged breathing of vapors from organic solvent or materials containing organic solvent is dangerous.
- Prolonged contact with organic solvents or materials containing organic solvents can have a toxic effect on the skin.

Masking

Masking is a process that is as important as the actual painting. It is also a very large project on a multi-colored paint scheme. A typical refinish project will be masked three times: once for stripper, once for the base coat and once for the trim. Depending on the trim design chosen, it may be partially masked several other times, once for each color in the trim package.

Figure 7-2-3 shows masking for the base color where everything that isn't being painted is masked. Once the base coat is finished and cured, the balance of the masking will be applied. In the case of polyurethane, there are re-mask time limits that must be observed, or the finish may lift or be marked by the tape.

Figure 7-2-3. Masking materials being applied to all areas that do not receive the base color coat of paint. *Photo courtesy of JRA Executive Air*

Figure 7-2-4. Suction-feed spray gun, with schematic

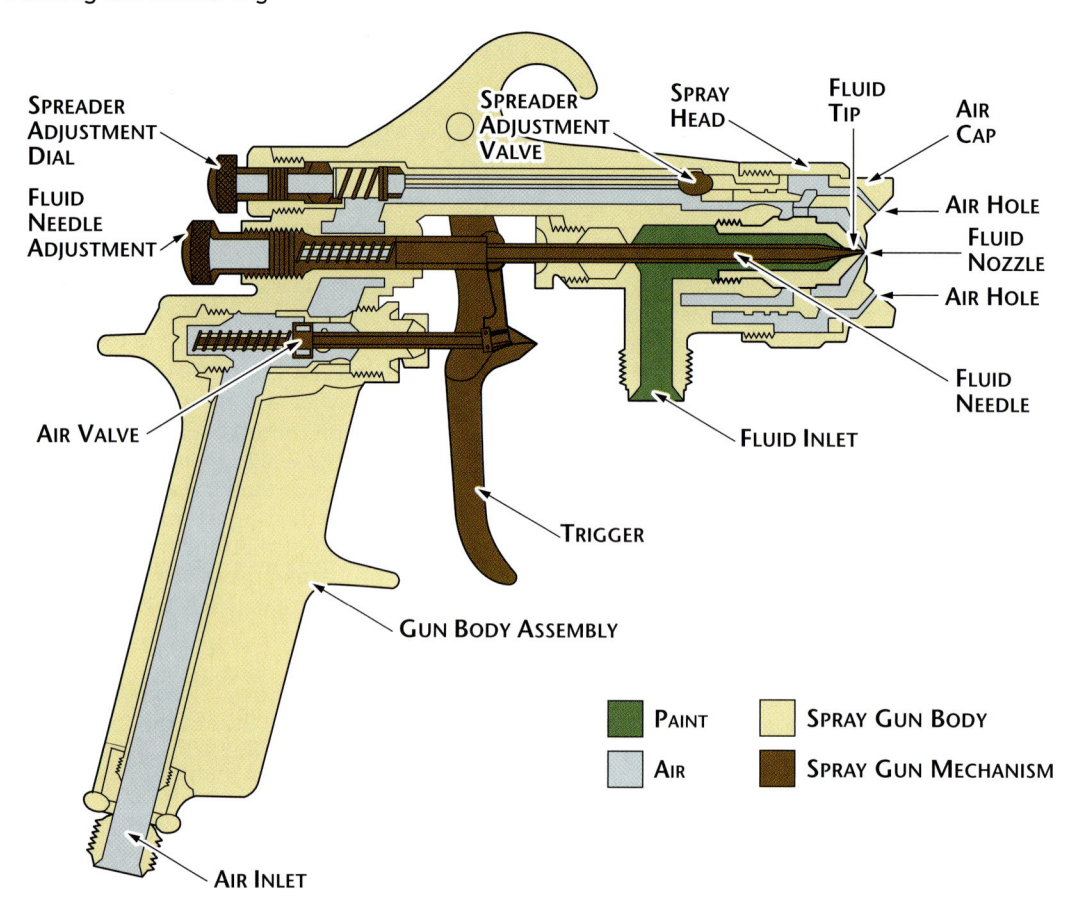

In general, a plastic masking tape, called fine-line tape, will be used where the color being applied will make an edge. Fine line tape does just as its name implies: it leaves a clean, fine line when removed. More generic masking tape can be used for the purpose of attaching the masking paper. Ordinary tape will not necessarily leave a good edge, and paint can soften it and bleed under the edge to spoil the line.

Removing masking tape properly, and at the right time, is just as important as applying it. The tape should be pulled off after the paint solvents have flashed off and the paint is still somewhat wet. Pulled to soon and the risk of the paint sagging is a problem, to late and fine little hair like strands stick to the tape and result in a uneven trim line that has to be re-touched. The tape should be pulled back on it's self with a smooth even motion. If, for any reason the masking tape is left on the surface for an extended period of time, before painting, it may be very difficult to remove and leave a residue which will have to be cleaned off after the paint has dried.

Painting Equipment and Maintenance Procedures

You will frequently use and maintain spray guns, air compressors and regulators. Like all precision tools, a paint gun cannot produce an acceptable finished product if it is not properly cleaned and maintained. Cleaning a paint gun is not one of those things that can wait. It must be done when it needs to be done.

Spray Guns

The spray gun atomizes the material to be sprayed. You direct and control the spray pattern by manipulating and adjusting the spray gun. Spray guns are usually classed as either suction-feed or pressure-feed. The types are divided by two methods:

1. The type of container used to hold the paint material
2. The method in which the paint is drawn through the air cap assembly

Suction-feed. The suction-feed spray gun (Figure 7-2-4) is designed for small jobs. The cup for the paint is connected to the spray gun by a quick-attachment fitting. The capacity of this cup is approximately 1 quart. The fluid tip of this type of spray gun protrudes through the air cap. The air pressure rushing past the fluid tip creates a low-pressure area in front of the tip. This causes paint to be drawn up through the fluid tip, where it is atomized outside the cap by the air pressure. This is one of the main reasons for checking thinned paint with a Zahn cup.

Pressure-feed. The pressure-feed spray gun is designed for use on large jobs, where a large amount of paint material is to be used. The paint material is supplied to the gun through a hose from a pressurized tank called a *pressure pot*.

This spray gun is designed to operate on high-volume, low-pressure air. This type of equipment eliminates the evaporation of the volatile substances of the mixture before striking the surface, because the paint and air are mixed in the tanks. In other words, a wetter coating is applied.

In actual practice, pressure-feed paint guns are rare. Instead, suction-feed guns are used with a pressure pot. For larger jobs requiring more material than can be easily supplied by a quart cup, they work well. There are a few rules to pay attention to when using a suction-feed/pressure pot combination:

- Use the lightest and longest hoses that are practical.
- Do not use the pot fluid pressure stated for a pressure-fed gun — it will be too high. Instead, use only enough pressure to ensure a constant flow of material to the gun: somewhere between 2 and 5 lbs. on the pot. Too much pressure will keep the spray pattern from working correctly.
- Always keep the hoses clean. Keep used thinner in a sealed can, so it can be used to do the initial hose cleaning. Finish with new, clean thinner.
- Keep the fluid needle packing in good shape, or it will leak paint.
- Always carry the hose over your shoulder, or it will drag on your work.
- Fluid needles and air caps come in different sizes. You may need one size larger.

Spray Gun Maintenance

Fluid leakage at the front of the gun is an indication that the fluid needle is not seating properly. This may be caused by a fleck of dried material in the nozzle, or the fluid needle packing may be too tight. It may also be caused by a bent fluid needle, a broken fluid needle spring or the wrong size fluid needle for the fluid tip.

Air leakage results from an improperly set air valve. This may be caused by a bent valve stem, broken spring or damaged valve or valve seat.

Jerky or fluttering spray is caused by an obstructed fluid passage, loose tip, damaged seat, or air in the fluid line. Air can be inducted into the line from several sources:

- A loose packing nut
- Dried packing
- Loose or damaged coupling nut
- Loose or damaged fluid tube
- Cup tipped too far. See Figure 7-2-5)

Faulty spray patterns, their causes and how to correct them are shown in Figure 7-2-6.

Cleaning a suction-feed spray gun. Spray guns should be cleaned immediately after each use. To clean a suction gun, empty the container, then pour a small quantity of thinner or suitable solvent into it. Draw the thinner or solvent through the gun by inserting the tube into the container of cleaning fluid. Move the trigger constantly to thoroughly flush the passageways and the tip of the fluid needle. Remove the air cap and soak it in solvent. If this action does not clean the small holes in the air cap, remove the paint material and use a toothpick or broom straw to clean the holes. Do not use wire or other metal objects. They will cause permanent damage to the air cap.

If you have a pressure pot attached, remove the air cap to clean the hose and pot. It will make thinner come out in a stream instead of a spray. The material can be collected in a can instead of sprayed around the shop. Reinstall the air cap for the final cleaning.

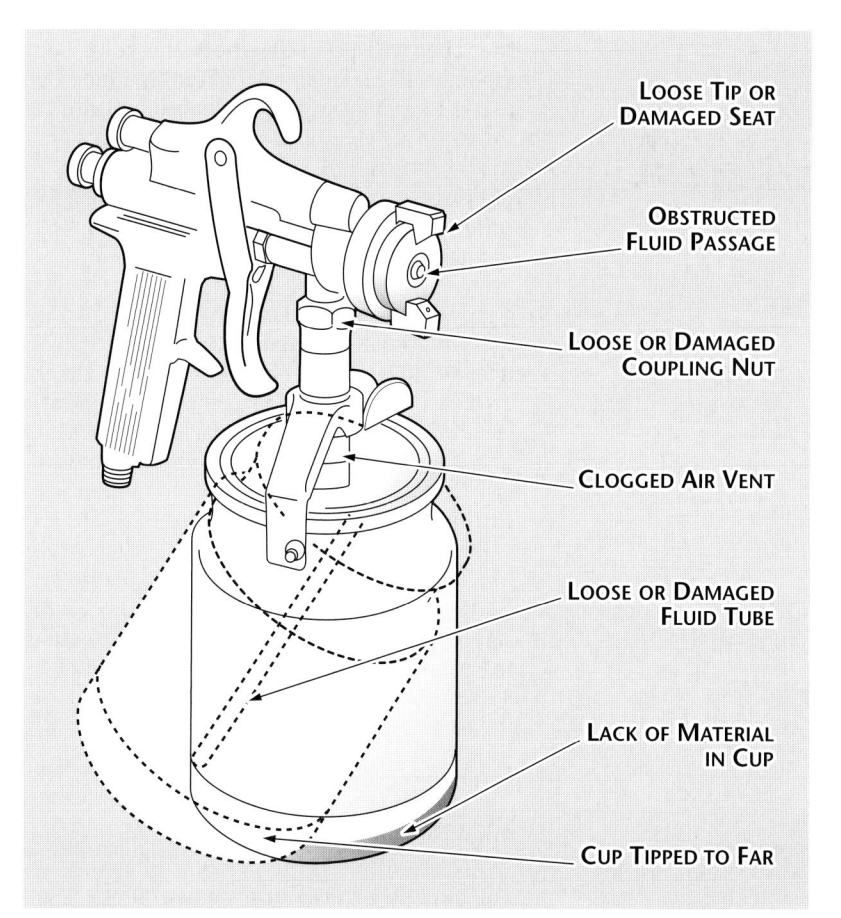

Figure 7-2-5. Causes of jerky or fluttering spray

7-12 | Painting and Refinishing

Cleaning a pressure-feed spray gun. To clean a pressure-feed gun, you should back off the fluid needle adjusting screw. Then, release the pressure from the pressure tank with the relief or safety valve. Hold a cloth over the air cap and operate the gun trigger. The cloth forces the spray material back into the pressure tank. Remove the fluid hose from the gun and the pressure tank. Attach a hose cleaner to the hose and run thinner or suitable solvent through it. Clean the air cap by using the same method as the suction gun air cap.

NOTE: *Do not immerse an entire spray gun in cleaning materials like solvents and thinners. These dissolve oil from leather pack-*

PATTERN	CAUSE	CORRECTION
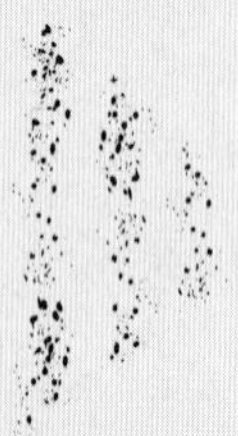	(A) Dried out packing around material needle valve permits air to get into fluid passageway. This results in spitting. (B) Dirt between fluid nozzle seat and body or a loosely installed fluid nozzle will make a gun spit. (C) A loose or defective swivel nut on siphon cup or material hose can cause spitting.	To correct cause (A), back up knurled nut C, place two drops of machine oil on packing, replace nut and tighten with fingers only. In aggravated cases, replace packing. To correct cause (B), remove fluid nozzle D, clean back of nozzle seat in gun body using rag wet with thinner, replace nozzle and draw up tightly against body. 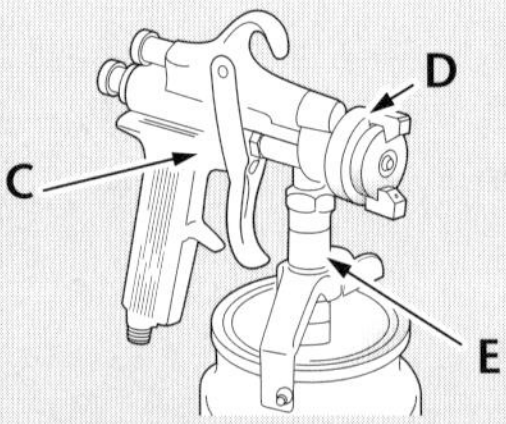To correct cause (C), tighten or replace swivel nut E.
	A fan spray pattern that is heavy in the middle, or a pattern that has an unatomized "salt-and-pepper" effect indicates that the atomizing air pressure is not sufficiently high.	Increase pressure from your air supply. Correct air pressures are discussed elsewhere in this instruction sheet.
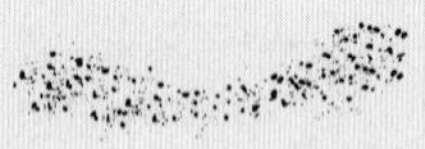	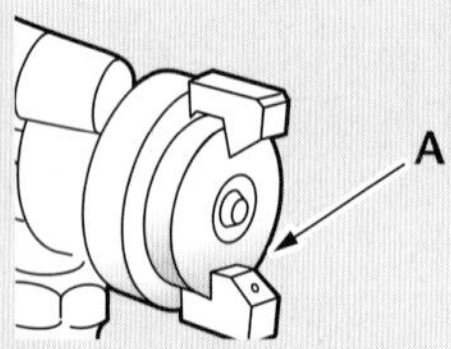 Dried material in wing port A restricts passage through it and produces a crescent. Full pressure of air from clean wing port forces pattern in direction of clogged side.	Dissolve material in side port with thinner. Do not poke in any of the openings with metal instruments.
	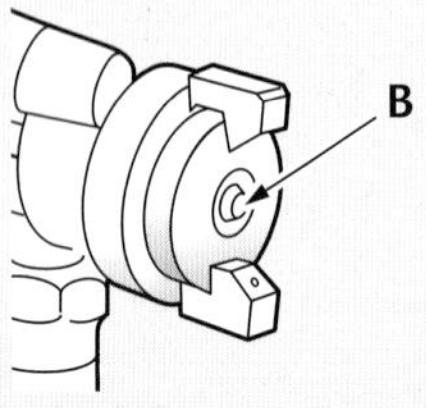 Spray pattern wider and heavier at either end is caused by dried material around the outside of the fluid nozzle. Tip B restricts the passage of atomizing air at one point through the center opening of air nozzle and results in pattern shown. This pattern can also be caused by loose air nozzle.	If dried material is causing the trouble, remove air nozzle and wipe off fluid tip, using rag wet with thinner. Tighten air nozzle.
	A split spray or one that is heavy on each end of a fan pattern and weak in the middle is usually caused by (A) too high an atomized air pressure, or (B) by attempting to get too wide a spray with thin material.	Reducing air pressure will correct cause (A). To correct cause (B), open material control to full position by turning to left. At the same time turn spray width adjustment to the right. This will reduce width of spray but will correct split spray pattern.

Figure 7-2-6. Faulty spray patterns, their causes and corrections

ings and cause the gun to have an unsteady spray.

The gun, fluid needle packing, air valve stem and trigger bearing screw require frequent lubrication. Remove the fluid needle packing before using the gun, then soften the packing with oil.

The fluid needle spring should be coated with grease according to the manufacturer's instructions. See Figure 7-2-7.

Air Compressors

To use a spray gun, you need a source of compressed air. Figure 7-2-8 shows one type of air

Figure 7-2-7. Spray gun lubrication point

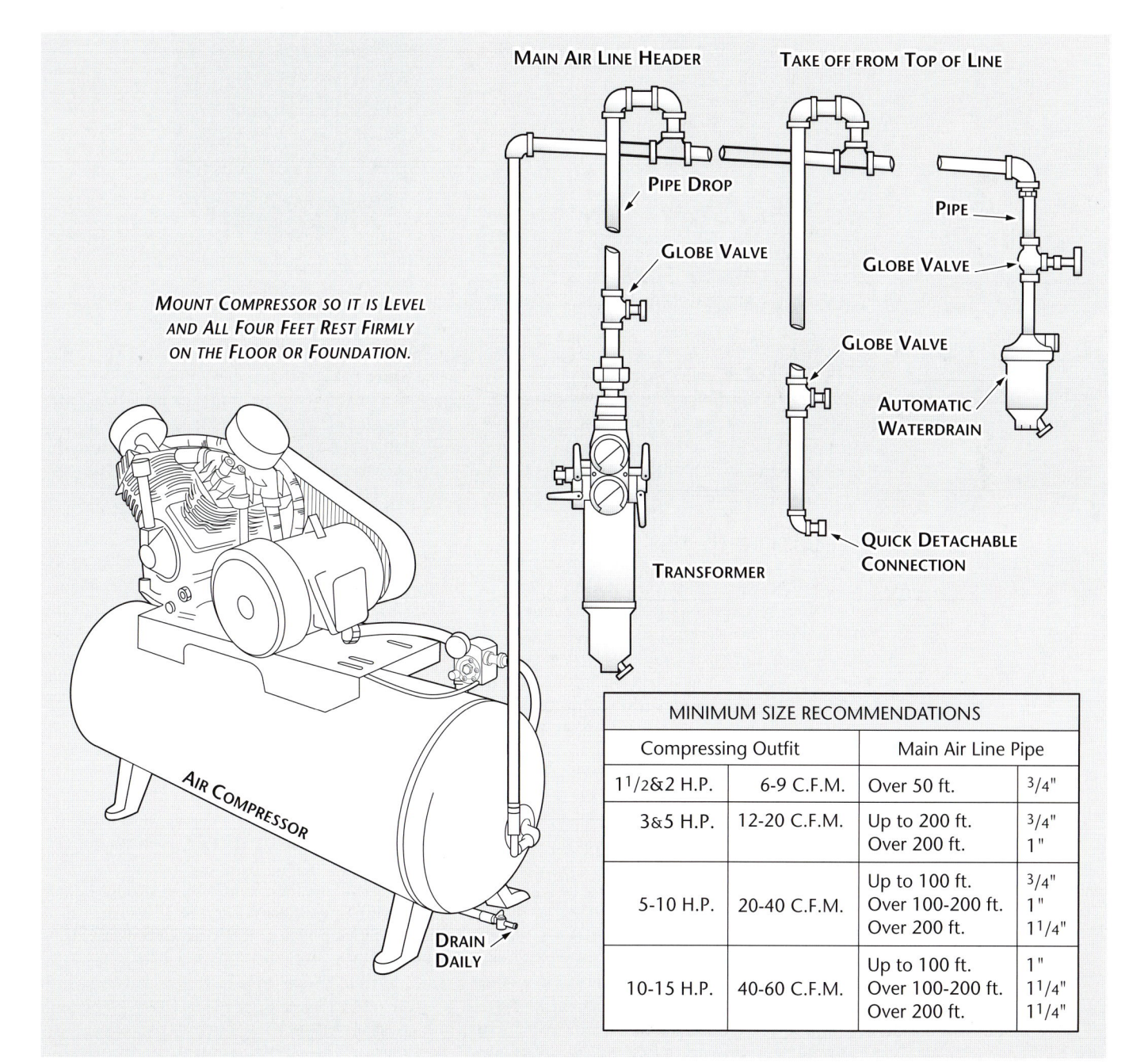

MINIMUM SIZE RECOMMENDATIONS		
Compressing Outfit		Main Air Line Pipe
1 1/2 & 2 H.P.	6-9 C.F.M.	Over 50 ft. 3/4"
3 & 5 H.P.	12-20 C.F.M.	Up to 200 ft. 3/4" Over 200 ft. 1"
5-10 H.P.	20-40 C.F.M.	Up to 100 ft. 3/4" Over 100-200 ft. 1" Over 200 ft. 1 1/4"
10-15 H.P.	40-60 C.F.M.	Up to 100 ft. 1" Over 100-200 ft. 1 1/4" Over 200 ft. 1 1/4"

Figure 7-2-8. Air compressors

Figure 7-2-9. A standard touch-up paint gun

Figure 7-2-10. Hobby-type paint gun

compressor: a stationary unit. There are also portable units. Both types are commonly used. The stationary unit consists of an electric motor, compressor, storage tank, centrifugal pressure release, pressure switch and mounting feet.

Touch-up Paint Guns

In addition to the standard spray equipment, special types have been developed for the occasional or small touch-up job. There are many types available. Figure 7-2-9 shows one that is commonly called a *touch-up gun*. In essence, it works just like a regular suction-fed gun, it's just smaller. It has all of the adjustments and thinning requirements of a full-sized paint gun. Other types are available from many suppliers. A good paint supply catalog will list several.

Hobby-type Paint Guns

There are many hobby-type paint guns. Most are of the constant-pressure type; they blow air all the time (Figure 7-2-10). Paint only comes out when the trigger is pulled. Constant-pressure guns are not a wise choice for an expensive refinish job. It is too easy to produce an unacceptable finish with them.

Air Regulators

The air regulator (transformer) is used to regulate the amount of pressure to the spray gun and to clean the air. The air delivered to the regulator always contains some oil from the compressor, some water caused by condensation, and many particles of dirt and dust.

Air regulators are equipped with a pressure valve and pressure-regulating screw to regulate the pressure delivered to the spray gun. They also prevent pressure fluctuations. The air must pass through a filter before it leaves the regulator. This filter is contained in the long, cylindrical part of the regulator and should be drained daily. Air regulators are also equipped with two gauges. One shows the pressure on the main line, while the other shows the pressure to the spray gun.

Spray Gun Technique

Proper spray gun technique reflects knowledge of the equipment and experience. The spray gun should be held so the spray is perpendicular to the area to which the finish is being applied. Ensure that the prescribed gun-to-work distance is maintained.

A distance of 6-10 inches from the gun to the work should be maintained when spraying epoxy-polyamide and polyurethane finishes. The gun should be held 8-10 inches from the work for lacquer and 6-8 inches for enamels. For a narrow pattern, the gun is held at the farther distances (10 inches for epoxy-polyamide and polyurethane, 10 inches for lacquer, and 8 inches for enamels).

A distance of less than 6 inches is undesirable, because the paint will not atomize properly, and an orange peel finish will result. A distance of more than 10 inches is equally undesirable. Dried particles of paint will strike the surface and cause dusting of the finish. Examples of correct and incorrect spray gun techniques are shown in Figure 7-2-11.

The distance the spray gun is held from the work is important; however, there are other factors to consider. Drying time and the size of the object to be painted, for example, determine how quickly the paint must be applied. Sometimes, more than one painter is required. See Figure 7-2-12. The manner in which the gun is held and operated is also important. See Figure 7-2-13. Move your arm and body with the gun to keep the spray perpendicular to the surface. Avoid pivoting and circular movements of the wrist or forearm, as this will cause the gun's position to vary too greatly: from too far away, to too close, then too far away again as it follows the arc.

Trigger the gun in order to avoid an uneven coat at the beginning and end of a stroke. Triggering is the technique of starting the gun moving toward the area to be sprayed before the trigger is pulled and continuing the motion of the gun after the trigger has been released.

Avoid too much overlapping on each pass of the gun, because an uneven coat will result. The rate of the stroke should produce a full, wet, even coat. Once the job is started, it must be completed without stopping.

Painting Order

Through experience, an effective sequence for painting an airplane has been developed. It aims to arrange start and stop points so there isn't a wet pass stopping beside a dry one, which would leave a rough overspray area. Actually, it can't be avoided, but a sequence can be ended in a place that won't show. At the same time, a standard sequence will let you arrange your stands and ramps in a safe and expedient order.

It is also a general practice to do the primer, tack coat and finish coat in different directions. The reasoning is that a thin versus thick spot will not develop because of the spray passes

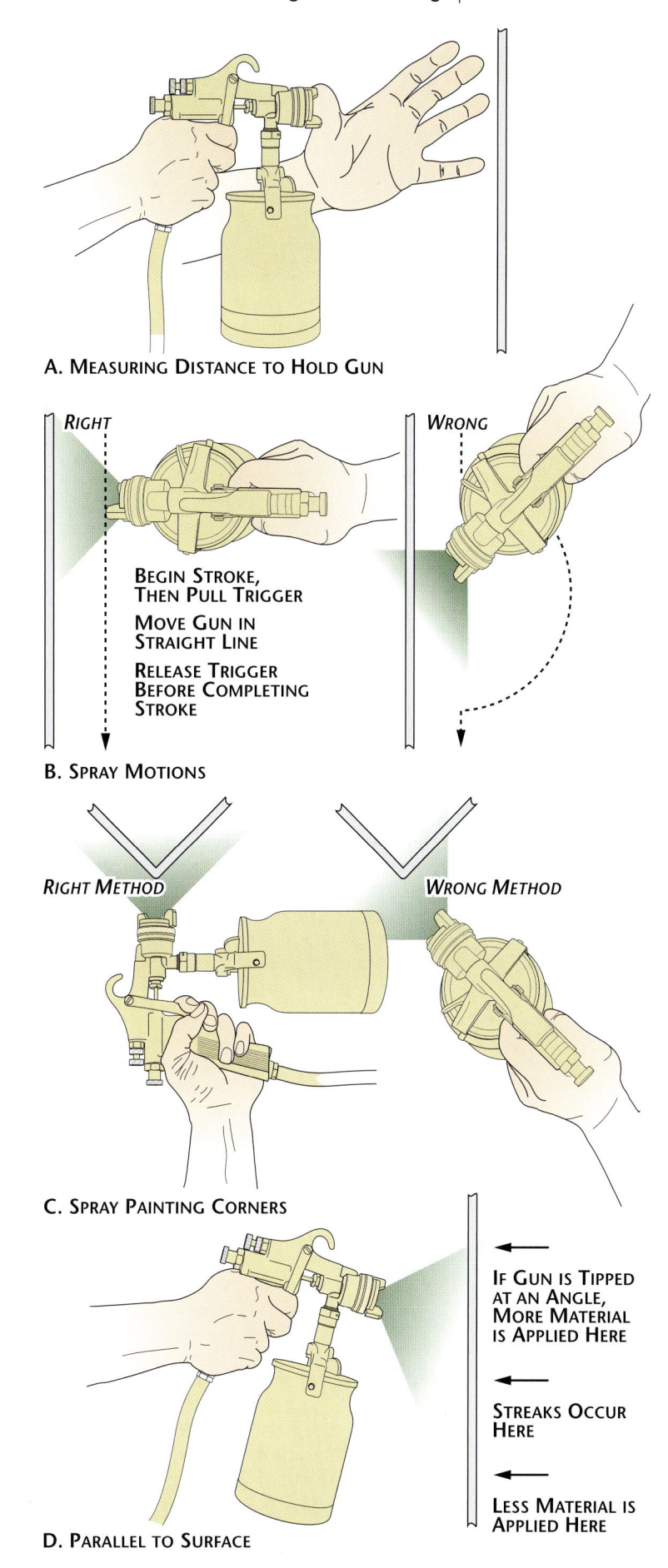

Figure 7-2-11. Examples of correct and incorrect spray gun techniques

Figure 7-2-12. On very large paint jobs, team spraying using two painters is the only way to cover the surface in the required time. One painter could never keep a wet edge to allow for seamless overlaps.
Photo courtesy of JRA Executive Air

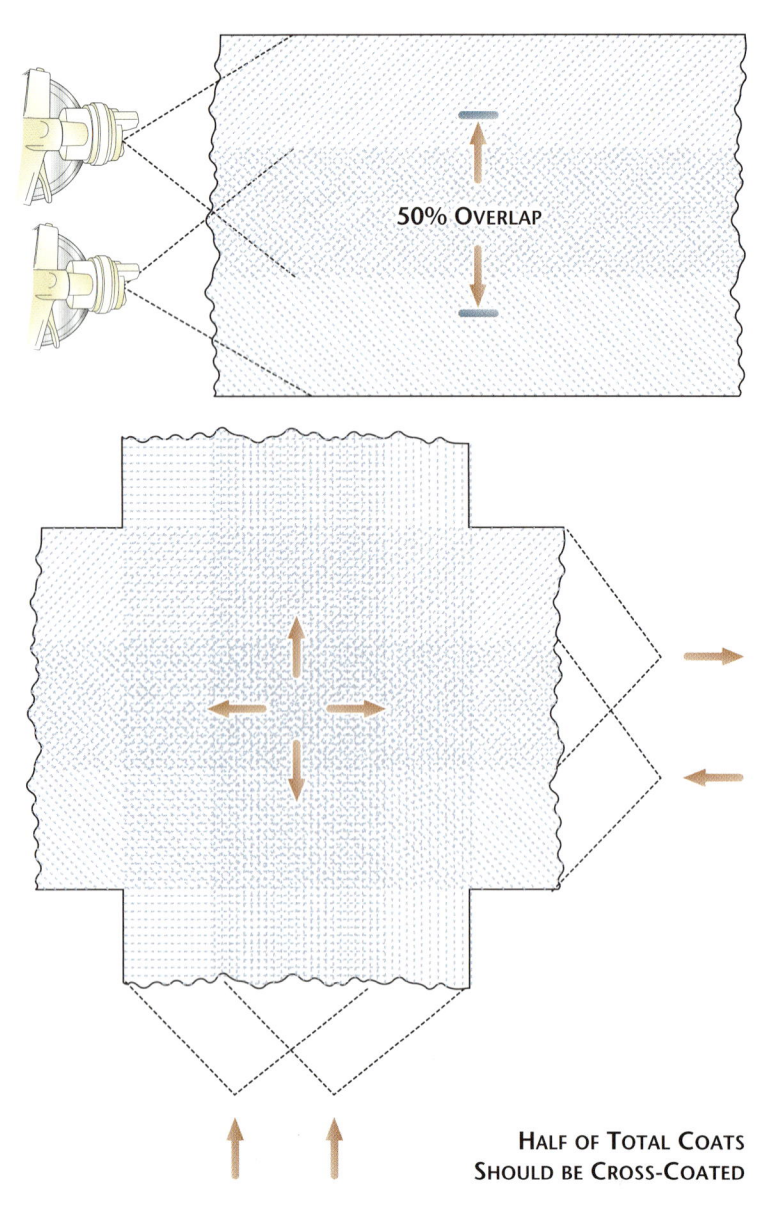

50% OVERLAP

HALF OF TOTAL COATS SHOULD BE CROSS-COATED

Figure 7-2-13. Correct methods of spraying

overlapping too many times. A good cross-coat sequence makes the point moot. Figure 7-2-14 is an example of a good painting sequence.

Trim

Once the base coat has dried, the trim can be masked and sprayed. Getting the trim lines uniform from side to side is a must. Careful measuring and patterns made from masking paper can be a big help.

Trim designs are generally a major part of any refinish operation. Because of the desire for sharp, clean lines, fine-line tape is a must. In the case of multiple colors of trim, several layouts may be necessary, as well as a studied painting order. The order will normally consist of the lighter colors being sprayed first, then masked, then the next darker color sprayed, etc.. See Figure 7-2-15.

N numbers. There is a definite size and style established in the FAA regulations for number size, placement and style. There have been some changes over the years, but the current regulation is frequently a test item for an A&P student and is explained in FAR part 45.23. FAR 45.29 explains what size markings should be.

Figure 7-2-16 shows the alphabet in the regulation layout. They are block roman letters and numbers that are the preferred shape. The old-style template for drawing these letters consists of the number eight with an I attached to it. From this template, all numbers and letters can be drawn. Another template in general use is made from a thin piece of clear acrylic. It is 12 inches long and 2 inches wide with divisions marked at 2, 4, 6, 8 and 10 inches, as well as a center line. Using this marking gauge, all letters and numbers can also be drawn, and with a little practice, fairly quickly. Both templates are shown in Figure 7-2-17.

Many different precut masks can be purchased that will eliminate the tedious masking that accompanies painting N numbers. For many of the highly sophisticated and stylized paint schemes used today, the boxy lettering just won't do. Following the size requirements closely, it is still possible to design a set of N numbers that actually looks good. If, however, you want to venture too far from the requirements, it would be good to run the choice by your local inspector for pre-approval. It is very difficult to redo them later.

Spray Gun Adjustments

Figure 7-2-18 shows the principal parts of a typical spray gun. The spreader adjustment dial is used to adjust the width of the spray pattern by varying the amount of air flowing through the air cap. When you turn the dial to the right, a round pattern is obtained. When you turn to the left, a fan-shaped pattern results.

As the width of the spray is increased, more material must be allowed to pass through the gun to get the same coverage on the increased area. To apply more material to the area, turn the fluid needle adjustment to the left. If too much material is applied to the surface, turn the fluid needle adjustment to the right. A proper spray pattern is a balance between the amount of fluid, the thickness of the paint, and the amount of air exiting the air cap. To get consistent results, use the Zahn cup during paint mixing.

In normal operation, the wings on the air cap are adjusted to the horizontal position. This provides a vertical fan-shaped pattern.

Spraying pressures. Normally, you will be concerned about spray-painting lacquer, enamel, epoxy and urethane materials. The correct air and fluid pressures used with these materials vary. There are several pitfalls of incorrect pressures, some of which are as follows:

- Excessive air pressure may cause dusting and rippling of the finish.
- Too little air pressure, coupled with excessive fluid pressure, causes orange peel. Check air hose length and determine the correct pressure drop.
- Excessive fluid pressure causes orange peel and sags.
- Too little fluid pressure causes dusting.

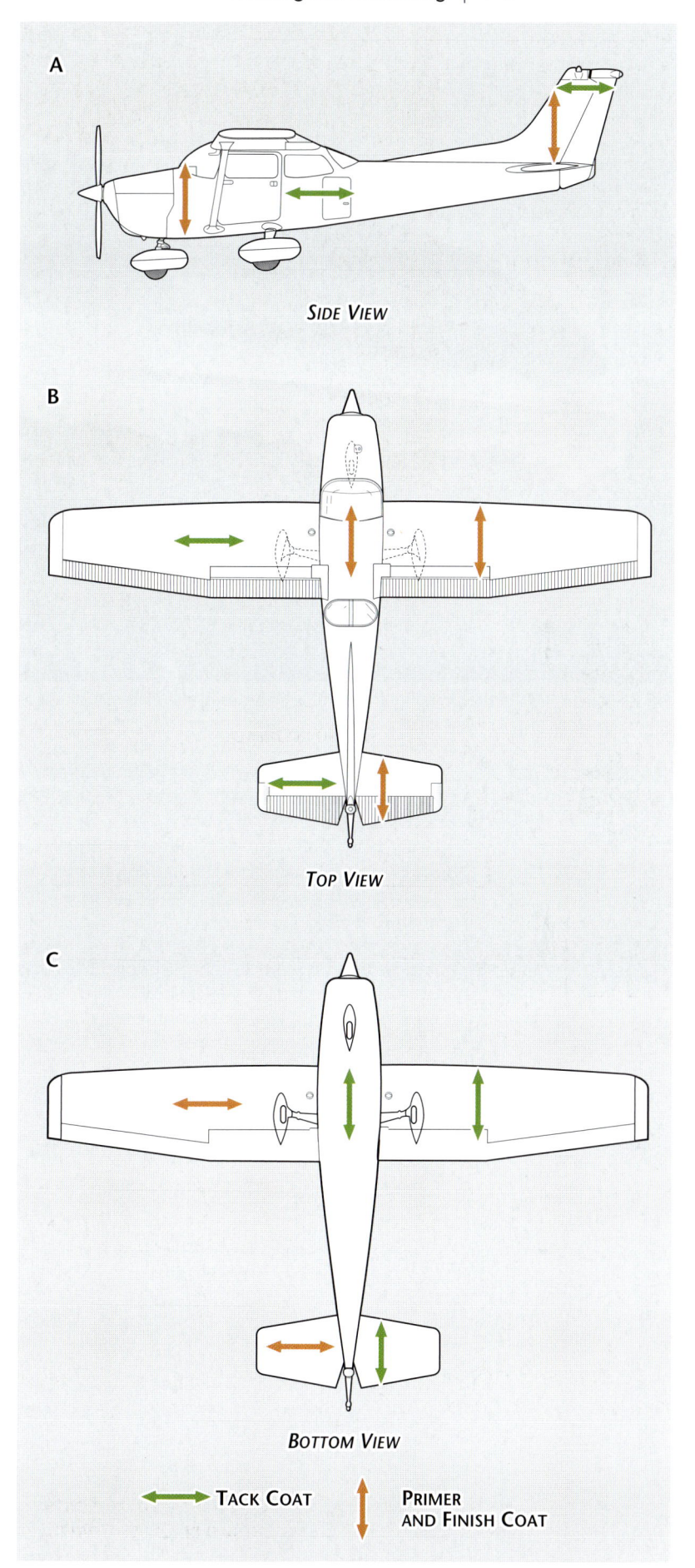

Figure 7-2-14. A painting sequence for a light single-engined airplane

Figure 7-2-15. While the actual painting of a trim design is relatively quick, the preparation can be very time consuming, taking several re-maskings.

Photo courtesy of JRA Executive Air

Airless Painting

Used principally by very large facilities for really large airplanes, airless and airless electrostatic painting is becoming standard for equipment finishing.

Airless painting equipment simply uses the pressure of the paint to cause the paint to create a spray pattern when forced out of a special orifice. Without using any pressurized air, there is very little, if any, overspray, and material wastage is reduced considerably.

Electrostatic equipment causes your work to actually attract the paint, virtually eliminating waste and overspray. As an added benefit, an entire job can use less paint.

To justify the cost of special commercial equipment, a facility has to do a lot of painting. Mostly, airless electrostatic painting is limited

Figure 7-2-16. The original Roman alphabet covered in the FARs

Storage of Materials

Containers used to hold paints, lacquers, removers, thinners, cleaners or any volatile solvents should be kept tightly closed when not in use. Care should be taken to store them in an OSHA-approved manner. The paint material should not be exposed to excessive heat, smoke, sparks, flame or direct rays of the sun. Wiping rags and other flammable waste material should always be placed in OSHA-approved containers. Waste containers should be emptied at the end of each day's work. Some chemicals, or combinations of chemicals, may spontaneously combust.

Sealants and Sealing Practices

Sealants are used to prevent the movement of liquid or gas from one point to another. They are used in an aircraft to maintain pressurization in cabin areas, to retain fuel in storage areas, to achieve exterior surface aerodynamic smoothness and to weatherproof the airframe. Sealants are used in general repair work to maintain and restore seam integrity in critical areas where structural damage or paint remover has loosened existing sealants.

Types of sealants. The physical conditions surrounding the seal govern the type of sealant to be used. Some sealants are exposed to extremely high or low temperatures. Other sealants contact fuels and lubricants. In such cases, it is necessary to use a sealant that has been compounded for the particular condition. Sealants are supplied in different consistencies and cure rates. Basic sealants are classified in three general categories:

- Pliable
- Drying
- Curing

Pliable sealants. Referred to as one-part sealants, these are supplied ready-for-use as packaged (Figure 7-2-19). They are solids and change very little during or after application. Solvent is not used with pliable sealants, thus drying is not necessary. Except for normal aging, they remain virtually the same as when they were packaged. They easily adhere to metal, glass and plastic surfaces. Pliable sealants are used around access panels and doors and in areas where pressurization cavities must be maintained.

Drying sealants. Drying sealants (Figure 7-2-20) set and cure by evaporation of the solvent. Solvents are used in these sealants to

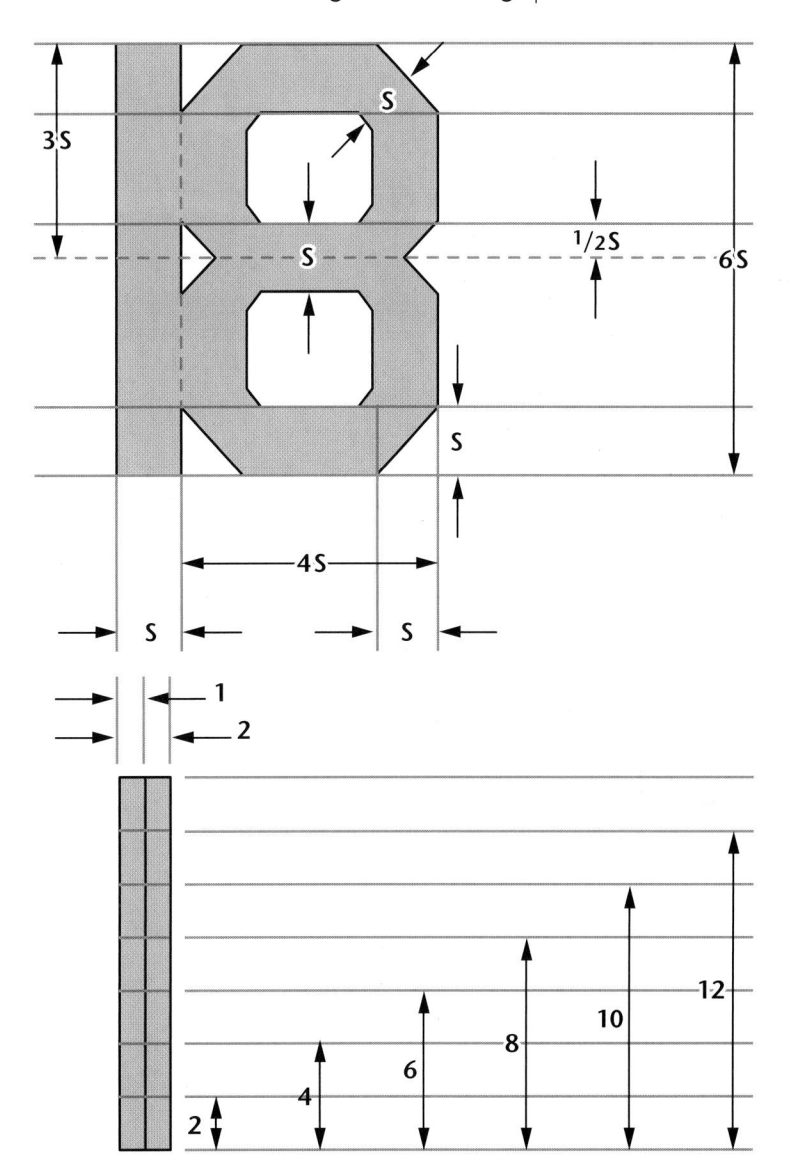

Figure 7-2-17. Letter templates for standard roman alphabet

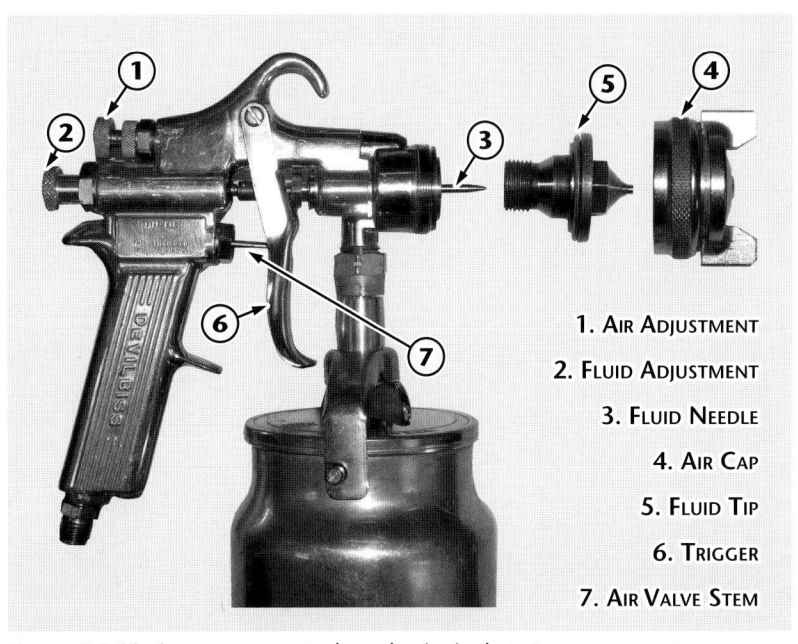

1. Air Adjustment
2. Fluid Adjustment
3. Fluid Needle
4. Air Cap
5. Fluid Tip
6. Trigger
7. Air Valve Stem

Figure 7-2-18. Spray gun controls and principal parts

Figure 7-2-19. This rubber and gasket adhesive is a general-purpose type. Flexible when cured, it is useful for most applications except upholstery.

- Sealant should be used within the application time limits specified by the sealant manufacturer.
- Sealant should not be applied to metal that is colder than 70°F. Observe the sealant manufacturer's temperature limits.
- Sealant should be discarded immediately when it becomes too stiff to apply or work. Stiff or partially cured sealant will not wet the surface to which it is to be applied as well as fresh sealant will. Consequently, it will not have satisfactory adhesion.
- Sealant should not be used for faying surface applications unless it has just been removed from refrigerated storage or freshly mixed.

While the use of sealants on aircraft surfaces has greatly increased over the past few years, application methods have been mostly through the use of brushes, dipping, injection guns and spatulas. Sealant spraying is a recent development. The MMM, SRM and the sealant manufacturer's information should all be followed.

When you are pressure-sealing an aircraft, the sealing materials should be applied to produce a continuous bead, film or fillet over the sealed area (Figure 7-2-22). Air bubbles, voids, metal chips or oily contamination will prevent an effective seal. Therefore, the success of the sealing operation depends upon the cleanliness of the area and the careful application of the sealant materials.

There are various methods of pressure-sealing the joints and seams in aircraft. The applicable SRM will specify the method to be used in each application.

Figure 7-2-20. De-icer cement is a special adhesive product used around the edges of de-icers to provide an electrical bond to the airframe. This prevents static electricity from building up and causing pinholes in the de-icers.

provide the desired application consistency. Consistency or hardness may change when this type of sealant dries, depending on the solvent content. Shrinkage during the drying process is an important consideration. The degree of shrinkage also depends upon the amount of solvent it contains.

Curing sealants. Catalyst-cured sealants (see Figure 7-2-21) have an advantage over drying sealants because they are transformed from a fluid or semi-fluid state into a solid by chemical reaction rather than by evaporation of a solvent. A chemical catalyst or accelerator is added and mixed just prior to sealant applications. Heat may be employed to speed up the curing process. When you use a catalyst, you should accurately measure and thoroughly mix the two components to ensure a complete and even cure.

Application of Sealants

The application of sealants varies according to time, tools required and the application method. The following restrictions apply to all sealant applications:

Figure 7-2-21. A typical two-part sealant, used with an applicator or fillet tool. Mix only the amount needed, as it has a limited pot life once combined.

Careful planning is necessary to close faying surface seals on large assemblies within the application time limit of the sealant. Once the sealant has been applied, the parts must be joined, the required number of bolts must be torqued and all the rivets driven within this time limit.

When insulating tape has been installed between the faying surfaces to prevent dissimilar metal contacts, pressure-sealing should be accomplished by fillet-sealing. Fillet-sealing is the spreading of sealant along the seam with a sealant injection gun. The sealant should be spread in approximately 3-foot increments. Before you proceed to the next increment, the applied portion of the fillet should be worked with a sealant spatula or tool. This working fills the voids in the seam and eliminates air bubbles. The leak-free service life of the sealant is determined by the thoroughness and care you use in working out the air bubbles.

After the sealant has cured to a tack-free condition, the fillet should be inspected for any remaining air bubbles. Such air bubbles should be opened and filled with sealant. When a heavy fillet is required, it should be applied in layers. The top layer should fair with the metal.

Injection-sealing is the pressure-filling of openings or voids with a sealant injection gun (Figure 7-2-23). Joggles should be filled by forcing sealant into the opening until it emerges from the opposite side. Voids and cavities are filled by starting with the nozzle of the sealant injection gun at the bottom of the space and filling as the nozzle is withdrawn.

NOTE: *A joggle is a joint between two pieces of material formed by a notch and a fitted projection.*

Rivets, Rivnuts®, screws and small bolts should have a brush coat of sealant over the protruding portion on the pressure side. Washers should have a brush coat of sealant on both sides. Split grommets should have sealant brushed into the split prior to installation, after which fillets should be applied to both the base of the grommet and the protruding tube in the pressure side.

Sealing compounds. Various sealing compounds are available, but only those chosen by the aircraft manufacturer should be considered. They will be listed in the AMM.

Figure 7-2-22. The reinforcement patches around these two fitting attachments were injection-sealed with a Semkit®-type sealant. Seam sealing is a necessary part of cabin pressurization systems.

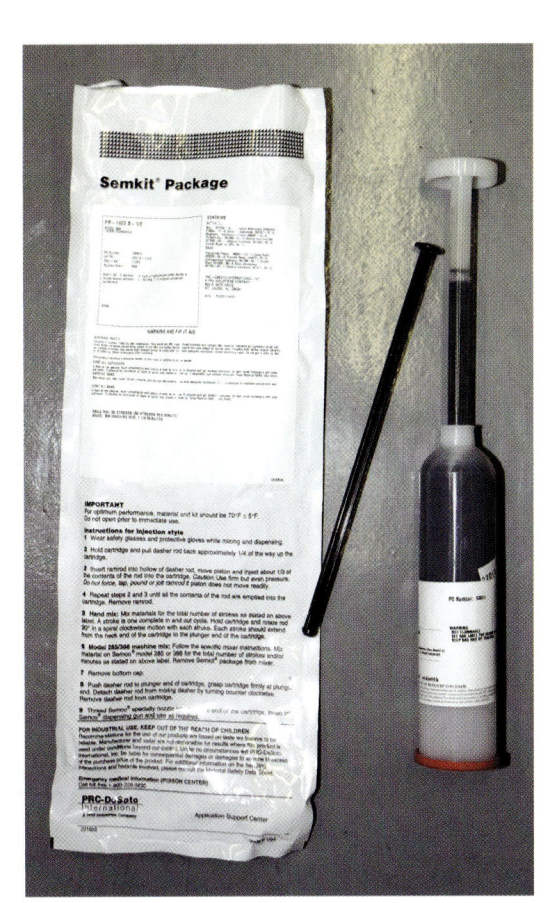

Figure 7-2-23. Semkits® are pre-packaged material kits that use a caulking gun-type applicator. The kit contains a plunger system for mixing.

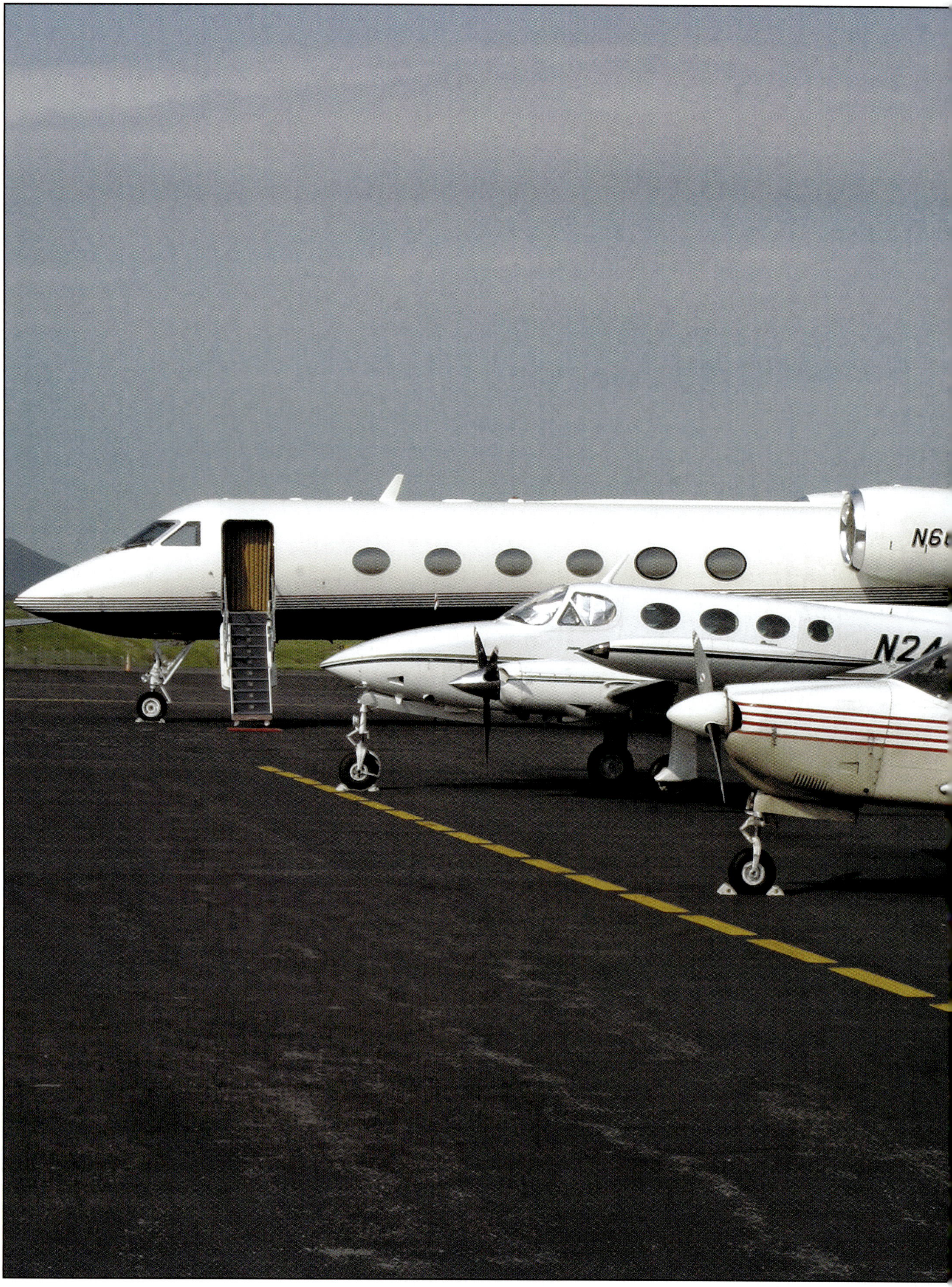

8

Assembly and Rigging

Section 1

Rigging and Assembly Data

This chapter includes both assembly and rigging since the subjects are directly related. Assembly involves putting together the component sections of the aircraft, such as wing sections, empennage units, nacelles, and landing gear. Rigging is the final adjustment and alignment of the various component sections to provide the proper aerodynamic reaction.

Two important considerations in all assembly and rigging operations are:

- Proper operation of the component in regard to its aerodynamic and mechanical function
- Maintaining the aircraft's structural integrity by the correct use of materials, hardware, and safetying devices

Improper assembly and rigging may result in certain members being subjected to loads greater than those for which they were designed. Proper adjustment of rigging can contribute to better balance in an aircraft and straighter flight.

Assembly and rigging must be done in accordance with the requirements prescribed by the aircraft manufacturer. These procedures are usually detailed in the applicable maintenance or service manuals. The Aircraft Specifications or Type Certificate Data Sheets also provide valuable information regarding control surface travel.

The rigging of control systems varies with each type of aircraft; therefore, it would be impractical

Learning Objectives

DESCRIBE
- Where rigging data is found
- Types of control cables
- Types of control cable fittings

EXPLAIN
- Principles of control surface balancing
- Measuring surface travel
- How mechanical linkages operate

APPLY
- Balance a control surface
- Install a control surface
- Inspect a flight control system
- Perform a rigging check

Left: A wide variety of airplanes will pass through a maintenance facility. At some point technicians will perform rigging and/or assembly operations on each type.

A24CE, Rev. 86		Page 5 of 39			
I - Model 200, Model A200C, Model 200C, Model B200, Model B200C (cont'd)					
Control Surface Movements	Wing flap	Maximum	35°		
	Aileron tabs	Up	15°	Down	15°
	Aileron	Up	25°	Down	15°
	Elevator tabs	Up	3° 30'	Down	13°
	Elevator	Up	20°	Down	14°
	Rudder tab	Right	15°	Left	15°
	Rudder	Right	25°	Left	25°
Serial Nos. Eligible	200:	BB-2, BB-6 through BB-733, BB-735 through BB-792, BB-794 through BB-828, BB-830 through BB-853, BB-871 through BB-873, BB-892, BB-893, BB-895, BB-912, BB-991			
	A200C:	BJ-1 and up			
	200C:	BL-1 through BL-36			
	B200:	BB-734, BB-793, BB-829, BB-854 through BB-870, BB-874 through BB-891, BB-894, BB-896 through BB-911, BB-913 through BB-990, BB-992 through BB-1313, BB-1315 through BB-1384, BB-1389 and up. See notes 23 and 24.			
	B200C:	BL-37 and up, BP-64 and up, BU-1 through BU-10, BV-1 through BV-10, BW-1 & up. See Note 23.			

Figure 8-1-1. A Type Certificate Data Sheet showing rigging data

to define a precise procedure. However, certain principles apply in all situations and these will be discussed in this chapter. It is essential that the aircraft manufacturer's instructions be followed when rigging an aircraft.

Rigging specifications are contained in the *Type Certificate Data Sheets*. These sheets are published on every aircraft that has been type certificated. See Figure 8-1-1 for a typical Type Certificate Data Sheet. These sheets contain several types of material about the aircraft and its performance. The area of particular interest in this portion of the text is the rigging specifications. Other material will be of interest in areas such as weight and balance. This information is revised as necessary by the Federal Aviation Administration (FAA). Normally it is revised as new models of the same aircraft are produced, or engineering changes are performed.

The same information concerning the aircraft is also contained in the manufacturer's maintenance manual. The manual will also include the procedures for rigging the controls to meet these specifications. Control surface travel is an inspection item for 100 hour and annual inspections. See Figure 8-1-1.

The assembly of aircraft today is quite limited and, aside from control systems, will only involve smaller aircraft. Many smaller general aviation aircraft are built in such a manner that wings and tail surfaces can be removed from the fuselage. This will probably only occur when a component has been damaged, or if the airplane must be trucked.

Larger aircraft are difficult to disassemble. Wing sections are normally assembled to the fuselage and the sections become an integral portion of the structure. Although these aircraft can have replacement assemblies installed, they will require special equipment, including jigs and structural tools, to ensure proper alignment. Depending on the airplane, the fixtures can be quite expensive and difficult to fabricate.

The replacement of wings on fully cantilevered aircraft leave few adjustments to be made to the wing, since they are normally bolted into the structure. The replacement of control surfaces will be more common than the replacement of wings and stabilizers.

Before any removal or assembly is undertaken the maintenance manual and structural repair manual must be consulted. From the manuals you can obtain the recommended methods of lifting, blocking, and supporting the various parts during assembly. This is very important because the sections are heavy and can seriously injure someone if not supported correctly. Some of these wings may have one small adjustment to set the twist in the wing. The eccentric front wing bushing of Cessna high wing airplanes is an example of that type of adjustment.

Section 2
Control Surface Balance

Principles of Balancing or Re-balancing

The principles that are essential in the balancing or re-balancing of the control surfaces are not too difficult to understand. The principles are exactly the same as in a weight and balance problem. Weight and balance is discussed in *Introduction to Aircraft Maintenance, Chapter 10, Weight and Balance*.

An out-of-balance condition can cause damaging flutter or buffeting of an aircraft and must be eliminated. This is best accomplished by adding weights either inside or on the leading edge of the tabs, ailerons, or in the proper location on the balance panels. When this is done properly, a balanced condition exists.

Re-balancing of Movable Surfaces

The material in this section is presented for familiarization purposes only, and should not be used when re-balancing a control surface. Explicit instructions for the balancing of control surfaces will be found in the service and overhaul manuals for the specific aircraft and must be followed closely.

Any time repairs on a control surface add weight fore or aft of the hinge center line, the control surface must be re-balanced. Any control surface that is out of balance will be unstable and will not remain in a streamlined position during normal flight. For example, an aileron that is trailing-edge heavy will move down when the wing deflects upward, and up when the wing deflects downward. Such a condition can cause unexpected and violent maneuvers of the aircraft. In extreme cases, fluttering and buffeting may develop to a degree that could cause the complete loss of the aircraft.

Re-balancing a control surface concerns both static and dynamic balance. A control surface that is statically balanced will also be dynamically balanced.

Static balance. Static balance is the tendency of an object to remain stationary when supported from its own center of gravity. There are two ways in which a control surface may be out of static balance. They are called underbalance and overbalance.

When a control surface is mounted on a balance stand, a downward travel of the trailing edge above the horizontal position (Figure 8-2-1) indicates overbalance. This is designated by a minus sign. These signs show the need for more or less weight in the correct area to achieve a balanced control surface as shown in Figure 8-2-1.

A tail-heavy condition (static underbalance) causes undesirable flight performance and is

A
CHORD LINE
PLUS (+) CONDITION
TAIL DOWN UNDERBALANCE

B
CHORD LINE
MINUS (−) CONDITION
NOSE DOWN OVER BALANCE

C
CHORD LINE
LEVEL HORIZONTAL POSITION
BALANCED CONDITION

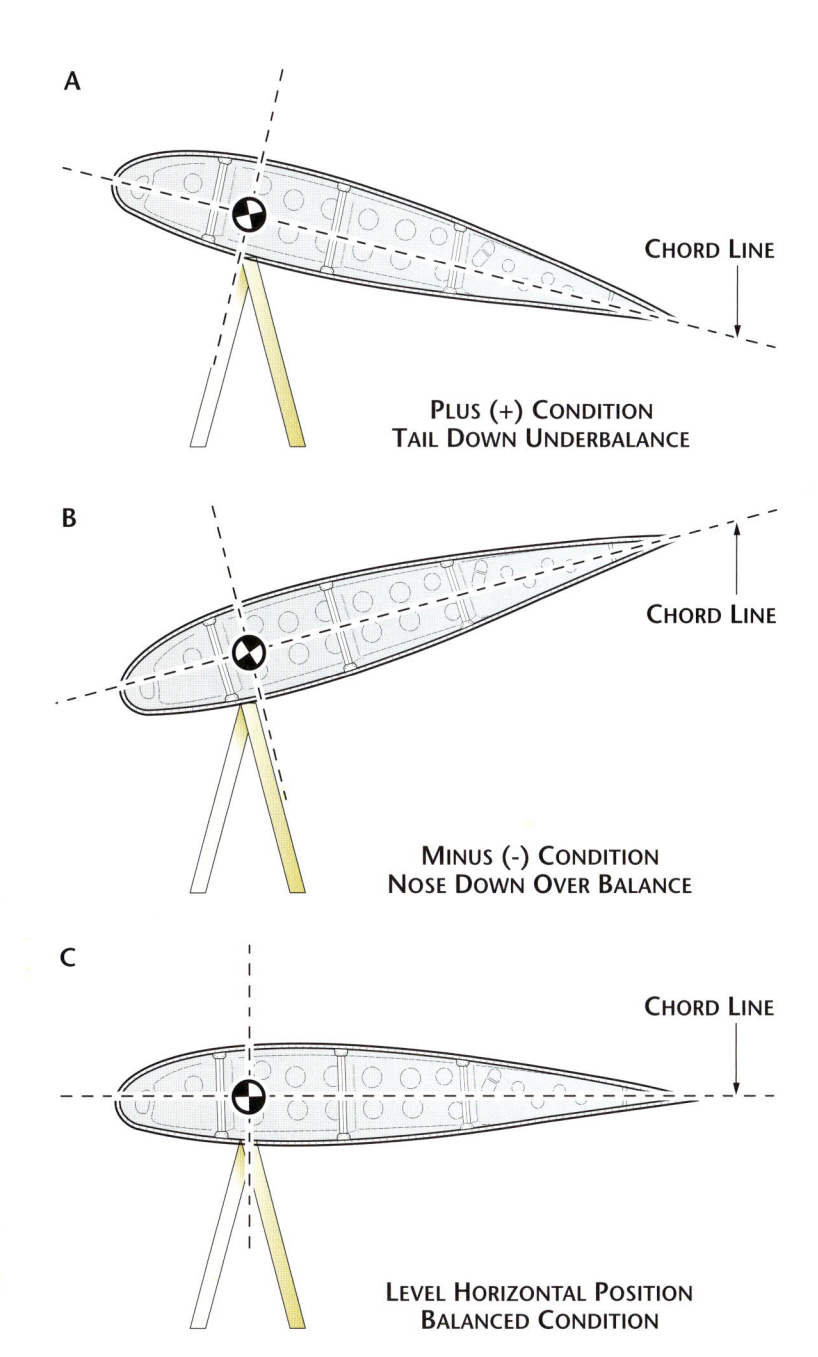

Figure 8-2-1. A control surface mounted on its balance stand

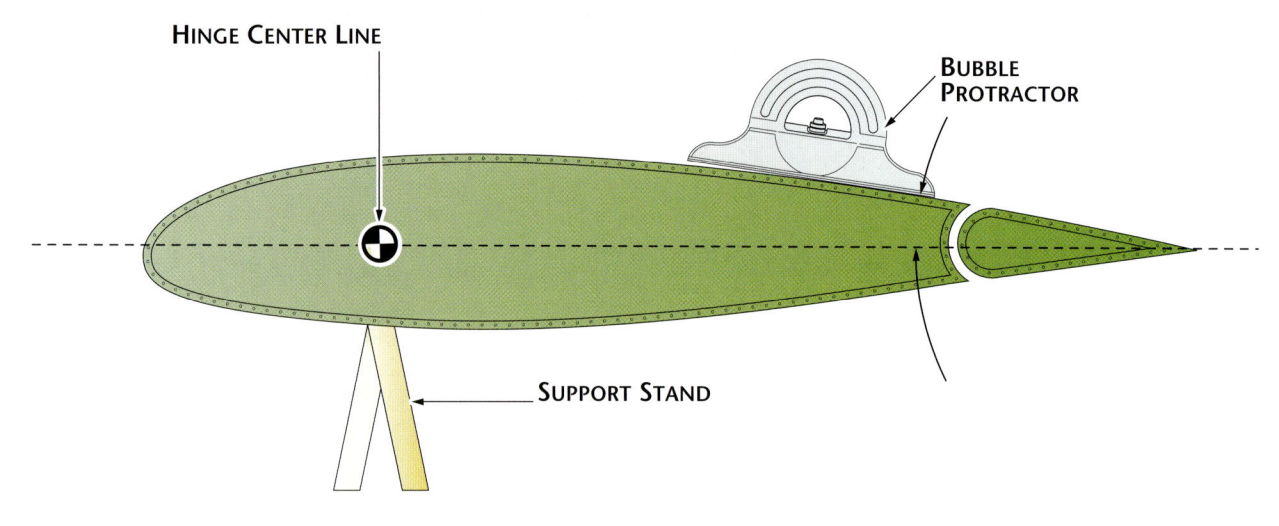

Figure 8-2-2. An aileron and its trim tab balanced in a level and streamlined position

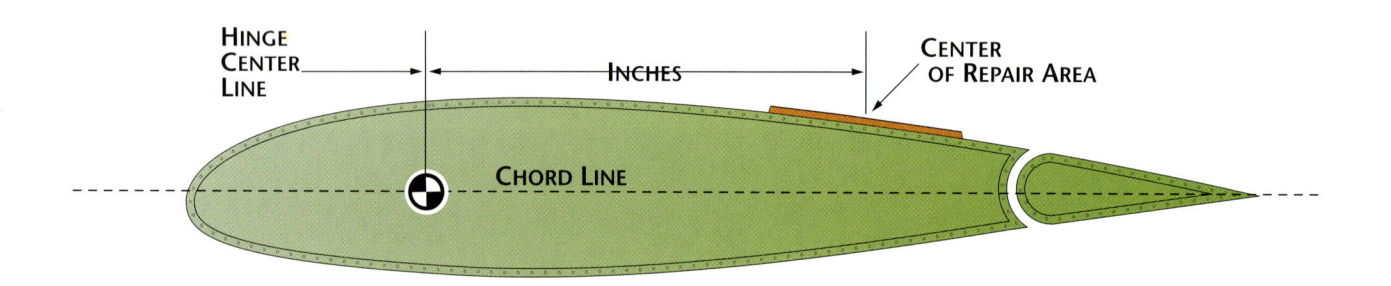

Figure 8-2-3. Calculation method measurements

not usually allowed. Better flight operations are gained by nose heaviness static overbalance. Most manufacturers design nose-heavy control surfaces.

Dynamic balance. Dynamic balance is that condition in a rotating body wherein all rotating forces are balanced within themselves so that no vibration is produced while the body is in motion. Dynamic balance as related to control surfaces is an effort to maintain balance when the control surface is submitted to movement on the aircraft in flight. It involves the placing of weights in the correct location along the span of the surfaces. The location of the weights will, in most cases, be forward of the hinge center line.

Trim tabs on the surface should be secured in the neutral position when the control surface is mounted on the stand. The stand must be level and be located in an area free of air currents. The control surface must be permitted to rotate freely about the hinge points without binding. Balance condition is determined by the behavior of the trailing edge when the surface is suspended from its hinge points. Any excessive friction would result in a false reaction as to the overbalance or underbalance of the surface.

When installing the control surface in the stand or jig, a neutral position should be established with the chord line of the surface in a horizontal position (Figure 8-2-2). Use a bubble protractor to determine the neutral position before continuing balancing procedures. Sometimes a visual check is all that is needed to determine whether the surface is balanced or unbalanced.

Any trim tabs or other assemblies that are to remain on the surface during balancing procedures should be in place. If any assemblies or parts must be removed before balancing, they should be removed.

Methods of Balancing

Several methods of balancing (re-balancing) control surfaces are in use by the various manufacturers of aircraft. The three most common methods are the calculation method, scale method, and balance beam method.

Calculation method. The calculation method of balancing a control surface is directly related to the principles of balancing discussed previously in the weight and balance section of this series. It has one advantage over the other methods in that it can be performed without removing the surface from the aircraft.

In using the calculation method, the weight of the material from the repair area and the weight of the materials used to accomplish the repair must be known. Subtracting the weight removed from the weight added will give the resulting net gain in the amount added to the surface.

The distance from the hinge center line to the center of the repair area is then measured in inches. This distance must be determined to the nearest one-hundredth of an inch (Figure 8-2-3).

The next step is to multiply the distance times the net weight of the repair. This will result in an inch-pounds (in-lbs) answer. If the in-lbs result of the calculations is within specified tolerances, the control surface will be considered balanced. If it is not within specified limits, consult the manufacturer's service manuals for the needed weights, material to use for weights, design for manufacture, and installation locations for addition of the weights.

Scale method. The scale method of balancing a control surface requires the use of a scale that is graduated in hundredths of a pound. A support stand and balancing jigs for the surface are also required. Figure 8-2-4 illustrates a control surface mounted for rebalancing purposes. The aircrafts maintenance manual will give the method for figuring corrections. Use of the scale method requires the removal of the control surface from the aircraft. The scale method is mostly reserved for large airplanes.

Balance beam method. A balance beam method is used by both Piper and Cessna Aircraft Companies. It consists of fabricating a

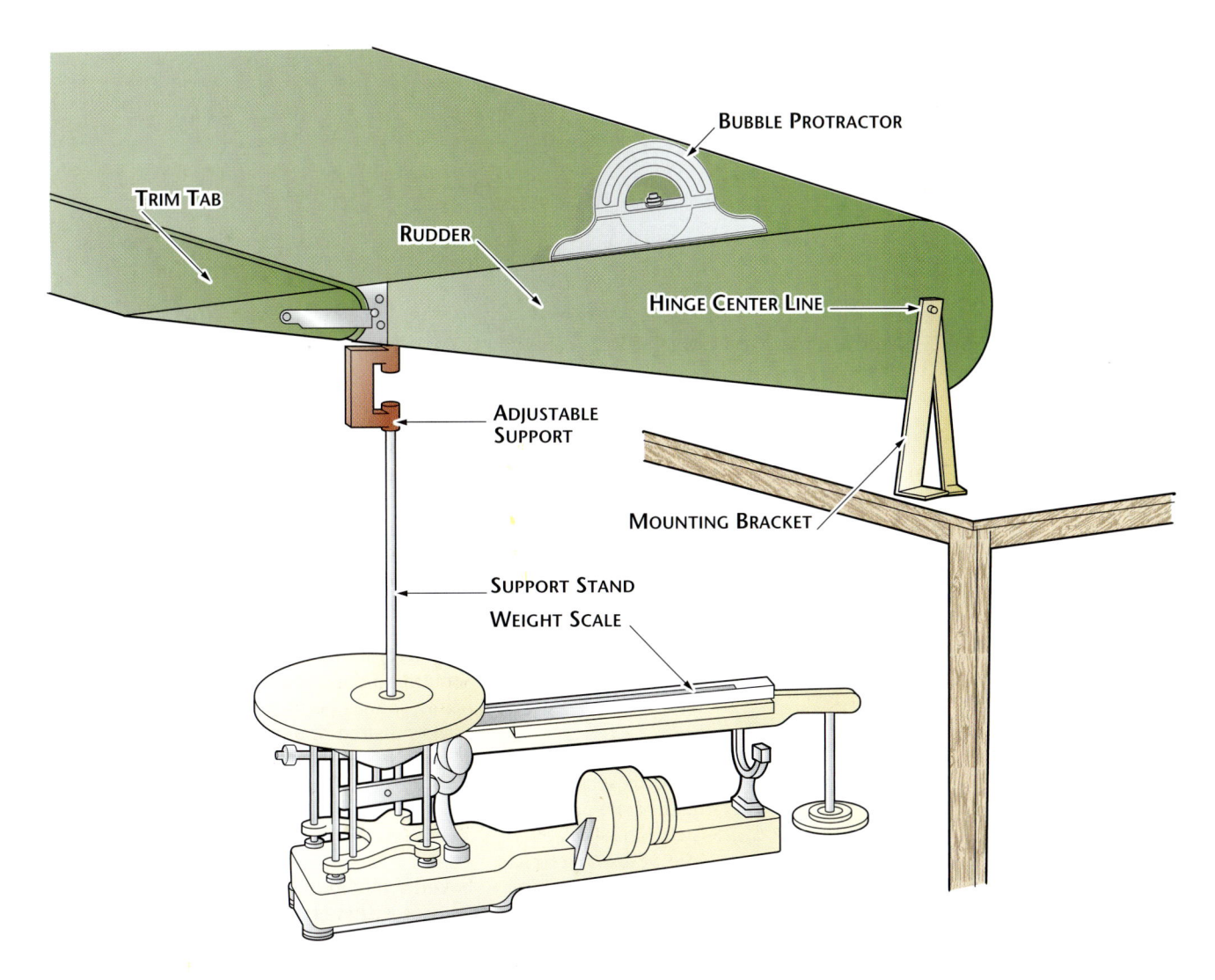

Figure 8-2-4. Scale method of checking weight behind hinge line

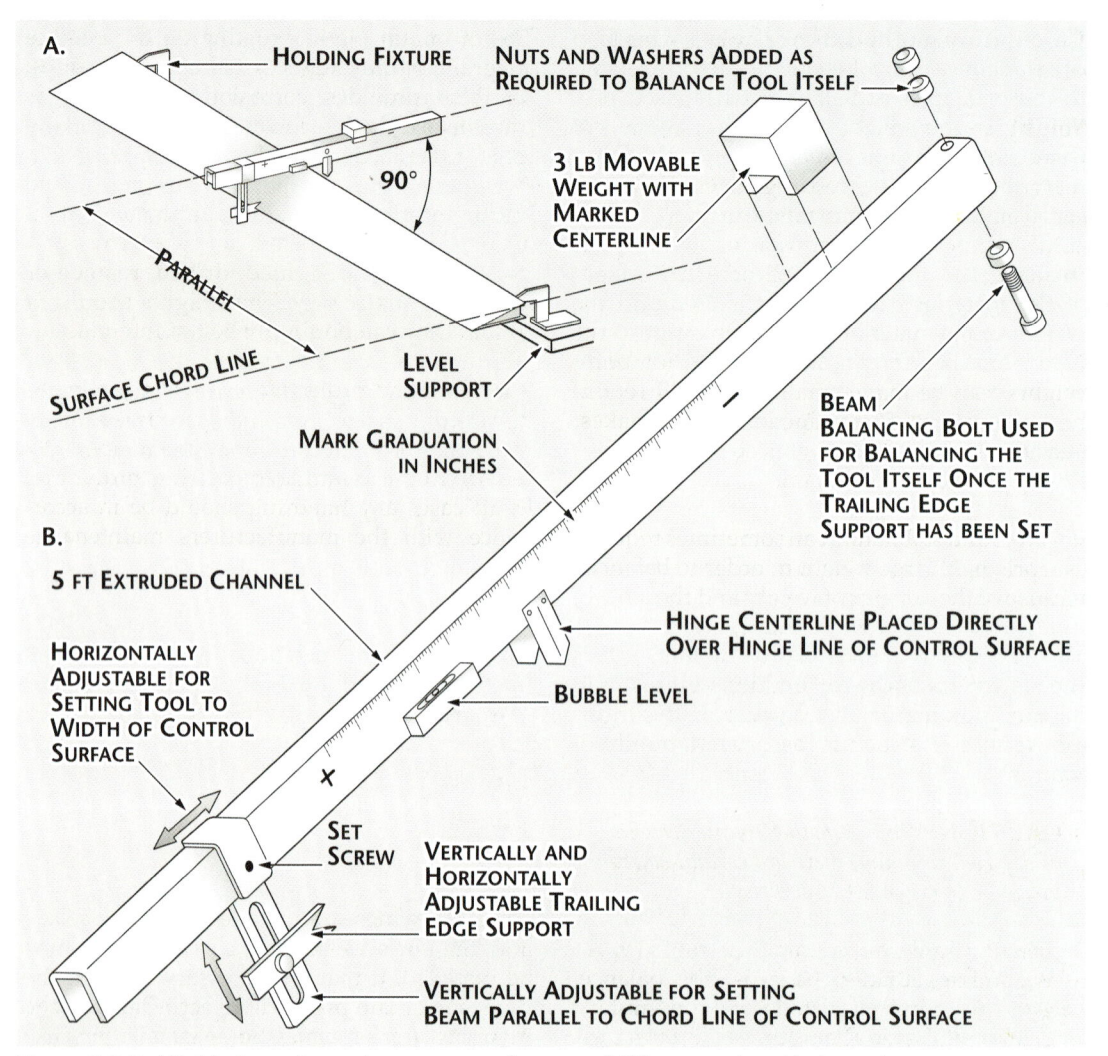

Figure 8-2-5. (A) A balance beam in use on an aileron and (B) a completed balance beam

balance beam with a sliding weight of a specific amount. See Figure 8-2-5. The aircraft maintenance manual gives specific dimensions to allow fabrication of this very specialized tool. It is also fairly easy to build.

Once the control surface is resting on the level supports, the weight required to balance can be established by moving the sliding weight. The maintenance manual will tell you what the balance point should be. If the surface is within tolerance, the balance is good. If it is out of tolerance the manual will explain where to add weight to bring it into tolerance.

A variation on the balance beam method is used by Beechcraft on the King Air line. Figure 8-2-6 shows the setup. It consists of level supports and a small bucket. When arranged as shown in Figure 8-2-6, the surface is balanced by adding water to the bucket until balance is achieved. Because the weight of the string is negligible, the bucket and its contents are simply weighed to establish the weight required to balance the surface.

Again, the maintenance manual will explain the necessity of adding or removing weight, and how much.

Control Surface Counterbalances

Aside from the aerodynamic balances designed into virtually all control surfaces, many surfaces

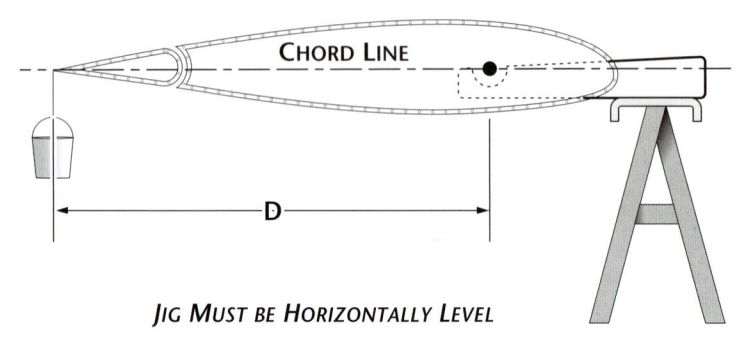

Figure 8-2-6. The King Air setup for measuring aileron balance

also use a weight system of physical counterbalances.

Weight construction. In ailerons many of these counterbalances are simply pieces of sheet steel riveted inside the leading edges. Some are lead weights that are installed in the aerodynamic counterbalance (portion of the surface ahead of the hinge line). Still others, particularly on large airplanes, use *depleted uranium* as a weight. Depleted uranium has a heavier mass than lead, therefore counterweights (or bobweights) can be made smaller and still retain the same weight. This reduction in size makes it easier to design the weights so that they are not exposed to the airstream.

Elevators and stabilators can sometimes require a surprisingly large weight in order to balance. Because of the amount of weight and the length of the arm, inspection of condition and attachment can be particularly important. Remember that a hard landing can produce a significant G force, thus making a twenty pound weight appear to the structure as several hundred pounds.

> **CAUTION:** *When handling counterweights of depleted uranium, there are certain safety precautions that must be observed.*

Depleted uranium is slightly radioactive. To minimize radiation hazards, the balance weights are cadmium plated during manufacturing. The depleted uranium would therefore normally pose no danger. That said, it should still be handled with caution. The primary hazard associated with the material is the harmful effect it could have should it enter the body. If the particles of the parent metal or its oxides are inhaled or ingested, they can be chemically toxic and cause a significant and long lasting irradiation of internal tissue.

The cadmium plating coating on the balance weights not only reduces radiation emissions, but also provides corrosion prevention, as unprotected depleted uranium corrodes fairly rapidly, producing a black, dusty oxide.

During installation, no penetration of the balance weights is permitted. The balance weights must not be sanded, filed, drilled, reamed or reworked in any way. The weights should fit so that they can be simply bolted into place.

Whenever the protective cadmium plating is breached, the weight could be removed from the aircraft or the part may be temporarily repaired by a cleaning/repainting procedure. In all cases any handling should be in accordance with the manufacturers maintenance manual.

Section 3
Control Surface Installation

Once the wings are installed on the fuselage and the surfaces balance checked, they may be installed. It may be necessary to shim the hinges to obtain proper fit in accordance to the manufacturer's manual. Some installations use special spacers or bearings with extended inner races to provide a working clearance between the attach points. If not installed correctly the surface can be damaged, or even jammed, during movement (Figure 8-3-1).

Before the aileron push-pull tube is installed, careful inspection of the control system

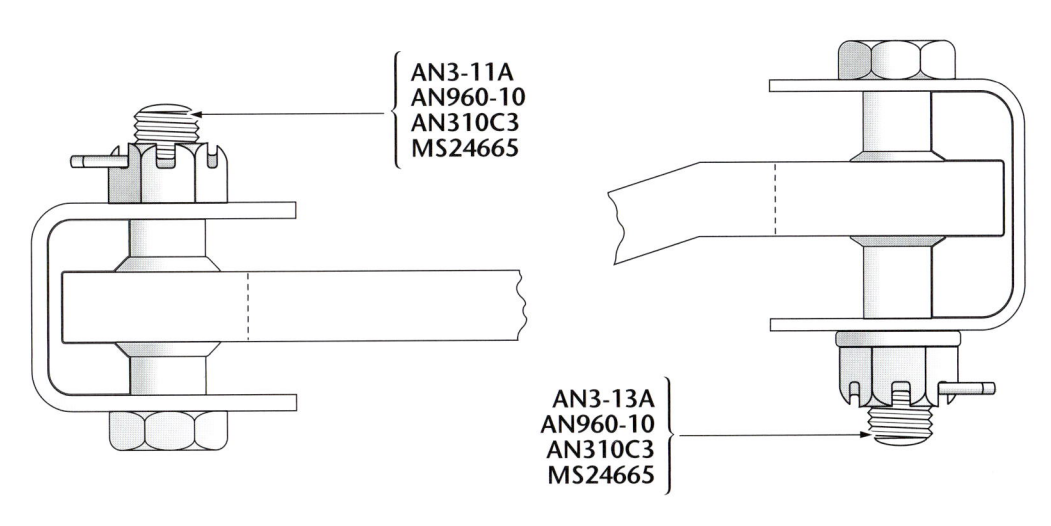

Figure 8-3-1. An example of the hardware used in control surface fitting and attachment.

8-8 | Assembly and Rigging

Ring Vernier Scale

Disk Degree Scale

Ring Adjuster

Disk-to-Ring Lock on Ring Engages Only when Zeros on Scales are Aligned

Ring-to-Frame Lock

Disk Adjuster

Frame

Ring

Disk

Corner Spirit Level on Frame

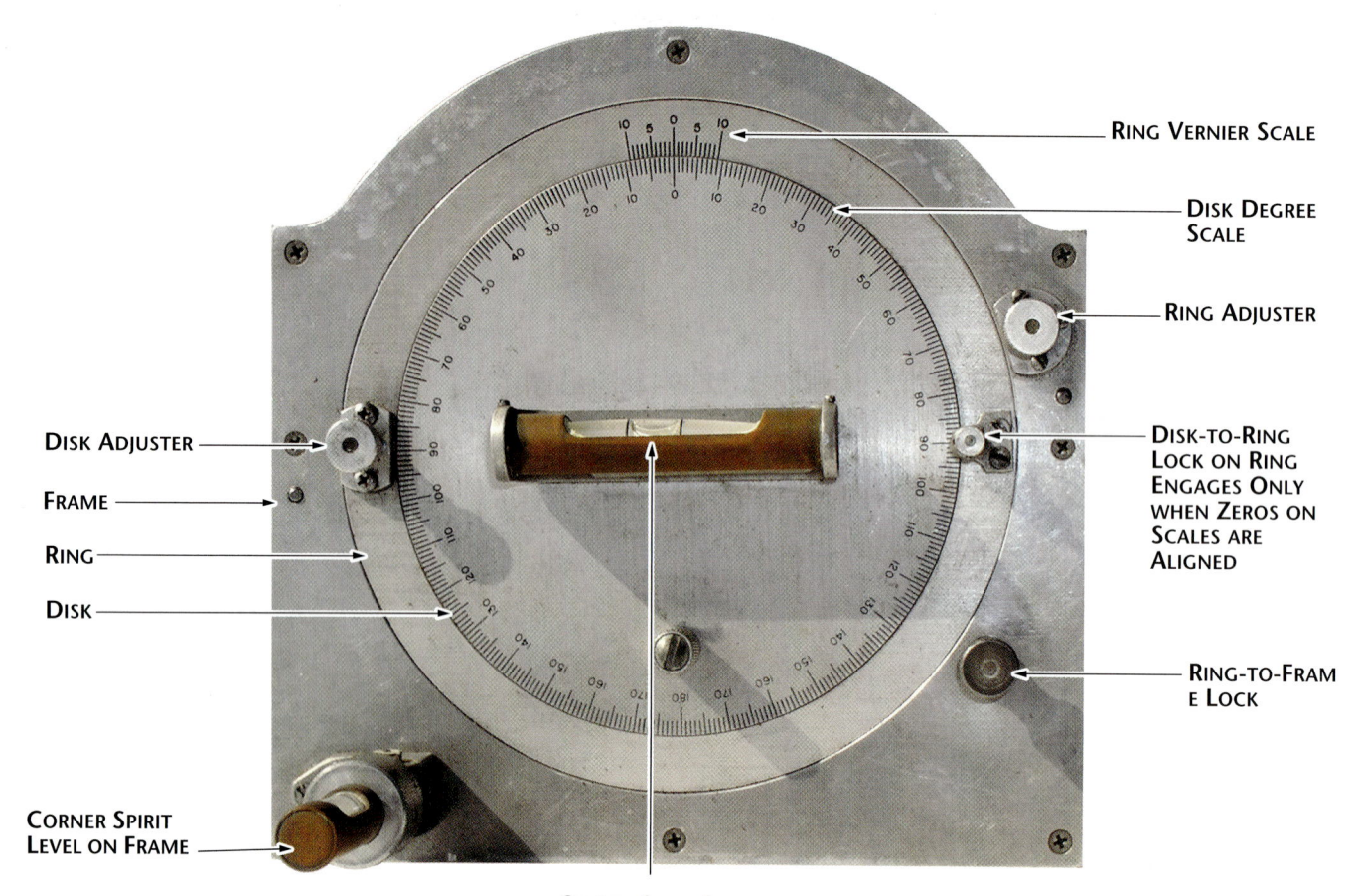

Center Spirit Level

1. With disk-to-ring lock in the deep slot, turn disk adjuster to lock disk to ring.
2. Move control surface to neutral. Place protractor on control surface and turn ring adjuster to center bubble in center spirit level (ring must be unlocked from frame).
3. Lock ring to frame with ring-to-frame lock.
4. Move control surface to extreme limit of movement.
5. Unlock disk from ring with disk-to-ring lock.
6. Turn disk adjuster to center bubble in center spirit level.
7. Read surface travel in degrees on disk and tenths of a degree on vernier scale.

Figure 8-3-2. A standard propeller protractor

should be made to determine that the cables are routed properly. It is easy to get a pair of cables crossed when they run under a floorboard, or over a headliner. Check that the quadrant chains on the control column have the proper number of links in each direction (centered).

Besides the direct cable, there will be a balance cable between the two ailerons. The balance cable is necessary because all cable controls must pull. When the control cable pulls a surface down, the balance cable pulls the surface on the other side up.

Once the cables are checked out, the aileron control tube may be hooked up. Hooking the pushrod up is another place where correct hardware installation is a must. Operating clearances are frequently close and the incorrect hardware can cause severe binding. Check the IPB for the correct hardware and it's stackup (order of installation).

Surface Travel Measurement

Once the ailerons have been correctly installed and the control system connected, they can be rigged.

The tools for measuring surface travel include protractors, rigging fixtures, contour templates, and degree plates, or fixtures.

Bubble protractors are the principal tools used for measuring angles in degrees. Unlike most other precision tools, protractors do not have a calibration or certification procedure. However, in the case of a bubble protractor there is a method to check it for accuracy. Do the following steps:

1. Place the protractor on a clean, flat, level surface.
2. Adjust the protractor to read 0°.
3. Mark the level surface where the ends of the protractor are located.
4. Look at the bubble and, using masking tape and a very sharp pencil, mark where the bubble falls.
5. Pick the protractor up and reverse it 180°, setting it down on the level surface and aligning the marks you just made.
6. Look at the bubble again. If the bubble aligns with the marks on the masking tape, the level is accurate.

If the bubble will not fall within the marks, sometimes the vial can be adjusted. If the tool will not allow for adjustment, get one that will.

One tool that can be used to measure aileron, elevator, or wing flap travel is the *universal propeller protractor* (Figure 8-3-2). Although the design is over fifty years old, they are still available today, and they are infinitely adjustable. Operation of a propeller protractor to measure control surface travel is covered in *Introduction to Aircraft Maintenance*, Chapter 4, Tools and Techniques.

Newer laser levels are available that can also do an excellent job in specific places. They are not ideal for finding level, but are very good at shooting a horizontal or vertical level line. They will be covered later in this chapter.

The actual rigging process for most ailerons requires the rigging to be done in the neutral position. The control column must be locked in neutral and the ailerons are normally set even with the trailing edge of the wing. On some aircraft the control column may be held in neutral by the gust lock. On others a board may be clamped between the two columns to hold the neutral position. The same procedure will work for centering rudder pedals; a short board and clamps.

Some aircraft are adjusted with both ailerons drooping a little below the trailing edge of the wing; particularly on cable operated systems. Once in flight the air load under the ailerons puts upward pressure on the surfaces and removes all the slack in the control cables. The aileron trailing edge and the wing streamline nicely. If this is required, it should be accounted for in the procedure. Another factor in establishing neutral that must be accounted for are the flaps. If the flaps are not all the way up the trailing edge position will be off. Therefore it is good policy to adjust the flaps first.

Once the positions are established, the cables may be tightened to the proper tension. Usually the balance cable and the direct cables will be tightened simultaneously because they are a closed loop. Therefore tightening or loosening one cable will also affect the other two. Generally the cables that hold the ailerons from dropping down are adjusted first. Rig the ailerons just a little bit higher than they need to be, then adjust the tension with the third cable.

After the cables are properly adjusted, the travel is checked. This can be accomplished using the tools previously discussed. Once the travel is established and the aileron stops adjusted, the rigging must be properly safetied. This includes the cotter pins in the hinge bolts or pins, counting the exposed threads on the turnbuckles, checking the thread engagement safety hole in the turnbuckle barrel, and of course, the safety wire.

The last step in any rigging process is to determine that the control surface movement is correct. Due to the fact that two cables go to each aileron they are very easy to rig backwards, and get the cables crossed. Several accidents have been caused by this oversight.

Flaps

Because of the wide variations in flap designs and the size of aircraft on which they are installed, a typical flap installation would be difficult to describe.

The simplest flap systems are manually operated. These may be actuated with the use of cables, torque tubes, or both, depending on the design. Most currently manufactured airplane designs have electric motor driven flap systems. These are usually driven by torque tubes and drive chain. A typical light aircraft flap system in its rigging position is shown in Figure 8-3-3.

Figure 8-3-3. Using a flap positioning tool on a King Air 90

Figure 8-3-4. A wire braced empennage on an older light airplane

Figure 8-3-5. A stabilator on a Boeing 717 showing the amount of total movement

Larger flap systems are operated by hydraulic power. These can use actuators, or be driven by hydraulic motors and torque tubes.

Empennage

External bracing. Brace wires are used on some of the older light aircraft to reinforce the stabilizer and vertical fin. These normally run from each side of the vertical fin to the stabilizer and from the stabilizer to the fuselage. See Figure 8-3-4 for a view. These require tension setting and the stabilizer must be kept level to avoid over-tension.

Cantilevered. The tail surfaces on most aircraft built today are bolted to the fuselage without any adjustments. Adjustments are not necessary unless the structure is damaged and repaired incorrectly. In this case adjustments may not be possible without additional repairs.

With a cantilevered vertical surface many airplanes use a moveable horizontal stabilizer, or *stabilator*. Stabilators are not just relegated to the small airplane segment. They are used on many transport category aircraft, as shown in Figure 8-3-5.

Most light aircraft stabilators are cable operated and use an arm/lever system to provide the actual control input. Most transport category systems use an electrically operated jackscrew. The jackscrew actuator(s) are controlled by a cable operated system of inputs.

Section 4
Control Cables

Most aircraft control systems use cable for control movements. Manufactured to federal specifications, the cable is made of either carbon steel or corrosion resistant steel. Corrosion resistant steel cable is not as strong as carbon steel cable, but will not corrode as rapidly. This is important in applications where outside elements are a factor.

The construction of the cable varies with the application. Basically there are three types of cable used. These are non-flexible, flexible, and extra flexible. Figure 8-4-1 gives a table showing the various specifications of different cables.

Non-flexible cable. The nonflexible steel cables are of the 1 by 7 or 1 by 19 construction according to the diameter. The 1 by 7 cable consists of six wires laid around a center wire in a counterclockwise direction. The 1 by 19 cable consists of a layer of six wires laid around a center wire in a clockwise direction plus twelve wires laid around the inner strand in a counterclockwise direction. Nineteen wires would be stiff and would not be suitable for making turns as would be required for control surface movement.

Flexible cable. The flexible cable is known as 7 by 7 cable. The 7 by 7 cable consists of six strands, of seven wires each, laid around a center strand of seven wires. This cable is capable of shallow bends but cannot make sharp turns over small pulleys.

Extra flexible cable. The 7 by 19 cable consists of six strands laid around a center strand in a clockwise direction. The wires composing the seven individual strands are laid around a center wire in two layers. Because of this construction the cable is easily bent to make turns and bend over pulleys. This cable is all pre-formed, meaning that the wires and strands are shaped prior to making the cable.

The 6 by 19 cable consists of six strands of 19 wires each, laid around a 7 by 7 cable core. This cable is found in nominal diameters of 7/16 inch to 1-1/2 inches, it is equal in corrosion resistance and superior in non-magnetic and expansion properties to the other cables.

Nylon-coated Cables

Nylon-coated cable is made by extruding a flexible nylon coating over corrosion-resistant steel (CRES) cable. The bare CRES cable must conform and be qualified to MIL-W-83420. After coating, the jacketed cable must still conform to MIL-W-83420.

The service life of nylon-coated cable is much greater than the service life of the same cable when used bare. Most cable wear occurs at pulleys where the cable bends. Wear is caused by friction between strands and between wires. In bare cable, this is aggravated by dirt and grit working its way into the cable; and the lubricant working its way out leaving dry, dirty wires rubbing against each other. In long, straight runs of cable, vibration work hardens

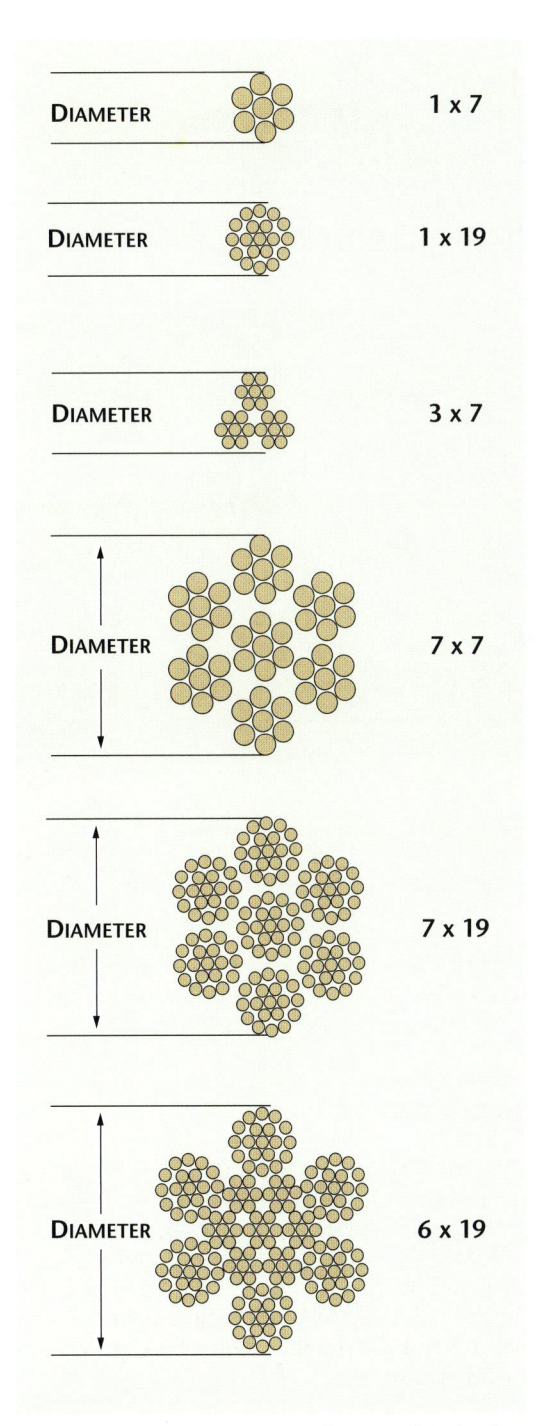

Figure 8-4-1. Cross sections of various kinds of cable

COPPER SLEEVE PART NUMBERS AND DIMENSIONS

Cable Size	Copper Oval Sleeve Stock No.		Manual Tool No.	Sleeve Length Before Compression (approx. inches)	Sleeve Length After Compression (approx. inches)	Number of Presses	Tested Strength (pounds)
	Plain	Plated*					
3/64	18-11-B4	28-11-B4	51-B4-887	3/8	7/16	1	340
1/16	18-1-C	28-1-C	51-C-887	3/8	7/16	1	550
3/32	18-2-G	28-2-G	51-G-887	7/16	1/2	1	1,180
1/8	18-3-M	28-3-M	51-M-850	9/16	3/4	3	2,300
5/32	18-4-P	28-4P	51-P-850	5/8	7/8	3	3,050
3/16	18-6-X	28-6-X	51-X-850	1	1 1/4	4	4,350
7/32	18-8-F2	28-8-F2	51-F2-850	7/8	1 1/16	4	5,790
1/4	18-10-F6	28-10-F6	3-F6-950	1 1/8	1 1/2	3	7,180
5/16	18-13-G9	28-13-G9	3-G9-950	1 1/4	1 5/8	3	11,130
			N 635 Hydraulic Tool Dies				
3/8	18-23-H5	28-23-H5	Oval H5	1 1/2	1 7/8	1	16,800
7/16	18-24-J8	28-24-J8	Oval J8	1 3/4	2 1/8	2	19,700
1/2	18-25-K8	28-25-K8	Oval K8	1 7/8	2 1/2	2	25,200
9/16	18-27-M1	28-27-M1	Oval M1	2	2 5/8	3	31,025
5/8	18-28-N5	28-28-N5	Oval N5	2 3/8	3 1/8	3	39,200

*Required on stainless cables due to electrolysis caused by different types of metals.

Table 8-4-1. Copper sleeve part numbers and dimensions

COPPER STOP SLEEVES AND DIMENSIONS

Cable Size (inches)	Sleeve No.	Tool No.	Sleeve	Sleeve	Tested Strength (pounds)
3/64	871-12-B4	51-B4-887	7/32	11/64	280
1/16	871-1-C	51-C-887	7/32	13/64	525
3/32	871-17-J (Yellow)	51-MJ	5/16	21/64	600
1/8	S71-18-J (Red)	51-MJ	5/16	21/64	800
5/32	871-19-M	51-MJ	5/16	27/64	1,200
3/16	871-20-M (Black)	51-MJ	5/16	27/64	1,600
7/32	871-22-M	51-MJ	5/8	7/16	2,300
1/4	871-23-F6	3-F6-950	11/16	21/32	3,500
5/16	871-26-F6	3-F6-950	11/16	21/32	3,800

Note: All stop sleeves are plain copper. Certain sizes are colored for identification.

Table 8-4-2. Copper stop sleeves and dimensions

the wires causing the brittle wires to fracture with eventual failure of the cable.

The nylon-jacket protects the cable in a threefold manner. It keeps the lubricant from oozing out and evaporating, it keeps dirt and grit out, and it dampens the vibrations, thereby, greatly reducing their effect on the cable.

Cable replacement. It is almost always better to replace a cable with one already fabricated, i.e. new. After allowing for material and fabrication cost, new cables are generally less expensive. They also fit correctly the first time.

Replace control cables when they become worn, distorted, corroded, or otherwise damaged. If spare cables are not available, prepare exact duplicates of the damaged cable. Use materials of the same size and quality as the original. Standard swaged cable terminals develop the full cable strength and may be substituted for the original terminals wherever practical. The smallest cable size for primary controls is 1/8 inch.

Cable Fittings and Splices

Woven splice. Originally the hand woven 5-tuck splice was used almost exclusively for aircraft cable. This method was very time consuming and produced only 75 percent of the original cable strength. The five-tuck splice is rarely seen except on some antique aircraft where efforts are made to keep the originality.

Nicopress process. The Nicopress process uses copper sleeves that are strong enough to allow the cable to be used at full rated cable strength provided a thimble is used.

Before undertaking a nicopress splice, determine the proper tool and sleeve for the cable to be used. Refer to Table 8-4-1 and Table 8-4-2 for details on sleeves, tools, and the number of presses required for the various sizes of aircraft cable. The tool must be in good working condition and properly adjusted to ensure a satisfactory splice.

To compress a sleeve, have it well centered in the tool groove with the major axis of the sleeve at right angles to the tool. If the sleeve appears to be out of line after the press is started, open the tool, re-center the sleeve, and complete the press.

Thimble-eye splice. Before undertaking a thimble-eye splice, initially position the cable so the end will extend slightly beyond the sleeve, as the sleeve will elongate somewhat

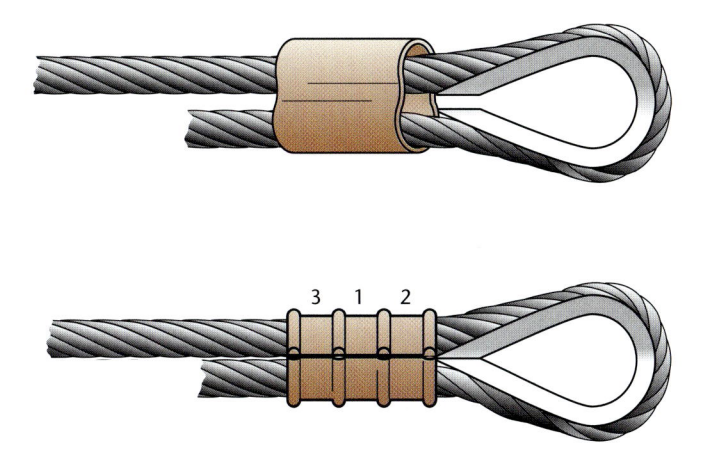

Figure 8-4-2. Compressing a copper sleeve: before and after

when it is compressed. If the cable end is inside the sleeve, the splice may not hold the full strength of the cable. It is desirable that the oval sleeve be placed in close proximity to the thimble points, so that when compressed, the sleeve will contact the thimble as shown in Figure 8-4-2. The sharp ends of the thimble may be cut off before being used; however, make certain the thimble is firmly secured in the cable loop after the splice has been completed. When using a sleeve requiring three compressions, make the center compression first, the compression next to the thimble second, and the one farthest from the thimble last.

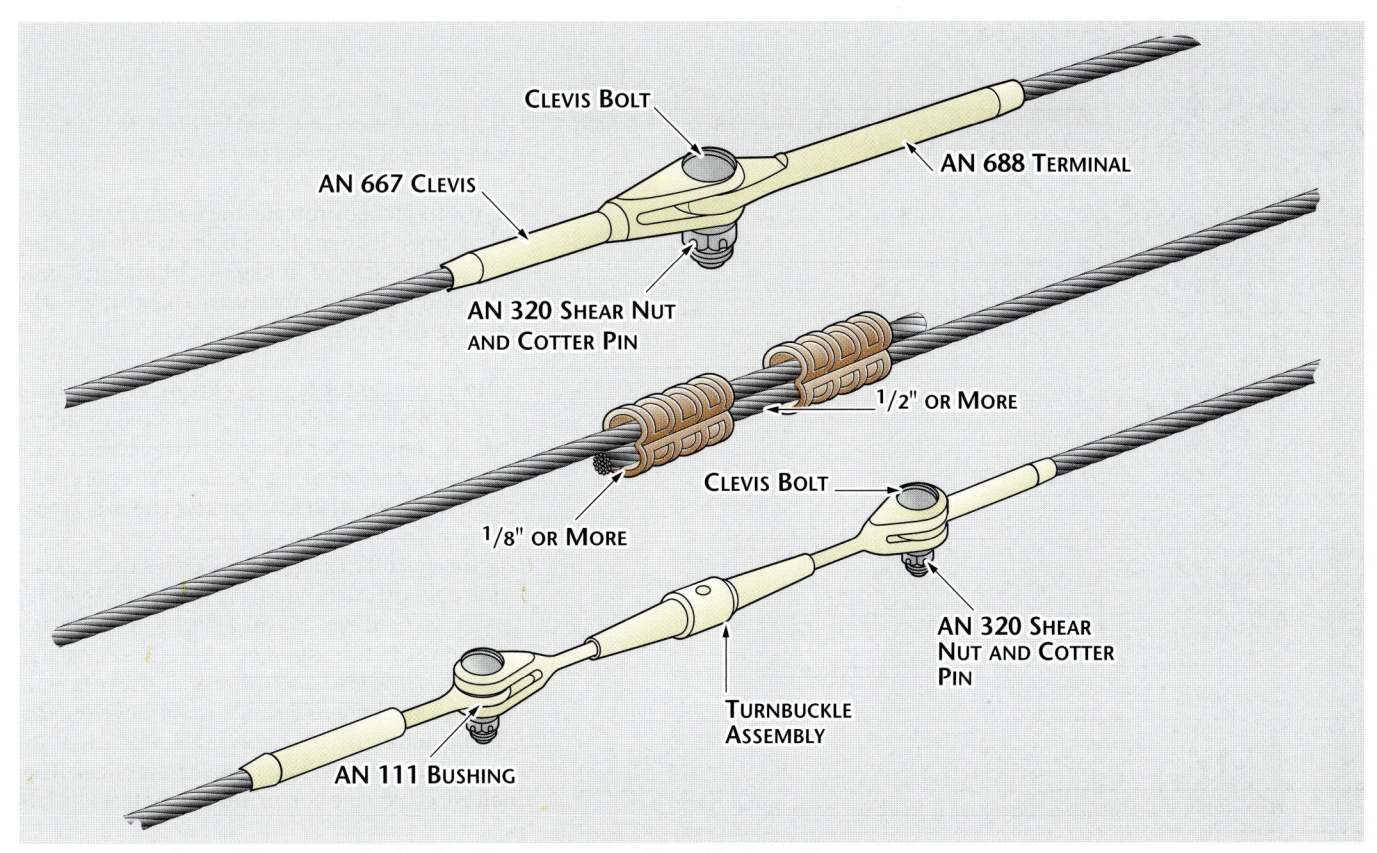

Figure 8-4-3. Three different methods of making an acceptable cable lap splice

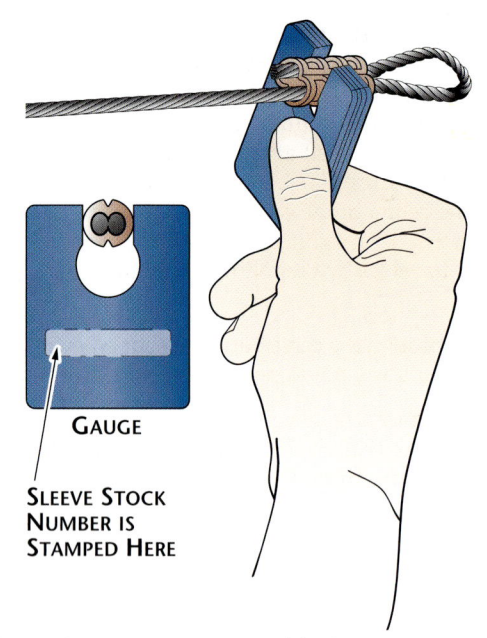

Figure 8-4-4. Using a gauge block to check sleeve compression

are installed in the same manner as nicopress oval sleeves.

> **NOTE:** *All stop sleeves are plain copper. Certain sizes are colored for identification.*

Terminal gauge. To make a satisfactory copper sleeve installation, it is important that the amount of sleeve pressure be kept uniform. The completed sleeves should be checked periodically with the proper gauge. Hold the gauge so that it contacts the major axis of the sleeve. The compressed portion at the center of the sleeve should enter the gauge opening with very little clearance, as shown in Figure 8-4-4. If it does not, the tool must be adjusted accordingly.

Other applications. The preceding information regarding copper oval sleeves and stop sleeves is based on tests made with flexible aircraft cable. The sleeves may also be used on wire ropes of other construction, if each specific type of cable is proof-tested initially. Because of variation in rope strengths, grades, construction, and actual diameters, the test is necessary to insure proper selection of materials, the correct pressing procedure, and an adequate margin of safety for the intended use.

Swage-type terminals. Swage-type terminals, manufactured in accordance with AN and MS standards, are suitable for use in civil aircraft up to, and including, maximum cable loads. When swaging tools are used, it is important that all the manufacturers' instructions, including "go" and "no-go" dimensions, be followed in detail to avoid defective and inferior swaging.

Lap splice. Lap or running splices may also be made with copper oval sleeves, turnbuckles, or swaged cable eyes. When making such splices, it is usually necessary to use two sleeves to develop the full strength of the cable. The sleeves should be positioned as shown in Figure 8-4-3. As in the case of eye splices, it is desirable to have the cable ends extend beyond the sleeves sufficiently to allow for the increased length of the compressed sleeves.

Stop sleeves. Stop sleeves may be used for special cable end and intermediate fittings. They

Cable Size (inches)	Wire Strands	BEFORE SWAGING					AFTER SWAGING	
		Outside Diameter	Bore Diameter	Bore Length	Swaging Length	Minimum Breaking Strength (lbs)	Shank Diameter*
1/16	7x7	0.160	0.078	1.042	0.969	480	0.138
3/32	7x7	0.218	0.109	1.261	1.188	920	0.190
1/8	7x19	0.250	0.141	1.511	1.438	2,000	0.219
5/32	7x19	0.297	0.172	1.761	1.688	2,800	0.250
3/16	7x19	0.359	0.203	2.011	1.938	4,200	0.313
7/32	7x19	0.427	0.234	2.261	2.188	5,600	0.375
1/4	7x19	0.494	0.265	2.511	2.438	7,000	0.438
9/32	7x19	0.563	0.297	2.761	2.688	8,000	0.500
5/16	7x19	0.635	0.328	3.011	2.938	9,800	0.563
3/8	7x19	0.703	0.390	3.510	3.438	14,400	0.625
Note: Use gauges in kit for checking diameters.								

Table 8-4-3. Straight shanked dimensions for swaged terminals

Assembly and Rigging | 8-15

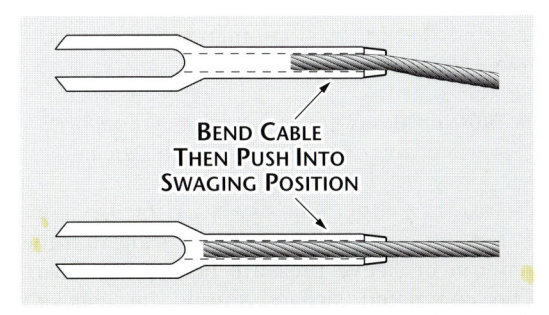

Figure 8-4-5. Cable insertion into swaged terminals

Observance of all instructions should result in a terminal developing the full-rated strength of the cable. Critical dimensions, both before and after swaging, are shown in Table 8-4-3.

Terminals. When swaging terminals onto cable ends, observe the following procedures:

1. Cut the cable to the proper length allowing for growth during swaging. Apply a preservative compound to the cable ends before insertion into the terminal barrel.

   NOTE: *Never solder cable ends to prevent fraying, since the presence of the solder will greatly increase the tendency of the cable to pull out of the terminal.*

2. Insert the cable into the terminal approximately 1 inch, and bend toward the terminal, then push the cable end entirely into the terminal barrel. The bending action puts a kink or bend in the cable end, and provides enough friction to hold the terminal in place until the swaging operation can be performed. Bending also tends to separate the strands inside the barrel, thereby reducing the strain on them.

   NOTE: *If the terminal is drilled completely through, push the cable into the terminal until it reaches the approximate position shown in Figure 8-4-5. If the hole is not drilled through, insert the cable until the end rests against the bottom of the hole.*

3. Accomplish the swaging operation in accordance with the instructions furnished by the manufacturer of the swaging equipment.

4. Inspect the terminal after swaging to determine that it is free from the die marks and splits, and is not out-of-round. Check for cable slippage in the terminal and for cut or broken wire strands.

5. Using a *"go no-go"* gauge or a micrometer, check the terminal shank diameter as shown in Figure 8-4-6 and Table 8-4-3.

6. Test the cable by proof-loading it to 60 percent of its rated breaking strength.

Swaged ball terminals. On some aircraft cables, swaged ball terminals are used for attaching cables to quadrants and special connections where space is limited. Single shank terminals are generally used at the cable ends, and double shank fittings may be used at either the end or in the center of the cable. Dies are supplied with the swaging machines for attaching these terminals to cables by the following method:

1. The steel balls and shanks have a hole through the center, and are slipped over the cable and positioned in the desired location.

2. Perform the swaging operation in accordance with the instructions furnished by the manufacturer of the swaging equipment.

3. Check the swaged fitting with a "go no-go" gauge to see that the fitting is properly compressed, and inspect the physical condition of the finished terminal. (See Figure 8-4-6.)

Cable slippage in terminal. Ensure that the cable is properly inserted in the terminal after the swaging operation is completed. Instances have been noted where only 1/4-inch of the cable was swaged in the terminal. Observance of the following precautions should minimize this possibility.

Measure the length of the terminal end of the fitting to determine the proper length of cable to be inserted into the barrel of the fitting.

Lay off this length at the end of the cable and mark with masking tape. Since the tape will not slip, it will provide a positive marking during the swaging process.

After swaging, check the tape marker to make certain that the cable did not slip during the swaging operation. See Figure 8-4-7.

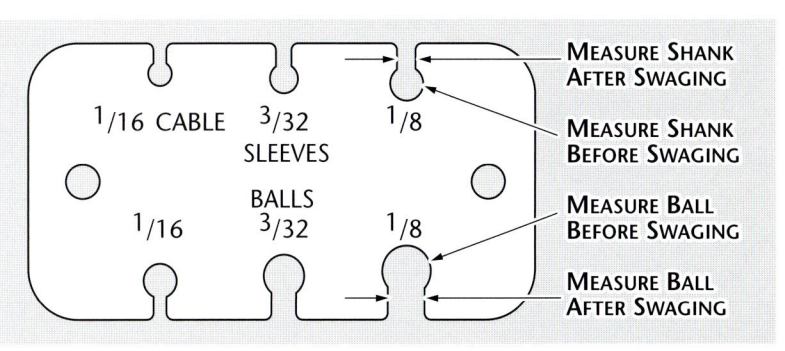

Figure 8-4-6. A go no-go gauge for swaging a ball terminal

Figure 8-4-7. Swaged terminal with slippage mark

(A) (B) (C) (D) (E)

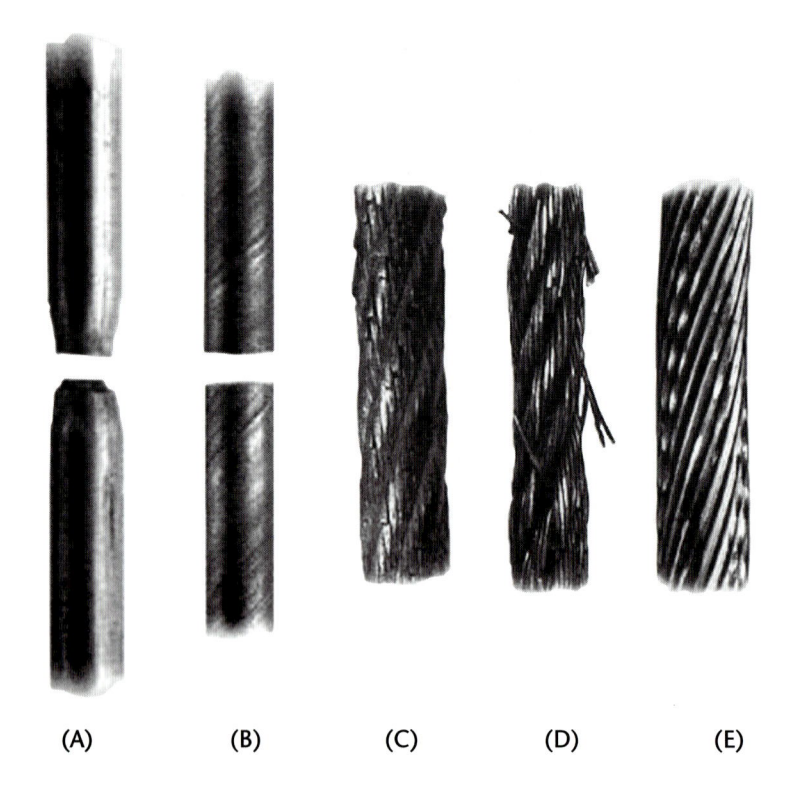

Figure 8-4-8. Typical cable wear patterns

Remove the tape and paint the junction of the swaged fitting and cable with red paint.

At all subsequent service inspections of the swaged fitting, check for a gap in the painted section to see if cable slippage has occurred.

Proof testing. When new cables are made using either the nicopress or swaged terminals, the cables should go through a *proof* or *load test*. This is conducted by slowly placing a load up to 60 percent of the rated breaking strength of the cable. Once this load is obtained it should be held for 3 to 4 minutes. A proof test fixture is not a normal fixture available to the average maintenance facility. They are time consuming to fabricate and operate. At the same time a cable proof test fixture must be completely safe to operate. A cable under several tons of tension can do severe damage should it come unfastened while under tension.

As part of the maintenance inspections of the aircraft, the control cables are inspected. This is done by rubbing the cables with a rag to indicate any broken wires. After the initial wiping of the cable, it can be visually inspected. Particular attention should be given to areas where the cable passes over fairleads, pulleys, and quad-

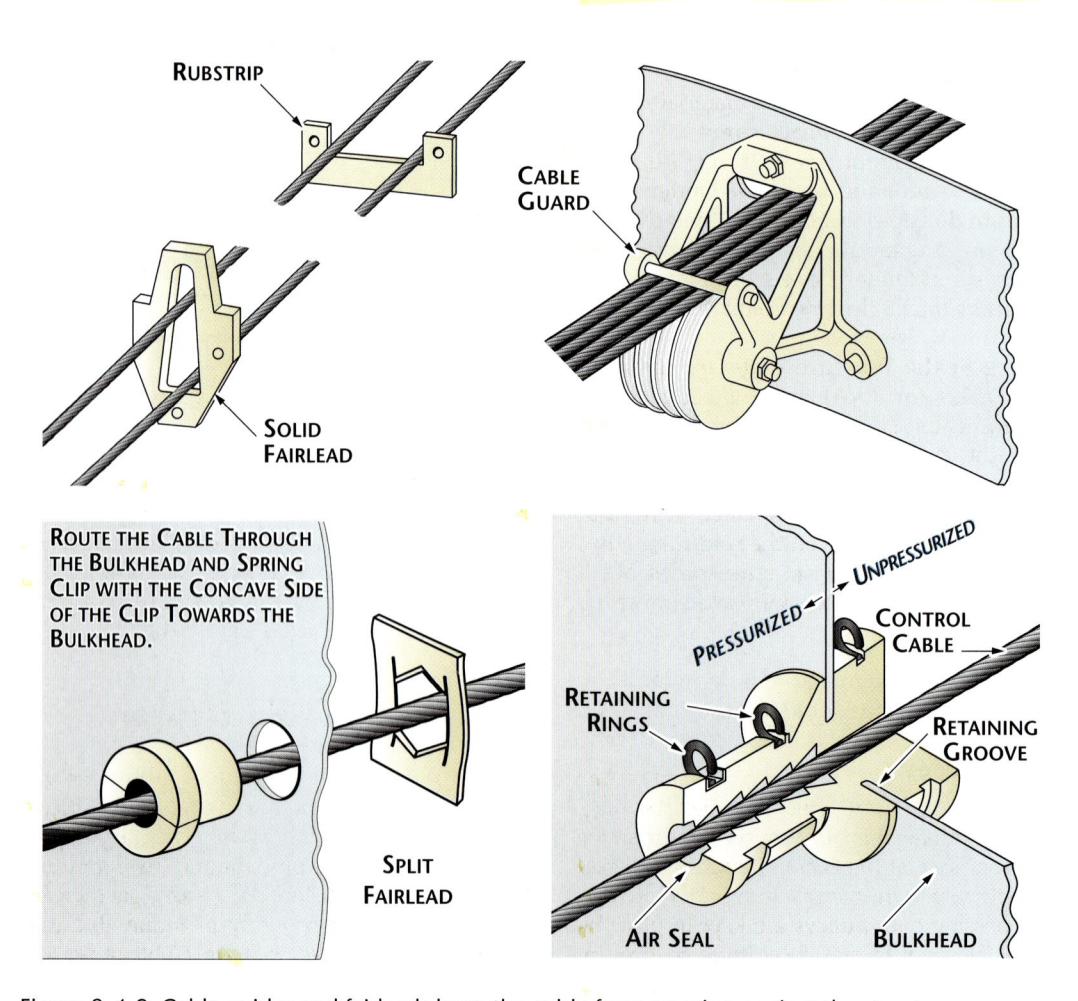

Figure 8-4-9. Cable guides and fairleads keep the cable from wearing against the structure.

rants for wear on the outside of the cable. Figure 8-4-8 shows typical wear patterns: (A) - tensile failure, (B) - fatigue break, (C) - repeated bending over pulley, (D) - fatigue failure, (E) - strand nicking - single strand broken out.

In addition to the wear factors on the outside of the cable, extensive wear can occur within the cable. This is caused by internal rubbing of the individual wires when the cable makes sharp bends around the cable. These areas cannot be seen by normal visual inspection.

Although wear is one of the factors that deteriorates the cable, it is also subject to corrosion. Special attention should be given to areas such as battery compartments, wheel wells, and lavatories where cables may pass through. Normally these are prime areas for corrosion which often occurs within the cable. The cables are often treated with Par-al-ketone to protect the cable from moisture and corrosion.

FAA AC 43.13-1B Change 1, Chapter 7 contains additional information on cable mechanics.

Cable Guides

Cable guides (Figure 8-4-9) consist primarily of *fairleads*, *pressure seals*, and *pulleys*. A fairlead may be made from a nonmetallic material such as phenolic, nylon, or a metallic material such as soft aluminum. The fairlead completely encircles the cable where it passes through holes in bulkheads or other metal parts. Fairleads are used to guide cables in a straight line through or between structural members of the aircraft. Fairleads should never deflect the alignment of a cable more than 3 degrees from a straight line.

Pressure seals. Pressure seals are installed where cables (or rods) move through pressure bulkheads. The seal grips tightly enough to prevent excess air pressure loss but not enough to hinder movement of the cable. Pressure seals should be inspected at regular intervals to determine that the retaining rings are in place. If a retaining ring comes off, it may slide along the cable and cause jamming of a pulley.

Control Cable Pulleys

Pulleys are used to guide, and to change the direction of, cable movement. Pulley bearings are sealed, and need no lubrication other than the lubrication done at the factory. Brackets fastened to the structure of the aircraft support the pulleys. Cables passing over pulleys are kept in place by guards. The guards are close-fitting to prevent jamming or to prevent the cables from slipping off when they slacken due to temperature variations.

EXCESSIVE CABLE TENSION

PULLEY TOO LARGE FOR CABLE

FROZEN BEARING

WEAR MARK

PULLEY MISALIGNMENT

WEAR MARK

CABLE MISALIGNMENT

NORMAL CONDITION

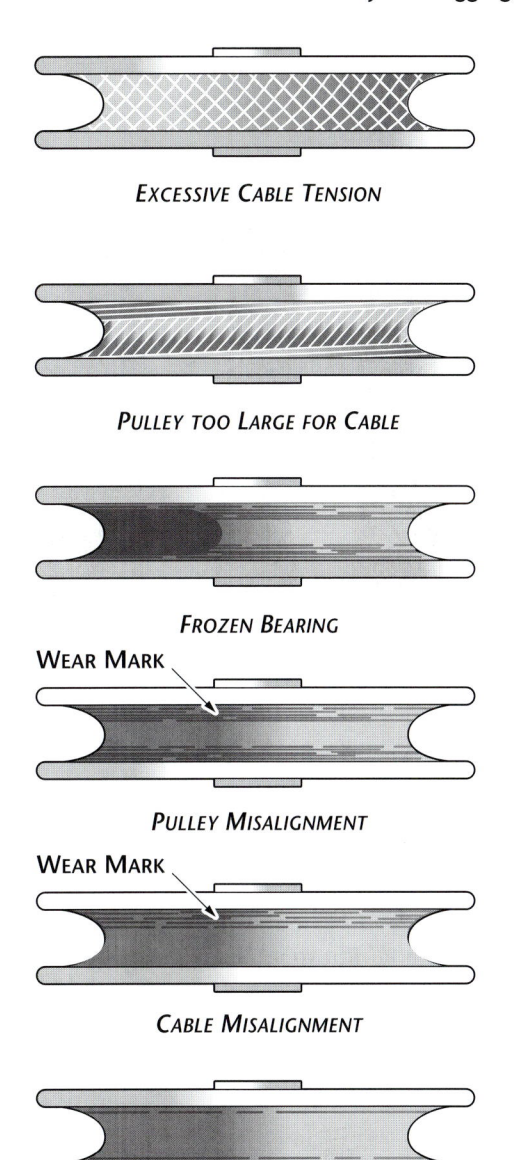

Figure 8-4-10. Control cable pulley wear patterns

In areas where pulleys are moved only a short segment of the total travel, they are often rotated at inspection. This is also a good time for a visual inspection of the pulley, since the wear factor is often an indicator of other problems. These problems can be identified by the pulley wear patterns (Figure 8-4-10).

Measuring Cable Tension

If control cables are rigged too tightly, the airplane will be heavy on the controls and difficult to fly. If too loose full travel will not be possible, and surfaces could flutter. To determine the amount of tension on a cable, a *tensiometer* is used. When properly maintained, a tensiometer is 98 percent accurate. Cable tension is determined by measuring the amount of force needed to make an offset in the cable between

8-18 | Assembly and Rigging

A

B

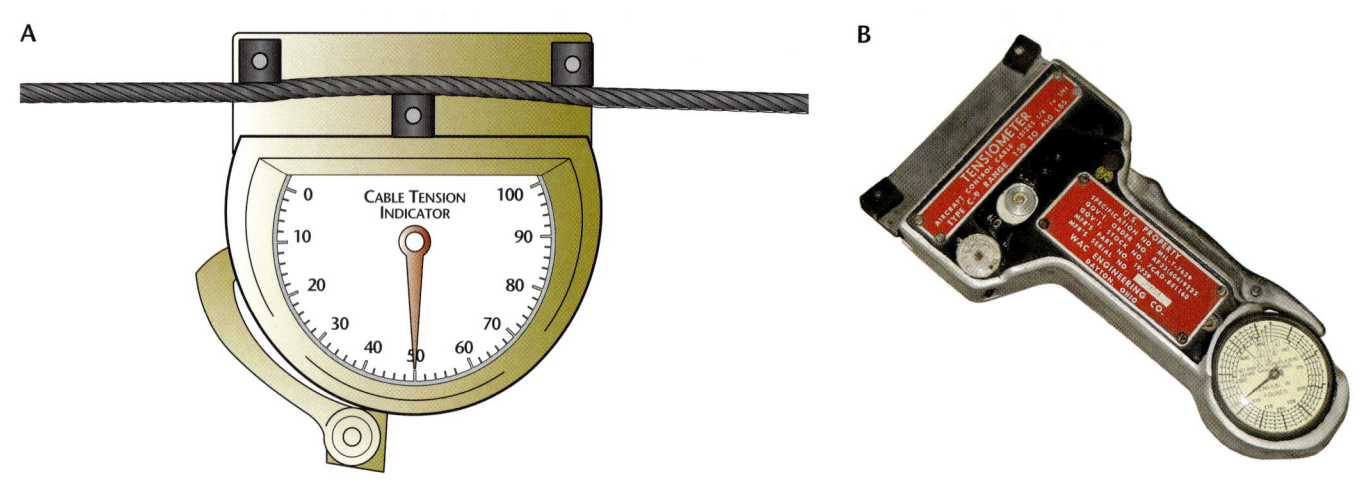

Figure 8-4-11. Cable tensiometers

two hardened steel blocks, called anvils. A riser or plunger is pressed against the cable to form the offset. Several manufacturers make a variety of tensiometers, each type designed for different kinds of cable, cable sizes, and cable tensions.

A cable tensiometer is illustrated in Figure 8-4-11A. This tool has different anvils that are matched to the different size cables. It can not be read directly; it has a chart that must be used to convert the dial reading to pounds of tension. See Table 8-4-4. For example: Using a No 2 riser to measure the tension of a 3/16 inch diameter cable a reading of 48 is obtained. The actual tension of the cable is 70 pounds. From the chart it can also be seen that a No 1 riser is used with 1/16, 3/32 and 1/8 cable.

A direct reading cable tensiometer is illustrated in Figure 8-4-11B. Before attempting to check a cable tension; the dial at the base must be turned so that the correct cable diameter is aligned with the pointer. Then with the handle all the way compressed against the body of the tool, place the cable between the anvils. Release the handle and then read the tension in pounds on the gauge.

When taking a reading, it may be difficult to see the dial. Therefore, a pointer lock is present on the tensiometer. Push it in to lock the

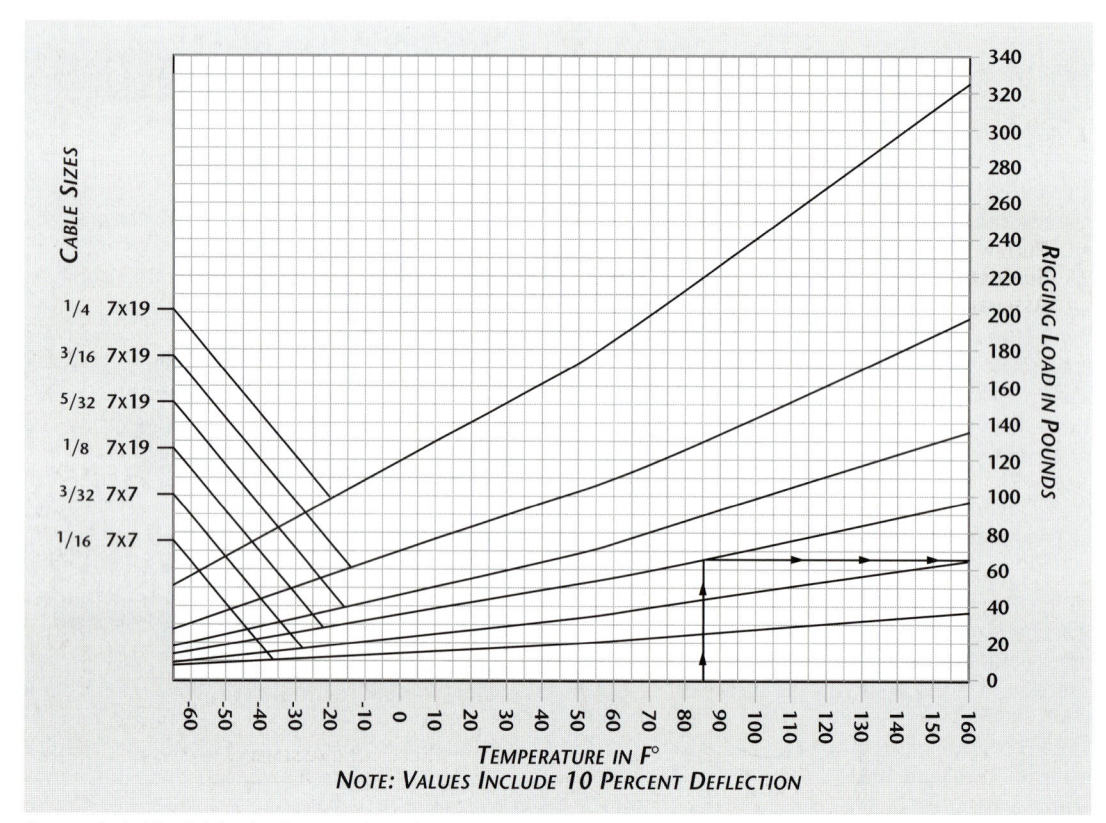

Figure 8-4-12. Cable rigging tension charts

TENSION	RISER NO. 1			RISER NO. 2		RISER NO. 3	
Tension (pounds)	Diameter			Diameter		Diameter	
	1/16	3/32	1/8	5/32	3/16	7/32	1/4
30	14	17	21	18	26		
40	20	24	28	24	32		
50	25	30	35	29	38		
60	30	35	42	34	43		
70	35	40	48	39	48		
80	39	45	54	43	53		
90	44	50	60	47	58		
100	48	55	65	51	62		

Table 8-4-4. Conversion of tensiometer reading to pounds

pointer. Then remove the tensiometer from the cable and observe the reading. After observing the reading, pull the lock out and the pointer will return to zero.

Cable rigging tension charts (Figure 8-4-12) are graphic tools used to compensate for temperature variations. They are used when establishing cable tensions in flight control systems, landing gear systems, or any other cable-operated systems.

To use the chart, determine the size of the cable that is to be adjusted and the ambient air temperature. For example, assume that the cable size is 1/8-inch in diameter, that it is a 7 by 19 cable, and the ambient air temperature is 85°F. Follow the 85°F line upward to where it intersects the curve for 1/8 inch cable. Extend a horizontal line from the point of intersection to the right edge of the chart. The value at this point indicates the tension (rigging load in pounds) to establish on the cable. The tension for this example is 70 pounds.

On many aircraft the rigging of the controls is simplified by the use of rigging pins to lock quadrants and bellcranks into their set positions. Some other rigging devices used to secure proper positioning include templates and fixtures.

Many larger aircraft have cable tension regulators (Figure 8-4-13) to maintain cable tension to the design factors. Most are spring-loaded pulleys or drums.

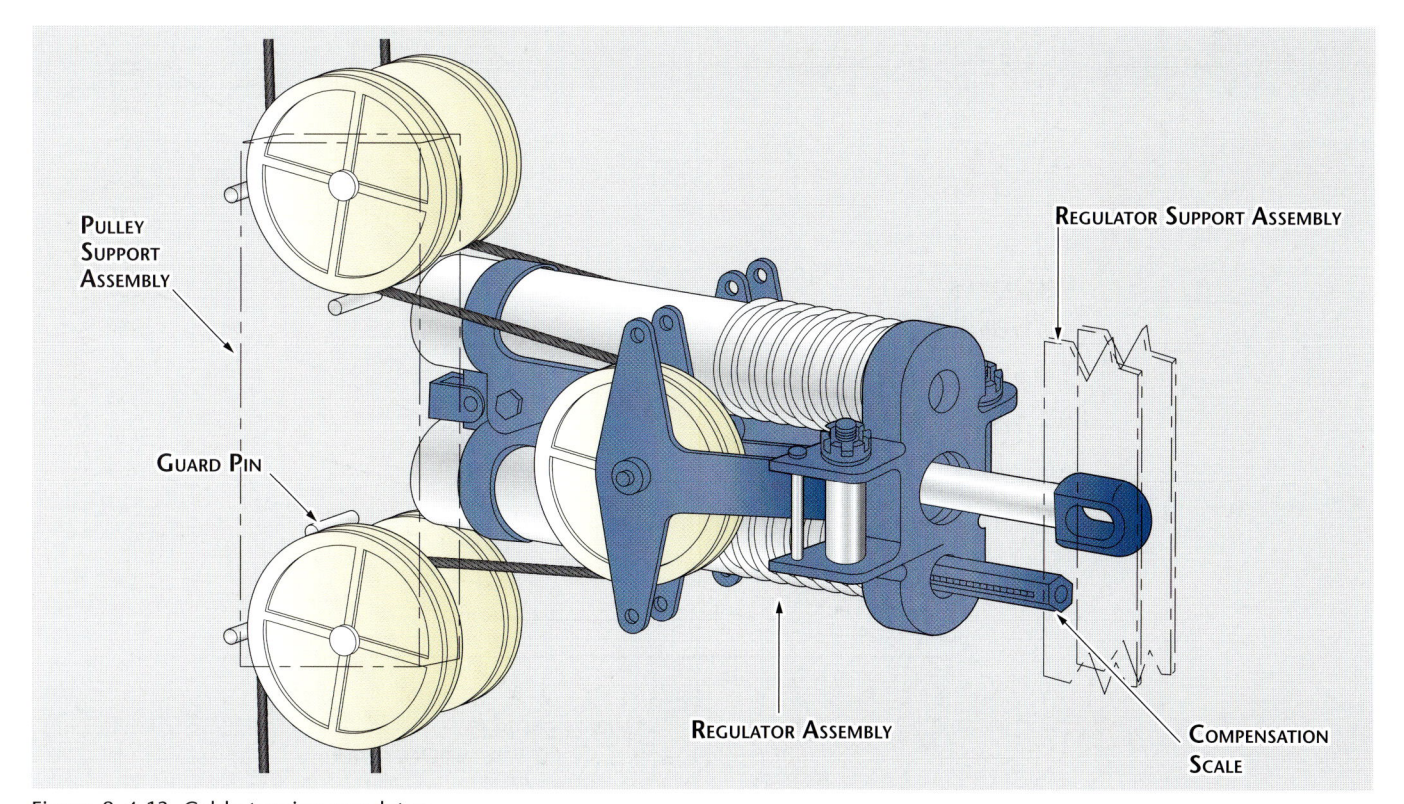

Figure 8-4-13. Cable tension regulator

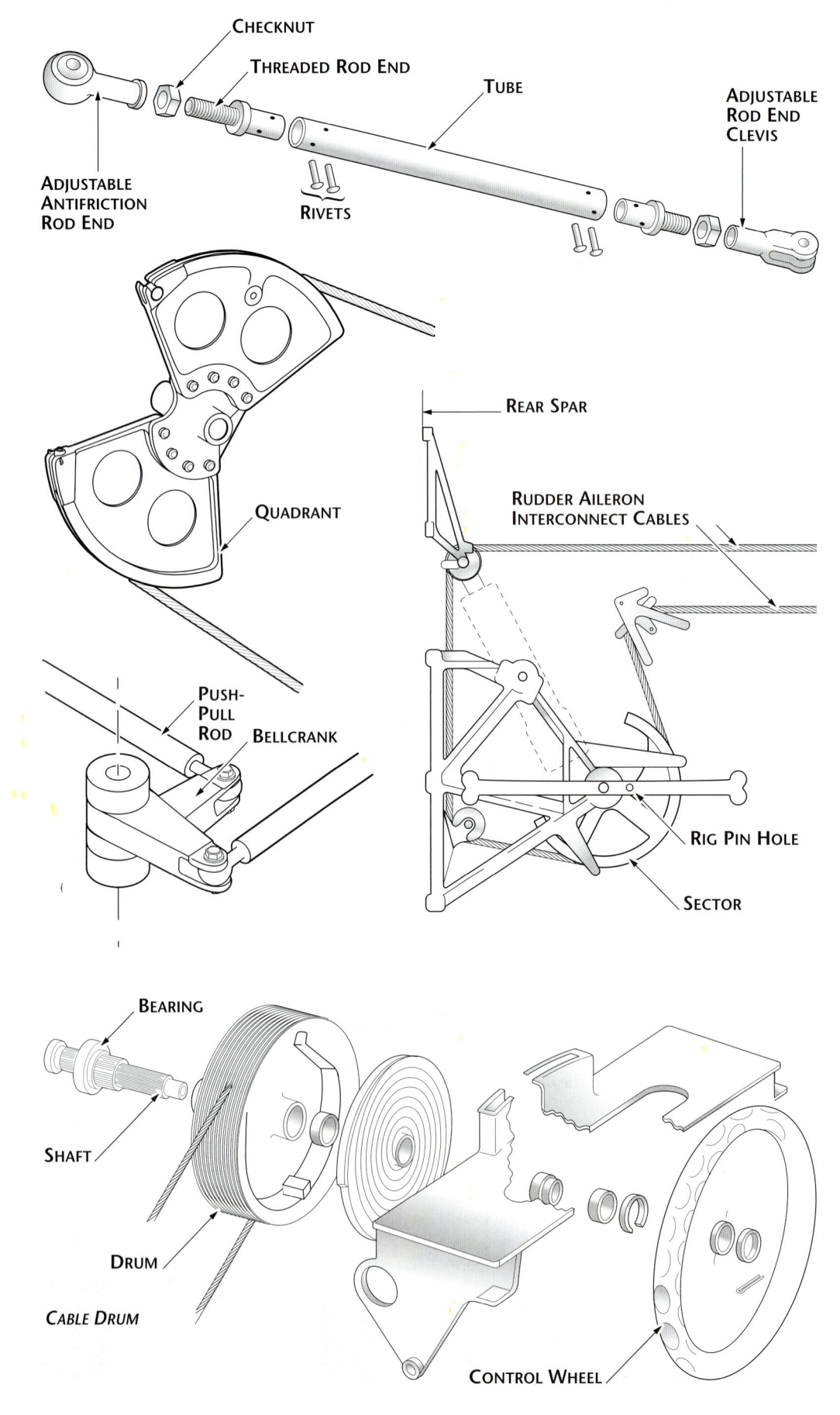

Figure 8-4-15. A torque tube system transmits a push-pull motion, with some sideways motion permitted, while cable systems can supply rotary motion for conversion to push pull systems.

Mechanical Linkage

Various mechanical linkages connect the cockpit controls to control cables and surface controls. These devices either transmit motion or change the direction of motion of the control system. The linkage consists primarily of control (push-pull) rods, torque tubes, quadrants, sectors, bellcranks, and cable drums.

Control rods. Control rods are used as links in flight control systems to give a push-pull motion. They may be adjusted at one or both ends. In some cases they are non-adjustable. The *rod end*, or *clevis*, permits attachment of the tube to flight control system parts. The checknut, when tightened, prevents the rod end or clevis from loosening.

Control rods should be perfectly straight, unless designed to be otherwise, when they are installed. The bellcranks and walking beams to which they are attached should be checked for freedom of movement before and after attaching the control rods. The assembly as a whole should be checked for correct alignment. When the rod is fitted with self-aligning bearings, free rotational movement of the rods must be obtained in all positions.

It is possible for control rods fitted with bearings to become disconnected because of failure of the peening that retains the ball races in the rod end. This can be avoided by installing the control rods so that the flange of the rod end is interposed between the ball race and the anchored end of the attaching pin or bolt, as shown in Figure 8-4-14.

Another alternative is to place a washer, having a larger diameter than the hole in the flange, under the retaining nut on the end of the attaching pin or bolt.

Torque tubes. Where an angular or twisting motion is needed in a control system, a *torque tube* is installed. Figure 8-4-15 shows how a torque tube is used to transmit motion in opposite directions.

Quadrants, bellcranks, sectors, and *drums* change direction of motion and transmit motion to parts such as control rods, cables, and torque tubes. The quadrant shown in Figure 8-4-15 is typical of flight control system linkages used by various manufacturers. Figure 8-4-15 illustrates a bellcrank and a sector. It also shows a cable drum. Cable drums are used primarily in trim tab systems. As the trim tab cvontrol wheel is moved clockwise or counterclockwise, the cable drum winds or unwinds to actuate the trim tab cables.

Rod end bearings. Rod end bearings are manufactured in two bearing types; *sealed bearing* and *uniball* types with both internal and external threads, or that are attached with rivets.

Figure 8-4-16 illustrates all three basic types of adjustable terminals, including internal and external threads, as well as an AN clevis fork.

Rod ends with external threads. The weakest link in this type of rod end is the threaded shank. If dropped, pried against, or used as a hand hold, the shank can be bent. Once bent the rod end is no longer airworthy. If it is not cracked, the threads at the bend have been stretched to the point that they will crack soon. They may not be straightened. Refer to Figure 8-4-17.

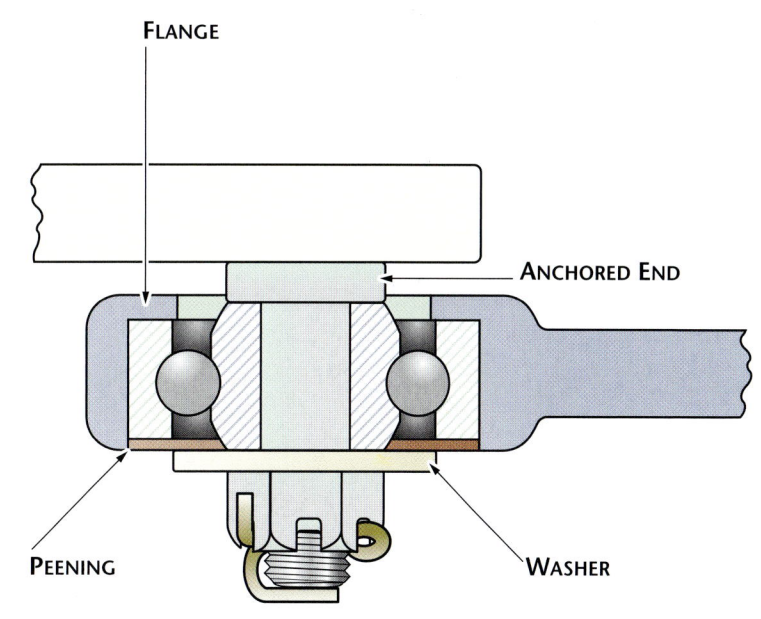

Figure 8-4-14. Control rod bearing installation

Figure 8-4-16. Three types of control rod adjustable terminals

Figure 8-4-17. Rod end bearing with typical damage to the external thread

8-22 | Assembly and Rigging

HYDRAULIC PRESS METHOD

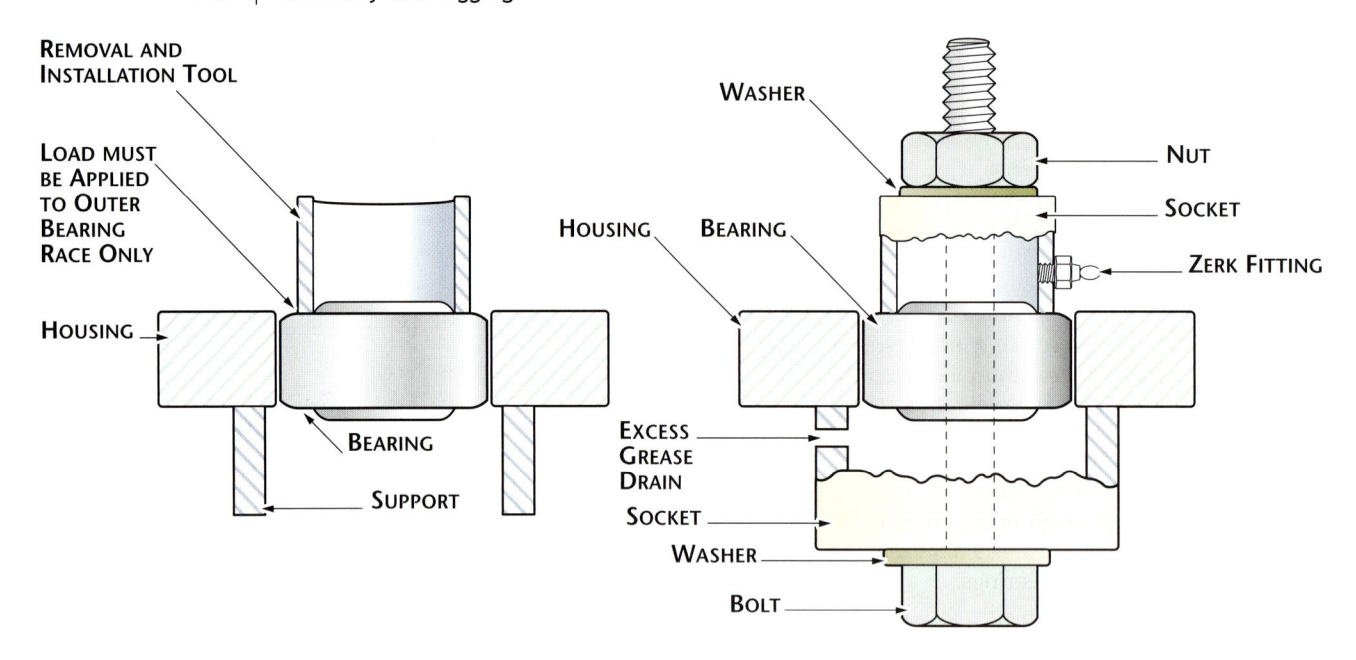

Apply the installing or removal load to the outer race of the bearing

Labels: REMOVAL AND INSTALLATION TOOL; LOAD MUST BE APPLIED TO OUTER BEARING RACE ONLY; HOUSING; BEARING; SUPPORT.

MECHANICAL PRESS METHOD

Combination lubrication, removal or installation tool

Labels: WASHER; NUT; SOCKET; ZERK FITTING; HOUSING; BEARING; EXCESS GREASE DRAIN; SOCKET; WASHER; BOLT.

Figure 8-4-18. These shop fabricated tools will ensure alignment during removal and installation. The sealed bearing can be relubricated through the zerk fitting.

(A)

(B)

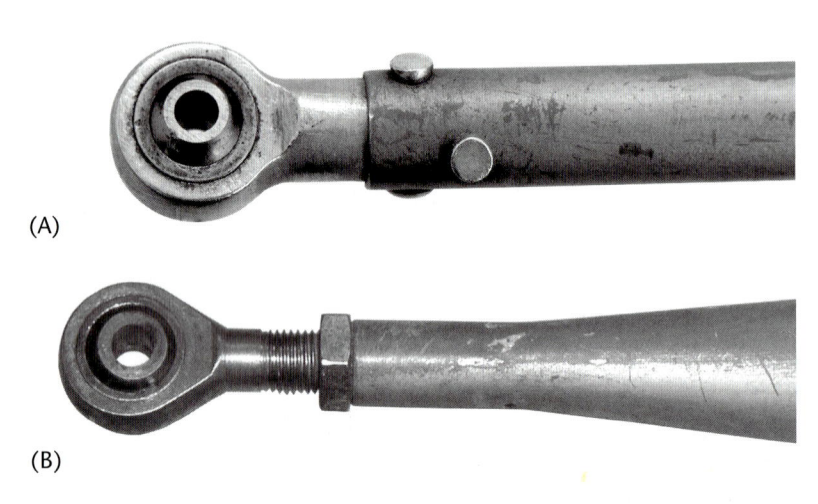

Figure 8-4-19. Examples of uniball rod ends. (A) is a riveted unit for fixed length torque tubes. (B) is an example of a external threaded adjustable rod end.

Figure 8-4-20. Sealed bearing rod ends have been in use for many years. When used to attach a control rod to an arm, a safety washer should be used.

Torque tubes with replaceable bearings. Some large torque tube controls have a fabricated boss that accepts a replaceable bearing. Figure 8-4-18 shows a cutaway installation that illustrates how to remove, replace, and re-lube these bearings.

There are three ways replaceable bearings are retained in the fitting:

- Normal press fit
- Normal press fit with staking
- Normal press fit with a retaining compound (Locktite or similar)

When pressing an old bearing out (or a new one in) it is paramount to keep the components square. Using a couple of sockets and a hammer is not an approved method. Any misalignment will overstress the fitting and cause it to develop a stress-induced crack, if it does not actually crack on the spot.

When retaining a bearing with only a press fit, everything should be clean and lightly lubricated before actually pressing the parts together.

If the bearing was previously staked, see the maintenance manual for an example of restaking. Place the new stakes 90° from the old ones and use edge spacing identical to the original installation.

If you suspect that a retaining compound was used, the maintenance manual will tell you what kind of compound, and what procedures to use.

Frequently both the bearing outer race and the hole it fits into must be primed before attempting installation. Without the proper primer the retaining compound will not adhere. Allow the primer to dry for the specified time interval before applying the retaining compound and pressing the bearing into place.

Uniball end bearings. A uniball has only three parts; a body, an inner race (usually brass or bronze), and a large inner ball with a bolt hole through it. Because of the clearance between the uniball and the race, dirt, dirty oil, and almost anything else can contaminate the bearing. They need to be cleaned and relubed regularly. Because of this same clearance they can be readily relubed. A cracked outer race, though uncommon, is the most frequent failure. Figure 8-4-19 has examples of different uniball rod end bearings.

Sealed bearing rod ends. These have a sealed ball bearing swaged into the body (Figure 8-4-20 The bearing portion is not replaceable. They are greased at manufacture and seldom is there a method to re-lubricate them. Lack of lubrication, causing a breakdown of the inner bearing balls and races, is the most common failure (in other words, rust). When the bearing fails it is possible for the entire inner race to depart the housing. If used to attach a control, the control movement would fail. To prevent failure a large area safety washer (AN 970) is used on the outside of the race.

A tool similar to the one used for bearing replacement can be fabricated. It will allow you to re-lube a rod end.

When an aircraft is washed, particular care should be given to rod ends. No direct spray gun pressure, and no high pressure water washes should be used on them. It is better to come back and clean them with a rag afterwards.

On inspection, these rod ends should be checked for the amount of thread engagement by inserting a piece of safety wire into the inspection hole. The threaded end of the rod should prevent the wire from passing through the hole. If the wire does go through the hole, readjustment of the rod end is necessary.

Stops

Adjustable and nonadjustable stops (whichever the case requires) are used to limit the throw-range or travel movement of the ailerons, elevator, and rudder. Usually there are two sets of stops for each of the three main control surfaces, one set being located at the control surface, either in the snubber cylinders or as structural stops, and the other at the cockpit control. Either of these may serve as the actual limit stop. However, those situated at the con-

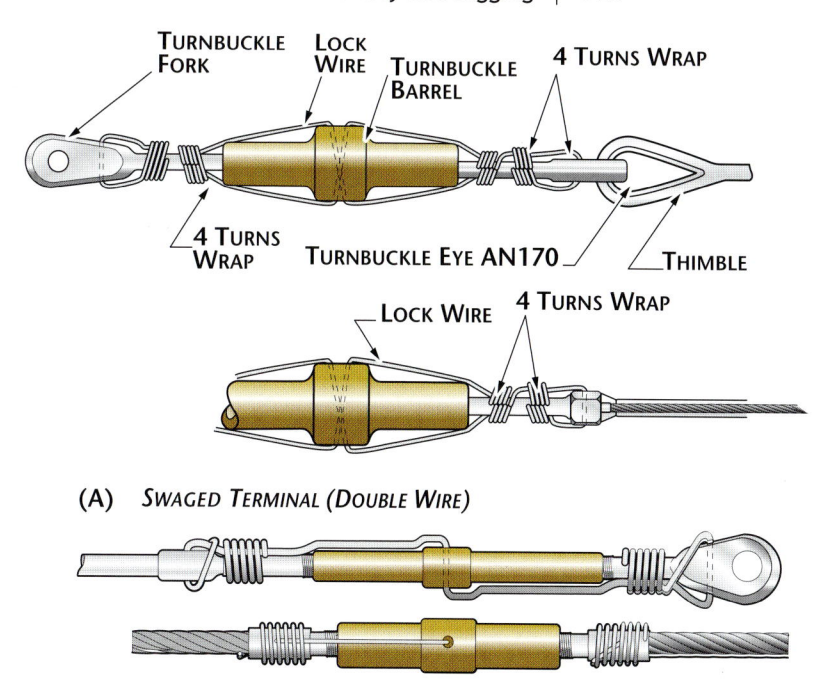

Figure 8-4-21. Methods of safetying turnbuckles

trol surface usually perform this function. The other stops do not normally contact each other, but are adjusted to a definite clearance when the control surface is at the full extent of its travel. These work as override stops to prevent stretching of cables and damage to the control system during violent maneuvers. When rigging control systems, refer to the applicable maintenance manual for the sequence of steps for adjusting these stops to limit the control surface travel.

Turnbuckles

The turnbuckle is a device used in cable control systems to adjust cable tension. The turnbuckle barrel is threaded with left-hand threads inside one end and right-hand threads inside the other. When adjusting cable tension, the cable terminals are screwed into either end of the barrel an equal distance by turning the barrel. After a turnbuckle is adjusted, it must be safetied.

In order for the turnbuckle to obtain the strengths of the cable it must be adjusted properly. This is no more than three threads exposed on each end of the turnbuckle. With this in mind, it may be necessary to adjust the cable at more than one location in order to obtain the proper length and tension.

Safetying turnbuckles. Each turnbuckle will require safetying to insure that the turnbuckle will not rotate and loosen. A chart in the maintenance manual will list the wire and method to be used on various cable sizes. The methods are shown in Figure 8-4-21A and B.

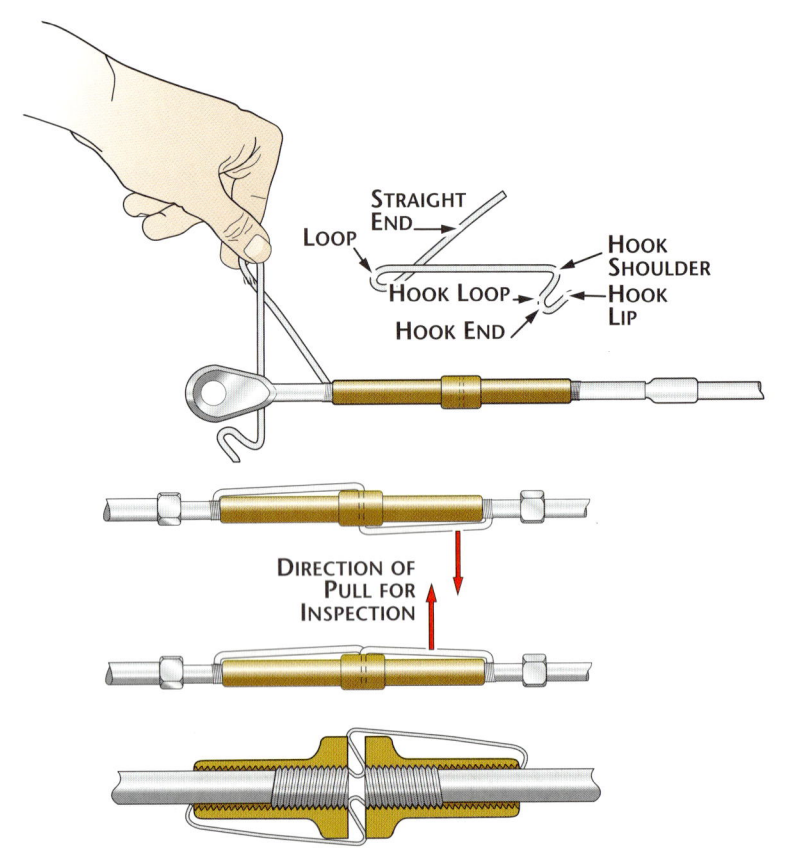

Figure 8-4-22. Installation of a spring steel turnbuckle lock clip

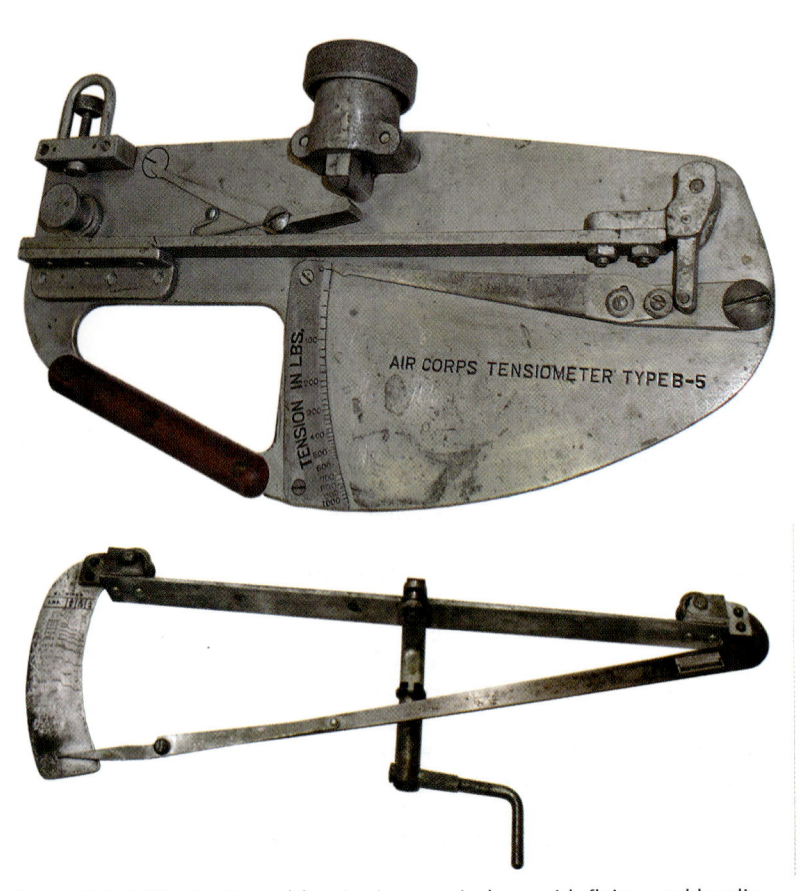

Figure 8-5-1. The basic tool for rigging an airplane with flying and landing wires is a tensiometer. Airplanes like the Stearman biplane cannot be rigged correctly without using a tensiometer.

On many aircraft today *a clip locking device* (*Stuke Lock*) is used in lieu of safety wire. Installation of a Stuke lock is shown in Figure 8-4-22:

1. After the turnbuckle is adjusted the groove on the terminals and the indicator notch on the barrel should be lined up
2. The straight end of the clip can then be inserted, locking the terminal to the barrel
3. The U shaped bend on the clip is then pushed into the hole until it turnbuckle barrel until it locks
4. Next lock the other side

When a control cable is properly rigged and the control is moved to each extreme, the control should hit its stops. It is important that springback exists when the controls are moved. This spring back indicates that the control has reached its stop prior to reaching any internal stops in the system. If hydraulic assist is a factor in a control system, the mechanical stops and movement must be carefully checked prior to hydraulic power being tested.

Section 5
Rigging Checks

Checking the relative alignment and adjustment of an aircraft's main structural components is called a rigging check. The name is a holdover from the days when an airplane required extensive rigging after assembly. Rigging required knowledge of an airplane's construction. In the days of biplanes, flying wires, and cabane struts, almost everything except the angle of incidence of the root of the lower wings was adjustable. Rigging could be a two or three day job if all was not well to begin with. It also required some very specialized tools (Figure 8-5-1).

Biplane rigging is a process that is best left to experts in the classic and antique segment of the industry.

Structural alignment. The position or angle of the main structural components is related to a longitudinal datum line parallel to the aircraft center line and a lateral datum line parallel to a line joining the wing tips. All rigging checks require that the aircraft be leveled. Only then will measurements be accurate.

The maintenance manuals of all airplanes will contain leveling instructions. Each airplane will be somewhat different. Even models of airplanes from the same manufacturer may not

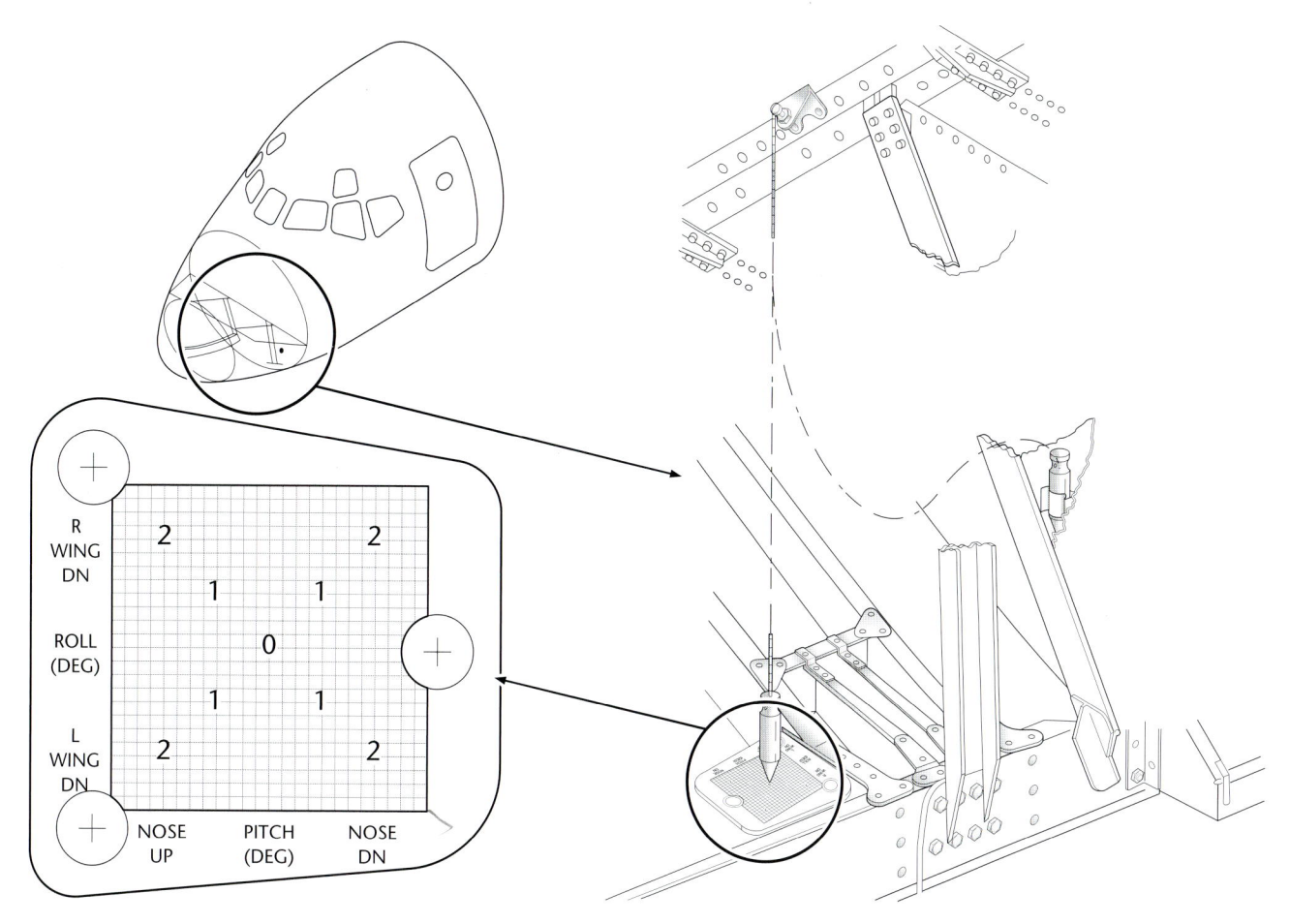

Figure 8-5-2. A grid plate for leveling a transport category airplane

be the same. Small aircraft usually have fixed pegs or blocks attached to the fuselage parallel to or coincident with the datum lines. A spirit level and a straight edge are rested across the pegs or blocks to check the level of the aircraft. This method of checking aircraft level also applies to many of the larger types of aircraft. However, the *grid method* is sometimes used on large aircraft. The grid plate (Figure 8-5-2) is a permanent fixture installed on the aircraft floor or supporting structure. When the aircraft is to be leveled, a plumb bob is suspended from a predetermined position in the ceiling of the aircraft over the grid plate. The adjustments to the jacks necessary to level the aircraft are indicated on the grid scale. The aircraft is level when the plumb bob is suspended over the center point of the grid.

Normally, rigging and alignment checks should not be undertaken in the open. If this cannot be avoided, the aircraft should be positioned with the nose into the wind.

The weight and loading of the aircraft should be exactly as described in the manufacturer's manual. Some transport aircraft can be loaded in a manner that exceeds the allowable jacking weight. In all cases, the aircraft should not be jacked until it is ensured that the maximum jacking weight (if any) specified by the manufacturer is not exceeded.

With a few exceptions, the *dihedral* and *incidence angles* of conventional modern aircraft cannot be adjusted. Some manufacturers permit small adjustments to the wing angle of incidence to correct for a wing-heavy condition. The dihedral and incidence angles should be checked after hard landings or after experiencing abnormal flight loads (severe turbulence) to ensure that the components are not distorted and that the angles are within the specified limits.

There are several methods for checking structural alignment and rigging angles. Special rigging boards which incorporate, or on which can be placed, a special instrument (spirit level or clinometer) for determining the angle are used on some aircraft. On a number of aircraft the alignment is checked using a transit and plumb bobs or a theodolite and sighting rods. The particular equipment to be used is usually specified in the manufacturer's manuals.

When checking alignment, a suitable sequence should be developed and followed to be certain that the checks are made at all the positions

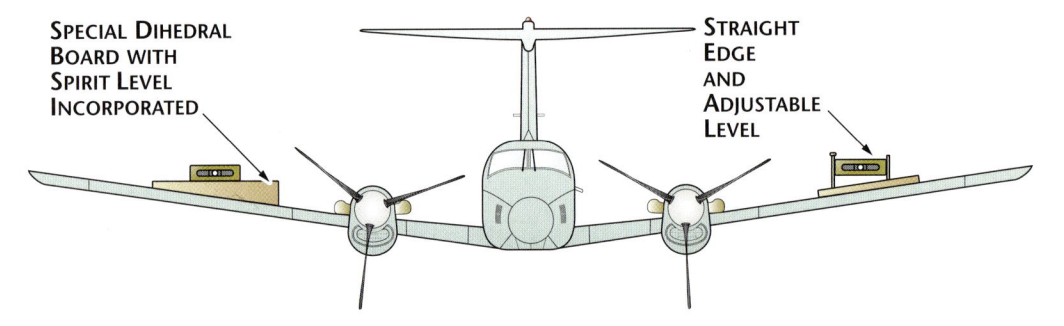

Figure 8-5-3. Different methods of checking dihedral

specified. The alignment checks specified usually include:

- Wing dihedral angle
- Wing incidence angle
- Engine alignment
- Horizontal stabilizer incidence
- Horizontal stabilizer dihedral
- Verticality of the fin
- A symmetry check

Checking dihedral. The dihedral angle should be checked in the specified positions using the special boards provided by the aircraft manufacturer. If no such boards are available, a straight edge and a clinometer can be used. The methods for checking dihedral are shown in Figure 8-5-3.

It is important that the dihedral be checked at the positions specified by the manufacturer. Certain portions of the wings or horizontal stabilizer may sometimes be horizontal or, on rare occasions, *anhedral* (negative dihedral) *angles* may be present.

Checking incidence. Incidence is usually checked in at least two specified positions on the surface of the wing to ensure that the wing is free from twist. A variety of incidence boards are used to check the incidence angle. Some have stops at the forward edge which must be placed in contact with the leading edge of the wing. Others are equipped with location pegs which fit into some specified part of the structure. The purpose in either case is to ensure that the board is fitted in exactly the position intended. In most instances, the boards are kept clear of the wing contour by short extensions attached to the board. A typical incidence board is shown in Figure 8-5-4.

When used, the board is placed at the specified locations on the surface being checked. If the incidence angle is correct, a clinometer on top of the board will read zero, or within a specified tolerance of zero. Modifications to the areas where incidence boards are located can affect the reading. For example, if leading-edge deicer boots have been installed, this will affect the position taken by a board having a leading edge stop.

Correcting for wing-heavy condition. On aircraft that have adjustments available, the angle of incidence can be used to correct for wing heaviness (pulling to one side when trying to fly straight and level). This is generally available only on high wing airplanes, particularly ones with lift struts.

The process is called *wash in* or *wash out*. If one wing is adjusted to a lesser angle of incidence, the wing is said to be washed out. The opposite, more angle, is a washed in wing. Washing in the heavy wing will produce more lift on that side, thus making a wing-heavy airplane fly straight and level.

Checking fin verticality. After the rigging of the horizontal stabilizer has been checked, the verticality of the vertical stabilizer relative to the lateral datum can be checked. The measurements are taken from a given point on either side of the top of the fin to a given point on the left and right horizontal stabilizers (Figure 8-5-5). The measurements should be similar within prescribed limits. When it is necessary to check the alignment of the rudder hinges, remove the rudder and pass a plumb bob line through the rudder hinge attach-

Figure 8-5-4. Tools for checking incidence are frequently fabricated as per instructions in the airplane's maintenance manual.

Figure 8-5-5. Checking a vertical fin

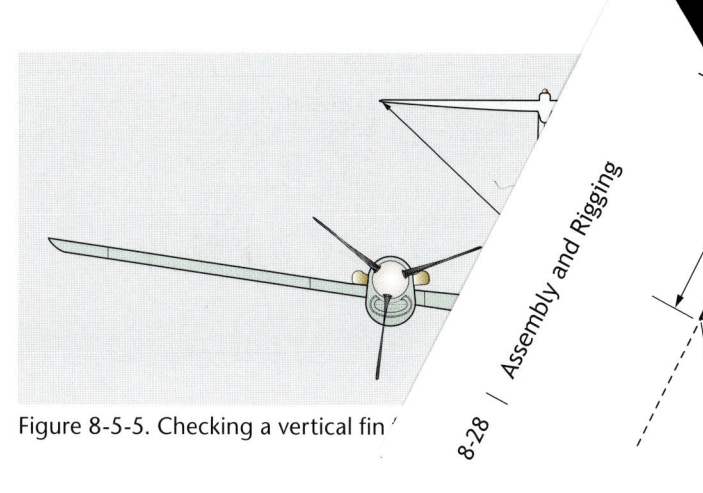

ment holes. To facilitate alignm[...]
same diameter as the rudder [...]
the head off with a hacksaw [...]
drill a string sized hole thr[...]
bolt. The line should pass c[...]
holes. Save the bolt for fu[...]
some aircraft have the le[...]
fin offset to the longitudinal c[...]
act engine torque.

Checking engine alignment. Engines
usually mounted with the thrust line parallel
to the horizontal longitudinal plane of symmetry. However, this is not always true. Some have
downthrust or sidethrust built in. Checking to
ensure that the position of the engines, including any degree of offset, is correct depends

points
When meas[...]
should be used [...]
sion. A 5-pound pull [...]

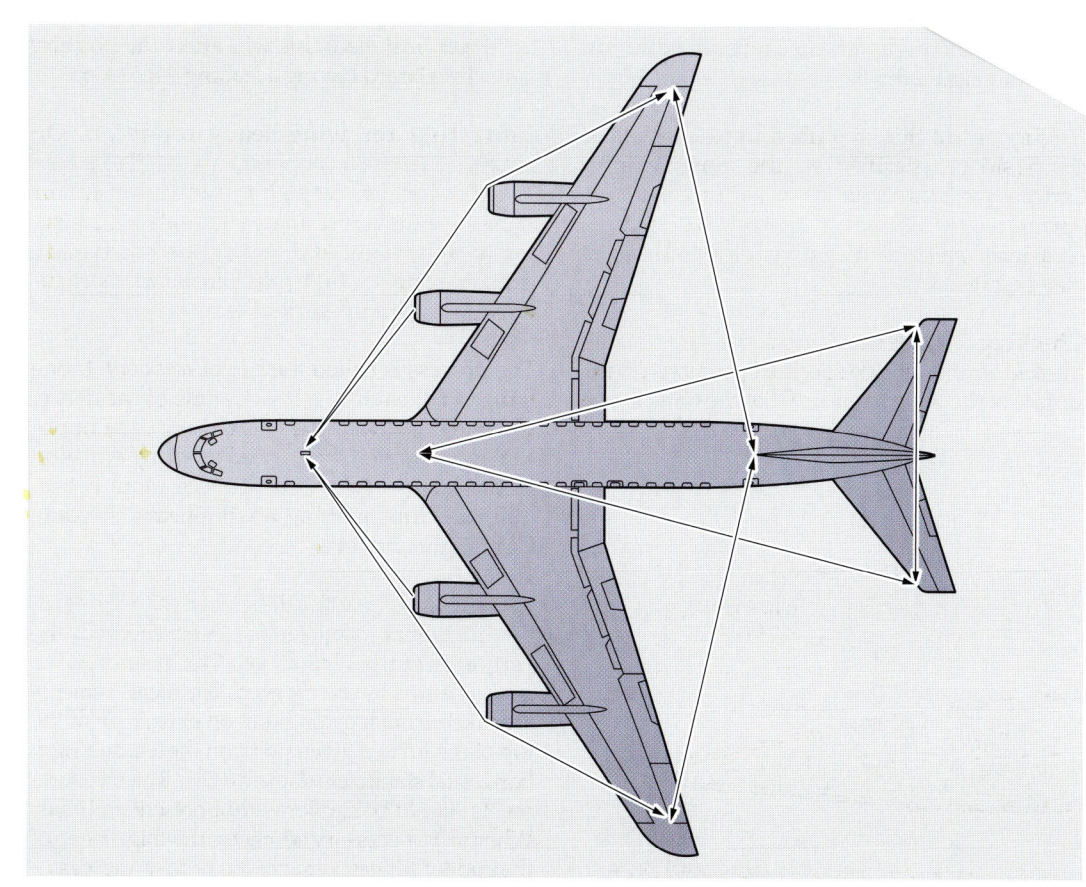

Figure 8-5-6. An example of a symmetry check

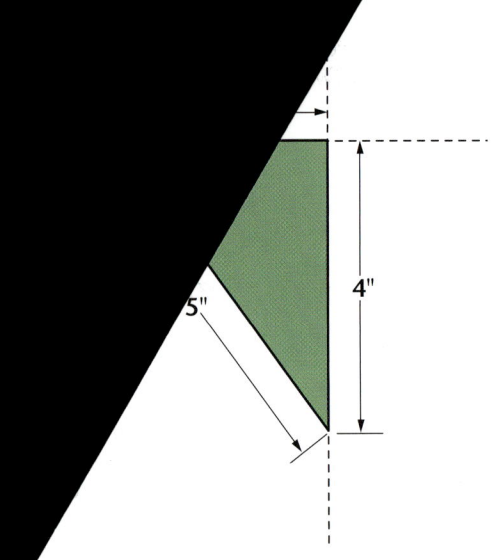

are marked from the fuselage line towards a wing tip, and 4 units are measured down the fuselage centerline, then the distance between the ends will be 5 units if everything is square. See Figure 8-5-7. In essence you are drawing a right triangle. For greater accuracy any multiple of 3-4-5 can be used, for instance, 6-8-10 or 12-16-20.

Adjustment of Control Surfaces

In order for a control system to function properly, it must be correctly adjusted. Correctly rigged control surfaces will move through a prescribed arc (surface-throw) and be synchronized with the movement of the cockpit controls.

Rigging any system requires that the step-by-step procedures be followed as outlined in the aircraft maintenance manual. Although the complete rigging procedure for most aircraft is of a detailed nature that requires several adjustments, the basic method follows three steps:

- Lock the cockpit control, bellcranks, and the control surfaces in the neutral position.

- Adjust the cable tension, maintaining the rudder, elevators, or ailerons in the neutral position.

- Adjust the control stops to limit the control surface travel to the dimensions given for the aircraft being rigged. The range of movement of the controls and control surfaces should be checked in both directions from neutral.

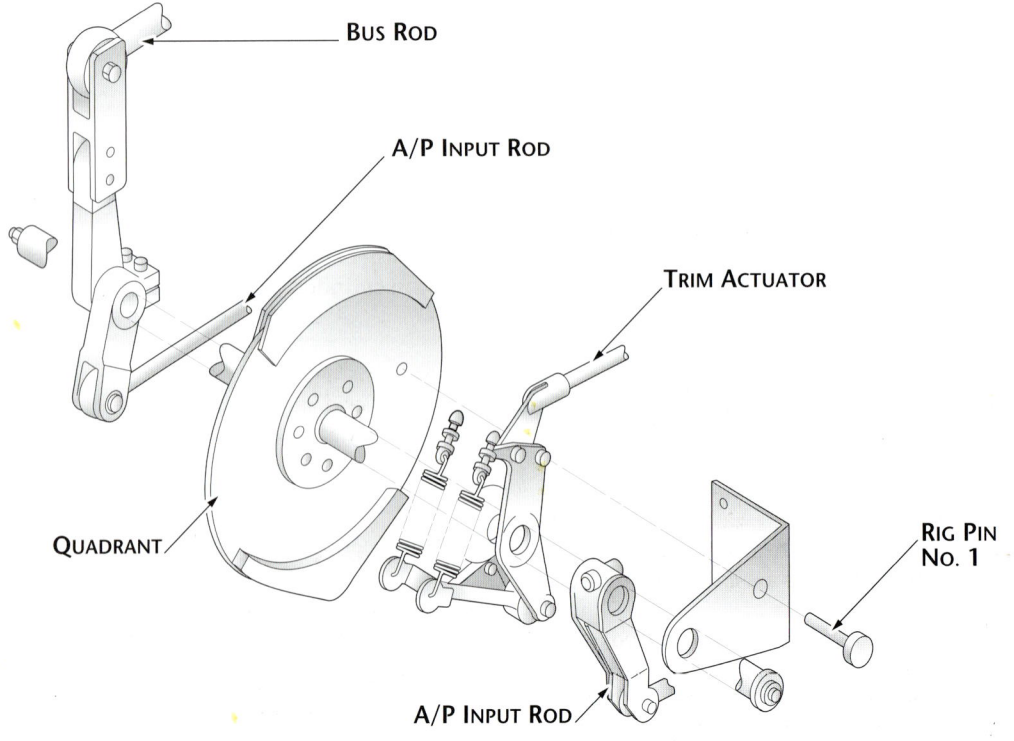

Figure 8-5-7. The 3-4-5 method of measuring a angle

Where large aircraft are concerned, the positions where the dimensions are to be taken are usually chalked on the floor. This is done by suspending a plumb bob from the checkpoints and marking the floor immediately under the point of each plumb bob. A laser level can be used to draw a straight line along the floor between the two plumb bob points. The measurements can then be established from different points in relation to the center line. If plumb bobs are dropped from each wing, a second laser line can be laid from tip to tip, crossing the fuselage center line. To check if the wings are square with the fuselage the carpenters 3-4-5 method can be used. When 3 units

Figure 8-5-8. A rigging pin in place

The rigging of the trim tab systems is performed in a similar manner. The trim tab control is set to the neutral (no trim) position, and the surface tab is usually adjusted to streamline with the control surface. However, on some aircraft the trim tabs may be offset a degree or two from streamline when in the neutral position. After the tab and tab control are in the neutral position, adjust the control cable tension.

> **NOTE:** *FAR23.677 states that a pilot must be able to determine the current position of the trim tabs as well as the neutral position of the trim controls for lateral and directional trim.*

Pins, usually called *rig pins*, are sometimes used to simplify the setting of pulleys, levers, bellcranks, etc., in their neutral positions. A rig pin is a small metallic pin or clip. When rig pins are not provided, the neutral positions can be established by means of alignment marks, by special templates, or by taking linear measurements. See Figure 8-5-8.

If the final alignment and adjustment of a system are correct, it should be possible to withdraw the rigging pins easily. Any undue tightness of the pins in the rigging holes indicates incorrect tensioning or misalignment of the system.

After a system has been adjusted, the full and synchronized movement of the controls should be checked. When checking the range of movement of the control surface, the controls must be operated from the cockpit and not by moving the control surfaces. During the checking of control surface travel, ensure that chains, cables, etc., have not reached the limit of their travel when the controls are against their respective stops. Where dual controls are installed, they must be synchronized and function satisfactorily when operated from both positions.

Trim tabs and other tabs should be checked in a manner similar to the main control surfaces. The tab position indicator must be checked to see that it functions correctly. If jackscrews are used to actuate the trim tab, check to see that they are not extended beyond the specified limits when the tab is in its extreme positions.

After determining that the control system functions properly and is correctly rigged, it should be thoroughly inspected to determine that the system is correctly assembled and will operate freely over the specified range of movement. Make certain that all turnbuckles, rod ends, and attaching nuts and bolts are correctly safetied.

If a control surface is properly balanced, rigged, and adjusted the most likely cause of any vibration sensed during the test flight would be too much play in the attaching hardware. If this occurs, recheck the control attach points for worn hardware.

Section 6
Hardware Installation and Safetying

There are special instances where hardware must be safetied in a specific manner. It is generally because of clearance required by a special design problem.

Most aircraft manufacturers have a Standard Practices section in their maintenance manuals. In all cases these are the final reference for the aircraft you are working on. However, for the most part standard nuts, bolts, screws, plugs, and turnbuckles have a standard method of being safetied. The following is a collection of normal procedures.

General Safetying Procedures

Because of the nature of flying, virtually all fasteners are safetied in some manner. More so than in any other mechanical endeavor. These practices are a safety device to prevent the disengagement of screws, nuts, bolts, snap rings, oil caps, drain cocks, valves, and other parts. The basic methods used in safetying are:

- Self-locking nuts
- Pal nuts
- Safety-wire
- Cotter pins
- Lock washers

Wire, either soft brass, steel or stainless steel is used on cylinder studs, control cable turnbuckles, and engine accessory attaching bolts.

Cotter pins are used on aircraft and engine controls, landing gear, and tailwheel assemblies, or any point where a turning or actuating movement takes place.

Self-locking nuts

Two types of self-locking nuts are currently in use, the all-metal type, and the fiber or nylon type.

- DO NOT use self-locking nuts on parts subject to rotation.

Assembly and Rigging

FINE THREAD SERIES	
Thread Size	Minimum Prevailing Torque
7/16-20	8 inch-pounds
1/2-20	10 inch-pounds
9/16-18	13 inch-pounds
5/8-18	18 inch-pounds
3/4-16	27 inch-pounds
7/8-14	40 inch-pounds
1-14	55 inch-pounds
1-1/8-12	73 inch-pounds
1-1/4-12	94 inch-pounds

COARSE THREAD SERIES	
Thread Size	Minimum Prevailing Torque
7/16-14	8 inch-pounds
1/2-13	10 inch-pounds
9/16-12	14 inch-pounds
5/8-11	20 inch-pounds
3/4-10	27 inch-pounds
7/8-9	40 inch-pounds
1-8	51 inch-pounds
1-1/8-8	68 inch-pounds
1-1/4-8	88 inch-pounds

Table 8-6-1. Minimum prevailing torque values for reused self-locking nuts

- Self-locking nuts should not be used with bolts or screws on turbine engine airplanes in locations where the loose nut, bolt, washer, or screw could fall or be drawn into the engine air intake scoop.
- Self-locking nuts should not be used with bolts, screws, or studs to attach access panels or doors, or to assemble any parts that are routinely disassembled before, or after, each flight. They may be used with anti-friction bearings and control pulleys, provided the inner race of the bearing is secured to the supporting structure by the nut and bolt.
- Metal locknuts are constructed with either the threads in the locking insert, out-of-round with the load-carrying section, or with a saw-cut insert with a pinched-in thread in the locking section. The locking action of the all metal nut depends upon the resiliency of the metal when the locking section and load carrying section are engaged by screw threads. Metal locknuts are primarily used in high temperature areas.
- Fiber or nylon locknuts are constructed with an unthreaded fiber or nylon locking insert held securely in place. The fiber or nylon insert provides the locking action because it has a smaller diameter than the

nut. Fiber or nylon self-locking nuts are not installed in areas where temperatures exceed 250°F. After the nut has been tightened, make sure the bolt or stud has at least one full thread showing past the nut. DO NOT reuse a fiber or nylon locknut if the nut cannot meet the minimum prevailing torque values. (See Table 8-6-1.)

- Self-locking nut plates are produced in a variety of forms and materials for riveting or welding to aircraft structures or parts. Certain applications require the installation of self-locking nuts in channel arrangement permitting the attachment of many nuts in a row with only a few rivets.

Finish identification. Several types of finishes are used on self-locking nuts. The particular type of finish is dependent on the application and temperature requirement. The most commonly used finishes are as follows:

- Cadmium-plating
- Silver plating
- Anodizing for aluminum
- Solid lubricant coating

Cadmium-plating. This is an electrolytically deposited silver-gray plating which provides exceptionally good protection against corrosion, particularly in salty atmosphere, but is not recommended in applications where the temperature exceeds 450°F. The following additional finishes or refinements to the basic cadmium can be applied:

- **Chromic clear dip.** Cadmium surfaces are passivated, and cyanide from the plating solution is neutralized. The protective film formed gives a bright, shiny appearance, and resists staining and finger marks.
- **Olive drab dichromate.** Cadmium plated work is dipped in a solution of chromic acid, nitric acid, acetic acid, and a dye which produces corrosion resistance.
- **Iridescent dichromate.** Cadmium plated work is dipped in a solution of sodium dichromate and takes on a surface film of basic chromium chromate which resists corrosion. Finish is yellow to brown in color (nominal gold color).

NOTE: *Cadmium-plated nuts are restricted for use in temperatures not to exceed 450°F. When used in temperatures in excess of 450°F, the cadmium will diffuse into the base material causing it to become very brittle and subject to early failure.*

Silver plating. Silver plating is applied to locknuts for use at higher temperatures. Important advantages are its resistance to extreme heat

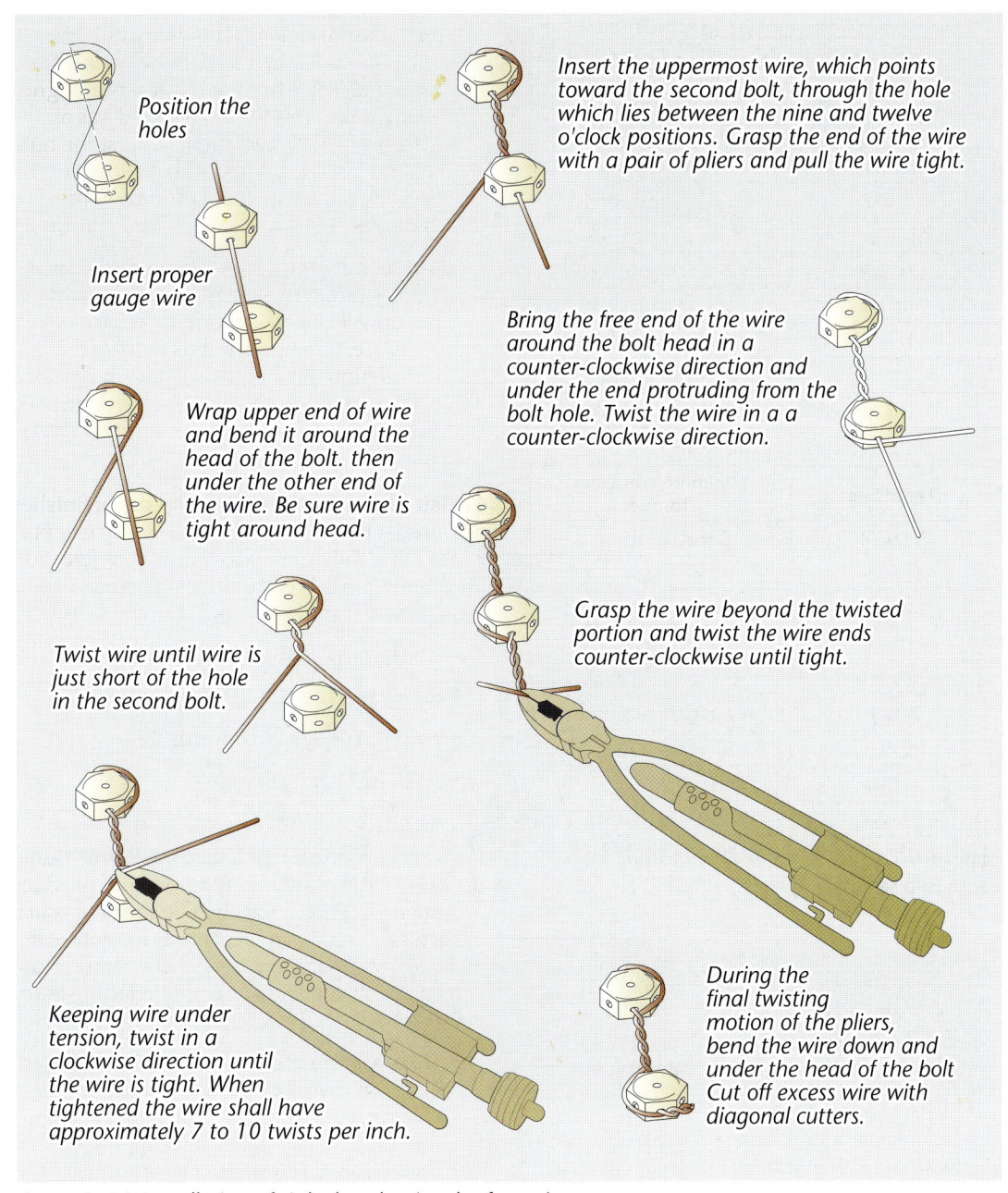

Figure 8-6-1. Installation of right-hand twisted safety wire

(1,400°F) and its excellent lubricating characteristics. Silver resists galling and seizing of mating parts when subjected to heat or heavy pressure.

Anodizing for aluminum. An inorganic oxide coating is formed on the metal by connecting the metals and anodes in a suitable electrolyte. The coating offers excellent corrosion resistance and can be dyed in a number of colors.

Solid lubricant coating. Locknuts are also furnished with molybdenum disulfide for lubrication purposes. It provides a clean, dry, permanently-bonded coating to prevent seizing and galling of threads. Molybdenum disulfide is applied to both cadmium and silver-plated parts. Other types of finishes are available, but the finishes described in this chapter are the most widely used.

Pal nuts

Pal nuts force the nut thread against the bolt or screw thread when tightened. These nuts should never be reused and should be replaced with new ones when removed.

Safety wire

Do not use stainless steel, monel, carbon steel, or aluminum alloy safety wire to secure emergency mechanisms such as switch handles, guards covering handles used on exits, fire extinguishers, emergency gear releases, or other emergency equipment. Figure 8-6-1 shows how to install safety wire. Some existing structural equipment or safety-of-flight

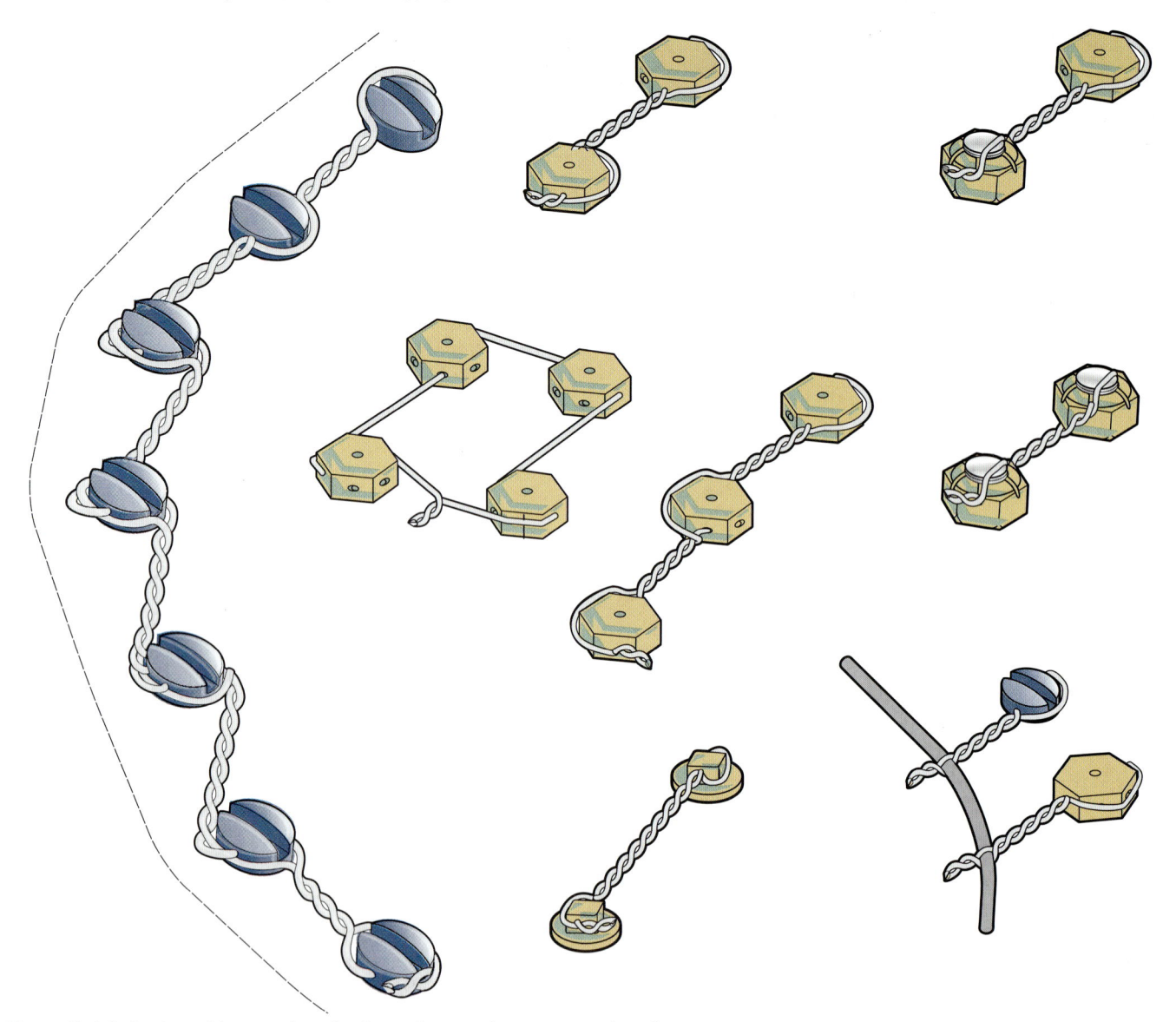

Figure 8-6-2. Real world examples of safety wire attachment on various fasteners

emergency devices require copper or brass safety wire (.020 inch diameter only). Where successful emergency operation of this equipment is dependent on shearing or breaking of the safety wire, particular care should be used to ensure that safetying does not prevent emergency operation.

There are two methods of safety wiring; the *double-twist method* that is most commonly used, and the *single-wire method* used on screws, bolts, and/or nuts in a closely spaced or closed-geometrical pattern such as a triangle, square, rectangle, or circle. The single-wire method may also be used on parts in electrical systems and in places that are difficult to reach.

Double-twist method. When using double-twist method of safety wiring, .032 inch minimum diameter wire should be used on parts that have a hole diameter larger than .045 inch. Safety wire of .020 inch diameter (double strand) may be used on parts having a nominal hole diameter between .045 and .062 inch with a spacing between parts of less than 2 inches.

Single-wire method. When using the single-wire method, the largest size wire that the hole will accommodate should be used. Copper wire (.020 inch diameter), should be used as a seal on equipment such as first-aid kits, portable fire extinguishers, emergency valves, or oxygen regulators. A secure seal indicates that the component has not been opened.

CAUTION: *Be careful not to confuse steel with aluminum wire.*

Installing safety wire. The general guidelines for installing safety wire are as follows:

- Always use new wire

- Use the same size and type of wire as used by the manufacturer

- Safety wire must be tight after installation to prevent failure from vibration

- Always install safety wire so it tends to pull each fastener tight

- Do not overstress the wire during installation. If twisted too tightly vibration may cause it to break

- Bend the cut end of twisted wire down to prevent being cut or punctured accidentally

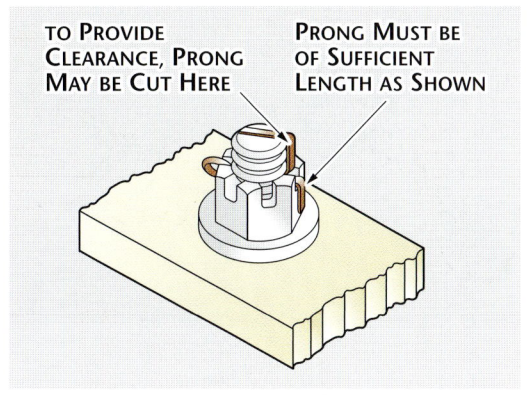

Figure 8-6-3. Cotter pin installation on a castellated nut

Wiring examples. Figure 8-6-2 shows a series of examples of actual wiring. Notice that each fastener is wired to it's counterpart so that any tendency to loosen by one fastener tends to tighten the other fastener. This is the basic premise of wire layout.

In some instances the twist between the second and third fasteners should be left hand (counterclockwise), and the pigtail may be left twist also. Sometimes this will help secure the loop in place around the fastener head and hold it down.

When there is a wire clearance problem, or when using castellated nuts, the wire is sometimes wrapped over the fastener instead of around it.

Frequently an engine accessory will have an eye cast into the case for the purpose of attaching safety wire. When using such an eye never use wire that is too small or allow the wire to become loose. To do so will accelerate wear on the eye and may wear it through.

Cotter pins

Cotter pins are produced in both carbon steel and stainless steel. Choose stainless steel when corrosion may be a serious factor or when the attracting properties of additional steel may affect instruments; near a magnetic compass for example.

Cotter pin safeties. After lockwire, the next most common method of safetying is by using cotter pins. Naturally, these can only be used on fasteners that have drilled shanks and use castle nuts, or on free fitting pins. Figure 8-6-3 shows an example of a cotter pin safety. Notice that the long end of the cotter is folded back a little past the bolt diameter and then turned down just a bit. This is to keep from gouging your arm while working on the airplane. The only reason to cut the long end even with the bolt end is for clearance. The short end of the cotter is trimmed so it will bend completely down beside the flat of the nut.

Control rods, fork ends on control cables, control surface hinge pins on older airplanes, and other connections that must be free moving, may use clevis pins as fasteners. To safety a clevis pin with a cotter you must always use a washer first (AN960 or AN960L), then install the cotter. This protects the trimmed ends of the cotter pin from contacting the structure and creating a jamming potential. Install the cotter as shown in Figure 8-6-4.

Lockwashers

Lock washers may be used with machine screws or bolts whenever the selflocking or castellated type nut is not applicable. Do not use lock washers where frequent removal is required, in areas subject to corrosion, or in areas exposed to airflow. Use a plain washer between the lock washer and material to prevent gouging of the surface of the metal.

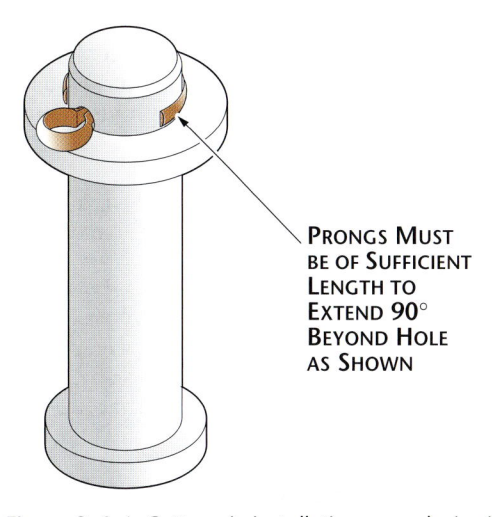

Figure 8-6-4. Cotter pin installation on a clevis pin. Always extend the legs of the cotter at least 90° past the hole on each side before trimming them.

Index Test

A

Achgelis, Gerd 1-3
adjustment of control surfaces 8-28
  rig pins 8-29
aerodynamic center of an airfoil 1-5
aerospace materials 3-1
aging 3-18
air compressors 7-14
Aircraft Maintenance Manual 5-5
air density 1-5
airfoil 1-1, 1-3, 1-4, 1-5, 1-23, 1-24, 1-26, 1-27, I-1, 5-16
  repairing 5-16
airfoil stability 1-5, 6-1. *See* helicopters
airframe structures 1-1, 1-3, 1-4, 1-5, 1-23, 1-24, 1-26, 1-27, 4-1, I-1, I-13
  airfoil
    leading edge repair 5-16
    trailing edge repair 5-18
  airplanes 4-2
  back-up 4-56
  beam 3-67, 4-6, 4-7, 4-36, 8-4, 8-5, 8-6, I-1, I-2, 4-6, 4-7, 4-36
    repair 4-36
  bulkheads 4-8
    repair 4-32, 4-34
  channels 4-35
    repair 4-35
  construction materials 4-2
  cracks 4-35
    stop-drilling 4-35
  damage
    classification 4-13
    evaluation 4-13
    inspection 4-13
    removal 4-13
    repair 4-13
      by insertion 4-13
      by patching 4-13
      by replacement 4-13
  dents 4-35
  empennages 4-7
  engine mount 4-4
  flight-control surfaces 4-8
    ailerons 4-8
    elevators 4-8
    flaps 4-8
    rudders 4-8
    trim tabs 4-8
  formers 4-8
    repair 4-32
  frame
    repair 4-36
  frames 4-8
  hat section
    splice repair 4-37
  helicopters 4-2
  inspection 4-11
    corrosion 4-11
    non-destructive 4-11
    protective coatings 4-11
    skin cracks 4-11
    skin wrinkles 4-11
    surface indications 4-11
  longerons 4-8, 4-10
    repair 4-29
  monocoque construction 4-2
  nacelles 4-4
  parts 4-4
  reinforced-shell construction 4-2
  repair 4-13
    angle 4-64
    bend-radius 4-61
    buckling 4-10
    channel 4-34, 4-61
    circular 4-24, 4-58
    corner 4-60
    creases 4-35
    dents 4-35
    excessive strength 4-10
    flange 4-59
    forming 4-10
    hat-section 4-64
    lightening hole 4-59
    maintaining original contour 4-11
    marking 4-24
      deburring 4-24
      hole finder 4-24
      pencil 4-24
      riveting 4-24
      transfer punch 4-24
    material selection 4-13
    minimizing weight 4-11
    oversize hole 4-65
    parts layout 4-13
    patch design 4-10
    patches 4-17, 4-18, 4-34
      closed-skin area 4-17, 4-18
      flush 4-17, 4-18
      lab 4-17, 4-18
      lap 4-17, 4-18
      open-skin area 4-17, 4-18
      scab 4-17, 4-18
    rectangular 4-58
    replacement material 4-10
    riveting 4-10
    safety 4-65
    strap 4-65
    stresses 4-10
    surface crack
      lap patch 4-17, 4-18
    Z-section 4-61
  repair vs. replace 4-56
  sections 4-4
  semi-monocoque construction 4-2
  spars
    angle repair 4-31
    repair by insertion 4-31
    repair by patching 4-31
    web repair 4-31
  stringer joint
    repair 4-36
  stringers 4-8
    cracks in radius of ends 4-29
    repair by insertion 4-26
    repair by J-section splice 4-29
    repair with formed angle 4-29
  wings 4-6
    box-beam 4-6
    I-beam spar 4-6
    mono-spar 4-6
    multi-spar 4-6
    ribs 4-6
      formed 4-7
      reinforced 4-7
      repair 4-31
      truss 4-7
Airframe Structures 4-1
airless painting 7-17, 7-19
alclad 3-17
aliphatic 7-7
alloys
  2xxx aluminum-copper 3-12
  7xxx aluminum-zinc alloys 3-14
  annealing 3-12
  designation 3-12
  heat-treatable 3-12
  heat treatment 3-12
  stress relief 3-12
alloy steel 3-24
all-wood airplanes
  Boeing Stearman 5-59
alphabet 7-18, 7-19
  templates 7-19
alumina 3-2
aluminum 3-2, 3-3
  alclad 3-17
  alloys 3-11, 3-12
    2xxx aluminum-copper 3-12
    7xxx aluminum-zinc 3-14
    annealing 3-12, 3-16
      full 3-16
      of castings 3-17
      partial 3-17
      stress-relief 3-17
    heat treatment 3-12
    stress relief 3-12
    wrought 3-12
  Bayer process 3-3
  casting 3-7
    die casting 3-7
      advantages 3-7
      gravity 3-7
      heat treatment 3-7
      low-pressure 3-7
      permanent mold casting 3-7

sand casting 3-7
clad 3-17
cladding
  alclad 3-17
extrusion 3-6
  applications 3-6
  shrink rules 3-7
foil 3-6
heat treatments 3-14
  quenching 3-14
  solution 3-14
history of 3-10
mining 3-3
plate 3-6
production
  cold-rolling mill 3-5
  hot-rolling mill 3-5
  ingot 3-5
properties 3-11
  altering 3-12
recycling 3-5
  rates 3-5
refining 3-3, 3-4
sheet 3-6
  marked 3-17
  shrink rules 3-7
  temper designations 3-11
aluminum alloy 4-2
  2014-T 4-2
  2024-T 4-2
  7075-T 4-2
aluminum ore 3-2
aluminum oxide trihydrate 3-2
AN. *See* Army-Navy standards
angle drills 3-48
angle of attack 1-4, 1-5, 1-8, 1-9, 1-10, 1-16, 1-17, 1-19, 1-24
angle of incidence 1-5, 1-6. *See also* Helicopters
annealing 3-12, 3-16, 3-18, 3-22, 5-51, 5-58
  cemented joints 5-51
  Plexiglas® 5-58
annular rings 3-62
anodized aluminum 8-30, 8-31
arm 3-49
artificial aging 3-16
ASP®. *See* fasteners
ASP® Fastener System 3-38
atmosphere 3-11
autogyro 1-1, 1-2, 1-21
autogyro principle 1-21. *See also* Helicopters
autorotation 1-17, 1-21, 1-24. *See* Helicopters

B

BA. *See* bend allowance
BACB30PT 3-39
back-drilling 4-24
  or transfer pins 4-24
bagging 5-23
balance beam method of balancing 8-5
balsa 5-60
band saws 5-53
bar folder 3-79

baseball stitch 2-10
basswood 5-59
bauxite. *See* aluminum ore
bauxite mining 3-3
Bayer process 3-3
  calcination 3-11
  decomposition
    seeding 3-11
  extraction 3-11
beaded collars 3-36. *See also* fasteners
  installation 3-38
bearing strength 3-2
bearing stress calculations 4-52
beeswax 2-12
Bell 47B 1-3. *See also* Helicopters
Bell Aircraft Company 1-3
  Bell 47B 1-3
Bellanca JE-1 6-2, 6-3
bellcranks 8-21
bend allowance. *See* sheet metal, bending
  finding 3-70
bend deduction. *See* material growth
bending 3-10, 5-47. *See also* forging
  bar folder 3-79
  clamping pressure 3-77
  deburring 3-77
  nose gap 3-78
    checking 3-79
  nose radius shims 3-77
  play 3-78
  radius and fillet gauges 3-77
  relief holes 3-81
  sheet metal 3-75
    box and pan brake 3-75
    cornice brake 3-75
    vise 3-75
  straight-line bends 3-82
  U-channels 3-79
bending sheet metal 3-63
bend radius 3-63. *See also* sheet metal
bend relief radius 3-79
bends 3-73
  closed 3-73
  flat layout 3-75
  open 3-73
bend tangent lines 3-65, 3-79, 3-80
Bernoulli's principle 1-4
bevel gears 1-33
bias 2-3
billets 3-6
birch 5-59
blank 3-80
bleeder materials 5-24
blowing 5-48
blushing 2-19
Boeing 3-39, 7-1
Boeing 747 3-9, 3-10
Boeing 757 7-1
Boeing Stearman 5-59
bonding jumpers 2-6
boron 5-18
box and pan brake 3-63, 3-75, 3-76, 3-79
box-beam wings 4-6
bracing. *See* welding

brake 3-77
  box and pan 3-76, 3-77
  cornice 3-76
    checking 3-79
  finger 3-77
  press 3-79
  setup 3-77
  sheet metal 3-77
  vise 3-76
brake reference line 3-67
brazing
  safety precautions 6-27
breather materials 5-24
Brinell tester 3-29
brittleness 3-2
BRL fastener 3-39
BRL fasteners. *See* PT® Fasteners
bubble balancing. *See* Helicopters
bubble protractors 8-8
bucker 3-57
bucking bar 3-55, 3-57, 3-58, 3-59, 3-62
bucking bars 3-59. *See also* riveting
bucktails 3-59. *See also* rivets
buffing 5-56
  Plexiglas® 5-56
bulkheads 2-5, 4-8
  installations 4-10
  repair 4-32, 4-34
"bullet" reamer 3-46
bumping 3-81, 3-86
  sandbag 3-88
butyate dope 2-2
butyrate acid 2-2
bypass indicator 1-35

C

cable fittings and splices 8-13
  lap splice 8-14
  stop sleeve 8-14
  terminal gauge 8-14
  thimble-eye splice 8-13
  woven splice 8-13
cable guides 8-17
  fairleads 8-17
  pressure seals 8-17
  pulleys 8-17
cable replacement 8-12
cable rigging tension chart 8-19
cable tension 8-17
  cable rigging tension chart 8-19
  tensiometer 8-17
cadmium plating
  removal of 6-17
cadmium-plating 8-30
calcination 3-11. *See* Bayer process
calculation of load 4-53
  maximum bearing load 4-53
  maximum rivet shear load 4-53
  maximum tear-out load 4-53
  maximum tensile load 4-53
calendering 2-3
camber 1-3, 1-4

cantilevered 8-10
capillary cementing 5-50
carbon steel 3-24. *See* welding
carburizing 3-27
    gas carburizing 3-27
    liquid carburizing 3-27
    nitriding 3-27
    pack carburizing 3-27
carburizing flame. *See* welding
Carpal Tunnel Syndrome 3-57
casehardening. *See* heat-treatment
castings. *See also* die casting
    die casting 3-7
      gravity 3-7
      heat treatment 3-7
      high-pressure 3-7
      inspecting 3-7
      low-pressure 3-7
      permanent mold casting 3-7. *See also* aluminum
    sand casting 3-7
cathode 3-4
caul plate
    materials 5-25
caustic soda 3-4. *See* Bayer process
cellulose 2-2
cement
    de-ice boot 7-19
    rubber and gasket 7-19
cementing 5-50
    annealing 5-51
    joining surfaces 5-51
    multiple applications 5-51
    Plexiglas® 5-50
    preparation for 5-50
    PS-18 cement 5-51
    soak cementing 5-51
center core 3-40
center of pressure 1-3, 1-5, 1-24
centrifugal force. *See* Helicopters
cetyl alcohol 3-43
Chadwick-Helmuth
    strobe-light tracking 1-13
chattering 3-48
chemical conversion treatment 7-5. *See* finishes
chill bars 6-16. *See also* welding
chip burner 1-37
chip detector 1-37
chord 1-3, 1-27
chrome-molybdenum steel. *See* welding
chromic clear dip 8-30
Cierva, Juan de la 1-2
circular hole saw 3-51. *See* hole cutters
circular saws 5-51
circumferential cracks 3-57
clad 3-17
cladding 3-17
clamping pressure 3-77
clamping rings 5-48
clamps 5-48, 5-63
    cabinetmakers' 5-63
cleaning 7-1
    pre-painting 7-2
    water break test 7-5

Clecos® 3-49
closed bends 3-72, 3-74, 3-75
cluster 6-3
coining 3-10. *See* forging
coin tap method 5-5
coint tap method 5-5
coke 3-4
cold beading 3-10. *See* forging
cold drawing 3-10. *See also* forging
cold flow 5-46
cold forging 3-10. *See* forging
cold forming 5-46
cold-rolling 3-5, 3-6
cold working 3-30
collars 3-30. *See also* fasteners
    beaded 3-36
      installation 3-38
    double-end 3-36
    identification 3-35
    part numbers 3-32
    removal 3-34
    shear-type 3-36
    tension pin-type 3-36
collective control 1-4
collective controls 1-34
color. *See* finishes
combining gearbox 1-33
COMPOSI-LOK® 3-39
compound curves 3-80, 3-91. *See also* forming
compounds
    sealing 7-21
compression. *See* stress
compression riveters 3-57
concave flange 3-83, 3-84
conductivity 3-2
Connie 7-1
construction materials 4-2
    aluminum alloy 4-2
contraction 6-3. *See also* welding
control cables 8-11
    cable replacement 8-12
    extra flexible cable 8-11
    flexible cable 8-11
    non-flexible cable 8-11
    nylon-coated cables 8-11
control rods 8-21
control surface balance 8-3
    dynamic balance 8-4
    methods of balancing 8-4
    principles of 8-3
    static balance 8-3
control surface counterbalances 8-6
    weight construction 8-7
      depleted uranium 8-7
control surface installation 8-7
control surfaces. *See* finishes
conversion coating 7-5
convex flange 3-83, 3-84, 3-85
core drills 3-46
cornice brake 3-63, 3-67, 3-75, 3-76, 3-79, 3-88, 3-90
corrosion 3-11, 4-17, 4-11
    treatment 4-17
corrosion-resistant steel 3-30

corrugating 3-81
Corsair 2-2
cotter pins 8-33
count 2-3
countersinking 3-46, 3-47. *See also* drilling
    back-countersink 3-48
    dies 3-56
    microstop 3-47
    press 3-56
    stop-countersink 3-47
    well 3-56
      draw die 3-56
countersink method 3-56
countersink well 3-39, 3-53, 3-55, 3-56
CoVan® 3-44
crazing 5-38
CRES. *See* corrosion-resistant steel
crimping 3-81, 3-82
    pliers 3-81
crimping pliers 3-81, 3-83
cryolite 3-4
crystalline alumina trihydrate 3-11
curving formed angles 3-82
cutting 5-51
    blades 5-51
    circular saws 5-51
    Plexiglas® 5-51
    unmasked 5-53
cutting torch 6-21. *See also* welding
cyclic controls 1-34

D

Daedalus 2-1
damage 4-11
    classification 4-11
    repairable
      Class V 5-31
      Class VI 5-31
      Class VII 5-31
    core
      honeycomb repair 5-9
    facing 5-9
    inspection 4-11
      coin tap method 5-5
    punctures 5-9
    repairing 5-9
    repair
      by insertion 4-13
      by patching 4-13
      by replacement 4-13
      chem-milled skin repair 4-17, 4-18
      corrosion treatment 4-17
      criteria 5-31
        aerodynamic smoothness 5-31
        strength restoration 5-31
      evaluation 4-13
      finishing repaired areas 5-12
      marking

deburring 4-24
  hole finder 4-24
  pencil 4-24
  riveting 4-24
  transfer punch 4-24
 parts layout 4-13
 removal 4-13
 repair tools 5-31
 rivet selection 4-17
 rivet spacing 4-17
 stressed skin repair 4-17, 4-18
  patches 4-17, 4-18
 tolerance 4-17
da Vinci, Leonardo 2-1
deburr 3-50, 3-76, 3-90
deburring 3-76, 4-24
decomposition 3-11. See Bayer process
 seeding 3-11
de-ice boot cement 7-19
denier 2-3
density 3-2
depleted uranium 8-7
die casting 3-7. See aluminum
 advantages 3-7
 gravity 3-7
 heat treatment 3-7
 high-pressure 3-7
 inspecting 3-7
 low-pressure 3-7
dies
 draw die 3-56
 heated 3-56
dihedral angle, checking 8-26
diluents 2-18
dimpling 3-55
 cracked
  circumferential cracks 3-57
  radial cracks 3-57
 hot dimpling 3-56
 inspection 3-56
 techniques 3-56
dollies 3-59. See bucking bars; See also riveting
dope 2-13
 application of 2-19
 butyrate 2-13
 diluents 2-18
 doping procedure 2-20
  multiple coats 2-20
 nitrate 2-13
 pigmented 2-13, 2-19
 plasticizers 2-18
 solvents 2-18
double-end collars 3-36. See also fasteners
Douglas fir 5-60
drag 1-1, 1-3, 1-4, 1-5, 1-9, 1-14, 1-16, 1-20, 1-21, 1-25
drag force 1-3, 1-14
drag wires 2-5
drape forming 5-47
draw die 3-56, 3-57
drill bushings
 standard holders
  arm 3-48
  Clecos® 3-49

  egg cup 3-48
  hole finders 3-49
  plate 3-48
  sheet holders 3-49
  standard 3-48
  strap duplicators 3-49
  transfer pins 3-49
 drill guides 3-48
 drilling 3-1, 3-42, 3-45, 3-46, 3-49, 3-50, 5-55
  "bullet" reamer 3-46
  chattering 3-48
  core drills 3-46
  countersinking 3-46
   back-countersink 3-48
   microstop 3-47
   stop-countersink 3-47
  CoVan® 3-44
  CS 3-42
  drill bushing 3-46
  extensions 3-44
  feed 3-42
  general rules 3-50
  holding the drill 3-45
  illustrated 3-45
  large holes 3-46
  lubrication 3-43, 3-44
   cetyl alcohol 3-43
   cutting oil 3-44
  normal 3-45
  piloted reamer 3-46
  Plexiglas® 5-55
  precise locating 3-45
  r.p.m. 3-42
  rules for 3-42
  safety 3-49
  SFM 3-42
  size chart 3-43
  sizes 3-44
  spars 5-62
  speed 3-42
  spiral chip 3-42
  starting 3-45
  step drills 3-46
  step reamer 3-46
  straight reamer 3-46
  surface feet per minute 3-42
  Taper-Lok® fasteners 3-42
 drills
  attachments 3-48
   angle drill 3-48
   drill bushings 3-48
    commercial threaded 3-48
    standard holder types 3-48
    tube 3-48
    TwistLock® 3-48
   drill guides 3-48
   drill stop 3-48
   snake drill 3-48
  bits 3-44
  core 3-46
  extensions 3-44
  holding 3-45
  sizes 3-44

   starting 3-45
   step 3-46
  drill stops 3-48
  driver 3-57
  drop hammer 3-80
  drop hammers 3-80
  drums 8-21
  dry Micro 5-6
  dry sump system 1-34
  ductility 3-2
  dynamic balance 8-4
  Dynamic Solutions, Inc.
   electro-optical tracking 1-13

E

eccentricity 3-61
Eckold sheet metal former 3-88, 3-90
Eddie-Bolt® 3-39. See also fasteners
Eddie-Bolt®2 3-39
edge gaps 3-62. See also riveting
edge joint. See welding
egg cup 3-48
elasticity 3-2
electrolyte 3-4
electro-optical rotor tracking. See Helicopters
empennage 1-3, 8-10
 cantilevered 8-10
 external bracing 8-10
 stabilator 8-10
empennages 4-7
 assembly 4-8
enamels 7-8. See also finishes
engine alignment 8-27
engine mount 4-4
 piston-engine mounts 4-4
 turbine-engine mount 4-4
English wheel , 3-91
epoxy
 zinc chromate 7-8
expansion 6-3. See also welding
external bracing 8-10
extraction 3-11. See Bayer process
extra flexible cable 8-11
extruded angles 3-82
extruding 3-6
extrusions 3-6. See also aluminum
 billets 3-6
 shrink rules 3-7
eyebrows 3-62. See also riveting
eyelets 2-12

F

fabric 2-1
 deterioration 2-4
 determining strength of 2-4
 doped
  determining strength of 2-4
 finish 2-1
 terms 2-3
  bias 2-3

Index | I-5

calendering 2-3
count 2-3
denier 2-3
fill 2-4
mercerization 2-4
pinked edge 2-4
ply 2-4
selvage edge 2-4
sizing 2-4
warp 2-4
warp ends 2-4
weft 2-4
woof 2-4
testing 2-4
using a punch tester 2-4
fabric covering 2-1
and static electricity 2-19
blushing 2-19
butyrate dope 2-2
coatings for 2-2
brush application of 2-19
covering materials 2-7
Dacron 2-7
Grade A cotton 2-7
specifications 2-7
fabric protection 2-6
finishes 2-3
Parts Manufacturing Authority (PMA) 2-3
polyurethane 2-13
thinners 2-13
glue 2-3
Parts Manufacturing Authority (PMA) 2-3
history of 2-1
materials preparation 2-6
Maule 2-3
nitrate dope 2-2
patches 2-20
doped-in 2-21
sewn-in 2-21
polyester 2-3
Supplemental Type Certificate (STC) 2-3
pre-covering
bonding jumpers 2-6
controls inspection 2-5
empennage inspection 2-5
fuselage inspection 2-5
rot cracks 2-5
splitting 2-5
inpsection 2-4
wing inspection 2-5
alignment 2-5
anti-drag wires 2-5
drag wires 2-5
procedures for 2-16
doping 2-16
installation 2-16
cotton fabric 2-16
linen 2-16
polyester fabric 2-16
shrinking 2-16
sizing 2-16
repair of 2-21
doped-in patch 2-21
panel

doped-in 2-21
sewn-in 2-21
patch 2-21
doped-in 2-21
sewn-in 2-21
sewn-in patch 2-21
tears in fabric 2-21
rib stitching 2-18
knot placement 2-18
spacing 2-18
seams
hand-sewn 2-9
machine-sewn 2-9
tapes 2-9
anti-tear tape 2-9
inter-rib lacing tape 2-9
reinforcing tape 2-9
surface tape 2-9
STCs 2-3
structural protection 2-6
synthetics 2-3
Supplemental Type Certificate (STC) 2-3
Technical Standard Order (TSO) 2-3
terms 2-3
bias 2-3
calendering 2-3
count 2-3
denier 2-3
fabric coverings 5-2
fairleads 8-17
fasteners 3-29, 4-38
70°-head radius lead-in bolt 3-39
ASP® fastener 3-39
ASP® system 3-38
BACB30PT 3-39
center core 3-39
collars 3-30
beaded 3-36
installation 3-38
double-end 3-36
fracture point 3-30
part numbers 3-32
recess 3-30
grip variation 3-30. See also fasteners
removal 3-34
safety 3-30
shear-type 3-36
tension pin-type 3-36
threads 3-30
wrenching flats 3-30
COMPOSI-LOK® 3-39
Eddie-Bolt® 3-38
Eddie-Bolt®2 3-39
Goodrich Rivnut® 3-39
head dishing. See also fasteners
head gap tolerances
head dishing 3-35
Hi-Lok® 3-29, 3-30, 3-39
Hi-Tigue® 3-30
identification 3-35
Light-Weight® 3-30, 3-31
Hi-Lite® 3-31
Very-Lite® 3-31
tools 3-35

Hi-Tigue® 3-30
Hi-Tigue® Hi-Lok® 3-39
hole preparation 3-32
holes for 3-32
grip gauge 3-32
preparation of 3-32
Huck bolts 3-36
installation tools 3-41
interference pins 3-29
Jo-Bolt®s 3-39
Jo-Bolts® 3-39
keyway preparation 3-41
Light-Weight® 3-30, 3-31
lockbolts 3-36
G.P. lockbolts 3-36
installation 3-37
pullers 3-38
pull-type 3-36
stump-type 3-36
OSI-BOLT® 3-39
OSI-LOK® 3-39
patterns 4-38
pins 3-30
finish codes 3-31
grip gauge 3-32
grip lengths 3-38
head 3-30
hexagonal recess 3-30
installation 3-33, 3-34
measuring 3-33
part numbers 3-32
pintail 3-37
protrusion limits 3-33
removal 3-34
shank 3-30
threads 3-30
transition area 3-30
PT® 3-38
PT® fasteners 3-39
RADIAL-LOK® 3-39
riveted joints 3-29
rivets 3-29, 4-56
acceptability limits 4-41
alloys 3-53
dimpling 3-55
edge distances 4-40
failure 4-51
flush-head 3-53
in bearing 4-51
installing 3-55
countersunk flush rivets 3-55
NACA rivets 3-55
protruding-head rivets 3-55
modified 120° countersink 3-55
modified universal-head 3-54
protruding-head 3-53
reduced flush-head 3-54, 3-55
selection 4-41, 4-56
shear stress calculation 4-50
sizes 4-56
spacing 4-39, 4-40, 4-41, 4-56
standard flush-head 3-54
universal-head 3-54
Rivnut® 3-39, 3-40

hole sizes 3-41
installation 3-41
installation tools 3-40
key 3-41
keyway preparation 3-41
notcher 3-40, 3-41
screws 3-29
screws in nutplates 3-29
sealing 4-49
sheet metal screws 3-29
SLEEVbolt® 3-41
SLEEVbolt® fasteners 3-41
ST1219-1CB 3-39
ST1219Y-1CA 3-39
Taper-Lok® bolts 3-41
Taper-Lok® fasteners 3-41, 3-42
Very-Lite® 3-31
VISU-LOK® 3-39
feeds and speeds 3-42
ferrous metals 3-10, 3-19
ferry permit 5-31
fiberglass
  types
    C-glass 5-4
    S-glass 5-4
fill 2-4
filler rod. See welding
fillet gauges 3-77
Filter 1-35
finger brake. See box and pan brake
finishes 7-1
  acrylic nitrocellulose lacquer 7-8
  chemical conversion treatment 7-5
  color
    most popular 7-1
  complete refinishing 7-2
    surface preparation 7-2
      caulking 7-2
      cleaning 7-2
      inspection 7-2
      sealing 7-2
  control surfaces 7-3
    rebalancing 7-3
  conversion coating 7-5
  curing sealants 7-20
  drying sealants 7-20
  drying time 7-6
  enamels 7-8
    safety precautions 7-8
  flaws
    fisheye 7-8
    orange peel 7-8
    rough surface 7-8
    runs 7-8
    sags 7-8
    streaks 7-8
    wrinkling 7-8
  injection sealing 7-21
  lacquer
    acrylic nitrocellulose 7-8
  leveling primer 7-6
  masking 7-1, 7-9
    for base coat 7-9
    for stripper 7-9
    for trim 7-9
  overcoating 7-5
    paint feathering 7-5
    scuff-sanding 7-5
  painting 7-1
    airless 7-16
    letters 7-20
    sequence 7-15, 7-16
      trim 7-15
    spray 7-16
      pressures 7-16
    touch-up 7-1
    trim 7-15
    N numbers 7-15
  paint removal 7-3
    HAZMAT 7-3
    media blasting 7-3
    media reclamation 7-3
    stripper 7-3
  polyurethane 7-2
    aliphatic type 7-6
    aromatic type 7-6
    catalyst 7-7
    isocyanate vapors 7-6
    "wet look" 7-2
  safety precautions 7-8
  sealants 7-19
    application of 7-20
    curing 7-20
    drying 7-20
    injecting 7-20
    pliable 7-19
    restrictions 7-20
  sealing compounds 7-21
  spray guns 7-20
    air regulators 7-14
    hobby-type 7-14
    touch-up 7-14
  stripper 7-4
  stripping 7-4
  thinning 7-6
  touch-up 7-5
    epoxy-polyamide 7-5
  treat and seal 7-5
  water break test 7-5
  "wet look" 7-1
  wet sanding 7-5
  Zahn cup 7-6
  zinc chromate primer 7-9
    thinning
      zoluol 7-9. See finishes
finishing
  final
    wet sanding 7-5
finish wheel 5-56
fin verticality, checking 8-26
fire extinguisher 3-18
fisheye 7-8
flag tracking. See Helicopters
flange 3-67
  concave 3-83
  convex 3-83
flanging 3-81
  nose ribs 3-85
  with crimps and beads 3-85
  with relief holes 3-85
flanging block 3-82, 3-85
flanging dies 3-81
flanging lightening holes 3-80, 3-81
flaps 8-9
flash tape
  materials 5-25
flat-sawn lumber 5-61
flat weld. See welding
flexible cable 8-11
flight-control surfaces 4-8
  ailerons 4-8
  elevators 4-8
  flaps 4-8
  rudders 4-8
  trim surfaces 4-8
FLOX 5-6
fluidised calciner 3-4
flush access door 4-23
flush-head pins 3-30, 3-35, 3-53
flushness variations 3-62
flush patch 4-42
fly cutter 3-51
Focke, Heinrich
  helicopter flight records 1-3
foil 3-6
Fokker
  monoplane 6-1
  The Spider 6-1
  Trimotor 6-1
Fokker, Anton 6-1
Fokker Dr. I 6-2
  as flown by the Red Baron 6-2
Fokker Dr. I triplane 6-2
Fokker D.VII 6-2
folding 3-79, 3-81, 3-82
  angular 3-79
  bars 3-79
  box 3-79
    bend relief radius 3-79, 3-80
    flanging 3-81
    flanging dies 3-81
    lightening holes 3-81
    relief holes 3-81, 3-82
forging 3-7
  cold forging 3-9, 3-10
  equipment 3-10
    hammers 3-10
    presses 3-10
    ring rollers 3-10
    upsetters 3-10
  impression die 3-9
  impression die forging 3-9
    tooling 3-9
  open die forging 3-9, 3-10
  seamless rolled ring forging 3-9, 3-10
  vs. casting 3-7
form block
  preparation 3-86
form block bumping 3-86
form blowing 5-48
formers 4-8
  repair 4-32

forming
  blank 3-80
  block bumping 3-86
  blocks 3-85, 3-86
  bumping 3-86
    procedure 3-86
    sandbag 3-86, 3-88
  compound curves 3-80, 3-91
    English wheel 3-91
    flanging lightening holes 3-80
  drop hammers 3-80
  flanges 3-86
    concave 3-86
    convex 3-86
  form block preparation 3-86
  hand forming 3-81
    bumping 3-81
    crimping 3-81, 3-82
      corrugating 3-81
      folding 3-81
      pleating 3-81
      pliers 3-81
    curving angles 3-81, 3-83
      stretching 3-81
    flanged angles 3-83, 3-84
      by stretching 3-83
      concave 3-83
      convex 3-83
    folding 3-82
    procedures 3-82
      straight-line bends 3-82
    shrinking 3-81, 3-84
    shrinking block method 3-84
    stretching 3-81, 3-82
    V-block 3-81
    V-block method 3-84
    work-hardening 3-84
  hydro press 3-80
  joggling 3-88
    dies 3-88
    stakes 3-88
  machines 3-88
    Eckold sheet metal former 3-89, 3-90
    piccolo sheet metal former 3-89, 3-90
    rotary 3-89, 3-90
    slip-roll 3-89, 3-90
  procedures 3-85
  shrinking 3-89
    tools 3-89
  stretching 3-89
    tools 3-89
forming blocks 3-84
forming curved flanged parts 3-84
forming flanged angles 3-83
  hand forming
    shrinking 3-84
forming procedures 3-85
forms 5-48
foundry 3-8
fracture point 3-30. See also fasteners
frame
  repair 4-36
frames 2-5, 4-8
free blowing 5-47

freewheeling unit 1-34
friction stir welding. See welding
FSW. See welding
full annealing 3-16
fuselage
  airplane 4-2
  helicopter 4-2

G

gaps between sheets 3-62
gas carburizing 3-27
gas metal-arc welding. See welding
gas tungsten-arc. See welding
gas tungsten-arc welding. See welding
gear train 1-34
gear type pumps 1-35
gliders 2-1
  Wright brothers' 2-1
glue 5-62
  joint 5-63
  types 5-62
  wooden structures 5-62
GMA. See welding
GMA welding. See welding
Golden Age of Aviation 6-2
Goodrich 3-40
Goodrich Rivnuts® 3-39
G.P. lockbolts 3-36. See lockbolts, groove-proportioned
grain deviation 5-62
grip gauge 3-32, 3-33
grip variation 3-30. See also fasteners
grommets 2-12
  flat washer 2-12
  installation of 2-12
  suction (seaplane) 2-12
groove-proportioned lockbolts 3-36
GTA. See welding
GTA welding. See welding
guides 3-48
gyroscopic precession 1-5

H

Hall-Héroult process 3-4
hammers 3-10. See also forging
hand-forming procedures 3-82. See forming
hand polishing 5-56
  Plexiglas® 5-56
hardening 3-24
hard maple 5-59
hardness 3-2, 3-27
hardness testers 3-27
  Brinell tester 3-28, 3-29
  indenters
    Knoop indenter 3-29
    Vickers indenter 3-29
  Knoop indenter 3-29
  microhardness testing 3-29
  Rockwell tester 3-29
    scales 3-28

Vickers hardness tester 3-29
Vickers indenter 3-29
Webster hardness gauge 3-29
hardware installation and safetying 8-29
hardwoods
  basswood 5-59
  birch 5-59
  hard maple 5-59
  mahogany 5-59
  oak 5-59
  white ash 5-59
  yellow poplar 5-59
hazards 5-35, 5-36
  equipment 5-35
  solvents 5-35
  waste disposal 5-37
HAZMAT 7-3
head 3-30. See also fasteners
head dishing 3-35. See also fasteners
header 3-58
head gap tolerances
  head dishing 3-35
heat blanket
  materials 5-25
heat forming 5-46
heat treatment
  annealing 3-12, 3-18
  quenching 3-18. See also heat treatment
  solution 3-14, 3-18. See also heat treatment
    precipitation-hardening 3-14
heat-treatment
  annealing 3-22
  carburizing 3-26, 3-27
    gas carburizing 3-27
    liquid carburizing 3-27
    pack carburizing 3-27
  casehardening 3-26
  hardening 3-24
  nitriding 3-27
  normalizing 3-24
  procedures 3-23
  tempering 3-24
  upper critical point 3-24
Heli-arc® welding. See welding
helical gears 1-33
helicopter 1-2, 1-3, 1-4, 1-5, 1-6, 1-7, 1-8, 1-10, 1-11, 1-12, 1-13, 1-14, 1-15, 1-16, 1-17, 1-18, 1-19, 1-20, 1-21, 1-23, 1-24, 1-28, 1-29, 1-31
Helicopters 1-1
  aerodynamics 1-3
    airfoils 1-3
    camber 1-3
    chord 1-3
    drag 1-3
    empennage 1-3
    lift 1-3
    tail rotor 1-3
    thrust 1-3
  algorithms and. See Helicopters
  and centrifugal force 1-6, 1-11
  anti-torque control 1-21
  autogyro principle 1-21
  autorotation 1-17, 1-21, 1-24
  Bell 47B 1-3
  Bernoulli's principle and 1-3

blades 1-30
  balancing 1-30
    chordwise 1-30
    spanwise 1-30
    trammeling 1-30
bubble balancing. *See* Helicopters
controlled descent 1-21
Focke-Wulf 61 1-3
history of 1-1, 1-3
  invention of 1-1
mast 1-11
  effects of stress on 1-11
rotor smoothing 1-12
rotor system 1-6, 1-8, 1-9, 1-10, 1-12, 1-15, 1-16, 1-17, 1-20, 1-22, 1-23, 1-31
  angle of incidence 1-6, 1-8, 1-9, 1-10, 1-12, 1-15, 1-16, 1-17, 1-20, 1-22, 1-23, 1-31
  forces acting upon 1-6
  hub drive 1-6
  plane of rotation 1-6, 1-8, 1-9, 1-10, 1-12, 1-15, 1-16, 1-17, 1-20, 1-22, 1-23, 1-31
rotor tracking 1-12
  electro-optical tracking 1-12, 1-13
  flag tracking 1-12
  perfect track 1-14
  strobe-light tracking 1-11, 1-13
  using vibration sensors 1-14
  value of 1-14
Sikorsky R-4 1-3
Sikorsky YR-4B/HNS-1 1-3
stress 1-10
  compression 1-10
  multiple 1-10
    bending 1-10
    shear 1-10
    torsion 1-10
tail rotor blades 1-30
  fiberglass 1-30
  metal 1-30
torque effect 1-21
vibration 1-12
VS-300 1-3
Helicopter Transmissions 1-31
hexagonal recess 3-30. *See also* fasteners
Hi-Lok® 3-29, 3-30
  identification 3-35
  installation 3-35
  Light-Weight® 3-30
  tools 3-35
Hi-Lok® fasteners 3-39
Hi-Shear identification charts 3-35
Hi-Tigue® 3-30
Hi-Tigue® Hi-Lok® fastener 3-39
HL. *See* Hi-Lok®
HLT. *See* Hi-Tigue®
hole cutters 3-51
  circular hole saw 3-50, 3-51
  fly cutter 3-50, 3-51
hole duplication 4-23
  back-drilling 4-23
  transfer pins 4-24
hole finder 4-24
  using a 4-24

hole finders 3-49
hole punches 3-50, 3-51
  turret punch 3-50
  Whitney hand punch 3-50
holes 3-32, 3-41
  preparation of 3-32
  spacing 4-38
hole saw 3-51. *See* hole cutters
honeycomb core 5-9
  repair 5-9
horizontal weld. *See* welding
hot bonding 5-20
hot oil 1-36
hot-rolling mill 3-5
HST. *See* Light-Weight®
Huck bolts 3-36
hydrolysis 3-11
hydro press 3-80

I

Icarus 2-1
impression die 3-9. *See* forging
impression die forging. *See* forging
incidence angles, checking 8-26
indenters
  Knoop indenter 3-29
  Vickers indenter 3-29
ingot 3-5
Inside dimensions 3-65
Inspect and Repair As Necessary 2-6
inspection 4-11
  damage 4-11
  non-destruction 4-11
  non-destructive 4-11
  pre-painting 7-2
instant-load moment 3-30
interference pins 3-29
  non-stressed holes 3-29
  stressed holes 3-29
intermediate shafts 1-35
internal stresses. *See also* welding
iridescent dichromate 8-30
isocyanates 7-7

J

J-chart 3-72
jig 4-13
jigs. *See* welding
Jo-Bolt® fasteners 3-39
joggle 3-87, 7-21
joggling 3-88
  dies 3-88
  stakes 3-88
joint. 6-3
joint preparation 5-63
joints 3-29. *See* welding
  variables 3-29

K

K-chart 3-67
kerf 6-22. *See also* welding
Kevlar® 5-18
Kevlar® fibers 5-18
key 3-41
keyway 3-41
  preparation 3-41
keyway preparation 3-41
Knoop indenter 3-29

L

lacquer 7-8
  acrylic nitrocellulose 7-8
lamina 5-25
landing in an emergency 1-34
layout and forming 3-63
layout method 3-80
lift 1-1, 1-3, 1-4, 1-5, 1-6, 1-7, 1-8, 1-9, 1-10, 1-11, 1-14, 1-16, 1-17, 1-19, 1-20, 1-23, 1-24, 1-26
lightening holes 3-81
Light-Weight® 3-30, 3-31
linen 2-2
liquid carburizing 3-27
load testing. *See* proof testing
lockbolts 3-33, 3-36
  G.P. lockbolts 3-36
  groove-proportioned lockbolts 3-36
  installation 3-37
  pullers 3-38
  pull-type 3-36
  stump-type 3-36
Lockheed L-749 7-1
longerons , 2-5, 4-10, 4-8
  installations 4-10
  repair 4-29
  warping 6-5

M

magnesium 3-18
  alloys 3-18
    aging 3-18
    annealing 3-18
    quenching 3-18
    solution heat treatment 3-18
    stabilizing 3-18
  hazards 3-18
mahogany 5-59
malleable 3-2
mandrel 3-41
manufactured-head variations 3-62
mark-off 5-48
masking , 7-4, 5-53. *See also* refinishing
material growth 3-67, 3-70, 3-71
matrix resin 5-20
Maule 2-3
mechanical linkage 8-21

bellcranks 8-21
control rods 8-21
drums 8-21
quadrants 8-21
sectors 8-21
torque tubes 8-21
media blasting 7-3
media reclamation 7-3
melting point 6-16. *See also* welding
mercerization 2-4
mercerized cotton 2-2
Mercer, John 2-2
metal inert-gas welding. *See* welding
metals 3-1
  primary 3-5
  secondary 3-5
metalworking 3-8
methods of balancing 8-4
  balance beam 8-5
  scale 8-5
methyl-ethyl-ketone 5-5
microhardness testing 3-29
Micro-Mesh® 5-42
microstop countersink 3-36, 3-47, 3-48, 3-60, 3-61, 3-62
MIG welding. *See* welding
military specification 3-52
MLD. *See* mold-line dimensions
modified 120° countersick rivets 3-55
modified universal-head rivets 3-54
mold-line dimensions 3-64, 3-71, 3-72
mold point 3-65, 3-67, 3-70, 3-71, 3-72
moment of force 1-12. *See also* Helicopters
monel 3-12, 3-19, 3-52, 3-54, 3-55, 3-56, 3-61
monocoque construction 4-2
mono-spar wings 4-6
MS. *See* Military Specification
multi-spar wings 4-6

N

NACA. *See* National Advisory Committee of Aeronautics
NACA riveting method 3-55
nacelle 4-5
NAS. *See* National Aerospace Standards
National Advisory Committee of Aeronautics 3-55
National Aerospace Standards 3-52
natural aging 3-15, 3-16
N-brace principal 6-2
nestling effect 3-55
neutral flame. *See* welding
neutral line 3-63, 3-64, 3-65, 3-66. *See also* sheet metal
Newton's Third Law of Motion 1-5, 1-21
Newton's Third Law of Motion 1-5, 1-21
nickel 3-19
  alloys 3-19
    Inconel® 3-19
    monel 3-19
nitrate dope 2-2
  and pigmentation 2-2
nitriding 3-27

N numbers 7-16, 7-17
  alphabet 7-17
noble fir 5-60
non-ferrous metals 3-10, 3-12
non-flexible cable 8-11
non-metallic structures 5-2
  advanced composites 5-17
    applications 5-18
    damage 5-26
    damage inspection 5-26
      visual 5-26
  boron fibers 5-18
  carbon fibers 5-18
  ceramic fibers 5-18
  graphite fibers 5-18
  hot bonding 5-20
  Kevlar® fibers 5-18
  matrix 5-20
  plastics
    transparent
      cleaning 5-39
      cold forming 5-46
      damage 5-41
      damage removal 5-43
      damage types 5-41
      edge finishing 5-46
      forming 5-46
      heat forming 5-46
      installation of 5-39
      mounting 5-46
      Plexiglas® 5-44
      repair 5-40
      restoration 5-41
      scratch removal 5-39
      surface restoration 5-43
  ply damage 5-6
    scarfed repair 5-6
  reinforced plastic 5-5
    repair 5-5
  resins 5-4
    epoxy 5-4
    polyester 5-4
  sandwich laminates 5-6
non-stressed holes 3-29
normalizing 3-24, 6-4. *See also* welding
normalizing temperature 6-5
nose gap 3-78, 3-88, 3-90
nose radius shims 3-76, 3-77
nose rib 3-85
  repair 4-31
nylon-coated cables 8-11

O

oak 5-59
oil canniing 3-61. *See also* riveting
oil cooler 1-37
olive drab dichromate 8-30
open bends 3-62, 3-72, 3-73
open die forging 3-10. *See* forging
open heads 3-62
orange peel 7-8
OSI-BOLT® 3-39

overaging 3-16
overcoating
  paint feathering 7-5
  scuff-sanding 7-5
overhead weld 6-15. *See also* welding
oxidizing flame. *See* welding
oxyacetylene welding. *See* welding
oxygen. *See* welding

P

pack carburizing 3-27
paint
  polyurethane systems 7-7, 7-8
    aliphatic 7-7
    application 7-8
    aromatic 7-7
    catalyst 7-8
    isocyanates 7-7
    pigmented material 7-8
    resin 7-8
  primers 7-7
    epoxy-polyamide 7-8
    leveling 7-7
    zinc chromate 7-8
  spraying 7-16
    pressures 7-17
  thinning 7-7
    Zahn cup 7-7, 7-17
    zoluol 7-8
painting , 7-1, 5-56. *See* finishes; *See also* refinishing
  airless 7-17, 7-19
  brush 5-56
  cleaning 7-2
  cleaning before 7-2
    water break test 7-5
  defects 7-8
    dark streaks 7-8
    fisheye 7-8
    light streaks 7-8
    orange peel 7-8
    rough surface 7-8
    runs 7-8
    sags 7-8
    wrinkling 7-8
  equipment 7-10
    maintenance 7-10
    spray guns 7-10
      air compressors 7-14
      cleaning 7-11, 7-12
      controls 7-19
      hobby-type 7-14
      maintenance 7-11, 7-12
      pressure-feed 7-10
      suction-feed 7-10
      technique for using 7-15
      touch-up 7-14
      troubleshooting 7-11, 7-12
  finishing
    wet sanding 7-5
  finish removal
    media blasting 7-3

masking 7-4, 7-8
materials
  storage 7-19
order 7-15
overcoating
  scuff-sanding 7-5
Plexiglas® 5-56
  brush 5-56
  spray 5-56
polyurethane
  application 7-8
preparation 7-1, 7-2
  chemical conversion treatment 7-5
  conversion coating 7-5
  masking 7-1, 7-4
primers
  epoxy zinc chromate 7-8
  zinc chromate 7-8
priming 7-7
  leveling primer 7-7
safety precautions 7-8
spray 5-56
spraying
  methods 7-16
  pressures 7-17
  team 7-16
stripping 7-4
surface preparation 7-2
thinning paint
  Zahn cup 7-6, 7-17
touch-up 7-1, 7-2, 7-5
  epoxy-polyamide 7-5
trim 7-16
  alphabet 7-17
  N numbers 7-16, 7-17
paint removal 7-3
  media blasting 7-3
paint remover. *See* finishes
paint stripper 7-3, 7-4
paint thinner 7-6
  Zahn cup 7-6, 7-17
pal nuts 8-31
panel
  doped-in 2-21
  sewn-in 2-21
partial annealing 3-16
Parts Manufacturing Authority 2-3
  materials 2-3
patches 4-10, 4-17, 4-18
  closed-skin area 4-17, 4-18
  doped-in 2-21
  flush 4-17, 4-18, 4-42
  lap 4-17, 4-18
    edge preparation 4-20
    for hole 4-20
  material selection for 4-43
  open-skin area 4-17, 4-18
  procedure for applying 4-20
  scab 4-17, 4-18
  sewn-in 2-21
  skin 4-46
  tape 4-26
path of rotation 1-6
patterns 3-82

peel-ply fabrics 5-24
Pegasus 2-1
perfect track 1-14
permanent mold casting 3-7. *See* aluminum
piccolo. *See* Eckold sheet metal former
piccolo sheet metal former 3-88
piloted reamer 3-46
pinked edge 2-4
pins 3-30, 3-31, 3-33, 3-38, 3-49
  finish codes 3-31
  identification 3-35
  installation 3-33, 3-34
  part numbers 3-32
  pintail 3-37
  removal 3-34
  tension
    grip lengths 3-38
pintail 3-37
pitch 3-4
pitch arms 1-6
plain butt joint. *See* welding
planetary gear system 1-33
plasma cutter 6-24. *See also* welding
plastic coverings 5-2
plasticizers 2-18
plastics
  Plexiglas® 5-44
plate 3-5, 3-6, 3-12, 3-48, 3-49
play 3-78
pleating 3-81
Plexiglas® 5-44
  annealing 5-58
    time and temperature 5-58
  blades for cutting 5-51
  buffing 5-56
  cementing 5-50, 5-51
    annealing 5-51
    Cement II 5-51
    joint preparation 5-50, 5-51
    methods 5-50, 5-51
      capillary cementing 5-50
      soak cementing 5-51
    PS-18 5-51
  characteristics 5-44
  characteristics of 5-44
  coefficient of thermal expansion 5-44
  cold flow 5-46
  cold forming 5-46
  cutting 5-51
    band saws 5-53
    masking 5-52
    saws to use 5-51, 5-52
      band saws 5-52
      circular saws 5-52
    unmasked 5-52, 5-53
  drilling 5-55
    cooling 5-55
    drill bits to use 5-55
    safety 5-55
  edge finishing 5-46
  finish wheel 5-56
  forming 5-46
    clamps 5-48, 5-50
    contour tolerances 5-48

    shrinkage allowances 5-48
  forming methods 5-47
    bending 5-47
    drape forming 5-47
    free blowing 5-47, 5-48, 5-50
      onto a form 5-48
    manual stretch forming 5-47
    plug-and-ring forming 5-47
  hand polishing 5-56
  heat forming 5-46
  mark-off 5-48
  mounting 5-46
  painting 5-56
    brush 5-56
    spray 5-56
  routing 5-54
  routing/shaping 5-54
  sanding 5-56
  shaping 5-54
  stress limits 5-44
  tapping 5-56
  thermal expansion 5-44
  threading 5-56
  trimming 5-54
  turning 5-54
plug-and-ring forming 5-47
ply 2-4
ply damage 5-6
pneumatic hammers. *See* rivet hammer
polyalkaline glycol 3-15
polyurethane 7-2, 7-8
  aliphatic 7-7
  application 7-8
  aromatic 7-7
  catalyst component 7-8
  isocyanates 7-7
  pigmented material 7-8
Port Orford cedar 5-60
pot 3-4
Pratt truss 6-2
  illustration of 6-3
precipitation hardening 3-15
pre-drive protrusion 3-59
press brake 3-78, 3-79
presses 3-10. *See also* forging
pressure indicator 1-36
pressure line 1-35
pressure pot 7-10
pressure regulators. *See* welding
pressure sealing 7-21
pressure seals 8-17
primer 7-7
  leveling 7-7
  thinning
    zoluol 7-8
  zinc chromate 7-8
primers
  epoxy-polyamide 7-8
  epoxy zinc chromate 7-8
  thinning
    zoluol 7-8
proof testing 8-16
protruding-head riveting method 3-55
protruding-head rivets 3-35, 3-53, 3-55

PS-18 cement 5-51
PT® Fasteners 3-39. *See also* fasteners
puddling rod. *See* welding
pulleys 8-17
pump outlet 1-35
punches 3-51
punch tester 2-4
    AC 43.13-1B 2-4

Q

quadrants 8-21
quantity indicator 1-36
quarter-sawn lumber 5-62
quenching 3-14, 3-15, 3-18. *See also* heat treatment

R

R-4 helicopter 1-3
radial cracks 3-57
RADIAL-LOK® 3-39
radius 3-77
radius and fillet gauges 3-76
radius gauges 3-31, 3-39, 3-51, 3-63, 3-64, 3-65, 3-66, 3-67, 3-70, 3-71, 3-72, 3-73, 3-76, 3-77, 3-78, 3-79, 3-80, 3-82, 3-84, 3-85, 3-86, 3-87, 3-88, 3-90, 3-91
ram air 1-37
reamers 3-46
    "bullet" reamer 3-46
    piloted reamer 3-46
    step reamer 3-46
    straight reamer 3-46
    tapered 3-46
rebalancing 7-3
recess 3-30. *See also* fasteners
recycling 3-5
    rates 3-5
red mud 3-4
reduced flush-head rivets 3-54
refinishing 7-1, 7-2. *See also* painting
    cleaning before 7-2
        water break test 7-5
    defects
        dark streaks 7-8
        fisheye 7-8
        light streaks 7-8
        orange peel 7-8
        rough surface 7-8
        runs 7-8
        sags 7-8
        wrinkling 7-8
    equipment
        spray guns
            controls 7-19
    finishing
        wet sanding 7-5
    finish removal
        media blasting 7-3
    lacquer
        acrylic nitrocellulose 7-8
    masking 7-4, 7-8

materials 7-19
    storage 7-19
media blasting 7-3
order 7-15
overcoating 7-5
    paint feathering 7-5
    scuff sanding 7-5
painting
    airless 7-17, 7-19
    trim 7-16, 7-17
        N numbers 7-16, 7-17
paint removal 7-3
paint stripper 7-3
preparation
    chemical conversion treatment 7-5
    conversion coating 7-5
    masking 7-4
primers
    zinc chromate 7-8
rebalancing 7-3
safety precautions 7-8
sealants 7-19
    application 7-19
    curing 7-19
    drying 7-19
    pliable 7-19
    two-part 7-19
spray painting 7-16
    methods for 7-16
    pressures 7-17
    team 7-16
stripping 7-4
surface preparation 7-2
thinning paint
    Zahn cup 7-6, 7-17. *See also* refinishing
touch-up 7-5
    epoxy-polyamide 7-5
re-hitting rivets 3-61
reinforced-shell construction 4-2
release fabrics 5-24
release films 5-24
replaceable bearings 8-22
resins 5-4
    epoxy 5-4
    polyester 5-4
retainer washer 8-29
ribs 2-1, 4-6
    formed
        formed 4-7
    reinforced
        formed 4-7
    truss
        formed 4-7
    wooden 2-1
rigging and assembly data 8-1
rigging checks 8-24
    dihedral 8-26
    engine alignment 8-27
    fin verticality 8-26
    incidence angles 8-26
    structural alignment 8-24
    symmetry 8-27
rigging specifications 8-2
rig pins 8-29

ring rollers 3-10. *See also* forging
rivet cutters 3-52, 3-53
rivet gun 3-33, 3-38, 3-52, 3-55, 3-57, 3-58, 3-63
riveting 3-1, 3-51, 3-57, 3-61
    bucking bars 3-59
    dollies 3-59
    in-close patterns 3-61
    oil canning 3-61
    rivet squeezers 3-57
    safety. *See also* riveting
    sheet discrepancies
        edge gaps 3-62
        eyebrows 3-62
        gaps 3-62
        gaps between sheets 3-62
        smiles 3-62
        voids around shanks 3-62
    team 3-57
        bucker 3-57
        driver 3-57
        tapping 3-57
    tools 3-57
        compression riveters 3-57
        pneumatic hammers 3-57
        rivet gun 3-57, 3-58
            comparisons 3-58
        rivet hammers 3-57
        rivet squeezers 3-57
        set-spring retainers 3-57, 3-58
    wrinkling 3-61
rivets 3-16, 3-51, 3-52, 3-53, 3-54, 3-55, 3-57, 3-59, 4-17, 4-24, 4-56
    accessibility 3-61
    alloys 3-53
    AQ 3-61
    bucktails 3-59
    code markings 3-53
    cutting 3-52, 3-53
    D 3-61
    DD 3-61
    dimpling 3-55
    driving as received 3-61
    edge distance 4-17
    flush-head 3-53
    heat treatment 3-16
    in bearing 4-51
    inspection standards 3-61
        annular rings 3-62
        below-surface heads 3-62
        cracks 3-61
        eccentricity 3-61
        flattened 3-61
        gaps 3-62
        limits 3-62
        manufactured head variations 3-61
        marred 3-61
        open heads 3-61
        sloped 3-61
        stepped 3-61
        upset head variations 3-61
    installing 3-55
        countersunk flush rivets 3-55
        NACA rivets 3-55
        protruding-head rivets 3-55

modified 120° countersink 3-55
modified universal-head 3-54
monel 3-61
part numbers 3-52
pre-drive protrusion 3-59
protruding-head 3-53
reduced flush-head 3-54, 3-55
re-hitting 3-61
removing 3-61
rivets
  shear failure 4-51
selection 4-17
shaver 3-61
shaving 3-59
shear stress calculations 4-50
sheet discrepancies 3-62
  edge gaps 3-62
  eyebrows 3-62
  gaps 3-62
  gaps between sheets 3-62
  smiles 3-62
  voids around shanks 3-62
shop head 3-52
sizes 4-56
spacing 4-17
standard flush-head 3-54
standard practices 3-59
terminology 3-52
types, illustrated 3-54
universal-head 3-54
upset head 3-61
rivet sets 3-58, 3-59
  flush 3-58
  non-flush 3-58
rivet squeezers 3-57
Rivnut® 3-40. *See also* fasteners
  hole sizes 3-41
  installation 3-41
  installation tools 3-40
  key 3-41
  keyway preparation 3-41
Rivnuts® 3-39
rocket fuel 3-12
Rockwell tester 3-29
  scales 3-28
rod end bearings
  external threads 8-21
  sealed bearing 8-21
  uniball bearings 8-21
rotary former 3-88
rotary machine 3-90
rotary wing 1-1, 1-24
rotary-wing aircraft 1-1
rough surface 7-8
routing
  Plexiglas® 5-54
Rumpler Taube 2-1
runs 7-8

S

safety 3-49, 3-62, 4-65, 5-12, 5-35
safetying procedures 8-29

cotter pin safeties 8-33
pal nuts 8-31
retainer washer 8-29
safety wire 8-31
safetying turnbuckles 8-23
safety wire 8-31
sags 7-8
sandbag bumping 3-87, 3-88
sandblasting 6-17. *See also* welding
sand casting 3-7. *See also* aluminum; *See* aluminum
sanding 5-56
  hand sanding 7-5
  Plexiglas® 5-56
  wet sanding 7-5
sandwich laminate damage 5-6
  repair 5-12
    materials 5-12
saw blades 5-53
scale method of balancing 8-5
scrap 3-5
sealants 7-19. *See* finishes
  application 7-19
  Semkit® 7-21
  types 7-19
    curing 7-19
    drying 7-19
    pliable 7-19
    two-part 7-19
sealed bearing 8-21
sealing 7-19
  compounds 7-21
  injection 7-21
  pressure 7-21
  procedures 7-19
  sealants 7-19
  sealant types 7-19
seals 4-46, 4-48
  defects 4-48
  hatch 4-48
  of hardware 4-49
  pressurization 4-48
    precaution 4-48
  removal 4-49
  repair 4-49
  replacement 4-49
  retainer 4-48
  types
    compounds 4-48
    rubber 4-48
    special 4-48
seamless rolled ring forging 3-10. *See* forging
seams 2-9
secondary meta 3-5
sectors 8-21
seeding 3-11
self-locking nuts 8-29
  anodized aluminum 8-30, 8-31
  cadmium-plating 8-30
  chromic clear dip 8-30
  iridescent dichromate 8-30
  olive drab dichromate 8-30
  silver plating 8-30
  solid lubricant coating 8-30, 8-31

selvage edge 2-4
semi-monocoque construction 4-2
Semkit® 7-21
setback 3-67, 3-68, 3-69, 3-73
SFM. *See* drilling, surface feet per minute
shank 3-30. *See also* fasteners
shape
  of repairs 4-11
shaping
  Plexiglas® 5-54
shaving rivets 3-60
shear 1-12. *See also* Helicopters
shear strength 3-2
sheet discrepancies 3-62
sheet holders. *See* Clecos®
sheet metal 3-63, 4-10
  bending 3-63
    allowances 3-65, 3-67
      finding 3-70
    bend radius 3-63
      minimum 3-64
    box and pan brake 3-63
    brake 3-63
    braking 3-63
    cornice brake 3-63
    neutral axis 3-65
    neutral line 3-63
    stresses from 3-65
    tangent lines 3-65
  buckling 4-10
  flats 3-69
    drawing sight lines 3-70
    finding length 3-69
    layout 3-70
  layout 3-63
  repair 4-10
    excessive strength 4-10
    forming 4-10
    patch shape 4-10
    replacement material 4-10
    riveting 4-10
  setback 3-67, 3-68
    finding 3-69
    formula 3-67
    K-chart 3-69
  stresses 4-10
  terminology 3-64
    bend tangent lines 3-65
    bend tangent lines (BTL) 3-65
    inside dimensions 3-64
    inside dimensions (MLD) 3-64
    mold line dimensions (MLD) 3-64
    total developed width (TDW) 3-65
      calculating 3-70
sheet metal former 3-90
sheet shear calculations 4-52
shop heads 3-52. *See* bucktails; *See also* rivets
short drive shaft 1-33
shrink allowance 6-5. *See also* welding
shrinkers , 3-90
  operation 3-91
shrinking 3-81, 3-82, 3-83, 3-89, 3-90
  shrinker 3-91
  tools 3-89

shrinking block method 3-84. *See also* forming
shrink rules 3-7. *See also* aluminum
sight lines. *See* brake reference line drawing 3-70
Sikorsky, Igor 1-3. *See also* R-4 helicopter
silver plating 8-30
sizing 2-4
skin cracks 4-11
skin repair 4-17, 4-18, 4-34, 4-41, 4-45
   layout 4-22
   longitudinal joint 4-38
   transverse joint 4-38
skin wrinkles 4-11
SLEEVbolt® fasteners 3-41
slip-roll former 3-88
slip-roll forming machine 3-90
slope 5-62
slug rivets 3-55
slurry 5-6
smelter 3-4
smelting 3-5
smiles 3-62. *See* eyebrows; *See also* riveting
snake drill 3-48
sniffer 5-25
   materials 5-25
soak cementing 5-51
sodium aluminum fluoride 3-4
sodium hydroxide , 2-2. *See* Bayer process
softwoods
   balsa 5-60
   Douglas fir 5-60
   noble fir 5-60
   Port Orford cedar 5-60
   spruce 5-60
   western hemlock 5-60
   white pine 5-60
soldering
   safety precautions 6-27
   silver 6-27
solid lubricant coating 8-30, 8-31
solution heat treatment 3-14, 3-18
solvents 2-18
spars 4-6
   angle repair 4-31
   repair by insertion 4-31
   repair by patching 4-31
   web repair 4-31
spiral chip 3-42. *See also* drilling
split-point drill 3-44
SPM. *See* Standard Processes Manual
sprag clutch 1-21. *See also* Helicopters
spray guns
   air compressors 7-14
   cleaning 7-11
   controls 7-19
   hobby-type 7-14
   maintenance 7-11
   pressure-feed 7-10
   pressures 7-17
   suction-feed 7-10
   technique for using 7-15
   touch-up 7-14
   troubleshooting 7-12
spruce 5-60

squashing 6-4. *See also* welding
squeeze riveter 3-56
SRM. *See* Structural Repair Manual
ST1219-1CB 3-39
ST1219Y-1CA 3-39
stabilator 8-10
stabilizer bar 1-5, 1-6
stabilizing 3-18
stakes 3-88
standard bushing holder 3-32, 3-37, 3-43, 3-48, 3-53, 3-54, 3-59
standard flush head rivets 3-54
standard practices 3-59
Standard Processes Manual 3-37
static balance 8-3
static electricity 2-19
steel 3-26, 3-58
   alloys 3-24
     chromium-molybdenum 3-24
     nickel steel 3-24
     stainless steel 3-24
   carbon 3-24
   determining the temperature of 3-26
   heat-treating 3-26
     procedures 3-23
   heat-treatment
     annealing 3-22, 3-24
     upper critical point 3-24
     tempering 3-24
step drills 3-46
step reamer 3-46
stop-countersink 3-47
stops 8-23
stop sleeve 8-14
straight-line bends 3-82
straight reamer 3-46
strain 1-12. *See also* Helicopters
Strain 1-12
strap duplicators 3-49. *See* hole finders
streaks 7-8
strength 3-1, 3-2
strength-to-weight ratio 3-2
stress 1-9, 1-10, 1-11, 1-12, 1-27
stress calculations 4-49, 4-50
   bearing 4-52
   rivet shear 4-50
   sheet shear 4-52
   tear-out 4-52
   tensile 4-50
stressed holes 3-29
stress relief 3-12
stress-relief annealing 3-16
stress risers 4-53
stretchers , 3-90
stretch forming 5-47
stretching 3-81, 3-82, 3-90, 3-91
   stretcher 3-91
   tools 3-89
stretching tools 3-90
stringers 4-8
   installations 4-10
   repair by formed angle 4-29
   repair by insertion 4-26, 4-27
   repair by J-section splice 4-27, 4-29

repair by patching 4-26, 4-27
stripper. *See* finishes
stripping 7-4. *See* finishes
   conversion coating 7-5
structural alignment 8-24
Structural Repair Manual 3-35, 3-37, 3-47, 3-50, 3-62, 3-72, 5-5
substitution 3-31, 3-37
Supplemental Type Certificate 2-3
surface feet per minute 3-42
surface travel measurement 8-8
   bubble protractors 8-8
   universal propeller protractor 8-9
swaged ball terminals 8-15
swage-type terminals 8-14
symmetrical airfoil 1-4
symmetry check 8-27

T

Table 7-2-1. Torch tip sizes 6-11
Table 7-2-2. Melting points of aircraft metals 6-18
Table 7-2-3. Approximate pressure for various tip sizes 6-22
Table 7-3-1. Current requirements for commonly used metals 6-32
Table 7-3-2. General operating data for aluminum 6-33
Table 7-3-3. Recommended post-weld heat treatments for austenitic stainless steels 6-36
Table 7-3-4. General operating data for stainless steels 6-37
Table 7-3-5. Ampere settings for MIG welding 6-39
tachometer generators 1-34
tail rotor blades. *See* Helicopters
Taper-Lok® bolts 3-41
tapes 2-9
   anti-chafe tape 2-10
   anti-tear tape 2-9, 2-11
   inter-rib bracing tape 2-10
   inter-rib lacing tape 2-9
   reinforcing tape 2-9, 2-10
     inter-rib bracing 2-12, 2-13
   specifications 2-10
   surface tape 2-9, 2-11
     application of 2-13
   uses 2-10
tapping 5-56
   Plexiglas® 5-56
TDW. *See* total developed width (TDW)
team riveting 3-57
tear-out calculations 4-52
Technical Standard Order 2-3
temperature indicating crayon 6-5. *See also* welding
temperature indicator 1-36
tempering 3-24
tensile strength 3-1
tensiometer 8-17
tension. *See* stress
terminal gauge 8-14
terminals 8-15
   cable slippage in 8-15

swaged ball terminals 8-15
swage-type 8-14
thermostatic 1-37
thimble-eye splice 8-13
thinners 2-13
thread 2-11
　coating 2-12
　hand-sewing cord 2-11
　machine-sewing cord 2-11
　rib-lacing cord 2-11
　　inter-rib bracing 2-12
　　sequence for using 2-11
　rib-stitching cord 2-11
　　application of 2-11, 2-12
threading 5-56
　Plexiglas® 5-56
threads 3-30. *See also* fasteners
through-bag connectors
　materials 5-25
thrust 1-1, 1-3, 1-4, 1-6, 1-10, 1-16, 1-17, 1-18, 1-19, 1-20, 1-22, 1-23
thrust force 1-3
TIG welding. *See* welding
titanium 3-18
　alloys 3-18
　　alpha 3-18
　　alpha-beta 3-18
　　beta 3-18
　conversion 3-18
tooling 3-9, 3-38, 3-46, 3-57. *See* forging
torque effect. *See* Helicopters
torque tubes 8-21
　replaceable bearings 8-22
total developed width (TDW) 3-65, 3-72
　calculating 3-70
touch-up 7-5
touch-up gun 7-14
touch-up painting
　epoxy-polyamide 7-5
toughness 3-2
tracking weights 1-30
transfer pins 3-49, 4-24
transfer punch 4-24
　using a 4-24
transition area 3-30. *See also* fasteners
treat and seal. *See* finishes
trim tabs 1-30
tube
　connections 6-3. *See also* welding
tubes
　diagonal 6-5
　horizontal 6-5
　vertical 6-5
tubing
　straightening bent 6-5
　　illustration of 6-5
tungsten inert-gas welding. *See* welding
turnbuckles 8-23
　safetying 8-23
turning
　Plexiglas® 5-54
turret punch. *See* hole punches
type certificate data sheet 8-2. *See also* rigging specifications

U
U-channels 3-79
uniball bearings 8-21
universal-head rivets 3-54
universal propeller protractor 8-9
upper critical point 3-24
upset head 3-55, 3-61
upsetters 3-10. *See also* forging

V
vacuum bagging 5-23
　materials 5-23
　　bag sealant tape 5-25
　　bleeder/breather material 5-23
　　caul plate 5-25
　　flash tape 5-25
　　heat blanket 5-25
　　peel-ply fabric 5-23
　　release film/fabric 5-23
　　sniffer 5-25
　　through-bag connectors 5-25
　　vacuum bagging films 5-23
vacuum pressure 5-23
V-block 3-81, 3-82, 3-83
V-block method 3-84. *See also* forming
vertical flight 1-2, 1-3, 1-10
Very-Lite® 3-31. *See also* fasteners
vibration 1-37
Vickers indenter 3-29
vise 3-75
　bench 3-75
Vise Grips® 3-34
VISU-LOK® 3-39
VL. *See* Very-Lite®
voids around shanks 3-62
von Richtofen, Manfred 6-2
VS-300 helicopter 1-3

W
warp 2-4
warp ends 2-4
Warren truss 6-2
　illustration of 6-3
wash in 8-26. *See also* wing-heavy condition
wash out 8-26. *See also* wing-heavy condition
waste disposal 5-37
water break test 7-5. *See* finishes
Webster harness gauge 3-29
weft 2-4
weight 1-1, 1-3, 1-6, 1-7, 1-10, 1-12, 1-14, 1-16, 1-29
　of repairs 4-11
welding 6-1, 6-7
　acetylene gas 6-8, 6-9
　　cylinders 6-9
　　fittings

　　left-hand threads 6-10
　　safety precautions 6-9, 6-27
　　storage 6-9
　backhand 6-14
　bracing. *See* welding
　　illustration of 6-7
　brazing 6-25
　　safety precautions 6-27
　　technique 6-25
　breaking the arc
　　illustration 6-34
　buckling 6-6
　butt welds 6-5
　carbon steel 6-18
　characteristics of a good weld
　　controlling 6-17
　chrome-molybdenum steel 6-18
　　preheating 6-19
　　TIG welding 6-19
　clusters 6-4
　　examples of 6-4
　corner joint 6-14
　cracking 6-21
　cutting torch 6-21, 6-22
　　illustration of 6-22
　　lighting 6-23
　　procedure 6-22
　　safety precautions 6-23
　expansion and contraction 6-3. *See* welding
　　chill bars 6-16, 6-17
　　controlling 6-16
　　　chill bars 6-16, 6-17
　　　illustration of 6-17
　　　jigs 6-16, 6-17
　　　preheating 6-17
　ferrous metals 6-17
　　flame cutting 6-21
　filler rod 6-18
　filler rods 6-11
　fillet welds 6-14
　flame 6-11
　　adjustment 6-11
　　carburizing 6-11
　　characteristics of 6-11
　　harsh vs. soft 6-11
　　neutral 6-11
　　oxidizing 6-11
　forehand 6-14
　friction stir welding 6-42, 6-43
　　advantages 6-44
　　disadvantages 6-44
　　equipment 6-44
　　illustrations 6-43
　　reliability 6-44
　　repairs 6-44
　　uses 6-43
　FSW 6-42
　gas metal-arc 6-27. *See also* MIG welding
　gas metal-arc welding 6-38
　gas-shielded arc welding 6-27
　gast tungsten-arc 6-27
　gas tungsten-arc 6-27. *See also* TIG welding; *See* welding

Index | I-15

gas welding 6-7
  equipment
    portable 6-7, 6-8
    setting up 6-13
    shutting down 6-13
    stationary 6-7
  oxyacetylene 6-7
  safety precautions 6-27
GMA 6-27
goggles 6-11
  lenses for 6-20
good vs. bad 6-47
groove welds 6-14
GTA 6-27
hazards 6-27
Heli-arc® 6-27
history of 6-1
hose 6-10
  oxygen vs. acetylene 6-10
inspection 6-44
  OEM parts 6-44
  visual 6-44
inspection of weld 6-36
internal stresses 6-4
joints 6-15
  butt joint 6-15
    double-bevel 6-15
    double-v 6-15
    single-bevel 6-15
    single-v 6-15
  corner joints 6-16
    illustrations of 6-16. See welding
  edge joints 6-16
    illustrations of 6-16. See welding
  lap joint
    double-fillet. See welding
    single-fillet. See welding
  plain butt joint 6-15
  tee joint
    illustrations of 6-16. See welding
kerf 6-22
lighters 6-10
magnesium alloy 6-21
magnesium alloys 6-36
melting point 6-16, 6-17. See welding
  listing of 6-17
  tee joint
    illustrations of 6-16
metal inert-gas 6-27
MIG welding 6-27, 6-38. See also gas metal-arc
  equipment 6-38
  filler metal for 6-38
  porous welds 6-41
  safety precautions 6-42
  sheilding gas 6-38
  techniques 6-40
non-ferrous metals 6-19
  aluminum 6-19
  beveling edges of 6-20
  melting point 6-19
  notching edges of 6-20
  preheating 6-20
  preparation of 6-19

puddling rod 6-21
technique 6-19, 6-20
  welding fluxes 6-20
  welding lenses 6-20
  welding rods 6-20
  aluminum alloys 6-19
oxygen 6-8
  caution 6-8
  cylinders 6-8
oxygen and 6-8. See welding
plasma cutter 6-24
positions 6-15
  flat weld 6-15
  horizontal weld 6-15
  illustration of. See welding
  overhead weld 6-15
  vertical weld 6-15
preheating 6-5
preparation for 6-17
  cadmium plating removal 6-17
  grease removal 6-17
  paint removal 6-17
  rust removal 6-17
  sandblasting 6-17
  scale removal 6-17
  varnish removal 6-17
pressure regulators 6-9
  illustration of 6-9
  single-stage 6-10
  two-stage 6-10
  working pressure 6-10
rewelding 6-17
safety precaution 6-27
sheet steel 6-6
shrink allowance 6-5
silver soldering 6-27
  flux 6-27
  illustration 6-26
  joints 6-27
    illustration 6-27
  preheating 6-27
  safety precautions 6-27
soldering 6-27
  safety precautions 6-27
stainless steel 6-19, 6-36
  current requirements 6-37
  filler rod for 6-37
  flux for 6-19
  inspection of weld 6-37
  preparation of metal 6-37
  techniques 6-19
  TIG welding 6-19
  torch adjustment 6-37
  welding procedure for 6-37
starting the arc
  illustration 6-34
stress 6-5
structural examples 6-3
subassemblies 6-5
temerature indicating crayon 6-5
TIG welding 6-27. See also gas tungsten-arc
  advantages 6-29
  application 6-29
  arc blow 6-34

breaking the arc 6-34
  illustration 6-34
  current requirements 6-33
  disadvantages 6-29
  effects of 6-33
  equipment 6-29
  filler rod for 6-33
  inspection of weld 6-36
  preheating 6-34
  preparation of metal 6-34
  procedures 6-33
  protective equipment 6-33
  starting the arc 6-34
    illustration 6-34
  torch adjustment 6-33
  vs. MIG welding 6-29
torch 6-10
  backfire 6-11
  cutting 6-22
    illustration of 6-22
    procedure 6-22
  flashback 6-11
  lighting 6-22
  tips 6-10
    cleaning 6-10
    comparison 6-10, 6-22
tube connections 6-3
tubes 6-6
tube warp 6-5
tubing clusters 6-45
tungsten inert-gas 6-27
two-torch method 6-5
western hemlock 5-60
wet Micro 5-6
wet sanding 7-5
wet sump system 1-34
white ash 5-59
white pine 5-60
Whitney hand punch 3-51. See hole punches
windmill effect 1-1
wing-heavy condition 8-26
wing ribs 4-6, 5-61
  repair 4-31
  repair by insertion 4-31
wings 4-6, 5-61
  box-beam 4-6
  I-beam spar 4-6
  mono-spar 4-6
  multi-spar 4-6
  ribs 4-6
  spars 4-6
wing spars 4-6, 5-61
  drilling 5-62
  gluing 5-62
wood 5-58
  commercial aircraft 5-62
  drilling spars 5-62
  finishing 5-63
  flat-sawn 5-60, 5-61
    vs. quarter-sawn 5-60
  gluing 5-62
    types of glue 5-62
  grain deviation 5-61, 5-62
  grain deviation (slope) 5-62

hardwoods 5-58
  basswood 5-59
  birch 5-59
  black walnut 5-60
  hard maple 5-59
  mahogany 5-59
  oak 5-59
  white ash 5-58
  yellow poplar 5-59
inspecting 5-63
purchasing 5-61
quarter-sawn 5-62
  vs. flat-sawn 5-60
repair 5-63
slope 5-62
softwoods 5-60
  balsa 5-60
  Douglas fir 5-60
  noble fir 5-60
  Port Orford cedar 5-60
  spruce 5-60
  western hemlock 5-60
  white pine 5-60
working with 5-60
wooden stringers , 2-5
wood structures 5-58
  drilling 5-62
  finishing 5-63
  gluing
    joint preparation 5-63
  hardwoods 5-58
    basswood 5-59
    birch 5-59
    black walnut 5-60
    hard maple 5-59
    mahogany 5-59
    oak 5-59
    white ash 5-58
    yellow poplar 5-59
  inspecting 5-63
  inspection 5-63
    moisture meter 5-63
  joint preparation 5-63
  repair 5-63
  softwoods 5-60
    balsa 5-60
    Douglas fir 5-60
    noble fir 5-60
    Port Orford cedar 5-60
    spruce 5-60
    western hemlock 5-60
    white pine 5-60
woof 2-4
work-hardening 3-83, 3-84
working pressure. *See* welding
woven splice 8-13
wrenching flats 3-30. *See also* fasteners
Wright, Orville 2-1, 2-2
  launch of glider 2-2
Wright, Wilbur 2-1, 2-2
  launch of glider 2-2
wrinkling 3-61, 7-8. *See also* riveting
wrought alloys 3-12

X

X axis 5-25

Y

yellow poplar 5-59
yield strength 3-2

Z

Zahn cup 7-6. *See also* finishes; *See also* refinishing
zinc chromate primer. *See* finishes; *See* primer
zinc plating
  removal of 6-17
zoluol 7-9. *See also* finishes

Corrections, Suggestions for Improvement, Request for Additional Information

It is Avotek's goal to provide quality aviation maintenance resources to help you succeed in your career, and we appreciate your assistance in helping.

Please complete the following information to report a correction, suggestion for improvement, or to request additional information.

REFERENCE NUMBER (To be assigned by Avotek)	
CONTACT INFORMATION*	
Date	
Name	
Email	
Daytime Phone	
BOOK INFORMATION	
Title	
Edition	
Page number	
Figure/Table Number	
Discrepancy/Correction (You may also attach a copy of the discrepancy/correction)	
Suggestion(s) for Improvement (Attach additional documentation as needed)	
Request for Additional Information	

FOR AVOTEK USE ONLY		
	Date Received	
	Reference Number Issued By	
	Receipt Notification Sent	
	Action Taken/By	
	Completed Notification Sent	

*Contact information will only be used to provide updates to your submission or if there is a question regarding your submission.

Send your corrections to:

- **Email:** comments@avotek.com
- **Fax:** 1-540-234-9399
- **Mail:** Corrections: Avotek Information Resources
  P.O. Box 219
  Weyers Cave, VA 24486 USA